D0023584

The Garland Encyclopedia of World Music

Volume 4

Southeast Asia

Volume 1
AFRICA
edited by Ruth M. Stone

Volume 2
SOUTH AMERICA, MEXICO, CENTRAL AMERICA, AND THE CARIBBEAN
edited by Dale A. Olsen and Daniel E. Sheehy

Volume 3
THE UNITED STATES AND CANADA
edited by Ellen Koskoff

Volume 4
SOUTHEAST ASIA
edited by Terry E. Miller and Sean Williams

Volume 5
SOUTH ASIA: THE INDIAN SUBCONTINENT
edited by Alison Arnold

Volume 6
THE MIDDLE EAST
edited by Virginia Danielson, Scott Marcus, and Dwight Reynolds

Volume 7
EAST ASIA: CHINA, JAPAN, AND KOREA
edited by Robert C. Provine, Yosihiko Tokumaru, and J. Lawrence Witzleben

Volume 8
EUROPE
edited by Timothy Rice, Christopher Goertzen, and James Porter

Volume 9
AUSTRALIA AND THE PACIFIC ISLANDS
edited by Adrienne L. Kaeppler and J. Wainwright Love

Volume 10
THE WORLD'S MUSIC: GENERAL PERSPECTIVES AND REFERENCE TOOLS

Advisory Editors
Bruno Nettl and Ruth M. Stone

Founding Editors
James Porter and Timothy Rice

The Garland Encyclopedia of World Music

Volume 4

Southeast Asia

Terry E. Miller and Sean Williams
Editors

GARLAND PUBLISHING, INC.
A member of the Taylor and Francis Group
New York and London
1998

The initial planning of The Garland Encyclopedia of World Music was assisted by a grant from the National Endowment for the Humanities.

Library of Congress Cataloging-in-Publication Data

The Garland encyclopedia of world music / [advisory editors, Bruno Nettl and Ruth M. Stone ; founding editors, James Porter and Timothy Rice].
p. cm.
Includes bibliographical references, discographies, and indexes.
Contents: v. 4. Southeast Asia / Terry E. Miller and Sean Williams, editors.
ISBN 0-8240-6040-7 (alk. paper)
1. Music—Encyclopedias. 2. Folk music—Encyclopedias.
3. Popular music—Encyclopedias. I. Nettl, Bruno, 1930– .
II. Stone, Ruth M. III. Porter, James, 1937– . IV. Rice, Timothy, 1945– .
ML100.G16 1998
780'.9—dc21

97-9671
CIP
MN

For Garland Publishing:

Vice-President: Leo Balk
Managing Editor: Richard Wallis
Director of Production: Anne Vinnicombe
Project Editor: Barbara Curialle Gerr
Copy Editor: J. Wainwright Love
Desktop publishing: Betty Probert (Special Projects Group)
Glossary and index: Marilyn Bliss
Music typesetting: Hyunjung Choi
Maps: Indiana University Graphic Services
Cover design: Lawrence Wolfson Design, New York

Cover illustration: A musician plays the *kajar*, a small pot gong that rests on a carved wooden frame. In Balinese gamelan music, this instrument maintains a strong regular beat that keeps the ensemble's complex layers of rhythm and melody together. (William Waterfall/Pacific Stock)

Parts of "The Indigenous Peoples (Orang Asli) of the Malay Peninsula" adapted from *Healing Sounds from the Malaysian Rainforest*, by Marina Roseman, 1991. Courtesy of University of California Press.

Printed on acid-free, 250-year-life paper
Manufactured in the United States of America

10 9 8 7 6 5 4 3 2

Contents

Audio Examples

The following examples are included on the accompanying audio compact disc packaged with this volume. Track numbers are also indicated on the pages listed below for easy reference to text discussions. Complete notes on each example may be found on pages 985–988.

About *The Garland Encyclopedia of World Music*

Scholars have created many kinds of encyclopedias devoted to preserving and transmitting knowledge about the world. The study of music has itself been the subject of numerous encyclopedias in many languages. Yet until now the term *music encyclopedia* has been synonymous with surveys of the history, theory, and performance practice of European-based traditions.

In July 1988, the editors of *The Garland Encyclopedia of World Music* gathered for a meeting to determine the nature and scope of a massive new undertaking. For this, the first encyclopedia devoted to the music of all the world's peoples, the editors decided against the traditional alphabetic approach to compartmentalizing knowledge from A to Z. Instead, they chose a geographic approach, with each volume devoted to a single region and coverage assigned to the world's experts on specific music cultures.

For several decades, ethnomusicologists (following the practice of previous generations of comparative musicologists) have been documenting the music of the world through fieldwork, recording, and analysis. Now, for the first time, they have created an encyclopedia that summarizes in one place the major findings that have resulted from the explosion in such documentation since the 1960s. The volumes in this series comprise contributions from all those specialists who have from the start defined the field of ethnomusicology: anthropologists, linguists, dance ethnologists, cultural historians, folklorists, literary scholars, and—of course—musicologists, composers, and performers. This multidisciplinary approach continues to enrich the field, and future generations of students and scholars will find *The Garland Encyclopedia of World Music* to be an invaluable resource that contributes to knowledge in all its varieties.

Each volume has a similar design and organization: three large sections that cover the major topics of a region from broad general issues to specific music practices. Each section consists of articles written by leading researchers, and extensive glossaries and indexes give the reader easy access to terms, names, and places of interest.

Part 1: an introduction to the region, its culture, and its music as well as a survey of previous music scholarship and research

Part 2: major issues and processes that link the musics of the region

Part 3: detailed accounts of individual music cultures

The editors of each volume have determined how this three-part structure is to be constructed and applied depending on the nature of their regions of interest. The concepts covered in Part 2 will therefore differ from volume to volume; likewise, the articles in Part 3 might be about the music of nations, ethnic groups, islands, or subregions. The picture of music presented in each volume is thus comprehensive yet remains focused on critical ideas and issues.

Complementing the texts of the encyclopedia's articles are numerous illustrations: photographs, drawings, maps, charts, song texts, and music examples. At the end of each volume is a useful set of study and research tools, including a glossary of terms, lists of audio and visual resources, and an extensive bibliography. An audio compact disc will be found inside the back cover of each volume, with sound examples that are linked (with a TRACK in the margin) to discussions in the text.

The Garland Encyclopedia of World Music represents the work of hundreds of specialists guided by a team of distinguished editors. With a sense of pride, Garland Publishing offers this new series to readers everywhere.

Preface

This volume of *The Garland Encyclopedia of World Music* covers one of the most diverse places on the planet, home to hundreds of millions of people. Yet Southeast Asia is considered by some to be utterly remote and inaccessible because of its perceived physical and cultural distance from the West. Numerous images of the region may come to mind. With these conceptions shaped partly by such dramatic fictions as *The King and I*, partly by colonial and wartime experiences, and partly by glorious travel footage on television and in magazines, Westerners of the twentieth century have been dazzled and confused by what Southeast Asia represents. Is it a tropical earthly paradise? A dense group of forests with landmines and former headhunters? A sweeping panorama of breathtaking terraced rice fields and volcanoes? Trance-dancing rituals, extraordinary wildlife, and incredibly crowded urban scenes? Southeast Asia is certainly all of these, but for the writers of this volume it is the music that has brought us together to explore and write about this extraordinary region.

Our authors hail from many parts of the world, but all share several things in common: an enjoyment of and respect for the musics and musicians of Southeast Asia, direct fieldwork and performing experiences, and a strong record of scholarship. We have tried to make these articles as accurate as possible, yet we recognize that we are limited not only by time and publication deadlines but also by the shifting, developing nature of music as we fix these words in print. And we have tried also to keep the language direct and straightforward. We want this volume to speak to the widest audience, from high school students to professors to interested readers from all backgrounds.

SOUTHEAST ASIA AND THE STUDY OF WORLD MUSIC

The island of Java was one of the first sites of research by Westerners in the young field of ethnomusicology in the early twentieth century. In fact, the Javanese gamelan orchestra was at one time virtually synonymous with the relatively new field of "world music." Worldwide knowledge of Southeast Asian musical traditions had been scattered and uneven for hundreds of years, but in the 1960s and 1970s the appearance of gamelan ensembles at colleges and universities in North America and Europe made them foremost in the minds of those interested in "exotic" music.

Mainland Southeast Asian musics, on the other hand, are still largely unknown in the West despite years of contact during wartime and following the exodus of more than a million refugees after 1975. Until the 1980s, only a few books and articles on Southeast Asian music were available in Western libraries. Since then, broader knowledge of and interest in Southeast Asian expressive culture have led to a large cohort of younger ethnomusicologists—the second and third generations of the field—discovering new excitement in Southeast Asia and exploring the region far beyond the limits of what might appear in a typical college survey of world music.

The traditional image of an encyclopedia includes catalogs of data, places, instruments, and names, with brief summaries of the most basic information. In *The*

Garland Encyclopedia of World Music, however, our goal is to reach beyond superficial descriptions to a broader grasp of the context, meaning, and issues affecting music and the lives of musicians. For example, we have written about the impact of war on Cambodian music, about the uneasy relationship between Islam and music in the islands, and about Southeast Asian responses to Western popular music. Yet no encyclopedia could possibly be complete in covering an area this diverse. The Human Relations Area Files name 151 separate ethnic groups in mainland Southeast Asia and 91 in island Southeast Asia. Although many of these groups have small populations, most have musical systems distinctive enough to warrant separate study. If we were unable to explore every musical system within Southeast Asia, we are nevertheless pleased to present the results of years of research on the part of so many authors.

Our goals for this encyclopedia include offering new perspectives on well-established Southeast Asian musics; providing a single source that can function as every scholar's first place to search; including resources for further exploration (such as the expanded bibliography, discography, and filmography at the end of the volume); and moving beyond the best known of the traditional musics to include dance, theater, popular, religious, ritual, and syncretic musics. Some musics that are only mentioned in passing here may leap to the fore as the "traditional" music of three generations hence, while some traditions (and the musics that go with them) are disappearing with their contexts and may be noted here for the last time. This encyclopedia is the first major resource to discuss upland and tribal traditions, as well as musics of some of the more remote islands.

Ironically, some of these very areas are the most rapidly changing of the entire region. As this volume goes to press, thousands of acres of Borneo's forests are burning out of control, destroying countless villages and gutting communities even as land is cleared for world-class golf courses, multinational hotels, and other development projects. Musical reactions to these and other events have been stunning to observe, from the development of Balinese rap to the gradual disappearance of Laotian repartee singing to a dazzling renewal of Cambodian classical performing arts. The nature of change as a constant in music has kept our work exciting and challenging, from blending Hans Oesch's fieldwork from the 1960s with that of Marina Roseman in the 1980s and 1990s, to adding the very latest on Filipino popular music in the mid-1990s.

We selected our contributors from both older and younger generations of researchers, all of whom emphasize different aspects of the area in which they worked. The editors of this volume have felt fortunate to work with authors not only from within Southeast Asia but also from the United States, Japan, Australia, and Europe. We deeply regret that two of the authors, Ruriko Uchida of Japan and Hans Oesch of Germany, died before this volume was finished. Both of these scholars specialized in the upland musics of mainland Southeast Asia and conducted extensive fieldwork in Thailand and Malaysia, respectively. Since the initial shaping of this encyclopedia, many new specialists in the area have established themselves. We wish to offer those people our apologies for not having been able to include their work, and we welcome the publication of their research in the future.

HOW THIS VOLUME IS ORGANIZED

In Part 1, we provide an overview of the entire region, focusing on issues of geography, diversity, and scholarship. We include a section on what to listen for in Southeast Asian music as a "first-stop" introduction to the area. In Part 2, the focus is on concepts common to the musics and cultures of the region as a whole. For readers interested in issues that cross national boundaries, such as colonialism, mass media, spirituality, and war, the articles in this section are important in gaining historical, political, and social perspective. For example, Wessing's article on bamboo, rice, and water covers the importance of these three near-ubiquitous features of Southeast Asian life, with examples from most of the region's nations. Deborah Wong and René Lysloff have combined their efforts in exploring the cultural politics of popular music in two nations: Thailand and Indonesia. The editors, Terry E. Miller and Sean Williams, have written jointly on the impact of multiple layers of influence on the region in the past two thousand years, whether it has been spiritual, colonial, or economic. These and other articles serve to link regions and their musics, to highlight their differences, and to place the musical details found later in the volume in a much broader cultural perspective.

Part 3 is by far the largest part of this volume. Its division into two main sections—mainland Southeast Asia and island Southeast Asia—reflects the important cultural and historical traditions that have shaped the region. Despite our presentation of discrete articles on each modern nation, readers will nevertheless find musical traditions and instruments that cross national and cultural boundaries (changing their local spelling and often their context as well). Terry E. Miller, responsible for editing the mainland articles, also undertook the enormous task of writing several of them. Other scholars for the mainland include Panya Roongrüang, Sam-Ang Sam, Amy Catlin, Patricia Matusky, Hans Oesch, James Chopyak, Ruriko Uchida, Marina Roseman, Deborah Wong, Phong T. Nguyễn, and Lee Tong Soon. In the island section, edited by Sean Williams, contributors include R. Anderson Sutton, Endo Suanda, Margaret J. Kartomi, David Harnish, José Maceda, Corazon Canave-Dioquino, Ramón P. Santos, Arnold Cabalza, Christopher Basile, René T. A. Lysloff, Janet Hoskins, Patricia Matusky, and Sean Williams.

Research tools

The editors do not expect readers to read the book from cover to cover. The amount of detailed information, with seemingly endless terms for genres, ensembles, and instruments, may overwhelm readers seeking a less comprehensive view. Each reader must glean the information needed for the moment, saving the remainder for times when more knowledge is required.

To help guide readers in their searches, we have provided outlines at the start of each article as well as numerous headings and subheadings. At the tops of many pages, we have placed important definitions as well as key excerpts from the text. To make further exploration and reading easier, we have followed several conventions. The list of References at the end of each article generally lists only those items actually cited in the article, but at the end of the volume readers will find a much more inclusive bibliography, discography, and filmography listing materials (mostly in Western languages) that are currently available in the West. There is also a comprehensive glossary with definitions of major terms and names, plus a useful index for locating topics. Maps appear near the beginning of most major areas, and photographs offer frequent glimpses of musical instruments, musicians, and musical contexts.

Musical examples

Some readers new to Southeast Asian music may be surprised to find that Western musical notation does not appear frequently in this volume. In most cases, standard notation is ill-equipped to handle the kind of tones, timbres, and musical motions that occur in Southeast Asian musics. Instead, contributors have often used local conventions to describe music (such as a numerical system for Indonesian gamelan), and these conventions are explained in each article. We recommend that you listen to the actual music rather than try to reproduce it on a Western instrument the way you could reproduce a reduced Mozart score.

Compact disc

An accompanying compact disc offers examples of some of the music of Southeast Asia. Because many fine recordings of the mainstream traditions are readily available (see the Discography), we have chosen important but under-recorded traditions for inclusion on the compact disc. Most of them are field recordings by the contributors to this volume and often represent the "first hearing" of these musics outside of their traditional context. A booklet of brief notes on the recordings is packaged with the compact disc inside the back cover of the volume; the notes themselves are duplicated on pages 985–988 of the text, preceding the index.

ACKNOWLEDGMENTS

Because work on this volume began in 1988, the people who have contributed to it over the years could staff an entire Central Javanese gamelan. For the first six years, however, Terry E. Miller was the sole coordinator; he commissioned articles, met with other volume editors in the series, and did the inital editing. He was joined in early 1994 by Sean Williams, who took responsibility for the sections on island Southeast Asia. We have worked (electronically, at least) side by side since then, dividing our duties and seeing our partnership enable the volume to move toward completion. Together, we wrote many of the articles in Parts 1 and 2, and we were pleased to see that our thoughts blended on paper. We were lucky to find diligent, expert authors who were willing to write their articles in a timely manner, put up with multiple stages of edits, re-edits, and copy edits, and in some cases delay their own projects in order to help us finish on time. We thank them for their years of patience and good humor in their dealings with us. The Southeast Asian musicians with whom we all have lived and worked—and whose original knowledge forms the core of this volume—deserve more appreciation, acknowledgment, and celebration than any of us could begin to offer.

We also want to acknowledge the efforts of our many assistants, including Scott Bullard, who spent many hours doing the intial copyediting. Later, Denise Seachrist and Andrew Shahriari, both of Kent State University, helped with numerous tasks, including entering edited material into computer files, searching for maps, copyediting, and making glossaries. We also thank Lawrence Rubens of Kent State University's audiovisual services department for converting Macintosh discs to PC format, often on short notice. Seán Johnson of The Evergreen State College helped with the island portion of the general reference section at the end of the volume, and the photographic services staff at Evergreen also deserve our acknowledgment for quick assistance. Our thanks go to Roy Hamilton and Gini Gorlinski, who examined several of the articles as outside readers, and to Janet Hoskins and Arnold Cabalza who contributed significant information to the Sumba and Filipino sections, respectively.

We are both grateful for the continuous assistance of Jacob W. Love, the volume's copyeditor, and Richard Wallis, the managing editor of the series. Jacob spotted endless details that kept us busy tracking down information for months, and Richard was both a no-nonsense advisor on nuts and bolts as well as a coordinator and occasional go-between for us and our contributors. Leo Balk and Barbara Curialle Gerr at Garland Publishing have each offered substantial support to our efforts, and we thank them for their time and energy. Philip Yampolsky took portions of the volume with him to some of the most remote regions of Borneo while completing his duties as an outside reader on time for us; we were impressed with his ability to send e-mail from nearly anywhere on the planet.

Finally, we want to express our genuine and heartfelt appreciation to our spouses, Sara Stone Miller and Cary Black, and to Sean's daughter Morgan (just an infant when Sean joined the project), who supported our long hours of work and endured our frequent excuses and absences on behalf of this volume. We are honored by their understanding and willingness to help us see this work through to completion.

We have done our best to prevent any errors from sneaking unnoticed into the final versions of the articles in this encyclopedia, but we recognize that a few may surface. We bear sole responsibility for these.

—Terry E. Miller and Sean Williams

Guide to Pronunciation

Thomas John Hudak

Listed below are approximate Engish equivalents to the sounds that appear in the Southeast Asian–language terms used in this volume.

GENERAL GUIDELINES

Unless otherwise indicated, vowels and consonants in Southeast Asian languages have the following English equivalents.

Vowels

Character	Pronounced as in English...
a	f*a*ther
ae, ac	b*a*t
e	b*ai*t
i	b*ea*t
o	b*oa*t
u	b*oo*t

Consonants

The consonants *p, t,* and *k* are unaspirated stops (without a puff of air) as in the English s*p*ill, s*t*ill, and s*k*ill. The consonant *c* is similar to the English sequence *t-y* in the phrase nex*t y*ear. The consonant cluster *ny* is similar to the English sequence *n-y* in the word ca*ny*on.

In contrast, *ph, th, ch,* and *kh* are aspirated stops (with a puff of air) as in the English *p*ill, *t*ill, *ch*ill, and *k*ill. The consonant *q* indicates a glottal stop, as in the sound that appears in the middle of the English sequence *oh-oh.* Glottal stops are also indicated in some languages with a ' symbol.

SPECIFIC LANGUAGE GROUPS

For names and terms in the articles listed below, exceptions to the general guidelines can be found in the appropriate chart. In all cases, vowels precede consonants, with both in English alphabetical order.

Khmer

For Khmer names and terms that appear in the article on the music of Cambodia, the following additional equivalents are suggested.

Character	Pronounced as in English...
ai	*ai*sle
ao	g*o*
au	c*ow*
ea	b*ai*t plus the vowel in b*u*t

Character	Pronounced as in English...
eu	b*u*t
ey	b*u*t plus the vowel in b*ea*t
ie	b*ea*t plus the vowel in b*u*t
oa	N*oa*h
oeu	n*ew* (with lips spread) + the vowel in b*u*t
ou	b*oo*t
uo	b*oo*t plus the vowel in b*u*t
Thailand	
aw	l*aw*
oe	but
ü	n*ew* (with lips spread)
u	b*oo*t
Burma	
ai	s*i*gn
au	s*ou*nd
e	b*e*t
ei	s*a*ne
o	s*aw*
ñ	(nasalizes the vowel that precedes it)
hy	*sh*ore
th	*th*aw
c, hc	*j*udge
k, hk	*g*ood
p	*b*ig
s	*z*oo
t	*d*o
Tones (shown with vowel *a)*	
a (unmarked tone)	low, level, long
à	high, long, falling toward the end
á	high, short, falling (with catch of breath)
a	high, short (with sharp catch of breath)
Laos	
ae	b*a*t
aw	l*aw*
oe	b*u*t
ou	b*oo*t
ü, eu	n*ew* (with lips spread)
x	*s*ing
Vietnam	
â	b*u*t
e	b*e*t
ê	b*ai*t
i, y	between b*ea*t and b*i*t
o	l*aw*
ô	n*o*
oa	*wa*nt
o	d*oe* (with lips spread)

Character	Pronounced as in English...
u	*new* (with lips spread)
d	*z*ero
d	*d*o
gi	*z*ero
nh	ca*ny*on
ph	*f*un
r	*z*ero
x	*s*on
Tones (shown with vowel *a*)	
a (unmarked)	midtone
á	high rising
à	low falling
a	falling, then rising
ã	high (with break in voice)
a	low (with break in voice)

Upland minorities

Akha people

ö	b*ai*t (with lips rounded)
ü	b*ea*t (with lips rounded)

Hmong

Final consonants indicate tone. Double vowels are nasalized.

b	high level
j	high falling
v	mid-rising
[no consonant]	mid-level
s	lower mid-level
g	low breathy
m	low glottalized ending
d	low rising

Lisu people

ü	n*ew* (with lips spread)

Indigenous people of the Malay Peninsula

ɛ	b*e*t
ə	b*u*t
ɨ	n*ew* (with lips spread)
ɔ	l*aw*
ɲ	ca*ny*on
ŋ	si*ng*
ʔ	oh-oh (glottal stop between syllables)

Indonesia

é	b*ai*t
è	b*e*t
eu	b*oo*k (with lips spread)
dh	*d*one

Contributing Authors

Christopher Basile
Monash University, Australia

Arnold Cabalza
University of the Philippines

Amy Catlin
University of California, Los Angeles, U.S.A.

James Chopyak
California State University, Sacramento, U.S.A.

Corazon Canave-Dioquino
University of the Philippines

David Harnish
Bowling Green State University
Bowling Green, Ohio, U.S.A.

Janet Hoskins
Monash University, Australia

Karl L. Hutterer
University of Washington, Seattle, U.S.A.

Margaret J. Kartomi
Monash University, Australia

Ward Keeler
University of Texas at Austin, U.S.A.

Lee Tong Soon
University of Pittsburgh, U.S.A.

René T. A. Lysloff
University of California, Riverside, U.S.A.

José Maceda
University of the Philippines

Patricia Matusky
Davis, California, U.S.A.

Terry E. Miller
Kent State University
Kent, Ohio, U.S.A.

Phong T. Nguyễn
Kent State University, Ohio, U.S.A.

Hans Oesch (deceased)
Basel, Switzerland

Panya Roongrüang
Kent, Ohio, U.S.A.

Marina Roseman
University of Maryland, College Park, U.S.A.

Sam-Ang Sam
Reston, Virginia, U.S.A.

Ramón P. Santos
University of the Philippines

Endo Suanda
University of Washington, Seattle, U.S.A.

R. Anderson Sutton
University of Wisconsin, Madison, U.S.A.

Ruriko Uchida (deceased)
Tokyo, Japan

Robert Wessing
University of Leiden, The Netherlands

Sean Williams
The Evergreen State College
Olympia, Washington, U.S.A.

Deborah Wong
University of California, Riverside, U.S.A.

Part 1
Introduction to Southeast Asia as a Musical Area

Most major Southeast Asian musics bear strong similarities to one another, crossing boundaries of culture, language, and land. But although bronze gongs, xylophones, and bamboo flutes link the musics of the region, there is nevertheless a remarkable diversity of peoples and musical styles. For centuries, the unique sounds and organizational systems of these musics have attracted outsiders—including dozens of scholars and the Western composers Debussy, Britten, and Reich.

Musicians of the restored court ensemble perform at the former Forbidden City in Huế, Vietnam. Photo by Terry E. Miller, 1993.

Southeast Asian Musics: An Overview

Terry E. Miller
Sean Williams

Scholars are trained to focus on significant details, and the deeper they go into a musical culture, the more they must deal with minutiae. The articles in Part 3, MUSICAL CULTURES AND REGIONS, as readers may rightly expect, go into detail about individual places, and for beginners this can be a daunting foray into a vortex of non-English words, technical terms, and conceptual diversity.

It would be good to have a broad view of the landscape before landing in any particular place. Then you could know the lay of the land—where the great rivers flow, where the mountain ranges divide regions, where the cities rise, where the main roads run. Such an overview is necessary for readers, but challenging to write, since no one knows everything. Nevertheless, we shall try to identify the most salient features of the Southeast Asian musical landscape.

REGIONAL ISSUES

The world is too large for holistic treatment; therefore, it is divided into continents and subcontinents. The subcontinent of Southeast Asia is also too large to be treated holistically; therefore, it is divided into two parts: mainland and islands. Within each division, the most obvious subdivision is the nation-state. Mainland Southeast Asia consists of seven nations (Burma, Cambodia, Laos, Malaysia, Singapore, Thailand, and Vietnam); island Southeast Asia consists of three (Brunei, Indonesia, the Philippines). Malaysia, extending into both divisions, is treated here as part of the mainland. Irian Jaya, the Indonesian province that occupies the western section of the island of New Guinea, is covered in the Oceania volume.

The national boundaries that demarcate Southeast Asia into its countries are recent and largely colonial inventions. Laos, a landlocked country, sandwiched among Vietnam, Cambodia, Thailand, Burma, and China, is a cobbled-together remnant of the spoils of war. The Republic of Indonesia came into being when Indonesians attained self-rule over the Netherlands East Indies. The Philippines was once a group of islands united in the name of a Spanish king's son, Felipe. Few of these countries developed an indigenous national consciousness before their national creation. Indeed, even within areas that have used the same linguistic and political systems for centuries, we have no reason to assume any kind of social, political, or musical unity.

The names of some nations (for example, Cambodia, Malaysia, Thailand) denote a dominant and mainstream culture, but the names of others do not. Culturally, the population of every country under consideration is far more complex than its national boundaries suggest. Consequently, it becomes problematic to describe everything within a country as particular to it: Filipino music, Thai music, Vietnamese music. Indeed, a term like *Indonesian music* suggests the existence of an artistic unity that represents all of Indonesia and no particular part or group. As with the commonly used term *African music,* there is not, in fact, any one Indonesian music; instead, there are Javanese musics, Balinese musics, Sundanese musics, and so on.

English terms that categorize musical types are rarely helpful when used outside the West (and can be misleading, even there). Applying such terms as *classical, folk,* and *popular* to musics in Southeast Asia can lead to frustration and misunderstanding because scholars only partially agree on what these terms denote. Other terms, such as *court, ritual, village,* and *mediated,* have been tried; some help, but some only raise further questions. Categories are rarely self-contained, because boundaries cannot be precisely established. Scholars are known for wringing their hands over terminology, for terminology speaks volumes about hierarchies, values, power, and other concepts of social relationships that affect music. Faced with the practical necessity of using the English language and denoting musical phenomena with specific terms, we step into the terminological minefield fully aware of its dangers, but having no guarantee of safety.

Lowland and upland peoples

Except for Singapore, all Southeast Asian nations have both lowland plains, usually drained by a major river, and upland areas, which may be either vast plateaus or rugged mountain ranges. Nearly every country or region discussed in this volume is tied in some way to the ocean, and some areas (especially in the island regions) are frequently rattled by earthquakes and volcanic eruptions. The way the land shapes and is shaped by its inhabitants has an impact on differences in musical production. Most nonmainstream minorities live in upland areas, and most of the dominant population lives in lowlands. Since most minorities differ in language and life-style from the dominant people, their musics are usually so different as to bear no comparison to those of the dominant people. Thus, it makes sense to treat minority musics separately.

Cultural differences affected by local geography lead scholars to a variety of questions about music and land. How has the isolation of upland tribes affected their choices in musical instrumentation? To what extent does the cultivation and consumption of rice have an impact on ritual performances? Does interisland commerce lead to musical trade among the islands? Is there any type of musical communication between upland and lowland peoples? Does the presence of volcanoes lead to the creation of certain types of musical performance? Each of these questions takes the physical geography of the region into account, and hundreds of others could be devised.

Regionalism

Each country of Southeast Asia displays diversity of culture and population. Each has more than one cultural region, even within the majority population. These are never completely discrete but may exhibit individuality in language (dialect or accent), central literary works, clothing, architecture, cuisine, musical instruments, and musical styles. In some countries (such as Thailand), a regional culture has been adopted

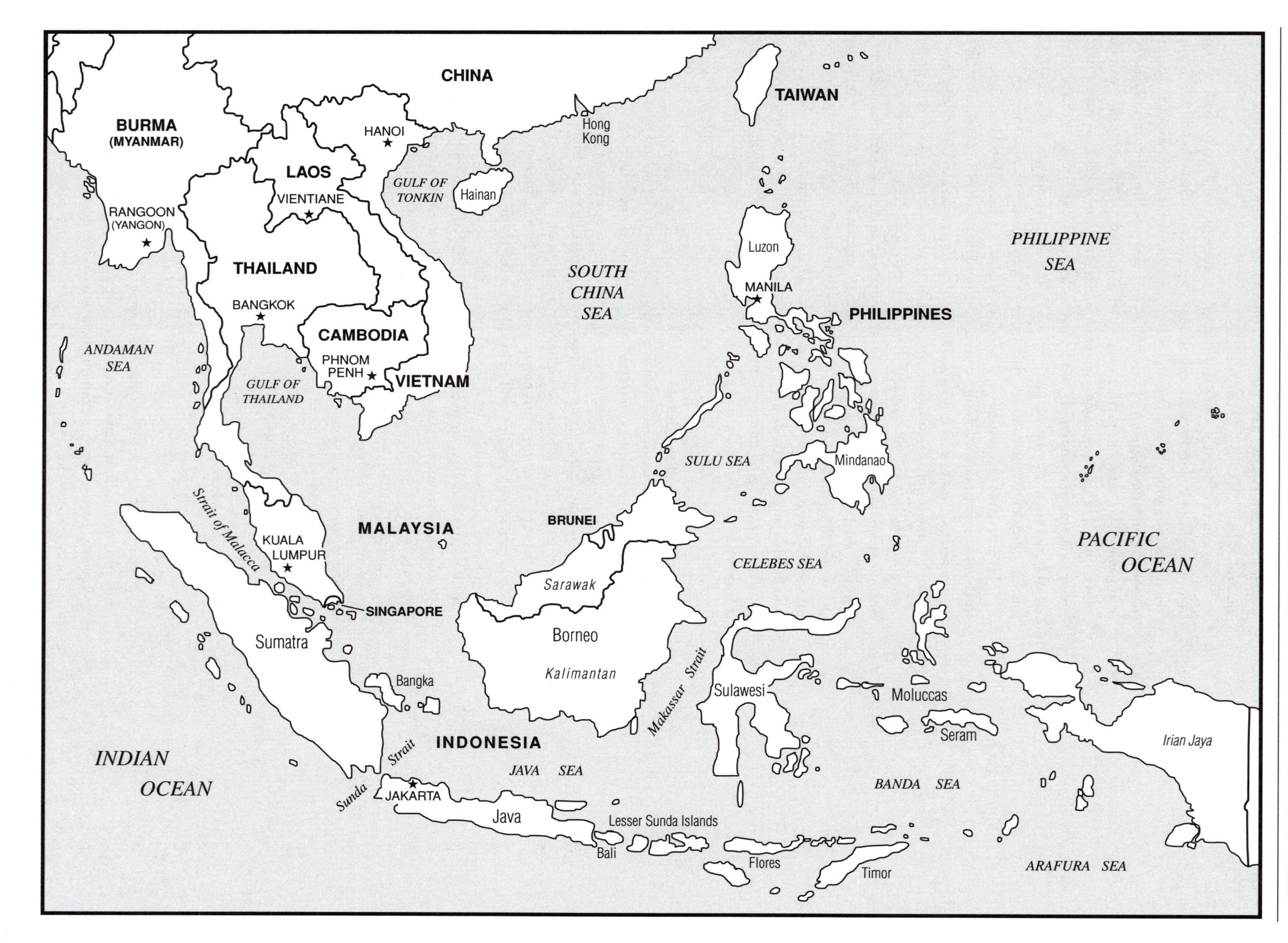
CHINA
TAIWAN
BURMA (MYANMAR)
HANOI
Hong Kong
LAOS
VIENTIANE
GULF OF TONKIN
Hainan
RANGOON (YANGON)
THAILAND
SOUTH CHINA SEA
Luzon
PHILIPPINE SEA
MANILA
BANGKOK
PHILIPPINES
CAMBODIA
ANDAMAN SEA
PHNOM PENH
VIETNAM
GULF OF THAILAND
SULU SEA
Mindanao
Strait of Malacca
MALAYSIA
BRUNEI
PACIFIC OCEAN
KUALA LUMPUR
CELEBES SEA
Sarawak
SINGAPORE
Borneo
Sumatra
Kalimantan
Bangka
Makassar Strait
Sulawesi
Moluccas
Seram
Irian Jaya
INDONESIA
INDIAN OCEAN
Sunda Strait
JAVA SEA
BANDA SEA
JAKARTA
Java
Lesser Sunda Islands
Bali
Flores
Timor
ARAFURA SEA

as the national culture. Whether the other regional cultures are viewed as challenges to the dominant culture or as complements to it depends on the time and place.

Regionalism is most likely to be tolerated, even celebrated, in countries that have achieved stability based on the "national" culture—true of both Thailand and Indonesia. Where such a consensus has not been reached, or where the lack of mass communications allows the maintenance of regional distinctiveness, all regions may be near-equals, or even rivals; in the latter case, regionalism works against nationhood and may consequently be suppressed. Regionalism is mainly an issue within the dominant culture, leaving minority groups largely on the outside.

Urban and rural

Asian cities reflect least the distinctiveness of "traditional" and especially regional culture. Many of the first centers of population in Southeast Asia were Hindu-Buddhist courts and commercial cities. The courts functioned as places to house the person in power with accompanying family, personnel, and regalia; the entire city would be laid out according to its relationship to the center. Many of these cities were inland. Commercial cities drew most of their population from those interested in profiting from trade; these cities tended to be located either at the crossroads of major inland trade routes or in ports. Commercial cities are laid out according to needs of access in relation to the market. Once Islam had become established in Southeast Asia, a kind of Muslim city developed, particularly in Malaysia and Indonesia; it included a large mosque located at the center of the city. Last, colonial administrative cities were created by various colonial empires, either on the foundations of other types of cities, or out of areas that appeared convenient for administration and commerce.

(opposite) Southeast Asia

Cities are the most modern places in a country, and the main cities are the most internationalized. The most modern cities of Southeast Asia are Singapore, Jakarta, Kuala Lumpur, Bangkok, Manila, and Hồ Chí Minh City (Saigon); the least modern include Rangoon (Yangon), Vientiane, Phnom Penh, and Hanoi (though Hanoi is rapidly changing). The largest cities often attract the regional poor, seeking opportunities. Money earned from urban wages is frequently channeled back to villages, and most urbanites maintain close ties to family and friends in villages. Cities, then, tend to develop pan-urban cultures, though pockets of regional populations sometimes maintain aspects of their culture. Urban populations have the greatest choices of musical styles, especially from the media, and are most thoroughly exposed to mass culture.

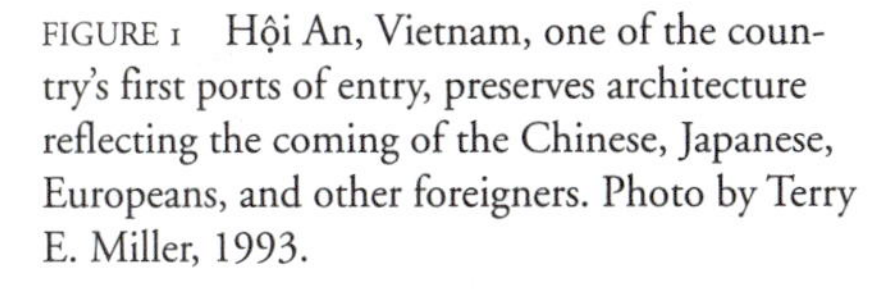
FIGURE 1 Hội An, Vietnam, one of the country's first ports of entry, preserves architecture reflecting the coming of the Chinese, Japanese, Europeans, and other foreigners. Photo by Terry E. Miller, 1993.

It is largely true that if you do not live in a city, you live in a village. Depending on the country's level of poverty or prosperity, village life may be slow to change (as in Borneo, Burma, certain areas of Indonesia, Laos, Cambodia, and Vietnam) or much affected by modernization (as in the Philippines, Malaysia, and Thailand). Some villagers with homes that once stood on the outskirts of Southeast Asia's cities now find themselves surrounded by factories, airports, bus terminals, and housing developments. Dispersed throughout many of the largest cities are village enclaves, complete with chickens, wells, tiny plots of cultivated land, and rural people (figure 2).

The poverty of village life tends to preserve its traditionality. At least in earlier times, village cultural life centered on cycles related to agriculture, religion, and the calendar. Songs and rituals are, or were, associated with various stages of agriculture (especially the growing of rice) and seasonal rituals and festivities. In general, musical activities ceased during the rainy season, which in Theravada Buddhist countries (Burma, Cambodia, Laos, Thailand) coincides with the Buddhist period of withdrawal, when rice requires little attention, allowing males to be ordained and to withdraw into a temple to earn spiritual merit.

Because this music originated in villages, where people must work year-round to maintain house, family, and food supply, it tends to be simpler than that found in cities, particularly in the mainland regions. Few music specialists support themselves through performance, and anyone with a modicum of talent may sing and play music. Musical instruments tend to be user friendly and simple, made from locally available materials (though exceptions occur).

The theme of courtship permeates village musics throughout Southeast Asia. Courtship was formerly ritualized and in places remains so. Males and females alternated performing various forms of repartee, creating veritable gender wars, based on wit and double entendre. The texts of repartee transmitted rural wisdoms, reminding listeners of their history, literature, role models, religion, and sometimes even "the facts of life." In its fundamental forms, ritualized courtship could be spoken (as with Lao *phanya*), but most forms involve some kind of heightened speech or song, with or without an instrument. In some places, certain performers grew so highly skilled that they became professional or semiprofessional entertainers, and the original function of courtship metamorphosed into a paid exhibition of talent.

FIGURE 2 In Yogyakarta, Java, small villages coexist with modern urban accouterments within the boundaries of the city. Photo by Sean Williams, 1989.

Classical, folk, popular

A tripartite division of music into classical, folk, and popular has limited validity in Southeast Asia. Each term creates dilemmas. *Classical* has connotations of sophistication, high value, being representative of the best of a culture and expressive of political and economic power, what Milton Singer has called Great Tradition of a culture. In Burma, Cambodia, and Thailand, scholars agree on what genres fit the classical category; for Laos, Malaysia, the Philippines, Singapore, and Vietnam, they do not. Substituting *court* for *classical,* as some writers do with Cambodian, Javanese, and Thai musics, is not necessarily better, for the music described as *court* was never restricted to a court and survives today—at least in Thailand and Cambodia—entirely outside the context of a court, even in villages.

Regardless of the term, "classical" musics have several traits in common. Musical instruments play a prominent role. Some are complex and highly decorated, and performance on them requires advanced technical skills. The repertory is usually extensive, requiring the undivided attention of musicians who must memorize complex works, practice long hours, and play for a variety of occasions, some ceremonial, some ritualistic, some for entertainment. These musics often require enough surplus wealth to allow the musicians to give their full attention to the art of music and to be relieved of any necessity of growing their food, providing their shelter, and securing their safety. Consequently, musics called classical are often associated with an aristocracy, or at least a wealthy elite. There is also a consensus among the wealthy elite that these musics best represent the culture of the nation to the outside world, whether the citizenry commonly listens to them or not.

Such definitions create few problems in categorizing some Burmese, Thai, Cambodian, and Indonesian musics as "classical," but elsewhere the issue becomes thorny. Though Laos has a "classical" music similar to that of Thailand, it is less extensive and sophisticated. Laos arguably has a classical music, but the tradition was damaged when the Pathet Lao (a Communist party) banned such "aristocratic decadence" in 1975, and the country's poverty and lack of an aristocracy prevent this kind of music from flowering beyond a minimal level. Vietnam's imperial court is long gone, and though its music survived until the 1970s, it was never widely known or played. Today, it has been revived, but more as a symbol of the city of Huế than as a symbol of the country. Malaysia, formerly a collection of sultanates, had royal music and entertainment, but these barely survive in isolated pockets. The term *Malaysian classical music,* like *Vietnamese classical music,* has no clear meaning. The Philippines has been so deeply Christianized that its current classical-music traditions are direct responses to Western European classical music; its nearest relative to other Southeast Asian classical traditions, the *kulintang,* is not locally promoted as a classical music.

For there to be folk music, there must be an identifiable group of people who constitute the folk. Urban people assume these folks are other people, usually villagers. If the term has any currency, it usually denotes the music heard in villages, frequently performed by nonspecialists, and usually associated with "functional" contexts, like rituals, festivals, and daily activities. The accessibility of bamboo for large portions of the rural Southeast Asian population has led to the prevalence of bamboo flutes, rattles, and other musical instruments. By a similar token, the need for inexpensive, easily available, lightweight instruments (such as small plucked lutes and Jew's harps) by certain inland and upland groups throughout Southeast Asia is understandable, considering the limits on resources, craftsmen, and portability. Villagers also perform on both flat and bossed gongs in what appear to be some of the most remote areas; however, the gongs and their methods of suspension tend to be less elaborate than in the courts or cities. Vocal music, wordplay, and poetic competition are strongly valued in most Southeast Asian rural traditions.

FIGURE 3 Villagers pump water in a quiet village in northeast Thailand. Photo by Terry E. Miller, 1992.

Important objects—including certain daggers, bronze drums, gongs, and masks—carry their own special kind of power and are believed to have an impact on people, places, and other objects.

In countries such as Cambodia, Laos, and Thailand, scholars make a clear distinction between classical and folk musics, but for Vietnam, no such distinction can be made. Since Vietnam does not have an agreed-upon classical music, Vietnamese musics are usually distinguished as traditional or modernized. Vietnam has the strongest Western classical-music tradition in mainland Southeast Asia, with Malaysia and Singapore running a close second and third, and its intellectual and cultural elite has received training in Western music in the conservatories of France, the former Soviet Union, and other Eastern European states. They prefer that Vietnam be represented by modernized compositions, leaving traditional music to fend for itself. At the same time, the kinds of traditional music being used to represent the nation to the outside world—water-puppet theater and chamber music—clearly derive from village culture. Folk songs may be sung by farmers in a rough voice, but they are also played by skilled amateurs (nonprofessionals) on finely decorated instruments in formal situations.

Whether derived from traditional indigenous music or influenced by outside cultures (especially the United States, Hong Kong, India, the Middle East, and Japan), the popular-music category is least debatable. Primarily disseminated through the media to almost all members of society, regardless of regional origin, income level, or degree of musical sophistication, this music has become predominant, or at least present, in people's lives. Not surprisingly, it is most developed in countries having the greatest wealth and urbanization—Thailand, Singapore, Malaysia, Indonesia, and the Philippines. Utilizing a creative combination of Western instrumentation and blended linguistic and musical features, it may be heard not only within the borders of such cities as Bangkok, Manila, and Singapore, but also in the remotest villages. It draws from a variety of traditions to appeal to the broadest number of listeners and therefore to become as commercially successful as possible. Vietnam's popular tradition derives from a movement to modernize the country, which led to the creation of both entertainment and revolutionary songs in Western style. Though Vietnam is considerably urbanized, it remains too poor to afford the music videos, spectacular pop concerts, compact discs, and slick nightclubs that make popular music powerful elsewhere. In other mainland Southeast Asian countries, the popular-music industry is modest, little more than a cottage industry of small shops copying small quantities of locally produced cassettes.

Networks of power and influence

Southeast Asian lands support millions of people, from kings and presidents to roadside vendors and beggars. Its alluvial plains and terraced hillsides are fertile ground for agriculture; indeed, most Southeast Asians are involved in agricultural endeavors. In addition to agriculture, every Southeast Asian country supports its own versions of governmental, economic, educational, religious, and legal systems. The diversity of systems within each nation reflects that nation's history, colonial ties, and current phase of modernization. What each country has in common with the others, however, is a local understanding of the concentration and dispersal of power.

In some areas of the world (particularly the West), power has often been measured by the strength of a nation's borders and that nation's ability to accumulate land. In Southeast Asia, power is usually centered in a person, a place, or an object. Strong, dynamic rulers who have gathered a large number of followers can wield power in a radiating field; those closest to the ruler have more power, while those farther away have less. Places such as Java's Borobudur or Cambodia's Angkor Wat are invested locally with the power ascribed to sacred sites that have withstood the ravages of time and wars. Important objects—including certain daggers, bronze drums, gongs, and masks—carry their own special kind of power and are believed to have an impact on people, places, and other objects.

Southeast Asian musical contexts tend to reflect the influences and behavior of persons believed to have some kind of power. Patrons of music might be responsible for owning and protecting an ensemble's musical instruments, for arranging performances, and for paying the musicians. The musical leader of an ensemble, however, might attract fellow musicians on the basis of outstanding musicianship. In Muslim countries or regions, a musician who has been to Mecca is usually considered purer and therefore more powerful than one who has not. In some cases, fame (as from a hit recording) confers power; however, it may be locally considered less enduring than power achieved through other means. As with Southeast Asian political leaders, power ascribed to particular musicians or patrons is fleeting and can shift to other people as circumstances dictate.

The traditional investment of inanimate objects with power has an impact on musical performance and functions as a determinant of musical hierarchies across Southeast Asia. This situation is more widely encountered in the islands than on the mainland. Within a typically stratified gong-chime ensemble, instrumentation usually includes one or more large gongs (or their equivalents), smaller gongs, a gong chime, multiple xylophones or metallophones, a set of drums, and stringed or wind instruments that serve an ornamental or melodic function. The gong or gong equivalent is the spiritual center of the ensemble. It acts as the periodic marker for the beginning, ending, and cyclic points within each performance. Ritual offerings, if

FIGURE 4 Java's eighth-century Borobudur temple, covered with detailed stone carvings, reflects the ruler's power as deriving from the gods themselves. Photo by Sean Williams.

they are made, are traditionally offered to the gong, which guides the entire ensemble. Though the gong typically has the easiest musical role to play (in terms of how it is struck during a performance), its spiritual weight is considerable. Instruments considered difficult to play may have little spiritual weight. In a musical performance, any Southeast Asian ensemble could probably do without many of the instruments that play a decorative function, but a performance without a gong is unthinkable.

Unresolved questions

Some fundamental questions regarding the musics of Southeast Asia, particularly their interrelationships, beg for resolution, but require evidence that is either unavailable or nonexistent. National pride sometimes clashes with conclusions suggested by the evidence. This is particularly true regarding questions of what is indigenous and what is acculturated. The following represent a sampling of these questions.

Identities

Who are the Burmese, the Cambodians, the Filipinos, the Indonesians, the Lao, the Malay, the Thai, and the Vietnamese? In prehistoric times, were there original and identifiable cultures directly related to those of today? Did these people migrate from somewhere, particularly an area of present-day China, to their present location? To what extent are these mainstream groups actually the result of the mixing of earlier groups and therefore the sum of their parts? For example, if the X people allegedly migrated from Yunnan, China, what happened to the indigenous people who were then occupying X's present-day lands? These questions are particularly pertinent in Thailand (and its Ban Chiang culture) and Vietnam (and its Đông Sơn and Hoà Bình cultures). If there is no "ethnic purity," how and when did the people who came to be called X develop a distinctive culture?

Authenticities

Relative to music, what is indigenous and what is acculturated? Outsiders, with their panoramic (but oftentimes superficial) views of Asian musics, are quick to see similarities among cultures, particularly in their organologies. They have few inhibitions about pointing out similarities that may or may not demonstrate relationships. Indigenous scholars and musicians, however, are more likely to assert the uniqueness of their own culture and may even resent the implication that their forebears borrowed this or that from another culture, particularly from a supposedly greater one. They are right to complain that outsiders often assume that "Indochina" had little culture of its own until it was "civilized" by Asia's two most prominent civilizations, China and India, and the term *Indochina* implies such. Why, they ask, could it not be the other way around? The fact that China and India can provide earlier documents does not, of course, prove their precedence.

In some cases, relationships are obvious, but the direction of the influence may not be. The hammered zither in mainland Southeast Asia appears to be of Chinese origin; some scholars believe that the Italian missionary Matteo Ricci took the instrument to China from Western Asia, but there is evidence that he visited Vietnam first. Many Southeast Asian two-stringed fiddles resemble those of China, but were they derived from China? Balinese, Burmese, Javanese, Khmer, Lao, Sundanese, and Thai classical dances might be dismissed as local manifestations of Indian dances because both traditions use a vocabulary of gestures of the hands, but whether this is true or not, the question is, To what extent did each culture modify the Indian system? Most of the musical cultures under discussion have cyclic metrical systems. Can we assume this trait came also from India because we know of the system of talas? or is this a logic with no single origin? Similarities do not prove relationships.

At least part of this debate, one that boils down to "originality" and "native creativity" versus "dependency" and "inferiority," is based on the false premise that the "great" donor nations themselves had invented the phenomena in question. Much of what is Chinese or Indian was earlier borrowed or acculturated from elsewhere too, and the original source—if there be one—could in some cases have been Southeast Asia.

Regardless of the source of its cultural artifacts, each country in Southeast Asia has evolved an individualized expression. Whether the Thai *saw duang* derives from the Chinese Chaozhou *touxian* or not, the former has a distinct shape, timbre, and playing technique separate from those of the latter. Even when a borrowed instrument remains unchanged, the musical style of the original culture seldom comes with it.

Retentions

Which cultures represent the earliest stages of culture in Southeast Asia? Eventually this question becomes an issue of whether the upland, minority, and usually marginalized peoples represent the earliest surviving stages of culture or merely echo the majority, dominant cultures. To say it another way: do the musical artifacts found in, say, the mountains of Vietnam indicate the earliest stages of Southeast Asian music? If so, then these instruments are most likely indigenous because these peoples show the least Indian, Chinese, or other outside influence. Since many speak distinct languages, did they precede the majority groups? And if this is so, did they formerly live in the lowlands and get forced into the uplands by newly arriving peoples?

If upland peoples preserve indigenous culture, then we can suppose that instruments like knobbed bronze gongs, bamboo and metal Jew's harps, bronze-drum idiophones, free-reed pipes and mouth organs, and vertically strung bamboo xylophones are fundamental to Southeast Asia. Can we further assume, then, that gong-chime ensembles, like the Thai *piphat,* the Cambodian *pinn peat,* and the Indonesian gamelan, developed from these organological layers? Can we assume that island Southeast Asia received its bronze instruments from the mainland? Does the presence of some of these allegedly original instruments on Borneo and beyond suggest an earlier transmission of culture, either over a prehistoric land bridge or by migrating sailors?

Conquests

If, as in the case of early Siam, the victors of war traditionally carried off much of the vanquished population, including entire musical organizations, thereby implanting new instruments, genres, and styles into their own culture, does this mean that Thai music reflects an earlier stage of Cambodian music? Was there also Cambodian influence in Lao court music because the Luang Phrabang court was established with the help of the Khmer? Did the Burmese acquire instruments similar to Thai instruments only after 1767, when the Burmese conquered Ayuthaya? Does current Balinese music sound anything like fourteenth-century Javanese music, which was at least partially transplanted to Bali?

Languages

Are there musical characteristics unique to language families? If we knew everything about all branches of a given language family (say, the Tai), could we find certain traits that are distinctively Tai? In the case of the Tai, we would want to know which branches are closest to the original Tai, the least influenced by outside cultures. Can we assume the groups living closest to a probably original homeland are the most conservative of related groups?

Each Southeast Asian music can be heard as a unique mixture of spices: some cuisines are spicier than others; some are an acquired taste.

Documentation

Do historical documents shed light on any of these processes? The writing of a history of Southeast Asian music has yet to occur. Historical documents are nonexistent in many cases and are often incomplete, undatable, or unreliable. Recording and preserving documents related to music seems not to have been a priority. Wars and the ravages of humidity, insects, fires, and floods guarantee that even where such documents exist, they are fragile. Often the most detailed and reliable documents were created by foreigners, especially Chinese visitors.

Iconographical evidence in stone carvings, murals, and other sources is valuable, though sometimes difficult to date. Unrestored paintings may show great deterioration, and restored paintings raise questions of authenticity, especially when the original had completely flaked away before the restoration. Early accounts written by Westerners, though invariably ethnocentric and sometimes condescending, shed valuable light in some areas, particularly organology, function, and the existence of certain genres, especially theatrical ones.

HOW TO LISTEN TO SOUTHEAST ASIAN MUSICS

This volume was not designed to be a sound-centered textbook, but we offer the reader a framework on which to become familiar with the musical sounds of the region. The compact disc included with the volume offers representative examples of music, but it is too limited to provide an ideal spectrum of sounds. For a fairly complete list of available recordings, the reader is referred to the discography at the end of the volume, with the caveat that not everything listed has equal value in representation, performance quality, recording quality, annotational quality, and accuracy. The following essay is intended to be a preliminary guide for listeners with little previous experience listening to Southeast Asian musics.

Two approaches to listening

One can respond to music on at least two levels, sensually and intellectually. Perhaps too often pedagogues take an intellectual, cognitive approach, insisting that listeners "understand," "know," and "appreciate" the music being heard. Ultimately, this is necessary, especially if one is to teach or explain the music to someone else. Such communication also requires the use of a technical vocabulary, which, though often denoting concepts that exist only in the mind, are customarily described in analogous terms—timbre, texture, melodic contour, and extramusicality. Even without this kind of knowledge, however, we can respond on sensual and emotional levels to the beauty and power of the music. This approach is not to be avoided if the novice listener has reservations about his or her ability to understand the sounds of these musics.

The sensual response

Music consists of vibrations, perceived as sound when transmitted through the ear to the brain. For sounds to be perceived as music, the listener must perceive them as an ordered process, playing out in real time. John Blacking defined music as "humanly organized sound" (1973:10). In a sense, then, music is a microcosm of order, which proceeds according to a known and perceivable plan. To go beyond this notion is to enter the realm of the intellect and its cognitive abilities—which leads to the intellectualization of music. Preceding this stage, however, is one where the listener may respond to music as a purely sensual experience, a series of sensed physical vibrations that feel good in the way a massage, a pleasant smell or taste, or a beautiful image feels good. One possibility is for the listener simply to let go, relax, and allow the vibrations to wash over without reference to cognitive knowledge. In doing so, the listener can appreciate Southeast Asian musics on one level, possibly the level on which many Southeast Asians appreciate it.

Who, having heard the heavy, golden, bronze instruments of a gamelan, can resist its siren call? This is music you can feel. Softly struck metal, slow rates of decay, clashing vibrations, produce a quality of sound that is nearly irresistible. No wonder that French composer Claude Debussy was enthralled on hearing and feeling the Javanese gamelan that in 1889 visited Paris! No wonder that so many Western educational institutions have purchased gamelans! No wonder that some Westerners go into voluntary exile in the land of the gamelan, or become obsessed with playing its music! And a consumer of music has choices: the power and stateliness of the Javanese gamelan's loud style, the dreaminess of its soft style, the hyperenergy of the Balinese *gong kebyar.*

Something can be said for an analogy between cuisine and music. Each Southeast Asian music can be heard as a unique mixture of spices: some cuisines are spicier than others; some are an acquired taste. Certain musics, such as Thai classical, Javanese court gamelan, and Lao *lam,* have a smoothness and consistency quite dissimilar to the pungent flavors of Burmese *hsaìñ,* Vietnamese chamber music, or Balinese gamelans. Just as some foods may not appeal to us on first tasting, some musics may not appeal on first hearing. Perhaps we could draw an analogy between

FIGURE 5 An intricately crafted mother-of-pearl design on a door at Bangkok's Wut Rajabophit illustrates the Thai penchant for symmetry within a totally decorated panel, a visual analog to the construction of Thai classical music. Photo by Terry E. Miller, 1992.

the feeling one gets from a cup of strong Southeast Asian coffee and listening to the nervous busyness of Toba Batak (Sumatran) melodies.

The intellectual response

Perceiving music is not only a holistic experience but also one that occurs out of sight and beyond touch—within the brain. Verbalizing music, what Charles Seeger called speech about music, partakes of an altogether different realm, language. To intellectualize about music, the listener must dissect the holism of sound systematically into constituent elements, all of which must be expressed in analogous terms or through physical demonstration. These elements of music are commonly listed as *medium* (what makes the sound), *melody* (an organized succession of tones), *rhythm* and *meter* (the organization of sounds in time), *texture* (the relationship among the music's constituent elements), *form* (structural organization), *timbre* (qualities of sound), and *extramusicality* (nonmusical meaning). We cannot possibly discuss all these elements in all the musics covered in this volume, but we do wish to point out certain of their more obvious challenges.

In-tuneness and out-of-tuneness are culturally learned norms. Westerners, not to mention many non-Westerners, have been conditioned to accept a twelve-tone, equal-tempered system of tuning as the norm of in-tuneness. Many Southeast Asian musics, however, use systems of tuning that are neither equally tempered nor organized in twelve steps. The fixed-pitch instruments of the Thai classical ensemble are tuned to seven equidistant tones, many of them out of tune in comparison with the Western system, but nonfixed-pitch instruments (such as bowed lutes and the voice) or flexibly pitched instruments (such as the flute) diverge even more, through portamentos and subtle ornamentation. Certain intervals in many Vietnamese scales diverge from any found in the Western equal-tempered system. Indonesian gamelans are uniquely tuned in nonequidistant steps. These systems of tuning contradict the Western notion that tuning is a natural process (equal temperament aside), based on the overtone series.

If anything is challenging to listeners unfamiliar with Southeast Asian musics, it is their timbres. Western ideas of pleasant and beautiful sounds may be encountered, but a great many instruments—including the human voice—produce sounds perceived as unpleasant and even ugly by some uninitiated listeners. It is difficult to describe timbres except by analogy, and using words like *nasal, raspy, strident, piercing,* and *clunky* may tell more about the listener's norms than about the music. Timbre may pose the greatest challenge to people meeting Southeast Asian musics for the first time.

As quoted above, Blacking's assertion that music is "humanly organized sound" presumes that music is organized. An understanding of all the constituent elements of music does not guarantee that the listener will perceive that organization, however. Formal order, though present, is often difficult or even impossible to recognize. Without detailed analysis from a fully notated transcription or a crystal-clear oral interpretation from an insider (or at least an informed outsider), there is little chance the listener can perceive the subtle recurrence of unifying motives or a sophisticated rondolike structure.

Knowing that music is organized raises a question: how is it created? Those accustomed to European-American traditions expect to find the name of a composer specified on a notated score. But the absence of scores—and in most cases, composers' names—does not mean the absence of composers. Musicians do play compositions throughout Southeast Asia, but these works are rarely notated, are performatively flexible, and are customarily transmitted orally.

The term *improvisation* comes immediately to mind as a second possibility for creating music. In English, that term implies a process that is free, loose, and unpredictable; in a negative sense, it is something musicians do when they cannot perform a composition or have forgotten one—a strategy for getting out of trouble, or worse, "faking it." In Asia, the term is normally associated with the concept of mode. In English usage, a mode is simply a scale that is neither minor nor major, as in the ecclesiastical modes of Europe (Dorian, Mixolydian, and so on). In Asian contexts, the term denotes a complex of elements, both musical and extramusical, that are together the basis for the creation—that is, composition—of music. These include pitch-based material, which can be ordered in ascending and descending patterns (scales); a hierarchy of tones, starting from or implying a resting point (the tonic); particular melodic and rhythmic motives appropriate to a particular mode; obligatory ornaments; cadential formulas; and a customary character or mood. Mode can govern anything from fully written composition to on-the-spot improvisation, the latter being simply a nonpermanent composition, created simultaneously with its first performance. As such, modal improvisation is not an expression of freedom, but a disciplined and bounded process. Possibly the most famous Asian modal system is embodied in the Indian terms *rag* and *rāga.*

In many traditions, mode has been a nonformalized, unarticulated, and intuitively practiced process. This is true in Lao and northeastern Thai music for the free-reed mouth organ (*khaen*). Northeastern Thai players customarily use five named modes (*lai sutsanaen, lai yai,* and so on), each preceded by the word *lai.* Though few players would explain this systematically, all will stay within a given set of constraints when spontaneously creating compositions in a given *lai.*

In the Javanese system, the term *pathet* embodies the concept of mode and governs the creation of relatively fixed compositions. Though only the skeletal structure of the composition is firmly fixed, the elements added in performance are also controlled by the conventions of a particular mode. Musicians in Java are well aware of their modal system, but Thai classical musicians, though they also operate within a modal system, are less aware of it, and do not articulate its conventions. Burma has modal systems too, and they are unusually complex because their terminologies vary according to the instrument, especially between the harp and *hsaìñ*-ensemble instruments.

Vietnam preserves Southeast Asia's fullest modal system, the *điệu* system, which governs the creation of fixed compositions and extended improvisations. Each mode consists of a set of tones, certain of which require ornamentation or vibrato. Each has a specific modal character or mood. Though ensembles play fixed compositions, each musician customarily warms up with a brief, free modal improvisation (*rao*) before all join together in playing the piece. Within the piece, each musician maintains the fixed structure but realizes the melody according to the mode and the idiom of the instrument.

Texture creates challenges equal to those of timbre. Southeast Asian ensemble musics may confront hearers with a seemingly chaotic matrix of sounds. Knowing that all performers are playing the same composition may even deepen the confusion, since it may sound more like each musician is playing a *different* composition simultaneously. These statements are more true of some Southeast Asian musics than others, but certain of them—Thai, Vietnamese, Indonesian, and especially Burmese—are particularly daunting to sort out aurally.

After listening to such an ensemble, we might draw an analogy with Southeast Asian traffic patterns. The degree of confusion varies from one city to another, and the rules of negotiation vary dramatically, but one can observe this phenomenon in virtually any Asian city choked with traffic—Bangkok, Hồ Chí Minh City, Manila, Jakarta. The roads have clearly painted lanes, but few drivers stay within them; they

In much Southeast Asian ensemble music, individual players are free to vary their parts each time they play a composition. The result may sound as chaotic as Bangkok's traffic appears, but both processes have a logic of their own.

FIGURE 6 Many busy intersections in Vietnam's Hồ Chí Minh City lack traffic controls, but drivers carefully negotiate to keep all four directions flowing at once. Photo by Terry E. Miller, 1993.

treat the lanes merely as suggestions. All manner of vehicles use every bit of pavement, even the sidewalks. The object is to arrive at a final destination, but normally this requires passing through periodic points of control—traffic signals, traffic police, and roundabouts. Between these intersections, each driver is free to use whatever space is open, weaving this way and that, cutting in, holding back, rushing ahead, to arrive at the next point of control, where all drivers must come together again before proceeding.

Much Southeast Asian ensemble music moves in this way. In Thai classical music, the composition consists of a skeletal structure whose tones regularly occur at points articulated by a pair of small cymbals (*ching*), which play two strokes, *ching* and *chap*. The *chap* falls on the last beat of each cycle, making Thai music end-accented, rather than front-accented, as is usual in Western music. These points are like the controlled intersections negotiated by Bangkok's traffic: the *chap*, at the end of each cycle, are more highly controlled moments than the other sounds. Between these points, however, individual players, working within the constraints of their own instrument's idiom, are free in most cases to vary their parts each time they play the composition. The result may sound as chaotic as Bangkok's traffic appears, but both processes have a logic of their own. And the rules vary from one city to another. Bangkok drivers would most likely get into trouble driving in Hồ Chí Minh City, where major intersections are sometimes without controls and all four directions proceed continuously. Not surprisingly, Vietnamese music is less clearly controlled, and sometimes the musicians seem to be apart in their beats.

Individual regions

These thoughts should make sense when read in conjunction with performances of various Southeast Asian musics. The following paragraphs offer more specific pointers for the most prominently known musics of each country.

Mainland Southeast Asia

Vietnam

Vietnamese music is played largely on instruments derived from China, modified to suit the Vietnamese musical aesthetic, but the two musical systems differ fundamentally. Vietnamese music is created within a modal system that allows both improvisation and composition. These modes often require ornaments or vibrato on specified tones, and indeed, one of the salient features of Vietnamese music is its ornateness.

Vietnamese chordophones have unusually high frets and loose strings, allowing for much bending of tones. Vietnamese music is also noteworthy for the syncopation of its rhythms, made all the clearer by a rhythmic instrument that marks certain beats in the cycle. In texture, there are often striking differences among instruments, in both melodic contour and rhythm. The pervasive bending of tones is especially expressive in the sadder, more minor-sounding modes, giving the music a somewhat plaintive flavor.

Thailand

Much has been said about the texture of Thai classical music and its seeming chaos upon first hearing. Though the listener may know intellectually that Thai music is actually highly organized, even square, he or she may not be able to hear the organization easily. First, one must listen for duple metrical organization, articulated by the cymbals (*ching*), with their constantly alternating *ching* and *chap* (some pieces use nothing but *ching*). One can also focus on the drums, which usually play regular cyclic patterns with little variation. These cycles provide a clear and rather rigid matrix, within which Thai composers and performers are required to play.

One can then focus on individual instruments. Unless a *piphat* or *mahori* is clearly recorded with a microphone on the larger gong circle (which plays the fundamental form of the composition), the listener will more likely focus on the leading instruments—the higher xylophone (*ranat ek*), or the higher fiddle (*saw duang*). The fiddle tends to play a fairly clear melodic form of the work, but the xylophone plays a variation of it, usually in constantly and evenly moving octaves. This motion, however, masks the articulation of phrases, and one sometimes wonders how the player could possibly memorize this seemingly random peregrination of tones, the aural equivalent of unwinding a large ball of string. If the ensemble includes a double-reed oboe (*pi nai*), its part is usually so different from those of the rest of the ensemble, so free in rhythm, so flexible in pitch, that the listener may wonder what it has to do with the work at all. Such are the challenges of listening to Thai classical music, especially the "high" repertory associated with ceremony. But actually, a great number of pieces are primarily organized as memorable melodic phrases; these constitute the "light classical" repertory and include some of the country's favorite pieces.

Cambodia

In comparison to the classical music of Thailand (especially the "high" repertory), Cambodian classical music seems simpler and easier to follow. This situation is due in part to less individual virtuosity and the fact that the double-reed oboe (*sralai*) plays a basic form of the melody rather than an elaborated one. Another easy way to distinguish Cambodian music from Thai is the former's tendency to unequal pairs of notes, a kind of dotted rhythm, which contrasts to the evenness of Thai rhythm.

To many, Cambodian village music, especially that for weddings (*kar*) and spirit-related ceremonies (*arakk*), is among the most attractive musics of Southeast Asia. The melodic inflections, especially those played by the reed instruments, have a bouncy, almost jazzlike feel, while the chest-resonated monochord (*khse muoy*) provides a distinctively resonant plucking sound.

Laos

The main challenge for outsiders wishing to listen to Lao (and by extension, northeast Thai) music is that the predominant genres (*khap* and *lam*) are closely bound to their lyrics. Though the melodies of *khap* and *lam* can be intriguing and the accompaniments attractive, the listener cannot fully appreciate Lao music without knowing the language and its dialects. It could be said about any music that hearing it live is better than hearing a recording, but this is especially true of Lao singing, in that the singers usually dance and often engage in suggestive horseplay.

The sound of the main Lao instrument, the *khene* free-reed mouth organ, is unusual in Asia because it produces vertical sonorities, not unlike chords. They do not function in a Western functional harmonic sense, but they do produce different degrees of tension and relaxation, providing a full-bodied, homorhythmic sound. Other instruments, including the plucked lute (*phin*) and the fiddle (*saw pip*), are rarer. The sound of the plucked lute is intriguing, especially when the player produces a succession of parallel fifths over a drone.

Regional Lao styles are distinguishable in melody and rhythm. Some, like that of the *khap ngeum,* sound rather dreamy because of their nonmetered, speechlike rhythms, but others are catchy in their rhythms, often reinforced by drums and small metal cymbals. Certain of them, especially *lam salavane* and *lam tang vay,* are so attractive that with little change they have become danceable popular types of song. In northeast Thailand, where central Thai influence is strong, the *lam* styles have been transformed into actual popular songs, accompanied by electrified local and standard rock instruments, brass instruments, and a set of drums. Indeed, since 1989, the rise of *lam sing,* a popularized form of *lam,* has been setting the pace for all sorts of other genres in Thailand.

Burma

On first hearing, Burmese classical music, especially that for the *hsaìñwaìñ* ensemble, resembles utter chaos. Western students, on first hearing Burmese music, are often unable to stifle looks of amazement, laughter, or verbal comments. This is because few other musics in the world exhibit such joyfully sudden shifts in rhythm, changes of texture and timbre, and a most disjunct melodic style. Thai and Cambodian classical musics (and their styles of dancing) could be described as smooth, continuous, and more or less relaxed, but Burmese music and dance are seemingly unpredictable, jagged, mercurial, and energetic. In this respect, the most similar (but somewhat tamer) style within Southeast Asia is the music of the Balinese *gong kebyar.*

Knowing cognitively how Burmese melody is constructed, like knowing how serial music is composed, does not necessarily mean that the listener can actually hear the process. In Thai classical music, the large gong circle plays the basic and straightforward version of the composition, as does the double-reed oboe in Cambodian classical music. These you can hear. But in Burmese music, nobody plays a coherent, intact version of any melody. Following a fixed structure that exists only in players' minds, even the lead musicians sound their instruments in an idiom comprising octave displacements, beat displacements, and other melodic "rearrangements."

FIGURE 7 The busy tinwork on Rangoon, Burma's Sule Pagoda suggests a Burmese aesthetic that is also heard in its music. Photo by Terry E. Miller, 1994.

Perhaps a visual comparison to the formal displacements of European cubist art will help the listener discern what has happened to the composition. A good way to understand this process is to ask a Burmese musician to play a familiar Western tune, as pianist Ù Ko Ko does on a recent compact disc, when he plays "When the Saints Come Marching In" (*Piano birman / Burmese piano* 1995:17). Perhaps two valid analogies to the process of displacement would be Schönberg's concept of *Klangfarbenmelodie,* in which the listener must connect disjointed bits of melody into a continuous whole, and Seurat's technique of pointillism, in which the viewer must connect discrete dots of color into a coherent image.

When listening to Burmese music, one cannot help but be struck by the distinctiveness and unblendedness of its timbres. Most Burmese solo instruments are individualistic, even unique in Southeast Asia—the set of twenty-one tuned drums, the harp, and the piano (at least as a "traditional" instrument). The sudden shifts in the music, which to foreigners can make it seem jerky and nervous, are also seen in Burmese dance, which, like the music, is energetic and kinetically sudden; it is unlike Thai dance, which (like Thai music) is smooth and continuous. That it also has a regular, underlying structure is confirmed in a repertory that requires two small idiophones to articulate cyclic patterns—a pair of tiny cymbals and a pair of hollowed-out wooden shells, hinged at one end.

Malaysia

On hearing Malaysian traditional music for the first time (such as the music for the royal coronation played on the double-reed oboe, or the accompanying music of the *ma'yong* theater played on the spike fiddle), one might be forgiven for confusing it with music from Western Asia. The melody flows continuously, using small intervals with little phrasal articulation while remaining within a narrow range. Nor does the cyclicality of its meter set it apart from Western Asian music, for the same is true there. What announces its Southeast Asianness is the presence of hanging gongs, which play on prescribed beats in temporal cycles.

Because Malaysia was colonized by Britain and remains multiethnic (Chinese, Indian, Malay), its music is also multiethnic, and the term *Malaysian music* covers a wide variety of somewhat unrelated styles. Some of them, such as for *ronggeng,* sound quite Western; others are purely Chinese. Some were borrowed from the popular-music traditions of Southern and Western Asia. "Malaysian" music, then, is the sum

kulintang Horizontal bronze gong-chime and ensemble

gamelan Stratified bronze gong-chime ensemble

colotomic structure The organization of music by periodic punctuation

rebab Two-stringed bowed spiked lute

gong kebyar Balinese dynamic, modern gamelan style

of its parts, but the music of the Malay is distinctive for blending Western and Southeast Asian traits.

Island Southeast Asia

The overall sound of island Southeast Asian music is often described as sonorous, probably referring to the fact that some of the most visible and audible music from the islands is performed on resonant bronze instruments, especially gongs. Indeed, a big portion of this music is played on stratified bronze ensembles, known collectively in Indonesia as gamelans and in the southern Philippines as *kulintang*. Variations on the basic gamelan and *kulintang* formats are common throughout the island nations and Borneo, and hundreds of different names are applied to what is basically a gong-chime ensemble.

In addition to gong-chime ensembles, thousands of other genres—European-style orchestras, indigenous vocal groups, solo instrumental performances—are spread across the islands of Southeast Asia, reflecting diverse musical priorities, contexts, and influences. While focusing on the sound and structure of the gong-chime ensemble, the reader should recognize that certain features of gong-chime music are readily applicable to other regional musics.

What makes a gong-chime ensemble? The basic component is a gong chime—a rack, usually horizontal, of small, tuned, bossed kettlepots. These pots may be laid out in a single row (as with the Filipino *kulintang* and the Balinese *trompong*), they may be arranged in double rows (as with the Javanese *bonang*), or they may be in a V- or U-shaped formation (as with the Sundanese *bonang*). Other main components of the ensemble are one or more hanging or horizontal bossed gongs, one or more drums (usually shaped like barrels, cones, or goblets), and xylophones made of wood or bamboo, or metallophones (especially bronze and iron). Many ensembles in the islands also have bamboo flutes, double-reed oboes, bowed lutes, or plucked zithers. The presence or absence of male or female singers varies according to repertorial requirements.

Gong-chime ensembles are often called stratified—a term that offers an indication of the musical texture. Within a piece of music, certain instruments have a punctuating function, said to be colotomic when they regularly mark temporal cycles. Much as a period (full stop) ends written sentences, the largest gong—or the instrument that has the function of that gong—ends musical sentences. Unlike most Western musics, island music of Southeast Asia tends to have a stronger emphasis on the last note of a four-beat pattern rather than the first note. Smaller hanging and horizontal gongs act as commas, occurring regularly at intervals that may be divided into two or four segments. Still smaller hanging or horizontal gongs may further punctuate a musical sentence. This texture then serves as the framework for the main theme, often played by large metallophones. Other instruments—including small metallophones, gong chimes, flutes, and zithers—may serve an elaborating function, decorating the main musical theme in dense musical patterns. The drum serves not only as the timekeeper and the keeper of the tempo, but as the instrument that usually outlines the form of the piece. Therefore, a stratified gong-chime ensemble has a four-part texture: colotomic gongs, a main musical theme, elaborating instruments, and drum patterns. Some ensembles (particularly in Central Java) may also have an "inner melody" performed on the rebab, which takes precedence over the more prominently heard main musical theme (Sumarsam 1975).

Much of island Southeast Asian music is performed cyclically. In the basic form of a cycle (Javanese *gongan*), each time the largest gong is struck, a cycle has been completed. In some pieces, several different cycles (each requiring the striking of a large gong) may be performed for the completion of a single, large-scale cycle. Once a cycle has been played, it may be repeated with variations on the elaborating instruments, or the piece may move on to a new cycle. The length of these cycles varies widely, from perhaps five seconds to many minutes. Individual variation from region to region and genre to genre determines the length of a cycle. What is often baffling to nonindigenous observers is the apparent lack of a sense of forward motion in this type of performance: how does the music move forward if the musicians keep repeating the same parts?

A partial answer to this question is that in many cases, the musicians use variation rather than exact repetition. The colotomic structure and the main musical theme may remain the same (at various densities), but the drummer and the musicians who play the elaborating instruments often spice up their playing with variations. The drummer may speed up or slow down the ensemble, allowing more open musical space for intricate rhythmic or melodic patterns to be performed. Small metallophones may be played in interlocking patterns or in a succession of melodic figures appropriate for certain types of performances. A flutist or an oboist may use ten or twenty cycles to complete a melody and may then use the same number of cycles each time to perform variations on the initial melody. Vocalists may perform when the colotomic instrumentation is quite sparse or (conversely) when it is dense enough to serve as a melodic outline on its own. Tension—and thus a sense of movement toward release—is created as the listeners learn to wait for the stroke of the gong at the end of each cycle. These and many more factors shape a different kind of listening experience for the uninitiated.

Island Southeast Asian music spans a continuum from note-for-note composition to improvisation. Tourists in Bali may be dazzled by promoters who claim that the intense, high-speed playing of the *gamelan gong kebyar* ensemble is totally improvised; however, *kebyar* musicians spend months working out intricate patterns and negotiating repertorial changes. At another extreme, a boy sprawled across the back of a water buffalo may improvise melodic figures appropriate to his culture and the capabilities of his bamboo flute without having to negotiate those patterns with anyone else.

Improvisation always occurs within certain musical contexts. In the gong-chime ensemble, neither the colotomy nor the main musical theme is improvised; however, the players of elaborating instruments and drums may choose from a variety of musical options: hundreds of short melodic phrases, ornaments, rhythmic flourishes, or minor variants. In the southern Philippines, the player of the *kulintang,* the instrument that functions as the primary carrier of the melody, works in a gradual ascending and descending progression through a series of patterns appropriate for each piece; the player has the option of repeating single patterns or groups of patterns. For solo instruments, the player's skill may be judged on the basis of improvisations, from the degree of the improvisations' appropriateness within the genre to the accuracy and fluidity of the melodic ornaments.

New listeners are also likely to notice the tonality of island Southeast Asian music. The term *pentatonic,* loosely and mistakenly applied to Asian music for decades, does not take into consideration either individual tonal variation, or the concept that Asian musics do not simply lift five out of the twelve tones of the chromatic scale and use them in music. The tuning of each ensemble in island Southeast Asia is internally coherent: all the instruments in a given ensemble are tuned to match each other. However, the instruments from one ensemble generally cannot play with those of another, because they do not use any standard tuning, such as equal temperament and A = 440. Though some master craftsmen may deliberately imitate either a prestigious or a commonly accepted tuning, variations in tuning between ensembles give each ensemble a unique sound and perceived temperament, such as "sweet" or "bright."

Informed islanders recognize good music on the basis of the ensemble's rhythmic coherence, dynamic balance among players, improvisational virtuosity, and improvisational appropriateness according to local modal rules, musicians' on-stage demeanor (said to be audible in their music), and seamless transitions from one section to the next. Good musicians know that if they play together long enough and listen closely to one another, all the above features will fall into place. Within the context of good music, all the joys and competitive urges that have a place in Southeast Asian society are given free rein, and informed audiences are free to appreciate musical events from the standpoints of both passion and reason.

A REPRESENTATIVE LIST

Knowing that students of Southeast Asian musics cannot possibly collect and know every kind of music, it is useful to ask what would constitute a must-know list of a Southeast Asian music-appreciation repertoire. Taking into consideration readily available recorded materials [see DISCOGRAPHY] and acknowledging the possibility of an idiosyncratic view, the editors offer the following list as both minimal and fundamental.

Burma

1. A composition played by a *hsaìñwaìñ.*
2. A composition for harp (*saùñ*).
3. A classical song for xylophone (*pa'talà*) and voice.
4. A classical composition played on a piano.

Thailand

1. A ritual or court composition played by the *piphat* ensemble.
2. A tuneful composition played by the *khrüang sai* or *mahori* ensemble with voice.
3. A virtuoso solo played on a xylophone (*ranat ek*).
4. Traditional village folk song of the *phleng phün ban* variety, with alternation of male and female soloists, each answered by a chorus of observers.
5. Traditional *lam klawn* accompanied by *khaen,* from the northeast.
6. The *salaw-süng-pi* ensemble of the north.
7. A song from the *manora* theater in the south.
8. An example of the music of any upland people from the north.

Laos

1. *Lam khon savan* from central southern Laos.
2. *Lam salavane* from southern Laos.
3. *Khap ngeum* from the Vientiane area.
4. *Khap thum* from Luang Phrabang.

5. Lao classical music from Vientiane.
6. An unaccompanied poem sung by the Hmong, followed by its rendition on a free-reed mouth organ.

Cambodia

1. A classical composition for the *pinn peat* ensemble with voice.
2. An entertainment song accompanied by *mahori* ensemble.
3. A village nuptial song (*phleng kar*).
4. Village vocal repartee with instrumental ensemble (*ayai*).
5. An excerpt of the narrative genre *chrieng chapey,* accompanied by a long-necked lute (*chapey*).

Malaysia

1. A song with choral response from *ma'yong* theater.
2. Music from a shadow play (*wayang kulit*).
3. Ceremonial music for a sultan played by a *nobat* ensemble.
4. Music for the *ronggeng* dance.

Vietnam

1. *Chèo* theater from the north.
2. *Tuồng* or *hát bội* theater from the central region.
3. A *ca trù* chamber song from the north.
4. A *ca huế* chamber song from the central region.
5. A *nhạc tài tử* chamber song from the south.
6. An accompanied folk song from any region.
7. An upland gong ensemble.
8. An upland free-reed gourd mouth organ.

Indonesia

1. Gamelan *pélog* or *sléndro* from central Java.
2. *Gamelan gong kebyar* from Bali.
3. *Tembang Sunda* from Sunda.
4. *Gondang* music of the Batak of Sumatra.
5. *Gendang raya* of the Iban of Borneo.
6. Bamboo flute (*saluang*) from Sumatra.
7. Tube zither (*sasandu*) from Roti.
8. Vocal duets (*berasi*) from East Flores.
9. Popular music (*dangdut*).

The Philippines

1. Plucked-string ensemble (*comparsa* or *rondalla*) of lowland Christians.
2. Flat gongs (*gangsa*) from the northern uplands.
3. *Kulintang* from Mindanao.
4. Dramatic opera (*sarswela*) of lowland Christians.

REFERENCES

Blacking, John. 1973. *How Musical Is Man?* Seattle and London: University of Washington Press.

Piano birman / Burmese piano: U Ko Ko. 1995. UM MUS, SRC Radio (Canada) UMM 203. Compact disc.

Sumarsam. 1975. "Inner Melody in Javanese Gamelan Music." *Asian Music* 7(1):3–13.

A Survey of Scholarship on Southeast Asian Musics

Terry E. Miller
Sean Williams

MAINLAND SOUTHEAST ASIA

Until the 1970s, published information about the musics of mainland Southeast Asia was sparse. In some areas, it was unreliable. Several facts explain this situation. First, the countries of the region had produced few native scholars. In some of these countries, music was not considered an academic discipline, and where it was, Western music tended to take precedence. Second, since the growth of ethnomusicology has been limited by academia's inability to create sufficient jobs for graduating ethnomusicologists, and since there are many countries and cultures in the world, academia has not produced enough scholars to cover all musical cultures. Because the pioneering program at UCLA focused on Indonesia, Western musical studies of Southeast Asia have been skewed toward the gamelan traditions of the islands. Third, war and oppression have made several mainland nations problematic for scholars. Until the 1990s, outsiders could barely get into Burma. Cambodia was completely disrupted by civil violence after 1975 and was basically closed to researchers until the late 1980s. Laos was closed to Western scholars from 1975 until 1990, and the ability to travel freely within the country was restored only in 1994. Vietnam was disrupted by war from the 1950s, and after 1975 was mostly closed to outsiders; since about 1990, policies there have been liberalized, and today the country is reasonably open to foreign scholars.

Before fighting and political chaos put several countries off limits, there had been even fewer ethnomusicologists, and few of them had been interested in mainland Southeast Asia. Thailand and Malaysia have remained mostly peaceful throughout the period, and for years, scholars have conducted research there with few or no restrictions.

The development of musical scholarship proceeded in three phases: *early, recent,* and *contemporary.* Few of the *early* writers on music knew anything of ethnomusicology; they were variously travelers, colonial officials, native-born (but Western-oriented) officials and academics, and in some cases armchair scholars working in Europe. *Recent* scholars include the generation first active in the 1960s, as ethnomusicology began to permeate academia, more in the United States than Europe. Some of them were composers seeking alternative ideas and sounds—musicians who ended up as scholars. With ethnomusicology programs firmly established throughout the United States, Europe, and (in limited ways) Southeast Asia, a *contemporary* generation of scholars, both Western and native-born, has begun to produce important work. The region, whose music had been so little known as recently as 1975 (when the author began teaching), has seen steady growth, but in fact, most of its musics, especially those of its minority peoples, have not been studied by academics.

A meeting of all scholars specializing in the musics of mainland Southeast Asia would not require a large room. Though the roster is growing, the scholar-to-population ratio is tiny, compared even with that of Indonesia. A comparable ratio in Western classical music would demonstrate how few people are working in mainland Southeast Asia. The number of scholars native to the region is likely to grow in Thailand, Vietnam, and perhaps Malaysia; but in Laos, Cambodia, and Burma, little change can be expected in the near future. With respect to the job market in the West, there are already too many ethnomusicologists, but with respect to the task, there are too few.

Vietnam

Of all the countries in mainland Southeast Asia, Vietnam has the longest tradition of musical scholarship. Documents written in Sino-Vietnamese (a form of classical Chinese, known only to the learned in Vietnam) go back hundreds of years. Until the 1990s, all scholars in this area were Vietnamese. The most prominent was Trần văn Khê, whose dissertation at the University of Paris, published as *La musique vietnamienne traditionnelle* (1962), remains the only comprehensive study in print. Phạm Duy, a composer of popular songs in Vietnam before 1975, published a book in 1975. Among the newest generation of scholars, most prominent is Dr. Phong T. Nguyễn, who has done comprehensive fieldwork in Vietnam since 1991. There are also numerous scholars in Vietnam, such as Mịch Quang, Hà văn Cầu, and Lư Nhất Vũ. Younger scholars include Dr. Lê Tuấn Hùng of Australia, Miranda Arana of the United States, and Barley Norton of the United Kingdom. Since 1991, Vietnam has opened itself to fieldwork, but cultural-service officers in the Ministry of Culture still maintain control over access.

Cambodia

Khmer music received little scholarly attention until the 1960s, when Alain Daniélou and Jacques Brunet of France contributed brief studies. Dr. Sam-Ang Sam, a Khmer native, has become the most active researcher, advocate, and performer of Khmer music living in the United States; his wife, Chan Moly Sam, while maintaining a career in teaching and performing Khmer dance, has contributed several valuable studies. Dr. Eileen Blumenthal has also studied Khmer dance, and Dr. Toni Shapiro and Dr. Kathy McKinley have recently become specialists in Khmer music. Research in Cambodia is difficult, mostly because of poor security and infrastructure.

Laos

Laos is likely the most underresearched country in mainland Southeast Asia. Nothing substantial was published before 1975, and from then until the early 1990s, the country was closed to most outside scholars. No scholar had specialized in this country's music until 1991, when Dr. Terry E. Miller received access to a broad spectrum of Lao musics recorded on site throughout Laos. Dr. Therese Mahoney has written a dissertation on Lao classical music, based on work in Vientiane in 1991–1992. Dr. Carol Compton has contributed scholarship on Lao singers' poetry, but not on their music. Two other scholars are likely to make contributions: Dr. Jarernchai Chonpairot of northeast Thailand, who wrote a dissertation on one Lao vocal genre;

and Mr. Phoxay Sunnalath of Laos, who has earned a master's degree in Thai studies and ethnomusicology in northeast Thailand.

Upland minority peoples

Though the remoteness of upland minority groups would suggest that their musics are the least studied, a fair amount of information has resulted from missionaries' efforts, especially in northern Thailand. The minorities of Burma remain little known, and only the Hmong (of Laos) have been studied in detail, mostly as immigrant communities in the United States, by Dr. Amy Catlin. The late Dr. Ruriko Uchida of Japan documented a great amount of music in upland Thailand and to a lesser extent Laos, and a compact disc of Karenni music (of the Thai-Burmese border) appeared in 1993. Dr. Gretel Schwörer-Kohl, a scholar at the University of Mainz, has begun to contribute work in this area. In Malaysia, the Temiar have attracted the most scholarly attention, and Dr. Marina Roseman has written extensively on their music. Before her work, the late Dr. Hans Oesch of Germany had done extensive fieldwork in upland Malaysia, and had produced commercial recordings for Bärenreiter. Upland Vietnamese groups were first documented by French officials and scholars, most prominent being Georges de Gironcourt with his work on upland and lowland musics, published as a single issue of the *Bulletin de la Société des études indochinoises* (1943).

Thailand

Compared to other areas, the number of scholars who have studied musics in Thailand is legion and growing. Some of them are Thai; indeed, Thai scholars comprised the earliest group. They included Phra Chen Duriyanga (born Peter Feit, son of Thai and American parents), Dr. Utit Naksawat, Montri Tramote, and Dhanit Yupho. Among Westerners, the primary scholar for Thai music for years was Dr. David Morton, a protégé of Dr. Mantle Hood and a faculty member at UCLA. His books, articles, and translations remain the foundation of Thai music studies. With his retirement, growing numbers of younger scholars from various countries began making contributions. In Thailand, they have included Dr. Jarernchai Chonpairot, Dr. Somsak Ketukaenchan, Professor Anant Narkong, and Professor Panya Roongrüang; in Japan, Dr. Yoko Tanese-Ito; in England, Dr. Francis Silkstone; and in the United States, Dr. Terry E. Miller, Dr. Pamela A. Moro, and Dr. Deborah Wong. Despite all this scholarly work, the musics of three of Thailand's four regions remain little known, and only that of the northeast has been extensively studied (by Dr. Terry E. Miller). With the rise of regional studies and the beginning of ethnomusicological study in Thailand, it is likely that more Thai scholars will appear on the scene.

Burma

Before Burma's government sealed the country from outside influence (around 1970), few outsiders had studied Burmese music. A Burmese scholar, Ù Khin Zaw, had published his most important work in the 1940s. After that, material on Burmese music became scarce, and with scholars either denied access or severely restricted, little work could occur. Dr. Judith Becker, Dr. Robert Garfias, and Dr. Muriel Williamson made significant contributions, but none specialized only in Burmese music. Since then, only Dr. Ward Keeler, an anthropologist, has worked extensively on Burmese music. With the founding of the University of Culture (in 1993) and its offering courses in Burmese music, more Burmese scholars may be able to offer their knowledge to the outside world.

Malaysia

Though Malaysia has been hospitable to research on music, only a few scholars have worked there. In the early 1970s, two nonmusic specialists, Mubin Sheppard and P.

L. Amin Sweeney, made useful contributions, and Dr. William Malm, a specialist in Japanese music, documented traditional theater in northeast Malaysia. The first person to specialize in the study of Malaysian music was Dr. Patricia Matusky (of the United States), who continues to contribute publications on the subject. Two younger scholars have now become active: in several books, Dr. Tan Sooi Beng has focused on theater and dance, and Dr. Margaret Sarkissian has focused on the Portuguese-derived music of Melaka (Malacca).

Singapore

Significant as an economic power in Southeast Asia, the city-state of Singapore is easily overlooked in reference to music. As a kind of cultural stew, its music(s) is (or are) difficult to define, and require(s) attention to questions of cultural change and interaction. Tong Soon Lee (of Singapore) is likely the first scholar to focus on Singapore's musical traditions.

ISLAND SOUTHEAST ASIA

Examining the existing ethnomusicological literature for island Southeast Asia is much easier than for the mainland, because island Southeast Asia has only two countries (Indonesia and the Philippines), plus one multinational island (Borneo). Furthermore, as this article will attest, the bulk of current research on music of the region has centered on Indonesia—specifically, the gong-chime court musics of Java and Bali. One of the most important aspects of this volume is that it tries to balance the wealth of information about mainstream Southeast Asian court traditions with important new work on places that are not so famous abroad. Each of these island areas has its own history of research, which can be explored in the bibliography at the back of this volume, and in the references at the end of each article.

In a dramatic contrast to the mainland, Indonesia, the Philippines, and Borneo have not been so deeply disrupted by war and postcolonial chaos. As a result of years of relative peace in the islands, both foreign and domestic researchers have had access to musicians, dancers, and actors in ways that would be impossible in, say, Burma. Though acquiring a research permit is a burdensome process, the average foreign researcher can be reasonably confident of working with local performers and scholars. It may always be the case that certain areas and people, such as the Baduy of West Java, are declared off limits to outside researchers; but most local officials recognize the potential benefits of allowing researchers to learn about and publicize the diversity of local arts.

As in musical studies of the mainland, most early outside scholars of the area were not professional ethnomusicologists, if only because the discipline had not yet been established. Instead, our earliest accounts of musical activity in island Southeast Asia come from travelers' accounts, colonial reports and diaries, notes written by missionaries and friars, and the occasional local scholarly treatise. Later sources came primarily in the form of master's theses and doctoral dissertations, most of which have remained unpublished but can be acquired through library loans. By the late 1970s, articles containing the essence of researchers' work had become the main form of publication for all of island Southeast Asia, and the trend continues, as the pace of publishing books begins to pick up momentum. Interested readers can look for relevant articles in issues of *Asian Music, Ethnomusicology, Indonesia, The World of Music,* and the *Yearbook for Traditional Music.* The following review of the literature is restricted to sources in English.

Huge areas within island Southeast Asia remain open for study. Among these are the broad range of Indonesia's Outer Islands, most of the upland and minority groups of the Philippines, and most of Borneo. The court traditions of Indonesia, a mainstay of Western scholarship for most of the twentieth century, remain a rich and varied source. As the shape of our field begins to shift, the level of our knowledge must also shift. Most ethnomusicologists know at least something about central Javanese and Balinese court traditions, but how many know about the diversity of Flores, or about the hundreds of Filipino genres found outside the *kulintang* traditions?

The late twentieth century has seen an upswing in the training and research of local ethnomusicologists, whose perspectives on their own music continue to add depth and breadth to research on the music of the islands. Collaborative research and publishing on the part of cultural outsiders and insiders is one of the field's most important new directions. Within the Philippines (where English is already a major language) and Indonesia (where Bahasa Indonesia is an easily learned lingua franca), ethnomusicology is likely to expand. The twenty-first century is certain to bring more musical information into the light of international publication than Jaap Kunst, Colin McPhee, and all the Spanish friars working in the Philippines ever dreamed of.

Indonesia

Two classic works of Indonesian ethnomusicology remain indispensable: *Music in Java,* by Jaap Kunst (1973 [1934]), and *Music in Bali,* by Colin McPhee (1966). Each of these ethnomusicologists wrote many other works, but these books are landmarks of the field. Written at the dawn of modern ethnomusicology, they differ dramatically from current scholarship in that they try to be comprehensive; they do not focus on a single style or genre but include as many styles and genres as possible. Both books, widely available in libraries, recall the period when Westerners discovered the elegance, logic, and beauty of Indonesian music—and realized that they could play it while studying it.

With the establishment of ethnomusicology as a discipline, Indonesian music was among the first non-Western musics to be brought to the United States and Europe. In particular, gamelans (ensembles of stratified gongs and gong chimes) began to be imported from the 1960s on, to the point that nearly every major university or college ethnomusicology program eagerly sought to purchase an ensemble. These ensembles were nearly always central Javanese court gamelans; more rarely, Balinese. In part as a result of emphasis on Javanese and Balinese court music, a large proportion of the first U.S and European graduate-student researchers in Indonesia worked in central Java and Bali.

Two important studies of the 1990s bring aspects of Javanese and Balinese music into more accessible prominence; these are R. Anderson Sutton's *Traditions of Gamelan Music in Java* (1991) and Michael Tenzer's *Balinese Music* (1991). What sets Sutton's book apart from other current works is that it moves away from a focus on the central Javanese court to recognize the diversity and the relationships among multiple Javanese traditions. Tenzer presents current Balinese music in a lavishly illustrated volume, which focuses on a specific genre of dance as its centerpiece; he also provides clues about how to understand Balinese music—information that makes his work accessible to nonspecialists.

Outside the library on central Java and Bali are works on west Java and Sumatra but surprisingly little else. West Java (also known as Sunda) has its share of unpublished doctoral and master's works. The most important book about the area is Wim Van Zanten's *Sundanese Music in the Cianjuran Style* (1989). It provides useful information about the Sundanese and focuses on the aristocratic music of the area. Almost no books with information about other genres have been published. The bulk of research and English-language discussion of Sumatra has been done in articles by

Margaret Kartomi of Monash University. Musical traditions of the Outer Islands of Indonesia (which include the Malukus, Sulawesi, Flores, Timor, and other areas) are so understudied that information about local music traditions is not readily available in any language. This situation is gradually changing as Indonesian and Australian scholars begin to cover more ground; for example, Christopher Basile's three years of research in Nusa Tenggara Timur are expected to yield more publications than the articles in this volume, which are among the only recent ones on the area.

The Philippines

Music of the southern Philippines ensembles (*kulintang*) became widely known among ethnomusicologists after the release of several discs of their music (on the Lyrichord label) and the establishment of several ensembles in the western United States. Usopay Cadar's M.A. thesis (1971) and doctoral dissertation (1980), both at the University of Washington, were among the first studies of *kulintang*; many ensuing works on the Philippines have focused on its traditions. The performance of Spanish-influenced Filipino music outside the Philippines usually occurs within immigrant Filipino communities.

As with Indonesia, most current studies of the performing arts in the Philippines are genre-specific. No book-length overview of Filipino music has been published, though individual scholars, including José Maceda and Usopay Cadar, plus Ramón Santos and Corazon Dioquino (two of the Filipino authors of this volume), have made important contributions. Some information appears on the liner notes of LP recordings and in journals specific to the Philippines, including *Filipino Heritage* and *Philippine Sociological Review*. This volume may inspire scholars, both from inside and outside the Philippines, to recognize the wealth of underexplored genres in the Philippines and to consider adding to the research on the subject.

Borneo

Some outsiders, misled by such adventure novels as *Into the Heart of Borneo,* have acquired stereotyped ideas about Borneo as the last bastion of twentieth-century headhunting. No musical ensembles from the island have pride of place in international ethnomusicology departments, and the glamor associated with mainstream Asian court traditions has passed Borneo by. The diversity of ethnolinguistic groups in Borneo has made even the creation of the Borneo survey article for this volume daunting, and the lack of recent research has kept available material inadequate.

Several scholars have made inroads in the area of music in Borneo; among them are Patricia Matusky and Virginia K. Gorlinski, whose doctoral dissertations are important area-specific resources. *Traditional Music and Drama of Southeast Asia* (Osman 1974), a useful volume, has several articles about the musical traditions of Borneo.

REFERENCES

Cadar, Usopay Hamdag. 1971. "The Maranao Kolintang Music: An Analysis of the Instruments, Musical Organization, Etymologies, and Historical Documents." M. A. thesis, University of Washington.

———. 1980. "Context and Style in the Vocal Music of the Muranao in Mindanao, Philippines." Ph.D. dissertation, University of Washington.

Gironcourt, Georges de. 1943. "Recherches de geographie musicale en Indochine." *Bulletin de la Société des études indochinoises* 17:3– 174.

Kunst, Jaap. 1973 [1934]. *Music in Java: Its History, Its Theory, and Its Technique.* 3rd ed. rev. and enlarged by Ernst Heins. 2 vols. The Hague: Martinus Nijhoff.

McPhee, Colin. 1966. *Music in Bali: A Study in Form and Instrumental Organization in Balinese Orchestral Music.* New Haven, London: Yale University Press.

Osman, Mohd. Taib, ed. 1974. *Traditional Music and Drama of Southeast Asia.* Kuala Lumpur: Dewan Bahasa dan Pustaka.

Sutton, R. Anderson. 1991. *Traditions of Gamelan Music in Java: Musical Pluralism and Regional Identity.* Cambridge Studies in Ethnomusicology. Cambridge: Cambridge University Press.

Tenzer, Michael. 1991. *Balinese Music.* Singapore: Periplus Editions.

Trần văn Khê. 1962. *La musique vietnamienne traditionelle.* Paris: Presses Universitaires de France.

van Zanten, Wim. 1989. *Sundanese Music in the Cianjuran Style: Anthropological and Musicological Aspects of Tembang Sunda.* Providence, R.I.: Foris Publications.

Part 2
Issues and Processes in Southeast Asian Music

Many are surprised to learn that the forging of bronze and iron, the cultivation of rice, and the domestication of farm animals began thousands of years ago among the peoples of Southeast Asia, independent of influences from India and China. Some of the largest—and most advanced—urban societies in the ancient world lived here. They developed large and complex musical ensembles as well as sophisticated theater and dance, created from within and yet adaptable to successive waves of outside cultural influences.

Vietnamese monks of the Mahayana Buddhist tradition in Hội An chant the sutras at an afternoon ritual. Photo by Terry E. Miller, 1993.

Southeast Asia in Prehistory

Karl L. Hutterer

It has been known for more than a century that Southeast Asia has had one of the longest histories of human settlement of any part of the world, rivaled only by East and South Africa and East Asia. Fossils of ancient hominids (human ancestors), discovered in Java in 1891 by the Dutch physician Eugene Dubois and classified by scientists as *Homo erectus*, played an important role in the early debates over human evolution. Since then, the Javanese sites have yielded a rich series of fossils, covering much of the history of the biological evolution of humankind. Unfortunately, that it has proven difficult to date the earliest human remains with confidence has resulted in a lively and continuing debate, which places their age anywhere from somewhat less than one million years to nearly two million years.

EARLY PREHISTORY

No other area of Southeast Asia has produced a record of hominid fossils as rich as that discovered in Java, though fragmentary finds have been made, notably in Vietnam and southern China. Together, these finds indicate that early hominids had spread from Africa into Asia by at least one million, and possibly two million, years ago, and dispersed over the whole Southeast Asian region.

None of the fossilized hominid bones has so far been found associated with artifacts, so we know virtually nothing about the culture and life of these pioneers. Archaeological research conducted during the first half of the twentieth century had tried, in the absence of clear stratigraphic information or other reliable methods of dating, to associate scattered finds of stone tools made of pebbles with the hominid fossils. On the basis of such speculation, the Harvard anthropologist H. L. Movius proposed a "chopper / chopping tool industry" as the earliest form of material culture in the region. This concept has been abandoned as unfounded in the light of more recent investigations. We do know that the earliest Southeast Asians lived when the earth was experiencing a series of major climatic fluctuations. During that period, commonly called the Ice Age (Pleistocene), several episodes of worldwide climatic cooling occurred. These episodes caused the formation of continental sheets of ice in the northern latitudes of Asia, Europe, and North America. The tropical latitudes of Southeast Asia, while remaining warm, likely experienced drastic shifts in rainfall patterns, and thus in forest cover. Also, the binding up of massive amounts of water in the northern sheets of ice resulted in a drop of worldwide sea levels, exposing in Southeast Asia a large, shallow shelf, extending from the continent toward Sumatra, Java, and Borneo. Thus, during the periods of climatic cooling, these islands were linked with the Asian mainland in a contiguous continental area. Though these must have been drastic changes in the ecology of the region, it is not known how they affected the development of hominid culture or how the early hominids adjusted to them.

The archaeological record improves dramatically by about forty thousand to fifty thousand years ago, with the regional appearance of biologically modern humans (*Homo sapiens sapiens*). Our evidence comes from a good handful of sites, mostly caves, in southern China, Vietnam, the Malay Peninsula, the Philippines, Borneo, and Sulawesi. It indicates the presence of small groups of people making their living by hunting and gathering, exploiting a broad range of resources from the tropical forests and savannas of the region. They used simple stone tools, some made of pebbles, most made of flakes. Few of these tools had highly refined and standardized forms, giving an image of primitiveness, particularly if compared with stone-tool technologies of a similar age in Europe or the Middle East. However, the Southeast Asian stone implements were likely used with an array of possibly quite sophisticated tools, made of wood and bamboo, to hunt and collect a broad spectrum of animals and plants from the tropical environment. The scantiness of the archaeological record suggests that, in stone-tool technology, local variations on the basic theme may have occurred, with somewhat more specialized forms in certain areas, as in northeast Borneo and southern Sulawesi. It is not known whether these variations reflect local cultural idiosyncrasies or an adaptation to specific environmental conditions or challenges.

Hoabinhian culture

In mainland Southeast Asia, the end of the Ice Age is clearly associated with a significant shift in cultural patterns. Starting roughly around fifteen thousand years ago, pebbles chipped into a variety of tools of characteristic shapes began to dominate stone-tool technologies. The new archaeological manifestation is known as the Hoabinhian culture or tradition, after the province (in northern Vietnam) where French scholars in the 1930s first observed it. Since this change in stone tools coincides more or less with the worldwide amelioration of climates toward the end of the last Ice Age, it is tempting to see it as a response to environmental change; however, that the technological change is seen over a wide area, which would have included a range of different environments, speaks against such an interpretation. Also, despite the technological shift, broad subsistence patterns do not seem to have changed much from the earlier period and continued to rely on the hunting and collecting of a broad range of wild resources from the seashore and the forest. Cultural patterns that seem characteristic of the Hoabinhian include human burial in a flexed position, and the extensive use of red ochre.

Vietnamese archaeologists distinguish three Hoabinhian phases: Son Vi, Hoabinhian proper, and Bacsonian. The Bacsonian is distinguished by the addition to the technological repertory of simple pottery and chipped stone axes whose cutting edges have been ground smooth. Next to southern China and Japan, Southeast Asia claims one of the oldest records of pottery manufacture. Research by Chester Gorman at Spirit Cave in northwestern Thailand in the 1970s suggested that Hoabinhian communities might have engaged in incipient forms of agriculture as long as ten thousand years ago; this claim, however, has not been sustained by subsequent research.

Hunters and gatherers have historically been involved in the collecting of highly prized forest products (including resins, beeswax, and aromatic woods) for the worldwide trade in exotic Southeast Asian raw materials.

Hoabinhian sites occur in three contexts: as caves, as wide scatters of stone tools in open areas, and as shell middens along the seacoast. The last are mounds built up from the discarded shells of shellfish collected for food. The Hoabinhian Period is clearly documented for all of mainland Southeast Asia, including the Malay Peninsula and Sumatra. There is some scattered evidence of tools of the Hoabinhian type in the Philippines and on the island of Borneo. The rest of island Southeast Asia does not seem to share in the Hoabinhian tradition; rather, the earlier tradition of stone-tool technologies based chiefly on the use of flake tools seems to continue without significant change for several thousand years beyond the Pleistocene.

THE BEGINNINGS OF AGRICULTURE IN MAINLAND SOUTHEAST ASIA

Not only the use of flaked stone tools but also the tradition of hunting and gathering survived in Southeast Asia for a long time. Hunting economies were not universally replaced by the development and spread of subsequent agricultural technologies and economies. Indeed, hunting and gathering are still practiced by some small tribal groups, even though they have adopted iron and other modern materials for their weapons. It does appear that, in the later prehistory and early history of the region, hunting changed from a primary subsistence activity to a more specialized economic endeavor, in which hunters focused mostly on the collecting of wild resources for trade with agricultural communities who provided in exchange manufactured products and starch staples. In many cases, hunters and gatherers have historically (and probably also in late prehistory) been involved in the collecting of highly prized forest products, including resins, beeswax, and aromatic woods, for the worldwide trade in exotic Southeast Asian raw materials. The further course of Southeast Asian prehistory does not involve a simple wholesale replacement of earlier traditions by subsequent innovations but resembles the development of an increasingly complex mosaic of interacting traditions.

In the Southeast Asian islands, stone-tool technologies probably tied to the continuing hunter-gatherer tradition show some peculiar innovations in some areas in the addition of more highly formalized and specialized stone tools around 7000 B.C. At various sites in the Philippines, Sulawesi, Java, and Timor, stone tools are found made of blades, elongated flakes with straight parallel sides, produced by a more sophisticated technique. In some cases, they are further worked to produce tiny cutting tools with one blunted edge, resembling European microliths. In southern Sulawesi, archaeologists also find small stone projectile points, some with serrated edges. The historical implications of these developments are unclear. Some of them persisted for a long time, in some cases well into the historic period, suggesting once more both coexistence and interaction between expanding agricultural communities and bands of hunter-gatherers.

Specifics about the beginning of agriculture in Southeast Asia, and with it the creation of more permanently settled communities, remain somewhat obscure. Much of the archaeological research on early agriculture in the region has focused on the elucidation of the history of the domestication and cultivation of rice, even though archaeologists recognize that Southeast Asian agricultural systems involve many indigenous crops, some of which may have preceded the emergence of rice as a dominant staple. Actual remains of prehistoric rice have been found in many sites throughout south China and Southeast Asia.

The oldest evidence for rice comes from Hemudu, a site in the Hangzhou Bay area of Zhejiang Province, and dates to 5000 B.C. At Hemudu, a thick layer of the remains of rice, including straw, husks, and seeds, is associated with agricultural tools, domesticated animals, and substantial houses, indicative of a permanent settlement. The period of the Hemudu settlement predates the time of the ethnic Han expansion to the south and represents a time when south China was occupied by populations related ethnically and linguistically to populations in Southeast Asia. The ethnic-minority nationalities of south China are the descendants of these inhabitants.

EARLY AGRICULTURAL COMMUNITIES

On the mainland of Southeast Asia proper, good evidence for early agricultural communities comes from well-studied sites in Thailand (including Ban Chiang, Non Nok Tha, and Ban Na Di in the northeast, and Khok Phanom Di and the Bang Pakong Valley in the Chao Phraya floodplain, near the coast of the Gulf of Siam) and in northern and central Vietnam. Though the evidence is indirect, studies of sediments containing prehistoric charcoal, pollen, and phytoliths (microscopic silica grains, found in plant structures) strongly suggest that rice cultivators were settled in the coastal area of the Gulf of Siam by at least the fifth, and maybe the sixth, millennium B.C.

The oldest direct evidence for settled agricultural villages comes from northeastern Thailand (the sites of Ban Chiang, Non Nok Tha) and northern Vietnam (the sites of the Phùng Nguyên Period), and dates back to at least 3000 B.C. or earlier. Most of the sites occur as low mounds, which rise from a meter to three meters above the surrounding plain and are the result of the activities of generations of early villagers. These farmers tended to settle on slightly elevated ground along the margins of floodplains. The remains of their villages include evidence of houses on stilts, cemetery areas, well-made pottery, and a variety of utilitarian and ornamental artifacts. The presence of burials and associated artifacts has helped archaeologists define cultural sequences and has allowed them to engage in tentative studies of demography and social organization.

In the early settlement phase (dating from the beginning of the third millennium B.C. to about 2000 B.C.), the technology of these villages was typically neolithic, marked by ground and polished stone axes and pottery, most of it decorated with cord impressions and occasionally incised designs. The dead were buried in extended position, lying on their backs, and usually accompanied by some pottery and occasionally other artifacts, including ornaments. In some cases, whole animals, or portions of animals, were buried with the dead, presumably as offerings.

There is indubitable evidence of rice and domesticated animals, including pigs, cattle, and dogs. The agricultural economy was complemented by some amount of hunting and exploiting of freshwater resources (fish and shellfish). There is considerable variety in the forms of pottery vessels, including utilitarian styles and others evidently meant for ritual or other special purposes. Clay spindle whorls indicate the practice of spinning and weaving. Ornaments include beads and bangles of shell and stone. At some sites, such as Khok Phanom Di, situated in a resource-rich estuarine environment, prehistoric villagers seem to have commanded considerable wealth.

During the second phase of settlement history, we can tentatively trace some broad social developments in northeastern Thailand. There is evidence for population growth, an expansion and intensification of agricultural systems, craft specialization (in the manufacture of pottery and bronze, the latter discussed below), some differentiation in the size and function of settlements, and distinctions in the way people were treated in burial. Together, the evidence suggests both an expansion of social systems and increasing complexity in their organization, particularly the emergence of social ranking. The second settlement phase is also associated with the appearance of bronze metallurgy, a prehistoric development often seen as a sign of social intensification.

Early metallurgy

Dating the first appearance of metals has been one of the thorniest and most controversial issues in Southeast Asian archaeology. Until the excavation of Non Nok Tha (in the late 1960s), it was thought that bronze and iron had been introduced to the region more or less simultaneously, late in the first millennium B.C. The work at Non Nok Tha, and at subsequent excavations at Ban Chiang and Ban Nadi, leaves no doubt that bronze metallurgy made its appearance in mainland Southeast Asia much earlier—at least by the late, and possibly by the beginning of the second millennium B.C.

Bronze manufacture apparently started out as a local village craft and is in evidence at most sites of that period. Recent excavations by Vincent Piggott at Non Pa Wai and other sites in central Thailand suggest that the manufacture and distribution of bronze artifacts may actually have involved a more complex system, with specialized communities smelting copper from ore and distributing it as ingots. Local artisans seem to have then remelted the copper with tin and cast it as bronze artifacts. The range of artifacts produced included axes, points of spears, fishhooks, bells, and bracelets. Many of them were cast by a fairly sophisticated process in bivalve molds made from sandstone.

Phùng Nguyên culture of Vietnam

Neolithic developments in northern Vietnam parallel fairly well those in northeastern Thailand. At the confluence of the Red and Black rivers, settled villages appeared toward the latter part of the third millennium B.C. Similar to their counterparts in Thailand, the archaeological sites form low mounds, located on slightly elevated ground along the margins of floodplains. Vietnamese archaeologists call the first phase of this development the Phùng Nguyên culture. Sites of this period are rich in stone adzes of a variety of forms, stone bracelets and other ornaments, and pottery. Many of the pots are decorated with incised parallel lines, filled with multiple impressions made by a small tool to create a typical design. Similar designs are found in sites of a comparable age in Thailand. Evidence of rice has been found in Phùng Nguyên sites. The working of bronze seems to have made its appearance toward the end of this phase, though extant bronze artifacts remain rare.

Around 1500 B.C., Phùng Nguyên culture was replaced by the Đồng Đậu culture, associated not only with a different type of pottery—vessels decorated with multiple parallel incised lines, rarely with impressions—but also with a great blossoming of the use of bronze. The bronze technology was quite similar to that of Thailand and involved the use of rather sophisticated bivalve molds. The range and style of bronze artifacts produced resembled, once again, those in Thailand, including socketed axes, points of spears, bracelets, and a variety of other ornaments. Around 1100 B.C., the Đồng Đậu culture was succeeded by the Gò Mun culture, which lasted until about the fifth century B.C.

There has been much discussion about the historical source of metallurgy in

Southeast Asia. Before the excavations in Thailand and Vietnam, it had been assumed that the knowledge of metals and their manufacture had been introduced to the region in protohistoric times from China or India or both regions. The early dates we now have for metal in Southeast Asia make this assumption more difficult to sustain, particularly since the early metal sites are not associated with other materials derived from these distant sources. Both the technology and the cultural forms it is associated with are quite different from the working of bronze and bronze artifacts found in either China or India and exhibit a strongly local character. Few archaeologists would suggest that bronze metallurgy in Southeast Asia represents an independent invention, but its historical sources remain obscure.

THE SPREAD OF NEOLITHIC CULTURES IN ISLAND SOUTHEAST ASIA

The introduction and spread of agriculture in island Southeast Asia is less well defined. There is, once again, considerable debate over dating. More importantly, few sites have yielded remains of cultivated plants, so the presence of agriculture is inferred on the basis of indirect evidence, including the presence of pottery and tools interpreted to be agricultural in function. The Southeast Asian islands also lack, for the most part, excavations of permanent village settlements until a much later stage of prehistory.

Nevertheless, it appears that agricultural communities first appeared in the north and spread from there to the south and east. The earliest sites are reported from Taiwan (again an area that was prehistorically in the Southeast Asian, rather than the Chinese, cultural sphere), with sites ascribed by K. C. Chang and others to the Ta-p'en-k'eng culture, sites of which date to 4300–2500 B.C., and are characterized by cord-marked pottery with incised decorations, polished stone axes and adzes, and chipped stone hoes. The Yüan-shan culture—related, but somewhat later–dates to 2500 B.C. and later. It is associated with globular vessels that are not cord marked but are occasionally decorated with punctations, incised patterns, and fine red or brown clay slips. Other artifacts include polished stone axes and adzes, chipped stone hoes, clay spindle whorls, and stone knives formally reminiscent of later metal knives used for harvesting rice. The Australian archaeologist Peter Bellwood has argued that the predecessor to the Ta-p'en-k'eng and Yüan-shan cultures is found in coastal south China, particularly in the culture represented by the Hemudu site (Bellwood 1985). Evidence for the presence of rice is reported from one site in Taiwan in the form of the impressions that grains of rice had made in pottery dating to ca. 3000 B.C. Foxtail millet may have been another important crop.

From Taiwan, Neolithic communities appear to have spread to the Philippines. Pottery with similarities to the ceramics of Yüan-shan has been found at Dimolit, a site on the coast of northeastern Luzon. Dating to between 2500 and 1500 B.C., this site also yielded the outlines of two small houses, with postholes and hearths. Other sites with similar pottery have been found throughout the Philippines, though they vary from each other in other details.

Red-slip pottery reminiscent of Taiwanese and Philippine wares have been unearthed in parts of Indonesia, including the Talaud Islands to the north of Sulawesi, in southern Sulawesi, northern Borneo, and Timor. The Timorese sites are of particular importance, as they have also yielded bones of pigs dating to about 3000 B.C., indicating husbandry in the context of a neolithic agricultural economy. Remains of the Tahitian chestnut (*Inocarpus* sp.), bamboo, and gourds have also been recovered from these sites.

Not so much is known about the early Neolithic cultures in the islands as about early farming communities on the mainland of Southeast Asia, particularly those excavated in Thailand and Vietnam. Bellwood believes that the appearance of

Though the late prehistory of Southeast Asia remains difficult to interpret, there is now ample evidence that indigenous peoples formed complex social and political systems before the rise of the earliest recognizable Hinduized states.

Neolithic cultures in the islands is due to an expansion of a distinctive and identifiable cultural group from the South China coast, the ancestors of the contemporary Austronesian-speaking peoples, who predominate in the Southeast Asian islands, and settled the farther Pacific reaches of Micronesia and Polynesia. These colonists, he believes, brought to Taiwan, the Philippines, and western Indonesia the cultivation of rice, millet, and sugarcane, the raising of pigs and dogs, and the crafts of weaving, making bark-derived cloth, and manufacturing sophisticated tools of polished stone.

More on the basis of evidence derived from historical linguistics than archaeology, Bellwood further argues that, as these populations moved into the southern Philippines and Borneo around 2500 B.C., they added from local sources a range of new items to their agricultural repertory, including yams, taro, breadfruit, bananas, the ingredients associated with chewing betel, and domestic fowl. In their marine technology, they added the sail to their canoes, which gave them greater mobility and aided them eventually in moving out into the wider Pacific. As they reached more equatorial areas, and particularly as they spread into eastern Indonesia, local environments proved less congenial to the cultivation of rice. Rice thus declined in importance as a crop and was completely abandoned in the settlement of the Pacific Islands.

The further development of Neolithic cultures in the islands is even less well defined. Sites have been recorded in the Philippines, Sulawesi, and Timor dating to 1500 B.C. and later, and containing pottery with incised and stamp-impressed decorations of broadly similar patterns. They include decorations of impressed dots, circles, and semicircles, sometimes applied within borders of incised lines. This pottery is reminiscent of Lapita ware, a ceramic ware typically associated with the settlement of the islands of the western Pacific around 1500 to 1000 B.C. by a population of highly efficient sailors, who clearly traced their cultural ancestry to somewhere in Southeast Asia.

Bellwood proposes either the Philippines or eastern Indonesia as the homeland of the people producing Lapita pottery, and thus of the Pacific Islanders. Recent excavations at the Bukit Tengkorak rock shelter in Sabah, northern Borneo, testify to the mobility and wide-flung contacts of late Neolithic communities in island Southeast Asia: besides pottery with Lapita affinities, the site yielded also obsidian flakes that, based on their chemical composition, were determined to have come from Talasea in the Bismarck Archipelago, about 6,500 kilometers to the east of Borneo. Talasea was a major source of obsidian for Lapita people, and Talasea obsidian is known to have been widely traded throughout the western Pacific. The finds in Sabah extend this network well into Southeast Asia.

THE COMING OF CIVILIZATION

The study of Southeast Asian civilizations has always been affected by the manifest dominance of religious, philosophical, and political systems derived from India and, to a lesser extent, China. Until after the 1950s, when modern prehistoric research was introduced to the region, it was not unreasonable to assume that what culture historians like to call civilizations were due in Southeast Asia almost entirely to derivation from the outside. In this interpretation, Indian and Chinese systems of statecraft and administration were seen as having been superimposed on unsophisticated local societies. Though the late prehistory of Southeast Asia remains difficult to interpret in many ways, there is now ample evidence that indigenous peoples formed complex social and political systems before the rise of the earliest recognizable Hinduized states.

By the end of the second settlement phase in northeastern Thailand, the treatment of select burials suggests strongly that local societies had become stratified. The presence of exotic artifacts in the form of nonlocal pottery and ornaments of marine shells indicates far-flung trading connections—which, in turn, attest to the presence of an elite social stratum interested in obtaining exotic goods to use as manifestations of power and to manipulate as instruments of social control. This developmental trend took one big step further in the third settlement phase, beginning sometime in the early first millennium B.C.

There is extensive evidence during this phase for social and political competition among communities, typical of systems on the way to coalescing into larger political organizations. This evidence includes indications of increased warfare, indicated by burials with decapitated heads. Among bronze artifacts, weapons became more common. Some villages appear to have been pillaged. The valleys of the Mun and Chi rivers of the southern Khorat Plateau, northeastern Thailand, saw the development of fortified sites surrounded by moats. There was at least a threefold division in the size of these sites, ranging from 15 to 20 hectares for the small sites to 68 hectares for the largest. This hierarchy of settlements suggests regionally organized political systems, beyond the level of autonomous agricultural villages, under centralized control.

Consistent with the evidence for political systems that expand in size and complexity was an increased sophistication of locally produced artifacts, including pottery covered with fine red slip or elaborately painted decoration, of which the painted wares from Ban Chiang have received by far the greatest fame. Indeed, although fine painted pottery has been found in most sites of that period, none has yielded ceramics in the numbers or of the elaboration as those recovered from Ban Chiang. The growing power of elites is indicated also by a great increase in the variety of exotic goods present, including beads of glass and carnelian, the latter an import from India. As part of an economy managed by central political powers and geared, in part, to an extensive trading network, salt was apparently produced from deposits in northeastern Thailand for trade to other parts of Southeast Asia and southern China. Toward the end of the phase, burial customs changed from inhumation to cremation, signaling a dramatic shift in one of the most central rituals.

One of the more important technological innovations of the late settlement phase involved the addition of iron to the metallurgical repertory, probably sometime between 600 and 500 B.C. It appeared first in the form of such bimetallic artifacts as points of spears with forged iron blades, to which a bronze socket was cast on. Iron artifacts became more common during the later part of the phase but never replaced bronze. At about the same time, excavations at the site of Ban Don Ta Phet in western Thailand revealed, besides iron implements, a large number of bronze artifacts that stand out for their variety and technological sophistication. Most of the artifacts have a high tin content, which produces a shiny, silvery metal (the Romans called a similar bronze *speculum*), brittle and difficult to work. Extremely thin-walled and often remarkably large, vessels were first cast in a lost-wax process, then forged, and eventually finished by being polished on a lathe. Many of them are decorated with

FIGURE 1 Bronze drum-gong in the collection of the Institute of Culture and Arts, Hồ Chí Minh City, Vietnam. Photo by Terry E. Miller.

engraved geometric patterns and figurative designs. There is also excellent evidence at Ban Don Ta Phet of trade interactions with distant India and northern Vietnam.

Vietnam

In Vietnam, the working of bronze blossomed greatly during the Gò Mun Period (from c. 1100 to 500 B.C.). Artifacts previously made of stone were now made of bronze, retaining their traditional forms. New types of bronze artifacts appeared and became standard items during the Đông Sơn Period, which followed. Pottery was more highly fired than during the previous periods, indicating improvements in manufacturing technology (and probably more sophisticated demands), and was decorated with incised curvilinear and rectangular lines.

The Phùng Nguyên–Đồng Đậu–Gò Mun sequence of cultural phases applies primarily to the Red River Valley. Vietnamese archaeologists report finding local variants of that sequence in other parts of northern Vietnam; however, all of them converge in the final phase of Vietnamese prehistory, the Đông Sơn Period (about 700 to 100 B.C.). The period takes its name from a site located on the banks of the Mã River in Thanh Hóa Province, where Olov Janse excavated parts of a large cemetery in the second half of the 1930s. Other Đông Sơn sites have meanwhile been found, and many have been excavated. They yield a rich array of bronze artifacts, some iron artifacts, personal ornaments of semiprecious stone, and pottery. Though technologically well made, the pottery of this period is little adorned. Much artistic effort, however, was lavished on bronze artifacts.

The most spectacular items in that regard are bronze drums, cast in complex piece molds and highly decorated, both on top and on the sides Đông Sơn (figure 1). The top (tympanum) always has a star in the center, surrounded by multiple concentric circles, filled variably with geometric motifs and stylized animals, particularly common among them birds identified as cranes. On the edge of the tympanum are often four frogs, cast in the round. The side (mantle) is normally decorated, in some cases with incised scenes of boats filled with fantastically dressed humans, sometimes brandishing spears or bows and arrows. Other decorations on drums show domestic scenes, processions, and what may be interpreted as ritual performances, which appear to include mouth organs and other instruments. Much valuable information about life during the Đông Sơn Period can be derived from the information on the drums, though the interpretation of the scenes, often highly stylized, is open to interpretation.

The information gleaned from the drums is of importance, however, because archaeological research on the Đông Sơn Period is deficient in two important kinds of evidence: few settlement sites are known for the period, so our knowledge almost exclusively derives from cemetery sites; and because of soil conditions, few traces of the bodies have survived with the graves, so the presence of a grave must often be inferred on the basis of clusters of artifacts. This deprives archaeologists of important evidence in the interpretation of the cemeteries. One significant settlement has been found in the site of Cổ Loa, which may furnish us with the earliest evidence of urbanism in Southeast Asia. The first phase of Cổ Loa as a central settlement is associated with Đông Sơn pottery, a large bronze drum, and many other bronze artifacts, and probably dates to 300 B.C. or earlier. The area defined by the outermost of three ramparts encloses some 600 hectares, though this probably represents an expansion sometime after the Đông Sơn Period.

In some of the richest graves of the Đông Sơn Period, one finds Chinese artifacts such as bronze mirrors and daggers (*ko*), and some of the graves themselves, particularly of the late Đông Sonian phase, are constructed of brick in a Chinese manner. This has sometimes been taken to indicate actual Chinese presence—and, indeed, the infiltration of the Đông Sơn social and political elite by Chinese immigrants, who may have come to Vietnam in advance of the general Han expansion. Han military expeditions into south China did lead to the formal annexation of northern Vietnam by the Chinese emperor Wu Ti in 111 B.C. and the creation of three commanderies: Chiao Chih (Tongking), Chiu Chen (Thanh Hóa), and Jenan (North Annam), though local administration remained for some time in the hands of traditional local authorities. However, an alternative, and probably better, explanation of the presence of Chinese artifacts in Đông Sơn sites is that they were obtained in trade from China by local lords. That Đông Sơn communities entertained an impressive network of trade over long distances is also indicated by the fact that Đông Sơn drums have been found scattered throughout mainland and island Southeast Asia, except the Philippines and Borneo. They can be traced as far as Burma to the west, and eastern Indonesia to the south.

The Dian culture of Yunnan

The Đông Sơn culture of Vietnam finds a parallel in the Dian culture of central Yunnan. There can be no doubt about the extremely close cultural relationship between the Đông Sơn and the Dian cultures, though the artifactual record recovered from burials of the latter is even more elaborated and spectacular than that for Đông Sơn. Once again, information about the Dian culture derives exclusively from several fabulously rich cemetery sites. No settlement sites have so far been identified or excavated, and nothing is known about the settlement pattern of that period. The richness of Dian bronze artifacts is hard to describe briefly. They include great drums of the Đông Sơn type—drums that, as with the Đông Sơn situation, are found distributed far beyond the Dian core area in the provinces of Guangdong, Guangxi, Guizhou, and Sichuan. Some of the drums in the Dian area—and many large containers, some of which have been found filled with cowrie shells—are topped with platforms or lids covered with elaborate scenes executed in figures cast in the round. They include market scenes, religious and political rituals with processions, and domestic scenes. Some of the lids are topped by martial scenes of men on horses, the finest ones being gilded. There is a profusion of bronze sculptures (representations of a longhorn, humpback type of cattle are common, as are attacking tigers and other wildlife), models of houses (replete with a full set of domestic activities), agricultural tools, and weapons (including daggers, swords, points of spears, maces, the release mechanisms for crossbows, and body armor). Many of the bronze artifacts are further decorated with ornamental motifs or scenes, either executed in low relief or engraved.

Together, the bronze artifacts furnish a remarkably detailed picture of Dian society. They attest to a highly stratified social system, which had the population and other resources to maintain an elaborate and expensive elite culture. Dian clearly emerged out of local roots and shared this trait with Đông Sơn and other, less well-known, local south Chinese Bronze Age cultures.

Both Đông Sơn and Dian leaders maintained trade interactions with distant areas, among them the Chinese empire. It may well have been this trade that brought the southern peoples and their polities to the attention of the Han. Several Chinese historical records surviving from that period provide useful, though often skewed, descriptions of the "Southern Barbarians." Sima Qian reports in his famous history that in 109 B.C. the Chinese emperor Wu Ti prepared to send troops to the south to conquer and destroy the barbarian kingdoms. The king of Dian submitted freely. He was rewarded by being entrusted with the continued administration of his territory, now however designated as the commandery of Yizhou, and was presented with a golden seal. A golden seal corresponding to the historical description has been found at the site of Shizhaishan.

The picture changed suddenly and drastically around 500 to 400 B.C., when both bronze and iron appeared simultaneously in the Philippines and in Indonesia, where the imported technology was adapted to local aesthetic and ceremonial needs.

The Sa Huynh culture in Vietnam

While Đông Sơn has a close cultural relationship to the north in the Dian culture, another Vietnamese bronze culture has been found to the south. It was documented first in a cemetery near the village of Sa Huynh on the coast of central Vietnam; other sites have been found, some predating Sa Huynh itself, once again illustrating a continuous local development. The Sa Huynh culture stands out by the fact that it practiced cremation. The ashes were interred in earthenware jars with finely made pottery, iron and bronze artifacts and various ornaments of semiprecious stone. The incised decorations of pottery found in Sa Huynh burial urns shares some similarities with various other prehistoric pottery in mainland Southeast Asia, including northeast Thailand and northern Vietnam, but it has its closest affinities in the Philippines. In addition, some personal ornaments found at Sa Huynh, interpreted as pendants and earrings, are encountered in virtual duplicate in the islands. The dean of Southeast Asian archaeologists, W. G. Solheim, II, proposed the concept of a Sa Huynh–Kalanay ceramic tradition, which he saw linked with a late prehistoric movement of Austronesian-speaking peoples from the coast of Vietnam to the Philippines. More recently, he suggested that the formal affinities may rather be the result of interactions with a group of Austronesian-speakers he calls Nusantao, who he believes were resident in the Southeast Asian islands and were a maritime-based people, engaging in the exploitation of marine resources and trade.

In all, the evidence indicates that throughout mainland Southeast Asia and southern China, the last millennium B.C. was a time when out of local farming communities arose larger social and political systems, which brought communities within a region together under centralized political leadership. This process was correlated with another development, the emergence of social stratification. It was further linked with the intensification of agricultural economies, with increasing craft specialization (and increasing artistic elaboration of elite material culture), the control of subsistence and craft economy by the central elites, and an ever-widening network of trade. In other words, we see the emergence of chiefdoms, first small and localized in their respective spheres of control, but over time growing in size and complexity. This development did not occur in synchrony across the subcontinent; rather, the cultural and social landscape of Southeast Asia remained, as it had been for some time, a mosaic of diverse components. Indeed, the degree of diversity intensified. The largest and most complex systems are seen in northern Vietnam and central Yunnan, where the development almost certainly crossed the threshold into state organization. The same may perhaps also be true for the Mun and Chi River area of northeastern Thailand, and possibly also for some other parts of the region, for which we still have insufficient archaeological evidence.

The important point is that we can observe the evolution of social complexity as an internal process. Typically of aristocracies and their political leaders, the Southeast Asian elites reached out to distant areas for trade and other interactions. It was this development that prepared for the next stage, signaling the dawn of history for the region, and entailing the importation not only of Indian and Chinese artifacts but also of religious ideas, social philosophies, and systems of political administration. It was with the tools of these intellectual imports that some Southeast Asian chiefs and princes then effected a further expansion of their powers and established the earliest historical empires of Champa and Funan.

PREHISTORY IN THE ISLANDS

Turning from the Southeast Asian mainland to the islands, we find that the archaeological record for the last two or three millennia B.C. is sparse and incoherent. We do know, however, that prehistoric communities in the islands did not share with their mainland counterparts an early involvement in bronze metallurgy. This situation may reflect the fact that there was no mechanism for transmitting the knowledge of bronze technology to the islands (possibly because of a lack of contact between the mainland and the islands), or that island communities were socially unreceptive to this technology. In the absence of evidence to the contrary, it appears that until the middle of the first millennium B.C., island societies remained organized in small, autonomous units, focused on subsistence economies based on agriculture and fishing. There was evidently a great deal of mobility among island societies during the last fifteen hundred years B.C., with far-flung exchange contacts, but it occurred in the context of a maritime-oriented subsistence economy.

The picture changed suddenly and drastically around 500 to 400 B.C., when both bronze and iron appeared simultaneously through many of the islands. In the Philippines, the source seems to have been Sa Huynh. This is suggested by other exchange goods and similar pottery shared with that site. In Indonesia, however, the source was more likely Đông Sơn, as the scattering of Đông Sơn drums throughout much of the archipelago suggests.

The occurrence of Đông Sơn drums in Indonesia raises a problem. Clearly, these artifacts must have been of enormous value, given the skill and labor invested in their manufacture and the long distance they traveled. How could small autonomous farming and fishing communities afford such treasures? Did they possess exchange goods of equal value to the Đông Sơnians? Or is the currently available archaeological record greatly understating the level of development of island societies in the late first millennium B.C.?

It is important to note that centers of metallurgy began to appear quickly in some parts of Indonesia, where the imported technology was adapted to local aesthetic and ceremonial needs. Some of the bronze artifacts made locally still retain a Đông Sơnian flavor, whereas others deviate greatly from the Đông Sơn model. Many of the artifacts are exceedingly elaborate, almost baroque in their ornateness. Their construction indicates that their function was almost certainly ceremonial or representational rather than utilitarian. These developments do indicate the presence of social and political systems above the village level during that period, when leaders could command the means for such specialized craft production.

There were several early, historically recognizable states in the islands, the largest and most expansionary of them Srivijaya. They are documented both through Chinese historical records and through inscriptions that survive from the sixth and seventh centuries A.D. The archaeological record is insufficient to link these historical empires with preceding prehistoric communities and political organizations.

ASIAN ART AND MUSIC IN PREHISTORY

Even though the archaeological record remains inadequate in many respects and is full of gaps, an ever more coherent picture of the ancient cultural development of the region has emerged over the past four decades. It tells us not only about the great changes that have occurred but also of long-term cultural-historical continuities. It demonstrates clearly a strong internal dynamic, in which Southeast Asia interacted with surrounding parts of the world as both a recipient of cultural innovations and a source of demographic, social, and cultural developments. We are now able to perceive deep, indigenous roots for the Hinduized and Sinicized historical civilizations of the region. Pursuing this generalized insight in a more specific context, can we trace the autochthonous prehistoric sources for the historic arts of Southeast Asia?

In investigating this question, we are highly constrained, not only by the facts that the number of well-excavated archaeological sites is remarkably small and the recovered materials are often poorly reported, but also by the peculiarities of archaeological preservation. In the decorative and figurative arts, our evidence is limited almost exclusively to ceramics and, for the last two millennia B.C. or so, to metal artifacts. Surely, prehistoric communities must also have expressed themselves artistically through wood, basketry, cloth, and other media. We know from contemporary ethnographic analogs that artistic endeavors in different media tend to share certain design principles and stylistic elements even though each medium also tends to be invested with a series of forms and motifs peculiar to it, and each is usually employed in specific and circumscribed contexts.

A review of the record of prehistoric pottery shows that many of the decorative motifs found among the early Neolithic communities throughout the region have endured over many millennia. Allowing for a large amount of local and subregional variability, we nevertheless find broad regional similarities and continuities. The elements of triangles, curvilinear designs, interlocking spirals, and concentric circles, the manner in which open spaces are filled in between major design elements, approaches to the way in which space is apportioned within a design, and other elements have endured into contemporary designs found on textiles, metalwork in the southern Philippines and Indonesia, and decorative woodwork. Within this broad generalization, art historians have tried, with varying degrees of success, to trace more specific historical and cultural relationships.

Until the late Bronze Age (ca. 500 B.C.), we have almost no records of Southeast Asian figurative art. Rare exceptions include small figurines of people and animals (cattle, elephants) made of baked clay from the earlier bronze period of northeastern Thailand and paintings on rocks found in many parts of the region but never well dated. We have, therefore, virtually no knowledge of the symbolic content of prehistoric Southeast Asian art. From ethnographic parallels and early historic accounts, we may assume that much of the content dealt with the animistic world of ancestors and natural spirits, some of which survives in contemporary tribal art and has not been completely superseded, even by the conversion of historic Southeast Asian civilizations to the great world religions. A fine example of this are the carved images of the thirty-seven natural spirits (*na'*), venerated in a chapel of the Swe Dagon pagoda in Rangoon, Burma.

The most elaborate artistic legacy survives in the bronzework of the Đông Sơn and Dian cultures of Vietnam and Yunnan. It includes a rich ornamental record, a wealth of individual figures, extensive scenes rendered by engraving or cast in low relief, and a large body of bronze sculptures. This art bears witness to specific artistic traditions, among them the textile art of the period. Many of the representations allow us to gain insights as to the rich ceremonial costumes of the period.

Music

Among the arts represented in the Đông Sơn and Dian record is music. Much discussion has taken place about the function and use of the drums themselves. Given the enormous effort, skill, and cost involved in their manufacture, it is logical to assume that they were made for, and closely associated with, powerful leaders. Some writers have claimed that the drums were seen as representations of the king or a paramount chief. By the same token, it is claimed that they were sacred instruments, invested with great supernatural powers.

We are fortunate in having, on the mantles of drums and in sculpted scenes, illustrations that show drums in use. Some show an individual drum under a platform in the aft section of a boat filled with warriors in ceremonial garb; in one sculpted scene on the lid of a cowrie-shell container from Yunnan, three drums are stacked on top of each other in the center of a grouping that seems to portray a human sacrifice; and several engraved scenes depict drums arrayed under a raised platform on which humans are placed with staffs, as if to play the drums. On a drum excavated at Cổ Loa, four players have their staffs alternately raised and lowered. These latter scenes are particularly interesting. While they do not exclude the possibility that bronze drums were beaten as isolated rhythmic instruments (as to call people to assembly or to war), they indicate that bronze drums were used in musical ensembles. Similar to the bronze gongs in Southeast Asian ensembles, Đông Sơnian drums come in a range of sizes. In 1990, Vietnamese archaeologists surveyed 115 drums found in Vietnam. The heights of the instruments ranged from 17 to 67 centimeters, and the diameters from 20 to 90 centimeters. Chinese archaeologists have studied scraping marks on the inside of Dian drums and believe that they are the result of tuning. All this suggests that individual drums were manufactured to conform to a specific pitch and that several drums could be, and were, combined into ensembles. Since each drum in such an ensemble seems to have been played by an individual musician, it is tempting to infer that this involved either a simple form of ostinato or that they were used in a way akin to bell choirs (figure 2).

FIGURE 2 Drawing of the tympanum (top) of a bronze drum-gong from Vietnam. From Nguyễn Văn Huyên and Hoàng Vinh, *Những Trống Đồng Đong Sơn Đã Phát Hiện Ở Việt Nam* (Viện Bảo Tàng Lịch Sử, 1975), p. 279.

Since each drum in such an ensemble seems to have been played by an individual musician, it is tempting to infer that this involved either a simple form of ostinato or that they were used in a way akin to bell choirs.

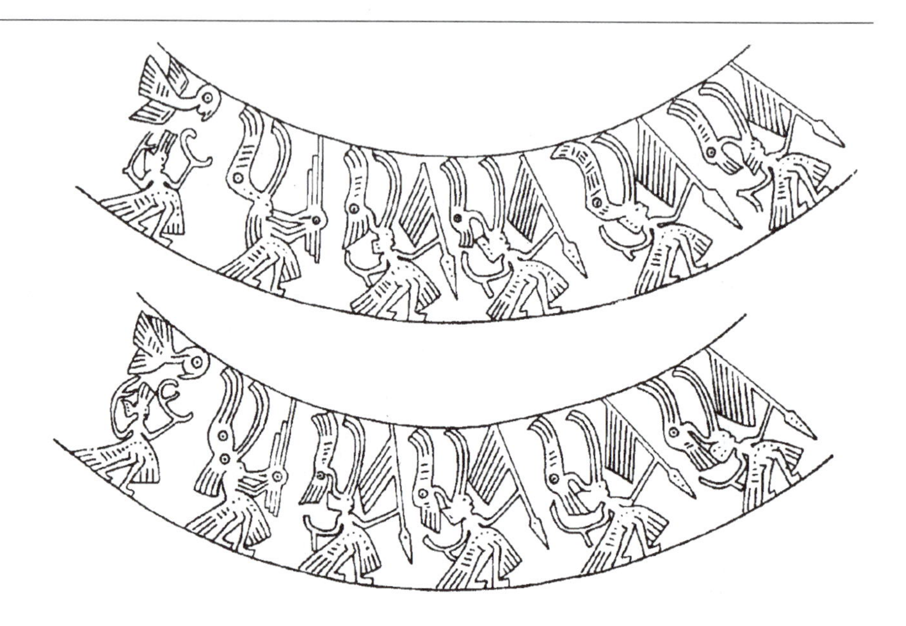

FIGURE 3 Detail of martial dancers and players of free-reed mouth organs, from a Vietnamese bronze drum-gong. From Nguyễn Văn Huyên and Hoàng Vinh, *Những Trống Đồng Đong Sơn Đã Phát Hiện Ở Việt Nam* (Viện Bảo Tàng Lịch Sử, 1975), p. 175.

Decorations on bronze drums show other musical instruments in use. Among them is an instrument strongly reminiscent of the contemporary Lao free-reed mouth organ (*khaen*), something that may be interpreted as hand-held cymbals similar to those now familiar from traditional Thai ensembles (*ching*), flutes, and bells. The mouth organs occur repeatedly, usually in the context of a row of dancers. Sculpted scenes from the Dian culture portray also several other instruments in action, in groups of musicians or groups of dancers and musicians. These instruments include hand-held drums and wind instruments related by Chinese archaeologists to the Chinese mouth organ (*sheng*). Examples of the latter have also been found as artifacts made of bronze in some of the Dian sites, at least one of them shaped like a calabash and adorned with a small cattle figurine. These instruments are less reminiscent of their Han counterparts than of similar wind instruments found today among south Chinese minorities (figure 3).

A full study of the musical traditions of the Đông Sơn and Dian cultures is yet to be carried out, but it is clear that there is a wealth of valuable archaeological information. The music of Southeast Asia appears to have ancient indigenous roots.

REFERENCES

Bellwood, Peter. 1985. *Prehistory of the Indo-Malaysian Archipelago.* Sydney, Orlando, London: Academic Press.

Higham, Charles. 1989. *The Archaeology of Mainland Southeast Asia.* Cambridge and New York: Cambridge University Press.

Bamboo, Rice, and Water

Robert Wessing

Three features that strike a visitor to lowland Southeast Asia are the roles played in daily life by bamboo, rice, and water. Bamboo seems to grow everywhere, and the peoples of Southeast Asia have been characterized as having bamboo cultures (Burling 1965:29). Bamboo serves as a building material, in crafts and household utensils, and as irrigation pipes, leading water into households and fields. Even the word by which we know it comes from Southeast Asia—the Malay *bambu.*

Water too seems abundant, especially to those from arid parts of the world. It flows alongside roads and paths to flood the fields of rice stretching to the horizon and patterning the lower mountainsides in their terraces, growing the crop that may be said to be the defining feature of life. Indeed, to a great part of the population of the area, to eat a meal is to eat rice, and a meal without rice is thought to be incomplete, leaving one dissatisfied. In fact, the eating of rice may be seen as one of the defining characteristics of being human; visitors are asked "if they are able to eat rice yet" and in some mythologies, spirits became human after consuming it (Terwiel 1994:18).

The presence of these features is set by the ecological conditions of the landscape, which contrasts mountain chains, valleys, and lowlands (Dobby 1961). In most of the islands, the landscape is simplified to a mountain-lowland contrast, without major continental rivers. The lowlands are often swampy, extended by riverine flooding. The climate is tropical, with distinct wet and dry monsoons in many places, bringing alternate periods of hot, dry weather and cool, rainy weather, the latter being the time of activity for subsistence agriculture. The mountains modulate the intensity of the rains, creating a mosaic of areas receiving heavy rainfall and areas receiving much less.

The floodplains of the major rivers were not the preferred areas of early human settlement, owing to their swampiness and the difficulty of clearing their land (Demaine 1978:49–50). Human habitations were mostly concentrated in areas of more moderate rainfall—along tributary rivers, where the land was more easily cleared for both settlements and agriculture. Although easier to cope with, rainfall in this environment could be insufficient, especially for wet-rice agriculture, leading to the need for a variety of schemes of managing water. The success of these is attested in some areas by some of the highest rural population densities in the world. The earliest settlers seem to have come primarily from the north (Huggan 1995:262), bringing a developed agricultural technology. The culture of these people was later influenced by ideas emanating from India—a script, literature, and religious concepts, which became adapted to meet local needs.

AGRICULTURE

Southeast Asian farmers cultivate a wide variety of crops, including roots, vegetables, fruits, beans, coconuts, ginger, and peppers. Alongside these, trees and bamboo are grown specifically for use as firewood and in construction. Bamboo is especially valued because it can be put to many uses (Austin and Ueda 1970). Its seeds can be eaten, and it figures in rituals, including those associated with rice agriculture.

The most important subsistence crop is rice, a plant so old that the origin and method of its first cultivation remain unknown. Its cultivation may have started as long as ten thousand years ago in an area ranging from the Ganges plains across northern Southeast Asia into southern China (Oka 1988).

Rice can grow in dry, rain-watered fields, and in wet, flooded ones. Some scholars believe dry planting was the earlier method; others think that the crop originated as a weed, associated with the cultivation of taro in wet gardens (Barrau 1965). In traditions of East Java, Kalimantan, the Philippines, and Taiwan, the cultivation of rice followed that of root crops (Mabuchi 1954), but since not all these crops are grown in wet fields, these traditions cannot answer this question. Since rice is quite adaptable, the perfect crop for Southeast Asia, both techniques may have developed simultaneously, in response to local conditions.

Whether grown on wet fields or dry ones, rice needs water. Where water occurs, either naturally or through irrigation, it is led to the fields; where it does not, as at higher elevations, the fields depend on rainfall. To be useful, water must be managed; uncontrolled water, as from floods, can devastate the crop. This trait led some observers to postulate hydraulic societies, in which grand systems of irrigation were controlled from the center by a despotic monarch. More recent analysis has concluded that such systems were constructed on smaller scales and adapted to varying needs and conditions, often crosscutting local political authorities.

The management and construction of these systems involves creating ditches, (bamboo) pipes, and floodgates, and developing the proper gradient of the field for a slow but steady flow of water. Each system demands cooperation among farmers to arrive at a reliable supply and an equitable distribution of the commodity; relationships between humans and water have indeed been called the defining feature of the region (Huggan 1995:263; Rigg 1992:1).

THE SPIRITUAL CONTEXT

Though many people in Southeast Asia are adherents of major religions (including Buddhism, Hinduism, Christianity, and Islam), people everywhere in the region believe the landscape is populated by spirits, the original owners of the land, water, and trees, and their cooperation is necessary for any enterprise, including agriculture, to succeed (Mus 1975). The spirits are related to humans; some people maintain that they originally were one group, which differentiated into humans and spirits. Natural spirits are one category, and ancestors are another; living humans may be seen as embodied spirits, which in some mythologies are said to have come about due to the spirits' eating rice. Spirits can imbue almost anything: rocks, rivers, and the forest are said to be owned or guarded by natural spirits, while ancestral ones guard their descendants' welfare.

Since these spirits are perceived to be touchy about their prerogatives, people perform rituals to ensure their cooperation. Offerings, sometimes including live sacrifices, are made to village guardians and to the more important spirits in the forest; ancestral spirits are invited to attend life-cycle rituals and are asked for their blessing.

Important to the welfare of the people, and central to beliefs about rice, bamboo, and water, is the spirits' control over the fertility of the fields and the crops, because without their cooperation no crops will grow. In Java, this fertility is sometimes seen as resulting from a marriage between the male sky and the female earth (Mabuchi 1954:71); in Malaysia, such a marriage also produced the first people (Hervey 1882:189). These perceptions are based on the observation that during the dry season, nothing grows on the land, which seems lifeless and barren; the coming of the rains turns the earth green once more.

Human sexual behavior is often taken as the model on which nature operates, and in Southeast Asia, sexual practices and taboos are part of the process of growing rice. These include adulterous men's exclusion from cultivation in Sarawak and a taboo on sexual intercourse during harvest among a variety of peoples. Since the emission of semen is seen as analogous to the flow of water, coitus might bring rain, which would ruin the harvest and chase away the spirit of the rice. Similarly, reports from Java, Burma, and Thailand tell of people actually or symbolically copulating in their fields to bring on the rains that will vivify the crops (Demaine 1978:51–52; Wilken 1912:41). Another method of ending a prolonged dry spell is bathing a cat, reversing the animal's natural proclivities, and, it is hoped, reversing the conditions of nature.

TRACK 1

Water, then, is seen as a source of life, controlled by spirits, reviving nature, and stimulating the growth of crops (figure 1). Because of its importance, the spirits controlling it are especially remembered at festivals and celebrations. During annual village-cleansing ceremonies in Java, in which social strains caused by daily frictions are ritually removed and harmony is restored, offerings are brought to the local source of water; this is often also the location of the village guardian spirit, remembered at family celebrations (including weddings and circumcisions), either at the source or at the place where the family usually obtains its water for daily use.

Irrigation water also receives special treatment, turning ordinary water into a fertility- or life-enhancing substance. In Java, people make offerings to this end at the

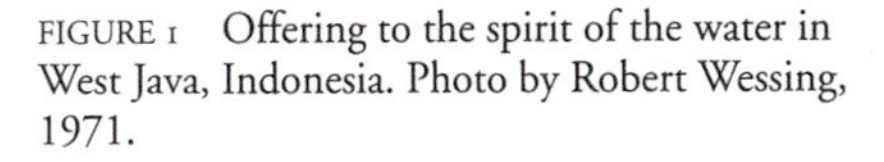

FIGURE 1 Offering to the spirit of the water in West Java, Indonesia. Photo by Robert Wessing, 1971.

Bamboo is seen as embodying the forces of growth and fertility and is closely linked with water and rice. It can sometimes be seen to grow: at least one variety can grow 30 centimeters a day.

place where the water enters the fields, while in Burma an image of a "lady of the weir" guards the water supply (Demaine 1978:61). The Chăm of Vietnam call her Patao Kumei, and credit her with the introduction of irrigation (LeBar et al. 1964:247). Sometimes the water is made to flow through graveyards, where it receives ancestors' blessing or is imbued by their spirit, linking the dead with their descendants and the fertility of their soil.

THE ORIGIN OF RICE

A variety of myths account for the origin of rice and for why people have to work to obtain it (Mabuchi 1954). The former have been classified into those where grain is obtained (1) from heaven or a place overseas; (2) from the underworld, sometimes brought by an ancestor; or (3) from the dead body of a (usually female) supernatural being or ancestor. Various versions of the latter type of myth usually refer to a time when rice was already in the world and readily available.

In one such myth, the kernels of grain were huge, fragrant, and sweet, and one kernel would feed a family. One day a widow, while building a barn, became annoyed when the abundance of rice hampered her work. She hit the grain with a stick, breaking it into pieces, which fell into both the forest and the water. The former became upland, dry rice, while the latter turned into wet-field rice. The grain became angry at being treated cruelly—and ever since, people have had to plant and nourish it (Tambiah 1970:351–354).

In most origin myths, rice originates from the body of a spirit, in Sundanese a spirit (*pohaci*) named Tisnawati, in some cases a goddess. The idea of a spirit or nymph is the more widespread. She is said to be vain and to like facial powder, perfumes, and mirrors, with which she is thought to primp—all traits more in keeping with spirits and nymphs than with goddesses (Hazeu 1901:90).

In a continuation of the myth, this spirit is killed and buried, and out of her body grows a variety of plants, among which are rice and sometimes bamboo. The spirit is often portrayed as coming from heaven to bathe in a pool, where a young man or a prince finds her. This man then hides her clothes, preventing her from returning to the sky. She consents to marry him, stipulating that no one may ever lift the lid of the cooking pot. When this is eventually done anyway, either by the young man or someone in their household, a single grain, an ear of rice, or a little girl is found there. The spirit, after leaving instructions about the planting and care of the grain, then dies or returns to the sky.

In other versions, the spirit emerges from a jewel at the bottom of the sea, or from a tear shed by a snake, traditionally categorized as a thing of the underworld. From there, she is transported to the sky. This transportation is the cause of her death, after which her body is brought to earth to be the source of rice (Hidding 1929).

In all these myths, the spirit of rice is originally associated with the underworld and water, the source of life. The spirit had to die before rice could grow—associating both the spirit and the rice with the ancestors, whose blessings are crucial to the maintenance of human society.

THE SPIRIT OF RICE

FIGURE 2 The mother of rice in West Java, Indonesia. Photo by Robert Wessing, 1971.

Rice is often spoken of as having a soul or as being identical to the spirit or goddess. Nash (1965:176) mentions a mother of rice, which sometimes seems identical to the Burmese soul of rice. The soul of rice should be understood in this context as a spirit, related to human spirits, whose essence is the growing power and nourishment of rice. The mother of rice is a number (often seven) of specially selected ears of rice, harvested before the rest of the crop, in which this essence is thought to reside. Never eaten, she may, in association with other selected portions of the harvest, be used as seed in the next cycle of planting (Kruyt 1903:398). The Minangkabau of Sumatra call this seed the heart of the rice (Cole 1945:263), and the Malays speak of it as the baby of rice, Seri Bumi (Essence of the Earth). Just as among humans, therefore, the essence (*semangat*) is passed on through the mother to the offspring, and without it the crop would fail (figure 2).

The Dusun of Kalimantan believe ancestral spirits can influence the rice for good or evil, depending on whether their descendants remember to venerate them (Liang 1985:90). More specifically, the Iban say there is a cycle in which ancestral spirits, in the form of a nourishing dew, bring the rice to life, and the spirit of the rice gives life to people, who, when they in turn become ancestors, give life to the grain.

Conceptions about the identity of the rice crop with the spirit vary considerably. Some observers state specifically that the two are identical. In West Java and Sulawesi, the spirit of rice only impregnates the crop (Kruyt 1935:109), while according to the Malays, rice is cared for and animated by spirits of the earth, who may be personified as the Islamized prophet Ketap or 'Tap (Endicott 1970:114). In Thailand, this caring and animating is done by Mae Phosop, variously called a goddess of rice, the guardian deity of mankind, and the mother of rice (Hanks 1972:97).

RICE AND BAMBOO

Bamboo is seen as embodying the forces of growth and fertility and is closely linked with water and rice. The ecological requirements of bamboo resemble those of rice grown on dry fields. It can sometimes be seen to grow: at least one variety can grow 30 centimeters a day. The Dusun pay homage to a sacred bamboo to assure fertility in general; yellow bamboo is thought to ward off evil influences. The tree is occasionally characterized as the container of the water of life or is used to catch the blessings given by the spirits of fertility.

Both in Taiwan and in India, myths tell how rice originated in bamboo. In Taiwan, bamboo was brought to earth by a man from heaven, who shortly after returned there (Mabuchi 1954:25). The Indian myth tells how king Rama's wife, Sita, had an extra finger on one hand, which she cut off and planted. From it grew a bamboo plant, which in its sections contained all kinds of grain, which became available to humankind through a hole in the bamboo, chewed there by a pig (Fuchs 1960:422).

In harvest ceremonies, some Sundanese make five holes in a bamboo; they then plug these holes with rice seed (ASS 1990:34). The people of Tengger, Java, do something similar during a ceremony at which they invoke ancestors and supernatural guardians (Hefner 1985:117, 123). In the Tanimbar Islands, some cooked rice is placed in three bamboos called seedlings, establishing the link between bamboo, (cooking) water, and rice, and enacting the local belief that cooked rice is the last step in a circle that includes young bamboo, water, and "old" (cooked) rice (van der Weijden 1981:193).

The seed of bamboo, which flowers only once and then dies, is edible, and both looks like and can be cooked like rice. Both in India (Fuchs 1960:68) and among the Chin of Burma (Lehman 1963:50) there is a belief that famine follows the flowering of bamboo, perhaps due to the close association between the two grasses; Lehman, however, makes a connection between rats attracted to the bamboo that then eat the rice. A reflection of the rice-from-bamboo myth may be found in the old Sundanese practice of planting bamboos with holes in them along the ricefields. The sound made by the wind playing through these holes is said to be music to entertain the spirit of rice (Wilken 1912:40). The Balinese are said to build musical irrigation tubes from bamboo, in which the water rushing through it makes a musical sound, entertaining the spirit of rice and encouraging growth.

The ceremony in which the Sundanese place rice in the bamboo is accompanied by a musical performance using tuned, shaken bamboo rattles (*angklung*), instruments essential to the planting and harvesting rituals in various areas of Indonesia (Baier 1986). In West Java, this music was formerly essential to securing an abundant crop, its music enchanting the spirit or goddess of rice, enticing her to come and bring prosperity on earth (Baier 1985:9) (figure 3).

THE GODDESS OF RICE

If the spiritual beliefs discussed above can be seen as dealing with village-level interests, with Sita we arrive at wider, state-level concerns, and with clear Indian religious influence on Southeast Asian beliefs. One of the consequences of Indian influence is that spirits are now called *widyadhari,* a kind of nymph or goddess, rulers of spirits. Their origin as Southeast Asian spirits remains clear from the traits ascribed to them—the previously mentioned love of powder and mirrors, and that the *widyadhari,* originally nymphs of mountains and the sky, are here associated with water and the underworld.

In Java and Bali, the Indianized goddess of agriculture is called Dewi Sri, a namesake of Sri, the Indian goddess of wealth, who has nothing to do with agriculture. In Thailand, she retained her original name, Mae Phosop. Sita is usually associated with a royal house rather than with agriculture, but both she and Sri are manifestations of the goddess Lakshmi, sometimes in Indian myth said to have been born in a plowed furrow, and sometimes during the churning of the ocean—stories that associate her with both agriculture and water (Dowson 1972:176).

FIGURE 3 Offerings to the spirit of rice (Dewi Sri) in West Java, Indonesia. Photo by Robert Wessing, 1971.

Sita is sometimes portrayed as being found as a princess or a maiden inside a mysterious bamboo, which only the king can cut down; at other times, she is discovered in a clump of foam, floating on the ocean. She and the king then marry and found a royal dynasty (Wessing 1990). In Java, this myth is expressed in the relation between the Goddess of the Indian Ocean, Nyai Roro Kidul, and prince Senopati, the founder of the royal house of Mataram in the 1600s. This goddess is often portrayed as having scales, relating her to the cult of the snake (*naga* in Indonesia, *nagi* in Cambodia), thought to be the original owner of the soil in much of Southeast Asia (Jordaan 1984). In ancient Cambodia, King Kaundinya is said to have made a source of water at the site of his capital by piercing the soil, creating a spring in the shape of the snake-princess Soma (Bosch 1951:127). He was said to cohabit nightly with this snake-consort to assure the fertility and the continuity of his realm (Gaudes 1993). In Java, the rulers of the principalities of Yogyakarta and Surakarta (the successors to Mataram) are said to continue the practice regularly with Nyai Roro Kidul.

Like Sita, Sri is associated with royal houses in her incarnation as queen to the god Vishnu, who appears as king. In Javanese tales (Rassers 1959:10–19), she

FIGURE 4 *Kaca-kaca,* uniting rice and bamboo in a representation of Mount Meru in West Java, Indonesia. Photo by Robert Wessing, 1971.

emerges from a magical jewel, brought from the bottom of the ocean to the heavens. She is adopted by the god Batara Guru, who falls in love with her. His advances rejected, he persists, and she consents if he can fulfill certain conditions, among which is to provide her with an instrument that will make music without being played (van der Weijden 1981:36). The affair ends tragically with Batara Guru's rape of Sri, who dies and is buried, to become the origin of settled life and certain plants (including rice, bamboo, and coconuts).

Sita and Sri are linked by bamboo, rice, water, and the Indianized royal house. One symbol of such a house is Mount Meru, the center of the universe and source of the cosmic power that maintains the state (figure 4). In Bali and West Java, this mountain is symbolized by a striking structure (in West Java called *kaca-kaca*)—a tall bamboo pole, from which a basket for rice is hung, realizing an integration of bamboo and rice (Wessing 1978:24). For life-cycle ceremonies, it is erected at the entrance, where musical performances take place; guests arriving for such an event need only look for the *kaca-kaca* to find their way. Kings often plow the first furrow of the season, and they are associated with spirits or sources of water. These sources are not always used for irrigation; Jordaan (1991) points out that they also supply life-giving holy water *(tirtha)* for the benefit of the state.

REFERENCES

ASS. 1990. "Bamboo among the Sundanese." *Voice of Nature* 81(May):34–37.

Austin, Robert, and Koichiru Ueda. 1970. *Bamboo.* New York: Walker Weatherhill.

Baier, Randal E. 1985. "The Angklung Ensemble of West Java: Continuity of an Agricultural Tradition." *Balungan* 2:8–16.

———. 1986. "Si Duriat Keueung: The Sundanese Angklung Ensemble of West Java, Indonesia." M.A. thesis, Wesleyan University.

Barrau, Jacques. 1965. "L'Humide et le Sec." *Journal of the Polynesian Society* 74(3):329–346.

Bosch, F. D. K. 1951. "Guru, Drietand en Bron." *Bijdragen tot de Taal-, Land- en Volkenkunde* 107:117–134.

Burling, Robbins. 1965. *Hill Farms and Padi Fields: Life in Mainland Southeast Asia.* Englewood Cliffs, N.J.: Prentice-Hall.

Cole, Fay-Cooper. 1945. *The Peoples of Malaysia.* Princeton, N.J.: Van Nostrand.

Demaine, H. 1978. "Magic and Management, Methods of Ensuring Water Supplies for Agriculture in South East Asia." In *Nature and Man in South East Asia,* ed. Philip Anthony Stott, 49–67. London: School of Oriental and African Studies.

Dobby, E. H. G. 1961. *Southeast Asia.* London: University of London Press.

Dowson, John. 1972. *A Classical Dictionary of Hindu Mythology and Religion, Geography, History and Literature.* London: Routledge and Kegan Paul.

Endicott, Kirk Michael. 1970. *An Analysis of Malay Magic.* Oxford: Clarendon Press.

Fuchs, Stephen. 1960. *The Gond and Bhumia of Eastern Mandla.* London: Asia Publishing House.

Gaudes, Rüdiger. 1993. "Kaundinya, Preah Thaong, and the 'Nagi Soma': Some Aspects of a Cambodian Legend." *Asian Folklore Studies* 52:333–358.

Hanks, Lucien M. 1972. *Rice and Man: Agricultural Ecology in Southeast Asia.* Chicago: Aldine.

Hazeu, G. A. J. 1901. "Nini Towong." *Tijdschrift voor Indische Taal-, Land- en Volkenkunde* 43:36–107.

Hefner, Robert W. 1985. *Hindu Javanese: Tengger Tradition and Islam.* Princeton, N.J.: Princeton University Press.

Hervey, D. F. A. 1882. "The Mentra Traditions." *Journal of the Straits Branch of the Royal Asiatic Society* 10:189–194.

Hidding, Klaas A. H. 1929. "Nyi Pohatji Sangjang Sri." Ph.D. dissertation, Rijksuniversiteit Leiden.

Huggan, Robert D. 1995. "Co-Evolution of Rice and Humans." *GeoJournal* 35(3):262– 265.

Jordaan, Roy E. 1984. "The Mystery of Nyai Lara Kidul, Goddess of the Southern Ocean." *Archipel* 28:99–116.

———. 1991. "Text, Temple and *Tirtha.*" In *The Art and Culture of South-East Asia,* ed. Lokesh Chandra, 165–180. New Delhi: International Academy of Indian Culture and Aditya Prakashan.

Kruyt, Albert C. 1903. "De rijstmoeder in den Indischen archipel." *Verslagen en Mededelingen der Koninklijke Akademie van Wetenschappen, afdeling Letterkunde* 4(5):361–411.

———. 1935. "De rijstgodin op Midden-Celebes, en de Maangodin." *Mensch en Maatschappij* 11(2):109–122.

LeBar, Frank M., Gerald C. Hickey, and John K. Musgrave, eds. 1964. *Ethnic Groups of Mainland Southeast Asia.* New Haven, Conn.: Human Relations Area Files.

Lehman, F. K. 1963. *The Structure of Chin Society.* Illinois Studies in Anthropology, 3. Urbana: University of Illinois Press.

Liang, Yap Beng. 1985. "The Traditional World-Views of the Indigenous Peoples of Sabah." In *Malaysian World-View,* ed. Mohd. Taib Osman, 76–130. Singapore: Institute of Southeast Asian Studies.

Mabuchi, Toichi. 1954. "Tales Concerning the Origin of Grains in the Insular Areas of Eastern and Southeastern Asia." *Asian Folklore Studies* 23:1–92.

Mus, Paul. 1975. *India Seen from the East: Indian and Indigenous Cults in Champa.* Translated and edited by I. W. Mabbett and D. P. Chandler. Monash Papers on Southeast Asia, 3. Clayton, Victoria: Centre of Southeast Asian Studies, Monash University.

Nash, Manning. 1965. *The Golden Road to Modernity: Village Life in Contemporary Burma.* Chicago: University of Chicago Press.

Oka, H. I. 1988. *Origin of Cultivated Rice.* Developments in Crop Science, 14. Amsterdam: Elsevier.

Rassers, W. H. 1959. *Pañji, the Culture Hero.* Translation Series, 3. The Hague: Martinus Nijhoff. Koninklijk Instituut voor Taal-, Land- en Volkenkunde.

Rigg, Jonathan, ed. 1992. *The Gift of Water: Water Management, Cosmology and the State in South East Asia.* London: School of Oriental and African Studies.

Tambiah, S. J. 1970. *Buddhism and the Spirit Cults in North-East Thailand.* Cambridge Studies in Social Anthropology, 2. Cambridge: Cambridge University Press.

Terwiel, Baas. 1994. "The Tale of the Giant Rice-Kernel and the Cursing Widow." In *Text and Tales, Studies in Oral Tradition,* 10–23. Leiden: Research School CNWS, Leiden University; CNWS Publications, 22.

Weijden, Gera van der. 1981. *Indonesische Reisrituale.* Basel: Ethnologisches Seminar der Universität und Museum für Völkerkunde. Basler Beiträge zur Ethnologie, 20.

Wessing, Robert. 1978. *Cosmology and Social Behavior in a West Javanese Settlement.* Papers in International Studies, Southeast Asia Series, 47. Athens, Ohio: Ohio University Center for International Studies, Southeast Asia Program.

———. 1990. "Sri and Sedana and Sita and Rama: Myths of Fertility and Generation." *Asian Folklore Studies* 49(2):235–257.

Wilken, G. A. 1912. "Het animisme bij de volken van den Indischen Archipel." In *De Verspreide Geschriften van Prof. Dr. G. A. Wilken,* ed. F. D. E. van Ossenbruggen, 3–287. Semarang: G. C. T. van Dorp.

Waves of Cultural Influence

Terry E. Miller
Sean Williams

To the extent that scholars can reconstruct a chronology and a history for Southeast Asia, the process is complex. People prefer to assert their national and regional identities. Often they do not see, and sometimes they even deny, that this individuality has resulted from a process extending back into the mists of history and prehistory, in which layer after layer of outside influence transformed, and was transformed by, the cultures that received it. We cannot speak of cultural purity in any sense, and the people of Southeast Asia recognize themselves as participants in multiple levels of society: as Southeast Asians, as citizens of a nation, as carriers of a regional tradition, as groups distinct from those of another province, district, village, or even family. It is therefore appropriate to understand that Southeast Asian cultures were formed from waves of cultural influence, from both nearby and distant societies.

An examination of Southeast Asian terminology easily shows how each language has absorbed words and writing systems from others, including those of India, China, Arabia, France, the United States, and Japan. The process is obvious in the case of musical instruments. Still, though terms for instruments (and even the instruments themselves) migrate easily, the musical styles to which they contribute are too individually expressive of a given people to travel. Anyone who dismisses Vietnamese musical instruments as simply Chinese does not understand that Vietnamese melodies, being modally based, require an entirely different approach to ornamentation and the bending of tones—which proves impossible to realize on Chinese instruments; hence, to embody the Vietnamese aesthetic, Vietnamese musicians modified Chinese-derived instruments with high frets, looser strings, and a different style of decoration.

In most Southeast Asian nations, people know that their culture has foreign origins, and they are aware of enclaves of resident foreigners, foreign invasions, and their own attraction to artistic foreignness. The Burmese repertory of classical songs includes *yòudayà,* songs said to have derived from Siamese taken to Burma after 1767, when the Siamese capital (Ayuthaya) was defeated. Many Thai classical compositions invoke one of the so-called twelve languages (*sipsawng phasa*). For example, the term *khaek* in the Thai composition "*Khaek Lopburi*" suggests a Malaysian or Indian origin, but it is actually a composition by Choi Suntarawathin. Similarly, the

organology The study of musical instruments

lithophone Stone xylophone

animism Religion that personifies natural elements

pa'talà Burmese suspended bamboo xylphone with twenty-four keys

ranat Thai xylophones

lanat Laotian suspended horizontal xylophone

roneat Khmer xylophones

jin in "*Jin Rua*" suggests a Chinese origin, but it is by Luang Pradit Phairoh. Vietnamese in Thọ Xuân Village in Thanh Hóa Province perform masked dances invoking the Cham, the Chinese, the Dutch, and the Lao. Sundanese vocalists in West Java occasionally intersperse rhymed couplets in Dutch, Japanese, or English with classical Sundanese couplets, primarily so audiences may enjoy the exoticism of those languages. Filipinos perform elaborate song-and-dance creations, celebrating the Spanish era of the Philippines. Awareness of foreigners and foreign cultures has been a part of Southeast Asia throughout its known history. Though its peoples have not been equally affected by foreign influences, few have remained isolated from them.

PRECONTACT MUSICAL SOURCES

Southeast Asia is distinctive for the uniqueness of each culture's response to outside influences, especially from India, China, and the West. The idea of assessing the region's precontact musical resources presumes that we can isolate them, but we cannot be sure we can. Nevertheless, a discussion of possible precontact resources is reasonable. Two topics, organology and animistic rites, include aspects most likely to have predated the coming of foreign religions, languages, and instruments.

Musical Instruments

Southeast Asia, or the areas from which the peoples of Southeast Asia originated, probably gave rise to types of instruments that did not derive from donor cultures. Some are unique to the subcontinent, some exemplify universal types, and some likely became modified into instruments found elsewhere. The most difficult questions to answer are who created these instruments, where the creation occurred, and when.

Since some instruments are associated with upland groups, which reflect little influence from India or China, their instruments probably represent the oldest organological layer. Many are found in both the mainland and the islands, suggesting a relationship. The direction of cultural diffusion is more likely from the former to the latter, but there is no way to determine whether this diffusion occurred during prehistoric periods (when land bridges between the areas arose), or whether it occurred by sea. Cultural diffusion may have proceeded from or through Taiwan to the Philippines as early as 3000 B.C. [see SOUTHEAST ASIA IN PREHISTORY].

Lithophones

The oldest extant Southeast Asian musical instruments are the lithophones unearthed in Vietnam since about 1950 (figure 1). Some nine or ten sets have been discovered, but they have attracted little attention from prehistoric specialists despite their having come to light nearly fifty years ago (Condominas 1952). Each set consists of eight to twelve narrow, variously shaped stones, each capable of producing a pitch when struck with a hammer. Since no one knows when they were made, by whom, or for what reason, it follows that we know nothing of the music played on them. They are

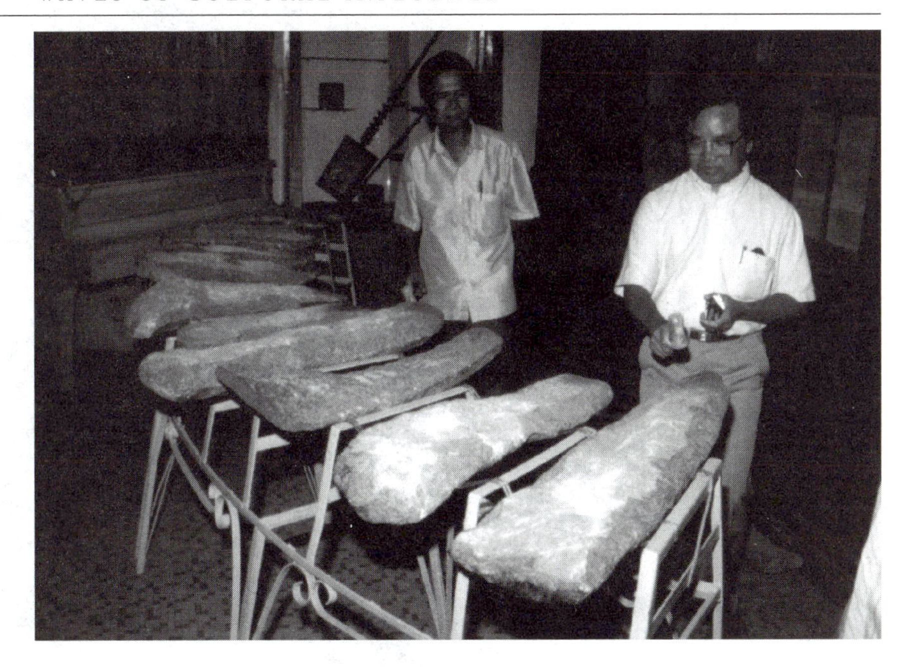

FIGURE 1 Lithophone discovered at Khánh Sơn, a village in the central highlands of Vietnam, in September 1979; now housed at Institute of Culture and Arts, Hồ Chí Minh City. Photo by Phong T. Nguyễn, 1991.

likely associated with some phase of the Hoabinhian culture, dating from ten thousand to a few thousand years ago. Ancient lithophones are still being discovered, and copies of them are being made on which newly composed music is performed.

Xylophones

Xylophones made of bamboo or hardwood, hung vertically from a post or set horizontally over a trough resonator, appear to have originated in Southeast Asia. Hanging bamboo xylophones, likely the oldest configuration, are primarily found in the mountains that straddle the borders of Vietnam, Cambodia, and Laos. Examples made of hardwood logs appear in Thailand's Kalasin Province (figure 2). Others appear in the Philippines and on various Indonesian islands, where they are played in both hanging and horizontal configurations.

The classical xylophones of lowland Burma (*pa'talà*), Thailand (*ranat*), Laos (*lanat*), and Cambodia (*roneat*) consist of hardwood or bamboo keys suspended on

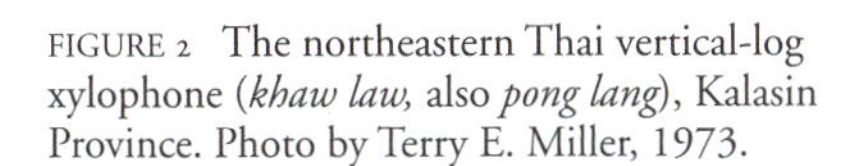

FIGURE 2 The northeastern Thai vertical-log xylophone (*khaw law,* also *pong lang*), Kalasin Province. Photo by Terry E. Miller, 1973.

FIGURE 3 A large hanging gong with boss, from Central Java. Photo by Sean Williams.

two cords over a wooden resonator. In Indonesia, Javanese gamelans include the *gambang,* with wooden keys lying flat on the edges of a resonator (for a comprehensive survey of Southeast Asian xylophones, see Miller and Chonpairot 1981). Highland groups in the Philippines use hanging bamboo or wooden keys. Whether the Southeast Asian xylophones spread to Africa with the migration of Malayo-Polynesian-speakers, as some think (Jones 1971), remains open to question.

Bronze instruments

Bronze metallurgy in the mainland dates to the early second millennium B.C. or before. Bronze instruments with keys, plus bossed and flat gongs, are distinctive to Southeast Asia. The boss, a large raised knob in the center of the gong, enables the instrument to be precisely tuned. Hanging gongs, most with bosses, are found widely in both mainland and island areas.

The uplands of the mainland are distinguished for their ensembles of individually held gongs. Lowland musicians play on sets of small, horizontally mounted gongs. In the islands, the great gamelans, especially those of Java, include the largest hanging gongs in Asia, and probably in the world (figure 3).

The most distinctive bronze instruments are so-called bronze drums, which have drum-shaped bodies with a flat bottom and top. At least 138 such instruments have been discovered since 1730 throughout Southeast Asia, including Vietnam, Yunnan Province (China), Thailand, Cambodia, Malaysia, Sumatra, Java, and some of Indonesia's lesser-known islands (including Luang, Roti, Salajar, and Sangeang). The historical specimens date to the Đông Sơn Period (late fourth century B.C.), but such instruments are still made and are occasionally used in Thai Buddhist temples. In Vietnam, artisans stand ready to make replicas for anyone willing to pay the price. While we know little of the drums' original use, the presence of sculpted frogs along the rims suggests a connection to ceremonies of rainmaking. The tops of some drums show figures that appear to be dancing and playing mouth organs.

Other widespread instruments

At least three other instruments appear to be indigenous: free-reed pipes and mouth organs, Jew's harps, and tube zithers. Though free-reed instruments are now used in East Asia, Europe, and the Americas, there is evidence that they spread to these areas from Southeast Asia. Within Southeast Asia, there are six types of free-reed instru-

FIGURE 4 A Hmong free-reed mouth organ (*qeej*) from central Laos. Photo by Terry E. Miller, 1973.

ments: a free-reed animal horn, a free-reed pipe with holes for fingering, a free-reed pipe and a gourd wind chest, a gourd wind-chest mouth organ, a Hmong mouth organ (figure 4), and a Lao raft mouth organ. A seventh, a rounded bundle of pipes in a circular wind chest, occurs in East Asia (for a complete survey, see Miller 1981).

Jew's harps, mostly of bamboo but some of metal, are found widely, more often than not used as disguisers of the voice (figure 5). Such instruments are distributed worldwide and are probably a universal type, suggesting multiple points of origin.

Bamboo tube zithers (figure 6) are less commonly used. They are most prevalent in upland regions, and are also found throughout Borneo and among some lowland Lao. There is reason to believe that the *valiha,* the tube zither of Madagascar (now the Republic of Malagasy) came with the Malayo-Polynesian-speaking peoples who migrated there from regions of Indonesia about A.D. 500.

Locally unique instruments

Throughout the subcontinent, instruments unique to one area or people are likely of ancient origin. Some are monochords. The Vietnamese *đàn bầu* has a single string, extending diagonally from a long, box resonator to a flexible wand at one end, allowing the player to bend the harmonics produced by plucking at the nodes. In the uplands of Vietnam, a bowed monochord stick zither (*k'ni*) is resonated through a string connecting the main string to the player's mouth. In lowland Cambodia and northern Thailand, monochordal stick zithers are resonated through a coconut shell placed on the player's chest.

The Lao, the northeastern Thai, and the Malay attach rattan-strung bows to large kites, which they fly during the cold, windy months; the air currents make the rattan vibrate, producing random successions of pitches (figure 7). Many rural Southeast Asians use bamboo to create music generated by the forces of nature, such as musical irrigation tubes, aeolian flutes (played by the wind), and the like.

Animistic rites

Foreign religions, and the cultures from which they sprang, have long been part of the cultural matrix that defines each people or country. Few of these religions are practiced in a "pure" form. The rites, practices, and beliefs associated with indigenous manifestations of animism are often absorbed into the major religions or coexist with them. Most Southeast Asians perceive no contradiction in honoring the Lord Buddha, a supreme deity, and a pantheon of spirits. Roman Catholics in Vietnam

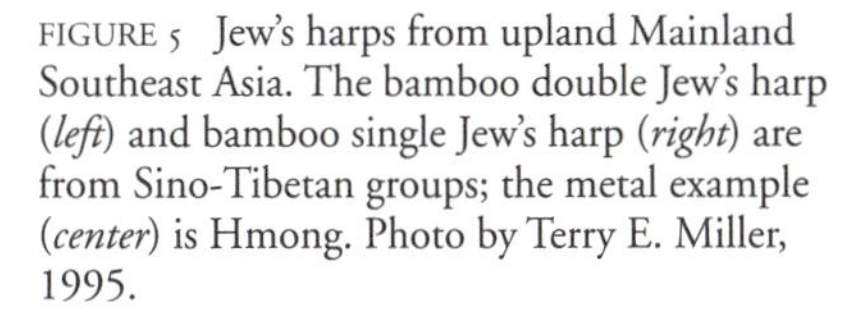

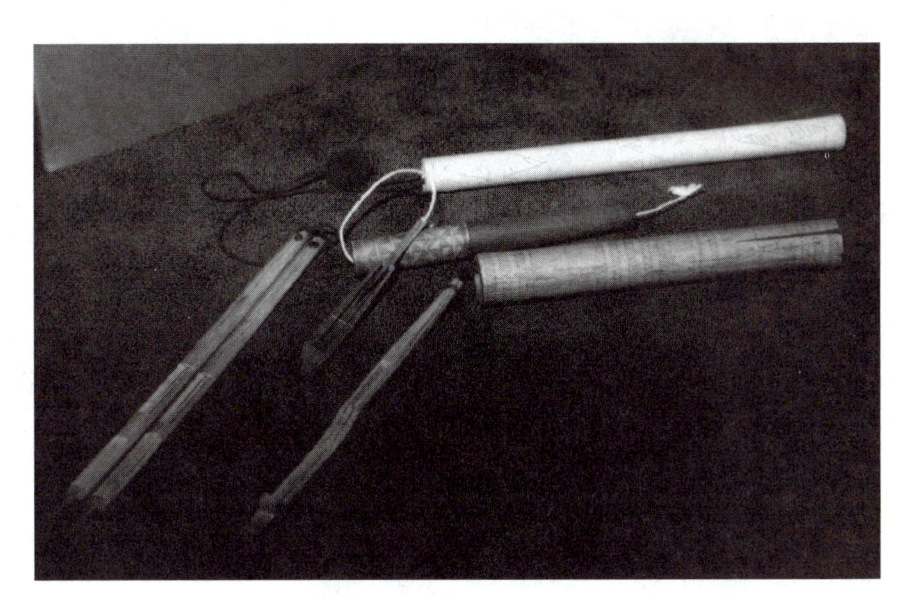

FIGURE 5 Jew's harps from upland Mainland Southeast Asia. The bamboo double Jew's harp (*left*) and bamboo single Jew's harp (*right*) are from Sino-Tibetan groups; the metal example (*center*) is Hmong. Photo by Terry E. Miller, 1995.

chầu văn Vietnamese possession ritual
mawlam Singer from northeast Thailand
khaen Free-reed mouth organ from northeast Thailand

FIGURE 6 Thảo Giang, a Bahnar minority member living in Pleiku, Vietnam, plays a tube zither (*ding goong*). Photo by Terry E. Miller, 1994.

often have altars for spirits. Muslims in Indonesia maintain remnants of the old pantheon of Hindu-Buddhist gods, some of whom derived from local forms of animism. The mixing of precontact animism with later "official" religions is the norm, not the exception, in Southeast Asia.

The kinds of animistic rites are legion, and we do not intend to discuss them systematically. Those that include some kind of heightened speech or music are fewer, though still numerous. We can mention only a few representative specimens.

In many areas, particularly the upland regions of Vietnam, Cambodia, and Laos, an annual sacrifice of a buffalo is an event of major importance. Music, particularly gong ensembles with dancing, plays a major role at these festivals. In Vietnam, mediums (*chầu văn*), accompanied by instruments and singing, go into trance to be possessed by spirits and thereby learn information that can help solve problems. Though the current government has banned such rituals, in isolated places they continue to occur, but the music can be performed alone as well.

Few upland peoples have been exposed to the major religions of their respective countries, and they continue to practice all manner of animistic rituals. The major exception is in areas where Christian missionaries have been active, but even there, old habits persist, sometimes reinterpreted into a Christian system of beliefs. In a Roman Catholic village near Kontum in Vietnam's central highlands, a visitor may nevertheless observe animistic funeral practices, including the traditional gong ensembles.

FIGURE 7 A musical bow (*sanu*) mounted on a homemade kite (*chula*), northeastern Thailand. Photo by Terry E. Miller, 1988.

FIGURE 8 A curing ceremony (*lam phi fa*) is accompanied by a free-reed mouth organ (*khaen*), northeastern Thailand, 1973. Photo by Terry E. Miller.

In northeast Thailand and Laos, when someone is ill and does not respond to treatment by a medical doctor, spirits are suspected to have caused the illness. Among the mediums who may intercede are *mawlam phi fa,* mostly females, who sing and dance around an altar of objects considered to be attractive to spirits, accompanied by a free-reed mouth organ (*khaen*). When possessed, the mediums behave as if they are the spirits inhabiting their bodies and provide an explanation for the victim's illness (figure 8). In Burma, Buddhist temples include shrines to a pantheon of thirty-seven spirits (*na'*). Of various origins, these deities are worshipped with music in a three-day ritual, *na'pwè,* which includes possession (Rodrigue 1992). In upland Malaysia, Temiar shamans go on spiritual journeys and dream songs—communications that tell the reasons for the community's problems (Roseman 1991).

In East Java, Muslim performers of hobbyhorse trance dancing become possessed by the spirits of horses. To the accompaniment of gongs, drums, and an oboe, they make horselike movements and commit potentially dangerous acts, like breaking and eating glass. In the Toraja area of Sulawesi, as part of elaborate funerals sending the spirit of the deceased to the next world, Roman Catholic Torajans join in large circles and dance. They leave an effigy (*tau-tau*) to guard the grave. In east central Flores, Roman Catholic Lio people maintain dwellings to house their ancestors' bones (figure 9). During seasonal agricultural festivities, they invoke these ancestors' spirits.

INDIAN CULTURE IN SOUTHEAST ASIA

The term *Indo-China,* though Eurocentric in character, correctly suggests the importance of Indic and Chinese influences on Southeast Asia. Assuming that Southeast Asian cultures *are* Indic or Chinese, however, would misrepresent reality. These civilizations did indeed influence the foundations of most civilizations in Southeast Asia, but in every case, those receiving the Chinese and Indic cultures transformed them into new cultures, in which visiting Indians and Chinese would likely still feel foreign. The cultural distinctiveness of every group that adopted and adapted the Indic and Chinese cultures, both historical kingdoms and contemporary nation-states, is what makes Southeast Asia one of the most colorful and attractive areas on earth. Yet there is truth to the statement that without the influences of India and China, Southeast Asia might be less distinctive.

FIGURE 9 An east central Flores house for spirits (left) echoes the shape of the volcanic cone seen to the right. Photo by Cary Black.

When we speak of India and Indian culture, we must differentiate between historical and contemporary influences. There is a world of difference between the culture of a state overseen by a Hindu-Buddhist god-king residing in a great temple and the culture of recent immigrants and their entertainments, especially Indian films and the ubiquitous genre of *filmi* songs. A visitor to Bali, Burma, Malaysia, Thailand, and Vietnam therefore finds both the great Indian-style temples of antiquity and recently built Hindu temples for merchants living in the neighborhood.

The study of early Southeast Asian history is daunting because the reader must sort out a bewildering succession of vaguely located and dated Indianized kingdoms. These historical kingdoms—including Angkor, Champa, Chenla, Dvaravati, Funan, Majapahit, Pagan, Pajajaran, Pegu, Srivijaya, and Sukhothai—speak to us through their mute statues, Buddha heads, and ruined temples, and we can feel something of their past as we visit their greatest monuments, the Angkorean temple complexes (Cambodia), the great Khmer temples at Phimai and Khao Phanom Rung (Thailand) (figure 10), the Chăm towers at Phan Rang (Vietnam), the vast expanse of temples at Pagan (Burma), and the great Javanese temples of Borobudur and Prambanan. These cultures were the foundations of modern Burmese, Cambodian, Javanese, and Thai civilizations.

FIGURE 10 Prasat Phanom Rung, the ninth-century, Indian-influenced Khmer temple on Phanom Rung Hill, Surin Province, northeastern Thailand. Photo by Terry E. Miller, 1988.

The place where this culture originated is not contemporary India, for great changes have occurred in both the South and the Southeast Asian subcontinents. About two thousand years ago, contact occurred primarily for two reasons—trade and religion. Some influence came to Southeast Asia indirectly, through China. Contemporary cultures of southern India more likely resemble the source than do those of northern India. Before this contact, small political entities probably dotted the landscape of Southeast Asia, ruled by local chiefs. The concept of a nation under a king descended from gods living at a temple representing a holy mountain is said to have come from India. The official religion of Southeast Asian kingdoms was usually a form of Hinduism, but Buddhism played a major role among the common people. The mixing of Buddhism and Hinduism with local forms of animism occurred widely and contributes to the individuality of Southeast Asian cultures. In fact, the magnificent Buddhist temple of Borobudur in central Java is only half an hour's drive from Prambanan, a great Hindu temple.

Over time, contacts with Indian culture and the intermarriage of culture-bearing

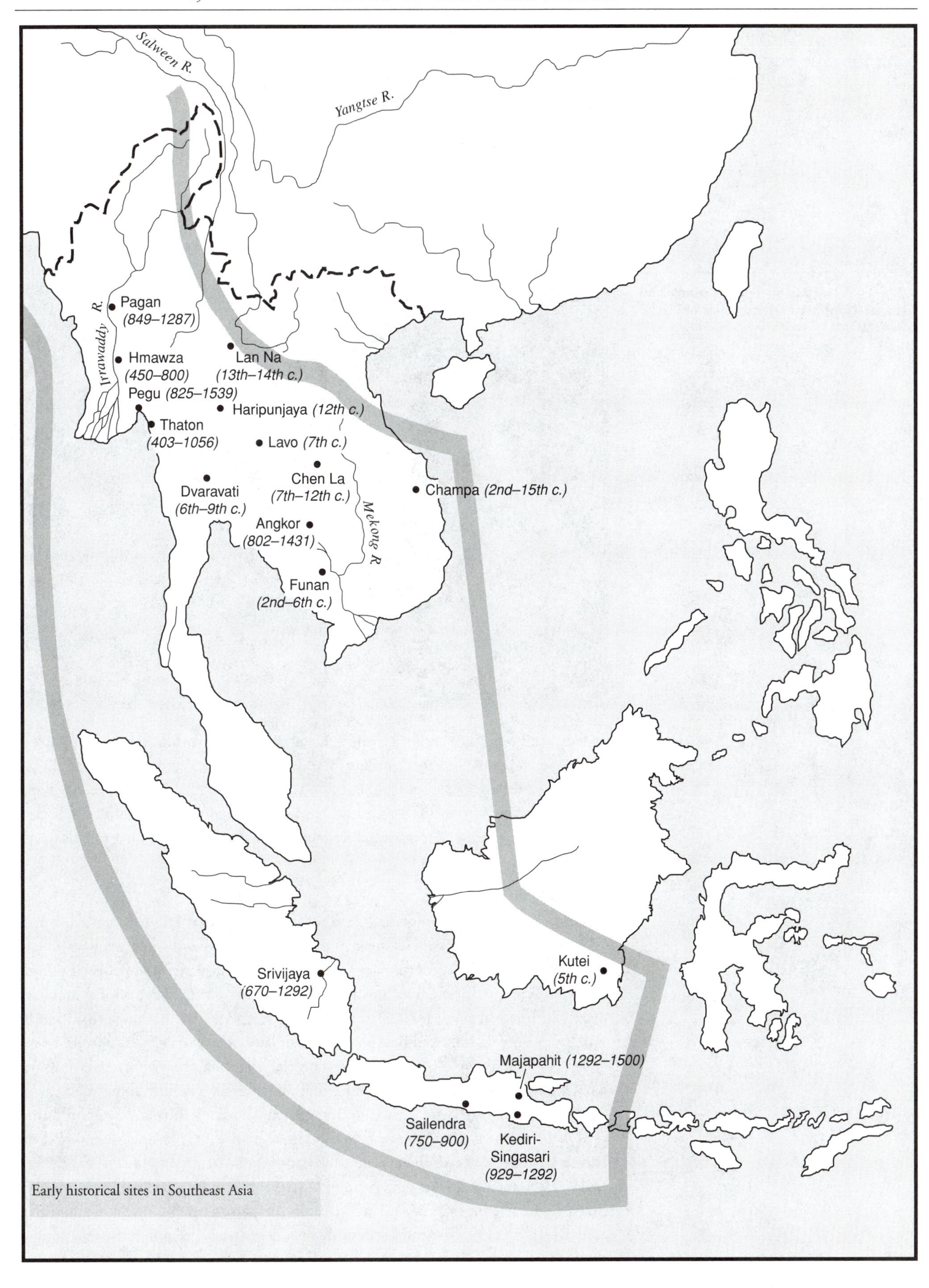

Early historical sites in Southeast Asia

Traditional literature is written on palm-leaf strips. Writers scratch the letters into the leaf, fill them with carbon powder, then bind the leaves with a cord or cords.

FIGURE 11 A *sukhwan* takes place around a holy-tree altar. Northeast Thailand. Photo by Terry E. Miller, 1973.

Indians with Southeast Asians transformed all those living within the radiating power of the sacred temple of the mountain. Those at the margins, especially people living at higher elevations, were least and last affected. Southeast Asian peoples received and adapted to their own needs many aspects of Indian civilization, including religion, architecture, sculpture, decoration, literature, language, scripts, farming practices, rituals, concepts—and music.

Spiritual matters

The essentials of this process include an understanding that Hinduism is not a unified and bounded religion but the sum of disparate parts, and when scholars invoke the general term *Hinduism,* they are likely referring to the systems of belief surrounding a particular deity, such as Shiva. While Hindu concepts, beliefs, and practices deeply influenced the leaders of the early Southeast Asian kingdoms, this kind of Hinduism survives only marginally on the mainland. A Brahman remains at the Thai court, responsible for rituals that maintain the kingdom's prosperity and stability. Though music is associated with these rituals, outsiders know little about it.

In areas of Thailand, Laos, and the Shan State of Burma, a *phram* (from *Brahman*) oversees the *sukhwan* or *bai si* ritual (figure 11). In heightened speech, before an altar of ritual objects, he calls back a person's *khwan* (a timid, spiritual essence, which tends to flee during times of stress or transition), which he figuratively binds to the person by tying threads around the person's wrist. At the Cambodian court, female dancers are seen as heavenly maidens (*apsara*), who link the kingdom to the gods. Thai classical musicians must be initiated through a series of *wai khru* rituals before altars bearing masks of deified Hindu and Buddhist figures from Indian religious literature, principally the *Ramayana,* the great pan-Asian epic. Indeed, the literary Rama himself is seen as an incarnation of the god Vishnu.

Bali, considered by many to be an earthly paradise, is the center of Hinduism in Indonesia. An unofficial system of castes (*tingkat* 'levels') still exists, and Hindu priests preside over local religious festivals, hundreds of which require artistic performance. The image of the god-king was much more powerful and prevalent before the twentieth century arrived in Bali, but many aspects of Hinduism are accepted and practiced on the island. People make offerings at all gateways, borders, and boundaries (such as crossroads, springs, doors, beaches, and volcanoes) and gateway events (such as births, deaths, and marriages). Most important, to be a Hindu in Bali means that creating art—music, dance, sculpture, painting—is a fundamental means of practicing one's religion.

Literacy, literature, and the imagination

The scripts of the Balinese, the Burmese, the Javanese, the Khmer, the Lao, the Shan, and the Thai, including local variants (like Sundanese and northern [*lanna*] Thai), derive from phonetic Indic scripts, which allowed these (non-Indic) vocabularies to be written and pronounced in their own ways. The transformations, however, are of such a magnitude that readers of modern Indic scripts can discern little. With them came a great deal of vocabulary, especially from Buddhist writings in both Sanskrit and Pali.

The more Indianized the culture, the more words of Indian origin in the language. Within Southeast Asian languages, the higher ranking the class of vocabulary, the more Indian-derived words it has. The levels of language reserved for Buddhism and for royal speech are so thoroughly Indian that learned individuals from Burma, Cambodia, and Thailand can converse using this vocabulary, though their everyday languages are quite different and mutually unintelligible. Multiple levels of language (with separate vocabularies for each level) occur in Javanese, Sundanese, and Balinese in Indonesia. Though some words are shared (or at least markedly similar) among the three areas, the least refined levels of each usually have the least in common.

Many early written documents were those of the court and its activities, but those with musical implications derive from religion (primarily Buddhism and Hinduism) and literature. Traditional literature and Buddhist sermons or Hindu tales and texts of chants were, and in some places continue to be, written on palm-leaf strips (figure 12). Writers scratch the letters into the leaf, and fill them in with carbon

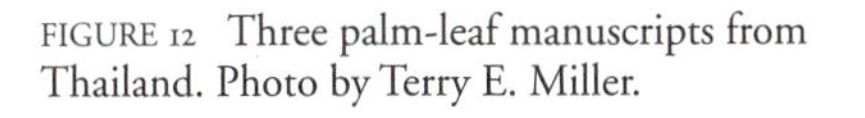

FIGURE 12 Three palm-leaf manuscripts from Thailand. Photo by Terry E. Miller.

powder (lampblack); they then bind the leaves with a cord or cords. In Thailand, these manuscripts preserve traditional stories, which serve as the foundations for preaching, solo narrative, and theater. Among them are a great number of local stories, stories of Buddha's birth (*jataka*), and the *Ramayana.*

Two Indian epics, the *Ramayana* and the *Mahabharata,* are central to the literature of all Indianized cultures. Since, like the (Nordic) *Ring of the Nibelungs,* the stories are long and complicated, only episodes can be told or acted at one time. Throughout Indianized Southeast Asia, the general population is familiar with the main characters and the basic plots. The *Ramayana*'s monkey-general, Hanuman, is as well known to Southeast Asian children as Mickey Mouse is to Western children. Dances, human theater, shadow-puppet theater, doll-puppet theater, and the decorative motifs that permeate society—all derive from these epics. In addition, the main characters of the stories are so well understood, that humans may formally or casually be called by the names of characters (as "He's a real Arjuna") in indication of their psychological makeup.

Musical influences

Trying to distinguish what *is* of Indian origin from what merely *resembles* it is the scholarly equivalent of walking in quicksand. Comparing the contemporary musical artifacts of Southeast Asia with those of India while seeking conclusions about a relational process that occurred possibly two thousand years ago can produce distorted results. Nevertheless, several topics require exploration, among them terminology, organology, musical process, and style. We must bear in mind several caveats: terms may travel apart from their objects, instruments may travel without their styles, similarities do not prove relationships, and proven relationships do not demonstrate the direction of transmission.

Terms and their objects

A great many Southeast Asian instruments bear Indian-derived names, but these instruments are not necessarily derived from India. Certain Indian terms are also found widely, denoting a variety of instrumental types in nearly endless verbal permutations. In Indian usage, the term *vīṇā* merely denotes stringed instruments, but Southeast Asian usage has transformed it into *phin,* referring to the northern Thai chest-resonated stick zither (*phin nam tao*) and multi-stringed stick zither (*phin phia*), and to the northeastern Thai-Lao plucked lute (*phin*).

Several lutes and board zithers derive their names from a common linguistic ancestor; they include the Sundanese boat-shaped zither (*kacapi*), the central Thai long-necked lute (*krajappi*), the Cambodian long-necked lute (*chapey*), a lute in the Philippines (*kudyapi*), and various lutes in Borneo and Sumatra (including the *sapeh,* the *safe,* and the *husapi*). The north Indian term *sitār,* which names a long-necked plucked lute, becomes *siter* in central and west Java, where it denotes small board zithers.

In seeking relationships between Indian and Southeast Asian instruments, we cannot be sure similarities between contemporary specimens proves a historical connection, but a few types seem clearly of Indian origin. Southeast Asian drums with laced heads are most likely of Indian origin, especially the pairs of long drums common to Malaysia (*gendang*), Indonesia (*kendang*), Thailand (*klawng khaek*), and Cambodia (*skor khek*). The Thai term *khaek* 'guest' denotes Malaysians and Indians. Indeed, these drums are somewhat similar to the Indian *tavil, pakhavaj,* and *mridanga,* and to the Sri Lankan *gata bera.*

Conical double-reed aerophones, including the Malaysian *serunai* and the Thai *pi chanai,* often bear a name related to that of the Indian *shenai.* But the Filipino

FIGURE 13 An East Javanese *terompet.* Photo by Sean Williams.

serunai is a set of small, tuned, metal plates in a frame, on which musicians practice for playing the *kulintang.* The Sundanese and east Javanese double-reed aerophone sidesteps the *shenai* name altogether, using the term *tarompet* or *terompet* (borrowed from a Western term reflected in Dutch as *trompet* and English as *trumpet*), though the instrument is clearly not a trumpet (figure 13). A more obvious relationship is seen between small Indian cymbals (*talam*) and those of the Burmese (*si*), the Thai (*ching*), the Lao (*sing*), the Khmer (*chhing*), and the Balinese (*cengceng*).

Dance

Southeast Asian dancers perform episodes from some of the same stories that Indian dancers do, and both traditions bear a major similarity: dancers tell stories gesturally; movements and poses represent encoded objects, actions, emotions, and ideas. For communication to take place, a connoisseur must know the dancer's codes, though in many cases a singer simultaneously performs the text. This is not to say that Khmer dance is Indian dance; clearly, it is not. Each Indianized Southeast Asian tradition of dance—Balinese, Burmese, Cham, Javanese, Khmer, Lao, Sundanese, Thai, and perhaps some in Malaysia—is distinctive, but all usually follow the same process of Indian dance, which differs strikingly from the concept of aesthetically pleasing but nonlexical movement ("pure dance") that predominates in some genres in the West.

Even in modern choreography, the reliance on Indian models is prominently in evidence. Choreographers recognize that to build bridges to their audiences, certain aspects of the dance should be based on familiar, Indianized material. The result often takes the form of a dance that reacts to or against Indian models of gestural expression and spatial orientation. In either case, the audience uses the prevailing mode of dance-based storytelling and gestures as its cultural referent.

Musical processes

There are two basic ways of playing music or singing: to reproduce a preexisting melody, with or without ornamentation and individual or idiomatic expression; or to create a composition while playing it, by following a set of conventions collectively called mode. India has both, and so does Southeast Asia. It is also possible to play fixed compositions that have been created according to the conventions of a given mode. Mode provides a musician with tonal material, a hierarchy of tones (allowing for the creation of tension and its release), typical melodic phrases and ornaments, and an emotional character. The Indian modal system (raga) is widely known and even more complex.

Metrically free modal improvisation, as heard in the *alap* of an Indian raga, is not the norm in Southeast Asia, but the Vietnamese system of modes (*điệu*) is nearly as complex as that of India. In Vietnamese chamber music, each musician usually warms up with a brief, unmetered improvisation (*rao*) before all begin the fixed composition. In addition, soloists improvise long and elaborate compositions based on modal principles. Another tradition of modal improvisation, though much simpler, is that of the northeastern Thai-Lao *khaen,* whose players improvise in two scalar systems, each having three modes (*lai*).

An analysis of the musics of Burma, Cambodia, and Thailand suggests an underlying modal system, but the classical traditions are almost entirely made up of fixed compositions, capable of shifting tonal centers throughout—what Western harmonic theory calls modulation and non-Western melodic theory calls metabole. The generation of melody in Malaysia, with arabesquelike streams of melody, spinning small intervals in a seamless web, points to Western Asian origins.

The system of *pathet* in central Java denotes not just a repertory of allowable tones but also a tonal hierarchy that defines a mood, a general character, or another nonmusical element. The tonal hierarchy sets up boundaries (clear in every musi-

Chinese influence on the cultures of Southeast Asia has been a factor for centuries, especially in Vietnam, a Chinese colony for more than a thousand years.

cian's mind) as to which melodic patterns, elaborations, and variations are appropriate. The correct performance of improvised elaborations and variations must be carried out according to the rules of individual *pathet.*

Indian influence is also likely where rhythmic-metrical cycles exist. The Indian system of talas, in which a closed cycle of beats underlies the melodic system (raga), is not unlike the cycles found throughout Southeast Asia, especially in classical musics. As in India, Southeast Asian drummers know individual drumstrokes by name and initially memorize a fundamental form of the cycle (but may improvise to a limited degree on it). In Burmese, Cambodian, Lao, and Thai classical traditions, small bronze cymbals mark the cycle; in Vietnam, a slit drum or castanet-like instruments mark certain beats. Cyclic meters distinguish Vietnamese music from Chinese, placing Vietnam within the Southeast Asian musical world despite its superficial similarities to that of East Asia.

It is difficult to say that the concepts of melodic modes and metrical cycles in Southeast Asia came directly from India, since both are found elsewhere (especially in Western Asia), but the similarities make the connection compelling. Aside from the process indicated by modal and cyclic construction, however, little else about Southeast Asian musical styles points toward India.

Contemporary Indian influence

Contemporary Indian culture exists in enclaves in Burma, east Java, Thailand, and Vietnam, and around 10 percent of the population of Malaysia is of contemporary Indian extraction. Many Indians in Burmese cities, brought there by the British during the colonial period, operate shops and restaurants. Most in Thailand migrated to open businesses, primarily fabric shops, but they also established temples and shrines, to which even the ethnically Thai pay homage. To our knowledge, except in Malaysia, Indian musics do not flourish within these communities, and where they do, they are not classical genres. The Malaysian *bangsawan,* a theater that mixed cultures to increase its popular appeal, traditionally had Indian elements, but modern, government-sanctioned *bangsawan* has largely been stripped of them.

Throughout Southeast Asia, theaters show Indian films, and shops sell cassettes of Indian *filmi* popular songs. The flood of popular Indian culture through films and their sound tracks has led to a spectacular local response in Indonesia. By the 1960s, Indonesian films based on Indian successes had caught the public imagination, and sound tracks featured *dangdut,* the genre that mimics the tabla, the flute, and the vocal ornamentation of *filmi.* Sung in Indonesian (more rarely in a local language), *dangdut* is the one musical genre that can be heard virtually anywhere in Indonesia. The elite consider it a music of the masses, but even the elite enjoy dancing to it when they let their guard down. Indian films and *filmi* remain popular in Indonesia, but they are outstripped by *dangdut,* with its use of the national language and Indonesian subjects.

CHINESE MUSIC IN SOUTHEAST ASIA AND ITS LEGACY

It would be hard to imagine Southeast Asia without the Chinese. The so-called Overseas Chinese vary from being unassimilated (and therefore easily noticed) to nearly assimilated. Although some Chinese had come to Southeast Asia by about 1600, most came from southern China during the nineteenth and twentieth centuries. They established businesses in the cities, major and minor. Many Southeast Asian cities retain a Chinese atmosphere, especially in their business sections. As in other parts of the world, many Chinese established restaurants, and the commercial cuisines of each country include Chinese dishes, modified to appeal to local palates. Because of success in business, the Chinese have come to dominate the economies of several countries, sparking resentment during tough times. As a result, they have been made scapegoats in times of stress and have suffered when local populations turned on them. Some fled, some suffered but survived, and some died.

Chinese influence on the cultures of Southeast Asia has been a factor for centuries, especially in Vietnam, a Chinese colony for more than a thousand years. Unlike the (mostly peaceful) relationship between India and Southeast Asia, that with China—especially for Vietnam—was violent. Many battles were fought, against both the Chinese and the Mongols, who controlled China during the Yuan Dynasty. Despite resentment toward the Chinese, the Vietnamese adopted Chinese ideographs long before converting to a romanized script, and the ability to read Chinese remains a requirement for Vietnamese scholars and religious people. The Vietnamese language is permeated with words of Chinese origin, much as Burmese, Khmer, Lao, and Thai are permeated with words of Pali and Sanskrit origin—and as English is permeated with words of Latin origin. As in these cases, it was a foreign religion—Mahayana Buddhism—that brought much Chinese culture to Vietnam (figure 14).

Chinese musical influence manifests itself in two ways: through the maintenance of genuinely Chinese musical genres, and through the apparent influence of those genres on Southeast Asian musics, both in style and in organology. Indeed, some Chinese musical activities in Southeast Asia are examples of survivals, for genres played in such places as Bangkok, Ipoh (Malaysia), and Hồ Chí Minh City are often older versions of types that have changed in the People's Republic of China. The following must be considered a tentative survey, since a systematic study of Chinese musics in Southeast Asia remains to be done.

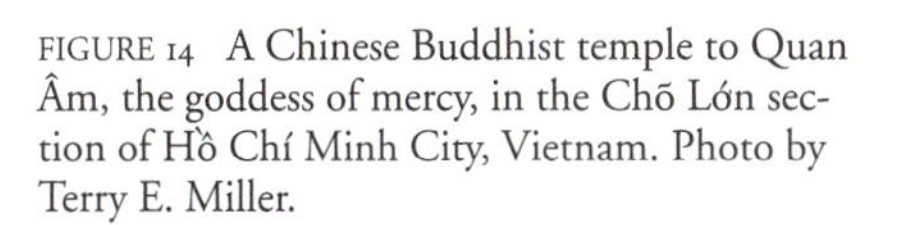

FIGURE 14 A Chinese Buddhist temple to Quan Âm, the goddess of mercy, in the Chō Lớn section of Hồ Chí Minh City, Vietnam. Photo by Terry E. Miller.

Vietnam

The Chinese are a prominent minority in lowland Vietnam, especially in the cities of the south, including those of the Mekong Delta. Visitors to these cities, especially the Chợ Lớn section of Hồ Chí Minh City, will find Chinese-descended people, spectacular temples, schools, restaurants, and shops. Today's Chinese population has little connection to the history of Chinese domination of the Vietnamese kingdoms. Of all Southeast Asian nations, Vietnam shows the most Chinese influence, modified to local tastes. The historical Vietnamese courts followed the Chinese model in both aesthetics and organization. The last series of Vietnamese emperors, the Nguyễn Dynasty, which governed in Huế from 1802 to 1945, established a "forbidden city" inside a larger walled city, the citadel. The court's musical establishment included Chinese-type ensembles, which played, at least in part, imported Chinese pieces.

Many of Vietnam's musical instruments originated in China. The *đàn tranh* zither is virtually identical to an older, sixteen-stringed *zheng,* the pear-shaped lute (*đàn tỳbà*) derives from the *pipa,* and the moon-shaped lute (*đàn nguyệt*) resembles both the *yue qin* and the *ruan.* Though these instruments appear to be Chinese, they have been modified to accommodate the Vietnamese musical system. Much of the latter requires tones outside the pentatonic tuning of the Chinese-derived instruments, plus ornaments peculiar to Vietnamese music. These can be realized only on instruments whose frets have been raised (to allow for the bending of tones) and whose strings have been made looser. These modifications make the instruments Vietnamese, not Chinese.

Today's Chinese population in Vietnam enjoys instrumental music at least as much as vocal music. It is played on familiar, unmodified instruments: a fiddle (*er hu*), a moon-shaped lute (*yue qin*), a pear-shaped lute (*pipa*), an oboe (*suona*), and various kinds of percussive instruments. Most Chinese music is played in private situations and cultural clubs, at funerals and festivals, and in theatrical performances for the linguistic communities, the Tiều (Chaozhou), the Quảng (Guangdong), and the Phước Kiến (Fujian). The Quảng and Tiều traditions are the most famous in Vietnam. After 1960 in Saigon, Quảng and Tiều musicians formed professional-level music clubs (*yue she*), where players rehearsed to play for fundraisers, commemorations, and funerals. Some Chinese instrumental pieces and melodies are known to Vietnamese musicians, who have adopted them into chamber music (*nhạc tài tử*) and theater (*cải lương*). These tunes are modally classified into a Vietnamese subcategory, *hơi quảng* 'Cantonese tunes'. Though Vietnamese and Chinese musicians share instruments and tunes, they cannot play together because Vietnamese musicians change the character of the Chinese tunes.

Thailand

At Ayuthaya, the former Siamese capital, Chinese music and theater existed by the 1600s, for several French visitors to the court—Bouvet, Chaumont, Choisy, La Loubere, Tachard—wrote at length about the Chinese entertainments they had to watch there (Miller and Chonpairot 1994:34–40). These entertainments included both Chaozhou and Guangdong opera. By the 1800s or before, street and restaurant performances of Chinese shadow-puppet theater also occurred in Bangkok.

Modern Thai cities include people of Chinese descent; some have lived in Thailand for only a generation, others for many generations. Most, constituting the vast majority of the country's shopkeepers, operators of hotels, and restaurateurs, engage in business and professional activities. Thai cities have at least one Chinese temple, plus Chinese organizations that organize festival activities and the hiring of opera troupes. The dominant Chinese-language group in Thailand is the Chaozhou (locally pronounced Taejiu), people who migrated from eastern Guangdong

FIGURE 15 A performance of Taejiu-language Chinese opera in Mahasarakham, Thailand, 1973. Photo by Terry E. Miller.

Province, in southern China. The internal business language of Thailand has been, and continues to be, Taejiu. But the Chinese-descended people have also taken Thai names, speak, read, and write Thai as their first language, and participate fully in Thai cultural life. Though the community retains Chinese music, Chinese students usually learn to play Thai classical music at school.

The Chinese temples and community organizations maintain at least three kinds of musical activity. First, numerous professional Taejiu opera troupes tour the nation's cities during most of the year, performing in eight-night runs in the traditional ritual setting, on a temporary stage facing the temple's main deity. This performance occurs around the deity's birthday. In many cities, the festival follows an all-day parade, involving student-musicians playing *daluogu* instruments (drums, gongs, cymbals) and sometimes *chuida* instruments (double reeds, side-blown flutes). The performances of operas occur each night, but during the day apprentice singers may have a chance to perform. Chaozhou opera requires a chorus of children, most of whom speak Thai-Lao as their native language. They come from the northeast and attach themselves to the opera troupe to get money. When grown up, they become the main actors and actresses; many do not speak Taejiu but can sing it. Fewer and fewer Chinese-Thai can understand Taejiu, and a simultaneous translation into Thai is sometimes read through loudspeakers (figure 15).

TRACK 2

Many temple clubs support a silk-and-bamboo (*sizhu*) club, which plays traditional Taejiu music. This style is distinctive for its use of a nasal-toned, two-stringed fiddle (*tou xian,* closely resembling the Thai *saw duang*) and a tradition of patterned rhythmic variations of the tunes. Local businessmen enjoy playing this music in its traditional setting, purely for their own enjoyment (figure 16). Some temples maintain Chinese-funeral musicians (*chuida* 'blowing and hitting'), who use a variety of melodic instruments, led by a *suona* and accompanied by percussion. Various Taejiu instruments imported from China are available at shops in Bangkok's old Chinese section, on New Road and Yaowarat Road.

Malaysia

Malaysia is a multiethnic country whose population is 31 percent Chinese. We should expect that Chinese music and theater would be performed there, but little information has been published on the subject. Most performances occur in ritual contexts—before a deity on the deity's birthday. Human theater is said to be per-

In Southeast Asia, the overwhelming majority of Muslims live in Indonesia, Malaysia, Thailand, the Philippines, and Brunei. Islam's position as the fastest-growing religion in the world is due in part to the rate of Southeast Asia's Muslim population's growth.

FIGURE 16 A Taejiu-speaking Chinese-Thai musician prepares for the rehearsal of a silk-and-bamboo ensemble in Khorat, Thailand. Photo by Terry E. Miller, 1988.

formed as it is in Thailand, and troupes from Thailand are said to perform in Malaysia. Puppet theater, however, is quite common, and has been documented. Three forms are maintained. The Hokkien-dialect glove-puppet theater was brought to Malaysia around the turn of the twentieth century. Small, boxlike stages are set up. The manipulators sit in the lower portion, working the puppets on a small stage above their heads. Musicians play lutes, fiddles, and perhaps a flute behind them. The performances of a Hokkien marionette theater are reserved for the Jade Emperor deity. There are also Chaozhou rod puppets (Stalberg 1984).

Nothing is known to have been written in the West about Chinese music or theater in Burma, Cambodia, or Singapore. The level of activity, if there is one, is probably modest, though Singapore likely has active Chinese musicians. The Chinese do not figure in Laos at all, and many Chinese-Cambodians either fled the Khmer Rouge or died.

Indonesia

To Indonesia, Dutch administrators brought Hokkien-speaking Chinese men (and later, Hakka and Chaozhou men) to establish commerce, and they offered marked political, educational, and economic advantages to men who migrated. These advantages bred resentment among local populations, which, in the months after the aborted coup of 1965, culminated in a large-scale massacre of at least five hundred thousand people, many of whom were Chinese-Indonesians. Though most Chinese-Indonesians are of mixed ancestry, local populations still consider them Chinese.

At least partially as a result of the troubles surrounding the massacre, public expressions of Chinese culture have been minimal. In the area around Jakarta (the national capital), local amalgams of Chinese and Indonesian music have developed. The main genre of Chinese-oriented music, *gambang kromong,* uses an eighteen-key xylophone (*gambang*), a ten-pitch gong chime (*kromong*), one or more two-stringed bowed lutes (*tehyan*), a side-blown flute (*suling*), and local percussion instruments, with singers and (for the modern repertoire only) optional Western band instruments (Yampolsky 1991). Though the ensemble once had a large number of Chinese melodies as part of its repertoire, the events of the mid-1960s have led to a gradual disappearance of these Chinese pieces and their replacement by local songs; nevertheless, the current ensemble performs at weddings and other Peranakan (mixed-blood, Chinese-Indonesian) cultural events.

The Philippines

The Chinese experience in the Philippines bears a marked similarity to that of Indonesia. Chinese merchants have maintained a presence in the Philippines for hundreds of years, ever since Manila developed as a center for Asian trade before the appearance of Spanish colonists. Even today, more than half the Chinese in the Philippines live in Manila. As in Indonesia, every urban center in the Philippines has numerous Chinese residents, who involve themselves in businesses and restaurants. Chinese men came to the country from Fujian Province (southern China). They intermarried with Filipinas and converted to Roman Catholicism; however, their complete integration with the Filipinos has not occurred. At the start of Spanish rule, the Chinese were forced to live together in limited areas; once that rule was relaxed, the Chinese continued staying together. In the twentieth century, younger generations of Chinese-Filipinos have begun to assimilate more closely with young Filipinos, and further cultural intermixing is likely.

Because Chinese expressions of cultural identity in the Philippines do not have to function in a post-massacre climate (like that of Indonesia), festive celebrations of boat races, weddings, Chinese operas, and Chinese New Year celebrations are common, accompanied by various types of music. Older Chinese immigrants still play in silk-and-bamboo ensembles. The far greater preservation of Chinese musical culture in the Philippines (especially in Manila) may reflect the government's tolerance of Chinese culture, plus the fact that many of the most important leaders of the Philippines (José Rizal and others) are or were of partial Chinese ancestry.

ISLAM IN SOUTHEAST ASIA

Islam, with roots in the Arabian peninsula of the seventh century, is based on God's teachings to the Prophet Mohammed. The basic Islamic system of beliefs includes the testimony of faith, *La ilaha illa Allah, Muhammad rasul Allah* 'There is no god but God, Muhammad is the messenger of God'. Being a Muslim also means believing in angels, prophets, scriptures, final judgment, divine decrees, and predestination. Muslims pray five times daily, facing the holy city of Mecca, and revere Friday as the holy day of the week. The five main elements ("pillars") of Islam include the testimony of faith (*shahada*), the ritual prayer (*salat*), almsgiving (*zakat*), fasting during the holy month of Ramadan (*sawm*), and the pilgrimage to Mecca (*hajj*). Prayers are held at local mosques; nearly every Muslim neighborhood in Southeast Asia includes a mosque, so the calls to prayer may sometimes be heard from the loudspeakers of more than thirty mosques simultaneously. Islam has two primary branches, the Shi'a and the Sunni; most of Southeast Asia's Muslims belong to the Sunni branch (figure 17).

In Southeast Asia, the overwhelming majority of Muslims live in Indonesia,

FIGURE 17 An Islamic mosque (*masjid*) in Penang, Malaysia. Photo by Terry E. Miller, 1973.

Malaysia, Thailand, the Philippines, and Brunei. Islam's position as the fastest-growing religion in the world is due in part to the growth rate of Southeast Asia's Muslim population. Indonesia has a majority Muslim population (about 90 percent). Though Muslims make up significant numbers in the populations of Brunei (68 percent) and Malaysia (47 percent), and lesser numbers in Thailand (4 percent) and the Philippines (4 percent), they do not comprise the entire ruling class of those nations. Islam in Southeast Asia is characterized by variety (rather than unity), because, over hundreds of years, the beliefs embraced by each ethnic group have become intertwined with Islamic beliefs.

Islam and music

Though relations between Islamic leaders and Muslim musicians have occasionally been problematic, most Southeast Asian Muslims regularly enjoy both instrumental and vocal music. Part of the congeniality between music and Islam in Southeast Asia reflects an Islamic adaptation to local customs concerning the performance of music. Spoken and chanted words, because of their links to Muhammad's reception of the word of God, are important to Muslims; as a result, vocal music and vocalists have always been regarded more highly than instrumental music and musicians. Furthermore, female vocalists are often granted a higher social (and sometimes, economic) status than male instrumentalists. As in many areas of the world, Southeast Asian musicians are sometimes regarded by religious authorities to be just short of respectability, and as Muslims themselves, musicians must tread a fine line between perpetuating their art and following their faith.

The type of music that receives the strongest censure from Islamic authorities is popular music [see POPULAR MUSIC AND CULTURAL POLITICS] because of its associations with dancing and drinking. Similarly, Islam officially discourages traditional musics associated with prostitution. Regional traditions of music, however, are accepted as part of local cultures to which Islam must adapt.

Certain instruments associated with Islam have become established in Southeast Asia. These include frame drums, huge barrel drums (used for the call to prayer), plucked lutes, and oboes (figure 18). These instruments have fit in with, and become absorbed by, local traditions, but the frame drums remain closely linked with an Islamic sound when used to accompany singing. Though Islamic music is a part of Southeast Asian culture generally, it has closer associations with Mecca and the roots

FIGURE 18 A huge Islamic barrel drum (*bedug*) from central Java, used to signal the call to prayer. Photo by Sean Williams.

of Islamic culture than some of the more locally derived traditions. Like the layers of religious influence that characterize many modern Southeast Asian systems of belief, Islamic music is yet another layer that enriches the spectrum of Southeast Asian music.

Indonesia

Before the full-scale introduction of Islam (between the 1200s and the 1600s), the systems of belief of the Indonesian peoples ranged from animism to Hindu-Buddhism. The kingdom of Majapahit (1200s to 1500s), essentially the last Hindu-Buddhist kingdom in Java, was the first Indonesian kingdom since Srivijaya (600s to 800s) to exercise control over trade routes. This power was significant to the entry of Islam because sea trade was the primary means of early Islamic penetration into Indonesia.

Though a large part of Indonesia was Hindu-Buddhist during the pre-Islamic period, not all residents of Hindu-Buddhist areas were exclusively adherents of an established religion. Locally dominant systems of belief were largely combinations of animist and Hindu beliefs. Hindu beliefs emphasized ritual actions and their correct execution and the charismatic image of the divine ruler. These aspects of worship became important contrasts to Islam; some aided in the conversion of locals to the new religion, while others altered the new religion substantially.

Though Majapahit rule remained dominant until the 1500s, Islamic influences had entered Indonesia centuries before. The first Muslims in Indonesia were probably traders from South Asia. Opinions about the precise location of their origin differ, but the area of Gujarat (western India) is commonly believed to have been the origin of Muslim traders to Indonesia and other parts of Southeast Asia. The adaptations of Islam to local conditions and beliefs in India had helped to pave the way for its adoption in Indonesia; it was brought to Indonesia by non-Arab Muslims, and it lacked the cultural unity that characterized its later development in West Asia. Arriving in Indonesia with individual traders first, and later with Sufis (a segment of Islam that emphasizes mystical practices and adaptation to local customs), Islam was absorbed into an already highly syncretic culture.

As early Muslim traders from India began to settle in Indonesia's coastal towns (especially in north Sumatra and the north coast of Java), being a Muslim gradually

Wayang, the drama that used characters from the old Hindu epics as heroes, simply developed a new offshoot, celebrating Islamic heroes. Since Islam discourages human representation, modifications were made to the puppets over time to make them appear less human.

became advantageous. Expansions in trade, made possible by increased contact between coastal Muslims and Indian traders, led to alliances with the Javanese merchant class. Once a substantial number of Muslim traders had begun to establish themselves in coastal areas (like Aceh, Banten, and Demak), a process of gradual incorporation with local communities took place. Intermarriage was effective because it ensured a steady supply of goods to a local administrator; it also increased traders' status and elevated them to positions of greater standing in the community.

The fall of Majapahit eventually occurred, at least in part, because Muslim communities in the coastal areas had grown in power. In the 1500s, the Mataram kingdom arose in Central Java. It differed from Majapahit significantly; it had borrowed Islamic elements that increased its influence locally. The adoption of Islam enabled it to subdue the local administrators in the coastal cities, who had previously used Islam as their main ideological weapon against Majapahit.

The kingdom of Mataram chose certain aspects of Islam to emphasize. First, as a means for maintaining traditional authority, it relied on earlier Hindu ideals of divine rulership and attention to ritual; it relied on charismatic leaders, not political platforms. Second, Islam in Indonesia in the 1500s and 1600s was permeated with individual interpretation. It was an almost secularized religion, in that it adapted to the social structure of the merchant cities, supporting the existing network of the distribution of power. In many ways, it was a means for continuing the traditional authority that had been in existence before its appearance; it was a justification for continued division of society based on ideological lines. Though Islam was a tool used by the elite for personal gain, it appealed to commoners, whom it made feel part of a larger community, not so spiritually subordinate to the upper classes as before, and united against non-Muslims.

FIGURE 19 A Javanese shadow-puppet figure (wayang). Photo by Sean Williams.

Two features of Indonesian life between the 1200s and the 1600s were important in the spread of Islam: the deliberate use of Hindu-Javanese forms of art as tools of propaganda, and the arrival of Sufism. Though the latter was far more important in terms of direct public influence, the former had a great deal to do with converting the local populace. Thus, wayang, the drama that used characters from the old Hindu epics as heroes, simply developed a new offshoot, celebrating Islamic heroes. Since Islam discourages human representation, modifications were made to the puppets over time to make them appear less human (figure 19).

Sufism was the main means by which Islam entered Indonesia. The influence of Sufis began in the 1400s and 1500s on a nonpolitical level; an individual would gather a group of followers and teach the mysteries of inner revelation and spiritual journeying. It was not until later that Sufis became more politically active; their earliest activities had been to settle in the formerly Hindu-Buddhist schools of the countryside. In a few years after Sufis entered Indonesia, many of these rural hermitages and monasteries became Islamic schools (*pesantren*).

When the Sufis migrated inland, the schools were a natural place for them to settle. They had already been welcomed by the coastal rulers, who saw an alignment with them as a means for gaining personal prestige, so they enjoyed essentially free rein when it came to attempts to convert inland people. Many students came to *pesantren* from remote areas, and upon their return they often set up schools of their own. Thus, the actual conversion of the Indonesians was hardly formal; it began as a mild overlay onto a variety of syncretic beliefs and did not undergo the far more rigid process of total acceptance that was supposed to be typical of the Arabian Peninsula.

Because Sufi teachings varied, a unified type of Islam was not established in Indonesia. Such religious diversity resulted in a wide range of types of Islamic practice, from extreme reformists to nominal Muslims; yet all exhibit some tendency derived in part from a Hindu-Buddhist heritage. Relations between the two groups have not always been friendly. Though Mataram used certain aspects of Islamic belief to its advantage, it was strongly Hindu in origin. Short-lived efforts to discourage Islam from developing occurred, but Java became almost entirely Muslim within a century. Islam flourished in the north Sumatran area of Aceh, where it remains one of the country's strongholds of traditional Islam. Aceh was one of the most powerful Islamic areas in the islands in the early 1600s, when it established centers of learning and attracted Muslim traders.

The Dutch colonists chose Java as the colonial capital. Relying on existing centers and routes of trade, they gradually altered the traditional relationships that had characterized the leadership of Java. Rather than looking to individual members of the Islamic hierarchy or to the charismatic leaders of inland communities, the Dutch selected members of the elite to serve as administrators. A major effect that this process had on Islam in Indonesia was that it limited communication between Indonesian Muslims and those outside the archipelago, discouraging political organization and leading to the development of a more internally coherent Islam within Java, in which the expansion of European and Chinese communities served to unite Muslims in both a system of belief and a life-style.

After intensive Dutch pressure, the Javanese elite began to loosen their grip on the idea of Islam as a unifying agent. In doing so, they lost their ideological hold on inland peasants. The result was a groundswell of interest in Islam from the lowest levels of society, which opposed the religious officials and reacted against their cooperation with the Dutch. At the same time (the mid-1800s), travel to Mecca was made easier, in part by developments in shipbuilding, and in part by the opening of the Suez Canal (1869).

With eased travel to Mecca and an increasing disparity between the local administration and the colonial administration, Indonesians focused on how other Muslim nations functioned. The number of Indonesians in Mecca increased dramatically in the late 1800s until they became the largest community there. Encountering their first foreign noncolonial city served as an inspiration for them to consider the realities of home rule and to recognize the political importance of establishing Islam as a single, nonsyncretic religion. Arabic and Egyptian writers had a profound influence on Indonesian nationalists who visited Mecca; they inspired an Islamic revivalist movement that continued into the twentieth century.

A reason for Islam's success in Indonesia has been its adaptation to local conditions. Every Indonesian is required to carry a personal identity card (*kartu tanda penduduk,* also KTP) which indicates the religion of the bearer, but the range of Islamic belief runs from fundamentalist to what some Indonesians jokingly call Muslim KTP ("I'm a Muslim only insofar as that is the religion printed on my personal identity card"). Not everyone prays five times a day, but nearly all Muslims fast during Ramadan. Some women cover all but their hands and faces, but others wear Western skirts and blouses. The flexibility of Islamic cultural practice reflects the Indonesian government's requirement of religious tolerance, written into the national constitution.

The conversion of Indonesia was a gradual process which took hundreds of years. Beginning with merchants and continuing with Sufis, the number of Muslims entering Indonesia peacefully increased from the 1400s on. In many cases, Indonesians carried on the process of conversion, particularly outside Java. In the late twentieth century, Muslim leaders are no longer synonymous with political leaders, and local attempts to agitate for the creation of an Islamic state are swiftly and severely put down by the government. Though the majority of Indonesians are Muslims, agreement on issues is rare and further unification unlikely.

Malaysia

The blend of Malay Muslims with Chinese and Indians in the population of Malaysia has led to a slightly different manifestation of Islam than in Indonesia, but its roots are similar. The Malay Peninsula was once called Malaya, but has been part of Malaysia since 1963, when the federation of Malaya, North Borneo, and Singapore was created (Singapore left the federation in 1965). The peninsula is quite close to the east coast of Sumatra, and the same merchants and Sufi mystics who traveled past Sumatra also stopped at Malay ports. Sea trade throughout the region was almost completely controlled by Muslims by the 1500s, and the expansion of Islam that characterized Indonesia's history during the past five centuries applies also to Malaysia.

The city of Melaka (Malacca), on Malaya's southwest coast, was a major center of trade, a base from which Muslims spread their influence along major routes. It was an extremely influential place in trade, culture, and religion, and though it fell to Portuguese rule in the early 1500s, it remained one of the most important cities in Malaysia. The presence of Sufis (who often came on board with traders) promoted the local expansion of Islam. They tended to shun politics, preferring to gather in rural schools to teach their disciples.

In the late 1800s, when the British came to govern Malaya, they did not discourage Islam. They were motivated primarily by economic and political goals. The British colonial experience in Malaya left intact the existing system of sultanates and general religious hierarchies. Because change so often begins in ports, it was appropriate that the beginnings of an Islamic reformist movement began in the Malay ports. These reformers were called the Kaum Muda (Young Group), as opposed to the Kaum Tua (Old Group) of religious conservatives, but their impact was felt much more strongly in the Dutch East Indies (soon to be Indonesia) than in Malaya. The nonreformist Muslims of the mid-twentieth century formed an alliance with the Chinese and Indian residents of the country as the colonial empire collapsed, and the Alliance Party won the elections in newly independent Malaysia.

The current Malaysian Islamic community is dominated by a conservative but adaptive majority, which recognizes the need for cooperation with the other two large groups of Malay society. That Muslims in Malaysia had to avoid both a fundamentalist and a heavily reformist movement to gain cooperation from the Indian and Chinese members of society meant that nationalism had to come before Islam. Though Malaysia and Indonesia both have pluralist societies, what differentiates them is that most of Indonesia's ethnic groups are Muslims, while it is primarily the Malays of Malaysia who are Muslim and therefore more culturally unified.

The Philippines

The Philippines, because of their location as an eastern point in a square including China to the north, Borneo and Sulawesi to the south, and Vietnam to the west, are particularly well suited to trade and communication. Most of the Muslims in the Philippines live in the southernmost islands—Mindanao, Palawan, and the Sulu Archipelago, which links the Philippines to northeastern Borneo. Though there were once more Muslims in the northern islands, since the 1500s the Spanish colonial effort resulted in a concentration of the Muslim population in the south, where Muslims have always been more closely oriented culturally toward the southwest than toward the north and their Christian fellow citizens.

The spread of Islam into Sumatra and the Malay peninsula led to its eventual establishment in the Sulu Archipelago on one of the routes from Melaka. The first real stronghold of Islam in the Philippines was the Sulu sultanate, dating from the mid-1400s. By the 1500s, the area of Maguindanao (on the western part of Mindanao) had become an Islamic area. Gradually, through trade and Sufism, most of the island became Islamic. Most of the country at that time comprised autonomous societies that traded with each other but lacked a unifying force. Only in western Mindanao and Sulu, where Islam had developed a strong presence, was there any semblance of a government whose influence extended beyond its immediate area.

In 1521, when the Spanish came to colonize and convert the Philippines, the Islamic populations of the south were the only ones able to resist encroachment into their territory and culture. As a result, Muslims of the southern Philippines maintain a strong cultural presence, despite an overwhelmingly Christian majority and the increasing presence of Christians in Muslim areas. In the decades just after World War II, the Bangsa Moro (Muslim Nation movement) has become a strong insurgent force and has grown in power.

Thailand

Thailand is mostly a Buddhist nation, but it has a small Muslim population of Malays, concentrated primarily in the southern peninsula. From the beginning, one of Thailand's main contacts with the Muslim world was through its networks of trade set up with the city of Melaka. When the Portuguese took over Melaka, trade with Muslims through that city was disrupted and replaced by Portuguese trade; however, the Muslim network continued for several more centuries, leading to the establishment of Muslim communities in various parts of the country.

The extension of Thai control onto its southern peninsula and its sharing a border with Malaysia have led to a greater concentration of Muslims in the south. Because of Muslim attempts to develop autonomously, Muslims have been at the forefront of Thai domestic difficulties during the twentieth century. In the early 1900s, the southern Patani sultanate was divided so its southern half would fall under British control and become part of Malaya, while its northern half would remain in Thailand. The outlawing of Malay and Islamic organizations and special schools in the 1940s and 1950s contributed to the isolation of the Muslim population. More recent attempts by the Thai government to exercise control over the area have resulted in Muslim resistance, aided by support from Muslims in Malaysia and other nations with large Muslim communities.

Brunei

The sultanate of Brunei occupies the northeastern part of Borneo. Like Malaysia, Brunei supports a large Chinese population (25 percent). It works closely with its Chinese community, but its government is more fundamentally Islamic than that of Malaysia. Brunei was an important stopover for Muslim traders and Sufi mystics during the early days of Islamic expansion into the area. Its location enabled it to become a major trading power by the early 1500s, when it controlled all of the island of Borneo and several smaller islands. Until 1971, it was a British protectorate, but

Certain countries, Burma and Singapore in particular, have sought to curb what they view as the excesses of Western culture. Others, especially the Philippines and Thailand, have been open to as much westernization as people desire.

because conversion to Christianity was not a motivating factor in the establishment of political and economic control, the British did not interfere with local religion.

Brunei enjoys a high standard of living; a large proportion of its Muslim population can afford the pilgrimage to Mecca at least once a year. Because of this contact with Arab culture, the Muslims of Brunei have been closely allied with Arabic Islam. Other Muslims in island Southeast Asia (especially Indonesia) tend to regard the Muslims of Brunei as being truer to Arabic forms and perhaps practicing a purer form of Islam because of the regularity of this contact.

THE WEST

Mainland Southeast Asia

Though all of Southeast Asia has been influenced from time to time by foreign cultures, and much of that influence has been acculturated into the identities of individual groups or nations, Western influence is in most ways more apparent, more recent, and perhaps more disruptive. Some of that influence has been imposed from the outside, particularly through colonialism and military occupation, but much of it has come about voluntarily, even enthusiastically. During colonial times, European influence was quite strong. In the postcolonial period, but particularly during the fighting in Vietnam, U.S. influence increased dramatically. Since then, however, at least part of what appears to be Western influence has actually come from Hong Kong, Japan, Singapore, (South) Korea, and Taiwan.

The dynamics of the relationships are complex, with emotions running the gamut from love to hate. Certain countries, Burma and Singapore in particular, have sought to curb what they view as the excesses of Western culture. Others, especially the Philippines and Thailand, have been open to as much westernization as people desire. In some places, Western (mostly American) popular culture dominates the scene, and American popular music has been widely available on pirated cassettes. The rise of the music industry in the urban centers of Southeast Asia is a major theme in the music histories of Indonesia, Malaysia, the Philippines, and Thailand [see POPULAR MUSIC AND CULTURAL POLITICS].

Vietnam

Vietnam's culture has undergone profound influence from at least two outside cultures, China and the West. During the late 1500s and early 1600s, Westerners—Dutch, French, Italians, Portuguese, Spanish, and others—entered Vietnam through the port of Hội An, just south of Đà Nẵng. Over the centuries, the Roman Catholic Church and the efforts of its missionaries wrought many cultural changes, some of which involved music. A group of Portuguese, French, and Spanish Jesuits and at least two Vietnamese converts created the system used for romanizing the Vietnamese language, but the French more cleverly used the church as a tool in efforts to make Vietnam a protectorate during the 1800s. This they did by converting those in power and granting power to those who converted. French-style Roman Catholic music, including Gregorian chant, came to Vietnam during the 1600s, and in one form or another, it continues to be sung.

The development of French schools, a preference for all things French by the Vietnamese elite, and the return of Vietnamese teachers and performers educated in France (and elsewhere in the West) brought to Vietnam the earliest and perhaps most complete Western musical establishment. Eventually this included conservatories, orchestras, opera performances, chamber music, and active composers. After people in the north turned to Eastern Europe for help, the conservatories and universities of such countries as the former Soviet Union, Bulgaria, Romania, the former Czechoslovakia, and (East) Germany began providing both European and Vietnamese teachers to maintain Vietnam's Western music. Despite the war and the feelings many Vietnamese have about Western culture, Hanoi still has an active symphony orchestra and a conservatory devoted to Western classical music. The conservatory in Hồ Chí Minh City continues to train performers of Western classical music.

The Vietnamese have been warm to returning Westerners, particularly Americans and French, but they have not become so enamored of American popular musical culture that it is replacing Vietnamese styles. The Vietnamese remain attracted to their own kinds of popular music, including modernized folk songs (*dân ca*). As the country modernizes, however, especially in the south (Hồ Chí Minh City is fast becoming a Vietnamese Hong Kong), American influence may grow. Within a few years, the local appreciation of popular music could change drastically.

Laos

With regard to westernization, there is little to say about Laos. Though the United States once had a strong presence (which influenced the nightclub scene in Vientiane), since 1975 the combination of poverty, isolation, and political conservatism has allowed for little growth in Western culture. Aside from a few clubs where rock may be heard, the Lao have few opportunities to develop aspects of Western culture. The French school is long closed and abandoned, foreign publications are unavailable, and foreigners maintain a low profile.

Cambodia

Whatever impact the West had on colonial and postcolonial Cambodia vanished under the Khmer Rouge, who stripped the country of its existing culture and killed or caused to die nearly 2 million people. Before 1970, when Prince Sihanouk and his wife ruled in Phnom Penh, the French atmosphere of the capital included performances of both classical and light European music. The nightclub scene included popular songs and dancing. The School of Fine Arts maintained a small Western orchestra. All this has vanished, and the continuing poverty of the country has precluded the reappearance of nearly everything except popular music in Phnom Penh.

Thailand

Ironically, as Western and modern Japanese influences have increased in Thailand, so has the strength of Thai classical music, though regional musics have fared less well. Never having been colonized, the Thai have viewed the West differently from their neighbors. Though the French had tried to convert King Narai and gain influence in old Siam during the late 1600s, their plan failed, and foreigners were kept at bay until the early 1800s. During that century and the twentieth, the Thai have done remarkably well at dealing with Western powers. Rather than resist westernization because of its association with colonialism, the Thai actually encouraged it after the

1932 coup d'état. The military régimes that followed encouraged the Thai to behave as they thought Westerners did—for everyone to wear shoes, for men to wear hats and ties, for husbands to kiss their wives when leaving and returning, and so on. Governments encouraged social dancing—and the cha-cha, the rumba, the tango, swing, and other dances became fashionable. The Thai created their own social dance, *ramwong,* done in a circle by men and women using simple gestures with their hands.

During the 1800s, foreign powers' brass bands made a strong impression, and from 1850 to 1900, the Thai court had its own band. Such bands became fixtures in schools and universities and continue to this day. Western classical music, however, penetrated Thailand slowly. Before about 1980, most classical music was performed by visiting Western ensembles, soloists, and members of the expatriate community. With the founding of the (semiprofessional) Bangkok Symphony Orchestra and various student orchestras, particularly at the College of Dramatic Arts and Chulalongkorn University, the country had at least a modest Western-music presence.

Western instruments—especially the piano, the violin, the guitar, and, more recently, all types of pop instruments, including synthesizers—have proven to be particularly popular in Thailand. As in the West, the children of cultured families are often expected to study piano or violin, but there is less prejudice against popular music, and many young people learn to play popular instruments. The Yamaha School in Bangkok is large and active.

The impact of the West is not so prominent in music as it is in all other aspects of modern Thai life, particularly in the cities. Not only Bangkok and Chiang Mai, the country's largest cities, but regional cities are rapidly showing evidence of affluence and modernization, some of it of Japanese origin, some American. This includes technology, popular music, fast food, films, shopping malls, life-styles, and a preference for English. Yet much of this kind of westernization appears to be superficial, retaining a particularly Thai character.

Burma

Outside the capital (Rangoon, now called Yangon), Western influence is a non-issue. Western influence gives the capital a slightly cosmopolitan air, but it feels more like the 1940s and 1950s than the present day. Having been colonized by the British, the Burmese have little love for their former masters and their culture, but the Americans are more fondly remembered for helping liberate Burma from the Japanese during World War II. Remnants of American efforts—including old military vehicles—still serve the Burmese. Though American pop culture must pass censorship committees, young Burmese are showing a particular fondness for it, including its music, but this kind of activity maintains a low profile.

Malaysia

At least superficially, the former British colony of Malaya (including Singapore) appears to be the most deeply Westernized country in mainland Southeast Asia. This situation has affected many aspects of modern Malaysian life, from its well-organized traffic to its educational system. Musically, Malaysia reflects the multiculturality of its population, and its affluence permits the importation of foreign films, recordings, and instruments. Western classical music is taught and performed in major urban areas, and earlier types of British ballroom music have helped mold such genres of dance as *ronggeng.*

Island Southeast Asia

Indonesia and the Philippines have been participants in a fairly positive relationship with the West in the latter half of the twentieth century, but that relationship was preceded centuries ago by violent conflict and colonization. The two countries differ markedly in their respective histories: Indonesia's was largely an economic colonization, but the Philippines' was religious. The lasting legacy of these forms of colonization has been the economic plundering of Indonesia and the almost complete Christianization of the Philippines.

Indonesia

By the late 1400s, Portuguese sailors had become famously successful as navigators, and by the 1500s, they had begun establishing bases in the Indian Ocean. European needs for Indonesian spices and the Portuguese willingness to procure those spices led to the development of routes that brought cloves, mace, nutmeg, and pepper to Europe. In 1511, the Portuguese established themselves in Melaka, a powerful center of trade, and their presence led to an almost immediate evaporation of trade from the area and the dispersal of Asian goods through other routes. Later in the 1500s, the Portuguese concentrated their efforts in the eastern Maluku islands—first Ternate, then Tidore, and finally Ambon. Some nonmilitary efforts at Christianization in Maluku left pockets of Portuguese Christianity which remain active, but the effort was not widespread across the archipelago.

The 1700s saw the struggle for dominance in the eastern Indonesian trade in spices, as the Spanish sailed down from the Philippines to Maluku and the English set up networks at various sites throughout the archipelago. The Dutch, who eventually gained control over the area, took a colonial approach that differed from that of the Portuguese. Rather than controlling the area from the center of the spice-growing area, the Dutch established a base in Batavia (now Jakarta) in 1619 and governed parts of the archipelago for the next three centuries. The initial motivation for the Dutch had been to take over the spice trade from the Portuguese, and after several years of infighting between competing Dutch shipping companies, the United East India Company (Vereenigde Oost-Indische Compagnie, VOC) was formed. The Dutch government gave the VOC near-autonomous governing power during the early years of its operation, and the VOC established the initial Dutch foothold in the area. The VOC fought against local Indonesians, English, Spanish, and Portuguese traders in the early 1600s. In 1619, on the appointment of Jan Pieterszoon Coen as governor general of the VOC, the definitive mark of Dutch colonialism began to be felt locally.

The 1620s saw a series of Javanese rebellions against the VOC, spearheaded by Sultan Agung of Mataram. The military losses the Javanese suffered helped solidify the VOC's presence in Batavia. Throughout that decade, Coen's method had been to use force to ensure the continuance of trade and its monopolization by the Dutch; later rulers followed his example. In a few decades, the Dutch had begun to exercise military control over a portion of the archipelago. By about 1800, the VOC had pulled away from the spice trade to concentrate its economic efforts on the cultivation of coffee and tea in the West Javanese highlands and elsewhere.

Internal power plays and corruption had weakened the power of the VOC, and it asked for financial assistance from the Dutch government. An investigation revealed severe mismanagement within the ranks of the VOC, and in 1800 the company's disarray led the Dutch government to dissolve its charter. Meanwhile in Europe, the Napoleonic wars had resulted in the French takeover of the Netherlands; the Napoleonic government sent Marshall Herman Willem Daendels to administer

The Dutch forged an alliance with the indigenous aristocracy, then put a large amount of activity and funding into cultural development. As a result, the courtly arts (particularly on Java) flourished throughout the 1800s.

the colony from 1808 to 1811. A strong reformer, he invalidated many preexisting VOC policies.

When the king of the Netherlands (William V) went into exile in England, he ordered that temporary control of what was then known as the Netherlands East Indies should be placed in the hands of the British. The transfer of power was accomplished in 1811, putting an end to Daendels's work and shifting it to Sir Thomas Stamford Raffles (who founded Singapore in 1819). This shift was designed to keep the archipelago out of French control; once the Napoleonic wars had ended, in the next decade, Dutch hegemony was restored. The Dutch forged an alliance with the indigenous aristocracy, and the Javanese people were governed through paid local administrators in an effort to maintain the most visible forms of traditional rule. Those leaders then put a large amount of activity and funding into cultural development; as a result, the courtly arts (particularly on Java) flourished throughout the 1800s.

In the 1830s, the Dutch set up in Java a system of forced-labor cultivation (*cultuurstelsel*), which garnered, for both the government and entrepreneurs, large profits in sugar, indigo, spices, tobacco, coffee, and tea. Only a small portion of non-rice-growing land was actually used for the intensive production of crops, yet it was enough to finance the Dutch navy and win tremendous profits for the Dutch over most of the 1800s. Though this system was gradually abolished, the new profits brought an increase in military expansion; by 1910, the Dutch had established varying degrees of control over most of the archipelago.

The Dutch had made few attempts to enhance the education or welfare of the Indonesian populace until early in the twentieth century, when the so-called Ethical Policy went into practice. The 1930s saw a large-scale reform of education and public welfare. An educated elite gradually established itself in Java; most were young men of the wealthier aristocratic families, who enjoyed the benefits of a Dutch-style education. Various local nationalist movements arose during the 1920s and 1930s, but none were yet led by individuals who could envision a truly all-encompassing nation, which would recognize the country's diversity. Sukarno, Indonesia's first president, had received a Dutch education and had spent several decades agitating for no less than total independence. He spent time in exile and under house arrest, as did some of his contemporaries.

In 1942, when Japanese troops invaded the area and took control from the Dutch, the myth of European superiority was irrevocably shattered. Though the Dutch tried to regain control of Indonesia after World War II, Sukarno rose to prominence again and proclaimed the independence of Indonesia on 17 August 1945. The practical achievement of independence took several more years, but Indonesia celebrates 17 August as its official day of independence. The Dutch ceded sovereignty to the Republic of Indonesia on 27 December 1949. After the revolution, the remaining Dutch were told to leave the country; Dutch-Indonesians were asked to choose their nationality. Those who chose to be "Dutch" migrated to Holland, where they and their descendants have at least partly integrated with Dutch culture. Since that time, the Dutch presence and their influences have receded considerably, having been replaced by a powerful sense of Indonesian nationalism and patriotism.

The Philippines

The Treaty of Tordesillas, signed in 1494, divided parts of the world into what would become Portuguese and Spanish territory, leaving the Philippines to Spain. The first colonizers arrived in the Philippines led by Ferdinand Magellan, who, though Portuguese, was funded by the Spanish. He left Spain with five ships in 1519 and arrived in the Philippines two years later. Though he did not survive to return to Spain, eighteen of his original 264 men did. Later explorers named the islands of Leyte and Samar Las Islas Felipinas after Felipe, son and heir apparent of Spain's King Charles I; by the end of the 1500s, Spanish navigators were calling the entire island chain the Philippines.

The first Western cultural influences came initially from Central America, because most sixteenth-century expeditions originated in Mexico, funded by Spain. Until Mexican independence (1821), the viceroy of Mexico was the chief administrator of the Philippines. Therefore, though the Spanish were officially in control of the Philippines, the nature of this relationship was such that the Spanish profited from one of their colonies through its control by another of their colonies. The economic balance among Spain, Mexico, and the Philippines was strictly maintained by the Spanish, and Manila became an outlet for trade goods purchased from other Asian countries.

In addition to functioning as a center of trade, the Philippines became the most Roman Catholic nation in Asia. Once military control was established, friars became the emblems of Spanish power in many small towns. Because religious colonization was more important to the Spanish than political rule, most of the Philippines' indigenous cultural traditions were either eradicated or subsumed within Roman Catholicism. By the twentieth century, only the southernmost islands and inland highlands remained non-Christian. Throughout its history in the Philippines, the Roman Catholic Church has been a center of power and influence, and its occasional clashes with the state have led to the continuing affirmation of separation between the two.

With the collapse of Spanish power in the Americas, the Philippines were forced to become more self-sufficient. By the 1830s, several ports were opened to the British, Europeans, and Americans. The improvement of trade and, by extension, the local economy, led to the rise of a local elite, which was joined by local religious leaders in a struggle toward independence. The first nationalist movement for reform was led by José Rizal (1861–1896), whom the Spanish exiled and later executed. In his footsteps followed a series of revolutionary leaders, including Emilio Aguinaldo, who declared independence in 1898.

The Philippines became a U.S. possession in the same year, when the U.S. Asiatic fleet smashed the Spanish navy in the Philippines. Aguinaldo had anticipated the arrival of the Americans as an opportunity for Philippine emancipation, but his hopes were dashed when an uninformed President McKinley ordered the "Christianization of the islands." Several years of an extremely bloody insurrection followed as the Americans established military control before setting up a civilian government and eventually a commonwealth.

In addition to the establishment of a democracy, the strongest and most enduring influence from the American colonization of the Philippines was the establishment of a widespread system of free education, with instruction in English. Through its policy of education, the language, values, and culture of the United States were broadly infused into the heartland of the Philippines. By the time the Philippines achieved independence (1946), the nation's people were a blend of a Malay foundation overlaid with Mexican Catholicism and American language and culture.

Implications for musical development

The colonial legacy of the Dutch, the Portuguese, the Spanish, and the Americans has had a strong impact on the musical cultures of the main archipelagos of Southeast Asia. In Indonesia, the Dutch approach—selecting local administrators to force economic cooperation from the people—led to the infusion of financial resources into the performing arts; many local administrators could afford to keep entire staffs of performers on hand to increase the local perception of power. Because the Dutch had no intention of eradicating traditional culture in the name of Christianization, the performing arts were allowed to thrive and expand in many cultural centers. The declaration of Indonesian independence led to the immediate disappearance of funding for these arts, causing a reshuffling of personnel and genres as priorities shifted.

In the Philippines, the primary intent of the Spanish was to Christianize the population, establishing a foothold for Spanish trade in the area. As friars and their schools developed into centers of power, local musical traditions faded, to be replaced by Spanish religious musical traditions. As reflections of a pre-Christian culture, indigenous traditions were no longer perceived as relevant. The eventual result of this was the virtual disappearance of all pre-Christian musical traditions in Roman Catholic areas. In contrast, Filipino Muslim and tribal peoples have continued to maintain unique forms of cultural expression.

In both island nations, current local traditions vie for economic standing with internationally marketed popular music and its local practitioners. Many of the articles in Part 3 of this volume include a discussion of how the dichotomy between local and international cultures affects the traditional performing arts, and some authors acknowledge that the rise of locally produced popular music has been an important step in the drive for modernization. In both Indonesia and the Philippines, however, the undercurrent of the colonial legacy remains an indelible part of national consciousness.

REFERENCES

Condominas, Georges. 1952. "Le lithophone préhistorique de Ndut Lieng Krak." *Bulletin de l'École Française d'Extrême-Orient* 45:359–392.

Jones, Arthur M. 1971. *Africa and Indonesia: The Evidence of the Xylophone and Other Musical and Cultural Factors.* Leiden: E. J. Brill.

Miller, Terry E. 1981. "Free-Reed Instruments in Asia: A Preliminary Classification." In *Music East and West: Essays in Honor of Walter Kaufmann,* ed. Thomas Noblitt, 63–100. New York: Pendragon.

Miller, Terry E., and Jarernchai Chonpairot. 1981. "The *Ranat* and *Bong-Lang:* The Question of Origin of the Thai Xylophones." *Journal of the Siam Society* 69:145–163.

Miller, Terry E., and Jarernchai Chonpairot. 1994. "A History of Siamese Music Reconstructed from Western Documents, 1505–1932." *Crossroads: An Interdisciplinary Journal of Southeast Asian Studies* 8(2):1–192.

Rodrigue, Yves. 1992. *Nat-Pwe.* Garthmore, Scotland: Paul Strachan-Kiscadale.

Roseman, Marina. 1991. *Healing Sounds from the Malaysian Rainforest: Temiar Music and Medicine.* Berkeley: University of California Press.

Stalberg, Roberta Helmer. 1984. *China's Puppets.* San Francisco: China Books.

Yampolsky, Philip. 1991. *Music of Indonesia 3: Music from the Outskirts of Jakarta: Gambang Kromong.* Washington, D.C.: Smithsonian / Folkways SFCD 40057. Liner notes.

Culture, Politics, and War

Terry E. Miller
Sean Williams

Art, particularly music, is rarely isolated from its time and place. Affected by events, it often reflects events in turn. When a revolution or a war breaks out, musicians can be deeply affected, and often, with other members of the population, they suffer injuries, lose their means of support, and even die.

Official controls over the arts have existed to some degree over long periods of time throughout most of the world, but the twentieth century has seen unprecedented attempts to control or inhibit the arts. Because music has communicative potential, particularly in narrative and theatrical genres, people in power often try to harness it for their own ends. Their efforts include manipulating the messages of music to influence people. Because singers can deliver messages efficiently to a broad spectrum of people, governments often want to use them for state purposes, but when they give voice to dissent, governments may subject them to censorship.

Even during peaceful times, music may be affected by developments in national cultural policies. The role that governments play in developing, controlling, and manipulating the arts is in some instances beneficial but in others detrimental. The following article provides an overview of important political events and issues embedded in Southeast Asian musics.

MAINLAND SOUTHEAST ASIA

Vietnam

As many have said, "Vietnam is a country, not a war," but for much of the world, especially the United States, Vietnam is synonymous with memories of a demoralizing military excursion, which scarred many people's memories. Americans easily forget that the suffering and disruption in Vietnam was, and continues to be, many times greater than that experienced in the West. Without attempting a history of the war, an explication of its roots and causes, or a psychoanalysis of its legacy, we intend to explore selected themes: the disruption of culture, music and theater as propaganda, the creation of a musical diaspora, and the cultural-political legacy affecting the Vietnamese arts today.

Colonialism brought European influence and the eventual founding of conser-

As the Republic of Vietnam approached its collapse (on 29 April 1975), thousands of people fled the country. These included some of the country's most prominent singers, actors, actresses, and musicians.

vatories with European-trained instructors [see VIETNAM: Modernization], but the traditional musical arts flourished according to local dynamics until the 1950s, when the war of resistance against the French heated up. After independence (in 1954), Vietnam divided into the People's Democratic Republic of Vietnam (the communist north) under Hồ Chí Minh and the Republic of Vietnam (the westernizing south) under a succession of presidents and generals. In both parts, music and theater served as weapons of propaganda and patriotism. The north followed the models of Russian socialist realism and Chinese revolutionism; efforts in the south were less systematic and ideological. In both parts of Vietnam, many songs with political texts urged people to resist the enemy (for a wartime account, see Brandon 1967).

In the south, musical life continued as best it could in both the cities and the countryside controlled by the government and the areas controlled by the National Liberation Front. In the latter areas, traveling troupes (*đoàn văn công*) performed on movable stages set up at night. From powerful secret transmitters, they broadcast songs, music, and theater, mostly with patriotic themes, urging people to overthrow the government. Many artists were arrested. Some were killed by napalm bombs. Some died in prison, including the infamous "tiger cages" on Côn Sơn Island. U.S. airstrikes in the north killed some of Vietnam's most expert performers and composers. Many of those in the north and the revolutionary zones of the south who survived continue to perform. One of them, composer Trần Hoàn, has become Minister of Culture and Information.

Though Saigon was relatively secure, random rocket attacks could and did kill musicians, actors, and actresses, with other members of the general population. In 1970, a rocket fell into a prominent theater during a *cải lương* performance, destroying the building and killing members of the cast and people in the audience. As the Republic of Vietnam approached its collapse (on 29 April 1975), thousands of people fled the country. These included some of the country's most prominent singers, actors, actresses, and musicians. Most resettled in France and the United States, where, over time, they built a Vietnamese music industry, which has been producing large numbers of cassettes, compact discs, and music videos, primarily of popular songs, but also of *cải lương*.

The current cultural policies of the Socialist Republic of Vietnam, formulated and executed from the Ministry of Culture and Information in Hanoi, have been selectively kind to the traditional arts. Though certain genres, particularly those of the south, have not received governmental support, some important genres have been revived and restored to extremely high artistic levels. These include the *chèo,* the *tuồng,* and water-puppet theaters, certain genres of folk song, and many ritual activities, for which the government has supported groups in purchasing instruments, costumes, and props. Though officials of the Information and Culture Service maintain a certain control over cultural activities under their purview, the traditional arts are generally allowed to flourish or decline on their own.

The major controversy over control and representation concerns a type of modernized "ethnic" music, *nhạc dân tộc cải biên* (figure 1), created at the Hanoi Conservatory along socialist models [see VIETNAM: Modernization]. Using modified instruments of both the lowland Viet and various central highland groups, *cải biên* has become an issue of both modernization and control, for the questions it raises include, who decides what "traditional" is to mean in modern Vietnam? and what kind of music should represent the national culture to the outside world? To the extent that politicians and officials, rather than artists, determine the outcome, this remains an issue of cultural politics.

The governments of both the Republic of Vietnam and the Democratic Peoples Republic of Vietnam tried to use music for propaganda, but the northern government (which became the national government after 1975) was harder on musicians. The *chầu văn* possession ritual was, and continues to be, banned, though it is said still to take place in private. The government prefers to send modernized troupes, instead of traditional musicians, to perform outside Vietnam.

Laos

During the fighting in Vietnam, Laos suffered far more than most outsiders realize. Incredible numbers of bombs were dropped over wide areas, particularly in the south, along the Hồ Chí Minh Trail. In some provinces, virtually every permanent building was destroyed, cluster bombs were spread over the countryside (where they continue to maim and kill), and many people, including musicians, died. During the war, the United States Information Service supported teams of northeastern Thai traditional singers (*mohlam*), who traveled widely in Laos singing anticommunist themes.

After 1975, when the Pathet Lao (communists) gradually gained complete power, what remained of the classical, courtly arts (music, theater, dance) in Luang Phrabang and Vientiane was disavowed because of its connection to the former régime and the aristocracy. Many traditional singers, including some of the country's most prominent *mohlam,* fled to the West. Those who remained were sent to "seminars" (reeducation camps), and their talents were harnessed to spread the news and views of the country's political establishment. In the later 1980s, the School of Fine Arts was reestablished in Vientiane, and ironically, the classical arts were used once again to represent Lao culture to the outside world. Though the government continues to retain traditional musicians within its system and controls foreign researchers' access to musicians, it now makes little propagandistic use of traditional singers.

FIGURE 1 The government-sponsored Đam San ensemble of Pleiku, Vietnam, performs *cải biên* for a visiting delegation on modified minority instruments. Photo by Terry E. Miller, 1994.

Burma

Burma, officially the Union of Myanmar since 1989, is administered by SLORC, the State Law and Order Restoration Council, a military junta that came to power after the failure of the revolution and elections of 1988 and 1989. With complete control of the media and all cultural activities, the generals have tried to keep Western influence to a minimum while supporting the traditional Burman arts. All newly composed music, all imported music, and all publications must pass through censorship committees; foreign observers, noting young Burmans' preference for the music of Michael Jackson and other American stars, can rest assured that every song has been inspected by the government and is clean of antistate messages. The Ministry of Education maintains secondary-level Schools of Music in Rangoon (now Yangon) and Mandalay, and in 1993 founded the University of Culture, a four-year college-level institution that teaches traditional Burman music, dance, theater, painting, and sculpture.

While the Burman arts are maintained in traditional fashion, those of the National Brethren—the non-Burman states, such as Shan State and Kachin State—have been manipulated for political purposes. Many of these states have been in long-standing rebellion against the central government and do not wish to be part of a united Myanmar. In the states themselves, traditional forms of dance and music continue to thrive, but the forms depicted in the media deliver messages of national unity through multiethnic collective dances, accompanied by popularized renditions of the original music. In this way, many otherwise traditional dances receive overt political interpretations in televised broadcasts.

Cambodia

The people of Cambodia suffered a worse fate than any other people in Southeast Asia during the twentieth century. Anyone who has seen the film *The Killing Fields* has confronted something of the horrors that befell the Cambodian people when the Khmer Rouge conquered the nation (in 1975) after the fall of the government headed by Lon Nol, whom the United States had supported. The Khmer Rouge sought to reinvent Cambodian civilization on a simple agrarian model. To do that, it had to destroy all sophisticated aspects of the culture, including most forms of music, theater, and dance. Some artists managed to flee the country, but a high percentage of the nation's cultural carriers were killed. Most musical instruments were destroyed, the National Library was stripped and its contents destroyed, and the National Museum's treasures were damaged or destroyed. An invasion by the Vietnamese army in 1979 stopped the Khmer Rouge from finishing the eradication of Cambodian culture.

During the reign of terror, artists were forced to create and stage spectacles glorifying the Khmer Rouge. Even after 1979, the new government adopted this form of theater for its own glory (figure 2). During the later 1980s, with help from nongovernmental organizations and at least one foreign government (Australia), efforts were made to rebuild the School of Fine Arts and to reassemble the troupes of dancers and musicians who had once been connected with Prince Sihanouk's palace. The arts have been so important in restoring the Cambodian people's spirits that they have received an unusually high priority. During the 1990s, the government has sent troupes of dancers and musicians—even actors and puppeteers—on worldwide tours, demonstrating the resilience of Cambodian culture.

The present Cambodian government has done little to use the arts for propaganda. In the late 1980s, the government's bookstore in Phnom Penh still offered cassettes of revolutionary popular songs, but on the streets, people preferred pirated copies of imported popular tapes from Thailand, the West, and elsewhere. Through

FIGURE 2 A tableau from a grand historical pageant held to celebrate the tenth anniversary of the overthrow of the Khmer Rouge, at Phnom Penh's National Theater in December 1989. Photo by Terry E. Miller.

all this, the present state of village musics and popular theatrical genres remains mostly unknown to outsiders, since researchers are prohibited from traveling to most parts of the countryside.

Thailand

War has not been an issue in Thai life since 1767, the light bombing of Bangkok during World War II notwithstanding. Cultural politics has played a role in the national development of music and theater, but not more than in most countries. In 1865, King Mongkut (Rama IV) of Siam, fearing the loss of "Siamese" culture to a growing preference for Lao (northeastern region) music, banned the performance of Lao music and dance in central Siam. The greatest interference in the arts occurred after the 1932 coup d'état, when a succession of military governments suppressed Thai classical music, preferring a policy of westernization. These governments encouraged Thai musicians to play classical music on Western instruments, and *ramwong,* a genre of Western-influenced social dance, came into being. The suppression of classical music lasted into the 1960s, but enforcement was gradually lifted. During the 1930s and early 1940s, some Thai musicians, fearing the loss of the classical repertory, began transcribing the music into staff notation. By 1941, some 475 pieces had been transcribed into parts or full scores. This collection of manuscripts was lost in a fire on 9 September 1960, but David Morton, then a student from the University of California at Los Angeles doing research on his dissertation, had microfilmed most of it. Some compositions were later published by the Fine Arts Department.

Since the 1980s, the Thai Ministry of Education has supported a growing number of music departments in the nation's system of education, and Thai students at all levels are exposed to classical and regional musics. Despite pressures from Thailand's increasing affluence, modernization, and urbanization, the classical arts are thriving. But these factors have had impacts in other ways [see THE IMPACT OF MODERNIZATION ON TRADITIONAL MUSICS].

Malaysia

A modernized, multiethnic state, Malaysia presents a useful example of how a well-meaning government has sought to establish a national culture that aims at simulta-

When the Indonesian government makes a decision about the use or misuse of the performing arts, that decision almost immediately has an impact on even the lowliest musicians, dancers, and actors.

neously unifying the country's ethnic groups and assuring the preeminence of the Malay (over the Chinese and Indian) segments of the population. As traditional contexts and patronage for such traditional arts as shadow theater (*wayang kulit*) and human theater (*ma'yong*) have changed, these genres have been restored to their allegedly original state and purged of modernisms and commercialisms. This process is most clearly documented in Tan Sooi Beng's study of *bangsawan* (1993), a formerly commercial and eclectic genre, restored to supposedly traditional Malay purity.

ISLAND SOUTHEAST ASIA

Indonesia

The Indonesian government has played a strong and consistent role in the music industry. Some of the most prominent performers are linked closely to the government, either by having a position in the military or civil service as their primary means of employment, or by being married or otherwise related to someone who does. The civil service is the largest employer of Indonesians, and most major political decisions by governmental leaders trickle down to the lives of civil servants and their families. Therefore, when the government makes a decision about the use or misuse of the performing arts, that decision almost immediately has an impact on even the lowliest musicians, dancers, and actors.

Indonesia's climate of religious tolerance (as set forth in Pancasila, its five principles for government) and its national motto (Unity in Diversity) allow for a broad range of performing arts and for the fostering of local traditions that do not have to follow nationalist models. Most people in power in Jakarta are Muslims, and the potential conflicts between Islam and music are well known [see WAVES OF CULTURAL INFLUENCE: Islam], but no one expects the Hindu Balinese to give up their blend of music, dance, and theater to conform to some kind of nationalist vision of the performing arts. Furthermore, the government recognizes that fostering diversity in the performing arts (through sponsorship of competitions) leads to local pride, believed to support general patriotism.

One of the strongest tools used by the government to control the performing arts is a national ban, or at least a national chill, on particular songs, dances, or artists. The government does not impose bans lightly. To ensure that the Indonesian performing arts reflect local pride and are neither offensive nor a potential embarrassment to Indonesian national consciousness and development, a body of consultants reads lyrics and studies danced and staged performances.

Because Indonesian leaders are aware of the role that Indonesia plays among nonaligned nations, some of the strongest attempts to control the performing industry have resulted from concerns about international embarrassment. In the late 1980s, after illegally duplicated copies of "We Are the World" (a recording intended to benefit victims of an Ethiopian famine) had gone on sale in Indonesia before the song's formal release in the United States, the government cracked down on the pirating of cassettes. Nearly overnight, thousands of cassette stores went out of business. (They opened up months later, with all new—and legal—cassettes, priced four times as high.) Most of the new cassettes were of international popular music, and local cassette industries were thrown into confusion as legal details were sorted out. The eventual result was that most of the cassette stores came back into business, local musics continued to be recorded, and—most important to the government—Indonesia was spared from further international humiliation.

The governmental use of the ban applies to individual songs and products, like illegal cassettes. Many songs have been banned by the government. If not banned outright, some are formally deprecated. Songs that have concerned the government have included "*Mandi Madu*" ('The Honey Bath') and "*Hati Yang Luka*" ('The Wounded Heart'), for different reasons. "*Mandi Madu*" is an extremely short, lively pop song in *dangdut* (Indian-film-influenced) style; its lyrics are sexually suggestive ("I'm wet, I'm wet, I'm wet"; "Spray me"; and so on). "*Hati Yang Luka,*" a song about spousal abuse, was perceived as being detrimental to national development because *lagu cengeng* or "weepy" songs like it supposedly lowered public enthusiasm for progress (for an examination of this song, see Yampolsky 1989).

The deprecation of a song by a governmental minister can result in a rise in the song's popularity. Both "*Mandi Madu*" and "*Hati Yang Luka*" were among the top hits at local government functions for several years after their official disapproval. Cassettes flew out of the stores as singers hurried to learn the songs so they could perform them in public. Other songs and artists have fallen out of popularity in a chilled climate of control and disapproval. Possible reasons for the variation in artistic responses to governmental concerns are the offender's position within the ranks of the military or civil service, the amount of money required to maintain a song's position on the air despite official disapproval, and the durability of the song or its performer.

In a national atmosphere tolerant of public prostitution and transvestism, it seems somewhat surprising that certain dances would also fall under government disapproval. However, the 1960s and 1970s were ripe periods for blending of Western influences and local elements, and governmental concern was strongest at those points. The popular dance known as *jaipongan* was developed in the 1970s, using movements from Sundanese classical and village dances, American break dancing, the choreography of Martha Graham, and martial arts. Female dancers' sexy use of their hips and the prevalence of dancing by couples led to talk of banning. Though dancing by couples had always been the standard fare at traditional performances by *ronggeng* (singer-dancer-prostitutes), bringing it out into the open and onto a formal stage was perceived as an embarrassment. The creator of the dance, the Sundanese choreographer-composer Gugum Gumbira Tirasonjaya, countered by opening dance studios throughout West Java; when a major politician's son was rumored to be interested in learning *jaipongan,* discussion of a ban subsided, and the genre rose in popularity.

No one in Indonesia (including the members of the government) is fooled into believing that banning or disapproving performances will lead to total compliance and the creation of strictly patriotic arts. The government recognizes the potential danger of political unrest, should such a harsh climate prevail. Although the Indonesian government is famous around the world for its restrictions on some of its greatest literary artists, cartoonists, and playwrights, performers are given much greater leeway to express themselves. Partly to maintain a peaceful climate and partly to occasionally jerk the reins, the government usually resorts to concerned disapproval of a song, style, dance, or performer, expressed in speeches, which are then widely cited in newspaper and magazine articles. The ways in which artists respond (through the use of metaphor, modification, or outright rebellion) keep the relationship between culture and politics a source for endless debates among performers, politicians, and the media.

The Philippines

Warfare has played an important role in the traditional musics of the southern Philippines, especially on Mindanao, where Muslim-oriented insurgents have fought the government since the 1970s. Though the insurgents are not known to have harnessed traditional music extensively for political purposes, the areas of the island under their domination have been virtually off limits to researchers. The affected musical traditions include some of the *kulintang* traditions, particularly of the Maranao branch.

Because the insurgency is located in a non-Christian region of an overwhelmingly Christianized nation, not just Muslims but Muslim performing artists (as bearers of Muslim culture) are suspect. Musicians in the Maranao region sometimes face official intimidation and harassment because of the musicians' public performances, and the families of musicians who have traveled abroad may face ill-treatment because of local assumptions about the channeling of foreign funds to the Muslim rebels. Public adherence to Islam and the performance of music enjoyed by Muslims provide the Philippine government with fodder for suspicion, surveillance, and persecution.

REFERENCES

Brandon, James R. 1967. *Theatre in Southeast Asia.* Cambridge, Mass.: Harvard University Press.

Tan Sooi Beng. 1993. *Bangsawan: A Social and Stylistic History of Popular Malay Opera.* Singapore: Oxford University Press.

Yampolsky, Philip. 1989. "*Hati Yang Luka*, an Indonesian Hit." *Indonesia* 47:1–18.

Popular Music and Cultural Politics

Deborah Wong
René T. A. Lysloff

Originally a branch of folklore, the study of popular culture has grown rapidly within the field of ethnomusicology since about 1980. Ethnomusicologists, while maintaining a firm footing within the world of traditional music, have noted the rise of popular musics throughout the world and have become interested in the processes of their growth, their meanings to modern societies, and their relationships to older types of music.

Southeast Asia provides fertile ground for the study of popular music, particularly in Thailand and Indonesia, where modernization and industrialization have had a profound impact on society. Each country article in Part 3 of this volume treats popular music to some extent, but Thailand and Indonesia have been chosen for more detailed discussion, with a focus on contextual and developmental issues. They are to be read as case studies. Other lively popular traditions, including those of the Philippines, Vietnam, and Malaysia, are not included here only because of limited space.

THAILAND

A comprehensive history of Thailand's popular musics has not yet been written. Thai scholars and critics have begun to write about them (mostly in Thai), but scholarship in Western languages is scattered and sketchy. These musical traditions, shaped by socioeconomic class and geocultural region, have absorbed Western musical influences in unexpected and thought-provoking ways.

What *is* Thai popular music? Excepting certain ritual repertories, Thai "classical" music has constantly absorbed melodies and influences from regional rural musics; for instance, the music of the urban street theater called *li-ke* is an exuberant mix of ritual dance-drama repertory and whatever popular songs are currently being heard. Thai music is characterized by borrowing among styles and genres—and even among regions, ethnic groups, and neighboring countries. Distinctions between high and low culture or classical and popular musics are therefore problematic in many contexts.

Nevertheless, after World War II, with the flowering of the recording industry

His Majesty King Rama IX (Bhumibol Adulyadej, reigning since 1946) is an enthusiast of jazz; he has been known to assemble bands at the palace and to sit in on sax and clarinet.

and the expansion of the urban middle class, new, mass-mediated musics emerged, created and disseminated via 78-, 45-, and 33 1/3-rpm records, and later by radio, cassettes, television, movies, and (most recently) compact discs. The emergence of these musics has everything to do with industrialization and Western influence.

Popular music history and genres

The first recordings of Thai music were made in the first decade of the twentieth century by European record companies. Between 1900 and 1910, the Gramophone Company made and issued ninety-seven records of Thai music. The German company Beka-Record G.m.b.H. recorded Thai music in 1905–1906 (Gronow 1981). These recordings captured a variety of styles and genres, from court and ritual musics to rural genres. Initially, foreign-made recordings were novelty items, targeted for the upper classes, but they were quickly replaced with recordings produced by and for Thais. Again, the history of the early recording industry in Thailand awaits writing, but several Thai labels had appeared by the 1920s and 1930s. Phonograph recordings were introduced by Westerners, but like many foreign influences, they seem to have been quickly appropriated and redefined by Thais.

Middle- and upper-class Thais have long been aware of American popular music. During the 1930s and 1940s, big band music made an impact. His Majesty King Rama IX (Bhumibol Adulyadej, reigning since 1946) is an enthusiast of jazz; he has been known to assemble bands at the palace and to sit in on sax and clarinet. Visits to the palace by Benny Goodman and Dizzy Gillespie have been memorialized in countless photographs, and the king has composed many big band songs, now widely available on cassette and compact disc.

Luk krung and *luk thung*

Big band music left other marks. One was *luk krung* (*luk* 'offspring', *krung* 'city'), a Thai version of big band jazz, featuring Thai compositions played on Western instruments. Until the 1960s, it remained popular among middle-aged urban Thais. As elsewhere, big band instrumentation was absorbed into emerging local genres (like highlife in West Africa). *Luk thung* was one of these. *Luk thung* (*luk* 'offspring', *thung* 'field') appeared in the 1940s and remains one of the most vital and commercially viable musics in Thailand. It has changed considerably since its appearance, but its style remains recognizable, and as a genre, it speaks to the rural and urban working class. It is closely related to the traditional rural musics of the ethnic Lao from northeastern Thailand, and these roots are especially obvious in the songs of the 1950s, where solo singers' vocal timbres—cultivating a pure tone and a rather constricted throat—resemble traditional *mawlam*; some songs employ *ching chap,* the small hand-held cymbals used as markers of time in much central Thai music. In addition to distinctly Thai or Lao characteristics, early *luk thung* songs often used a backup band of Western trumpets, saxophones, trap set, and other spinoffs from big band instrumentation.

Despite these intercultural influences, *luk thung* was, and remains, one of the most distinctly Thai popular musics, not only in style but also in its aesthetics and social implications. It speaks to the working classes, and its lyrics address not only the daily realities faced by farmers but also the experiences of rural working peoples who migrate to Bangkok searching for work. The genre thus appeals not only to farmers but also to workers in factories and drivers of taxis. In this sense, *luk thung* is intensely political: it maps out a decades-old process of labor migration, and it speaks an emotional language of displacement and nostalgia. Though its lyrics may address everything from love to military service to a rural temple fair, its style alone evokes working-class experience.

Luk thung was the first genre sustained and then driven by the recording industry. First disseminated as 45-rpm records, it became "big business" when the cassette industry boomed in the 1970s. Its development as a genre closely parallels the development of the entire recording industry, now a multimedia entertainment enterprise. The contemporary star system is emblematic of this transformation: singers and bands are created through cassette albums, videos, broadcasts on radio and television, and concerts. Each new form of technology has played a central role in the development of the genre. Today, *luk thung* singers make music videos, are featured in weekly television shows, and star in films. Still, live performances continue to play an important role in making a singer, and road tours are central to a singer's success (Marre 1985 and 1994 [1983]).

The business of *luk thung* reflects tensions between performers, recording companies, radio DJs, and the public. In the late 1980s, 70 percent of the promotional budget for a new *luk thung* album was usually assigned to radio promotion, and the other 30 percent divided between television and print media. The *luk thung* market has long been dominated by a few recording companies, but singers' contracts are far from standardized. A singer recording for the first time may not receive any fee at all, nor are royalties guaranteed. More established singers may receive anywhere between U.S. $200 and $4,000 for a ten-song cassette album, and then might choose between lump sum or per-tape-sold royalties—but these arrangements and figures vary widely among companies.

Luk thung is only one of several kinds of popular music in Thailand. It is a working-class music that crosses rural-urban lines, but *luk krung* and *string* are distinctly urban and middle class. Ubonrat notes "the overall market share between the three main genres in the Thai popular music industry is approximately 40:20:30 for *Luktoong, Lukkroong,* and *String* respectively" (Ubonrat 1990b:64). *Luk thung* therefore has a slight edge in the market. Both *luk krung* and *string* are emblematic of the growing middle class in Bangkok, and both are part of a larger category of pop music known as *phleng thai sakon* (*phleng* 'musical piece', *sakon* 'Western'), Western-style Thai pop. *Luk krung* is soft in sound and affect; it has been compared to Western crooners' music. *String* is closer to rock and roll; its cassettes are slickly packaged, with bold graphics, vaunting Western youth aesthetics: its singers often wear jeans, leather jackets, and sunglasses, and may cultivate a cool, disaffected persona. To Western ears, though, the music sounds unrebellious. Vocal and instrumental timbres tend to be soft and sweet; a supporting wash of synthesizer sound is common. The American influence of rock, pop, blues, and country is clearly discernible, strongly mediated by Thai sensibilities of softness, sweetness, and control. Whereas a Western listener is apt to describe both *luk krung* and *string* as saccharine, young urban Thais are more likely to find *luk krung* romantic, moving, and a bit old fashioned, and to view *string* as self-consciously modern. Western-style Thai pop is thus a mixture of apparently contending agendas: transnational in its origins and its relation to other Asian urban popular musics, it encompasses an array of distinctly Thai popular musics.

Songs for life

The fields (*thung*) and the city (*krung*) denote musical landscapes and class as well as metaphoric realms, but another kind of popular music bridges these domains. The music of social criticism and opposition, known as *phleng phua chiwit* 'songs for life', is seen by Thais as a separate genre of popular music. Songs for life originated with the band Caravan in the early 1970s: musicians and intellectual activists, they were at the center of the student demonstrations that first toppled the dictatorship of Thanom Kittikachorn in 1973 and were then violently suppressed in the political crackdown of 1976 (Caravan 1978). Caravan's songs quickly became symbols of the democracy movement; in 1976, Caravan fled into the countryside with hundreds of other activists and continued to perform via underground broadcasts from the Communist Party of Thailand. It is hard to overemphasize the impact of their songs; now, several decades later, the most famous are still known by most Thais, whether farmers or office workers (Myers-Moro 1986).

A second band, Carabao, has had a more prolonged effect on Thai cultural politics. The name *Carabao* evocatively refers both to Caravan as its ideological parent and to the water buffalo, a symbol of Southeast Asia's farmers. Carabao's icon (featured on all their cassette albums and on fans' T-shirts) is a water-buffalo skull, with sweeping horns. One of Thailand's longstanding popular-music groups, Carabao released some ten albums between 1981 and 1990, when the group disbanded.

Both Caravan and Carabao have made creative use of traditional rural instruments and vocal timbres, but their overall styles are strongly informed by American musics of protest. Caravan favored the acoustic guitar folk rock of Bob Dylan and Joan Baez; Carabao cultivated electric guitars and a harder-hitting style. Like Caravan, Carabao's songs consistently addressed the experience of farmers and their lives of poverty and exploitation, but Carabao's political commentary was impressively far reaching. Little escaped their critical eye: their songs addressed prostitution, Thai consumerism, government-approved suppression of dissent, American imperialism, and much more. Whereas Caravan's songs were broadcast clandestinely, Carabao was commercially successful, and when certain songs, including "*Prachathipatai*" ('Democracy'), were banned from the airwaves, cassette sales went up (Hamilton 1993:519). Censorship is real and constant in Thailand, but the cassette industry is (so far) less subject than radio or newspapers to direct interference.

Caravan and Carabao are not the only examples of oppositional Thai music; they are merely the most famous. Social criticism has also emerged from popular regional musics, especially from northern Thailand. The singer-composer Charan Manophet, the band Salaw (the *salaw* is a two-stringed northern Thai bowed instrument), and a children's group called Nok Lae represent regional resistance to what is perceived as the cultural imperialism of central Thai language and government. Nok Lae perhaps represents cooption more than resistance: this group featured some eight boys and girls, all younger than twelve years old, who performed wearing the clothes of northern Thai ethnic minority groups (including the Karen, the Akha, and the Hmong). During 1985–1986 or so, Nok Lae was hugely popular in Bangkok and was immediately absorbed into advertising: their Colgate commercials were ubiquitous for more than a year. What they represent, and to whom, is another question. Their innocence and cuteness was capitalized on, and it could be said that they represent the infantilization of highland minority peoples, packaged for urban Thais. Still, by emphasizing northern Thai language, clothes, and musical instruments, these groups have sometimes directly (more often obliquely) suggested that Thai culture itself is a contested arena in which regional identities may gather political force.

Dissemination, ownership, and cultural politics

Songs move through Thai society in many ways. Thai popular musics are formally disseminated through a series of multimedia links in which television, radio, and cassettes are interlocking businesses. These networks, however, have limited scope: for linguistic reasons, Thai popular musics are virtually unmarketable outside Thailand—unlike, for instance, Chinese-language popular musics, which have a transnational diasporic market. The insularity of the Thai popular-music market therefore encourages informal circulation.

Nightclubs and restaurants play an important role in a less controlled kind of dissemination, in which small bands perform not only their own numbers, but also whatever songs are popular at the time. Such bands usually play one- to two-hour gigs, and may perform at several nightspots in a single evening. They learn new songs by listening to cassettes and by buying inexpensive music magazines featuring current popular songs, complete with lyrics and chords.

The rise of karaoke bars has enabled anyone to perform. Hits are therefore almost instantly absorbed into a far-flung network of live performance. Big hits are likely to show up in other kinds of live performance: shadow puppeteers in Southern Thailand and urban *li-ke* performers interweave popular *luk thung* with traditional repertory. In addition to boxing matches, movies, and other events, festivals at Buddhist temples have live music, in which local bands perform current hits. We can regard such circulation as the mark of an open-ended music system, in which consumer-performers take active roles in dissemination, or we can see this phenomenon as the ultimate cooption of the consuming public by entertainment conglomerates. Hits may be designed for mass-mediated dissemination, but they quickly move into what might be called a mass-mediated oral tradition.

Rapid industrialization and a growing urban middle class have begun to transform traditional concepts of entrepreneurial ownership. Even within Southeast Asia, Thailand is infamous for piracy—of software, pharmaceuticals, Gucci handbags, Nike sneakers, Rolex watches, and cassette tapes. Western musical copyrights were long ignored, and tourists could load up on pirated versions of albums released only a few days earlier in the United States or Europe, often for little more than U.S. $2 per album. Thai popular-music albums were also pirated (though to a lesser degree), and Thai musicians are beginning to assert copyright protection for their own products. Trade sanctions and severe clampdowns on music and video piracy have, to some extent, boosted sales of Thai materials, though 80 percent of the Thais surveyed by a Bangkok newspaper in 1993 felt that piracy should be suppressed (Pennington 1993). It may well be that the transnational entertainment industry, in concert with other cultural forces, has helped to begin changing ideas of ownership (Wong 1995 [1989–1990]) and may point to the closeness of the connections between finanscape and ideoscape (Appadurai 1990)—to global economies of capital, aesthetics, and commercial authority.

Thai musicians and consumers continue to grapple with the implications—economic, moral, and ideological—of Western musical influences. Thai rap, for instance, had a limited impact in 1992–1994 or so, though during those years it was wildly popular among urban teenagers. If anything, Thai rap was a style: rap kids (*dek rap*) were seen in Bangkok malls, sporting baggy jeans, baseball caps worn backward, and occasionally break dancing to cassettes playing in their Walkman headphones. Thai producers of music and critics agreed that Thai rap was a distant cousin

Japanese pop is part of Bangkok mall culture; second- and even third-generation Thai-Chinese sometimes listen to Cantopop; cassettes of South Asian *filmi* are easily found in most Thai towns and cities; and all of this is framed by Western musical influences.

to its American relative. Almost completely divested of social criticism, most Thai rap was about broken romance, and it rarely used "rude words." Though it featured sampled music, driving rhythms, and recited vocals, its resemblance to American rap ended there. Bangkok newspaper columnist and music critic Khunthong Assunee said Thai rap "is just a fashionable trend. . . . Thai musicians don't have an in-depth understanding of rap music and its origins. Thai rap songs don't contain any worthy messages like American rap songs do" (Rakkit Rattachumpoth and Sirimas Chaianuchpong 1993). Whether Thai rappers *should* emulate their American counterparts is an open question, but Thai consumers apparently voted with their wallets: in 1993, more than one hundred thousand copies of a new album by the leading rapper Jetarin Watthanasin were sold in less than a month and eventually sold more than eight hundred thousand copies—as compared with Michael Jackson's *Dangerous,* an album that in Thailand sold 840,000 copies, of which an estimated eight hundred thousand were pirated (Pennington 1993).

The effects of Western popular culture on Thai society concerns Thais from all walks of life. Western influence is charged with widely different effects: on the one hand, modernization is admired and sought by many Thais; on the other hand, Western popular culture is often viewed with dismay, and even distaste, as emblematic of lax morality and a loss of values. Michael Jackson's Bangkok concert in 1993 prompted extended public discussions of these issues in newspapers, on the radio, and on television. Juvenile delinquency, public expressions of sexuality, and a general loss of Thai cultural awareness were often cited as looming issues. The chair of the government's Committee on Religion, Art, and Culture suggested that it was time to conduct a survey exploring the influence of Western pop or rock culture on Thai youth. Other public figures were more skeptical about the supposed cause-and-effect influence of Western popular culture on Thai young people. The magazine editor Tiva Sarachudha questioned the hypocrisy of denouncing Madonna's performances and costumes while allowing the red-light district Patpong to exist: "In terms of revealing costumes, Madonna's outfits cannot compete with some worn by *luk thung* dancers," he said. Samapol Piwapongsiri, a radio announcer popular among teenagers, suggested that American rock concerts and Thai cultural identity were neither endangering nor endangered: "That attitude looks down on our youngsters. Please have some trust in them" (Pattara 1993).

All this raises the question of who is listening to what, and why. Ubonrat (1990a) looked closely at female factory workers' consumption of popular culture (music, radio, movies, and so on) in the greater Bangkok area and found that *luk thung* was their favorite music, but songs for life and *luk krung* also played significant roles in their recreational listening and in events like weddings and union meetings. One professor of music who grew up in a rural area but now teaches Thai classical music in a Bangkok university loves *luk thung* songs from the 1950s to 1960s and owns a fair number of such cassettes. More research on listening habits is clearly needed, but it would seem that dichotomies between rural and urban, working class and middle class do not entirely define who listens to what, let alone why.

Thai popular musics, their audiences, and the intersections of each with the world outside Thailand's borders is lively territory. Japanese pop is part of Bangkok mall culture; second- and even third-generation Thai-Chinese sometimes listen to Cantopop; cassettes of South Asian *filmi* are easily found in most Thai towns and cities; and all of this is framed by Western musical influences or, some might say, musical imperialism. None of these issues is unique to Thailand. What is special to Thai popular musics is the dynamism of its social arena, into which outside elements are constantly introduced but are then reshaped into something for and by Thais.

INDONESIA

Popular music is not new to Indonesia, but the extent of its geographical diffusion and social penetration is relatively recent. Innovations in media technologies have made both foreign and domestic popular music widely accessible and affordable to Indonesia's working class, urban poor, and rural peasantry. Here, by *popular music,* I mean a kind of music arising out of industrialized society and enjoyed by the urban poor and working class, as well as the middle and wealthy classes. Some Indonesian popular music predates industrialization but will be discussed in conjunction with those that arose concurrently with, and are presently disseminated through, media technologies.

In the development of popular music, radio and cinema (and later TV) have obviously been important, but the Indonesian state has controlled the broadcast media and film industry by regulating the influx of foreign (mainly Western) movies and curtailing popular resistance to the dominant political ideology. Radio and TV news, for example, remain under the strict control of the government and serve primarily for propaganda. As for film, in 1994 the government banned the movie *Schindler's List,* arguing that it contained explicit sexual scenes, and since the director (Steven Spielberg) would not permit any editing, it was not allowed to be shown in Indonesian theaters. However, there may also have been political (that is, anti-Semitic) motivations behind the ban. Ironically, the movie was already widely known to Indonesia's upper and middle class, many of whom had purchased video or laser-disk copies brought into the country illegally.

The cassette industry

The introduction of cassette technology has had a dramatic impact on Indonesia, both socially and economically. It marked the beginning of a shift of media control from the state to private enterprise, bringing into being a highly lucrative commodity industry. In Indonesia, cassette technology is hard to separate from popular music, since the latter could hardly exist without the former. Coming into widespread use by the mid-1970s, cassette recorders have provided small-time entrepreneurs with affordable means to distribute pirated U.S. and European popular music to people who would be otherwise unable to afford legitimately produced vinyl disks (see Yampolsky 1987:2). Furthermore, cheap, battery-powered cassette players (and the commercial cassettes they played) brought popular music to even the most remote villages, those without electricity. At the same time, the inexpensive cassette led to a market expansion of popular groups from Indonesia's own urban centers (particularly Jakarta), whose audiences were previously limited to the middle and upper classes. Finally, cassette technology gave rise to a flourishing domestic industry, which has marketed cassettes of rural or small town popular and traditional musics to targeted local consumers. For Indonesia, specifically Java, this has profoundly affected both traditional and popular musical forms.

Genres of popular Indonesian music

Research on the popular music of Indonesia is still rather spotty, focusing primarily on specific regions and genres. R. Anderson Sutton, in a key study on recent developments in the cassette industry of central Java (1985), examines both the implications for traditional musicians and the possible ramifications for (Western) scholarly research in Javanese traditional music. In another work, he discusses the role of the media in shaping the performing arts (1991). A major study by Philip Yampolsky (1987) focuses on the Indonesian national recording company, Lokananta. Though largely an annotated discography (and cassettography), this work provides an insightful history of Lokananta's development from a minor transcription service for the national radio station of Indonesia, Radio Republik Indonesia (RRI), to a major national recording studio. However, Yampolsky points out that Lokananta has increasingly focused on the gamelan music of central Java, leaving most traditional musics and popular genres to privately owned recording companies.

An article by Martin Hatch (1989) provides an overview of genres, styles, and trends. Hatch organizes his writing around three main categories of popular Indonesian music: *kroncong, dangdut,* and pop. He also identifies several subcategories, some by regional variations and others by stylistic traits. However, since genres often overlap in style, repertoire, and instrumentation, categories such as these are problematic. Furthermore, Indonesian popular music continues to change, and some of these categories may no longer be applicable, say, ten years from now. Nevertheless, Hatch's approach provides a useful survey of most of the genres heard today. His main categories (and, to a lesser extent, some of the subcategories) are discussed individually and in more detail below.

Kroncong

The term *kroncong* may have originally referred to a guitarlike instrument brought to Indonesia by the Portuguese, or it may be an onomatopoeic word derived from strumming on the guitar. Another possibility is that it originally denoted the jingling of the tambourine or the ankle bells that accompanied, with the guitar, sixteenth-century Portuguese dances. Present-day usage of *kroncong* usually denotes both a repertory of music and the ensemble that plays it. A modern *kroncong* ensemble is made up of one or more singers (though most songs are for solo voice) accompanied by ukulele, banjo, guitar, cello, double bass, violin, and flute. Hatch (1989:54) calls *kroncong* a new Indonesian music, perhaps in contradistinction to the traditional music of the Javanese or Balinese gamelan. However, *kroncong* is hardly new, having originated in sixteenth-century contact with Portuguese traders who established themselves in coastal settlements throughout the territory of what has become Indonesia and Malaysia. In the 1800s, it was firmly established in Indonesia's port cities, particularly Jakarta in West Java. By the turn of the twentieth century, it had traveled inland to areas surrounding the traditional cultural centers of central Java, and had begun to come under the influence of gamelan music.

By the end of World War II, two genres of *kroncong* were in existence: *kroncong asli* 'original *kroncong*' and *langgam kroncong* '*kroncong* song', now usually known as *langgam jawa* or *langgam jawi* 'Javanese song'. In an extensive study, Bronia Kornhauser (1978) provides a detailed history of *kroncong,* with an analysis of several songs. What is perhaps most important about this study is that it describes the history of cross-cultural contact (in this case between the West, specifically Portugal, and indigenous Indonesian peoples) and how this resulted in a unique form of musical expression. The study is also significant because it appeared when the study of acculturated (hybrid, syncretic) and popular musics was not yet considered entirely legitimate by many ethnomusicologists. For example, Jaap Kunst (1973:3–4) has little good to say about *kroncong.* While positive views are found in later works of Heins (1975) and Becker (1975)—Heins was first in pointing out the romantic and (post)colonialist notions of authenticity and native purity behind Western scholars' lack of interest in *kroncong*—Kornhauser's study is by far the most comprehensive.

A useful companion to Kornhauser's work is the Smithsonian / Folkways recording (SF 40056) *Music of Indonesia 2: Indonesian Popular Music,* compiled by Philip Yampolsky (1991). The notes, also written by Yampolsky, include a concise history of *kroncong.* Two of the songs Yampolsky collected ("*Kroncong Morisko*" and "*Kroncong Kemayoran*") are also discussed by Kornhauser and represent examples of old-style *kroncong* (*kroncong asli*), in which vestiges of early Portuguese musical contact are evident.

The banjo and the ukulele, playing alternating and interdependent parts, are reminiscent of particular Javanese gamelan instruments (*kethuk* and *kempyang*) in the *kroncong* genre known as *langgam jawa.* Indeed, instruments of the gamelan are also suggested in other parts, including the elaborate guitar figuration (the metallophone or xylophone, *gendèr* or *gambang*), the rhythmic and percussive plucking of the cello (the drum, or *kendhang ciblon*), the continuous melody of the violin (the rebab, a bowed lute), the interpolative flute part (*suling,* a bamboo flute), and the extremely slow-moving bass (gong or other punctuating instruments). Furthermore, the singing of *kroncong* by women, particularly in *langgam jawa,* is deliberately made to resemble that of the *pesindhèn* (solo female singer) in gamelan music. Texts are most commonly sentimental, their most common theme being lovesick yearning. A typical example is "*Ngimpi*" ('Dreams'), by Gesang, transcribed and translated (by René Lysloff) from the singing of S. Mulyani:

Who is not disappointed
Awakening suddenly from a nap
Flustered and groping
Finding only a pillow
Turning your head left and right
Hugging your knees in loneliness
Desperately trying to remember
What was just a dream
The only comfort being
No one else knows [of your loneliness]
The dream I had last night
Seemed as if it were true
There [in my dream] we met
And I felt happiness
I was devoted to him alone
As if it were in the past
Indeed it was another time
When we said our vows
But, sadly
I opened my eyes and awoke
I would have been relieved
Were there someone who understood
According to what [most] people say
Dreams are only the blossoms of sleep
But others will more honestly admit
Dreaming can make you feel the sadness of longing.

kroncong Eurasian colonial-based popular music of Indonesia

dangdut Hindi film-influenced popular music of Indonesia

orkes melayu Malay songs with stringed instruments

ronggèng Female professional singer-dancer tradition

While maintaining the general texture and style of *kroncong,* some ensembles have experimented with different instrumentation, such as employing a gamelan or a full Western orchestra. A style known as *pop kroncong* is characterized either by the use of electric organ, synthesizer, or trap set—or by performing Western or Indonesian pop tunes accompanied by traditional *kroncong* instruments. An amusing example of the latter type is "*Debalik Pelangi*" ('Behind the Rainbow'), on the recording *Madu Dan Racun* by Sundari Sukoco, sung to a melody made famous by Judy Garland in the classic film *The Wizard of Oz.*

Dangdut

Perhaps the most dramatic example of the relationship of media, culture, and the state is the Indonesian popular music known as *dangdut.* As Peter Manuel (1988:210) notes, there is little about *dangdut* that is distinctly Indonesian in style, aside, perhaps, from the language. Similar to *kroncong,* it is an acculturated music. However, it emerged not out of direct cultural contact but as a result of exposure to foreign media—Indian film and the Western popular-music industry. Indian film, popular throughout Indonesia for several decades, left its musical imprint on an already acculturated Malaysian music known as Malay orchestral music (*orkes melayu*), a predecessor to *dangdut,* which had made its way to Indonesia via Sumatra. *Orkes melayu* can be traced to the first decades of the twentieth century, but its earlier history remains unclear. One Indonesian *dangdut* specialist argues that it is rooted in an ancient female dancer-singer tradition known as *ronggèng* (Nizar 1994). Played by ensembles made up of drums (*gendang*), lutes, bass, harmonium, bamboo flute, acoustical guitar, and sometimes brass, the music of *orkes melayu* became extremely popular in Indonesia and Malaysia during the 1950s and early 1960s, and many artists were famous in both countries.

William Frederick (1982) argues that, following the debacle of 1965 (in which Indonesia was deeply shaken by the murder of six military leaders and the chaos that followed), Indonesia opened up to the West and was flooded with U.S. pop, rock, and country. With a combination of the more traditional *orkes melayu* and *kroncong* with the sounds of electrified Western pop and rock, the way was paved for a more lively and provocative style of music. By 1975, largely through the personality and music of singer-musician Rhoma Irama (born in 1947 as Oma Irama), the term *dangdut* came to be used to describe the new Indonesian popular music. Present-day *dangdut* groups use instruments found in most Western rockbands (electric guitars, bass, trap set, synthesizers, and so on). What distinguishes *dangdut* from other forms of popular music is its rhythm: emphatic fourth and first beats in 4/4 meter. This rhythm is the source of the name *dangdut* (rest-rest-*dang-dut,* rest-rest-*dang-dut,* and so forth), suggesting two different kinds of drumstrokes. Peter Manuel (1988:211) argues that this rhythm derives from the North Indian *kaherva,* a meter often heard in Indian film music.

The lyrics of *dangdut* are also interesting. Unlike the relentlessly upbeat ethos of most mainstream Indonesian pop or the heavy sentimentality of many *kroncong* songs, *dangdut* has a rich variety of themes, ranging from Islamic moralizing to erotic love—and even blunt social and political criticism. Rhoma Irama's song "*Nafsu Serakah*" ('Insatiable Greed'), taken from the sound track to his 1980 film *Perjuangan dan Do'a,* as translated by William H. Frederick (1982), comments on the chasm between the poor and the rich:

> All over this part of the world
> We hear the drumbeats answering each other.
> All over this part of the world
> So many dead lie scattered everywhere.
> It's all the result of insatiable greed.
> People who lust, in the cunning, for power
> Will do anything and think it's all right.
> Have we now returned to the law of the jungle
> With the strong oppressing the weak?
> A small group of power-hungry people
> Fill the world with suffering.
> Stop aggression, stop tyranny,
> When will we ever see justice done?
> Almost everywhere in the world
> We hear the cries of a restless humankind.
> Almost everywhere in the world
> Human beings are falling prey to their own kind.
> The reason is that man has forgotten his Creator
> And turned religion into little more than an addendum.
> Men have begun to worship material things.

Because performances can be, as in the case of Rhoma Irama, a fantastic synthesis (or juxtaposition) of Arabic, Asian, and Western elements, not only in terms of music, but in stage appearance, this text may seem at odds with the style of *dangdut.* A shrewd manipulator of his public persona, Rhoma Irama made himself larger than life, even as he became a national icon for Indonesia's poor. He is widely known as a devout Muslim who believes in social justice and protecting human rights. As Frederick notes (1982:112),

> To the Western eye the result seemed, and still seems, to be so much ripped-off kitsch. . . . How successful it all was in the public eye can be gauged by the rapid development of a dangdut dance craze that set kampung and village alike to rock, and by an explosion of dangdut fashions in the wake of [Irama's group] Soneta innovations: tiger-print velvet slacks, silver lamé bell-bottomed trousers, calf-length white leather boots with brass heels and toe guards, and ultimately an eye-poppingly romantic, Arabian Nights–like Islamic couture (*busana Islam*).

Excepting the characteristic rhythm, some of the more recently recorded *dangdut* hits are difficult to distinguish from other popular musics. A style that arose in the late 1980s, known as *disco dangdut,* emphasizes dance. The texts also reflect a general movement away from the serious social commentary of Rhoma Irama toward the more mainstream and less controversial theme (and variations) of true love. Yet some songs are delightfully silly. One, "*Ayam*" ('Chickens'), lists varieties of game hens, chickens, roosters, and other forms of poultry, even the long-haired *ayam malam* (nighttime roosters, punks who go out at night and cause trouble). An important trait of the overall texture of *disco dangdut,* in addition to synthesized instrumentation, is the inclusion of sampled vocal calls and soundbites, sometimes in interlocking rhythmical patterns. This trait often subverts potentially oppressive sentimentality in many songs, making them playful—and perhaps more important, danceable.

Though *dangdut* music is basically dance music, social dance between the sexes is usually discouraged, and is even prohibited in many parts of Indonesia, especially in small towns and rural areas. Female singers of *dangdut* troupes usually gyrate alone on stage while their young, almost exclusively male, fans dance below. Nevertheless, as popular culture (Western values) collides with traditional norms, these women find themselves in the center of growing controversy. Attention has been focused on *dangdut* because of its featured female performers' dress and movements. Dancing provocatively in tight miniskirts while singing suggestive words, dancers often get blamed for a perceived decline in the morals of Indonesia's youth. In the editorials of central Java's major newspapers, moralists charge that *dangdut* and other genres featuring female dancers "smell of pornography" (*bau porno*), that their artistic values have given away to brazen eroticism and Western commercialism. In the summer of 1994, Indonesian governmental authorities and religious leaders took action to force performers of *dangdut* (female dancers and singers) to clean up their act. Normally one of the major attractions of *sekaten* celebrations (marking the birth of the Prophet Mohammed), *dangdut* was banned outright from Yogyakarta and strictly controlled in Surakarta. Ironically, though moralists argue that such "pornography" in Indonesian popular culture arose out of Western influence, *dangdut* may have originated in a much older tradition of erotic female dance, known throughout much of Indonesia and parts of Malaysia as *ronggèng* or *tayuban.* (Another possibility is that *dangdut* arose out of the Islamic-influenced tradition of male singing and dancing known as *gambusan.*) Studies of village forms of dancing, such as *ronggèng* and related traditions, suggest that eroticism and prostitution (whether real or imagined) have a long history in rural female dancing (Hughes-Freeland 1993; Sutton 1984).

Indonesian pop

In overall sound, Indonesia's mainstream pop strikingly resembles its Western equivalent: simple melodies and rhythms in duple meter, accompanied by functional harmony played on guitars, electric keyboards, and drums. Songs are usually light in character, sung by either male or female vocalists, with texts in verse-and-refrain form, relating to youthful love. An important trait of the pop scene in Indonesia is that songs are written by one person and then usually performed by another. A good example is the 1986 megahit "*Madu dan Racun*" ('Honey and Poison'), written by Arie W. and Jonathan Purba and performed by the group Bill & Brod. Typically, the lyrics are about the vagaries of female love:

> *Verse:*
> You're so beautiful, you're so sweet, and you're very spoiled,
> Always bashful, your spirit tender, behind your uncertainty,
> In the haziness of your doubt, through the curtains of your clouds,
> I see your two hands behind your back.
>
> *Refrain:*
> Honey is held in your right hand,
> Poison is held in your left hand. . . .
> I just cannot know which one you'll reach out to me,
> I just cannot know which one you'll reach out to me.

Philip Yampolsky (1989:14) argues that regional pop (*pop daerah*) is differentiated from national *pop Indonesia* mainly by language; if regional musical elements are included, these have only a superficial role:

> The essential gesture of assimilation is achieved by using the regional language in the national music idiom, but certain genres go further and reinforce this gesture by musical means, incorporating features of the regional music, such as a typical rhythmic pattern, or a distinctive local instrument. There are sharp limitations, however, on what kinds of regional music instruments can be used, since they must be compatible with the overall Western style—which means, in practical terms, that they must be capable of being tuned diatonically, or else they must be percussion instruments of indefinite pitch.

"*Madu dan Racun,*" however, was so popular it quickly became performed and recorded in other musical styles and genres, ranging from *kroncong* to Javanese and Balinese gamelan. In the region of Banyumas (in western Central Java), not only was the text translated into the provincial language (Javanese), but the music was adapted to traditional instruments and their system of tuning—rather than the reverse, as Yampolsky argues.

In other parts of Java, too, musicians are experimenting with fusions of national pop and regional musical traditions. A study by Sean Williams (1989–1990) provides an overview of modern popular music in West Java (Sunda). Williams identifies Sundanese characteristics in popular music by language (as distinguished from the Javanese and Indonesian languages), instruments, systems of tuning, and other melodic and rhythmic features. Such regional pop styles are often recorded either by local small-time entrepreneurs or by large recording companies for specifically targeted regional markets.

Regional popular music need not necessarily have any recognizable Western elements. An article by Peter Manuel and Randal Baier (1986) focuses on the West Javanese popular genre known as *jaipongan.* Truly indigenous regional popular music, it is rooted in an older Sundanese folkloric music known as *ketuk tilu,* a traditional genre performed by a female singer-dancer accompanied by spike fiddle (rebab), three pot gongs (*ketuk tilu* 'three ketuk'), hanging gong, hanging metal plates (*kecrèk*), and two barrel drums. The modern *jaipongan* ensemble is similar to *ketuk tilu,* but the drummer now uses up to six drums instead of two, and the ensemble includes, in addition to the other instruments, one or more *saron* (a metallophone struck with a hard beater), a *degung* (gong chime), and sometimes a *gambang* (xylophone).

In most cases, regional pop tends to emulate or imitate the national popular style by taking on, as Yampolsky argues, the national music idiom. Some regional pop styles, as we have seen with "*Madu dan Racun,*" incorporate songs into local traditions. In the case of *jaipongan,* the reverse has occurred: Indonesian pop songs often take on the style of *jaipongan*—especially the virtuosic drumming and the underlying, repetitive, three-pitch *ketuk* percussive patterns (high-low-medium-low, and so on). In other words, *jaipongan* began as a regional folkloric music but evolved into a major popular music genre and a powerful influence on the national pop scene. *Jaipongan* as a regional music became "nationalized" into a style through the replacement of Sundanese texts with those in Indonesian and the use of Western instruments (electric guitars and keyboards) and melodies with functional harmony.

As Indonesia continues to modernize, its pop songs reflect growing sophistication in national and global concerns. Most groups still sing sentimental songs of young love, but some explore larger themes, sometimes more controversial ones. A

Songs about social ills are often attacked for being the cause of the problems they describe. The government's response to "*Hati Yang Luka*" was a clumsy attempt to reassert its control over cultural values and the media.

few even blunder into sensitive political or social issues, running afoul of governmental and national notions of morality. As Philip Yampolsky reports (1989), one Indonesian pop song, "*Hati Yang Luka*" ('A Wounded Heart'), written by Obbie Messakh, sung by Betharia Sonatha, and subsequently covered by others, raised a storm of controversy in the late 1980s because it and others like it were seen by Indonesia's Ministry of Information as weakening the spirit of Indonesia's people. As far as music is concerned, "*Hati Yang Luka*" is uninteresting and typical of *pop Indonesia* ("Indonesian Pop"): it is performed in Western light popular musical style (known in the past as "bubblegum") with a simple melody, accompanied by functional harmony in duple meter by guitars, keyboards, drums, and synthesized instrumentation. It belongs to a type of song disparagingly called *lagu cengeng* 'weepy songs', known for sad and overly sentimental lyrics, concerned with unrequited love, separation, betrayal, and so on. The following lyrics, to "*Hati Yang Luka,*" however, deal with marital problems, even physical abuse, and this may have been too close to real life in Indonesia (Yampolsky 1989). All but the last four lines of the text are sung by a woman (as the wife), and the last four lines are sung by a man (as the husband).

Again and again I try
always to give in
for the sake of our marriage
although sometimes it hurts
See the red mark on my cheek
the imprint of your hand
You often do this when you are angry
to cover up your guilt
Am I like that bird over there
for sale
so you can do what you like to me
and hurt me
If we really break up
it won't be Fate that caused it
Maybe it's better this way so you can be satisfied
and spread your love around
Just send me home to my mother
or [and?] my father
Once, with a handful of gold [bridal wealth]
  you asked me to marry you
Once, we made vows in front of
  witnesses—*huwo huwo*
Now that's all over with
swallowed up by lies—*huwo huwo*

Now all that's left is the story
of a wounded heart
Let it be, let it be
you are sad tonight
Perhaps tomorrow you will find happiness
with someone else.

The governmental overreaction to "*Hati Yang Luka*" is similar to the hysteria over gangsta rap in the United States in the mid-1990s. Songs about social ills are often, and sometimes with considerable leaps of faith, attacked for being the cause of the problems they describe. Yet the real reason behind the ban on "*Hati Yang Luka*" likely has more to do with power and the resistance to that power. By "resistance" I do not necessarily mean that, by addressing men's beating their wives, "*Hati Yang Luka*" was resistive. Yampolsky (1989:4) notes that "within three months of the original issue the music industry had begun a blizzard of secondary versions, follow-ups, and remakes." It was perhaps the *popularity* of the song (and the theme of a man's beating his wife) that brought its ban about. In other words, the pleasure derived from vicariously experiencing marital strife through the media is, in itself, a kind of resistance to Indonesia's traditional patriarchal norms and values, where such family problems should not be scrutinized and discussed publicly. The multitude of recordings inspired by the song represent the patriarchy's loss of control over so-called traditional values, and perhaps even the recording industry. The harshness of the response was the method through which the government clumsily attempted to reassert its control over cultural values and the media.

Contemporary Javanese rock

Like hard rock in the United States, Indonesian rock sounds grittier than other popular genres, carries a more powerful beat, and has more obvious ties to traditional blues. It was, from its inception, an amplified music, featuring the electric guitar, often with a distorted timbre, and a hard-edged vocal part with texts that often self-consciously resisted conventional morals and standards. Finally, a musical seriousness surrounds rock: musicians are serious about the way they play rock, and fans are serious about the way they listen to it. In contrast to most mainstream pop artists, rock performers usually compose their own music, and their songs are usually self-consciously progressive, sometimes even radical. While the commodity-oriented pop scene discourages innovation, rock musicians search for ways to establish their individuality. A good band carves out its own particular style, maintaining the loyalty of its fans as it continues to develop.

The term *rock* as a musical designation may be new to Indonesia, since Hatch (1989) uses the term *pop berat* 'heavy pop' to denote it. However, progressive elements and hard rock are found as far back as the 1970s in the music of Harry Roesli, and *rock* is now the standard term used in the Indonesian popular press. Guruh Sukarno Putra (the son of Indonesia's first president) and his group Guruh Gypsy recorded rock incorporating Balinese gamelan. Until recently, however, rock remained on the periphery of the Indonesian popular-music scene. Though Guruh Gypsy never reached the sustained popularity in Indonesia that Led Zeppelin achieved in the United States, they were important in establishing a progressive fusion of rock with jazz and Western harmony with gamelan timbres.

Similar fusions have continued to interest Indonesian listeners and inspire further experimentation by musicians. The award-winning experimental jazz group Krakatau modified the West Javanese five-tone *saléndro* scale into what members describe as a ten-pitch microtonal system (from the liner notes to the cassette album,

Mystical Mists). Combining state-of-the-art digital electronic equipment with traditional West Javanese instruments, Krakatau produces a unique sound, mixing jazz rhythms, traditional music, and spacey new-age effects. The group Gong 2000, however, combines hard rock with Balinese gamelan to create a music reminiscent of Guruh Gypsy but with more of an edge. It is clear from the liner notes to their latest album, *Laskar* (probably released in 1993), that the musicians are trying to create a uniquely Indonesian kind of rock, one that draws inspiration from regional traditions.

Youthful rebellion and resistance in Indonesia generally is most commonly expressed in music in terms of style rather than content. Most Indonesian rock groups, such as Gong 2000, Sket, and Slank, have a hard-edged sound and the rock "look" (shoulder-length hair, open and gaudy shirts, leather jackets, jeans), but their lyrics are tame, with the usual themes of love and teenage angst. Gong 2000 goes further, and in their most recent album includes songs with cautionary texts addressing "safe" social themes—themes too broad to be considered sensitive by the state, like pollution, ecology, preserving traditional culture, and so forth.

The band Swami, especially artists Iwan Fals and Sawung Jabo, have produced sometimes overtly political songs. Iwan Fals, in particular, has run afoul of the Indonesian government because of the social commentary in several of his songs (see Piper and Sawung Jabo 1987:32). Their music resembles that of other Indonesian rock groups, though the overall quality is considered better. The narrative texts are clearly rooted in the contemporary folk style established by ballad singer Ebiet G. Ade in the late 1970s and continued by Leo Kristi into the 1990s. Iwan Fals also preserves the protest element of Indonesian contemporary folk music, said to be modeled after the songs of Bob Dylan. With Sawung Jabo, his political idealism and sincere concern for Indonesia's poor and disenfranchised has won him loyal fans among intellectuals, while the hard rock music of Swami has gained him a broad following from the younger generation. Like many other rock musicians, he and Sawung Jabo express the anxieties of Indonesia's youth over their environment, their society and government, and their own cultural identity. Though many of their songs are rebellious, sometimes even politically subversive, most are filled with a profound love of country and disgust at violence. The message of their music is clear: they seek political and social change through reformation, not anarchy.

Other trends

Intense marketing of pirated cassette copies of popular music from throughout the world (though mostly the West) has had a major impact on Indonesia's popular music. Local and nationally known artists continue to pay close attention to the global pop scene. Some try to create unusual hybrid forms through the blending of local and foreign styles, such as combining elements of reggae with *dangdut,* as did Fahmy "Sharp" Shahab and Hetty Sundjaya in their 1990 album, *Kopi Dangdut.* Others try to emulate specific genres, for both their musical interest and their social messages. Indonesian rapper Iwa-K has found a small but loyal audience among urban youth. Two of his songs, in English, demonstrate an astounding knowledge of hard-core rap, but he puts a personal stamp on his other songs by singing them in the Indonesian language and exploring themes related to both traditional and contemporary Javanese culture. The title song from his 1993 album, *Topeng,* addresses the hypocritical masks worn by people every day. The cover of the album depicts Iwa-K standing in the dead of night behind a low brick wall fringed by barbed wire, with flames licking up into the sky behind him. Sporting a shaved head and wearing dark sunglasses, he holds a traditional Javanese mask (*topeng*) in one hand. In the light of the flames, he looks almost threatening, vaguely like a south-central L.A. rapper.

However, this illusion is immediately dispelled by the traditional Javanese mask he holds in his hand. Like his music, the cover photo makes the connection between two different cultures: traditional Java and African-American hiphop.

As in the United States, Indonesian pop has made strong inroads into other media forms, particularly television. In 1962, the Ministry of Information established TVRI (Televisi Republik Indonesia), and since the Palapa satellite was launched in 1976, its programming has been broadcast throughout the archipelago. Today, television sets are found even in the most remote villages. Many people may be too poor to own a set, but they likely have access to one. In 1991, the state permitted the privatization of broadcast (and cable) television, later giving rise to several stations, new in 1994: RCTI (Rajawali Citra Televisi Indonesia, transmitting out of Jakarta), TPI (Televisi Pendidikan Indonesia, Jakarta, Indonesia's educational channel), SCTI (Surabaya Citra Televisi Indonesia, Surabaya), and AN-TEVE (Andalas Televisi, Lampung).

With newspapers and radio, television functions as an important propaganda arm of the state. Thus, while allowing private TV and radio stations, the state maintains strict control over some aspects of the broadcast media. All news is directly relayed from the state television and radio stations. The Ministry of Information carefully scrutinizes all media, including film and print media, for any items that may be considered deleterious to the Indonesian state and its people. Various magazines and newspapers, films, and television shows have been censored or banned altogether for these and other reasons, including pornography and publicizing subjects critical of the state (or otherwise controversial).

As in the United States, popular music has become a basic aspect of broadcast television. A large part of popular music television in Indonesia consists of broadcasts of U.S. music videos. Though Indonesia has no music TV channel, it does boast several programs devoted solely to music videos, both foreign and domestic. Some of the domestic videos are simply taped performances, for example, a crooner in soft focus; others imitate the fantastic narratives found on MTV and VH1, using similar camera angles and fast cuts. Still others depict elaborate stage shows of singing and dancing à la Janet Jackson or Madonna—albeit with tamer movements and lyrics. One might see hiphop moves alongside *jaipongan*-style dancing (arms held out with elaborate movements of the hands) to the accompaniment of *disco dangdut.* Much of this borrowing of styles of singing, dance movements, dress, overall look, and so forth, has had a direct impact on domestic popular culture generally, with resultant spinoff industries, mainly in the urban centers, related to dance clubs, fashion, and cosmetics.

Further research is needed for understanding the impact of media technology and Western popular music on Indonesia. The debate on cultural imperialism is far from over and must be considered in the light of the most recent technological developments, such as computers and computer games, digital media technology, the World Wide Web, parabolic antennas, and satellite TV. All these developments will have direct cultural implications and, for better or worse, may bring about the transformation or even the demise of many traditional musics and cultural practices.

REFERENCES

Appadurai, Arjun. 1990. "Disjuncture and Difference in the Global Cultural Economy." *Public Culture* 2(2):1–24.

Becker, Judith. 1975. "Kroncong, Indonesian Popular Music." *Asian Music* 7(1):14–19.

Bill and Brod. 1985? *Madu & Racun.* Jakarta, Indonesia: Dian Records. Cassette.

Caravan. 1978. *Thailand: Songs for Life, Sung by Caravan.* New York: Paredon Records. LP disk.

Frederick, William H. 1982. "Rhoma Irama and the Dangdut Style: Aspects of Contemporary Indonesian Popular Culture." *Indonesia* 34:103–130.

Gong 2000. 1993? *Laskar.* Jakarta: Konser Musik / P. T. Metrotama Musik. Cassette.

Gronow, Pekka. 1981. "The Record Industry Comes to the Orient." *Ethnomusicology* 25(2):251–284.

Hamilton, Annette. 1993. "Video Crackdown, or the Sacrificial Pirate: Censorship and Cultural Consequences in Thailand." *Public Culture* 5(3):515–531.

Hatch, Martin 1989. "Popular Music in Indonesia." In *World Music, Politics and Social Change: Papers from the International Association for the Study of Popular Music,* ed. Simon Frith, 47–67. Manchester: Manchester University.

Heins, Ernst. 1975. "Kroncong and Tanjidor: Two Cases of Urban Folk Music in Jakarta." *Asian Music* 7(1):20–32.

Hughes-Freeland, Felicia. 1993. "*Golèk Ménak* and *Tayuban:* Patronage and Professionalism in Spheres of Central Javanese Culture." In *Performance in Java and Bali: Studies of Narrative, Theatre, Music, and Dance,* ed. Ben Arps, 88–120. London: School of Oriental and African Studies, University of London.

Iwa-K. N.d. *Topeng.* Musica MSC 7941. Cassette.

Kesengsem. [N.d.] Various artists. Klaten (Java), Indonesia: Kusuma Recording K.O.K. 007. Cassette.

Kornhauser, Bronia. 1978. "In Defence of Kroncong." In *Studies in Indonesian Music* 104–183. Monash Papers on Southeast Asia, 7. Clayton, Victoria: Monash University.

Krakatau. 1994? *Mystical Mist.* PT Aquarius Musikinda APC AQM 16-4 P9603. Cassette.

Kunst, Jaap. 1973 [1934]. *Music in Java: Its History, Its Theory, and Its Technique.* 3rd ed. Revised and enlarged by E. L. Heins. 2 vols. The Hague: Martinus Nijhoff.

Manuel, Peter. 1988. *Popular Musics of the Non-Western World.* New York: Oxford University Press.

Manuel, Peter, and Randal Baier. 1986. "Jaipongan: Indigenous Popular Music of West Java." *Asian Music* 18(1):91–111.

Marre, Jeremy. 1985. "Two Faces of Thailand: A Musical Portrait." In *Beats of the Heart,* 198–214. New York: Pantheon Books.

———. 1994 [1983]. *Two Faces of Thailand: A Musical Portrait.* Newton, N. J.: Shanachie Entertainment. 60-minute VHS video.

Myers-Moro, Pamela. 1986. "Songs for Life: Leftist Thai Popular Music in the 1970s." *Journal of Popular Culture* 20:93–113.

Nizar, M. 1994. "*Dangdut: Sebuah Perjalanan*" (Dangdut: a journey). Five-part series. *Citra* 221–225.

Pattara Danutra. 1993. "Fear over Negative Effects of Western Concert." *Bangkok Post,* 5 September.

Pennington, Philip. 1993. "Keeping in Tune with the Times." *Bangkok Post,* 5 September.

Piper, Suzan, and Sawung Jabo. 1987. "Indonesian Music from the 50's to the 80's." *Prisma* 43(March):25–37.

Rakkit Rattachumpoth and Sirimas Chaianuchpong. 1993. "Rap Beats Out the Competition." *Bangkok Post,* 27 April.

Shahab, Fahmy "Sharp," and Hetty Sundjaya. 1990. *Kopi Dangdut.* Dian Records. Cassette.

Sutton, R. Anderson. 1984. "Who Is the Pesindhèn? Notes on the Female Singing Tradition of Java." *Indonesia* 37(April):119–133.

———. 1985. "Commercial Cassette Recordings of Traditional Music in Java: Implications for Performers and Scholars." *The World of Music* 27(3):23–43.

———.1991. *Traditions of Gamelan Music in Java.* Cambridge Studies in Ethnomusicology. Cambridge: Cambridge University Press.

Ubonrat Siriyuvasak. 1990a. *The Dynamics of Audience Media Activities: An Ethnography of Women Textile Workers.* Bangkok: Chulalongkorn University, Women's Studies Programme.

———. 1990b. "Commercialising the Sound of the People: *Pleng Luktoong* and the Thai Pop Music Industry." *Popular Music* 9(1):61–77.

Williams, Sean. 1989–1990. "Current Developments in Sundanese Popular Music." *Asian Music* 21(1):105–136.

Wong, Deborah. 1995 [1989–1990]. "Thai Cassettes and Their Covers: Two Case Histories." In *Asian Popular Culture,* ed. John Lent, 43–59. Boulder, Colo.: Westview Press, 1995.

Yampolsky, Philip. 1987. *Lokananta: A Discography of the National Recording Company of Indonesia, 1957–1985.* Madison: Center for Southeast Asian Studies, University of Wisconsin.

———. 1989. "Hati Yang Luka, an Indonesia Hit." *Indonesia* 47:1–17.

———, ed. 1991. *Music of Indonesia 2: Indonesian Popular Music.* Smithsonian / Folkways C-SF 40056 (cassette), CD-SF 40056 (compact disc).

The Impact of Modernization on Traditional Musics

Terry E. Miller
Sean Williams

It has been widely believed that, at least until the twentieth century, the rate of musical change in Asia has been extremely slow. Western music histories have tended to place non-Western music at the beginning of a chronological history in the "Ancient and Oriental" category, assuming that even living "Oriental" music had changed little since "Ancient" times. But even from current knowledge of Asian musical histories (knowledge that remains limited in important ways), we can surmise that change was always a factor, and when calamity struck, as when a population was carried off to a conqueror's kingdom, radical change could and did occur. From a closer perspective, however, we can see that indisputably the twentieth century has been an age of nearly cataclysmic change, much of it stimulated by contact with the West. These factors may be considered under the heading of modernization.

LOSS OF TRADITIONAL CONTEXTS

Just as species of plants and animals disappear when their habitats are disrupted or vanish, musics require a habitat for their continued existence. As with species of flora and fauna, some musical genres are hardier than others, more able to cope with changes, but the most vulnerable of them simply vanish. Musics performed in concert settings for attentive audiences are less likely to perish in the face of modernization than musics closely linked to functions that may disappear, such as agricultural practices, rituals, and festivals.

Whether musics survive the loss of their contexts also depends to some extent on general attitudes toward tradition, preservationism, and national or local identity. Prosperity and modernization do not necessarily degrade traditional musics, but poverty tends to preserve old ways by limiting options. Nothing destroys cultural habitats more quickly or thoroughly than factional violence, revolution, and war, processes that Southeast Asia has experienced on a grand scale.

The following paragraphs provide case studies illustrating particular kinds of challenges to traditional musics.

Changes in agricultural practices

Throughout Southeast Asia, numerous musical genres, mostly vocal, are (or were) associated with the stages of growing rice. In Thailand, these songs were categorized

phleng phün ban Village songs from Thailand

angklung Indonesian tuned, shaken bamboo rattles

phleng luk thung Popular music genre from Thailand

FIGURE 1 A remote *lao thüng* village in Salavane Province, Laos, is largely insulated from all aspects of modernization, especially because of poverty. Photo by Terry E. Miller, 1991.

as local songs (*phleng phün ban,* also *phleng phün müang*). Before the arrival of modern agricultural practices (which, through mechanization, required fewer workers), members of village communities worked together in the fields. During breaks in work, in the heat of the day or after work, they enjoyed engaging in vocal repartee, pitting the best male singers against the best female singers in a contest of wits; allied onlookers often provided choral responses. In musical terms, this repartee blended antiphonal and responsorial patterns. The songs differed in text and melody according to the stage of work—transplanting, cutting rice, threshing, husking, raking. Few musical instruments were involved; most were markers of rhythm (figure 1).

As Thailand prospered after World War II, its financial wealth was first concentrated in the cities, especially Bangkok. Over time, the government constructed a fine system of highways, electrified villages, beamed radio and television into the country's remotest corners, and encouraged farmers to use gasoline-powered tractors instead of water buffaloes. People no longer worked the fields communally. By the 1960s in central Thailand (later in other areas), these songs had nearly vanished, their contexts gone. They survive only in the memories of a few elderly singers, in archives, and in refined scholastic versions, performed in costume for special events.

In Indonesia (especially on Java), traditional music associated with growing rice included the use of tuned bamboo rattles (*angklung*), whose sound was pleasing to the goddess of rice, Dewi Sri. Since the mid-1970s, *angklung* have been co-opted as tools for Western-style classes in music. Now often tuned diatonically, rather than in the village-style *saléndro* tuning (more or less equidistant), the instruments are used

FIGURE 2 By 1988, the commercial production of audio cassettes was largely limited to small shops with boom box cassette duplicators in Phnom Penh, Cambodia. Photo by Terry E. Miller.

to teach an array of Indonesian patriotic songs and Western pieces, including the "Blue Danube" waltz and "Danny Boy." The rituals traditionally used to perpetuate the agricultural cycle and the *angklung* music that went with the rituals have mostly been abandoned, replaced by chemical pesticides and fertilizers.

Urbanization

During the twentieth century, some Southeast Asian cities—Bangkok, Jakarta, Manila, Saigon—have grown into megacities. As rapidly growing populations in the provinces ran out of land to divide or found few local opportunities, heavy migrations to the cities occurred. Cities have the best and worst of what the world offers, including everything modern. Peoples from various areas are mixed together, and rustic identities give way to urban ones.

Musics formerly heard in distant villages are drowned out by new sounds, especially those of the media, but sometimes this situation in turn gives rise to new and vibrant types. In Thailand, where vast numbers of young men and women from the north, northeast, and south have migrated to Bangkok, the areas are remembered in *phleng luk thung*—pop songs, to be sure, but hybridizations, blending regional instruments and stylistic traits into modern urban sounds, which blare from shops, cars, and corners (figure 2). Music videos invoke objectified images of rural life: fishing nets, farmer hats, agricultural tools, costumes, and behaviors. The modern city gives rise to modern musics.

In Manila, the primary urban center of the Philippines, migrants find their way into an intensely heterogeneous society with a broad overlay of Spanish colonial and American popular culture. Regional and rural traits that make rural migrants stand out (and thus be less employable) are quickly abandoned. In the coastal cities of Borneo, discoveries of oil have led to the creation of large company towns, complete with discos and modern conveniences. In this kind of urban climate, options for the perpetuation of local Dayak culture are nonexistent.

Changes in control over the musics performed

In northeast Thailand during the early 1970s, the most popular entertainments were repartee singing (*lam klawn*), accompanied by a free-reed mouth organ (*khaen*), and two kinds of local theater (*lam mu* and *lam phlün*). All drew on traditional poetry, its metaphors, narratives derived from Buddhist stories (*jataka*), and a reserved stage manner.

From the World War II period onward, a high percentage of northeastern youths migrated to Bangkok, and as Bangkok became more prosperous, so did many formerly poor northeasterners. Used to bright lights and modern sounds, these youths returned to their home villages for holidays. Though the grandparents preferred older-styled entertainments, the grandchildren preferred modern ones. Since the younger generation also had plenty of money, they hired what they wanted to hear. By the mid-1980s, the two theatrical genres had mostly been transformed into a succession of popular songs, backed by an ensemble that included brass and electrified instruments, a set of drums, and (to maintain a link with the past) a *khaen*. Even if the older generation did not prefer this kind of entertainment, by not having money they lost control over performances to those who did have money.

In West Java, local governments have long prided themselves on their support of Sundanese performing arts. In the late 1980s, however, the central (primarily Javanese) officials in Jakarta declared that support to be a waste of funds. Older, aristocratic Sundanese genres, including *tembang Sunda* and gamelan *degung klasik,* had to be largely abandoned in favor of cheaper, Javanese-approved pop acts. Central Javanese court gamelans still play for national-government events such as important affairs of state and the visits of international dignitaries; locally, control over who performs for regional events is no longer entirely in the hands of the regional government.

Loss of regionality

Before Southeast Asia had modern nation-states, it had courts, surrounded by towns and villages. In the distance were other power centers, but no precise boundary between them existed. Because of isolation, preserved by poor or nonexistent roads, little communication, and linguistic differences, regionalism continued to be a factor, even after nation-states had established boundaries and had begun building pan-national cultures.

Regionalism remains most pronounced in the least wealthy—therefore least modernized—nations, particularly Burma, Laos, and Vietnam. Though Vietnam was reunified in 1975, regional differences among the south, the center, and the north remain strong. Throughout Southeast Asia, one should (and in some cases, must) go to a particular region to hear its music in context.

Regionalism in Thailand, among the most modernized of Southeast Asian nations, has undergone drastic change since the early 1970s. Then, the regional cultures were looked down upon. An educated northeasterner would prefer to behave as a (central) Thai. The study of northeastern music and theater was considered of little value. Each region's people nursed stereotypes about the peoples of the other regions.

Since the mid-1970s, as the country prospered and the government encouraged the formation of a strongly unified national culture based on that of the central region, the distinctiveness of the regional cultures weakened. Ironically, as they weakened, they became more attractive. As the nation became more tightly unified and fears of regional secessions receded, the Thai could celebrate the colorfulness of the north, northeast, and south. The country's universities developed programs in regional studies, and much money has poured into schools designated as regional centers. Yet the decline of the regional cultures seems irreversible. In the northeast, with the dominance of central Thai media, the local language is vanishing, and with it the vocal arts that depended on traditional poetry. In the north, where regionalism has become especially weak, civil servants wear local clothing styles on Fridays, but little local architecture survives. On Thai television, troupes of supposedly regional per-

FIGURE 3 The modern urbanite has access to every form of modernization at Bangkok's six-story Mah Boon Krong Shopping Center. Photo by Terry E. Miller, 1988.

formers act like rustics, wearing mannered farmers' clothes, but play modernized versions of the old music. The homogenization of Thai culture is proceeding rapidly because there are national media, a national network of roads, a unified group of universities, national newspapers, and the requirement that all government business be transacted in (central) Thai (figure 3).

The Philippines is one of the most modernized of the Southeast Asian countries; its literacy rate is extremely high, and an educated populace speaks several international languages, including English, in some of the remotest villages. An advanced network of communication and transportation, aided by a recovering economy, has led to a countrywide push to leave the excesses of the Marcos era behind, in a general effort toward prosperity and unity. With marked exceptions (such as the Muslim-led rebellion in the South and certain upland groups in central Luzon), the populace is moving toward homogeneity. Any celebration of regional culture has been replaced by generic images of rural life (water buffaloes, rice terraces, and so on), which result in the simultaneous distancing and romanticizing of the regions' peoples into an exotic rural "other," to which few want to belong.

Changes in patronage

The classical arts, because of their complexity and expense, have depended most on the patronage of the wealthy and powerful. Local aristocracies, including the courts of kings and extended royal families, formerly made classical music and theater possible in Burma, Cambodia, Indonesia, Laos, Malaysia, Thailand, and Vietnam. Before achieving independence from the Dutch (who heavily subsidized the aristocracy),

In the master-disciple arrangement, the hopeful student must prove his or her worth to the master, who transmits the art gradually, unsystematically, and over a long period of time.

many court musicians in Java could count on lifetime employment; after independence, many had to leave their positions and seek nonmusical employment in the cities just to support themselves and their families. Today, only Cambodia retains a king and palace, and Malaysia rotates a kingship among the surviving sultans. Since independence, central Java's sultans have retained a revered status but little genuine political power.

In all these countries, including Cambodia and Malaysia, the classical arts are patronized by a government-supported system of education. Schools operate differently from the old court music establishments, with fixed schedules, credit classes, and the codification of the arts through textbooks and collective instruction.

Wars

Wars have always been part of human life, and wars have always affected the arts. During the late twentieth century, however, two events have shaken mainland Southeast Asia to its core. The reign of terror of the Khmer Rouge, from 1975 to 1979, nearly obliterated the entire Khmer culture. At least 2 million people perished, including a high percentage of the country's artists, dancers, actors and actresses, makers of instruments, and musicians. Enemies had formerly come from without, but in 1975, enemies came from within, perpetrating another twentieth-century holocaust.

Warfare in Vietnam, which raged after World War II, when the Viet Minh challenged the French, resulting in a protracted conflict involving the United States, severely disrupted the arts. Partisans and ideologues harnessed the arts for political purposes, and many individual tragedies occurred. In Laos, provinces were bombed back into prehistory, and with the destruction of towns and villages went the loss of many musicians' lives. The modernizations of warfare enhanced human efficiency in disrupting human life [see CULTURE, POLITICS, AND WAR].

INSTITUTIONS FOR THE TRANSMISSION OF MUSIC

Virtually all Southeast Asian musics have been created and transmitted orally since time immemorial, and the most important institution for transmission has been the master-disciple relationship. In this arrangement, the hopeful student must prove his or her worth to the master, who transmits the art gradually, unsystematically, and over a long period of time to the student, who usually lives in close proximity to the master and who may work as a kind of servant. In this system, money plays a minor or even nonexistent role. The only contract is the unspoken bond of respect between student and teacher.

During the twentieth century, according to the level of development within a given country, new forces have required new methods for transmission. With the growth of cities, an increase in the pace of life, and the decline or elimination of the courtly and aristocratic systems of patronage, the transmission of music has changed.

FIGURE 4 The National Conservatory of Music of Hồ Chí Minh City, Vietnam, formerly the Saigon Conservatory. Photo by Terry E. Miller, 1991.

Modernization has led to the institutionalization of musical pedagogy through the rise of conservatories, colleges, and universities, professional teaching studios, and lessons for pay. A culture's most ancient kinds of music do not always lend themselves to the new environment. The most usual response is for the music to change to fit the institution rather than vice versa. Each country has found its own solution to these dilemmas.

Mainland Southeast Asia

Formerly, each country's most sophisticated music was created and transmitted through a court or an aristocratic musical establishment. Over time, the monarchies either ended (Burma in 1886, Vietnam in 1945, Cambodia in 1970, and Laos in 1975) or saw their power and wealth curtailed (Thailand and Malaysia). Each nation's court music, dance, and theater survived only if a new governmental bureau was created to support it or if educational institutions assumed the role—both of which have long been the patterns in Europe.

The Vietnamese followed the French example by creating conservatories in the European style, mainly to teach European classical music, but they included departments of traditional music (figure 4). There was a tendency, however, to make the music fit the institution; consequently, traditional Vietnamese music came to be notated on staves and is taught systematically, as are piano and violin. Students from the conservatories, if they learn anything at all about traditional music, learn little of the improvisational art central to the older styles. In Saigon, students have long been able to study traditional instruments and theater, but in Hanoi, teachers trained at Eastern European conservatories had the upper hand, and most of what is taught as traditional is really a modernized ethnic music (*nhạc dân tộc cải biên*). Some traditional music is transmitted through these institutions, but in rural areas the old master-disciple system remains the primary method (figure 5).

In Cambodia, the continued transmission of court music passed to the École des Beaux Arts during the mid-twentieth century, but during the reign of the Khmer Rouge, the school and its properties were destroyed, and most of its teachers and students were exiled or killed. The school, refounded a few years after the Khmer Rouge were expelled, has continued to grow. It first became the University of Fine Arts and then, with the resumption of the monarchy, it became the Royal University of Fine

FIGURE 5 Young students study traditional drumming at the former Saigon Conservatory of Music. Photo by Terry E. Miller, 1970.

Arts. Classical music, dance, theater, and instrument making are once again being taught to the next generation of Cambodians (figure 6).

The Lao experience has followed a similar pattern. With the fall of the monarchy and the exile of most of its artists (to the United States and France), the court music of Luang Phrabang, the royal capital, ended. In Vientiane, the former administrative capital (and after 1975 the only capital), the École des Beaux Arts, founded in the mid-1950s, came under the strict control of the communist government. For years, Lao classical music, considered a symbol of the former régime and its alleged decadence, was excluded, but by the early 1990s it had again resurfaced as a national expression. Consequently, a national educational institution again transmits the classical music and dance of the Lao.

Because Thailand has avoided the twin plagues of colonialism and war, its patterns of music transmission have undergone a more normative change, driven mostly by the diffuse forces of modernization. But even in formal institutions (including schools at all levels), the age-old *wai khru* ritual remains the norm. The term *wai* 'to

FIGURE 6 Students study Khmer classical dance at the University of Fine Arts, Phnom Penh. Photo by Terry E. Miller, 1988.

FIGURE 7 Masks and other ritual objects on a *wai khru* altar at the School of Dramatic Arts, Roi-et, Thailand. Photo by Terry E. Miller, 1988.

greet' denotes the customary courtesy of putting one's hands together and bowing slightly; *khru,* derived from the Indic word *guru,* denotes the teacher or master. The intention of the ritual is to bond disciple to master—and to the master's artistic lineage, which extends to the original teachers, the pantheon of Hindu and Buddhist gods. In the basic ritual, the student brings a modest collection of ritual objects (candles, flowers, a white cloth, coins, incense) and presents them to the teacher, who blesses the student, and now allowed to touch the student, provides a ritual first lesson, in which the teacher grasps the student's hands and plays a beginning motive, usually on the gong circle (*khawng wong yai*). At different stages, more elaborate rituals may occur. Even in public schools, students perform a large-scale *wai khru* once a year for their teachers. After this ritual bonding has occurred, the teacher willingly transmits the special knowledge of the art (music, dance, boxing), and the student willingly receives it. Even with Bangkok's pace of life increasing and the teaching of music having become a regularly scheduled affair (not unlike teaching in the West), the *wai khru* remains essential to the transmission of any traditional art (figure 7).

With the disbanding of the royal music establishment after the 1932 coup d'état, nationwide responsibility for these arts passed to the Fine Arts Department (Krom Silapakon), which oversees educational institutions, official ensembles, and publications. Though Thai musical arts, especially classical music, fell on hard times from the 1930s to the 1960s, they have undergone a sustained recovery since the early 1970s. As late as the mid-1970s, music was not considered a serious academic subject, and only one college was offering a degree in music. Since then, most of the country's universities and colleges have created degrees in music, both Western and Thai. The country's most prestigious university, Chulalongkorn, now offers degrees in both Western and Thai music through the Faculty of Fine Arts and offers degrees in both Western and Thai music education through the Faculty of Education. Srinakharinwirot, Mahasarakham, and Mahidol universities offer graduate degrees in Thai Cultural Studies, including Thai music. The Fine Arts Department supports both the postsecondary School of Dramatic Arts and ten high schools for the arts throughout the country; at these institutions, students learn both classical Thai music and the music and dance of the region (figure 8).

Also since the early 1970s, there has been a complete change of attitude toward Thai regional studies. Ironically, as the regions' cultures have declined because of the prevalence of the central-Thai-dominated media and the spread of a generalized

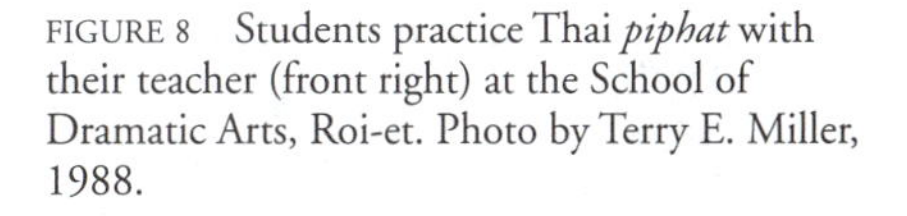

FIGURE 8 Students practice Thai *piphat* with their teacher (front right) at the School of Dramatic Arts, Roi-et. Photo by Terry E. Miller, 1988.

Foreigners began to study the music of the Philippines from early in the twentieth century, and by the 1930s several Filipinos had become involved, primarily with the aim of using it in teaching and composition.

national culture, the Ministry of Education has founded a major institute for regional studies in each region, offering a graduate degree.

Similarly, modernized Malaysia has worked to create a national culture by institutionalizing its traditional arts. Though the sultans still support modest establishments for court music, including the gamelan of Trengganu State, the central government has the greatest responsibility for the preservation of traditional music.

Burma's government, too, maintains secondary schools for the arts (including music) in Rangoon and Mandalay. In 1993, it founded the University of Culture in Rangoon to offer advanced degrees in music, dance, sculpture, and painting (figure 9).

Island Southeast Asia

Indonesia has had a nationally supported system of high-school education in music since 1950, when the Konservatori Karawitan Indonesia (Indonesian Conservatory of the Traditional Arts) was established in Surakarta, Java. Since then, a handful of similar institutions have been founded in large cities across Java and on several of the other major islands. College-level instruction in music and dance was established in the early 1960s at the Akademi Seni Karawitan Indonesia (Indonesian Academy of Traditional Arts); branches arose in major Indonesian cities, all now called Sekolah Tinggi Seni Indonesia (Indonesian University of the Arts). Students attending these institutions look forward to education in most of the major Indonesian court musics, with an emphasis on local traditions. Instruction is also offered in Western musical

FIGURE 9 The first-year class at Burma's University of Culture practice playing harp and xylophone while others sing and play rhythmic percussion. Photo by Terry E. Miller, 1994.

notation and theory, and dance is regularly featured. Outside these institutions, most major universities in Indonesia offer a major in music or dance, varying between Western classical music and Indonesian music.

Some professors at Indonesia's top performing-arts institutions have been educated in the West (particularly in the United States) and offer training in ethnomusicology and fieldwork. Occasionally a visiting artist from another world-music tradition is invited to give a lecture or demonstration. The University of North Sumatra (Universitas Sumatera Utara) now offers a master's degree in ethnomusicology and features visiting faculty from the United States and other countries in addition to its own trained staff. As more students have graduated from these institutions and either pursued advanced work in the West or continued involvement in music at the local level, the local acceptance of music as an academic discipline has risen. A drawback to this system is that many of the finest musicians of Indonesia do not themselves have advanced degrees, so they are not the ones hired to teach in institutions. Among them, the older methods of guru-disciple relationships still thrive. Pay is now sometimes offered to them, but some, out of pride and respect for the old ways, refuse to accept it.

In the Philippines, the earliest formal music education was offered in religious institutions, first at St. Scholastica's College in 1906. During the next several decades, other schools—the Conservatory of Music of the University of the Philippines, the Academy of Music of Manila, the Centro Escolar University, the Music Department of Santa Isabel College, the Lyric Music Academy, the Schola Cantorum—followed. All offered training in Western classical-music traditions, with visiting faculty from Europe and the United States. Through the 1990s, musical education in the Philippines has concentrated on the Western classical traditions, though the early emphasis on hiring faculty from other countries has lessened sharply, now that the Philippines has sufficient numbers of highly educated musicians and music teachers.

Foreigners began to study the music of the Philippines from early in the twentieth century, and by the 1930s several Filipinos (among them Antonio Molina, Justice Norberto Romualdez, Francisco Santiago) had become involved, primarily with the aim of using it in teaching and composition. With the addition of new courses on world-music traditions at a variety of institutions and the decision of pianist and composer José Maceda to study anthropology and ethnomusicology in the United States (where he received his Ph.D. degree in 1954), the study of ethnomusicology gained new ground in the Philippines. Maceda has worked to establish local programs in ethnomusicology, and many scholars have done fruitful work as a result of his efforts and inspiration.

REVIVAL MOVEMENTS

The term *revival movements* suggests at least two possibilities. First, there is the reestablishment and restoration of genres that have recently been lost, through neglect, war, poverty, or modernization (figure 10). Second, there is the revival of earlier styles, long forgotten. Both processes have occurred in Southeast Asia, and at least one such movement—the restoration of music, dance, and theater in Cambodia—has been fundamentally important to an entire nation.

Mainland Southeast Asia

Warfare and revolution have been extremely damaging to traditional music systems of mainland Southeast Asia. This effect was especially strong in Cambodia and Vietnam. During the reign of terror (1975–1979), the Khmer Rouge might have succeeded in eradicating Cambodian culture had the Vietnamese not invaded. By the

FIGURE 10 AVT, a traditional-popular group from Saigon, Vietnam, regrouped after the war in the United States. Here, they perform at the 1980 Festival of American Folklife in Washington, D.C. Photo by Terry E. Miller, 1980.

mid-1980s, after liberated areas had been stabilized and survivors had begun to enjoy a somewhat normal life, the first moves were made to restore music and dance. A high percentage of the nation's musicians and dancers had been killed or had fled abroad. Those who remained began reviving these arts. By 1989, the tenth anniversary of the Vietnamese invasion, young troupes from the reestablished Royal University of Fine Arts could again dance in the yet unrestored dance pavilion of the palace in Phnom Penh (figure 11). Within a few years, troupes of dancers, musicians, and shadow puppeteers began touring the United States and Europe. Though these institutions have been revived, their future hangs on the country's ability to overcome continuing political chaos, corruption, crime, and a lingering Khmer Rouge.

During the war in Vietnam, Hanoi was heavily damaged, and many of its artists were killed by American bombs, but since 1975 the government has restored, through official support, many of the nation's most important performance genres, including water-puppet theater, *chèo* and *tuồng* theaters, and many local traditions of

FIGURE 11 Young dancers from Cambodia's Royal University of Fine Arts perform in an unrestored dance pavilion at the royal palace. Photo by Terry E. Miller, 1988.

FIGURE 12 In Huế, Vietnam, the grand court dances that formerly entertained the emperors of the Nguyên Dynasty were in the early 1990s restored on a small scale by independent artists, faculty, and students from the Huế Conservatory, especially for tourist shows at hotels. Photo by Terry E. Miller, 1993.

ritual and chamber music. The most stunning restoration has occurred in Huế, the former imperial capital, which sustained heavy damage during the Tết offensive (February 1968). Vietnam's last emperor, Bảo Đại, had abdicated in 1945, but the court-music establishment had continued there, with governmental support. The chaos that preceded the Tết invasion made fleeing the city advisable, but the ensemble's leader was killed crossing the Perfume River. For twenty-five days, after the National Liberation Front attacked the city, they occupied it and the walled citadel with its inner Forbidden City. The armies of the United States and the Republic of Vietnam then drove them out, at a tremendous cost of property and lives. By late 1969 or early 1970, the court ensembles were reestablished. They continued to perform for state occasions until April 1975, when the advancing armies of the north approached Huế. Again the musicians fled, and the ensemble remained silent for eighteen years until March 1993, by which time the four or five survivors had trained a new generation of players to perform the old repertoire. About the same time, students and faculty from the Huế Conservatory, with other artists, restored as best they could other kinds of court entertainments, including dances that they perform mainly in hotel lobbies for visitors, with much smaller troupes than those of the old court would have had. Like conservatory students generally, whether they specialize in Vietnamese or Western music, the performers play from notation on staffs (figure 12).

Malaysia has systematically restored many of its traditional genres, mostly since the 1970s. In 1971, when ethnomusicologist William Malm documented the *ma'yong* theater of Kelantan Province, it was barely surviving by becoming a quasi-popular form of entertainment. Partly because of Malm's attention, a movement to restore *ma'yong* to its former elegance began. Other genres, including *bangsawan* theater, have similarly received restoration, but sometimes they have been restored to a state that had never before existed.

The restoration of historical practices has occurred on a limited scale in Thailand, associated with a single ensemble, Fong Naam. Because this ensemble has recorded numerous compact discs since 1990, its efforts are well known, even in the West. Interpreting the work of Montri Tramote, a Thai scholar and composer, Fong Naam has recorded pieces using historical but obsolete ensemble configurations and has revived one extinct instrument, a crystallophone (struck glass-key idiophone, *ranat kaeo*). Some of the restorations are based on evidence that other scholars inter-

New compositions divide into two types: those using traditional instruments and procedures and those adding nonindigenous instruments and using Western compositional devices.

pret differently. Some of Fong Naam's recordings purport to arrange traditional pieces in chronological order—a dubious task, considering how little is known about the dating of Thai compositions.

Island Southeast Asia

One of the tasks taken on by the Indonesian Department of Education and Culture (Departemen Pendidikan dan Kebudayaan) has been to catalog the performing-arts traditions of each province of Indonesia. Lists of hundreds of ensembles are compiled and filed in departmental offices. However, some listed genres may not be practiced any more. Genres once performed in an area may be listed because they might be performed again, even if knowledgeable musicians have died. A tremendous amount of local pride is invested in the traditions encapsulated in these lists. The establishment of higher institutions of music education has led to a resurgence of interest in certain styles among students and in the occasional performance of these styles (including, for example, west Javanese *topèng banjet*) as newly packaged village traditions for hotels and tourists. But generally, styles that have little commercial value—by having no colorful costumes, no "pleasing" sound, no possibility of being sold in mass quantities on cassette—do not get revived.

Borneo has been devastated through widespread strip mining, logging, and drilling for oil, with other development such as the clearing of thousands of hectares of tropical forest for the construction of a luxury golf course. Huge trucks rumble through villages once reachable only by canoe, and foreign products are everywhere. In the wake of this development, traditional practices that required music are now disappearing rapidly. Though some people have tried to encourage local revivals of moribund arts, neither the funds nor the organization is yet in place for such revivals to happen.

In the Philippines, a nationwide nostalgia for the quaint customs of the colonial past (with none of the brutality or subjugation) has led to a revival of Spanish-era musics, dances, and costumes. These revived traditions have spread to the United States, where the Filipino-American community enjoys Filipino-Spanish music and nineteenth-century Filipino ballroom dances. In the Philippines, troupes stage large-scale events for hotels and other tourist destinations, but many Filipinos themselves enjoy these performances.

COMPOSITIONAL INNOVATIONS

The idea of traditional composition mainly pertains to the still-evolving classical musics of Southeast Asia, the most fertile fields being Burma and Thailand in mainland Southeast Asia and Java and Bali in island Southeast Asia. New compositions divide into two types: those using traditional instruments and procedures and those adding nonindigenous instruments and using Western compositional devices. The latter are easy to recognize. The former are often indistinguishable from older-stratum compositions. In Cambodia and Laos, conservation (rather than innovation) has been the goal.

The idea of traditionality appears to leave little room for composers, but composers, whether known or unknown, have always existed. Perhaps the greatest difference between composers in the West and those of much of Southeast Asia is that the former write their music into notation, impose their personalities and visions on their works, and receive social acclaim from the popular appreciation of those works. From the 1600s through the 1800s, European composers allowed their contemporaries to complete their compositions in performance, especially through a kind of stylistic improvisation, but this trait has always been part of traditional Asian composition. It is not necessarily true, however, for "modern" Asian composers, trained in Western-style music.

Most Southeast Asian composers remain anonymous—a situation not difficult to understand since few compositions are written down and those that are usually are notated in a minimalistic, skeletal fashion (Hood and Susilo 1967; Miller 1992; Myers-Moro 1990). Indigenous notations other than staff notation occur in Burma, Indonesia, the Philippines, Thailand, and Vietnam; but it is rare to see musicians performing from notation. The role of the traditional composer is more to provide a distinctive framework to be fleshed out by musicians.

Fundamentally in Southeast Asia, musicians have had two ways to make music: by playing preexisting melodies or compositions and by simultaneously composing and performing according to the requirements of a modal system. Modal systems are found to lesser and greater extents in most Southeast Asian countries, especially in Vietnam, northeast Thailand, Laos, and Indonesia. Even where composition occurs, it is often governed by a modal system. When musicians perform preexisting compositions, they may often realize their own version of the melody within the confines of several variables, including the modal system, the idiom of their instrument, the style of their school, and perhaps their regional idiosyncrasies.

Innovative composers in mainland Southeast Asia

Twentieth-century compositional innovations are quite limited within mainland Southeast Asia. Innovations are most likely to occur in places where modernization in the arts is advanced, where musicians have obtained compositional training outside of Southeast Asia, and where a musical establishment can perform new kinds of works. Burma has innovative traditional composers who write for the nation's premier ensembles, but the country has remained too poor and isolated to develop a modernistic stream of composition. Laos, with its small population and lack of wealth, has given rise to little in the way of modern composition, other than a few popular songs. Cambodia, too, has seen little innovative composition, though one native-born Cambodian, Chinary Ung, having left his country for training in the West, has written many modern compositions, few having anything to do with Cambodia. Vietnam, with a longer tradition of Western conservatories, has European-trained composers writing traditional symphonies, concertos, and operas in conservative European styles, but the expatriate composer P. Q. Phan writes in an avant-garde style. Only Singapore and Thailand have produced composers seeking ways to join their Asian musical heritage with Western techniques and styles (Ryker 1991). Vietnam has produced a socialist-inspired modern music that purports to be traditional.

Thailand

A clear distinction cannot be made between "modern" and "traditional" composition in Thailand. Rather, they are two ends of a continuum. Though all Thai classical music is composed, the names of composers from before the early 1800s are rarely known. Except for the most serious of *naphat* compositions (which must be played exactly as taught), performers have latitude in realizing a composition according to their instrumental idioms and their abilities. What the composer created was a title and a skeletal structure, which he transmitted orally to other musicians, who preserved the composition in their memories. Composers sometimes added to existing compositions; sectional composition, especially those called *phleng thao* (in three tempo levels), have sometimes resulted from the work of two or more composers.

From the mid-1800s at the latest, the names of composers are known, and it is possible to compile lists of works for most composers, though the dates of composition are missing, and there never were manuscripts. Most composers served the court as performers and composers, not unlike the situation in Europe before about 1800, when J. S. Bach, Telemann, and Haydn, for example, were both performers and composers. Some Thai composers—again as in old Europe—were members of the royal family. Most of their works are perceived as "traditional" and "classical" works, but some are modern or Western. Prince Nakorn Sawan (1881–1944), whose full royal name was Chao Fa Grom Pra Nakorn Sawanworapinit, composed the famous traditional piece "*Khaek mon bang khun phrom*" and wrote the Mekla waltzes, said to be the first original Thai work for symphony orchestra. Prince Narit (1863–1947), composer of several of Thailand's most beloved compositions (including "*Khamen sai yok*" and "*Phraya sok*"), also created the *Cinderella Suite,* based on a Western story. The nation's most celebrated composer, Luang Pradit Phairoh (1881–1954), creator of much of today's standard repertory, was not an innovator in the Western sense.

The most clearly innovative composers are mostly young and active. They include Boonyong Gatekong (b. 1920), Panya Roongrüang (b. 1947), Dnu Huntrakul (b. 1950), and Somtow Sucharitkul (b. 1952). Other than Boonyong, who is mostly traditional in orientation, most composers combine in some way both Thai and Western instruments, with or without the use of Thai melodies. Ironically, Thailand's most famous modern composer is the American-born and -educated Bruce Gaston (b. 1946), who has lived in Thailand since the 1970s. A member of the traditional ensemble Fong Naam, he composes in a fresh, modern idiom, blending Thai traits with Western classical, jazz, and popular styles, played by a mixture of Thai and Western instruments. One of his works, the *Chao Phraya Concerto,* created jointly with Boonyong, requires prepared and electronically extended piano, Thai ensemble, four Western ensembles, and electronics. Panya Roongrüang has composed extensive works combining vast numbers of Thai and Western instruments. His melodic material is borrowed from both Thai and Western sources, and many of his compositional practices derive from Thai traditions. His works include the extensive *Chao Phraya Suite,* unrelated to Gaston's work.

Burma

In Burma, new compositions for the classical *hsaìñwaìñ* ensemble continue to be composed and performed. Many are notated in a skeletal form for each instrumentalist. Newer compositions tend to be virtuosic, displaying subtlety of orchestration through the use of individual instruments and contrasted groups. Because they are played entirely on Burmese instruments, most outsiders assume they are traditional rather than modern; indeed, they are both.

Singapore

Music in Singapore, since 1965 an independent, business-oriented city-state, is almost entirely the result of the city's most prevalent traits: modernization and multiculturalism. Having been a British colony, Singapore experienced Westernization to a greater degree than any other place in Southeast Asia except the lowland Philippines.

Consequently, several modern musical institutions were founded after World War II, including choirs, orchestras, theaters, and schools. Support for the arts is modest, but private and public funds allow composers to create new works, though they must earn their livings in other areas, principally teaching. Among the most active composers are Samuel Ting Chu San, Shen Ping Kwang, Kam Kee Yong, Bernard Tan, and Leong Yoon Pin. Some composers are seeking to bring together the musics of Singapore's disparate communities by combining sounds derived from the city's Malay, Chinese, and Indian heritages.

Vietnam

The term *nhạc dân tộc cải biên* 'modernized music' denotes a new genre of composition in Vietnam. It originated during the 1950s among conservatory musicians trained at institutions in the former Soviet bloc (particularly Russia, Bulgaria, Romania, and [East] Germany), where socialist aesthetics held sway. They brought back a socialist vision of folkloric music remarkably congruous with revolutionary compositions being created in China before and during the Cultural Revolution (1966–1976). During the 1970s and 1980s, *cải biên* became the official music used by the government to represent Vietnam, both to the outside world and within Vietnam.

Cải biên is played on a combination of modernized instruments of Vietnamese, upland, and Western origin, some of which have been electrified and all of which have been given chromatic, equal-tempered tunings to facilitate virtuosity, harmony, changes of key, and colorful orchestrations. Even the prehistoric lithophone has been copied, and new works have been written for it. The performers dress in various kinds of nativistic costume, affect joyous, peasantlike attitudes, and consciously show off their skills through programmatic compositions created primarily at the Hanoi Conservatory.

Cải biên offers audiences an exciting repertory of composed, programmatically titled, harmonically based, virtuosic music, often with voice and dance, blending traits from late-nineteenth-century Eastern European romanticism with newer kinds of Asian and Western popular music. Although one cannot object to the composer's right to create such a music, problems occur when this music is represented to both the Vietnamese and the outside world as traditional, while the older and still living types are excluded from both the conservatory and the media. With official encouragement, ethnomusicologically ignorant recording teams from Europe, the United States, and Japan have recorded albums of such compositions, which they have disseminated on compact discs as traditional. Cultural officials have preferred to send *cải biên* troupes on international tours because nonspecialized audiences find the music attractive. The conservatory has preferred to teach this kind of notated music because it fits the institution better than traditional music transmitted from master to disciple, because traditional musicians do not have advanced degrees, and because it better realizes the government's goals of modernizing Vietnam along socialist models.

Musical composition in island Southeast Asia

Indonesia

Composing in the court and aristocratic ensembles of Indonesia has taken two main approaches: in the older approach, a composer creates a main melody and a title, and the musicians of the traditional ensemble realize the composition for the composer; in the newer approach, all parts may be written out (or no indication of form may be given at all), and various blends of styles may be used. Most new compositions in Indonesia (usually called *kreasi baru* 'new creations') have come out of the institu-

There is no doubt that Debussy was much taken by the sound of the gamelan. He wrote, "Javanese music is based on a type of counterpoint by comparison with which that of Palestrina is child's play."

tions of music training, but some composers have developed new works outside institutional contexts. Both faculty and students at institutions are expected to develop new creations, using both traditional and nontraditional forms and instruments. These creations are performed at the school, for a largely school audience; not many of the older, more conservative musicians from the community attend. New creations are almost always reviewed in local newspapers and discussed eagerly by younger musicians. Occasionally an innovation catches on outside the academy.

In Java, composers in all the major cities (including Jakarta, Bandung, Surakarta, Yogyakarta, Surabaya, Semarang, and Banyumas) are working to expand the boundaries of traditional Javanese and Sundanese musics. The central Javanese composers Hardjosoebroto, Martopangrawit, Nartosabdho, and Wasitodiningrat worked primarily within the traditional compositional style, creating the main musical themes and vocal lines for gamelan performances but also adding to and modifying earlier works. Groundbreaking Sundanese composers Nano Suratno and Gugum Gumbira create new works constantly, for performance and further development, both inside and outside the Sundanese academic world, respectively.

The Balinese composer Lotring was one of the first early-twentieth-century innovators to expand Balinese ideas about the creation of new forms and new works. He used approaches like selecting melodies and rhythms and recontextualizing them in different genres, or switching systems of tuning, or simply opening up the boundaries between genres (Tenzer 1991:55). Since his work in the 1920s and 1930s, hundreds of Balinese composers have followed his lead, and the current climate of competition-driven composition has caused composers to create at a dizzying pace.

The Philippines

Because in the twentieth century the Philippines has had a strong Western orientation, compositional trends in the West have been reflected in the Philippines. Many foreign composers and performers visited the Philippines, either as guest faculty at local institutions, or as performers for the musical societies that are a part of Filipino life [see ART MUSIC OF THE PHILIPPINES IN THE TWENTIETH CENTURY]. Many composers in the early twentieth century used Western forms to highlight Filipino melodies, as in Antonino Buenaventura's works; others created musical theater based on local themes, such as Juan Abad's "*Mabuhay Ang Pilipinas*" ('Long Live the Philippines'). In the late twentieth century, Francisco Feliciano, Bayani de León, José Maceda, Ramón Santos, and others have run the gamut of compositions, from the Western classical idiom (concertos, choral and orchestral works) to works as much outside the boundaries of traditional Western forms as any being produced in the United States or Europe.

The influence of Southeast Asia on Western composers

Exoticism, the fascination with anything from outside one's normative experience, is a theme that runs through Western cultural history from the 1700s or before.

Clearly, European expansion, colonialism, and the experiences Europeans had in far-off, "exotic" places stimulated the exoticism seen in painting, architecture, decoration, furniture, fashion, and, to a slight extent, music. In this regard, Southeast Asia has played an important role, but one that is not well understood by observers who, though knowing Western music, do not know the music of Southeast Asia. This limitation has led to unfounded generalizations, which have become part of the unquestioned folklore of Western music history.

With regard to Southeast Asian music performed abroad, exotic Western composition began after 1889, resulting from the Grand Universal Exhibition in Paris, where musicians from Asian countries appeared. This, in fact, was not the first time, for Thai musical instruments had been seen in Europe in 1869, but they then had no known influence on European composers. Claude Debussy was not alone in hearing a Javanese gamelan, nor was this ensemble the only "exotic" ensemble he heard; a Vietnamese ensemble played too, but evidently he was not much attracted to its sound. There is no doubt that Debussy was much taken by the sound of the gamelan: he wrote, "Javanese music is based on a type of counterpoint by comparison with which that of Palestrina is child's play" (quoted in Sorrell 1990:2). But there is no justification for later writers' assertions that he *imitated* gamelan structures and sounds in his music. Some observers hear gamelan music in the second movement of his string quartet, in the symphonic poem *La Mer,* and even in the arguably Southeast Asian "Pagodes" from *Estampes.* The timbral effect of combining flute and harp in *Nuages* may imitate the struck-ringing effect of the gamelan. A twenty-four-piece Javanese gamelan was brought to Chicago for the World's Columbian Exposition in 1893, then left to decay in the Field Museum until its restoration in 1977. Whether American composers were influenced by its music remains to be ascertained.

Island Southeast Asia has always had a greater attraction to Westerners than the mainland part. David Morton, the first Western scholar to focus on Thailand, was a composer before becoming an ethnomusicologist, but there are no known overtly Thai compositions by him. Chinary Ung, a Cambodian by birth, has written a piece with a Cambodian title (*Mohori*), but it is not otherwise Cambodian in sound. More obscure is Paul Hindemith's one-act opera *Das Nusch-Nuschi,* op. 20 (1920), written for Burmese marionettes in an only slightly exotic style, having nothing to do with Burmese music. Even more obscure is Iannis Xenakis' use of the Lao *khaen* as one of the sources of sounds for his *musique concrète* composition *Bohor I* (1962). While Rodgers and Hammerstein's 1956 film version of their 1951 musical *The King and I* tries to appear Thai, and even includes some Thai dialogue, both the Buddhist chant and all the accompanimental music for the presentation of the dance-drama "Small House of Uncle Thomas" is an example of Rodgers' "orientalism," which invokes the sound of Thai music only through the use of xylophones. Boublil and C.-M. Schonberg's *Miss Saigon* (1989) paid homage to the stereotype that "Southeast Asia" means a gamelan, and the opening to the musical sounds vaguely like a gamelan in the way that Steve Reich's works do. Through a friend, Schonberg sampled Asian percussion and even a Vietnamese zither (*đàn tranh*) for the synthesizers, but chose to use a Japanese vertical bamboo notch flute (*shakuhachi*) to represent Kim, the Vietnamese heroine.

The gamelans of Java and Bali have long attracted composers' attention. Colin McPhee and Mantle Hood were composers before becoming Balinese and Javanese music specialists, respectively. McPhee's toccata for orchestra, *Tabuh-Tabuhan* (1936), was written after he had spent four years in Bali. Francis Poulenc's Concerto in D Minor for two pianos (1932) includes a lengthy passage that clearly reflects Indonesian inspiration, but its source is uncertain. Other composers have traveled to

Indonesia and consequently written music echoing their musical experiences. Benjamin Britten visited Bali in 1956 and composed in the same year a Balinese-inspired opera, *The Prince of the Pagodas*, which includes passages that were explicit attempts to approximate the sound of a Balinese gamelan. Lou Harrison has been involved with various Asian musics since the early 1940s and in recent years has composed for American gamelans. His work *Double Music* (1941), which he created jointly with John Cage, suggests the sounds of a gamelan, but in later years Harrison wrote gamelan-inspired works for Western instruments (including *Concerto in Slendro*, 1961), works that combined gamelan with Western instruments (including *Three Pieces for Gamelan with Soloists* [horn and violin], 1978–1979, and *La Koro Sutro*, 1972), and new works for gamelan alone. Some of the latter have been written for what is called the American gamelan, ensembles innovative in design and only loosely based on Indonesian models, using such nontraditional materials as aluminum and polyvinyl chloride pipe.

Many so-called minimalist composers—especially John Adams, Philip Glass, Steve Reich, and Terry Riley—were growing up at the height of the first wave of interest in world music in the United States, the early 1960s. During that period, some musicians traveled to foreign countries (Riley studied African drumming at the University of Ghana), and others studied on the West Coast, a hotbed of Asian music in America. Many of their works suggest the influence of the Balinese gamelan, though transformed by their ideas of phase change and additive processes. Reich's *Music for Mallet Instruments, Voices and Organ* (1973) is clearly gamelanlike. Finally, Wendy Carlos, who, chasing a solar eclipse, traveled to Bali about 1985, became fascinated by the gamelan music she heard. Her "Poem for Bali" (on her 1986 album *Beauty in the Beast*), created entirely on a synthesizer, reproduces gamelan sounds and styles.

REPRESENTATION

Before Southeast Asians were conscious of their respective images in foreigners' eyes, each culture created and performed its own music. Occasions where music served to represent the culture were rare, limited to state ceremonies for visiting dignitaries or performances by an ensemble traveling to the West. In the age of media and tourism, however, the issue of representation is of paramount importance, for through it, peoples show themselves to others. No one wants to be seen in a negative light, but the ability to manipulate the message by controlling the medium is limited. Representation is an issue in audio and video recordings (figure 13), musical presentations for tourists (figure 14), and for troupes traveling abroad to perform at festivals, fairs, and similar situations.

FIGURE 13 Burhan Sukarma (*left*) and Rukruk Rukmana record traditional Sundanese *tembang Sunda* accompaniment for an elderly singer (Pa Cucu, not pictured), who wished to pass on an older style of performance to the next generation. Photo by Sean Williams, 1987.

Relative to the question of what music best represents a nation or culture, there are at least two views: (1) that of the representatives of the culture itself, and (2) that of outsiders, including academic ethnomusicologists, who reduce a culture's music to one or two selections for survey courses.

Mainland Southeast Asia

In mainland Southeast Asia, the degree of consensus on representation tends to correlate with the degree of consensus on what constitutes the classical music of the society. The presence of a generally agreed-upon classical music settles the issue, but when there is no consensus, disputes are likely.

Burma

Few would disagree that Burma has a classical music, embodied in the *hsaìñwaìñ,* though the harp (*saùñ*) and the songs it accompanies could be considered classical

FIGURE 14 Foreign visitors can commission virtually any sort of traditional performance. Here, in a hotel, a tourist has arranged a special appearance of *gamelan suling* (bamboo-flute ensemble) by a group from Ubud, Bali. Photo by Tom Ballinger, 1984.

too. Part of its appeal is visual, since the instruments' frames are intricately carved and brilliantly painted in gold. The musicians' virtuosity overcomes the shock most outsiders experience on hearing the ensemble for the first time. The government supports three large cultural troupes, including such ensembles, and they regularly tour outside Burma.

Thailand

Though few Thai regularly listen to music played by the Thai "classical" ensembles (*piphat, mahori, khrüang sai*), preferring various kinds of popular music for everyday listening, there is a consensus that this kind of music represents Thai culture at its best and most impressive. The performers' dignity, the visible beauty of their instruments, and the fullness of the sound communicate grandeur, elegance, and sophistication. Most travel videos designed to attract foreign visitors, including those made in Thailand, overlay the classical music in scenes of dance, theater, and ceremony with innocuous, synthesized background music. Evidently there is concern that complexity of sound and strangeness of timbre might outweigh the appeal of the dancers' costumes and the beauty of the instruments' appearance.

Laos

To the extent that Laos represents itself to the outside world, its policies have undergone great change since 1975, when the royalist government was eclipsed by the Pathet Lao. At first, the classical arts (music, dance, theater) were banished as symbols of a decadent past and a discredited aristocracy. The music of the common people—principally *lam,* but also *lam rueang,* a theater adopted from northeast Thailand—were to represent the Lao spirit. But since about 1990, cultural policy has again favored the classical arts, and the government has sent a troupe of masked dancers on foreign tours. In this respect, the government's choice of music clashes with the view held by many outsiders—that *lam* better represents the soul of the Lao people.

Cambodia

Having nearly lost their culture to the Khmer Rouge, the surviving Khmer people made clear their preference for a nationally representative music—classical dance and

pinn peat Khmer classical ensemble
ma'yong Malaysian human theater
wayang kulit Theater using leather shadow puppets
bangsawan Theater shows of the Malay nobility

the accompaniment of the *pinn peat.* Though this ensemble was originally a royal entertainment, there have long been village troupes. One of the principal cultural activities in Khmer refugee camps in Thailand was the study of classical dance and music, taught by survivors. The same has been true in the United States and Europe among the Khmer population. The present Cambodian government consistently sends classical troupes to perform outside the country. For outsiders choosing an example to represent Cambodia, recordings of classical music predominate.

Malaysia

For many years, outsiders' views of traditional Malaysian music were bounded by available recordings. These featured two kinds of theater that flourished in Kelantan Province in the northeast: human theater (*ma'yong*) and shadow-puppet theater (*wayang kulit*). They also featured examples of the Malaysian gamelan and coronation musics. Since then, the Malaysian government has sought to develop and systematize the traditional arts according to its views of an ideal multicultural society.

Some older Malaysian genres, such as *bangsawan,* a once popular theater, have undergone traditional restoration, which amounts to the reinvention of a form that never really existed. For tourists, the government has recreated a form of Portuguese music among a community in Melaka (Malacca) said to have descended from the Portuguese. Therefore, it is difficult to ascertain which music can with reasonable authenticity represent Malaysia to the rest of the world.

FIGURE 15 A Hồ Chí Minh City instrument shop sells not only traditional instruments but also an accordion and souvenir miniatures of instruments. Photo by Terry E. Miller, 1991.

Vietnam

Representing Vietnam musically to the outside world has proved controversial, at least to many outsiders. The Southeast Asian country most deeply influenced by European socialist or Marxist cultural policies, Vietnam formerly sought to manipulate outsiders' impressions by sending troupes to perform highly choreographed and modernized forms of so-called traditional music. This is most clearly seen in the *JVC Video Anthology of World Music and Dance,* where most selections feature a virtuosic government-sponsored troupe performing on a foreign stage. Even within Vietnam, controversy concerns whether the modernized music (*nhạc dân tộc cải biên*) created at the Hanoi Conservatory under socialist influence better represents Vietnam's artistic soul than what most outsiders consider to be truly traditional.

This problem has been most acute in the compact discs that have appeared since Vietnam reopened to the Western world. Many recording companies have sent professional recording engineers to Vietnam to obtain recordings, and government representatives have consistently provided them with troupes performing modernized ethnic music. At the same time, the Vietnamese government discovered that the country's water-puppet theater, with its non-Westernized traditional music, had great appeal, and these troupes have become the country's cultural ambassadors. Outsiders, in selecting a music to represent Vietnam, are most likely to choose one of the older, regional types of chamber music or the recently restored court music of the imperial city of Huế.

Island Southeast Asia

In island Southeast Asia, the three regions of Indonesia, the Philippines, and Borneo pose different issues of representation. While Indonesia's representational tours and recordings are created for the purposes of presenting the nation to uninformed outsiders, performers in the Philippines highlight their colonial heritage for people of Filipino descent. Borneo, with its current rapid destruction of the ecosystem and the cultures attempting to survive in that ecosystem, has very few mechanisms in place for representation.

Indonesia

Representative troupes of performers from Indonesia have been visiting foreign countries for more than 100 years, since the Grand Universal Exhibition in Paris (1889). Throughout the latter half of the twentieth century, the Indonesian government has recognized the importance of sending performers abroad as goodwill ambassadors. The enthusiastic welcoming of these groups in Japan, Australia, the United States, and Europe assures continued tours of this kind.

Most tours involve classical performers of Balinese, Sundanese, or central Javanese gamelans; however, the 1991 Festival of Indonesia tour to the United States brought a variety of performers from outside the mainstream gamelan traditions, most of them heard by American audiences for the first time. Other tours—to the Netherlands, Great Britain, Malaysia, Saudi Arabia, and other destinations—have expanded understanding and appreciation of nongamelan traditions.

Mounting a tour is exceedingly difficult. Musicians face heavy expenses getting a passport (U.S. $100 and up, more than some musicians make in a year), and may meet obstacles getting permission to leave the country or enter another. Some musicians chosen for a tour are selected not for the excellence of their musicianship but for their connections, possession of a passport, or other nonmusical reasons.

The Philippines

Many Filipinos consider themselves more European than Asian. For proof, they point to the high literacy rate and general level of worldliness, open communication, and transportation that characterize Manila at the end of the twentieth century. Hundreds of years of Spanish (and later, American) influences have given most current lowland Christians the sense that their colonial heritage is closer to their true identity than any indigenous culture eradicated in the colonial effort. As a result, the Filipino culture used for national representation is largely Spanish-oriented, with Filipino forms of Spanish originals, often linked to Roman Catholicism. String ensembles accompany dances derived from late-nineteenth- and early-twentieth-century styles. Rural Filipino culture is often represented through the use of two pairs of bamboo poles, arranged in a cross and clapped together while dancers step lightly in and out of the pairs. Because the differences among Spanish-derived music, Muslim-oriented *kulintang* music, and upland music are striking, the styles are not often placed together on the same stage.

TOURISM

Tourism for much of the non-Western world has been a two-edged sword: one side provides jobs and hard currency; the other brings great numbers of visitors, some of

FIGURE 16 Dancers and musicians perform for tourists in a Bangkok restaurant that offers a Thai meal followed by demonstrations of music, dancing, fighting with swords, and boxing. Photo by Terry E. Miller, 1988.

whom behave insensitively and through their patronage encourage seamy activities, including prostitution, drugs, and gambling. In parts of Southeast Asia, tourism is so important it is responsible for at least part of the country's prosperity. Two Southeast Asian countries—Thailand and Indonesia, especially Bali—have been havens for tourists. Malaysia, the Philippines, and Vietnam are attracting fewer visitors. Cambodia, Laos, and Burma attract few, for various reasons. In each case, tourists can expect to see so-called cultural shows, offered by hotels, restaurants, or government agencies. What is shown, how it is shown, and why it is shown are all issues begging for discussion.

Culture for sale

For most non-Southeast Asians (not just Westerners, but even East Asians), the lands and peoples of Southeast Asia are exotic. Travel posters and books play up the bright colors of markets, clothes, temples, and palaces, all inhabited by smiling natives. Travel videos provide clips of endless festivals, parades, displays of tropical fruit, wild animals, and performances, especially dance. Rarely do they show the musicians, and often they substitute newly composed, unoffensive music for the original music, fearing, one assumes, that the real sounds, possibly too harsh or strange, would repel the potential visitor. The countries most successful at tourism have done so in part by offering themselves as exotic—a treat for visitors' eyes, palates, and video cameras (figure 16). Bangkok, one of the most Westernized of Southeast Asian cities, recently advertised itself as "the most exotic destination in Asia." Once the visitors arrive, those representing travel companies, ministries of tourism, and "culture centers" usually know what to do to start the artesian well of money flowing.

Though the locals appreciate the flood of foreign currencies, they are often less pleased with the visitors' behavior. For most visitors, two weeks in a Southeast Asian paradise represent a deserved vacation, a relief from the workplace and from a colder climate. Being on holiday, they dress down. But in the local world, whose inhabitants dress conservatively in business or work clothes or school uniforms, the visitors' individualistic outfits, odd hairstyles, skimpy clothing, and rubber sandals make *them,* rather than the locals, seem exotic.

Tourists' encounters with the genuine—a great temple, a great palace—may

FIGURE 17 A Western tourist photographs dancers of the sacred *rejang* in Tenganan, Bali. In earlier times, outsiders were often prohibited from watching such ritual performances. Today, even the most sacred rituals are flooded with domestic and international tourists and representatives of the media. Photo by Tom Ballinger, 1984.

become problematic. At Bangkok's Temple of the Emerald Buddha and former palace, incorrectly dressed visitors are now given makeshift skirts and shoes to wear, rather than be turned away (the former practice). In Bali, visitors are requested to wear narrow scarves around their waists when entering temples; menstruating women or people with wounds are requested not to enter at all (figure 17).

Genuine but packaged culture

Experiencing traditional culture on its own terms and in its original context is, as any researcher knows, a challenge that can be overcome only through diplomacy, development of an effective network of friends, and discretion. There is no way for daily busloads of visitors to have this kind of experience. Therefore, it has proven better to offer such parties more or less genuine experiences in controlled atmospheres, some of which *are* genuine (as in the Imperial Palace in Huế, Vietnam) and some of which are ersatz (Thailand's Rose Garden). For visitors to Thailand who cannot make the trip to the country's important historical sites, the Ancient City (an open-air museum-park) offers scaled down reproductions of the great temples and palaces from Ayuthaya, Sukhothai, and elsewhere. Visitors to Jakarta are advised to go to Taman Mini, an amusement park with life-size representations of the people, art, architecture, clothing, and other cultural artifacts from each of the country's twenty-seven provinces.

A question planners have to face in each country is this: do you give visitors what *they* want to see, do you give them what *you* want them to see, or do you give them what you *think* they want to see? Most officials and travel agents have discovered that audiences want a variety of brief, visually exotic presentations that will fill their photo albums and video anthologies. Full-length theatrical performances, long instrumental suites, text-dominated vocal genres, and context-dependent genres (such as ritual music) are avoided. Few visitors have a solid foundation in the country's history and culture (despite the availability of better and better travel guides), and most of those on vacation really do not come to be educated. The answer: provide entertainment (figure 18).

The most usual venues for such entertainment are hotels, restaurants, and historical sites. The best shows present meritorious artists, even faculty and students of nearby educational institutions, in the performance of serious musical and theatrical segments. The worst employ a troupe of mediocre performers who try to be everybody, from dancing farmers to courtly musicians.

To attract more tourists than neighboring communities, villagers stage decontextualized performances of local music and dance at guest houses, where the proprietors speak fluent English and serve American-style meals.

FIGURE 18 Neighborhood children provide Sundanese and diatonic Western music on *angklung,* and dance *jaipongan* for tourists at Saung Angklung, on the outskirts of Bandung, West Java. Photo by Cary Black, 1988.

Visitors to Hanoi are offered nightly performances of Vietnam's water-puppet theater in a comfortable venue with live, traditional music. Visitors see and hear only a series of vignettes rather than complete stories, but the performances are genuine and tastefully done. Similarly, visitors to the Forbidden City within the Citadel of Huế hear restored court music played by surviving masters and a new generation of disciples. The government pays these performers out of gate fees. In hotel lobbies, a troupe of students and teachers from the Huế Conservatory regularly presents to tourists performances of restored versions of court dances, songs, and other genres. Their show sometimes follows an "imperial" dinner, for which a couple is selected to act as emperor and empress, be dressed in imperial regalia, and be served in grand fashion.

At the Inya Lake Hotel or at open-air restaurants around that lake in Rangoon, Burma (or Yangon, Myanmar, as it is now called), foreigners can nightly see variety shows of Burmese instrumental pieces, dances, and marionette plays, with athletic displays, folkloric performances, and popular songs. Many of the performers are moonlighting professionals (figure 19).

Most of the dancers and players in Bangkok's restaurants are faculty and students from the country's most prestigious institutions. While in Vientiane, visitors may enjoy a sukiyaki dinner across the street from the Lan Xang Hotel while listening to Lao classical music played by faculty members from the School of Fine Arts.

In areas like Borneo and the farthest reaches of eastern Indonesia, the traditional performing arts have begun to be encouraged and supported by local governments in

FIGURE 19 Skilled artists perform a segment of a marionette show for tourists at Rangoon's Karaweik Restaurant, a gigantic concrete reproduction of a royal barge situated in the Royal Lake. Photo by Max Miller, 1986.

an effort to attract cultural tourism. On Biak, tourists from Honolulu used to stagger off an airplane at 4:30 A.M., go through immigration and customs, and view an early-morning staged performance of local traditions before their plane took off again for Bali. The performance was entirely out of context, but the musicians got paid. In both central Java and Bali (Sanger 1988), the tourist machine is well run, and visitors can always expect to see excellent performances every night and sometimes during the day. Bandung, the Sundanese regional capital, has begun to feature tourist performances at restaurants and hotels, but most of the best music and dance occurs for private events only.

In the Philippines, performances of local traditions, particularly in upland areas, have increased as tourism has become a part of the local economy. To attract more tourists than neighboring communities, villagers stage decontextualized performances of local music and dance at guest houses, where the proprietors speak fluent English and serve American-style meals.

Give them what you think they want to see

In virtually all cases, someone has to decide "*what* is displayed, *how* it's packaged, and *who* controls the representation" (Sarkissian 1994:34). This statement suggests that messages delivered through performances can be, and almost invariably are, manipulated. Sarkissian has studied the cultural show offered to visitors to Melaka (Malacca), Malaysia, a city conquered in 1511 by Portuguese sailors, some of whom stayed on and married into the local population. Working from the thesis that "tourist performances become cultural texts, constructions, stories people *choose* to tell about themselves," Sarkissian demonstrates how, with government encouragement, the State Economic Development Corporation of Melaka has turned imaginatively recreated but ersatz performances of Portuguese folk art into a local cash crop. Evidently, visitors are happy to accept the premise that old Portuguese culture survived in Melaka and that the performers are simply behaving as they normally do; indeed, they do behave that way, every Saturday evening.

During the fighting in Vietnam, U.S. soldiers on leave in Bangkok (and the usual civilian tourists) visited one of Thailand's first "cultural centers," Thailand in Miniature or Timland, a theme park offering a one-stop look at the farming of rice,

FIGURE 20 At the national radio studio in Denpasar, Bali, the hosts of a popular program invite listeners to phone in their favorite traditional songs or poems to share with an island-wide audience. New poetry is also welcomed, and the hosts and other listeners comment on—and critique—the correct use of melodies and prosody. Photo by Richard Wallis, 1995.

animal husbandry, boxing, music, dance, fighting with swords, making lacquerware, weaving, and other types of crafts. Thirty years later, such parks are far more sophisticated, and even include a recreated "floating market" to replace the real one that used to flourish in Thonburi, across the river from Bangkok proper.

Unconventional visitors

Guidebook series, including the *Rough Guide*, the *Travel Survival Kit*, and *Insight*, cater to a class of visitors who dislike people who buy package tours, stay in expensive hotels, and eat at American fast-food outlets. Wearing cutoffs and backpacks, guidebook-toting visitors walk around Asian cities and trek through the countryside, camera (if any) hidden away. Some seek music, theater, and dance on its own terms. But can they find it? If they arrive at the right time (not, for example, during the rainy season, when outdoor performances cease), they may encounter it at a temple fair, at a New Year's street celebration, in association with a ritual (the *phleng korat* singing in Khorat, Thailand, near the shrine to Khun Ying Mo), or in an ordinary public theater. A local radio station may be a surprise setting for a performance of high-quality traditional music (figure 20). But finding it will not be easy, especially if they do not know the local language.

Visitors who do find such performances, however, will be rewarded with exceptional experiences, in which they themselves may become a focus of attention. Other members of the audience may be so impressed that they seek someone who speaks English or French or German or Japanese to interpret for them. Visitors may be offered an opportunity to go backstage, to meet the performers, and to make friends who will lead them to further (and usually less obvious) performances. Visitors may learn of Bangkok Bank's Friday afternoon performances of traditional theater or music at one of its branches, of chanting for a special Buddhist ritual, or of a local temple fair where several traditional theatrical troupes are to compete.

Even casual visitors with limited funds and a nonrenewable short-term visa can experience the genuine. But this outcome requires a flexibility that package tours' schedules usually preclude. The best recommendation may be to travel alone; people will be curious and likelier to strike up a conversation than if they observe visitors

FIGURE 21 The Balinese have reinvigorated the art of singing classical literature with public competitions among poetry-reading clubs. Participants are judged on posture, gestures, ensemble style, and adherence to musical and textual requirements. Traditionally, such singing took place only within the contexts of religious and life-cycle rituals. Photo by Richard Wallis, 1995.

busily photographing them. If you must take a tour, go in the smallest group possible (no more than five people) with someone comfortable in the local language.

COMPETITIONS

Though ethnomusicologists prefer to observe and document musics in their original "cultural contexts," by the later twentieth century many of these contexts had vanished—and in some cases, the musics along with them. Some forms of music, dance, and theater, however, survived by going on stage. Instead of being a homemade entertainment created by villagers in the fields during breaks in work, a folk song genre may move to a stage, where performers pretending to be villagers render fixed, costumed, choreographed versions of formerly extemporized songs. Not too distant from this phenomenon has been the development of competitions, usually for trophies, sometimes for money. Though not a major issue in mainland Southeast Asia, these competitions are common enough (particularly in Indonesia) that they deserve discussion (figure 21).

With data lacking from most areas, we are restricted to a limited body of experience. Competitions have long been, and continue to be, a mainstay in the northeastern region of Thailand, where singers (*mawlam*) accompanied by a *khaen* perform in repartee fashion and in theatrical genres. Competitions involving both types have occurred since no later than the early 1970s: Mahasarakham hosted an annual festival every February, when nearly a dozen theatrical troupes competed simultaneously on the grounds of the provincial government. The judges were required to use comprehensive criteria, but audiences tended to prefer troupes with the brightest lights and the loudest amplification. Indeed, troupes not having a powerful system could not even be heard. Besides the troupes' sound systems, a central area featured more individualized performances (solos, demonstrations of archaic genres, small groups), but all competed with the carnival rides and food shops, which also had sound systems. The annual competitions ceased after 1974, because with the democratization of Thailand came the growth of political parties. The members of the organizing committee, all running against each other in the election, could no longer cooperate in mounting a competitive festival.

Smaller-scale competitions, many sponsored by Mahasarakham University,

FIGURE 22 Two of Burma's great artists, Yi Yi Thant (voice) and Ù Myint Mauñ (harp), record classical songs for broadcasting on radio before a national classical-song competition. Photo by Terry E. Miller, 1994.

FIGURE 23 In Malang, East Java, a masked male dancer goes into "trance" during a trance-dancing competition; the number five is displayed on the front of his costume. Photo by Sean Williams, 1987.

continue. In the early 1990s, one contest brought Thai-Khmer ensembles from the Thai provinces bordering Cambodia. Some have featured performers of *lam sing,* the latest fashion in "traditional" repartee-song, using a high percentage of pop songs. Competitions among the classical ensembles of the nation's universities and colleges, usually held in central Thailand, have also occurred.

Burma offers a unique event each November, a national competition in Burmese classical song. To prepare for this event, the country's most important singers record much of the repertory, which the radio then broadcasts, allowing potential competitors to record the songs and learn them (figure 22).

In Indonesia, competitions are one of the strongest motivating forces behind the perpetuation of both the traditional and popular performing arts. Competitions are usually sponsored by major national corporations (especially cigarette companies) and by local, regional, and national governments (figure 23). Every imaginable aspect of the performing arts can be a part of the competition—from the accuracy of ornaments, to the beauty of costumes, to the choice of lyrics. Winners often achieve tangible rewards, including a big sum of money, recording contracts, and promises of an international tour, plus the genuine respect and jealousy of their peers. Most juries have the potential of being suspected of bending the rules, but enough are honest that musicians and audiences really believe in and enjoy the tension and excitement generated by competitions. Drawbacks include the rapid standardization of once-flexible repertories and styles of performance, alterations to genres for stage performance, and problems in creating professionals out of still-raw amateurs. However, for firing up local enthusiasm in the performing arts, especially among people who might stray from traditional values, competitions are usually perceived as important, necessary, and beneficial.

REFERENCES

Hood, Mantle, and Hardja Susilo. 1967. *Music of the Venerable Dark Cloud.* Los Angeles: Institute of Ethnomusicology, University of California, Los Angeles. LP disk.

Miller, Terry E. 1992. "The Theory and Practice of Thai Musical Notations." *Ethnomusicology* 36(2):197–222.

Myers-Moro, Pamela. 1990. "Musical Notation in Thailand." *Journal of the Siam Society* 78(1):101–108.

Ryker, Harrison, ed. 1991. *New Music in the Orient.* Buren, Netherlands: Frits Knuf.

Sanger, Annette. 1988. "Blessing or Blight? The Effects of Touristic Dance-Drama on Village-Life in Singapadu, Bali." In *Come Mek Me Hol' Yu Han': The Impact of Tourism on Traditional Music,* ed. Adrienne L. Kaeppler, 89–104. Kingston: Jamaica Memory Bank.

Sarkissian, Margaret. 1994. "'Whose Tradition?': Tourism as a Catalyst in the Creation of a Modern Malaysian 'Tradition'." *Nhac Viet* 3(1–2):31–46.

Sorrell, Neil. 1990. *A Guide to the Gamelan.* Portland: Amadeus Press.

Tenzer, Michael. 1991. *Balinese Music.* Singapore: Periplus Editions.

Part 3
Music Cultures and Regions

Each of Southeast Asia's ten nation-states, by virtue of geography and history, has developed a distinct culture despite broader traits that link them. Though the character of each nation is strongly influenced by a single majority culture, regional variations within provide for an impressive variety of dialects, both linguistic and musical. By understanding their musical sounds and practices, we gain a greater sense of how Southeast Asians organize and express their views of the world.

Music cultures throughout Southeast Asia use small pot-shaped gongs that are struck on their central bosses. Sometimes, they are held singly by individual musicians; more often, they are placed on a long rack and played by one or more players. Frame drums accompany the gongs in this ensemble from the island of Sumatra in Indonesia. Photo by H. Kartomi, 1985.

HALLS
MENTHO-LYPTUS
TABLETS

Majority Cultures of Mainland Southeast Asia

The arts of each of mainland Southeast Asia's seven nations are uniquely expressive. Yet they result, in part, from a long and continuing progression of foreign influences on local traditions. Despite many cataclysmic events throughout history, each nation's expressive culture has persisted and continues to adapt to the pressures of modernization. With growing urbanization have come new, popularized genres that blend local and outside influences to create a voice for the region's fastest-growing segment of the population—urban youth.

The blind *khaen* player Thawng-khun Sia-run performs in an obscure northeastern Thai village. Photo by Terry E. Miller, 1973.

Introduction to the Musics of Mainland Southeast Asia

Terry E. Miller

Nation-states do not necessarily define human cultural groups, but by virtue of their individual histories they deeply affect all ethnic groups living within their borders. Because of the vagaries of history (wars, colonialism, migrations), linguistic groups rarely live simply and cleanly within current, internationally recognized boundaries. Though the majority of lowland Khmer-speakers live within the borders of Cambodia, significant populations live in Thailand and Vietnam. To a great extent, those outside Cambodia have long been disconnected from mainstream Cambodia and were therefore unaffected by the Khmer Rouge, who devastated Cambodia's culture from 1975 to 1979.

Articles focused on nation-states do not tell the entire story of the musics heard within the national borders. In every case, the nation-state is a complex of linguistic and ethnic groups and cultures. Such terms as *Thai music, Lao music,* and *Burmese music* are as problematic as the term *African music:* no one type of music is Thai, Lao, Burmese, or African. Rather, there are *musics* (plural) in Thailand, Laos, Burma, and Africa. At least in mainland Southeast Asia, terms like *Thai, Lao,* and *Burmese* denote the more or less unified majority, mainstream cultures of their nation-states. Their musics tend to dominate because of their numbers, their visibility, and their variety.

The deeper one digs into the musical cultures of the countries described in this volume, the more complex matters become. From a distance, each country may appear homogeneous, unified, and susceptible to the handy reductionism required in encyclopedias. On closer examination, however, each country is complex. Each has cultural regions, minority ethnic groups, and numerous historical strata, some ancient, some modern. From the (emic) viewpoint of the indigenous population, further subdivisions within each cultural region may extend down to the village level, and although these may numb outsiders trying to make sense of a more generalized experience, they may have great significance to insiders. Just as some Western observers may view each album produced by a given band as virtually a style period, so might the people of northeast Thailand distinguish among provinces and among districts of each province. From the viewpoint of Western pedagogues, a seminar on the string quartets of Beethoven makes perfect sense, but a seminar on the *phleng thao* of the Thai composer Luang Pradit Phairoh is overly specialized; in Thailand,

Mainland Southeast Asia

however, the reverse may be true. Any study of music—particularly one intended for readers living outside the cultures under study—must have a clear sense of how "deep" one is to descend into the bottomless realm of difference.

In this section, we have striven to provide a basic musical ethnology of each nation-state, and though ethnomusicology has since the mid-1970s moved away from descriptive methodologies toward theoretically based ones, we have concluded that a descriptive foundation—a musical road map—must be comprehended before one can delve into the diverse and often thorny issues of interpretation. Interpretive theories, especially of the school of deconstructionism, can be heavily subjective and therefore susceptible to challenge and revision. We are hopeful that the following articles will be more stable and less trendy.

The lengths of the articles reflect several factors, especially proportion of population and current knowledge. Burma, for example, is geographically larger than Thailand but receives far less space. The reader must understand that Thailand has been continuously open to researchers, who may travel anywhere within the country, and that several scholars specialize in that country's music—but until the 1990s, Burma was virtually closed to researchers. It has a far less developed infrastructure (inhibiting travel within the country), and no ethnomusicologists known to us specialize in Burma alone. All authors have agreed that the space given them is inadequate; all could have written much more.

The following articles, then, reflect the current state of knowledge, but even as this volume goes to press, the nation-states covered in this section (actually, the topics of the entire volume) continue to be actively researched, in many cases by the authors who have written here. New researchers have established themselves since the period 1989–1990, when the volume was commissioned.

This volume appears at an auspicious time for research in mainland Southeast Asia. In 1994, Burma began allowing visitors to stay for a full month, rather than a single week. The same year, Laos suspended its restrictions on internal travel, though obtaining a visa still poses a challenge. Thailand, Singapore, and Malaysia remain open, as they have been. Though parts of Cambodia are still off limits and dangerous, researchers travel freely to and from Phnom Penh. Since 1993, Vietnam has given visiting researchers relative freedom to seek out music and theater, and since 1994, people of all nationalities have again been permitted to visit its central highlands. The articles that follow, then, represent the state of knowledge at the beginning, rather than the end, of what promises to be the most productive period of musical research in Southeast Asian history.

The Khmer People

Sam-Ang Sam
Panya Roongrüang
Phong T. Nguyễn

KHMER LIVING IN CAMBODIA

The word *Khmer* designates the majority ethnic group in the Kingdom of Cambodia —a people usually known to the outside world as Cambodians. In the Khmer language, the nation was traditionally called Kampuchea, but because of the Khmer Rouge reign of terror from 1975 to 1979, when the country was called Democratic Kampuchea, that term gained such notoriety that the word *Kampuchea* is now avoided. During the years of Khmer Rouge rule, the Khmer people suffered famine, mass killings, loss, separation, distrust, disgrace, and shame. In Southeast Asia, no other country's culture has suffered so extensively, its people's psyches so deeply scarred, and the lives of so many of its musicians, makers of instruments, and dancers wasted. Because the word *Kampuchea* continues to haunt the Khmer people, the Westernized term *Cambodia* is preferred. Here, *Khmer* denotes the main ethnic group and its cultural expressions.

Cambodia occupies an area of 181,040 square kilometers, about the same size as the state of Washington. Today's Cambodia, with official but artificially drawn boundaries, belies the fact that lowland Khmer live across its borders with Vietnam and Thailand, and that upland Khmer live across the border in Laos and Vietnam. Excepting for the mountainous areas along the Lao and Vietnamese borders, most of Cambodia is flat, dominated by extensive forests and open plains, where wet-rice cultivation is the norm. The country is drained by two major rivers. The mighty Mekong, more than a kilometer wide at the capital, Phnom Penh, flows from southern Laos through Cambodia on the way to its delta in Vietnam, where it divides into nine branches. Starting from the Great Lake in western Cambodia, the Tonle Sap River flows southeast to join the Mekong at Phnom Penh, where the Basakk River adds to the flow. Cambodia is a land whose culture is closely related to the water on which its people depend.

Cambodia's 1994 estimated population of 9,752,466 has grown rapidly since 1979 (Grainger 1995), when the Khmer Rouge, accused of murdering or starving more than two million people, were overthrown. Though the birthrate remains high at 2.87 percent, life expectancy remains low (just over forty-nine years) because medical care is minimal and life remains difficult for most Khmer. Ninety percent of the

Cambodia

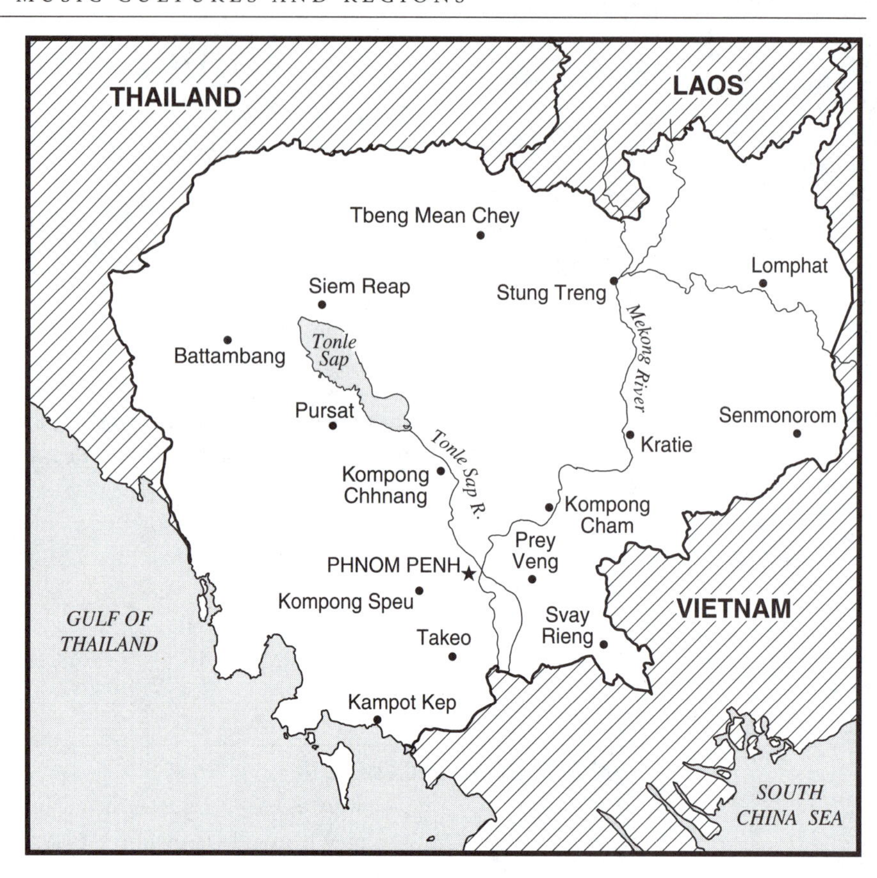

population is ethnically Khmer (lowland and upland); Vietnamese constitute about 5 percent and Chinese about 1 percent.

Cambodia received nominal independence from France in 1949 and full independence in 1953. Until 1975, Francophile culture retained a certain dominance among sophisticated, urban Khmer, but because Phnom Penh's entire population was driven to the countryside in 1975 and many were consequently killed or starved to death, the French cultural heritage is now largely gone. Literacy is estimated at only 35 percent. Phnom Penh's control of many of the country's twenty provinces is tenuous because of continued Khmer Rouge strength, and the government's treasury is too small to address national needs for medical care, schools, infrastructure, and communications.

Since 1953, the country's name has changed six times. Below are the official names by which Cambodia has been known from independence to the present.

Khmer Names	*English Names*	*Periods*
Preah Reacheanachakk Kampuchea	Kingdom of Cambodia	1953–1970
Sathearanakroat Khmer	Khmer Republic	1970–1975
Kampuchea Pracheathipatey	Democratic Kampuchea	1975–1979
Sathearanakroat Pracheameanitt	People's Republic of Kampuchea	1979–1989
Roat Kampuchea	State of Cambodia	1989–1993
Preah Reacheanachakk Kampuchea	Kingdom of Cambodia	1993–present

Historical overview

Migrations into the mainland regions of Southeast Asia from the north continued well into historic times. The ancestors of the Khmer came with earlier waves that followed in the wake of the proto-Malays. The Khmer are closely related to the Mon, who settled further to the west, but of whom only small pockets survive in Thailand and Burma.

According to conventional history, based largely on Chinese sources, when the Khmer arrived in present-day Cambodia, two powerful states had already been established there by people of Malay stock: Champa, controlling part of central and southern Vietnam, and Founan (Funan), in the southernmost part of Vietnam and most of present-day Cambodia. Founan was at the height of its power at the end of the 400s.

It is believed that one of Funan's vassals was the Khmer state of Chenla, situated in present-day northern Cambodia and southern Laos. By about the mid-500s, Chenla had overcome Founan and reversed the pattern of overlord and vassal. About A.D. 627, it absorbed Founan during the reign of Isanvarman I, who married a princess of Champa and extended his domain westward until it bordered the Mon kingdom of Dvaravati (*Southeast Asia* 1969:2:104). Before the end of the reign of Jayavarman I (656–681), Chenla was showing signs of breaking up. Civil war followed his death, and the country split into two parts: Land Chenla (northern part) and Water Chenla (southern part). Khmer power suffered an eclipse for more than a century.

The Khmer, like the people of Founan and Champa, absorbed many aspects of Indic culture, including the Hindu-based concept of the *deva raja* 'god king' and the great temple as a symbolic holy mountain. Though Khmer kingdoms waxed and waned and were eventually eclipsed, the Khmer penchant for building stone temples throughout their kingdoms left monuments by which today's people can sense the power and cosmic order of their ancient forebears. King Jayavarman II (802–830) revived Khmer power and built the foundation for the Angkorean Empire, founding three capitals (Indrapura, Hariharalaya, and Mahendraparvata), whose archaeological remains reveal much about his times.

The first great expansion of Khmer power occurred during the reign of Suryavarman I (1002–1050). After winning a long civil war, he turned his force eastward and subjugated the Mon kingdom of Dvaravati. Consequently, he ruled over the greater part of present-day Thailand and Laos, plus the northern half of the Malay Peninsula. Cambodia became a great empire; the temples of Angkor, an archaeological treasure replete with detailed bas-reliefs showing many aspects of the culture (including some musical instruments), remain monuments to Khmer culture (see figures 1 and 2). After the death of Suryavarman II (1113–1150), who built Angkor Vatt, Cambodia lapsed into chaos until Jayavarman VII (1181–1218) ordered the construction of a new city. He was a Buddhist, and for a time Buddhism became the dominant religion in Cambodia. As a state religion, however, it was adapted to suit the *deva raja* practice, with a *Buddha raja* being substituted for the former Hindu-derived *Shiva raja* or *Vishnu raja*.

The Siamese Tai became increasingly powerful in the valley of the Chao Phraya River. In 1238, they captured Sukhothai and soon established a powerful, independent kingdom (*Southeast Asia,* 2nd ed. 1969:2:105). The rise of the Tai kingdoms of Sukhothai (1238) and Ayuthaya (1350) resulted in almost ceaseless wars with the Khmer, leading to the destruction of Angkor in 1431, when, through the treachery of two Buddhist monks, the forces of Ayuthaya captured Angkor itself. The Tai are said to have carried off ninety thousand prisoners, many of whom were likely dancers and musicians (Blanchard 1958:27). The period after 1432, with the Khmer people bereft of their treasures, documents, and human bearers of culture, was one of precipitous decline. In 1434, King Ponhea Yat made Phnom Penh his capital, and Angkor was abandoned to the jungle. During the following century, King Ang Chan

mohori Court ensemble for entertainment music

chrieng chapey Narrative accompanied by long-necked lute (*chapey*)

chapey dang veng Long-necked lute with two to four strings

ayai Repartee singing accompanied by small ensemble

(1516–1566) transferred the capital to Lungvek (Lovek), but it was captured in 1594 by the Siamese. To stem Siamese and Vietnamese aggression, Cambodia appealed to France for protection in 1863 and became a French protectorate in 1864. During the 1880s, with southern Vietnam and Laos, Cambodia was drawn into the French-controlled Indochinese Union. For nearly a century, the French exploited Cambodia commercially and exercised power over Khmer politics, economics, and society.

During the second half of the twentieth century, the political situation in Cambodia became chaotic. King Norodom Sihanouk proclaimed Cambodia's independence in 1949 and ruled the country until 18 March 1970, when he was overthrown by General Lon Nol, who established the Khmer Republic. On 17 April 1975, the Khmer Rouge, led by Pol Pot (alias Saloth Sar), came to power and virtually destroyed the health, morality, education, physical environment, and culture of the Khmer people. On 7 January 1979, Khmer forces under Heng Samrin, augmented by Vietnamese forces, ousted the Khmer Rouge. After more than ten years of painfully slow rebuilding with only meager outside help, United Nations intervention resulted in the Paris Peace Accord (23 October 1992), which created the conditions for general elections, leading to the formation of the country's current government and the restoration of Prince Sihanouk to power as king in 1993. The Khmer Rouge continue to control portions of western and northern Cambodia, and security outside the capital remains problematic.

Music in Cambodia

A distinction must be made between "music in Cambodia" and "Khmer music." The former embraces all ethnic groups within the national boundaries, and the latter is limited to the majority, lowland Khmer. The northern provinces of Rattanakiri and Mundulkiri include hilly plateaus, home to the Pnong (Phnorng), an upland Mon-Khmer speaking group, and in the southwest, along the Koulen and Cardamom ranges live the Kuoy (Kui), Por, Samre, and other upland Mon-Khmer speakers, whose musical expression emphasizes gong ensembles, drum ensembles, and free-reed mouth organs with gourd wind chests. In the west, around the Great Lake (Tonle Sap) live Chăm, Chinese, Vietnamese, and other lowland minorities, but the extent to which these groups maintain their traditional musics is little known.

The musical landscape

The Khmer musical mansion has numerous rooms, and though all are connected by doors and hallways, each represents a distinct genre and must be taken on its own terms, yet within the larger structure. The following overview reflects commonly accepted Khmer categories, expressed in closely equivalent English terms.

A fundamental division separates traditional and modern musics in Cambodia.

Traditional musics are vastly more extensive in variety than modern ones, though the latter are dominant in the lives of many Khmer, especially those living in urban areas. Within the traditional category are three subcategories—court, folk, and religious. The last, consisting mostly of chant, is not music, strictly speaking, but it has musical qualities. Each subcategory has further subdivisions.

Court genres

The term *court* is preferred over *classical,* since the music, theater, and dance of this type were originally exclusive to the court and expressed its wealth and power. Some genres described as court are, however, derived from court styles but performed by commoners. Nevertheless, the court genres, being especially sophisticated, represent the highest developments in the Khmer performing arts.

Court music includes ceremonial music played by the court ensemble (*pinn peat*). It also includes dramatic genres, the human ones also involving dance. The term *lkhaon* embraces all dramatic subgenres (court and folk), but only two are court genres. The term *lkhaon kbach* denotes two genres, both performed exclusively by females: dance-drama and isolated dances created on a theme. Second, there is *lkhaon khaol,* an all-male dance-drama performed in mask. Several varieties of shadow plays (*lkhaon sbek*), though styled for the court, are not necessarily found at the court.

Folk genres

The term *folk* has been chosen to denote genres associated with ordinary people, most of whom live in villages and practice farming. Most of these genres have (or had) a practical function, and were performed in conjunction with calendrical festivals, Buddhist festivals, and rites of passage. The folk genres are further subdivided into ceremonial, theatrical, functional, dance, solo instrumental, and religious groups.

Ceremonial genres include music for weddings (*kar*), funerals (*khmaoch*), spirit ceremonies (*arakk*), and ordinations (*bambuoh neak*). In addition, the long-drum ensemble (*chhaiyaim*) is usually employed to entertain at festivities and to lead parades.

Folk theater is of several types, including *yike, basakk,* and *mohori* (which are still active), *ape* (which, though revived, remains extremely rare), and *pramotey* (a genre known to have survived only until 1975). The term *functional* is used to group three otherwise unrelated genres that remain widespread: *chrieng chapey,* a solo narrative accompanied by a long-necked lute called *chapey dang veng*; music for boxing; and repartee-song, accompanied by instruments and involving solo male and female voices (*ayai*).

Folk dance broadly denotes both older, traditional dances known to rural peoples, and a long and growing list of folk-style dances created in urban schools, especially the Royal University of Fine Arts. The four traditional dances are *trott, chhaiyaim,* the peacock of Pursat, and the wild ox. Between 1965 and 1975, eleven folk-style dances created on rural themes included the harvest dance and the gum-lac-pounding dance (named for a black insect product used to blacken the teeth), which have entered the repertoire. Since 1979, dozens more have been created, about ten of which have been widely accepted.

A final category accounts for solo folk-instrumental music, among which the *sneng* (free-reed buffalo horn) and the *slekk* (a leaf buzzer, played in the mouth) are best known.

Religious and other genres

The category of religious music primarily embraces chant performed in Buddhist temples, both individually and by groups, and special chants (*saraphanh*) associated with the festival celebrating the birth, death, and rebirth of the Buddha, sung by both monks and lay people. Because Hinduism came to Cambodia before the other major religions and was the official religion of the court, it continued to affect religious practices even after the arrival of Buddhism, though both religions were influenced by the animistic practices and beliefs of the original Khmer. A few royal ceremonies of Hindu origin continue to survive at the court and include music. Buddhist chant is exclusively vocal, but some Hindu rites involve instruments, including the conch trumpet.

The second major division, modern and Western, includes both Western classical music and a plethora of types of popular songs, some Khmer derived, some of Asian origin, and some showing greater degrees of Western influence. Western classical music was never more than a fragile plant in Cambodia, requiring the special support of the court and the university. During the Khmer Rouge period, it completely disappeared, but it has been gradually revived at the Royal University of Fine Arts since 1979.

Popular songs have long appealed to Khmer of all kinds, but they are associated more with cities than with villages. *Mohori* songs are folk music that has been modernized, and the term *traditional popular songs* denotes a genre of slow, sentimental ballads featuring Western combo instruments and a vocal style that combines attributes of both Western and Khmer songs. There are also categories for songs with Latin beats, plus other kinds of songs having foreign melodies. As in the West, the Khmer have been quick to catch on to popular-song videos, which have attracted a following, both in Cambodia and among overseas Khmer in the West.

Though the Khmer people make up the majority of the population of Cambodia (estimated in March 1995 to be 96.17 percent), the remainder (370,463 persons) comprise twenty-one minority ethnic groups officially sanctioned by the Ministry of the Interior. These vary from the nearly extinct Kachok with six people and the Saoch with seventy-two, to the Chăm with slightly more than two hundred thousand (Grainger 1995). Some of these groups live in the upland areas of northeastern Cambodia bordering Laos and Vietnam; others live among the Khmer majority in lowland areas. Other minorities include the Vietnamese and Chinese. The musical traditions of these twenty-one groups are extremely varied and mostly unrelated to each other or to those of the mainstream Khmer.

Historical perspectives

Khmer music reflects both geographical and historical relationships to neighboring cultures. The Indianization of Southeast Asia nearly two thousand years ago included the area that became Cambodia and deeply influenced lowland peoples, especially the ruling elites. In later periods, Chinese, French, Vietnamese, and Cham also came, each leaving a mark. The early port near the Mekong Delta, known as Óc Eo to the Viet and called by later observers a crossroad of the arts, was the most likely point of infusion. The Khmer absorbed diverse influences from these peoples—language, concepts, systems of writing, literature, religion, styles of art, musical instruments, and possibly styles of instrumental performance. But the Khmer absorbed and adopted foreign cultures to suit their own traditions and tastes, resulting in a distinctly Khmer cultural blend.

Travelers from India offered the Khmer languages, systems of writing, the concept of a god-king, literature, styles of art (especially sculpture), Hinduism and Buddhism and their rituals, musical instruments, and likely the concept of cyclical time. The Chinese introduced cuisine, an alternate form of Buddhism, musical instruments (two-stringed fiddles and hammered dulcimers), and the theatrical style which the Khmer adapted into *basakk* theater. Europeans, especially the French, brought Roman Catholicism, technology, and much musical influence, including notation, classical European music and instruments, and popular music, which the Khmer adapted into modern music (*phleng samai*).

Little is known of the prehistoric period before the coming of Indian traders and missionaries. Upland Mon-Khmer speakers living in the mountains straddling Vietnam, Cambodia, and Laos, where Indianization made little penetration, probably preserve the oldest strata of Khmer culture. Animistic rites require music. The bronze gong ensembles and dancers of the Pnong in Rattanakiri and Mundulkiri provinces are associated with the ritual sacrifice of buffalo (*kapp krabey phoeuk sra*). Other dances, such as the Peacock of Pursat (*kngaok Posatt*) and the Wild Ox (*tunsong*), preserved by the Por of Pursat and Kamopong Chhnaing provinces, likely derived from rituals. Other musical instruments, including the *sneng* (used on elephant-hunting expeditions) and the *ploy* (a free-reed mouth organ with gourd wind chest), are survivals from the earliest periods.

Indianization occurred during the Funan-Chenla period (first to ninth centuries), when the Khmer juxtaposed prehistoric animistic rituals with those of Hinduism, the coexistence of which continues among villagers. Court rituals were created. The blowing of a conch (*saing*) by a Brahmin priest created a propitious vibratory environment for divination and propitiation and to signal the sovereign's arrival.

Khmer civilization reached its peak from the ninth to the fifteenth centuries. The great temple-city of Angkor marked the apex of Khmer glory. In it stand gigantic masterpieces symbolizing the union of celestial and earthly beings. Carved on the walls of the great temples are figures of celestial dancers (*apsara*) with musical instruments: the angular harp (*pinn,* figure 1), circular frame gongs (*korng vung,* figure 2), suspended barrel drums (*skor yol*), small cymbals (*chhing*), and a quadruple-reed oboe (*sralai*). These are believed to have developed into the *pinn peat,* the ensemble now used to accompany court dances, masked plays, shadow plays, and religious cere-

FIGURE 1 The extinct Khmer harp (*pinn*) as depicted in a late-twelfth-century relief from the Bayon at Angkor Vat. Photo by Terry E. Miller.

It is possible for novice listeners to distinguish Khmer musics from those of neighboring cultures. Just as the nontonal Khmer language has a totally different sound from tonal Thai, the two musics have entirely different characters.

FIGURE 2 A twelfth-century version of the gong circle (*korng*) with seven gongs, pictured at Angkor Vat. Photo by Terry E. Miller.

monies. Among Khmer ensembles, the *pinn peat* is the most important legacy of the period of Angkor.

In 1431, Angkor was looted by conquering Siamese armies, abandoned, and overrun by vegetation. The Khmer king and his court fled, and the capital was moved to Lungvek. Once again, in 1594, Lungvek was sacked by the Siamese. Little is known of this period, the most obscure in Khmer history. This second eradication shocked and weakened the Khmer. Music and its functions were deeply affected, and a new style of melancholic and emotional music is said to have emerged.

The period from 1796 to 1859 saw a renaissance of Khmer music. King Ang Duong, the greatest of the monarchs of this period, ascended the throne in 1841 in the capital, Oudong. Under his rule, Khmer music and other forms of art were revived and began to flourish again.

For Khmer traditional arts, the twentieth century has been a period of conservation, preservation, and revival. Forms of art surviving from the past were carefully conserved under the eyes of traditional masters. At the beginning of the century, foreign influences resulted in new forms of art. Chinese theater is now presented in a modified Khmer form, *basakk*. Islamic-influenced theater appears in a modified form, *yike*. As in the early period, we see the modification of imported forms into

Khmer style. Costumes, languages, performing styles, décor, song, and music of the Chinese and the Muslims were Khmerized to suit local needs and tastes.

Cambodia's music culture in relation to that of Southeast Asia

Initial observations may lead to the conclusion that Khmer culture is closely related to Siamese culture (the southern branch of the Tai people). This conclusion appears more obvious with court or classical musics than with folk or village musics, which differ widely. The main difficulty occurs when observers assume that the Khmer were influenced by the Siamese and others, rather than vice versa. Superficially, Siamese influence on Khmer court music appears stronger than the reverse, but in fact, Khmer influence on the Siamese is far deeper.

Khmer culture was well developed and already deeply affected by Indic culture in the 1200s, when the Tai established their first historical kingdom, Sukhothai. For several reasons, not the least being the Siamese attacks on the center of Khmer civilization (Angkor) and the consequent forced migration of Khmer people (including those learned in the arts) to Siam, the Siamese absorbed much from the Khmer, including vocabulary, a system of writing, architecture, art, Buddhism, musical instruments, repertory, and dance. The old, formal script of central Thailand, called *dua khawm*, is a Khmer script, and the "royal" language used at the court to this day is a form of Khmer. While the details of the relationship are not always clear or certain, there is little disputing that the Khmer profoundly influenced the Siamese.

Much of the apparent similarity in classical music and dance-drama stems from the nineteenth and twentieth centuries, when Siamese musicians, dancers, and composers were sent from the court in Bangkok to aid the Khmer in restoring their arts. Though the Khmer absorbed repertory and aspects of theater and dance from the Siamese during this period, they changed these arts in ways—sometimes obvious, sometimes not—to suit the Khmer temperament.

In terms of sheer sound, without considering subtle aspects known only to specialists, it is possible for novice listeners to distinguish Khmer musics (both court and folk) from those of neighboring cultures. The gentle, long-short (dotted) rhythms in Khmer court music obviously differ from the usually continuous and even rhythms of Siamese court music. Folk musics, especially *phleng arakk* (music for worship of spirits) and *phleng kar* (wedding music), are distinctive in timbre (especially from the chest-resonated monochord and reeds, both free and double) and syncopated rhythms. Just as the nontonal Khmer language has a totally different sound from tonal Thai, the two musics have entirely different characters (for further details, see Miller and Sam 1995).

Some scholars have been tempted to lump Khmer court music with other gong chime music cultures in Southeast Asia. Since the circular frame gongs neither lead nor dominate any Khmer ensembles, the gong chime idea does little to explain the Khmer tradition. Additionally, applying the Indonesian term *gamelan* to Khmer ensembles—as was done in a compact disc in 1994—only adds to the confusion. Khmer musics reflect the particular character and circumstances of the Khmer people, their history, and their individual predilections.

Review of research

Despite occasional articles in the *New York Times* on current political events in Cambodia and the exposure Khmer Rouge atrocities garnered through the film *The Killing Fields,* Cambodia remains little known to most of the world. Its arts, though occasionally in the spotlight during cultural tours from Phnom Penh or performances given by overseas Khmer, are similarly little known. Before 1970, many tourists visited Cambodia, mostly to see Angkor's treasures, and during their visits they usually watched demonstrations of Khmer dance and music. After 1970, tourism declined, and from 1975 until roughly 1990, it ceased.

Research in Cambodia has been slight, not only because of limited access and continuing problems with security and health, but also because few non-Khmer have taken an interest in local music, dance, and theater. Readers who depend on previously published materials, both written and recorded, particularly those by non-Khmer, may fall prey to the misunderstandings and distortions in these documents, perpetuated by outsiders with little knowledge of the country's traditions.

The most important primary source for research remains indigenous Khmer musicians, but they prefer to learn and play music rather than verbalize about it. Transmission of the arts from the older generation to the younger requires concentration and unlimited time on the part of students, but in Cambodia a high percentage of the masters died during the reign of terror, and those who survive are elderly. If they do not pass their knowledge to the younger musicians before death, a segment of the country's cultural treasure will disappear. For years after the Khmer Rouge were overthrown, however, everyone was too poor and too concerned about survival to devote much time, energy, and material to studying music. Nevertheless, because music and dance have meant so much to so many Khmer, in terms of national identity and as a link to a glorious past, the restoration of these arts often took precedence over more mundane matters.

Non-Khmer writers have tended to see Khmer musics as mere regional variations among "typical" mainland Southeast Asian musics, viewing the classical tradition in the same breath as that of the Thai, and comparing village musics to others of similar format in Laos, Vietnam, and Thailand. It would be unfortunate to dismiss Khmer classical music as part of the larger gong chime musical culture of the subcontinent without pointing out its uniqueness. Southeast Asia is not a melting pot of musics but a salad, where each vegetable retains its individual flavor. Contemporary Khmer musicians feel strongly about this issue and wish their music to be appreciated on its own terms.

Khmer music scholars in Cambodia have never been plentiful, but some have published significant materials. When communicating with the outside world, they formerly used French, but today French is declining and English is gaining preference. Most publications on music by the Buddhist Institute are in Khmer, however, and since few outside scholars who have paid attention to Khmer music are fluent in Khmer, this material has largely remained unknown. Many publications in European languages are problematic and full of errors and misunderstandings; they sometimes reflect Eurocentric or Thaicentric bias. A great deal of information has been passed from one scholar to the next without being critically examined, especially relative to the assumption that Khmer tuning, like Thai tuning, is equidistant.

Until the 1980s, three writers have tended to dominate discussions of Khmer music—two French (Alain Daniélou, Jacques Brunet) and one Vietnamese (Trần Quang Hải). Though Daniélou's work goes back to 1957 and Brunet's to 1969, and their audio recordings are of fine quality and continue to be important, their writings express profound misunderstandings of the subject. Trần's overview of the subject (1980) is inadequate for many reasons. Trần assumes and asserts that most Khmer musical and theatrical genres derived from elsewhere—*mohori* from Thailand, *yike* from Java, *roam vung* from Laos. The Khmer view their arts, no matter how similar to those of their neighbors, as uniquely expressive of the Khmer spirit.

The *JVC Video Anthology of World Music and Dance* has similar problems and inaccuracies. The section on Cambodia presents unrepresentative excerpts. Better videotapes have been commercially produced, and are available at Southeast Asian

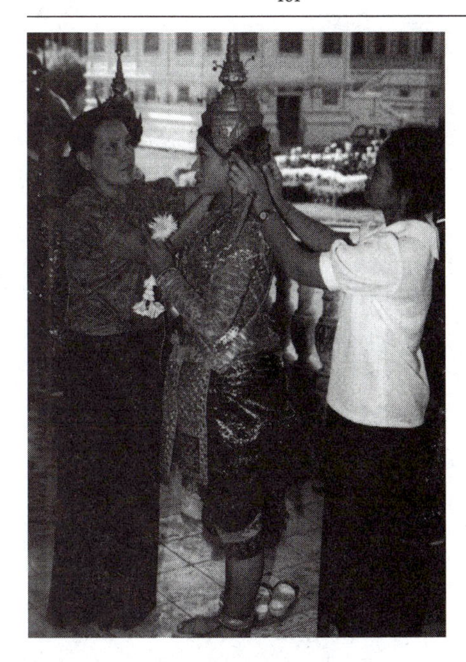

FIGURE 3 Two teachers help a dance student of the Royal University of Fine Arts prepare to perform at the smaller dance pavilion of the palace. Photo by Terry E. Miller, 1988.

grocery stores across the United States and in other countries where mainland Southeast Asians live.

The study of Khmer music

Both native Khmer students and visiting researchers doing fieldwork and wishing to study traditional Khmer music would normally have to find a master, become an apprentice, and learn the art over time. Khmer music has been passed orally from one generation to the next through rote teaching, with little verbalization. To transmit Khmer music, dance, and theater in a formal setting, the government supports one national institution—a school known in French as the Université Royale des Beaux Arts (Royal University of Fine Arts). The university was established in 1965 under the patronage of His Royal Highness Prince Norodom Sihanouk. The Khmer Rouge régime devastated and closed it, but it reopened on 27 January 1981 under the direction of Chheng Phon. It has five faculties: Archaeology, Architecture, Choreographic Arts (Folk and Court Dances and Theater), Music (Classical Western and Traditional Khmer Musics), and Plastic Arts (figure 3).

Each school year, the Faculty of Choreographic Arts recruits about forty to fifty new students, chosen on the basis of two important factors: educational background and talent. The dance department holds two classes daily, a morning session from 7:00 to 11:00 (devoted to dance training), and an afternoon session from 2:30 to 5:00 (involving general studies, including mathematics, history, and Khmer literature). The Faculty of Choreographic Arts offers two degree levels, the first being a four-year program leading to a *Diplôme és Arts* in Court and Folk Dances, Theater, and Circus. During their senior year, prospective graduates in court dance are required to choreograph a new dance; those who expect to graduate in folk dance must learn a repertoire of twenty-one dances.

The second level, which lasts three years and leads to a *Baccalauréât és Arts*, requires a review of the first-level dance repertoire and creation of new dances. At this stage, students work closely with their teachers, the typical ratio being one teacher to five students. Once a week, students report to their teachers on their development, exchanging ideas and receiving comments. Once a month students present their works to a committee for evaluation and feedback, insuring that new creations fit the artistic guidelines.

Musical Instruments

Classification

Khmer organology follows a single-step scheme. At the most general level, Khmer musicians use a tripartite division: *kroeung damm* 'percussion instruments', *kroeung khse* 'stringed instruments', and *kroeung phlomm* 'wind instruments'. The Khmer system of classification derives from the verb that denotes the action of making the sound. In Khmer, *leng* 'to play' applies to all instruments. Each division is associated with a more specific verb, like *damm* 'to hit, to strike' for idiophones and membranophones, *kaut* 'to bow' or *denh* 'to pluck' for chordophones, and *phlomm* 'to blow' for aerophones. *Kroeung damm* include both idiophones and membranophones. Since both groups are struck, both involve the same verb—*damm.*

In the Sachs-Hornbostel system, Jew's harps are classified as idiophones, or more specifically, plucked linguaphones since they have vibrating tongues. Khmer musicians, however, classify Jew's harps as aerophones. They see this category as logical because an instrumental tongue is played inside the mouth. Khmer musicians refer to all reeds (free reed, single reed, double reed, and quadruple reed) as tongues (*andat*)

chhing Small, thick metal cymbals connected by a cord

chhap Medium-size cymbals, thinner than *chhing*

krapp Pair of bamboo wooden clappers

roneat ek Higher-pitched xylophone, with twenty-one keys

because all of them are played in the mouth. Moreover, they use the verb *phlomm* 'to blow' to denote the playing of these instruments.

In Khmer logic, it is also possible to classify instruments in other ways. The two-stringed fiddle (*tror so*) can be classified as a stringed instrument (*kroeung khse*), a bowed instrument (*kroeung kaut*), or an instrument used in the *mohori* ensemble (*kroeung mohori*). The high-pitched xylophone (*roneat ek*) can be classified as a struck instrument or performance technique (*kroeung damm*), an instrument of the *pinn peat* ensemble (*kroeung pinn peat*), an instrument of the *mohori* (*kroeung mohori*), a leading instrument (*kroeung noam*), or a traditional instrument (*kroeung dantrey buran*).

Whereas the Sachs-Hornbostel system is based on theory, the Khmer system is based on performance. The Khmer system was created to serve neither organology nor museology, but only for the practical making of Khmer music. Thus, it derives from the culture, from within, instead of from without. Both music theory and practice, including ideas of organology, are passed subconsciously in an unsystematic way from master to pupil during music lessons and performances.

In functional terms, the Khmer conceive of instruments as being primarily religious or secular. Playing techniques are associated with music and therefore affect musical style—which leads to other kinds of classifications. The following kinds of description summarize this sort of thinking.

1. Physical materials and playing characteristics
2. Role, such as leading (*ek*)
3. Musical style, such as running (*roneat rut*)
4. Ensemble context, such as *arakk*, *kar*, *pinn peat*, *mohori*
5. Controlling action, such as mouth with aerophone and Jew's harp
6. Size, such as *tauch* and *thomm*
7. Status, such as court and folk
8. System of beliefs, such as religious or otherwise sacred, or secular

The musical instruments of Cambodia are made from clay, hide, bamboo, gourd, other plants, silk, horn, wood, iron, copper, brass, and bronze. Instruments are arranged below according to the Sachs-Hornbostel system of classification.

Idiophones

Concussion idiophones

The term *chhing* is likely onomatopoeic for the sound a pair of thick, bowl-shaped cymbals produces. Made of an alloy of iron, copper, and gold mixed with bronze, each measures about 5 centimeters in diameter. Paired cymbals are joined by a cord that passes through a small hole at the apex of each. The player holds one cymbal in each hand and strikes them together to produce open and closed sounds—*chhing* and *chhepp*, respectively. To produce the open sound, the cymbal in the right hand strikes the other with an outward sliding motion; to produce the closed sound, the player strikes and holds both cymbals together, dampening the sound. The *chhing* and *chhepp* strokes mark unaccented (O) and accented (+) beats respectively during performance, and consequently the *chhing* functions as the timekeeper of entertainment, theater, and dance ensembles.

The *chhap* is a pair of cymbals larger in diameter but thinner than *chhing*. They are most commonly used in the *chhayaim* and *basakk* ensembles.

The *krapp* is a pair of clappers made of bamboo or hardwood in different sizes and shapes; they are used by men or women. There are several kinds of *krapp*. Among them, the *krapp kou* (pair of clappers) used in the *chhaiyaim* ensemble and Khmer folk dance (*robaim krapp*), and *krapp phuong* (similar in shape to an open fan) used by vocalists and mistresses of the dance to keep time for their students, are most important.

The *pann,* a struck wooden slit drum of Chinese derivation and name, serves mainly in the *basakk* ensemble to reinforce the beats.

Struck idiophones

Roneat is a generic term in Khmer referring to xylophones or metallophones—bar idiophones, with bars of bamboo, wood, or metal. The name *roneat* derives from *roneap* 'bamboo strips'. Khmer xylophones have bars suspended with cords over both trough-shaped and boat-shaped resonators, evidently indigenous to mainland Southeast Asia. Miller and Chonpairot (1981) have documented the known histories and speculated on the origins of three such instruments: the Burmese *pa'talà*, the Thai *ranat*, and the Cambodian *roneat.*

Khmer xylophones have bamboo or wooden bars strung together along two cords running through holes in each bar and suspended on two hooks on the upper ends of the resonator. The maker takes care to ensure that the bars are spaced so they can vibrate freely. Each bar is tuned by attaching to the ends of its underside some *pramor,* a mixture of lead, beeswax, and rosin (*mrum, sab*). Khmer musicians practice both "rough" and "fine" tunings. The former aims merely at finding approximate pitches; the latter finely adjusts the required pitches. Khmer musicians prefer to fine-tune their xylophones with lumps of *pramor*, which also keep the sound from ringing too long.

Roneat ek (combining *roneat* 'xylophone' and *ek* 'one, first, leader' to mean 'first xylophone' or 'leading xylophone') is also known as *roneat rut* 'running xylophone' (figure 4). Its role is to start a piece and to cue the others, but contrary to what many Khmer musicians think, it does not play the melodic line. Instead, it plays variations of the melody, whose actual form is realized by a vocalist or oboist. The *roneat ek* plays octaves, less commonly fourths or fifths. Its twenty-one hardwood or bamboo bars provide a three-octave range, but because it is played in octaves (between the left and right hands), its working range is only two octaves.

The resonator of the *roneat ek,* about 115 centimeters long and about 56 centimeters high, sits on a raised square base 14 centimeters high. Its bars are cut equally in width, in different lengths and thicknesses. Thicker bars produce lower pitches; thinner ones produce higher pitches. The bars vary in length from about 37 centimeters at the bottom to 27 centimeters at the top. The width of each bar is about 7 centimeters, and the thickness is about 1 to 1.5 centimeters.

The player beats the bars with two mallets having thick disk heads. Musicians

FIGURE 4 An informal ensemble, consisting of xylophone (*roneat ek*), metallophone (*roneat dek*), two gong circles (*korng vung tauch, korng vung thomm*), and two drums (*skor thomm, sampho*), plays at Tonle Bati Temple, south of Phnom Penh. Photo by Terry E. Miller, 1988.

use two kinds of mallets to strike the bars, according to the context and function of the music and whether the playing is indoors or outdoors. For indoor performances, soft mallets are used; but at outdoor performances, hard mallets are used. The handles of the mallets are about 40 centimeters long, soft disks are about 4 centimeters in diameter and 3 centimeters thick, and hard disks are 3.3 centimeters in diameter and 2 centimeters thick.

Roneat thung is better called *roneat thomm* 'large xylophone' because its resonator and bars are larger and longer than those of the *roneat ek,* and its range is lower. The rectangular trough resonator, about 125 centimeters long, is supported on four short legs. The ends of both *roneat ek* and *roneat dek* are flat and straight, but those of the *roneat thung* are curved slightly outward. The *roneat thung* has sixteen bamboo or wooden bars, measuring about 47 centimeters long at the lower end to 38 centimeters at the upper end. Each bar is about 6 centimeters wide and about 2 centimeters thick.

Only soft mallets are used to play the *roneat thung*, either indoors or outdoors. The handles of those mallets are about the same length as those of the *roneat ek*, but their disks are larger and thicker. Each measures about 4 centimeters in diameter and about 3.5 centimeters thick. The range of the *roneat thung* partially overlaps that of the *roneat ek*, their highest notes being an octave apart. Because of differences in style, the sixteen bars of the instrument permit a range of music of over two octaves, a range greater than that of the *roneat ek*. The role assigned to the *roneat thung* is to counter the melody, especially in rhythm. The *roneat thung* plays a line almost identical to that of the *korng thomm*, except in a vivacious, funny, comic fashion (*lak*). The *roneat ek* plays continuous octaves, but the *roneat thung* plays a highly syncopated form with many single notes, plus fourths and fifths.

The *roneat dek* is the higher-pitched metallophone, whose origin remains obscure. For Thailand, Morton concluded that metallophones had appeared in the mid-1800s, perhaps modeled after the Javanese *saron* and *gendèr* (1974:62, 190). The *roneat dek* has twenty-one bronze bars. Because of their weight, the bars cannot be suspended on cords but are laid in stepwise order on pads over a rectangular trough resonator. The resonator itself, about 1 meter long, is supported by four short legs. In shape and size, the bars resemble those of the *roneat ek*, but they are tuned by scraping or filing away part of the metal. The player uses a pair of mallets similar to those of the *roneat ek* but with disks of wood or the hide of a buffalo. The style of playing is identical to that of the *roneat ek.*

The *roneat thong* is the lower-pitched metallophone among Khmer bar idiophones. Its sixteen bars are made of a mixture of bronze and copper (bronze for bright sound and copper for long life). Now obsolete, it was formerly used only in palace ensembles.

The Khmer word *korng* 'gong' is generic for all gongs, whether flat or bossed, single or in a set, suspended on cords from hooks, or placed over a frame. Their history can be traced in part from the epigraphy and iconography of the Founan-Chenla and Angkor periods, for many can be seen in carvings on the walls of ancient Khmer temples. Among the minority ethnic groups inhabiting the highlands, several types of *korng* are the predominant instruments.

The Khmer have two sets of bossed gongs—*korng vung tauch* and *korng vung thomm*—arranged on circular frames, both used in the *pinn peat.* The individual bossed gongs differ in size and are made of bronze. Each is suspended horizontally from leather thongs passing through holes in the metal and placed over a rattan frame about 30 centimeters above the floor. The gongs are arranged with the lowest pitch to the player's left and the highest to the right; the player sits in the middle of the frame. Each gong is tuned to its required pitch using *pramor*, a mixture of mud and lead (*samna phuok*), the chaff of rice (*kantuok*), and beeswax (*kramuon khmum*) slightly different from that used to tune xylophones. This material is applied within the underside of the boss. For this application, the gong must be untied and turned over and its boss must be heated; when cool, it can be tied back into the frame and played.

The player of a *korng* uses two mallets to strike each gong on the boss. There are two types of mallets, soft and hard. Soft mallets are for indoor use; hard mallets, for outdoor use. Each mallet has a handle about 15 centimeters long and a disk padded with cloth or the hide of an elephant.

The *korng vung tauch*, or simply *korng tauch*, is the smaller (higher-pitched) set of gongs, the ovular frame of which measures about 110 centimeters from left to right. The number of bossed gongs varies, and musicians differ on the correct number. Some say sixteen, some claim eighteen, some even mention twenty-one. The equivalent Thai instrument has between sixteen and eighteen, a minimum of sixteen being required; sometimes the other two are untuned dummies, but on modern instruments they are normally tuned and used. The *korng tauch* is normally used only in the *pinn peat vung thomm* (*pinn peat* of greater instrumentation) which needs two *korng.* As with the *roneat ek*, the *korng tauch* plays melodic variations in continuous notes divided between both hands.

Korng vung thomm or *korng thomm* denotes the larger and lower-pitched circle of gongs, similar to the *korng tauch* but larger in size, both gongs and frame. The latter measures about 1.2 meters from side to side. Since *korng tauch* and *korng thomm* overlap in range, identical pitches are normally identical in size. The *korng thomm* plays a line almost identical to that of the *roneat thung*, but it is steadier, with less syncopation.

The *korng mong* is a single, suspended bossed gong played with a padded stick, larger in size than those used in circular frames. It has several uses, as in the *korng skor* and *chhaiyaim* ensembles that are used in temples to signal mealtimes and to call a gathering for a temple ritual. In the *korng skor,* this gong informs friends and relatives in the village that an ill person is about to die; consequently, using it in the wedding ensemble is taboo.

The *khmuoh* is a flat gong played with a closed fist, open palm, or padded stick.

angkuoch Jew's harp of bamboo or iron

kroeung damm Khmer classification term for percussion instruments

skor arakk Single-headed goblet-shaped drum of clay or wood

skor thomm Pair of large barrel drums

skor chhaiyaim Long, vase-shaped single-headed drums

It is primarily used in wedding ceremonies to signal the arrival of the bride and the bridegroom, but it is also part of the *basakk* theater ensemble.

Plucked idiophone

The *angkuoch*, also called *kangkuoch*, is a Jew's harp similar to other such instruments found in Southeast Asia and Oceania. In Cambodia, it has long been used by keepers of cattle and others, both as a solo instrument and sometimes to accompany a vocalist. In the Sachs-Hornbostel system, it is classed as a plucked linguaphone within the idiophone category, but in Khmer thinking it is a wind instrument because Khmer musicians use the verb *phlomm* 'to blow' to describe its playing action.

The Khmer *angkuoch* is usually made of bamboo or iron. When made of iron, it has an outer frame (commonly 10 to 15 centimeters long by 1 centimeter wide) in which a movable vibrating tongue, wider toward the attached end, is curved upward at the free end. The frame follows the outline of the tongue. Those of bamboo are similar, but the tongue does not curve.

The player holds the *angkuoch* firmly, usually in the left hand between the thumb and the index finger, and sets part of the frame between the lips, keeping the jaw somewhat open to allow the oral cavity to amplify and modify select overtones among the vibrations of the device. The right index finger sets the tongue into vibration with soft, backward strokes. Various pitches can be obtained by altering the shape of the oral cavity, and by inhaling and exhaling to change timbres. Traditionally, Jew's harps served as disguisers of the voice for courting couples to communicate and serenade one another privately.

Membranophones

Drums

In Khmer, drums are classed as struck instruments (*kroeung damm*). The Khmer use drums merely to accompany singing and dance, and do not attribute to them any magical, spiritual, or ritual significance. *Skor* is a generic term denoting practically all membranophones, including those listed here without the prefix *skor*.

The *skor arakk*, also known as *skor dey* 'clay drum' or *skor dai* 'hand-held drum', is a single-headed goblet-shaped drum, its body made of baked clay or wood and its resonator of snakeskin, lizardskin, or calfskin. The *skor arakk* is made in different sizes, according to its use. Traditionally, it is used in the *arakk* (spiritual ceremony) ensemble, from which the instrument takes its name, but it can also be found in the ensembles for *kar* 'weddings', *mohori* 'entertainment', and *ayai* 'alternate singing'.

Skor thomm 'big drum' denotes a pair of large barrel drums, the largest Khmer membranophones. They are played for a great variety of occasions, from informal gatherings to formal dances. According to carvings on Angkorean temples, these drums were used in military ensembles, and were likely called military drums (*skor toap*). They were used to encourage and signal troops, telling them when to march, rest, retreat, or mount an assault (Pich 1970:29). The *skor thomm* had a prominent function in traditional Khmer society, being found in pagodas, district headquarters, and schools. In pagodas, they announced times for prayer and eating; in district headquarters, they called people to come to meetings; in schools, they signaled class times, recesses, and dismissals.

Skor thomm are made of a light but strong wood, such as *chreh*, *koki*, or *tnaot*. First, the log is cut into a piece about 50 centimeters long, which is then carved with a slight bulge at the center and a slight taper at both ends. The diameter at the center is about 46 centimeters and at the ends about 40 centimeters. Then the solid block is hollowed for its entire length to a thickness of about 1 centimeter, and two rows of small holes (one row near the rim of each head) about 4 centimeters from the edges are drilled. When the membrane is positioned, small bamboo or wooden pegs are hammered into these holes to tighten the hide, but during the past few decades nails have been substituted for pegs, and drilling is not necessary.

The heads are normally of oxhide, but buffalo hide is also used; both skins require treatment before use. The fresh hide is boiled in water with salt, betel, and citron to remove the hair, to make the hide soft and strong, and to prevent stretching. Then the maker of the drum covers the ends of the body with the treated hide while it is wet, secures it with pegs or nails, and lets it sit for at least two weeks (or even longer than a month) before it can be played. The finished drum must be able to produce two untuned sounds: a low tone (*toung*) and a high tone (*ting*). Khmer musicians refer to this duality as *chhloeuy knea* 'to answer each other'. The hide of the side that produces the lower sound is thicker and remains looser than the other, whose hide is thinner and fastened more tightly. Finally, a metal ring about 3 centimeters in diameter is screwed into the body at the center of the bulge so the drum can be hooked to a wooden stand while being played. Normally, *skor thomm* are played in a pair with two unpadded wooden sticks, each about 35 centimeters long; they are tilted obliquely against stands, leaving only one head playable and the other vibrating freely.

Skor chhaiyaim are long, vase-shaped drums, used mainly in the *chhaiyaim* ensemble, associated with religious and traditional ceremonies such as the flower ceremony (*bonn phka*) and the fundraising ceremony (*bonn kathinn*). According to older musicians, such ensembles have been maintained in Khmer villages for many centuries. In performance, drummers wear clown masks to create a comic atmosphere, enlivening the celebration. Each of the four drums that make up an ensemble is supported on the players' shoulders by strips of cloth, and the single heads are beaten with the hands. The four drums are also grouped into two sets, one pair producing a higher tone and the other pair a lower tone. To adjust the pitch, tuning paste is placed on the center of the head.

The *skor yike* is a large frame drum with a head of the skin of a crocodile, a *tunsang* (a kind of large lizard), or an ox. Eight drums, seven of the same size and the larger, conical *skor chey* 'victory drum' (played by the troupe's leader, the teacher), make up the *yike* ensemble. Casually playing and stacking them are forbidden.

The *skor klang khek* are long, two-headed drums in conical shape with heavy leather lacing. Since they are regarded as suspended drums, they are also called *skor yol* 'suspended'. When associated with the funeral ensemble (*klang chhnakk*), the number of drums per ensemble varies according to the rank of the deceased. A king's funeral requires sixteen drums (eight of gold and eight of silver), plus three oboes; for commoners, three drums and one oboe suffice. The ensemble most often plays the piece "*Klang Yaun.*" Today, this ensemble is preserved only in the royal palace in Phnom Penh.

There is some confusion concerning terminology associated with the *klang chhnakk.* Some call it *klang khek,* the title of a piece they also play. In addition, *skor klang khek* is incorrect because *skor* means 'drum' in Khmer and *klang* the same in Thai, but *khek* suggests an Indian origin. Therefore, its name—*skor klang khek*—involves a redundancy.

The *skor chey* has a conical body made of hardwood with two calfskin or goatskin heads, of unequal size, laced with leather thongs or rattan strips. In an ensemble, the drums are usually played as a pair, one male and one female. Players use their bare hands or (less commonly) sticks.

The *sampho* is a small, two-headed barrel drum with a bulge near the center, tapering to each head. Its body, made of any of several kinds of wood (*khnaor, kakoh, raing,* or *beng*), is hollowed from a solid piece of wood, and its ends are covered with the hide of a calf tightened with gut, or sometimes with rattan strips. For easy carrying, a rattan or gut handle is woven into the top of the bulge, and the drum is permanently attached to a wooden stand in a horizontal position. The *sampho* has a length of about 49 centimeters and a height (including its permanently attached stand) of 50 centimeters. At the center bulge, the drum is about 35 centimeters in diameter, the larger head 28 centimeters, and the smaller 25.

The most important drum in Khmer music, the *sampho* is closely associated with the *pinn peat,* in fact as its leader. It is equally important for accompanying the solo playing of an oboe in freestyle-boxing pieces and "*Salauma,*" a tune used for the actions of fighting. The *sampho* has a variety of rhythmic patterns appropriate to its function. When used in an ensemble without dancing, it plays a fixed eight-beat cycle in *muoy choan* (the first-level rhythmic pattern) or a sixteen-beat cycle in *pi choan* (the second-level rhythmic pattern). When accompanying a dance or a *sbek* (shadow-play) performance, it uses a special pattern (*laim* 'dance'), specific to the piece it accompanies.

Beyond its leading role and uniquely among Khmer instruments, the *sampho* is considered by Khmer musicians to be sacred and spiritual. According to Khmer belief, the membranes can be attached only on a Thursday that is a *guru* day. As part of this process, a ceremony is conducted and offerings are made to Preah Pisnukar, a spiritual architect and god of construction, asking for blessing and good sound (Pich 1970:30). Known for centuries from its carved depictions at various Angkorean temples, it maintains both ritualistic and entertainment roles to this day.

The player uses both hands to strike the heads of a *sampho*. Because the drum must produce both lower and higher tones, one head is larger than the other. The heads, their centers painted black, are tuned with a paste (*bay sampho* 'rice for *sampho*') that is a mixture of cooked rice mashed with ashes from burned branches of palm or coconut midribs, but new bread will also do. The thicker and heavier the paste, the slower the vibration of the parchment and the deeper the tone.

The *sampho* controls the tempo and regulates the preestablished rhythmic cycles. Therefore, it is considered the leading instrument in the *pinn peat* and the instrument of the teacher (*krou*). Surprisingly, many Khmer musicians regard it as a simple instrument, easy to play, and thus neglect it. This attitude sometimes results in the oversimplification of rhythmic patterns, or even in the use of just one simple rhythmic pattern for almost every piece. Consequently, the *sampho* has tended to lose its proper role and become an accompanying instrument.

The *thaun* is a single-headed, goblet-shaped drum similar to the *skor arakk,* but it has a shallower head area and a slimmer body. Like the *skor arakk*, its body is made of clay or wood, and its head is made of the hide of a calf, or of goatskin or snakeskin, laced to the body by leather thongs, rattan strips, or nylon cord. Its primary use is in *mohori,* where it is paired with the *rumanea*. In performance, the player lays the drum horizontally on his lap and strikes it softly with bare right-hand fingers, playing an interlocking pattern with the *rumanea.*

The *rumanea* is a single-headed, shallow, wooden frame drum with a calfskin membrane nailed to the body. Like the *thaun,* with which it is paired, its primary use is in the *mohori.* The player holds it vertically on his left leg, with the *thaun* on the lap, and strikes its head softly with bare left-hand fingers.

Mirliton

The mirliton (*slekk*) is a simple, natural leaf of a tree. The player selects a leaf that is stiff and thick enough to vibrate freely—especially the leaves of *lumpuoh*, *puoch*, or *kravann* trees. The player picks a leaf, folds it along its length, places it between his lips, and blows over the folded edge. Such temporary instruments can be used in the wedding ensemble (*vung phleng kar*), but they are most often played solo.

Chordophones

Harp

The *pinn*, an angular harp prominent in Cambodia during the Angkor period, is known only from carvings on the walls of several temples around Angkor (figure 1). It is not known today, nor has it been revived; nevertheless, the Khmer court-music ensemble (*pinn peat*) takes its name from it. The word *pinn* is likely related to the Sanskrit *vīṇā*, which may have derived from the Egyptian *vin* (Sachs 1940:224).

Zithers

Khmer musicians consider the *khse muoy* (also *say diev,* both terms meaning 'string one' or 'one string') one of the oldest musical instruments in Cambodia. The resonator is half of a round, dried gourd, the open side of which is placed against the player's chest. The body-fingerboard, a stick about 90 centimeters long, is securely attached with wire to the round side of the gourd. A single string of steel or brass runs along the fingerboard from a carving at the lower end to a tuning peg at the upper end. To pluck the string, the player wears a metal or bronze plectrum on his index finger, or more frequently, on his middle finger. The *khse muoy* is used mainly in traditional *arakk* and *kar* ensembles.

The *krapeu,* also known as *takhe*, *takkhe*, and *charakhe*, is a three-stringed zither (figure 5). This instrument is zoomorphic, constructed in an abstract shape of a crocodile (*krapeu*). The other terms suggest a Thai origin, for Thai *charakhe* means 'crocodile', but whether *takhe* and *takkhe* mean the same or refer to a large lizard called *thukay* is uncertain. Beneath the resonator box are three or five legs to raise the instrument off the floor and permit its sound to project. Along the neck are twelve high, graduated frets of ivory, bone, bamboo, or wood. There are three strings, the highest one (*khse ek*) made of gut or nylon, the middle one (*khse kor*) also made of gut or nylon, and the lowest (*khse bantor*) made of metal. The melody, restricted to the upper two strings, is played by a plectrum made of ivory, bone, animal horn, or wood, tied to the player's index or middle finger. The third (lowest) string serves as a drone.

The *khimm* is a small hammered zither with two rows of bridges, played with two lightweight beaters. It is believed that the Khmer *khimm* was brought to Cambodia by the Chinese, who used it in their theater ensembles. In Cambodia, it was modified for use in the Khmer *basakk* theater. The *basakk* ensemble uses two sizes of *khimm*: high pitched (*khimm tauch*) and low pitched (*khimm thomm*). While the former plays the melody line, the latter plays a partly harmonic bass version. It is also commonly used in the *mohori* and *kar* ensembles.

The *tror khmer*, also known as *tror khse bey* 'three-stringed fiddle', is among the oldest of Khmer musical instruments. Its body is made from the dried shell of a coconut, cut in thirds and covered with a snakeskin resonator.

FIGURE 5 A zither (*krapeu*), one of a handful of palace instruments that survived the Khmer Rouge reign of terror. Photo by Terry E. Miller, 1988.

Lutes

The term *tror* is generic for bowed lutes, including spike fiddles. Some types of *tror* may derive from Chinese bowed lutes (*hu*), which came to Cambodia at the turn of the twentieth century with the Chinese theater called *hi* (Pich 1970:21). Khmer musicians have adopted and modified them into Khmer instruments and use them in several ensembles, including the *arakk*, the *kar*, the *mohori*, the *yike*, the *ayai*, and the *basakk*.

The *tror Khmer*, also known as *tror khse bey* 'three-stringed fiddle', is among the oldest of Khmer musical instruments. Its body is made from the dried shell of a coconut, cut in thirds and covered with a snakeskin resonator. It is smaller than its nearest relative, the Thai *saw sam sai*, and the Javanese rebab, whose body is wood, not coconut. The *tror Khmer* is used principally in the *arakk* and *kar* ensembles. Its bow is detached, in contrast to two-stringed Khmer fiddles, which place the hairs of the bow between their strings. The bow (*chhak*) is made of bamboo or wood, with horsehair or nylon (*say*). Like Western players of stringed instruments, Khmer musicians put rosin on their bows. The tuning of this instrument (from low to high) is A–D–G (approximate tempered pitches).

The *tror chhe*, also known as *tror ek*, is a two-stringed fiddle with the hairs of the bow passing between the strings. Its cylindrical resonator is made of bamboo, wood, or ivory, with a snakeskin resonator on the front. The two strings (*khse ek* 'higher' and *khse kor* 'lower') are made of metal and tuned in perfect fifths (D–A). Among the fiddles, the *tror chhe* is the highest in pitch. Its name is thought to be onomatopoeic.

The *tror so tauch* is a two-stringed fiddle similar to the *tror chhe,* but larger and tuned G–D. It is used in the *arakk,* the *kar,* the *mohori,* and the *ayai* ensembles as the lead instrument.

The *tror so thomm* is yet larger than the *tror so tauch*, and its tuning is D–A. Its use is similar to that of the *tror so tauch,* except that it does not play a leading role.

The *tror ou* is a low-pitched, two-stringed fiddle that differs from the previous three in that its strings are made of gut, nylon, or metal, its resonator is the shell of a coconut, with a calfskin resonator, and it is tuned C–G. Some resonator boxes have beautiful designs carved into the back.

The *tror ou chamhieng* is a two-stringed fiddle with a turtleshell body. This instrument is used exclusively by Cham people living in Cambodia.

Two other fiddles (*tror kandal* or *tror thomm* 'large fiddle') are used exclusively at the Royal University of Fine Arts. The *tror kandal* is tuned G–D, but the *tror thomm* is tuned D–A. These instruments were recently developed at the university as an experiment and to extend ensemble tessitura downward. Consequently, they are unknown outside the university.

The *chapey dang veng* is a lute with a long neck which curves backward at the top (figure 6). The body of the resonator (*snauk*) is made of a specific wood called *raing*, the fingerboard (*dang*) is made of *krasaing*, the resonator cover (*santeah*) is a thin piece of wood called *khtum*, the bridge (*kingkuok*) is of *thnung*, and the frets are carved from bone. There are either two strings or two courses of two strings, each made of gut or nylon. The Khmer have a saying regarding this instrument:

Snauk raing,	The resonator box made of *raing,*
dang krasaing,	the fingerboard made of *krasaing,*
santeah khtum,	the piece of thin wood made of *khtum,*
kingkuok thnung,	the bridge made of *thnung,*
khtung chha-oeung.	the frets made of bones.

Though the *chapey dang veng* is used in the older forms of the *arakk* and *kar,* it is most commonly used in epic singing (*chrieng chapey*), in which the singer accompanies himself on this instrument.

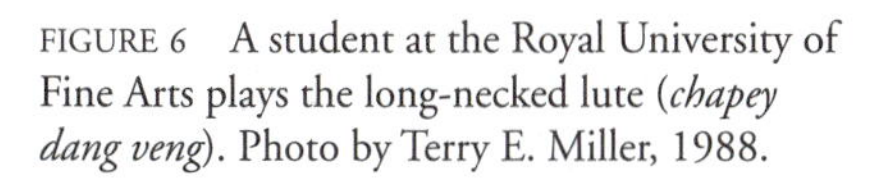
FIGURE 6 A student at the Royal University of Fine Arts plays the long-necked lute (*chapey dang veng*). Photo by Terry E. Miller, 1988.

Aerophones

Flutes

The *khloy* is an end-blown duct flute made of bamboo, wood, plastic, or metal, used in the *mohori* and *kar* or as a solo instrument. It has two sizes: smaller, higher-pitched (*khloy ek*) and larger, lower-pitched (*khloy thomm*). Each normally has six holes for fingers and one hole for a thumb, but some have seven holes for fingers and others have no hole for a thumb. A hole drilled between the highest hole and the duct opening may be covered with a membrane made of rice paper or bamboo. When used, it provides a bright, slightly buzzy timbre. Most Khmer players of aerophones, including those who play the *khloy,* master circular breathing, which enables them to produce a continuously flowing melody. Students learn this technique early in their study, soon after acquiring their instruments.

Reeds

The *sneng* is an aerophone made of the horn of a buffalo or an ox. Though found in different sizes, most are about 39 centimeters long. The horn is open at both ends, which serve as holes for fingering. At about the middle of the horn is a rectangular hole, over which a bamboo free reed is placed and sealed with beeswax. The player inhales and exhales into this hole. The *sneng* plays two notes a perfect fourth apart—the smallest range of all Khmer wind instruments. It is used by keepers of cattle, firewood collectors, and bee collectors, especially to signal the time for a meal or for returning to the village. It is most commonly used both during elephant-hunting expeditions and for the *arakk* ceremony, playing the piece "*Bangkauk Sneng,*" which invites a spirit to come and preside at the ceremony.

The *ploy*, also called *m'baut,* is a free-reed mouth organ with a gourd wind chest, found among upland Mon-Khmer speakers in Boutoy District, Mondulkiri Province, and among the Por and Kuoy in Kampong Chhnang, Pursat, and Siem Reap provinces. The number of bamboo pipes varies from five to seven. Each pipe, which pierces the bottom of a dried gourd wind chest, has one hole for fingers and a free reed, and sounds when a player inhales or exhales through the hole for blowing and covers the hole for fingering. Similar instruments are found in the mountains straddling the borders of Cambodia, Laos, and Vietnam.

The *pey pork* is a side-blown pipe with a bronze free reed placed over a hole about 2 centimeters from the upper end (figure 7). The tube is of wood or bamboo (*pork*); the term *pey* denotes several types of reed instruments. The player places the mouth over the section with the reed and holds the instrument almost horizontally. The seven holes for fingers and the one hole for a thumb produce seven pitches in an octave with a range of slightly more than an octave. The *pey pork* is used in the *arakk* ensemble to play, among others, the piece "*Surin*" to invite a spirit to come to the ceremony. It is mostly used as a solo instrument, or to accompany a vocalist.

The *ken*, a free-reed mouth organ in raft form, closely associated with lowland Lao speakers in Laos and northeast Thailand, is also found in northwestern Cambodia, an area once part of the Lao principality of Champassak [see LAOS and THAILAND]. In Cambodia, the *ken* is used to accompany a regional folk dance called by the same name.

The *pey prabauh* (also known as *pey a*) has a wood or bamboo body about 30 centimeters long (figure 8). The double reed (*loam, andat*), nearly 8 centimeters long and positioned into the upper end of the body, is made of an aquatic plant called *prabauh,* from which the instrument takes its name. At the base, the reed is rounded to fit into the body, and at the upper end (where it is played), it is shaved thin to

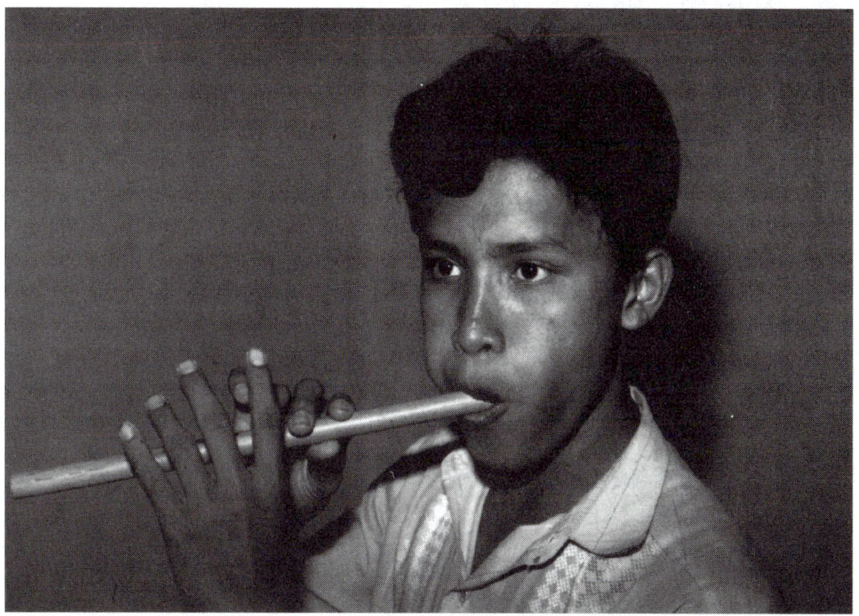

FIGURE 7 A Royal University of Fine Arts student plays a free-reed pipe (*pey pork*). Photo by Terry E. Miller, 1988.

FIGURE 8 A Royal University of Fine Arts student plays a double-reed pipe (*pey prabauh*). Photo by Terry E. Miller, 1988.

vibrate. Along the body is one membrane-covered hole and seven holes for fingering. The *pey prabauh* is principally used in the *arakk* and *kar* ensembles, where it functions as the standard by which the other instruments are tuned. In structure, it resembles the Chinese *guan*, the Korean *piri*, and the Japanese *hichiriki*.

The *sralai* is a quadruple-reed oboe with a slightly bulging body. Early iconographical evidence of it is seen in bas-relief carvings at Angkor. It is of central importance in *pinn peat,* the ensemble that accompanies court dances, masked plays, shadow plays, religious ceremonies, and boxing matches. It comes in two sizes: small (*sralai tauch*), and large (*sralai thomm*). There is also a *sralai* with a flared bell (*sralai klang khek,* of Javanese origin).

The body is made of various hardwoods (*kakaor, beng, neang nuon*) or ivory. The maker is conscientious about the wood he uses. When cutting a tree, he carefully distinguishes the top from the bottom, because constructing an instrument upside down would make it hard to blow; the upper end (with the reed) must be the top end of the tree.

The bodies of the *sralai tauch* and *sralai thomm* are carved with a bulge at the center and slight flaring at both ends. The inside is hollowed in a slightly conical shape. Sixteen pairs of rings are carved around the bulge, between which six holes for fingering are bored—four in one group on the upper end, two in another on the lower end—separated by a noticeable space. These rings add beauty and help prevent the fingers from slipping. The space between the two groups of holes also serves as a standard of measurement for the length of the reed. The *sralai tauch* varies in length from 31 to 33 centimeters, each end having a diameter of about 3 to 4 centimeters. The length of the *sralai thomm* varies from 40 to 42 centimeters, each end having a diameter of about 4 centimeters.

The reed has two parts: the tube and the tongues. The tube, made of bronze, brass, or sometimes silver, is tapered so that the end that fits into the top of the oboe is a little larger than the other end, to which the tongues are fastened. This lower (larger) end is also wound with thread for a tight fit when inserted into the instrument. The reed is made of the leaf of a palm, cut into four small tongues and fastened to the tube with thread. The length of the *sralai tauch* reed is about 5.5 centimeters, and the length of the *sralai thomm* reed is about 7 centimeters. When

sralai klang khek Small wood or ivory double reed with flared bell

saing Conch shell trumpet

Angkor Vat Temple-city in Cambodia, center of ancient Khmer civilization

aerophone Instrument in which vibrating air produces sound

played, the entire reed (tube and tongue) is placed in the mouth, with the lips resting against the oboe.

A complete *pinn peat* includes both a *sralai tauch* and a *sralai thomm*. This orchestration is more common in villages and at the Royal University of Fine Arts for accompanying masked plays and shadow plays; at the palace, only the *sralai thomm* is used. Sometimes it is replaced by a duct flute. If both sizes are used, the *sralai tauch* takes all solos, but when only one *sralai* is needed, the *sralai thomm* is preferred over the *sralai tauch,* for its range.

Sralai klang khek means 'oboe used in the *klang khek* [funeral] ensemble', but it is also called Javanese oboe (*sralai chvea*) and Javanese wind instrument (*pey chvea*). Its body, made of either wood or ivory, is carved from one or two pieces. The reed resembles those of the *sralai tauch* and the *sralai thomm*, and there are seven holes for fingers and one for a thumb. The *sralai klang khek* is most often used in funeral and boxing ensembles.

Trumpets

The conch (*saing*) is perhaps the oldest wind instrument in Cambodia. Used only by Brahmin priests, it served at certain court functions to signal the sovereign's arrival. In Thailand, "Brahmin priests still serve . . . at certain court functions and are a curious survival in a Buddhist court. They originally came to Ayuthaya from Angkor after the Thai conquest of the Khmer capital, and the Ayuthayan kings, seeking to take over the mantle of the Khmer empire and legitimize their claims to power, took over the rites as well" (Smithies 1971:72). The *saing* produces only a single pitch.

A theoretical description of Khmer music

Discussing Khmer classical music in English from technical and theoretical viewpoints requires a kind of translation that can easily distort what Khmer musicians understand. Khmer musicians articulate few of the elements Western scholars normally study, and therefore there is no way to verify a description in Western terms and concepts. Khmer musicians transmit their music by rote, with minimal discussion. Each understands what he or she does in a phenomenological way, but not within the context of a general theory. Khmer musicians do not need music notation or isolated scales, these requiring a scholar who wishes to communicate such matters to people outside the tradition. Consequently, there is some friction between the writer's Khmer (emic) view and his Western-trained, ethnomusicological (etic) view.

System of tuning

Perhaps the most troublesome issue is tuning, for this forms the basis of the system. Since Khmer classical music has received less investigation than Thai classical music, and the two traditions are superficially similar, it has been assumed that what is true of Thai music is also true of Khmer music. In fact, this is not the case (Miller and Sam 1995).

The conclusion that both Thai and Khmer tunings consist of seven equidistant pitches is based on a faulty understanding of the tradition. Though fixed-pitch instruments—primarily xylophones, metallophones, and tuned gongs—may be tuned equidistantly (171.4 cents), this practice is a compromise to allow for playing pieces centered on different pitches. This functional equidistance may be true of Thai music, but not of Khmer music, for Khmer musicians of a given ensemble play primarily at only one level of pitch. Because equidistance is neither necessary nor desired, there is no problem with the Khmer system of tuning being nonequidistant. Such nonequidistance is easily heard with reference to aerophones, chordophones, and the voice, but their intervals are difficult to measure. Because of this, scholars typically measured the xylophones, metallophones, and tuned gongs as references, which resulted in overgeneralizations.

Most Southeast Asian aerophones (those of the Khmer in particular) produce varied intervals, closer to Western semitones and tones than the generally supposed equal interval. This point is reinforced by the fact that Khmer musicians of a given ensemble must begin and end a piece on predetermined pitches, for starting and ending on another would produce not an equal transposition of the original pitch level but a different mode.

Khmer tuning is done according to aesthetic preference, but basing the intervals on the ensemble aerophone is widely practiced (figure 9). When this changes, so does the tuning. How musicians tune their instruments is important in the study of the system of tuning. Though Khmer musicians tune their instruments by ear, the concept of perfect fifth and octave is constant. Pitches between these are adjusted to suit the overall context of the music being played. Some musicians continue to retune their instruments time and time again before concerts, after trying out a given piece. In short, one leader's xylophone will likely exhibit a tuning different from another's. Each leader imposes his or her tuning on the ensemble. Khmer vocalists also do not sing equidistant intervals. As a result, traditional Khmer music has been played on Western instruments with a degree of satisfaction, using a modern music ensemble called modern *mohori* (*mohori samai*). Except for the *thaun-rumanea* pair of drums, this ensemble uses all Western instruments (flute, violin, banjo, mandolin, guitar, accordion, organ, violoncello) to play traditional Khmer music. Of these instruments, only the violin and violoncello allow for the use of a non-Western tuning pattern.

It is hard to generalize about Khmer tuning, as each instrument and ensemble has to be individually measured, and one must discard notions pertaining to musics

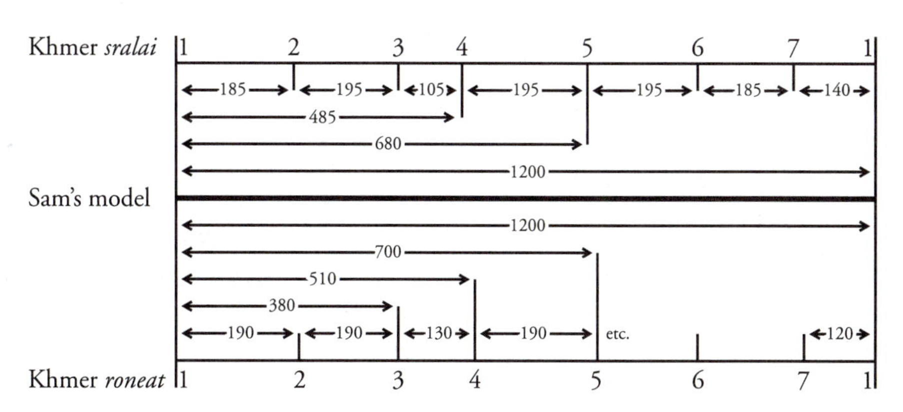

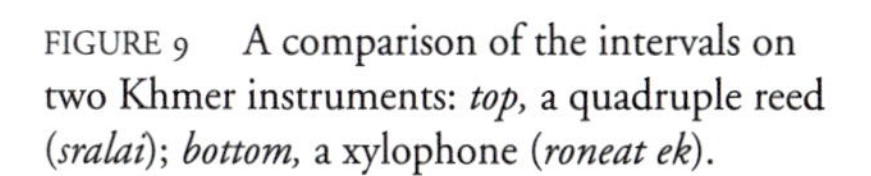
FIGURE 9 A comparison of the intervals on two Khmer instruments: *top,* a quadruple reed (*sralai*); *bottom,* a xylophone (*roneat ek*).

of other cultures while looking at Khmer music. From the outside, some musical aspects and approaches might appear the same, but from the inside, they are quite different. These include the Thai *thao* and Khmer *thav*, the Thai-Khmer metrical levels (*chan dio / muoy choan, song chan / pi choan, sam chan / bey choan*), and the way Thai, Laotian, and Khmer musicians tune their instruments.

Khmer music compromises between the ideal and the actual. In terms of tuning, *the ideal* is expressed in an individual tuner's tuning of a given instrument, as when using perfect fifths and octaves, whereas *the actual* is the result of many individually tuned instruments and the resulting blended sound of the ensemble. This kind of compromise occurs in performance, the construction of instruments, and their tuning. The intervals produced by the fixed-pitch percussion, the winds, and vocalists are divergent, but in making music they all blend and compromise with one another to produce a sound that is uniquely Khmer.

Scale, key, mode

Scale

The term *scale* normally denotes the presentation of the tonal material of a composition or group of related compositions in ascending and descending order. These pitches are drawn from the total system of tuning, and are consequently fewer in number. On the concept of scale, there are no written sources by Khmer musicians. Not surprisingly, then, there is no Khmer term for "scale." *Musique Khmère,* a book published in French by teachers at the Royal University of Fine Arts, shows several scales, but does not discuss them; elsewhere, it mentions pentatonic and heptatonic scales, but again with no discussion. Daniélou (1957) discussed Khmer scales, but tried to explain them in terms of Indian music without providing justification for this claim: he believed four things: (1) the Khmer borrowed the *ghandhara-grama* scale from India; (2) the Khmer have a semitone scale without the fifth and augmented fourth; (3) the Khmer borrowed the pentatonic scale from the Chinese; (4) and the Khmer scale is a tempered heptatonic one because the system of tuning is. For Daniélou, the pentatonic scale was necessarily Chinese, whereas the heptatonic scale may possibly have been Khmer, replacing the pentatonic one. He divided Khmer compositions into "ancient" and "traditional." The oldest stratum of pieces was based on an ancient scale, later replaced by the Chinese pentatonic scale. Therefore, there were three scales—ancient (Khmer, the oldest), pentatonic (Chinese), and heptatonic (apparently Khmer). These conclusions cannot be taken seriously because there is little or no evidence to support them.

Surviving music reveals that there are two scales in Khmer music: one pentatonic (or more precisely, anhemitonic pentatonic, consisting of five pitches devoid of semitones) and one heptatonic (having seven pitches with approximate semitones and tones).

Key

The word *key* as applied to Khmer music refers to centering music on a given xylophone or metallophone bar, a given gong, or a given aerophone fingering, not to the concept of key in the Western sense. The Western pitch G, used as the normal "key" of the *pinn peat,* refers to bar 6 on the *roneat* and gong 6 on the *korng* (counting from top to bottom, highest to lowest). In the *mohori* ensemble, the general pitch is C. Consequently, Khmer musicians of a given ensemble play pieces only at the designated level.

The traits of the Khmer scalar system can be summarized as follows:

1. The availability of pentatonic and heptatonic scales derives from the tuning of Khmer instruments.
2. The central pitch of a scale remains constant; for *pinn peat,* it is G; for *mohori,* it is C (or vocal range of vocalists—male or female).
3. Pentatonic and heptatonic scales have differing numbers of fundamental pitches used in a given piece—five pitches in the former and seven in the latter. The structure of the anhemitonic pentatonic scale can be expressed as 1–2–3–5–6–8 or G–A–B–D–E–G, with the fourth and seventh degrees available as passing tones. The structure of the heptatonic scale makes all seven pitches equally important.
4. Since there are only two types of Khmer scales, there are only two distinct intervallic structures. That of the pentatonic is M2–M2–m3–M2–m3, and that of the heptatonic is M2–M2–m2–M2–M2–M2–m2.
5. Since the tuning is nonequidistant, the 1–2–3–5–6–8 pattern, for instance, can begin only on a single note or key, and not all five or seven without changing the interval set. More precisely, *pinn peat* musicians traditionally play pieces only in G. If one changes the central pitch, the scale is different because the intervals are changed. Beginning a pentatonic scale on A would result in an intervallic structure of M2–m2–M3–M2–m3, which would sound wrong.

Partly because all *pinn peat* music is played in what sounds like the G scale, Khmer pieces sound the same to many listeners. However, some pieces, such as "*Lo*" and "*Rev*" switch tonal levels, or (to use harmonic language) modulate. In Khmer music, this phenomenon, known to ethnomusicologists as metabole, is simple (figure 10). First, it does not require the harmonic preparation and resolution typical of Western modulation. Second, it does not shift key or tonality, but simply jumps to a new tonal level, usually a fourth or fifth above or below the original level. Third, a piece played at the new level of pitch is perceived to be the same as one played at the previous level in terms of length, tonal progressions, and structure, except that instrumental ranges might require a different melodic motion, usually involving octave displacements. Fourth, metabole in Khmer music occurs only after a piece has completed a full cycle.

There is no standard pitch in Cambodia, so instruments are not necessarily built at the same level. The "key" of G, the central pitch of *pinn peat* music, is referenced to a certain bar of the xylophone or the gong, or to the fingering on an aerophone. It is possible to encounter two ensembles tuned a tone apart, but this tuning does not

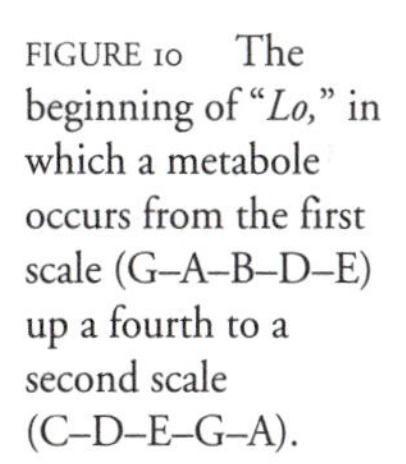
FIGURE 10 The beginning of "*Lo,*" in which a metabole occurs from the first scale (G–A–B–D–E) up a fourth to a second scale (C–D–E–G–A).

Khmer musicians do not find it necessary to talk about their music. For them, it is more important to play well and have a large repertoire. When Khmer musicians are learning a piece, their teachers tell them exactly how to play it, and they do not ask why.

mean that one ensemble is being played in G and the other in, say, A. In transcribing the music, one cannot account for this difference by transcribing the music of the first ensemble in G and the other in A, for A means a different central tone, a different set of intervals, a different fingering for the aerophone. Indeed, the "standard" pitch (G) varies a great deal from one part of the country to another, so that G in one place may actually be higher than A in another. The same is true of the *mohori,* whose central tone (C) can vary by at least a tone. Therefore, a given pitch named by a Western letter is relative, and is not equivalent to the parallel Western tone.

Mode

Whereas the term *scale* is a conceptual abstraction or reduction based on analysis, the term *mode* or *melody type* denotes a complex of traits related not only to melody, but to actual practice. Mode is the basis for melodic composition, improvisation, and embellishment, consisting of such factors as tonal material, a hierarchy of tones, and typical melodic movement and phrasing. It may include extramusical aspects relative to proper performance context, time, mood, or (as with the Indian raga) even magical powers. As with scale, there is no Khmer term for mode, and Khmer musicians do not verbalize it; yet the concept exists, though transmitted in a nonsystematic manner.

The basis of Khmer modes apparently lies in a set of five, six, or seven tones in a hierarchical system of tonal relationships. The modes neither have names, nor convey articulated feelings (like the modes of, for example, Burma, India, Indonesia, Korea, Thailand, and Vietnam). Khmer modes are based on the same set of tones, but with different finals. The hierarchy in Khmer mode correlates points of rest, final tone, tones at the endings of cycles and phrases, and cadential resolutions, all essential to the identification of mode because they govern the basic structure of a piece.

Mode in *pinn peat* music is difficult to separate from scale, whose central tone is the constant G, to which all finals (including G itself) relate. Mode, therefore, is recognizable according to its final in relationship to the principal tone of the scale. Because modes are based on different finals, they manifest different intervallic structures; each set of intervals is distinctive to a particular mode. Five modes are generated from the pentatonic scale (G–A–B–D–E), and seven are generated from the heptatonic scale (G–A–B–C–D–E–F), each with a different final. Thus, it is theoretically possible to have altogether twelve modes, but in practice there are fewer.

Khmer modes are identified by their final tone, rather than being generated as a set of intervals from the same starting tone, as in classical Indian music. However, Khmer musicians create new modal structures by shifting the tonal emphasis from one tone to another within the same tuning or scale. Consequently, Khmer musicians are careful when starting and ending a piece. If starting on an inappropriate tone, the piece will end on the wrong final, also putting it in the wrong mode, because it affects the intervallic modal structure. Thus the five- and seven-tone scales, when starting and ending on different tones and appearing in different orders, are capable of producing various modes.

Khmer musicians do not find it necessary to talk about their music. For them, it is more important to play well and have a large repertoire. Knowing how to start and end a piece properly (with regard to pitch, ambitus, and level) is much more important than knowing what the scale or mode is. When Khmer musicians are learning a piece, their teachers tell them exactly how to play it, and they do not ask why. They trust their teachers to have the requisite knowledge and experience. The "traditional" way is right, provided one has been properly taught; one need not theorize beyond that. Ethnomusicologists feel an obligation to theorize to find order and logic in Khmer music, but as far as Khmer musicians are concerned, doing this neither makes one a better musician nor does it increase musical knowledge.

For this study, fifty Khmer musical pieces were randomly sampled to find the frequency of the following modes, expressed here in percent:

Mode	Percent
G–A–B–D–E–G	26
G–A–B–C–D–G	2
G–A–B–C–D–E–G	2
G–A–B–C–D–E–F–G	8
D–E–G–A–B–D	14
D–E–F–G–A–B–C–D	10
B–D–E–G–A–B	2
B–C–D–E–F–G–A–B	2
A–B–D–E–G–A	10
A–B–D–E–F–G–A	2
A–B–C–D–E–G–A	8
A–B–C–D–E–F–G–A	2
E–G–A–B–D–E	4
E–F–G–A–B–D–E	6
E–F–G–A–B–C–D–E	2

Texture

Khmer music is melodically based and does not depend on vertical sonorities. Its texture is usually regarded by ethnomusicologists as heterophonic, or as Hood (1982) and Morton (1976) prefer to call it, polyphonically stratified. The linear character of the melody flows according to the scale and mode, but each composed melody has its individual character.

Though specific compositions can be reduced to a generic version (as is presented, for example, in a single-line transcription), in fact, an abstract and underlying structure known to the musicians is more important. Each instrumentalist or vocalist has a characteristic way of realizing this structure, creating a different idiomatic version. Depending on the instrument, the idiom of this structure has specific patterns and a greater or lesser density according to the degree of ornamentation. The development of an intricate melodic line through variation technique not only avoids repetition and monotony, but allows players to exhibit their skills by improvising (figure 11). Beginning players, though, play simpler versions than experienced players.

In a solo rendition, the texture of Khmer music is monophonic, though in the case of xylophones and gong circles numerous octaves, fourths, and fifths produce polyphony that differs completely in function from Western harmony. When many musicians play together, the texture results from the simultaneity of many distinct versions of the same melody. More than one pitch occurs at any given moment, but

Within the cycle, stronger beats are articulated by the *chhep* stroke (symbolized as +), played on the small cymbals, and weaker beats on the *chhing* stroke (indicated by o): o + o +.

FIGURE 11 The first four measures of "*Chinaroeur*" as performed by a singer, with six possible instrumental variations.

these sonorities result more from chance and instrumental idioms than from an intention to play polyphonically.

Beats, rhythms, cycles

Most Khmer compositions are in duple meter, customarily transcribed as 2/4 or 4/4 time. In notation using staffs, accented or strong beats occur at the beginning of a measure. In Western music, phrases can begin either on a downbeat or on an upbeat that leads to a downbeat; thereafter, the same pattern of hierarchical accents (main beat, secondary beat, interior beats, and so on) repeats itself to the end of the phrase or piece. Khmer music, however, is organized in rhythmic or metrical cycles, the last stroke of which is the strongest. These cycles coincide in length with melodic phrases—meaning that Khmer music, like Thai music, appears to be accented at the ends of phrases.

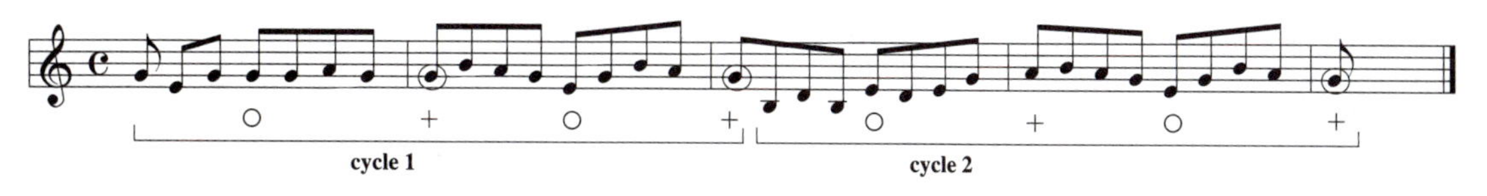

FIGURE 12 Two *chhing* cycles played in relation to a melody, O indicating the unaccented, undamped sound (*chhing*) and + indicating the accented, damped sound (*chhap*).

Within the cycle, stronger beats are articulated by the *chhep* stroke (symbolized as +), played on the small cymbals, and weaker beats on the *chhing* stroke (indicated by o): o + o +. Parallel to both melodic phrase and *chhing* cycle is a cyclic pattern of drumming. The final beat of a cycle does not always coincide with a stressed drumstroke. As in many other Asian musics, Khmer drumstrokes are onomatopoeic: sounds verbalized as *choeung, chapp, ting, tup, teung,* and *theung* are obtained by striking the head of the drum at different places and with different strokes, closed or open. Though the last stroke of the cycle is the most stressed and the melodic tone at that point the most important structurally, musicians do not accentuate this fact by playing louder or harder. Drums also serve as leaders in Khmer music ensembles, setting tempi and keeping time. Yet to many Khmer musicians, drums are only supportive of other pitched instruments and are therefore secondary. Consequently, few Khmer musicians make the drum their main instrument of study.

It is important to understand that the tones falling at the end of each cycle—that is, on its strongest beat—together constitute the skeletal or abstract form of a melody, and pitches falling on secondary beats begin to flesh out the melody. The final beats are also important to the texture, for here all instruments reunite on a unison or an octave. Between these points, musicians have greater latitude to fill in according to the scale or mode and the idiom of the instrument.

Because a melodic phrase ends on a strong beat, the phrase must begin on a weak beat, similar to an upbeat in Western music. This requirement can be easily seen in transcriptions on staffs (figure 12).

Oral tradition, in the Khmer musical context, lends itself to flexibility, variability, and embellishment. Musicians in an ensemble have in mind a collective melody, which no one person plays, more like the generic melody mentioned above than the abstracted one based on skeletal tones. The collective melody serves as a guideline for the musicians to follow from beginning to end, and it holds them together as an ensemble. An analogy to it would be the network of roads on a map, potentially directing a band of travelers to a common destination. Each traveler is free to choose a route, but because musical playing in ensembles is a collective process, the musicians—the travelers—must periodically meet at agreed-on locations before taking off again. In this manner, the travelers keep together as a band. Only with the collective melody can a Khmer ensemble realize the common goal of playing a composition.

Levels of tempo

Khmer music has three kinds of cycles, differentiated by length but each having four strokes on the *chhing*. The first level (*muoy choan*) is half the length of the second (*pi choan*), which in turn is half the length of the third (*bey choan*). If a first-level phrase lasts four measures, a second-level phrase lasts eight, and a third-level phrase lasts sixteen (figure 13).

Though the intervals between *chhing* strokes and their coincidental structural tones vary, the musicians maintain melodic activity, weaving distinctive phrases around the structural tones. Obviously, first-level melodies have less filling in than third-level ones (figure 14).

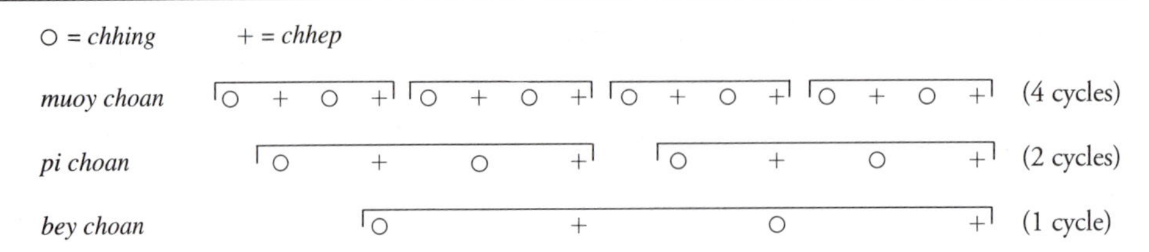

FIGURE 13 The *chhing* strokes for the three levels of tempo: *muoy choan, pi choan*, and *bey choan.*

FIGURE 14 The first two measures of each tempo of "*Chvea Srok Mon,*" showing melodic relationships.

The drum or drums appropriate to a particular ensemble or genre execute a specific pattern associated with the prescribed metrical level (*choan*). There are two classes of rhythmic patterns for the *sampho*, probably the most important drum in the *pinn peat:* (1) patterns associated with the three tempo levels, and (2) pieces and patterns known as music for drumming (*phleng skor*) or music for dancing (*phleng laim*), usually used with dance and theater pieces. Each of these pieces has its own cyclic pattern.

Similarly, pieces in the Khmer repertoire are grouped according to the three tempo levels, and according to *laim* and *skor*. They include "*Toch Yum Muoy Choan,*" "*Toch Yum Pi Choan,*" "*Chvea Srokk Mon Bey Choan,*" and "*Prathomm.*" Pieces in a given group, such as "*Toch Yum Pi Choan,*" must be accompanied by the *pi choan* drum pattern because the melody was constructed using that length cycle.

Rhythm

People who listen to Khmer music may notice a tendency for musicians to render melodies in a kind of long-short, nearly dotted rhythm, while Thai music is even in rhythm. This trait clearly distinguishes Khmer music from Thai, though many other aspects appear similar or the same. As one moves westward toward Thailand, this rhythmic feature becomes less and less pronounced; musicians from Siem Reap, for example, play nearly even rhythms.

Court music, dance, and theater

Until Western ideas and practices came to Cambodia, music graced nonmusical contexts, be they spiritual or nuptial ceremonies, boxing, the shaving of hair, or ordination. It was seldom that music, with the exception of *mohori*, was rendered merely for the sake of listening. Music was intended primarily to accompany dance and theater performances and national and religious ceremonies.

Ensembles and genres

Vung phleng pinn peat

The *vung phleng pinn peat* is the main court ensemble. Besides playing music alone, it accompanies court dance, masked plays, shadow plays, and religious ceremonies. Out of the traditional context (as in concert halls), it can perform alone, without an extra-musical context. It is thought to be more than one thousand years old because reliefs of its instruments—oboes, gongs, cymbals, drums—-were carved in stone at Angkor Vat.

TRACK 3

Considered to have the loudest sonorities of all Khmer ensembles, its full instrumentation includes two oboes (*sralai tauch* and *sralai thomm*), two xylophones (*roneat ek* and *roneat thung*), one metallophone (*roneat dek*), two gong circles (*korng tauch* and *korng thomm*), one pair of small cymbals (*chhing*), two drums (*skor thomm* and *sampho*), and vocalists (*naek chrieng*). A small *pinn peat* consists only of the low-pitched oboe, the high-pitched xylophone, the low-pitched circular frame gong, one drum, one pair of small cymbals, and vocalists.

The *pinn peat* repertoire is called drum music or dance music. It has been called action tunes: each tune, with its prescribed drum pattern, accompanies a particular action on stage, executed by a dancer, an actor or actress, or a puppeteer. "*Punhea Doeur*" is for a human march, "*Prathomm*" is for monkey actions, "*Krao Nak*" is for monkeys marching into battle, "*Krao Nai*" is for demons going into battle, "*Phlekk*" is for the movements of birds, "*Lo*" is for floating on water, "*Cheut Chapp*" is for combat, and "*Aut*" is for expressing grief. When there is no action (as in religious ceremonies), the repertoire is treated the same as when it is used for dance or theater performances. Because this ensemble is the basis for Khmer classical music, its repertoire and traits are discussed at greater length elsewhere in this article (figure 15).

FIGURE 15 In the foreground, a *pinn peat* with two female singers accompanies dance in the smaller dance pavilion at the palace. Photo by Terry E. Miller, 1988.

Vung phleng mohori

The term *mohori* denotes both the ensemble and its repertoire (figure 16). Its origin and history are unclear. Morton (1976:102) documented the existence of a Thai cognate, *mahori,* at least as early as the Ayuthaya Period (1300s to 1700s), though Prince Damrong (1931:3) had asserted that the Thai *mahori* was of Khmer origin. The Khmer word *mohori,* more generally, is the name of a bird. With reference to music, it denotes a large ensemble composed of many kinds of instruments, but today it is applied more specifically to a small ensemble of wind, stringed, and percussion instruments, whose ideal instrumentation is high-pitched xylophone (*roneat ek*), low-pitched xylophone (*roneat thung*), duct or fipple flute (*khloy*), high-pitched two-stringed fiddle (*tror chhe*), medium-high-pitched two-stringed fiddle (*tror so tauch*), medium-low-pitched two-stringed fiddle (*tror so thomm*), low-pitched two-stringed fiddle (*tror ou*), three-stringed zither (*krapeu*), hammered dulcimer (*khimm*), small cymbals (*chhing*), and two-piece set of drums (*thaun-rumanea*). In practice, the instrumentation varies from ensemble to ensemble, depending on patronage and ownership. The *mohori* of the Royal University of Fine Arts in Phnom Penh, for instance, has many players because it is patronized by the state and can afford to employ many musicians. In its performances, instruments are doubled, tripled, and even quadrupled. Sixteen instruments constituted the *mohori* of the Royal Palace in Phnom Penh: *roneat ek, roneat thung, korng tauch, korng thomm, tror Khmer, tror ou, tror chhe, khloy, skor arakk, chapey dang veng, krapeu ek, krapeu thung* (now obsolete), *thaun, krapp, chhing,* and *rumanea* (Pich 1970:4).

Mohori music has a lighter character than *pinn peat* music. Its repertoire includes lullabies, songs of love, sentimental pieces, and descriptive or narrative pieces.

FIGURE 16 A *mohori* ensemble. Photo by Sam-Ang Sam.

Other Khmer music ensembles (such as the *arakk*, *kar,* and *pinn peat*) function in religious contexts, but the *mohori* functions in secular contexts. It is played at banquets, accompanies a *mohori* play, and performs for folk dances of recent origin—the bamboo clappers' dance (*robaim krapp*), the pestle dance (*robaim angre*), and the harvest dance (*robaim chraut srauv*). It may also be heard in the evening after dinner, merely for entertainment and self-enjoyment. At such times, it is often called concert music.

Mohori music has a lighter character than *pinn peat* music. Its repertoire includes lullabies, songs of love, sentimental pieces, and descriptive or narrative pieces. Khmer music is traditionally bound to be played in a certain key, starting on a prescribed bar of a xylophone. The *pinn peat* repertoire is traditionally rendered in what resembles the Western key of G (or *roneat* bar 6, counting from the top), but the *mohori* repertoire is played in the key of C (or *roneat* bar 3). Not being aware of this, and not taking into account the divergent tunings of the various instruments (for example, *tror chhe* is tuned D–A; *tror so tauch,* G–D; *tror so thomm,* D–A; and *tror ou,* C–G), some musicians start a piece in a key other than C, which then makes the playing of some instruments, such as the two-stringed fiddles, difficult.

The usual performance pattern in *mohori* music calls for the vocalist and ensemble to alternate performing each section. The vocalist, accompanied only by drums (*thaun-rumanea*) and cymbals (*chhing*), sings one or two verses, followed by the ensemble playing the same sections of music.

With the introduction of Western culture to Cambodia, a hybrid ensemble and repertoire, known as modern *mohori* (*mohori samai*) or fake or modified *mohori*

(*mohori khlay*), emerged. This ensemble, having its base in cities and large towns, is a mixture of Khmer and Western instruments—*khloy, chhing, thaun-rumanea*, violin, banjo, guitar, keyboard, and accordion. The repertory, of traditional origin, is used for entertainment.

Repertoire

Regarding repertoire, David Steinberg wrote: "About 1939 a scholar estimated that only three hundred melodies were used. . . . Some of these songs undoubtedly are very old, carried orally from one generation to another since there is no Khmer musical notation system" (1959:262). In 1985, however, Chheng Phon, Cambodia's former Minister of Information and Culture, estimated that 1,080 pieces of Khmer music were known. Regardless of which figure is closer to reality, a large number have surely been lost. Some are known only by their names. This situation results from the lack of musicians who could learn them all through oral transmission, the paucity of audio recordings that preserve Khmer music, the absence of musical notations, the presence of a negative attitude toward transcriptions, and the fact that many musicians who knew hundreds of pieces died before they could transmit this legacy to their pupils. Obviously, the Khmer Rouge reign of terror further eroded the potential repertoire. Nevertheless, living Khmer musicians have tried to retain a few hundred pieces.

The Khmer repertoire includes *descriptive* and *sentimental* categories, with typical examples indicated:

Descriptive
- *Omm Touk* 'Row a Boat'
- *Khyall Bakk Cheung Phnum* 'The Wind Blows at the Foot of a Mountain'
- *Krapeu Kantuy Veng* 'Long-Tailed Crocodile'

Sentimental
- *Veacha Pha-Em* 'Sweet Words'
- *Sdech Saok* 'A King Weeps'
- *Ora Sakor* 'Stormy Chest'

The repertoire also includes *national accents,* compositions that have either generic names or titles preceded by nationalities, meaning "in the style of" or "in the accent of" Khmer, Lao, Mon, Phoumea (Burmese), Chvea (Javanese), Chenn (Chinese), Baraing (French), and Arabb (Arabian). These pieces are not compositions borrowed from the cultures in question, but each has a certain character, style, and general manner appropriate to each, at least as understood by Khmer musicians. Besides melodic style, their identity is often signaled by the drum(s) and other percussion; for example, pieces in the *chenn* accent use Chinese percussion. The national accents include these:

Khmer
- *Khmer Pothisatt* 'Khmer from the Province of Pursat'
- *Khmer Krang Phka* 'Khmer String Flowers'
- *Khmer Chraut Srauv* 'Khmer Harvest Rice'
- *Khmer Tbanh* 'Khmer Weave'
- *Khmer Yol Tong* 'Khmer Swing'
- *Khmer Doeur Prey* 'Khmer Walk Through the Forests'

Lao
- *Lao Chhaom Chhan* 'Lao Look at the Moon'
- *Lao Stouch Trey* 'Lao Fish'

Lao Phlomm Slekk 'Lao Blow the Leaf'
Lao Bek Srokk 'Lao Flee the Country'
Mon
Mon Choh Touk 'Mon Board the Boat'
Phoumea
Phoumea Doeur Yoeut 'Burmese Walk Slowly'
Phoumea Ho 'Burmese Whoop'
Phoumea Chakk Kangkep 'Burmese Spear a Frog'
Chvea
Chvea Srokk Mon 'Javanese from Mon Country'
Chenn
Chenn Se 'Chinese Medical Doctor'
Chenn Damm Dek 'Chinese Ironsmith'
Chenn Chha 'Chinese Fry'
Chenn Chapp Changkeh 'Chinese Grab the Waist'
Baraing
Baraing Srav Puor 'French Pull the Robe'
Baraing Nakk Phlett 'French Fan'
Arabb
Arabb Thvay Por 'Arab Wish'

Pieces are often associated with specific occasions or situations within a drama. For instance, only "*Klang Yaun*" is used to accompany a boxing match because of its unique power to put boxers into the right mood and to pace the fight. Similarly, "*Cheut Chapp*" and "*Salauma*" accompany combat scenes during performances of court dances, masked plays, and shadow plays.

To perform a piece properly, musicians must understand it thoroughly. They must know the nature and style of the piece and the instrument (its comfortable range and style), to which they must apply their own skill and creativity. A musician shows his skill by playing his instrument stylistically, providing proper octave displacements conforming to its range in the realization of a melody, and interpreting the piece according to its proper character and sentiment.

A special trait of Khmer music centers on the notion of *bamphley* 'to cheat, to alter, to change'. At the general level, it denotes an action by which a person (magician, goldsmith, seller of meat) cheats his audience or customers. The action of *bamphley* is to make things appear different from their original forms. In music, *bamphley* denotes the action of embellishing a melodic line. A given piece is not rendered the same each time it is played; it can be heard in renditions from the simplest to the most complex. The embellishment stamps the quality of performance as excellent or mediocre.

Many factors contribute to the variations within a rendition: (1) a piece, particularly a short one, is usually repeated several times, and to avoid monotony, the players provide embellishment; (2) musicians have great freedom to interpret their lines; and (3) musicians' creativity and inspiration are different every time they play.

Court dance

History

Dance has been associated with the court of Cambodia for more than a thousand years. An ancient inscription of Vat Kdey Trap (a temple in Ba Phnom, a historical city southeast of Phnom Penh), of the Chenla period (500s to 800s), mentioned the first offering of a dozen sacred dancers to the local sanctuary (Groslier 1965:283). These sacred dancers (*apsara*) were first carved on the walls of Phnom Bakheng Temple during the reign of King Yasovarman (887–900). Some 1,737 such figures carved on the walls of the Angkor temples reflect a period of history in which Khmer performing arts reached their greatest expression. It is also believed that the *apsara* handed down to the Khmer the secrets of choreography (Thiounn 1930:29). The most powerful Khmer sovereign, King Jayavarman VII, is said to have consecrated 615 dancers at the Ta Proum Temple, 1,000 at Preah Khan, and 1,622 at the rest of the temples founded in the Khmer empire (Thierry 1963:361). In the Angkor compound, gigantic masterpieces symbolize the union of celestial and earthly beings. The concept of god-king included dance and dancers as a sacred part of the role of worship. Offerings were made with dancing, chanting, praying, and music.

After the Siamese attack in 1431 and the fall of the Angkor Empire, the Khmer declined in power. The Khmer empire was once again sacked by the Siamese in a second conquest in 1593, which severely weakened the Khmer. Each time the Siamese captured and carried off, to their new kingdom of Ayuthaya, prisoners of war, treasures, important documents, scholars, artists, musicians, and dancers. The period from after the decline of Angkor to the 1700s was obscure with regard to Khmer dance.

A renaissance of the Khmer performing arts, especially dance and music, occurred during the period from 1796 to 1859 during the reign of King Ang Duong. Under his rule, Khmer court dance was revived and restored. Court dancers then included both men and women, but because female dancers could achieve the ideal curves to a greater degree than male dancers, they soon came into ascendancy at the court. King Ang Duong divided the male and female dancers into two groups. This division resulted in the development of two separate forms of dance: female group or court dance and male group or masked play. The men's form came to be supported primarily by the local government or wealthy patrons outside the court, and since those days, it has thrived in the countryside. Khmer court dance is thus regarded as a female tradition. Women perform the roles of king, queen, prince, princess, and demon, and only the role of monkey is played by men. Costumes, headdresses, masks, movements, and gestures identify the characters.

In 1906, under the reign of King Sisowath, a troupe of some one hundred Khmer court dancers toured Europe for the first time. Since Cambodia's independence, Khmer court dance has gained widespread popularity through subsequent tours and participation in international festivals and conferences. It has also spread beyond the palace walls to the Royal University of Fine Arts campus in Phnom Penh. After 1970, court dance underwent change in both image and status.

From 1975 to 1979, there was virtually no dancing in Cambodia. The Khmer Rouge had no interest in preserving and maintaining the art and chose to make Cambodia an absolute agrarian society, devoid of art and religion. In 1979, when the Heng Samrin régime drove out the Khmer Rouge and took control of Cambodia, the priority then was survival, not the restoration of art. Most artists, dancers, and musicians were tired and often physically and mentally ill from the heavy labor, malnutrition, and inhumane punishment imposed by the Khmer Rouge, and thus they could not continue their artistic practice.

The 1980s marked the beginning of a new era in the history of Khmer court dance. Thousands of Khmer had sought refuge in other countries. Many were resettled in Japan, Australia, France, Switzerland, Canada, and the United States; some remain in refugee camps along the Khmer-Thai border. Whether dancers are resettled or in camps, the court-dance tradition is open to the populace. In Khmer communities across the United States, for instance, troupes were formed to offer instruction to

Dancers are trained from age five or six in the royal palace. They strive to realize the concept of extreme curvilinear lines in the hands, arms, torso, and feet—the ultimate goal of Khmer court dance.

FIGURE 17 A court dance is performed in the smaller dance pavilion of the palace. Photo by Terry E. Miller, 1988.

Khmer children. In this environment, court dance can reasonably be viewed as "people's dance" or "traditional Khmer dance."

In 1995, court dance returned to the rehearsal hall, under the close supervision of Her Royal Highness Princess Norodom Buppha Devi and expert teachers Chhieng Proeung, Khan Chea, Sam On Soth, Kong Ros, Theay Em, and others (figure 17). They practice every morning at the Chann Chhaya dance pavilion and go to the northern campus of the Royal University of Fine Arts for classes on general subjects, such as Khmer language and literature and Khmer history and geography.

Training

Dancers are trained from age five or six in the royal palace. Traditionally, they traveled beyond the palace walls only when accompanying the king. They learned a repertoire that includes romances, myths, pure and narrative dance pieces, stories from legends, the *cheadakk* (*jataka*), and regional epics, such as *Preah Chinnavung*, *Preah Chann Korup*, *Preah Vessandar*, and *Reamker*. Dancers strive to realize the concept of extreme curvilinear lines in the hands, arms, torso, and feet—the ultimate goal of Khmer court dance. *Chha banhchauh*, or the "mother of postures," constitutes the 4,500 gestures of pure dance. They are the basis and foundation of all Khmer dance and performing arts involving postures, movements, and gestures. Students undergo strenuous training, perfecting their bodies. Every day, starting in the early morning, they go through routines of bending their waists, elbows, wrists, and knuckles.

There are three types of dance in the court form: pure dance, thematic dance, and dance-drama. Pure dances are composed of those movements in the "mother of postures" or "dance alphabets" that serve as the basis and foundation of Khmer dance. Pure dance movements are also seen in the transitional dance phrases when dances are accompanied by instrumental music. In the performance of court dance, dancers act out plots using the *kbach* language of dance (a system of gestures that denote meanings), all of which is articulated by the chorus during vocal renditions. The performance thus comprises the alternation of vocal and instrumental performances.

The costumes of Khmer court dance include gorgeous masks and headdresses and elaborate jewelry worn on the neck, forearms, wrists, and ankles. The jewelry is made of precious stones, gold, silver, or brass, depending on who the patron is.

Repertoire

The *Reamker (Fame of Preah Ream)*, the Khmer version of the Indian epic *Ramayana*, has long been the principal theme for court dance. It permeates Khmer culture. The culture's classic story, it has served as a main theme for the visual and performing arts in Cambodia for centuries. Its story concerns conflicts between good and evil, involving heroes and heroines. Its monkeys and demons have divine powers that allow them to fly, lift mountains, and so on. Its main characters include these:

1. Preah Ream, the highest-ranking king and most important male character, Sita's husband and Preah Leak's older brother, heir to the throne of Ayuthaya
2. Reap, also known as Tossakann (Ten Arms), King of Lanka, the highest-ranking demon and most important demonic character
3. Kumphaka, Reap's younger brother, the Viceroy of Lanka
4. Hanuman, Preah Ream's ally, the White Monkey, the most important monkey
5. Sita, Preah Ream's wife, the highest-ranking and most important female character
6. Bunhakay, Reap's niece
7. Tossaroth, Preah Ream's father

Normally, only excerpts from the entire story are performed. The favorite ones are

The rearing of Sita by Reap
The exile of Preah Ream, caused by Preah Bat Tossaroth
The encounter of Reap with Preah Ream and Sita
Chasing the golden stag
The abduction of Sita
The battle between Preah Ream and Reap
Hanuman and Suvann Machha, a mermaid
Sita and the ordeal by fire

Music to accompany court dance

Khmer court dance, a compound art, includes dance, mime, song, and music. Music is fixed to fit formalized movements and gestures, which depict each type of action: crying, walking, and flying. Dance is traditionally accompanied by a *pinn peat.* A chorus sings texts that tell the story while dancers express the plot through movements and gestures. The *pinn peat* music sets the tone and mood and provides appropriate background sonorities for the dance, while the chorus reinforces and echoes dance movements, gestures, and dramatic expressions. They unveil the story through texts, describing what is seen on stage. In the time of King Sisowath, there were twenty-four singers, two first female singers, and two readers (Thiounn 1930:51).

The *pinn peat* provides support for court dance by introducing new actions and connecting them; it signals changes of scenes and ends them; it projects the rhythmic patterns for the dancers' footwork. When the music slows down, it gives dancers a feeling of relaxation, and when it accelerates and increases in intensity to the climax, it sharpens the dancers' actions. This is because the *pinn peat* is the one element that links the dance performance by providing cues. *Pinn peat* music also evokes a specific value, feeling, and atmosphere be it a royal cortège, a march of a demonic army to the palace, a battlefield scene, or a happy return of the monkey army, or whether a character is in grief or joy. All this can be recognized through the music in the *phleng laim* or *phleng skor* repertoire, pieces associated with specific actions, scenes, or emotions.

The *pinn peat* functions in specific ways to lead the dance and support the dramatic tension of the entire presentation. Each instrument, particularly the drums (*sampho, skor thomm*), provides detailed dynamics and nuances for the dance.

Masked play

The Khmer masked play (*lkhaon khaol* or *lkhaon bett muk* 'covered-faced theater') has become an endangered performing art because most old masters died during the Khmer Rouge régime (1975–1979), and there has been insufficient support for the troupes to continue the tradition. Occasional performances are mounted by the Royal University of Fine Arts and the Department of Arts and Performing Arts. In earlier times, masked-play troupes were found only in the provinces of Battambang and Kandal. The genre has been relatively neglected by scholars, both Khmer and non-Khmer.

During the 1600s, troupes of female and male dancers graced the courts of Cambodia. In addition, at some pagodas where *Ramayana* manuscripts were preserved, male troupes consisting of the novice monks began performing masked plays (Thiounn 1930:31). Like court dance, the masked play is a compound performing art, joining together dance, mime, song, music, and—most important—narration. Only three masked-play troupes were in existence in Cambodia before 1975—two in Battambang Province and one in Kandal Province. The fate of the Khmer masked play is of great concern, particularly because the Khmer Rouge killed so many artists, and its current condition is uncertain.

It is believed that the Khmer masked play developed at the same time as court dance (*Le Théâtre dans la vie khmère* 1973:7)—a time, according to Samdech Chaufea Thiounn, as early as the 1500s (1930:31). Leclere noted the early existence of male troupes (1912:31). Thai sources on the masked play confirm its existence around the same time. Prince Dhani Nivat wrote: "The dance drama and the masked play are not mentioned earlier than the late seventeenth century though they might have existed prior to that" (1973:117). According to Sem (1967:157, whose work, concentrating particularly on the Vat Svay Andet troupe in Kandal Province, is the most extensive study on the Khmer masked play), the masked play was introduced into Cambodia by King Ang Duong in the mid-1800s; "however, the tradition itself is much more ancient, and seems to have been practiced during the Angkor period." Two troupes, one female and one male, were at the court of Oudong. The former was considered the principal one, but the latter, after the death of King Ang Duong, was dispersed from the court to the homes of governors and wealthy patrons.

Masked-play performances are seasonal, ritualistic, and associated with village beliefs. They were typically performed at night during the Khmer New Year (13–15

April) or during the day of the ceremony to worship spirits (*pithi sampeah krou*), to attract rain, or to save villagers from illness. The *Reamker* traditionally served as the only story on which masked-play performances are based, but in the 1980s, new themes were created by faculty of the Royal University of Fine Arts, the Department of Arts and Performing Arts, and the provincial troupe of Kampong Thom Province. Only episodes based on fortunate themes were selected for performance. Perceiving the *Reamker* as an interplay between real life and spiritual life, villagers refused to perform scenes of separation or death, fearing this would attract bad luck. The deaths of secondary characters, however, were tolerated. Often seen performed, for example, is the death of Kumphakar, whose defeat signifies the liberation of water from the sky, which had been blocked by the gigantic demon's body. Time and time again, the presentations of masked play develop the same theme, stressing the battle between good and evil. After many years, the episode of Kumphakar remains the favorite, since it plays a role in agrarian rites, especially ones appealing for rain during a drought. The following are the mostly commonly staged episodes:

Kumphakar and the barrage of water
The battle of Kumphakar and Preah Ream
The death of Kumphakar
The return of Kumphakar
The combat of Veyareap and Preah Ream
Preah Ream in search of Sita

Accompaniment for the masked play is provided by a *pinn peat.* In contrast to the court ensemble, which primarily accompanies court dance, the village *pinn peat* accompanies village plays for religious ceremonies and the masked play or *lkhaon khaol.*

Shadow play

Before movies, television, and videos, the Khmer watched and enjoyed shadow plays. With the advent of modern forms of entertainment, these plays have declined in popularity, becoming a nearly forgotten art. Occasional performances are offered in theater contexts for tourists or on international festival stages by members of the Royal University of Fine Arts and the Departments of Arts and Performing Arts. The all-night performances of the past have given way to presentations lasting thirty minutes or less.

There are three kinds of shadow plays in Cambodia: small shadow plays (*sbek tauch* 'small leather'), large shadow plays (*sbek thomm* 'large leather', also called *ayang*), and colored shadow plays (*sbek poar* 'colored leather'). Khmer are also making puppets as souvenirs to decorate the homes and offices of wealthy Khmer and foreigners.

Small shadow plays

In performance, the puppets for these shadow plays are placed between a light and the back of a white cloth. They have articulated arms and jaws. Accompaniment is provided by a *pinn peat.*

Large shadow plays

The large shadow play is a compound art, having dance, mime, song, music, and narration. The puppets may be as tall as 2 meters and weigh as much as 7 kilograms each. They are translucent and do not have articulated arms or jaws (figure 18). Each is mounted on two sticks and handled by a male puppeteer, who also dances. Puppeteers hold the puppets firmly against a white screen lit by the flame of torches or burning coconut shells.

Before movies, television, and videos, the Khmer watched and enjoyed shadow plays. With the advent of modern forms of entertainment, these plays have declined in popularity, becoming a nearly forgotten art.

FIGURE 18 Large shadow puppet (*sbek thomm*). Courtesy of Sam-Ang Sam.

Though shadow puppetry is a common artistic medium in many parts of Southeast Asia, the Khmer large shadow play is matched only by the Thai *nang yai*. Like the court dance and masked play, the large shadow play draws its essence from various dimensions, one of which is the *Reamker* epic. In villages, performances typically continued all night. Though the forms of present performances have been modified, especially through the use of electric lights instead of a flame, the characters remain identical. The most commonly performed episodes are

Sukhachar
The death of Intrachitt
The floating maiden

This genre exhibits a unique combination of dance and puppetry because during the performance the puppeteers dance while manipulating the puppets. Occasionally, puppeteers leave the screen and dance with the puppets in their hands or sometimes even without the puppets. For accompaniment, these actions require specific musical pieces: "*Cheut*," "*Cheut Chapp*," "*Cheut Chhoeung*," "*Krao Nak*," "*Krao Nai*," "*Trakk*," "*Tayay*," "*Lo*," "*Aut Tauch*," "*Aut Thomm*," "*Phlekk*," "*Prathomm*," "*Khlomm*," and "*Sdech Yeang*."

Before the war in Vietnam and the devastation of Cambodia, there existed in Cambodia two large-shadow-play troupes, one in Battambang Province and the other in Siem Reap Province. The former and its 130 puppets were patronized by Lok Mchah, owner of the masked-play troupes discussed above. The latter, with 150 puppets, was maintained in the village of Ta Phul under the direction of Nap Chum, the troupe's narrator. Today, only a few sets are known to exist: one at the Musée Guimet in Paris, one at the Department of Arts and Performing Arts in Phnom Penh, and another in Siem Reap.

The large shadow play was originally an all-male tradition, but in the early 1970s, when it was brought to the Royal University of Fine Arts, this changed. The performances there included female puppeteers because male dancers were few. This was particularly necessary when a troupe of limited size traveled internationally.

Colored shadow plays
The colored shadow play is little known today. It survives mostly in the memories of older Khmer and in a manuscript of a Khmer colored shadow play. Twenty-six colored puppets remain in the collection of the Department of Arts and Performing Arts in Phnom Penh. In contrast to the small and large shadow plays (performed at night or in a dark setting), the colored shadow play was performed during the day.

Folk music

Ceremonial music
Home and family remain important anchors in the lives of the Khmer people. Most ceremonies that mark Khmer life's passages—birth, the shaving of hair, marriage, illness, death—take place in a home. Seasonal celebrations held in the temple include annual temple festivals; the Rains Retreat, during which young Khmer men take vows to be monks and novices for a brief period; commemorations of the Buddha's birth and death; and the anniversary of the Buddha's first teachings. Temple fairs are among the most exciting events in traditional Cambodia, occasions to meet friends and community members, taste different foods, see many kinds of entertainments, purchase art objects and souvenirs, and feel fully a part of the Khmer culture.

The temple (*vat*), a place where monks lived, studied, and conducted Buddhist rituals, remains central to traditional Khmer society. It was also an educational center for villages. Funerals were held in it. Most rituals and festivals included music, especially funerals for an important personage, when performances of dances, masked plays, and shadow plays were usually included.

Spirit-worship ceremony (arakk)
Arakk is a ceremony for the worship of spirits, during which a medium attains trance to identify the cause of an illness. In the 1200s, there were "sorcerers who practice

FIGURE 19 A spirit-ceremony ensemble (*vung phleng arakk*). Photo by Sam-Ang Sam.

their arts on the Cambodians" (Chou Ta-Kuan [1993]:35). This ceremony remains prevalent in Cambodia because most people live in rural or remote areas, where hospitals and modern medicines are scarce. Consequently, people rely heavily on traditional healing methods, which use roots, leaves, the bark of trees, and fruits as medicines, with the intervention of mediums. In Khmer animism, people believe their happiness is determined by the spirits that live around them. Therefore, when a villager becomes ill, people believe the spirits are angry. In this situation, to heal the ill person, friends and relatives invite a medium to go into trance to tell the cause of the illness. Such a ceremony is known to be *banhchaul roup* 'enter to body' or *banhchaul arakk* 'enter the guardian'.

The ceremony is preceded by consultation with a village elder, someone who has knowledge of the existence of spirits and their powers. Then they search for the right medium. Mediums may be male or female, and they are already known in the community. In many cases, mediumship is hereditary. Finally, an *arakk* ensemble is engaged and the required offering objects secured. With the preparations completed and the arrival of the predetermined date, the ill person is brought to the place where the ceremony is to be performed. Then the spirit ensemble (*vung phleng arakk*) begins to perform for the medium and the spirits (figure 19).

The spirit ensemble consists of a musical bow (*khse muoy*), a three-stringed fiddle (*tror Khmer, tror khse bey*), a long-necked lute (*chapey dang veng*), a double-reed pipe (*pey prabauh*), goblet drums (*skor arakk, skor dai*), small cymbals (*chhing*), and vocalists (*neak chrieng*). Outside of an ensemble situation, two other instruments, a single free-reed pipe (*pey pork*) and an animal horn (*sneng*), can serve as solo instruments during the opening ceremony and invitation of the great teacher (*krou thomm*), named Samdech Preah Krou or Samdech Poan.

The *arakk* is conducted in three phases: opening (invitation), ritual (trance and interrogation), and closing (thanks). To begin it, the piece "*Surin*" is played to invite the great teacher to come and preside over the ceremony (figure 20). At this time, a single free-reed pipe is played to accompany the giving of offerings to the Samdech Preah Krou, who speaks through a medium. Arrangements are then made to soothe the spirit—Dambang Dek (Iron Stick), Srey Khmao (Black Lady), Neang Tey Sangreng, Kantong Khiev, or others. If the great teacher fails to respond and does not come to the ceremony, a follow-up piece, "*Bangkauk Sneng,*" is played on the animal horn. Both of these pieces are unmetered.

FIGURE 20 "*Surin,*" a spirit-ceremony tune with actions.

After the interrogation, when the causes of the illnesses are known, the ensemble plays the piece "*Ke*" and offerings are made, thanking the spirits and closing the ceremony.

Wedding ceremony (kar)

Weddings are exciting and important events in Khmer life. Each couple expects to be married only once in a lifetime. The traditional Khmer wedding originally lasted seven days and seven nights. Later, it was reduced to three days and three nights. Today, because of limited family financial resources and time, it is conducted within a single day and night. A long and elaborate wedding is now perceived as wasteful and impractical.

Courtship usually begins when a young man, using metaphors derived from nature (sky, moon, trees, birds, animals), makes remarks on a young girl's beauty. As in traditional Khmer society generally, it is unseemly to speak of love directly. As the relationship develops, the prospective marriage will be the subject of gossip among friends, relatives, and neighbors. This ultimately leads to formal negotiations and an engagement. The future in-laws investigate each other's families before making a serious commitment. They might consult an astrologer to read dates and signs of birth, luck, and the fortune of the prospective couple.

The usual age for marriage in Cambodia is about twenty to twenty-five for men and sixteen to twenty-two for women. In earlier times, it was the bridegroom's family who chose the bride. Much careful negotiation, at first through intermediaries, and the offering of ceremonial courtesy characterized the early part of the proceedings, which could extend over a long period of time. Today, emancipation is the general rule, and young people make their own decisions about marriage.

When the date set for marriage has arrived, the ceremony is conducted. Throughout the entire event, ritual haircutting, the blackening of teeth, the tying of thread, dancing with swords, rolling mats, and holding scarves occur, and a nuptial music ensemble plays almost continuously.

The *vung phleng kar*, the most popular of all Khmer music ensembles, can be found in virtually every village, town, and city in Cambodia, and even in Khmer refugee communities in the United States (figure 21). Playing in this ensemble was formerly reserved for old, serious male musicians; young musicians were not allowed to play this music because the Khmer perceived wedding ceremonies and music as

A death is announced to relatives, friends, and neighbors through the playing of music, and music permeates the Khmer funereal rituals. Each phase of the funeral and its rite requires an appropriate funeral ensemble.

FIGURE 21 A wedding ensemble (*vung phleng kar*). Photo by Sam-Ang Sam.

bestowing a blessing. Those who practiced the tradition closely even went so far as to hire only old musicians who were not blind or handicapped (Pich 1970:6). The original instrumentation was a leaf (*slekk*), a double-reed pipe (*pey prabauh,* which served as a tuning standard for the ensemble), a musical bow (*khse muoy*), a three-stringed fiddle (*tror Khmer*), a long-necked lute (*chapey dang veng*), small cymbals (*chhing*), goblet drums (*skor arakk*), and a vocalist (*neak chrieng*).

The more contemporary instrumentation includes a duct flute (*khloy*), a three-stringed zither (*krapeu*), a medium-high-pitched two-stringed fiddle (*tror so tauch*), a low-pitched two-stringed fiddle (*tror ou*), a hammered dulcimer(*khimm*), small cymbals (*chhing*), a goblet drum (*skor arakk*), and a vocalist (*neak chrieng*).

Among the action tunes played by the *kar* ensemble are the following: "*Hom Rong*" is played in the evening before the ceremony as an official opening and to invite the guardian spirits to bless the bride and bridegroom and the wedding quarters, and to ask permission to use the place. "*Angkor Reach*" or "*Nokor Reach,*" whose title invokes the ancient Khmer kingdom, is played so that the couple will recall their past. "*Sarika Keo*" is played for the haircutting at one or two o'clock on the second day. "*Preah Thong*" is for the thread-tying and scarf-holding ceremonies. "*Kang Soy*" is associated with ancestral worship, the offering of blessings, and wishes for prosperity and longevity.

Funerals

Funerals are the saddest of all ceremonies. In the Khmer tradition, a death is announced to relatives, friends, and neighbors of the departing member of the family

FIGURE 22 A funeral ensemble. Photo by Sam-Ang Sam.

and community through the playing of music, and music permeates the funereal rituals. A funeral ceremony is divided into phases: predeath, precremation, procession to the crematory, the cremation, and the postceremony or death anniversary. Each phase of the funeral and its rite requires an appropriate funeral ensemble, variously called *vung phleng korng skor, vung phleng klang chhnakk, vung phleng pinn peat*, and *vung phleng klang khek*.

The *korng skor* is known under different names, depending on the region, as in Pursat Province, where it is called *vung phleng kantrimm ming* or *vung phleng maung krum* (Pich 1970:7). This ensemble performs only when a person dies or when a corpse is dug out of the grave for a ceremony (figure 22). The instrumentation includes two large, bossed gongs (*korng thomm,* one "male," sounding *moung,* and the other "female," sounding *ming*), a large, double-headed barrel drum (*skor thomm,* which sounds *toam, toam*), circular frame gongs (*korng vung*), and a pipe (*pey*). The percussive pattern is *moung, ming, moung, ming, toam, toam, toam, toam, moung*. For the Khmer, these sounds convey a sad and melancholic feeling. On hearing them, villagers know that there has been a death, or a corpse is being dug out of its grave.

Traditionally, after a person dies, the corpse is kept in the house for one, two, or three days—a decision that reflects the financial resources of the family. If the deceased is a head monk, his corpse could be kept for three to six months before the cremation ceremony is performed. For a king, it could be six months to a year. If the death was caused by a contagious disease, the corpse would be kept at the temple for a shorter period of time to prevent the disease from spreading to other members of the family or community.

The *klang chhnakk,* sometimes incorrectly called *vung phleng klang khek*, is used when the corpse is kept at home or in the temple, during the procession when the corpse is carried to the crematorium, or during the cremation. Formerly, the ensemble performed on the backs of elephants as a military band to encourage the army in battle. In the ensemble's name, *klang* means 'drum' and *chhnakk* is a derivation of *chhneah* meaning 'victory.' Thus, *klang chhnakk* or *klang chhneah* means 'victory drum'. Though other instruments are now added, the term means 'ensemble of victory drums'. The instrumentation of this ensemble includes *sralai klang khek, skor klang khek thnakk,* and two *skor sangna.*

When it is time to take the corpse to the crematory, the ensemble *vung phleng klang khek* accompanies the procession. *Klang* means 'drum' and *khek* means 'Javanese'; thus, *klang khek* means 'Javanese drum'. The *klang khek* ensemble consists of one pair of large, bossed gongs (*korng thomm*), a pair or pairs of long double-headed conical drums (*klang khek*), and a so-called Javanese oboe (*sralai klang khek*).

Ancestral-worship ensemble (vung phleng pey keo)

At the royal palace, the *vung phleng pey keo* ensemble performed during the ritual *bonn sen daun ta* 'ancestral worship' during the *bonn phchum benn* (soul day) ceremony. Today, it seldom performs. It includes high-pitched xylophone (*roneat ek*), low-pitched circular frame gongs (*korng vung thomm*), a long-necked lute (*chapey dang veng*), a duct flute (*khloy*) or a double-reed pipe (*pey prabauh*), a three-stringed fiddle (*tror Khmer*), and two goblet drums (*skor arakk*). The ensemble also includes a lead vocalist, who takes charge of opening the ceremonial manual, and three vocalists who take a subordinate role. The repertoire of the *pey keo* ensemble is similar to that of the *arakk*. Some of its pieces include "*Ak Yum,*" "*Bampe,*" "*Krom Neay,*" and "*Surin.*"

Other festivals

In Cambodia, ceremonies called *bonn* take place year-round, but only some require a musical ensemble. When music is required, it functions as a background by creating an appropriate ambience. Among the ceremonies using music are the flower ceremony (*bonn phka*), the fundraising ceremony (*bonn kathinn*), the ancestral or soul-day ceremony (*bonn phchum benn*), the boat-rowing ceremony (*bonn omm touk,* more commonly known as the festival of water), and the New Year's ceremony (*bonn chaul chhnaim*).

Royal plowing ceremony (bonn chroat preah naingkoal)
The ceremony of royal plowing, or the opening of the sacred furrow, is the first of the traditional agrarian festivals. On an auspicious day determined by astrologers at the palace, the king formerly traced the first furrows in the capital's sacred fields of rice, inaugurating the season of plowing. Today, the ritual is performed by a male designated as the King of Meakh, who guides the yoke and plow, followed by a female designated as the Queen Me Hour, who sows seeds. After thrice circling the field, the procession stops at a chapel where Brahmins invoke the gods' protection. The sacred cows are unharnessed and guided to seven silver trays containing rice, corn, beans, and other edibles. Based on their choice, predictions are made for the coming year. If they choose the cereals, the harvest will be good. If they eat herbs, cattle diseases are to be feared. If they drink water, rain will be abundant and peace will reign. But if they drink alcohol, trouble will break out in the kingdom.

New Year (bonn chaul chhnaim)
The Khmer New Year begins with the tenth Chinese moon in the month of Kaddoeuk. The New Year festival spans three days, 13–15 April, after the end of the harvest season. The actual time and date are determined by astrologers, who calculate the exact moment when the new animal protector (tiger, dragon, snake, and so on) arrives. The Khmer spend the entire month preparing for the celebration, cleaning and decorating their houses with candles, lights, star-shaped lanterns, and flowers and making an altar for offerings to the Tevoda goddesses for the coming year. During the first three days of the lunar year, people travel to pagodas to offer food to the monks. They pray for prosperity and good health, and show appreciation to their parents and elders. Resolutions are made, debts are paid, and gifts are exchanged. Then they make music, dance, and play traditional games, such as catch the baby eagle (*chapp kaun khleng*), throwing the ball of scarves (*chaol chhuong*), hiding the scarf (*leak kanseng*), and tug of war (*teanh proat*). This is a joyous festival, in which Khmer renew themselves and ward off misfortunes in preparation for the upcoming year (figure 23).

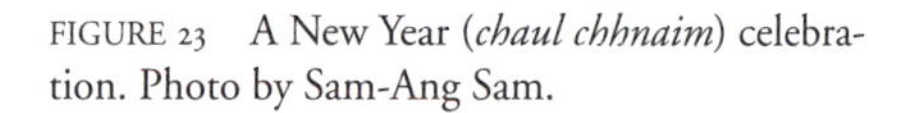

FIGURE 23 A New Year (*chaul chhnaim*) celebration. Photo by Sam-Ang Sam.

Spirit-commemoration festival (bonn dakk benn *or* bonn phchum benn)
The spirit-commemoration festival occurs in September to honor the spirits of the dead. For fifteen days, villagers take turns in bringing food to the temples for the monks. On *bonn phchum benn,* the fifteenth day (coinciding with the full moon), all villagers dress in their finest clothes and go to the temple, and children offer food to the monks. Prayers are offered to release the ancestors from sin and to allow them to pass on to a better life. According to Khmer belief, those who do not follow the practices of *phchum benn* receive curses from their angry ancestors.

Fundraising festival (bonn kathinn)
Another major religious festival in Cambodia, one lasting for twenty-nine days after *bonn phchum benn,* is *bonn kathinn.* This festival is celebrated in the month after the end of the Rains Retreat, when new saffron robes and other necessary goods are offered to the monks. People of towns and the countryside process to the *vatt* where the monks are waiting to exchange their old saffron robes for new ones. The ceremony brings spiritual merit to both lay people and the monks.

The king's birthday
His Majesty Preah Bat Samdech Preah Norodom Sihanouk Varman, King of Cambodia, was born on 31 October 1922 in Phnom Penh. Every year, His Majesty's birthday is celebrated in regal fashion, and the nation joins in to honor the king. The royal palace is open to the public, festivities take place throughout the capital, and a grand fireworks display is organized at sundown along the Tonle Sap River.

Independence day
Cambodia achieved independence from France on 9 November 1953, which anniversary is marked each year by a gala parade in front of the royal palace. The spectacle includes floats, marching bands, and other presentations highlighting the nation's achievements.

Festival of water (bonn omm touk)
The three-day festival of water (*bonn omm touk*) draws tens of thousands of people to the riverbanks to celebrate the flow of the river by watching a festive cavalcade of competitive boat races. The finish line is symbolized by a gate that retains the water. Once the line is cut, water flows down the Mekong, commencing the fishing season. Other traditional ceremonies include midnight meals of pounded rice and the full-moon celebration with its lighted flotillas and fireworks in the evening.

Flower ceremony (bonn phka)
The flower ceremony (*bonn phka*) is organized to raise money to support a local monastery, especially to construct new buildings. Sometimes it is organized to raise funds in support of another monastery in another village. It is one of the most joyous celebrations for the Khmer. People donate money to the event according to their wealth and kindness. Traditional music of the *pinn peat* is played, and the long-drum ensemble called *chhaiyaim* (whose performers wear comical clownlike masks) performs to enhance the celebration.

National festival (bonn cheat)
Bonn cheat is a national celebration in honor of the nation. Unlike other festivals and celebrations (which are community or village oriented), this one is organized by the government. In Cambodia from the monarchy to the republic, and from communism to socialism and back to the monarchy, celebrating *bonn cheat* never ceased. The

lkhaon Generic term referring primarily to theater or play

yike Village theater genre of Cham origin

tror ou Two-stringed fiddle with coconut resonator

basakk Village theater genre of Chinese origin

time of the event has changed according to the régime. Today, the government celebrates it on 7 January, the date when the current régime expelled the Khmer Rouge and regained control of the country.

Theater

Lkhaon is a generic term referring primarily to theater or play. Over time, several types of theater—including *lkhaon yike, lkhaon basakk, lkhaon mohori, lkhaon ape, lkhaon pramotey,* and *lkhaon niyeay* (spoken)—were found in Cambodia. Khmer court dance (*lkhaon kbach* 'theater of movements', from *lkhaon* 'theater' and *kbach* 'movements') is also classified as a type of theater. Today in Cambodia, such theater performances are virtually nonexistent, with the exception of occasional performances offered by theater groups of the Royal University of Fine Arts and the Department of Arts and Performing Arts. This decline is due partly to the impact of video productions that are easily available at minimal cost. Consequently, these theater genres face extinction.

Yike

Yike theater consists of dancing, acting, miming, narration, songs, and music. By the end of the 1800s, it had attained great popularity and was performed in every province across the country. It used to be performed in the palace for the king, his family, and their guests. Today, it has lost its prestige and royal patronage, and is confined to villages and the Royal University of Fine Arts.

According to Khmer sources, *yike* originated among the Chăm, whose kingdom in present-day Vietnam finally fell to Vietnamese armies in the 1600s. Several thousand Chăm were resettled in Cambodia, where they formed a close-knit community, the so-called Chamtown. *Yike* was transmitted to the Khmer through intermarriage and as a result of wars between the two groups. The Chăm widely used drums in religious contexts. In Islamic religious ceremonies, the Chăm gathered in a circle and played the drums, interspersed with chanting and praying.

This pattern among the Chăm was the foundation of the Khmer *yike.* Performers sat in a circle and got up to perform when their turn came; on finishing, they went back and sat down in their original places. Initially, the audience simply sat around the performers. Later, performers added a curtain for a backdrop, and after a character finished performing, he or she went behind it. Eventually the event became a fully staged dramatic performance, including several scenery cloths. One Chăm trait that has survived in it is a headband (*robai*) worn by dancers.

The scenery, props, and décor are largely symbolic. At first, a bedlike riser was placed on stage to symbolize a house, a palace, a mountain, or a forest, depending on the situation. Later, a door was added to symbolize the house, or a pillar for a palace—as seen, for example, in *Tum Teav* (a story like that of Romeo and Juliet). Performances at the Royal University of Fine Arts include moving clouds, flowing streams of water, waves, rain, and lightning. Lighting has also evolved, starting with torches, then using fish-oil lamps (*changkieng thma sa-oy*), petroleum lamps (*maing song*), and finally modern fluorescent lighting. King Norodom introduced a style of scenery that mixed Khmer and Western conventions representing, for example, a mountain or forest, or simply a cloudy sky. Traditionally, a *yike* performance lasted all night. University performances, however, last only two hours, presenting only the key elements of the plot.

Yike music emphasizes drumming, singing, and dancing over speaking. Each ensemble uses two to thirteen drums. Over time, it was found that the vocalists sang more in tune when accompanied by melodic instruments, and at some point two such instruments made their way into the ensemble—the *tror ou chamhieng* (half of the shell of a coconut, low-pitched, two-stringed fiddle) and later, the shawm.

Yike traditionally performed *jataka* (Buddha birth stories). Later, popular themes joined the repertoire. Scenes and stories are performed by three roles: a narrator, clowns, and dancers, all using singing. Performances begin with an invocation (*hom rong*) because Khmer performers believe ghosts, spirits, and witches live around the stage. Thus, it is natural for them to invite the supernaturals to come and bless the stage, the performers, and the performance. It also serves as a warmup and signal to the performers. The form of the *yike* is smooth and tender. There are four kinds of stage movements: (1) invocation movements (*kbach hom rong*); (2) walking movements (*kbach doeur*), which vary according to whether a character or group is good or evil; (3) movements giving way to the song (*kbach banhchoun chamrieng*); and (4) fighting or combat movements (*kbach chbaing*).

The *yike* repertoire has altogether eighty-five songs, divided into two groups: solos (*chamrieng tol*) and refrains (*chamrieng bantor*). The former are slow, whereas the latter are faster and more rhythmic. Each song, because it serves a particular situation, is a kind of tune with actions, representing, for example, comedy, the opening invocation, sadness, and grief. Originally, the leading vocalist, usually the group leader and/or teacher, began the song. A commonly used poetic meter used in *yike* songs is *patya vatt* 'sixteen syllables' as seen in the following text:

Kun toeuk thla chreah.	Look at the clear water.
Sampong phka treng.	The treng flowers are all over.
Satt hoeur praleng,	Birds fly and play with one another,
chhieng chhap machha.	Catching fish.

This meter is the same as that associated in scripts used by the Chăm for chanting and praying.

Basakk

Lkhaon basakk remains a popular form of theater in Cambodia. It owes its origin to a type of Chinese theater called *hi* (*xi* in Mandarin), which was introduced in 1930 to the Basakk River region, from which it takes its name (Jacq-Hergoualc'h 1982:10). Chinese influence is obvious in the music, songs, musical instruments (especially the cymbals and woodblocks), costumes, makeup, and acrobatics. In *basakk,* the actors and actresses improvise their roles according to a scenario under the guidance of a director who knows the story well (figure 24). The musical ensemble comprises *tror ou chamhieng, khimm tauch, khimm thomm, pann, lo,* and *khmuoh*. The stories include Tipp Sangvar (a name), Rattanavung (a name), and Kandanh Panhchapoar (Five-Colored "Dreadlocks").

FIGURE 24 A painted-face character from a *basakk* theater performance. Photo by Sam-Ang Sam.

Functional repertoires

Narrative (chrieng chapey)

Chrieng chapey (figure 25) is a male-dominated, vocal, narrative-entertainment genre. In earlier times, it was performed from dusk to dawn, yet kept the audience laughing throughout the night. *Chrieng chapey* is performed by a male vocalist who accompanies himself on a long-necked lute (*chapey dang veng*). The words *chrieng chapey* mean literally 'sing the lute' (*chrieng* 'to sing' and *chapey* 'lute'). Before 1975, the vocalist drew his repertoire from popular legends, such as *Preah Chinavung* and *Hang Yunn,* but more contemporary events—such as describing Khmer Rouge atrocities, liberation from the Khmer Rouge, and so on—have been added.

Repartee (ayai)

Ayai is a kind of repartee singing, usually the alternation of a man and a woman, accompanied by an ensemble of the same name. Vocalists perform for hours, improvising on short, topical themes, which are sometimes discussed and agreed on before the performance, but are otherwise created spontaneously in performance. Singers of *ayai* perform an unaccompanied line of text, immediately followed by a small ensemble of strings and a flute playing standard patterns. This art requires talent, fast thinking, a good voice, some acting ability, and mastery of Khmer poetry. Sung phrases conform to set poetic meters, often in a twenty-eight-syllable stanza, consisting of four phrases of seven syllables each. Intellectuals and the elite consider *ayai* to be a low-class entertainment for common peasants. This attitude is partly due to the bawdiness of the language. In traditional Cambodia, polite young women were not allowed to watch such a performance.

Boxing (pradall)

Boxing is considered the number-one sport in Cambodia, soccer being second. Before 1975, boxing matches were organized almost weekly at the Olympic Stadium in Phnom Penh. Like the Thai, the Khmer prefer freestyle boxing, in which boxers use fists, elbows, heads, knees, and feet to hit and kick their opponents. Though the boxers wear gloves, some matches result in death.

Khmer freestyle boxing is normally accompanied by the music ensemble called *vung phleng pradall* or *vung phleng klang khek*, consisting of an oboe (*sralai klang*

FIGURE 25 At the Central Market in Phnom Penh, a singer of epics sits on the street, playing a *chapey* (long-necked plucked lute). Photo by Sam-Ang Sam.

FIGURE 26 The Cambodian "fishing dance." Photo by Sam-Ang Sam.

khek), drums (*skor klang khek* or *sampho*), and small cymbals (*chhing*). The music is unique and can be immediately recognized by any Khmer familiar with boxing. The music is in two parts: for the invocation and for the fight. The former invokes a spirit (*krou* 'teacher') to concentrate the boxers' minds and to give them confidence. Music for the first part is played slowly in *rubato* style; the oboe plays the melody, accompanied by a *sampho* playing strokes at important structural points in the melody. The second part is faster and in meter. As the rounds progress, the music accelerates, stopping only at the end of a round or when a boxer is knocked out. During an exciting fight, the audience joins in by clapping their hands in rhythm with the *sampho.*

Folk dance

Because written documents pertaining to Khmer dance are lacking, the origin of Khmer folk dance is obscure. Some masters of dance believe that folk dances are as old as the Khmer people. Khmer folk dance is solely of peasant origin and use and is considered a part of the peasants' lives (figure 26). It has its deepest roots and flourishes among the rural people, who dance in the village common or on a rough stage built under the spreading trees and shielded by their shade, creating a beautiful setting. Among villages, there is a spirit of intimate understanding and candor among both performers and spectators.

Nature has been a major inspiration for folk dances, coupled with customs, traditions, and beliefs, all of which are interrelated. Dance is not merely an optional luxury; it is a way of life. The subjects of Khmer folk dance are various, indicating how important a role dance plays in the social, religious, and sociological life of the people.

Various types of folk dance are intended to satisfy a need for security and happiness through their relationship to belief, tradition, and recreation. The religious form of dance emerges from the customs and beliefs that give value to miracles, nature, the soul, witchcraft, and animism. This form of dance is best represented by dances called the Peacock of Pursat and the Sacrifice of Buffalo. The traditional form emerges from traditions practiced by peasants and farmers. This kind of art is usually performed during traditional ceremonies, and is best represented by the *trott,* a dance performed during the Khmer New Year in April, marking the transition from the old year to the new. When there is a drought, the *trott* is performed to ward off the evil spirits which, in Khmer belief, are causing the drought. Recreational forms of danc-

Nature has been a major inspiration for folk dances, coupled with customs, traditions, and beliefs, all of which are interrelated. Dance is not merely an optional luxury; it is a way of life.

ing are sometimes called peasant's art or people's art. After the harvest, peasants gather to perform village dances that express their spontaneous joyfulness after the completion of their work, as exemplified by the *krapp* and the pestle dances. The most popular folk dances are those of more recent origin. They include the coconut-shell dance (*robaim tralaok*), the bamboo-clapper dance (*robaim krapp*), the pestle dance (*robaim angre*), and the cardamom-picking dance (*robaim beh kravanh*).

Though Khmer court dance is distinguished by movements (*kbach*), the beauty and value of Khmer folk dance are seen in the choreography (*krala*). There are six salient elements observable in Khmer folk dance: (1) music, (2) song, (3) rhythm, (4) movements and gestures, (5) choreography, and (6) costumes. Court dance is a product of the royalty and aristocracy, but folk dance is of the commoners. Thus, it is closely related to peasants' lives, with themes rooted in those people's agricultural activities.

Historically, Khmer folk dances divided into three groups: (1) the original dances of the upland minority ethnic groups, accompanied by their ensembles, in particular, the Kuoy fighting dance (*robaim veay Kuoy*) and the Sacrifice of Buffalo dance (*robaim kapp krabey phoeuk sra*); (2) dances performed for traditional ceremonies, such as the *trott* (*robaim trott*); and (3) more recent creations, accompanied by the *mohori* ensemble, such as the bamboo clappers' dance (*robaim krapp*), the pestle dance (*robaim angre*), and the fishing dance (*robaim nesat*). Since 1979, with the ascendance of the Heng Samrin government, former members of the Royal University of Fine Arts and Department of Arts and Performing Arts have reestablished the university and department so that Khmer culture could revive. During this time, some two hundred folk dances have been created as part of their efforts to expand the folk-dance repertory and to create requirements for the degree programs at the university. Few of these dances have proved effective enough for inclusion into the permanent repertoire. Only about ten among them—including the mortar dance (*robaim tball kdoeung*), the new Cham dance (*robaim cham thmey*), and the cardamom-picking dance (*robaim beh kravanh*)—have achieved permanent status.

The musical accompaniment for folk dance varies. Drums and oboe are used to accompany *robaim veay kuoy*, but a gong ensemble accompanies the Sacrifice of Buffalo. For ambience and effect, the large frame drum often replaces the goblet drum. One can observe such a situation in the fishing dance (*robaim nesat*), the crossbow dance (*robaim sna*), and the Cham dance (*robaim cham*). The Peacock of Pursat (*robaim kngaok posatt*) is accompanied by a drum, a fiddle, and a singer, but only drums and a singer accompany the *trott* dance.

Solo instrumental music

Though practically any instrument can be used for playing solo, only a few instruments in Cambodia are considered solo instruments. Such instruments, tending to have timbres and intensities that are incompatible with other instruments in an ensemble, include the conch (*saing*), the Jew's harp (*angkuoch*), the leaf (*slekk*), the single free-reed pipe (*pey pork*), the free-reed horn (*sneng*), and the chest-resonated monochord (*say diev*).

The *slekk* is merely a leaf from a tree, of which the most favored are *lumpuoh, puoch,* and *kravann.* One can simply pluck the leaf from a tree and play. The player places the leaf against the lower lip by folding the leaf to curve upward. Blowing the air out against the folded end makes the leaf vibrate against the upper lip, creating the sound. Different pitches can be obtained in the same way as in whistling. In a normal context, players of leaves are not necessarily considered musicians. People play leaves while walking to the fields of rice and while watching their cattle. Besides its principal function as a solo instrument, the leaf is sometimes heard (but rarely) in the wedding ensemble.

Another solo instrument is a bamboo Jew's harp (*angkuoch, kangkuoch*). It is restricted to solo playing because it is too soft to be heard in an ensemble. Today it is no longer popular, and few people know how to play it. People often say its main function is to serenade a lover, usually a man courting his girlfriend. In practical courtship, men and women speak to one another directly because it takes too much time to fall in love with one another using the *angkuoch* as a disguiser of speech. Using such an instrument, the man must first get the woman's attention to listen to his Jew's harp; second, she has to figure out what he is saying through it.

The free-reed horn (*sneng*) is made of a buffalo horn or oxhorn open at both ends. On one side of it, a small, rectangular hole is carved, and over it a bamboo free reed is placed. The instrument produces only three pitches (E, G, A, or ascending intervals of a minor third and major second). Among Khmer aerophones, this has the smallest range. It was used in an elephant-hunting expedition by hunters to attract wild elephants. The most commonly heard piece played on the free-reed horn is "*Bangkauk Sneng.*" In the deep forests while a hunter approaches wild elephants, he plays the instrument, whose seemingly magical sounds are thought to have a powerful effect on elephants. On hearing such a sound, elephants turn and charge at it, giving the hunter an opportunity to catch and tame them. Besides its function in hunting elephants, "*Bangkauk Sneng*" is played in the *arakk* ceremony to invite a spirit to possess a tranced medium.

The conch (*saing*), devoid of any holes for fingering, is a solo instrument used only by Brahmin priests in religious events, such as the ancestral-worship ceremony and the plowing ceremony, and to signal the sovereign's arrival. It produces only one tone.

The free-reed pipe with holes for fingering (*pey pork*) is normally a solo instrument because of its timbre, though it was formerly a member of the wedding ensemble. The most commonly heard pieces played on it are "*Surin,*" "*Banloeu Prey Veal,*" and "*Thngai Trang Kroluoch.*" When accompanying a vocalist, the pipe plays whatever the vocalist chooses to sing.

The chest-resonated monochord (*say diev*), since it appears in the bas-relief carvings on the walls of Cambodia's temples at Angkor, is among the oldest Khmer musical instruments. Because of the slightness of its volume, it has more commonly served as a solo instrument or to accompany a vocalist, though it formerly appeared in the wedding ensemble. Its solo repertoire includes mostly wedding songs, such as "*Hom Rong,*" "*Lum-ang Thnung,*" "*Sarika Keo,*" and "*Phatt Cheay.*"

Music in Khmer religious contexts

The state religion of Cambodia is Theravada Buddhism, to which most of the population subscribes. During the period of the Khmer Rouge, Buddhism ceased to function, many temples were destroyed, and most monks and novices were killed. As a consequence, the survivors have borne the responsibility of restoring Buddhism and its practices. Since 1979, it can again be said that Buddhism provides the moral fiber of the Khmer life-style but includes tenets derivative of Hinduism and animism. Buddhists believe that life is a series of cycles of death and rebirth, during which the individual passes through a succession of incarnations. Depending on the person's conduct in previous lives, a new incarnation may be of a higher or lower status. Buddhists strive to perfect their souls to be released from the cycle of death and rebirth and attain the state of enlightenment (nirvana).

In traditional Khmer society, men must enter the monkhood for at least three months during their lifetime, often at the age of twelve or thirteen. During this time, they learn Buddhist philosophy and social morality, and practice chanting. The temples where they study are centers of Khmer life, not only for prayer but also for education, medical care, and administrative organization. Since the 1950s, Buddhist education has been systematically organized to include modern knowledge from the primary level to the university level. Buddhist knowledge can be acquired at Buddhist institutions, including the High School of Pali, the Buddhist Institute, and the Buddhist University. The monks who reside in these temples are at the highest spiritual level for achieving nirvana. They wear distinctive saffron robes, shave their heads, and set out each morning to collect food from local people.

Though Buddhist scriptures, classical literature, epics, fables, books of games, and dance manuals all may be written in prose, most are written in verse. For dance and theater, poetic writings are adapted and set to song and music. The category of religious music embraces primarily chanting of the Buddhist scriptures and reciting poems rendered by monks and lay people at the temple or at home. Ordinary chanting (*saut thoar*) is rendered simply by monks and lay people, within a narrow range and in an intertwined texture, which seems chaotic on first hearing. The texts of the chants, usually in Pali (the sacred language of Theravada Buddhism), are rarely understood by either the practitioners or the listeners. This fact has led to debates over whether Khmer should become the language of Cambodian Buddhism so that all may understand. Some monks have offered chanting in Khmer, but it is not yet widely accepted.

Another category of Buddhist performance, the recitation of poems (*smaut*), is distinguished in style from both chanting and singing. *Smaut* occupies a position between chanting and singing, but unlike the former may be accompanied by a solo instrument such as a free-reed pipe, a duct flute, or a fiddle. For the Khmer, *smaut* is both powerful and didactic, even entertaining. It sets the mood and creates a religious atmosphere. It usually appears at various points in the sequence of a ritual. For example, a kind of *smaut* called *saraphanh* is associated with festivals celebrating the birth, death, and rebirth of the Buddha.

Musically, the distinctions among chanting (*saut thoa*), reciting (*smaut*), and singing (*chrieng*) are not well expressed in the English terms. Khmer recitation is actually considered sweet, melodious, and musical, but it differs from song because it is in the rhythm of speech (also called rubato style) rather than strict pulsation or meter. Consequently it is considered a separate category from both chant and song.

There are several styles of *smaut*, and each has its own name: *pileap, roah, pradao, piporanea, smaut metri ba, smaut kumar ba, smaut trai leak*, and so forth. Following is an example of a *smaut* text set in *pathya vat* 'sixteen syllable' meter.

Khnhomm saum bangkum	I salute
champuoh Preah Puth,	the Lord Buddha,
trung kung khpuoh phott	who resides in the highest
leu trai loka.	of the tri-worlds.

Neam Preah Kodamm	The name is Preah Kodamm
baramm sasda,	the Supreme,
chambang leu moha	who is greater
neak prach taing lay.	than all sages.

The main themes used in *smaut* are from the *tripitaka* (Buddhist scriptures) and *jataka* (Buddha birth stories); these form the basis of the Buddhist precepts, which in turn are central in shaping Khmer lives and families. The texts are written entirely in the vernacular, or are mixed with Pali and Sanskrit.

Temples were centers for the practice and preservation of this kind of art. Originally practiced and preserved there, the *smaut* later penetrated the primary schools and even the Royal University of Fine Arts (Faculty of Choreographic Arts), where it has become an important component of the school's stage presentations.

Foreign and modern music

Classical Western music

Before 1975, the music faculty of the Royal University of Fine Arts offered courses in classical Western history, theory, and composition. Instructors from France and Germany were sometimes brought in, but few had more than a superficial knowledge, and their teaching lacked depth. Only the university maintained a chamber orchestra and a symphony orchestra; concerts were rare.

Popular music in Cambodia

Popular music in Cambodia has its roots in the songs brought by French colonialists during the nineteenth and early twentieth centuries. In addition, many wealthy Khmer sent their children to France, where they heard European popular songs. By the 1950s, Khmer forms of popular music had developed, partly from songs believed to have been introduced by Filipinos, for the genre was first called "music from Manila" (*phleng Manil*). This genre, which rose in the 1950s, peaked in the mid-1960s to the mid-1970s, particularly with the nationally recognized figure Sin Sisamouth, the so-called Cambodian Elvis. Popular music in Cambodia virtually disappeared from 1975 to 1979. The Khmer Rouge, believing it symbolized the decadence of urban residents, intellectuals, aristocrats, and the capitalistic and domineering classes of society, killed most pop-song writers, composers, and singers active before 1975.

Popular music, a product of the city, is heard mostly at nightclubs, private parties, weddings, sporting events, and social dances, and in restaurants. At home, people in all levels of society listen to it on radio and cassettes, and occasionally on television. Since the early 1980s, Khmer music videos have become popular. Even members of the royal family were known to listen to popular music, and King Sihanouk formerly played pop songs on the saxophone. Sometimes Khmer court dancers and musicians played backup music for pop singers. Though classical music is revered as the national music, most prefer to listen to popular music. Even so, pop musicians have a low social status, and popular music is not considered a serious career and is not studied formally. Indeed, it is put in the same category with alcohol, illegal drugs, and illicit sex.

During the period of the monarchy (before 1970), most songs dealt with themes of love. From 1970 to 1975, the period of the republic, themes of revolution critical of the monarchy appeared. From 1975 to 1979, there were no popular songs, but after the expulsion of the Khmer Rouge, themes of revolution, heroism, and liberation came to dominate. Even current hits continue these themes, plus those of sepa-

> Virtually all the earth's people have experienced war, famine, revolution, and neglect. But no known population in Southeast Asia has suffered more deeply than the Khmer, whose existence and culture were nearly snuffed out by the Khmer Rouge from 1975 until 1979.

ration and sadness, because too much has happened for most people to think again about love.

Khmer popular bands, *mohori samai* 'modern *mohori*', use only Western instruments. Earlier, these included banjo, metal flute, cello, violin, and accordion, but more recently, so-called standard bands are made up of electric lead guitar, rhythm guitar, electric bass, keyboards, and a drum set (the standard sets used in bands in the West, but smaller).

Pop songs are classified by their rhythms and styles of dancing. *Roam vung* is a dance in a circle, *roam kbach* is a dance that echoes gestures from temple dances, *saravane* derives from southern Laos, and *laim leav* is also derived from Lao singing. The *roam vung* is danced by a couple around a table covered with flowers. Khmer versions of the bolero, the cha-cha, and the twist use Western rhythms. Khmer can hear cassettes of American pop stars singing hard rock and heavy metal, but Khmer bands do not yet play these styles. Among the best-liked Western artists are Carlos Santana, the Beatles, and the Rolling Stones.

About 90 percent of pop songs follow a fixed melodic format, basically ABCB. Two stanzas (A and B) are sung, followed by a refrain (C), then by a third stanza using the same melody as B. All the known lyricists are men; women only sing. Sometimes Khmer pop singers borrow Western songs but substitute pertinent Khmer lyrics. At parties made up of guests of mixed ages, musicians play many kinds of songs to please everybody, some Western, some Khmer or Lao. Usually slow songs are followed by fast ones. The most popular rhythms danced to in the late 1990s include the rumba, the bossa nova, the waltz, and the foxtrot. Even though the music is popular, musicians seldom earn much money; further, they must avoid overtly political lyrics, especially those critical of the régime, or face jail.

Epilogue: the destruction and reconstruction of the Khmer performing arts

Virtually all the earth's peoples have experienced war, human-caused famine, revolution, neglect, and other types of madness that cause suffering and death. At various times in history, victors have carried off conquered peoples to their own country, where the vanquished peoples have come to influence their conquerors, often in profound ways. But no known population in Southeast Asia has suffered more deeply than the Khmer, whose existence and culture were nearly snuffed out by the Khmer Rouge from 1975 until 1979.

Under the wily Prince Sihanouk, Cambodia had remained neutral in the war between the Republic of Vietnam (south) and the Democratic People's Republic of Vietnam (north), the former supported primarily by the United States, the latter by the Soviet Union and other communist countries. Though the north Vietnamese and their southern allies (the National Liberation Front) entered Cambodia to move men and arms to within striking distance of south Vietnam, their havens there were not threatened until the spring of 1970, when both American and Vietnamese troops invaded. This event led to a coup d'état in which Prince Sihanouk, absent from the country at the time, was deposed and a Khmer general named Lon Nol installed as leader. The Khmer Rouge had existed for years, but their strength increased after 1970, and five years later, when the Lon Nol government was near collapse from ineptitude and corruption, the Khmer Rouge struck, on 17 April 1975. At last able to realize their intellectually based plan to rid the country of its traditional culture and return it to its simple agrarian roots, the Khmer Rouge emptied Phnom Penh, swollen to nearly 3 million, and marched its inhabitants into the countryside. Of an estimated 2 million people who then died, the Khmer Rouge murdered most, and the rest succumbed to disease, starvation, and hardship. Nearly 1 million people avoided death by fleeing the country.

The Khmer Rouge targeted intellectuals and other carriers of Khmer traditions. Among the casualties were most of Cambodia's musicians, dancers, teachers, and makers of instruments. In December 1988, Chheng Phon, Minister of Information and Culture, estimated that 90 percent of the country's playwrights, researchers, artists, and theorists were killed or lost, and that the remaining 10 percent were deeply traumatized. He further estimated that 70 percent of the material culture of the Khmer had been destroyed, among it much of the contents of the National Museums, the entire National Library, virtually everything of the educational system (including the universities), and most documents.

On 7 January 1979, dissident Khmer Rouge and an allied army of Vietnamese invaded Democratic Kampuchea and drove the Khmer Rouge from power and into exile in the countryside, where they remain. The process of reconstruction began, but the destruction was so extensive and the resources so limited (most governments refrained from recognizing the government because of the Vietnamese occupation) that progress was slow. Though court music and dance were closely associated with the former elite, they were also seen to represent the heart and soul of the Khmer people and their culture, and consequently the restoration of dance, music, and drama were seen as high priorities. This process moved forward through the efforts of Chheng Phon and other energetic Khmer, who, with the surviving teachers, rebuilt the Royal University of Fine Arts and the court-music system. Many foreigners, especially Bill Lobban of Australia (in Cambodia from 1987 until 1993) and Dr. Toni Shapiro of the United States, worked tirelessly to rebuild, document, and encourage.

The traditional Khmer arts used to be performed for recreation, entertainment, custom, and tradition. Today, they are more likely to serve politics. New themes have been created to suit the political policies of the régime in power. Political leaders, usually with little knowledge of the arts, use them as vehicles to assure their ascendancy.

The Khmer have one of the oldest and richest traditional cultures in Southeast Asia. With the introduction of Western culture to Cambodia, traditional cultural practices have gradually diminished as the Khmer came to see the older cultural patterns as useless and a waste of time. Traditional ceremonies, entertainments, festivals, and games were simplified, shortened, and even eliminated. Some genres, including *lkhaon ape, lkhaon pramotey,* and *sbek poar,* are known only in peoples' memories. Though urban residents describe *arakk* ceremonies as superstitious and regard them as things of the past, for many living in the countryside they remain part of life. Wood and stone guardians and other images connected with spirit worship and ceremony are still found throughout Cambodia, and belief in them remains alive among Khmer living outside the country.

The mass media are largely responsible for the growth of popular music and the fading away of traditional music. This change coincides with the increasing neglect of Khmer musicians and the populace. With the explosion of technology and the increased importation of Western culture, particularly rock, fewer and fewer youngsters in Cambodia understand, appreciate, or practice their traditional culture. Poor economic conditions have also contributed to the decline of traditional culture.

In modern Khmer society, traditional music has a minor place in concert halls, during dance and theatrical performances, and in a few ceremonies. The duration of Khmer weddings, which formerly lasted seven days and nights, has been reduced to barely one day. In the past, music was played almost continuously, but now it has been cut to a few hours or a single morning. Not surprisingly, many old Khmer musicians have given up playing music since the rewards are meager, and they have had to choose more lucrative professions to support their families, which naturally take precedence over the preservation of traditions. Traditional musicians have an even lower status than pop musicians, who themselves are paid badly.

There may be no other country in the world whose people have more strongly attached their lives to the arts as symbols of their soul and identity. Among the refugee communities in the United States, the Hmong are known for their needlework and the Vietnamese for their popular music, but the Khmer are known for their commitment and dedication to the classical performing arts. Reflecting this image, Khmer refugees have worked to rebuild their culture for almost two decades, both in refugee camps and after 1975, when resettled in the United States and France. Such rebuilding has largely depended on a handful of devoted artists. In new Western environments and settings, where they find no Khmer monasteries, temples, palaces, schools, and universities (sites that once passed on the knowledge of the traditional arts), Khmer artists have had to find other methods, often at their own expense, to see that their arts, which are so dear to them, survive.

—Sam-Ang Sam

KHMER LIVING OUTSIDE CAMBODIA

The legal borders of Cambodia, drawn under European colonial rule, reflect the political situation of the nineteenth and twentieth centuries. Just as non-Khmer ethnic groups (including the Chăm, the Lao, and the Vietnamese) live in Cambodia, many Khmer live outside Cambodia, especially in northeast Thailand and southern Vietnam. Because these groups have been separated from mainstream Khmer culture, they were little affected by the Khmer Rouge upheaval in Cambodia from 1975 to 1979.

—Terry E. Miller

Khmer music in Thailand

The Khmer in Thailand speak both Thai and Khmer. Khmer is not usually written, but when written, it is done phonetically in Thai. The romanizations used here derive from Thai, but romanizations used above appear in parentheses on first use.

The border between Thailand's northeast region and Cambodia is created by the Panom Dongruk mountain chain, forming the edge of a plateau on the Thai side, with a lower plain on the Cambodian side. Because of warfare, most of the Khmer population on the Thai side, which now numbers more than half a million, immigrated from Cambodia to three provinces—Buriram, Sisaket, Surin—centuries ago. Most are bilingual, speaking both Khmer and Thai, but some groups among them speak only minimal Thai. Traditionally they are farmers, growing rice and other crops and keeping a ritual structure on the ground beneath the house. Their music consists of ancient traditions brought with them and still maintained, plus a central-Thai-influenced Khmer classical music.

The main kind of Khmer-Thai music is *kantrüm.* A *thum-mong* ensemble serves for funerals. Only Buriram Province has a village *mahori* ensemble, and both

Buriram and Surin provinces have a village form of *piphat.* Both ensembles differ in many respects from both Thai and Khmer classical ensembles of similar names.

Musical instruments

Idiophones

The *kapkaep* combines traits of concussion idiophones and scraped idiophones. It is made of one or two pieces of hardwood, about 30 centimeters long and 2 centimeters wide, with teeth cut into one side and bottlecaps attached at one end to make jingling sounds. With a round stick, 30 centimeters long, the player scrapes or beats the main piece(s). Holding the main piece(s) with one hand, the player beats or scrapes it or them with the round stick in the other hand. Players sometimes dance.

Krab are hardwood concussion idiophones, usually played as two pairs. Each piece is about 1 centimeter thick, 4 centimeters wide, and 12 centimeters long. Holding pairs in each hand, the player strikes one piece against the other to provide a piercing, concussive sound. Players often dance.

The *ching* is a pair of small, thick-rimmed cymbals, handmade from metal alloys. It differs from its central Thai namesake by being larger and flatter, and looks more like the *chap* than the *ching.* This instrument is found only in the same area as the *takay* (zither) in Buriram Province.

The *mong* (also *mung*), a large single gong made of a metal alloy, is beaten with a soft mallet. The gong is about 1.5 centimeters thick and 50 to 60 centimeters in diameter. It is most commonly used for signals in a monastery, but people bring it with a large drum to funeral ceremonies.

Membranophones

The *kantrüm* is a drum named after its sound. Because this drum is played mostly in one particular ensemble, the name of the ensemble is also *kantrüm.* The drum is made in pairs, a larger, deeper-toned female, and a smaller, higher-toned male. From softwood, the drums are carved into an elongated goblet shape, with a waist and one head, covered usually with calfskin (the best instruments have female lizardskin). The membrane is stretched tightly by cords that pass through holes at its edge. The diameter of the head is about 20 to 25 centimeters, and the length is about 50 to 60 centimeters. Both players beat the drums barehanded.

The *toom,* a barrel drum carved of hardwood, has two heads covered with cowskin, nailed to the body. The face of each drum is about 60 centimeters in diameter, and the body is about 70 to 75 centimeters long. Its name derives from the sound emitted when wooden sticks hit the head. This drum provides a single, low-pitched, loud tone, and traditionally it signals time at Buddhist monasteries.

Chordophones

The term *trua* denotes two kinds of bowed lutes, one having a wooden resonator and the other a coconut-shell resonator. Those with wooden resonators come in three sizes: small (*trua-ji*), medium (*trua-ek*), and large (*trua-thom*). All have snakeskin heads. A wooden bow is strung with horsehair or nylon, which passes between the two metal strings. A medium-sized *trua* is about 60 centimeters long, with the others proportionally larger or smaller. Since they are locally made, or even homemade instruments, sizes are not standardized. The strings are tuned to an approximate fifth.

The coconut-shell fiddle (*trua-ou*) has two metal strings, a cowskin resonator on the front, and carvings with holes on the back. Its bow, passing between the strings, resembles that of the other *trua.*

Another kind of *trua,* rarely encountered, has a hollowed-out turtle shell, whose

pey-aw Cylindrical, double-reed aerophone
sralai Quadruple-reed aerophone with bulging shape
khloy End-blown duct flute of bamboo
kantrüm Village Khmer ensemble in northeast Thailand

FIGURE 27 A lute (*japey*) in the *mahori khmer* ensemble. Photo by Panya Roongruang.

end is covered with the skin of a snake. Like the ordinary wooden *trua,* it has two strings. The Chăm in both southern Vietnam and Cambodia also have such an instrument, which some say originated with the Chăm.

A floor zither (*takay* 'crocodile') is carved and hollowed from softwood into a crocodile shape. Two strings stretch over ten bridges along the body from the tail to the tuning pegs on the head. Between the thumb and index finger, the player holds a plectrum made from the horn of a buffalo, and with it plucks the strings. Little known, this zither is found mainly in Koktachai Subdistrict, Müang District, Buriram Province.

The *japey* is a two-stringed softwood lute. It has ten frets, placed on a fingerboard attached to a large, round, hollow body, which has many small holes (figure 27). Two metal strings stretch from the bottom of the body over a bridge and frets to tuning pegs at the end of the neck. The strings, tuned to a fifth, are plucked with a small, thin, plectrum made from the horn of a buffalo. Little known, this lute is confined to the same subdistrict as the *takay.*

Aerophones

The *pey-aw* (also *pey a* and *pey praboh*) consists of a short bamboo tube with a large double reed cut from *mai-aw,* a soft bamboo of genus *Arundo.* The playing end of the reed tapers into a flat, thin shape; to keep this shape, a flat brace of two bamboo sticks girdles it. A rounded base of a reed is put into the upper end of the body, which has seven holes for fingers and one for a thumb. The *pey-aw* is about 25 centimeters long and 2 centimeters in diameter.

FIGURE 28 A *kantrüm* ensemble in Surin Province, Thailand. Photo by Terry E. Miller.

The *sralai,* a quadruple-reed aerophone with a bulging wooden body, is also central to Cambodia's *pinn peat* ensemble. Like the Cambodian *sralai tauch,* the body is about 30 centimeters long, with six holes for fingering. It is identical to the central Thai *pi nawk,* and musicians are likely to use an instrument of Thai origin. Today, it is found only in Koktachai District, Buriram Province.

The *pi-ngyen* (also *pey pok, pi-triang,* and *pi-phuk*) is a bamboo free-reed pipe with holes for fingering. Near the mouthpiece, a small, thin metal free reed is inserted over a hole, and the player covers it with the mouth. Like the equivalent instrument in Cambodia, it has seven holes for fingers and one for a thumb, and the tube is about 30 centimeters long and 2 centimeters in diameter.

The *pi-ankong* (also *pi-jaruang* and *pi-jarong*) resembles the *pi-ngyen,* but is longer and thicker and sounds about one octave lower.

The *khloy,* a bamboo fipple flute with six holes for fingers and one for a thumb, is identical to the Khmer *khloy* and the Thai *khlui.* Like the latter, it has a hole between the upper end and the holes for fingering, but this hole is covered with tape, unlike the Khmer *khloy,* which preserves the buzzing timbre.

Ensembles

Kantrüm, the most famous and most widespread ensemble, gets its name from the sound of the dominant drums in the ensemble (figure 28). The number of instruments depends on the occasion and how many people and instruments are available. The ensemble typically consists of a pair of *kantrüm* drums and a *kapkaep,* plus a *trua* (sometimes one size, sometimes both large and smaller sizes), a *trua-ou,* and a *pey-aw.* Other aerophones, including a *pey-jariang,* a *pey-pok,* and a *khloy* can be added.

Traditionally, performers sat in a circle and faced each other, but today, because of central Thai influence and tourism, they more commonly perform on a stage and face the audience. The ensemble performs pieces in succession. Each piece repeats several times without announcement because village audiences know the pieces; this process can last for several hours. Besides instrumental music, the Khmer have vocal music and several types of dance, including the clapper dance (*kapkaep*). *Kantrüm* is played for many occasions, but not funerals. In Cambodia, the equivalent ensemble (*vung arakk*) is associated with spiritual ceremonies.

FIGURE 29 A *mahori khmer* ensemble. Photo by Panya Roongrüang.

The *mahori khmer* ensemble, sometimes called *mahori koktachai* (after the subdistrict where it is thought to have originated), is found primarily in this subdistrict (figure 29). The founder of the ensemble came from Cambodia and settled his family at Koktachai subdistrict about 1920. An entirely different kind of *mahori* is found at the temple in Na-Som Village, south of Surin, a government-designated cultural village, which voluntarily agreed not to modernize. The ensemble there includes fiddles (*trua*), a *sralai,* a *takay,* a *japey,* a pair of *krab,* and a pair of *kantrüm.* The texture of the music is polyphonically stratified. Each instrument plays different realizations of the same melody. In performance, one of the leading instruments, a *sralai* or a *trua,* begins alone and is then joined by the others. The player of the *krab* may dance when the ensemble is playing, sometimes joined by two other dancers.

Na-Som Village also houses a *beepat khmer* at the temple. This ensemble consists of a *roneat tauch* with twenty-three keys, a *kong vung thomm* with sixteen gongs, a *sralai,* a pair of *skor thomm,* plus *chhing* and *chhap.* Its repertoire, at least in title, suggests a central Thai origin, though some of these pieces are also played in Cambodia.

The funeral ensemble (*thum mong*) consists of a *thum,* a large gong (*mong,* also *mung*), a *pi-jaruang,* and a *pi-phuk,* if available. After someone dies, the players borrow the drum and the gong from the monastery and join with players of *pi* and other local instrumentalists. Music is played throughout the night until the corpse is taken to the monastery for a ceremony and cremation.

Genres

Singing (*jariang*), a narrative vocal genre, may be accompanied by either a solo instrument or an ensemble. The instrument that normally accompanies *jariang* is the *japey*—in which case the performance is called *jariang-japey.* The singer plays an introduction on the *japey,* sings a stanza, and repeats the same melody on the *japey,* and so on. The texts are of many types, including *jataka* (stories of Buddha's birth), Buddhist doctrine, and courtship. According to respondents in the Surin area in 1973, a singer of *jariang* from Surin in 1953 began using the northeast Thai *khaen* to accompany his singing, calling the genre *jariang brün.*

Kantrüm music, a genre of compositions sometimes played apart from the ensemble of the same name, is the best known Thai-Khmer music. A *mahori khmer* may play both instrumental and vocal music of the *kantrüm* type, but the pattern of drumming changes according to the character of the melody. Besides being played for listening, *kantrüm* accompanies dances for pleasure (including *ruam un-re* and *kanob-ting-tong*), and *jol-ma-muad* for the spiritual ceremony. Other famous tunes include *kaew-naw, cherb, jerng-mui, olanai,* and *jol-tang.* Besides the traditional *kantrüm,* a popular form has been created in the Surin area; though modernized, it retains much of the character of the older form.

Players of *mahori khmer* at Koktachai Subdistrict in Buriram Province know many old types of tunes (*phleng boran*) that *kantrüm* musicians do not know. Some *mahori khmer* tunes, such as "*Klom*" and "*Pleng ching,*" resemble certain central Thai tunes, and others sound like combinations of two or three such pieces. Whether they are pastiches or not, they have become typical of the *mahori khmer* repertoire in Thailand.

—Panya Roongrüang

Khmer free-reed mouth-organ music in northeast Thailand

The northeast Thai-Lao free-reed mouth organ (*khaen*), well known to Khmer-speakers in Thailand, often accompanies the singing of *chariang* (compare *chrieng chapey* in Cambodia proper). Though players of *khaen* may have a repertoire of many titles, all are played in a single mode, *lai nyai.* Some titles, like "*Mamuat*" ('Spiritual Ceremony'), allude to function, and others, like "*Dam rai yule dai*" ('The Elephant Shakes Its Trunk'), are programmatic. Some northeastern Thai players of *khaen* learned to imitate Khmer musicians, using titles like "*Jariang khamen*" (*khamen* being the Thai pronunciation of *khmer*) and "*Sui khayom hua chang*" ('A Sui Plays Music [the *khaen*] Seated on the Head of an Elephant'). The word *Sui,* properly *Soai* or *Kui,* denotes a subgroup of Mon-Khmer–speakers straddling the border.

—Terry E. Miller

Khmer music in Vietnam

Before the coming of the Viet, the Nam Bo Plain in the basin of the Đồng Nai and Mekong rivers was where Mon-Khmer peoples created an obscure kingdom, Óc Eo. During the 1600s and 1700s, by which time the Việt had conquered this region, the surviving Khmer continued to live in villages among the Việt and later-arriving Hoa (Chinese). Somewhat isolated from the main Khmer kingdoms at Angkor and later Phnom Penh, their culture has interacted with the Vietnamese and Chinese cultures. Because of this isolation, they did not suffer during the Khmer Rouge reign of terror that racked Cambodia from 1975 to 1979. Their population today is estimated at eight hundred thousand.

The Khmer in Vietnam maintain a musical culture that includes vocal and instrumental music, plus dance and dance-drama. All their cultural activities, especially those involving music, are centered in village Buddhist temples. In Sóc Trăng Province and nearby areas, the typical ensemble (*pânpiêt,* and *pinn peat* in Cambodia) consists of boat-shaped xylophones and metallophones (*rôniết*), gong circles (*khôngvông*), a drum (*xămphô*), an oboe (*xralây*), and a pair of small cymbals (figure 30). Other ensembles play for ritual ceremonies and weddings.

Khmer folk songs in Vietnam have been extensively researched. They include songs of boating (*ôumtouck*), metered songs of love (*lâm*), unmetered songs of love (*xaccrova*), nuptial songs (*pleng ka*), lullabies (*bompê kon*), and children's songs (*bot chriêng kômara kômarây*). These songs—whether sung in paddies, on roadways, under palms, at work, chasing birds, rowing boats, at weddings, or during festivals—reflect the people's environment and lives.

Most sumptuous are the theatrical genres *rồbăm* and *yùkê,* performed in the courtyards of Buddhist temples during festivals, when hordes of people assemble. The *rồbăm,* a masked-dance theater, performs stories such as *Riểmkê,* the Khmer ver-

The Khmer in Vietnam maintain a musical culture that includes vocal and instrumental music, plus dance and dance-drama. All their cultural activities, especially those involving music, are centered in village Buddhist temples.

FIGURE 30 In Sóc Trăng province, Vietnam, a *pinn peat* ensemble performs. Photo by Phong T. Nguyễn.

FIGURE 31 Theater (*rồbam*) played by the Khmer in Sóc Trăng Province, Vietnam. Photo by Phong T. Nguyễn.

sion of the *Ramayana.* Each character, wearing a painted mask, performs complex choreographic patterns. *Rồbăm* is accompanied by an ensemble of drums, an oboe, gongs, and cymbals. The performance of a complete story can last up to twenty nights (figure 31).

In contrast, the *yùkê* (also *lakhôn bassắc*) incorporates a patchwork of stories from folkloric, popular, and modern traditions. Begun in Tra Vinh Province in 1940, it has followed the modernizing trends of Viet reformed theater (*cải lương*), popular in the same areas of southern Vietnam. Modeled after *cải lương, yùkê* places much importance on singing, and modifies the traditional Khmer ensemble by adding stringed instruments, a Western drum set, scenery, and stage lighting. Plays have spoken dialogue and spontaneous jokes. The traveling *yùkê* troupes of Trà Vinh, Sóc Trăng, and Cần Thơ provinces have performed widely in cities and villages of the Mekong Delta.

Nontheatrical dances include a dance of courtship (*lâmthôn*), a dance in a circle (*rom vông*), a stylistic dance (*rom kbách*), a Sarawan [place-name] dance (*rom sarawan*), a peacock dance (*rom ca-ngok*), and a coconut dance (*rom tà-lok*). Some dances associated with rituals of possession and weddings require extensive training.

—Phong T. Nguyễn

REFERENCES

Blanchard, Wendell, ed. 1958. *Thailand: Its People, Its Society, Its Culture.* New Haven, Conn.: Human Relations Area Files.

Chou Ta-Kuan. [1993]. *The Customs of Cambodia.* 3rd ed. Bangkok: Siam Society.

His Royal Highness Prince Damrong (Rajanubhap). 1931. *Siamese Musical Instruments.* 2nd ed. Bangkok: The Royal Institute.

Daniélou, Alain. 1957. *Musique du Cambodge et du Laos.* Pondichéry: Publications de l'Institut Français d'Indologie.

His Royal Highness Prince Dhani Nivat. 1973. *The Khon.* 5th ed. Bangkok: Fine Arts Department.

Grainger, Mathew. 1995. "Government Approves Study of Ethnic Minorities." *Phnom Penh Post,* 10 August, 8.

Groslier, Bernard-Philippe. 1965. "Danse et musique sous les rois d'Angkor." *Felicitation Volumes of Southeast Asian Studies* 2:283–292.

Jacq-Hergoualc'h, Michel. 1982. "Le Roman source d'inscription de la peinture khmère à la fin du XIXe et au debut du XXe siècle." *Bulletin de l'École Française d'Extrême-Orient* 126:3–10.

JVC Video Anthology of World Music and Dance. Produced by Ichikawa Katsumori. Tokyo: Victor Company of Japan.

Leclere, Adhemard. 1912. *Cambodge: Contes, légendes et jatakas.* Niort: Imprimerie Nouvelle G. Clouzot.

Miller, Terry E., and Jarernchai Chonpairot. 1981. "The Ranat and Bong-Lang: The Question of Origin of the Thai Xylophones." *Journal of the Siam Society* 69:145–163.

Miller, Terry E., and Sam-Ang Sam. 1995. "The Classical Musics of Cambodia and Thailand: A Study of Distinctions." *Ethnomusicology* 39(2):229–243.

Morton, David. 1974. "Vocal Tones in Traditional Thai Music." *Selected Reports in Ethnomusicology* 2(1):89–99.

———. 1976. *The Traditional Music of Thailand.* Berkeley: University of California Press.

Musique Khmère. 1969. Phnom Penh: Imprimerie Sangkum Reastr Niyum.

Pich, Sal. 1970. *Lumnoam Sangkhep ney Phleng Khmer* [*A Brief Survey on Khmer Music*]. Phnom Penh: Éditions de l'Institut Bouddhique.

Sachs, Curt. 1940. *The History of Musical Instruments.* New York: Norton.

Sem, Sara. 1967. "*Lakhon Khol* au village de Svay Andet, son rôle dans les rites agraires." *Annales de l'Université des Beaux Arts* 1:157–200.

Smithies, Michael. 1971. "*Likay:* A Note on the Origin, Form, and Future of Siamese Folk Opera." *Journal of the Siam Society* 59:33–64.

Steinberg, David. 1959. *Cambodia: Its People, Its Society, Its Culture.* New Haven, Conn.: Human Relations Area Files.

Le Théâtre dans la vie khmère. 1973. Phnom Penh: Université des Beaux Arts.

Thierry, Solange. 1963. *Les Danses sacrées.* Paris: Sources Orientales.

Thiounn, Samdech Chaufea. 1930. *Danses cambodgiennes.* Phnom Penh: Bibliothèque Royale du Cambodge.

Trần Quang Hải. 1980. "Kampuchea." *The New Grove Dictionary of Music and Musicians,* ed. Stanley Sadie. London: Macmillan.

The World and Its Peoples: Southeast Asia. 1965. 2nd ed. New York: Greystone Press.

Thailand

Terry E. Miller

Delimiting a description of Thai music to that which is found within the borders of the contemporary Kingdom of Thailand, although simplifying matters, would not accurately reflect the true state of things. The term *Tai* denotes a complex of separately named ethnic groups speaking related tonal languages, called by linguists Tai-Kadai. Three major Tai peoples are distinguished: the Siamese (or Central Thai), the Lao, and the Shan. However, some linguists (Lebar et al. 1964) divide the Tai peoples into six groups:

1. The Western Tai include the Ahom and Hkamti Shans of Assam, the Chinese Shans of central and western Yunnan, and the Burmese Shans, especially numerous in Shan State and known among the peoples of Thailand as Tai Yai (Great Tai).
2. The Southern Tai include the largest and most famous groups: the Siamese Tai of the central Thai plain, the Khorat Tai of the Khorat plateau in Nakhawn Ratchasima Province (northeast of Bangkok), and the Tai of southern Thailand. Seen as a unified people by anthropologists, these groups show significant differences in their music.
3. The Central Mekong River Tai include two groups found primarily in southern China, especially Yunnan Province: the Nüa and the Lu. The Khün are found in Shan State, and the Yuan live in northern Thailand. The largest group is the Laotian Tai—or simply Lao—living in northeastern Thailand and throughout Laos.
4. The Central Upland Groups include the Black Tai (of Laos and Vietnam), the White Tai (of northern Vietnam), the Red Tai (also of northern Vietnam), and three groups found primarily in Laos: the Neua, the Phuan, and the Phuthai.
5. The Eastern Groups include enclaves of Tai-speakers in southeastern China and northern Vietnam: the Chung-Chia, the Chuang, the Tho, the Trung-Cha, the Nùng, and the Nhang.
6. The term *Kadai* was created by linguist Paul Benedict to denote four small

groups of Tai-speakers in southeastern China and on the island of Hainan: the Li, the Kelao, the Laqua, and the Lati.

These groups total perhaps 75 million people, of which the Siamese Tai (about 35 million) and the Laotian Tai (about 20 million) constitute the largest parts. Of the remainder, the largest group is the Chuang, numbering about 18 million. Although each of these groups is presumed to have music distinctive to a greater or lesser degree from the others and from non-Tai, little is known about the musics of the minority groups. The musics of the Siamese Tai and the Laotian Tai have been well documented.

HISTORY

For the present study, establishing a comprehensive history of the Tai peoples is neither possible nor necessary. It is likely that the original Tai gradually migrated from southern China, especially the southeastern areas, but an old theory—that the allegedly Tai kingdom of Nanchao in Yunnan was pushed south by the Mongol invasion of China in the 1200s—has largely been discredited. The wide distribution of the Tai over several million square kilometers suggests that their history is extremely complex, and attempting to sort it out here would not necessarily help explain the musics of contemporary Tai peoples. David K. Wyatt, whose book *Thailand: A Short History* offers the best summary of recent thinking, writes: "The modern Thai may or may not be descended by blood from the late-arriving Tai. He or she may instead be the descendant of still earlier Mon or Khmer inhabitants of the region, or of much later Chinese or Indian immigrants. Only over many centuries has a 'Thai' culture, a civilization and identity, emerged as the product of interaction between Tai and indigenous and immigrant cultures" (1984:1).

The first historical Tai kingdoms were at Chiangmai and Sukhothai in modern-day Thailand, both founded in the 1200s. The rise of Ayuthaya, founded in 1350, gradually eclipsed the others. This period saw the final destruction of the Khmer Kingdom at Angkor by Ayuthaya in 1431, the golden age of the Tai court culture, and penetration by Europeans in the 1600s. The French, among others, had designs on the Kingdom of Siam (as they had on other areas of Southeast Asia), but plans to convert the king to Roman Catholicism and gain control of his kingdom came to naught: Siam remained a neutral, independent buffer state between the British colonies of Burma and Malaya and the French Indochinese colonies (Laos, Cambodia, Vietnam). The Burmese destroyed Ayuthaya in 1767, but the Siamese reestablished a court at Thon Buri (opposite modern Bangkok) the same year, and moved the capital to Bangkok in 1782.

The current era, called Rattanakosin, has been unified by the succession of nine kings, each called Rama, of the Chakri dynasty. Westernization began during the reigns of King Mongkut (Rama IV, ruled 1851–1868) and King Chulalongkorn (Rama V, ruled 1868–1910). A bloodless coup d'état in 1932 ended the absolute monarchy, and in 1939 the name of the country was changed to Prathet Thai (Land of the Free), westernized as Thailand. The current monarch is His Majesty Bhumibol Adulyadej (Rama IX), who ascended the throne in 1946.

The cultural diversity of Thailand

Though all Tai peoples are culturally interrelated, the citizens of modern Thailand, focusing on the peoples within their national borders, know little of the Tai peoples of Burma, Laos, Vietnam, and China. Because little musical research has been accomplished among Tai peoples outside Thailand and Laos, the focus of this article

Thailand

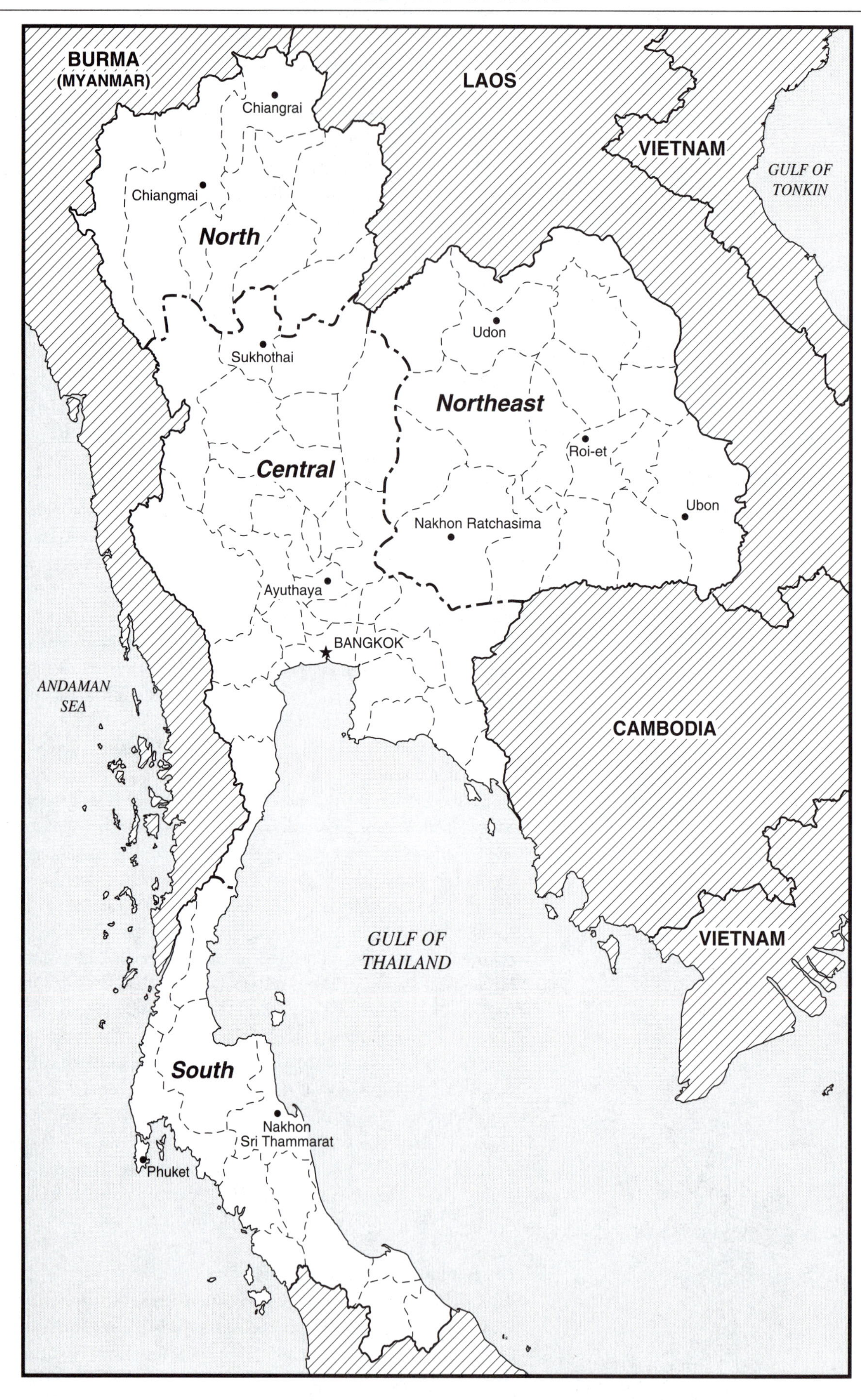
BURMA
(MYANMAR)
LAOS
VIETNAM
GULF OF
TONKIN
Chiangrai
Chiangmai
North
Udon
Sukhothai
Northeast
Roi-et
Central
Ubon
Nakhon Ratchasima
Ayuthaya
BANGKOK
ANDAMAN
SEA
CAMBODIA
GULF OF
THAILAND
VIETNAM
South
Nakhon
Sri Thammarat
Phuket

will be on these two nations. I shall use the terms *Tai* to denote the linguistic group at large and *Thai* to denote the people living within Thailand.

The modern Kingdom of Thailand is bordered by Burma, Laos, Cambodia, and Malaysia and has a land area of 511,770 square kilometers, roughly equal to Spain or to Nevada and Utah combined. Its estimated population (July 1994) is 59,510,471 persons, of whom 19.5 percent are urban. The growth of the population slowed in the late twentieth century and is now only 1.3 percent a year. Governed as a parliamentary democracy, the country is organized into seventy-three provinces, including Bangkok. Each province is divided into districts, subdistricts, and villages. In mainland Southeast Asia, only the people of Malaysia, with an income of U.S. $7,500 per capita, are more prosperous than the Thai, whose income is $5,500 per capita. This figure stands in marked contrast to Thailand's neighbors: Vietnam, $1000; Burma, $950; Laos, $900; and Cambodia, $600.

The four cultural regions

The Thai understand their country as having four cultural regions: center, south, north, and northeast. Each is distinguished from the other in dialect, diet, housing, decorative motifs, literature, and especially music. Though the dialects are interrelated, people from one region tend to have trouble understanding people from another. This is especially true with regard to the texts of songs. The language of the Siamese Tai in central Thailand, known commonly as Thai, has become the official language of the country; it is the language of the national media, officialdom, and schools. As a result, regional dialects declined dramatically in the late twentieth century, despite government-sponsored efforts to reinvigorate regional culture. Each region has a major research center, and numerous students and faculty specialize in local culture, but the forces of modernization and media-induced unity will likely marginalize regional distinctions.

Central Thailand consists of a vast plain emanating north from the capital, Bangkok (known to the Thai as *Krungthep Mahanakhawn* 'City of Angels'), with the Chao Phraya River at its center. Besides Bangkok, central Thailand's thirty-five provinces include the ancient cities of Ayuthaya, Lopburi, Sukhothai, and Nakhawn Pathom. Prominent among its musics are the classical court tradition, various repartee songs, and theatrical genres (*lakhawn chatri* and *li-ke*).

Southern Thailand's fourteen provinces occupy the peninsula extending along the Burmese border to the Malaysian border. The southernmost provinces, Yala and Narathiwat, were originally Malay sultanates, and consequently the typically southern Thai culture is mostly found farther north, especially in Nakhawn Si Thammarat and Phatthalung provinces. The two most prominent musical genres of this region are shadow-puppet theater (*nang talung*) and human theater (*manora*).

Northern Thailand, consisting of the nine provinces in the northwestern bulge bordering Laos and Burma, centers on Chiangmai, Thailand's second largest city. In addition to the Thai population, these provinces are home to significant numbers of upland peoples unrelated to the Thai linguistically and whose music is treated elsewhere in this volume [see MUSIC OF UPLAND MINORITIES IN BURMA, LAOS, AND THAILAND]. Northern Thai music is distinct for one ensemble (*salaw süng pi*), the fingernail dance, and the candle dance.

Northeastern Thailand's seventeen provinces are on the Korat Plateau, extending to the Mekong River, bordering Laos and Cambodia. Culturally diverse, this region includes the Korat Tai (around the city of Nakhawn Ratchasima, known also as Korat), the Khmer-dominated provinces along the Cambodian border, and the mainstream culture of the remaining provinces, known among the Thai as Isan (a Pali-Sanskrit word meaning 'northeast'), whose culture is essentially the same as that of the lowland Lao in Laos. Around Korat, where the language is closer to Siamese Tai than to Laotian Tai, the main musical genres are *li-ke* and a kind of repartee-song. In the three provinces bordering Cambodia, the main language is Khmer, and the distinctive musical genres are one traditional ensemble (*kantrüm*), a narrative type, and two classically based ensembles. The most distinctive Isan genres are highly developed forms of repartee called *lam,* accompanied by the region's most famous instrument, the *khaen,* a free-reed mouth organ. In Laos, lowland Lao music is closely related to the music of northeast Thailand.

Village and court

In Thailand, as in most Southeast Asian countries, a basic distinction is to be made between village and court. Traditions of the latter were originally associated with the ruling elite, their ceremonies, and their entertainments, while those of the former were part of rural life and closely associated with a cycle of festivals related to agriculture and Buddhism. Village traditions in Thailand are often based on the idea of repartee, a stylized courtship ritual between male and female singers.

With the increasing importance of modern urban life centered in Bangkok, a more fundamental distinction is to be made between traditional musics (both court and village) and modern music—primarily popular songs, disseminated both live and through the media. In spite of the growth of popular culture, classical music, dance, and theater remain strong because of their importance for Thai identity—internally, externally, and for rituals and other formal events. At the same time, these classical arts, formerly reserved for the aristocracy, are primarily transmitted through both private and public schools and universities, allowing anyone, regardless of background, access to them.

When Europeans visited Ayuthaya in the 1600s, they noted the existence of foreign communities, especially Chinese. Early writers, such as La Loubere, Gervaise, and Bouvet, described performances of Chinese musical theater. Most ethnic Chinese, who came to dominate the business sector of the Thai economy, likely arrived during the 1800s and 1900s. Consequently, most cities have community organizations that sponsor performances of locally produced Chinese theater and maintain clubs for amateur musicians who play traditional silk-and-bamboo music. Many of these are situated at Chinese temples. Most Chinese in Thailand speak Chao-chou (called Taejiu in dialect), and their music is distinctive from other kinds of Chinese music, but small enclaves of other dialects, such as Guangdong (Cantonese), are found, some retaining a distinctive musical expression. Thailand remains a good place for observing traditional Chinese music and theater in functional contexts.

Thai musics in international contexts

Most Thai musics are similar in some way to musics found among their neighbors, whether in structure, instruments, or scale. It would be a mistake, however, to conclude that Thai musics are merely derivative of other cultures or that neighboring musics derive from the Thai.

Because the great cultures of India and China have long and documented histories and because they played such an important role in the development of Southeast Asia, it is sometimes assumed that they provided the foundations on which Thai music was created. Clearly some phenomena, especially instruments, are of Chinese or Indian origin, but similarities in tuning, scale, texture, or rhythmic practices do not necessarily prove a relationship. The pattern may, in fact, be precisely the reverse, or there may be no relationship at all.

Since it can be argued that little is unique to any defined culture, its identity derives not from uniqueness of the constituent parts but from the combination of them. This is true of Thai musical culture. Whether the construction of Thai classical music is similar to that of Chinese music does not matter; in sound and spirit, Thai classical music is obviously different from Chinese music. Whether patterns of drumming in Thailand are cyclic (as in Indian drumming) does not matter; the Thai patterns are different from those of India. Whether Thai musicians express themselves on the same instruments used by their neighbors does not matter; Thai musical expression is strikingly different from that of Thailand's neighbors.

Consequently, the musics of Thailand must be viewed both as individually expressive of the Thai people and yet as having complex but sometimes uncertain relationships with those of surrounding cultures.

Terminological concerns in cross-cultural analysis

Translating certain musical terms from Thai to English may inadvertently invoke inappropriate associations. It has been usual to refer to the music associated with the court, ceremony, and certain kinds of theater in central Thailand as classical (*phleng thai düm*)—a concept borrowed from the West. In this case, most of the associations are appropriate, for Thai do acknowledge this music to be "of the highest class; most representative of the excellence of its kind; having recognized worth" (*Webster's New Universal Unabridged Dictionary*). Similarly, it is thought of as "music that conforms to certain established standards of form, complexity, musical literacy." I therefore maintain the usage of the term *classical.* And just as classical music in the West is cultivated by a minority, so is Thai classical music known to and appreciated by the few. The term *court music* is less satisfactory in that the music under study was not restricted to court, and today it functions almost entirely outside the court.

Review of research

The scholarly study of music in Thailand has gathered momentum since the early decades of the twentieth century, dependent on the development of the field of ethnomusicology in the West and the overcoming of a reluctance in Thailand to include music among subjects fit for intellectual study. The first comprehensive study of Thai classical music in a Western language appeared only in 1976, and surveys of Thai music in the Thai language remain largely untranslated and inaccessible to most non-Thai.

Most publications by Thai scholars on Thai music have been short, and few have gone beyond the basics of the classical tradition, leaving the village traditions virtually unknown. Most writers have been government officials, some of them members of the royal family, but today university professors are publishing numerous studies. Few articles are technical; many concentrate on extramusical matters, like dance, ritual, and theater. The early writers included Phya Anuman Rajadhon, who wrote as a folklorist; His Royal Highness Prince Bidyalongkorn (Bidyalankarana); His Royal Highness Prince Dhani Nivat, who concentrated on theater; and even His Majesty King Vajiravudh (Rama VI), who wrote an article on theater and a book on dance-drama poetry.

Writers focusing on music are few. Of those publishing in European languages, His Royal Highness Prince Damrong (Rajanubhap) was among the first, with brief articles on musical instruments and dance from the 1920s and early 1930s. Booklets by the European-trained musician Phra Chen Duriyanga (born Peter Feit) in the Thai Culture Series "Thai Music" and "Thai Music in Western Notation," though limited in scope to the basics of one ensemble, have been widely circulated. Dhanit Yupho, late Director General of the Fine Arts Department, while concentrating on theatrical matters, published an important study of musical instruments, which David Morton translated into English. Another Director General, (Luang) V. Vichitr

"Finally the scene was closed with a kind of Chinese tragedy which bored the spectators and us in particular, who were obliged to attend all these shows. . . . We saw only burlesque dances and ridiculous farces . . . with horrible masks and contortions of one truly possessed." (1685)

Vadakarn, published in 1942 a brief historical survey, "The Evolution of Thai Music," now out of print. In many ways, the most significant writer has been Montri Tramote of the Fine Arts Department, whose main study, *Sap-sang-khit,* a study of musical vocabulary derived from a television series, remains untranslated. His commentaries on specific Thai compositions, published in *Silapakorn Magazine,* also remain untranslated.

Since about 1970, there has been an upsurge in writings about Thai music, some of it aimed at the student-textbook market and some in English. Exceptional are Utit Naksawat's writings, Jarernchai Chonpairot's study of Thai composers based on original research (rather than a recycling of earlier writings), and Panya Roongrüang's *History of Thai Music* (1973) and his *Thai Music in Sound* (1990), in both English and Thai, which includes three audiocassettes with examples extensively illustrating the text. At least in the past, Thai scholars were reluctant to question critically the writings of respected seniors, especially members of the royal family. The number of Thai trained in serious musical scholarship remains small but is growing.

The few studies of Thai music published by Westerners before David Morton's pioneering work barely deserve notice. Frederick Verney's pamphlet *Notes on Siamese Musical Instruments* is useful not only for its descriptions and line drawings but also for its forward-looking attitude. Writing about the pitfalls of Western musical ethnocentrism, Verney concludes, "To appreciate the music of the East it would be necessary to forget all that one has experienced in the West" (1885:5). Two German pioneers in ethnomusicology, Carl Stumpf and Erich M. von Hornbostel, recorded a Siamese ensemble visiting Berlin in 1900. Stumpf's study of Siamese theory (1901) and Hornbostel's formal analyses of the transcriptions (1920), though misguided (by today's standards), are pathfinding studies in the field.

No technically comprehensive study of Thai classical music existed until the 1960s, when David Morton, a student in ethnomusicology at the University of California, Los Angeles, went to Thailand to conduct research for his dissertation. Published as a book in 1976, his work remains the primary source for the analytical study of Thai music. In addition, he published numerous articles and the translation of Dhanit Yupho's study of instruments. In the later years of his career, Morton emphasized composition and other matters, leaving the study of Thai music to a new generation of scholars.

Historical sources

Historical sources of European and American origin going back to the 1500s provide glimpses of the instruments, the genres, and the practices of earlier periods. Most betray some prejudices on the writers' part, those of the 1800s being the most strident. The earliest of them, Fernão Mendes Pinto's *Peregrinacão* (1614), reporting observations made in 1548, mentions processions and instruments. The most valuable descriptions predating the 1800s come from the later 1600s, when French missionaries, in league with Phaulkon, the Greek adviser to King Narai, attempted to convert the king and thereby subvert the kingdom. First published during that period, several books—Bouvet 1963 [1685], Choisy 1687, Gervaise 1688, and Tachard 1686—include information on theater and ceremonial music. By far the most significant was Simon de La Loubere's *Du Royaume de Siam,* first published in French in 1691 and in English in 1693. La Loubere devotes an entire chapter to music, describing numerous instruments and genres; he includes line drawings of several instruments, plus a song transcribed into staff notation with phonetically spelled text. Following the failure of the French efforts at colonization, few foreigners traveled to Siam or wrote about it until nearly 150 years later.

Nineteenth-century sources become numerous from about 1820 on. The most important of them are by Sir John Bowring (1969 [1857]), John Crawfurd (1967 [1828]), George Finlayson (1826), Charles Gutzlaff (1834), Edmund Roberts (1837), W. S. W. Ruschenberger (1970 [1838]), and Frederick Arthur Neale (1852). Thai music was heard in Europe as early as 1869, when a Siamese exposition went to Paris and Le Havre. The most important event, however, was probably the London Inventions Exposition of 1884, where several British scholars took note of Siamese music. Alexander J. Ellis examined Siamese instruments while researching his landmark article (1885a) on tuning, in which the cents system was first used. Frederick Verney, secretary to the Siamese legation, published an insightful pamphlet, *Notes on Siamese Musical Instruments* (1885), and A. J. Hipkins included several Siamese specimens in his *Musical Instruments Historic, Rare, and Unique* (1945 [1888]). In Berlin in 1900, Erich M. von Hornbostel and Carl Stumpf were the first researchers to record a Siamese ensemble; they published two major analytical studies of the recordings (Hornbostel 1920; Stumpf 1901).

Before 1932, classical music was essentially an accouterment of court life, restricted to the nobility. Visitors from abroad were often provided performances of music and theater; some found the music agreeable, and others found it excruciating. Seventeenth-century French missionaries saw not only Siamese music and theater but also Chinese. An exasperated Jesuit astronomer, Père Bouvet, wrote: "Finally the scene was closed with a kind of Chinese tragedy which bored the spectators and us in particular, who were obliged to attend all these shows. Mr. Constance [Phaulkon] had condemned us to remain to the end, and Mr. Ambassador [Simon de La Loubere] had made us refrain from returning [to our quarters] before him . . . but we saw only burlesque dances and ridiculous farces . . . with horrible masks and contortions of one truly possessed" (1963[1685]:132–133). According to these writers and several before and after them, music was played to accompany the king's processions as he walked from place to place, to entertain the king when he awakened, ate, and retired, and to accompany certain ceremonies, both at court and in temples.

The nobility were not necessarily passive hearers of music. Some acted, some performed music, and others composed classical works. King Rama I (ruled 1782–1809) wrote major poetical works, and King Rama II (ruled 1809–1824) devoted considerable energy to play writing, acting, and improving drama in general. King Mongkut (Rama IV) restored the custom of appointing a second king, in this case his brother, Prince Chutamani, with the title Phra Pin-klao. The second king, who had a special fascination for things Lao, played the Lao free-reed mouth organ (*khaen*) for Sir John Bowring in 1855. The seventh king of this line, Prajadhipok (ruled 1925–1935), the last absolute monarch, composed some now-famous classical compositions. The reigning monarch, Bhumibol Adulyadej (Rama IX), is known for his jazz-style compositions and for his abilities in playing jazz clarinet and saxophone. His daughter, Princess Sirindhorn, having studied Thai classical instruments, has encouraged respect for this ancient music.

With the end of absolute monarchy came the end of the musical establishment at court. As musicians and actors lost their official positions, they were sometimes fortunate enough to find a new wealthy patron who maintained to some extent the old system. Great musicians received royal titles both before and after 1932 and were consequently respected, though few attained wealth as a result. Others found support in the newly developing educational system. Indeed, the College of Dramatic Arts was formed to continue the classical tradition of music and theater. Since 1975, it has founded nine branches in all four cultural regions—essentially high schools for the arts—where both classical and regional traditions are taught to students aged twelve to eighteen, who also study the standard curriculum. The college is a part of the Department of Fine Arts, which oversees antiquities and their preservation and study, publications, and many kinds of performances.

Democratization

The most significant change, however, was the democratization of classical music, making it available to any interested citizen. The educational system has become the bastion of Thai classical music, a place where anyone, even villagers from a poor province, can study with traditional masters. Musical study leading to college and university degrees is a recent development, thanks to a growing appreciation of the arts as legitimate academic areas. Baccalaureate degrees, with majors in Thai or Western musics, can be obtained from Chulalongkorn University, Srinakharinwirot University, Mahidol University, and Mahasarakham University, all but the last based in Bangkok. Several colleges also offer music majors, and Bansomdej Chaopraya Teacher's College was the first to offer a music degree.

Nevertheless, it would be difficult to argue that classical music plays more than a minor role in the musical life of the modern Thai. Increasingly affluent and rapidly growing, Bangkok's population primarily listens to various kinds of popular music, some more Thai in style than others, heard through the media (radio and television), on inexpensive cassette tapes and music videos, and in live performances. The people of smaller cities and villages tend to follow Bangkok's lead, though in the less developed areas of the kingdom, nonclassical traditional musics remain important.

The most commonly heard performances of classical music take place within educational contexts and in places where tourists receive a sampling of Thai culture, both in restaurants and major parks (such as the Rose Garden). Though classical music is therefore rarely heard and its performers only modestly rewarded, the Thai people sense that this kind of music has something to do with Thailand's soul and identity. Just as many nonprofessing Christians still prefer to be married and buried within a church, Thai who otherwise never listen to classical music usually choose it to represent the beauty of their culture to non-Thai.

General observations on Thai classical music

Some classical musicians have achieved a certain prominence as soloists, but Thai music is primarily ensemble-oriented—unlike, for example, Indian music, where star soloists predominate. Since little improvisation beyond idiomatic ornamentation occurs in the music, master performers are respected more for their extensive repertories, subtle ornamentation, and lineage than for virtuoso techniques. This is not to say that solo playing is not cultivated—a few flashy musicians succeed in their careers—but that this aspect is secondary to the ensemble, in which the individual's sound is subordinated to the mixture.

It could be argued that this factor has contributed to the decline of Thai classical music in an age where Thai popular musicians and ensembles attract audiences on the basis of individual appeal, and both Western classical and popular musicians individually achieve star status. Recordings are promoted as much for the pieces as for the performers; and sometimes the names of the ensemble and the musicians are omitted entirely. This contrasts to the featured-artist factor in Indian music, the virtuoso factor in contemporary traditional Chinese music, and the recording-star factor in Western classical music—all of which contribute to the strengths of their respective traditions.

The traditional mode of training was time consuming but thorough. The student may have lived in the home of the master, spending many hours a day in study and supervised practice. Masters taught everything by rote, showing students a phrase at a time and asking them to repeat it. As each phrase was mastered, the piece was repeatedly played from the beginning to that point. Gradually, entire pieces were learned. Neither notation nor note taking was permitted; discussion and questions were unusual. Over time, the student's repertoire increased. Even today, these methods prevail among traditional masters and in the College of Dramatic Arts and its branches. Even young musicians can play hours of difficult music entirely from memory. Nevertheless, as the pace of Thai life has quickened, less and less time remains for this sort of teaching. In Bangkok, students may have to settle for carefully scheduled lessons once or twice a week.

Notation (discussed in detail below) is a recent phenomenon, from about the third decade of the twentieth century. Though the Fine Arts Department has published classical music transcribed into staff notation, the notations used by Thai students are much simpler, being either tablature or pitch notation, the latter indicated either by arabic numerals or Thai initials of the solfège system. Students learning string music are the most likely to use notation, and most of the published collections are for these instruments.

About 1987, Chanok Sakarik, a descendant of the revered composer and teacher Luang Pradit Phairoh and a cofounder of a school for traditional music in Bangkok, developed a computer-graphics program to teach young students the basics of several classical instruments. The student observes, as in the case of the xylophone, the proper keys being struck while the music is played by the unit's synthesizer. This kind of blending of modern technology and children's fascination with computers to maintain the traditional arts has proven effective at the school, where students come for only limited periods on certain days of the week.

Musicians observe obligatory conventions of etiquette. It is customary to remove one's shoes when entering a home or a temple; students also do so in many public-school classrooms. Since Thai instruments are played on the floor, the removal of shoes before entering an instrument room is requisite. Instruments must be treated with respect, and consequently rough treatment—or even stepping over them—is forbidden. Students were traditionally required to keep their heads below their master's, even to the point of crawling into the room. Today, that custom is not so strictly followed, but it is still polite to keep one's head below the heads of important people. Before playing, students will fold their hands in the praying position (*wai*) and perform a brief *wai khru* ritual in remembrance of their teacher and their teacher's lineage. Before public performances, entire ensembles or dramatic troupes perform more elaborate rituals.

MUSICAL INSTRUMENTS

Thai instruments are fairly extensive, and their sources are varied. According to early European descriptions, over the past four hundred years the body of available instruments has gradually expanded, while a few instruments became obsolete. In contrast to the Chinese, the Thai have proven quite conservative with regard to their instru-

ching Pair of small, thick metal cymbals connected by a cord

chap Medium-size cymbals, connected by a cord, flatter and thinner than the *ching*

krap Several kinds of percussion idiophones

ranat ek Higher xylophone, with twenty-one keys

ranat thum Lower-pitched xylophone, with seventeen or eighteen keys

ments in resisting the urge to "improve" them. Consequently, the technologies of most instruments remain those of a distant past.

Thai musicians have a basic system for classifying instruments. The most comprehensive catalogue of instruments by a Thai scholar is Dhanit Yupho's *Nangsü khrüang dontri thai,* published by the Fine Arts Department in 1957 and translated into English as *Thai Musical Instruments* by David Morton (1960). A new edition, combining both versions, was published in 1987 in honor of the author's eightieth birthday. Dhanit classifies fifty-six instruments of both classical and regional origin in three groups: percussive instruments (subdivided into instruments of wood, metal, and leather), wind instruments, and stringed instruments (subdivided into plucked and bowed).

This survey follows the Sachs-Hornbostel system, which differs only slightly from Dhanit's. Regional instruments are treated under separate headings below.

Idiophones

Concussion idiophones

1. *Ching.* Two identical brass cymbals with thick walls and the shape of a shallow teacup are joined with a cord which passes through a hole in the center of each. They come in two sizes, one set being 5 centimeters in diameter, the other 6 centimeters. The name of the instrument is onomatopoetic, describing the undamped sound produced when the cymbals are struck together; the damped sound is described as *chap.* The function of the instrument is to provide an audible beat, marking the accented and unaccented beats in accompanying both instrumental and vocal music. Its origin is uncertain, since similar instruments are found both in China (*shing*) and India (*kaitala*).

2. *Chap.* Onomatopoetic in name, the *chap* cymbals are also of brass, flatter and thinner than the *ching.* Two sizes are distinguished: the *chap lek* 'small *chap*', measuring 12 to 14 centimeters in diameter, and the *chap yai* 'large *chap*', about 23 to 26 centimeters in diameter. The former are joined with a cord like the *ching,* but the latter are separate; their function is to play syncopated rhythmic patterns within the colotomic structure.

3. *Krap* 'castanets'. Again onomatopoetic for its *krap-krap-krap* sound, three specific types of *krap* 'castanets' are distinguished: *krap khu, krap phuang,* and *krap sepha.* Rarely heard, the *krap khu* 'pair of castanets' consist of either two pieces of a bamboo tube split lengthwise, or two pieces of wood carved like bamboo halves. Their usual length is about 40 centimeters and their width about 3 to 4 centimeters. The *krap phuang* 'cluster castanets' is a bundle of five thin pieces of hardwood or ivory 21 to 22 centimeters long, alternating with six sheets of brass enclosed in two flared wooden or ivory end pieces. A wire passes through one end of all the pieces, as if it were a fan. The instrument is held in one hand and struck into the open palm of the other, caus-

ing the pieces of wood and brass to crack together. Its usages in the past were evidently for signaling, whereas in the twentieth century it was used in rarely heard types of songs: boat songs (*phleng rüa*), garland-of-flowers songs (*tawk soi*), and *sakarawa* poems. The instrument bears a distant similarity to the Korean *pak,* used to signal the beginning and end of certain court compositions. Finally, the recitation castanets (*krap sepha*) consist of two polished hardwood bars 18 to 21 centimeters long. Each bar's cross-section resembles that of a loaf of bread, 2 centimeters across the bottom, 4 centimeters high, and 3 centimeters across a rounded top. To create a distinctive rhythm with the chant, the reciter holds a pair in each hand, either rolling them together or alternating them; they are also now used in some classical ensembles.

Struck idiophones

Bar idiophones

Two kinds of bar idiophones are found: xylophones (*ranat ek* and *ranat thum*) and metallophones (*ranat ek lek* and *ranat thum lek*).

4. *Ranat ek.* The foremost xylophone, *ranat ek* 'first' or 'principal', is distinctive to mainland Southeast Asia. As described by Dhanit,

> The present model of the *rana-t ay-k* [*ranat ek*] has twenty-one keys. The lowest-toned key is 38 centimeters long, 5 centimeters wide and 1.5 centimeters thick. The keys decrease in size and become thicker as the tones become higher. The highest-toned key is 30 centimeters long. The keys are hung on a cord which passes through holes at each of the nodes of the keys—7 to 9 centimeters in from the end of each key. This "keyboard" is suspended over a boat-shaped body from metal hooks on the end pieces—two on each end. The distance between the two end pieces is 120 centimeters. (Dhanit 1987:17)

The keys are of hardwood or bamboo. The *ranat,* although widely believed by Thai musicians to be an original Thai instrument, is not described in the literature until 1826 (Finlayson); thereafter, it is normally included in lists of instruments. Neale (1852:235) asserts that the *ranat* is of Burmese origin, and the best players of his time were Burmese. Indeed, the *ranat* and the Burmese *pattala* are nearly identical. Thai scholars usually reject this theory, asserting that the Burmese more likely copied the *ranat* as early as the 1500s but used the *ranat thum* idiom. The existence of *yòudayà* songs in the Burmese repertoire, said to have come from Ayuthaya, suggests Siamese influence rather than vice versa. The *ranat* idiom is continuous: even notes are played in octaves, using two kinds of mallets, soft and hard, depending on the ensemble. A twenty-one-key instrument has a range extending from G (below middle C) to f′ above the staff according to Thai conventions with staff notation.

5. *Ranat thum.* Larger and lower in range than the *ranat ek,* the *ranat thum* measures 126 centimeters along the keyboard, with the seventeen or eighteen keys ranging in size from 42 by 6 centimeters at the lower end to 35.5 by 5 centimeters at the upper. Unlike the *ranat ek*'s curved wooden resonator supported on a square base, the *ranat thum*'s resonator is parallel to the floor, supported on four feet. Dhanit writes that this instrument was created during the period of King Rama III (1824–1851), with keys of hardwood or bamboo. The idiom is quite unlike that of the *ranat ek:* broken octaves and syncopated rhythms—considered playful by the Thai—predominate. This instrument acts as a foil to the *ranat ek,* playing around the main notes of the melody rather than reinforcing them. Only soft mallets are used. The range of the instrument (E to f′) partially overlaps that of the *ranat ek,* but the thicker bars and heavy mallets differentiate its timbre.

6. *Ranat ek lek* or *ranat thawng.* Created during the reign of King Rama IV (1851–1868), the *ranat thawng* 'gold' is the equivalent of the *ranat ek* in heavy brass, iron, or bronze keys and having the same range. These bars rest directly on felt strips on the horizontal resonator. The origin of the instrument is uncertain, but it likely succeeded the little-known and short-lived *ranat kaeo,* a crystallophone, recently revived by the Fong Naam Ensemble in Thailand. Others suggest it was inspired by Javanese gamelan instruments, but in fact there is no gamelan equivalent. Its function is to double the *ranat ek* in large ensembles, but because of its weight it is difficult to move and consequently not often seen.

7. *Ranat thum lek.* Designed by Phra Pin-klao, the brother of Rama IV, the *ranat thum lek* 'iron' (usually of bronze) doubles the *ranat thum* in idiom and range, though it may have as few as sixteen keys. Similar to the *ranat thawng* but having larger and fewer keys, it is sometimes played with mallets consisting of hard, untanned buffalo-hide discs on the ends of sticks.

Gongs

8. *Khawng.* Thai gongs of the present period all have rims and bosses and are struck with a padded beater. Bossless rimmed gongs have been unearthed in the northeast region in the area of That Luang and along the Mekong River and are still found among upland Mon-Khmer groups in southern Laos. *Khawng* may be suspended within a frame or held in one hand suspended on a cord. The term *khawng* is thought to be onomatopoetic. The instruments are distinguished by several names, usually indicating size and function. Some gongs serve in classical ensembles to mark accented beats; others serve in village ensembles for a kind of ostinato or are beaten alone in processions. (a) *Khawng mong* vary in diameter from 30 to 45 centimeters and give the sound *mong.* Since they were beaten during the day to indicate the hours, the term *chua-mong* 'hour' is derived from the sound of the gong. (b) *Khawng chai* refers to gongs measuring up to 80 centimeters in diameter, which have the sound *mui* (called *khawng mui*) or *hui.* The term *chai* is thought by Dhanit to have derived from the *chayakunta,* an Indian gong. (c) *Khawng meng* and *khawng kratae* refer to small gongs, about 19 centimeters in diameter, with 1-centimeter-thick metal struck with a piece of wood. The former term applies in funeral ceremonies in the *bua loi* ensemble, while the latter applies to a small gong used to call the watches at night. (d) *Khawng khu* 'pair of gongs' are thick walled but suspended horizontally on cords passing through four holes in the rim in a rectangular wooden box. One has a lower sound (*mong*); the other, a higher sound (*meng*). The *khawng khu* is rarely heard outside southern Thai theater. (e) *Khawng rao,* now nearly obsolete, was formerly used in *rabeng,* a kind of sung entertainment. It consists of three gongs—large, medium, small—suspended vertically within a wooden frame, all facing to one side. Today, it may join the large *mahori.* (f) *Wong khawng chai* were created during the reign of King Rama V as part of an ensemble to accompany *dükdamban,* a newly created kind of theater. The instrument consists of seven large-diameter gongs suspended vertically in a circular wooden frame of seven panels, but counting the opening, the overall shape is an octagon. The player, seated in the middle, strikes the appropriate pitch at certain accented points in the melody. Today, both the theatrical genre and the instrument are rare.

9. *Khawng rang.* Obsolete and probably never widely used, the *khawng rang* consisted of eight small gongs of successively smaller diameter (from left to right), suspended horizontally on cords or rawhide thongs along a wood-and-rattan frame. The eight pitches, constituting a complete Thai "scale" plus the upper octave, made the instrument capable of realizing melodies. The shape of the *khawng rang* suggests the southern Philippine *kulintang* and more distantly the Javanese *bonang.* Though rarely

used in central Thailand, it may be used in the *thum-mong* funeral ensemble by Khmer-Thai in northeastern Thailand.

10. *Khawng wong yai.* Meaning gongs in a circle (*wong*), this instrument is of two sizes, larger (*yai*) and smaller (*lek*). The former is the original instrument and before the creation of the latter (during the reign of King Rama III) was simply called *khawng wong.* A smaller version of the *khawng wong yai,* made for the *mahori* ensemble, is softer in tone to balance the strings. The instrument consists of sixteen brass-bossed gongs horizontally mounted on an oval rattan frame (its width is greater than its depth) with wooden posts, each gong suspended by a leather thong through four holes in the rim. The player enters the frame through the rear gap; sitting cross-legged, he strikes the boss with a pair of disc mallets, the soft ones of wood covered with cloth, the hard ones of untanned buffalo hide. The gongs range in diameter from 17 centimeters on the player's far left to 12 centimeters on the player's far right and span a range from D to e′. Each is tuned through the placement of lumps of beeswax and powdered lead into the underside of the boss. The musical function of the *khawng wong yai* is to play the *luk khawng,* the least dense version of the melody, sometimes conceived as the basic form of the melody, and students customarily begin with this instrument. The idiom consists primarily of octaves, fourths, fifths, and single-note playing. Apparently one of the oldest surviving instruments, it was widely mentioned in the literature from the period of the French missionaries (late 1600s). La Loubere provided a drawing of it but showed inverted cup-shaped gongs sitting atop wooden posts and struck like a bell, doubtless an inaccuracy on the artist's part. Much earlier, semicircular frames with eight or nine gongs were carved in the walls of Angkor Vat, a thirteenth-century temple in Cambodia (Morton 1976:10).

11. *Khawng wong lek.* For the smaller oval, eighteen gongs vary in diameter from 13 centimeters on the player's far left to 9.5 centimeters on the right and have a range one octave above that of the *khawng wong yai.* As noted above, the *khawng wong lek* was created during the reign of King Rama III and like its sister instrument also comes in a smaller size for *mahori* ensembles. Unlike the *khawng wong yai,* the part played by the smaller instrument is denser, more melodic and active, exhibiting many stereotyped ornamental figures. Consequently, only advanced performers play it.

12. *Khawng mawn.* So similar and yet so different, the *khawng mawn* consists of fifteen or sixteen gongs mounted in a beautifully carved wooden frame shaped like the letter U with a single pedestal. The largest gongs are to the player's left, and a humanlike figure, a god's face (*na phra*) is carved on the frame. Since the 1800s, these have also been differentiated into larger (*yai*) and smaller (*lek*), like the *khawng wong.* Their usage is restricted to the Mawn (often spelled Mon) ensemble, which, while seeming to be ethnic (the Mon, a minority in western Thailand and Burma, predated the Thai in the present area of the kingdom), is played by Thai classical musicians primarily for funerals (figure 1).

13. *Mahorathük.* The bronze idiophonic drum—it is not a membranophone—has for years been widely studied as an archaeological artifact. Unearthed in most countries of both mainland and island Southeast Asia, the bronze drum is primarily a mysterious instrument of the distant past. Having a flat metal head from about 25 to 65 centimeters in diameter mounted on a drumlike body, flared at the top, it is struck with beaters. Most of these drums have decoration on both body and top—especially four frogs, leading to the speculation that they were beaten to induce rain. In old Siam, the *mahorathük* was beaten with two padded beaters for special ceremonies, especially in relation to royalty. Certain Buddhist temples also used them with a conch-shell trumpet to summon monks for morning and evening services and to mark the initial lighting of candles. Today, only a few temples in Bangkok retain them, and they are rarely heard.

The largest Thai classical drum is the *klawng that*, *klawng* being a generic term for drum and *that* the specific type. However, the *taphon* is the most significant drum because it is considered quasi-sacred and must therefore be kept in a high place.

FIGURE 1 A player of the Mon gong circle (*khawng mawn lek*) within a *piphat mawn* ensemble at a Bangkok temple where funerals occur regularly. Photo by Terry E. Miller, 1988.

Slit drums

14. *Kraw.* The *kraw* is a section of bamboo, closed at each end by a node and having a lengthwise slit. It was beaten as a signal, as when a headman called villagers to a meeting. In some theatrical pieces, one is used on stage for signaling. The length and diameter vary, the larger ones being more resonant.

15. *Krong.* Similar to the *kraw* but up to 2 meters long, the *krong* consists of several sections of bamboo, with the slit running throughout or in sections. This instrument was beaten to accompany certain kinds of singing and dance, but it was also used within a *piphat* for military scenes in the large shadow-puppet theater.

Shaken idiophones

16. *Angkalung.* Neither described in Dhanit nor usually considered a Thai instrument, an *angkalung* consists of two pieces of bamboo, each tapered at one end, set into a bamboo frame so that when the entire frame is shaken, the tubes make a sound. The smaller tube sounds the octave of the larger. *Angkalung* are made in multi-octave sets, with seven pitches to the octave. First imported from Indonesia during the early to mid-twentieth century and then made locally to conform to the Thai tuning system, they are widely played in schools, in the manner of Western hand-bell choirs.

Membranophones

Single-headed drums

17. *Thon* or *thap.* This inverted-vase- or goblet-shaped drum, with body of clay or (less commonly) wood, is related in shape to drums from North Africa and Western Asia, like the Arabic *darabuka* and the Persian *dombak.* The head, directly laced to a metal ring at the waist of the body, cannot be tuned. Two specific types are distinguished. The wooden *thon chatri,* measuring 36 centimeters long and 20 centimeters in diameter at the head and played in pairs, is specifically meant for the ensemble that accompanies southern Thai human and shadow-puppet theaters. These drums are also used with central Thai classical ensembles to accompany certain kinds of songs. The *thon mahori* is slightly larger in diameter (22 centimeters) and length (38 centimeters), with a clay body and a head of any of various materials (calfskin, goatskin, snakeskin). The body is sometimes highly decorated with gold, silver, lacquer, mother-of-pearl, or pieces of colored glass. Both types are played by the right hand, leaving the left available to influence the tone by covering the open end. Today, the *thon* is associated with the *rammana* in classical ensembles, and when a single player handles both, he or she plays the latter with the left hand. The *thon*'s history in Thailand is unknown, but it was described and pictured by La Loubere in 1691.

18. *Rammana.* This is a shallow, conical, wooden drum with a single head of calfskin tacked directly to the body—a method of fastening that suggests a Chinese origin, though the Chinese are not known to have had a drum of this type. The usual *rammana,* sometimes called *rammana mahori,* has a head 26 centimeters in diameter and a body 7 centimeters deep. The head is raised slightly from the rim of the body by a cord (*sanap*), and consequently the head of the *rammana* can be tightened by wedging paper into this opening. This drum is used with the *thon* in *mahori* and *khrüang sai.* The 50-centimeter-diameter *rammana lam tat,* with a 12.5-centimeter-deep body, has a head fastened to a metal ring around the narrow part of its body with rattan or cane strips. Its use today is restricted to central Thai repartee-songs (*lam tat*) and village percussive ensembles.

Double-headed drums

19. *Klawng that.* The largest Thai classical drum is the *klawng that, klawng* being a generic term for drum and *that* the specific type. Each of its heads, measuring some 46 centimeters in diameter, is attached firmly to the wooden body with metal tacks, or less commonly with pegs of wood, ivory, or bone. Barrel-shaped, the body is a hollowed-out piece of hardwood. Dhanit asserts that only since the reign of King Rama II has a pair of drums been used, each tilted toward the player by an X-shaped support that passes through a metal ring attached to the side of the body. The player strikes the heads with two padded drumsticks. Though Dhanit claims the heads can be tuned by weighting them with lumps of cooked rice and ash, usually they are not. The *doom,* the drum giving the higher pitch, is considered the male or husband (*dua phu*), and the *dawm,* with the lower pitch, is the female or wife (*dua mia*). As is true of several other Thai drums (like the *taphon* and the *sawng na*), a round black patch is in the middle of each head, and a black ring is painted around the rim, both derived from a natural sap. The *klawng that,* having an aggressive sound, is restricted to *piphat,* especially for theater. In 1691, La Loubere called the drum a *clong,* and suggested that even then such drums were played in pairs, contradicting Dhanit's claim.

20. *Taphon.* The *taphon* is the most significant drum because it is considered quasi-sacred and must therefore be kept in a high place. An asymmetrical barrel drum with the larger head (25 centimeters in diameter) to the player's left and the smaller head (22 centimeters) to the right, it is played with the hands. The body, 48

centimeters long, is carved from solid teak or jackfruit, and the edges of the heads are sewn with twisted strands of cane. Leather thongs run the length of the body, from one head to the other alternately, through the cane loops. These thongs are so closely spaced that the wooden body cannot be seen. More thongs to a width of 7 to 8 centimeters encircle the bulge in the body, and a handle is attached to it. The drum is attached horizontally to a wooden stand with thongs. Evidently, this was not always so, for La Loubere (1691) described it as hung around the player's neck. Like the *klawng that,* it has both a black patch and a black rim stripe of sap, and before playing, the player must tune the larger drumhead by weighting it with a mixture of cooked rice and ash. The *taphon* is used almost exclusively in *piphat.*

21. *Taphon mawn.* Like the *taphon,* the *taphon mawn* is mounted horizontally on a stand, but it is much larger, with neither a handle nor an extra band of thongs around the middle. The body, 74 centimeters long, appears more cylindrical in shape, though there is still a slight bulge near the larger head (51 centimeters in diameter), struck by the player's left hand; the smaller head is 37 centimeters in diameter. The black circle, the rim stripe, and the head weighting described above apply here. The *taphon mawn* is used exclusively in *piphat mawn* and for *mawn* compositions in *piphat.*

22. *Klawng taphon.* Rarely seen, the *klawng taphon* consists of two *taphon,* mounted at a 45-degree angle on a wooden stand, with the larger heads facing the player, who strikes them with padded sticks similar to those used to play xylophones. Designed during the reign of King Rama V by Prince Narit for *dükdamban,* a now nearly obsolete kind of theater, this instrument is sometimes used in *piphat mai nuam,* a softer version of the hard-mallet ensemble (*piphat mai khaeng*), to replace the *klawng that.*

23. *Klawng khaek.* The modifier *khaek* suggests vaguely an Indian, Muslim, or (according to Dhanit) Javanese origin. Indeed, nearly identical drums are found in Malaysia (*gendang*) and Java (*kendhang*), and the Indian *mridangam* is similar. The Thai *klawng khaek* is a pair of drums with carved wooden bodies, 58 centimeters long, nearly conical in shape, but having a slight bulge near the larger head. The larger head, to the player's right, is about 20 centimeters in diameter; the smaller is 18 centimeters wide. The heads, of calfskin, are held onto the body with a thick leather hoop or ring; widely spaced leather thongs loop around them. Another thong, encircling the drum near the bulge, can be slid back and forth to tighten or loosen the heads and consequently to affect the tone. The drum with the higher pitch, considered more authoritative, is male (*dua phu*), and the one with the lower pitch is female (*dua mia*). Two players are required to realize interlocking patterns; while the player of the male drum rests the larger (right) head on his raised knee, the player of the female drum holds it horizontally on his crossed legs. All four heads are played with the fingers and palms, but none is weighted for tuning. Though Dhanit conjectures that the drum is old, it appears only in non-Thai literature in the early 1800s. The *klawng khaek* are sometimes used in *piphat* for informal occasions and more routinely in *mahori.* With the conical double-reed aerophone (*pi chawa*), however, they are requisite in the accompaniment to Thai boxing.

24. *Klawng malayu.* Similar to the *klawng khaek* but shorter (54 centimeters) and of greater diameter (20 and 18 centimeters), the *klawng malayu* pair, as their name suggests, is borrowed from Malaysia, for these drums are identical to *gendang,* both in shape and in manner of playing. The larger head is struck with a right-angled stick and the smaller head with the hand. Their use was evidently restricted to funeral ensembles and earlier to processions; today, they are rarely heard.

25. *Klawng chana.* Similar to the *klawng malayu* but shorter (52 centimeters) and of greater diameter (heads 26 and 24 centimeters) and also played with a stick in

FIGURE 2 A military procession in the murals at Wat Phra Keo, Bangkok (early 1800s). *Left to right (lower row): klawng chana, pi chawa, klawng yao, trae ngawn,* and *sang; (upper row) trae ngawn* and *sang.* Photo by Terry E. Miller, 1988.

one hand, the *klawng chana* were higher in pitch, decorated with colorful designs. Their usage was restricted to military processions (figure 2) and later to certain funeral ceremonies. They are virtually obsolete.

26. *Boeng mang.* A single drum of nearly cylindrical shape with a carved wooden body about 54 centimeters long, the *boeng mang* is now seldom seen. At one time it preceded the *klawng chana* in military processions. The name of the drum is Mawn (Mon). The heads, measuring 16 and 17 centimeters in diameter, have the usual black circles and stripes, but only one head was weighted (tuned).

27. *Boeng mang kawk.* In *piphat mawn,* an observer is likely to encounter *boeng mang kawk,* a set of seven *boeng mang,* hung vertically in a semicircular wooden frame about 116 centimeters wide and 66 centimeters high. The heads are tuned with rice and ash to produce the seven tones of the tuning system, and each drum is played with the hands by a person seated on a stool or chair within the frame. The drums can be used to reinforce the colotomic structure provided by the *taphon mawn,* but they can also play melodies that in the hands of a highly skilled player can become virtuoso solos. The instrument is related to the Burmese or Mon *patt waiñ,* whose twenty-one smaller drums of graduated sizes are hung within a complete circle.

28. *Sawng na.* Functionally, the conical *sawng na* 'two faces' replaces the *taphon* in *piphat* for *sepha* recitation. From 55 to 58 centimeters long, the *sawng na* has heads that are joined with closely spaced leather thongs, similar to those of the *taphon.* Varying in diameter from 20 to 24 centimeters, the heads are loaded with rice and ash to attain the desired pitch. Dhanit reports that the *sawng na* came into use during the reign of King Rama II.

Aerophones

Flutes

29. *Khlui.* The *khlui,* a vertical block flute, has six to seven holes for fingering on the upper side and a hole for the thumb on the lower (with the opening for the duct). Instruments made of bamboo have a pierced node about 2.5 centimeters from the lower end, but *khlui* are also made of hardwood and plastic; once, some were made of ivory. On the player's right side, near the thumbhole, is another hole, formerly cov-

The *pi* is likely one of the oldest of Thai instruments, for it is mentioned by name by La Loubere (1691), but *pi* alone can refer to any reed instrument.

ered with a thin membrane of bamboo skin and vibrated in sympathy with the main column, similar to that heard on the Chinese *dizi,* a side-blown flute. Thai normally cover the hole with tape or paper, and it no longer has a function, though the Cambodian equivalent (*khloy*) retains the membrane. In addition, four holes near the lower end are said to affect the tone; a piece of cord is often tied through them. The *khlui* is made in three sizes: *khlui lip* (36 centimeters long, 2 centimeters in diameter, pitched in d), *khlui phiang aw* (45 centimeters long, 4 centimeters diameter, pitched in c), and *khlui u* (60 centimeters long, 4.5 centimeters diameter, pitched in G). The *khlui u* has only six holes for fingering on top. Neither the *khlui lip* nor *khlui u* are commonly used, nor is the even more obscure *khlui kruat,* slightly shorter than the *khlui phiang aw.* The pitch of each instrument matches one of the modes or scales, and depending on the "key" of the piece and the ensemble, players choose a particular instrument.

Reeds

30. *Pi.* The double reed (*pi*) is distinctive in shape and peculiar to Thailand and Cambodia (where it is known as *sralai*). Externally the carved wooden body flares slightly at the ends, while the middle bulges with fourteen pairs of lathed rings. Six holes for fingering on the top and a single hole for the thumb on the bottom are within these rings. The bore is slightly conical. A metal tube (*kam phuat*) is placed into the upper end, sealed into the *pi* with cotton thread. Onto this tube are tied four small palmyra-palm-leaf pieces in two double layers; when played, they are turned vertically (sometimes horizontally) within the player's oral cavity, not held between the lips. The *pi* comes in three sizes: (1) the *pi nai* (40 to 41 centimeters long and 4.5 centimeters in diameter, pitched in G) is used in *piphat* almost universally now, but it was designed to be used inside (*nai*) the palace, where a softer sound was desired; (2) the *pi klang* (37 centimeters long and 4 centimeters in diameter, pitched in A) was formerly used in the large shadow-puppet theater (*nang yai*); (3) the *pi nawk* (31 centimeters long and 3.5 centimeters in diameter, pitched in c), which has the most piercing tones of the three, was intended for performances outside (*nawk*) the palace. Obviously, the *pi* is a significant member of *piphat,* since it constitutes part of that ensemble's name. The *pi* idiom, with its flexible pitch, sliding between fixed pitches, and flowing rhythm, contrasts markedly with the other instruments of the ensemble, all having fixed pitch and played with attention to the beat. The *pi* is likely one of the oldest of Thai instruments, for it is mentioned by name by La Loubere (1691), but *pi* alone can refer to any reed instrument.

31. *Pi aw.* Virtually extinct in Thailand, the *pi aw* was a 25-centimeter-long bamboo tube without nodes, wrapped at the ends with metal bands and having seven upper holes for fingering and one for the thumb. Into the upper end was inserted a large double reed of cane about 5 centimeters long, sealed into the tube with thread. Formerly used in the string ensemble (*khrüang sai*), it was replaced by the *khlui*

(Dhanit 1971:73). It is retained both inside Cambodia and among the Khmer of northeast Thailand.

32. *Pi chanai.* Now virtually obsolete, the *pi chanai* was formerly used in royal processions and probably in other ensembles. Its length, 19 centimeters, consists of two parts: a wood or ivory conical tube with seven upper holes for fingering and a lower hole for the thumb, plus a flared wooden bell 7 to 8 centimeters in diameter. The reed resembles that of the *pi,* with four palm-leaf pieces tied to a metal tube, but with a metal or coconut disc on the tube between the player's lips and the body of the instrument. Probably related to the Indian *shahnai* and the Malay *sarunai,* the *chanai* is likely one of the earliest surviving instruments of the Tai peoples.

33. *Pi chawa.* The *pi chawa,* ostensibly from Java (*Chawa*), is similar to the *pi chanai,* but the conical wooden tube, again with seven upper and one lower holes for fingering, is 27 centimeters long; with the wooden bell (7 to 8 centimeters in diameter), it measures 38 to 39 centimeters long. Also like the *pi chanai,* it has a disc on the tube between the four-piece reed and the body. This instrument is associated with the *klawng khaek.* Formerly used in royal and military processions, it is now heard primarily as accompaniment to boxing, in certain funeral ensembles, and for episodes from the *Inao* story in *lakhawn* drama.

34. *Pi mawn.* The largest of the three conical *pi,* that of the Mawn (Mon) has a wooden body 50 centimeters long and a metal flared bell another 23 centimeters long, joined loosely to the body with cord. As with the previous two instruments, the reed tube (8 to 9 centimeters long), with four palm-leaf pieces, includes a disc on which the player rests his lips. Because of the weight of the instrument, some players rest the bell on a chair or the floor. Its primary use is in *piphat mawn,* which, though of Mon origin, is played by Thai musicians, especially for funerals.

Horns

35. *Trae.* Onomatopoetic, the word *trae* denotes two horn-type instruments of metal, *trae ngawn* 'curved' and *trae farang* 'French' (generalized as 'Western'). The former consists of two pieces, a conical section measuring 22 centimeters long with a 3-centimeter-wide mouthpiece similar to that of the modern trumpet or horn at one end and a wider bell section 28 centimeters long and 7 centimeters in diameter, with a cord tied between the two sections. The *trae farang* is in fact the valveless trumpet of Europe from the Renaissance and Baroque periods. An old name, *trae wilundah,* is evidently derived from "Holland," whose traders were among the first to penetrate old Siam. Both types of *trae,* with the *sang* (see below), were associated with processions and royal ceremonies for visiting dignitaries. Today, they are heard as part of an occasional state function.

36. *Sang.* The conch, polished and opened at one end to be played as a trumpet, is widely distributed, but for the central Thai, its origin was likely India, where the conch was associated with ceremony. Among the Thai, it was associated with dignified ceremonies and played with the two types of *trae* described above. As in India, in Thailand the instrument is considered to have magical and sacred properties.

Chordophones

Lutes

37. *Krajappi.* Somewhat flamboyant but now rarely seen, the *krajappi,* a plucked lute, measures 180 centimeters from top to bottom. The somewhat oval, flat body is 44 centimeters long, 40 centimeters wide, and 7 centimeters thick; the tapered neck, which curves back beyond the tuning pegs, is 138 centimeters long. Four gut strings, attached to four lateral pegs, run over eleven frets on the neck and over a wooden

bridge and are attached to a tailpiece; treated as two courses, they can be tuned variously, as to g and d (to match the *saw duang*) or c′ and g′ (to match the *saw u* at the octave). The player plucks the strings with a plectrum of horn, bone, or tortoiseshell. The word *krajappi* is likely derived from the Pali-Sanskrit word for tortoise and relates to chordophones, both similar and dissimilar, found elsewhere (such as the *kacapi,* the zither of several Sundanese ensembles). The shape of the instrument bears greater resemblance to certain instruments of China (like the *ruan*) and Vietnam (like the *đàn nguyệt*) than to those of India. The *krajappi* was formerly an important member of *mahori* and *khrüang sai,* but it is nearly obsolete. In Cambodia, where it is called *chapey dang veng,* it is still used to accompany narrative singing (*chrieng chapey*).

38. *Saw sam sai.* The name of the instrument literally means bowed lute or fiddle (*saw*) with three (*sam*) strings (*sai*). Elegantly rounded and triangular, its body consists of the lower half of a special coconut with three bulges and the opening covered with a goat or calfskin resonator. Wooden and fretless, the neck is 24 centimeters long and has three lateral tuning pegs; the portion below the body measures 19.5 centimeters and tapers into a metal spike. When disassembled, the neck consists of three pieces, one of which goes through the body. Three gut strings, tuned A–d–g, are anchored through a hole in the hollow lower piece, run over an arched ivory or plastic bridge, disappear through a hole into the neck just below the tuning pegs, and fasten inside. A thick, round head weight of enamel or lacquer (formerly, silver, or even gold, with diamonds), called *thuang na,* is stuck to the membrane to deaden unwanted frequencies. A separate, S-shaped, wooden bow stick 86 centimeters long has horsehair tied at the tip and extends to the handle. Seated on the floor with legs to the left, the player turns the fiddle on its spike, resting the neck of the instrument on his shoulder, holding the bow underhanded and stationary. While bowing, he stops the strings to the neck. The *saw sam sai* is both a solo instrument and the leader of the *mahori,* the only ensemble in which it plays. Rarely seen is a smaller version, the *saw sam sai lip.* Evidently the oldest of the Thai fiddles, the *saw sam sai* was described by La Loubere: "They have very ugly little *Rebecks* or Violins with three strings, which they call *Tro*" (1969[1693]:68). The parallel instrument in Cambodia is called *tror Khmer,* and a Mon fiddle slightly resembling a violin is the *tror.* The Thai instrument also resembles the Malay and Javanese *rebab,* which have two strings and a name borrowed from Western Asia.

39. *Saw duang.* The higher-pitched of the Thai two-stringed fiddles, the *saw duang* has a cylindrical body of wood (sometimes ivory) 13 centimeters long and 7 centimeters in diameter. Dhanit asserts that originally the body was a section of bamboo, but because the body is conically carved inside, we cannot be sure. A wooden neck 70 centimeters long pierces the body near the python or boa resonator, while the rear is left open. The two strings, tuned g and d′, are attached to the slightly protruding neck below the body and run over a small bamboo bridge to two rear pegs near the top. A loop of string about two-thirds up the neck pulls the strings toward a fretless neck, defining the playing area and putting the requisite tension on the string. The bow hairs, passing between the strings, are pulled against the lower string and pushed against the upper, while the left hand touches the strings without pulling them against the neck. The *saw duang* is not mentioned or described in non-Thai sources until Verney's pamphlet of 1885, which includes a line drawing showing the bow separate and omitting the neck loop. The *saw duang* may have been derived from one of the Chinese bowed lutes (*hu qin* and *er hu*). Chinese theater was commonly played at the Siamese court of Ayuthaya in the 1600s when La Loubere and others visited there, and Chinese Thai throughout Thailand maintain both amateur silk-and-bamboo ensembles (*sizhu*) and professional theatrical troupes. Since most

Chinese in Thailand originated in the Chao-zhou district of Guangdong province in China, their fiddle, the *tou xian,* with its conical inside shape and strident tone, is the most likely candidate as the model for the *saw duang.* The latter is widely heard today—in the *mahori,* as the leader of the *khrüang sai,* and as a solo instrument.

40. *Saw u.* The lower-pitched two-stringed bowed lute consists of a large, round coconut, one side of which has been cut away and covered with goat or calfskin, 13 to 15 centimeters wide. The rear portion has holes to let the sound out, with a carving, usually of Hanuman, the white monkey of the *Ramayana* story. As with the *saw duang,* the two gut strings, tuned c and g, are attached at the lower end to the base of a neck 80 centimeters long and pass over a bridge of tightly rolled cloth to two rear pegs; similarly, a cord loop pulls the strings toward the neck, and the bow hairs pass between the strings. The *saw u* as we know it does not appear in any pre-twentieth-century sources, though Hipkins and Verney both illustrate a "saw oo" that is essentially a larger version of the *saw duang,* that is, with a cylindrical body. Hipkins further calls both of these "Saw Chine, or Chinese fiddle" (1945[1888]: pl. XLII). While many Thai believe the word *u* to be an onomatopoetic descriptor of the sound of the instrument, it more likely derives from the Chinese word *hu.* The nearest Chinese equivalent for the Thai *saw u* is the *yeh hu* with coconut body, but its membrane is wood, not skin. Instruments with coconut bodies would seem to be exclusive to tropical or near-tropical areas (from southern China southward), and the Thai-Cambodian form is distinctive to these cultures.

Zithers

41. *Ja-khe.* The name of the Thai zither is derived from *jarakhe* 'crocodile' and likely relates to the Mon equivalent, *mi gyaung,* also meaning crocodile, which has realistic zoological features; the Thai *ja-khe* has only the abstract animal form. Although played on the floor like a zither, it is arguably a lute, since the body and neck are differentiated, and some Thai assert that it was derived from the *krajappi.* The *ja-khe* measures 130 to 132 centimeters long, divided into a "head" portion (52 centimeters long, 28 centimeters wide, 9 to 12 centimeters deep) and a "tail" portion (81 centimeters long, 11.5 centimeters wide). The entire body is supported by five legs, 8 centimeters high. Along the neck of the hardwood body are eleven high frets, graduated from 2 centimeters in height near the center to 3.5 centimeters in height at the three lateral tuning pegs. There are three strings, tuned C–G–c, but most playing occurs on the upper two. The player fastens a 5-to-6-centimeter-long ivory or bone plectrum to the right index finger by wrapping the plectrum's silk cord around the finger and bracing it with the thumb and middle finger. Considered difficult to master, strumming involves rapid back-and-forth motions while the left hand stops the strings on the frets. A thin piece of bamboo is inserted under the strings on the bridge, causing the strings to vibrate slightly against the metal bridge, giving the instrument its characteristic timbre. A member of both the *mahori* and *khrüang sai,* the *ja-khe* was not mentioned in the literature until Turpin's secondhand account (1771), where he calls it a crocodile. Finlayson, writing in 1826, mistakenly called it a *tuk-kay,* after a well-known lizard whose cries give it its name. The *ja-khe* is also commonly played alone (figure 3).

42. *Khim.* Ironically, the *khim,* a hammered dulcimer, is probably the most popular of Thai instruments but also the most clearly of recent and Chinese origin. Derived from the Chaozhou Chinese *yang qin,* the *khim* is a small, butterfly-shaped (trapezoidal) dulcimer, 86 centimeters on the longer side, 56 centimeters on the shorter, and 34 centimeters wide. It has two sets of bridges and fourteen courses of strings, some with four strings, some only three. Its tuning is seven tones, with the lowest set on the right (A–g), a medium and overlapping set in the middle (e–d′),

Earlier called *phinphat*, the *piphat* is the most important ensemble of Thailand. Traditionally, all players were male, and the ensemble accompanied masked plays, nonmasked dance plays, long narratives, and various rituals or ceremonies.

FIGURE 3 Students at Chulalongkorn University, Bangkok, have a group lesson: *left to right, ja-khe, ranat thum, saw duang.* The teacher is at the far right. Photo by Terry E. Miller, 1988.

and the highest set on the left (b–a′). Used primarily for solo playing and much favored by female players, the *khim* can also be added to the *khrüang sai* and the *mahori.* To give it added resonance, the instrument is raised from the floor on a small stand, and the player sits crosslegged or with legs to one side. Played alone, the instrument has a full sound because many sonorities (thirds, fourths, fifths, and octaves) accompany the otherwise monophonic melody. Actually a metallophone (idiophone), the recently introduced *khim lek* (metal dulcimer) is configured exactly like the normal *khim,* but with thin, flat, aluminum keys, resembling the European-American glockenspiel. Such instruments are inexpensive and durable and do not need tuning—and are therefore believed ideal for children.

ENSEMBLES

In importance, the ensemble far outweighs the instrumental solo and is at least the equal of the vocalist. A singer, though crucial in telling a story in drama or conveying the words of nontheatrical songs, is rarely accompanied by an ensemble, but alternates with it. The history and development of ensembles in early Siam is not known with certainty, but the thinking of Thai scholars Prince Damrong, Dhanit Yupho, and others—much of it traditional rather than documented information—is summarized by Morton (1976:101–114).

Over time, the names and instrumentation of most ensembles have been standardized, but an observer is as likely to encounter an ensemble that in some way violates the published standards as to find one in rigid conformity. Each ensemble includes at least one aerophone (a flute or a double reed), which determines the pitch in which the music is played. Here, the standard contemporary ensembles will be described first, followed by a discussion of what is known of their history.

Thai ensembles perform seated on the floor, players sitting crosslegged or with legs to the left. Positions for each instrument are fairly standard, but when accompanying theater (where space is limited), musicians may seat themselves differently. Except for some student ensembles using stringed instruments, musicians play from memory, not notation. Men traditionally wear high-collared, white, military-style jackets (after British colonial styles) and wraparound trousers (*jong kraben*). Women often wear colorful wraparound trousers, a tight-fitting top, and a large sash over the left shoulder.

Piphat

Earlier called *phinphat* (the equivalent Khmer ensemble is still called *pinn peat*), the *piphat* is the most important ensemble of Thailand. Traditionally, all players were male, and the ensemble accompanied masked plays (*khon*), nonmasked dance plays (*lakhawn*), long narratives (*sepha*), and various rituals or ceremonies. The inclusion of the *pi* quadruple reed is what normally makes this ensemble distinctive, but variants use other aerophones. The standard *piphat* uses hard mallets (*mai khaeng*) and is described in three sizes; four other types are also called *piphat.*

Piphat khrüang ha

Literally 'five instruments', this ensemble actually includes six if both drum and cymbals are counted separately (figure 4):

One *pi nai*
One *ranat ek*
One *khawng wong yai*
One *taphon*
One pair of *ching*
One set of *klawng that*

Piphat khrüang khu

Literally 'pairs of instruments', this ensemble includes nine instruments with an optional tenth:

Two *pi* (*pi nai* and *pi nawk*, though today the latter, being nearly obsolete, is replaced with a second *pi nai*)
One *taphon*
One pair of *ching*
Two *ranat* (*ranat ek* and *ranat thum*)
Two *khawng wong* (*khawng wong yai* and *khawng wong lek*)
One pair of *klawng that*
Optionally, one *mong*

Piphat khrüang yai

Literally 'large [group of] instruments', this ensemble includes thirteen instruments, with another optional one:

Two *pi* (as above)
Two *ranat* (as above)
Two metallophones, *ranat ek lek* and *ranat thum lek*

FIGURE 4 A *piphat khrüang ha* with *ranat thum* added in performance at the Siam Society, Bangkok. *Left to right: khawng wong yai, taphon, ranat ek, pi nai,* and *ranat thum.* Photo by Terry E. Miller, 1972.

Two *khawng wong* (as above)
One *taphon*
One pair of *ching*
One pair of *chap lek*
Optionally, one pair of *chap yai*
One *mong*
One pair of *klawng that*

Piphat mai nuam
Literally 'soft mallets' (opposed to the above, presumed to be *mai khaeng* 'hard mallets'), this ensemble is a softer-sounding ensemble. In it, the fipple flute (*khlui phiang aw*) replaces the *pi,* and a coconut-body fiddle (*saw u*) is added.

Piphat nang hong
This ensemble developed from the *bua loi* and *klawng khaek* (see below), combining those with certain classical instruments. Its usage is restricted to playing specific pieces, such as those of *khaek* (Muslim, Malay, Indian) accent.

Two *ranat* (*ek* and *thum*)
Two *khawng wong* (*yai* and *lek*)
One *pi chawa*
One pair of *klawng malayu*
One pair of *ching*
Two pairs of *chap* (*yai* and *lek*)
One *mong*
One pair of *krap sepha*
Optionally, one *ranat ek lek* and one *ranat thum lek*

Piphat mawn
The *piphat* of the Mon people of western Thailand and Burma, this ensemble is actually played by Thai. The repertory, primarily pieces in *mawn* (Mon) accent, is most often heard at funerals. Some small ensembles based in the funeral sections of certain Buddhist temples omit the *boeng mang kawk.*

Two *ranat* (*ek* and *thum*)
Two *khawng mawn* (*yai* and *lek*)
One *pi mawn*
One *taphon mawn*
One *boeng mang kawk*
One pair of *ching*
Two pairs of *chap* (*yai* and *lek*)
Set of three *khawng* in a frame
Optionally, one *ranat ek lek* and one *ranat thum lek*

Piphat dükdamban

This ensemble, created during the latter half of the nineteenth century by Prince Narit to accompany a theatrical genre that proved short-lived, lives on through occasional instrumental performances. This grouping is distinguished by the presence of the flute, a fiddle, and the seven-sided stand of gongs (*wong khawng chai*), which is quite expensive and therefore rarely heard.

Two *ranat* (*ek* and *thum*)
One metallophone (*ranat ek lek*)
One *khawng wong yai*
One *saw u*
One *khlui*
One *wong khawng chai*
One pair of *ching*
One *taphon*
One pair of *klawng khaek*
One pair of *klawng taphon*

Mahori

The word *mahori* originally meant "instrumental music" but later came to denote an ensemble that specifically includes melodic idiophones, chordophones, and a flute. The three-stringed fiddle (*saw sam sai*) is the leader of the *mahori,* the only ensemble in which it plays. Earlier, the main function of the *mahori* had been entertainment, but later it replaced the *piphat* in accompanying *lakhawn,* a genre of dance-drama. To reduce the volume of sound, the three possible pairs of melodic idiophones are ideally smaller than those used in the *piphat,* but ensembles lacking the extra instruments can easily use normal models.

The Fine Arts Department still illustrates two early forms of the *mahori* (called *mahori boran* 'old *mahori*' and *mahori khrüang hok* 'six-instrument *mahori*'), but they are obsolete. The evident rigidity with which the modern ensembles are presented belies a more casual approach to forming these groups in reality. In short, a "pure" *mahori* is less likely to be encountered than one that merely mixes chordophones and idiophones.

Mahori boran

The 'old ensemble', this consisted of four instruments:

One *saw sam sai*
One *krajappi*
One *thon*
One *krap phuang*

The word *mahori* originally meant "instrumental music" but later came to denote an ensemble that specifically includes melodic idiophones, chordophones, and a flute.

FIGURE 5 A small *mahori. Left to right: ching, khlui phiang aw, ranat ek, saw duang, khawng wong yai, saw sam sai, saw u, ja-khe, rammana,* and *thon.* Photo Fine Arts Department, Bangkok, 1960.

Mahori khrüang hok

The 'six-instrument *mahori*' (with seven instruments in all) includes the instruments of the *mahori boran,* plus three more:

- One *khlui*
- One pair of *ching*
- One *rammana*

Mahori wong lek

The 'small ensemble', using nine instruments, is in contemporary use (figure 5):

- One *ranat ek* (*mahori* size for this and all melodic idiophones)
- One *khawng wong yai*
- One *saw sam sai*
- One *saw duang*
- One *saw u*
- One *ja-khe*
- One *khlui phiang aw*
- One pair of drums (*thon* and *rammana*)
- One pair of *ching*

Mahori khrüang khu

Literally 'instruments in pairs', this ensemble uses nine paired instruments and one *mong*:

Two *ranat* (*ek* and *thum*)
Two *khawng wong* (*yai* and *lek*)
Two *saw sam sai*
Two *ja-khe*
Two *saw duang*
Two *saw u*
Two *khlui* (*phiang aw* and *lip*)
One pair of drums (*thon* and *rammana*)
One pair of *chap lek*
One *mong*

Mahori khrüang yai

Literally 'large [number of] instruments', this ensemble includes all instruments in the ensemble above, plus the following:

Two metallophones (*ranat ek lek* and *ranat thum lek*)
One pair of *chap yai*
One additional *khlui* (*khlui u*)

Khrüang sai

This is a string ensemble (*khrüang* 'instruments', *sai* 'string'). Its history is unknown, but its lineage appears fairly recent, possibly from only the twentieth century. Its function is not clearly defined, since it has not been closely associated with either theater or dance. Its basic instrumentation is fixed, consisting of the two-stringed bowed lutes and zither plus flute, but instruments of diverse origin have been included at times; one of them, with *pi chawa,* is detailed below. Other possibilities include harmonium, accordion, and violin.

Khrüang sai khrüang lek or khrüang sai wong lek

A small ensemble (figure 6), this consists of

One *saw duang*
One *saw u*
One *ja-khe*
One *khlui phiang aw*
One pair of drums (*thon* and *rummana*)
One pair of *ching*

Khrüang sai khrüang khu

An ensemble in pairs, this includes

Two *saw duang*
Two *saw u*
Two *ja-khe*
Two *khlui* (*khlui phiang aw* and *khlui lip*)
One pair of drums (*thon* and *rummana*)
One pair of *ching*
One pair of *chap lek*
One *mong*

Khrüang sai pi chawa

Having some characteristics of the *khrüang sai,* this ensemble can also be seen as an expanded *klawng khaek*:

FIGURE 6 A small *khrüang sai* ensemble. Left to right: *khlui phiang aw, saw duang, ching, ja-khe, thon, saw u,* and *rammana.* Photo Fine Arts Department, Bangkok, 1960.

One *saw duang*
One *saw u*
One *ja-khe*
One *pi chawa*
One *khlui phiang aw*
One pair of *ching*
One pair of *klawng khaek*

Khrüang sai phrasom

This refers to basic string-and-flute ensembles, to which various instruments may be added, including *khim,* accordion, violin, and so forth.

Other ensembles

Two Thai ensembles, *klawng khaek* and *bua loi,* are most likely of Indonesian and Malaysian origin, respectively. Prince Damrong offers speculation as to their introduction and early use in Siam (Morton 1976:112). They are primarily associated with boxing and sword fighting and possibly with scenes from the Javanese epic *Inao* as presented on the Thai stage.

Klawng khaek

One *pi chawa*
One pair of *klawng khaek*
One pair of *ching*
Optionally, one *khawng meng*

Bua loi

One *pi chawa*
One pair of *klawng malayu*
One pair of *ching*
Optionally one *khawng meng*

Historical ensembles

Considerable speculation about the development of Thai ensembles has been offered by Thai scholars, especially Prince Damrong, but little documentation exists to prove these assertions conclusively. At least two ensembles now obsolete can be seen in photographs from the early 1900s. One of them, *mahori boran* (see above) has already been described. The second, *khap mai* 'to recite with a beat', consisted of one *saw sam sai,* one singer, and one *ban thaw,* a drum known in India as *damaru.* The latter are small, hourglass-shaped drums with two laced heads and a stick handle attached to the waist; a string with a ball at the loose end strikes the heads alternately as the player twists the handle.

Early European sources provide little help before the mid-1800s, since the earliest writers listed only individual instruments and failed to mention groupings. Crawfurd's account (1967[1828]:333) lists the members of "a full Siamese band" as gong circle [*khawng wong*], xylophone [*ranat*], *saw sam sai, krajappi,* flute [*khlui*], flageolet [*khlui lip*?], *ja-khe,* cymbals [*ching*], and castanets [*krap*?]; he does not mention drums. Bowring, the first to describe a *piphat* ("Pe pat"), oddly includes in the list the *boeng mang,* a drum associated with the *piphat mawn.* He also describes an early *mahori* ("mahari") that includes a xylophone, a gong circle, a three-stringed fiddle, a lute (*krajappi*), a flute, *ching,* and a *thon rummana* set of drums (1969[1857]:148–149).

Verney's pamphlet (1885) is the first source to list the instrumentation of specific ensembles. He includes both a "mahoree," which then included "1 Chapee" (*krajappi*), and a "bhimbhat" (*piphat*) which strangely included three flutes and no double reeds. His "klong khek" (*klawng khaek*) included three *pi chawa,* a pair of *klawng khaek,* one pair of *ching,* and oddly, two *saw sam sai.* Finally, "Lao Phan," an ensemble said to be from the north (but actually from the northeast), included two *khaen,* two *khlui,* two "fiddles," two "alligators" (*ja-khe*), a pair of drums (*thon rummana*), and a pair of *ching.*

CONTEXTS FOR CLASSICAL MUSIC

Though Thai widely acknowledge the importance of classical music, both as a symbol of their culture and as an art expressive of what it means to be Thai, few actually choose to listen to it. Opportunities to hear it remain scarce, and with few economic incentives to encourage its study and practice, this situation is not likely to change soon. Alas, classical music better represents the past than the present, and its status is reinforced by the apparent lack of development in the tradition since the early 1900s. Thai classical music is more a museum piece, maintained as a living specimen in what David Morton has called a hothouse environment, than a vital part of modern Thai life. It was not always so, though classical music was during its heyday almost exclusively for the aristocracy, never a music of the people.

Making a living as a traditional classical Thai musician is at least a possibility, even in modernized Bangkok. Besides opportunities for teaching in publicly and privately supported education, from elementary school through university, the public still demands that musicians perform at temple rituals and private ones. The demand is greatest after *awk phansa,* the end of the Buddhist season of abstinence and penitence, that is, from October until the beginning of the next cycle, *khao phansa,* in late July.

Tourism also provides opportunities for both part-time and full-time employment, at restaurants and theme parks, and in hotels. At certain temples, *piphat mawn* are kept busy providing music for funerals. Making a living playing classical music is less lucrative than playing popular music, but for serious musicians, the satisfaction of maintaining an important element of Thai culture and delving deeply into a music with deep historical roots and a vast repertoire may offset the financial disadvantage. In this sense, Thai classical musicians are little different from their counterparts playing Western classical music.

"Sometime after all were thus placed, a great Noise of Trumpets, Drums, and many other Instruments was heard, and then the throne was opened, and the King appeared sitting on it." (1688)

Historical contexts

Most early European sources mention Thai making music as part of court activities, though accounts as to what ensembles or instruments were used remain vague. According to early documents, music accompanied the activities of the king (and likely other noblemen) throughout the day and wherever he went. When the king traveled by land, his subjects were forbidden to gaze on his person, and warning them was a group of musicians that preceded the procession. A Mr. Glanius, writing in 1682, notes:

> All along the way nothing is to be heard but Fifes, Drums, Flutes, and other instruments, which make a passable Harmony. . . . His Majesty's subjects were permitted to see his person only during the *kathin* procession in October, when all lay people, including the royal family, were expected to take gifts and new robes to Buddhist monks. When the King proceeded by water, several boats of musicians followed. (p. 112)

A seventeenth-century writer noted further: "When he goes by land, the procession is led by two hundred Elephants, each attended with three armed men; these are followed by many Musitians with Gomnies [?], Pipes and Drums, and a thousand men richly armed, and provided with Banners. . . . [and] by many Servants loaden with fruits and presents for the Sacrifice, accompanied with a sweet consort of Musick" (Schouten 1663[1636]:128).

The king's daily activities were accompanied by music: "Sometime after all were thus placed, a great Noise of Trumpets, Drums, and many other Instruments was heard, and then the throne was opened, and the King appeared sitting on it" (Tachard 1688:167). Others noted how musicians played fanfares outside the audience chamber according to events within. Gervaise affirmed that the King of Siam, like many crowned heads of Europe, needed music to encourage sleep: "then [he] goes to sleep lulled by vocal and instrumental music" (1688:117).

Coronation ceremonies were occasions for much music, but before the 1800s few foreigners actually saw these. In 1851, at the coronation of King Mongkut, after the chief astrologer performed the naming ceremony, "priests or astrologers" blew conchs "and beat gongs and drums" (Bowring 1969[1857]:424). Likewise, the funeral of the king and likely of other dignitaries was occasion for music. Mendes Pinto, who likely witnessed the funeral of King Yot Fa in 1548 in Ayuthaya, wrote that the burning of the king's body "was accompanied with so horrible a din of cries, great Ordnance, Harquebuses, Drums, Bells, Cornets, and other different kinds of noyse, as it was impossible to hear it without trembling" (1692:276).

The instruments used on these ceremonial occasions became largely obsolete with the cessation or simplification of royal functions, especially after 1932. A few such rituals persist. Untrained observers often mentioned drums, but the type remains obscure. Dhanit describes the *klawng chana* as the most likely drum for early processions and funerals. Though many writers use the term *flute,* the instrument in question is more likely a double reed, the *pi chanai.* Allusions to trumpets suggest both the curved, metal *trae ngawn* or the straight *trae farang* (of European origin). Some mention the conch (*sang*) specifically, but others may have dismissed it as a trumpet.

Contemporary contexts

After the coup of 1932, not only was the court-music establishment disbanded and its musicians sent out to fend for themselves, but the nonroyal leadership, favoring Western manners and customs, discouraged and even forbade the performance of traditional classical music. Officials encouraged the performance of classical music on Western instruments, and the Fine Arts Department, newly founded to oversee cultural matters, created a Western orchestra. This department published disc recordings of these adaptations as late as the 1960s, and some remain available on cassettes. During the dark years (1932 to the 1960s), classical music lost its context and nearly disappeared.

Though the College of Dramatic Arts, a division of the Fine Arts Department, continued to teach and produce both classical music and theater, performances were presented only periodically in the National Theater. Music was not considered an acceptable academic area in Thai higher education until the 1970s. Before then, most musical activities were extracurricular, organized by students' clubs. Gradually music has become an acceptable major, and now it is possible not only to study music at many Thai universities and colleges, but to choose a major in Western or Thai classical music. Consequently, universities and other educational institutions have become the primary haven for classical music in Thailand, just as they are in the West for its classical music. Further, while some classical music was taught at the primary and secondary levels, it remained peripheral until the founding (in the 1970s) of ten branches of the College of Dramatic Arts (Pattalung and Nakhon Sri Thammarat in the south, Chiangmai and Sukhotai in the north, Roi-et and Kalasin in the northeast, and Lopburi, Ang Thong, Chantaburi, and Bangkok in the central region). These residential "high schools for the arts," with students aged eleven to eighteen, offer a normal curriculum plus substantial study of dance and music. Both classical types of music and theater and local genres are taught at each, and students, sometimes with faculty, offer public performances, locally and nationally. Thanks to these schools and the postsecondary College of Dramatic Arts in Bangkok, performances of classical music and theater have not only become more common, but are now offered throughout the country. Chulalongkorn, Srinakharinwirot, and Mahidol Universities, which created majors in Thai classical music and employed skilled teachers, regularly offer public performances. In sum, Thai classical music now thrives within the educational system, appeals to a moderately large audience, and maintains a high standard of skill, representing a remarkable comeback from the late 1930s, when all seemed about to be lost.

Classical music is also found outside academia. Ensembles are sometimes hired to play for temple fairs, the Western New Year, and other festive occasions (figure 7). Several Buddhist temples in Bangkok specialize in funerals, and there an observer is likely to encounter a *piphat mawn* performing throughout the day as a background to funerals and processions, though at some temples other ensembles also play music of Chinese origin for Chinese funerals. Television and radio occasionally offer programs of classical music and theater. A ubiquitous and all-too-predictable venue for classical music is the tourist restaurants in Bangkok and theme parks outside (such as the Rose Garden and Ancient City). The typical show, lasting about thirty minutes, includes

khon Classical masked theater, based entirely on *Ramayana*

lakhawn Various types of dance-drama

Ramakian The Thai version of the Indian *Ramayana* epic

nang yai Classical large shadow-puppet theater

FIGURE 7 A mixed ensemble of *ranat ek, saw duang, saw u, klawng khaek, ching,* and *krap khu* play music at a shrine behind Bangkok's Wat Benchamabophit, the Marble Temple. Photo by Terry E. Miller, 1988.

scenes from masked drama and dance-drama (both accompanied by an ensemble that is rarely "pure"), followed by simulations of boxing and sword fighting, accompanied by at least an imitation of the *klawng khaek.* The instrumentalists may play alone during dinner.

Classical music is an important element in theater, which by definition brings together music, dance, acting, and story. Human theater takes two important forms, masked drama (*khon*) and dance-drama (*lakhawn*), and puppet theater has two rarely seen genres, *nang yai* 'large shadow-puppet figures' and *hün krabawk* 'doll puppets'. Each requires a classical ensemble. In addition, two narrative genres, much cultivated in the past, are now rarely seen—*sepha* 'recitation with *krap*' and *thet mahachat* 'reciting the story of Prince Wetsanton'. In these genres, a *piphat* punctuated the presentation but did not accompany it.

Khon

Khon, the masked drama based entirely on the Thai version of the Indian epic *Ramayana* (Thai *Ramakian*), almost certainly derived from the large shadow-puppet theater. In the latter genre, male puppeteers dance beneath their puppets in front of a cloth screen. According to Thai records, about 1515 the Ayuthayan monarch Rama Tibodi II organized for his twenty-fifth birthday numerous performances, including one in which the puppeteers first pantomimed the actions of the rawhide figures above them. They are said to have worn heavy makeup and played in front of, rather than beneath, the screen. Later the puppets were discarded, and *khon* evolved as an

FIGURE 8 Several members of the monkey army, led by Hanuman (second from right), appear in a *khon* performance of part of the *Ramakian* in Roi-et. Photo by Terry E. Miller, 1988.

independent human genre. La Loubere in the late 1680s witnessed what he called *Cone,* but he claimed that it was accompanied by a violin and "some other instruments." *Khon* received notice from numerous later writers, with Ruschenberger's description of a performance being the most complete, albeit ethnocentric, written up to that point (1970[1838]:82–83). Several kings of the Bangkok period were personally involved in theater, and the *khon* versions of the *Ramakian* written by Rama I and Rama II are significant; that by Rama I is the only complete version, but the one by Rama II is considered more suitable for the stage. After 1932, *khon* was maintained exclusively by the Fine Arts Department, with occasional presentations at the National Theater, but since the 1980s *khon* performances by students at both secondary and baccalaureate institutions have become usual.

Originally played by an all-male cast, *khon* was later influenced by the *lakhawn* dance-drama and began to include female performers. Gradually, the divine and human roles shed their masks in favor of makeup, leaving only demons and simians wearing them. Masked or not, the actors neither speak nor recite, leaving this function to the reciter (*khon puk*), seated offstage. The exception to this rule is the comedians, who speak from the stage. The reciter's texts consist of two kinds of poetry, *kham puk* in *khap* form, and for dialogue, a kind of rhythmic prose in *rai* form. Close coordination between dancer and reciter was of utmost importance. Neither kind of poetry, since each contains many archaic and formal words, is easily understood by the audience.

Because a complete performance of the *Ramakian* (figure 8) would last many days, episodes called *chüt* lasting a few hours are normally given. The term *chüt,* meaning 'set', derives from the practice in *nang yai* of collecting a set of puppets for a given scene. Performances were formerly given in the open air on the ground, but when on a stage, it was open on three sides with the ensemble and reciter in front or to one side. The actors' costumes are quite elaborate, with strict traditions of costume, color, and mask for individual characters. Stage properties are restricted but include a dais, bows, arrows, royal canopies, and other objects. The most elaborate is the war chariot, which must be moveable.

Accompanying *khon* is the *piphat* with hard mallets (*mai khaeng*), originally said to have been the small grouping—*piphat krüang ha*—consisting of *ranat ek, khawng wong yai, pi nai, ching, taphon,* and *klawng that.* The player of the *ranat* is the melodic leader, but the *taphon* must carefully coordinate with the dancers. The melodic members of the ensemble, silent during dialogue and recitation, accompany stage action, drawing from a repertoire of tunes appropriate to a specific action (*pleng naphat*), such as fighting, making love, or fleeing. In addition, there are pieces for processions. The performance may be preceded by a group of instrumental pieces in the form of an overture (*homrong*). During the 1800s and 1900s, when the influence of the feminine *lakhawn* was felt on the rough and masculine *khon,* singing came to be interpolated, but its performance required offstage singers seated with the reciter.

Nang yai

There are two kinds of shadow-puppet theater in Thailand today: small puppets with articulated limbs (called *nang talung* in the south, *nang bra mo tai* in the northeast); and, in central Thailand, the large puppets (*nang yai*), related to the classical *khon* and accompanied by the same *piphat* and repertoire.

The origin of the latter genre is conjectural, but two theories are current: (1) that shadow theater originated in India and was transmitted to the Thai from Java via the Malay peninsula; (2) that shadow theater traveled from India to Java and was transmitted to the Khmer kingdom of Angkor by Jayavarman II in 802 and then to the Thai after the fall of Angkor in the 1400s. Indeed, the Khmer have a nearly identical form of theater called *sbek thomm.* The earliest mention of *nang yai* in historical records is from the Palatine Law of King Boromtrailokanart of 1458. Eighteenth-century European writers mention puppet theater, but La Loubere and Bouvet apparently refer to marionettes, though Tachard writes, "These illuminations were accompanied with the Noise of Drums, Fifes, and Trumpets" (Tachard 1688:213).

Cut from cowhide, the puppets measure from 100 to 200 centimeters high and 50 to 150 wide; most require the hide of a single cow, but some require those of two cows. Rather than represent a single character, each is a tableau showing one or more characters, with its scenic context, in a particular pose or scene (like "Duel between the white monkey and the black monkey" and "Hanuman wrecking Totsagan's garden"). Each puppet is supported by two (rarely one) wooden poles protruding to 30 to 60 centimeters below. These are held in performance by a male manipulator, who, while displaying a puppet, moves gracefully, as if dancing.

In performance (figure 9), a screen of white cloth about 16 meters long and 6 meters high with decoration around its border is stretched across the stage, and a

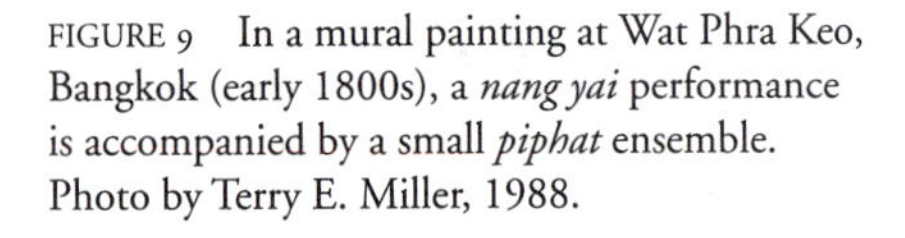

FIGURE 9 In a mural painting at Wat Phra Keo, Bangkok (early 1800s), a *nang yai* performance is accompanied by a small *piphat* ensemble. Photo by Terry E. Miller, 1988.

bonfire (now electric lights) is prepared behind it. The manipulators assemble puppets in sets (*chüt*), as a performance requires from one hundred to three hundred puppets. An elaborate *wai khru* ceremony to honor the troupe's teacher and various deities precedes the actual performance, the first part requiring the sponsor to present three candles and a small amount of money to the troupe's leader; one of the lit candles is placed on the *taphon*. Then the ensemble plays an overture (*hom rong*) of six pieces. Two other candles are then lighted by the manipulators in honor of Vishnu and Siva, and the ensemble plays appropriate pieces. Then follow the manipulators' invocations to the master of the troupe, in three sections: to King Dasaratha and the hero, Rama; to the *rüsi* or *rishi,* a hermit and seer who possesses magic knowledge, to the Buddha, to Anirudh (genii of forests, streams, and mountains), and to the Old Master; finally, magic words to protect the troupe in competition. Then, as the fire is lit from behind, the ensemble plays a march leading to a duel between white and black monkeys. Only then does the excerpt from the *Ramakian* chosen for that evening begin.

The story is told by offstage reciters in a kind of heightened speech. The instrumental ensemble accompanies periods of action by playing standard action tunes while the manipulators move in time with the music. (His Highness Prince Dhaninivat has argued that at some point the manipulators put down the puppets and began dancing as the actors, creating the human theater *khon*.) These genres share many similarities in music, story, and action. Though *nang yai,* like *khon,* plays the story of Rama exclusively now, during the late 1700s and early 1800s it also presented adaptations of the story of *Inao.*

According to some early Siamese documents, performances used to occur during late afternoons and early evenings before the screen, but without the fire lit. Dancing to *piphat* accompaniment, the manipulators depicted with brightly colored figures the celestial dance of the goddess Mekhala as she teased the demon Ramasun with a jeweled ball.

Today in Thailand, only three troupes still perform *nang yai,* and only three complete sets of puppets exist (a fourth collection, of two hundred, is in the Ledermuseum in Offenbach, Germany). The Fine Arts Department troupe rarely performs, and the other two, both based at Buddhist temples, have few opportunities to perform. The troupe from Wat Ban Don, Rayong Province, has 250 puppets, and the troupe at Wat Kanon in Potharam District, Ratchaburi Province, has 323, both sets being more than a hundred years old. A rare public exhibition of puppets and an extended performance by the troupe of Wat Kanon was given at the River City Shopping Complex in October 1988—the first major recognition of this seemingly dying genre.

Lakhawn

The term *lakhawn* is usually glossed 'dance-drama', but with various modifiers it refers to specific genres, each associated with a particular region and audience. It is distinguished from *khon* by its emphasis on singing and graceful dance. The literature on *lakhawn,* none of which relates directly to musical issues, tends to be confusing, with variant explanations of the origins and usages of certain terms and reconstructions of history based more on speculation than on solid evidence.

Three aspects must be taken into account: historical developments, the influence of the Fine Arts Department from 1934 to the present, and *lakhawn* in contemporary Thai life.

Historical developments

Two possible origins for *lakhawn* can be posited, one from southern Thailand, another from the Khmer after the fall of Angkor Vat; both may have contributed to the

That a dance-drama called *lakhawn* already existed in the 1600s is attested by La Loubere, who clearly described a performance of a type later to be called *lakhawn nawk.*

resulting genres that attained their peak of development in the years before 1932. While the Khmer retain elaborate and graceful dances obviously similar in style to those of Thailand, we cannot be sure of the relationship five hundred years ago. There is more concrete evidence that central Thai *lakhawn* was influenced by troupes from the south playing a genre of theater called *manora, nora,* or *manora chatri.* These terms derive from a *jataka* story, *Suton Manora* (Sanskrit *Sudhana Manohara*), the most important story played. Prince Damrong writes that during the 1800s numerous *manora* troupes were brought to Bangkok to settle and perform, but he also claims that *manora* occurred as early as the funeral of the father of King Rama I. As late as 1920, at least ten *manora* troupes were said to be living in the Lan Luang area of Bangkok (Ginsberg 1972:170). These southern troupes gradually changed in language, manners, and music to suit the central Thai taste and came to be called *lakhawn chatri.* Because *manora* used an all-male cast and the oldest genres of central Thai theater called *lakhawn* were male, Thai scholars (including Dhanit Yupho) argue that the reformed *manora* in central Thailand (that is, *lakhawn chatri*) formed the basis for later genres called *lakhawn* (that is, *lakhawn nawk* and *lakhawn nai*). Nevertheless, aspects of Khmer dance already present at the Thai court must have merged with the newly rising theatrical genres.

That a dance-drama called *lakhawn* already existed in the 1600s is attested by La Loubere, who clearly described a performance of a type later to be called *lakhawn nawk.* This reference casts doubt on the assertion that *lakhawn* developed only in the 1800s, from southern influence:

> The Show which they call *Lacone,* is a Poem intermixt with Epic and Dramatic, which lasts three days, from eight in the Morning till seven at Night. They are Histories in Verse, serious, and sung by several Actors always present, and which do only sing reciprocally. One of them sings the Historian's part, and the rest those of the Personages which the History makes to speak; but they are all Men that sing and no Women. (1969[1693]:49)

The next known mention of *lakhawn* in non-Thai literature is Bowring's account from 1857, describing an all-female troupe and ensemble.

In addition to *lakhawn chatri,* there were two other types, *lakhawn nawk* and *lakhawn nai. Nawk* is interpreted by various writers to mean one of two things: 'outside', as in 'outside the court', that is, of the common people, and 'countryside', as in *ban nawk* 'rural villages', meaning that *lakhawn nawk* came from rural regions, perhaps the south. It is believed that *lakhawn nawk* preceded *lakhawn nai,* identified with royal houses and refined audiences. *Nai* means 'inside', as in 'inside the palace', and may be a shortened form of *lakhawn nang nai* 'dance-drama of the inside ladies'. In the beginning, *lakhawn nawk* was played exclusively by males and *lakhawn nai* by females, but at some later time the distinctions became blurred, and mixed casts appeared. Dhanit Yupho offers the Thai view of the differences:

> In the case of Lakon Nok the aims are quick action and humour. But often the humour is obscene and indulged in longer than it should be. Even the characters who are royalty makes jokes and move on intimate terms with the courtiers, sometimes against the etiquette of the court. So, the text of the Lakon Nok plays has to be brief and colloquial in style and leave openings for the actors and actresses [sic] to introduce their own jokes on a large scale. The acting, too, has to be lively and natural in the manner of ordinary people though there may be slight exaggerations for the sake of artistic effect. The vocal and instrumental music must be quick in movement in order to harmonize with the general character of the Lakon Nok.
>
> Lakon Nai, on the other hand, places a great importance on dancing, even when that may made [sic] the action of the play slow, because, in this kind of drama, graceful and langourous movements are held to form the essence of the art. The Lakon Nai does not favour coarse humour, and it attempts to preserve the traditional customs and manners. The writers of the Lakon Nai have to choose their words carefully, adopting poetical expressions and excluding vulgarisms. The music has to be tender and slow unlike that of the Lakon Nok in order that the performers may display their skill in dancing to the full and imitate the elegant movements of royalty as befits the Lakon Nai which originated in the court. Thus the Lakon Nai aims to display, at one and the same time, at least sweet vocal music, fine poetry, good instrumental music and graceful acting which form the best elements of Thai theatrical art. (Dhanit 1963:93–94)

Traditional *lakhawn* was played before a plain curtain, with only a bench for a prop, everything being symbolic. There were no scene divisions. Actors and actresses had exposed faces, except for certain special characters, such as animals. But during the reign of Rama V, a period of Westernization, dramas came to be divided into scenes, and scenery was introduced.

The stories played by both kinds of *lakhawn* were varied but made little use of the *Ramakian.* Traditional stories included *Khun Chang Khun Phaen* and *Khrai Thawng,* set by old Siam's best dramatists. During the reign of King Boromokot (1733–1758), at the end of the Ayuthaya Period, Javanese *Panji* stories became popular at the court and were staged as plays in *lakhawn* style under the Thai name *Inao.* Both Rama I and Rama II wrote (or had written) settings of the *Inao* stories, but those by the latter have proven more effective for the stage. The version by Rama II, posthumously published in 1921, has 1,294 pages and 20,520 stanzas.

Little is known of the music of the *lakhawn. Lakhawn chatri* likely began with southern instruments but is said to have changed to a central Thai ensemble at some point. The hard-mallet ensemble originally accompanied both *nawk* and *nai,* but at some point the soft-mallet ensemble replaced it. Eventually, the *mahori* sometimes replaced the *piphat.* Both dance and singing were important, the dances being set to specific pieces (*phleng*). For stage action, there was additional use of the action tunes used in *khon.* The vocal parts were performed by an offstage chorus, since the actors or actresses could not manage it while acting; they could, however, speak during dialogue.

The influence of the Fine Arts Department

Thai theater and music reached their zenith during the reign of King Rama VI but declined dramatically after 1932, when the Royal Institute, which oversaw the arts, was transferred from the Bureau of the Royal Household to the Department of Fine Arts. That year also saw an economic crisis stemming from the Great Depression. In the years immediately after World War II, the Fine Arts Department moved to restore the glory of Thai music and theater—arts that had fallen to the point of

FIGURE 10 *Lakhawn chatri* performed in a ritual context near the great Phra Pathom Chedi temple in Nakhon Pathom, west of Bangkok. Photo by Terry E. Miller, 1973.

imminent extinction. Eventually, the Department revived all three varieties of *lakhawn*. These were collectively called *lakhawn ram* 'dance' in contradistinction to the newly created *lakhawn phut* 'spoken'. Both traditional and new stories were staged. *Lakhawn chatri* performed both *Manora* and *Rothasen*. *Lakhawn nawk* presented such tales as *Suwannahong*, *Kaeo Na Ma*, and *Sang Thawng*; and *lakhawn nai* presented the traditional *Inao*, *Sawit-tri*, and scenes from the *Ramakian*.

To describe newly staged versions of *lakhawn*, three new terms appeared: *lakhawn dükdamban*, *lakhawn puntawng*, and *lakhawn rawng*. The first is said to have been based on old themes, but the accompaniment (*piphat dükdamban*) made it musically distinct. This ensemble, like the soft-mallet ensemble, uses *saw u* and *khlui* but adds the seven-toned gong set (*wong khawng chai*) peculiar to this ensemble. *Lakhawn phanthawng* is described by Dhanit as "a mixture of themes resembling the old *lakhawn nawk* more than any others" (1963:75). *Lakhawn rawng* denoted a play in which singing permeated the performance in the manner of Western opera. Performances of these types are now quite rare.

Lakhawn *in contemporary Thai life*

Performances outside the control of the Fine Arts Department exist, but terminology is confusing. The original *lakhawn nawk* is said to have died out shortly after World War II. People widely believe, too, that it combined with the southern genre *li-ke* to create the modern folk-theatrical form of that name. *Li-ke* as a central Thai village genre is widespread.

At certain temples, however, theatrical performances variously called *lakhawn chatri*, *lakhawn rawng*, and simply *lakhawn* still occur. All are associated with Buddhist temples or Hindu shrines and therefore have a religious function. On a permanent stage within the grounds of Bangkok's *lak müang*, a Hindu-derived shrine for the pillar considered the exact center of the city, a theatrical genre called *lakhawn rawng* is performed daily. Citizens come to the *lak müang* asking for help, for lucky lottery numbers, for a mate, for children, and so forth. If they are successful, one of the possible responses is to sponsor a segment of a *lakhawn* performance. The audience consists of rougher sorts, who come and go while the stories are performed by troupes of modest talent. Dialogue, action, singing, and dancing occur, all accompanied by a small hard-mallet ensemble (usually without a *pi nai*). Similar kinds of theater occur at certain Buddhist temples, like the Phra Pathom Chedi in Nakhawn Pathom (figure 10).

In Bangkok, an open-air shrine to the Hindu god Brahma, founded in 1956, stands at the corner of Ploenchit and Rajadamri Roads, where *lakhawn* dance occurs daily. While worshippers light incense and ask for favors, four or six young women dance and sing at the four corners of the area surrounding the figure of the deity. Accompaniment consists of a *ranat ek,* a *taphon,* and sometimes a *ching.* In a custom called *ram khe bon,* patrons fulfilling their vow to Brahma pay a substantial amount of money for the dance. As a result, the shrine derives goodly sums of money, which it gives to charity.

Finally, performances of traditional *lakhawn nai,* sometimes mixed with *lakhawn nawk,* are given by students and faculty of the branches of the College of Dramatic Arts and other schools.

Hün

Seldom seen and never widespread, *hün krabawk* is nevertheless a theater of Thailand's only remaining non-shadow-type puppets. Evidence that rod-type puppets with moveable arms manipulated from below were once somewhat common is found in the National Museum, where several sets with figures about 30 centimeters high are displayed. These may have been commissioned by the second king in the mid-1800s to perform Chinese-style theater. Of greater certainty is that in Sukhotai in 1892, a prince observed bamboo-rod puppets said to have been copied from puppets brought from Hainan Island, off the southeastern coast of China. He brought one back to Bangkok, where it was copied, and the first *hün* troupe was founded in 1893, with another in 1899. Evidently iron sticks, used to move the arms, were added only in 1899. One troupe remains, performing a variety of stories, including Sunthon Phu's classic *Phra Aphai Mani* and the *Ramakian.* All performers are seated within a raised stage behind a curtain, the manipulators holding the puppets outside the screen with outstretched arms.

The complete ensemble, if used, is said to be a soft-mallet *piphat* ensemble with *khlui* and *saw u,* but a smaller ensemble is also common. The story is told by a group of some six or seven women reciting the words while each keeps an audible beat with a pair of long concussion sticks (*krap khu*). Action is accompanied by the ensemble using standard action tunes (figure 11).

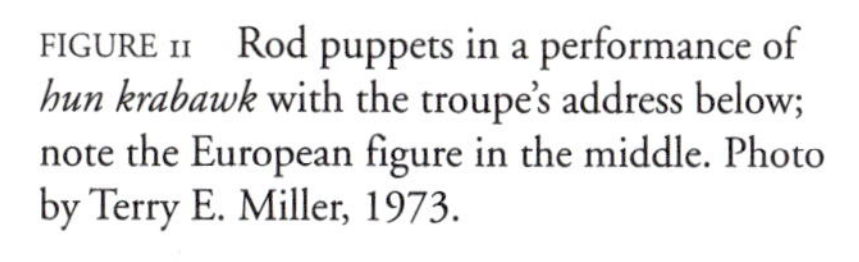

FIGURE 11 Rod puppets in a performance of *hun krabawk* with the troupe's address below; note the European figure in the middle. Photo by Terry E. Miller, 1973.

wai khru Ritual ceremony to honor one's teacher

sepha Narrative genre accompanied with *krap*

thet mahachat Preaching/chanting the story of Prince Wetsandon, the Buddha-to-be

tham khwan Ceremony to restore a person's spiritual essence

Wai khru

The ritual of *wai khru* (*khru,* from *guru*), which greets or honors teachers, is of fundamental importance in Thai culture. Through it, those who learn any art, both nonmusical (like boxing) and musical (including making instruments, dance, singing, and instrumental performance), establish a lifetime relationship through their teachers to their teachers' teachers, finally to the Hindu-Buddhist cosmology, which oversees these arts. Indeed, even teachers in public schools and university professors are so honored. Of greatest importance in this pantheon are the *thewada* or *deva* who created music and transmitted it to humans. Rituals are held on Thursday, because each day is associated with a planet, and Thursday is reserved for Phin Pharyhatsa-baudii, the Thai equivalent to Jupiter, but Sunday is also acceptable.

Wai khru are of many levels and types. When a student is accepted by a teacher, whether privately or in a formal school, the student is expected to perform a beginning-level ceremony, which requires only modest offerings—candles, cloth, incense, flowers, and coins. High-level ceremonies take place before a multilevel altar, on which are placed the masks of the gods and certain main characters of the *Ramakian.* Various offerings—rice, candles, cigarettes, whiskey, a boiled chicken, an egg, a pig's head—are also placed there, each with its own significance (the pig's head, for example, is for the demon king Totsagan). The student is led in repeating lines in Pali, the sacred language of Theravada Buddhism. The *wai khru* concludes with a ritual first lesson, when the student is taught (in the case of *piphat*) the first few notes of the piece "*Phleng Tra.*" Dr. Deborah Wong has written extensively on this subject (1991).

In addition to the ritual objects, the best musical instruments available are displayed at the altar. In a ceremony that can last up to three hours, a hard-mallet *piphat* ensemble performs high-level compositions (*phleng naphat*) in alternation with a ritualist, who chants auspicious texts in Pali. Each piece has a function, marking a ritual event in the process. Toward the end, female dancers perform before the altar to honor teachers of dance.

Sepha

A nearly extinct narrative genre now revived at Chulalongkorn University, *sepha* existed to tell just one story, that of *Khun Chang Khun Phaen,* Mr. Chang and Mr. Phaen. The story is believed to be based on fact—that its hero, Khun Phaen, was born in 1485, had five wives, and was sent by King Ramadhipati II of Ayuthaya (1491–1529) to lead a punitive force against the king of Chiangmai, a rival. Strangely, Mr. Chang, whose name appears first in the title, is a minor character. The literary version that serves as the basis of the recitation evidently dates back to the reign of King Rama II but is the work of many different writers and revisions. First published in 1872, it has appeared in revised editions since.

Sepha was performed as entertainment for guests at various occasions, like housewarmings and birthdays, but especially tonsure ceremonies. Because of conjugal difficulties in the story, it was not considered auspicious for marriages. Two or more reciters, either male or female, were invited to tell in heightened speech (*khap*) the story of Mr. Phaen, each accompanying himself or herself with two pairs of wooden castanets (*krap sepha*). Each reciter played a role, or if there were too few reciters, each played more than one role, as in old-fashioned radio plays. Because the recitation was tiring, both to the performers and audience, it was customary to interrupt the recitation with music played by a *piphat.* His Highness Prince Bidyalongkorn described in 1940, when the genre was nearly dead, the process of signaling the ensemble to play:

> When a reciter wants a pause to take breath, or for a drink or a cigarette, he brings a passage of the rhymes to a close by singing it—not merely reciting. The orchestra, knowing the signal, strikes up, playing the tune indicated by the singer. Needless to say, the loud Thai orchestra would drown the man's voice if he continued to sing, so he lights a cigarette, or takes a drink, or even goes out for a breath of air. (1981[1940]:45)

Later, as the genre died out, the *piphat* retained for solo performance the repertory associated with *sepha* but without the recitation. This repertoire is of the type most commonly heard in live performance and on recordings outside the theater.

Thet mahachat

Thet is a verb meaning 'to preach' in heightened speech, and *mahachat* means 'the great birth'—the human, penultimate life of the Lord Buddha, just preceding his enlightenment. *Chat* is short for *chatok,* or the story of Buddha's birth, from the Pali *jataka.* It is customary in central Thailand to recite the life of Prince Wetsanton, the Buddha-to-be (bodhisattva in the Mahayana tradition), as an exemplary life to be copied.

Taking place in October, before the rice is harvested, the festival is held in the preaching hall (*sala*) of the local temple (*wat*), beginning early in the morning and lasting until midnight. The original text was entirely in Pali; it is now customarily recited in Thai, with some Pali stanzas interspersed throughout, but these cannot be understood by most laity. The story is broken into thirteen chapters (*kan*), each sponsored by a particular person or family, which brings gifts to the temple. Though this is a religious story and festival, talented monks (*phra*) recite the story in an entertaining fashion, sometimes adding humor and intonations much enjoyed by the less stodgy of the laity. The fifth chapter, concerning Chuchok, an aged Brahmin mendicant and his young but shrewish wife, permits much humor and therefore attracts the largest audience.

At the end of each chapter and before the following one, a hard-mallet *piphat* ensemble customarily plays from a standard repertoire. Those who know the pieces can detect which chapter is about to start, even from a distance. Today, such complete performances are rare, but recordings have been produced of the *piphat* music alone, now often played through a public address system in place of live musicians.

Tham khwan

The ceremony to call back and bind the spiritual essence *khwan,* symbolized in the tying of threads around the wrist (which has Hindu roots), pervades Buddhist Thailand. Though rare in southern and central regions, in contrast to the north and northeast, the central *tham khwan* included a *piphat* to perform music at auspicious moments. Since the ceremony could be performed for commoners and royalty alike, the musicians could also vary from local village musicians to those of the court. The custom of using a *piphat* is long forgotten, but *Rüang Tham Kwan,* a suite (*rüang*) of *piphat* pieces, remains, published in score by the Fine Arts Department.

THE STRUCTURE OF THAI CLASSICAL MUSIC

Devising a systematic description of the structure of a musical tradition is a common ethnomusicological goal. The approach derives from the study of Western classical music, necessarily making use of terminology that, although generically English, was created to denote phenomena sometimes particular to the Western tradition. Thai musicians have terms for numerous phenomena, but it would be risky to say that they have a comprehensive theory of Thai music and certainly not according to Western theoretical concepts. While the Thai view is adequate for Thai musicians, the following explanation seeks to answer questions inherent in the Western view.

Pitch materials

Controversy swirls around the problem of Thai tunings, specifically whether the tones of the Thai system are equidistant or not. The issue, however, is primarily limited to instruments with fixed pitches, the *ranat* and the *khawng wong,* which have seven bars or gongs per octave. The voice, aerophones, and most chordophones make use of intonations between those of the fixed-pitch instruments, and these are difficult to accommodate in any system; indeed, the gliding commonly played on these suggests a continuum of sound, rather than a series of specific levels of pitch. Thai equidistance, like that of the West, may represent a practical compromise over the more flexible and complex system that is reality. Neither Western nor Thai string ensembles necessarily play in equidistance, since it, certainly for the West, would produce undesired beats in polyphony. Consequently, any discussion of equidistance and nonequidistance concerns only certain members of the Thai instrumentarium.

The earliest scientific measurements of pitch made on Thai instruments were done in 1885 by the English phonologist Alexander J. Ellis. His specimen was a *ranat ek* with nineteen bars in the South Kensington Museum, London. The results vexed him because intervals varied from 45 to 258 cents. He concluded, "This scale is quite enigmatical. The second Octave, of which only the beginning was measured, quite disagrees with the first" (1885a:506–507). When musicians from Siam arrived with their instruments a few months later, Ellis carefully measured their *ranat ek* and *ranat ek lek* and found intervals on the first varying from 127 to 219 cents and on the second varying from 160 to 200 cents. But these instruments had just arrived after a long trip and a change of weather. Ellis consulted with Prince Prisdang, the Siamese envoy, who

> told us that the intention was to make all the intervals from note to note identically the same. This would give the above division of the Octave into seven equal intervals, each containing 171.43 cents. In order to test the correctness of this information, I made a finger-board for my dichord . . . on which I could play such a scale, and I played it before the musicians at the Siamese Legation. They unanimously pronounced the scale good. I then played the scale I had heard from the Ranat Ek, and they said it was out of tune. This experiment may be considered decisive. The ideal Siamese scale is, consequently, an equal division of an Octave into seven parts, so that there are no Semitones and no Tones, when the instrument is properly tuned. (1885b:1105)

Both the museum specimen and the newly arrived instruments had lost bits of the lead-and-beeswax mixture normally used to weight the bars and gongs. The same problem may well hold true for contemporary instruments, just as an exacting measurement of most pianos sitting around a Western conservatory would reveal deviations from equidistance. Thai tuners, like many tuners of pianos, set the temperament by ear, not with a mathematically calibrated machine. One tuner's in-tuneness may vary from another's. Furthermore, instruments are not continuously checked and retuned. If bits of tuning wax fall off Thai instruments, or the weather causes strings on a piano to deviate from their set tension, instruments go slightly out of tune, but both Western and Thai musicians tolerate a certain deviance from the ideal before feeling the need to correct the situation. Consequently, there is truth to the assertion, which has become the conventional wisdom of Thai music, that the system of tuning consists of seven equidistant pitches—but it is also true that in reality it is not exactly so. The question then turns on the significance of the discrepancies.

Reviewing Morton's book, Paul Fuller (1979) used the research of Thai physicist Somchai Thayarnyong to take issue with the theory of equidistance. Somchai argues that not only are the instruments in fact not equidistant, but proof of the meaningfulness of the differences is clear from the fact that Thai musicians play in specified levels (in Western terms, keys) according to the situation—that is, *li-ke* is different from *khon*. Somchai relates that the musicians shift levels to "keep the temper and mood according to the original of the play." This evidence may be misleading, however, for pieces are played at specific levels according to the kinds of instruments used. Especially to accommodate the aerophones, each ensemble therefore has its normal level or levels of pitch.

Further proof of *practical* equidistance is found in the fact that fixed-pitch instruments can be reconfigured in more than one ensemble. A given piece played by a hard-mallet *piphat* ensemble at its level will shift down one pitch when played by the *piphat mai nuam*, *khrüang sai*, and *mahori* because the aerophone of the *piphat* ensemble is the *pi nai* and that of the latter three is the *khlui phiang aw.* Though *mahori*-size xylophones and gong circles exist, not every ensemble can afford them. Consequently, the same instruments usually have to serve both ensembles, meaning the same piece can be played on the same instruments at different pitch levels. Furthermore, after a tuner finishes his work, someone plays a test piece, starting on each of the seven possible pitch levels.

Traditional teachers of *piphat* instruments do not use any notation in transmitting the music to their students, but teach by rote, note by note. Sometimes the initial Thai letters for the Western *do–re–mi* system are written with chalk on the keys (a system to be explained shortly), but references to Western letters are not part of the system. And yet, Thai have been transcribing classical music into Western staff notation since the 1930s, not for pedagogical purposes, but for publication and analytical study. Most transcriptions have been published by the Fine Arts Department in books, magazines, and pamphlets. A project to preserve Thai music in transcription (begun in the 1930s, but never completed) made use of staff notation. The relationships among the notational systems used in Thailand (staff, solfège, and cipher), with the variables of ensemble type and aerophone, are quite complex. Morton's statement that G is the home level of the *piphat* is correct (see Miller 1992), but where is G?

The system to be described was created by the Fine Arts Department for its transcriptions into staff notation. Obviously there is a major discrepancy between the twelve semitones implied by the staff and the seven tones of the Thai system. *Piphat* music is transcribed in G major, with one sharp in the signature, and the notation suggests semitones and tones within the scale; the reader must understand that in fact there are only Thai tones of roughly 171 cents, and consequently F and F-sharp represent the same bar or gong, depending on "tonal" context. Pieces transcribed in F major or B-flat major, however, become confusing to read, because if a passage shifts

A xylophone from one Thai ensemble placed in another ensemble may or may not be in tune in the new setting, for ensembles are tuned together rather than to a national standard.

FIGURE 12 Chart showing *ranat ek* and *khawng wong yai* pitches for *piphat* and *mahori* or *khrüang sai*, respectively.

ranat ek

bar no.	1	2	3	4	5	6	7	8	9	10	11	12	13	14	15	16	17	18	19	20	21
mahori	G	A	B	c	d	e	f	g	a	b	c′	d′	e′	f′	g′	a′	b′	c″	d″	e″	f″
piphat	F	G	A	B	c	d	e	f	g	a	b	c′	d′	e′	f′	g′	a′	b′	c″	d″	e″

khawng wong yai

gong no.	1	2	3	4	5	6	7	8	9	10	11	12	13	14	15	16
mahori	E	F	G	A	B	c	d	e	f	g	a	b	c′	d′	e′	f′
piphat	D	E	F	G	A	B	c	d	e	f	g	a	b	c′	d′	e′

(or modulates), the usage of the flats and naturals changes, preserving the appearance that the melody is in a major scale.

The question remains, where is G (or F or B-flat) on an actual instrument? The master of *piphat* teaches by striking certain gongs of the *khawng wong* for the student, who imitates that action. When one compares a transcription of a given piece to the orally given instructions, one deduces that G is the fourth and eleventh gongs (counting from left to right) on the *khawng wong yai*, and the second, ninth, and sixteenth bars on the *ranat ek*. A master of *mahori*, however, in teaching the same piece would ask the student to strike G on the third and tenth gongs of the gong circle or first, eighth, and fifteenth bars of the xylophone. In short, a *piphat* piece notated in G major is played one tone lower if transferred to the *mahori* or the *khrüang sai*, but both are in G; the reason for the shift has to do with the different aerophones and their tuning. The *pi nai* is comfortably played starting from the fourth gong, while the *khlui phiang aw* is played starting on the sixth. The sixth gong in *piphat* terms is B-flat, but in *mahori* it is C in relation to the staff notation (figure 12).

Unlike in the West, which acknowledges one standard pitch (A = 440 hertz), in Thailand the standard is more variable. A xylophone from one ensemble placed in another ensemble may or may not be in tune in the new setting, for ensembles are tuned together rather than to a national standard. Morton, testing numerous xylophones in Thailand, found that the fifth bar from the left on the *ranat ek* varied from 277 hertz to 289.3 hertz (1976:28). It is also true that off-the-shelf aerophones vary in pitch level too, and finding, for example, a *khlui* to match the fixed instruments is requisite. Compared to Western pitch, then, the fourth bar, notated as B(-flat) for *piphat* and tuned at approximately 262 hertz, is roughly equivalent to C; in *mahori* pitch, it is also written as C. Consequently, the notated pitch of *mahori* music roughly approximates that of Western pitch, while *piphat* music is one tone higher.

Other notational systems have been used in the written literature to convey Thai music, among them two different usages of solfège, a series of roman numerals, and two series using arabic numerals. Certain of these systems seem needlessly complicat-

FIGURE 13
Example of metabole in a Thai classical melody.

ed, often contradictory, and sometimes idiosyncratic; but some, having been used long enough to become established, must be understood, despite their imperfections (Miller 1992).

Scale

As seen on fixed-pitch instruments, the Thai system of tuning has seven tones in the octave, functionally equidistant, though the voice and nonfixed-pitch instruments use tones beyond these seven. The term *scale* denotes an abstract series of tones derived from the system of tuning, presented in ascending order and forming the basis of a given composition or class of compositions.

In Thai music, five fundamental tones, forming a pentatonic scale, are the basis of most compositions. The pattern is three consecutive tones, a skipped tone, two consecutive tones, and a skipped tone, or, 1–2–3–5–6. Many compositions, however, use six or seven tones. Morton offers two reasons for these seemingly extra scalar entities: their use as passing notes on weak beats; and their use during a temporary shift of tonal center—a phenomenon known to ethnomusicologists as metabole, avoiding the Western term *modulation*. Exceptions occur. Compositions in the *mawn* or *khaek* accents routinely use six fundamental tones (figure 13).

Mode

The term *mode* has been used in both musicological and ethnomusicological literature to denote numerous phenomena, from abstract scales (the major, minor, Gregorian modes) to highly developed systems that form the basis for improvisation and composition (the Indian ragas). The term is especially troublesome when applied to Thai music. Morton's study devotes considerable space to concepts of mode (1976:115–179). His analysis, based on written versions of classical compositions, is far too detailed to repeat here, but he concludes that several factors considered essential in defining mode by ethnomusicological standards exist in Thai music. Among them is the use of a nonequidistant supply of tones (a so-called gapped scale), a hierarchy of tones in which the first is a finalis, a cadential formula (5–6–5–3–2–1), and a fifth polarity in which double phrases ("couplets") end on 1 but the first phrase tends to end on 5 (1976:178–179).

The closest Thai equivalent to "mode" is *thang*, a term that can mean different things in different contexts: the melodic idiom of a particular instrument, as *thang ranat ek*, as opposed to *thang saw duang*; the overall style of a particular teacher or school, as *thang Luang Pradit Phairoh*; a national melodic style, as *thang mawn* (Mon) and *thang khaek* (Indian or Malay), plus the drum patterns associated with them; the pitch level of a composition as played on instruments. The last usage relates most closely to mode. Each of the seven fixed pitches has a name, and each can be pitch 1 for a scale, conceived either as seven successive pitches or as a pentatonic scale in the 1–2–3–5–6 pattern. The following summarizes the essentials of the system of *thang* based on *piphat*-pitch names.

Thang nai is notated as G, the fourth gong on the lower gong circle and second bar of the upper xylophone and is the pitch of the *pi nai.* Consequently it serves for all ensembles and theatrical genres requiring the hard-mallet ensembles: *lakhawn nai, lakhawn nawk, khon,* and *nang yai.*

Thang klang is notated as A, the fifth gong and the third bar, and is the pitch of the *pi klang,* now virtually obsolete. This was the pitch level for the hard-mallet ensemble, which accompanied both *khon* and *nang yai* during the 1600s and 1700s, when the *pi klang* was used. It is also the pitch level for the soft-mallet ensemble as well as for the (rarely heard) *mahori mawn*; as with *mahori* compositions generally, its music would be written in B-flat instead of A, but the same bars and gongs are struck as when notated in A for *piphat. Thang klang* is also called *thang luk ot* because a class of lament-type compositions called *ot* are played in this *thang.*

Thang phiang aw bon is notated as B-flat, the sixth gong and fourth bar, and is the pitch of the *khlui phiang aw.* Consequently this mode is the pitch level of the soft-mallet *piphat* ensemble, the *mahori,* and the *khrüang sai,* ensembles that use *khlui phiang aw,* though in staff notation the tone C serves for the latter two. It is also the pitch level for the standard hard-mallet *mawn* ensemble (*piphat mawn mai khaeng*) and for the even rarer *piphat nang hong,* which uses *pi chawa.*

Thang kruat or *thang nawk* is notated as C, the seventh gong and fifth bar, and is the pitch level of the (little-used) *pi nawk.* Formerly, when *lakhawn nawk* used *pi nawk,* its compositions were played at this level. In addition, some compositions for *sepha* played by the hard-mallet ensemble are in *thang kruat. Kruat* means 'pebbles' or 'coarse sand'.

Thang klang haep is notated as D, the first gong and sixth bar, but exists more in theory than in reality. For *piphat,* it is rarely used. Since the now rare *khlui lip* is at this level (though notated in E-flat), there is the suggestion of use, but *khlui lip* is not a primary aerophone in any ensemble. The term *haep* means 'harsh' or 'grating'.

Thang chawa is notated as E-flat, the second gong and seventh bar, but is rare. It is the pitch level of the *pi chawa,* the primary aerophone only for the *khrüang sai* with *pi chawa,* notated as F. It is also an alternate pitch level for the *piphat mawn mai nuam.*

Thang phiang aw lang is notated as F, the third gong and first bar, and is the pitch level of the now rare *khlui u* (notated, however, as G). It is the pitch level for numerous ensembles. At written F, it is used by *piphat mai nuam* and *piphat dük-damban,* ensembles that use *khlui,* and by *piphat mawn mai khaeng.* At written G, it serves for *mahori* and *khrüang sai.* It is also known as *thang nai lot,* 'one pitch below *thang nai*'.

Colotomy

The concepts of meter, rhythm, and tempo are not clearly demarcated in Thai: the word *jangwa* serves in various contexts for all three. The term *jangwa saman* 'general rhythm' refers to the feeling of beat, even the pulses of the heart. A description of meter, rhythm, and tempo would be incomplete without an additional factor, involving melody. We shall call it rhythmic density, but it necessarily involves melodic density.

Rhythmic density is articulated in Thai classical music by a small pair of brass

FIGURE 14 Patterns for *ching* in the three *chan*. A circle indicates *ching*, a cross indicates *chap*, and a circle and a cross together indicate *siang tok*, the final and more accented *chap* stroke.

○ = *ching* stroke + = *chap* stroke ⊕ = final stroke (*siang tok*)

sam chan	○	+	○	⊕	(1 cycle)
sawng chan	○ +	○ ⊕	○ +	○ ⊕	(2 cycles)
chan dio	○ + ○ ⊕	○ + ○ ⊕	○ + ○ ⊕	○ + ○ ⊕	(4 cycles)

cymbals (*ching*), which provide an audible beat throughout a given composition. The rhythm defined by the *ching* is called *jangwa ching*. The *ching* play two strokes: an undamped, unaccented stroke, sounding *ching*; and a damped, accented stroke, sounding *chap*. The symbol "+" in notation indicates *chap*, and "o" indicates *ching*. In a high percentage of Thai compositions, *ching* and *chap* alternate, with *chap* always at the end—meaning that Thai music is both duple in meter and accented at the end. There are exceptions. Some action tunes and other special compositions require only the sound of *ching* throughout, though they remain duple. A few pieces are in 7/4 time, with an unusual pattern resulting. Pieces in Chinese accent (*samniang jin*), again duple, use a four-beat cycle with beat 1 open: ——, *ching, ching, chap*.

Furthermore, the *ching* pattern is conceived in cycles of four strokes, which parallel the cycles of drumstrokes (*nathap*). The four-stroke cycle ends on the second *chap*, which has greater importance than the first; coinciding with an important structural melodic pitch, *siang tok*, it serves as the cycle marker. In Thai notational systems, *ching* and *chap* fall before the bar. Modifying staff notation to have the accent before the bar has proved extremely confusing, and consequently, when Thai music is so written, the accent falls after the bar.

Three rhythmic densities (or tempo levels, *chan*) are common in Thai music: *chan dio* 'first level', *sawng chan* 'second level', and *sam chan* 'third level'. The third level is the least dense (the strokes are farthest apart), and the first is the most dense (the strokes are closest together). The relationship among them is proportional: a pattern in the second level takes half as much time as one in the third level, and a pattern in the first level takes half the time of the second (figure 14).

Two more *chan*, though rarely heard, exist. *Khrüng chan* 'half level' takes half the time of the first, and *si chan* 'fourth level' takes twice as much time as the third. In practice, the *ching* plays *chan dio* for *khrüng chan* and *sam chan* for *si chan*.

There is a third rhythmic concept, *jangwa nathap*, patterns related to drums in the *thap* (or *thon*) category. The strokes made by Thai drums, like those of many other Asian drums, bear names. Paralleling a given *ching* is a pattern that can be articulated on drums through these strokes. The words vary from drum to drum—and to a limited extent from teacher to teacher and school to school. Those presented here derive from the tradition of the College of Dramatic Arts.

Generally speaking, there are two major sets of drum patterns, but supposedly national patterns exist, as do numerous other patterns particular to small groups of compositions or even to individual ones. Since the patterns can be quite different from one drum type to another, the presentation of all possible patterns is beyond the scope of this study. Discussion is limited to the sets *nathap propkai* and *nathap sawngmai*. Each is a set of three patterns, one for each of the three rhythmic densities (*chan*). A *propkai* pattern takes twice the time of its equivalent pattern in *sawngmai*; if the former's third level takes eight measures in notation, the latter's third level takes four. Figure 15 shows each of these with the appropriate *ching*.

The third level of *sawngmai* and the second level of *propkai* are equally long, but the patterns associated with them differ. Because the time intervals between strokes in the third level are long, players lose a feel for the beat, so *ching* players usually dou-

nathap Cycle of drum strokes
nathap propkai Longer set of three drum cycle patterns
nathap sawngmai Shorter set of three drum cycle patterns
klawng khaek Two-headed conical drums; ensemble for boxing and theater
thon Wood or clay single-headed, goblet-shaped drum
rammana Wooden frame drum with single head

nathap propkai

sam chan				○ |				+ |				○ |				⊕ |
sawng chan		○		+ |		○		⊕ |		○		+ |		○		⊕ |
chan dio	○	+	○	⊕ |	○	+	○	⊕ |	○	+	○	⊕ |	○	+	○	⊕ |

nathap sawngmai

sam chan				○ |				+ |				○ |				⊕ |
sawng chan		○		+ |		○		⊕ |		○		+ |		○		⊕ |
chan dio	○	+	○	⊕ |	○	+	○	⊕ |	○	+	○	⊕ |	○	+	○	⊕ |

FIGURE 15 *Ching* stroke patterns in each *chan* for *propkai* and *sawng mai* systems.

ble the stroke rate in *propkai.* This doubling makes distinguishing *propkai* from *sawngmai* dependent on recognizing the drummed pattern. Which pattern occurs in a particular composition is a matter of custom, not choice. These patterns, with predictable phrase lengths, duple meter, and symmetry, reveal the classicality of Thai music, its restraint and balance—traits that harmonize with other kinds of traditional Thai behavior.

While the *ching* provides the basic articulation of the cyclical metrical system, other idiophones can be used to reinforce it and add spice to the sound. Either or both kinds of *krap*—the wooden, castanetlike *krap sepha* or the fanlike *krap phuang*—reinforce the *chap,* sometimes both within the four-stroke pattern, sometimes only on the final, accented stroke. A single-bossed gong, *khawng mong,* can also be struck at this point. The medium cymbals, *chap lek,* may also be used, but their role is far more complex. Two strokes are used: *dawk,* striking the edge of one cymbal vertically against the inside of the other; and *chae,* rattling the cymbals together, face to face. The pattern includes syncopation, which, in the hands of a player who improvises variants, may become somewhat complex (figure 16).

The drums used to play the standard cycles include the *taphon,* the *sawng na,* the *klawng khaek,* and the *thon rammana* (a pair, one laced and the other tacked). A second category of drums, usually defined as having tacked heads rather than lacing

FIGURE 16 *Chap lek* patterns compared with those for *ching, mong,* and *krap.*

* = vertical stroke on *chap lek* - = horizontal stroke on *chap lek*

ching pattern for *sawng chan*	○	+	○	+ |	○	+	○	+
chap lek pattern	* *	-	-	- |	* *	-	-	-
krap pattern		x		x |		x		x
mong pattern				x |				x

(though the *thon* is an exception to the rule), is called *mai klawng.* Drums of this category, played with sticks, produce patterns particular to specific pieces.

The following strokes constitute the basic vocabulary of the *klawng khaek* and the *thon rammana.* The former have a total of four heads, but the latter have only two. The *thon* is the wife (*mia*) and the *rammana* the husband (*phu*). With the *klawng khaek,* the wife has a slightly lower pitch than the husband.

Thang: an undamped stroke on the center of the wife drum's head by closed right-hand fingers.
Ting: same as the preceding, but on the husband drum's head.
Ja: an undamped stroke on the wife drum's rim by two or three left-hand fingers.
Jo: same as the preceding, but on the husband drum's rim.

An unnamed stroke is a damped stroke on the wife drum by the right-hand fingers (figure 17).

Besides these standard sets, individual pieces have many special patterns (*nathap phiset*), which can be categorized into three groups. First are patterns for the action-related tunes of the masked theater and dance-drama, some of which have complex, changing tempos. They are called *nathap taphon klawng* since they are played on the *taphon* and the *klawng that.* Second are national patterns for language-tune pieces (*phleng pasah*), such as specific *nathap* for Burmese, Lao, Cambodian, Malay, Mon, and Chinese tunes. Last are *nathap* for dances that specifically require the expression of particular moods.

Because constant repetition of the same pattern would become boring for both players and listeners, drummers play variants of the basic patterns, but these do not deviate much in style or brilliance from the basic patterns. The Thai drummer is a timekeeper, reinforcing the cycle in subservience to melodic instruments; virtuoso display, as heard among Indian tabla drummers, is unknown in Thai music. Variations played on drums of the *thap* or *thon* category are called *sai,* and those of the *mai klawng* category are called *len mai.*

Excepting the idiom of the *ranat thum* (lower xylophone) and solo work on the *ranat ek,* the rhythms of Thai music are simple, compared to those of India and Vietnam. Three characteristics account for most rhythmic activity in melody. First, continuous notes (notated as quarters, eighths, or sixteenths) are common, especially in motivically constructed melodies, music for *piphat,* and versions for particular instruments, especially *ranat ek.* Second, unequal patterns—notated as dotted, but realized in a proportion closer to 2/1 than 3/1—characterize certain instruments, such as the *ja-khe.* Third, syncopation occurs mainly in certain stereotyped and idiomatic ornaments on specific instruments, such as the *sabat* on *ranat thum* or *khawng wong lek,* but the *ranat thum* allows extraordinarily complex improvisation, which defies transcription. Syncopation can also occur in certain polyphonic passages, discussed below under the heading of texture.

The changes in rhythmic density as articulated by the *ching* are not to be confused with the concept of tempo. A *piphat* playing *sepha*-repertoire music—played alone, originally to permit the reciter time to rest—may be inclined to play as fast as the skills of the leader (*ranat ek*) allow, but music of *lakhawn* will usually be played more slowly, to fit the character of the dance. A solo *ranat ek* will usually play rapidly, but a solo *khlui* or *saw* will play more slowly, to allow more extensive and subtle ornamentation. The vocal section of a composition is usually sung more slowly than the instrumental section is played. The tempo will slow at the end of a section that leads back to the singer, as it will from the fast to the slow sections in a solo piece—a phenomenon called *thawt.* The concept of accelerating tempo has no term but is

FIGURE 17 Drum strokes (*thon* and *rammana* or *klawng khaek*) in each *chan* for *propkai* and *sawng mai* systems. (Note: accent at beginning of measure.)

Nathap propkai drum strokes and *ching* strokes:

Drum strokes: t = *ting* th = *thang* j = *jong* ja = *ja*

Sam chan

ching

```
                                         o                 +                          o                   +
drum strokes - - th t - j - ja - j - ja - j | j - - - - - j - ja - j - ja - j | ja - t - t - th t th t th - t - j - | ja - t - th - t - t - th - th - t - | th
```

sawng chan

```
           o              +                o                +
- - th t - j - | ja - j - ja - j - | ja - t - th - t - | t - th - t th t - | th
```

chan dio

```
      o         +          o          +
- - t | th - t - | - - th - | t th t - | th
```

Nathap sawngmai drum strokes and *ching* strokes:

sam chan

```
           o              +                    o                   +
- - th t - j - | ja - j - ja - j - | ja - t - t - th t | th t th - t th t - | th
```

sawng chan

```
     o         +         o          +
- t - | j - t - | t - - - | th - t - | th
```

chan dio

```
  o     +       o     +
- j - | t th | t - | th
```

expressed as *reo khün*; there is some tendency to accelerate tempos in instrumental music, especially in the three-part *phleng thao,* which successively presents the same basic melody in each of the three rhythmic densities.

Melody

Thai classical music is based on melody, but melody is manifested not in an abstract, ideal form (*thang phün* or *thang kep*) but in many individual realizations according to the idiom of the instrument or voice realizing the melody (*thang khrüang*). Notated versions of Thai compositions are of two types, actual transcriptions of individual parts and generic abstractions. The former appear in scores, the latter in tune collections for no particular instrument.

Morton's analysis shows that, broadly speaking, Thai melody has two possible characters: motivic and lyrical. Older compositions, especially for *piphat,* tend to be motivically constructed; they are difficult for beginners and outsiders to remember and recognize. Consequently, theatrical music (such as action tunes) and the longer suites appropriate to ceremonial occasions show a motivically based melodic style. The individual, idiomatic realizations of the melody tend to be quite diverse. Newer compositions, especially those identified with the *sepha* tradition, are distinguished by long, flowing phrases. They are more easily remembered, and individual idiomatic realizations tend to resemble each other closely. Lyrical melodies lend themselves to generic presentation, whereas motivic melodies can be reduced only to structural abstractions.

Thai melodies tend to be far more conjunct than disjunct. Though gaps appear between pitches 3 and 5 and between 6 and upper octave 1, these do not violate the contiguous pattern of the pentatonic scale. Intervals larger than a Thai fourth (as between pitches 2 and 5) occur infrequently. However, both abstract and idiomatic realizations may exhibit intervals of a sixth, a seventh, or an octave, but these primarily result from octave displacements required by limitations of instrumental range (in idiomatic versions) and avoidance of extreme ranges (in abstract versions). Figure 18 shows a conjunct version of the beginning of "*Kamen Sai Yok*" ('Sai Yok Waterfall, in Cambodian accent'), followed by the realization on *saw duang,* whose lowest written pitch is G.

The regular and symmetrical phrases seen earlier in the colotomic structure are also characteristic of the melodic structure. The clarity with which the resulting

FIGURE 18 "*Kamen Sai Yok,*" first section, in generic form and with octave displacements to accommodate *saw duang,* tuned g and d′.

The melodic idiom taught to beginners is simpler than that of advanced players, and ensemble idioms are simpler than solo idioms. A catalogue of all possible characteristics available to a soloist on each instrument would constitute a small book.

phrases are articulated, however, varies; motivic melodies, being based on short units, have less feeling for phrase than do lyrical ones. Some lyrical melodies have phrases that in an abstract version would end with long, sustained pitches. Thai music, like Western classical music of the Baroque period, prefers restlessness over repose, and instrumentalists normally play stereotyped filler material (*luk thao*) in place of these long notes.

A discussion of fundamental structure and ornamentation inevitably leads to the matter of idiom (*thang*), and idiom begs the question of texture. Idiom also raises questions about pentatonicism, since some instrumental idioms appear hexatonic or even heptatonic. Each instrument has a unique character in its realization of a melody, for even lyrical melodies are based on a series of structural pitches that fall on the strokes of the *ching*. Further, there is a hierarchy of structural pitches, with *chap* being more important than *ching*, and the final *chap* in the cycle is more important than the first. The individual instrumental realizations can be so different from each other that the relationships are obscured, but they nevertheless exist in the structural pitches or skeletal melody.

Thang depends on two variables: the instrument and the teacher (or school). Additionally, the melodic idiom taught to beginners is simpler than that of advanced players, and ensemble idioms are simpler than solo idioms. A catalogue of all possible characteristics available to a soloist on each instrument would constitute a small book, but the basic traits, taught to ensemble players of modest skill, are fewer and can be summarized.

Khawng wong yai: Considered the basic and least dense of the parts (and called *luk khawng*), it consists primarily of broken and simultaneous octaves, broken and simultaneous fourths, and some brief passages in single notes, notated primarily in eighth-note values. When the upper range is exceeded, the right hand holds to a pitch while the left hand continues upward. In many pieces, the player must dampen notes by touching the beaters to the bosses after striking them.

Khawng wong lek: Denser and more challenging than the lower *khawng wong*, this part consists primarily of continuous sixteenth notes, played singly and shared between the hands. Two techniques distinguish it, however—the replacement of either the second or fourth pitches in a four-pitch group with pairs of thirty-second notes, and the *sabat* technique, in which a note is approached from below by two quick, consecutive notes.

Ranat ek: This part consists of continuous sixteenth notes played in octaves, but when the right-hand part exceeds the range of the keyboard, it holds one pitch while the left-hand part continues to play upward. This style (*kep*), characteristic of motivic music, contrasts with *kraw,* the style for lyrical melodies, in which long notes are sustained with tremolo (alternation of the beaters).

Ranat thum: Potentially the most challenging and complex part, this idiom is considered somewhat playful and humorous, analogous to one use of the bassoon in the Western orchestra. It involves both simultaneous and broken octaves and fourths but has a tendency to use single notes, with greater rhythmic variety than found in other parts, especially syncopation. Indeed, advanced performers play spurts of notes, often anticipating the main pitches but resting on the main beats.

Ranat ek lek and *ranat thum lek:* These parts are essentially the same as those of the wooden or bamboo equivalents, but the *thum lek* part may be simpler.

Pi nai: The most difficult part to transcribe and describe, it includes much portamento and realization of the melody out of time with the fixed-key instruments. In addition, it has much subtle ornamentation, consisting of slides to main notes, fill-ins between main notes, and so on. Published transcriptions look much simpler and more regular than actual realizations.

Saw sam sai: Considered the most challenging of the bowed strings, its part tends to be highly ornamented, with occasional double stops, possible since the bow is separate. An expressive realization in string music is called *thang wan* 'sweet version'.

Saw duang: Realized in a single-note melody with simple rhythms, the density varies from the beginner's version (*thang thamada* 'ordinary') in more or less continuous eighth notes, to a version twice as dense, with sixteenth notes (*thang kep*), to one with passages in thirty-second notes (*thang kep khayi*).

Saw u: This part is essentially the same as *saw duang,* but the contour of its version may vary considerably, in part because of idiom and range.

Khlui: Although beginners tend to play a simple version with simple rhythms, skilled performers are inclined to play around the main melody, falling behind and catching up or anticipating. Many subtle and quick ornaments characterize the *khlui* idiom, and longer notes may be realized with accelerating repetitions of the pitch. The *khlui* is often heard above the rest of the ensemble, seemingly in its own rhythmic and melodic world.

Ja-khe: Although long notes on the *ja-khe* can be sustained through tremolo, the usual nature of the idiom is continuous pairs of notes written as dotted sixteenths or thirty-seconds.

Voice: Because the singer must realize the words of a tonal language while taking into account the main structural pitches of a melody, the vocal part may vary radically from the instrumental version—so much so that in some cases no apparent relationship will be seen or heard. Indeed, a second stanza with a different pattern of lexical tones can alter the melody dramatically. The vocal part is highly ornamented (sometimes to realize the linguistic tones, sometimes as style) and includes much portamento; the singer avoids a clear pulse, giving it a flowing feeling.

Thai vocal melody is distinguished for its melismatic continuations of words and free vocalization to vocables, the former called *üan sot saek* and the latter simply *üan.* The voice is usually accompanied only by rhythmic percussion, but in some styles both voice and instruments sound simultaneously. Factors that affect how a given syllable will be realized melodically include the lexical tone, the degree of the scale, the national accent (*sam-niang*) of the melody, and the school of the singer. An extremely complex process of realization, intuitive for traditionally trained singers, it has been analyzed by Yoko Tanese-Ito (1988).

The most demanding idiom is found in solo playing (*thang dio*), but solo performance is secondary to ensemble performance. Besides extremely fast tempos, solos include the most advanced techniques, greater rhythmic variety and complexity, and a high density of notes. Accompaniment is usually limited to drum(s) and *ching*.

Texture

Defining the texture of Thai classical music leads through arguments over whether "polyphonic stratification" or "heterophony" is the better descriptor. Those who see a closer relationship with other so-called gong-chime cultures of Southeast Asia, particularly Java and Bali, argue for the former term, while those who see more similarity with Chinese music argue for the latter. Since the argument is one of semantics, both views are correct, at least partly so. Observed similarities do not necessarily result from the influence of either Indonesia or China. Heterophonic practices exist throughout the world, and especially in Asia.

Categorizing Thai music as part of the Southeast Asian gong-chime culture seems too simple, for only the hard-mallet *piphat* ensemble, including one aerophone and two wooden and melodic idiophones, comes close to being a gong-chime ensemble. A direct relationship between island Southeast Asia and Thailand (and by extension Burma, Cambodia, and Laos) cannot be assumed, despite historical contact, for neither xylophones nor tuned gongs are peculiar to either region, and both are used by the least developed and least influenced peoples of mainland Southeast Asia. Ensembles with strings are clearly not "gong chime." Similarly, relating Thai music to Chinese silk-and-bamboo (*sizhu*) music, clearly heterophonic (with slight variants in performance because of differentiated instrumental idioms), is of limited help, for Thai texture is more complex than that.

The answer lies somewhere between the two, in a distinctly Thai musical world. *Piphat* music of theater and ceremony tends to be motivic and the differences in idioms among the instruments rather great; but *piphat* music in *sepha* style tends to be more lyrical, with slighter differences among the instruments. The former is comparable to polyphonic stratification, and the latter is comparable to heterophony. Beyond that, Thai music exhibits passages that are nearly polyphonic, not the result of chance combinations but stemming from compositional processes (discussed below). Broadly speaking, then, the texture of Thai classical ensemble music is heterophonic in that each musician realizes the preexisting melodic structure in the idiom peculiar to his or her instrument or voice. In some styles, these differences are greater than in others, but the concept of simultaneous variants nevertheless holds true (figure 19).

Antiphonal textures and actual polyphony frequently occur in ensemble music, much of the latter being actual counterpoint, all of it intended, none the result of improvisation. The ensemble divides into "high" and "low" instruments, but the factor of prestige must be taken into account. For example, in a *piphat* ensemble, the "high" instruments are *ranat ek, khawng wong lek,* and *pi nai,* and the "low" instruments *khawng wong yai* and *ranat thum.* The "high" instruments lead. In the *mahori* ensemble, the *saw sam sai* is a "high" instrument, based not on range but on prestige. Otherwise, *saw duang, ja-khe,* and *khlui* are "high," while *saw u* is "low." The divided ensemble plays both *luk law* and *luk khat. Luk law* is of two types: *law tam,* in which the lower instruments repeat what the higher instruments played, and *law taw,* in which the lower instruments complete a line begun by the higher instruments. Some compositions include passages of counterpoint that resemble what is called stretto, or even canon, in the West. In *luk khat,* the two groups answer each other in quick succession, overlapping at phrase endings, but in *luk lüam* the two groups are offset by only one sixteenth note, producing true stretto (figures 20 and 21).

FIGURE 19 The idioms (*thang*) of *piphat* instruments, from a Fine Arts Department score for the beginning of "*Sathukan,*" from the *Evening Prelude* or *Homrong yen.*

FIGURE 20
Antiphonal and contrapuntal patterns in Thai classical compositions: *a, luk law luk tam*; *b, luk nam luk taw*; *c, luk khat*; and *d, luk luam.*

Form

Morton included under "form" what is included here under "genres." Though form is part of the definitions of several genres, the comments here are more narrowly concerned with internal construction than with overall plan.

The underlying structure of any melody, motivic or lyrical, is defined by the pitches that fall on the strokes of the *ching,* with the hierarchy from most important to less important being from the final *chap,* to the secondary *chap,* to the *ching,* to beats between these strokes. These pitches unify the often radically different realizations based on instrumental idiom, vocal-textual realization, and rhythmic-density level. Formal analysis of motivic compositions without first isolating these pitches is

FIGURE 21 *Luang na* counterpoint in a coda where the ensemble divides into two groups, one finishing before the other.

difficult, but with lyrical melodies it is much easier to recognize the recurrences of tuneful phrases.

Thai composers, unlike their Western counterparts, work easily within the bounds of tradition, creating new works from an old mold rather than establishing personal identities through stylistic uniqueness. Tradition offers Thai composers many conventions, which they rarely violate, giving a certain unity to Thai classical music as a whole. Formal organization is usually bounded by established colotomic structure, with its regularity of phrase length, balancing of symmetrical phrases, and duple meter. Greater degrees of freedom, with phrases of flexible length and non-metered passages are mostly restricted to *phleng naphat,* both high *naphat* and action tunes.

Many compositions are constructed of two or more sections (*thawn*). Typically, the vocal version is performed first and only once, immediately followed by the instrumental version, which repeats. The instruments customarily overlap the last several beats with the vocalist and then continue into the next vocal phrase. If the text has more than one stanza, the pattern repeats. Instrumental tempos are usually faster than vocal tempos. Sections are usually related motivically, but by and large, multisectional compositions are through-composed. Though binary compositions maintain unity, ternary compositions do not exhibit ABA form. The same rhythmic density (*chan*) is maintained throughout a section and often throughout a piece. Works entirely in the second or third level of density are common, but works entirely in the first level are not known to exist. A few works are composed to begin in the third level and go without break into the second. Works having all three levels, pieces called *phleng thao,* are more fully described below.

A major factor in Thai melody is unity, achieved at the level of motive in some compositions and at the level of phrase in others. It is achieved by many devices, among them immediate repetition, the return of earlier material in later parts of a composition (especially a return to the opening material at the conclusion), melodic sequence, and motivic unity (figure 22).

Many compositions end with a coda (*luk mot*), appended to the main composition and normally unrelated to it melodically. Codas tend to be drawn from a preexisting group, are often performed contrapuntally with a divided ensemble, accelerate to the fastest tempo of the piece, and end on a pitch other than pitch 1, 3, or 5 of the pentatonic scale (usually pitch 2). Further, the coda's final pitch must coincide with the end of a rhythmic cycle and its *chap.*

Extramusical relationships

Functional compositions, such as those for theater, have extramusical relationships. Most other works have titles that suggest some kind of programmatic relationship, though some compositions (such as *tayoi*) appear to be abstract.

FIGURE 22 *"Lao Siang Thian,"* first section.

The meanings of the titles may be expressed in the vocal text, when there is one. For example, the title of the well-known *"Khamen Sai Yok,"* composed by His Royal Highness Prince Narit in 1888, mentions a place in Kanchanaburi Province (the *Sai Yok* waterfall) and describes the beauty of the scenery of the area, the animals, their sounds, and the sounds of water. The extended instrumental work *"Khlün Kratop Fang"* ('Sounds of the Surf'), by King Prajadhipok, attempts to depict in music the ebb and flow of the waves. The king used much divided-ensemble back-and-forth answering, with passages of counterpoint and even hocket, creating a kind of Thai version of Debussy's *La Mer.*

A great many Thai compositions allude to animals: *"Aiyaret"* ('Elephant'), *"Jarakay Hang Yao"* ('Long-Tailed Crocodile'), *"Nok Khao Khamae"* ('White Cambodian Dove'). The last includes the sounds of a bird (usually played on the *khlui*), but few such compositions depict their titles realistically.

Improvisation

Impromptu composition simultaneous with performance, as in India (*raga*) or Vietnam (*rao*), does not exist in Thai classical music. Students are taught by rote to play specific versions (*thang khru*) of particular pieces. In certain kinds of repertoire, especially high *naphat* compositions, the version learned cannot be varied, but in most other literature a certain amount of flexibility in performance regarding the details of instrumental idiom (*thang khrüang*) is permissible, especially as the player gains experience and maturity. Though Morton has argued that a sense of modality exists in Thai music, it exists for the purpose of creating new compositions worked out in advance rather than in live performance. Thus, Thai musical improvisation exists only in idiomatic realizations, which might better be described as improvisatory rather than improvisations.

Composers and repertoire

Thai classical music is a composed tradition, but the place of the composer and the method of transmission are different from those of the Western tradition. Most Thai compositions from the 1800s and 1900s are attributed to known composers, and those from earlier times are considered anonymous. Composition continues. But Thai composers normally write nothing on paper: they compose elaborate tunes and structures in their heads. The fleshing out of the composition occurs in performance, when the composer, acting as teacher, orally transmits the composition to other players. Sometimes the composer teaches each instrumental part by rote, sometimes by playing the *luk khawng* version on the *khawng wong yai* from which other players derive their own parts according to the idioms of their individual instruments. As a consequence, the process of realizing a composition into sound is shared among all players of the ensemble. The stylistic details are flexible, and patterns of individual ownership and copyright have not developed.

Three studies of Thai composers have been published, all in Thai. Jarernchai Chonpairot's *History of Thai Musicians* appeared in 1970, Panya Roongrüang included composers in his *History of Thai Music* in 1973, and the Fine Arts Department published its *Biographies of Accomplished Artists* in 1978. Even so, the Thai composer's place in the world of classical musical remains obscure. Performers are often uncertain of the composer's identity, but it is also true that classical musicians have not until the late twentieth century begun taking academic courses that include the history of Thai music.

The names of Thai composers are potentially confusing. Since 1913, Thai have been required to have surnames, but it remains customary both to address and alphabetize people by their given names. Most Thai also have informal names, and these are sometimes part of the name by which a composer is known. Further, from the time of Rama V and Rama VI, Thai kings have bestowed both ranked titles and honorific names on notable citizens—recognition confined to the individual, not passed to the next generation. King Rama VI also bestowed these on musicians and dance-drama actors, though he at first excluded women from the system. The most famous of these titled musicians (figure 23) is also Thailand's most famous composer, usually known as Luang Pradit Phairoh (1881–1954). His given name was Sorn (Arrow), and his family name Silapabanleng (Performing Arts), but Rama VI conferred on him both the title Luang (approximately 'Sir') and honorific name Pradit Phairoh ('Beautifully Creative'). Other musicians received names meaning, for example, 'Recite Sweet Words', 'Be Adroit at Music', and 'Beautiful-Sounding Fiddle'. Musicians not having such titles and names are normally addressed as teacher (*khru*) or professor (*ajan*).

FIGURE 23 Thailand's most famous composer, Luang Pradit Phairoh, appearing on a postage stamp on the occasion of his centenary, 1981.

The daughter of Luang Pradit Phairoh, Khunying (Madame) Chin Silapabanleng, also a highly regarded musician, established the Luang Pradit Phairoh Foundation, now maintained by her children. Besides offering musical training to youngsters, the foundation has published the complete works of the master, in both cipher notation and solfège. In addition, Chanok Sakarik, Ajan Chin's nephew and the master's grandson, has created a computer program with graphics and sound to teach basic instrumental techniques; it runs on an inexpensive and locally available Japanese computer. The master's compositions include the most widely heard works in the repertory, including "*Hom Rong Aiyaret*" ('Elephant'), "*Hom Rong Patom Dusit*" ('First Level of Heaven'), "*Mawn Ram Dap*" ('Mawn Sword Dance'), "*Lao Siang Thian Thao*" ('Oracle of Light, Lao Accent'), "*Khamen Phuang*" ('Garland'), and "*Saen Kham Nüng*" ('Recalling').

Some composers were royalty. King Prajadhipok (Rama VII, ruled 1925–1935) composed "*Khlün Kratop Fang*" ('Sounds of the Surf'), "*Ratri Pra Dap Dao*" ('Starlit

When royalty visited other royalty, they often took with them their musicians, who engaged in friendly contests with the host's musicians. Each ensemble tried to stump the other.

Night'), and *Khamen La Aw Awng*" ('Refined One'). Prince Narit composed Thailand's most famous composition, "*Khamen Sai Yok*" ('Sai Yok Waterfall'), in 1888. Others were commoners too young to have received honorific names from Rama VI. The most famous of them was Nai ('Mr.') Montri Tramote (d. 1995) of the Fine Arts Department, who besides being a prolific composer (including "*Som Sawng Saeng*" ['Moonlight'] and "*Kaek Doi Maw*" ['Indian Beats the Pot']) was Thailand's foremost music historian. He and others composed additional variations (rhythmic densities) to preexisting anonymous works.

Repertoire

The Thai repertoire has been organized in several ways. Under "Forms and Compositional Techniques," Morton discusses several of the most important genres. Tanese, following Fine Arts Department thinking, organizes the repertoire into two major groups: *phleng naphat,* associated with the theater; and *phleng mahori,* independent of the theater. But Panya Roongrüang offers a more detailed list, of ten categories:

1. Naphat

Considered the most serious of all Thai musics, *phleng naphat* are the instrumental compositions associated with both theater and ritual ceremony. Because they are so important, musicians may not change even a single note from what the teacher transmitted. *Naphat* are of two types: ordinary and high, they are differentiated according to the kind of role whose action they accompany—ordinary ones for human or unimportant persons, high ones for gods and royalty. Because in the masked theater, the large shadow puppet theater, and dance-drama they accompany specific characters, actions, and situations, they are often called action tunes and have been compared to Wagnerian leitmotifs. These actions include military marching, traveling, fighting, changing bodies, drinking, eating, sleeping, and greeting or inviting. Apart from their use in theater, they can be played independently, organized into suites (see category 2). Unity is vaguely achieved through a common mood, similar titles, or in some cases a single rhythmic density. *Phleng naphat* are also played during *wai khru,* ceremonies to honor teachers.

2. Phleng rüang

Though *rüang* means 'story', a *phleng rüang* is a suite of pieces that is not linked to a story. These pieces consist of three types of compositions in their most complete form: *phleng cha* (slow pieces) in *sam chan, phleng sawng mai* (medium-tempo pieces) in *sawng chan,* and *phleng reo* (fast pieces) in *chan dio.* Each group is organized into a section under its own title. Of twenty-nine *rüang* transcribed into staff notation, nineteen included pieces in all three rhythmic densities; the remainder had pieces in a single density, or in two cases two densities. Suites usually begin with slower pieces and end with faster ones. Individual compositions vary in length from about sixteen measures to the extreme of 684 measures (for "*Tao kin phak bung*" ['Turtle eats *phak bung*']), with the average being, according to Morton, forty to sixty measures. There is also a special category of ceremonial or ritual suites called *phleng ruang pitikan,* which includes *Homrong yen* (published by the Fine Arts Department as the '*Evening Prelude*') with twelve pieces, the *Homrong chao* ('*Morning Prelude*') with five pieces, the *Homrong klang wan* ('*Afternoon Prelude*') with fourteen pieces, the *Homrong thet* ('*Preaching Prelude*') with six pieces, the *Phleng ruang tham khwan* ('*Prelude for the Ritual to Call Back the Spiritual Essence*'), and the *Homrong thet* [*mahachat*] ('*Prelude for Preaching the Great Life of the Buddha*') with thirteen pieces, one for each chapter of the story and used as an interlude to its chanting. The first piece of these ceremonial suites is "*Satugan,*" meaning a Buddhist greeting, which is also the first serious piece a *piphat* musician learns.

3. Homrong

Homrong literally means 'overture', but some works so designated are actually suites. One group precedes theatrical performances, another musical performances. The *Homrong sepha* suite formerly preceded a performance of the *sepha* narrative genre, but after *sepha* became obsolete, such "overtures" shifted function to preceding a concert of instrumental music. Overtures for the masked theater (*khon*), called *homrong kan sadaeng,* are the most important, plural because they are differentiated by time of day: morning with nine pieces, noon with fourteen pieces, and evening with five pieces. There are also overtures for dance-drama (*lakhon*), large shadow-puppet theater (*nang yai*), and the rod-puppet theater (*hün krabawk*).

4. Phleng tap

Shorter suites, consisting mostly of melodious compositions, are called *phleng tap.* There are two kinds, though, depending on whether the suite is purely instrumental or interspersed with singing. The former, called *tap phleng,* bring together several pieces, either in the same "key" (*thang*) or in the same tempo level. For the latter, called *tap ruang,* the music may not be unified—and may even include *naphat* pieces—but they are used within a sung story, such as the *Ramakian.* The number of pieces in a suite varies from four to thirty-four in the manuscript collection of the Fine Arts Department, but five or six is most usual.

5. Phleng thao

Perhaps the most intriguing in structure are the *phleng thao,* from a term meaning 'a set in graduated sizes' (e.g., of bowls). In music, it refers to a composition that is played continuously in three rhythmic densities, *sam chan* (third), *sawng chan* (second), and *chan dio* (first), with or without singing. They originated during the mid-1800s and reached their zenith during the first three decades of the twentieth century. When royalty visited other royalty, they often took with them their musicians, who engaged in friendly contests with the host's musicians. Playing special and clever arrangements of known tunes, each ensemble tried to stump the other, for failure to detect the tune embedded in the new arrangements meant loss of face.

The *phleng thao* grew out of the practice of taking a preexisting (later, a newly written) melody and both expanding and contracting it. The original melody was in *sawng chan,* the augmentation in *sam chan,* and the diminution in *chan dio.* The structural pitches occurring on the *ching* and *chap* strokes were preserved in the longer and shorter versions, but in the former extra filler notes had to be added and in the latter notes were removed. The results were more sophisticated than this might sound, however, for in the hands of a good composer, each level had its own melody and character, though the ending of each section is typically related melodically. If the *sawng chan* melody—the original—had sixteen measures, *sam chan* had thirty-two and *chan dio* eight. The number of *ching* strokes per level remained the same, but their rate of speed doubled, going from the third to the second and from the second to the first. Without the *ching* patterns to identify the level, an experienced listener can still recognize the *chan,* even though the density of melodic pitches does not change; what changes is the rate of *structural* pitches.

Luang Pradit Phairoh's famous composition *Lao Siang Thian Thao* ('Oracle of Light, in Lao Accent') will illustrate these principles. The most important pitches are those occurring on the *siang tok,* the final *chap* of the four-stroke cycle. In section 1, these are G–G–G–G–A–C–A–C; in section 2, G–D–G–D–A–C–A–C. Figure 24*a,* section 1, of the *sawng chan* version, shows how these structural pitches (circled) are embedded into the melody, while figure 24*b* shows the same relative line in section 2 in all three *chan* in order to see how the same structural pitches occur in melodies of different densities.

6. Phleng yai

The *phleng yai* category, meaning 'great pieces', includes extended ensemble compositions requiring solid memories and playing skills adequate to negotiate as many compositional devices, many of them polyphonic, as the composer can muster. These include the techniques discussed earlier under texture, such as *luk law* and *luk kat,* the *thayoi* pattern, where a phrase is not only passed between high and low instruments, but is reduced in length by half, two times in succession. *Phleng yai* are constructed in multiple sections, each in a different mode (*thang*). Examples of *phleng yai* include works such as *Khaek Lopburi* ('Lopburi [city], in Khaek accent'), *Choet Jin* ('Long Trip, in Chinese accent'), and any *thayoi* compositions.

FIGURE 24 *a, Lao Siang Thian Thao, sawng chan,* section 1, with structural pitches (G–G–G–G–A–C–A–C) circles; *b,* the first line of *sam chan, sawng chan,* and *chan dio,* section 2 compared, with structural pitches (G–D) circled.

7. Phleng dio

Works for solo instruments are called *phleng dio.* They are created to show off a performer's skills and memory, but they also allow the performer to exhibit both virtuosic and subtle playing. A melody will be presented in at least two forms, *thang wan* 'sweet version' (also called *thang ot*) and *thang kep* 'fast, continuous version' (also called *thang phün*). The former versions are slower, tuneful, and variable in duration; the latter are faster, played in continuous even notes. Favorite solo pieces include "*Grao Nai*" ('Military March'), "*Phaya Sok*"('Royal Sorrow'), and "*Choet Nawk*" ('Giant's March').

8. Phleng la

These are special pieces to end a concert, since *la* means 'goodbye'. Indeed, the ceremonial suites and overtures usually end with the *phleng naphat* "*La.*" But in a special kind of *phleng la* (called *dok* 'flower'), a vocalist sings a passage of longing and wishing farewell, followed by a highly ornamented instrumental solo, which imitates the vocal style. In a *piphat,* the *pi nai* plays the solo; in a *mahori,* the *saw sam sai* plays it; and in a *khrüang sai,* the *saw u* plays it.

9. Phleng kret

Miscellaneous pieces, including portions of longer works and suites played separately, are called *phleng kret.* Mostly they are in the *sawng chan* tempo level, but some have been extended to *sam chan.* Among the former compositions are three especially well known examples, with singing sections. "*Lao Kum Hawm,*" recorded in 1900 by Stumpf and later analyzed by Hornbostel, has three sections totaling eighty-eight measures, too long for *thao* treatment. The other two, "*Lao Duang Düan*" ('The Moon, in Lao accent') and "*Lao Dumnün Sai*" ('Walking on the Sand, in Lao accent'), are shorter, but still too long to be a *phleng thao.* Extremely rare is *si chan,* the fourth rhythmic density, whose structural pitches would be separated by twice the time of the third density. Though others may now be known, only one was known to Morton—Luang Pradit Phairoh's augmentation of Prince Narit's "*Khamen Sai Yok,*" the original entirely in the third density. Each of the two sections is thirty-two measures long, making each section of the fourth density sixty-four measures long. The composer, however, used the drum and *ching* pattern for *sam chan* with his extended version, changed the patterns of the original from *sam chan* to *sawng chan,* and composed a short version (*chan dio*) of sixteen measures per section, making a complete *phleng thao.*

A class of compositions has titles that begin with a descriptor of culture: *Khamen* 'Khmer', as in "*Khamen Sai Yok,*" and *Lao,* as in "*Lao Siang Thian.*" These works are considered to have a national accent (*samniang*), and it has long been customary to play many of them as a suite, *Awk Pasa* ('Out of Language', or 'Language Suite'). The original tune for a composition so designated may or may not have come from the culture denoted but is at least considered to be in the style of that culture. The most common tunes are "*Lao,*" "*Khamen*" (Cambodian), "*Khaek*" (Muslim, Malay, or Indian), "*Mawn*" (Mon), "*Khaek-Mawn,*" "*Jin*" (China), and "*Phama*" (Burma), but others are possible, including "*Jawa*" (Java), "*Yipun*" (Japan), "*Farang*" (Western), and "*Yuan*" (Vietnam). Of the common ones, "*Khaek,*" "*Lao,*" "*Phamah,*" and "*Jin*" are notated on C (C–D–E–G–A scale), "*Khamen*" on F, and "*Mawn*" on B-flat. A factor that makes these Thai-created pieces seem more exotic is the use of instruments peculiar to each culture, especially drums and other percussion. In playing *samniang jin* (Chinese), one might hear Chinese *luogu* (percussive) instruments and a Chinese bowed lute, such as the standard *er hu* or Chaozhou *tou xian* playing with a mixed Thai ensemble.

For non-Thai, the vocal sections of Thai classical compositions are perhaps the hardest parts to understand, for the words are strung out in long melismas, the intonation is complex, and the timbre is nasal, totally unlike vocal timbres in the West.

10. Phleng hang khrüang
Literally an 'instrumental tail', these are short, sometimes playful pieces, mostly in *chan dio.* They can be attached to longer pieces as a kind of coda. Coming at the end of a long, serious work, they are like a sweet dessert. They also permit the ensemble, or individual members, to exhibit their skills in solo renditions. Whether a named *phleng hang khrüang* is used or not, it is customary to end long works with one of many standard *luk mot* codas. They gain speed rapidly and before the end the ensemble divides, allowing the high instruments to race the low instruments to the *siang tok,* beating them by one beat.

For non-Thai, the vocal sections of Thai classical compositions are perhaps the hardest parts to understand, for the words are strung out in long melismas, the intonation is complex (using portamento and pitch levels quite outside those of the xylophones and gong circles), and the timbre is nasal, totally unlike vocal timbres in the West. Singers normally begin the composition, accompanied only by *ching* and drum(s). During the last few beats of the section, the leader of the ensemble parallels the singer and then launches into the instrumental version of the same section, usually at a faster tempo. The vocal versions are generated from the same set of structural pitches as the instrumental versions, but the melodic result is usually quite different. There is also another kind of singing, however, when the vocalist sings along with the ensemble. Though considered part of the category of popular songs, some classical songs were transformed in the mid-1900s by setting new syllabic texts (one note, one syllable). This style is called *nua tem.*

Notation

Thai music, especially *piphat* music, is normally taught orally through rote memory, but the use of notation has become common with the two-stringed fiddles (*saw duang* and *saw u*), the *ja-khe,* and the *khim.* Sometimes notation is used to convey a generic version of a melody and to require individual instruments to convert it to their idioms. Besides staff notation, Thai musicians have used two kinds of notation—tablature and pitch notation. For the latter, they use two symbolic schemes (numbers and solfège), but for tablature, they use only numbers. These notations appear in published collections of music—some generic, some for specific instruments, and in some instrumental tutors. All are prescriptive, for even tablatures leave out many idiomatic details, especially ornamentation. Teachers who use notation often require their students to make their own copies from the teacher's repertory. Some have been reproduced by inexpensive means (like mimeograph); others have been published.

All Thai notations exhibit a convention that confuses anyone accustomed to staff notation: the accented beat (downbeat in Western terms), coinciding with the *ching* strokes, falls just before the bar. Within a measure there are four beats, usually transcribed as four sixteenth notes. Two eighth notes would normally require

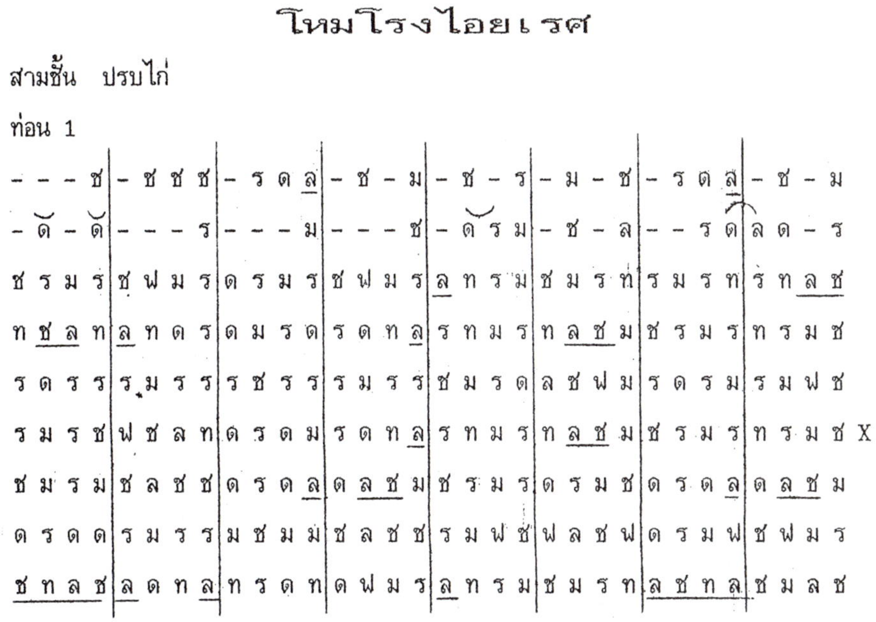

FIGURE 25 An example of Thai solfège notation.

โหมโรงไอยเรศ

สามชั้น ปรบไก่

ท่อน 1

- - - ช | - ช ช ช | - ร ด ล | - ช - ม | - ช - ร | - ม - ช | - ร ด ล | - ช - ม
- ด - ด | - - - ร | - - - ม | - - - ช | - ด ร ม | - ช - ล | - - ร ด | ล ด - ร
ช ร ม ร | ช ฟ ม ร | ด ร ม ร | ช ฟ ม ร | ล ท ร ม | ช ม ร ท | ร ม ร ท | ร ท ล ช
ท ช ล ท | ล ท ด ร | ด ม ร ด | ร ด ท ล | ร ท ม ร | ท ล ช ม | ช ร ม ร | ท ร ม ช
ร ด ร ร | ร ม ร ร | ร ช ร ร | ร ม ร ร | ช ม ร ด | ล ช ฟ ม | ร ด ร ม | ร ม ฟ ช
ร ม ร ช | ฟ ช ล ท | ด ร ด ม | ร ด ท ล | ร ท ม ร | ท ล ช ม | ช ร ม ร | ท ร ม ช X
ช ม ร ม | ช ล ช ช | ด ร ด ล | ด ล ช ม | ช ร ม ร | ด ร ม ช | ด ร ด ล | ด ล ช ม
ด ร ด ด | ร ม ร ร | ม ช ม ม | ช ล ช ช | ร ม ฟ ช | ฟ ล ช ฟ | ด ร ม ฟ | ช ฟ ม ร
ช ท ล ช | ล ด ท ล | ท ร ด ท | ด ฟ ม ร | ล ท ร ม | ช ม ร ท | ล ช ท ล | ช ม ล ช

hyphens between the pitch numbers, and a dotted eighth three hyphens, but many versions leave these out. Seeing only two numbers, the user assumes they are even eighth notes; a single number indicates a full quarter note. These notations, however, are not designed to convey complex rhythms—which, as part of the idiom, are left to oral transmission.

To use these notations, the player must know the conventions that are implied but not indicated. How does the notation relate to the pitches of the instrument? Where is 1 or *do?* Tablatures do not indicate pitch, but the player must know the tuning of the instrument, plus how the numbers relate to the frets or holes for fingering. Such notations have been used since only the 1940s, but since individuals like to create idiosyncratic ones (which they may hope will become the nation's standard), an amazing variety is available in print. The details of their theories and methods go beyond this article's scope (see Miller 1992), but a few are shown above and below.

1. Solfège notation (figure 25). The initial letters of the Western *do–re–mi* syllables written in Thai constitute a kind of pitch notation. Since this style cannot show much rhythmic detail, and there is no way to differentiate octaves, it is of limited clarity.

2. Number notation (pitch). Used generically, this notation works similarly to solfège, in that the numbers 1 to 7 indicate the seven pitches of the fixed-tuning system. Again, there is no way to differentiate octaves.

3. Number notation (tablature). Tablatures must distinguish strings, frets, or fingers. In the case of two-stringed-fiddle notations, a horizontal line separates the lower and upper strings, and 0 indicates the open string, 1 the first finger, and so on. Sometimes slurs for bowing are indicated. In the case of the *ja-khe* and the *khim,* there are two horizontal lines to accommodate the three strings (for *ja-khe*) and three bridge sections (for *khim*).

4. Luang Pradit Phairoh Foundation number notation. In the complete works of the master, the editors used numbers 1 to 9 to indicate the first-position pitches for *saw duang,* and parallel to that, the solmization initials in the roman alphabet. The introduction provides a way to play the same melodies on the *saw u,* but the solfège equivalents differ (figure 26).

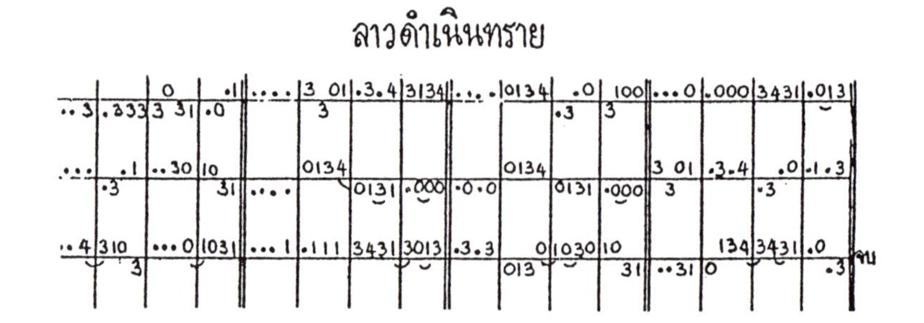

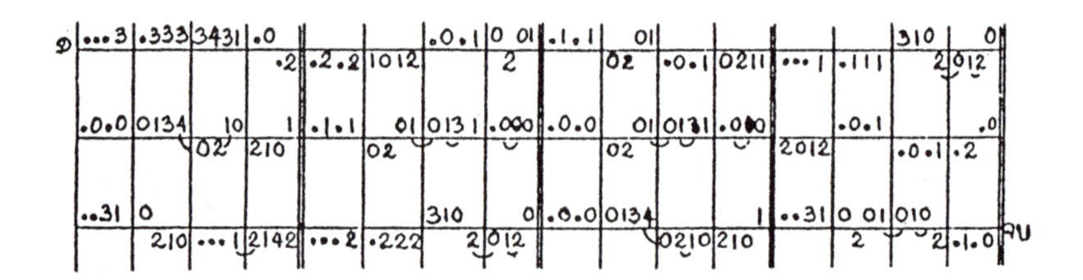

FIGURE 26 Examples of *saw duang* and *saw u* notations.

THAI MUSIC HISTORY

Reconstructing Thai music history is particularly challenging for three reasons: few documents have survived the ravages of time, insects, weather, and war; the scholarly study of Thai music, particularly its history, is a recent phenomenon in Thailand, and few have attacked the problem; and there are problems in dating many of the surviving documents, particularly iconographical evidence.

Traditional Thai musicians share a kind of oral history that challenges the modern scholar who insists on documentation. For them, truth remains in the beholder's eye. Promising but admittedly ethnocentric sources of information have been the written reports of European and American travelers, emissaries, missionaries, and others who observed Siamese music firsthand, going back to the 1500s (Miller and Chonpairot 1994).

Written sources

The earliest known document concerning Thai music is a fourteenth-century Buddhist cosmology, *Trai Phum Phra Rüang* (also spelled *Traiphum P'a Rüang*), rewritten from an Indian document entitled *Traibhumikatha* in 1345 by Lu T'ai (also called Payah Lithai and Lidaiya). Included in the list are human and earthly instruments, but none of them can be related to present-day instruments, except possibly the *saw pung daw,* which some Thai believe refers to the *saw sam sai.* Inscriptions in stone from the Sukhothai Period have offered little information, but the study of these sources continues. Unlike in Cambodia, where bas-relief carvings at Angkor depict numerous instruments, no public buildings built in Thailand before about the eighteenth century bear depictions of musical instruments or performances.

The earliest European account with mentions of music was written in 1505 by the Bolognese traveler Ludovico di Varthema, but since he visited Tenasserim, now in Burma, its value is limited. More interesting is Mendes Pinto's *Peregrinação,* published in Portugal in 1558 but based on his 1548 trip to Siam.

The greatest number of useful sources stem from France's effort, between 1662 and 1688, to convert Pra Narai, King of Siam (at Ayuthaya), to Roman Catholicism and thereby attain control over his kingdom. The most detailed accounts of music and instruments were written by Nicolas Gervaise and Simon de La Loubere; the former includes an attempt to transcribe a Siamese melody, and the latter includes both a song (figure 27) and drawings of several instruments. After 1688, when the French

FIGURE 27 A Thai song, "*Say Samon,*" transcribed by Simon de La Loubere during his visit to the Siamese court at Ayuthaya in 1688 and published in his book *Du Royaume de Siam* (1691).

attempt failed, European visitors all but disappeared from Siam until late in the 1700s, after the Burmese had sacked and destroyed Ayuthaya, and the Siamese had reestablished their kingdom at Thonburi, then Bangkok.

Between 1810 and 1820, an increasing number of visitors, more of them ambassadors than missionaries, visited Bangkok, and many of them published books with chapters or sections on music. Oddly, some of the most biased and ethnocentric descriptions of Thai culture come from this period. An exception to this trend was Anna Harriette Léonowens' *The English Governess at the Siamese Court* (1870), the basis for Margaret Landon's *Anna and the King of Siam* (1944), in turn the basis for Rodgers and Hammerstein's Broadway musical *The King and I* (1951)—a piece still banned in Thailand because of its allegedly barbaric treatment of King Mongkut and his son Chulalongkorn.

By about 1900, detailed, scholarly treatments of Thai music and theater had begun to appear, most of them written by European scholars who had worked with Siamese musicians visiting Europe for various expositions. Exceptionally detailed was the work of the Italian Col. G. E. Gerini, who published a fine book on Thai arts and crafts in 1912. A visit by Siamese musicians to the London Inventions Exposition in 1885 led to three important studies: A. J. Ellis's "On the Musical Scales of Various Nations" (1885a), detailing the tunings of instruments from many parts of the world, including Siam, using cents; A. J. Hipkins's *Musical Instruments Historic, Rare, and Unique* (1945 [1888]), with color illustrations of several instruments; and Frederick Verney's pamphlet *Notes on Siamese Musical Instruments* (1885), with systematic descriptions and drawings of many instruments. Verney was also notable for his view that understanding Siamese music required giving up one's assumptions about music based on European experiences.

In 1900, a delegation of Siamese musicians traveled to Berlin, where Carl Stumpf and Erich M. von Hornbostel made what is likely the first recordings of Siamese music; most of their cylinders survived the world wars and remain in the Berlin Phonogram Archive. In 1901, Stumpf published his analytical study "Tonsystem und Musik der Siamesen," and in 1920, Hornbostel published his "Formanalysen an siamesischen Orchesterstücken." Both articles were based on the recordings made in 1900. These analyses, while thorough, now seem old-fashioned

In many ways, Thai classical music remains extremely conservative, and though innovation occurs, its scale is small compared to the modernization that has occurred in China, Indonesia, and Malaysia.

and Eurocentric; because they were done in Germany by scholars who knew little of Thai culture, they tell us nothing of performative contexts.

Iconographic sources

Little survived the destruction of Ayuthaya, but David Morton (1976) pictures two supposedly Ayuthaya-Period items that depict instruments—a carved wooden bookcase, now in the National Museum, and a painting, dated about 1730. Whether their dating is accurate cannot be determined, however.

The interior walls of numerous Thai temples of the eighteenth and nineteenth centuries and later are covered with murals, some depicting instruments and making music in processions, ensembles, theater, and rituals. Though some of them have been published, no systematic search has been made. Even with such an inventory, dating the paintings remains a problem. For example, the Temple of the Emerald Buddha (*Wat Phra Keo*), Bangkok's royal temple, is surrounded by a vast wall, the interior side of which is roofed over to protect murals of the entire *Ramakian* story, painted during the reign of King Rama III. Numerous panels depict musical scenes in detail. They likely reflect the state of music at the time, but many had severely deteriorated before restoration began (in the 1980s), and we cannot be sure all details presently visible in them are accurate. Nonetheless, iconographic documents are a rich source for reconstructing the past.

The modern period

In many ways, Thai classical music remains extremely conservative, and though innovation occurs, its scale is small compared to the modernization that has occurred in China, Indonesia, and Malaysia. Is Thai music a museum piece? is it, as David Morton puts it, a "hothouse plant"? Composition continues, though most new works deviate little from tradition. Works that combine Thai and Western instruments have been created, most notably by Panya Roongrüang, but they do not appear to be sweeping the country. Popular songs developed out of the classical tradition, using the same melodies, but this is a new development, quite apart from classical music.

Bruce Gaston, an American composer and musician, who formed the group Fong Naam, is composing works that blend jazz and popular idioms with Thai classical traits, but Gaston also plays in another Fong Naam group—which, for the most part, is a strictly traditional *piphat.* Their CD releases represent some of the best recordings ever made of classical music, but a few selections also represent a new trend—historicism. Fong Naam revived the *ranat kaeo,* a crystallophone, said to have preceded the *ranat ek lek.* They also recorded literature using an ensemble that omits the *khawng wong yai,* considered by many other musicians to be without a basis.

From the 1930s to the 1950s, the government severely suppressed classical music, and rural genres were disappearing on their own. Since the 1960s, remarkably, classical music has become stronger, even as the popular-music industry has become a big business. The greatest growth has come in educational programs. Until about 1980, music was rarely treated as more than an extracurricular activity in schools—primary, secondary, and postsecondary. In many schools, Thai music remains extracurricular, but the founding of the regional *nathasin* (high schools for the arts) throughout Thailand has led to an unprecedented growth in the teaching of music, both of classical and regional genres, and degree-granting programs have become strong in several universities and colleges.

Outside of education, a greater awareness of Thai traditions has also developed. Most notably, Bangkok Bank built an auditorium and established a continuing series of programs each Friday in Bangkok, when academic specialists present practitioners of all sorts of traditional music and theater, both classical and folk.

Though most Thai do not choose to listen to classical music (preferring, instead, the sounds emanating from radios and televisions), people acknowledge the propriety of having classical music in conjunction with ceremonies and rituals and representing their culture to the outside world. It appears safe to say that, because the traditional contexts are intact, the future of Thai music is bright, and classical musicians will find opportunities for employment.

THE PLACE OF BUDDHISM IN THAI MUSIC

The importance of Buddhism in the traditional musical life of Thailand cannot be overstated. Besides the significance of chant itself, the temple is the focus of festivities where musical and theatrical events take place, the source of the literacy that serves as the basis for theatrical and narrative stories, and sometimes the patron of musical ensembles. The calendar of Buddhist festivals parallels the agricultural cycle, providing regular activities that require music; Buddhist rites themselves also provide opportunities for making and hearing music.

Thai Buddhism, including its texts and rituals, has received extensive attention from both Thai and non-Thai scholars, but the musical aspects of chant and preaching remain little studied. B. J. Terwiel's *Monks and Magic* (1979) analyzes religious ceremonies in central Thailand and includes useful sections on chanting and preaching. S. J. Tambiah's works, especially his *Buddhism and the Spirit Cults in North-East Thailand* (1970), treats Buddhist rites in some detail, though certain information applies only to that region. Kenneth E. Wells's *Thai Buddhism: Its Rites and Activities* (1975) provides a good introduction to Buddhism as it actually operates in modern-day Thailand, with translations of most of the sacred texts.

Background

Since the history of Thai Buddhism is readily available and of minimal importance to this study, only certain points need be borne in mind. Buddhism and Hinduism both entered the area of Thailand over a period of several hundred years, beginning about five hundred years after the passing of the Lord Buddha (543 B.C.). The magnificent *chedi* at Nakhon Pathom, west of Bangkok, whose original Dvaravadi structure is believed to date from about A.D. 500 (it is now covered with a 115-meter-high structure built by King Rama IV in 1860), is believed to be the oldest Buddhist structure in Thailand. The Dvaravadi were Mon-Khmer-speaking Buddhists who helped transmit this faith to later cultures.

As for the Thai, Hinduism eventually declined. It survives in a few rituals, while the Theravada (or Hinayana) Buddhist tradition supplanted the Mahayana, which had come first; little of Mahayana Buddhism remains in modern practices. Consequently, both Sanskrit and Pali, the latter the sacred language of Theravada Buddhism, profoundly affected the Tai languages, central Thai more than the others.

Buddhism can be viewed in two ways: first, as a philosophy of life based on the doctrine of the Buddha; second, as a syncretistic popular religion practiced by ordinary people more attuned to its festivities and social activities than to its deeper meaning, who see no contradiction in maintaining traditional animistic practices.

A split into sects, which occurred during the reign of Rama IV (King Mongkut), has implications with regard to style of chanting. The king reformed Buddhist practices by regularizing the orders for certain services, established or revived certain sacred festivals (like *Wisaka bucha,* the day celebrating the birth, enlightenment, and death of the Lord Buddha), raised the standards of Buddhist scholarship, and reestablished relations with the Sinhalese Monastic Order in Sri Lanka. His was a back-to-basics movement, meant to purify the *sangha* (community of monks and novices) by refocusing its attention on doctrine. In the late 1830s, the king-to-be himself had become the abbot of Wat Bovoranives-Voravihan in Bangkok near the palace and had founded a new order, which he called *Dhammayuttikai* (or *Dhammayut* for short), meaning 'Order Adhering to the Dhamma'. The mainstream came to be called *Mahanikai* ('Great Assembly'), but Mongkut called it the Order of Long-Standing Habit. The new sect was maintained under Mongkut's son, Prince Vajirananvaroros, who in 1893 officially organized the Dhammayut Order and made himself head of those monasteries that embraced its doctrines and practices. While the distinction between Dhammayut and Mahanikai temples will not be apparent to casual observers, and monks from one sect may worship with monks of the other, there are distinctions in rules, behavior, the pronunciation of Pali, and styles of chanting. According to Wells (1975:26), in 1969 there were 24,198 Mahanikai temples with 180,184 monks and 108,996 novices, and 1094 Dhammayut temples with 9703 monks and 5931 novices.

The temple (*wat*) is the focus of the Buddhist life and associated secular social activities, not the least of which are music and theater. Temples vary in size and grandeur, from Bangkok's Wat Pra Keo (Temple of the Emerald Buddha, the royal monastery near the Grand Palace) and Wat Phra Jetubon (or Wat Po, Temple of the Reclining Buddha, nearby)—monumental compounds, encompassing several major buildings and perhaps dozens of smaller edifices—to humble village temples with only one or two wooden buildings.

The compound of any fairly important monastery will include most of the following structures: a *chedi* (stupa), a high, pointed or rounded structure over sacred objects, such as a bone, a hair, or a tooth of the Lord Buddha; a *wihan* (Pali *vihara*), a hall for preaching; an *ubasot* or *bot,* for rites of the *sangha*; a *sala,* a public hall for preaching; *kuthi,* dormitories for monks; an open tower, housing a large metal bell or a large, barrel-shaped drum for signaling, or both instruments; and a sacred bodhi tree (*Ficus religiosa*). Both the *wihan* and the *bot* have images of Buddha, in front of which chanting takes place. Most ceremonies and chanting open to the laity occur in the *sala.* The drum and the bell announce to resident monks and the public the times of rituals and meals. Many temples also have a library for sacred palm-leaf manuscripts, plus a crematorium.

Tourists by the tens of thousands visit the major temples of Bangkok and Chiangmai, renowned for their color and architectural grace, but few notice the small temples found in every neighborhood and village, where the vast majority of Thai practice their faith.

Occasions for chanting

Certain Buddhist festivals can be the cause of musical performances, both on the temple grounds and elsewhere. The following are among the most likely to include music.

1. *Songkran,* the traditional new year, on 13 April, celebrating the end of the dry season and the imminent return of the rains.

2. *Awk phansa,* the end of the Buddhist Rains Retreat (*khao phansa*), occurs in October on the fifteenth day of the waxing moon. A three-month period when agricultural work is heavy and musical performances are avoided, this period ends with relief, merrymaking, and making music.

3. *Kathin,* between the full moons of October and November, centers around the community's gift of new robes and other gifts to the monks. Two-day events usually occur on weekends, when a village, a neighborhood, a school, or a government agency provides food for the monks the evening before and then processes to the temple or through the village bearing the gifts the next day. The procession will likely include dancers and musicians (such as a *klawng yao*), and theatrical troupes may be hired to entertain at night.

4. *Loi kratong,* the festival of lights, occurs on the full moon of November, when villages and towns organize parades culminating with the launching of tiny, candle-filled boats, and large, electrically lighted floats on rivers, canals, and lakes.

5. Temple fairs, intended to raise money to help maintain buildings or build new ones, usually occur during the dry months (November to March). Admission to the temple grounds is charged, but most entertainments are free to watch.

6. Music may occur in conjunction with other occasions, such as ordinations, marriages, funerals, the king's birthday (5 December), New Year's Day (1 January), and so forth.

Monks and their activities

Thai Buddhism is centrally organized into a monastic order (*sangha*) under a supreme patriarch in Bangkok, but the structure becomes looser the farther from Bangkok and other cities you go. Monks are forbidden by the 227 precepts, specifically precept 7, from singing, dancing, playing music, and watching drama, dance, and other secular entertainments. While some talented monks entertain and thrill audiences with acrobatic displays of vocal technique, modestly described by their verbs as chanting (*suat*) and preaching (*thet*), the monetary rewards they accept go to the temple treasurer, who may offer the monks paper chits with which to make purchases.

The leader of a monastery with resident monks is the abbot (*jao a-wat*). Ordained monks are formally called *bhikkhu,* but normally called *phra,* and must be older than nineteen. Those in robes under that age are novices (*nen*). Below them are aspiring novices, temple boys (*dek wat*), who help in the temple while learning the basic rules of monastic behavior. A committee of laymen oversees secular activity and maintains the buildings. The minimum permissible number of monks and novices is five with twelve being the average in 1958. Large temples have between fifty and five hundred residents. Service in the temple is considered meritorious for both the monk or novice and his family, and every Buddhist male in Thailand is expected to spend some time in robe before age twenty.

Chanting is the responsibility of both monks and novices, led by the abbot, but since the repertoire of chants takes time to learn and the minimum period one may retreat to the temple is one week, many will learn only some chants or parts of them. Only a small percentage of monks can fully understand the sacred texts in Pali. Consequently, many who chant and even some who preach know not what they are saying.

The sacred texts were traditionally written on long strips of dried palm leaf using a sharp stylus, the letters filled with lampblack and the leaves joined with cords at two points. Today, texts are more likely to be read from printed palm leaves or mod-

During services, the abbot selects the texts to be chanted, cueing the chapter with the first words. All, including the abbot, face the image of Buddha, kneeling. They chant some passages with heads bowed to the floor, muffling the sound.

ern books. Traditionally, the texts were written in sacred alphabets peculiar to each region of Thailand. Central Thai monks learned *dua khawm,* closely related to Khmer; northeastern Thai monks learned *dua tham,* and northern monks read *dua yuan* (also called *dua müang*)—none of which were intelligible to lay persons. Today, with palm-leaf manuscripts out of fashion and the old scripts known only to scholar-monks, most monks read from books using Thai letters and an orthography peculiar to Pali. Three published collections include the basic chant texts: *Suat mon chabap luang* (Royal Book of Chants), more than five hundred pages long; *Jet tam nan* (Seven Stories); and *Sip sawng tam nan* (Twelve Stories). All are available in ordinary bookstores, the latter two in inexpensive paper editions. The collection of seven can be used by anyone, but the collection of twelve is reserved for royal and state ceremonies. None includes melodic notation or other indication of the chant.

Routines of chanting

Chanting takes place both inside and outside the temple compound, both in the presence of lay persons and in private, both collectively and individually. The daily routine is altered both during the penitential season and on holy days (*wan phra*), which occur four times a month, when the laity bring food to the temple, hear the chanting of the sacred canon and hymns, and hear blessing chants.

Ordinarily a monk's or novice's routine begins before sunrise, soon after which he and his brethren go forth, each with an iron begging bowl (*bat*), accepting donations of food from the citizenry. The monks chant, eat, then assemble in the *bot* or *wihan* to chant the morning service (*tham wat chao*). A large temple drum beaten at 11 A.M. signals that lunch must be eaten before noon, but chanting does not occur in conjunction with the noon meal.

The remainder of the day is spent at study, at work, and at leisure until dusk, when the monks reassemble for the evening service (*tham wat yen*). The length of each service—from twenty minutes to an hour— depends on how many chants are chosen by the abbot, who leads the chanting. Some are obligatory, but he may draw from or ignore a substantial body of other chants, including some that may reflect on the events of the day.

Ordinary texts are found in the *Jet tumnan* and *Sip sawng tam nan.* Ideally, each monastery is to have both services; in reality, many have only the evening service, and some observe that only occasionally outside the penitential (*khao phansa*) period. During the three months of withdrawal, a great deal more chanting takes place than usual, with extra services at 4 A.M. and 9 A.M., in the early afternoon and just before sunset (figure 28).

Types of chant

Chanting texts privately by the *sangha* is simply called *suat,* and other types are reserved for the laity's hearing, specifically chants for general and meritorious use

FIGURE 28 The abbot (at left) and two other high-ranking Buddhist monks lead evening-service chanting at Ubon's Wat Thung Sai Müang. Photo by Terry E. Miller, 1988.

(*suat hai ngan mongkon*), and chants for funerals (*suat hai upamongkon,* also *awamongkon*). Pali is understood only by educated monks who have spent years studying it. There are also chants for ordination (*suat nak*), for the robe-giving festival (*suat kathin*), and for miscellaneous occasions. Breechah Pintawng, one of Thailand's most senior scholars, distinguishes chants as short chants (*suat san,* with near syllabic text setting), and long chants (*suat yao,* more melodic and melismatic).

Easily discerned stylistic differences distinguish the chants of the Dhammayut sect from those of the Mahanikai sect. The former describes its chant as being in *makot* style, while the latter uses *sang yok* style. The differences, more in rhythm and phrasing than in melody, will be described below. During services, the abbot selects the texts to be chanted, cueing the chapter with the first words. Certain chants are in responsorial form and are not to be confused with this kind of prompting. All, including the abbot, face the image of Buddha, kneeling. They chant some passages with heads bowed to the floor, muffling the sound. Lay people may observe the chanting, but do not participate.

Learning the chants first requires the monk or novice to memorize the texts, a process accomplished over time. Inexperienced members are permitted to use their copies of the *Jet tam nan* when no laity are present but must chant from memory when they are. Many chant only the passages they know, remaining silent during the remainder, leaving to the most experienced the task of keeping the service going. Monks are expected to spend considerable amounts of time alone, memorizing and practicing the chants, but most learning actually takes place through experiencing it. The pitch level is set by the abbot, and no instruments of any kind are customarily used, excepting the temple drum (or bell) and a large hanging bossed gong, which on special occasions in major temples marks important points in the text.

Because Pali is a nontonal language, chants in Pali may theoretically be chanted on a single tone, but in fact this rarely happens. The resulting melody can be rationalized in several ways. First, melodic inflections occur to relieve the boredom of a single pitch. Second, melodic inflections occur because the texts are written in Thai letters, some of which have built-in tonal inflections. Inflections also occur out of habit, or to express feelings. While the same text will not necessarily be chanted the same way in every temple, customary patterns unify the Thai tradition.

The available body of recorded chants demonstrates two melodic tendencies—one in which a reciting pitch alternates with a pitch either a tone or a semitone below and the reciting pitch alternates with a lower fourth. The following scale patterns, expressed in pitch letters, summarize the scalar formations found thus far (reciting pitch italicized).

Group I	Group II
1. F–*G*	1. D–*G*
2. F–*G*–A	2. D–*G*–A
3. F–*G*–B-flat	3. D–*G*–B
4. F–*G*–A–B-flat	

Chants using scales in Group I have been found to be more common than those of Group II.

The *sang yok* style, used in the vast majority of temples (those of the Mahanikai sect), is distinguished by its slow tempo, the alternation of two durational values in a two-to-one ratio, a tendency to evenness, and an unsystematic approach to phrasing. The *makot* style, used only in Dhammayut temples, is faster in tempo and given to clear and systematic phrasing, with a greater variety of durational values, transcribed as quarter, eighth, and sixteenth notes. Though meter is absent, quarters may be juxtaposed with sixteenths, giving passages a syncopated feeling. Some passages also sound rushed, giving the *makot* style a feeling of restlessness, in contrast to the *sang yok* style. Figure 29 contrasts three versions of the text *Namo tatsa phakhawato arahato samma samphutthatsa* 'We worship the Blessed One, Arahat, Supreme Lord Buddha'. Chanted thrice, this text occurs frequently in all services.

Preaching *(thet)*

Preaching (*thet*) is too vast a subject to treat in detail here, for most preaching now is in the vernacular, which leads to a plethora of regional variants. The chanting of sermons also varies—from austere intonation on a single pitch to virtuoso displays with generous melismas, for sermons, unlike chants, are delivered by individuals. Monks highly skilled in using the voice become virtual performers of sermons, called on to preach at distant temples.

Preaching normally occurs on holy days, when the laity gathers with lighted candles and incense to hear a learned monk, seated in a large, wooden chair. The people sit before him, legs to their left, hands folded in front of them. In times past, sermons were written in Pali on palm leaves in one of the learned alphabets. Few understood the words, but their efficacy was realized simply by being transformed into sound.

FIGURE 29 Three ways of intoning the *namo* chant in Pali.

After 1850, some Thai words were introduced into preaching; and since 1940, sermons have been written entirely in the Thai alphabet, with most of the words in Thai (Terwiel 1979:119–120).

In delivery, preaching has two basic styles. Ordinary theological sermons (*thet thammada*) are chanted primarily on a single pitch, with inflections down one pitch and up a minor third, similar to Pali chant. A second category, story-sermons (*thet nitan*), have greater appeal to listeners because they are in the regional vernacular and are often the same stories seen on stage. In a study of Buddhism in northeastern Thailand, Tambiah classifies these sermons into three types: (1) *batom sompot,* which tell the life of the Lord Buddha, including his previous lives (*jataka* stories); (2) *thet bun phrawet* (called *thet mahachat* in central Thailand), the story of Prince Wetsandon, the penultimate life of the Buddha before enlightenment, told once a year during a daylong festival; and (3) *thet nitan phün müang,* local stories, drawn from regional literature. Through these stories, by example, the people learn Buddhist morality and behavior (Tambiah 1970:125–127).

Story sermons are delivered in a more melodic fashion than ordinary sermons, but like chant, they hover around a reciting pitch. Because the language is tonal, melodic inflections are closely coordinated with the contours of ordinary speech.

The preaching of the story of Prince Wetsandon occurs during a multi-day festival from late October to early November in central Thailand and in late February to early March in the northeast. Read from palm-leaf manuscripts written in Thai letters but having dialectal differences according to region, the story is divided into thirteen chapters (*kan*), fourteen in the northeast. Traditionally, the central Thai *thambun mahachat* required a classical *piphat* ensemble to play between each chapter. The northeastern version includes four sections unknown to the central Thai, two telling the story of the travels of Pra Malai (who visited heaven and hell and returned to tell mortals about them), and two stories that serve as introductory and concluding chapters. Chanting takes place in the temple meeting hall (*sala*), with each monk seated on the preaching seat amid the people. Offerings are presented by families who sponsor individual chapters. Some monks preach in a simple fashion on a few pitches, but some exhibit great technical skill through the beauty of their voices and their ability to execute ornate melismas (figure 30).

The northeast also has *thet lae,* preaching in which monks deliver *klawn*-type poetry in a highly melodic fashion, similar to singing, but not so designated because of the traditional proscription on monks' singing. Parts or all of Prince Wetsandon's story can be told in memorized *thet lae* poetry rather than chanted from a manuscript, and through this, the story can be told in a few hours rather than the usual twelve to fourteen. There is also *thet lae* for general teaching and even entertaining, though the underlying purpose is still to teach the people how to behave properly. In central Thailand, however, the term *lae* denotes a kind of popular song with a religious text sung by lay singers (figure 31).

Finally, all the regions but the south have a kind of lay singing that occurs in the *sala* in conjunction with festivals called *saraphan* or *suat saraphan.* Troupes of female singers reverently entertain people using religious poetry set to a simple repeated melody drawn from a standard repertory of several dozen tunes. Many villages have one or more troupes, and occasionally a temple will sponsor a *saraphan* contest, in which a dozen or more troupes compete (figure 32).

The *Sukhwan* ritual

The Thai and the Lao have a Hindu-derived ritual intended to preserve or restore the health of a person undergoing life changes or a rite of passage. It is properly called *sukhwan* or *tham khwan* in Thai and *sukhuan* in Lao, though when performed for

The *khwan* is said to be a timid spirit, inclined to flee at times of stress. Its loss may cause afflictions and misfortunes, and its flight must be checked before the crisis if possible.

FIGURE 30 Preaching (*thet*), from the story of Prince Wetsandon, chapter 10, in northeastern Thai.

monks, it is called *ba si* or *bai si.* Its purpose is to retain or call back the *khwan,* variously glossed as 'psyche', 'morale', and 'spiritual essence'. Some have likened it to the Christian concept of the soul, but Thai informants who understand that concept consider this idea incorrect. A person has thirty-two individual *khwan,* representing

FIGURE 31 A talented monk (in raised chair) chants *thet lae* at a *kathin* festival in Barabu. Photo by Terry E. Miller, 1973.

various parts of the body, and the ceremony concerns them collectively. The *khwan* is said to be a timid spirit, inclined to flee at times of stress, danger, and important changes of status, or even during a long trip. Its loss may cause afflictions and misfortunes, and its flight must be checked before the crisis if possible. The rite is conducted in a variety of situations, including marriage, ordination, promotion, pregnancy, and childbearing, before a long trip, at the beginning of the Buddhist penitential season, before an important enterprise, for the sick and dying, for reintegrating people into the community after a period of time in prison or military service, and after a bad omen, such as a lightning strike.

The ritualist who summons the *khwan* is a *maw khwan* or *phram* (*pham* in Lao), the latter derived from Brahman. This person is typically an older and respected male, a householder, formerly a Buddhist monk, and literate in learned scripts. Many began their study of *sukhwan* while they were robed monks living at a temple, but robed monks do not conduct the ritual. The *phram*'s texts are traditionally written—actually incised—in one of the learned alphabets on palm-leaf strips. His texts are not considered secret, and he may exchange texts or share them with outsiders; indeed, some collections have been published in Thailand. There is no requirement of a singing voice, for though the ritual is chanted, the verb that describes the process is *sut* 'to chant', not a word for 'to sing' (*rawng* or *lam*).

The ceremony may be performed in the temple meeting hall (*sala*), in a home, outdoors, or wherever necessary and appropriate. The *phram* and other participants seat themselves around ritual offerings intended to attract the *khwan*. A conical-tiered altar object (*pha khwan*) is decorated and surrounded by other offerings, including boiled eggs, bananas, flowers, candles, money, lumps of glutinous rice, and lengths of string. Reciting from memory or from a manuscript, the *phram* intones auspicious words, beginning with the threefold *namoh* chant, in Pali. Then follows

FIGURE 32 A *saraphan* melody from the northeast.

FIGURE 33 The temple's abbot ties a string on the wrist of a newly promoted monk in northeast Thailand. Photo by Terry E. Miller, 1974.

the vernacular text appropriate to the occasion. At the conclusion of the chanting, the *phram* begins tying strings around the participants' wrists, including onlookers if they desire. Thus, it is not uncommon to encounter Thai and Lao people with pieces of string tied around their wrists. The tying of the string symbolically binds the *khwan* back into the person (figure 33).

Recitation varies in style from man to man, especially with regard to scalar pattern. Some use as few as three pitches, others as many as six. There is close coordination between the melodic inflections and the tones of the words.

In central Thailand, elaborate ceremonies were formerly accompanied by a *piphat* that played music throughout the ceremony. No instruments of any sort are involved in *sukhwan* ceremonies elsewhere in Thailand. The ceremony is still common in northern and northeastern Thailand and in Laos but has become rare in central Thailand, identified with the more traditional villages only.

REGIONAL THAI CULTURE

Historically, the Kingdom of Siam only gradually became modern Thailand as it expanded into areas formerly under Khmer, Lao, Malay, Mon, and (in northern Thailand) Tai control. Borders were loosely defined, and these outlying areas acknowledged allegiance to the court in Bangkok more than they were administered directly. Until railways and highways were built to the south, north, and northeast, these regions were quite isolated from central Thailand (the original Kingdom of Siam) and consequently developed and maintained distinct cultural patterns.

As Siam, changing into Thailand, became concerned about national unity (both political and cultural), central Thai culture remained dominant. As late as the 1970s, regional cultures—their languages, diets, and musics—were considered inferior and were simply left alone. In each region, people spoke the local languages at home, but had to use central Thai, the official language, in school and in government business. For years, insurgencies in the northeast and the south kept large areas off limits to control by and influence from the central government, but gradually, as the so-called communists saw what had happened in Cambodia, Laos, and Vietnam, these areas were pacified, and to make certain the peace would hold, the government began developing them. During the 1960s and 1970s, the highway system began to reach formerly remote areas, the media (both radio and television) began penetrating into every electrified town and village, and increasingly urban centers became more uniform, more central Thai. At the same time, great numbers of people from the regions migrated to Bangkok seeking work, and they brought back home the wonders of modern Bangkok whenever possible. During the 1980s, electrification throughout rural Thailand and improvements to the roads allowed these influences to spread throughout the kingdom, even to distant villages bordering Thailand's poverty-stricken neighbors, Malaysia excepted.

For a decade (the 1970s), the modernization that made research and travel possible in the distant regions converged with their lively and distinct cultures, but little musical research was accomplished. This result was due in part to an attitude that regional cultures were unworthy of study. As young people from the villages entered regional colleges and universities, they began the process of adopting central Thai culture. Those who went to Bangkok encountered Western and Japanese cultures. Over time, modernization and Thailand's booming economy, which brought prosperity even to the poorest areas, eroded regional cultures to the point that they began to disappear.

Old central Thai culture—that found in villages—declined dramatically, even during the middle years of the twentieth century. Communal farming changed to individual work, leaving most genres of folksong without a context. That same process affected the other regions more slowly, but at this writing the transformation is nearly complete. Even architecture became more uniform throughout the country's villages, and in the 1980s a craze for Spanish-style homes began changing the appearances of towns and some villages. Popular music of many kinds has become dominant, not only because the media are filled with it, but because young people, having more money than their elders, hired the *luk thung* troupes they preferred over the *li-ke* or *mawlam* troupes their parents preferred.

It seems ironic that a dramatic decline in regional culture has paralleled a similarly dramatic rise in the study of regional culture. Not only did the Fine Arts Department found high schools for the arts in each region (which taught both Thai classical and local musics), but one university in each region was designated to be the center for the study of that region's culture, complete with large, new buildings and operating budgets. But these institutions can do nothing to reverse the decline of local culture. In the north, there has been a move to keep local culture alive by designating Friday for the wearing of regional costumes, by preserving buildings exhibiting selected regional symbols, and by establishing touristic villages, where old patterns are maintained from 8 A.M. to 5 P.M., with shows every two hours. The process of preserving a culture by objectifying certain aspects of it—as exhibited in these villages, restaurant shows, and souvenir shops—is also part of its death throes.

Even the northeast, the most conservative and least developed economically, is succumbing. The decline of the local language, *phasa isan* 'northeastern language', is so sharp that classes in it are now offered in a few schools. Genres traditionally sung in it cannot survive in a world where few understand it. Consequently, these genres are changing over to central Thai lyrics. Depictions of *isan* culture have become stereotyped, even when done by northeasterners. Before people were conscious of regional culture, performers dressed variously in central Thai, Western, or local styles, but today they wear the most obvious and colorful local styles available. Performers now exaggerate naïve rural patterns of behavior, whereas they formerly tried to mask the humility of their backgrounds; rice-farming culture is now hip. Music videos of northeast-based pop songs invoke images of old *isan* through such symbols as costumes, fishnets, rice boxes, the *khaen,* and other now-exotic paraphernalia. Whereas northeast culture was formerly rated lower than any other, today it is all the rage.

Consequently, much of the following material on music in Thailand's regions is

The songs progress from a call to an answer to a greeting to various kinds of courtship poetry, much of it heavily laden with insults and mockery, sexual and otherwise. In short, it is a verbal war of the sexes.

more about the past than the present. Most of this music survives, but little of it is easy to find. Only the northeast has developed a strong, modern voice, with roots in the old traditions.

Central Thailand

Central Thai village life, like village life throughout Thailand and Southeast Asia generally, is centered on agriculture, wet rice being the main crop. Though the tightly knit village remains, the communal aspects of farming have all but disappeared since the 1940s and with them most traditional musical genres that depended on this context. Consequently, village song is largely a matter of history, and the few remaining performers are elderly. Literature on the subject is meager, and most of it is restricted to the poetry, with little or no mention of song.

The most thorough village song study in a Western language remains Prince Bidyalankarana's paper, read before the Siam Society in 1925 and reprinted numerous times since. Even at this date, the context for village song was changing rapidly, as agriculture shifted from communal, volunteer labor to hired labor with distant markets in mind. Today's central Thai farmers are more likely to work alone, using tractors and trucks, than in a group using animals and hand tools. The music that accompanies work is supplied by the radio or cassette tape.

Village songs

The term denoting these songs is *phleng pün ban* 'songs of the village'. When roads were poor or nonexistent, groups of villages tended to be isolated from each other, giving rise to endless variants in terminology, melody, and practices. Certain traits underlie virtually all of them, however. The following nine were enumerated by Duangjai Thewtong (1984), focusing on the folk songs of Ban Pohuk in Ratburi Province.

1. Most songs alternate male and female singers (repartee) and soloist and a chorus of onlookers (call and response).
2. Songs are sung without melodic instrumental accompaniment; some genres use simple idiophones.
3. Two types of poems occur: improvised poems and memorized traditional poems.
4. Improvised texts use the vernacular with many double entendres, while memorized poems use refined language, even "royal" vocabulary.
5. Whether the words are serious or not, the manner of performance and attitude are lighthearted.
6. Sexuality, normally repressed in ordinary conversation, is given free reign, both in direct and indirect statements.
7. All aspects, textual and melodic, are orally transmitted.

8. Melodies coincide in length with the lines of the poetry, realize the lexical tones of the words, and rarely exceed a single octave in range. Styles of ornamentation vary from place to place. The scales used are typically pentatonic, but often concentrate on three pitches. Since there are no instruments of fixed pitch with which to compare them, it is difficult to ascertain any exactly ideal pitches, especially since portamento and near-speech intonation are inherent to the style. Transcription into staff notation has proven nearly futile.
9. Rhythm and meter vary on a continuum from free-speech rhythm to strict metrical organization, always duple.

Songs occurred in conjunction with both agricultural and festival cycles. Most were sung in conjunction with harvesting and threshing, which occur in December and January, and at festivals occurring during the last three months and first month of the year, though certain songs associated with specific ceremonies could be sung any time. Some writers on the subject have given the impression that half the villagers were born poets, but those skilled in repartee song received some kind of training. Males (*phaw phleng*) or females (*mae phleng*) skilled in repartee song became prominent within village society. Aspiring singers asked to be trained and became students through the *wai khru*; indeed, performances, even in informal contexts, usually began with a *wai khru* song. While formal training was common, it was not required, since others learned the songs through repeated hearing as members of the chorus of onlookers (*luk khu*).

The nearly universal format is courtship—genuine in an informal context, feigned in a formal one. Following the *wai khru,* the contents progress from a call to an answer (*bot krün*) to a greeting (*bot pra*) to various kinds of courtship poetry, much of it heavily laden with insults and mockery, sexual and otherwise, thinly disguised under a surface meaning; in short, it is a verbal war of the sexes. Finally, one performer may propose marriage to the other, suggest the other run away from his or her spouse, or even have to fight for the woman against a second man. The performance ends with a farewell poem (*bot chak*).

Some specific types are distinguished by name. The following are considered the most important and pervasive.

1. *Phleng phuang malai* 'garland songs' are sung in a circle with males and females separated, sometimes accompanied by hand clapping. The lead singers (*phaw phleng* and *mae phleng*) incorporate danced movements, but the chorus (*luk khu*) does not. This type is performed at Buddhist festivals, ordinations, or any time people gather.
2. *Phleng rüa* 'boat songs', now extinct, were sung during the high-water season (October and November) in the late afternoon and evening, when boatloads of men and women gathered at a quiet spot on a river or canal. The soloists, who played a pair of *ching,* each occupied a boat surrounded by their chorus of supporters, some of whom played wooden castanets (*krap*), medium cymbals (*chap*), or a goblet drum (*thon*).
3. *Phleng lamtat* 'cutting songs' are sung throughout the year. They survive through professional singing groups, hired to entertain. The singers divide into two groups of two or three persons each according to sex, and all wear costumes consisting of traditional wraparound trousers (*jong kra-ben*) and a colorful old-style shirt. While *lamtat* tunes are in the majority, a presentation may include other types of song, such as *phleng phuang malai* and *phleng i-saeo.* Accompaniment is provided by a group of three or four persons playing a large, flat drum with a single tacked head (*rammana lam tat,* as distinguished from

FIGURE 34 *Phleng khorat* performed near the shrine of Khun Ying Mo in Nakhon Ratchasima Province (Khorat). Photo by Terry E. Miller, 1988.

the smaller, classical *rammana*), *ching, chap,* and *krap.* Performances last from dusk until dawn.

4. *Phleng propkai* or *phleng top bai,* similar to *phleng phuang malai,* are sung at Buddhist festivals, ordinations, and other occasions. Nearly extinct, these songs emphasized sexual language considered to be obscene and could therefore be performed in private for a spirit in return for a favor. They are considered the basis of the *nathap propkai* in classical music.
5. *Phleng choi* are thought to have originated in *phleng propkai* too, but serve for the most intense competition and are sung at a faster tempo, with clapping as the only accompaniment. As in *lamtat,* the players divide into two competing teams, one of each gender. Like *phleng lamtat, phleng choi* have survived in a commercial context.
6. *Phleng khorat* are sung in and around the city of Nakhon Ratchasima (commonly called Khorat) by pairs of unaccompanied singers. Today, they are primarily heard in the city near the shrine to Khun Ying Mo, the female figure who once defended the city against invaders. Part of the ritual activity at the shrine involves promising to hire singers if the wish is granted. Consequently, singers perform during both day and night in an area near the shrine, according to how many people pay for segments; audiences come and go (figure 34).
7. *Phleng kio khao* 'rice-cutting songs' were sung in the fields, both during work and especially during breaks. The poems combined references to cutting rice and courtship, for they were originally work songs.
8. *Phleng i-saeo* are similar to *phleng lamtat,* but are faster and require greater skill at improvising poems. In contemporary commercial performances, they are accompanied by *ching, krap,* and drums, but the original accompaniment consisted only of *krap.*
9. *Phleng hae nangmaeo* 'procession carrying a female cat' is a rainmaking song sung after the *songkran* festival in April if the rains have not started. Sung during a procession in which a cat is carried on a stretcher, the singers—often drunk—plead for rain, and beat drums and gongs.
10. *Phleng songfang,* associated with dehusking the rice during harvest, were sung for relaxation in the threshing area. A similar type of song for the same purpose was called *phleng song khaw lam phuan.*

11. *Phleng phanfang* were sung when the rice straw was separated from the grain.
12. *Phleng song khaw lam phuan* were sung when the chaff was removed from the grain, in central Thailand accomplished by having cattle tread the rice.
13. *Phleng chak kradan* were sung when the grains of rice were raked into piles with a long board.
14. *Phleng rabam* or *phleng rabam ban rai* suggests an association with dance, and some simple gestures are part of most performances. *Phleng rabam* are sung in a circle for a variety of occasions.
15. *Phleng ram pha khao san* originated in Patum-thani province and were sung by groups of women in boats as they made their way to the Buddhist temple collecting donations for the monks.
16. *Phleng den kam ram kio* originated from cutting rice. Performers therefore carry a sheaf of rice in one hand and a sickle in the other.
17. *Phleng phitsathan* were associated with courting while gathering flowers for a Buddhist temple. When the singers entered the preaching hall (*sala*), the men and women sat opposite each other and began singing, the theme being a request for blessings.

Village song has died out because its context has disappeared. In the 1980s, Bangkok Bank established an archive into which have been placed numerous recordings of village songs performed by elderly (and often now deceased) singers. In 1987, a troupe of elderly singers was discovered in Ban Phanom Tuan, Kanchanaburi Province, and a great variety of songs recorded, including types not described here. The texts, with extensive commentary and photographs, have been published in Thai. This project is a landmark in Thai ethnomusicology, for until the 1980s few paid any attention to these supposedly primitive songsters.

Li-ke

Among ordinary Thai, both in the cities and villages, especially in central Thailand, but also in other regions, *li-ke,* a kind of theater, retains enormous popularity. Inexpensive to hire, troupes often perform at temple fairs or in conjunction with other festivities, such as an ordination, on the temple grounds, in the street, or even to attract people for the opening of a new market. *Li-ke* is sometimes seen on television or heard on radio. Nonetheless, it is considered entertainment for the unsophisticated; the gaudiness of its costumes and the ostentation of its jewelry are seen as symbols of poor taste.

Li-ke performances take place on temporary stages erected for the occasion, with or without seats for the audience. A series of scenic drop cloths provided highly stereotyped locales, separating the actors on stage from those in waiting. Behind the scenes, the personnel get in costume, apply makeup, and perform a *wai khru* before their performance, which, beginning in the afternoon or the evening, lasts several hours and sometimes most of the night. A small ensemble is seated on stage right. Modern performances are loudly amplified from microphones hanging from the stage and near the instrumentalists. The audience, far from being passive, responds audibly to what is happening on stage, interacting with the comedians. Enamored members of the audience may interrupt the performance to place garlands and large-denomination bills on handsome actors and beautiful actresses.

Originally the troupes were all male, but since the early 1900s have included women. Each member plays a stock role: leading male, leading female, second male, second female, parent, king, queen, antagonist, comedian. Their costumes are fanciful, intended to suggest the royalty of most characters:

li-ke Central Thai theater for the common people

Khun Chang Khun Phaen Well-known story, often used in *li-ke*

awk khaek Malay-derived opening for *li-ke*

klawng yao Long, single-headed village drums

> Fantasy is to be found in the costumes, where imaginative bad taste is allowed to run riot. Never were jewels so gaudy or colours so clashing. The men uniformly wear bouffant breeches (the pleats of which give them constant concern during the performance) held up with brocaded belts and have a fancy throw-over garment. . . . They wear a flashy earring, a headband as a sign of rank and they all sport prominently Japanese watches with no concern for anachronism. (Smithies 1971:41–42)

Musical accompaniment is provided by classical instruments, as few as a *ranat ek,* drums (such as *taphon*), and metal idiophones (*ching, chap,* and others) for small troupes; or a small *piphat,* usually without *pi nai,* for more formal ones. Nothing so formal as action tunes, as found in the classical theaters, governs music in *li-ke,* where any sort of tune, be it classical or otherwise, may accompany action. The actors and actresses speak dialogue and declaim poetry in a form of heightened speech closer to chant than to song, but whose style is not unlike that of some central Thai village songs. As in village songs, the vocal timbre is quite nasal (figure 35).

The stories played in *li-ke* run the gamut from famous classical stories in nineteenth-century literature (such as *Khun Chang Khun Phaen*) to newly created stories based on highly conventional themes. Plots are created in an improvised fashion, from a scenario rather than a script but using many previously memorized blocks of dialogue and poetry. Improvisation in *li-ke* is more a matter of rearranging than creating anew. The comedians, whose humor may be both topical and in response to the audience, are the freest actors.

FIGURE 35 *Li-ke* on a temporary stage in the street in Mahasarakham; the musicians are on a raised, enclosed platform on stage right. Photo by Terry E. Miller, 1992.

The history of *li-ke,* despite extensive research by several Thai scholars and Smithies, remains unclear. The term clearly derives from one or more Malay terms—*di-khe* or *yi-khe*—which denoted a ritualistic form of song performed by men and boys in a circle, accompanied by large drums (*rammana*). Since southern Thailand is partly Malay, a clear connection to the Thai exists. Indeed, even modern *li-ke* performances open with a brief section chanted in mannered Thai called *awk khaek* 'Muslim [or Malay] opening'. It has been assumed that the Thai copied aspects of the original Malaysian *di-khe* about 1880, turning it gradually into a form of narrative theater.

Another possibility exists, however, for *li-ke* clearly resembles both the now obsolete *lakhawn nawk* (the rough version of the refined dance-drama) and what is called *lakhawn chatri.* The earliest mention of this kind of theater in Western literature dates from 1898, when Ernest Young describes *yeegai,* a kind of theater said to have originated in the Malay states (1898:170). Thompson in 1910 mentions *eekays* as being performed by men and boys (1910:173). But Gerini's description from 1912, while repeating the Malay-origin theory, compares it with *lakhawn* [*nawk*] (1912:84). Exactly how modern *li-ke* relates to Malay ritual is unclear, but it is apparent that while a term was borrowed from the Malay, the style of theater seems to be based on central Thai *lakhawn nawk* with perhaps more modern influences; Smithies suggests that Chinese theater in Thailand has added a visual influence.

Long-drum ensembles

The drums called *klawng yao* 'long drum' or *klawng hang* 'tail drum' are typically found in ensembles marching in all kinds of processions associated with festivities, religious and secular. The members of the troupe include drummers (usually male) and dancers (usually female). Serious troupes strive for consistency of costume. They usually consist of people from a particular village, school, or some other organization.

The *klawng yao,* carved of hardwood, has a single head. Its upper 40 percent is shaped like a deep kettle, the head attached with leather thongs or cord to a ring at the bottom of a rounded body. The head, with a black circle painted on it, must be tuned with lumps of rice and ash so that all drums in the group have the same pitch. The lower 60 percent of the body is narrow, in a slight hourglass shape. A wooden ring at the bottom end enlarges the base. A strap allows the player to suspend the drum from his shoulder, and a colorful cloth skirt envelops the laced section of its body. Drums vary greatly in size, with a 20-centimeter head and 75-centimeter length being average. The player uses his hands to strike the head; but if inclined to virtuosity, he may use his fists, elbows, knees, heels, or head.

A full ensemble includes at least two and preferably far more *klawng yao,* plus players of *ching* and *chap, krap, khawng mong* of various sizes, and a large *rammana,* suspended from a pole carried by two men. A great number of cyclic patterns are possible, some involving much syncopation, but a regular pulse is normally maintained by the *khawng mong* and the *krap.* Variations occur in performance, but players do not stray far from the basic patterns. Most patterns also involve leader-chorus singing, preceded by a series of three yodels from the leader (figure 36).

At least two terms denote additional types requiring *klawng yao* accompaniment: (1) *phleng yoi,* because their texts are about courtship and require a division of singers into groups of males and females, relate to *phleng phün ban* (noted above). Each male performer has a scarf, which he wraps around a female dancing partner; (2) *kra thua thaeng süa* occur during public processions, especially for ordinations and weddings. Four performers dress according to their roles: a tiger, a hunter, the hunter's wife, and the hunter's son, acting out a simple skit during the procession.

Dhanit and other Thai believe *klawng yao* came to the Thai from the Burmese as

FIGURE 36 Patterns for central Thai *klawng yao*.

ching	+	o	+	o	+	o	+	o
mong	x	x	x	x	x	x	x	x
drums	*ta*	*tung*	*ta*	*tung*	*ta*	*tung*	*tung*	---
	pa	—	*pleng*	—	*pa*	—	*pleng*	—
	—	*tung*	*ta*	—	*tung*	—	*tung*	—
	bom	—	*bom*	—	*bom*	—	*bom*	—
	tung	*tung*	—	*tung*	*tung*	—	*pa*	—
	ta	*tung*	*tung*	—	*ta*	*tung*	*tung*	—

a result of contact during the wars in the 1700s, but others assert that it did not arrive before the reign of King Rama IV. The Burmese *òzi* is clearly similar, but so is the Cambodian *skor chhaiyaim.* Having spread to other regions of Thailand, *klawng yao* is particularly prominent in the northeast.

Southern Thailand

The neatly drawn border between Thailand and Malaysia masks the history of the peninsula, for the Thai province of Pattani was once a center of Malay civilization. The fourteen provinces comprising the south (*phak tai*), which extend down the peninsula beyond Prachuap-Khirikhan Province, have a colorful and complex history. To about A.D. 600, the area was part of Funan and from the 700s to the 1200s was ruled from Sumatra by the Srivijaya Empire, which profoundly influenced the region. The Khmer influenced the northernmost provinces until the rise of the Tai at Sukhothai in the 1200s, when the peninsula came under their control. After the fall of Ayuthaya (1767), the region was briefly independent, but King Taksin regained control and gradually expanded the borders until an agreement with the British established the modern border. The culturally most important city is Nakhon-Sri-Thammarat, founded in A.D. 550 and known to the Malay as Ligor. It was here that Theravada Buddhism from Sri Lanka first established itself on the Southeast Asian mainland.

The south is distinctive for its architecture, dress (men often cover their heads and wear sarongs), diet, language, and arts. Buddhism is the dominant religion, but the southernmost provinces have many mosques. A significant successionist insurgency has continued for years, as has unrest associated with the Chinese population. Unlike the north, which has a developed tradition of instrumental music and little theater, the south is known for its theatrical genres, both human and puppet. The theatrical traditions have been researched slightly, but music in the region has received scant scholarly attention.

Musical instruments

The southern instrumentarium is limited, and most types are found elsewhere in Thailand, albeit sometimes with a different name, but a few are distinctive to the region.

1. *Pi ka law* or *pi haw,* a conical double reed with a wooden body about 33 centimeters long, has seven holes for fingering and one for the thumb. The player pushes his or her lips to a disc-shaped gourd, with the reed within the oral cavity. The bell, often a separate piece of wood, is wound with thread for use at funerals. Thai sources suggest its use is restricted to funerals and lifelong

Buddhist ordinations, but either this instrument or a closely related one, the *pi chawa,* is used in theater.

2. *Pi nai,* the classical Thai double reed, is used for both human and puppet theater.
3. *Saw* fiddles, the classical Thai *saw duang* and *saw u,* sometimes now replace the double reed in theatrical performances.
4. *Khawng khu,* a pair of bossed metal gongs, are tuned either a fifth or a sixth apart and suspended horizontally in a small wooden box, each struck with a padded stick. The gong pair is used in both human and puppet theaters.
5. *Khawng fak* or *mong lek fak,* a pair of metal bars measuring 5 by 20 by 1.5 centimeters suspended horizontally in a wooden box, are tuned a fifth or a sixth apart and are played with a pair of small mallets. In theater, this instrument has the same function as the *khawng khu.*
6. *Krap, krap phuang,* or *krap chak,* a vertical stack of six to ten thin pieces of hardwood, 1 by 23 by 4 centimeters, strung together and mounted on a thick wooden base, which has a vertical rod piercing each piece. The player grabs a handle on the topmost piece and moves it up and down during human theater (*nora*).
7. *Klawng nang* or *klawng chatri,* a pair of small barrel drums, each with two tacked heads 20 centimeters in diameter and 25 centimeters high. Tilted forward by an X-shaped stand of crossed sticks, the drums are struck with two sticks. A small version of the central Thai *klawng that,* this drum pair is used in both human and puppet theater.
8. *Phon,* a large barrel drum, has two tacked heads, about 50 centimeters in diameter and 50 to 55 centimeters high, suspended horizontally from a metal ring and beaten with a pair of sticks. It is used exclusively in Buddhist temples for ceremonies.
9. *Püt,* a conical drum about 50 centimeters long, has leather lacing and heads measuring 23 and 26 centimeters in diameter, each of which is tuned with a mixture of cooked rice and coconut ashes (*khi püt*). It is played with both hands, with the *phon* in temples.
10. *Thon,* a pair of wooden drums 30 and 33 centimeters long, respectively, has a slightly conical shape, leather lacing, and heads measuring 13 and 15 centimeters, respectively. The player strikes one head with his hand and the other with a small curved stick. The *thon* is not to be confused with the central Thai *thon,* a goblet-shaped, single-headed drum.
11. *Thap* or *thon chatri,* a hardwood, goblet-shaped drum, has a single head, similar to the central Thai *thon* (also called *thap*), 33 centimeters long, 18 in diameter at the widest place, and 13 at the head.
12. *Khawng mong yai,* a single bossed gong 75 centimeters in diameter at the front and 70 at the back, has a 20-centimeter rim and a knob raised 5 centimeters, struck with a padded stick. Other sizes of *khawng* are sometimes also used.

Ensembles

Only two distinctly southern ensembles have been identified, and one of them accompanies both human and puppet theaters.

1. *Ka law* ensemble, used in Buddhist temples for ceremonies, funerals, ordinations, *kathin* processions, and other similar occasions, consists of the *pi ka law,* large and small *thon,* and three *khawng mong.*
2. The ensemble for human theater and puppet theater is the same: *pi chawa* or *pi nai, khawng khu, thap, ching,* and *klawng nang.* A *krap chuk* may be added to

manora Type of southern Thai theater named for the leading character

nang talung Southern Thai shadow-puppet theater

nang pra mo thai Northeast Thai shadow-puppet theater

the ensemble used in *nora* theater. In either, a *saw u* (less commonly a *saw duang*) may take the place of the double reed.

Genres

Only three genres, two major and one minor, are found in the south, but the former two are distinctive and in the minds of many Thai symbolize the arts of the region.

Human theater

Research published in Western languages on southern Thai human theater (*manora,* or *nora,* or *manora chatri*) has been limited to two articles, one by René Nicolas (1927) and a second by Henry D. Ginsberg (1972); beyond listing instruments and providing general comments, neither has much to say about music. Materials published in Thai are also quite limited, and none are known to focus on music. A few recordings of the music and song were published in the early 1970s and transferred to cassette tape in the 1980s, but few documents are available for study.

The term *manora,* usually shortened to *nora,* refers to a famous story of Indian origin. Manora (in Sanskrit, Manohara), a heavenly bird-maiden, comes to the earthly plane and marries a human prince, Suthon (in Sanskrit, Sudhana). They become separated, and Suthon seeks to travel to her realm to regain her. While this story was likely the first story or at least the most widely used and likely had ritual associations, it is hardly ever seen, and the repertoire is now based on twelve other stories, including several classics of Thai literature (*Sang Thawng, Khun Chang Khun Phaen,* and *Phra Aphai Mani*).

Traditional *nora* troupes were quite small and until the early 1900s were all-male, with female roles taken by boys; females are now normal members of the troupe. There were three basic characters: a hero, a heroine, and a comedian, plus a troupe leader, helpers, and musicians, about twelve in all. Large troupes added extra actors, dancers, and workers, and could total twenty-five to thirty persons. Financial rewards were modest, since performances were largely confined to the three dry months (from March to May), the rest of the year being too rainy to allow more than sporadic local performances. Life in the troupe was tiring, for performances lasted from evening until perhaps 4 A.M., and soon the troupe had to pack up for the trip to the next venue.

Nora is often described as dance-drama, but the emphasis is on dance rather than on drama. The main characters are dancers, considered to be heavenly birdlike creatures (*kinnara*), and the costume includes wings and a tail. The comedian, however, is called a hunter (*phran*), for the third character in the *manora* story was Bun, a hunter. A full performance includes several hours of dancing and singing interspersed with rhyming comic verse in southern dialect accompanied by instruments. The play took place only after this routine. As early as the 1960s, the less traditional—and, ironically, the most successful—troupes had begun to include regionally based popular songs (*phleng luk thung*), and by 1972, they retained little that was old, emphasizing the popular songs over what remained of the drama.

Before modernization, a traditional performance took place either by day or by night. The usual occasion was a fair, but sometimes wealthy individuals sponsored troupes in conjunction with weddings, funerals, or fulfilling a vow (see below). The performance took place originally on mats laid on the ground, but performances today typically use temporarily raised wooden stages with lights and amplification. It was formerly customary to engage at least two troupes in competition.

To attract an audience, the ensemble played an extended overture (*homrong*), lasting up to an hour. Opening the performance is an invocation (central Thai *wai khru,* southern Thai *kat khru*), which can last up to thirty minutes. The leader of the troupe usually performs this role, intoning texts to sanctify the event, honor the troupe's teachers, and summarize the legend of the origin of *nora.* One unusual aspect of the performance has tended to guarantee the transmission of these texts: after the reciter completes each line, the chorus (of instrumentalists, *luk khu*) repeats his words in chant, filling out the rhythmic cycle. Following the invocation, the troupe performs solo dances, songs, and short skits. The main story, if one is performed, comes only after several hours of this sort of entertainment. The leading player's entrance is delayed, making his appearance the high point of the night.

Nora formerly had associations with magic and ritual, for the master of the troupe might also perform *khwan* ceremonies, exorcisms, topknot ceremonies, and ordinations. The master was also thought to have the power both to help others attract mates and to lure young women into his lair. To protect his troupe during competition, he learned magic formulas called *mon* (from *mantra*) in Pali, Sanskrit, or imitations of those languages.

Performances also occurred as fulfillments of vows made to a spirit asked for a favor—a custom called *kae bon.* The *nora* troupes that migrated to Bangkok in the 1800s and evidently merged with central Thai *lakhawn nawk* to form *lakhawn chatri* were often hired to fulfill vows. At the *lak müang* shrines in Bangkok and the Phra Pathom Jedi in Nakhon Pathom, this custom continues. These *lakhawn chatri* troupes, however, are now accompanied by a small *piphat* and sing in Central Thai.

Without expert studies of *nora* music, all observations must be considered preliminary. The ensemble depends on three primary instruments, the double reed (*pi chawa*) for melody, and the gong pair (*khawng khu*) and drum (*klawng chatri*) for rhythm. In modern performances, a bowed lute (*saw duang* or *saw u*) may substitute for the double reed. The instrumental melody is founded on the seven basic tones of the double-reed instrument, the resulting scale being nonequidistant, but because of pitch bending and rapid ornamentation, difficult to measure. The music that accompanies dance is drawn from a repertoire of more or less fixed tunes and rhythmic patterns realized on the drum(s), while the gong pair maintains a rapid pulse by alternating tones. Some recitation is delivered in speech rhythm over the regular instrumental pulse, but the usual declamatory style is in duple meter with much syncopation. Recitation centers on a single pitch, with intonations rising to a pitch between a semitone and a tone and then falling one tone. Recitation is accompanied by at least the drum and the gong pair. When the chorus repeats the reciter's words, its texture may be heterophonic.

Shadow-puppet theater

Shadow-puppet theater (*nang talung*) is found from Greece to Indonesia, and from China to Malaysia. Northeast Thailand has a small-sized shadow-puppet theater (*nang pra mo thai*). In the south, a similar theater is one of two preeminent theatrical genres, but in central Thailand, it is extremely rare.

The word *nang* 'leather' denotes the puppets, but because modern movies are also played against a screen, both are called *nang.* The modifier *talung* refers to the southern Thai city of Pattalung in the center of an important area for shadow theater, though the city of Nakhon-Sri-Thammarat is equally important. Some southern Thai, claiming that shadow-puppet theater started in Kuan Prao Village (near Pattalung), call the genre *nang khuan.*

Like other types of southern musical culture, few studies exist in either Thai or Western languages. Most accessible is an article in English by Michael Smithies and Euayporn Kerdchouay (1972), but this, like all known studies, provides little information about music. Similarly, little is known of the history of shadow-puppet theater in Thailand, or of its relationship to similar phenomena in Malaysia (*wayang kulit*), Indonesia (*wayang kulit*), and Cambodia (*nang sbek tauch*). Early writers on old Siam had nothing to say about any genres from the south, mentioning shadow puppets as possibly coming "from the Country of *Laos*" (La Loubere, 1969[1693]:47) or being of Chinese origin (Tachard 1688:213).

Shadow-puppet theaters are temporary structures set up on the grounds of temples, schools, or governmental offices. A wooden platform is built on four wooden posts between 2 and 2.5 meters off the ground (some are now built on oil drums), with additional posts supporting full side walls, a half back wall (over which people climb to enter and leave), and a roof that slants downward from front to back. The front is partially covered with a tightly stretched, thin, white cloth, 2 meters high and 4 meters wide. Besides the name of the puppeteer and perhaps a sponsor, advertising commonly covers up to one-third of the screen. Into a freshly cut banana stalk, placed horizontally behind and below the screen, are stuck the puppets' bamboo spines. Formerly, light was provided by a kerosene lamp, but with electricity (provided until recent years by portable generators), a lamp is substituted. In either case, a piece of tin covers the back of the light, protecting the puppeteer's eyes. The electricity that powers the light also runs an amplification system, which, like most systems used in village entertainments, is turned to a painfully high level. In villages where security was poor, the puppeteer reportedly had to sit on corrugated iron to avoid having knives stuck into him from below.

The personnel inside this space include the master puppeteer (*nai nang* 'leather man'), his assistant or apprentice, and five or six musicians, all of whom sit on the floor. The instruments used in shadow-puppet theater are essentially the same as in *nora,* but the *ching* is quite prominent. Until a specialized study is done, little can be said about this music, except that it shares some characteristics with that of *nora.* The melodies of the *pi chawa* (or now, the *saw duang* or the *saw u*) are typically melismatic, and those of the double reed use seven tones. In available recordings, the *ching* and the *khawng khu* maintain, with the drum, a steady, duple metrical organization; the puppeteer chants texts on three or four pitches (a reciting tone with inflections up two tones and down about one semitone). Dialogue is spoken; only invocations are chanted. Action is accompanied by fixed melodies appropriate to specific actions. To attract an audience, in place of the original overture (*homrong*), popular music may well precede the performance, and instruments other than the traditional ones—a drum set, or an individual conga—may augment the ensemble

Made of calfskin, shadow puppets are of two types: a thicker set in vivid colors for daytime use without a screen; and a thinner set, formerly in subdued earth tones, now in vividly painted colors, which allow the light to pass through. Nearly two-dimensional, each side-view figure is attached to a thin bamboo spine about 28 centimeters long. The figures vary in size, with main characters (such as Rama) measuring around 20 centimeters high and 7 wide. A full set numbers between 150 and two hundred, but only forty or fifty are used during any given performance. Each puppet represents only one character, not a scene (as in central Thai *nang yai*). Characters are both traditional and modern (for modern stories), dressed in the latest fashions, with prominent hairdos, jewelry, and watches. Each character has one movable arm, attached to a separate and thinner stick, but comic characters, invariably painted black, may have two movable arms, a moveable jaw, and visible genitals. Color symbolizes certain characters: Phra Ram (Rama) is green, and his brother, Phra Lak, is red. The collection of puppets is kept in a folder of plaited bamboo until needed, when the puppet's bamboo spine is stuck into the banana stalk. If the figure is placed against the cloth, its shadow (and colors) are seen by the audience; away from the screen, it cannot be seen.

A performance begins with an invocation performed by a character called the *rüsi,* a hermit-magician. Second, Phra Isuan (Siva) appears, as does a young, crownless prince, who pays respects to (animistic) gods, to angels (*thewada*), local spirits, sponsors, and local officials. Finally, a comedian appears, announcing the story. The main story in southern shadow theater was traditionally the *Ramakian,* or more usually, episodes from it, with many local interpolations. But several hundred other stories are available, including some of the great Thai classics, like *Phra Aphai Mani.* During the 1960s, the United States Information Service, in cooperation with the Thai government, produced an anticommunist, antisuccessionist film of a *nang talung* performance that was shown in sensitive southern villages during the height of antigovernmental activities there. The language of the royal characters is central Thai, but the comedian always speaks in southern dialect, making jokes—both salacious and otherwise—about local characters and habits not criticized directly in ordinary speech.

A nighttime performance typically begins about 9 P.M., after people have returned from the fields, bathed, and eaten. It lasts until midnight, when a temple drum signals a break of one hour. About 1 A.M., it resumes, and proceeds until dawn. The audience for the first part is mostly children, the story line simpler, and the humor more restrained; during the second part, the audience is mostly adults, the story line more complex and the humor risqué. A troupe may be hired for many occasions, including a Buddhist merit-making festival (*tham bun*), housewarmings, ordinations, weddings, and funerals. They may also appear at temple fairs, where admission is charged to raise money for the temple. Sometimes at a fair, a shadow-puppet troupe is paired with a *nora* troupe and Thai boxing, but there is also a tradition of having contests where up to twenty shadow-theater troupes may appear on the same field, the prize being awarded to the one with the largest audience. As Smithies points out, audiences can be bought, making the results unreliable.

Daytime performances are rare. The thicker puppets were used without the screen, and the audience could see the puppeteer and the musicians. The season for performances is the dry period from April to July, which precedes the Buddhist penitential season, when performances are traditionally forbidden.

Li-ke ba, li-ke khaek dang, li-ke bok

A little known genre, evidently related to central Thai *li-ke,* is briefly described in a recent Thai publication, *Folk Music and Traditional Performing Arts of Thailand* (1987?). Formerly played by an all-male cast, but now mixed, the genre is based primarily on one story about an Indian trader and his wife. There are three characters: Khaek-dang, Yayi (his wife, a Thai), and a court official. Musical accompaniment is provided by a *pi chawa,* two *rammana* of central Thai origin, a *khawng mong* gong, and a pair of *ching.* Certain resemblances to the local *nora* are apparent.

Northern Thailand

The nine provinces comprising the northern bulge of the kingdom border Laos on

Northern Thai music is rarely heard today, and certain common instruments have become virtually extinct since the mid-1970s, when their last masters died.

the north and east and Burma on the west—an area better known as the Golden Triangle because of its production of opium. Lowland culture centers around Thailand's second largest city, Chiangmai, but numerous upland ethnic groups unrelated to the Thai live in the hills and mountains. The region was part of the Dvaravati kingdom of Haripunchai (modern Lamphun) until 1281, when Mengrai, a Tai prince, conquered it and created the Kingdom of Chiangmai around a new capital, founded in 1296. His kingdom, Lan-Na-Tai (Million Tai Ricefields), expanded into modern-day Laos, but in 1556 the Burmese captured Chiangmai and held it until 1775, when King Taksin recaptured it, making it part of modern Thailand.

Northern Thai culture is distinct from that of central Thailand in many ways, including dialect, script, literature, diet, architecture, and the arts. Whereas the epic story forming the cultural foundation of central Thailand is the *Ramakian,* in the north the analogous foundation is *Phra Law.* To what extent the Burmese and Lao cultures have influenced that of northern Thailand is difficult to isolate, but the regional music (*phleng phün müang*) is distinct from that of other regions of the kingdom, and from those of neighboring countries. Beyond lists of instruments and genres, little musical research on the region has been published, leaving theoretical matters uncertain.

What distinguishes northern Thai music are certain instruments unique to the region, the extensive and distinctive ornamentation of melody, and the heterophonic texture of ensemble music. In cultural programs featuring regional arts, northern Thailand is typically represented by the fingernail dance (*fawn lep*) rather than by instrumental music. Northern Thai music is rarely heard today, and certain common instruments have become virtually extinct since the mid-1970s, when their last masters died.

Musical instruments

1. *Pi chum,* a bamboo pipe with metal free reed and seven holes for fingering. Placing the mouth over the reed (mounted on the side near the upper end) and holding the instrument almost horizontally, the player exhales, ideally using circular breathing. *Pi chum* come in four sizes: *pi mae* 'mother *pi*', 40 centimeters long and 2.5 in diameter; *pi klang* 'medium *pi*', 30 centimeters long and 2 in diameter; *pi koi* 'little-finger *pi*', 20 centimeters long and 1.5 in diameter; and *pi tat* 'cut *pi*', 15 centimeters long and 1.5 in diameter.

2. *Süng,* a hardwood or teak plucked lute, about 80 centimeters long, with a round body, a fretted neck, and four metal strings in two courses, tuned in either a fourth or a fifth, plucked with a piece of animal horn. *Süng* can be made in two other sizes, larger (*yai*) and smaller (*lek*) (figure 37).

3. *Salaw* or *thalaw,* a bowed lute with a coconut resonator on a spike, three strings (formerly silk, now metal), forward tuning pegs, and a separate bow. *Salaw* are

FIGURE 37 A traditional northern Thai ensemble plays in a village home. *Front to rear: süng, salaw,* and *khlui.* Photo by Terry E. Miller, 1994.

made in three sizes: large (*yai*), medium (*klang*), and small (*lek*), about 80, 60, and 50 centimeters long, respectively. The last two have only two strings, the *lek* tuned in a fifth, and the *klang* in a fourth; the *yai,* with three strings, is tuned up a fifth and a fourth.

4. *Tung tung,* a small, bamboo tube zither, used primarily as a toy. It consists of a section of bamboo cut between nodes, with a sound hole; two strips of bamboo skin, raised on pegs, are plucked, but have no predetermined pitch.

5. *Phin nam tao,* a monochord with a half gourd or coconut-shell resonator and attached stick supporting the string, played against the chest, which also acts as resonator. It is now virtually extinct. The softness of its timbre restricted it to personal use. Its origin is uncertain, but similar monochords were found in India and ancient Cambodia (at Angkor), and the instrument has similarities with certain African monochords. The half gourd is attached through its stem near one end of a stick some 78 centimeters long. A single silk string or brass wire stretches from a 25-centimeter-long tuning peg at the end of the stick near the gourd to the other end, which curves upward and is often highly decorated. The string is tightly secured to the stick near the gourd with a piece of cord (*rat awk* 'squeeze the chest'). The player, always male, must bare his chest, against the left side of which, using his left hand, he presses the gourd. The left hand stops the string while the right hand plucks, producing harmonics. The player may alter the timbre by raising the gourd away from and back onto the chest. Players usually accompanied their own singing with this instrument.

6. *Phin phia,* also a chest-resonated stick zither with a half gourd or coconut-shell resonator, but with two or four strings. The stick is longer than that of the *phin phia,* measuring slightly more than one meter, but the tuning pegs are shorter, about 18 centimeters long. Similarly, the player used it to accompany his singing as he walked to court his girlfriend.

7. *Teng thing,* a two-headed asymmetrical barrel drum with lacing mounted horizontally on a stand, similar to a *taphon.* The heads measure 36 and 30.5 centimeters in diameter, and the barrel is 91 centimeters long.

8. *Klawng düng nong* or *klawng ae,* a long single-headed wooden drum with a slightly waisted body. The upper 40 percent includes the head, with leather lacing fastened to a ring; the lower 60 percent has a series of turned rings. There are three sizes: small (*noi*), 1.5 to 2 meters long with a head 50 centimeters in diameter; medium (*klang*), 2.5 to 3.5 meters long with a 70-centimeter head; great (*luang*), 3 to 4.5 meters long with a 1-meter head (figure 38).

9. *Klawng u je,* similar to the *klawng düng nong* but smaller, being about 1.5 meters long with a single head 18 to 20 centimeters in diameter. They resemble the *klawng yao,* used elsewhere in Thailand.

10. *Klawng pu ja,* a two-headed cylindrical drum with leather-thong lacing, about 2 meters long, with heads about 1 to 1.2 meters in diameter, mounted horizontally and beaten with two sticks. Two similar, but much smaller, drums (*luk tum*) are placed horizontally on the drum at one end. These drums were formerly used to signal news of war but now serve exclusively in Buddhist temples to signal the people.

11. *Klawng chum,* a two-headed barrel drum with closely spaced leather thongs. There are two sizes, the smaller being 70 centimeters long with heads of 20 centimeters and the larger being 9 decimeters long with heads of 40 centimeters.

12. *Talot pot,* a two-headed tubular drum with leather lacing and a strap for suspending from the neck. The drum is 1 meter long, with heads measuring 30 and 20 centimeters, respectively.

13. Gongs. There are two types of gongs: the bossed *khawng,* identical to that of

FIGURE 38 The longest Thai drums, *klawng ae,* on carriages in Chiangmai. Photo by Terry E. Miller, 1973.

central Thailand; and the *pan* or *phan,* a flat gong, used in Buddhist temples. The former type come in at least four sizes: *khawng ui, khawng mong, khawng kratae,* and *khawng noi,* 50 to 60, 30 to 35, 25, and 20 centimeters in diameter, respectively.

14. Cymbals. There are two sizes of cymbals: the *sa-wae* and the *sa-wa,* 15 and 30 centimeters in diameter respectively, equivalent to the central Thai *chap lek* and *chap yai*, respectively.

Certain central Thai instruments are also used. These include the dulcimer (*khim*), the fipple flute (*khlui*), and the conical oboe (*pi chawa*).

Ensembles

TRACK 8-4

A small number of ensembles have names and are more or less standardized, but other possible groupings without specific names may be encountered. Those which are standardized follow:

1. *Penja duriyang* 'five instruments'—*pi mae, pi klang, pi koi, salaw, süng*—is used for festive occasions, dances, and processions.
2. *Wong dontri lanna wong yai* 'large northern ensemble' consists of three *süng,* three *salaw,* a drum, wood castanets, *khlui, ching,* and *pi chum.*
3. *Pi chum* may have three, four, or five members. The basic ensemble uses *mae, klang,* and *koi,* the medium adds the *dut,* and the (obsolete) large ensemble used a size called *pi koi lek.* The *pi chum* ensemble primarily accompanies the singing of *saw.* In a three-member ensemble, the *pi mae* has the leading part, the *pi klang* the so-called sustaining part, and the *pi koi* the so-called contrasting part. An enlarged ensemble (*pi chum ha* 'five') uses the basic three *pi chum* plus *süng* and *salaw.* In Phrae and Nan provinces, an ensemble of three *süng* (one each of the three sizes) accompanies singing.
4. *Khrüang pra kom* 'northern percussion ensemble', consists of *klawng düng nong* (or *klawng aeo*), *talot pot, sa-wae* (and possibly *sa-wa*), *khawng mong,* and *khawng ui.* Its primary use is for festive processions.
5. *Klawng u je* consists of a drum, a gong, and *sa-wa.*
6. *Klawng chum* consists of six large drums, one small drum, two northern oboes (*nae*), and two *khawng.*

The occasions for music included courting, weddings, housewarmings, ordinations, processions, the *loi krathong* festival, the *thet mahachat* festival (reading of the life of Prince Wetsandon), and funerals. Many of these contexts have become rare, or have disappeared or changed to mediated music, but the percussion ensembles primarily associated with temples are likely to be used now and then at temples preserving them.

Genres

1. *Khao* denotes a narrative genre, the heightened-speech reading of long stories from palm-leaf manuscripts, some of northern origin, others widely known, such as the story of Prince Wetsandon. Although similar to *an nangsü* reading in the northeast, *khao* is appropriate for many occasions (not only funerals) and though normally for solo voice is on occasion accompanied by the *süng*. The melody of *khao* derives from the lexical tones of the text, articulated to seven distinct scalar tones spanning an octave.

2. *Saw.* A repartee genre with at least one male and one female singer, *saw* is performed from about 10 A.M. to 5 P.M. A stage singer is called *chang saw,* meaning someone skilled at performing *saw.* The texts, partly memorized and partly extemporized (to allow topical comments), are sung to standard melodies adapted for the particular texts. Although the topics may be local and satirical, even bawdy, they also include discussions of ethics, history, and episodes about folk heroes drawn from northern epics. *Saw* is said to accomplish at least three purposes: instructing the young about love and sex, teaching the moral code of Buddhism, and transmitting the contents of traditional northern literature. All take place in the general context of feigned courtship. Accompaniment is provided by one of three possible ensembles—*pi chum sam* 'three [sizes of] *pi chum*', *pi chum si* 'four *pi chum*', and *pi chum ha* 'five *pi chum*'—plus *süng* and *salaw.* In Phrae and Nan provinces, *saw* is accompanied by three sizes of *süng. Saw* melodies are sometimes called *tham-nawng,* the term for melody used elsewhere in Thailand, and sometimes *rabam.* At least twelve melodies, most of them from a specific area, are identified by name. Pentatonic, the melody is supported by an accompaniment of densely woven heterophony. Singers of *saw* are commonly hired to entertain guests at ordinations and other celebrations associated with Buddhism and for housewarmings.

3. *Saw lakhawn* or *lakhawn saw.* The only type of theater found in northern Thailand, *saw lakhawn* is played from a scenario much like that of central Thai *Li-ke,* and the troupe consists of stock character roles: two male lovers competing for the lead female, parents, and a comedian. The stories are various, including northern epics such as *Phra Law, Nai Ai,* and *Noi Chai-yah.* Performances last from about 9 P.M. to 2 A.M.

4. *Joi.* Until the mid-twentieth century, courtship required the male to visit his lover at her home, engage in ritual dialogue based on poetry called *aeo sao,* and sing terse poetry, both serious and risqué, called *joi* (less commonly *saw siang yao* '*saw* with melismas' or *ram lam nam* 'singing a story with dance'). The three known standard melodies of *joi* require more extensive ornamentation (*üan*) than is usual in *saw. Joi* can be sung unaccompanied but was formerly accompanied by *phin phia* and later by *süng* or *salaw.*

5. *Fawn phi* 'spirit dance', a communal spirit ceremony done once a year in April or May, is organized around a small building filled with hanging pieces of multicolored cloth. During the day, music is provided by an ensemble, and participants eat, drink, and become possessed as they bury their faces in a piece of hanging cloth and swing from it. Around 5 P.M., diviners kill a chicken and predict the future according to how the entrails fall.

In the view of most people of the northern region, to listen to Westernized popular songs (*phleng sakon*) is to be modern, but to listen to local, traditional music is to be backward, only for the old and poor.

6. Dance. The north is famous for the grace of its dances and martial displays, also called dances. The former, performed in pairs, are typically accompanied by an ensemble of drums, gongs, cymbals, and double reed. The most important dances follow.

Fawn thian 'candle dance' was originally sacred in character but has lost this quality. Each dancer has a lighted candle in each hand, and naturally the dance must be performed at night.

Fawn lep 'fingernail dance' is danced usually during the daytime for festivals and ceremonies. Each dancer wears 15-centimeter-long brass fingernails on the four fingers of each hand.

Fawn ngio 'Shan dance' derives from dances of the Tai-Yai (or Shan) and includes the use of scarves.

Fawn man kam boe or *man mui chiang ta* 'butterfly dance' mixes aspects of northern and central Thai and Burmese dances. This dance, which also uses scarves, ends with the dancers in a formation that supposedly resembles a butterfly.

Fawn man mong khon also mixes aspects of northern, central, and Burmese dancing. It is distinguished by a faster tempo, a distinctive costume (including a long skirt and a long-sleeved blouse), and a unique hairdo (partly in a central knot on the head, partly flowing over the left shoulder).

Fawn dap 'sword dance' can be danced by men or women, each holding a sword, at times gripped by their teeth. Accompaniment consists of drums, gongs, and medium-sized cymbals.

Fawn joeng 'combat dance' is only for men. Barehandedly wielding swords, they display combat ability. Accompaniment is the same as for the *fawn dap*.

Fawn top maphap 'teasing dance', which precedes the *fawn dap* in a performance, is done by barehanded males, who tease and anger their opponents by clapping each other's hands and striking their bodies. Accompaniment is the same as for the *fawn dap*.

Musical style

A comprehensive description of northern Thai musical style is premature because little information is available on the tradition, but some traits are evident. The seven-tone system of tuning appears nonequidistant, and pitches can be arranged in an ascending order of tones and semitones that approximates a Western major scale. Most melody is pentatonically based, with scales beginning both on pitch 1 (1—2—3—5—6) and pitch 6 (6—1—2—3—5); however, the remaining pitches may be used in a passing function, especially pitch 7. Melodies appear to exhibit a polarity between a tonic and its fifth (1 and 5, or 6 and 3), these pitches being emphasized over the others (figure 39).

Instrumental melody varies in idiom, with some (like *khlui* and *salaw*) using extensive ornamentation. The most complex melodies are those realized on *pi chawa*,

FIGURE 39 Two northern Thai melodies.

where intonations outside the basic seven and portamento make analysis difficult. Most melodies are fundamentally fixed, especially those played by ensembles, but variation bordering on simple improvisation occurs in solo playing. When two or more instruments play together, heterophonic texture occurs.

All observed melodies, with the exception of *khao* recitation, are organized colotomically into duple meter articulated by drums, gongs, and cymbals. The structure is cyclic, though in a simplified fashion, but determining whether meter is end accented, as is central Thai classical music, is difficult. Rhythms tend to be simple, and syncopation is rare.

Northern Thai music has for many reasons been disappearing. Thailand's prosperity, especially emanating from Chiangmai, has brought modern entertainment to the region. In the view of most people of the region, to listen to Westernized popular songs (*phleng sakon*) is to be modern, but to listen to local, traditional music is to be backward, only for the old and poor. There are fewer and fewer players of the instruments, especially of the *phin nam tao* and the *phin phia,* both of which are virtually extinct. The greatest threat to vocal music is the loss of the northern dialect, *lanna thai.* The texts of *saw* have gradually changed to central Thai, at least in part—which affects both the relation with the melody and the listeners' comprehension, and consequently traditional literature is being forgotten. Whereas vocal genres were transmitted orally, they are now becoming more literate, but with the loss of literacy in *lanna thai* script, texts are forced into central Thai writing, with changes in pronunciation and tone.

Northeastern Thailand

Seventeen provinces make up the northeastern region, *phak isan.* Covering 170,226 square kilometers and constituting fully one-third of Thailand's territory, this area borders Cambodia on the south and Laos on the east and north, primarily following the Mekong River. Geographically, the region is a plateau, which receives less rainfall than the rest of the country, resulting in frequent droughts and greater poverty than elsewhere.

The region was under Khmer domination before the Tai gained ascendency and vanquished the great Angkorian empire in the 1400s, attested by many Khmer ruins, including the magnificent temples of Khao Phanom Rung in Buriram Province and Pimai in Nakhon Ratjasima Province. Culturally, most of the people of the northeast are Lao, sharing one language, literature, diet, and music with the people across the Maekong in the nation of Laos. Their being divided results from history. Earlier, the Siamese armies defeated the Lao kingdoms, gaining authority over the northeast, but later, in the 1800s, the French blocked an expanding Siamese kingdom, which logically would have included the Tai-speakers of present-day Laos and Vietnam.

Three separate cultural subgroups are distinguished in the northeast. The majority are Lao-speakers who occupy thirteen provinces, all but those along the southern tier of the region. Three provinces—Buriram, Surin, Sisaket (Srisaket)—are home to a majority of Khmer-speakers. Third, Nakhon Ratchasima Province is the center of the Thai-Korat population, whose language is close to central Thai. In addition, there are several smaller subgroups, most notably the Phuthai, related to the Lao, plus various Khmer-speaking groups: the So and the Saek in the upper northeast and the Kui, the Soai, and the Sui along the southern border.

Unlike the music of other Thai regions, that of the northeast has been extensively studied. The music of the Lao majority has been treated in detail in numerous articles and several books, by both Terry E. Miller and Jarernchai Chonpairot of Mahasarakam University. Professor Chonpairot has also studied the music of the Phuthai as part of a team of Thai scholars led by José Maceda. The study of Khorat-area music and that of the Khmer began in the mid-1980s and continues. In comparison to other regions of Thailand, the northeast can be said to be the most conservative musically. The influx of Western-style popular music emanating from Bangkok has been countered by modernized versions of local genres, some of which are tremendously popular.

Though efforts have been made to increase tourism in the northeast, it has long had the fewest tourists of any region. Without a central city rich in attractions, it has remained a low-density tourist area, and consequently cultural villages, cultural shows, and other objectifications of culture have not appeared to a great extent. Formerly disdained as a place of backward people, poverty, and bad-smelling food, the northeast has become chic for many Thai, however—a place of happy rice farmers, singing and dancing in colorful local costumes, with the country's most exciting popular songs (*luk thung* and *lam sing*).

Musical instruments

Northeastern instruments remain rich and largely distinct from those of the rest of Thailand, but one instrument, the free-reed mouth organ (*khaen*), is preeminent. Consequently, the *khaen* will be treated separately from the following list of instruments.

1. *Phin* (also *süng*). Though the term *phin* derives from the Indian term *vīṇā,* it denotes a plucked lute of unknown origin. The body of the instrument is made of wood, but the shape of the resonator varies widely: round, oval, rectangular, or waisted (imitating a guitar). Dimensions vary widely too, with resonators from 2 to 3 decimeters in width (or diameter) and overall length from 6 decimeters to more than 1 meter. The instrument has two to four metal strings (three being most common), which pass over a series of frets to lateral tuning pegs. Some instruments are plain, being homemade by craftsmen of limited skill, but others are beautifully finished, sometimes with an elaborate carved neck piece beyond the tuning pegs. A standard three-stringed instrument has at least four commonly used tunings: (1) big mode (*lai yai*), A–e–a; (2) small mode (*lai noi*), A–d–a; (3) head-falls-off-the-pillow mode (*hua tok mawn*, A–a–a; and (4) old-time-*lam-ploen*-theater mode (*lam ploen samai boran*), A–a–e′. The player plucks the strings with a small piece of horn held in the right hand. The *phin* can be played alone in combination with the *khaen* and percussive instruments, and especially in this combination to accompany a genre of theater called *lam ploen.* Techniques include the playing of single-line melodies, melody with the lowest string used as a drone, and (in the case of the fourth tuning) melody played parallel with the middle string, resulting in parallel fifths over a drone. Its repertory, partly improvised and partly fixed, derives from that of the *khaen,* though individual players use idiosyncratic titles. During the past twenty years, electrified *phin* have become common (figure 40).

FIGURE 40 A *klawng yao* ensemble prepares to parade at a Roi-et temple following the abbot's birthday observation; note the electrified *phin,* with its amplifier and speakers on the cart. Photo by Terry E. Miller, 1994.

2. *Saw pip* or *saw krabawng.* Saw denotes a bowed lute, and *pip* or *krabawng* denote metal cans. The *saw pip* is thus a homemade bowed lute with a body made from a discarded metal container, square or cylindrical, such as for kerosene, Hall's lozenges, or Ovaltine. Two metal strings run over a bridge along a stick neck to two rear tuning pegs. As on the central Thai *saw duang,* the strings are acoustically shortened with a string loop about two-thirds up the neck, but the bow can be separate or can pass its horsehair or nylon between the strings. The strings are tuned in a fourth or a fifth. Unlike the *khaen* and the *phin,* the *saw pip* is of recent origin, probably during the 1930s. It can be played alone, in combination with the above-mentioned instruments, and (in the 1930s) as part of the ensemble that accompanied a now defunct genre of theater called *maeng tap tao.* Its repertory, largely improvised, derives from that of the *khaen* (figure 41).

3. *Sanu* or *tanu.* This is a musical bow with a strip of rattan, palm leaf, or plastic held by pieces of rope or cord. The bow, which may vary widely in size, is attached with cord to a large traditional kite (*wao*) and launched during the windy season (November to January), usually at night. The wind vibrates the strip, causing random pitches to sound. Changes in wind speed alter the pitches and create rhythms, resulting in a kind of melody that may vary in range up to a fifth or more. Alternately, a person may swing the bow around in circles at the end of a rope (see figure 7, p. 60).

FIGURE 41 Thawng-khun Sia-run plays a *saw pip* made from a Hall's lozenge can. Photo by Terry E. Miller, 1973.

4. *Saw bang* or *saw krabawk,* a two-stringed bowed tube zither, is found among the Phuthai people in the provinces of Kalasin, Mukdahan, and Sakon Nakhawn, where it joins an ensemble that accompanies boxing, singing, and dancing. It consist of a section of shaved bamboo about 7 centimeters in diameter, cut to include two nodes, with 5 or 6 centimeters extra on the lower end and 14 centimeters on the upper. Overall length varies widely, from around 45 centimeters to 60 or more. Two metal strings stretch from the lower end, where they pierce the bamboo skin and are secured with small pegs, over a bridge to two rear crisscross tuning pegs at the upper end. A strip of rattan pulls the strings to the body near the pegs, defining their acoustic length. A sound hole is cut in the rear of the body. A bow, consisting of a curved bamboo stick and horsehair, is separate from the instrument. The strings are tuned in unison, but only one is stopped in performance, creating melody and drone; alternately, the strings can be tuned in a fourth or a fifth.

5. *Phin hai.* Developed in 1979, the *phin hai* consists of two or three graduated

saw pip Northeast Thai bowed lute with metal can body

wot Circular bamboo panpipes in northeast Thailand

hun Northeast Thai Jew's harp

pong lang Northeast Thai vertical xylophone of logs

sizes of ceramic jars (similar to pickle crocks) with a thick rubber band stretched over the open top of each. The player strikes the rubber band with the hand, producing low pitches, which function rhythmically rather than melodically. The instrument plays in various ensembles to accompany dancing and certain genres of singing, such as *lam phanya yoi.*

6. *Wot.* Originally a toy, the *wot* became a musical instrument for adults during the 1970s. It consists of six to nine bamboo tubes about 7 to 18 centimeters long, clustered around a tapering piece of bamboo 28 centimeters long. Each tube is closed at the tail end and cut off at an angle at the upper (which is open), with a rounded lump of beeswax or, more commonly, *khisut* (a black insect product, pliable in warm weather), to guide the air over the ends of the tube. Originally this panpipe was attached to a string and whirled around to produce random sounds, but now players hold it in their right hand, turning it while blowing, to produce pentatonic melodies.

7. *Pi luk khaen* 'reed child mouth organ'. This is a Phuthai free-reed pipe with five holes for fingering. A tiny metal free reed near the upper end is covered by the player's mouth. Stopping various holes produces six pitches: G, A, B, C, D, E. A small hole between the sound holes and the reed is covered with a membrane of bamboo skin or plastic. The instrument can be played alone or in small ensembles that accompany both dancing and singing.

8. *Hun* (in Korat, *hia*). This is the northeastern Jew's harp. Made of bamboo and measuring 12 to 15 centimeters long and about 1.5 to 2 centimeters wide, it has an end section with a vibrating tongue, which may be a separate piece attached to the main piece with *khisut.* As with all Jew's harps, the player uses various shapings of the mouth to emphasize particular overtones, producing melodies within the lower notes of the overtone series. It is played alone, and its music is more rhythmic than melodic, but unlike Jew's harps of the upland peoples in the region, it is not used as a disguiser of speech or for courting.

9. *Pong lang* or *khaw law.* The original *khaw law* was a simple vertical xylophone with at least seven and sometimes as many as fourteen logs, hung from a tree or post and struck with beaters. These instruments were kept at home but were mostly used in small field huts, where farmers could while away the time by playing simple melodies. Respondents could document them back only to about 1900, primarily in Kalasin Province. The term *khaw law* derives from a village headman's signal box, which consisted of a single log or section of bamboo (between unpierced nodes) with a slit. The term *pong lang,* which actually denotes a large metal bell mounted in a wooden frame and strapped to the back of a lead cow, derives from "*Pong Lang,*" the title of a famous piece of programmatic music played on both the *khaen* and *khaw law*—a piece that imitates the rhythm of the *pong lang* bell as the cow sways from side to side. By the early 1970s, the *khaw law,* already known exclusively as *pong lang,* was becoming known outside Kalasin and appeared in dance-accompaniment ensembles. After that, it became so widely known that it must now be considered a stan-

dard northeastern instrument. It consists of twelve solid, hardwood logs of graduated length, strung on two strands of rope (with knots holding the logs in place), with the longest log hung at the top of a frame and the lower end hooked to the base. Sizes vary, but one specimen's longest log was 54 centimeters and its shortest, 29; another specimen varied from 53 to 23. Each log is about 6 centimeters in diameter. The center portion of each log is shaved thinner, both front and back, for tuning and resonance. Tuned pentatonically (A–c–d–f–g–a–c′–d′–f′–g′–a′–c″), it is often played by two musicians, one seated on the left (playing melody with two beaters), one seated on the right (playing drones with one or two beaters). The repertoire earlier consisted of improvised pieces similar to those for *khaen,* but in today's usage, within ensembles to accompany dance, fixed melodies are prevalent (Miller and Chonpairot 1981) (see figure 2, p. 57).

10. *Mai kap kaep* or *krap khu.* Similar to the central Thai *krap sepha,* the northeastern castanets consist of two pairs of flat pieces of wood about 12 centimeters long, 5 wide, and 1 thick, one pair for each hand. Their primary usage was in a now extinct genre of singing, *mawlam kap kaep,* in which the player accompanied himself.

11. *Pang hat,* a Phuthai flat metal gong about 40 centimeters in diameter, struck with a padded beater, is used in ensembles to accompany processions and dances.

12. Cymbals. The central Thai pair of *ching* is called *sing* in the northeast, and the *chap* is called *saeng.* The latter comes in several sizes.

13. *Klawng seng, klawng jing,* or *klawng tae.* Primarily associated with the Phuthai, these pairs of two-headed, conical drums, made of hollowed tree trunks covered with cowhide and secured with leather straps between heads, are used both in processions and to accompany dancing. They are also used at festivals, especially in contests (*jing*) during the rocket festival (*bun bang fai*). Two drummers, each beating a pair of suspended drums with hardwood sticks covered with lead sheeting, compete to attain the higher pitch and louder volume (figure 42).

14. *Klawng yao* or *klawng hang.* The single-headed long drums of the northeast are essentially the same as those of central Thai village music.

15. *Klawng tum.* This two-headed drum, 40 centimeters long and 30 in diameter, with leather lacing, is primarily used in processions and in dance-accompaniment ensembles among the Phuthai. The name of the drum is said to be onomatopoetic.

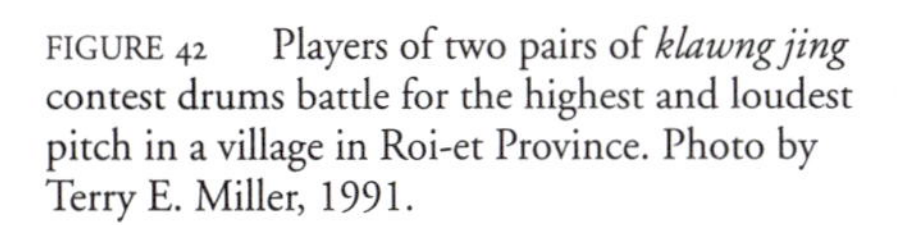
FIGURE 42 Players of two pairs of *klawng jing* contest drums battle for the highest and loudest pitch in a village in Roi-et Province. Photo by Terry E. Miller, 1991.

16. *Klawng dung,* a single-headed drum about 80 centimeters in diameter, with a shallow body 20 centimeters wide, and leather lacing resembling the *rammana lam tat* of central Thailand, is played with the hands in the *klawng yao* ensemble.

17. *Thon din phao.* Similar to the central Thai *thon,* with a single head, the northeastern *thon din phao* is smaller and shaped differently (a deeper waist) and is more elongated. Sizes vary, with a larger drum 13 centimeters wide and 30 long, and a smaller one 7 centimeters by 20. The head is of either snakeskin or frog skin.

There are no fixed melodic ensembles in the northeast comparable to those of the central region, but mixed ensembles of local instruments have developed since the 1970s. Minimally, there have been *khaen* and *phin,* the melodic instruments accompanying old *lam mu,* but all newly created melodic instruments have achieved acceptance into ensembles; these include the *pong lang,* the *wot,* the *phin hai,* and the *saw pip.* Ensembles of *klawng yao* have existed for as long as anyone knows, but at least by the 1980s players added an electrified, amplified *phin* to that group. Since long-drum ensembles normally parade around a village or town, enterprising musicians have created for the *phin* small pushcarts carrying a car battery, an amplifier, and speakers (see figure 40).

Genres

Among Lao-speakers in the northeast, the primary kind of music is vocal, called *lam.* The term, sometimes misunderstood by central Thai to mean 'dance' (central Thai *ram,* since /r/ is often changed in pronunciation to /l/), refers to singing in which a flexible melody is coordinated with the lexical tones of the poetry and differs from *rawng* or *lawng* (*hawng* in Lao), meaning 'to sing a fixed melody such as a popular song or the national anthem'. A skilled person is called *maw,* and consequently a singer is a *mawlam,* though the term has come to denote singing or a genre of singing; the latter usage may be shortened to simply *lam.* Most kinds of *lam* are accompanied by a *khaen,* with or without other instruments. Most genres are nontheatrical.

In 1973–1974, when I initially researched northeastern music, the region was just opening to the modern world. A highway had been built from Bangkok to Nong Khai, but the region had virtually no paved roads anywhere else until about 1970. The genres seen and recorded in 1973 were as purely northeastern as they could be, since before then the media were mostly local (radio and recordings on disc), and influences from central Thailand had come only in bits and pieces. A great number of traditional genres flourished at that time, though some of them were fading into oblivion. Change has probably always been a factor in the northeast, but since 1974 the degree of change in traditional music and theater has been breathtaking.

At first the popular songs of the *phleng luk thung* variety—which not only express the feelings and culture of each region but do it with the instruments and idioms—came from all four regions; but over time, those from the northeast prevailed, and others fell into obscurity. The region's population is significant and growing, and with many migrant workers from the northeast living in Bangkok, the market for up-to-date songs was expanding. Over time, northeastern songs became popular among Thai of all regions, much as U.S. country music expanded from the upland South to national and international popularity. *Luk thung* shows, supported by the younger generation (with its relative wealth, earned in the big city), became so popular in the 1980s that they threatened to eclipse traditional singing and theater. By the end of that decade, the *mawlam* began fighting fire with fire, developing a new kind of *lam* for the 1990s—*lam sing.* Traditional in format, its contents accommodated the times by blending *luk thung* with traditional material, but accompanied

FIGURE 43 An abstraction of a *klawn* stanza, showing required Thai tone marks. The check mark stands for *mai tho*; the vertical, for *mai ek*.

Line 1	___	___	___	✓	¦	___	___	___	___
Line 2	___	___	___	(none)	¦	___	___	___	✓
Line 3	___	___	___	✓	¦	___	___	___	' (b,g,d)
Line 4	___	___	___	✓	¦	___	✓	___	(none)

by electrified instruments and a trap set. At the time of this writing, *lam sing* is sweeping Thailand, forcing older genres to accommodate it. Nevertheless, *lam sing* cannot be fully understood without the knowledge of its predecessors.

Many cultural phenomena in the northeast, including music, are interrelated. The poetry used in singing is nearly identical to that found in traditional literature written on palm-leaf manuscripts, a type called *klawn* or *kawn,* consisting of four-line stanzas, each having seven basic syllables, with a given pattern of tonal signs and patterns. The rhyme scheme also follows a complex pattern, which unifies different lines. Figure 43 shows the required tonal signs.

Singers' poetry often differs from standard written literature through a prevalence of prefixes, suffixes, and additional syllables, which subdivide the basic syllables (beats) of a line. In virtually all cases, singers learn their poetry from written sources provided by their teachers, and consequently the *lam* tradition is based on memorized poetry with minimal improvisation.

Several nontheatrical genres of *lam* consist of male-female alternation (repartee) but without the chorus(es) of supporters common in central Thai village songs. Though not sung or recited, courtship poetry (*phanya*) appears to be the basis for these genres. Until the period of modernization, ritual courtship was common in northeastern villages, as elsewhere in Thailand. Among the Lao, boys and girls were expected to memorize subtle poetry, replete with double entendres, to be used in the war of wits and sexuality. Questions and insults had to be answered, and someone without an appropriate poem lost face. *Phanya* is virtually extinct, however, but the main genres of *lam*—*lam klawn* and *lam sing*—are essentially staged reenactments of ritual courting.

The stories used in theatrical genres and excerpted in nontheatrical genres derive from traditional Lao literature, originally recorded on palm-leaf strips in thick books (*nangsü phuk* 'book in a pile'), using *thai noi,* the old Lao alphabet. These stories are used in vernacular Buddhist preaching (*thet nithan* 'story preaching'), some of which are localized *jataka* stories. Besides entertaining, they teach people how to behave and thus serve to transmit the worldview of the Lao from generation to generation. The composers of singers' poetry continually rewrite these tales for different contexts.

The singing of *lam* also relates to a nearly extinct tradition of reading epic-length stories in poetry from palm-leaf books at wakes (*ngan hüan di* 'good house party'). This custom, called simply *an nangsü* 'reading a [palm-leaf] book', was done aloud in heightened speech, more or less on specific pitches that form a pentatonic scale related to one of those used in singing.

The khaen *as the basis of a theory of northeastern Thai music*

A full understanding of each particular genre and the *khaen* is not possible without reference to theoretical factors. The pitch-name system used here, proposed in the early 1970s by Jarernchai Chonpairot of MahasarakhamUniversity, has been adapted in many schools, including the School of Dramatic Arts, Roi-et. It is based on the *khaen,* whose music informs northeastern theoretical thinking and terminology, but pitches are relative, since *khaen* are built in many lengths and consequently have no absolute fundamental pitch comparable to A = 440.

Typically, a beginner on the *khaen* receives basic instruction informally from a friend or a relative but after that is mostly left alone to evolve a personal style based on what he hears from others.

The basic tuning of northeastern Thai music is fundamentally different from that of central Thailand. It has nonequidistant steps approximating the Western pattern of tones and semitones. The measurement of pitches on the *khaen* is limited in accuracy because the reeds are subject to weather-caused changes and because slight differences in wind pressure can alter the pitch by a noticeable number of cents. Nonetheless, the pitches of two *khaen* measured in 1974 showed variance from equal-tempered degrees to be plus or minus 16 cents (Miller 1985:215). Other instruments of fixed pitch (like the *pong lang*) follow the same system of pitches, and since the *khaen* accompanies most genres of singing, singers also sing in this intonation. The latter factor is different from classical singing, where vocal music is considerably subtler in pitch than that of fixed-pitch instruments.

The *khaen* (also spelled *kaen, khene, ken, can,* and *khen*) is the most important instrument of northeastern Thailand and of the Lao generally, but as a bamboo free-reed mouth organ it is related to many other types in Southeast and East Asia. Its form—that of a raft, not a bundle—sets it apart in this region.

Khaen are made in four standard sizes with regard to the number of pipes: six, fourteen, sixteen, and eighteen. Among the Phuthai, one sometimes encounters instruments with eight or ten pipes, and in Laos the *khaen* of the Phuan differs in the arrangement of pitches. The pipes, traditionally measured in a forearm's length (*sawk*), can vary from around 40 centimeters (for a small *khaen* of six pipes) to between 4 and 5 meters long. The latter are now obsolete, with the approximately 1meter length being standard. It is not necessary for *khaen* to have any standard length because they are normally played alone and must comfortably match just one singer's voice. *Khaen* of various numbers of pipes are distinguished by a number, but the system has one inconsistency. A *khaen* with six pipes is *khaen hok* 'six *khaen*', but those with fourteen, sixteen and eighteen pipes are called *khaen jet* 'seven *khaen*', *khaen paet* 'eight *khaen*', and *khaen kao* 'nine *khaen*', respectively, referring to pairs of pipes. In Laos and northeast Thailand until the 1950s, the *khaen jet* was standard, but now *khaen paet* has become standard. The *khaen hok,* usually described as a child's toy, may show an early form of the instrument; the *khaen kao* primarily accompanied a genre of singing now nearly extinct, and consequently the instrument is rarely seen.

With the *khaen paet* a point of reference and the lowest pitch designated A (to avoid sharps and flats), an examination of the arrangement of pitches, standard for all instruments, shows no apparent logical pattern (figure 44). Though the pitches occur in a series of seven, the scales of most of the repertoire are pentatonic. Because it is difficult to play more than three successive pipes, the pitches have been arranged to balance the pitches of each scale between the hands while avoiding more than three successive pipes—an arrangement comparable in concept to that of a QWERTY typewriter keyboard. Each pipe has a name, but few players know all their names, and there is no other fixed way to communicate information about individual pipes.

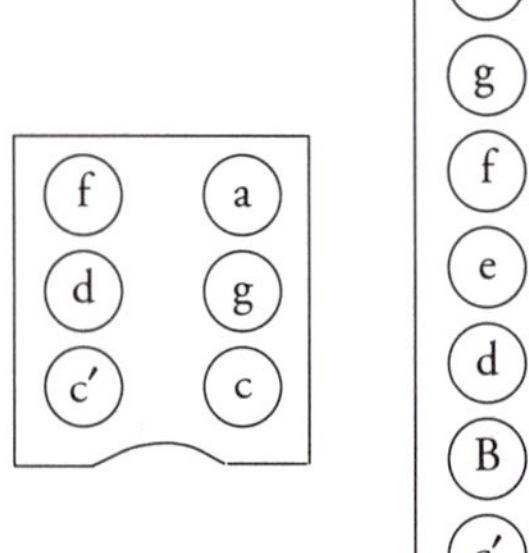

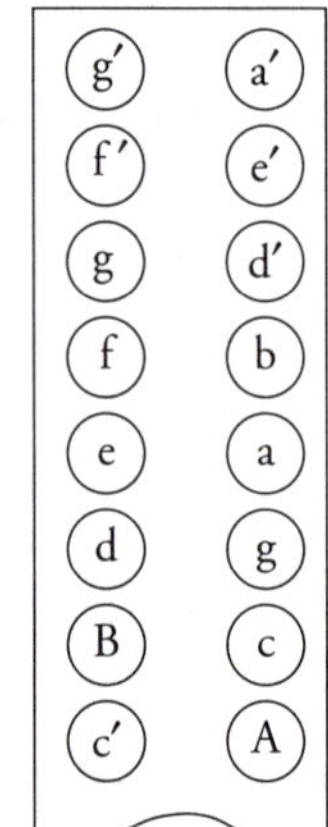

FIGURE 44 Arrangements of pitches of *khaen hok* and *khaen paet.*

The lack of notation is not unusual, but the fact that few players of *khaen* have had any formal study (except those who study at the College of Dramatic Arts branches in Roi-et and Galasin) is surprising. Typically, a beginner receives basic instruction informally from a friend or a relative but after that is mostly left alone to evolve a personal style based on what he hears from others. Many players therefore tend to be eclectic, clearly distinguishing the style of one province or generation from another. *Khaen* playing is exclusively male, except in modern schools, where some female students learn to play it. In villages, only men play it. The instrument itself is considered female, however.

The *khaen* consists of thin bamboo pipes (*mai ku khaen*) whose nodes are pierced with a red-hot poker. They are arranged in two parallel rows in raft form. From front to back, the tallest four pipes are nearest the player, and each succeeding pair are shorter than the preceding pair. The pipes are fitted into a hollowed-out wind chest (*tao* 'breast', 'gourd') carved of hardwood with a hole for blowing (*ru pao*) and sealed into place with *khisut*. The rows are separated by thin bamboo dividers at the bottom and near the top, and the pipes are tied with a natural grasslike material (*ya nang*) at the bottom, upper middle, and top. A series of holes for fingering (*ru nap*) are burned into the outside of the pipes above the wind chest, but the first pair, played by the thumbs, has its holes on the front; the last pair's holes, played by the little fingers, are lower than the rest, which are otherwise even in height.

Each pipe has a small metal free reed of copper-silver alloy (*lin khaen*) mounted over a hole (*ru lin*) cut in the pipe. Facing the outside of the instrument, these are enclosed within the wind chest and are activated into vibration only when the hole is covered. The complexities of this relationship were first clearly explained in detail by Laurence Picken et al. (1984). The player inhales and exhales alternately through the wind chest while holding the chest in his palms. The thumbs control row 1; the index fingers, rows 2 and 3; the middle fingers, rows 4 and 5; the ring fingers, rows 6 and 7; and the little fingers, row 8. Slight shifts in this pattern are required in one mode and in isolated passages elsewhere. The player tilts the instrument to the left, his lips pressed firmly to the mouthpiece.

Khaen music is improvised, based on *lai,* a simple modal system. There are five named *lai,* but an unnamed sixth mode completes the system. Several basic programmatic pieces, also improvised, are known to all players, and many others may be known locally or individually.

Two pentatonic-scale patterns form the basis of *khaen* music—and by extension, singing. No fixed term designates them, but many players would understand the distinction based on the terms *san* and *yao,* because those patterns are associated with named types of singing. The two scalar systems are shown in figure 45.

For singers, there are only the scales, but for *khaen* players, there are specific modal manifestations of these scales, the *lai* mentioned above. Each *lai* begins on a different pitch, three based on the *san* pattern, three (including the unnamed one) on the *yao* pattern. They are called *lai sutsanaen* 'melody of love', *lai po sai* 'left-thumb mode', *lai soi* 'fragmented mode', *lai yai* 'big mode', and *lai noi* 'little mode'. Their relationships, with the unnamed mode on E, are shown in figure 46.

Each *lai* has one or two drones, which reinforce the fundamental or starting

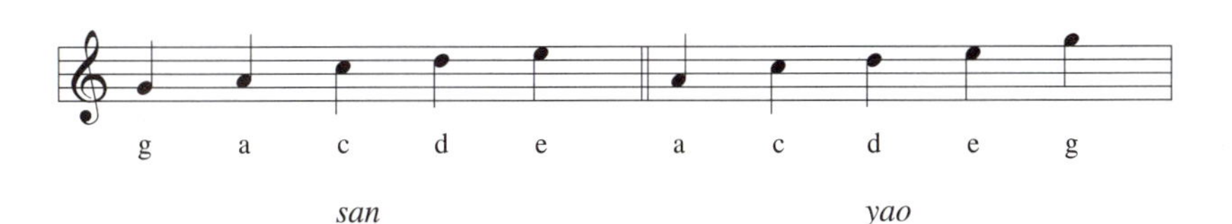

FIGURE 45 The *san* and *yao* scales.

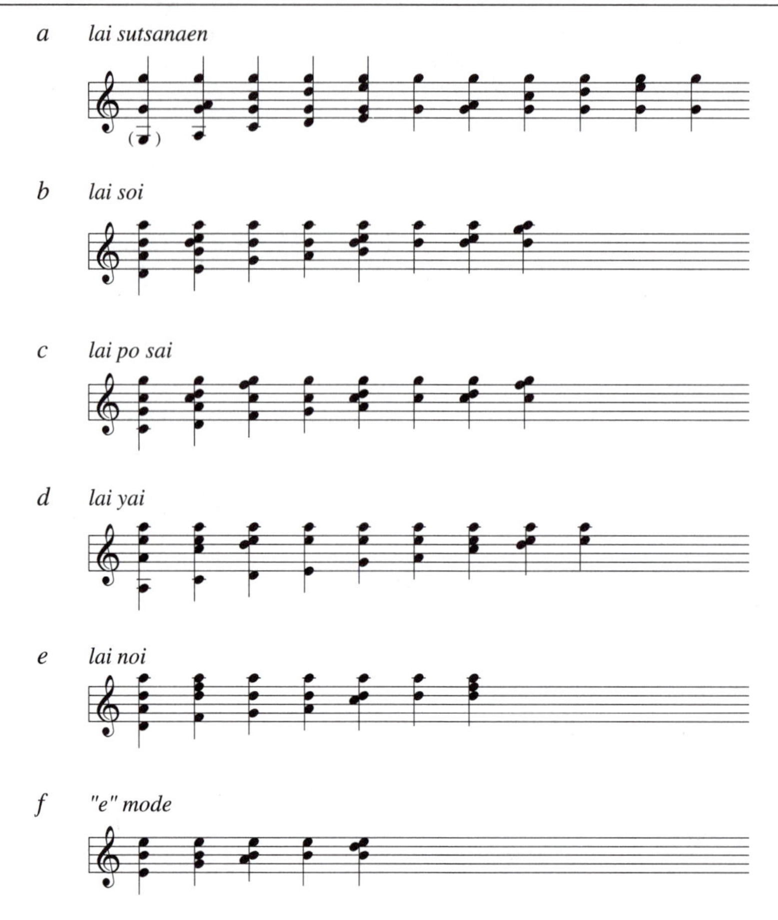

FIGURE 46 The six modes (*lai*) for *khaen* and their sonorities. The last is an unnamed mode on E.

pitch at the octave and fifth (only the octave in one case), these held during play either with fingers or small pieces of *khisut.* Unlike the drones of bagpipes, they do not necessarily sound continuously, because they respond to any tonguing used. Furthermore, each degree of the scale, heard normally as the lowest sounding pitch, is realized with a specific sonority, giving *khaen* music polyphonic texture in addition to the drones (figure 46).

The basic repertoire required of a *khaen* player consists of improvisations in each of the five standard modes. Such spontaneous compositions may last from a minute to any length desired. As an accompaniment to singing, the patterns may be maintained for hours. The modes based on the *san* scalar pattern are normally in meter, but those of the *yao* pattern may be in either meter or speech rhythm. The usual metrical organization is duple, but here and there in an improvisation, a measure having a triple division of beats may occur, perhaps by design, perhaps through error. Most playing consists of unequal pairs of notes, varying from dotted (proportion of three to one) to triplet (two to one). Some *khaen* music can therefore be transcribed into compound meter (like 6/8 time) rather than duple (like 2/4 time). Tempos vary widely, according to the player's ability and generation, the older generations having played more slowly. Among professional players, a tempo of quarter note = 70 (with primary movement in eighths and sixteenths) would be considered slow, while fast players could range up to quarter note = 152. The latter in continuous sixteenth notes would produce more than six hundred melodic tones per minute.

Genres of lam

The vocal music of the Lao in both northeast Thailand and Laos is centered on its texts, the language of which is Lao. Two activities common to human communities worldwide give rise to the various kinds of *lam*: storytelling and courtship.

FIGURE 47 A *khaen* player accompanies a singer of *lam phün* in an informal performance. Photo by Terry E. Miller, 1973.

The telling of traditional stories, including localized *jataka* stories (Buddha birth stories from Indian literature), has been mentioned earlier in reference to chanted sermons and the reading of palm-leaf manuscripts at wakes. These stories were sung by *mawlam* accompanied by *khaen* and acted out and sung by troupes of humans (*lam mu* and *lam ploen*) and puppets (*nang pra mo thai*).

The second pattern—courtship—ritualizes gender relationships in various kinds of repartee, which can include tender love poetry, descriptions of nature, Buddhist lessons, excerpts from old stories, challenges, insults, mockery, and sexual innuendo. This is a pattern found throughout mainland Southeast Asia, particularly in Thailand. Repartee in most other places (like central Thailand) was highly dependent on function and context, but repartee *lam* is staged and requires only the context of a festival.

Lam phün

Already in decline in the 1940s, *lam phün* 'story' required but one singer and a *khaen kao* (of eighteen pipes) for the performance of an epic-length tale lasting up to several nights. Most of the stories were localized *jataka,* such as *Thao Kalaget, Thao Suriwong,* and *Naphak klai-kradon,* but one—*Wiangchan* (Vientiane)—was historical, telling the story of the rise and fall of the Lao capital, Vientiane. In a variant called *lam rüang* or *lam hüang* 'story', the performer changed parts of the costume to represent the characters of the plot. *Lam phün* is sung in the *yao* scale but using a sixth pitch, resulting in a scale of A–B–C–D–E–G, while the *khaen* accompanies in *lai yai* or *lai noi* (figure 47).

Lam klawn

Until its precipitous decline in the late 1980s, *lam klawn* was the most widespread and popular repartee genre in the northeast, indeed, the most representative of all genres. A pair of singers—one male, one female, each accompanied by his or her own player of a *khaen*—alternated from about 9 P.M. until daybreak, feigning a developing courtship through memorized *klawn* poetry. Though the poems were learned in advance, their order was determined by the developing conversation. Singers asked questions of each other, from the personal (how old are you? are you married? would you like to run away with me?) to the intellectual (questions of geography, history, Buddhism, literature, and so on). Some singers engaged in double entendre with sexual innuendo; singers could sing thoughts that ordinary people could not politely say. Female singers tended to start and finish their careers while young, but male singers continued into middle age or later, and a few highly respected female singers continued into their later years.

The singing progressed in three stages, each distinguished by its scale, rhythmic-metrical qualities, and poetic content. *Lam klawn* began with "short" style (*lam thang san*), sung in the *san* scale, accompanied on *khaen* by any of the *san*-scale modes (*lai sutsanaen, lai po sai,* or *lai soi*), depending on the singer's range. After a short ABA introductory section in speech rhythm, the main poem began, using the *klawn* form, sung in duple meter. Singers took turns extending up to thirty minutes throughout the night, until about 5 A.M. Then the *khaen* switched to a *yao*-scale mode (*lai yai* or *lai noi*), but kept a steady beat while the singer proclaimed the poetry in speech rhythm. This section, "long" style (*lam thang yao*), tended to be more introspective, invoking such images as the sound of thunder (which implied rain and the continuation of life), the tender side of love, and the pain of parting. After about fifteen to thirty minutes without break, the *khaen* continued in the same mode but changed to the patterns for *lam toei.* In this section, faster-paced and metrical, the poems became lighter, even humorous, bringing the performance to an end about 6 A.M., when

lam Lao/northeast Thai term for text-generated song

mawlam Traditional northeastern Thai singer

lam klawn Northeast Thai repartee song accompanied by *khaen*

lam sing Modern form of *lam* in northeast Thailand

everyone still in attendance would return home to begin a long day of work. Before electrification, the coming of the media, and excellent roads, entertainments in villages were rare, well worth the loss of sleep.

Performances occurred in conjunction with calendrical rites: the New Year (Thai and Western), Buddhist festivals (such as *gathin*), and rites of passage (such as ordinations). The main season for performances extended from mid-October to February or March, when the weather became too hot and festivals rare. Few performances took place during the rainy season (beginning in May) and none during the penitential season. *Mawlam* associations were formed to act as singers' booking agents. A successful singer's income could make him or her rich (compared with ordinary people), but not so rich as Bangkok's popular singers or movie stars.

Luk thung were already in existence by 1970, but *lam klawn* was strong and well supported by villagers. The old pattern of youths' migrating to Bangkok for work grew to a virtual exodus, since the northeast remained poor, the fields were getting overworked, families were growing rapidly, and land was insufficient for the new generation. The youth were successful in Bangkok and brought back home their newly acquired wealth and tastes. They wanted modern entertainments—and could pay for them. *Luk thung* shows increased and succeeded in crowding out *lam klawn,* which, though it enjoyed a brief revival in the late 1980s, went into a steep decline by 1990 and has virtually disappeared since (figure 48).

FIGURE 48 A pair of *mawlam klawn,* each with *khaen* player, perform on a temporary stage in Mahasarakham. Photo by Terry E. Miller, 1973.

Lam phanya yoi

A little known genre, *lam phanya yoi* came from the area of Mukdahan along the Mekong River bordering Laos. This genre, closely related to *lam khon savan* across the river, likely gave rise to a more widespread style, *toei hua non tan.* During the later 1980s, *lam phanya yoi* became quite popular throughout the northeast, partly for the loud amplification of its electric *phin* and drum set. Today, to survive, it has begun incorporating *luk thung* and calls itself *lam phanya yoi sing.*

Lam sing

As late as 1989, few had heard of *lam sing,* but within a few years, it had not only eclipsed all other genres of *lam* but had become the rage all over Thailand. Though it is modernized, it retains its traditional roots in the repartee format and the use of *khaen.* Associated with motorcycle and car racing, the term *sing* implies speeding, something fast and modern. From obscure beginnings about 1985 in Chaiyapoom Province, it blossomed in the area of Khon Kaen City after 1987, under Mawlam Ratdri Siwilai, a female *lam klawn* singer who switched to the new style. To teach this genre, both she and her brother operate schools.

Lam sing is accompanied by a *khaen,* an electric *phin,* and a drum set. Musically it consists of a traditional element earlier called walking in the forest (*dün dong*)—a passage in Khon Kaen style *lam klawn* (*thang san*), when the melody switched to the *yao* scale but remained in meter. In *lam sing,* it is called *lam dün* and attains a modern sound through its accompaniment. However, singers incorporate *luk thung* songs into the performance, and this is what made *lam sing* so powerful: it retained the traditional repartee format and the traditional poetry but brought in a modernized accompaniment and its nemesis, the pop song, which had nearly eclipsed traditional singing. In addition, the youthful in the audience danced in styles seen in *luk thung* shows. Within a short time, *lam sing* has taken back the night in northeast Thailand. It attracts large audiences and is widely available on cassettes. It compromises on language, using central Thai for most *luk thung* songs and even in some *lam* texts (figure 49).

Lam mu

Theater in northeastern Thailand dates only to the 1950s, and because travel was so difficult then and isolation made it impossible for anyone to have comprehensive

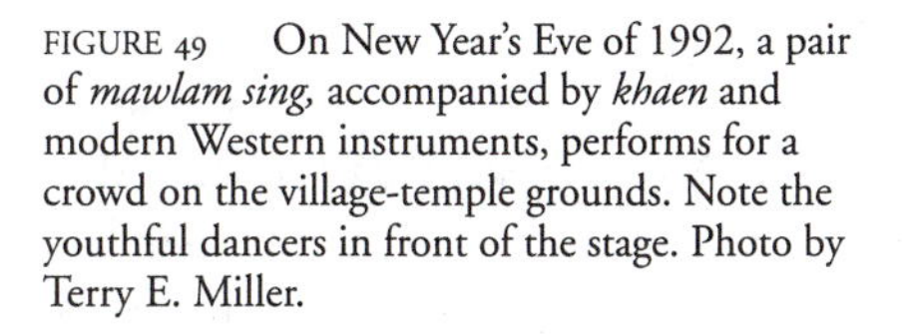

FIGURE 49 On New Year's Eve of 1992, a pair of *mawlam sing,* accompanied by *khaen* and modern Western instruments, performs for a crowd on the village-temple grounds. Note the youthful dancers in front of the stage. Photo by Terry E. Miller.

knowledge, reconstructing this history has proved difficult. Central Thai *li-ke,* sometimes performed in localized versions, provided one influence, especially for staging, costumes, and scenery; *lam phün* provided the stories. Two kinds of theater developed: "collective" singing (*lam mu*) and "spontaneous" singing (*lam ploen*), both of which appeared soon after 1950 but in different areas.

Lam mu developed gradually by using raised wooden stages with multiple backdrops, adding lighting and amplification and adopting the latest fashions in costume alongside those of *li-ke.* Accompaniment was provided by a *khaen,* but by the 1970s a drum set was sometimes used with styles of song other than the usual *lam thang yao.* The stories performed were the same Lao epics and *jataka* stories sung by *mawlam phün,* read in *an nangsü,* and preached in *thet nithan.*

Troupes averaged about twenty-four persons, including actors, actresses, musicians, and staff. All actors and actresses played stock roles, including leading male and female, second male and female, parents, the enemy of the leading male, comedian, servants, and miscellaneous roles. Unlike *li-ke* (which improvised on a scenario), *lam mu* was played from a fully written script, though comedians could improvise topical routines. Consequently, there was little acting, with those engaged in singing or dialogue congregating around the hanging microphone, while the others tended to stand around with nothing to do. Most troupes were formed by young villagers seeking an opportunity for fame and fortune and a relief from the drudgery of farming rice and parenting children. Some became successful and wealthy, but most were rarely engaged and made little money. As with *lam klawn,* troupes could be engaged through *mawlam* associations, and all performances were free to audiences, since they were hired by donors, individual or collective (figure 50).

Between the mid-1970s and the late 1980s, *lam mu* underwent a transformation that involved greatly enlarging the troupe, adding numerous pop songs, adding Western brass and electrified stringed instruments, and especially in creating the *hang khrüang,* a troupe of young female dancers. The performance began with hours of pop songs danced by the *hang khrüang* and sung by star singers, followed only late in the night by some semblance of the story. With some troupes having more than one hundred musicians, singers, dancers, and stagehands (*khawn-woi* 'convoy') and requiring large trucks and buses, their cost became prohibitive, and consequently performance sites are surrounded by fences and an admission is charged. Young people dance near the stage, sometimes getting drunk and disrupting the performance with fights.

Lam ploen

Though *lam ploen* had a separate origin from *lam mu,* they soon came to resemble each other, visually but not musically. *Lam ploen* used not only *khaen* and *phin* but also a drum set and congas. Singing consisted of two types, a speech-rhythm introduction accompanied only by *khaen* and *phin* and the main body of the poem in meter, accompanied by all instruments, in the *yao* scale. The introduction, often performed behind the curtain, included the stock phrase *buet pha kang* 'open the curtain'. Like troupes performing *lam mu,* troupes performing *lam ploen* used stock characters and played from a script but tended to have more dancing because of the prevalence of drumming. Both kinds of theater traveled to Laos, but never took root there, though southern Lao singers can still perform excerpts from old-style *lam ploen* out of context.

In northeastern Thailand, *lam ploen* followed the same route as *lam mu*—expanding the troupe, adding Western instruments, electrifying instruments, and especially having a *hang khrüang* dance to *luk thung*—and as a result, these genres became nearly indistinguishable. Both of them have experienced decline in the

FIGURE 50 A performance of *lam mu* on a temporary stage on temple grounds in Mahasarakham. Photo by Terry E. Miller, 1973.

1990s, as they became too expensive and audiences shifted their attention to *lam sing,* which had most of their attractions but was much cheaper to produce.

Nang pra mo thai

Least known and little encountered is northeastern shadow-puppet theater. In the early 1970s, the last time it was closely studied, most troupes had derived their performance from a combination of central Thai music combined with southern Thai small puppets, but using northeastern comic characters speaking the local language. Accompaniment was provided, therefore, by a homemade xylophone (*ranat ek*), a drum, and cymbals, and the main story was the epic of Rama. A few troupes were entirely northeastern, using *khaen,* speaking and singing in the local language and playing a local story, especially the Lao epic *Sang sin sai.*

Lam phi fa

Though most Thai are Buddhists, they see no contradiction in maintaining age-old beliefs in spirits, both natural and human-derived ones. There are many local ways to deal with the world of spirits. Most involve an intermediary who either communicates with the spirits or becomes possessed by them. Only one kind involves music. It is known variously as *lam phi fa* 'sky spirit', *lam phi thaen* (the sky spirit's proper name), *lam thai thüng* 'group of spirits', and *lam song* 'to possess, to enter'. All the ritualists are women, who sing accompanied by a male *khaen* player. A *mawlam phi fa* troupe is called when someone remains ill and cannot be cured by a medical doctor (traditional or modern), and spirits are suspected. The troupe, consisting of anyone who has previously been cured in such a ritual, takes around a tray of ritual objects intended to attract spirits. While the *khaen* plays continuously in one of the *yao*-scale modes, the women sing loosely in *lam thang yao* style.

POPULAR MUSIC IN THAILAND

Thailand's rapidly expanding economy has produced astounding affluence, especially in the cities, which, for sophistication, rival those of Korea, Malaysia, and Taiwan. This is especially true of Bangkok, a city slowly choking to death on its own success—gridlock traffic jams; air, water, and noise pollution; and a reputation for vice.

Perhaps because the Thai never experienced colonization and therefore had no

By the 1950s, there were popular songs using both Thai classical and newly composed melodies accompanied by Western instruments. Sung by young men and women backed by a combo, these pieces were associated with the wealthier and most Westernized segments of Thai society.

axes to grind with Westerners, the Thai have had a long-running love affair with Western culture, originally from both Europe and the United States, later the Westernized popular culture of Hong Kong, Japan, and Taiwan. The development of popular music in Thailand can be traced to the introduction of Western music during the 1800s, especially from Great Britain and the United States (see POPULAR MUSIC AND CULTURAL POLITICS).

Brass bands

During the first half of the 1800s, Western military bands evidently accompanied some of the foreign missions sent to Bangkok. By 1874, the court was supporting a military band:

> After the parade His Majesty's own brass band played for us. There were sixteen instrumentalists, led by a sergeant major, a mere youngster seven or eight years old and three feet in height; indeed, none of the members of the band were more than twenty years of age; their uniform was the same as that worn by the guards. They played in remarkably good time and tune, first the "Siamese National Hymn," a rather pretty composition; and, second, a very familiar western waltz. Afterwards another band of musicians, who were older, but had had less practice, were ordered out, and they rendered a piece of dance music tolerably well. (Vincent 1874:152–153)

When Russian and German princes visited Siam in 1890 and 1899, respectively, they were welcomed by Siamese military bands. J. G. D. Campbell, who came as an educational adviser, wrote (1902:123) about the use of Western music in schools:

> [T]he creditable performances, too, by Siamese bands indicate that they cannot be altogether without aptitude for European music; though the boys and girls in the schools show such little evidence of talent for it that it is hardly worth the trouble of teaching them, and few of the Siamese who have been in Europe seem to have acquired any taste or love for it.

W. A. Graham (1912:467) said Bangkok supported several fine military bands whose performance of European tunes was quite acceptable by Western standards.

Prince Krom Phra Nakhawn Sawan Waraphinit, Supreme Commander of the Siamese Navy, was thoroughly trained in European music. Not surprisingly, the most important military band was that of the Siamese navy, whose musicians learned both performance and theory, but other military units also had bands. In the early 1900s, a Thai-American musician, Peter Feit, son of a German-born music teacher and a Thai mother, went to Bangkok, where, as a civil servant to the court, he received the honorific title Phra Chen Duriyanga. His monograph *Siamese Music in Theory and Practice as Compared with That of the West* (1947), a rationalization of Siamese music in Western terms, remains in print; many readers have assumed the author to be a native-born Thai musician.

The military-band heritage, while continuing in its own right, was also the starting point for both classical Western music and Thai popular music. Western classical music exists in modern Thailand, but it is restricted to the Bangkok elite and the expatriate community. The Bangkok Symphony Orchestra offers a brief season of concerts, supplemented by visits from foreign ensembles. It was not until the late 1970s that music degrees became established in a few universities, offering concentrations in both Western and Thai musics. Piano and violin remain favorite instruments; the Yamaha Corporation, a Japanese manufacturer of musical instruments, offers piano instruction at its franchised schools.

One result of the 1932 coup was a government-sponsored preference for Western culture over Thai culture. Besides requirements to wear hats and socks, and for men to kiss their wives when leaving for work, this program included the encouragement of social dancing, out of which grew *ramwong,* a circular social dance, using Thai-derived gestures of the hands, accompanied by Westernized Thai music. It remains the obligatory ending to Thai Night celebrations abroad.

In the early 1900s, military bands played arrangements of Thai classical compositions, but Western instruments (such as the pump organ, the accordion, the violin, and the piano) also joined the string ensemble (*khrüang sai,* then called *khrüang sai prasom* 'mixed ensemble'). To accommodate differences in concepts of tuning and pitch, performers considered the organ's B-flat key a Thai C, but differences between the seven-tone equidistance of Thai tuning and the twelve-tone equidistance of Western tuning remained problematic. Military-derived wind ensembles played for silent movies, often using action tunes (borrowed from Thai traditional theater), but the *khrüang sai prasom* played Westernized (that is, harmonized) Thai melodies during changes of reels. Brass bands also played for ballroom dancing.

The development of the modern popular song

An important development leading to Thai popular song was the composition of new texts for Thai classical melodies, resulting in what were called *phleng thai nua tem.* Unlike classical singing (which is melismatic), this new type had one syllable per note—syllabic text setting. By the 1950s, songs using both Thai classical and newly composed melodies accompanied by Western instruments were known as city-people songs (*phleng luk krung*). Mainly slow ballads crooned by young men and women backed by a combo that might include a violin, a saxophone, a trumpet, an accordion, and an electric organ, these pieces were associated with the wealthier and most Westernized segments of Thai society and accompanied ballroom dancing.

The "classical" form of the *phleng luk krung* was created by a small group of composers, the most important being Suntarapon, an employee of the Public Relations Department, whose name became synonymous with the genre. These old-style *phleng luk krung* are still favored by a small segment of Thai society, but with the rapid increase of the population and the growing affluence of the younger generation, American and British styles of popular music have come to the fore.

In the 1960s, British musicians such as Cliff Richard and the Shadows influenced Thai pop to the point that this music was known in Thai language as *shadow.* After that, American influence became dominant. The pirating of American recordings onto cheap cassette tapes quickly spread every new development from the West. A great array of magazines focusing on popular culture in general or popular music in particular are sold to the newly affluent younger generation, and some shops offer nothing but photos and other mementos of their latest heartthrobs. Generally known as *phleng sakon* 'modern songs', the current styles represent every American style from country to rap, though usually with a Thai flavor that removes their hard edges.

Social and political unrest since the mid-1970s—related to the Communist movement, uprisings against oppressive dictators, and the mass migration of country folk to Bangkok and the resulting growth of slums—gave rise to songs for life (*phleng phua chiwit*), a socially conscious genre, akin to the music of American folk styles of the 1950s and 1960s. The songs composed and performed by two groups in particular—Caravan and Carabao—commented on disillusionment with contemporary Thai society, environmental issues, political matters, and materialism.

For years, to impoverished sons and daughters living in the remote provinces of the north, the south, and the northeast, Bangkok looked like a pot of gold at the end of a rainbow. There they found work as taxi drivers, maids, and vendors, and in even less desirable occupations. Their musical heritage, the traditional musics of each region, became the basis for modernized songs generically known as *phleng luk thung* 'country-folk songs'. Looked down upon as rustics by their employers, homesick migrants could assert a kind of regional identity and pride through these songs.

Though *phleng luk thung* were created from the traditional musics of all regions, those of the northeast came to dominate. Being the poorest and most disparaged region, the northeast had the most to gain. Its people, more than others, knew both the poverty of their home villages and the slums in which they lived. Their songs came to have meaning for all Thai of similar experiences, and that success raised the prominence of northeastern *phleng luk thung* to a par with *phleng sakon.* As these now well-heeled youth returned to their home villages during holidays, they came to dictate musical taste, since they had the funds. With the rise of larger and larger touring *phleng luk thung* troupes and their dancing girls during the 1980s, the local traditional genres—*lam klawn* and its related theatrical genres, *lam mu* and *lam phloen*—declined or adapted to the situation by using more and more *phleng luk thung* (figure 51).

Traditional *lam klawn* had a brief burst of popularity in the late 1980s. About 1987, a modernized form, *lam sing,* was created by a singer in Chaiyapum as direct competition to *phleng luk thung* troupes. *Sing* means 'racing', or weaving a car with a loud stereo through Bangkok traffic, and its musical namesake not only goes fast but also features *khaen,* an electric *phin,* a drum set, and congas. The format and func-

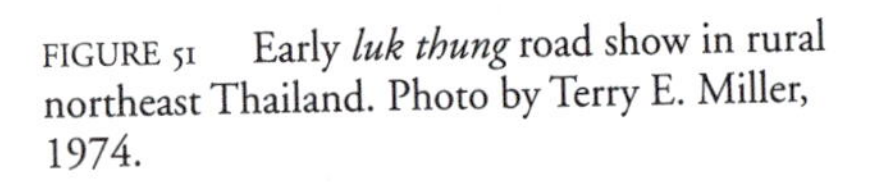
FIGURE 51 Early *luk thung* road show in rural northeast Thailand. Photo by Terry E. Miller, 1974.

tion—repartee between a pair of male and female singers—is traditional, but the mixing of traditional *lam* with *luk thung* and overall sound is modern and consequently attracts young people, including those who work in Bangkok.

Everyday life in modern Thailand is seemingly dominated by popular culture. Popular music is heard throughout the country—in hotels and restaurants, on the radio, on temporary stages in remote villages, on cassette tapes, and in music videos. And yet when Thai represent themselves and their culture to outsiders—tourists visiting the Rose Garden or their hosts at American universities—they universally choose Thai classical music, whether they otherwise prefer to listen to it or not. Thailand's heart may beat to the sounds of rock and modernized regional music, but its soul rejoices in its classical tradition.

REFERENCES

His Royal Highness Prince Bidyalankarana. 1926. "The Pastime of Rhyme-Making and Singing in Rural Siam." *Journal of the Siam Society* 20:101–127.

———. 1941. "Sebha Recitation and the Story of Khun Chang Khun Phan." *Journal of the Siam Society* 33:1–22.

Bouvet, Père. 1963 [1685]. *Voiage de Siam du Père Bouvet,* edited by J. C. Gatty. Leiden: E. J. Brill.

Bowring, John. 1969 [1857]. *The Kingdom and People of Siam.* Kuala Lumpur: Oxford University Press.

Campbell, J. G. D. 1902. *Siam in the Twentieth Century.* London: Edward Arnold.

Choisy, [François Timoléon,] L'Abbé de. 1687. *Journal du voyage de Siam fait en 1685 et 1686 par M. l'Abbé de Choisy.* Paris: Chez Sebastien.

Crawfurd, John. 1967 [1828]. *Journal of an Embassy from the Governor-General of India to the Courts of Siam and Cochin China.* Kuala Lumpur: Oxford University Press.

Dhanit Yupho. 1957. *Nangsü khrüang dontri thai* (Book of Thai musical instruments). Bangkok: Fine Arts Department.

———. 1960. *Thai Musical Instruments.* Translated by David Morton. Bangkok: Fine Arts Department.

———. 1963. *The Khon and Lakon.* Bangkok: Fine Arts Department.

———. 1971. *Book of Thai Musical Instruments.* 2nd ed. Translated by David Morton. Bangkok: Fine Arts Department.

———. 1987. *Nangsü khrüang dontri thai / Book of Thai Musical Instruments,* combination reprint of Dhanit Yupho 1957 and 1971, with new illustrations. Bangkok: Fine Arts Department.

Duangjai Thewtong. 1984. "Village Music in Central Thailand: A Field Study of Mooban Pohuk." M.A. thesis, Kent State University.

Ellis, Alexander J. 1885a. "On the Musical Scales of Various Nations." *Journal of the Society of Arts* 33:485–527.

———. 1885b. "Appendix to Mr. Alexander J. Ellis's Paper on 'The Musical Scales of Various Nations' read 25th March, 1885." *Journal of the Society of Arts* 33:1102–11.

Finlayson, George. 1826. *The Mission to Siam and Hue the Capital of Cochin China in the Years 1821–2.* London: John Murray.

Fuller, Paul. 1979. Review of *The Traditional Music of Thailand,* by David Morton. *Ethnomusicology* 23(2):339–343.

Gervaise, Nicolas. 1688. *Histoire naturelle et politique du Royaume de Siam.* Paris: Claude Barbin.

Gerini, G. E. 1912. *Siam and Its Productions, Arts, and Manufactures.* N.p.: no publisher.

Ginsberg, Henry D. 1972. "The Manohra Dance-Drama: An Introduction." *Journal of the Siam Society* 60:169–181.

Glanius, Mr. 1682. *A New Voyage to the East-Indies,* 2nd ed. London: H. Rodes.

Graham, W[alter]. A[rmstrong]. 1912. *Siam: A Handbook of Practical, Commercial, and Political Information.* London: Alexander Moring.

Gutzlaff, Charles. 1834. *Journal of Three Voyages along the Coast of China in 1831, 1832, & 1833.* London: Frederick Westley and A. H. Davis.

Hipkins, A. J. 1945 [1888]. *Musical Instruments Historic, Rare, and Unique.* London: A. and C. Black.

Hornbostel, Erich M. von. 1920. "Formanalysen an siamesischen Orchesterstücken." *Archiv für Musikwissenschaft* 2:306–333.

Jarernchai Chonpairot. 1970. *Prawat nakdontri thai* (Lives of Thai composers). Bangkok: privately published.

La Loubere, Simon de. 1691. *Du Royaume de Siam.* Paris: Jean-Baptiste Coignard.

———. 1969 [1693]. *A New Historical Relation of the Kingdom of Siam.* Kuala Lumpur: Oxford University Press.

Landon, Margaret. 1944. *Anna and the King of Siam.* New York: John Day.

Lebar, Frank M., Gerald C. Hickey, and John K. Musgrave. 1964. *Ethnic Groups of Mainland Southeast Asia.* New Haven, Conn.: Human Relations Area Files Press.

Léonowens, Anna Harriette. 1870. *The English Governess at the Siamese Court.* Boston: Fields, Osgood.

Mendes Pinto, Fernão. 1663 [1558]. *The Voyages and Adventures of Ferdinand Mendez Pinto* [*Peregrinação*]. Translated by H. C. Gent. London: J. Macock.

Mendes Pinto, Fernão. 1952–1953 [1614]. *Peregrinação* [*Texto primitivo, inteiramente conforme á primeira edicão (1614) versão integral en Português moderno por Adolfo Casais Monteiro*]. Lisbon: Sociedade de Intercâmrio culturai. Rio de Janeiro: Livraria-editora.

Miller, Terry E. 1992. "The Theory and Practice of Thai Musical Notations." *Ethnomusicology* 36(2):197–222.

———. 1985. *Traditional Music of the Lao: Kaen Playing and Mawlum Singing in Northeast Thailand.* Contributions in Intercultural and Comparative Studies, 13. Westport, Conn., and London: Greenwood Press.

Miller, Terry E., and Jarernchai Chonpairot. 1981. "The Ranat and Bong-Lang: The Question of Origin of the Thai Xylophones." *Journal of the Siam Society* 69:145–163.

———. 1994. "A History of Siamese Music Reconstructed from Western Documents, 1505–1932." *Crossroads* 8:1–192.

Morton, David. 1976. *The Traditional Music of Thailand.* Berkeley: University of California Press.

Neale, Frederick Arthur. 1852. *Narrative of a Residence at the Capital of the Kingdom of Siam.* London: Offices of the National Illustrated Library.

———. 1985. *Narrative of a Residence at the Capital of the Kingdom of Siam.* Bangkok: White Lotus.

Nicolas, René. 1927. "Le Théâtre d'Ombres au Siam." *Journal of the Siam Society* 21:37–51.

Panya Roongrüang. 1973. *Prawat kan dontri thai* (History of Thai music). Bangkok: Thai Wattana Panit.

———. 1990. *Thai Music in Sound.* Bangkok: author. Book and three cassettes.

Picken, L. E. R., C. J. Adkins, and T. F. Page. 1984. "The Making of a *Khāen:* The Free-Reed Mouth-Organ of North-East Thailand." *Musica Asiatica* 4:117–154.

Pratuan Charoenchitt, ed. N.d. *Dontri phün ban lae silapa kan sadaeng khawng thai* (Folk music and traditional performing arts of Thailand). Bangkok: Office of the National Culture Commission, Ministry of Education.

Roberts, Edmund. 1837. *Embassy to the Eastern Courts of Cochin-China, Siam, and Muscat; in the U.S. Sloop of War Peacock.* New York: Harper and Brothers.

Ruschenberger, W. S. W. 1970 [1838]. *Narrative of a Voyage around the World, during the Years 1835, 1836, and 1837.* 2 vols. London: Dawsons of Pall Mall.

Schouten, Joost. 1663 [1636]. *A True Description of the Mighty Kingdoms of Japan and Siam.* Translated by Roger Manley. London.

Smithies, Michael. 1971. "Likay: A Note on the Origin, Form, and Future of Siamese Folk Opera." *Journal of the Siam Society* 59:33–64.

Smithies, Michael, and Euayporn Kerdchouay. 1972. "Nang Talung: The Shadow Theatre of Siam." *Journal of the Siam Society* 60:377–387.

Stumpf, Carl. 1901. "Tonsystem und Musik der Siamesen." *Beiträge zur Akustik und Musikwissenschaft* 3:69–138.

[Tachard, Guy.] 1686. *Voyage de Siam des Pères Jésuites.* Paris: Senueze et Horthemels.

Tachard, Guy. 1688. *A Relation of the Voyage to Siam Performed by Six Jesuits.* London: J. Robinson and A. Churchill.

Tambiah, S. J. 1970. *Buddhism and the Spirit Cults in North-East Thailand.* Cambridge: Cambridge University Press.

Tanese-Ito, Yoko. 1988. "Taikoku koten kakyoku ni okeru kasi no seichou to uta no senritu tono kankei" (The relationship between speech tones and vocal melody in Thai court song). D.M. dissertation, Tokyo National University of Fine Arts and Music.

Terwiel, B. J. 1979. *Monks and Magic: An Analysis of Religious Ceremonies in Central Thailand.* 2nd ed. Bangkok: Curzon Press.

Thompson, P. A. 1910. *Siam: An Account of the Country and the People.* Boston: J. B. Millet.

Turpin, M. [François Henri]. 1771. *Histoire civile et naturelle du Royaume de Siam . . . jusqu'en 1770.* 2 vols. Paris: Costard.

Verney, Frederick. 1885. *Notes on Siamese Musical Instruments.* London: William Clowes and Sons.

Vichitr Vadakarn, (Luang) V. 1942. *The Evolution of Thai Music.* Bangkok: Fine Arts Department.

Vincent, Frank, Jr. 1874. *The Land of the White Elephant.* New York: Harper and Brothers.

Wells, Kenneth E. 1975. *Thai Buddhism: Its Rites and Activities.* Bangkok: Suriyabun.

Wong, Deborah Anne. 1991. "The Empowered Teacher: Ritual, Performance, and Epistemology in Contemporary Bangkok." Ph.D. dissertation, University of Michigan.

Wyatt, David K. 1984. *Thailand: A Short History.* New Haven, Conn.: Yale University Press.

Young, Ernest. 1898. *The Kingdom of the Yellow Robe.* Westminster, England: Archibald Constable.

Laos

Terry E. Miller

Since the majority populations of both the Lao People's Democratic Republic (hereafter, Laos or PDR Laos) and northeastern Thailand are culturally related, their musics have much in common. But because of different political histories, the Lao-speakers in each area have become distinct in many ways, including in music. The Lao of Laos are economically far poorer than the Lao across the Mekong River, whose orientation is toward Bangkok, its modernization, and its dramatic growth.

Laos is a landlocked, mostly mountainous nation of 236,800 square kilometers. It shares a long, mountainous border with Vietnam on the east, and an equally long border with Thailand on the west and southwest, with the Mekong River marking about half of the boundary. Formerly, the Lao controlled part of what is now Cambodia in the south, and Lao-speakers lived there at least until 1975. In the northwest, Laos shares borders with China and Burma in an area known as the Golden Triangle.

Less than 4 percent of the land is arable, with much of the remainder in forest or meadow, mostly on hills or mountains. Consequently, Laos has always had a low population density. With an estimated 1996 population of about 4.9 million, the population density is only twenty persons per square kilometer. The Lao government estimates income at about U.S.$135 per capita, qualifying Laos for Fourth World status—among the world's poorest nations. This status is reflected in Lao life expectancy: fifty years for men, fifty-three years for women.

Most of the nation's people live in the lowlands (primarily in the Vientiane plain), along the Mekong River, and in isolated pockets in valleys and along tributary rivers. Because Laos became part of French Indochina in the late 1800s, its cultural-political orientation was francophile, isolating it from its neighbor, Siam (now Thailand), which was under Siamese, not northeastern Lao, dominance. Because of border disputes with Thailand following the 1975 Communist coup, the free interchange of culture and commerce normal when Laos was the Kingdom of a Million Elephants was severely restricted, leaving Laos economically isolated from the Thai, yet dominated by their media; Thai television and radio stations reach deeply into Laos. Although musical culture in Laos remains conservative, the main factor resisting rapid modernization on the Thai model is simple poverty.

Despite an exceptionally low population density, the musics of Laos are strikingly diverse. Isolation, stemming from both linguistic and geographical barriers, preserves these differences.

Ethnically, Laos is a multicultural mosaic, consisting of 50 percent lowland Lao and 50 percent upland Tai, Mon-Khmer, and Tibeto-Burman language groups. Theravada Buddhists, the lowland Lao remain the dominant people despite the Communist Party's claims to equality for all people. Although some upland groups are said to be Buddhist, most are animist. Buddhism appears to be weak in Laos, with limited activity at even the greatest temples.

The Lao view their population in three groups: *Lao Lum,* lowland Lao; *Lao Theung*, the tribal Tai and Mon-Khmer, who dwell at lower or mid-elevations; and *Lao Sung*, mostly Hmong and Yao, who usually live at the highest elevations. These terms were created by the Socialist government to replace the derogatory term *Kha* (slave), formerly reserved for uplanders.

After 1975, the new Socialist government reorganized the country into sixteen provinces (*khwaeng*) and one municipality (*kampheng nakhon*), Vientiane, the capital. The nation's largest city, with a population officially just under half a million, Vientiane is one of the world's quietest and least densely populated capitals. Two other cities are quite modest in size: the former royal capital at Luang Phrabang, and Savannakhet. Infrastructure is primitive by any standards, and communications among population pockets limited or nonexistent. The nation has about 13,000 kilometers of roads, only 4,000 kilometers of which are described as all-weather; there are no railroads. While many provinces lack electricity, or have it for only a few hours per day in the provincial capitals, Laos is a major exporter of electricity from its Ngeum River dam. A newly constructed bridge over the Mekong at Vientiane, opened in 1994, ended Laos's historically islandlike isolation, created by rivers and mountains. Because of the factors above, Lao music has remained regional, and shows little outside influence.

Lao has no comprehensive term corresponding to *music* in English. Sanskrit-derived terms such as *dontri*, *turiya*, and *maholi* appear in old Lao literature but are primarily limited to court instrumental music. The modern term *dontri* continues to denote Lao classical music and Western music of any kind, but other kinds of traditional "music" are denoted with verbs differentiating their manner of performance: *khap* 'to recite', *lam* 'to sing', *kom* 'to lull', *suat* or *sut* 'to recite ritualistically', *seung* 'to chant responsorially', *wao* 'to court or speak', *an* 'to read a manuscript in heightened speech', and so forth.

Despite an exceptionally low population density, the musics of Laos are strikingly diverse. Isolation, stemming from both linguistic and geographical barriers, preserves these differences. Musically, Laos is among the least-researched nations in the world—not surprisingly, considering its linguistic diversity, the natural inhibitors to travel and communication, underdevelopment, its being virtually closed to outsiders from 1975 until about 1990, and governmental restrictions on everyone's movements (most especially researchers') until 1994. Add to this the fact that few scholars have paid attention to Lao music, and it is no wonder that a Lao-music bibliography

Laos

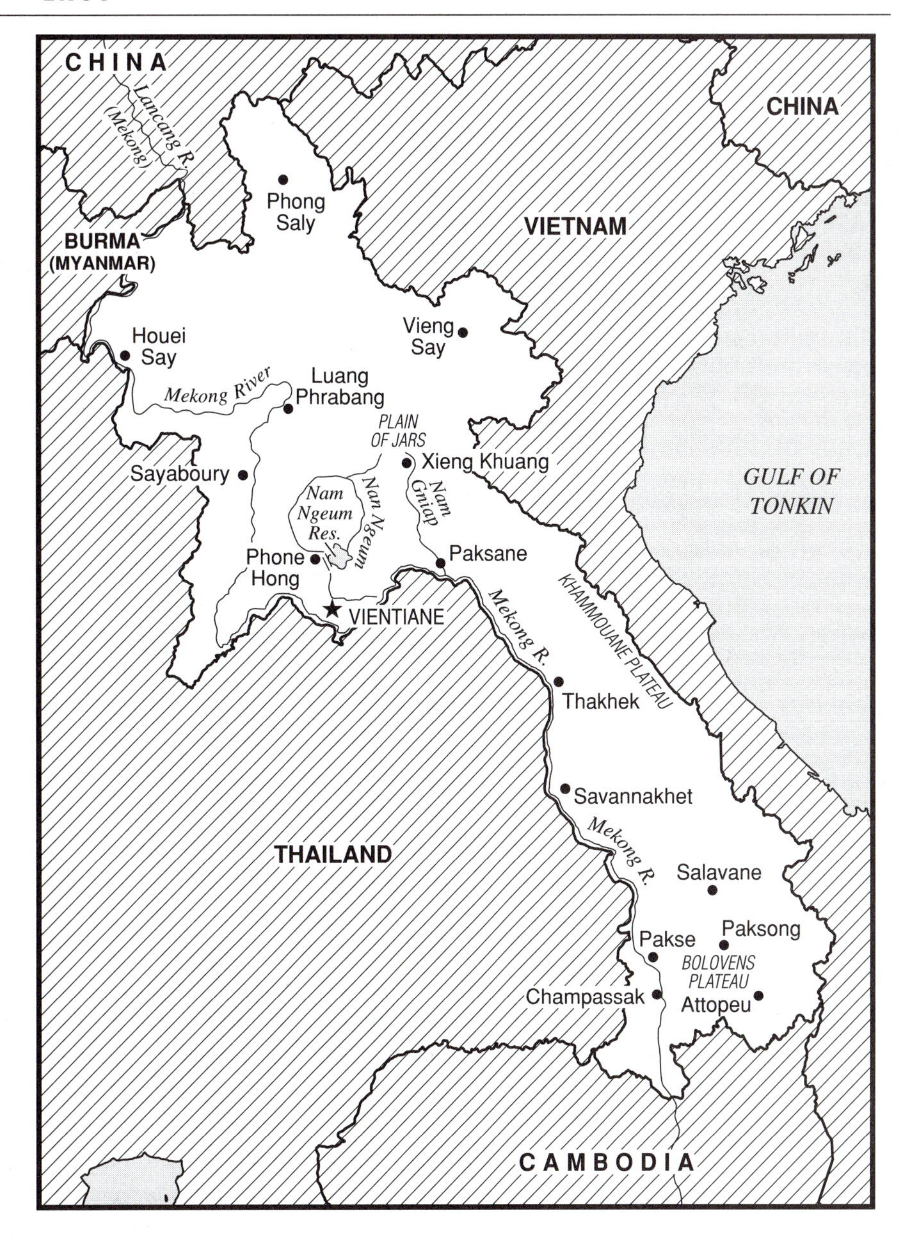

would be brief indeed. Within Laos there are few scholars, with only one approaching the status of a music specialist. From outside Laos, a few French visitors and officials wrote brief articles, most often of a romanticized nature, during the colonial period (before 1949), and only a few others have written anything on the subject since. I was the first to have done systematic fieldwork in Laos (1991), and one American student, Therese Mahoney, has researched the contemporary classical music of Vientiane. Dr. Jarernchai Chonpairot, a Thai scholar from northeastern Thailand, has written a dissertation (1990) on one Lao vocal genre, *lam khon savan.* Some years earlier, Dr. Carol Compton published a detailed study (1979) of a poetic text of *lam som* from the Champassak area. Consequently, this article remains incomplete and often tentative.

At this point, it remains impossible to write a comprehensive overview of upland musics, for no upland group's music has been studied systematically on site. The issue is further complicated by the fact that many ethnic groups only live partially within Laos: many, especially the Tai-speaking groups, straddle the borders with Vietnam and the People's Republic of China. Cultural policies in the latter have affected music and dance, but the border area between Vietnam and Laos is extremely remote. The Hmong constitute a significant minority in Laos, but they also live in China and Thailand, making nation-based studies problematic. Certain groups, such as the Kmhmu, have been studied extensively by anthropologists, none of whom has undertaken a systematic treatment of music. Few recordings are commercially available. Consequently, the emphasis in this study is lowland Lao music.

This article follows a French-derived romanization with modifications by R. Marcus. This, however, creates a problem when comparing Lao terms with those used in northeast Thailand [see THAILAND], since the latter are romanized differently. Both spellings appear in the glossary and the index.

NONCLASSICAL MUSIC

Instrumental music

In Laos, most classical and village instruments—those of the upland minorities excepted—have parallels in Thailand. The classical instruments differ little from those of Thailand, and village instruments have counterparts in northeastern Thailand, a culturally Lao region.

Though fipple flutes (*khui*), plucked lutes (*phin, kachappi*), and fiddles (*so, so i*) are found here and there—more in the south than in the north—the free-reed mouth organ (*khene*) is the predominant melodic instrument in rural Laos. Whereas the instrument with sixteen pipes predominates in Thailand, the *khene chet* with fourteen tubes was usual in Laos until the late twentieth century. Variants of the *khene* are used by specific groups: the Kmhmu use one with twelve pipes and an extended tail on the wind chest; the Phuan people in Xiengkhuang, and possibly the Kmhmu there and elsewhere, use one with fourteen pipes—one of which is mute—and having its own order of tones (figure 1). When the lowland instrument has eight pairs, the highest pair is g′ (L–8) and a′ (R–8). L–2 of the Phuan instrument is mute. Though *khene* are made in Laos, respondents in the 1970s reported that most instruments used in Laos were either imported from northeastern Thailand or made by makers from that region (figure 2).

Related to the *khene* is the single free-reed pipe with holes for fingering, used by Thai Dam (Black Tai, so called because of the prevalence of black in their clothing). It has two sizes, larger (*pi luang*) and smaller (*pi bap*). Similar instruments are found elsewhere in Laos but are uncommon. In northeastern Thailand, these pipes are associated with the Phuthai, who earlier migrated from southern Laos.

Idiophones and membranophones are few but important. The vertical slit drum (*dung lung*), famous in northeastern Thailand (where it is called *pong lang*), is rare in Laos. Variously shaped two-headed laced drums played with the hands are called *kong*, and the smaller and larger cymbals similar to those of classical Thai music are pronounced in the Lao manner (as *sing* and *sap*). Single-headed longdrums called

FIGURE 1 The order of tones in three Lao free-reed mouth organs. Transcription by Terry E. Miller.

Lowland Lao *khene*		Phuan *khene*		Khmu *khene*	
Left	Right	Left	Right	Left	Right
f′	e′	f′	d′	e′	d′
g	d′	g	d′	g	d′
f	b	f	a	f	a
e	a	e	a	e	g
d	g	d	g	d	c
B	c	–	c	c′	A
c′	A	c′	A		

FIGURE 2 Three musicians from Salavane in southern Laos play music for *lam salavane* on, left to right, the *khene*, the *phin*, and the *so i*. Photo by Terry E. Miller, 1991.

kong nyao are commonly seen in processions. An idiophone distinct to the southern Lao is a clapper-scraper (*mai ngop ngep*); the player claps together two hinged pieces of wood about 30 centimeters long and scrapes a block of wood over the teeth cut into the lower piece.

Manufacture and tuning

The manufacture of instruments occurs on a small scale in isolated villages throughout the country. In Vientiane, private shops make mostly poor-quality instruments for sale to tourists in overstocked and underpatronized souvenir shops. On Luang Phrabang Road, the Lao government operates a small factory, State Enterprise of Cultural Production, where young craftsmen make *khene*, classical bowed lutes and xylophones, *phin*, drums, and guitars (*gida*), sold in their shop, or to other shops.

The tuning of traditional Lao music, like that of northeastern Thailand, is based on the *khene*, which has seven tones per octave, in intervals that match closely those of Western diatonic tuning: A–B–c–d–e–f–g. Higher tones on the *khene* duplicate these at the octave. Though few players of *khene* in Laos commonly use the theoretical terms known to players in northeastern Thailand, the same principles apply. Thus, northeastern Thai theoretical terminology will serve in reference to Lao styles.

Two basic pentatonic scalar systems derive from this tuning: one, called the *san* scale, sounds major, and is expressible as starting on G (G–A–C–D–E); the other, called the *yao* (sometimes pronounced *nyao* in Lao) scale, sounds minor, and is expressible as starting on A (A–C–D–E–G). On a *khene,* the *san* scale can be played in three modes, and the *yao* scale can be played in two. In northeastern Thailand, *san* modes (with starting tone in parentheses) are called *lai sutsanaen* (G), *lai po sai* (C), and *lai soi* (D), and *yao* modes are called *lai yai* or *lai nyai* (A) and *lai noi* (D) [for a fuller explanation of *khene* music, see THAILAND: Northeastern Thailand].

Styles of playing

As in northeastern Thailand, Lao players of *khene* sometimes play solo, but they do so less commonly and with less virtuosity than across the Mekong. Terminology used for titles varies widely. Among Lao players, *thang* 'style, way' replaces *lai*, and qualify-

khene Free-reed bamboo mouth organ, main instrument of Laos

lam Traditional vocal genres of southern Laos

khap Traditional vocal genres of central and northern Laos

seung pong fai Responsorial singing in the streets during the rocket festival

ing terms may refer to regional vocal genres (such as *thang savannakhet*), techniques (such as *thit sut noi* 'to plug' [with *khisut* wax] high d′ or a′), function (such as *pheng nang thiam*, for a spirit-related ceremony), or allude to extramusical images (such as *mae hang kom luk* 'the widow sings a lullaby to her child').

Solo playing named after regional genres is usually an accompaniment style played alone, but the patterns performed are inconsistent among players. The titles of Lao music for the *khene* show little consistency from region to region. One player in Salavane differentiated twelve local styles, according to ethnic group, technique, and even the stories they were said to represent. Players were also aware of, and often played, the styles of northeastern Thailand, including *lot fai tay lang* 'the train runs along the track'—clearly imported, since Laos has no railroads.

The primary function of the *khene* is to accompany singing. It is said that a fully qualified player must know thirty-two varieties of song but that knowing fifteen to eighteen is acceptable. Each regional vocal genre has a distinct accompaniment in mode, rhythm, and melodic traits, but variations among players are normal. To accommodate the tessituras of male and female voices, players must be able to accompany in at least two modes of each scale (*san* and *yao*). Rather than using the modal names known in northeastern Thailand, Lao players call the lower-pitched mode of each scale *nyai* 'great' and the higher-pitched mode *noi* 'small'.

Vocal music

The names of regional vocal genres are preceded by either *khap* or *lam*, but though both denote song, neither is used in reference to singing Lao classical music or Westernized music. Most genres called *lam* or *khap* are in repartee: in a battle of the sexes, alternating male and female singers feign courtship, or even trade insults.

Chonpairot believes the old Thai term *khap lam nam* 'to sing' was shortened to *khap* in northern Laos, and to *lam* in both southern Laos and northeastern Thailand; Lao scholars believe the difference is determined by the kind of poetry used, *lam* using *kon on* (with seven syllables per line) and *khap* using *kon khap* (with four or five per line). Since a skilled practitioner is called *mo*, a singer is *mokhap* or *molam*, and a player of a *khene* is *mokhene*.

Rituals

Two types are known in southern Laos, *lam phi fa* and *lam soen*, each associated with rituals of healing and possession. *Lam phi fa* 'singing [to invite the] spirit of the sky' (also called *lam phi thai* and *lam phi thaen*) occurs when a patient who does not respond to either traditional or modern medicines is thought to have become ill because spirits have been offended. Ritualists, usually older women accompanied by a *khene*, sing to invite the offended spirits to enter their bodies and reveal the cause of the illness, while the patient observes. The ritual occurs in a home around an assortment of ritual objects (*khreuang bucha*), and may last several hours. A *molam seun* (a ritualist) ministers to a sick person whose *khuan* (a kind of soul or spiritual essence) has left. Singing the melody of the genre *lam som*, the ritualist uses magic formulas to call this essence back.

An important ritual, practiced in many rural areas of Laos, is the sacrifice of the buffalo. Charles Archaimbault (1991), who has published a detailed study of the sacrifices of various ethnic groups in the Xiengkhuang (or S'ieng Khwang) area, says little about music associated with the rite. Jacques Brunet (1992 [1973]) included on a compact disc an example of music from the sacrifice at Vat Phu (south of Champassak) which has a small ensemble of hand-held gongs, some beaten with the hands, some with sticks, accompanying a vocalist-ritualist. This ritual, part of the spring festival, is attended by lowland Lao and uplanders from the Boloven Plateau, and entertainment music is provided by the classical *piphat* of Champassak.

Of animistic origin, the rocket festival (*pong fai*) is important in much of southern Laos and northeastern Thailand. During the hot, dry months preceding the monsoon rains—April, May, sometimes as late as June—villagers prepare long, highly decorated, powder-filled rockets (essentially phallic symbols), which they launch to break the clouds and tell the deity of the sky (*phayah thaen*) to send rain. Associated with the festival are parades, which include both dancing accompanied by long drums (*kong nyao*) and responsorial singing in the streets, often by drunken revelers begging for whiskey and money; this genre is *seung pong fai*.

Entertainment

The Lao have at least twelve named and widely acknowledged regional genres, some designated by a provincial name (such as *lam salavane*), some after a village (such as *lam tang vay*), and some after an ethnic group (such as *khap thai dam*). Five genres whose names are preceded by *khap* are found in the north, mostly in pockets separated by rugged mountains. In these areas, infrequent communication results in distinctness and specialization: singers of one *khap* genre do not normally sing any other. The *khap* genres are *khap ngeum* (after the Ngeum River Valley, north and northeast of Vientiane), *khap thum luang phrabang* (from the former royal capital of Luang Phrabang), *khap phuan* (named for the Lao Phuan, a branch of the lowland Lao, living in Xiengkhuang Province), *khap sam neua* (after the village of Sam Neua, Houaphanh Province), and *khap thai dam* (after the "tribal Tai" living in north-central Laos).

Seven genres with names preceded by *lam* are found in the south. Since these genres originate in the lowland areas along or near the Mekong River and its major tributaries, intercommunication is possible. As a result, southern Lao singers usually know more than one local genre and *lam klawn*, a northeastern Thai genre, called *lam kawn* or *lam tat* in Laos. Before 1975, because musicians could travel freely between Laos and northeastern Thailand, genres from the latter area became known in Laos. After 1975, with thousands of Lao in northeastern Thai refugee camps, the converse became true.

These genres are *lam sithandone* (or *lam siphandone*), from southern Champassak Province (before 1975, named Sithandone Province); *lam som,* from the same area; *lam saravane,* from Saravane Province; *lam ban xok,* from a village of that name a few kilometers from the city of Savannakhet; *lam tang vay,* after a village 95 kilometers southeast of Savannakhet; *lam khon savan,* from Savannakhet Province; *lam mahaxay,* after the town of Mahaxay, Khammouane Province; and *lam phu thai,* after the Phu Thai people, living in various parts of the south. *Lam sithandone* and some genres from the Savannakhet area most closely resemble genres found in northeastern Thailand.

Besides regional genres, three other genres occur but less commonly. In *lam nithan* (also called *lam puen* and *lam leuang*), a soloist accompanied by a *khene* sings epic-length tales, especially those derived from Buddhist *sathaka* (stories of Buddha's previous births), such as *Kalaket.* The term *lam leuang* once meant the same but later denoted a theatrical genre from northeastern Thailand, also called *lam mu.* Troupes from the northeast formerly crossed the river to perform, and a few troupes were also formed in Laos. Through the addition of pop songs and troupes of dancing girls, mostly in place of the original story, *lam mu* in the northeast has changed beyond recognition, but the Lao government has preserved *lam leuang* theater to promote socialist policies. Evidently, northeastern *lam ploen* troupes also came to Laos, for many southern singers still perform old-style *lam ploen* outside theatrical contexts. Few still remember its origin as theater and do not know that the genre has since changed beyond recognition in the northeast. *Lam kae* 'answering singing' denotes a format wherein singers question each other on subjects including Buddhism, history, and other kinds of knowledge. *Lam top phanya* denotes local genres sung only by a man and answered by a woman who speaks (*wao*) poetry of courting (*phanya*).

Performances of traditional music occur in conjunction with several kinds of events, including calendrical and Buddhist rites and national festivals. Among the most important are *bun song kan* 'water-throwing festival' during the fifth lunar month (April), *bun bang fai* 'rocket festival' during the sixth lunar month (May), *bun kathin* 'festival of presenting gifts to monks' during the twelfth lunar month (November), for ordinations, temple fairs, the New Year, and certain national holidays. Other important events where singers may be hired include the rite celebrating a new house, weddings, cremations, ceremonies for the deceased, and *bun phawet*; the latter is a festival in which the life of Prince Vetsandone, the penultimate life of the Buddha before enlightenment, is read in heightened speech over a one- or two-day period.

The principles that govern the creation of *khap* and *lam* are virtually the same as those pertaining to northeastern Thai *lam.* Poetry is composed in four-line stanzas in *kawn* form, with a fixed lexical-tonal pattern. The coordination of melodic pattern and lexical tone is necessary for full comprehension, but in practice, singers do not rigidly apply melodic formulas: they allow musical phrases and their individuality to override total coordination. Whereas northeastern Thai *lam klawn* has three sections—*lam thang san, lam thang yao, lam toei*—each Lao genre uses just one basic melodic pattern throughout the performance. In performance, some singers restrict themselves to a single local genre (the normal pattern in northern Laos), but southern Lao singers typically offer two or more types, including *lam klawn.* Since the Lao spoken in each region of Laos varies in tonal pattern, any one singer has difficulty knowing many tonal patterns. Consequently, the Lao distinguish between singers who are of the tradition and singers who have learned it as outsiders. Tonal inflections allow native speakers to detect when a singer is not of the region.

Lao singers traditionally perform in smaller, more intimate settings than do northeastern Thai singers. As was true until the mid-twentieth century in the northeast, many Lao singers still perform seated, executing the simple gestures of the dance (*fon*) from the waist up. The player of the *khene* is seated behind or to one side of the singer. Much slower than genres from across the Mekong, Lao genres give singers time to think of variant patterns to individualize the memorized poems. Average Lao singers repeat their poems with little or no change, having learned them by rote rather than from written form; but the most skilled can create poetry as they sing. Since Lao genres also permit breaks between couplets or stanzas (covered by the *khene*), singers have time to formulate new lines. A typical example, whether sung alone, or as part of a round in alternation with a singer of the opposite sex, lasts from about three to ten minutes.

The traditional singer (*molam*) holds a special position in Lao society, not as a professional but as a person knowledgeable about culture, history, behavior, Buddhism, stories, and courtship. Villagers, however, are somewhat ambivalent about the status of *molam*, since their feigned courtship on stage opens opportunities not available to ordinary people. However, unlike the case in Thailand, few Lao *molam* have achieved star status, and consequently the "stigma of the stage" is only nominal. Also in contrast to the northeastern Thai singers, Lao *molam* receive low monetary rewards, are (or at least were) often illiterate, and have few opportunities for performance, stemming in large part from the low population density and limits on travel.

During the civil war in Vietnam (which involved Laos), the Lao army gave *molam* the rank of sergeant, to teach and entertain troops. In Vientiane, the Lao Military Radio Station broadcast *lam* of many kinds with government propaganda embedded in the texts. The use of *lam* to propagate policies in Laos goes back at least to 1957, when the United States Information Service recruited singers and players of the *khene* from northeastern Thailand to mock the Pathet Lao in the earthy images of *lam* poetry.

Regional genres

Since Lao singers perform specific, named regional genres, each genre is distinct in some way. For the novice listener, most of the southern *lam* types may sound alike. Each type, however, is distinguished in several ways, some of which—including regional tonal inflections and subtle ways of handling text—are unlikely to be noted by outsiders. The following descriptions focus on musical elements discernible to any sensitive listener. These include accompanimental instruments, whether accompaniment or voice is declaimed or metrical, scale or mode; typical melodic motives; and other idiosyncratic features. Most descriptions are based on an adequate number of samples, but some of the northern genres are so underresearched that few samples exist. Commercial tapes available in Laos provide a poor substitute for on-site recordings, especially since *khap* recordings are scarce.

Lam sithandone. Also called *lam siphandon* 'four thousand islands', this genre is most similar to Ubon-style *lam klawn* in northeastern Thailand. Only the *khene* has been found to accompany this type, playing any of the *san*-scale modes (discussed above) in a manner indistinguishable from the style of players in northeastern Thailand—that is, using a sixteen-pipe instrument and in meter. The singer, however, declaims the poetry, though brief passages become regular in accent. Each time the singer begins a round, an introduction, usually with stereotypical phrases, descends melismatically to a cadence on the tonic, the lowest and final tone of the scale. Then the singer leads into the main body of the poem from the tone a sixth above the "tonic," rising a fourth. What makes this passage striking is its suggestion of a shift to the *yao* scale. Indeed, throughout, the singing emphasizes these tones (figures 3 and 4).

Lam som. Said to be named after a river and found on and around Khong Island in the Mekong in southern Champassak Province, *lam som* is the rarest of the Lao genres. In the 1970s, when Carol Compton did fieldwork, only four or five singers

FIGURE 3 Typical passages in *lam sithandone*, in *lai soi* mode: *a*, accompaniment; *b*, voice in declamatory rhythm. Transcription by Terry E. Miller.

The traditional singer (*molam*) holds a special position in Lao society, not as a professional but as a person knowledgeable about culture, history, behavior, Buddhism, stories, and courtship.

FFIGURE 4 Male and female singers, accompanied by a *khene*, sing *lam sithandone* in the old recording studio of the former building of the United States Agency for International Development in Pakse, Laos. Photo by Terry E. Miller, 1991.

were known to be active (Compton 1979). By 1991, *lam som* evidently survived in the repertoire of only one singer, Duangpheng, a female *molam* living in Pakse. Of all the southern *lam* types, only *lam som* does not appear on commercial cassettes. Like *lam sithandone,* which shares the same area, *lam som* is accompanied only by a *khene*, which plays slow, metrical patterns in a variant of the *yao* scale, having a sixth tone, one just above the tonic (A–B–c–d–e–g); in northeastern Thailand, this is called *lai nyai lam phoen*, after the narrative genre it accompanied. The singer, however, declaims the text in rhythms that rarely relate to those of the *khene*. Both singer and accompaniment emphasize tones A, B, and d at cadences, imparting a quality that makes *lam som* immediately distinctive (figure 5).

Lam salavane. Salavane Province's population includes many Mon-Khmer upland groups, principally the Loven (also called Boloven, the name of the plateau), the Lovae, and the Tau-oi, plus some lowland Lao. In lower elevations along the major rivers, the Mon-Khmer population has adopted the lowland Lao life-style. *Lam salavane* is a Lao-language genre, sung by both Lao and Mon-Khmer but derived from Mon-Khmer styles. Instrumental accompaniment varies from solo *khene* to an ensemble that includes lute, fiddle, flute, drum, and other small percus-

FIGURE 5 Typical introductory patterns for *khene* in *lam som*. Transcription by Terry E. Miller.

FIGURE 6 Typical accompaniment patterns in *lai noi* for *lam salavane.* Transcription by Terry E. Miller.

FIGURE 7 Typical accompaniment patterns in *lai noi* for *lam ban xok.* Transcription by Terry E. Miller.

sive instruments, which play steadily moving metrical patterns in a *yao*-scale mode. A drummer (apparently requisite in this genre) strikes the drumhead on the first, second, fourth, and fifth beats of an eight-beat rhythmic cycle.

TRACK 6

The genre is further distinguished by a melismatic vocal introduction, usually rising from the fifth scalar degree to the upper "tonic," and cascading downward, or sometimes starting on the upper "tonic," dropping a fourth, and returning to the "tonic" via a semitone below—a tone that does not exist on the *khene.* The body of the poem is declamatory, and each stanza tends to follow a descending contour. *Lam salavane* is one of the most popular types from southern Laos. With its catchy drumming, it has often been transformed into popularized arrangements, especially in the song "*Tia long, salavane, tia long*" ('Slow Down and Relax, Salavane', figure 6).

Lam ban xok. Though denoted separately, *lam ban xok* (named after a village) may either be a predecessor of *lam khon savan* or a variant of it. And both types are the likely origins of the northeastern Thai *toei hua non tan* and *lam phanya yoi,* sung just across the Mekong. Accompaniment is rarely less than *khene,* drum, and small cymbals, but some recordings add an electric bass guitar. A metrical accompaniment using the *san* scale (in *lai sutsanaen* or *lai po sai* modes) supports a declaimed vocal line, which may approach regular accents. Stanzas tend to begin high and cascade to a tone one, three, or four tones above the "tonic." Gaps, during which the ensemble continues to play, are especially long. Distinguishing *lam ban xok* from *lam khon savan* is challenging because the essential differences are subtle: a more declamatory character for the former, the tones preferred at the ends of the third and fourth lines of poetry, and the accompaniment patterns. Functionally, *lam ban xok* is different: people do not dance to it, singers are not hired specifically to sing it, it is associated with ceremonial occasions, and it is described as serene and reserved (figure 7).

Lam tang vay. The name of a village in Savannakhet Province, *tang vay* means 'rattan chair' because this village is known for its rattan crafts. Lowland Lao sing this genre, but its derivation is said to be *Lao Theung,* the Mon-Khmer people who live at higher elevations in the area. Some people differentiate between lowland (*tang vay nam* 'water') and upland (*tang vay khok*). Further, some claim that *tang vay* was formerly a *khap* style that over time changed to *lam.* Originally accompanied by a free-reed pipe (*pi*) or a flute (*khui*), with a gong, a drum, and sometimes a scraper (*mai ngop ngep*), it is now normally accompanied by *khene,* a lute (*kachappi*), a fiddle (*so*), and percussion. The metrical, ostinato-like accompanimental pattern, basically | AAGG | F–D– |, supports a vocalist who metrically sings eight-beat phrases, each of which tends to descend. Because the melodic patterns are relatively fixed, *lam tang vay* is one of the easiest of the Lao genres to recognize (figure 8).

Lam khon savan. Derived from the name of the city Nakhon Savannakhet, *lam khon savan* is probably the most important of the southern Lao genres. Unlike those of most genres, singers of this genre have for generations been considered professionals, but formerly the female counterpart was a *phanya* reciter, recruited locally and paid little or nothing; today, however, the woman is normally a *molam.* This genre

FIGURE 8 Typical patterns in *lam tang vay*: *a, b,* accompaniment in *lai noi*; *c,* vocal pattern. Transcription by Terry E. Miller.

has been the specialty of one of the most famous singers of Laos, Molam Bountong, a man also known as Molam Indong, formerly of Savannakhet, now of Murfreesboro, Tennessee (United States). His musical partner was Phimmasone, a woman who settled in Paris, depriving Laos of its most famous *lam khon savan* pair.

Each singer opens his or her section of a round with a short introduction in *hai* form, followed by the long middle section made up of stanzas of *kon* poetry and a closing section consisting of three short phrases. Accompaniment is provided minimally by a *khene*, but all the instruments normally encountered in central southern Laos may be used, including the *mai ngop ngep*. The metrical accompanying motives, sometimes ostinato-like, support a predominantly metrical vocal line, often distinguished by short-long patterns and syncopations, particularly at the ends of phrases. Though the singing uses the *san* scale, and the *khene* plays any of its (three) modes, a few players have been known to use a *yao*-scale mode. As with other styles of this region, the vocal melody usually descends through the stanza, and excepting the end of a section avoids the "tonic." According to Chonpairot (1990:186), each singer tends to develop a personal melodic outline, which varies throughout the performance to conform to the lexical tones. *Lam khon savan* is closely related to, and easily confused with, *lam ban xok* and *lam mahaxay* in Laos and *toei hua non tan* and *lam phanya yoi* just across the Mekong in Thailand (figure 9).

Lam mahaxay. This genre is named after the town of Mahaxay, 45 kilometers east of Thakhek, Khammouane Province, on the road to Vietnam. Because of similar accompanimental patterns and mostly metrical singing, it is easily confused with *lam khon savan*. A distinguishing feature is each phrase's scalar descent to the "tonic." The metrical accompaniment is normally an ensemble of *khene*, *kachappi*, *so*, *mai ngop ngep*, and other percussive instruments, using the *san* scale. The vocal contour clearly descends, often from a long or melismatically ornamented high note (figure 10).

Lam phu thai. The term *Phu Thai* 'Thai people' is a lowland Lao or Thai term for upland Tai-speakers, such as the Red, White, or Black Tai, who migrated from northeastern Laos and northwestern Vietnam to lowland Laos and northeastern Thailand. Many evidently live, or lived, around the town of Mahaxay, where they became acculturated to lowland Lao ways, and some of them migrated into northeastern Thailand. Thus, the term refers not to a linguistically distinct Lao subgroup but to acculturated uplanders living among lowlanders. These people practice true *phu thai* singing, but the Lao genre called *lam phu thai* is mostly sung by ethnic Lao "in the style of" the *phu Thai*.

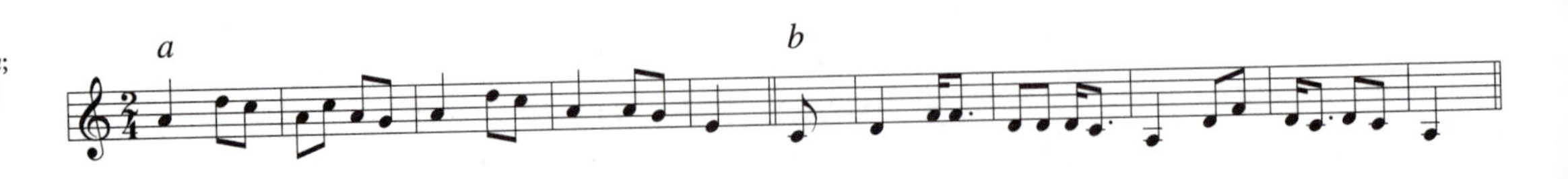

FIGURE 9 Typical patterns in *lam khon savan*: *a,* accompaniment, in *lai sutsanaen*; *b,* vocal pattern in *lai po sai*. Transcription by Terry E. Miller.

FIGURE 10 Typical motives of accompaniment in *lai soi* for *lam mahaxay*. Transcription by Terry E. Miller.

FIGURE 11 Typical patterns of accompaniment in *lai noi* for *lam phu thai*. Transcription by Terry E. Miller.

FIGURE 12 Typical vocal phrase of *khap ngeum*, sung in free rhythm.

As in other central-southern Lao genres, the accompaniment can be an ensemble of *khene*, lute, fiddle, drum, and percussion, playing metrically in a *yao* scale, especially *lai noi*, which allows for tones below the "tonic." The singing, however, is more declamatory than metrical. It has descending contours, and often opens with a melisma on the first syllable. Many lines of text follow a fixed rhythmic pattern (figure 11).

Khap ngeum. Though found in the environs of Vientiane but especially along the Ngeum River around the town of Tourakham, the style of *khap ngeum* suggests a northern origin. Other than classical music, no other musical style is associated with the capital, but much of the present-day population came there from throughout Laos after the 1975 coup and the flight of Vientiane's population to Thailand. The people who sing *khap ngeum* likely descend either from migrants from northeastern Laos (especially Houaphanh and Xiengkhuang) or from conquered upland peoples brought by the lowland Lao to the vicinity of Vientiane. North of the area where the majority live, the Ngeum River has been dammed to generate electricity, much of which is exported to Thailand.

Khap ngeum is accompanied by a *khene* alone. Though the version with sixteen pipes may be used, the two highest pairs are ignored, suggesting that originally a *khene* with fourteen or twelve pipes was used. Though the playing of the *khene* can be related to a standard mode, usually *lai noi*, neither the patterns nor the drones and sonorities are like those of ordinary *lai noi*. The accompanist plays in rapid arabesques, often trilling between two tones a third apart. The singer slowly and deliberately declaims lines of text, often separated by long pauses (figure 12). Phrases tend to begin on the fifth or seventh tone and descend to the third, with sectional endings descending to the "tonic." Listeners are expected to add cascading-fourth melismas at the ends of sections to encourage the singer. Because of the slow delivery and the gaps between lines or sections, singers can more easily improvise poetry and comment on immediate events, such as the visit of ethnomusicologists. Typically, the woman answers in *phanya*, but today, some women sing instead (figure 13).

Khap phuan. Formerly called *khap xieng khuang*, this genre is properly named after the Lao subgroup called Phuan, who dwell in the Xiengkhuang area. Living on the Plain of Jars (a cool, rainy plateau), in villages among Thai Dam, Lao Sung (especially the Khmu), and Lao Theung (mostly Hmong), the Phuan are roughly equivalent to the lowland Lao elsewhere. A few recordings are available, but *khap phuan* is unusual in that the woman answers in unaccompanied heightened speech in rhythms, scale, and tempo different from those of the man.

Accompaniment is provided by the *khene* in Phuan tuning (figure 14). The player's metrical pattern typically lasts four beats, each somewhat accented as he plays the

khap ngeum Repartee song of the Ngeum River basin near Vientiane

khap phuan Repartee song of the Phuan Lao of Xiengkhuang Province

khap sam neua Vocal music of the upland Lao of Houaphanh Province

khap thai dam Repartee song of the Black Thai minority

FIGURE 13 Male and female singers, accompanied by *khene*, sing *khap ngeum* on a covered veranda in Tourakham Village, north of Vientiane. Photo by Terry E. Miller, 1991.

"tonic" and octave of a *yao*-scale mode, either *lai nyai* or *lai noi*. The male singer's melody, in meter, is simple and syllabic; it often returns to the "tonic." Lexical tones are clearly realized, especially falling tones, sung to a glissando. The female singer's response was performed at a tempo slightly more than twice that of the male to a four-tone scale related to the "tonic," one tone above and two below (expressed in *lai noi* tones, A–C–d–e). Her rhythm was nonmetrical but steady in two durations, one twice the length of the other (figure 14).

Khap sam neua. The genre most remote from mainstream Laos originates in extreme northeastern Laos (Houaphanh Province, near the town of Sam Neua) and across the border into northwest Vietnam. Speaking a Tai language different from lowland Lao, the Neua people who inhabit this area are evidently the singers of *khap sam neua* and are thus more like "tribal Tai" than lowland Lao. The *khene* used to accompany has no more than fourteen pipes, and perhaps as few as ten. It follows the

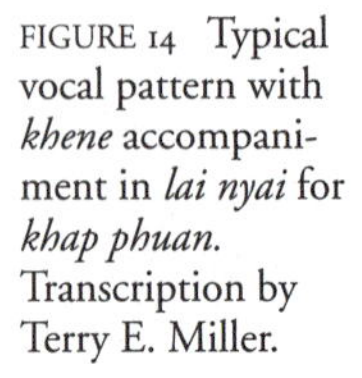

FIGURE 14 Typical vocal pattern with *khene* accompaniment in *lai nyai* for *khap phuan*. Transcription by Terry E. Miller.

a

b

FIGURE 15 Typical patterns in *khap sam neua*: *a*, vocal cadence; *b*, accompaniment in *lai noi* mode.

nonmetrical vocal line closely, without drones but with multiple tones. Using the *nyao* scale restricted to the range of a seventh, the singer completes the first line of a couplet on the third and the second line on the "tonic." Each line has a descending contour, and stanzas end with a distinctive cadence—a double alternation of "tonic" and the tone below. In the available recordings, the female singer's accompanist appeared to use a *khene* with fewer pipes than the male singer's (figure 15).

Khap thai dam. The genre most different in style from any Lao style—that of the Thai Dam—does not require travel to their traditional home in remote areas of northern Laos and northwestern Vietnam but can be heard in Des Moines, Iowa, where a large community of Thai Dam from Laos resettled after 1975. The Thai Dam do not use the *khene* but prefer a smaller free-reed pipe (*pi bap*), or a larger one (*pi mon*). While the singer declaims the poetry to somewhat indistinct steps of the *yao* scale (such as d–f–g–a–c′–d′), the *pi* plays only five tones: four in that scale, and one not in it (c♯–d–g–a–d′). Their rhythmic relationship is so free that it is difficult to detect any correspondence. Portamentos occur in both voice and instrument, especially at the ends of lines. Since one recording was of an unaccompanied performance, it is justifiable to conclude that *khap thai dam* is probably closer to *phanya* in heightened speech than to *lam* as understood by lowland Lao (figure 16).

Khap thum (luang phrabang). Historically a separate principality, later the royal capital and the location of the most important Buddhist temples of Laos, Luang Phrabang (named after the *phrabang,* an important image of Buddha) is sited at the junction of the Mekong and Khan rivers in remote central-northern Laos. The hills and mountains that surround the city on all sides are home to numerous upland

FIGURE 16 Male and female singers, accompanied by a free-reed pipe (*pi*), sing *khap thai dam* on an open porch in Ban Ban, a village east of Phonsavan, Xiengkhouang Province. Photo by Terry E. Miller, 1991.

FIGURE 17 Male and female singers, instrumentalists, and a chorus of onlookers enjoy an impromptu performance of *khap thum* in Luang Phrabang City. Photo by Terry E. Miller, 1991.

groups, many of which migrated into the area during the last couple of centuries. Originally part of the unified Kingdom of Lanxang (Kingdom of a Million Elephants), Luang Phrabang became a separate kingdom in 1707 as a result of a civil conflict and remained independent of Vientiane until 1946, when King Sisavang Vong of that city became the first king of reunified Laos. Luang Phrabang is the location of the now-vacant palace where the late King Savang Vatthana supported musicians, dancers, and actors, who performed Lao classical music, dance, and theater until 1975, when the Pathet Lao overthrew the coalition government and deposed him. Classical music ceased to be performed, and the instruments became museum pieces in the palace, but the classical tradition deeply affected the nature of *khap thum* (figure 17).

Stylistically, *khap thum* has little relation to the other Lao types described above but is a local counterpart to the court tradition in repartee form. Instrumental accompaniment is provided by various combinations of court instruments. Some are quite close to the formal *sep noi* or *maholi*, which consists of xylophone (*lanat*), gong circle (*khong vong*), fiddles (*so i, so u*), flute (*khui*), drums, and large and small cymbals. Many of these may be omitted, and other instruments, such as the dulcimer (*khim*), may be added. The ensemble plays a composed melody in duple time, while male and female soloists alternate, singing a more or less fixed melody, different from that of the ensemble. At the end of a couplet, a chorus of hand-clapping listeners completes the line with a single-tone response. Because male and female voices differ in range, the ensemble shifts between two tonal levels. The scale is pentatonic in the form of 1–2–3–5–6, with some passing use of 4. At the end of a performance or major section, the ensemble finishes alone with a standard type of coda (*luk mot*), similar to those found in Thai classical music.

Khap thum is therefore a type of song, closer to being a tune than the melodies of traditional *lam* and *khap*, which are only partially fixed. Other melodies also exist, and they can be performed by the same groups. Similar in format but different in its melody is *salong sam sao*. Another, called *an nangseu* 'to read a (palm-leaf) book', is performed by a single singer; in northeastern Thailand, however, this term denotes the reading of stories written in palm-leaf manuscripts in heightened speech closely allied with the lexical tones (figure 18).

FIGURE 18 Typical melodic patterns in *khap thum*: *a,* instrumental introduction; *b, c,* vocal patterns; *d,* cadential pattern for voice. Transcription by Terry E. Miller

Though *khap thum* clearly has classical foundations, its style and context are casual and close in spirit to that of village *lam*. As it did not depend for survival on court functions, it persists for festive occasions among ordinary urban people. Because of its instrumentation, classical players in Vientiane perform it as a lighter alternative to classical compositions.

Other genres. Though Laos has a small population, its ethnic makeup is extremely diverse. Because of rough terrain, lack of development, and difficulties in travel, these musics are likely to remain obscure. Among the little-known regional genres that are virtually undocumented are *khap meuy,* from Khammuane, east of Vientiane; *lao phay,* from Pongsaly; *khap ngom,* from the Luang Phrabang area; *khap haw,* a Chinese-derived type from Pongsaly; *khap lam,* from the areas of Champassak and Bolikhamsay; *khap maen,* from near Vientiane; *khap ong ga,* from Pongsaly; *eua ba*; and *joi yuan*.

General observations on nonclassical vocal genres

The foregoing data reveal patterns that suggest groupings of regional genres and possible common origins for these groupings, leading to eight preliminary conclusions:

1. The *khap* genres of the north differ stylistically from the *lam* genres of the south, and as groups they are separated by a vast area—much of Khammuane, all of Bolikhamsay, and much of Xiengkhuang provinces—for which there is little musical information.
2. Three *khap* genres (*ngeum, phuan, sam neua*) exhibit similarities with regard to accompanimental patterns, the khene used, and its relationship to the singer's melody. There are likely other local types, not yet documented, which are close in style to one or more of these.
3. The *lam* genres of central southern Laos (*ban xok, khon savan, mahaxay, phu thai, salavane, tang vay*) are typically accompanied by a small ensemble rather than solo *khene*, though the latter instrument alone is acceptable when other performers are unavailable. Each has distinctive melodic patterns, especially in the accompaniment, which differentiate them. Three of them (*khon savan, mahaxay, ban xok*) may be descendants of a common ancestor. *Salavane* is perhaps most different, since it is performed by acculturated Mon-Khmer, rather than lowland Lao, and *phu thai* is based on the singing of "tribal" Thai.
4. Melodies of the same central-southern Lao genres consistently exhibit descending contours, but those of the remaining two southern genres (*sithandone* and *som*) do not.

Nonclassical theater virtually did not exist in Laos until around the 1940s and 1950s, when three genres from Thailand began crossing the Mekong, mostly to border areas.

5. The latter two southernmost *lam* genres use solo *khene* accompaniment and are similar to styles in northeastern Thailand, which also use solo *khene.*
6. All southern Lao genres have metrical accompaniment, but only *tang vay, khon savan,* and to a lesser extent *mahaxay* have metrical vocal lines. The most strictly metrical is *tang vay.*
7. Southern Lao singers normally perform more than one genre, even four or five, but northern singers perform only one.
8. Two genres are radically different from all others, and point to separate origins: *khap thai dam* is more correctly "tribal" Tai, rather than lowland Lao; and *khap thum* is related to court music.

The foregoing describes those genres particular to the Lao, but southern singers in particular have for many years learned and performed styles from northeastern Thailand. Besides the survival of the old-style *lam ploen* theater music from the northeast, Lao singers perform complete *lam kon* cycles, called in Laos *lam tat* or *lam kon isan.* Singers perform it standing (unlike Lao genres, which they perform seated). Lao singers report that their audiences expect them to devote a substantial portion of a concert to styles from northeastern Thailand. Though the genres of both regions are broadly Lao, those from Laos itself reflect the conservative regionalism of the Lao, while those from Thailand reflect the emergence of a dynamic, modernized musical culture under strong influence from Bangkok. In the past, northeastern Thai singers knew little of the Lao styles, but after musicians appeared in refugee camps and began recording cassettes, there has been a modest vogue for Lao styles among northeastern Thai singers. As a result, Lao singers, both within and without Laos, tend to prefer northeastern Thai style when singing for non-Lao audiences.

Theater

Nonclassical theater virtually did not exist in Laos until around the 1940s and 1950s, when three genres from Thailand began crossing the Mekong, mostly to border areas. The development of these genres began with a central Thai theater called *li-ke,* which used classical instruments, heightened speech, and song, all in central Thai style, with colorful costumes, realistically painted backdrops, and spontaneous action based on a scenario rather than on a fully written script. When *li-ke* came to parts of northeastern Thailand (around 1930) and began penetrating the northeast, local performers began founding troupes that both imitated *li-ke*, especially its visual aspects, and transformed the music into a northeastern Thai and Lao style, using *khene* and *lam.* These developments occurred in isolated pockets over a period of at least two decades, but Lao informants report that *li-ke* reached Laos between 1947 and 1950 from Khorat, Thailand, and that the original members of that troupe were involved in founding the Natasin Fine Arts School in Vientiane in the mid-1950s.

At about the same time (from the early 1930s), a solo narrative genre accompanied by a *khene,* found both in Laos and northeastern Thailand— *lam ploen* (written "poen" in Lao)—was transformed into *lam leuang*, where the singer acted out various parts through gesture and costume. This development is said to have begun in Laos, and then became known in the northeast by about 1932. In 1952, a troupe of actors in Khon Kaen province, Thailand, began performing stories using a fully written-out script sung to Lao music, and called the genre *lam mu* 'collective singing'. By 1956, they had embraced stage conventions from *li-ke* and thus brought together the various influences of *li-ke, li-ke lao*, and *lam leuang*. The genre came to be known both as *lam mu* and *lam leuang.*

Until 1975, both northeastern Thai and local troupes continued to perform *lam leuang* in Lao border cities. I observed a Lao performance in Vientiane in 1973 by a troupe working from a scenario, rather than from a script. During the preceding years, *lam mu* and *lam kon* had been politicized as the government, working with the United States Information Service, commissioned troupes to perform propaganda pieces, and paid *molam* from Thailand to sing anticommunist texts in Laos. Since *lam leuang* theater was intended for the less sophisticated, whether living in cities or villages, it was an effective vehicle for spreading policies and influencing thinking.

During the civil war, around 1969, the Pathet Lao, operating in Viengsay (a "liberated zone"), began developing *lam leuang* into a medium for spreading communist ideas. This they called *lakhawn lam*, essentially a theater of songs with themes of justice and liberation. Since 1975, the government in Vientiane has maintained the troupe, the only one in Laos. Before classical genres were revived, the government held up *lakhawn lam* as the people's theater, as opposed to the decadence of elite classical genres.

CLASSICAL MUSIC

The ensembles and theatrical genres associated with the court at Luang Phrabang and the Fine Arts School in Vientiane have long been called classical. The Lao term *peng lao deum* 'Lao traditional compositions' differentiates this tradition from that of *lam.* Though similar in style and function to related traditions in Thailand and Cambodia, the Lao version, for various reasons, remained more modest, and the court context ceased to exist in Laos after 1975.

Whereas treatments of the classical traditions of Thailand and Cambodia can be matter of fact, since both continue independent of each other, finding a neutral place from which to explore Lao classical music is more challenging. Thai musicians offer one set of conclusions from their perspective, based both on musical evidence and feelings of Thai nationalism, but the view from Laos is more complex, being caught up in prerevolutionary and revolutionary politics, historical relationships, and feelings of Lao nationalism. The Lao had an early relationship with the Khmer since Fa Ngum, the first king of unified Lan Xang (ruled 1353–1373), had been raised in exile at Angkor. The Lao-Khmer relationship has been relatively peaceful, though part of present-day Cambodia was once under the control of the Lao principality of Champassak.

Historical relations between the courts of the Lao and the Siamese (the Tai of the Chao Phraya Valley, in present-day central Thailand) have been more difficult. The Lao and the Siamese are better viewed as historical and linguistic cousins than as big brothers and little brothers, because in earlier times their kingdoms were not nearly so disparate in power and wealth as they came to be in the 1900s. After 1828, when Bangkok's armies invaded Vientiane, destroyed it, and forcibly resettled much of the population in central Thailand, relations have become imbalanced in Thailand's favor, compounded when Laos became a French protectorate. Clearly, many Lao today resent modern Thai power, wealth, and the fact that Laos, being landlocked, depends on Thailand for access to goods and a route for exports. Both the communist victory in 1975 and the weakness of the Lao economy make resistance to Thai hegemony an issue of Lao survival.

On the matter of Lao classical music, two viewpoints have developed. At one extreme is the view that the Lao tradition is merely a provincial version of a superior Thai one; at the other extreme is the view that Lao classical music is independent of Thai music. Neither view is realistic, but ascertaining the truth is obstructed by a lack of evidence and by potential distortion from Thai or Lao centrism. A comparison of mid-to-late twentieth-century traditions suggests clear influence from Thailand, but historically it is difficult to know if this was always the case. Readers of recent writings on Lao classical music may sense a preference for a theory of Khmer, rather than Siamese, Thai origin. Since Fa Ngum's wife was Khmer, some writers (especially Viravong 1964:37) assert that the Khmer ruler sent musicians and dancers with other craftspeople, Buddhist monks, and revered statues of the Buddha soon after 1353. Since we know little of Khmer music in the 1300s, and nothing of Lao music of that time, we cannot draw any conclusions concerning early historical relationships.

Even when unified as Lan Xang, the Lao kingdom consisted of several small, isolated centers of power, which became virtually independent principalities during the 1700s. Presumably each court had music, dance, and theater in accordance with its wealth, but none was completely isolated from Siamese influence (earlier from Ayuthaya, later from Bangkok). The tradition of Luang Phrabang, most removed from Bangkok physically, survived until 1975, when the King of Laos, Savang Vatthana, abdicated. The royal dancers and musicians were resettled in Nashville, Tennessee. They tried to keep their tradition alive but offered only a few performances. The National Council for Traditional Arts arranged the filming of *The Last Dance,* a documentary of their last known performance.

Vientiane's tradition seems to have disappeared, at least temporarily, when Siamese troops sacked the city in 1828 and exiled the population to central Thailand. A classical tradition reemerged into prominence in the mid-1950s with the founding of the Natasin School (or National School of Dramatic Arts). After 1975, most of the Natasin staff was resettled in Des Moines, Iowa, but they too have failed to maintain the tradition. After 1975, the Natasin School continued with a new staff. The third principality was Champassak, in the deep south, whose history is interwoven with that of the Siamese. A classical ensemble descended from the court survives in a village setting there and was investigated in 1991 by the author.

Classical music (*peng lao deum*) served varied purposes at the court. It provided entertainment and atmosphere at festivities and ceremonies and provided appropriate music within rituals. It accompanied theater and dance and entertained foreign guests on state occasions. Some have viewed it as the great tradition of the Lao, one of the highly developed court traditions of Southeast Asia, in contrast to the alleged little tradition of *lam* and *khene*. In the minds of the ruling elite, classical music became a symbol of Lao civilization, a projection of Lao power. Under the communist government, however, it was criticized as symbolizing an elitist, bourgeois society. Only gradually since the 1980s has the role of classical music changed from a symbol of decadence back to a symbol of Lao identity.

Musical instruments

The earliest physical evidence of Lao classical instruments is found on the gilded carvings in relief covering the exterior front wall of Vat Mai in Luang Phrabang, dated variously between 1796 and 1820. The ensemble of musicians includes a xylophone (*lanat*), a gong circle (*khong vong*) having at least eleven gongs, a small horizontal drum on a stand (*taphone*), a two-stringed bowed lute with coconut body (*so u*), small cymbals (*sing*), and two barrel-shaped drums played with sticks (*kong that*), plus a small mouth organ (*khene*) and a reader of a palm-leaf manuscript. Painted on the ceiling of the portico in gold on a red background are human figures playing other kinds of instruments, including a lute, a small drum, and conical double-reeds. We cannot be sure that either the reliefs or the paintings on the ceilings date to the building of the temple.

The Lao customarily divide instruments into four categories: *tit* 'plucked', *si* 'bowed', *ti* 'beaten', and *bao* 'blown'. The main classical instruments are distinct from those used in *lam* (except *khap thum*), but a few overlap, such as the flute (*khui*), certain drums, and two kinds of cymbals: *sing*, the smaller type; and *sap*, the larger. All have Thai classical equivalents.

Plucked instruments

Kachappi (Thai *krajappi*), a two-, three-, or four-stringed, fretted, plucked lute, whose body is usually rounded.

Bowed instruments

So i (Thai *saw duang*), a two-stringed fiddle, with cylindrical body and snakeskin resonator.

So u (Thai *saw u*), a two-stringed fiddle, with coconut body and calfskin resonator.

Beaten instruments

Lanat (Thai *ranat ek* and *ranat thum*), xylophones, the higher called *lanat ek mai* with twenty-one bars of wood or bamboo, the lower one called *lanat thum mai* with seventeen or eighteen bars of wood or bamboo.

Khong vong, gong circles, the higher called *khong vong noi* or *khong wong ek* with eighteen bossed gongs, the lower called *khong vong nyai* with sixteen gongs, suspended horizontally on leather strips in a rattan frame open at the rear (through which players must enter and exit). Thai terms are the same, but *nyai* is pronounced *yai*.

Khim (Thai *khim*, from Chao-zhou Chinese *yang qin*), a dulcimer with two sets of bridges.

Kong taphone (Thai *klawng taphon*), an asymmetrical-shaped, two-headed barrel drum, mounted horizontally on a stand, and played with the hands.

Kong that (Thai *klawng that*), a pair of Chinese-style barrel drums, with tacked heads mounted obliquely on a stick frame, beaten with two sticks.

Sing (Thai *ching*), small cup-shaped metal cymbals, beaten in open (*sing*) and damped (*sap*) strokes to mark cycles in classical compositions (and for rhythmic effects in *lam*). There are two sizes: small (*noi*) and large (*nyai*).

Sap (Thai *chap*), thin, disklike, metal cymbals, which play syncopated patterns in opposition to the *sing*.

Blown instruments

Pi kaeo (Thai *pi nai*), a quadruple reed instrument, carved of wood with a bulbous shape.

Khui (Thai *khlui phiang aw, khlui lip*), a fipple flute of bamboo, with seven holes for fingering and one rear hole for the thumb, made in two sizes, the larger (lower) simply *khui*, the smaller (higher) *khui lip*.

Ensembles

Two ensembles are usually named, but they had different names in Vientiane and Luang Phrabang. The ensemble associated with ritual, formal, state occasions, the-

piphat/sep nyai Lao classical ensemble with xylophones, gong circles, and oboe

maholi/sep noi Lao classical ensemble of strings and flutes

khon Classical masked drama primarily playing the story of Rama (*Ramakian*)

ater, and dance is called *piphat* in Vientiane (after Thai usage), and *sep nyai* in Luang Phrabang. It consists of one or two xylophones, gong circles, and, depending on whether hard or soft mallets are used, an oboe (hard) or flute (soft). The exact make-up of the ensemble is flexible: some have one xylophone and two gong circles, some neither oboe nor flute, and so on. The second ensemble is called *maholi* in Vientiane (again the same as the Thai term *mahori*), or *sep noi* in Luang Phrabang. The instrumentation of this group is quite flexible. It includes virtually any of the instruments listed above, except the oboe, in greater and smaller groupings that include the bowed strings.

Although the ensembles discussed here are otherwise not distinct from those of the central Thai, the Lao have made them more Lao by adding the *khene,* an indigenous instrument. Adding the *khene*, however, raises the question of tuning. *Khene* are tuned to have seven tones in an octave, with both semitones and tones, similar to but not influenced by Western diatonic tuning. Classical instruments of fixed pitch (xylophones, gong circles) were traditionally tuned in seven equidistant tones, though since the instruments were tuned by ear, the intervals between the tones are never mathematically equal. The chordophones are flexible in pitch. There is, then, a tuning discrepancy between classical instruments and the *khene,* which musicians either hear as harmless or eliminate by retuning the xylophones and gong circles (a time-consuming procedure). Thus, the *maholi* or *sep noi* ensemble often has one or two *khene* playing, but they are played melodically, without the drones customary in village music.

Regional styles

Though a unified kingdom at its founding, Lan Xang included three widely dispersed centers of power connected by the Mekong River: Champassak in the south, Vientiane in the center, and Luang Phrabang in the north. In the early 1700s, the kingdom broke into three princedoms. It remained divided until the 1800s, when the French reunified Laos as part of Indo-China. As a consequence, three separate court-music traditions developed, all similar to each other and to those of Cambodia and Thailand.

Over time, local idiosyncrasies developed. The court at Champassak vanished as the Thai gained power in that area, and part of its territory was ceded to Cambodia, but a classical ensemble persists in a village near Champassak, now little more than a village itself. Luang Phrabang became the royal capital and the king's residence, while Vientiane became the administrative capital. After 1975, however, with the king's abdication, court music at Luang Phrabang ceased to function, and the city lost its royal status.

Luang Phrabang

Because Fa Ngum founded the court that became Luang Phrabang and possibly brought Khmer musicians and dancers there, a Khmer origin for the Luang Phrabang tradition has been asserted. Luang Phrabang was no more isolated than other centers of power in early Laos, since it was on the banks of the Mekong River; but by modern standards, it is quite isolated. The upriver trip from Vientiane was long, dangerous, and only seasonally possible, and overland travel over the mountains was difficult even in peacetime. Today, the only realistic way to reach the city is by air. It is surrounded by hills and mountains, inhabited mostly by non-Lao upland groups. Before 1975, villagers of Lao Lue origin living in a nearby village called Ban Phanom were recruited to perform at the court. After Laos became independent (in 1954), King Sisavang Vong created a full-time palace ensemble of the older players, who provided music for rituals, festivals, dance, and theater, both at the court and in villages around Luang Phrabang. The most important function of the troupe was to perform at the *bun pi mai*, the Lao New Year, held in mid-April.

Assessing how glorious the court tradition really was is difficult. Though no evidence of large-scale ensembles remains, there was classical dance, the masked drama called *khon* (which performs only the Thai version of the Indian *Ramayana*), and a hand-puppet theater. The latter was reported to have originated about 1930; it performed both the story of Rama and a Lao epic, *Sang Xin Xay*.

Comparing pre-1975 recordings of the Luang Phrabang tradition with the living tradition in Cambodia, however, proves nothing with regard to history. After the fall of Angkor, Khmer court music was devastated; it was restored in part with the help of the Siamese in the 1800s and 1900s. Khmer and Thai classical musics have much in common, especially in repertoire, that can be traced to these relationships. Recordings available from Luang Phrabang suggest neither Khmer influence nor anything particularly distinct from the present Thai tradition. Jacques Brunet's recordings document modest performances, using small numbers of instruments without the *pi*. The repertory is of Thai origin, since the compositions are by known composers, and the style of playing is in even-note values, not the long-short pattern of the Khmer. An excerpt of *khon* masked drama was narrated in Thai, not Lao.

After the Luang Phrabang musicians fled the country, only the instruments remained. They are housed in the palace museum, silent. Classical music, however, is said to remain alive in several private homes. Among them is that of Houmpheng Boupha (b. 1920), who had played classical music as a boy. In the 1950s, he began teaching his children to play classical instruments; later, he taught his grandchildren. His family's activities continue, though on a modest level.

Vientiane

Vientiane's tradition may be younger, having returned to prominence only in 1956 as the Natasin School (or National School of Dramatic Arts), with help from the United States Agency for International Development. Its purpose was to promote Lao national identity through music, dance, and theater, and one important function was performances for visiting foreign dignitaries. Its most important regular function was playing at *bun that luang*, a festival held in December at the city's most famous temple, built originally in 1566, destroyed in the later 1800s, and rebuilt with French help in the 1930s. The school officially opened in 1959 with ten teachers, trained in Bangkok from 1956 to 1959. Consequently the Vientiane tradition began largely as a copy of that of Bangkok.

As part of the school's purpose of promoting Lao nationalism, choreographers created new dances illustrating characteristic life in Laos both among the lowland Lao and upland groups—dances such as the *fon ha pla* 'fishing dance', the *fon phao lao* 'ethnic dance', and five "friendship dances." Instrumental teachers created ensembles that combined *khene* with other instruments for accompaniment. Brunet published two recordings from Vientiane, one of *khong vong* and *so u,* the other mixing *so i, khui,* and *khene* in performing *Pheng Paeh,* a Thai composition learned by all beginners and played as a warmup in rehearsal. In 1975, most of the Natasin staff, with much of the city's population, fled to Thailand, and the musicians resettled in Des Moines.

Neither a wealthy nor a highly respected institution (because some people said the faculty and students could only play music or dance), the Natasin School barely survived the change to communist rule, which condemned the arts of elites and elevated those of "the people"; consequently, the friendship dances and other dances depicting the life of "the people" survived. Thai influence was eliminated, the costumes from Bangkok lost, and in 1992 the name changed to the National School of Folkloric Music and Dance. By 1991, however, the government was seeking better relations with the noncommunist world, and wished to send troupes to international artistic events. In that year, as intergovernmental relations grew warmer, Princess Sirindhorn of Thailand visited Laos and promised to send an ensemble of instruments. Later, the princess donated a new set of costumes to the Lao school. The Lao developed an elaborate, classical-derived performance from the Lao *Pha Lak Pha Lam* (but using both classical and Lao instruments) and has presented it in Thailand.

In the 1990s, the institution moved to better quarters, rebuilt its staff from former students, and has begun to be used internationally again by the Lao government to promote Lao cultural identity. According to a teacher at the school, there are ensembles of *piphat, maholi,* and *khene vong* (mouth organs), and training in *khon, lakhon* and various genres of Lao *lam*. The staff was said to include fifty-five teachers, who, to 150 students ranging in age from thirteen to eighteen, teach these subjects plus ballet, piano, violin, saxophone, and guitar. Of the teachers, five teach *khene,* three teach *kachappi,* eight teach *piphat,* and ten teach *maholi.* The numbers of faculty and students varies at times, and these figures may be inflated. The school has established some eight or nine troupes, which, for festivals, birthdays, marriages, funerals, and ordinations, perform throughout the city and elsewhere in Laos, sometimes in restaurants.

Champassak

Champassak, along the Mekong in southern Laos, was in the 1700s and 1800s the court center of one of the three principalities that eventually combined into modern Laos. Little remains of Champassak besides village homes, old colonial buildings, and a few minor temples; but before 1975, because the Angkor-period Khmer temple called Vat Phu is located eight kilometers to the south, Champassak was the center of tourism in southern Laos.

Champassak's history during the last two centuries is complicated by the fact that it was not a state (with defined boundaries) but a court center (with shifting spheres of influence), and after 1778 became more a vassal of the Thai than of the Lao. The continuing presence of a classical instrumental ensemble made up of farmers living in surrounding villages is remarkable, but its history is difficult to ascertain. Since virtually nothing is known of Lao court music before the twentieth century, we cannot say whether this ensemble represents a survival of Lao or Thai traditions (or possibly Khmer traditions influenced by the Thai). The ensemble's repertory is essentially Thai, but the last known teacher who worked with the ensemble is said to have come from Cambodia in 1967 and to have stayed three months.

The ensemble, called a *pinpat,* consists of at least seven musicians, all male, who play xylophone (*lanat ek*), gong circle (*khong vong*), oboe (*pi*), plastic soprano recorder (called *khui lip*), horizontal drum (*tapon*), pair of barrel drums (*kong that*), and small cymbals (*sing*). In 1994, the players' ages ranged from eighteen to eighty-

FIGURE 19 The *pinpat* ensemble of Champassak performs in the otherwise empty lobby of a hotel in Champassak City. Photo by Terry E. Miller, 1991.

three. The tradition continues to be passed orally from father to son, for the youngest member, who plays xylophone, learned from his father, who plays a gong circle (figure 19). The ensemble plays periodically for local festivals, but the most important event of the year is the annual buffalo sacrifice, held at Vat Phu.

Champassak and Luang Phrabang (in the case of *khap thum*) show how an elite music moves to the realm of the nonelite. But in Vientiane, classical music remains largely a hothouse plant in a climate where *lam* is typically Lao. From another perspective, the Lao are proud of their ability to play complex compositions, mount theatrical productions, and train graceful dancers, just as the classical Western tradition exists in the United States and is more than just an echo of Europe.

The Lao accent and Lao identity

Some observers note the existence of Thai classical compositions in the Lao accent (*samniang lao*), all by Thai composers. Among them are some of the most famous titles in the repertoire—"*Lao siang tian,*" "*Lao duang düan,*" and "*Lao jarün sri.*" Some Lao believe these to be Lao melodies adapted by Thai composers. For evidence, they point to the thousands of Lao forcibly exiled in central Thailand after the destruction of Vientiane. Though some supposedly Lao melodies were possibly derived from the songs of the Lao, most were derived from the music of northern Thailand around Chiangmai, an area commonly called Lao by the central Thai. Nonetheless, the Lao prefer to play compositions in the Lao accent.

A question remains: how is Lao classical music distinctively Lao? There is no single, absolute answer, only perspectives. Thai musicians would rightly note that the original teachers at Vientiane's Natasin School were trained in Bangkok, that the Luang Phrabang repertoire heard in available documents is also Thai, that the Lao do not have a known distinct body of Lao compositions by Lao composers, and that performances of theater and dance followed Thai models. In addition, there is no evidence that these (living or recently living) Lao traditions have any direct connection to the performing arts of the distant past.

The Lao, however, would likely emphasize all aspects that differ from the Thai tradition in any way—the addition of *khene* to ensembles, the Lao variant of the Thai *Ramakien* called *Pha Lak Pha Lam*, and the use of some Lao tunes. Lao resistance to perceived Thai superiority in both power and culture, not to mention the geographi-

Poverty makes it difficult for musicians to purchase the equipment necessary for playing popular music. Ironically, there may be more popular-music activity among Lao youth in the West than in Laos itself.

cal relationship of a landlocked country to one with ports, results in motivation for honing a distinct identity. That Thailand avoided colonialism and Laos did not, plus the communist victory in Laos (which completed the country's economic collapse), has given the Lao a perspective on life different from that of the Thai. Perhaps the truest thing a neutral outsider can observe is that classical music in Laos, though clearly derived from Thai, has distinct cultural and political meanings to the Lao, both in the past and present.

POPULAR MUSIC

Before 1975, Vientiane was known for its nightlife, including popular types of music performed in hotels and clubs, but after the change of government in 1975, Vientiane (and all of Laos) fell on austere times. Until about 1990, there was virtually no free enterprise, and the drabness of daily life was only occasionally broken by festivities. For anyone with a radio or television, however, the Thai media were always available, and because the Thai media along the Mekong remain stronger than the radio stations and single television station in Laos, all owned by the government, Lao popular culture is essentially borrowed Thai popular culture.

At least since 1991, a few government-owned clubs have offered live popular music, and young people increasingly want to learn to play modern pop instruments. The few stores selling audiocassettes offer mostly unauthorized copies of tapes imported from Thailand, with a few of Lao traditional musics.

The most prevalent form of distinctly Lao popular music is modernized renditions of the traditional, regional genres, a Lao parallel to Thailand's *luk thung* songs. Some genres are more flexible in this regard than others; indeed, of the northern (*khap*) genres, only *khap thum* lends itself to this treatment. Most *lam* genres from the south work well. The change involves the use of an electric guitar, an electric *phin,* or a synthesizer with an electric bass guitar, a set of drums, and new poetry. The Thai Dam minority, said to be more prosperous than most other Lao, have had their own popular songs for more than twenty-five years.

Two factors hold back the development of popular music in Laos. First, the power of the Thai media will continue to overwhelm the minuscule Lao popular-music industry for years to come. Second, poverty makes it difficult for musicians to purchase the equipment necessary for playing popular music. Opportunities for learning how to compose, arrange, and play modern instruments are also limited. Ironically, there may be more popular-music activity among Lao youth in the West than in Laos itself. As times change, however, there is likely to be more popular music, not less; but whether genres independent of Thailand develop remains to be seen.

LAO MUSIC TODAY

The fall of the coalition government in 1975, and the resulting flight of tens of thousands of ethnic Lao, Hmong, Khmu, and other minorities (first to camps in

Thailand, then to permanent resettlement in the United States, France, Canada, Australia, and other countries) have created a musical diaspora. Some resettlement officials tried to keep classical musicians from Vientiane and Luang Phrabang together in the camps near Nongkhai, Thailand. Eventually, the Luang Phrabang group resettled in Nashville, Tennessee, and the Vientiane group from the Natasin (Fine Arts) School resettled in Des Moines, Iowa; but after individuals began taking jobs, group cohesion broke down, and neither group was able to sustain performances in its new homeland. Though both national and state arts agencies targeted them for help, the results were few, and Lao classical music in the United States hardly survives.

The *lam* tradition, however, was carried by some of the country's finest singers, particularly Bountong Insixiengmai (living in 1997 in Nashville, Tennessee) and his cousin Khamvong Insixiengmai (living in 1997 in Fresno, California), a recipient of a National Heritage Award from the National Endowment for the Arts in 1992. Of Southeast Asian refugees in the United States, the Lao communities have had the greatest difficulty in sustaining cohesion, and consequently regular performances of Lao *lam* have not occurred. Indeed, Lao singers have not been able to maintain strong partnerships. Several skilled players of *khene,* most notably Khamseung Syhanone, live in the United States.

Musicians who remained in the newly established People's Democratic Republic of Laos after 1975, especially those who specialized in *lam,* were required to work for the government and sing its messages, but the government found that *molam* were less than reliable and would return to traditional material when out of officials' earshot. Currently, musicians may be hired privately, and they have primarily returned to the traditional themes of Buddhism, love, and lore. Some musicians, because they were closely associated with the former régime, were sent to reeducation camps (called seminars), and classical musicians in particular suffered because their art was called the music of the aristocracy.

Today in Laos, though musicians are mostly free to perform, little money is available for hiring them. Poverty prevents the radical change that is sure to come if the country achieves a measure of prosperity. The Lao hear modern popular music on Thai radio and television every day, and since many people favorably view the modernization of traditional music, only the lack of money holds back conversion to electric guitars, sets of drums, and other symbols of modernization and Western freedoms. Indeed, in the United States, the World Music Institute (New York) has issued a cassette of "pure" Lao music, performed by Khamvong and his partner, Thongkhio; but their commercial release for the Lao community included an electric guitar and a set of drums. Since the specifically Lao genres have had difficulty holding their own for many years in the face of more energetic styles of *lam* from northeastern Thailand, the genres that have expressed the distinctiveness of Lao sensibilities are in danger of being snuffed out by styles from abroad. Preservationism will not be able to stem this tide.

Before a complete picture of music in Laos can be drawn, a great deal of fieldwork must be conducted. Even now that the government has lifted its controls on in-country travel, the remaining obstacles are formidable. There is as yet no national inventory of musicians. Consequently, researchers are uncertain where to go. With overland travel either rough or dangerous or both, one is limited to flying to isolated airstrips serviced by Lao Aviation, which offers only semischeduled flights on small, overloaded planes. Facilities for guests are few and spartan, and the local rental of vehicles can be expensive. Researchers have to be prepared to work in areas without electricity, with no way to recharge batteries. Medical care is minimal. Laos has a tremendous variety of ethnic groups, and until their individual musical systems, often linked with little-studied languages, can be documented in depth, our knowledge of music in Laos will remain incomplete.

REFERENCES

Archaimbault, Charles. 1991. *Le sacrifice du buffle a S'ieng Khwang (Laos).* Paris: École Française d'Extrême-Orient.

Brunet, Jacques. 1992 [1973]. *Laos: Traditional Music of the South.* Auvidis / UNESCO D 8042. Compact disc and commentary.

Chonpairot, Jarernchai. 1990. "Lam Khon Sawan: A Vocal Genre of Southern Laos." Ph.D. dissertation, Kent State University.

Compton, Carol. 1979. *Courting Poetry in Laos: A Textual and Linguistic Analysis.* De Kalb: Northern Illinois University. Special report 18.

Viravong, Maha Sila. 1964. *History of Laos,* translated by the U.S. Joint Publications Research Service. New York: Paragon Book Reprint Corporation.

Burma

Ward Keeler

Officially called Myanmar, Burma borders five other nations: Bangladesh and India on the west, China on the north, and Thailand and Laos on the east. Burma's landmass—657,740 square kilometers—is slightly smaller than that of Texas. Of a total population of 44,277,014 (July 1994 estimate), 68 percent are Burmese (also called Burman), nine percent Shan, 7 percent Karen, 4 percent Rakhine, 3 percent Chinese, 2 percent Mon, 2 percent Indian, and 5 percent "other." Areas dominated by the Burmese are called provinces whereas those of the "National Brethren" are states. Burmese culture predominates in seven provincial divisions (Irrawaddy, Magwe, Mandalay, Pegu, Rangoon, Sagaing, Tenasserim), and non-Burmese tend to dominate in seven states (Chin, Kachin, Karen, Kayah, Mon, Rakhine, Shan). Some of these states have been in rebellion against the central government since 1948, when Burma gained independence from Britain. Consequently, research in these areas has been extremely limited. Nationwide, the predominant religion is Theravada Buddhism, but sizeable groups of Christians and Muslims exist.

Burma is the only nation in Southeast Asia bordering both India and China, countries thought to be the sources of Southeast Asia's religious and artistic traditions. Burmese music is clearly indebted to India for some instruments, but surprisingly little evidence of direct influence survives, and still less of Chinese influence. Burmese music therefore supports a recent scholarly trend, which stresses the indigenous roots of Southeast Asia's cultural traditions, rather than seeking origins elsewhere. Indeed, Burmese music has obvious affinities with other mainland Southeast Asian traditions, particularly that of Thailand; yet even in this regard, Burma is remarkable for the distinctiveness of its heritage.

Burmese music can be divided into two styles: an outdoor type and an indoor, chamber type. Listeners unaccustomed to Burmese music are as likely to be taken with the elegance and quiet of the chamber-music style as they are to be put off by the raucousness of the outdoor style; yet, though the instrumentation and playing of the two styles differ, the principles underlying the music and the repertoire played in either style are much the same.

In part because Westerners find Burmese music less immediately alluring than some other musical traditions of Southeast Asia, and in part because entry into

Burma (Myanmar)

Burma for Western researchers has been difficult since the early 1960s, outsiders know much less about Burmese music than about, say, Javanese, Balinese, or Thai music. Only five ethnomusicologists—three Western, two Japanese—have conducted sustained research in Burma since 1945. The following remarks are therefore provisional.

Each of Burma's ethnic groups has its own language and musical traditions. The ethnic Burmans, native speakers of Burmese, have enjoyed some degree of political preeminence within a region roughly corresponding to the present nation since the days of Pagan, the kingdom that ruled from a city by the Irrawady in Upper Burma in the tenth through the twelfth centuries. The regions peopled by non-Burmans but under Burman control have undergone varying degrees of political and cultural incorporation. The following account refers to Burmese music, using the adjective most familiar to English-speakers, but the reference is only to the traditions of the ethnic Burmans, not to all residents of Burma.

HISTORY

The earliest documentary reference to Burmese music is found in China, in a Tang Dynasty chronicle. It gives an account of a troupe of musicians and dancers sent to the Chinese court by the Pyu, in Lower Burma, in the 800s. Only some of the fourteen types of instruments described in the chronicle seem to correspond to anything now known in Burma, most notably one of the two harps and perhaps the "lizard-head zithers." None of the instruments mentioned resembles any instrument in the modern Burmese outdoor ensembles. It is unclear whether contemporary instruments were not yet in existence, or were simply not thought suitable by the Pyu for a mission to a royal court (Becker 1967, 1980).

FIGURE 1 A Mon fiddle (*tayò*) in the Museum of History, Rangoon. Photo by Terry E. Miller, 1994.

A few instruments known to have existed are now either lost or no longer in widespread use. A bowed fiddle (*tayò*) has been replaced by the Western violin; how the mouth organ (*hnyìñ*) was played is no longer known; it is not even known for sure what one instrument was (its name, *sàñdeyà,* is now applied to the piano); the "crocodile-shaped zither" (*mì jaùñ*) is no longer used by Burmans, though the Mon still have such an instrument (Garfias 1985) (figures 1 and 2).

Burmese written references to music are sparse until the 1700s. With the coming of the Koùñbauñ dynasty, the royal court began to sponsor advances in performing genres, and court musicians' contributions to the tradition of the performing arts greatly expanded the musical repertoire. The courts supported two types of ensembles, one (called *anyeíñ tìwaìñ*) to accompany an entertainment featuring women who danced and sang, and another (called *htwe'tomuçì tìwaìñ*) for royal ceremonies and processions.

It was the practice in Southeast Asia that a triumphant army did not long occupy a vanquished kingdom. Instead, conquerors physically removed many of its inhabitants, forcing them to settle in the invading army's homeland, where their

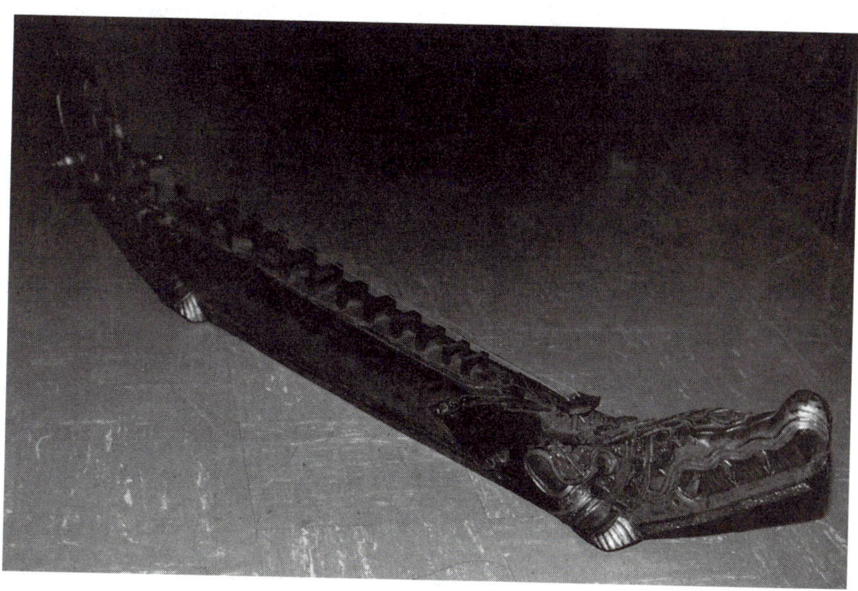

FIGURE 2 A Mon zither (*mì jaùñ*) in the shape of a crocodile. Photo by Terry E. Miller, 1994.

labor could be put to use. Artists' labor was as likely to be exploited in this way as anyone else's. Burmese claim that many of their artistic traditions developed out of Siamese-Thai courtly arts brought to them by artists obliged to move to the Burmese capital when Ayuthaya fell to invading Burmans in 1767.

One of the most notable of the Koùñbauñ musician-statesmen, Myáwadi Mìñçì Ù Sá (or Wuñçì Ù Sá), born in Upper Burma in 1766, was important in the assimilation of Thai arts into Burmese culture. He combined a military career with musical activity. In addition to composing classical songs, he took advantage of being on a royal commission at the end of the 1700s to learn, from aging Thai artists removed from Ayuthaya long before, the Siamese-court versions of the *Ramayana* and *Inao,* a tale of palace intrigue. He wrote Burmese versions of these stories, composing songs and music, enriching the Burmese courtly arts. The vagaries of military fortunes and courtly intrigues brought him both high and low, but he was honored just before his death, in 1853, by King Mindon (Williamson 1979a).

The classical repertoire continued to grow throughout the 1800s, but with the end of the era of Burmese kings in the late 1800s, the corpus of classical compositions ceased to develop further. Instead, Burmese and Western musical styles have become increasingly hybridized.

TYPES OF ENSEMBLES

The distinction between outdoor and indoor music in Burma corresponds to that between loud, vigorous music, and soft, chamber music. Outdoor ensembles come in many varieties, most named for their respective drum types. The *hsaìñwaìñ,* or simply *hsaìñ,* is the most commonly used outdoor ensemble; it consists of drums, gongs, and aerophones. A chamber-music ensemble may consist of as few as one vocalist and one instrumentalist (either a harp or a xylophone), plus the vocalist's bamboo clapper and hand-held cymbals. The instruments within each of these ensembles can be distinguished by whether they have fixed pitches, or whether they can be easily retuned. During the twentieth century, and increasingly since the late 1970s, musicians often combine Burmese and Western instruments, creating a broad spectrum of musical styles, from a largely classical Burmese style that incorporates the piano and violin to a more Western popular style.

That indigenous Burmese ensembles are distinguished by categories of placement (outside or inside) may reflect a distinction, common in Southeast Asian palaces, between the inner quarters and the outer, more public areas. In many Southeast Asian courts, music suitable to the former was refined and subtle; music suitable to the latter, loud and impressive. (Similar distinctions are made among Vietnamese and Chinese ensembles.) But today, with the Burmese courts long gone, the "outside style" refers to public performances of dance, plays, and rituals using *hsaìñ* (or combinations of *hsaìñ* instruments with electronically amplified Western ones) and smaller-scale outdoor ensembles. The "inside style" applies to intimate gatherings of a few aficionados of classical music and brief, weekly classical-music programs shown on Burmese television. Many performances that incorporate Western pop music cannot be readily categorized according to the outside-inside distinction at all.

In the following, the word *hsaìñ* denotes the most common outdoor ensemble, and the phrase "chamber ensemble" denotes any configuration of instruments playing in a small group with a vocalist: the latter type usually includes a singer (or singers who take turns singing individually) accompanied by one instrumentalist, either a harpist or a xylophonist. Occasionally, both a harpist and a xylophonist accompany a singer, but this accompaniment is considered a modern innovation.

FIGURE 3 Two Burmese dancers (after Frost and Strickland 1927: between pp. 56 and 57).

Hsaìñwaìñ

The most important and frequently heard ensemble in Burma is the *hsaìñwaìñ,* or simply *hsaìñ.* It includes from six to ten performers. At a minimum, it includes a drum circle, a gong circle, a bass drum, large cymbals, a smaller set of cymbals, and an oboe. The first three instruments are placed in a row in front, with the others set behind them. If enough players are at hand and the instruments are available, it can also include gong racks, a set of side drums, one or more stick-beaten drums, and a large bamboo clapper. The *hsaìñ* accompanies all types of theatrical performances, of which Burmese are great devotees, and it is also played on ritual and religious occasions, such as spirit-propitiation rites, pagoda festivals, boys' entries into a temple as novices, girls' ear-piercing ceremonies, and so on (figure 3). Officials' visits take on pomp from the presence of a *hsaìñ,* as does an important funeral.

The name of the ensemble comes from the words *hsaìñ,* possibly meaning 'cords for hanging jars or pots', or 'to suspend by cords', and *waìñ,* meaning 'circle' or 'circular'. Two of the most important instruments, the drum circle and the gong circle, are constructed in just this way: small drums in the first case, or gongs in the second, are suspended from a circular frame.

Instruments of the ensemble

Drum circle

The *pa'waìñ* (*pa'* 'drum', *waìñ* 'circle, circular') consists of twenty-one tuned drums hung vertically by cords from a circular wooden frame. The frame, about a meter tall, is elaborately decorated with colored glass and gold paint. The drums, held away from the frame by cane, vary from 13 to 41 centimeters high. They have two heads, but only the upper one is struck. The *pa'waìñ* is tuned by loading the center of the head with a paste of boiled rice and ashes; the more *pa'sa* added, the lower the tone. One of the most imposing instruments in the ensemble, it is divided into eight sections, with a circumference of about five meters. The player of the drum circle, *hsaìñ hsaya* (*hsaya* 'master'), sits in the middle on a small stool. Only his head and shoulders are visible from outside the frame, but while he plays, his whole body bobs and weaves (figure 4).

An instrument resembling the drum circle can be seen in Indian temple reliefs, and Indians tune their drums by the same method as Burmese tune the *pa'waìñ.* The instrument is probably one of a few Indian instruments that survived in Southeast Asia beyond the period of Indian cultural dominance. A similar instrument is found in Thailand in the *piphat mawn* (*mon*) ensemble, but it has only seven tuned drums. Only since about 1920 has the drum circle included twenty-one drums; previously, they numbered nineteen.

Properly called the *pa'waìñ,* the drum circle is usually called the *hsaìñ,* so in everyday speech the names of this instrument and the whole ensemble are the same. This usage attests to the importance of these drums among the several in the ensemble, as does the fact that the player of the drum circle is the troupe's leader. Except when the *hsaìñ* is accompanying a singer or a dancer, the player of the drum circle determines what piece is to be played and when. He is also responsible for hiring and firing players in the ensemble, and for setting up engagements. Most *hsaìñ* are known by the name of the drum player who is their leader: the name of the ensemble, with the drum player's name prominently displayed in gold lettering, is usually emblazoned across a cloth backdrop used in performance.

Gong circle

The gong circle (*cìwaìñ, cì* 'copper, bronze'), consists of twenty-one small, graduated,

pa'waìñ Set of twenty-one tuned drums in a large, circular frame

cìwaìñ Set of twenty-one graduated bossed gongs mounted horizontally in a circle

maùñsaìñ Set of eighteen or nineteen bossed gongs on wooden frames in five rows

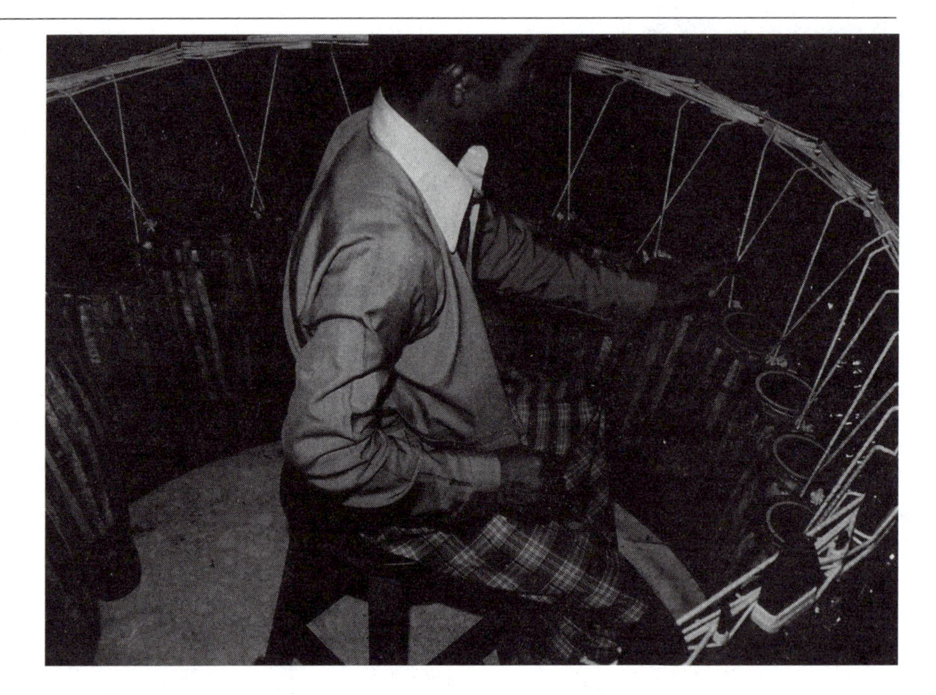

FIGURE 4 The Burmese drum circle (*pa'waìñ*) of twenty-one tuned drums. Photo by Terry E. Miller, 1994.

knobbed gongs set on a circular rattan frame resembling that of the drum circle. The gongs are struck with two beaters, formerly made of a soft wood, now made of wood with rawhide tips. To obtain the best tone, the player must strike the gongs at an angle. In the upper range (but not in the lower range), the gongs are damped with the fingers. Players tune the gongs by using beeswax to make lead filings adhere to the inside of the bosses of the gongs: the more filings added, the lower the pitch (figure 5).

The wooden frame is not so large as that of the drum circle: it is slightly smaller in circumference, and only about half as high. The instrument is placed near the drum circle, in the front row of the ensemble. Musicians usually learn to play it before going on to the *pa'waìñ.*

The number of gongs in the *cìwaìñ* has increased: in the early 1800s, they numbered only seventeen; by 1939, they numbered nineteen; and today, there are twenty-one.

Gong rack

The gong rack (*maùñsaìñ*) consists of eighteen or nineteen small, graduated, knobbed gongs, secured by cords to wooden frames divided into five rows (figure 6). The gongs are flatter and larger than those of the gong circle, and their tone is lower. Their sound differs, too, because they are made of a different alloy than is used for the gongs of the gong circle. This alloy gives them a less resonant, somewhat tinny

FIGURE 5 The Burmese gong circle (*cìwaìñ*). Photo by Terry E. Miller, 1994.

sound. All but the largest of the frames are set flat; the largest one is propped upright. The introduction of the gong rack seems to date from the 1920s or so (Becker 1980:475).

Miscellaneous drums

The *pa'má* (*pa'* 'drum', *má* 'main') is the largest drum of the ensemble, a barrel drum suspended from a wooden beam, often decorated with a dragon's head, inlaid glass, and gold paint. Both the size of the drum and the dimensions of its supporting structure make it a conspicuous feature of the ensemble. The *sakhúñ,* another double-headed horizontal drum, rests on a rack.

The word *hcau'loùñpa'* (*hcau'* 'six', *loùñ* 'counting word for objects', *pa'* 'drum') refers to these two drums plus smaller barrel drums, of various sizes, each standing on one drumhead (figure 7). The smaller drums are tuned to either the tonic or the fifth degree of the mode in use, or to other important pitches of the mode. Tuning is achieved either by using paste (*pa'sa*) or by tightening the drumhead to raise the pitch. The drumheads are struck by three or four fingers of either or both hands. The tone varies according to where the drumhead is struck and with what degree of force. The drumhead is sometimes damped with the palm, sometimes not.

The body of each drum is made by hollowing out a single teak log, with one end larger than the other; the larger drumhead is struck. Strips of hide secure the drumheads to the drum, and the crisscrossing strips over the body of the drum give it a striped look. The drums are arranged in order of size, the largest on the player's left, in a slight curve.

FIGURE 6 The Burmese gong rack (*maùñsaìñ*). Photo by Terry E. Miller, 1994.

Oboe

The multiple-reed oboe (*hnè*) is made of a conical tube of acacia or other hardwood, bored through the center. It has seven holes for fingering on its anterior side, equidistant from each other, plus a hole for the thumb on the underside, and a copper bell loosely attached to the end of the tube by means of a red cord. The bell does not amplify the sound; it appears to be primarily decorative, and the instrument can be played without one. The reeds are made of a toddy-palm leaf that has been soaked, and then smoked for months, folded, and cut so as to make six concentric layers; if the instrument is used frequently, the reed must be replaced every two or three months (figure 8).

The oboe comes in two types: larger, *hnè c̱ì* (*cì* 'large, great'), and smaller, *hnè ḵaleì* (*kaleì* 'small'). The former is about 45 centimeters long, the latter about 30 centimeters. The larger oboe serves in compositions of a slower tempo and greater digni-

FIGURE 7 A set of Burmese drums used to accompany dance. Photo by Terry E. Miller, 1994.

FIGURE 8 The Burmese multiple-reeded oboe (*hnè*). Photo by Terry E. Miller, 1994.

ty; it was always used on royal ceremonial occasions. The smaller oboe serves for quick and merry pieces, including those played for folkloric rituals. In performing softer music, particularly if accompanying singers, an oboist may substitute a bamboo, end-blown fipple flute (*palwei*), which has the same pitches and same fingering as the oboe. Both instruments have two-octave ranges, starting at about middle C on the larger, and at the G above on the smaller. Only fairly recently have the two oboes come to be pitched a fifth apart in this way. About the time of World War II, they were still pitched a fourth apart, and earlier still, only a third apart (Okell 1971:25).

Though the oboe seems to have come from India, and though its reedy sound reminds Westerners of West Asian music, it bears no special relationship to the Muslim community in Burma. The earliest surviving written reference to it is in a late-fifteenth-century poem, though an earlier Pagan inscription refers to what is likely a wind instrument of some sort (Okell 1971:25).

Other instruments

In the *hsaìñ* ensemble, small cymbals (*sì*) are played with the *byau'*, a small block of wood with a slit in it, struck with a stick. *Sì* and *byau'* together articulate colotomic structure. The large metal cymbals in the *hsaìñ* can be called either *yak̲wìñ* or *lak̲wìñ* (figure 9). The *wale'hkou'* are large bamboo clappers, made from a section of a large type of bamboo. The *hsaìñ* ensemble includes one large, hanging, bossed gong (*maùñ*).

Relations among instruments

The timbre of each instrument determines its role in the *hsaìñ*. The oboe, ubiquitous in all outdoor ensembles (not just the *hsaìñ*), stands out for its reediness and extremely rapid variations. It carries the melody clearly, though the complexity of its variations can obscure the melody more than a vocal part would, and its sound tends to dominate any ensemble. The drum circle and gong circle also play idiomatic variants of the melody, but because of timbre and the fact that they can sound two notes simultaneously, they do not sketch the melodic line quite so clearly.

Burmese musicians say the gong circle should normally be less prominent than the drum circle; they view it as an accompanying instrument. Since the upper octaves of the drum circle do not resonate as much as the upper gongs of the gong circle, the

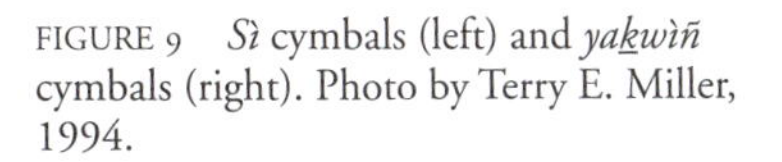

FIGURE 9 *Sì* cymbals (left) and *yak̲wìñ* cymbals (right). Photo by Terry E. Miller, 1994.

A specific tune and rhythm are associated with each spirit, and people who attend *na' pwè* with any frequency know after a few moments of music which spirit is about to be invoked.

latter are damped immediately after being struck. In the lower range, however, where the drums are more powerful, they do not risk being drowned out by the gongs, and the latter are not damped.

The one time the gong circle is not subordinate to the drum circle is at the outset of a performance. Tuning the drum circle is a time-consuming process, and during that time, the gong circle leads the *hsaìñ,* playing *yòudayà* songs and other classical compositions. Indeed, the gong circle provides the standard tuning for the ensemble.

The drums of the *hsaìñ* ensemble are integrated in performance according to two principles: the larger the drum or set of drums, the deeper its pitch or pitches; and the more rarely it is struck, the more important a role it plays in maintaining the rhythmic pattern, and the less it contributes to the melodic line of the song. The largest drum, at one extreme, is the *pa'má,* and the drum with the greatest range is the drum circle. The latter has virtually no control over the rhythm of the ensemble, but is prominent in playing the melody (figure 10).

Though certain instruments can play two notes simultaneously, Burmese musicians do not distinguish between a melodic part and a harmonizing part secondary to it. True, the upper range of such instruments is used for playing something like a basic melody of a composition, and the lower range plays either the same note an octave lower, or a concordant note. But the overall effect is not one of harmony. Instead, two-part instruments play lines that may at times be identical, at times distinct, but both of which relate to an underlying basic melodic line, which every instrument approximates. This kind of texture, known as heterophony, is as typical of the drum circle and gong circle in the *hsaìñ* as it is for the harp and the xylophone in chamber ensembles. In fact, it is true in most Burmese uses of the piano.

Occasions for use; repertoire

The *hsaìñ* ensemble accompanies many kinds of performances (figure 11). Increasingly, electronically amplified or acoustic Western instruments are mixed with the Burmese ensemble.

One context in which no Western instruments are likely to be mixed with Burmese is the spirit-propitiation rite called *na' pwè,* for which a *hsaìñ* will be hired to accompany mediums, most of them transvestites (of either sex), who dance to invoke spirits (*na'*), and then dance as the spirits take possession of them. A *na' pwè* begins, like a traditional marionette performance, as the *hsaìñ* gives a musical depiction of the threefold destruction of the world, swept by wind, fire, and flood. Then a devotee appears and sings a series of verses, dedicating offerings to the spirits and calling to witness the stage itself, the local spirit, and the people in attendance. She then sings the song of Indra, who in Burma is considered the king of the spirits. He speaks through her to say he is joining the celebration, then to say that he has enjoyed himself and is returning to his heaven. After this, the series of songs invoking individual spirits begins, lasting several hours into the night (K 1981).

FIGURE 10 An exceptionally ornate carved wooden stand for drums at Rangoon's University of Culture. Photo by Terry E. Miller, 1994.

A specific tune and rhythm are associated with each spirit, and people who attend *na' pwè* with any frequency know after a few moments of music which spirit is about to be invoked. As in many other contexts, the musicians will often banter with some of the people dancing. Much of this interaction consists of punning, and much is bawdy. It is unclear whether it is the ritual nature of the event that makes *na' pwè* more resistant to Western musical influence than other kinds of performances, or simply the slightly unfashionable, somewhat licentious reputation they have among Burmese who disapprove of the ritual on both theological and moral grounds.

In full-scale theatrical performances (*za' pwè*), the *hsaìñ* accompanies actors as they sing, and provides a musical commentary on much of the action. Most of this music derives from the classical collection of texts, the *Maha Gitá*. The *hsaìñ* also plays an overture at the opening of the performance, interludes between scenes, and closing music at the end. When actors sing, they enter into something like a dialogue with the drum circle. The actor sings a verse of music, and then the player of the drum circle replicates as closely as possible the embellishments the actor has used. The actor then sings another verse. This pattern is occasionally broken, however: the *hsaìñ* may play music evoking a different context as an interlude after the vocal part, rather than simply repeating that part, to suggest another dimension of the scene.

The ability of the *hsaìñ* to evoke a particular mood or context is central to its role in a performance. Most traditional Burmese music is basically vocal music, and even when no singer voices the words, the text of a composition, or at least its gist, is

FIGURE 11 A village *pwé* (after Frost and Strickland 1927: between pp. 62 and 63).

present in people's minds. Musicians playing the standard repertoire can count on spectators' ability to make the appropriate associations to the music. Much of this is conventionalized, so that in scenes marked by grief, the *hsaìñ* plays a certain composition (*ngouhcìñ*); for fight scenes, another (*leìhcìñ*); for scenes of longing, yet another (*hmaiñ*), and so on. Aside from evoking specific emotions, certain compositions are appropriate to particular situations; a hero meditating in a forest calls for one tune; certain compositions are available for use when an evil king makes his entrance; and so on. But variation is possible, and the *hsaìñ* can even weave thematic material together, so a flying horse's entrance can be accompanied musically by the theme for another character combined with strains of the music used in royal days to ready horses for battle (Garfias 1975b:8).

It is possible for the *hsaìñ* to play alone, especially in modern compositions. Called *bala hsaìñ* (*bala* 'bare, naked'), this kind of performance is rare, but it gives players an opportunity to display their virtuosity. In this context, the player of the drum circle is not beholden to someone else—either the vocalist, a spirit medium in the *na' pwè,* or the actor in a *za' pwè.* The musicians must try to hold people's attention by their remarks and jokes, and by the speed, intricacy, and variety of their playing. Players of drum circles have been observed at such a performance playing a particular tune several times over, identifying each rendering as the way one or another famous predecessor had played it (John Okell, personal communication).

There is one exception to the rule that the player of the drum circle is the leader of the *hsaìñ.* A genre called *anyeíñ* brings together musicians, women who sing and dance, and clowns. In the days of Burmese kings, this was a royal entertainment. Now it is a popular one, less elaborate and costly than a *za' pwè,* and more easily arranged on short notice, since it involves fewer players and few or no props. (This trait makes it appropriate for funerary occasions, such as observing a distinguished monk's death, which Buddhist doctrine enjoins people to perceive as a happy event, even as they mourn the monk's passing.) In an *anyeíñ* troupe, the leader of the ensemble is the xylophonist, not the player of the drum circle, who plays a much reduced version of the *pa'waìñ*—which may really be a *hcau'loùñpa'* set slightly expanded (John Okell, personal communication). The xylophonist organizes the troupe. The musical repertory of *anyeíñ* is distinct from that of *za' pwè.* The musical side of the performance is often somewhat diminished by the clowning that goes on between, and even during, musical numbers.

FIGURE 12 A long drum (*òzi*), used in village ensembles. Photo by Terry E. Miller, 1994.

Other outdoor ensembles

In Burma, as in much of Southeast Asia, drums are the defining element of many ensembles: both the ensemble and the repertory are denoted by the name of the constituent drum. Only in the style of chamber music does the percussive pattern become so reduced as to allow the elimination of drums. In it, a vocalist articulates rhythmic structures with a wooden clapper and hand-held cymbals.

Òzi

Òzi are goblet-shaped drums, about 25 centimeters across the head. An *òzi* is made by hollowing out a single block of light wood about a meter long. It is played vertically, resting on the drummer's chest and suspended by a cord from the drummer's neck. It is tuned to the fundamental pitch (*thañ hmañ*) by the application of paste (*pa'sa*) to the center of the drumhead. The *òzi* is played with cymbals, bamboo clappers, and often a bamboo flute or an oboe. The drummer and others sing and dance, playing a repertory of tunes specific to the *òzi* ensemble. *Òzi* are used on occasions that call for a procession of some kind, including pagoda festivals (figure 12).

Doùpá

Doùpá are small, double-headed drums, about 75 centimeters long. Their heads, made of cowhide, are of different sizes, the right one larger than the left one, measuring about 25 and 18 centimeters in diameter respectively. The right head is tuned to the fundamental pitch (*thañ hmañ*), the left to a pitch either four or five degrees higher; tuning is achieved with paste. *Doùpá* are played suspended horizontally across the chest, usually in an ensemble that includes large cymbals, an oboe, and large bamboo clappers. They may also accompany singers, who improvise texts to the rhythm of the drums. *Doùpá* are played in villages on festive or other important occasions.

Bouñcì

Bouñcì, like *doùpá,* are double-headed drums, and they are likewise played suspended horizontally across the chest. However, they are somewhat larger, about a meter long. They are usually played in pairs, on the occasion of rice-planting festivals, pagoda festivals, or other important events. They may be joined by an oboe, large cymbals, and large bamboo clappers, or they may play in a complete *hsaìñwaìñ.* The most famous is named after the city of its origin, Shwebo, Upper Burma, once the seat of a Burmese dynasty. Shwebo drums are said once to have measured 1.3 meters long and 37 centimeters across the face of one, 40 centimeters across the face of the other; today's drums are cut shorter.

Byò

Unlike the drums mentioned above, all of which are struck with the hands, *byò* are stick-beaten; made of teak, they are slightly larger than *doùpá,* are played in pairs, and are accompanied by a smaller drum, *palou'tou'.* Used in any ensemble, they are usually accompanied at least by a large oboe and cymbals. The ensemble plays on such occasions as a boy's becoming a Buddhist novice, and at the close of ceremonies and performances.

Sito

All the drums mentioned above are associated with rural Burma, at least in origin. *Sito,* however, are associated with royalty, as the name suggests (*si* 'drum,' *to* 'royal'), and in keeping with their special status, they are Burma's largest drums. They measure close to 1.25 meters long and 50 centimeters in diameter, and are double headed

saùñ Burma's arched harp, the last surviving harp in Asia

pa'talà Xylophone with twenty-four bamboo keys suspended over a wooden resonator

sì Two small hand-held cymbals shaped like bells

wà Clapper of spoon-shaped bamboo pieces

FIGURE 13 The Burmese chime (*cìsi*) played in a procession at Rangoon's Shwe Dagon pagoda. Photo by Terry E. Miller, 1994.

but played on one side only, struck with a stick. During the days of Burma's kings, they were played at all royal ceremonies. Since the fall of the last Burmese kingdom in 1885, they have been played on important ceremonial occasions, in company with one or more large oboes, gong racks, cymbals, and clappers. Their history is illustrious: they were mentioned in an inscription from the Burmese kingdom of Pagan in 1190.

Sporting-event ensembles

Two types of Burmese sporting events may be accompanied by a small ensemble consisting of gongs, an oboe, and drums. These events are Burmese boxing and a game called *hcìñlòuñ,* in which people standing in a circle use their feet, heads, and torsos, but not their hands, to keep a rattan ball in the air; their aim is grace and agility. Most games of *hcìñlòuñ* are simply neighborhood pickup matches; but occasionally, exhibitions are put on as part of neighborhood celebrations or pagoda festivals, and at these exhibitions, a small musical ensemble will accompany the playing.

Indoor ensembles (chamber music)

The chamber ensemble, unlike the *hsaìñ,* is likely to be heard by small gatherings of people—probably musicians themselves—who enjoy its qualities. It is also heard on state-run radio and television. It affords women more opportunities for music making than the *hsaìñ.* Women may learn to play the harp, and female vocalists are probably more numerous than male. Otherwise, women can take part in musical performances only as actresses, singers, or dancers, either in *za' pwè* or *anyeiñ*.

Chamber music usually combines one vocalist and one instrument, either the arched harp or the bamboo xylophone. The bamboo flute (*palwei*) can join either of these instruments. Piano and guitar are sometimes used in modern styles of chamber music.

Arched harp

Burmese consider the arched harp (*saùñ*) their most prestigious instrument, associated with the refinement and sophistication of the old royal courts. It consists of two parts: a resonator, carved from a hollowed piece of hardwood; and the curved root of an acacia tree, set into the resonator to provide a long, graceful arch. (The root, which should widen toward the end to resemble a leaf of the sacred *bo* tree, must be found in that shape in nature.) The design gives the instrument an unusually elegant form, resembling a swan arching its neck.

The top of the resonator is covered with deerskin. The fourteen strings of the modern harp are stretched between a slightly curved bar on the resonator and the lower portion of the arch. Some of the strings are of twisted silk, and some of them are now of nylon. The strings can be tightened or loosened with tuning cords whose tassles hang down from the arch. A small wooden loop is attached to the front of the resonator to secure the harp during tuning. The instrument is covered with three coats of lacquer to conceal the seams between the various parts of the instrument, giving it a smooth, even surface. It may be decorated with gold leaf, semiprecious stones, and lacquer designs.

Four holes are cut in the deerskin membrane. The moment these openings are made is considered astrologically influential over the harp's future performance. As one opens these holes, one asks spirits to take up residence in the resonator, and one must treat the instrument with the respect that heirlooms and other valuables often elicit in Southeast Asia (Williamson 1968, 1975a).

The harpist sits cross-legged, with the resonator placed on the right thigh and the arch against the left one. The right elbow rests on the top of the resonator while the thumb and index finger of the right hand pluck the strings. The left thumb presses the strings to modify the pitch (figure 14).

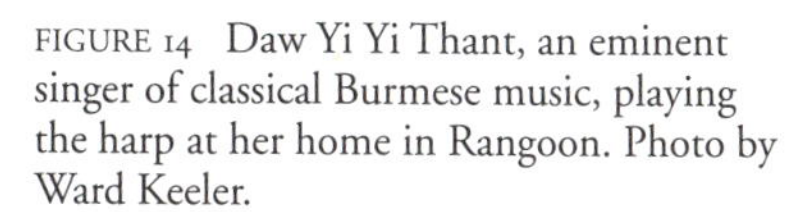

FIGURE 14 Daw Yi Yi Thant, an eminent singer of classical Burmese music, playing the harp at her home in Rangoon. Photo by Ward Keeler.

The harp reached Burma from India. Burmese assume that the images of harps seen in reliefs in Pagan depict the ancestor of their modern arched harp, but the pictorial evidence points to an origin in the harps of southern coastal India. The images of Pyu harps in Lower Burma show an intermediate form between the Indian ancestor and the modern Burmese *saùñ,* which resembles these Pyu harps much more than the ones pictured in Pagan (Becker 1967:18).

A fresco from the Ava dynasty (1364–1555) shows a harp with a curved arch and eleven strings. The great musician and statesman of the Koùñbauñ dynasty, Myáwadi Wuñc̱ì Ù Sá, seems to have increased the number of strings to thirteen from seven; Deiwá Eiñda Ù Mauñ Mauñ C̱ì (1855–1933), the last court harpist, added the fourteenth string, the shortest and therefore highest in pitch. Some harpists have begun using a sixteen-stringed harp, but this version is not universal (Williamson 1975a:111, 1980:482). During his exile after the fall of Upper Burma to the British, the last Burmese king, Thibaw, summoned Ù Mauñ Mauñ C̱ì to India to play for two royal ceremonies, including his daughter's wedding. Perhaps the king felt that the ceremony would be lacking without the traditional royal entertainment.

The history of this harp suggests development toward an ever more complex, virtuoso style, perhaps inspired by Thai musicians said to have influenced Burmese music after the fall of Ayuthaya. At present, the harpist plays in accordance with the tempo set by the hand-held cymbal and the bamboo clapper (both under the singer's control), but the harpist may either follow the vocal line or diverge from it. In any case, the harpist must remain within a general range, the *tì ḵwe'* (*tì* 'to play an instrument', *ḵwe'* 'area, patch'), determined by the tune and mode of the composition (Williamson 1980:482–484).

Pa'talà

The alternative major instrument of a chamber ensemble is the bamboo xylophone (*pa'talà*). (The term probably derives from the Mon words for a percussion instrument and a box or chest.) The contemporary *pa'talà* consists of twenty-four bamboo slats suspended over a resonating chamber. The slats narrow progressively as one moves up the scale, toward the player's right. Twine passing through holes at either end of each slat links the slats. Their range covers three full diatonic octaves, plus two notes on the treble end. Makers tune each slat by shaving its underside: shaving the middle lowers the tone; shaving the ends raises it. The *pa'talà* is played by two padded beaters (figure 15).

The earliest evidence for the instrument comes from the Kalyani Inscription (1400s) and a literary reference of the 1500s. The *pa'talà* resembles several Southeast Asian xylophones, including the Thai *ranat* and the Khmer *roneat.*

Hand-held cymbals

The *sì* consists of two small, hand-held cymbals shaped like bells. Between the thumb and the forefinger of the right hand, a vocalist holds one bell steady, its mouth upturned. A string links this bell to another one of the same size and shape, held and manipulated by the other fingers of the same hand. In performance, the latter bell strikes the former at set intervals.

Clapper

A hand-held clapper (*wà*) is made of bamboo. The vocalist holds it in the left hand, rapping it against the thigh at set intervals, in coordination with the *sì,* to control the tempo (figure 16).

FIGURE 15 Secondary students at the Fine Arts Department school in Rangoon practice xylophone (*pa'talà*). Photo by Terry E. Miller, 1994.

PERCUSSIVE PATTERNS

Burmese music typically includes a wide array of percussive instruments—drums of many shapes and sizes and gongs spanning several octaves. But the most important percussive instruments in any ensemble that includes vocalists are the diminutive cymbals (*sì*) and the bamboo clapper (*wà*), held in the singer's hands. Using these, the vocalist controls the tempo.

Most classical songs begin with a nonmetered section, which leads to a fixed meter for the greater part of the composition until a final coda, when nonmetered music returns. The meter is articulated by the *sì* and the *wà* in one of three cyclic rhythmic patterns, each with eight beats. In the following three patterns (after Becker 1980:479), x is *sì* and o is *wà*.

Phrasal beats	*1*	*2*	*3*	*4*	*5*	*6*	*7*	*8*
Pattern 1		x		o		x		o
Pattern 2		x		x				o
Pattern 3				x		x		o

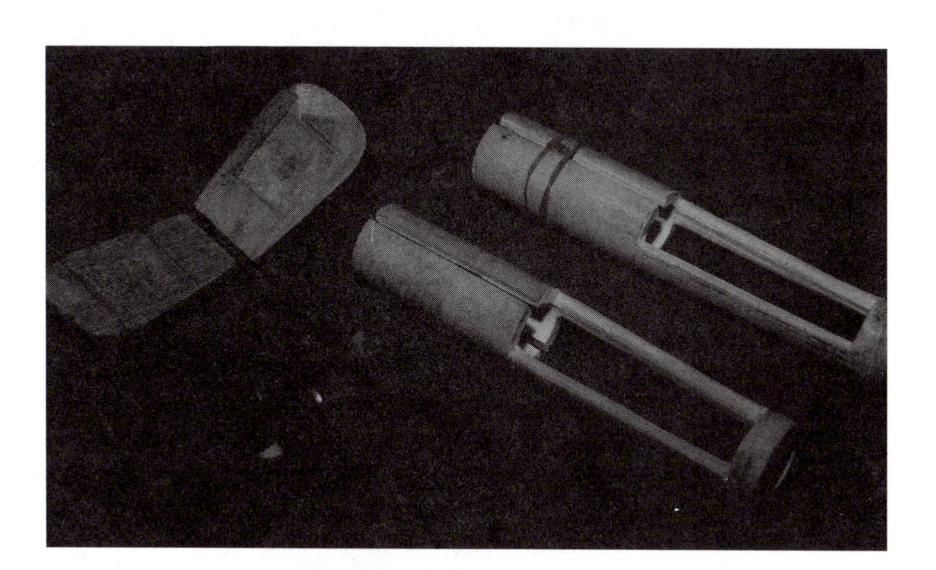

FIGURE 16 Two forms of Burmese clappers (*wà*). Photo by Terry E. Miller, 1994.

A good singer should maintain an almost nonchalant air, singing variations that bear little obvious relation to the steadiness of the *sì* and the *wà*. But the singer still has a responsibility to keep the beats in good order.

Because there are many more types of song than rhythmic patterns, there is no one-to-one correspondence. Furthermore, though most songs within a single type will use the same rhythmic pattern, not all do. Most *coù* songs are in pattern 1, and most *yoù-dayà* songs are in pattern 2.

A point of some confusion is whether the *wà* marks the first or the final beat of a four-beat cycle. It is agreed that it marks the strong beat, and the *sì* marks weaker beats. However, Burmese musicians state that the *wà* should be written as the first beat of a bar, whereas Westerners point out that it is sounded at the final, culminating beat, and so should be noted as the fourth beat. This problem is all the more vexing in that a composition can begin on either *sì* or *wà.* The first song a student learns begins with a little exercise, two lines in which one sings the words *sì* and *wà,* striking each of them in time to the appropriate word. The song is in duple time, and the first line begins with *sì.* The first line of the poem itself, however, begins on *wà.* Then again, some songs begin not on *wà,* but on *sì.* It appears true, however, that every composition ends on *wà,* usually held off in much the same way that the final gong in a Javanese gamelan composition is briefly delayed.

To confuse matters further, the symbols by which *sì* and *wà* are noted on a page appear to be reversed in Mandalay and Yangon. In the above table, I have changed Becker's notation to conform to Mandalay usage. The symbol for *wà* looks like the way the word is written in Burmese, with a central circle indicating the initial /w/ sound.

In analyses of the "First Thirteen *Coù* Songs" (1975b) and a *bwé* song (1979b), Muriel Williamson documented the integration of vocal and harp parts with reference to *sì* and *wà* patterns 1 and 2. In the *coù,* the meter is duple, and a typical couplet consists of sixteen beats divided into eight measures (*walaśì*). The singer, accompanied by the harpist, sings the first line of the couplet during the first four measures. In the second line, the singer completes a cadential formula (*thañ çá̱*) in three measures. The harp then completes the cadence in the eighth measure. In the *bwé* song, the metric pattern, called *nayiṣì* (pattern 2 above), is quadruple. The singer's line runs ostensibly from the first *sì* through the second in each phrase, though embellishments may cause it to extend through the silent beat. The fourth beat, however (on which the *wà* falls), is reserved for the harp, which confirms the singer's cadence. The singer continues into beat four only to add dramatic emphasis, or to reinforce the cadence.

Judith Becker (1968), analyzing Southeast Asian percussive patterns, has helped clarify the principles at work in Burmese music. She finds throughout Southeast Asia the pervasive use of eight-beat and sixteen-beat phrases, phrases in which odd-numbered beats are little stressed, and even-numbered beats are stressed in a hierarchical pattern that reserves the greatest emphasis for the final beat of the phrase. In many Southeast Asian ensembles, a gong marks this beat. (In Burmese chamber music, the clapper marks the end of a phrase.) The degree of emphasis a beat receives is set by the number of percussive instruments—drums, cymbals, gongs, clappers—that sound. Both percussive patterns and melodic contours support the sense of completion at the end of eight-beat or sixteen-beat phrases.

The structure provided by these rhythmic patterns is a foil to the variations and embellishments played by members of the ensemble. Much of the artfulness of Burmese music lies in how a singer, a harpist, or another instrumentalist plays around a steady beat. A good singer should maintain an almost nonchalant air, singing variations that bear little obvious relation to the steadiness of the *sì* and the *wà*. But that nonchalance must never lead the singer to compromise a responsibility to keep the beats in good order.

VOCAL MUSIC

TRACK 7

Burmese music is essentially vocal: most compositions are settings of poetic texts, although not always performed with a vocalist. The repertoire of songs divides up into types. The name of a type may be that of a poetic form; it may refer to the pattern of its rhythmic accompaniment; or it may refer to some circumstance, historical or cultural, connected to a set of compositions.

The Burmese musical modes and the principal types of song exemplifying them are:

1. hnyìñloùñ
   - coù
   - bwé
   - thahcìñh̲k̲añ
2. au' pyañ
   - pa' pyoù
   - lòká na' thañ
   - leìdwei thañ ga'
3. palè
   - yoùdayà
   - talaìñ
   - moñ
   - bòle
   - thañzàñ
4. myìnzaìn
   - teìda'
   - shi'hsebo
   - deìñ thañ

The classical repertoire, consisting of the above types of song and called *thahcìñ c̲ì* (*thahcìñ* 'song', *c̲ì* 'great'), developed over several centuries. The earliest song, "*Bauñ Là Coù,*" the sixth of a set known as the "First Thirteen *Coù* Songs," reputedly describes a king's passage up the Irrawady to Tagaung in about 1370. Two other songs in that set are also believed to have originated in the 1300s. The first five *coù* of the set, in the order in which they were eventually arranged, are believed to date from the early 1700s: four of them are attributed to Wuñc̲ì Padeitháyas̲a, a royal minister born during the Toungoo dynasty, about 1672. The last five are attributed to Myáwadi Wuñc̲ì Ù Sá (Williamson 1975b).

Coù, bwé, and *thahcìñh̲k̲añ* are all old songs of the royal court, celebrating the king, other notables, events, and places. *Pa' pyoù* songs, composed later, quote these songs while incorporating new elements. They are the most numerous of the classical songs in the repertoire. The special popularity they enjoyed at court suggests a kind of play among the cognoscenti, people knowledgeable enough to appreciate references to, and variations on, the canon. These songs are considered particularly difficult, requiring a thorough knowledge of the repertoire to be performed correctly (Garfias 1975b:12) (figure 17).

FIGURE 17 Instrumental version of last *coù* song published by the Ministry of Culture in 1960 (excerpt). Provided and edited by Robert Garfias.

Yoùdayà songs are traditionally thought to have been brought to Burma at the time of the Burmese sack of Ayuthaya (1767), though contemporary Thai apparently hear nothing familiar in them. (*Yoùdayà,* the Burmese version of *Ayuthaya,* is the word with which Burmese label the country and people of Thailand.) *Moñ* and *talaìñ* songs, far fewer, are also thought to derive from a non-Burman source—the Mon people, living in Lower Burma, Thailand, and Cambodia.

Deìñ thañ songs are used in propitiating spirits (*na'*). Like several of the smaller groups of types of song, they are short, strophic songs whose melody changes slightly to conform to the text.

Language and music

Poetic forms are distinguished by both meter and rhyme, though either or both of these constraints can vary in rigidity, reflecting the period in which a text was composed. In the earliest known Burmese poems, the number of syllables per line and the pattern of the rhymes are strictly regular, but by the 1600s, greater flexibility and complexity were permitted. Consequently, many songs do not display perfectly regular line length, but since the same melodic line is not applied to different verses, this irregularity is not so problematic as it would be in Western compositions based on repeating melodies with a series of substituted lyrics.

The language of the texts is both archaic and allusive; many Burmese have difficulty understanding the songs. Burmese who do not care for classical music cite this lack of intelligibility to explain why it bores them; aficionados, however, though they may have little more sense of the songs' meaning, are not daunted by the obscurity of the language, and are satisfied to have some minimal notion of a song's meaning. Famous pieces in the repertory are familiar from their contexts: without knowing the meaning of certain words, one can appreciate that a particular theatrical song played whenever a horse appears has to do with horses.

Linguistic and musical tones

An intriguing, but as yet too little researched, question is how the phonetic constraints of Burmese, a tonal language, are reconciled with the tonal variations of the melodic lines to which words are set. The Burmese language has only two distinct tones, but syllables are further differentiated by voice quality, duration, and the presence or absence of a final glottal stop. The result yields five possible types of syllables: high, short, "creaked" (with a slight final glottal occlusion); high and heavy (in final position, falling); high with a full glottal stop; low, though sometimes pronounced as a rising tone; and toneless.

Williamson (1981) examined the relations between Burmese types of syllables and the shape of melismas in a classical *bwé* song, seeking to find which syllables are likely to be pronounced on two or more notes, and whether melismas end on the same, a higher, or a lower pitch. She found that low-tone syllables are the most flexible, so melismas can end in any of the three possible ways, though in the important cadential positions, melismata on low-tone syllables fall. High stopped syllables are also flexible. High heavy-tone syllables do not have melismas that end higher than they begin, though they may rise before falling. High, creaked tones are the least flexible; they are sung consistently to falling thirds (or rarely seconds) in a melodic pattern called *dyáñ,* which one learns by name in the first *coù* song. Indeed, this type of syllable receives remarkably consistent musical treatment: no matter what the shape of the melody up to a given point, it is usually sung on the notes *thoùñp̱au'* to *ngàp̱au'* (6 to 4; in the mode *hnyìñloùñ,* this would be about A to F) or *thoùñp̱au'* to *leìp̱au'* (6 to 5; in *hnyìñ loùñ,* A to G). Robert Garfias (1981) suggested it would otherwise be particularly difficult to distinguish high creaked syllables, which in speech are pronounced with a brief, strong pulse, from high, heavy syllables, since any musical setting is likely to cause syllables to be held longer than is usual in speech.

Syllables and music

A related and even more difficult question is how types of syllables and their musical settings relate to each other in a series, that is, not simply the melodic handling of single syllables, but the relation between types of syllables and pitches in phrases. In speech, what indicates the tone is not the absolute pitch of any one syllable, but whether it is higher or lower relative to the preceding tone. The relationship is likely to be compromised by virtually any musical phrase. How is intelligibility maintained?

No single participant in an ensemble sings or plays "the song" in an isolable, repeatable form. Instead, each member of the ensemble plays variants.

Williamson provided part of the answer in noting that in cadential positions, high and heavy tones are likely to be set to falling melismas. Okell remarked that in the first *coù*, the phrase *tò p̱iñ tò loùñ* ends with a high-tone syllable, *loùñ*, but on a lower note than the preceding syllable, indeed on the same note as the low-tone syllable *p̱iñ*. In speech, this would suggest that *loùñ* was instead a low tone. A musician explained that to avoid that suggestion, one sings the final syllable starting from a higher note, only then falling to the cadential, lower pitch. The higher note at the outset accords with the word's high, heavy tone, which the lower pitch, required by the cadence, contravenes. This comment implies that melismas make possible an approximation of the proper tonal relations between syllables in succession, at least enough to assure moderate intelligibility, despite the vagaries of the tune.

Nevertheless, the types of syllables and musical-pitch relations probably risk reducing intelligibility for those unfamiliar with a particular composition. A middle-aged Burmese man living in the United States, overhearing his teenage daughter's Burmese pop music, asked whether the performers were singing in Burmese or in English. Part of his confusion was due to the poor quality of the sound of Burmese recordings, but it also reflected the way the melodies compromised the tonal relations between syllables.

What is a Burmese tune?

Given that there is no standard system of notation for Burmese music, and that anthologies contain only the texts of songs, the question arises of just what it means to "know" a particular composition. No single participant in an ensemble sings or plays "the song" in an isolable, repeatable form. Instead, each member of the ensemble plays variants. To uncover their basis, Williamson elicited three sung versions of a single *bwé* song, one of them with a harp accompaniment played by the singer. She then extracted an underlying, unembellished tune, which she labels the basic tune, one that only a beginner, if anyone, would ever learn. The crucial elements of this tune, she concludes, are the initial pitches and the cadential formulas for each stanza and line, and for any important part-line break in the poem (Williamson 1979b).

Still, there is a basic melodic shape more specific than that list of constituent parts suggests. A Japanese ethnomusicologist who asked for similarly alternative versions of the same piece demonstrated the consistency of melodic shape (Tokumaru 1980:72). True, this was an elementary piece of the repertoire, the first of the "First Thirteen *Coù* Songs," one used only for pedagogy. As Williamson claimed, vocalists, oboists, and players of drum circles enjoy considerable freedom to embellish and vary a musical line, provided they stay within the parameters of the particular song's tonal levels and rhythmic constraints. Williamson also observed (1981) that one common area of divergence in different singers' renderings of a single composition lies in the frequency with which they use melismas instead of stationary syllables (sung on one note only), and in the complexity and range of those melismas.

It is useful to compare Williamson's concept of basic tune with Sumarsam's account of an inner melody in Javanese gamelan composition (1975). This inner melody, played by no single instrument or singer, is still present in the participants' minds as they play. The comparison points to one clear contrast. The neophyte in Java can play the *balungan,* sometimes translated 'nuclear melody', on one of the technically simpler instruments; and once memorized, that sequence of notes provides a guide to the pitches of nodal points (ends of phrases and of gong periods) in the composition. It does not provide a guide to the tune of the composition, however, dispersed among the voice, the rebab, and other lines, all of which are open to embellishment and variation. Although Burmese music offers the learner no easy aid to a piece comparable to the Javanese *balungan,* the basic melody of a Javanese or a Burmese composition—what a musician hears as constant or distinctive in a composition—seems elusive in similar ways.

One other comparison with Java is perhaps appropriate. Williamson found that all three singers she recorded used the same figures at certain dramatic points in the song, despite the ostensible freedom for variation inherent in Burmese performances (Williamson 1979b). Similarly, in Java, a particular composition will often contain some crucial figure not open to the same degree of variation as the rest of the piece. This figure is not indicated in the piece's *balungan*: it is simply learned from a teacher, or is assimilated by the musically alert as an intrinsic element of the composition.

P. A. Marano reported (1900) that Burmese favored high tenor voices in men and deep contralto voices in women. Those preferences still seem to hold, particularly in the classical repertoire. Vocal range is not much stressed, however. If a singer finds that a song is reaching beyond the limits of his or her range, sudden octave displacement up or down can be done without embarrassment.

A few songs are sung without accompaniment, a few more are sung with the *si̱to* ensemble, and others are sung with the various folk ensembles mentioned above; however, it was hard, already in the 1960s, to find people who could still sing those folk songs (K 1981). Much more common is for a singer to be accompanied by a harp, a xylophone, or sometimes a *hsaìñ* ensemble, the musicians repeating each sung verse.

Burmese musicians say the accompaniment to a singer should be fairly simple. The repeat, however, affords musicians an opportunity to display their skill at improvising complex variations. In *anyeíñ,* the repeat accompanies the singer as she executes a dance, and in this, as in all contexts, the rhythms are livelier than in the initial rendition (figure 18).

TUNING

The Burmese scale—or perhaps more accurately, the Burmese system of tuning—consists of seven notes to the octave. Burmese who are familiar with Western music theory often compare their scale to the C-major scale. The pitches of the scale are given one set of names for instruments in the *hsaìñ* ensemble and a different set of names for instruments in the chamber ensemble. In the case of the *hsaìñ* instruments, pitches are named after the fingering positions of the oboe. The tonic is called *thañ hmañ* (*thañ* 'sound, note', *hmañ* 'correct'), the note obtained by open fingering. The rest of the pitches are named not in ascending order, but in descending order, as obtained if one covers each of the seven holes of the oboe in order, proceeding from the top to the bottom of the cylinder.

The names of the tones make this model clear: the second note of the Burmese scale, called "two holes" (*hnapau'*), meaning that two holes are covered, is the seventh degree; the third note, "three holes" (*thoùñpau'*), corresponds to the sixth degree.

FIGURE 18 *Na'* song in version for *hsaìñ* or chamber ensemble (excerpt). Transcribed and provided by Robert Garfias.

Garfias suggests that the descending order is explained by the fact that Burmese melodies tend to follow a descending contour (Garfias 1975a:39). The reversed order of the notes from Western practice sometimes causes confusion.

In the chamber-music ensemble, a different set of names applies. The two sets of names are as follows:

chamber music	*degree*	*hsaìñ*
hnyìñloùñ	tonic	thañ hmañ
palè	seventh	hnapau'

chamber music	*degree*	*hsaìñ*
duraká	sixth	thoùñp̱au'
pyidopyañ	fifth	leìp̱au'
au' pyañ	fourth	ngàp̱au'
myìñs̱aìñ	third	hcau'pau'
hcau'thwenyúñ	second	hkuni'pau'

In the *hsaìñ* system, the series starting with *thañ hmañ* can refer to both a fixed series, in which *thañ hmañ* corresponds approximately to the Western C, *hnapau'* approximately to the Western B, and so on, and to a movable series, in which *thañ hmañ* denotes the fundamental pitch in each mode. In the chamber-music repertory, the series *hnyìñloùñ,* and so on, remains fixed, and a secondary set of movable names of tones (*tya, tei, tayò*) applies to the fundamental, seventh, and fifth degrees. Furthermore, *hsaìñ* musicians and players of chamber music usually tune differently: harpists and xylophonists tend to tune their instruments to a fundamental pitch close to D, but *hsaìñ* musicians tune *thañ hmañ* closer to C-sharp (Garfias 1980b).

How closely the Burmese scale actually corresponds to the Western diatonic scale is somewhat vexed, however. It seems clear that in the classical tradition the seventh and third degrees were somewhat lower, and the fourth degree somewhat higher, than their Western equivalents. However, three factors complicate matters. First, instruments with fixed tuning have different intervals than those with variable tuning. Second, measurements of the tunings of different ensembles in Burma show that even fixed-pitch instruments do not share precisely the same intervals (Khin Zaw 1940). And thirdly, the impact of Western music in Burma has apparently fostered a shift away from indigenous tuning toward Western diatonic tuning.

Because the seventh and third degrees of the Burmese scale are slightly lower than the Western ones, and the fourth degree is slightly raised, the Burmese scale gives a Westerner the impression of having equidistant intervals, much like those of Thai classical music. Garfias has warned us not to assume this to be the case, however, on the grounds Burmese musicians do not speak of equidistance as the ideal, nor do measurements demonstrate it (1980b:480).

As in Java and Bali, there seems in Burma to be a generally agreed-on tuning, with considerable tolerance for variation. The intervals among the fixed-pitch instruments need not, therefore, conform to a single standard.

Variable-pitch instruments and singers can make finer adjustments in intervals in accordance with the mode of a particular composition. They may not use precisely the same tuning as the rest of an ensemble. Tomoyoshi Otake has suggested that the analogy of the Javanese gamelan is instructive. Javanese music has an ideal five-tone *sléndro* scale, with some narrower and some wider intervals. Where the wider and narrower intervals occur depends on the starting pitch, which differs for each of three modes (*pathet*). Javanese singers and the stringed instrument, the rebab, can adhere to the ideal scale no matter what the mode, but the fixed-pitch instruments cannot, and the compromise in Java is to tune the latter according to a nearly equidistant scale.

In Burma, Otake (1980:57–58) has suggested there is once again a single ideal scale, but differing modes entail similarly diverse starting pitches and consequently differences in where narrower and wider intervals fall. As in Java, a compromise between the ideal scale and the fixed-pitch instruments is reached, though in Burma the pitch discrepancies are greater than in Java.

This analysis may explain the fact that, in two modes (*hnyìñloùñ* and *au' pyañ*), the fourth degree is slightly higher on the xylophone than as sung by the vocalist, and

Burmese audiences seem to tolerate pitch discrepancies to a surprising degree. These discrepancies make possible subtle and pleasurable play on modes, particularly in small ensembles.

in another mode (*pyidopyañ*), the seventh degree on the xylophone is slightly lower than that of the voice: the singer can make adjustments that the xylophonist cannot.

There are further complications. One possibility is that the vocalist who sings a fourth slightly lower than the xylophone and a slightly higher seventh is following not so much the constraints of the particular mode as the pull of the Western diatonic scale. Even if that is not so, Otake's explanation, based as it is on the physical constraints of the fixed-pitch instruments, may be unnecessarily reductive. He noted discrepancies between the pitches of voice and harp on the one hand, and between other instruments on the other, in the chamber ensemble. In the *hsaìñ,* he noted similar discrepancies between the drum circle and the oboe on the one hand, and the fixed-pitch instruments on the other. He also mentioned that both the harpist and the vocalist are likely to be influenced by the intervals of the fixed-pitch instruments. Yet Garfias observed that, in a chamber ensemble, the pitches of voice and harp could differ, and in the case of the *hsaìñ,* that the pitches of the voice, the oboe, and the flute could differ from those of the drum circle. In such cases, the harpist or player of a drum circle follows the tuning of the fixed-pitch instruments, even though either could easily follow what Otake called the ideal scale, as employed by the vocalist and either aerophone. This practice suggests that the discrepancy in pitches is attributable not simply to the contrast between fixed-pitch and variable-pitch instruments, but to a deliberate aesthetic choice, one that Garfias (1975a:49) found noticeable in the lightly ornamented parts of the singer's or aerophone's lines.

The piano may offer a perspective that would make Burmese pitch discrepancies appear less strange. Western violinists are known to remark that when playing the piano one cannot distinguish between an A-sharp and a B-flat—and they impugn the musicianship, indeed the ears, of pianists on those grounds. A violin is a variable-pitch instrument, a piano a fixed-pitch one, and that in performance they will often play slightly different pitches is something Westerners have no difficulty accepting. It may be that Westerners exoticize Burmese musical traditions unduly if, forgetting about the disparities between violin and piano in their ensembles, they overemphasize the significance of pitch discrepancies among the *hsaìñ* or the chamber-music instruments in Burma (figure 19).

If a Burmese harpist and a Burmese vocalist hit slightly different pitches, the effect is not likely to be as jarring as if a Western vocalist and an instrument with sustainable notes, such as flute or piano, hit and held slightly dissimilar pitches. No indigenous Burmese instrument except the oboe and the flute can sustain notes in this way, and there is no evidence that these two instruments use a tuning distinct from a vocalist's. It would be useful to know whether Burmese vocalists can maintain pitches distinct from those of a piano when the piano is played with Western tuning, but in fact the piano does not often sustain notes for any length of time when played in the Burmese style.

Burmese audiences seem to tolerate pitch discrepancies to a surprising degree.

FIGURE 19 The composer Ù Ko Ko plays traditional accompaniments on an electric piano with a violin, also playing traditional music. Photo by Terry E. Miller, 1994.

Garfias has suggested that these discrepancies make possible subtle and pleasurable play on modes, particularly in small ensembles. The tolerance for these discrepancies is most evident in large ensembles, especially when Burmese play Western instruments, or Western instruments in tandem with Burmese ones, as in *za' pwè*. It seems impossible, especially when a *hsaìñ* plays with Western instruments, to attain anything remotely like uniform tuning, and Westerners are unlikely to find the result pleasurable. That such mixed ensembles are popular in Burma should probably dissuade outsiders from concluding that Burmese are unaware of these discrepancies, and instead encourage analysts to ask what other criteria determine how Burmese derive pleasure from their music.

A possible analogue might be found in the realm of dance. The Western ballet tradition places enormous stress on the perfect coordination of the corps de ballet: several dancers, and sometimes every dancer, should make precisely the same movements at precisely the same instant. In Southeast Asian dance, dancers are less preoccupied with simultaneity, and spectators look for the style with which a particular dancer executes his or her movements, even in a group. Drawing an analogy between uniform movement in dance and uniform pitch in music, one might at least entertain the notion that much the same aesthetic approach, more individualizing than homogenizing, underlies the Burmese approach to music. The way that vocalists and the more prominent instruments in an ensemble give voice to diverse variations on a melodic line supports this suggestion.

The matter of the Burmese scale appears even more complex in the light of claims that Burmese singers are losing the ability to distinguish Burmese scales from the Western diatonic scale. In 1978, at a seminar on Asian music held in Japan, two respected Burmese teachers of the harp, one from the State School of Music and Drama in Rangoon, the other from the school of the same name in Mandalay, were asked to play the Burmese scale on the harp as it occurs in the *myìñsaìñ* mode, and then to sing it. The teacher from Rangoon, Ù Sein Pe, sang the scale with the fourth degree raised about half a tone above the fourth degree of the Western diatonic scale, thereby reproducing the note as it occurs on the xylophone. Ù Myint Maung, who frequently remarks on the loss of the Burmese scale, played and sang it like the Western diatonic scale. However, in performance, he tended to raise it to almost the same pitch as that of the xylophone. The incident was reported without commentary (Emmert and Minegishi 1980:57). Perhaps the reason for the disparity between Ù Myint Maung's demonstration and how he played the scale in performance was that he wished to demonstrate how most contemporary musicians would play the scale, but in performance he adhered to the traditional tuning. Also unclear, however, is whether "in performance" referred to the harp accompanying a vocalist alone, or the harp playing with the xylophone—a modern but no longer unusual practice, in which case Ù Myint Maung's pitch might simply have been pulled toward that of the xylophone.

Burmese treatment of the piano would appear at first sight to support Ù Myint Maung's claim that the Western diatonic scale has triumphed over the Burmese scale in most circumstances. Though Burmese formerly tuned the white keys of the piano to the Burmese scale to use it to accompany vocalists much as indigenous instruments do, in the course of the twentieth century this practice has been abandoned, and now a Western tuning is used. Yet the existence of sharps and flats on the piano provides notes beyond the standard C-major scale Burmese take as equivalent to their own, and Burmese pianists use the black keys in different ways according to which mode a composition is in, even when two modes have the same starting pitches. Although these notes are not available on most Burmese instruments, they may correspond to sung notes and sound quite unusual to Western ears. It appears, therefore, that the diatonic scale has not completely supplanted the Burmese one.

Actually, the Burmese playing of pianos is in itself somewhat surprising to Western ears. To Burmese, notions of a harmonic accompaniment to a melodic line often matter but little; instead, one hears the piano played in much the same way as the Burmese harp or the Burmese xylophone, the two parts playing a melodic line in support of the vocalist's line, but not really harmonically subordinate to it. One cannot preclude the possibility that a vocalist could maintain disparate tuning even when accompanied by the piano.

An essential relationship in Burmese music is that between any pitch and its concordant, called its *mei'* 'friend, pair,' a fifth below it or a fourth above it. Instruments that can play two parts often play a note and its *mei'* simultaneously, but a *mei'* can alternate with the main pitch in melodic, and especially cadential, patterns. Burmese cadences can cause a Westerner some surprise, since cadences on the fundamental pitch do not ordinarily sound completed to Western ears, but do to Burmese ears.

MODES

Burmese musical terminology appears to have no general word meaning mode, but there are named modes for both *hsàin̄* and chamber ensembles, and the concept is basic to traditional Burmese music. Burmese modes are susceptible to analysis with reference to both ends of Powers' scale-tune continuum. Modes are distinguished according to their fundamental pitches, and the pitches receiving greater or lesser stress in a composition: there is a "hierarchy of pitch relationships" (Powers 1980:377). At the same time, modes typically have recurring melodic formulas, shorter or longer passages that musicians exploit in improvisation and that listeners recognize as specific to particular modes. As it happens, Western scholarship on the subject divides neatly into accounts that emphasize scalar considerations (Garfias, Williamson) and those that emphasize melodic constraints (Becker).

Although every mode is based on five tones, all seven tones are used in all the available modes. The same heptatonic series of pitches is employed, classically with the raised fourth and lowered third and seventh degrees mentioned above, in every mode. In each mode, however, at least two tones are avoided in positions of stress, and in one mode (*hkunithañc̱i*) three tones are so avoided. These secondary pitches do appear, but in unstressed positions and primarily in the higher registers. Stressed positions are defined by rhythmic patterns. Cadences are particularly important to the identification of a specific mode.

Modes and the names

Just as there are two series of names of tones, one applied to the *hsaìñ,* the other to the chamber ensemble, so there are two sets of names for the modes. Each set, furthermore, admits of certain variations. Unfortunately, the published sources do not agree on what the names of the modes are. Burmese agree that the chamber-music ensemble has seven possible modes, of which only four are commonly used. Four names of tones from the chamber-music system of tuning do double duty as the names of these most commonly used modes. They are *hnyìñloùñ, au' pyañ, palè,* and *myìñs̱aìñ.* The remaining three are *pyidopyañ, duraká,* and *hcau'thwenyúñ.*

The names of the nine named modes in the *hsaìñ* ensemble, their fundamental pitches, and their approximate Western equivalents, as set forth by Garfias (1975a), are provided below.

mode	*fundamental tones*				
thañ yoù hcau'pau'	I	III	IV	V	VII
	C	E	F	G	B
hkunithañc̱i	I	III	IV	V	VII
	G	B	C	D	F
pa'saboù	I	II	III	V	VI
	C	D	E	G	A
tahcañ pou	I	III	IV	V	VI
	C	E	F	G	A
ngàp̱au'	I	II	III	V	VI
	F	G	A	C	D
hsi' cì	I	II	III	V	VI
	B	C	D	F	G
ngàp̱au' au' pyañ	I	III	IV	V	VI
	F	A	B	C	D
leìp̱au' au' pyañ	I	II	III	V	VI
	G	A	B	D	E
thañ yoù hnapau'	I	II	IV	V	VI
	B	C	E	F	G

Some musicians consider IV a secondary tone in the mode *hkunithañc̱i,* leaving only four primary ones (Garfias 1975a:44).

All but two of these modes (*thañ yoù hnapau'* and *ngàp̱au' au' pyañ*) can be reduced to two general sets, according to what the secondary pitches (S) are and what the intervals between the primary pitches are (after Garfias 1975a:44):

Type 1	1	S	3	4	5	S	7
Type 2	1	2	3	S	5	6	S

Tahcañ pou and *hnapau'* are exceptional cases, the former really a subset of *pa'saboù,* and *hnapau'* only rarely performed. However, since the starting pitches of the com-

mode Collection of musical elements forming the basis for improvisation and composition

fixed-pitch instruments Instruments, such as xylophones and gong circles, whose pitch cannot be changed during performance

variable-pitch instruments Instruments, such as fiddles and flutes, whose pitch is infinitely controllable during performance

yòudayà Genre of classical songs said to be derived from the Siamese at Ayuthaya

monly used modes differ, each mode feels distinctive to Burmese musicians, and despite the parallels in the structure of intervals that analysis reveals, this systematization does not figure in Burmese understandings of their music.

Not all modes are equally represented in either the *hsaìñ* repertory or the repertory of chamber music. The compositions most frequently played by *hsaìñ* are in the modes *thañ yòu hcau' pau', hkunithañci, ngàpau',* and *pa'sabòu.*

How the modes of chamber music relate to *hsaìñ* modes is unclear. *Hnyìñlòuñ* in the repertory of chamber music seems to correspond to *thañ yòu* in the *hsaìñ* repertory, *palè* to *pa'sabòu,* and *myìñsaìñ* to *ngàpau'* (Garfias 1980a:479). Garfias did not actually specify such equivalences systematically, however. Becker followed Khin Zaw's equivalences (1940), but the latter's modal names do not correspond to those of Garfias' list. Garfias stated that Burmese musicians are amenable to dividing modes into two basic types: the *hnyìñlòuñ* type in chamber music and the *thañ yòu* type in *hsaìñ,* on the one hand; and on the other, the *palè* type in chamber music and the *pa'sabòu* type in *hsaìñ.* However, the relations between *hsaìñ* and chamber music modes require clarification.

The modes imply changes in the tuning of variably pitched instruments. The drum circle and the harp must be retuned for each mode. Of twenty-one drums of the drum circle, the highest eleven are still tuned consecutively to all seven pitches of the scale, no matter what the mode. The secondary pitches in a specific mode occur in passing in the melodic variations that the drummer plays. In the lower registers, the drums are tuned to the five primary pitches of the mode, and the secondary pitches are not available. The harp's strings are tuned to the five main pitches of each mode, and the secondary tones are attained by pressing strings with the fingers of the left hand. The fixed-pitch instruments cannot simply eliminate the secondary pitches from the lower register, as the drum circle does; but in performance, players easily pass over such pitches (Garfias 1975a).

Modal melodic units

Becker (1969) emphasized melodic formulas rather than scalar constraints. Noting that Burmese nonmusicians can distinguish the modes with ease, she attributed this facility to the recurrence of melodic patterns specific to particular modes. The existence of a store of such patterns for each mode explains musicians' fluency in creating new compositions in performance.

Becker drew on melodic patterns to demonstrate how Burmese sort their songs into types, each associated with a particular mode. However, it is hard to discern the criteria by which songs are constructed, and how their various sections are perceived to be linked, particularly since the musical setting for each verse is unique, and in the course of a song there is no return to an earlier melody or verse. Becker suggested that modal regularities, conceived primarily in terms of recurring melodic formulas, bind together parts of a particular song, and songs of the same type one to another.

To support her assertions, Becker sought out the smallest repeating musical units in four songs of a single type, *coù,* in the mode *hnyìñloùñ.* These segments, consisting of brief sequences of a few notes, recur with sufficient frequency to distinguish themselves from random sequences of tones. Segments link to form longer patterns, which also repeat in the corpus. In a hierarchy of constituent units, patterns combine to form phrases, phrases combine to make verses, and verses combine to form songs. At each level, sets of equivalent—and so presumably mutually substitutable—units are discernible.

Shape is primary in determining what constitutes a category of segments. Segments having a falling fourth are likely to be treated as equivalent and interchangeable, but functions are also taken into account: whether units begin a sequence or instead approach a cadence can cause units of similar shape to fall into different categories. Certain regularities appear in segments according to their function: opening patterns tend to be somewhat static, using open octaves more than other patterns; and cadential patterns emphasize the tonic.

As a song progresses, Becker found a tendency to draw on melodic patterns from earlier verses, imparting a kind of aesthetic unity while maintaining links between the particular song and its mode. But what Becker sought finally was a set of syntactical rules for the combination of melodic formulas in any given mode—an ambitious project requiring exhaustive analysis of a large corpus of songs. Failing that, she pointed to melodic patterns that recur in the analyzed *coù* songs, and noted that in another, parallel analysis of *yoùdayà* songs (in the *palè* mode), she had discerned still other, distinctive melodic patterns, ones not characteristic of the *coù* songs.

On the basis of these studies, Becker concluded that melodic patterns specific to particular modes are what enable Burmese to identify the mode of composition. They also provide musicians with a storehouse of available patterns to combine and recombine as best they can. This process occurs virtually every time they play, inasmuch as they need never duplicate a performance precisely.

Margaret L. Sarkissian pointed out that Becker's analysis would have proved more convincing had she demonstrated her conclusions with reference to songs of another type within the same mode, and to songs of a different mode. For example, would one find similar or different melodic patterns in *bwé* and *thahcìñh̲k̲añ* songs, which are also in the *hnyìñloùñ* mode? In the absence of comparative data, it is hard to establish what depends on modes, what depends on the type, and what, if anything, is likely to be shared in the Burmese song repertoire (Sarkissian 1986:14). This question is all the more pressing in view of the fact that the *coù* that Becker analyzed form part of a thirteen-song set, the "First Thirteen *Coù,*" studied and even performed as a cycle in Burma. It seems possible, in the absence of confirming evidence, that the repeating patterns Becker discerned are typical of this cycle of songs, but not necessarily of *coù* more generally, or of the mode *hnyìñloùñ.*

An especially important element in any song, it appears, is the transition from starting to ending pitches. Musicians distinguish songs within a single mode by reference to just such a movement: they speak of songs in *thañ yoù* mode as *thañ hmañ–thañ hmañ c̲á* (*cá* 'to fall') if they both begin and end on the pitch *thañ hmañ,* but *thañ hmañ–hcau'pau' cá* if they begin on *thañ hmañ* and end on *hcau' pau'* (Garfias 1975a:49).

In an analysis of the "First Thirteen *Coù,*" Muriel Williamson (1975b), too, discerned many repeating patterns in these songs: a typical form of introduction, frequently repeated musical phrases, and in *coù* four through thirteen, essentially similar precodas (approaches to the coda), and coda. But she focused on the progression through levels of pitch (tonal centers) in the course of each *coù,* and above all on the cadences to each stanza. Levels of pitch are defined by open fifths, consisting of a root and the fifth below it, its *mei' thañ.* The modulations from one level to another, *thañ pyaùñ* (*pyaùñ* 'to move'), occur within one tuning, not from one tuning to another. At the end of each stanza, the vocal line cadences on either (in the earlier songs) a tone one step above the fifth that defines the level, or (in the last five songs) on a tone one step below that level. The harpist follows each vocal cadence with an *atò,* a cadential formula confirming the root and fifth. The name of the pitch above the fifth provides the name of the *atò*; *hcau'pau' tò* is the cadence on the principal fifth 3–7, and *ngàpau' tò* is that on the fifth 4–1.

On the basis of this study of tonal centers and cadences, Williamson (1975b:155) discerned a consistent form in all *coù* songs, characterized by the use of specific tonal centers at important points in the music. The principal fifth 4–1 (*ngàpau'*) typically characterizes one stanza, with a downward modulation to 3–7 (*hcau'pau'*) or its concordant 7–4 (*hnapau'*), followed by a return to *ngàpau'* (4–1). The pattern of movement from and back to *ngàpau'* may be repeated according to the length of the poem. There will also be an important section in *tapauk* (1–5), with the typical precoda and coda, also in *tapauk.*

Williamson linked the recurrent levels of pitch in her analysis to the melodic patterns Becker had discovered, saying a vocabulary of patterns typical of each level functions in making the transition from one level to another. In addition, the patterns within one level or one transition type are interchangeable, but Williamson implied that they are not substitutable between one pitch level and another.

While promising, Williamson's analysis dealt with a particular cycle of songs, and readers cannot be sure whether these patterns are generalizable to all *coù,* to all songs in *hnyìñloùñ* mode, or only to the *coù* in the studied cycle.

Becker's and Williamson's studies both made valuable suggestions about how to approach Burmese modes, but further confirmation is needed for their conclusions to stand. This is particularly clear because the usual links between type and mode do not always apply. In a few cases, two songs of the same type are in different modes. Burmese musicians attending a seminar in Japan in 1978 mentioned that some *yoùdayà* songs are in the *hnyìñloùñ* mode, but most are in the *palè* mode, whereas some *pa'pyoù* songs are in the *palè* mode, though most are in *au' pyañ* (Emmert and Minegishi 1980). Each such anomalous case would probably have to be accounted for individually, but until this is done, assertions about the defining traits of types and modes must remain provisional.

Another topic that deserves further research is how modes are handled in the more modern compositions—pieces that do not entirely break with Burmese musical traditions. Such compositions do not stick to one mode. Are modes completely extraneous to their makeup? Or is there simply more freedom in their treatment?

External constraints on modes

Research on modes in other societies, such as in India and Java, indicates that modes may be linked to criteria that determine when a particular mode is appropriate, or in what order compositions in different modes should be played. The matter has not been carefully addressed in Burma (Sarkissian 1986). In the theater, there seems to be no structured ordering of modes: compositions are played according to their thematic links to moments in the story as it unfolds. In other contexts, however, there do appear to be some patterns.

Garfias mentioned in passing (1975b:10) that in the course of a night at a *na' pwè,* one mode shifts to another, and then to a third, and that a fourth mode will have been used during the orchestra's playing in the afternoon, before the beginning of the *na' pwè.* He did not specify what the modes are. Khin Zaw remarked that only a song of the *pa' pyoù* type can be played after a *coù,* and that one may not have a *yoù-*

dayà or a *bòle* song in such circumstances (Khin Zaw 1940:415). However, it is not clear whether this is because the latter songs are of the mode *palè,* while the former are of the mode *au' pyañ,* or because of other aspects of these types. Khin Zaw also remarked that a *pa' pyoù* song must be followed by a postlude called a *than pyan* (*than* 'sound,' *pyan* 'return') to return to the tonic.

The lack of a consistent modal progression during a dramatic performance poses certain practical difficulties. The drum circle must be retuned for each mode, but retuning takes time, as the player of the drum circle must apply paste to several of the drumheads, and keep checking for pitch as he does so. To fill the time, clowns engage in banter with the musicians. Dramatic tension is not served by this practice, but dramatic tension is a Western concern, not a Burmese one. However, if the composition to be played is not long enough to warrant retuning the drum circle, the *hsaìñ hsaya* may simply omit certain pitches, substituting others.

TRANSMISSION AND CHANGE

The classical music tradition in Burma is maintained in two forms, written and oral. The written portion consists of the words of about five hundred songs. These have been collected in two anthologies, *Maha Gitá* and *Gitá Withòdani,* published in editions readily available in Burma. The contents of the two anthologies are largely similar, though some texts appear in only one or the other, and variants occur among some. The anthologies do not show how the texts are set to music, and the layout of the texts on the page does not suggest divisions into verses and stanzas—which readers must discern on the basis of the rhymes.

Since Burmese music does not have a consistent or a widely known system of notation, outsiders may wonder how its repertory of compositions can be transmitted from one generation to the next. The solution has been to embed the music-learning process in a larger social context, and to develop a vocabulary of oral conventions by which specific musical figures could be identified. The transmission of the musical tradition in Burma has always been marked by personal relationships between musicians and their apprentices. In the past, a young musician would go to live at the home of an established master—usually the leader or manager of an orchestra—for two or three years. In accordance with patterns for acquiring any desired skill in Southeast Asia, the apprentice would be available to do odd jobs around the house, and would accompany the troupe to its performances. Occasionally, the master would give the apprentice a lesson (Okell 1964). To what extent the pattern of live-in apprenticeship applied to female students is unclear.

When a master gave a lesson, he would usually teach tryout pieces (*asàñ*), brief compositions without a fixed beat, demonstrating a particular mode's important pitches. A student's later ability to improvise correctly depended on this knowledge. Another means to ease study was the existence of three versions of a tune, graded in difficulty, from the simplest (*acè* 'widely spaced'), to one of middling difficulty (*ala'* 'middle'), and finally an intricately embellished version (*asei'* 'densely packed'). But probably most important was the apprentice's experience listening to the ensemble perform. This enabled him to become familiar with tunes before learning to play them. He would eventually do so, but only after he had mastered the tune would he go to his teacher for guidance on fine points (figure 20).

Beside troupes to which aspiring musicians could attach themselves, the traveling theatrical troupes, most based in Rangoon or Mandalay and managed by the male romantic lead (*mìñthà* 'prince'), were important in transmitting Burmese music. They visited the towns of Upper and Lower Burma, especially in the central zone, during the cool, dry months from October to April. Local musical groups then imitated their music. At the same time, audiences learned the repertoire well enough to

In modern-dress plays, the Burmese *hsaìñ* is largely overshadowed by Western instruments (including electric guitars, amplified violins, electronic keyboards, trumpets, and snare drums) playing in alternation with or even simultaneously with the Burmese instruments.

FIGURE 20 Secondary students at the Fine Arts Department school in Rangoon study the Burmese harp. Photo by Terry E. Miller, 1994.

associate many important compositions to specific contexts. Such shared associations are essential to the effectiveness of the tradition's use of evocative themes.

Such touring troupes still exist, but it is uncertain to what extent they maintain the classical repertoire. Increasingly, the parts of the performance dealing with old-style historical and religious subjects (those linked to the classical repertory), are shortened or even omitted in favor of pop-music concerts at the start of a performance and dancing in mixed style, followed by modern-dress plays. In the last, the Burmese *hsaìñ,* while still present, is largely overshadowed by Western instruments (including electric guitars, amplified violins, electronic keyboards, trumpets, snare drums) playing in alternation with or even simultaneously with the Burmese instruments. To what extent the new-style performances maintain the traditional repertoire, adapt it, or abandon it, and whether younger audiences know the classical repertoire well enough to respond to musical allusions, are points deserving of research. The marionette (*you'theì*) tradition, which drew on the same repertory as the traditional *za' pwè,* has not taken on these modern forms, but it has become virtually extinct (figure 21).

In town, too, many people study music in private lessons, rather than through apprenticeship, though lessons are more likely to be exchanged for gifts and services than for cash, which would offend the dignity of some highly regarded musicians.

The establishment of the state schools offered students an alternative way to get musical knowledge. Administered by the Fine Arts Department, a unit of the Ministry of Culture, four schools at the secondary level (two each in Rangoon and Mandalay) enroll pupils. Each city has a school of music and drama and a school of

FIGURE 21 Two marionettes displayed in the Museum of History, Rangoon. Photo by Terry E. Miller, 1994.

FIGURE 22 A teacher at the University of Culture demonstrates a horse marionette. Photo by Terry E. Miller, 1994.

painting and sculpture, said to have opened in 1954. The school of music offers classes in Burmese music and its history, and instruction in voice, harp, piano, xylophone, and ensemble instruments. In September 1993, the department opened the University of Culture, a baccalaureate-level institution with degrees in music, theater, painting, and sculpture. Each freshman class in music would have fifty students, so after four years the university would have two hundred. Besides studying Burmese music, they would receive instruction in other world musics (figure 22).

Pedagogy

Most students first study singing, then an instrument. The first instrument taken up is usually the bamboo xylophone. A student of either voice or xylophone begins by learning the "First Thirteen *Coù*" songs. The first three are in the "widely spaced" style; the rest are usually taught in the "middle" style (Okell 1964). The whole cycle teaches the beginner a basic vocabulary of musical phrases, which recur in other *coù* songs and other compositions.

The range of information that needs to be conveyed orally if one is to transmit a Burmese composition without simply playing it is considerable, particularly since some instruments play two synchronous tonal lines. Remarkably enough, Burmese musicians have developed a system of solfège that manages to represent rhythm, melody, and the correct strokes—whether separate or simultaneous—and their pitches on two-part instruments (Garfias 1981). In the first *coù* song, the beginning student already memorizes, as part of the text of the song, the names of the three most important pitches of a mode: the fundamental (*tya*), the seventh degree (*tei*), and the fifth degree (*tyò*). One also learns the names of a melodic pattern of a falling third (*dyáñ*), a ninth built on the fundamental of the mode (*htañ*), and a fifth (*htouñ*). Syllables are available to name virtually all possible combinations of sounds (Garfias 1981, Williamson 1975b).

The basic vocal line and the instrumental accompaniment of a composition are closely tied. For example, the falling third in the vocal part of the first stanza of the first *coù* imposes a specific figure on the xylophonist, a figure always associated with that vocal pattern in the repertoire. Indeed, the basic structure of the accompaniment to any song is fixed by oral tradition. Nevertheless, players have room for ornamentation, provided that they know the constraints of the meter and mode.

Since the tradition has long been transmitted orally, passed down through lines of masters and their pupils, it is not surprising that variant versions of many songs exist, and that proponents of one variant or another defend them tenaciously. Given that modernity is understood by virtually all bureaucracies as equivalent to standardization, it is not surprising that the Burmese Ministry of Culture has attempted to establish "correct" versions of all songs. It remains to be seen how successful these efforts will be at eliminating rival traditions.

Westernization, the media, cultural policies

Perhaps the greatest threat to the continued transmission of Burmese music lies not in the absence of a system of written notation, but in Burmese interest in Western music. That interest dates back to the nineteenth century and remained strong even in the face of official disapproval during General Ne Win's rule.

Burmese responses to Western music must be understood in the context of Burma's history, particularly in relation to colonialism, as these tinge all of Burma's problematic relations with the outside world. The Burmese mix of defensiveness, imitation, and eclecticism is no doubt common to cultural developments in many postcolonial societies. Yet Burmese responses start from Burma's own musical traditions, and so give the results a particular cast. In fact, Burmese have found several means of bridging the gap between their own and Western music. In some cases, they have chosen to use a Western instrument such as the piano to accompany classical or neoclassical Burmese songs in a way resembling that of indigenous instruments. In other cases, they have forged new styles of singing that incorporate much about Western popular music, often choosing to accompany a single song with alternating Burmese and Western instrumental backups. In these modern songs with their mélange of styles, modes are no longer consistent within a composition. Finally, since the 1980s, Western pop has appeared ready to displace Burmese music entirely from popular tastes. Actually, to call this music "Western" is tendentious. Much of the most popular music in Burma today consists of pop music sung in Burmese but with fairly generic tunes, similar to those of Thailand, Indonesia, and Hong Kong.

Another practice common throughout Southeast Asia is to take popular Western hits and dub them in national languages. Comparing a few Burmese and Indonesian versions of the same Western original suggests that Burmese renderings are more successful at maintaining a jazzy or bluesy feeling. This difference may be attributed to the greater amount of syncopation and generally freer variations in Burmese singing. Regardless of origin, all songs intended for media dissemination, private (via cassette) or public (television, radio, public performance), must first be approved by official committees. Even songs originating in small, private studios undergo this process.

People have long decried the imminent loss of Burmese musical traditions. In a book published in 1900, the author of an appendix on Burmese music bemoaned how Western influences were driving out Burma's own music (Marano 1900). It is difficult, at this point, to determine just how many vocal and musical styles have been altered since then. In the late 1930s, an urgent appeal was made to the government to finance the recording of some of Burma's renowned older singers and musicians, lest their knowledge die with them. The establishment of state-supported art academies has encouraged the continued training of musicians and dancers schooled in the classical traditions. An unfortunate consequence of those schools' founding was that regional variations in the musical repertory were eliminated in favor of uniform teaching, and much of the dancing that students learn in the two academies is of a hybrid sort.

The state television station broadcasts brief programs of classical singing one evening a week, plus occasional dance performances. These, with performances by the two large state-supported National Cultural Troupes (Naiñ Ngañ T̲o Yiñ Ceì Hmú Ahpwé) and a smaller one, are in some respects the purest expressions of Burmese classical musical traditions one can find in Burma. Though these troupes' performances of Burmese music, dance, and theater are quite conservative, if highly abridged, those representing the National Brethren (including Chin, Kachin, Mon, Shan) are usually considerably altered, and a patriotic message is often imposed on them.

Probably the long-term result of pop's increasing popularity in Burma will be the confinement of the classical repertoire to a tiny segment of the population devoted to its pleasures, much as has occurred with classical music in the West. Commercial recordings of classical music are already difficult to find, despite the proliferation of cassette-shops in the cities. Enthusiasts with the necessary equipment record songs off radio and television as best they can. In recent years, the government has sponsored a nationwide competition for singers of classical songs and their accompanists each November in Rangoon. In preparation, during the months prior to the competition, the country's FM radio station broadcasts performances of much of the repertoire of classical songs by established performers.

Most performances in Burma use elaborate sound systems, though of poor quality, turned to a high volume. A *za' pwè* troupe usually has four or five loudspeakers arrayed across the front of the stage, and the actors stand stage front and center through most of a scene to remain near the microphones. Music ensembles, too, are highly amplified; only rehearsals and small gatherings of friends are exempt from the rule of intensely distorted sound. Popular taste seems to have grown so accustomed to this sound that it is deliberately cultivated. Consider, for example, a recording session by an ensemble commissioned to record a tape of classical music for use at the funeral of an important monk. The recording took place in a house converted into a recording studio, suprisingly well equipped for a country with little access to modern technology. Instruments were distributed in different rooms, with a mixer to coordinate them. In the front room, however, with several instruments and microphones, were placed two large loudspeakers through which the music was broadcast while the recording proceeded. This imparted a fuzzy, amplified sound to the recording, something the recording engineers apparently found desirable.

Musicians in Burmese society enjoy only limited respect unless they attain unusual renown, and even then they are regarded with some suspicion by the proper denizens of society. An accomplished Burmese harpist may enjoy some measure of prestige; the members of a *hsaìñ* troupe do not. The modest payment musicians receive does not, of course, explain their devotion: art and camaraderie are the only rewards they can count on. It is true that the cultural phenomenon of the media star has become more common with the rise of pop. But for all the celebration of Burmese culture in the pronouncements of the state and among older people, it is unclear to what extent young people will feel moved to learn traditional musical forms.

Musicians in Burmese society enjoy only limited respect unless they attain unusual renown, and even then they are regarded with some suspicion by the proper denizens of society.

REFERENCES

Becker, Judith. 1967. "The Migration of the Arched Harp from India to Burma." *Galpin Society Journal* 20:17–23, pl. v–vii.

———. 1969. "Anatomy of a Mode." *Ethnomusicology* 13(2):267–279.

———. 1980. "Burma: Instrumental Ensembles." *The New Grove Dictionary of Music and Musicians,* ed. Stanley Sadie. London: Macmillan.

Emmert, Richard, and Yuki Minegishi. 1980. *Musical Voices of Asia: Report of Asian Traditional Performing Arts 1978.* Tokyo: Heibonsha.

Frost, Helen, and Lily Strickland. 1927. *Oriental and Character Dances.* New York: A. S. Barnes.

Garfias, Robert. 1975a. "Preliminary Thoughts on Burmese Modes." *Asian Music* 7(1):39–49.

———. 1975b. "A Musical Visit to Burma." *World of Music* 17(1):3–13.

———. 1980a. "Burma: Classical Vocal Music." *The New Grove,* ed. Stanley Sadie. London: Macmillan.

———. 1980b. "Burma: Theory." *The New Grove Dictionary of Music and Musicians,* ed. Stanley Sadie. London: Macmillan.

———. 1981. "Speech and Melodic Contour Interdependence in Burmese Music." *College Music Symposium* 21(1):33–39.

———. 1985. "The Development of the Modern Burmese Hsaing Ensemble." *Asian Music* 16:1–28.

K [Khin Zaw]. 1981. *Burmese Culture: General and Particular.* Rangoon: Sarpay Beikman.

Khin Zaw. 1940. "Burmese Music: a Preliminary Enquiry." *Journal of the Burma Research Society* 30(3):387–460.

Marano, P. A. 1900. "A Note on Burmese Music." In *Burma,* ed. Max Ferrar and Bertha Ferrar, appendix C. London: Sampson Low, Marston.

Okell, John. 1964. "Learning Music from a Burmese Master." *Man* 64:183.

———. 1971. "The Burmese Double-Reed 'Nhai'." *Asian Music* 2(1):25– 31.

Otake, Tomoyoshi. 1980. "Aspects of Burmese Musical Structure." In *Musical Voices of Asia: Report of Asian Traditional Performing Arts 1978,* ed. Richard Emmert and Yuki Minegishi. Tokyo: Heibonsha.

Powers, Harold S. 1980. "Mode." The *New Grove Dictionary of Music and Musicians,* ed. Stanley Sadie. London: Macmillan.

Sarkissian, Margaret L. 1986. "Aspects of Mode in Burmese Music." Manuscript.

Sumarsam. 1975. "Inner Melody in Javanese Gamelan Music." *Asian Music* 7(1):3–13.

Tokumaru, Yoshihiko. 1980. "Burmese Music: A Brief Discussion of its Present Situation." In *Musical Voices of Asia: Report of Asian Traditional Performing Arts 1978,* ed. Richard Emmert and Yuki Minegishi. Tokyo: Heibonsha.

Williamson, Muriel. 1968. "The Construction and Decoration of One Burmese Harp." *Selected Reports in Ethnomusicology* 1(2):45–72.

———. 1975a. "A Supplement to the Construction and Decoration of One Burmese Harp." *Selected Reports in Ethnomusicology* 2(2):111–115.

———. 1975b. "Aspects of Traditional Style Maintained in Burma's First 13 Kyò Songs." *Selected Reports in Ethnomusicology* 2(2):117–163.

———. 1979a. "A Biographical Note on Myáwadi Ù Sá, Burmese Poet and Composer." *Musica Asiatica* 2:151–154.

———. 1979b. "The Basic Tune of a Late Eighteenth-Century Burmese Classical Song." *Musica Asiatica* 2:155–195.

———. 1980. "Burma: Harp." *The New Grove Dictionary of Music and Musicians,* ed. Stanley Sadie. London: Macmillan.

———. 1981. "The Correlation Between Speech-Tones of Text-Syllables and Their Musical Setting in a Burmese Classical Song." *Musica Asiatica* 3:11–28.

Peninsular Malaysia

Patricia Matusky
James Chopyak

The Federation of Malaysia consists of peninsular Malaysia and the states of Sarawak and Sabah on the north shore of Borneo [see THE INDIGENOUS PEOPLES (ORANG ASLI) OF THE MALAY PENINSULA and BORNEO]. Extending southward from the mainland of Southeast Asia and the Isthmus of Kra, the landmass of peninsular Malaysia separates the South China Sea from the Indian Ocean. Lying on a sea route from China to Europe, it has received many different peoples, who have stopped to conquer, settle, and trade. The racial mixture of the country reflects continual migration to and from the peninsula.

Orang asli 'original peoples' inhabit tropical forests in the interior mountains of the peninsula. Some have settled on farmlands, but most are hunter-gatherers. Near the foothills and on the coastal plains are the Malay peoples, who for centuries have inhabited and ruled the peninsula. By the second or third century, Indian traders had carried Hinduism and Mahayana Buddhism to the peninsula, overlaying with alternate beliefs the animistic practices of the Malay peoples. By the mid-1200s, Arab traders and missionaries had brought Islam to the peninsula. By 1400, the town of Malacca, on the west coast, had become an important center of government, trade, and religion.

Early in the 1500s, European colonialism began. Around 1511, Portuguese adventurers captured Malacca. In 1641, the Dutch conquered it. Finally, in 1786, the British established colonial rule throughout the peninsula, which lasted until the mid-1900s. With British colonization came migrations of southern Chinese peoples, who engaged in commerce and worked the tin mines, and of Indian peoples, who found positions in the civil service and worked on rubber and palm-oil plantations.

Earlier known as the Federation of Malaya, then as Malaysia, this nation consists of two parts, peninsular and insular, the latter comprising Sarawak and Sabah on the island of Borneo far to the east. The nation's 1994 population was estimated at 19,283,157. In 1990, the ethnic composition of peninsular Malaysia was about 61.5 percent Malay and other indigenous groups, 30 percent Chinese, 8 percent Indian, and 0.5 percent other nonindigenous. The urban centers of the country, the largest of which lie along the west coast (with Kuala Lumpur as the federal capital) support a mixture of ethnic groups, of which Chinese and Indians form the largest segment.

Peninsular Malaysia and Singapore

Malay peoples dominate federal and local governments, the agricultural areas and small towns along the east coast, and to some extent those along the west coast.

The performing arts of each main ethnic group in the country have remained distinct and separate for the most part. The aspects of Indian music that have entered the milieu of traditional Malay musical practice stem from Indian influence during the first centuries of the Christian era. Indian musical practice has had little effect on traditional Malay rural and court musics, but North Indian styles have influenced some twentieth-century urban theatricals. Malay music shows little influence from Chinese immigrants. Two notable exceptions are urban *bangsawan* theatrical music (Tan 1993) and the *joget gamelan* court music, nurtured in the early 1900s by a Chinese wife of a sultan of Pahang (D'Cruz 1979).

RURAL TRADITIONS

The musical traditions of the rural and semiurban areas take a variety of forms, including traditional theatrical genres and other kinds of storytelling, plus music for royal ceremonies, the martial arts, life-cycle events, and religious occasions. Other important forms are music associated with the cultivation of rice and traditional healing, and music for general entertainment.

Theatrical music

Village musical-theatrical genres, including shadow plays and dance-dramas, encompass vocal and instrumental music, plot, improvised monologue and dialogue, and dance. All such genres in Malaysia have developed through an oral tradition in which knowledge passes from one generation to another by word of mouth and rote learning. No written history or theory exists, but myths and legends recount the origin of traditional theatrical genres.

The performers of theatrical instrumental music are exclusively men, who from an early age attach themselves to a particular troupe performing a specific theatrical genre. Boys aspiring to be musicians in a shadow-play troupe informally join a troupe, and for several years play alongside experienced musicians. (The puppeteers and the actors of some dance-drama genres, however, undergo a formal apprenticeship.) Musicians also find opportunities to perform with other troupes, even troupes performing different theatrical forms. Since modern and Western music are becoming the preferred medium, and the number of those playing traditional music is not increasing, the movement of musicians among troupes keeps the local supply of performers adequate, though only barely. The mobility of musicians over the years has led to some sharing of musical repertoires and instrumentation among regional theatrical genres.

The music of traditional Malay theatricals is usually performed by small, percussion-dominated orchestras, which typically consist of several drums, a gong chime, one or more hanging, knobbed gongs, and a single, nonpercussive, melodic instrument (an aerophone or a chordophone). The orchestra plays as needed to accompany the drama. In each theatrical genre, these pieces comprise specific repertoires of music. Pieces to express mood or emotion, information, and intent are vocal numbers with instrumental accompaniment. Purely instrumental music usually accompanies dance or movement of some kind. In the shadow-puppet theater, all puppet movements require musical accompaniment—as do gestures with hands, steps, and swift strides in dance-dramas.

Shadow-play and dance-drama performances tell one story over successive nights. To ensure a successful performance, the first night requires a special opening ritual, the *buka panggung* 'opening of the stage'. For shadow plays, the puppeteer conducts the ceremony; for major dance-dramas, a traditional medium or shaman (*bomoh*) does. The puppeteer or shaman reads special prayers and presents offerings of prepared foodstuffs, including rice, eggs, and betel. Uttering special recitations to elements in the unseen world, he ritually bathes in incense the musical instruments and (for shadow plays) the puppets.

The *buka panggung* leads into a standard set of musical pieces that preface the story. Those performed are unique to each individual dramatic genre, but all pay homage to otherworldly beings and introduce the main characters or types of roles in the drama. On subsequent nights, the standard set of musical pieces opens the show, and the drama continues.

Shadow-puppet theater

The shadow-puppet theater (*wayang kulit*), a popular form of theater for centuries, continues to be performed. In peninsular Malaysia, it takes any of four types: *wayang kulit Jawa, wayang gedek* (or *nang talung*), *wayang Siam* (or *wayang Kelantan*), and *wayang melayu* (or *wayang Jawa*).

Wayang kulit Jawa

This is the *wayang purwa* of Indonesia, performed by peoples of Javanese descent living along the southwest coastal areas in Johore (see JAVA). The languages of the stories are Malay and Javanese. The accompaniment is the Javanese gamelan, which in Malaysia consists of *saron* (*demung, barung, peking*), one or two *bonang, gambang, ketuk, kenong, kempul,* and *gong agung* (*gong kumbang*). The orchestra uses the *sléndro* system of tuning. Bronze, brass, or iron are used to make the metal idiophones; the large knobbed gongs, the *kenung,* and the *bonang* are often shaped from metal barrels. Occasional substitutions for the knobbed gongs (including the *gong agung, kenung,* and *kempul*) are tuned, rectangular-shaped, brass keys (or slabs), each suspended above a wooden box resonator.

Wayang gedek

The southern Thai form of shadow play, which uses leather puppets, is performed by Thai peoples living along the northern border regions of Malaysia. The Thai language, mixed with the local Malay dialect, relates the stories, while the musical accompaniment comes from an ensemble of Thai fiddles, drums, knobbed gongs, and cymbals. Influence from the Thai *nang talung* in the northwest regional Malay shadow play is evident in the mixture of the local Thai and Malay dialects and the common use of dramatic and musical repertoires, stock characters, and puppet design. The ensemble strikingly resembles that of the Thai *manora* dance-drama and the Malay shadow play of the northeast coast, utilizing (in the state of Kedah, for example) two goblet-shaped drums (*gedumbak*), one stick-hit barrel drum (*geduk*), one oboe (*serunai,* a quadruple-reed aerophone), a pair of finger-held cymbals (*kerincing*), and a pair of small, knobbed gongs set in a wooden box and struck with padded beaters (Ku Zam Zam 1983).

Wayang Siam *and* wayang melayu

These forms are the indigenous types of shadow theater, with distribution in the north- and east-coast regions. As products of Malay culture, both forms are performed by Malay peoples in regional dialects. The *wayang melayu* was formerly performed in court as entertainment for aristocrats (see below); but having lost its royal patronage, it is nearly extinct. In contrast, the more popular of these forms, the *wayang Siam,* with many regional styles, has always been performed in the rural and semiurban areas of the north, by and for the common people. It is folk theater, performed mainly for entertainment. Formerly, it was also played for major ritual functions, such as the *pelepas niat* 'fulfillment of a vow', *pelimau* 'ritual bathing of a student puppeteer or musician', *sembah guru* 'paying homage to one's teacher', and *semah angin* 'adjustment of the puppeteer's "wind" [emotions]'.

The *wayang Siam* and the *wayang melayu* are performed in a small, raised hut (*panggung* 'stage'), of which one wall is a white screen (*kelir*). A lamp hangs before the screen, on which, as the puppeteer (*dalang*) relates a story, the puppets cast shadows. The puppeteer takes all roles in the story, manipulates the puppets, cues the ensemble to begin and end musical pieces, and sings the requisite vocal pieces. The ensemble—drums, gongs, cymbals, oboe—is also in the hut, just behind the puppeteer. As in most Malay traditional theatrical forms, a single story usually takes several nights to complete. The dramatic repertoire of the *wayang Siam* comes from the oral Malay version of the *Ramayana* epic (the 'root' or main story, rarely performed), the *Panji* stories, Malay folktales, and stories of local themes and events (Sweeney 1972).

The ensemble for the *wayang Siam* is mainly percussive: pairs of *tetawak,* large, hanging, knobbed gongs, struck on the knob with a padded beater; *canang,* small, knobbed gongs, suspended horizontally in a wooden rack, struck on the knobs with padded sticks; *kesi,* small hand-held cymbals, struck together; *gedumbak* and *gendang,* double-headed, elongated barrel drums, tuned and hit with hands; *geduk*; and one *serunai* 'oboe' (figures 1, 2). Each instrument has large and small sizes, metaphorically called mother (*ibu*) and child (*anak*), respectively.

The musical repertoire, involving some thirty-five pieces, provides an appropriate tune for any dramatic situation encountered in the stories. Specific musical pieces

FIGURE 1 The *wayang kulit Siam* stage (inside view) with the *gendang, gedumbak,* and *geduk* drums ready for performance. Photo by Patricia Matusky.

serve only to accompany the appearance of the major puppets. Other tunes accompany and signify battles and other violence, hunting and crouching in ambush, walking (by both refined characters and country bumpkins), giving news, sleeping, and so on. A core group of pieces called "*Dalang Muda*" ('The Young Puppeteer') appears in a fixed prologue of music, song, and action, usually performed by a deputy or apprentice. Four musical pieces accompany the appearance of an old sage, the descent of the demigods (*dewa panah*) from the heavens, the battle of the demigods, and their ascent to their otherworldly realm. After the battle and the rituals, the second half of the prologue uses five more pieces to introduce the major characters (Matusky 1993). A special musical number brings the puppeteer to the stage, and the main story of the evening begins.

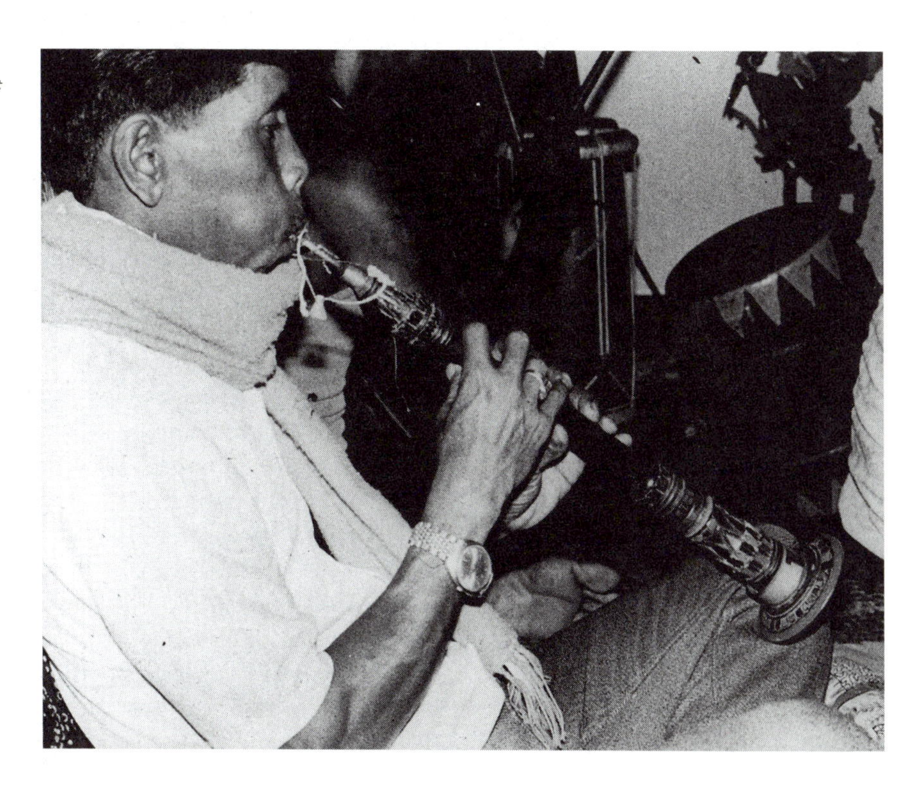

FIGURE 2 The quadruple-reed oboe (*serunai*), the main melody instrument in the *wayang kulit Siam* and *gendang silat* ensembles. Photo by Patricia Matusky.

The most elaborate of the dance-dramas, and possibly the oldest, is the *mak yong,* believed to have originated in the northeast state of Kelantan and the southeastern Thai provinces of Patani and Narathiwat.

The movements of the puppets require specific music, played by the orchestra on cue from the puppeteer. The music features a dense, highly ornamented melody, played by the oboe or sung by the puppeteer. The tuned drums provide a percussive, melodylike counterpoint, while the gong chime, hanging gongs, and cymbals mark the colotomic units of the pieces.

Dance-drama

Traditional dance-dramas are performed primarily in the rural areas of the northwest- and east-coast regions. They include *mak yong, mek mulung, hadrah, mak yong laut,* and *rodat.* In the extreme north, Thai and Thai-related forms, such as *manora* and *jikay,* are performed by troupes of Thai and Malay peoples. The island of Penang, off the northwest coast, is home to two additional urban theatricals: *bangsawan* (an acculturated form, incorporating Indian, Western, and other elements) and *boria.*

Mak yong

The most elaborate of the dance-dramas, and possibly the oldest, is the *mak yong,* believed to have originated in the northeast state of Kelantan and the southeastern Thai provinces of Patani and Narathiwat. Written sources suggest the *mak yong* flourished in the villages of these regions during the late 1800s. Briefly in the early 1900s, the court of the Kelantan sultanate gave this genre royal patronage. In the early 1900s, *mak yong* troupes carried the form to other parts of peninsular Malaysia, Medan, Sumatra, and the Riau-Lingga islands of Indonesia.

The *mak yong* is usually performed on a roofed platform, raised a meter off the ground. The central area of the platform serves as the area for acting (*gelenggang*). The musicians sit along its northeast edge. Actresses not actively participating in the drama during the performance also sit there, serving as the chorus.

The actors wear elaborate costumes, but use few props—as is typical of traditional Malay theater. The dramatic repertory of the *mak yong* consists of twelve tales, featuring the adventures of local heroes (Ghulam-Sarwar 1976). Villagers say the story "*Dewa Muda*" ('The Young Demigod') serves as the root story from which the other tales evolved. The *mak yong* also shares some dramatic and musical repertoire with other regional theatricals, including the *wayang kulit* and the *manora.* All *mak yong* stories are told through dialogue, singing, and dancing by the major roles, including the king (*pak yong*) and queen (*mak yong*), two clown-servants (*peran*), and the *tok wak* (an astrologer or expert of some kind). A small group of ladies-in-waiting serves as the chorus. The roles of king, queen, and retinue are always played by women; men perform only the clown-servant parts.

The primary function of the *mak yong* is entertainment, but formerly it also graced high rituals. Rarely performed, these rituals include the *semah angin* and *sembah guru* (as noted also in the Malay shadow play), the *menyambut semangat* (requesting good performances), and *puteri-mak yong* (for healing).

FIGURE 3 From the *makyong* theater, the salutation dance before the bowed lute (rebab), with the *gendang* drums and *tetawak* gongs in the background. Photo by Patricia Matusky.

The basic *mak yong* orchestra is a percussion-dominated ensemble consisting of two *gendang,* two *tetawak,* and a three-stringed rebab as the main melodic instrument. The performance of specific pieces, such as the dance *tari ragam,* occasionally adds certain instruments from the Malay shadow-puppet theater and the *manora*; these instruments may include the *serunai* oboe, the *geduk* drum, and the *canang* gongs.

Just as in other traditional Malay theatrical genres, music is an integral part of the performance. Pieces in the repertoire are distinguished as either drummed pieces (*lagu paluan-paluan*) or sung pieces (*lagu nyanyian*). The drummed pieces accompany the entrance and exit of the actors from the stage and provide traveling music. More numerous are the sung pieces: the ritual opening music for dance (*menghadap rebab*); pieces for giving news, expressing intent, and covering other sensitive situations; lamentations; lullabies; and invocations of power for extraordinary feats or events. A standard musical opening of every performance consists of five basic pieces, each with a specific function. The piece "*Pak Yong Turun*" ('The Pak Yong Descends') accompanies the entrance of the troupe onto the stage; "*Menghadap Rebab*" ('Salutation to the Rebab') pays homage to the rebab (figure 3); two song-dances (*sedayung*) introduce the king and queen; and the "*Pak Yong*" once again sings an appropriate piece for character self-introduction, which begins to set the scene (the piece "*Ela*" often serves this purpose). Once these pieces have ended, the clown-servants herald the beginning of the story. The musical pieces have highly florid melodic lines, either sung by one of the major characters or played on the rebab, while two drummers play interlocking rhythms on the *gendang.* The melodies and percussive patterns fit within a time-organizing gong unit, played on two *tetawak* (Matusky 1994).

Mek mulung

The *mek mulung* theater is found only in the northwest state of Kedah. Like the *mak yong,* it features a repertoire of stories told through spoken dialogue, song, and dance. Its history is obscure, but old performers look to the ancient kingdom of Patani as its place of origin. Some of its conventions and repertoire and its supposed place of origin show some similarities to (and perhaps influences from) the local *mak yong* (now obsolete). The *mek mulung* is performed mainly for entertainment, but formerly a special ritual performance (*berjamu* 'feasting [of spirits]') was occasionally carried out to propitiate the otherworldly elements important to the genre. The stories of the

FIGURE 4 The *mek mulung rebana* drums, with the *serunai,* hanging gong, and *kecerek* concussion sticks (*right background*). Photo by Ghulam Sarwar Yousof.

mek mulung treat local events and legends, the most important of which, "The Young Demigod," carries the same title as the root story of the *mak yong.*

Performances of *mek mulung* take place at ground level in a roofed, hutlike stage, closed only at the back wall. A small, circular area at stage center serves as the area for acting, and the musicians sit at the edge of the stage near the back wall. The major character, *pak mulung,* is a king; other roles are princes (*raja muda*), princesses (*puteri*), and four clown-servants (*peran*). In contrast to the *mak yong,* men play all roles, both male and female. The costumes are plain. As in other Malay and Thai-related theatricals of Kedah and Perlis, the clowns wear red masks over the top half of their faces. When not actively engaged in the action, the princes, princesses, and clowns sit at the edge of the stage, serving as a chorus.

The musicians are exclusively male, and their instruments are predominantly percussive. Two large *rebana* 'hand-hit frame drums' (*gendang ibu*) and two small *rebana* (*gendang penganak, gendang peningkah*) play interlocking rhythms. The ensemble includes one medium-sized, hanging, knobbed gong (struck on the knob with a padded beater), several pairs of *cerek* (wood or bamboo sticks, struck together), and sometimes one *mong* (a single, small, knobbed gong, placed horizontally in a wooden frame, hit on the knob with a stick). A small oboe, the only melodic instrument in the ensemble, complements these instruments. The musicians also sing (figure 4).

A small repertoire of musical pieces accompanies specific dramatic situations. Villagers say some of the drumming patterns (and perhaps other musical elements) are shared with another theatrical, *hadrah,* found in the same region (Mohammad Ghouse 1979:361–367). As in the shadow play and *mak yong,* a *mek mulung* begins with a standard prologue of music, song, and dance. The opening of the show is fixed in content and form. It includes a lengthy introductory instrumental piece, "*Pembukaan*" ('Opening'); a greeting, "*Bertabik*" ('Greeting'), sung in responsorial style with orchestral accompaniment; a salutation, "*Puteri Nak Bangkit*" ('Princesses Appear'), sung in responsorial style by the young prince and two or three princesses; "*Puteri Berjalan*" ('Princesses Walk'), a dance in a circle by the royal retinue; and the introductory song and dance by the king, "*Pak Mulung Nak Bangkit*" ('King Appears'), sung in responsorial style. Finally, the clowns come to the stage, and the story begins. If a second evening is needed to complete the story, it begins with the five standard opening pieces of music and dance.

The style of singing the *mek mulung* is predominantly syllabic, with little vocal ornamentation. The *rebana* drums, producing high and low pitches, provide accompanying rhythms in duple meter. The *cerek* mark time on even-numbered beats, and the gong marks the end of four-beat segments.

Hadrah *and* rodat

These forms of Malay theater grew from the tradition of singing Islamic religious verses (*zikir*) in praise of God and the prophet Muhammad. The singing was, and is, accompanied by an ensemble of *rebana,* on which the singers beat rhythms. Occasionally, a full story is danced. Both the *rodat* and the *hadrah,* having lost most of their religious significance, are secular genres, performed at weddings, after harvests, and at public festivals.

In the 1800s, the *hadrah,* featuring the singing of *zikir* with drum accompaniment, was brought to Penang by Indians from Bengal and Nagore. Performers established troupes in Perlis and Kedah, where the form further evolved and is still performed. Dances were added, and both Malay and Hindustani songs were interspersed in performances. Historical dramas and legends are also enacted as a main part of the performance; between episodes or scenes, female impersonators perform popular Malay and Hindustani songs.

Mainly all-male troupes perform *hadrah.* A performance takes place on a temporary stage, at ground level or raised, with a simple dropcloth at the rear. Typically, props are minimal. Actors in male roles wear the traditional *baju melayu* ('Malay suit': headgear, long-sleeved shirt, trousers, and a *samping* cloth, tied at the waist); those in female roles wear the Malay women's sarong and *baju kebaya* 'Malay-style blouse'.

At the foot of the stage, the musicians sit facing the actors, playing drums and a knobbed gong. The orchestra consists of eight or more large *rebana,* with jingles (*kerincing*) inserted in their bodies (*gendang hadrah* '*hadrah* drums'); one somewhat smaller *rebana,* with a deeper frame and no jingles (*gendang peningkah*); and one small, hanging, knobbed gong, hit on the knob with a padded beater. Using high and low pitches, produced by hitting the drumhead at the center or near the rim, the *hadrah* drums and the *gendang peningkah* play interlocking rhythms, usually in four- or eight-beat units, to accompany the singing. The knobbed gong punctuates the drumming at regular four- or eight-beat intervals.

The drummer who directs the singing and drumming is the leader (*kalifah*). He is usually the solo vocalist. The other drummers sing the choral parts as they play. A typical piece begins with an opening text and melody (the *kepala lagu*), sung by the leader and repeated by the chorus. The leader and the chorus then sing responsorially, the chorus in unison. Contemporary performances use a repertoire of about fifty songs—in Arabic, Urdu, and Malay (Mohammad Ghouse 1979:418). The singing of both solo and choral parts is predominantly syllabic, with virtually no vocal ornamentation.

Like the *hadrah,* the *rodat* was originally a religious event, in which verses were sung to the accompaniment of rhythms played on frame drums (see below). In the 1800s, traders from Aceh (north Sumatra) traveling to Sambas (in Borneo) and then to the east coast of the peninsula may have brought *rodat* to Terengganu. By the early 1900s, several all-male troupes performed the original style of singing the *zikir* with frame-drum accompaniment. In the 1930s, however, performances included dancing by men and transvestites. After 1945, women replaced the latter, and troupes got bigger, until a given troupe had three separate groups of performers: the male singer-dancers (*pelenggok*), the female singer-dancers (*mak inang*), and the musicians (*pengadis*).

The *rodat* was originally performed to celebrate Muhammad's birthday and Malay weddings. With the addition of dancing and the singing of popular Malay and Hindustani songs, and especially with the addition of women to the troupes, performances became popular at secular events, such as the harvest celebration, the sultan's birthday, and festivities for Malaysian National Day, 31 August.

mak yong Former courtly theater featuring female actresses and male comedians

hadrah Derived from Islamic singing, a kind of secular theater accompanied by drums and a large gong

rodat One kind of Islamic-derived theater, originally associated with Muhammad's birthday

jikay Comic theater derived from Islamic *zikir* and southern Thai theater

manora Southern Thai theater featuring a half-bird, half-human creature, performed in northern Malaysia

Performances of *rodat* take place on a simple stage at ground level, with a curtain serving as a backdrop. The *pelenggok* sit and perform on the stage in front of the curtain. The *pengadis* sit downstage (at the front edge of the stage), facing them. The *mak inang* appear on stage only when performing their songs and dances. As in the *hadrah,* the costumes are simple. The *pelenggok* wear the *baju melayu,* and the *mak inang* wear the traditional Malay long skirt and long-sleeved blouse. The musicians wear usual street dress.

In a typical performance, eight to twelve chapters (*fasal*) from the *Book of Verses* (*Kitab Zikir*) are sung in Arabic in antiphonal style between two groups of men, the *pelenggok* and the *pengadis.* No story is enacted. One drummer leads the singing and drumming and signals changes of tempo and rhythm. During the singing of the first two chapters, the leader, with frame-drum accompaniment, sings an opening line of text, which the entire *pengadis* group repeats. In alternation with the musicians, who continue to provide rhythmic accompaniment, the *pelenggok* then begin to dance and sing specific verses. The singing of subsequent chapters is periodically interspersed with popular Malay and Hindustani lyrics and melodies, sung by the *mak inang.*

Rhythmic accompaniment comes from the *tar,* small frame drums. As with their *hadrah* counterparts, jingles are set into their bodies. However, no laces are used to secure the drumhead; the skin is stretched and secured by a metal rim. The ensemble uses no gongs. The drumming patterns, in several timbres, are typically four beats long. They accompany a vocal line essentially syllabic in style, with little or no ornamentation.

Jikay *and* mak yong laut

The *jikay,* also known as *dikey* or *likey,* is believed to have originated in the late 1800s in the singing of *zikir* among the Malays living in the present-day southwest Thai provinces. After the late 1800s, it developed into secular theater with many regional styles, and it was eventually brought southward to Perlis and Kedah, and to Langkawi Island, where it is still occasionally performed. Through song, dance, and improvised dialogue, local legends are enacted, with considerable emphasis placed on slapstick comedy, song, and dance.

The opening rituals, similar to those in other forms of traditional Malay theater, are carried out before the presentation of a local story. Both men and women take the roles of stock characters. The stage is usually a raised platform with a simple drop cloth at the rear. The actors enter from behind the curtain to stage center, where the dramatic action, song, and dance take place. The musicians, an all-male group, sit downstage, facing the actors. The actors and actresses wear traditional dress, and the musicians wear normal street attire.

Like all Malay theatrical orchestras, the ensemble that accompanies the *jikay* is dominated by percussion. A complete orchestra includes *rebana* (with no jingles), in large, medium, and small sizes; one tambourine; one hanging, knobbed gong, hit with a padded beater; five or more pairs of *cerek*; one pair of *kesi*; one oboe, which may be the Malay *serunai* or the Thai *pi*; and one violin (*biola*). Smaller ensembles consist of the basic three *rebana,* two pairs of *cerek,* and a violin.

The musical repertoire is small. Only a few pieces introduce an act or episode and accompany the dances. Specific pieces are used only by certain types of characters. The vocal melodies, usually unornamented, are accompanied by the violin, which either plays in unison with the voice, or provides countermelodies against it. The drums provide the rhythms of the musical pieces, and the *cerek,* the gong, and the cymbals mark the time.

Like the *jikay,* the *mak yong laut* is believed to have its origins in the Malay villages of the southwestern Thai provinces. It was brought southward to Perlis, where a group of Malay and Thai peoples performed it as village theater. It remains an intimately localized form of theater. Nevertheless, its staging and other theatrical conventions resemble those of the *jikay.* Stories of local interest are presented through dialogue, song, and dance. The influence of Thai culture and the blending of Thai and Malay elements are evident in the lyrics, which mix both the southern Thai and local Malay dialects.

The orchestra accompanying the *mak yong laut* consists of two *rebana,* in large and small sizes, with no jingles, of the type using rattan laces to secure the skin to the body; one large *rebana,* with the skin tacked to the body; two *tetawak*; four or more pairs of *cerek*; and one violin, formerly a three-stringed rebab. The musical style closely resembles that of the *jikay.*

Manora

A dance-drama of the rural southern Thai peoples, the *manora* (*menora*) is performed by groups of Thai and Malay peoples throughout the northern Malay states, including Penang Island. Depending on the geographical area, a mixture of the local dialects and the southern Thai dialect is used. A performance may occur for special religious occasions at Thai and Chinese Buddhist temples (Tan Sooi Beng 1988), or for secular festivities, as for the sultan's birthday and state holidays.

In north Malaysia, the *manora* has a variety of regional styles. The basic features of a performance include a lengthy invocation, a dance by the main character, and a play or skit. The invocation consists of a dance of stylized poses and gestures, alternating with rhymed verses. The text, responsorially chanted by the dancer and the members of the orchestra, tells the story and recounts the genealogy of the performer's teacher. The dramatic repertoire of the *manora* involves twelve basic stories, related to a tradition of central Thai stories. These stories are performed by men and women, with one or more clowns.

The stage for the *manora* may be at ground level or on a raised platform, with a painted scene as backdrop. Action takes place in front of the backdrop. The musicians sit along one edge of the stage, facing the actors. The *manora* character wears an elaborate costume, featuring a pinnacled, crownlike headpiece; a beaded shirt; trousers; feathers from a bird's tail; bangles on the arms; long, arched, silver fingernails; and a cloth that hangs from the waist. The source of the genre can be found in southern Thai folk legends and in the *jataka* tales about the lives of the Buddha. In the *jataka* stories, the *manora* character is identified with the heavenly bird (*kinnara*) named Manohara (Ginsberg 1972:63).

Within the complex of *manora* styles of Malaysia, the eastern regional style found in Kelantan and Terengganu incorporates much use of the Malay language and a play performed in the *mak yong* style. This stylistic type, locally known as *manora-mak yong,* utilizes a fairly large orchestra, incorporating musical instruments and pieces from both genres. A complete orchestra includes, from the core *manora* orchestra, the Thai *pi,* two *thap* (Malay *gedumbak*), one *klong* (Malay *geduk*), two *mong* (Malay *canang*), one pair of *ching* (Malay *kesi*), and several pairs of *cerek.* On Malaysia's east coast, this ensemble would be supplemented by the Malay oboe (replacing the Thai *pi*), one three-stringed rebab, two *gendang,* and two *tetawak.* Only the core instruments of the *manora* ensemble are used during the first part of a performance, including the invocation, sung in southern Thai dialect. As the story or dramatic episode commences, using predominantly the local Malay dialect, the added instruments come into play, and the performance becomes distinctly *mak yong* in style.

In the northwest regions of Malaysia, the *manora* does not incorporate other local theatrical forms, but adheres to the invocation-play or comic-skit dichotomy in a distinctly north Malaysian musical style. The play or comic skits that fill out an evening's performance invariably include male and female actors, with one or more clowns in red masks, similar to those used in the *mek mulung* and *jikay,* and in the *awang batil.* The plays or skits feature at least one well-known *manora* actor and are told in a mixture of Thai and the dialect of the audience.

Music is used in several ways. A musical piece signaling the beginning of the *manora* is characteristic of all regional styles, as is a ritual presentation of prayers and offerings. The main dancer and the orchestral musicians chant the invocation responsorially, accompanied by *mong, ching,* and *cerek.* In contrast, the invocatory dances are accompanied by a full orchestra, with the *thap* and *klong* providing repeated four- or eight-beat rhythms, the *pi* playing the melody and the idiophones marking underlying four-beat temporal units. On the east coast of the peninsula, where the *tetawak* usually join the orchestra, the large hanging gongs, with *mong, ching,* and *cerek,* mark the specific structural beats of a gong unit. This unit (or *gongan*), as found in the east-coast *wayang kulit* and *mak yong,* establishes the musical form.

The musical pieces found in the dramatization of a story or comic skit in the second half of the performance of a *manora* usually accompany the performers' entrances and exits. The musical pieces also signal the beginning of an act, and the vocal numbers often set the mood or give information about the story. On the east coast of the peninsula, where the *manora* often combines with the *mak yong,* pieces from both the *mak yong* and the *wayang kulit Siam* are used.

Dance

Barongan *and* kuda kepang

The dances *barongan* 'demon' and *kuda kepang* 'hobbyhorse' may stem from the totemistic worship of natural spirits in the ancient animistic religion of the Javanese peoples. Both forms involve music and trance-dance. In Malaysia, the *barongan* may serve as a prelude to the performance of the *kuda kepang.* Using elaborate masks and other props, these dances are performed where peoples of Javanese descent have lived since the 1300s or before: the states of Johore, Negeri Sembilan, Malacca, and Selangor.

The origin myths of both forms show a fusion of animistic and Islamic elements. In the Malaysian context, stories of the worship of animal spirits are mixed with tales of Islamic prophets and the propagation of their faith. According to some legends, the *barongan* involves a tiger dancing with a peacock on its back. Hence, the most commonly used mask in Malaysia incorporates a tiger's physiognomy, with peacock feathers and other decorations. Likewise, the origin myths of the *kuda kepang* tell of the propitiation of animal spirits, but emphasize the feats of Arabian Islamic warriors, who went to battle in a frenzied, trancelike state. Other stories tell of an old woman who snatched the corpse of a famous Islamic warrior as she rode his horse

(Mohammad Ghouse 1979:114–115). In remote villages of the southwestern regions of peninsular Malaysia, the propitiation of the spirits, the trance-dance, and the use of bamboo figures of horses are central elements in the *kuda kepang*. In urban settings, this dance sheds these elements and is performed by groups of male dancers, using the bamboo horse figures, as colorful entertainment at public festivities.

In a village context, a performance begins with the appearance of the demon, who, using dance movements, stalks and spars with a dancer representing a prince on horseback by carrying the figure of a horse. Later, a clown replaces the demon, and improvised comic imitation of the dance with the prince concludes the first part of the performance.

The demon's dance is accompanied by a small ensemble: one *gendang*, a small barrel drum (*tipung*), one oboe (*selumprit*), one *mong*, and a *kenong* (a gong chime, two knobbed gongs, set on a wooden rack). The oboe carries a continuous, unbroken melodic line, while the double-headed drums provide percussive rhythms. The *kenong* and the *mong* mark the rhythmic-temporal (or colotomic) unit.

The *barongan* is immediately followed by the *kuda kepang*, a trance-dance that requires nine or more dancers, carrying bamboo hobbyhorses. A shaman (*pawang*) leads the group. He recites prayers and incantations and offers prepared foodstuffs, drinks, and flowers to spirits present for the dance. By cueing changes in tempo, rhythms, and dance movements, he directs the dance. As the *pawang* cracks a whip, the dancers jump, emphasizing movements of their legs and feet. As the dancers become possessed by the spirit of a horse, they go to the *pawang* for food and drink, until he brings them out of trance.

As the *kuda kepang* begins, a change in orchestral instrumentation occurs. The dance of the horses is accompanied by percussion, for which the *kenung*, sometimes replaced by the *saron demung*, and the *mong* continue to play the colotomic unit. The *gendang* provides the main rhythms. A second cylindrical, stick-hit drum, a *jidur*, is often struck in unison with the *mong*. Finally, some bamboo *angklung*, of only two or three pitches, play a brief melodic-rhythmic pattern, which repeats continually throughout the dance.

Randai

The Minangkabau peoples of West Sumatra perform this type of theater. It incorporates acting, dance, song, instrumental music, and *pencak silat*, the Malay art of self-defense (see below). The Minangkabau peoples who settled in Negeri Sembilan carried *randai* to the west coast of peninsular Malaysia. Its repertory has roots in the *kaba* and the *tambo alam minangkabau*, traditions of storytelling in which poetical narration and the singing of songs were accompanied by a three-stringed rebab, or by any kind of percussive implement or instrument, such as a matchbox containing a few wooden matches dropped onto a hard surface in a regularly recurring beat (Mohammad Anis 1986:17–19). Later, acting was introduced, and stories dramatized legends and historical events.

A celebration of a major event to benefit a given community, such as completing the harvest or erecting a school building, provides a reason to hold a performance of a *randai*. Women play female roles in costumes appropriate to the characters. All men in the troupe wear the traditional *silat* costume: a long-sleeved shirt, loose-fitting trousers, a tied waistband, and cloth headgear. The martial arts are important in *randai*, and a performer must be highly skilled in them, for the movements of *pencak silat* are the basic gestures and footwork of the dance. The *randai* was formerly performed specifically for events associated with traditional customs (*adat*), such as weddings and circumcisions. The troupes were all-male ensembles, with female roles played by men dressed as women.

The performance of *dabus*, with roots in Sufi traditions, was believed to be a way to reach a higher state of consciousness and ultimately to attain unity with God.

A performance can occur in any setting—from a temporary raised stage to a ground-level area outdoors; in the hall of a school or in another building. Performances feature singing and dancing in a circle (*randai*) with the audience gathered around. Once the dancers have entered the area of the stage, they sing in unison, as in a circle they perform a sequence of dance movements. When the dance is over, they sit on the ground, and a short drama or episode is enacted in the middle of the circle. The dramatic episode is followed by another dance in a circle. Short dramas or episodes and dances in a circle accompanied by songs alternate to the end of the performance.

The dancers' entrance to, and exit from, the performing area is accompanied by music played by a *taklempong pacik,* an ensemble consisting of five small, knobbed gongs, played by three men (Mohammad Anis 1986:25). Each player holds one or two of the gongs in one hand and beats them with a stick held in the other. A double-headed drum (*katindiek*) or a single-headed drum (*adok*), and an oboe, may join in.

At intermissions, music is played by a *taklempong* (or *caklempong*), a large ensemble, consisting of at least three gong chimes of different sizes, all tuned to the same diatonic scale. The melody-carrying gong chime, the *gereteh* (*gerteh*), is made up of fifteen tuned, small, knobbed gongs, in double rows in a wooden frame. The *tingkah* and *saua* each consist of eight small, knobbed gongs, in a single row on a wooden rack. All gongs are hit on the knob with a pair of sticks. The *tingkah* and *saua* play similar short rhythms in chordal structures, which repeat throughout a piece. The higher notes of the chord are played on the *tingkah*; the lower pitches, on the *saua.* In addition to the gong chimes, the ensemble may include an oboe, which carries the main melodic line. Electric guitars and a set of drums are occasionally used, as are a *katindiek,* an *adok,* and a small frame drum (*rabano*) (Mohammad Anis 1986:56). This ensemble also accompanies some traditional dances of the area, including dances with candles (*tari lilin*) or plates (*tari piring*), which dancers hold while executing intricate movements with their arms and hands.

Dabus

The performance of *dabus* (among the Minangkabau in Malaysia and Sumatra called *bermain dabus, berdabus,* and *dabuih*), with roots in Sufi traditions, was believed to be a way to reach a higher state of consciousness and ultimately to attain unity with God (see SUMATRA). It was brought to the peninsula from Aceh (Sumatra) by seafarers around the 1700s and also by the Minangkabau immigrants who settled in Negeri Sembilan and Malacca. Peoples of Bugis descent, who perform *dabus* in Perak, say the form originated during Muhammad's lifetime (Mohammad Ghouse 1979:140).

Dabus, an Arabic word, means 'iron awl with a handle'. In Malaysia, it names the dance, perhaps formerly a dervish dance, performed with sharply pointed iron awls (*anak dabus*); when the dancers shake the awls, metal rings or jingles attached to the handles sound. The *dabus* may be seen and heard at weddings and other life-cycle events and on national holidays.

A performance takes place on a temporary stage at ground level. The group, all men, wear the *baju melayu.* In Arabic, they sing *berzanji,* verses in the *Kitab Berzanji,* the book of verses praising God and Muhammad. As they begin to sing, the dancers, each carrying an *anak dabus,* begin to dance. After reaching a trancelike state, they stab their bodies and arms with the *anak dabus* and do other extraordinary feats without physically injuring themselves. Constant repetition of the sung parts and repetitive movements of legs and feet sustain the trancelike state (Mohammad Ghouse 1979:143–151).

A basic ensemble consists of several small- and large-sized *rebana* and one hanging, knobbed gong. Some groups add an oboe to accompany the beginning of the singing. The patterns of drumming usually repeat in four-beat units. The gong punctuates certain beats within the unit, plus the final beat of the pattern. The drummers sing responsorially in a predominantly syllabic style, with a few short melismas. Early in a performance, a soloist sings a phrase of text, and the chorus answers him with a refrainlike passage; later, they repeat a short melody over and over, loudly and in unison.

Tari inai

Formerly a court dance, the *tari inai* (*tarinai, terinai*) is associated with traditions of towns and villages in the northern states. It is performed in Perlis for weddings, circumcisions, processions, state ceremonies, and public festivities. At court, a solo male danced the original version; in the 1990s, groups of young women perform it—particularly at weddings, during the application of henna to the bride's hands and feet.

The dance involves supple movements of the arms and hands, with the dancer sitting or standing. There is little footwork, and some pieces feature a lighted candle held in the dancers' hands. The music is played by a small ensemble, the *gendang tarinai* (also *gendang keling*). Veteran performers of the music say this orchestra and its repertory originated in the Middle East during Muhammad's lifetime and was used both there and in India to muster Islamic soldiers during times of battle. The ensemble was brought to Malaysia by Indian musicians; hence the Malay name *gendang keling* 'Indian drums' (figure 5).

FIGURE 5 "*Gendang keling*" drums, with the *serunai* and two hanging gongs (far left) for the *tarinai.* Photo by Patricia Matusky.

a 16-beat

b 32-beat

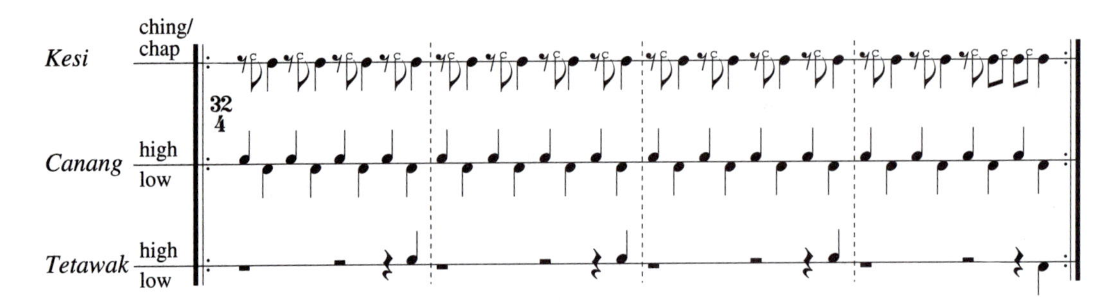

c 16-beat

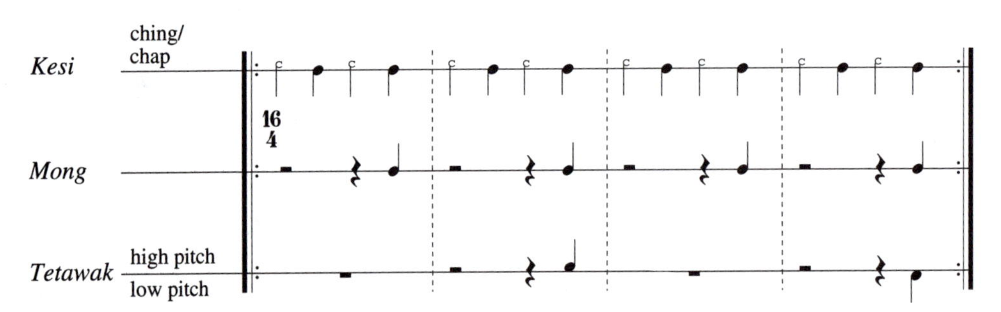

d 4-beat

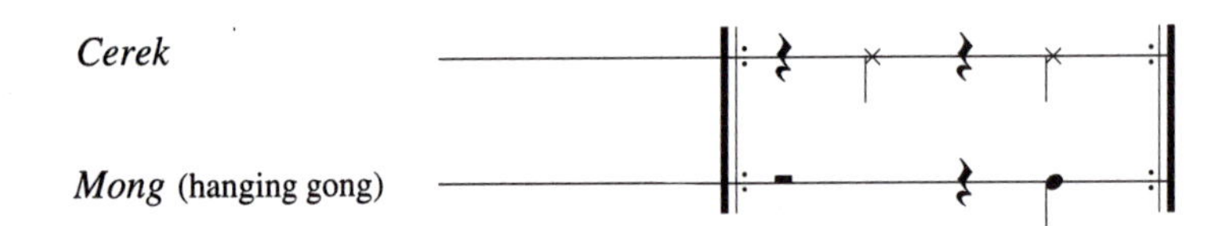

FIGURE 6 Rhythmic-temporal (gong) units in traditional theater and dance music: *a,* sixteen-beat gong unit from *makyong* and *tarinai* pieces; *b,* thirty-two-beat gong unit from *wayang kulit siam,* "Menyembah"; *c,* sixteen-beat gong unit from *wayang melayu,* "Jubang"; *d,* four-beat gong unit from a *mek mulung* piece.

The ensemble consists of two *gendang* (struck with a straight rattan beater, or with an out-curved stick on one drumhead and the hand on the other), one or two oboes, and a pair of hanging, knobbed gongs, providing a high and a low pitch. Complex interlocking rhythms played on the drums complement the charm of melodies played on the oboe. The hanging gongs mark the regular rhythmic-temporal units underlying the oboe and *gendang.* If two oboes play a rendition of a single piece, their melodies alternately imitate each other, or a phrase played on one oboe sounds against a dronelike tone played on the other.

Stylistic features of theatrical music

The ensembles for traditional Malay theater and dance are small, chamberlike orchestras. They are mainly percussive. The texture of nearly all theater musics has two or three layers of polyphonic sound: a rhythmic-temporal unit (colotomic unit, or more specifically a gong unit), a drummed pattern of rhythms, and a melodic line, voiced or instrumental. These layers, as they progress through time in a seemingly linear way, join together, and present a logical and coherent totality, by means of a repeated rhythmic-temporal unit, played by specific instruments.

In the *wayang Siam* and *wayang melayu,* the *mak yong,* the *joget gamelan,* the *main puteri,* and the *tarinai,* time-marking bronze, wood, or bamboo idiophones provide the fundamental layer of sound, the rhythmic-temporal unit. These musics utilize large, hanging knobbed gongs, with smaller gongs, cymbals, and concussive bamboo sticks. Their basic structural entity is the gong unit (*gongan*), a cyclically recurring temporal unit of a set number of beats. The lowest-pitched hanging gong of the orchestra always marks its end, as shown in the *tetawak* part of figure 6*a–c*. By marking specific internal beats, smaller higher-pitched gongs, cymbals, and concussive sticks binarily subdivide this unit. These markers of time, with the large gong(s), give the music specific formal structure. When only one large hanging gong appears in an ensemble, its tone marks the end of a two- or four-beat colotomic unit (figure 6*d*).

Another important layer in the musical texture is the rhythms the drums play. The numbers and kinds of drums depend on the theatrical orchestra and musical piece. Most drums usually play in an interlocking style, effected by two or more drummers. To produce composite rhythms (figure 7), specific drums play particular timbres at specific times. Usually four or eight beats long, these rhythms repeat to fill the time of the gong unit in which they occur. They are accented at the end, and rests typically occur more frequently at the beginning; rhythmic activity becomes more dense from the midpoint to the end. A reiteration of the lowest timbre (vocalized as *duh* or *dong*) provides the greatest stress on the penultimate and final beats (figure 7*b–c*).

The third stratum of musical sound, the melody, is usually played by a single wind or stringed instrument, or vocalized by one or more singers. The shadow-play traditions provide examples of either a single instrument or a vocalist carrying the melody; an exception is the *wayang melayu,* which melodically employs a two-stringed rebab and a *canang* (see below). In most pieces of *wayang Siam,* the oboe plays the melody. A typical melody has predominantly stepwise motion and a high degree of ornamentation, including trills, grace notes, appoggiaturas, and triplet and sixteenth-note passages (figure 8*a*). These ornaments strongly contrast with periodic, sustained, dead tones, sometimes three beats or more in duration. To play the oboe, performers use a circular or continuous technique of breathing; hence, a melodic line, once begun, does not stop until the music does. The same trait typifies oboe melodies for the *gendang silat* and, to some extent, the *tarinai.* The scales used in theatrical musics tend to have a pentatonic or hexatonic core of primary pitches, with microtonal intervals and secondarily added pitches (figure 8*a–b*).

The music of many of the dance-drama genres and healing rituals relies on the voice as the main carrier of the melody. In these genres, if a melody instrument is present, it is usually the rebab, which typically plays heterophonically with the voice (or voices). In *mak yong* pieces, the melodies provide clear examples of heterophony between voice and rebab, and among several voices. They have long, melismatic passages featuring trills, turns, slides, grace notes, appoggiaturas, wide tremolos, and the glottal stop (figure 8*b*). Rests punctuate the melodic phrases, which typically spin out in lengths of two or four beats in slow tempi. The melodies of other dance-drama genres are not so ornate and do not require a highly trained vocal technique. Normally, in vocal music of all dance-drama genres, nasalization and emphasis in the upper register produce a thin and sometimes strident voice quality.

Music for storytelling

Storytelling in Malay culture includes the use of stylized language, singing, chanting, instrumental accompaniment, and sometimes drama. In past generations, professional storytellers related romances (*penglipur-lara*), often accompanying themselves

a 4-beat pattern, repeated

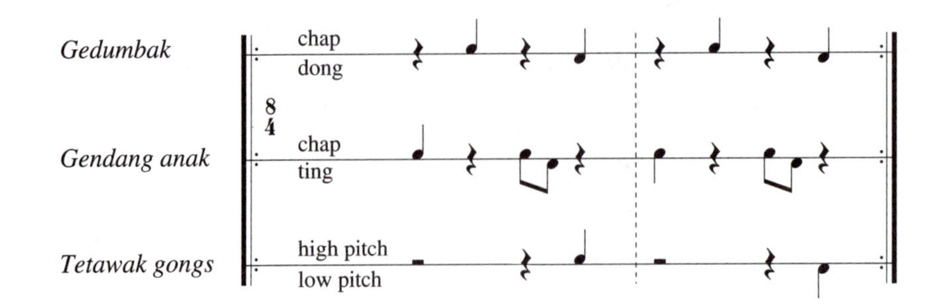

b 8-beat pattern

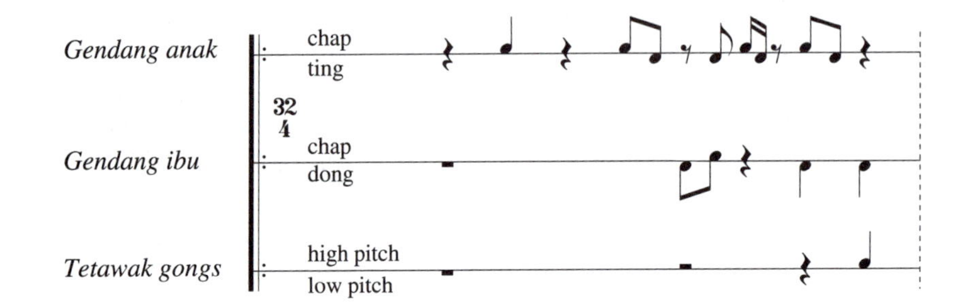

c 4-beat pattern

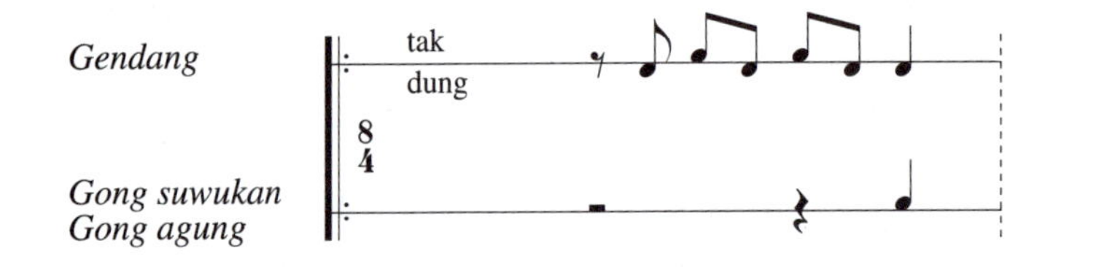

d 4-beat pattern

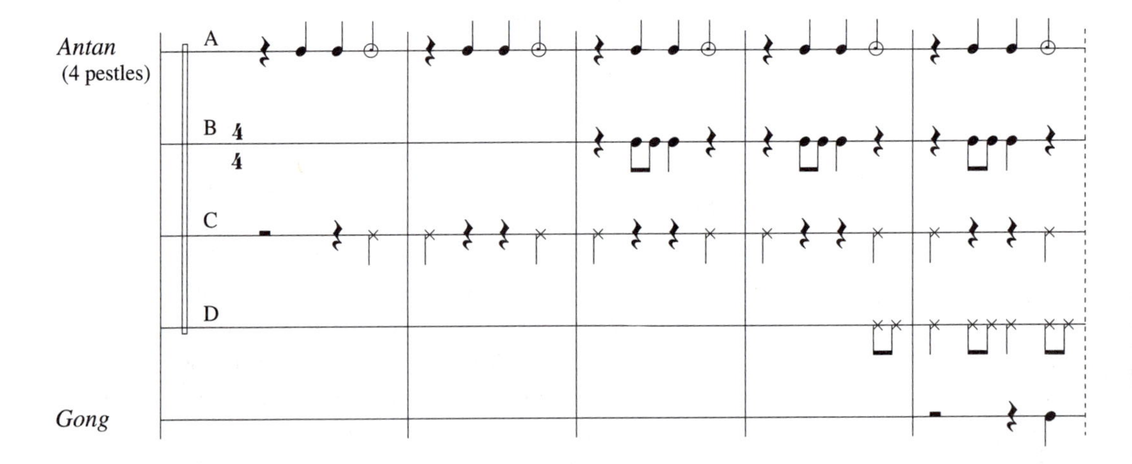

FIGURE 7 Interlocking rhythmic patterns in music for traditional theater and dance: *a,* a drum pattern from the *wayang kulit Siam* piece "*Pak Dogol*" (four-beat pattern, repeated); *b,* drum pattern from the *mak yong* piece "Sedayung mak yong" (eight-beat pattern); *c,* drum pattern from the *joget gamelan* piece "Perang" (four-beat pattern); *d,* percussive pattern from the *tumbuk kalang* piece "*Tiga Beranak*" (four-beat pattern).

instrumentally. As late as the mid-1900s, the art of storytelling was widespread in the northern Malay states and as far south as Selangor. By the 1990s, however, in both rural and urban areas, published texts, film, television, and modern drama had begun to hold greater interest, and many of the old storytellers had died, taking their art with them.

Regional genres were known by specific names, derived from the main (or root)

FIGURE 8
Melody in traditional Malay musics: *a,* excerpt from the *wayang kulit Siam* piece "*Pak Dogol*"; *b,* excerpt from the *mak yong* piece "*Menghadap Rebab.*"

FIGURE 8 (*continued*) *c,* excerpt from *rebana besar* performance.

story, or from a hero in the most popular story of the genre. In the northwest states, the genres were *jubang linggang, selampit,* and *awang batil* (also *awang belanga*). The *jubang linggang* and the *selampit* involved song and recitation, without instrumental accompaniment. The *awang batil* used an overturned brass bowl (*batil*), on which the storyteller beat out short, repeated rhythms to accompany and complement his recitation. Sometimes he would wear a mask, representing the character about whom he was speaking. The well-known *selampit* and *awang batil* veterans who still performed during the 1980s died in the early 1990s.

In Selangor, a narrative tradition known as *kaba* was performed by and for Minangkabau peoples living in the region. A three-stringed rebab may originally have accompanied the storyteller, but a violin has replaced it. Some narrative traditions, such as those found in Terengganu and Pahang, are unnamed. In those states, storytellers sing tales by improvising texts to repeated melodic lines, sometimes accompanying themselves by beating rhythms on a *rebana.*

Probably the most musically complex of the extant traditions of storytelling was found in Kelantan. The storyteller (*tok selampit*) was often a blind man who sang tales (*tarikh selampit*) as he accompanied himself on a rebab. The rebab doubled or imitated the vocal part, either playing in unison with the voice or repeating the vocal melody. The parts played on the rebab were melodically dense, with considerable sixteenth- and thirty-second-note movement. The melodies were usually ornate, with many grace notes, slides, and other embellishments. In both the voice and rebab parts, the melodic range was narrow, and microtonal intervals were common. Textual phrases began in syllabic style, but ended in long melismas. In many traditions, the music acted as a catalyst to enable the storyteller to develop his story (Sweeney 1972:60). The rebab melody in the *tarikh selampit* served to cue the storyteller for a specific starting pitch, and melodic phrases played on the rebab between the lines of sung text gave him time to collect his thoughts, prepare for the next line of text, or simply to rest.

Music for healing

Traditional Malay medicine encompasses various kinds of ritual ceremonies, intended to communicate with the world of spirits to determine whether the nature of an illness is physical or psychological. In such ceremonies, the aim is to summon and exorcise the spirits causing the illness. A ritualist serves as a medium, and a small ensemble often provides the musical component. Known by different names, healing rituals appear in different forms. The *main saba* (a curing ceremony, incorporating dance around a *saba* tree) and *main lukah* (a fishermen's curing ritual performed in Pahang) are regional types using song, dance, and drumming. The *main puteri* (*peteri*), another form that extensively uses music, is found in Kelantan and Terengganu (Malm 1974).

In the *main puteri,* a medium (*tok puteri, tok teri, bomoh*) becomes possessed by the spirits causing an illness. The performance of vocal and instrumental pieces helps him enter a state of trance. A trance-dance (*tarian lupa*) is a prominent feature of the ceremony. An assistant, the *tok minduk,* plays the rebab as he converses and sings in dialogue with the medium (figure 9).

An early form of the orchestra accompanying this ceremony consisted of two *redap* drums (also *rebana riba*); a large, hand-hit *rebana,* held upright in the lap; a three-stringed rebab; and a *batil,* struck with a pair of sticks. The orchestra used in Kelantan is larger, perhaps because of the occasional performance of the *main puteri* with the *mak yong* (resulting in a hybrid form, *main puteri–mak yong*). The contemporary *main puteri* orchestra of Kelantan includes the core *mak yong* orchestra (a rebab, a pair of *gendang,* and a pair of *tetawak*), plus two or more *canang,* a pair of *kesi,* and sometimes an oboe.

The dialogue between the *tok minduk* and the *tok puteri* is sung in a slow tempo, with long gong units (marked by the knobbed gongs), long rhythmic patterns in the drum part, and a vocal line featuring a basically syllabic style of singing. The rebab accompanies the vocal lines of both singers by either playing heterophonically with the voice or reiterating short melodic phrases as ostinatos. The trance-dance sections feature the repetition of brief gong units and short drummed rhythms, a fast tempo, and the reiteration and emphasis of the running beat by the small gongs and the hand-held cymbals.

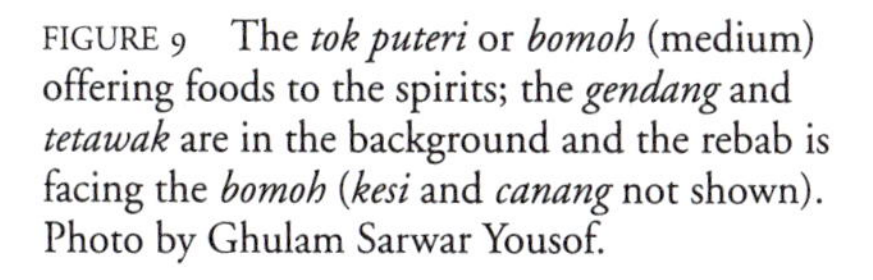

FIGURE 9 The *tok puteri* or *bomoh* (medium) offering foods to the spirits; the *gendang* and *tetawak* are in the background and the rebab is facing the *bomoh* (*kesi* and *canang* not shown). Photo by Ghulam Sarwar Yousof.

silat Martial arts–derived dance with drum accompaniment

gendang Two-headed, leather-laced drum with slightly bulging body

rebana Single-headed, round frame drum, sometimes with spokes

main pulau Type of song performed by women weeding dry rice fields

tumbuk kalang Folk song derived from rice-pounding songs

Music for the martial arts

Stemming from *silat* or *pencak silat,* the Malay art of self-defense, some dancelike forms have evolved. Though performed in peninsular Malaysia in a variety of styles as a competitive event among men, the *silat* also occurs as a fight-dance, performed by both men and women in Kelantan. As scenes of battle or other rituals preface the traditional performance of some theatrical genres, a highly stylized form of the martial arts in dancelike form sometimes precedes a dramatic performance—even in the milieu of Malay urban theater. The ensembles that accompany the *silat,* whether in its competitive martial-arts style or as a dance, are the *gendang silat* in the northern states, and the *caklempong* in the southern states.

Gendang silat

A small orchestra, the *gendang silat* provides highly dynamic music to accompany the movements of *silat* in north Malaysia. It consists of one hanging knobbed gong, one oboe, and two *gendang.* Two drummers play the latter. They hit the small drumhead with the hand and the large drumhead with an outcurved stick. Throughout the *silat* exhibition, an oboe provides a lively melodic line in eighth- and sixteenth-note movement, and the *gendang* play loud rhythms in interlocking style, accenting specific beats. On every other beat, the knobbed gong is struck with a padded beater. The music begins in a slow tempo and accelerates until the performance climaxes in a near frenzy.

Pencak silat

This style of the martial arts, exhibiting either armed or unarmed movements of self-defense, was brought by Minangkabau peoples, who migrated to peninsular Malaysia before the 1900s. The *pencak silat* is accompanied by the *caklempong* ensemble: one *caklempong,* two *rebana* (with a deep frame and no jingles), and one hanging, knobbed gong. The *caklempong* carries the melody, structured in short, repetitive phrases. In some *pencak silat,* choral parts feature recitation, which takes the form of short, narrow-ranged, melodic phrases continually repeated throughout a performance. Two drummers play rhythms on the *rebana,* and the knobbed gong marks the end of each four-beat rhythmic unit.

Music for work, life-cycle events, general entertainment

Work

Since rice and fish are staple foods throughout the peninsula, the major occupations in villages are agriculture and fishing. Along the coast, fishing and related activities are the predominant kinds of work for most of the year. Typical occupational activities—catching fish, maintaining boats, hauling nets, repairing nets—are sometimes accompanied by songs with rhythms and tempi that match the motions of the work.

In inland communities, the growing of rice and vegetables preoccupies most rural dwellers. Though music and song are usually heard after the harvest of the crops, some communities carry on musical activities to accompany the work of planting and caring for the crops during the growing season. Women in some remote villages of Pahang, as they weed dry ricefields, perform *main pulau,* songs to whose rhythms they step slowly in a circle (Mohd. Taib Osman 1982:58). A leader, who stands in the middle, directs the singing and guides the work from one part of the field to another. To lighten laborious activity, fishermen and farmers make rhythmical motions of the body and incorporate songs into their work.

In Negeri Sembilan, the *tumbuk kalang* (or *antan tumbuk kalang*) is played by peoples of Minangkabau descent. Formerly it was one stage of processing rice. It stems from the activity of pounding (*tumbuk*) the rice in a mortar (*lesung*) with a wooden pestle (*antan*). Before industrial methods were used in processing rice, two or three people parched newly harvested grains, put them into the well of the mortar, pounded them, and winnowed the chaff from the edible grains. The ancient activity of pounding rice by two or three people who, sequentially in rhythm, stamped their poles into the well of the mortar, led to the stamping of the pestles on various parts of the mortar to achieve a variety of timbres produced in specific rhythms. Eventually, the stamping became enhanced by clapping and the singing of work-related songs in the form of *pantun,* four-line stanzas that were, and still are, sung responsorially, with each singer alternating every two or four lines of text.

Villagers perform the *tumbuk kalang* only as entertainment, and they no longer pound rice during the performance. Performers are mainly groups who live on government farming schemes, such as projects of the Federal Land Development Authority. The performances may be heard after the harvest of rice, during performing-arts festivals, on the occasion of a visit of dignitaries to a village, or at special school festivities. Performance settings vary widely. In villages, playing often begins in the late evening and concludes after dawn.

The ensemble features a hardwood mortar with a cup-shaped well in the middle of its top surface. It sits securely on a base (*kalang*); the top surface, shaped in a long, narrow rectangle, may be stamped in the central well, on either side of it, or on the outer walls. The location for stamping and the size of the pestle affect the timbre. The rhythms produced by three or four pestles interlock, as each player produces a specific timbre at a specific time. The pestles begin stamping in staggered entrances, and the rhythms are typically four beats long, with a knobbed, hanging gong marking the end of each four-beat unit (figure 7*d*). The pieces often begin with a short, improvised prelude on the flute; a *rebana* and a small *caklempong* sometimes join in. The instrumental parts accompany the singing of the *pantun,* which a soloist and a chorus may sing responsorially. (Two singers may sing the vocal part, alternating verses.) When dance is added, the resulting performance is a *taridra.* The dancers are men and women, whose gestures and steps reflect the topic of the song being sung. A song about planting rice, for example, would require text and movements suggesting hoeing, sowing, replanting the seedlings, harvesting the mature stalks, and pounding the rice.

Life-cycle events

Life-cycle events, including the major rites of passage, are usually associated with *adat* (customary law and practice) ceremonies, some of which are highly elaborate and communal. Music, often an integral part, is performed by both skilled and semi-skilled members of a community. Life-cycle events that make extensive use of music and religious recitation include weddings and circumcisions.

The circumcision (*berkhatan*) ceremony usually follows the chanting of *berzanji.*

Also, in the southern states, the ensembles playing *kompang* music with the chanting of *zikir* accompany processions as part of the ceremony. The drumming is performed on the *kompang,* a hand-beaten frame drum. It has a shallow, hardwood body and a single tacked head, sometimes with metal jingles inserted into the frame. The drummers may chant religious texts, and in some social contexts they chant secular texts, but the emphasis is on the drumming, which is in interlocking style, effected by two or more groups of players. As the lead drummer beats the cues for abrupt changes in tempo, levels of volume, and rhythms, the drummers produce sharp contrasts in timbre. The extreme range of high and low timbres in the drumming, the loud volume, and the fast tempi offer a dynamic accompaniment to the ceremony or procession.

In the northern peninsular states, *hadrah,* the chanting of religious texts at a circumcision, is accompanied by rhythms played on the *rebana.* An ensemble of *rebana* provides percussive accompaniment, but chanting is the focus. Unlike the *kompang,* the *rebana* uses rattan laces to attach the skin to the frame and has no jingles. The construction of and playing technique on the *rebana* result in a mellow, resonant sound, which allows the sung texts be heard with clarity.

In the regions inhabited by peoples of Minangkabau descent, the *bongai* (also *rentak kuda*) is often performed for a circumcision, a wedding, and entertainment after the harvest. It features repartee between two people who sing *pantun* responsorially. A group of some eight men and women perform this genre. The first performer sings a statement. A second singer answers by composing and singing another *pantun* in response; the first singer (or a third singer) then takes up the singing of another statement; and so on. Typical themes of the *pantun* are love, comedy, teasing, and innuendo. The *bongai* is accompanied by a small *caklempong* ensemble: one gong chime (*gereteh*), one oboe, one *rebana* or *gendang,* and one hanging, knobbed gong. It may also be played during national holidays and is sometimes heard during child-associated life-cycle ceremonies.

Weddings call for the performance of musical genres, including the *kompang* or the *hadrah,* as the bridegroom is escorted to the bride's house. The solemn singing of *zikir* in regional styles and the witty entertainment of *bongai* (in Minangkabau communities) may also be heard. Another genre performed especially for weddings is the *tari inai* (*inai* dance), played during the applying of henna (*berinai*) to the bride's hands and feet (see "Dance," above). Especially in urban areas, weddings also feature the latest hits, played by a Western pop band, or by an *asli* ensemble.

Events involving childhood and the stages of development in a child's life are often marked by musical performance. In some parts of the peninsula, the first cutting of the baby's hair (*potong rambut*) and the first time a child's feet touch the ground while it learns to walk (*jejak tanah*) are occasions for the performance of *maulud,* verses praising Muhammad and statements on exemplary behavior (Mohd. Taib Osman 1974:214–215). In some Minangkabau communities of Negeri Sembilan, the *bongai* is also performed in celebration of the *potong rambut.* Lullabies are commonly sung to small children, and children's songs teach proper social conduct and behavior. Most traditional children's songs use diatonic scales with piano or guitar accompaniment.

General entertainment

Music that serves for entertainment occurs in the theatrical genres noted above. After harvests, audiences enjoy listening to *rebana ubi, kertok kelapa, kacapi, seruling,* and *dikir barat,* particularly in the northern states (figure 10; see figure 14). In Kelantan, after the harvest of rice, the men of one village often play sets of *rebana ubi* drums in competition with the men of another. The *rebana ubi* is an extremely large, considerably modified version of the *rebana.* It has a wooden, conical body, with a single

FIGURE 10 Teams competitively play *rebana ubi* drums. Photo by Patricia Matusky.

drumhead measuring nearly a meter in diameter. For the head, makers of drums usually employ water-buffalo hide, which they attach to the body by thick rattan laces sewn into the hide and looped around a large rattan ring at the base of the body. They tighten the skin with wooden wedges, which they hammer into the space between the ring and the body. Drummers, one or two to a single drum, beat the instrument by hand or with a padded beater. They play interlocking rhythms whose names are often the titles of pieces in the repertoire of *wayang Siam.* (The actual musical relationship of *rebana ubi* pieces and shadow-play pieces is unclear.) Some villages own as many as ten *rebana ubi.*

Another type of ensemble featuring the interlocking playing technique is known as *kertok kelapa* (or *kertok kayu*). The *kertok kelapa* is made from a hollow coconut shell secured on a wooden base. A slab of bamboo or wood of a specific thickness and length is laid across the opening at the top of the coconut and is struck with a wood stick by a single player. A number of these percussive instruments are struck, with each player beating his instrument at specific times to produce resultant melodic-rhythmic patterns.

For solo entertainment, a single player strikes and plucks a tube zither (*kacapi*), producing a combination of percussive rhythms and short melodies plucked on strings. Imitating music from shadow plays or other theatrical genres, the performer simultaneously plays the parts of two or three different instruments. Another instrument that plays melodies for individual enjoyment in intimate settings is the end-blown flute (*seruling*).

A favorite choral vocal form found in the northeast states is the *dikir barat,* in which men sitting in a circle sing verses of popular, nonreligious texts. A soloist begins a piece with an introductory text, sung on a lengthy, improvised melody in free rhythm. A performance in responsorial style follows. Unison choral singing answers the soloist, in strictly duple rhythm. A *rebana kercing* (*rebana* with jingles) usually provides rhythms, and a hanging, knobbed gong marks the end of every two- or four-beat unit. The clapping of hands, gestures of hands and arms, and the swaying of the body enhance the performance. Though probably stemming from the religious singing of *dikir* (as the name of the genre suggests), the *dikir barat* is entirely secular. Two or more groups of men from different villages often perform it competi-

In the *boria*, the song-dance routines usually begin with an orchestral introduction, using popular Western music for dancing. Rumbas and cha-chas have been favorite openers.

tively. Audiences rate them by their skill in improvising lyrics, their vocal style, and their movements and showmanship.

Traditional urban musical-theatrical genres

Begun in Penang Island, the *boria* and the *bangsawan* are the products of nineteenth-century urban culture in peninsular Malaysia. Both forms incorporate spoken dialogue, songs, and dances.

The boria

Formerly in Penang, at fun-filled New Year's celebrations during the first ten days of Muharram, men traditionally performed the *boria.* Troupes of twenty or more gathered under the leadership of a composer-manager, the troupe's lead singer. Each year, the troupe selected a theme (such as Arab warriors, European traders, or Chinese shopkeepers) around which their costumes and comic improvisations revolved. For their performances, troupes expected monetary remuneration. In the early 1900s, they wandered from one neighborhood to another, performing in people's yards, or in the halls of clubs and associations.

A typical performance is in two parts, consisting of a short comic sketch and a song-dance routine. The sketch, acted by four or more men playing rural people, often highlights local events and domestic situations. In the late 1900s, it sometimes served as a vehicle for political propaganda. The song-dance routines usually begin with an orchestral introduction, using popular Western music for dancing. Rumbas and cha-chas have been favorite openers. The accompanying ensemble varies in instrumentation from one troupe to another. The main melodic instrument has consistently been the violin. Players optionally add various Western, Malay, or Indian drums, plus Chinese cymbals. The lead singer and the chorus alternately sing twelve or more verses, featuring a set routine of gestures and steps. The troupe then goes to its next location, where it gives a similar performance.

The bangsawan

This genre is more formalized in performance and repertory. Brought by performers from Bombay in the late 1800s, it developed as an adaptation of Parsi theater. Plays about romances and situations concerning Malay royalty became locally known as nobility (*bangsawan*). Eclectic, the repertoire features Hindustani and Arabian legends, Chinese romances, English dramas, and Malay legends (Tan 1993). Some troupes have as many as fifty actors, plus musicians and a manager.

In its early days, the *bangsawan* stage was a temporary, roofed platform, raised to ease viewing, with a backdrop near the rear. Later, troupes adopted the Western indoor proscenium stage with elaborate backdrops—a convention still in use. The cast consists of several stereotyped roles: the hero, the heroine, the leading lady, comedians, a king, a queen, and villains (Ghulam-Sarwar 1987:7–17). The costumes are elaborate.

FIGURE 11 The *ronggeng* ensemble for *bangsawan* and other syncretic genres, including (left to right) tambourine, knobbed gong, two *rebana,* violin, and accordion. Photo by Tan Sooi Beng.

Spoken dialogue alternates with song and dance. At first, the musical pieces came from different sources, including older American pop-dance styles (such as the cakewalk and the Charleston), Spanish dances, and other popular musics from Western Europe and India. The original orchestral instruments were the harmonium and the tabla, instruments of Parsi theater. As the form and its repertoire evolved, the instrumentation changed. The musicians optionally used a piano, a flute, a violin, and a *rebana.* In the late 1900s, in an effort to make the music more Malay, orchestras began featuring a violin, an accordion, a *rebana,* and a knobbed gong (Tan 1988:255) (figure 11). Since the 1970s, the music has featured the rhythms and melodies of the *asli* repertoire—a syncretic musical tradition, emerging from Malay urban and semiurban culture, featuring multiple elements (Western, Arabic, Indian) and incorporating aspects of indigenous Malay music.

Musical traditions at court

Since the founding of the earliest Kedah court (in the 400s), documentary evidence of musical performance in peninsular courts has survived. Passages describing ceremonial orchestras and ensembles for theatrical entertainment appear in historical texts, such as *Al-Tarikh Salasilah Negeri Kedah,* the *Sejarah Melayu,* and the *Hikayat Patani.* Accounts of the *asyek* dance (*tari asyek*) and of the ensembles of musical instruments seen and heard at Malay courts also appear in published reports and articles, such as those of Peter Floris and Frank Swettenham, European traders of the 1600s and 1700s, respectively. Later documents attest to a gamelan and a retinue of dancers in the courts of Pahang and Terengganu, and personal evidence tells of lavish and sophisticated productions of the *mak yong* at the court of the early-twentieth-century Kelantan sultanate.

Royal patronage was once generous, but after World War II it almost completely ceased. The *nobat* remains the only musical tradition still viable at court. The other musical-theatrical genres once performed there—the *wayang kulit melayu,* the *mak yong,* the *tari inai*—survive only as traditions among the folk, and some are nearly extinct. These and other traditional forms are fast losing their significance, for they compete in a society bounded by the strictures of orthodox Islam on the one side and the influence of television, films, and changing values on the other. One traditional dance-drama (*joget gamelan*) has taken on the status of a national art. This has been possible in part because of the support the Terengganu state government has given the genre and the use of the genre in the development of modern dance-drama in urban contexts.

Shadow-play music

The *wayang kulit melayu* (also *wayang melayu* or *wayang Jawa*) is the shadow theater performed under court patronage in Kelantan and Kedah and formerly in the Patani sultanate. As entertainment for aristocrats, it was performed only in palaces. During the late 1800s and early 1900s, Malay courts sent puppeteers to Java to learn their art, and they returned with manuscripts of stories from the *Mahabharata* and the knowledge of playing techniques in the Javanese style. Malay puppeteers used Hindu stories and cowhide puppets in Javanese design, but told the stories in local Malay dialects. As in traditional folk theatricals, the *buka panggung* opened every performance, and the raised, enclosed, hutlike stage identical to the folk shadow-play stage continued to serve for the *wayang melayu* at court. By the 1990s, royal patronage had ceased. Though puppeteers and musicians still live in Kelantan, performances are rare, and the form is nearly extinct.

The orchestra that accompanies performances features a set of six or more bronze idiophones: one *canang,* one *mong,* one pair of *kesi,* and two *tetawak.* Of these, the *mong,* the *kesi,* and the *tetawak* mark musical time, while the *canang* and a two-stringed rebab provide melodies. A pair of *gendang* adds rhythms. The musical repertoire was formerly large, but only about twenty pieces survive. As in the *wayang Siam,* these pieces— sung and instrumental—accompany specific kinds of action, emotion, mood, and intent. Just as the borrowing of musical repertoire occurs among village theatricals, so borrowing occurs in regional court musics. The only extant musical piece for the *asyek* dance appears in the *wayang melayu* for the entrance and walking movement of a princess.

Music for dance and dance-drama

Asyek *dance*

Two forms of Malay music for dance or dance-drama without speech or song developed in the court tradition. One of these, *tari asyek,* is believed to have originated in the court of the Patani sultanate. It was performed exclusively by female dancers as entertainment for royalty, especially for the sultan. The dance and its music are still known among performers in Kelantan. It is occasionally performed as part of public festivities for the sultan's birthday and other national celebrations.

Slow-paced, the dance stresses intricate movement of the arms, hands, and fingers. The dancer may sit or stand. In the 1800s and early 1900s, the dance was accompanied by several *gedumbak* (*gedumbak asyek*) and one boat-shaped xylophone (*gambang*)—all played by women. A rebab, played by a male musician of the court, completed the ensemble (Mohd. Taib Osman 1974:211). In the mid-1990s, however, orchestras were all-male; they included three *canang,* two *gendang,* and one hanging gong (Malm 1974:9). Other instruments—an oboe, a *geduk,* and a fourth small gong—could participate (Mohammad Ghouse 1979:443). Only one piece ("*Jubang*") survives. It has a structure of two eight-beat melodic phrases, played on the *canang.* The drums complement the melody with a repeated eight-beat rhythm. A single stroke on the hanging gong marks the end of the melody.

Joget gamelan

The second major tradition of dancing at court is *joget gamelan* (also *gamelan terengganu* or *gamelan pahang*). This style, with roots in the central Javanese traditions of court gamelan and dance, was known at the court of the rulers of Riau-Lingga. In the early 1800s, through a marriage between the royal families of the Riau-Lingga Islands (in Indonesia) and Pahang, the gamelan, with its music and dance, was taken to the Pahang court. A century later, through a marriage between the Pahang and Terengganu royal families, the gamelan and its retinue of musicians and dancers moved to the sultan's palace in Terengganu, where it continued to develop under the patronage and tutorship of the sultan and his wife. The *joget gamelan,* as it became known, was entertainment only for royalty at such court functions as installation ceremonies, birthday celebrations, engagements, and weddings, and for state visits. During World War II, and for two decades thereafter, its activity ceased; only in the 1960s was the tradition revived. Under the sponsorship of the Terengganu state government, it continued to develop. In the 1990s, it is a national art, danced and heard as entertainment at state ceremonies.

The surviving repertory of music and dance is not large. Essentially interpretive, its pieces may serve in a variety of dramatic situations. Many dance-dramas in the traditional repertory are based on the *Panji* stories, and other dramas are drawn from folktales. A given story is told through the medium of dance. Each piece has specific musical accompaniment. The dancers are exclusively women, who perform both male and female parts in elaborate costumes appropriate for the character or scene depicted.

Played only by men, the orchestral instruments are one *gendang,* two *saron* (*barung* and *peking*), the *kerumong* 'gong chime', one *gambang,* the *kenong* (a set of five large, pot-shaped gongs), and the *gong suwukan* and *agung* (large, hanging gongs, of high and low pitches, respectively). The large gongs and *kenong* mark musical time, while the *gendang* provides rhythms. The nuclear melody of a piece is played on the *saron barung,* while the *peking,* xylophone, and gong chime ornament it (D'Cruz 1979).

Ceremonial music

Nobat

For several hundred years, the *nobat* and its music have graced the regalia of the Malay sultanates. The concept originated in the Middle East and developed in Islamic societies from southern Spain to India. In about the twelfth century, the sultan of Pasai, Sumatra (who had received the *nobat* from Middle Eastern sources), introduced it to the ruler of Malacca. Subsequently, the *nobat* was used to install the first sultan of Kedah (Ku Zam Zam 1985:177), where it is still used today. The Malay sultanates that own and use this orchestra as part of their regalia are Kedah, Perak, and formerly Selangor on the west coast, and Kelantan on the east.

Social status in feudal Malay society distinguished between commoners and rulers, and the *nobat* was a major element in signifying aristocratic rank. In effect, the orchestra validated the sultan and his sultanate: the sound of the music was symbolically equivalent to his presence. The *nobat* still provides music for court ceremonies. All the stages of a royal marriage require, as accompaniment, specific music played by the royal orchestra, as do the activities involved in the installation of a ruler. In addition, to announce the time for Muslims to pray, the Kedah *nobat* is played at specific hours throughout the day. The orchestras of most of the former Malay sultanates are rarely heard. The Kedah *nobat,* the most active in its home state, usually plays for the installation of the national king.

The instrumentation of late-twentieth-century *nobat* includes one oboe (*serunai*); one trumpet (*nafiri*); two *gendang,* one drumhead, hit with the hand and the other with a stick; one kettledrum (*nehara,* alternately, *nahara* and *nagara*), hit with a pair of rattan sticks; and sometimes one knobbed gong, hit with a padded beater. The Kedah *nobat* formerly had a second oboe and two pairs of cymbals. In addition, the orchestra includes a cane staff (wrapped in yellow cloth, signifying royalty), believed to have magical powers and used to lead the ensemble. The instruments of the *nobat* command respect and honor. Legends say they have magical powers, and musicians observe taboos to protect their purity. Wrapped in yellow cloth

musiqa Arabic word denoting music as distinct from chant

Qur'ān The Islamic canon of Muhammad's writings, intended to be chanted

azan The Islamic call to prayer, chanted five times daily from a minaret

zikir Vocalized religious chants, usually accompanied by drumming

covers, all stay in a special place in the palace. In Kedah, the ensemble is stored and played in the *nobat* hall (*balai nobat*), a building built for the purpose. The instruments are played only by a group of specially trained musicians, who pass down their knowledge to their sons or other male relatives, or to other individuals chosen by the sultan. Two of the musicians serve as leaders of the orchestra (*kalau besar* and *kalau kecil*), each with specific responsibilities for teaching new players and maintaining the orchestra.

Musicians learn a repertoire of twenty or more instrumental pieces (*man*). A traditional system of notation (*daî*) records individual pieces. Specific instruments and methods of playing are symbolized by letters of the *jawi* script, derived from Arabic (Ku Zam Zam 1985:181). Some pieces, having broad functions, enhance court ceremonies; others, having more specialized functions, highlight festive ceremonies, sensitive or emotional events, and solemn occasions. Pieces are sectionalized, usually into four parts or movements. The oboe carries a melodic line, and the *gendang* provide basic rhythms, in unison or in interlocking style. The *nehara* plays steady beats and cues changes in melody, rhythm, and tempo. The knobbed gong punctuates the rhythms at regular intervals of time, and the *nafiri* periodically produces a sustained tone, enriching the texture.

Music and religion

To speak of music associated with religion among the Malay peoples of peninsular Malaysia is to speak of two different attitudes and paths of development. The first is based on pre-Islamic religious beliefs, rooted in animism and overlaid with precepts from Buddhism and Hinduism. Vestiges of these beliefs survive in the opening rituals of some theatrical forms and in healing rituals and related forms propitiating beings from the world of spirits.

The second main path of development is associated with Islam, a religion many peninsular Malays adopted in the early 1300s. Within its sphere, musical practice was, and still is, bound with orthodox definitions of appropriate musical sound. In Malaysia of the 1990s, the Muslim notion of appropriate musical sound rested to a large degree on sectarian interpretations of context and function. The segment of the population that practices the musical forms found throughout the peninsula takes a less rigidly conservative view. Disregarding context and function, the definition of music used in the West—denoted by the Arabic term *musiqa* (derived from Greek *mousikē*)—does not apply to Islamic religious sounds (al-Faruqi 1985:6).

Consequently, excluding *musiqa,* Malay society considers chanting the Qur'ān the highest form of art involving sound. It may be rendered in a solo or unison choral format, unaccompanied. At the annual Qur'ān-reading competition (held in Kuala Lumpur), crowds listen to highly skilled chanters, both male and female. The chanting mixes syllabic and melismatic styles. Vocal embellishments involve glottal stops, single and double grace notes, slides, turns, and wide tremolos.

FIGURE 12 Singing a form of *zikir* accompanied by hand-hit *rebana ubi* drums. Photo by Patricia Matusky.

Another form of cantillation that excludes *musiqa* is the call to prayer (*azan, adhan*), vocalized five times a day from minarets. It is always chanted by a man, the *muezzin*, usually amplified by loudspeakers. To reach a wide audience, government television channels broadcast it nationally.

Several kinds of chant (*nazam, berzanji, marhaban*) are appropriate forms of cantillation. In these forms, religious texts in Arabic praise Muhammad, amplify religious teachings, or prescribe proper Islamic behavior. In Terengganu and Pahang, only women perform the *nazam*. In various regions, only men perform the *berzanji* and the *marhaban*.

Other forms of vocalizing religious texts (*zikir*) involve some degree of *musiqa*, including drumming. The most notable drum used to serve this function is a frame drum. Ubiquitous in peninsular Malaysia, it features in many distinct regional styles. In the south, *kompang* is a frame drum with a shallow body and a single skin, tacked onto a wooden frame; some sets incorporate metal jingles in the frame. A similar drum with jingles (*rebana kercing, tar*) is found in the northeast. In contrast, the central and northern states feature a frame drum whose makers attach a single skin to a wooden body by means of laces sewn into the skin and looped around a thick rattan ring at the base. To tighten the skin, they insert wooden wedges between the ring and the frame. This drum is the *rebana*, and on some models a rattan ring (*sedak*), inserted inside the drum (between the skin and the body), tightens the drumhead. The *rebana* has a variety of sizes, with considerable variation in the diameter of the head and the depth of the frame. Found mainly in small ensembles, it accompanies the singing or reciting of religious texts, in regional styles variously called *zikir rebana, zikir pahang, dikir beredah, hadrah, rebana besar*, and *rebana kercing*. The sung texts are in Arabic or Malay and may be religious or secular. In most regional styles, each person in a given group takes turns singing parts of the verses in slow tempi, against unison drumming on the *rebana*.

Formerly in Kelantan (and possibly still in its remote regions), *rebana besar*, a popular type of *zikir* performance, featured a large *rebana ubi*, hit with the hands (figure 12). The drummers sing Arabic or Malay verses praising Muhammad or commenting on moral behavior. A player opens a verse by singing a rhythmically free phrase in melismatic style; to complete the verse, the chorus sings in unison (figure

8*c*). The choral style of singing is distinctly syllabic; ornamentation occurs only in the soloist's part. Unison drumming in duple meter and slow tempo provides accompaniment.

Religious genres that include elements of *musiqa* are considered appropriate in the proper social and religious setting. In a religious context, Muhammad's birthday (Maulud-an-Nabi), fasting at Ramadan (Puasa), leaving on a pilgrimage to Mecca, and celebrating the conclusion of Ramadan or the pilgrimage (Hari Raya Puasa, Hari Raya Haji) are formal Islamic rituals during which people sing *zikir.* These genres also serve in *adat* ceremonies, for they may be performed in celebration of life-cycle events, such as the first cutting of a baby's hair, and rites of passage, such as weddings or circumcisions.

URBAN-BASED FOLK MUSIC

Traditional Malay culture has often been noted for its eclecticism. Many of the world's important cultural and religious influences have passed through this region, so it is no surprise that Malay music and musical instruments reflect diverse influences.

The music that developed among the ordinary people of Malaysia is distinct from that of courtly traditions. It is the music that has interacted with, and been a reflection of, the mainstream culture of the west coast of peninsular Malaysia. These musical genres have had a much greater impact on Malaysian music in the twentieth century than any other traditional musical forms. They occur in many geographic variants, depending on the performers' places of origin.

Musical instruments

No single instrumentation is standard in urban Malay traditional musics. Instrumentation varies from one genre to another, from one place to another, and from one era to another. What is described here are the most common instruments, but exceptions and variations occur.

Most traditional Malay ensembles include at least one melodic instrument, at least one instrument to provide rhythmic accompaniment, and at least one instrument serving a colotomic function: marking off certain points in time. When more than one melodic instrument is present, the focus is usually on a melodic line, accompanied by countermelodies based on it. Melodies characteristically utilize embellishments (*bunga* 'flower'), which carry over into contemporary musical forms. Traditionally, these melodies and countermelodies are performed heterophonically, not implying any sense of Western functional harmony.

Melodic instruments

The violin is one of the most widely used Western instruments in performances of traditional Malay music. Brought into Malaya by the Portuguese more than four hundred years ago, it is held by Malaysian musicians in the same manner as in the European tradition. The flute is also commonly used as a melodic instrument. Locally constructed bamboo instruments were formerly used, but in the twentieth century, metal European flutes have almost replaced them. In some performances, a plucked, pear-shaped lute (*gambus*) serves as a melodic instrument; the Malay variant of the Arab *'ud,* it closely resembles its Arab ancestor. The guitar is now sometimes used with, or to replace the *gambus*. The harmonium, and more recently, the accordion have also developed roles as melodic instruments; though added only since the 1940s, the accordion is widely used in traditional performances.

FIGURE 13 Three men play the single-keyed *kertok kelapa* coconut xylophones. Photo by Gerald Moore.

Rhythmic instruments

Two basic types of membranophones are used for rhythmic accompaniment: two-headed, barrel-shaped drums and single-headed, frame drums. These instruments come in many sizes and styles of construction. The most widely used are the *gendang* (lashed two-headed drum, resembling the Javanese *kendang*) and the *rebana* (a single-headed frame drum, resembling the Arab *tar*). The Indian tabla is also used in genres influenced by music from India.

Colotomic instruments

The main instruments formerly used to mark off points in time were knobbed bronze gongs resembling bronze gongs found in other parts of Southeast Asia. Most of the gongs used in Malaysia today are believed to have been made in either Java or Sumatra. They come in various sizes, between 30 and 60 centimeters in diameter.

Genres of West Malaysian popular music

Asli *and* dondang sayang

The Malay word *asli* is the most widely used term in reference to traditional music. This word can be glossed 'original, real, genuine, aboriginal' and derives from the word *asal* 'beginning, root, source, place of birth'. In its generic sense, the term *asli music* often serves in Malaysia to denote any music considered old or traditional. The term has numerous specific musical designations.

The term *asli* also denotes a particular musical genre that dates from the 1600s or 1700s. Though regional variations occur, this genre is widely acknowledged to have developed from *dondang sayang* 'melody of love' of the Malaysian Chinese community in Melaka. The primary difference between *dondang sayang* and *asli* is that the text in *dondang sayang* is improvised; in *asli,* it is composed in advance. One particular melody, "*Dondang Sayang,*" is always played as the principal melody in *dondang sayang* performances. Since a great deal of improvisation and playing of variant melodies and countermelodies occurs in both *dondang sayang* and *asli,* and since these genres are closely related in many of their basic musical traits, the distinctions between them are not always clear. Each stanza of most *asli* songs and *dondang sayang* performances is in binary form (AB). The melodies usually move in minor and major

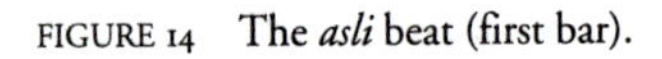

FIGURE 14 The *asli* beat (first bar).

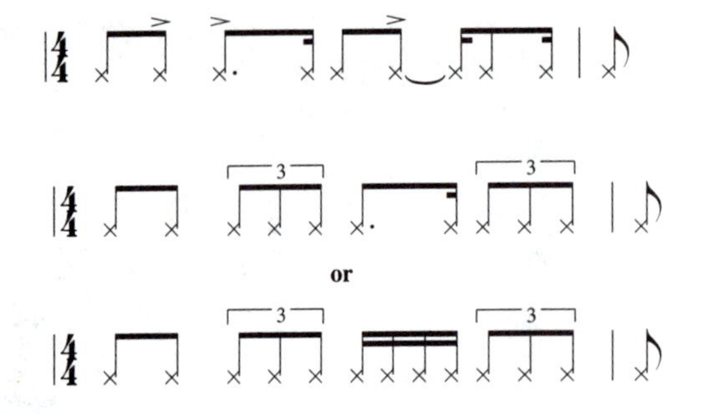

FIGURE 15 Two common examples of the second four beats of the eight-beat accompanying *asli* rhythm.

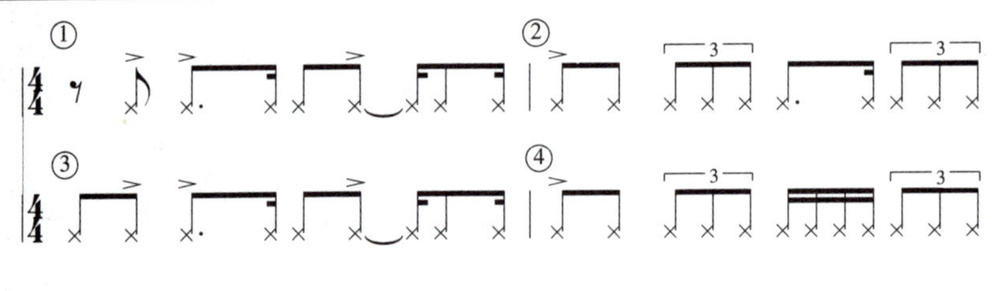

FIGURE 16 A typical accompanimental pattern in a sixteen-beat section of an *asli.*

FIGURE 17 The first eight notes of the *asli* "*Seri Mersing*" with an accompanying *asli* beat.

seconds. As a result of chromaticism, tonal implications often seem to shift and can be best termed ambiguous.

Typical rhythms

Asli can be identified primarily by rhythmic accompaniment, consisting of eight-beat phrases or cycles, usually notated as two bars of 4/4 time. Traditionally, this accompaniment is performed by a *rebana* or a *gendang.* The first four beats of each pattern are fixed (figure 14). The second four beats are usually improvised within the constraint that their rhythm must not be inconsistent with the style and feel of the first four. More rhythmic movement usually occurs toward the end of each bar (figure 15).

The *asli* rhythmic cycle repeats throughout a performance of *dondang sayang* or an *asli* (figure 16). The beat is usually played at a tempo of about one beat per second. This tempo is so closely identified with the *asli* beat that Malaysian composers commonly use the term *asli* to indicate it.

Though other traits of the *asli* genre include the actual form and text of the songs, the accompanying rhythm is the most important identifying factor. This trait can be seen in the melody of an *asli,* which can be transformed to be used in other traditional genres, primarily by changing the accompanying rhythmic pattern (figure 17).

The traditional ensemble for performing an *asli* normally consists of either a *rebana* or a *gendang,* a knobbed gong, a violin, and sometimes a harmonium. The most common alterations to this are the substitution of an accordion for the harmonium and the addition of a flute to play countermelodies. This combination is usually regarded as traditional, but any group of instruments—orchestras, jazz bands, even rock bands—may play an *asli.*

Other traits

An identifying trait of *asli* and *dondang sayang* is that the singer does not usually sing the principal melody. The violin and the flute play that melody while the singer sings a short, highly improvised variant of it. If two melodic instruments are used, one often alternates between the melody and an improvised countermelody. The principal melodic instrument often improvises highly ornamented variants of the melody, with the basic melody only vaguely implied.

A harmonium or an accordion sometimes plays several notes at a time, serving more as a drone than as harmony. The three basic parts—drum, violin, voice—are all rhythmically independent, though they stay within the framework established by the basic eight-beat pattern. The gong serves a colotomic function, marking off the music into temporal units, emphasizing specific drumbeats.

Other uses of the term asli

Asli langgam 'stylized modern tune' is often called *asli* for short. This is a musical development of the middle of the twentieth century. The singer sings the melody from the beginning to the end of the song, with the violin in a less embellished style. The term *asli* also names a vocal style, the most commonly used one in traditional Malay music. The style associated with *asli* and *dondang sayang* is apparently the origin of this term, but the singing of *asli* is not restricted to use in only these genres. Often the term describes any highly ornamented vocal style. Performances by someone considered to be a singer of *asli* usually include songs from other genres. This style is commonly believed to be a mixture of older Malay traditions with Arab and Indian influences.

Texts

The texts of *asli* and *dondang sayang* are related to the Malay *pantun* in form, style, and rhyme. This poetic form has greatly influenced the lyrics of most other genres. It is the most widely known and most popular Malay poetic form. In its fundamental form, it has four lines, each eight syllables long, rhyming *abab*: the first line rhymes with the third, and the second line rhymes with the fourth. The earliest surviving written reference to it appears in *Sejarah Melayu* (The Malay Annals), which date from the 1400s, but it is recognized as a much older phenomenon. Like the *dondang sayang,* it is believed to have originated in Melaka. The term *pantun* has been traced to other languages; likely cognates are the Javanese *atuntun* 'connected in lines' and the Tagalog *tonton* 'to speak in a certain order'.

Pantun can be spoken, recited, or sung, for a variety of social occasions. Often they are performed in a competition to determine who can create the best ones. Traditionally, such competitions have played a part in courting among young Malay men and women. Competitions may involve small or large groups, and may in part be presentational, and in part participational. Professional dancing girls sometimes engage in creating *pantun* with male observers, challenging them with flirtatiousness. In addition to creating new examples in an impromptu manner, participants employ respected *pantun*, which people remember and repeat as sayings and proverbs.

For nonnative speakers of Malay, especially those unfamiliar with the form, the meaning of individual *pantun* can be difficult to fathom. The greatest difficulty is in the first two lines, because the meaning often becomes clear only in the last two. Furthermore, the connection between the two pairs of lines is expected to be obscure, subtle, and esoteric. The first two lines can be thought of as a general and vague preparation for the final two, which can serve as either the logical conclusion to the first two, or as a surprise, depending on the creator's intention. The ability to create good *pantun* is highly respected, but it is less important in Malaysian society than it once was.

A Malaysian *pantun* commonly begins with a reference to nature or a place within Malaysia. The text is always secular. Its topics are love and personal relationships. The term *pantun* can loosely refer to any four-line poem or lyric. The following is a famous Malaysian *pantun.*

Apa kena padi-ku ini,	What ails my ricefield so fine,
Sini sangku, sana pun goyang?	Entangled here, there on the move?
Apa kena hati-ku ini,	Whatever ails this heart of mine,
Sini sangku, sana pun sayang.	Entangled here, there in love.

A. W. Hamilton explained this text: "The effect of a fitful breeze on a field of growing rice is likened to the gusts of a conflicting passion of the heart" (1982 [1941]:96).

Joget *and* ronggeng

The terms *joget* and *ronggeng* denote the most famous and popular traditional Malaysian dance, often called the unofficial national social dance. The word *joget* has two literal meanings: 'dance' and 'dancing girl'. In its earliest usage, it probably denoted female courtly dances and dancers in the state of Pahang. The instrumental ensemble that accompanied the dance was known as a *joget gamelan.* This ensemble still exists in Pahang and Trengganu but is not related to the *joget* discussed here.

The form of the *joget* was influenced by Portuguese and Malaysian-Portuguese dancers and musicians from the time of the Portuguese occupation of Melaka, four hundred years ago. Until the early twentieth century, it was known by the name *ronggeng.* With the creation of *joget modern,* the term *joget* generally replaced the term *ronggeng* as the name of the genre. The *joget modern,* in its original form, used European (modern) instruments in an outdoor dancehall-like setting. Since unmarried women's taking part in such affairs was considered improper, men paid to dance with professional female dancers (*joget*). It is widely believed that one of the main reasons for the popularity of the *joget* is that it is a social form of dance, in which male and female performers move flirtatiously around each other.

The traditional *joget* was accompanied by an ensemble essentially the same as the *asli* band: a violin, a knobbed gong, a flute (optional), and at least two *rebana* or *gendan. Joget* music is fast. It emphasizes duple- and triple-beat divisions, both in alternation and simultaneously. This rhythm resembles that of many European 6/8 dances, like the tarantella and the fandango; however, the *joget* is commonly notated in 2/4 time. Since this rhythm also appears in Arabic, Iranian, and Indian music, and since these cultures have had a heavy impact in Malaysia, not everyone credits the development of this musical form to Portuguese influences.

The most important identifying musical trait of this genre is a constant rhythmic feeling of two against three, achieved in various ways (figure 18). The melody usually alternates between duple and triple meter. The gong serves a basic colotomic function by playing on the first beat of each 2/4 bar, and the larger drums usually play a basic triple pattern, emphasizing the first and second beats. The other drums usually alternate their improvisations between triple and duple patterns.

The simultaneous and alternating duple and triple sections occur in the melodies of separate parts in each measure and in the melody of one part in successive measures. *Joget* follows a three-part (ABC) form. Its lightheartedness is expressed in lyrics based on the *pantun* form. Usually the A and B sections of the *pantun* correspond to the *a* and *b* sections of music, and the C section is instrumental.

The *joget* form and rhythm have been used in contemporary popular music and in other modern forms. Therefore a *joget,* like an *asli,* can be heard performed by almost any combination of instruments in any style, ranging from rock to symphonic

FIGURE 18 An idealized example of a typical *joget*.

music. What makes performances *joget* is their lightheartedness, their accompanying rhythm, and their form.

Masri

The term *masri* denotes the music associated with a dance of the same name (figure 19). The music can be performed slowly or quickly, and is most often accompanied by one or two rhythmic patterns. The melodies are believed to display a particularly prominent Arab influence, especially in an implied tonality, seeming to shift between major and minor modes.

Inang

The dance *mak inang* (from *inang* 'wet nurse') exemplifies the most difficult Malay musical genre to characterize. The term refers not to any specific musical element but to a style of performance. As a result, many different rhythms are often labeled, or mislabeled, as *inang,* and there is a considerable amount of overlap between *inang* and other genres. No set rhythm is always labled *inang,* but some rhythms tend to be commonly used to accompany *inang* dances. Malaysians hear an influence of Hindustani music on *inang,* especially when a vocal part is included. Sometimes even a fast-paced *masri* rhythm can be called an *inang.* In fact, the song "*Mak Inang*" is usually performed as a fast *masri.*

Zapin

The *zapin* is believed to have been an Arabic dance, which en route to Malaysia absorbed influences from Indian dances. Accordingly, the *gambus* and the harmonium are used widely in performing it. The *gambus* part stands out. The rhythm of the melody closely relates to the rhythm played by the drums (figure 20). Strongly accented rhythms are a feature of *zapin.* This pattern is often associated with specific scalar degrees. Most commonly, it reinforces the tonic and the dominant.

Keroncong is probably the oldest form of popular Malaysian music. It is thought to have originated in the music of the sixteenth-century Portuguese colonies in the Moluccas (Maluku) and Batavia (Jakarta).

FIGURE 19 A *masri* melody and rhythm can be played slowly or quickly.

Ghazal

The Malaysian ghazal, a new genre of traditional Malay music, originated in the state of Johore in the southern part of the Malay peninsula in the late 1800s. The Malaysian version of the ghazal is different from, but related to, the ghazal as found in parts of the Middle East and northern India. It is also believed to have gained some Portuguese influence en route to Malaysia. As with the *inang,* the term *ghazal* sometimes denotes a style of performance, and can even be applied to a music-making party, a session that includes ghazals and other traditional musical forms.

The main pulse of a Malaysian ghazal is about twice as fast as *asli* tempo. A basic accompanimental rhythm, called ghazal rhythm (figure 21), is more a rhythmic framework than a strictly followed accompanimental pattern.

The typical instrumental ensemble used in performing ghazals includes a violin, a guitar, a *gambus,* a tambourine, maracas, two tablas, and a harmonium. A Malay

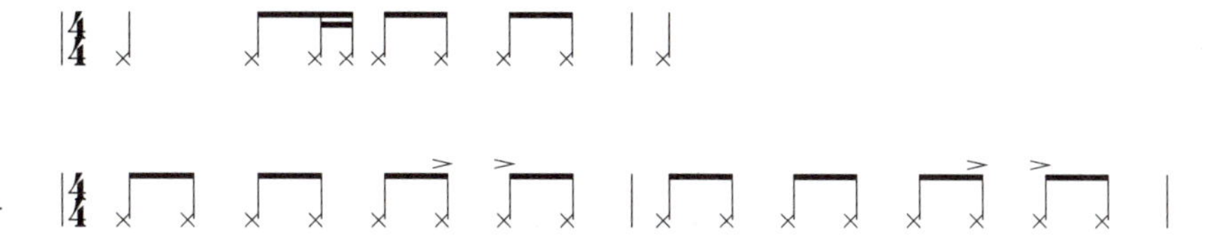

FIGURE 20 In a *zapin,* the rhythm of the melody closely relates to the rhythm played by the drums.

FIGURE 21 The basic Malaysian ghazal rhythm is more a rhythmic framework than a strictly followed accompanimental pattern.

rebana or *gendang* (or both) sometimes supplement(s) or replace(s) the second tabla. The violin plays the basic melody. The guitar and the *gambus* provide countermelodies. The harmonium usually plays countermelodies and occasional major and minor thirds. The player of the tabla usually uses one hand to keep the basic ghazal pattern going and improvises elaborations with the other hand. The vocal style and melodies used for the ghazal are virtually identical to those of *asli.* Because of these similarities, a song begun in an *asli* style may suddenly double in speed and shift to a ghazal-accompanying pattern. Such songs can be called by either term or qualified as a style of either.

Keroncong

Keroncong is probably the oldest form of popular Malaysian music. It is closely related to, and widely believed to derive from, Indonesian *kroncong.* It is thought to have originated in the music of the sixteenth-century Portuguese colonies in the Moluccas (Maluku) and Batavia (Jakarta). In Malaysia, *keroncong* is mainly associated with the former colony of Malacca (Melaka). It is not so much a musical form as a style of performance. An *asli langgam* becomes a *keroncong langgam* when performed in *keroncong* style. *Keroncong* is no longer regarded by most Malaysians as a form of popular music.

Dangdut

Dangdut is another example of Hindustani-influenced music in Malaysia. Though the term itself originated in Indonesia, the style of music it denotes originated in Malaysia. Hindustani music has long influenced many types of music in the Malay Peninsula. Perhaps as a result, no single name has been used to denote Hindustani-influenced music in Malaysia; however, when one of these forms traveled to Indonesia, it became known (by the mid-1940s) as *orkes melayu* 'Malay orchestra'. In the early 1970s, the name *dangdut* (imitating the sound of the tabla, used as an accompanying instrument) replaced the term *orkes melayu* in Indonesia. By 1980, the term had come to Malaysia.

In common usage, *dangdut* denotes virtually any vocal or instrumental popular music that uses a tabla and electric guitars. The melodies most commonly are a Malay-Indian mixture. *Dangdut* has no set rhythmic pattern, so the rhythmic patterns of *inang,* a loosely defined traditional genre, are most often used.

Pan-Malaysian folk songs (lagu-lagu rakyat)

Pan-Malaysian folk songs do not constitute a single specific musical genre, but this term is important, since it denotes the most famous and widely heard songs that can be thought of as traditional music in Malaysia. Most of these songs are essentially diatonic, though they do not always follow traditional Western harmonic progressions. Detailed histories do not exist for most of these songs, but they have been influenced by European music. These songs are widely recognized and accepted as part of Malaysia's and even Indonesia's national or regional identity. Some of them are identified with particular regions within Malaysia or Indonesia.

Lagu-lagu rakyat melodies and lyrics usually have no fixed versions, but exist in widely accepted variants. The genre has no identifying musical traits, though many people believe that these songs may have originated as *asli* performed in *bangsawan*. Most of the songs are strophic. Some, like "*Rasa Sayang Eh,*" have fixed choruses with improvised *pantun* verses.

European music

Muzik klasik 'classical music' and *muzik seriosa* 'serious music' are the most common Malaysian terms used for Western classical or serious music. *Muzik klasik* has been associated with the largest urban areas of the Malay Peninsula: Ipoh, Kuala Lumpur, Penang, and Singapore, but even rural towns today have piano-oriented private music schools, which follow a British syllabus. The music is by European composers or Malaysian composers, written in Western classical music formats.

The earliest classical-music societies were formed by expatriate communities in urban areas, but today many of these same societies are made up primarily of Malaysians. Amateur symphony orchestras have played in Malaysia since the 1940s, and several chamber-music societies are active. Every year, an estimated five to ten thousand Malaysian students sit for the ABRSM (Associated Board of the Royal School of Music, London) music exams in piano. *Muzik klasik* is also supported by the Malaysian Ministry of Culture, which, in addition to supporting traditional ensembles of Malay music and dance, has formed a National Youth Orchestra.

Brass bands

Throughout the twentieth century, European brass bands have played important roles in Malaysian society, affecting both traditional and contemporary musics. The Selangor State Band, begun by the British to provide public and private popular entertainment for colonial officials and their families, was the first military-style wind band in Malaya.

Since there were not enough Western-trained musicians in Malaysia in 1894, when the band was founded, the British contracted to import the entire sixty-four-member Manila Band from the Philippines to form this band. Within a few years, similar state bands, also comprised of Filipino musicians, were established in the Malaysian states of Perak and Penang. Though the bands consisted of civilians, they were usually associated with local police regiments. The Malayan Police Band, begun in 1905, included musicians from India and the Philippines. Many of these musicians settled in Malaya, married, and had children who often became musicians. The musicians and their descendants have had an enormous affect on music in Malaysia. They formed Malaysian dance and cabaret bands in the early 1900s, performed in *bangsawan* theaters, and even played for Malaysian productions of Chinese opera.

Today, Malaysia's capital, Kuala Lumpur, is the home for Army, Navy, Air Force, and Police Bands. Regional military bands also exist. For decades, most urban secondary schools and some rural schools have had brass bands. The Police Band's recording of the Malaysian national anthem, "*Negara Ku*" ('My Country'), begins and ends each day's broadcast on television and radio. Meanwhile, the official bands maintain a busy schedule of live public and ceremonial performances throughout the year. In addition to the national anthem, nine of Malaysia's states have anthems. These are the states with royal families, and the anthems serve a ceremonial purpose, marking the sultan's arrival and departure at official functions. In this sense, the state anthems have replaced the older ceremonial orchestras (*nobat*), considered part of a sultan's regalia.

Music in contemporary West Malaysian society

In the last half of the twentieth century, Malaysian music was intertwined closely with government policies on national culture and the mass media. This connection has affected the survival and promotion of various genres and the development of contemporary music. The policies for a national culture state that Malay culture and Islam are its basis, but that room must be allowed for influences from other racial and religious groups. The existence of a national culture is intended as both a reflection of national unity and an aid to its promotion.

The impact of the modern mass media on music in Malaysia cannot be overstated. As in many other rapidly developing nations, people are most likely to experience music through commercial recordings and broadcasts. The effects of the media, coupled with the desire to create a national culture, have had the greatest impact with the creation of Radio Television Malaysia (RTM), whose coverage has included semiclassical music, popular songs, jazz, and traditional Malay, Chinese, and Indian musics.

The founding of the RTM Orchestra (1961) was one of the most important events in contemporary Malaysian music. The orchestra developed along the lines of a dance band rather than a symphony orchestra, though it has been supplemented to perform works in symphonic styles. It has performed as an accompanying ensemble for singers and is one of the primary sources of contemporary instrumental music in Malaysia. It and smaller ensembles (consisting of its personnel) have provided much of the music broadcast by RTM.

Throughout this period, the RTM Orchestra, regarded as the premier musical organization in the country, was a trendsetter, which the commercial-music industry emulated. Each branch of the Malaysian military has established its own dance-style orchestras patterned after it, as have the city of Kuala Lumpur and other major urban centers. For broadcasts through its first two decades, RTM relied primarily on its own recordings and live performances of Malaysian music. Since the 1980s, it has increasingly relied on the commercial recording industry for many of its broadcasts.

A wide variety of music is available to people in Malaysia. In addition to music from other countries (which people follow extensively), Malaysian popular music has a variety of styles, some of which have been influenced by traditional genres. In the 1950s, songwriters took Western popular-music idioms and gave them Malay lyrics and a Malay feel. They were trying to write popular songs that were appropriate to modern Malaysian life. This they accomplished by borrowing rhythmic and stylistic aspects of famous folk songs. Thus, the traditional genres *asli, joget, zapin, inang,* and *masri* have directly influenced the development of Malaysian popular music.

Accordingly, as Western instruments and Western musical concepts (most noticeably, functional harmony) have begun to change contemporary performances, popular-music styles have had an impact on traditional Malaysian forms, which can now be heard performed by ensembles that use almost any combination of instruments. Even performances by highly regarded traditional musicians not uncommonly have a violin, traditional drums, and a gong supplemented by electric guitars, a piano, and synthesizers. The colotomy of the gong in some traditional ensembles is played by an electric bass guitar, which may also provide implied functional harmonies.

Throughout Malaysian history, instruments and other aspects of foreign music were often adopted and adapted to local situations. This phenomenon has continued in popular music. As a result, many international trends in popular music have surfaced in Malaysian popular music. Malaysian rock has been conservative. Throughout the 1960s and early 1970s, a modified rock combo accompanied most singers. In the 1970s and early 1980s, most popular albums tried to achieve an orchestral sound for accompaniment—widely assumed to be an influence of the RTM Orchestra. Guitar-dominated bands (*kugiran,* from *kumpulan gitar ran-cak* 'lively guitar group') became common in the late 1960s and early 1970s. Most mem-

Malaysian popular music is the most important musical genre in Malaysia. Though based on Western or international pop-music styles, it can be seen as representing a true expression of contemporary Malaysian culture.

bers began as self-taught part-time or totally amateur musicians who played for parties, dances, and nightclubs. Many bands play a mixture of traditional and modern Malay songs, plus Western-style popular songs and rock.

Since the mid-1980s, Malaysian rock bands have developed large, loyal followings. They still play a variety of styles, ranging from heavy metal to middle-of-the-road or easy-listening styles. The most common style can be best described as Malay balladry. Some musicians try to project a Malaysian image by utilizing the rhythms found in traditional genres. As in earlier history (with *keroncong* and *lagu-lagu rakyat*), some styles—and even specific songs and performers—are active participants in both Malaysian and Indonesian musical cultures.

Malaysian popular music is the most important musical genre in Malaysia. The annual national talent time (Bintang RTM) features only popular songs, and national popular-song competitions (such as Pesta Lagu Malaysia) have occurred since Malaysia became independent. Televised specials to celebrate religious and national holidays use popular songs much more than any other musical genre. Malaysian songs for Hari Raya (a Muslim holiday celebrating the end of Ramadan) are performed in conservative popular styles.

As Malaysia has become more prosperous and economically advanced, the commercial-music industry has become locally more important. Malaysian popular music, though based on Western or international pop-music styles, can be seen as representing a true expression of contemporary Malaysian culture. More Malaysians listen to it than to any other musical style, and it is the only kind of music composed, arranged, performed, marketed, and followed by all the ethnic groups in Malaysia.

REFERENCES

D'Cruz, Marion Francena. 1979. "Joget Gamelan, a Study of Its Contemporary Practice." M.A. thesis, Universiti Sains Malaysia.

al-Faruqi, Lois Ibsen. 1985. "Music, Musicians and Muslim Law." *Asian Music* 17(1):3–36.

Ghulam-Sarwar Yousof. 1976. "The Kelantan Mak Yong Dance Theater, a Study of Performance Structure." Ph.D. dissertation, University of Hawai'i.

———. 1987. "Bangsawan: The Malay Opera." *Tenggara* 20:3–20.

Ginsberg, Henry D. 1972. "The Manohra Dance-Drama: An Introduction." *Journal of the Siam Society* 60:169–181.

Hamilton, A. W. 1982 [1941]. *Malay Pantuns.* Singapore: Eastern Universities Press.

Ku Zam Zam, Ku Idris. 1983. "Alat-Alat Muzik Dalam Ensembel Wayang Kulit, Mek Mulung dan Gendang Keling di Kedah Utara" (Musical instruments in the shadow play, *mek mulung,* and *gendang keling* ensembles of North Kedah). In *Kajian Budaya dan Masyarakat di Malaysia,* ed. Mohd. Taib Osman and Wan Kadir Yusoff, 1–52. Kuala Lumpur: Dewan Bahasa dan Pustaka.

———. 1985. "Nobat DiRaja Kedah: Warisan Seni Muzik Istana Melayu Melaka" (Nobat of the Kedah sultan: a musical heritage of the Malay Malacca sultanate). In *Warisan Dunia Melayu, Teras Peradaban Malaysia,* ed. Abdul Latiff Abu Bakar. Kuala Lumpur: Biro Penerbitan GAPENA.

Mohammad Anis Mohammad Nor. 1986. *Randai Dance of Minangkabau Sumatra, with Labanotation Scores.* Kuala Lumpur: University of Malaysia.

Mohammad Ghouse Nasaruddin. 1979. "The Desa Performing Arts of Malaysia." Ph.D. dissertation, Indiana University.

Mohd. Taib Osman, ed. 1974. *Traditional Drama and Music in Southeast Asia.* Kuala Lumpur: Dewan Bahasa dan Pustaka.

Malm, William. 1974. "Music in Kelantan, Malaysia and Some of its Cultural Implications." In *Studies in Malaysian Oral and Musical Traditions,* 1–49. Michigan. Papers on South and Southeast Asia, 8. Ann Arbor: University of Michigan Press.

Matusky, Patricia. 1993. *Malaysian Shadow Play and Music: Continuity of an Oral Tradition.* Kuala Lumpur: Oxford University Press.

———. 1994. "Music of the Mak Yong Theater of Malaysia: A Fusion of Southeast Asian Malay and Middle Eastern Islamic Elements." In *To the Four Corners,* ed. Ellen Leichtman, 25–53. Warren, Mich.: Harmonie Park Press.

Sweeney, Amin. 1972. *Ramayana and the Malay Shadow Play.* Kuala Lumpur: National University of Malaysia Press.

Tan Sooi Beng. 1988. "The Thai Manora in Malaysia: Adapting to the Penang Chinese Community." *Asian Folklore Studies* 47(1):19–34.

———. 1993. *Bangsawan: A Social and Stylistic History of Popular Malay Opera.* Singapore: Oxford University Press.

Vietnam

Phong T. Nguyễn

The Socialist Republic of Vietnam (Cộng Hòa Xã Hội Chủ Nghĩa Việt Nam) occupies the coastal area of mainland Southeast Asia from China in the north to Cambodia in the south, and shares its western border with Laos. These borders were established in the 1600s after a long process of expansion southward. The area of Vietnam—331,689 square kilometers—roughly equals those of Malaysia, New Mexico, and Norway. The country is narrow and elongated: its distance from north to south is some 3,444 kilometers, but at some points it is only 50 kilometers wide. A highway and a railway furnish transportation from one end of the country to the other, but they are not modern enough to overcome the country's regionalism. Vietnam has fifty provinces, which can be grouped into three cultural regions: the north, the center, and the south. Each is distinct in language or accent, character, attitude, and music.

The population of Vietnam, 73,103,898 (estimate, July 1994), can be divided into the Việt and fifty-three upland minorities. The Việt, who primarily inhabit lowland areas, are called urban (*kinh*), and the minority ethnic groups, tending to occupy highland and mountain areas, are called high (*thượng*). Among the upland groups are the Mường, the Thái, the Hmông, the Mán, the Bahnar, and the Jarai, speaking languages from three families, Austroasiatic, Austronesian (Malayo-Polynesian), and Tai. The language of the Việt and that of their cousins the Mường belong to the Austroasiatic group. In addition to the upland minorities (about 10 per cent of the population), Chinese live mainly in the urban areas. Life expectancy is about sixty-five years.

Most Việt are Buddhists, primarily of the Mahayana sect, but notable percentages are Chinese Buddhist-Taoist, Roman Catholic, Muslim, and Cao Đài (an indigenous religion). Vietnamese multiculturalism has resulted in a complex intertwining of musics. To date, however, most musical research has focused on the Việt.

Thousands of years ago, people who settled in what is now Vĩnh Phú Province in northern Vietnam laid the foundations for present-day Vietnamese music and culture. Since then, Vietnam's history can be delineated musically into both folk and artistic strata. Folk songs (or more precisely, peasants' songs) and narratives sung by different ethnic groups depict long histories. Research has revealed that the

Vietnamese performing arts are rooted in antiquity: the origins of rivers, oceans, and mountains, and indeed the meaning of life, are described in the legends of peoples inhabiting Vietnam, and archaeological discoveries have authenticated many legendary specifics.

HISTORY

The Văn Lang Period (2879–258 B.C.)

Archaeologists have found it difficult to document music in the days of the Thẩm-khuyên *Homo erectus* and the Kéo-làng *Homo sapiens* in northern Vietnam, but discoveries regarding the lithic culture of Hòa Bình and Bắc Sơn and the bronze culture of Đông Sơn provide evidence of music and dance in prehistoric Vietnam (Phan, Hà, and Hoàng 1989). This period corresponds to the historical Văn Lang era under the Hùng kings (2879–258 B.C.), an era recalled in traditional oral narratives and royal annals.

Vietnam

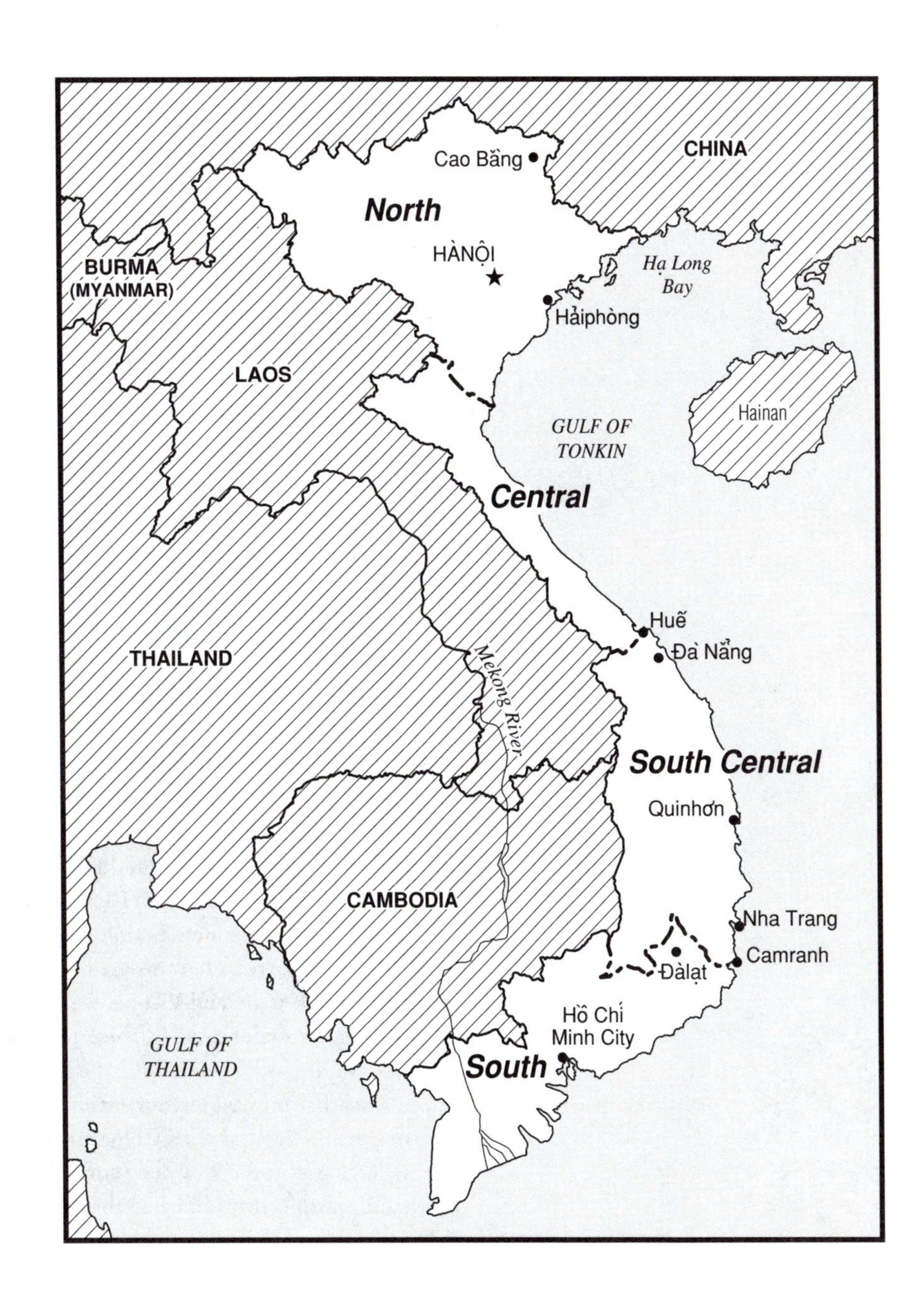

Musical instruments found in Vietnam, including bronze drums, bells, and lithophones, and the images depicted on these instruments, provide valuable historical clues. Several sets of lithophones from Ndut Lieng Krak, Khánh Sơn, and Bác Ái villages—the music of which remains unknown—date back to this era, extending from the third to the first millennium B.C. These lithophones were likely played by ancestors of the highlanders who live in the Trường Sơn mountains, near the border with Laos and Cambodia.

The discovery of these lithophones and bronze gong drums confirms a direct connection between Vietnamese music and that of Southeast Asia in general. Vietnamese lithophones may have been precursors of Southeast Asian xylophones, such as the bamboo xylophones called *t'rung* in Vietnam and *ch'lung* in Indonesia. The Đông Sơn bronze gong drums are of major significance, as they were distributed throughout Southeast Asia and southern China. Other instruments of archaeological import are bells, cluster bells, and stone chimes. Pictures of other instruments—mouth organs, drums, clappers—are engraved on some bronze gong drums, and some scholars believe these engravings represent an early theatrical performance on a boat. Indeed, forebears of the present-day theatrical genres *chèo* and *múa rối nước* may well be represented there.

Many Vietnamese scholars regard the Đông Sơn period (700–100 B.C.) as a foundation of their culture, but relating that period to later ones has proved impossible. This gap in the history of Vietnamese music reflects foreign invasions and changes in political leadership, from the Triệu kingdom (179–111 B.C.) to the Chinese Western Han (after 111 B.C.).

After the Văn Lang Period (258 B.C.–A.D. 939)

After 258 B.C., the dearth of descriptions of music has led some scholars to speculate that indigenous music became an integral part of customary festivals and religious ceremonies and was therefore kept secret. However, religious processions in Giao Châu (now northern Vietnam) in the first and second centuries featured Indian-derived musics. Though Vietnam was under Chinese political administration at that time, no Chinese musical forms were acknowledged to have existed in Vietnam until at least a thousand years later. This view may be attributable to the erroneous belief that music of that era in Vietnam had been completely subsumed by Chinese music, and therefore did not require separate study.

Buddhism and Indian culture were introduced to Giao Châu by ship-borne merchants, who helped establish thriving commercial relations with Western Asia as early as the first century (Nguyễn 1982). In the second century, envoys of Roman emperor Marcus Aurelius (reigned A.D. 161–180) arrived in the coastal city of Vinh. Vietnam then served as the eastern terminus of maritime trade from the West. Indian Buddhism, therefore, was known in Giao Châu, and in the second century became an important religion there. Buddhist books, the only reliable records that survived the Chinese-Vietnamese wars (110 B.C.–A.D. 938), reveal musical activities—mostly concerned with Vietnamese Buddhist liturgy—in the second century. Temples were built, Sanskrit texts were translated, and communities of monks were organized. Indian, Central Asian, and Vietnamese Buddhist monks translated sung texts (sutras) into Chinese; in later periods, these texts were used in East Asia. Music from this period onward was known both in the Buddhist liturgy and by peasants. Therefore, it is probable that musical instruments from India and Central Asia were brought into Vietnam before replicas from China arrived overland.

A large gap in the knowledge of musical events in Vietnam occurs between the sixth and ninth centuries, when the country was in the midst of resistance against Chinese domination. One noteworthy incident is recalled. The Tang Dynasty

(618–907) hosted a Vietnamese orchestra, with other foreign ones, at its imperial court. From then on, Vietnamese music remained part of Chinese palace activities until the 1800s, when the Qing Dynasty finally canceled it.

Vietnam won its independence from China in 938. Music, dance, and theatrical genres were major entertainments at Vietnam's royal palace. From 985, annual water-puppet-theater performances and boat races were held to celebrate the king's birthday. In the tenth century, Lady Phạm Thị Trân, an artist who taught songs and dance to the army, was named national lady artist (*ưu bà*) by the court.

Buddhist dynasties

The Ngô, Đinh, and earlier Lê dynasties (939–1009) served as a transition to the more prominent reigns of the Buddhist zealots and kings of the Lý and Trần dynasties (eleventh to thirteenth centuries). Vietnamese consider this a golden age of music and culture. A royal decree in 1025 assigned a music director (*quản giáp*) to supervise the music guild (*giáo phường*). This person was in charge of all musical activities at the national level. A kind of vocal chamber music began to evolve in the royal court, and an illustrious female singer, Đào Thị, received an award from the king. As a result, many singers thereafter were named in her honor, and the phrase "songs of Lady Đào" (*hát ả đào,* Sino-Vietnamese *đào nương ca*) became synonymous with the musical genre she performed.

Kings of the Lý and Trần dynasties were renowned for their musical artistry. They performed dances, wrote liturgical songs, and composed music. A hundred-singer royal chorus was formed in 1011. King Lý Nhân Tông (1066–1127), a leader in powerful and prosperous times and himself a dancer, composed music and choreographed dances. Artists were highly esteemed, and in 1041 at least one hundred musicians and singers received awards and promotions from the court.

After many years of neglect, water-puppet plays were again treated to full productions, with a full complement of musicians, singers, and dancers. The Lý and Trần dynasties were generous, humane, and culturally far reaching; even in those days, they made an impact on the cultures of Laos, Champa, India, and China. As noted in accounts engraved on stelae at Sùng Thiện Diên Linh, many foreigners attended national festivals in honor of King Lý.

Music from Laos and Champa was regularly performed for Vietnamese kings as a tribute. The song style *ải lao,* still practiced in festivals for Saint Dóng, is believed to be the first foreign music presented to Vietnamese kings during the Lý period. Hundreds of singers and dancers captured during victories over Champa performed, and by all accounts were well treated, in the royal palace. Having acquired an extensive knowledge of foreign music, King Lý Thánh Tông (1052–1072) composed songs reminiscent of Chăm music. Though the music of India was little known to most Vietnamese of the day, an Indian monk named Du Chi Bà Lam was noted for teaching Buddhists the art of mantric cantillation.

Foreign elements were also assimilated into theatrical performances at the Trần court. In a thirteenth-century battle with Chinese invaders, the soldier Li Yuan Ki (in Vietnamese, Lý Nguyên Cát) was captured. Until recently it was widely believed that his skills as an actor were so apparent that he was granted a pardon and subsequently treated as a guest artist. Therefore, it was thought that he introduced Chinese stories, costumes, roles, and acrobatics into Vietnamese theater. There are no detailed accounts of the era's songs and instrumental adaptations, however, so it is impossible to document a complete transference of Chinese theatrical arts to the Vietnamese in the 1200s.

Various forms of performances did not cease when music halls were built and outdoor festivals and Buddhist ceremonies were organized on a national level. Thus,

chèo Predominant form of human theater in northern Vietnam

tuồng Court theater genre of central and south-central Vietnam

tiểu nhạc Vietnam's court ensemble of strings and winds

đại nhạc The oboe-dominated ritual ensemble of Vietnam's court

hát bội The southern Vietnamese term for *tuồng* court theater

during the Trần Dynasty, Vietnamese music—in a variety of incarnations—became broadly popular.

Lê and Nguyễn dynasties

The beginning of the 1400s witnessed a shift in political power to the Lê family (fifteenth to eighteenth centuries). This shift was accompanied by a movement toward a more Confucian society, with heavy Chinese influences at the royal court. As a result, popular forms of music began to break away from the courtly arena, and rigid Confucians insisted that the elegant music (*nhã nhạc*) of the court be clearly distinguished from the vulgar music (*tục nhạc*) of commoners. This distinction became even more noticeable at the end of the later Lê Dynasty, when some forms of music previously presented at royal palaces, halls, and outdoor festivals were consigned to villages and provinces. Water-puppet plays, certain kinds of theater, and dances, once the sole province of royalty, devolved into popular entertainments. Meanwhile, the court embraced new kinds of music. By decree, the court orchestra adopted the instrumentations of the Ming court of China. The leader of this change was Lương Đăng, a minister who brooked no opposition. A philosopher and political strategist named Nguyễn Trãi was executed for dissidence on this issue and others.

A result of the legal code of 1437 was the collapse of theatrical genres such as *chèo* and *tuồng* and folk dances, all of which had received support from the Đại Việt court during the Lý and Trần Dynasties and flourished through the first quarter of the 1400s. From that year, all forms of theater were prohibited by King Lê Thái Tông, much influenced by Confucian aesthetics. Musicians and singers, with their offspring, were not permitted to take national civil-service examinations.

From 1680 to 1740, the later Lê Dynasty forbade any full-scale musical performances like those characteristic of the previous dynasty. The Nguyễn, whose court was at Huế in central Vietnam, however, began to restore ritual music to the Confucian temples and temples of the royal family. The Commission on Music permitted the string-and-wind ensemble (*ty bã lệnh*) and the ritual ensemble (*nhạc huyền*), which later came to be known as the small ensemble (*tiểu nhạc*) and the large ensemble (*đại nhạc*), respectively. Like court orchestras in other East Asian countries, these ensembles featured many instruments of Chinese lineage and were classified as civil or military. They also had conductors.

The string-and-wind ensemble had two three-stringed lutes, two two-stringed fiddles, two two-stringed coconut-shell fiddles, two moon-shaped lutes, two pear-shaped lutes, two oboes, two small drums, two one-headed drums, one hourglass-shaped drum, one three-gong set, and one coin clapper. The ritual ensemble had one large drum, one small drum, one large stone chime, twelve small stone chimes, one large bell, twelve small bells, one wooden idiophone (*chúc*), one wooden tiger-shaped idiophone (*ngữ*), two *cầm* zithers, two *sắt* zithers, two small vertical bamboo flutes, two transverse bamboo flutes, two long transverse bamboo flutes, two mouth organs, and two ocarinas. The large ensemble included twenty large drums, eight trumpets, four large gongs, four small gongs, four conch trumpets, and four water-buffalo horns.

The Nguyễn kings favored music and literature. The role of Confucianism seemed to diminish at the heart of the kingdom, and musical activities were given a chance to revive. This artistic rebirth saw the royal court again embrace various kinds of music and dance, including the royal chorus, chamber music, theater, ethnic music, ethnic dances, and the Buddhist liturgy. Musics of the Chăm and the highlanders were also presented to the kings. King Tự Đức and various princes and princesses were prominent songwriters and musicians. Their contributions to present-day chamber music (*ca huế*) and songs show how influential this genre was.

In the 1800s, the greatest musical honor bestowed by the Nguyễn court and its mandarins was on the theatrical genre called *hát bội* in the south and *tuồng* in the north. Nightly performances of *hát bội,* with highly sophisticated theatrical techniques and long stories, were presented inside the royal palace. Some stories lasted more than one hundred nights and involved hundreds of characters. The most remarkable playwright of this period was Đào Tấn, a court dignitary, governor, teacher of theater, poet, and Buddhist devotee. *Hát bội* reached the height of its popularity around 1900.

Reform movements in the twentieth century

The Nguyễn Dynasty ended in 1945, when Emperor Bảo Đại abdicated. Traditional music was severely affected by World War II and by the ways of life that had developed in urban areas. Since the late 1800s, music of the French colonialists (from sources as varied as the military, the Roman Catholic Church, and nightclubs) and many European instruments had made their way into Vietnam. However, despite the war and the influx of foreign music, traditional music survived. Beginning around 1900, a reform movement spread throughout the country, starting with *cải lương* 'reform, innovation', a new form of theater that originated in the south.

Between 1920 and 1945, the whole country was in the midst of modernization. Following the example of *cải lương,* people created new theatrical troupes, of which *ca kịch huế* 'Huế theater troupes' in Huế and *bài chòi* in Bình Định are examples. Some artists of *chèo* in the north also embraced modernization, calling this either *chèo cải lương* 'reformed *chèo*' or *chèo văn minh* 'modernized *chèo*' to capture urbanites' attention.

In the cities, music students in French colonial and Roman Catholic schools began to embrace the Western system of music. They composed Vietnamese-language songs, first called modernized music (*nhạc cải cách*), then new music (*tân nhạc*), with accompaniment based on tempered scales and Western rules of harmony.

Despite many moves toward reform and modernization, the country lapsed into yet another war—first a war of independence against the French, then a civil conflict, which resulted in the loss of many lives and a country divided into north and south for twenty years. Unification occurred in 1975 under a socialist régime.

Music in yearly cycles

The Indian calendar was replaced by a modified Chinese calendar in the first century, during the period of Han annexation. Some of the singing and dramatic genres presented during the lunar New Year festival (in February) may have originated with the Hùng kings (third millennium B.C.); other such forms date from the first century. In Phong Châu, homeland of the earliest known culture in Vietnam (dating back fifteen thousand to twenty thousand years), the rite of the god of rice is celebrated on the twelfth day of the first lunar month. At midnight, local leaders sketch out a sequence of ritual services, songs, and plays, endowing the new day with ritual significance.

FIGURE 1 A festival in Lim village, Hà Bắc Province. Photo by Phong T. Nguyễn.

The preliminary plans are then expanded into a full schedule of events. Comic plays present farmers and craftsmen in a humorous light. Similar festivals are organized in many parts of the country, albeit in different forms. Indeed, musical events are based on yearly agricultural cycles; festivals are sponsored to express wishes for, and celebrations of, successful harvests. Music is associated with both work and entertainment throughout the cycles of the lunar year.

To many observers, Vietnam is at its most beautiful in the spring and fall. Spring usually begins in late January or early February. The cycles of the year commence on the first day of the Vietnamese New Year, the beginning of spring. Both spring and fall provide opportunities for relaxation and fun; the most important festivals are held in the countryside during these periods of good weather. Men and women enjoy singing folk songs and ritual music to celebrate these seasons, and temples resound with joyous songs, dances, processions, and games. These events last for several days; in some areas, celebrations may last a whole month (figure 1).

Besides performances associated with seasonal celebrations, national and religious festivals are organized according to a special schedule. Important holidays include *thuợng nguyên* 'full-moon day of the first month (of the lunar year)', *trung nguyên* 'full-moon day of the seventh month', *trung thu* 'mid-autumn', and *hạ nguyên* 'full-moon day of the tenth month'. Musical performances are coordinated with ritual ceremonies in Buddhist temples (*chùa*), shrines of traditional deities (*đền*), and village temples serving as communal houses (*đình*). The *trung thu* is not only a children's festival, but also an opportunity for other games and competitions. In Thái Bình, Thiền Quang Temple (also called *chùa Keo*) hosts three days of liturgical ceremonies, Buddhist chanting, and traditional music contests, boating contests, dances imitating the rowing of boats, and water-puppet theater.

Music is also an integral part of most daily activities, whether rocking a baby, praying at a holy place, attending a wedding or a funeral, honoring the anniversary of a loved one's birth or death, or just enjoying personal entertainment. Some of these events are marked by their own specific cycles: a death is followed by a sequence of rituals starting with the funeral and ending two years later; a local deity may be commemorated once a year on a specific date.

Dramas and concerts are performed regularly, but most such entertainments occur during the holidays. From village to village, particularly in the spring and fall, the daily calendar is packed with traditional festivals. Most of them honor local gods or national heroes, but some occur simply because people love to gather and sing. In any event, music is inextricably bound up with customary and cultural activities. In popular minds, many indigenous customs are rooted in an antiquity shared with both East and Southeast Asia, but the music and songs attached to these customs bear a uniquely Vietnamese stamp.

MUSIC THEORY

Vietnamese scholars have not thoroughly and conclusively addressed questions of music theory. The difficulty lies in the fact that, even though Vietnamese music is nationally and culturally unified to a great extent, regional styles and ensembles exhibit striking differences. A general formality and customary manner of presentation are typical of all Vietnamese music, but no all-embracing theory can be applied to the genres found from north to south.

However, certain conventions—some quite strict—can be observed in Vietnamese musics. Whether oral or written, they make up a music theory. Included are several systems of instruction in music, developed by respected regional masters whose "theories" are based on those of their elders. To validate a student's played version of beats, measures, rhythms, pitches, and ornamentations, a demanding music teacher may well ask a student, "Who is your teacher?" In this way, the prevalent, yet informal, music theories remain relatively uncorrupted. Good teachers must therefore agree on certain conventions to preserve the character of a specific region's music.

Thus, the term *Vietnamese music theory* should properly be pluralized and considered within the contexts of three distinct geographical regions: north, central, and south. In each region, various ensembles and theatrical genres are created according to specific rules. Methods of learning and instrumentation vary greatly from one region to another, and musicians from different regional ensembles do not play together.

Vocal music dominates many musical performances. Since Vietnamese is a tonal language with distinct regional variations, the traditional songs of a particular region are best understood only within their regional contexts. Oral instruction is more the rule than the exception, and the conversion of known musical notations (whether onomatopoeic or Chinese *gongche pu*) into an orally transmissible form is common. Notation is used primarily by students—for the sake of memorization.

Before the twentieth century, books discussing music focused mainly on history, performative customs, and descriptions of instruments. Manuscripts of theoretical instructions, though extensive and helpful in many ways, were often limited to a specific kind of music practiced by a small community. From the 1700s on, Chinese *gongche pu* began to be used, primarily by musician-scholars in central and southern regions (figure 2). Being Vietnamized to fit the scalar tones, it was soon transferred to a solfège system, which helped music students to memorize syllables through oral transmission. It does not, however, serve as a standard notation (figures 3 and 4).

Vietnamese music theories are especially valuable resources as a result of their use of visualization, audiation, and oral explanation by teachers within a given area. The primary requirement for musical success is, as one would expect, a keen ear: a good student can readily distinguish tiny gradations of pitch. Such an ability is not inherent, however; some students need to hone their skills through repeated listenings. This practice is passed from one generation to the next, with an exacting and rich terminology. For related musical genres, there are three basic traditions—north, central, south. Among them, scales, ornamentation, and lyrics vary widely and can be more locally identified.

In Vietnam, it is difficult to define performances as either purely folk or purely artistic, as most performances bear traits of both traditions.

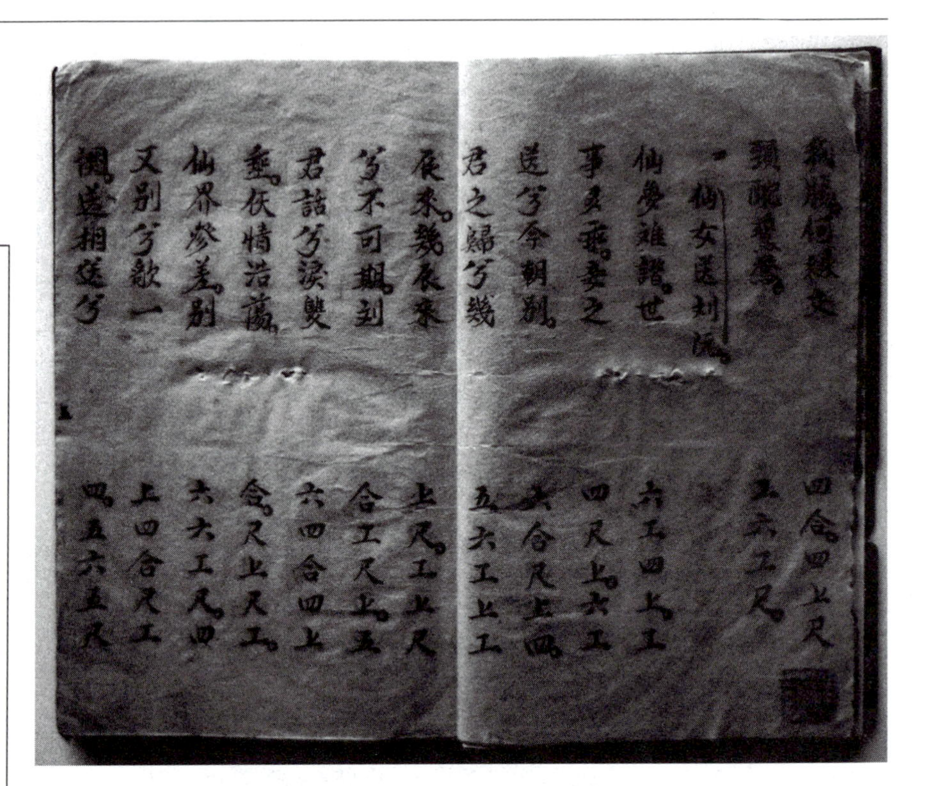

FIGURE 2 Old notation in Chinese characters. The song is "*Tiên Nữ Tống Lưu Nguyễn*" ('The Fairies Say Farewell to Lưu and Nguyễn'). The lyrics (*above*) and schematic music (*below*) are read from top to bottom, right to left. Each vertical line has five words, which correspond to five musical notes.

Xuân Tình
(*Spring Love*)

Lớp I
(*Section I*)

Câu
(*Phrase*)

1. ___ Cống cống ___ xừ
2. Xừ ___ xê cống xàng
3. Xang xụ xê ___ hò
4. Xê ___ hò hò xang
5. Xang xụ xê ___ hò
6. Xê ___ hò ___ hò xang
7. Xang cống cống ___ xừ
8. Xừ ___ xê ___ cống xàng
9. Xang xụ xê hò
10. Xê ___ hò ___ hò xang
11. Xang xụ xê xụ
12. Xụ cống cống xang
13. Xê xề xề liu
14. Liu ___xề ___ xề liu

FIGURE 3 Notation in romanized characters from the 1950s. The piece, "*Xuân Tình*" ('Love in Spring'), is notated in a skeletal manner. In each four-measure phrase, the weak beats are underlined, and the strong beats are doubly underlined.

Vietnamese ethnomusicologists have speculated about whether folk songs adhere to any discernible music theory or theories. In Vietnam, it is difficult to define performances as either purely folk or purely artistic, as most performances bear traits of both traditions. Still, even if it is not possible to establish definitely that folk songs reflect one or more theories, observers can at least note theoretical ties between artistic and folkloric musics in Vietnam. This connection may be explained by the fact that peasants who sing folk songs may also be amateur, semiprofessional, or professional musicians, actors, and actresses. Professionalism is manifested when, for example, a village ritualist performs his songs and dances in an organized and reserved manner.

Forms of presentation

Traditionally in many Vietnamese genres, the performance of songs and other music is realized first in speech rhythm, then in meter. This form of presentation embodies the socioaesthetic philosophy that things must be done in a courteous order: first nonmetric, then metric; first slow, then fast; first new, then familiar. This results in a gradual, orderly introduction of the soundscape. It is important to involve both kinds of metrical organization in presenting a mode in chamber music; a complete performance must include both of them. The nonmetric introduction is denoted by a

FIGURE 4 (opposite) Musical tablature for zither, created by Dr. Nguyễn Văn Bửu (1956:47). The three levels correspond to the three octaves of the zither as viewed from above by the player: the upper row is for the lowest octave, the center for the middle octave, and the lower row for the highest octave. Glides, presses, and other tonal changes are indicated with arrows and plus signs.

TỨ ĐẠI OÁN

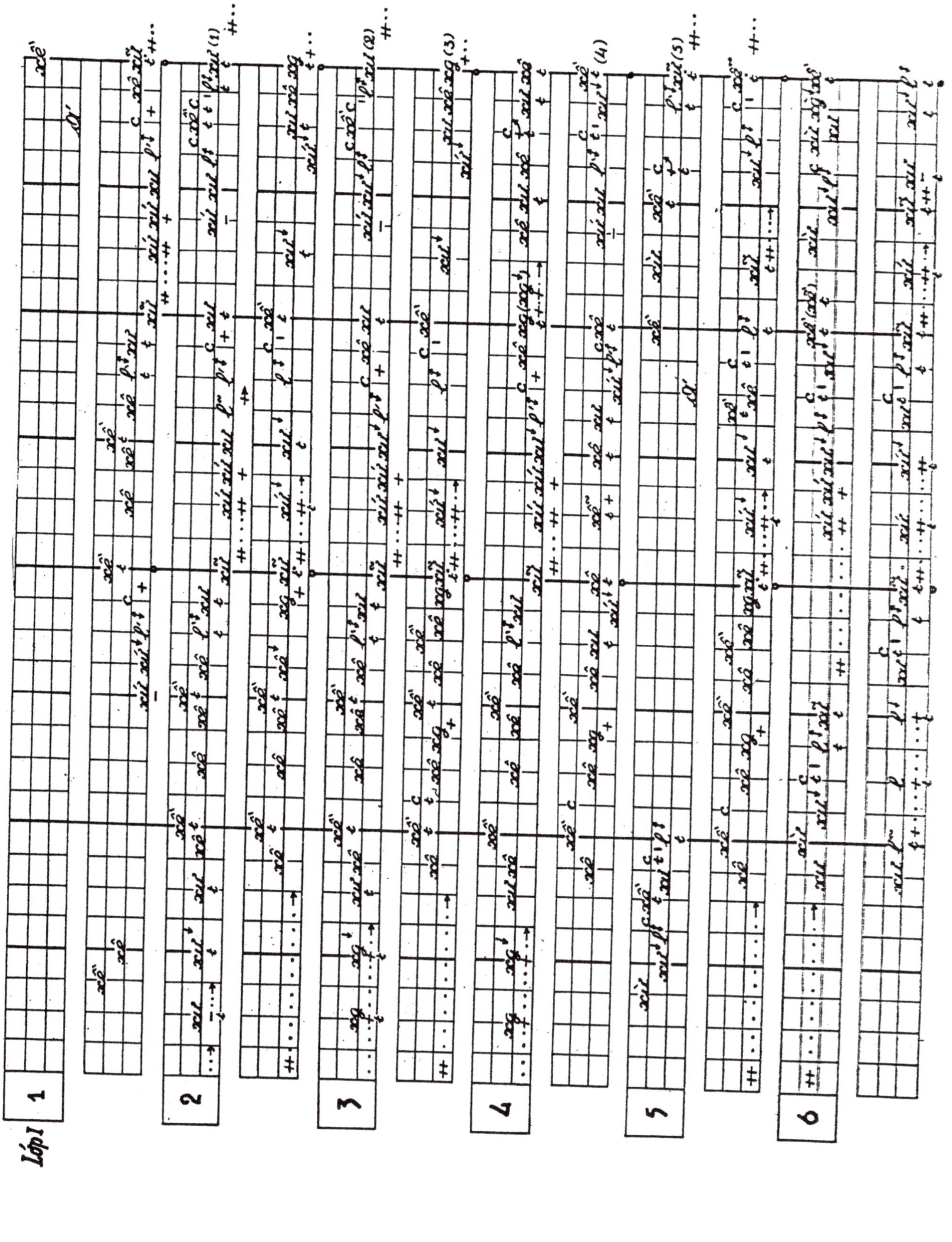

Lớp I

1

2

3

4

5

6

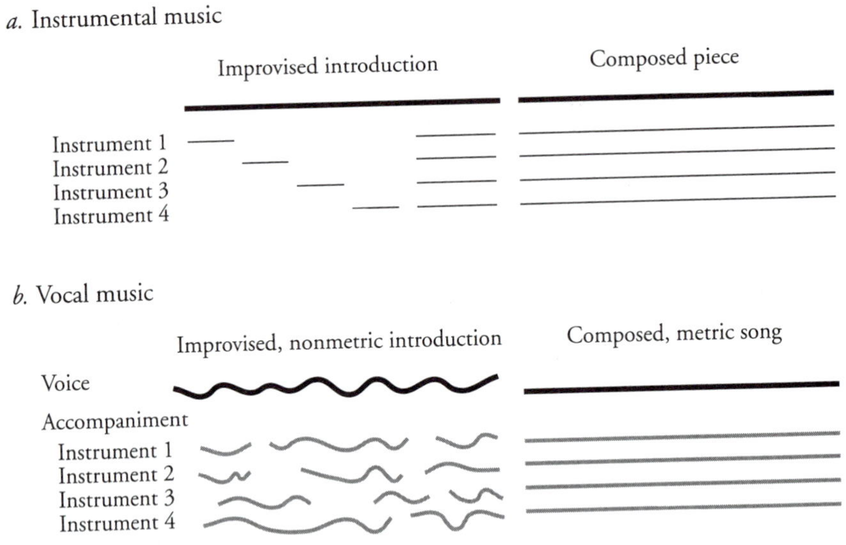

FIGURE 5 Forms of presentation in music.

a. Instrumental music

Improvised introduction — Composed piece

Instrument 1
Instrument 2
Instrument 3
Instrument 4

b. Vocal music

Improvised, nonmetric introduction — Composed, metric song

Voice
Accompaniment
Instrument 1
Instrument 2
Instrument 3
Instrument 4

variety of terms used in different contexts, more for voice than for instrumental ensemble, depending on musical genres or styles. For instrumental music, *rao* 'announcement' or *dạo* (pronounced *zow*) 'promenade', and for voice, an introductory recitative (*nói lối* 'speaking the way'), *nói sử* 'telling a story', *ngâm* 'sung poetry', *vãn* 'complaint', *vĩa* 'edge, side', *bỉ* (derived from *vỉ* or *vĩa*), and other terms, denote this introduction.

In a typical chamber-music ensemble, a song or instrumental piece is performed in one of three forms: (1) a short, improvised, and nonmetrical introduction followed by composed music; (2) an improvised, nonmetrical poetic song accompanied by instruments; (3) an improvised, metrical song accompanied by instruments.

The voice, prominent in Vietnamese music, can be part of the improvised introduction. In *nói lối,* a poem is sung and accompanied nonmetrically throughout, and a *ngâm* has no introduction. Improvisation, elaboration, and variations are employed in both metrical and nonmetrical sections. The metrical part is oftener a schematic composition than a fully realized one (figure 5).

For the introduction, a short song is sometimes used instead. This use happens only in *cải lương* or modern *vọng cổ,* songs called *tân cổ giao duyên* in southern Vietnam. An improvised solo (or several solos played consecutively) commonly occur in the introduction, followed by a chorus. In instrumental ensembles, the instruments improvise consecutively before playing the metrical piece together.

In a more complex form, metric and nonmetric musical interchanges occur during long songs, including *ca trù* chamber songs, and in theatrical music. The insertion of shorter or longer free-rhythm sections varies from one song or genre to another, most frequently in theatrical songs.

A feature common to Vietnamese traditions is heterophony, in which several versions of the same melodic lines are superimposed. To create a timbral play, three, five, or eight instruments together display their distinctive timbres, highlighted by syncopated rhythmic cells. This noncomposed character makes room for improvised melodies and rhythms derived from the conventional notes of an instrumental piece, a song, or both. Though the music is monophonically based, musicians in ensembles may hear a kind of polyphony of instrumental improvisation played contrapuntally. This tendency makes Vietnamese music heterophonic.

Scales and modes

The Vietnamese concept of mode involves a rich combination of elements constituting the basis for a complete performance. It must therefore cover both the musical rules and the extramusical meanings of a given piece of music. In certain performances, including peasants' songs and folk-ritual music, mode is simplified, but in more sophisticated genres and performance styles, the concept of mode becomes paramount. Extensive oral explanations of the theory of mode are offered to students by teachers of chamber, theater, ritual, religious, and court music as a part of the customary training.

There is room to believe that this modal conceptualization, probably nurtured from time immemorial, is based on combined notions of both exact and flexible pitches, melodic patterns, specific ornamentations, timing, quality and type of vocal sound, and particular modal sentiments. The totality does not, however, contradict the idea that performances of modes must comprise all these features individually. For the music to be modally effective, three basic elements must be employed: sentiment, scale, and ornamentation.

Ethnomusicologists sometimes say this process is comparable to that utilized in Indian ragas or the *maqamat* of the Arabic world, but details of the modes in Vietnam differ in pitches, forms, structures, instrumentation, and types of audience; mental processes also differ.

Terminology

It is not easy to find a nationally accepted term equivalent to "mode." Some scholars have considered *điệu* (also called *điệu thức* or *thức điệu*)—a term used not only in music, but also in art and literature—equivalent to "mode." This generalization has, however, occasioned controversy because *điệu* admits to variant meanings, including 'fashion, way, manner, melody, song, piece, rhythm'. Indeed, it would not be wrong to state that there are some forty-six different *điệu* in *ca trù,* twenty in *ca huế,* and eighty in *nhạc tài tử,* chamber musics of the north, the central region, and the south respectively. Each *điệu* has a distinctive modal expression, which can be understood as a mode or type of song, and each has seemingly endless variations. Ethnomusicologists in Vietnam are still working toward a unified definition of terms to be used at the national level. The major difficulty they face is that, for several generations, musicians of different subcultures have defined concepts and meanings in ways meaningful only to themselves; therefore, to have a clearer picture of what a mode may mean in Vietnamese music as a whole, it is necessary to understand the meanings of the following terms used within prominent genres.

Cung, a term employed for *ca trù,* expresses a mode that involves a specific vocal type and rhythm. *Giọng* 'voice' is an alternative for what we may understand as mode. There are five recognized modes: *nam* 'south, soft', *bắc* 'north, rigid', *huỳnh* 'yellow, bright', *pha* 'mixture, uncertain', and *nao* 'slanting, happy variance'. This tradition includes the concept of *thể* 'modal category', a term that has a broader meaning than *cung.*

Làn điệu refers to the aria, type of melody, or style of song that contains most features of a mode. This term is often used in *chèo,* a theatrical genre, and in *hát quan họ,* a courtship folk song, both of the northern region.

Điệu, a term commonly known to musicians and singers in the central region and the south, is somewhat equivalent to "mode"; however, because of the generalized meanings of *điệu,* the term *hơi* is locally preferred. *Hơi* 'breath, air, nuance' may describe either the meaning of a mode or a specific nuance, distinguishing one mode from another by means of specific ornamentations. A musician playing a wrong ornament may destroy a mode. Therefore, the combined term *hơi-điệu* is used for clarity's sake. The meanings of these terms are also shared by Vietnamese actors and religious singers.

An extensive repertoire of traditional pieces and songs in both chamber and the-

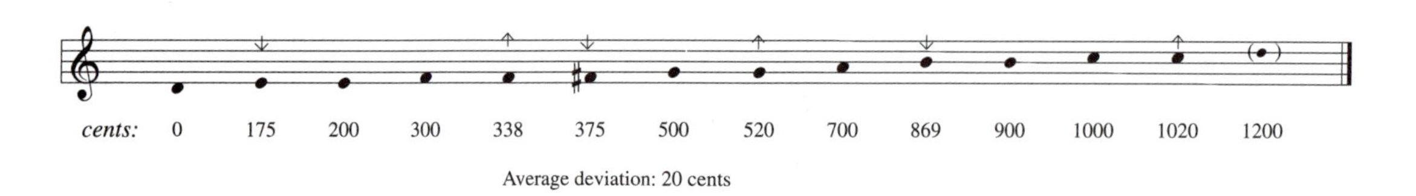

FIGURE 6 The tonal material of Vietnamese music.

atrical music requires executing the modes with subtlety and consistency. This process calls for four basic skills: organizing tonal materials in a hierarchical pattern, displaying ornamentation, using specific melodic patterns, and preparing modal sentiments for a given song or piece. For an accomplished musician, the last skill is the most important, in that the musician must shape the sentiment before realizing it through the appropriate expressive mode.

Scales

A scalar system plays a preliminary role in all musical performances. It varies according to the genre, subgenre, or social context in which a song or instrumental piece is constructed. Convention dictates that, in Vietnamese music, there is no such thing as absolute pitch. The fundamental tone of a scale may be chosen to fit the voice of a singer or the acoustic capacity of an instrument; thus, for best results, singers and musicians need to tailor solutions to individual needs. Other scalar tones are then proportionally derived from this fundamental pitch. The total number of possible tones is considered to be twelve and constitutes a theoretical system of tuning. Vietnamese scales use fewer than twelve tones in virtually all cases.

A variety of scales, all bearing the same tone numbers, do not necessarily display the same values between intervals. A great many tones in Vietnamese scales do not have Western equivalents; rather, variations in the size of Vietnamese intervals may be compared to those used in other Southeast Asian music. Generally, whole-tone intervals range between 165 to 175 cents. Intervals of less than a quarter tone or a semitone are heard when modulation or transmigration of scale units occurs.

Last, the tones or number of tones used has sociocultural connotations. Many lullabies and ritualistic songs (including Buddhist cantillations and religious chants) have two- or three-tone scales. The scales of chamber music and theatrical pieces have five to seven tones. Having more tones permits the transmigration of scalar units, also known as metabole.

The scheme of figure 6 shows all possible tones existing in Vietnamese music, based on a general study. To ease the comparison of intervallic values, the tone D is treated as the fundamental tone.

In art music, three categories of tones make up a scale: obligatory tones are fundamental, and they provide the structural framework of the piece or song; additional tones, which may be added to the initial scalar unit, may or may not lead to the transmigration of scalar units; passing tones, heard only a few times during the piece or song, are especially applicable in music built on a clearly established pentatonic or hexatonic scale.

Pentatonicism has long been discussed by learned Vietnamese musicians and ethnomusicologists. Some musicians interpret the five tones as corresponding to the five material elements conceived in Chinese philosophy: earth, metal, wood, water, and fire. For some, that many musical instruments are fretted or tuned to a five-tone scale lends credence to the concept of pentatonically based music. Moreover, these tones are associated with the Chinese pentatonic scalar degrees.

Explanations based on this tempered pentatonicism encounter problems trying to account for instrumental pitches constantly restructured outside the pentatonic system in performance. These pitches can be obtained by pushing on the string beyond the frets to get a note of higher pitch (figure 7*a*). Any given fret can therefore produce multiple pitches, depending on how firmly a musician presses the string (figure 7*b*).

Traditional Vietnamese music is thus not restricted to a five-tone system of tuning, but is expanded by additional tones produced by pressing on the strings. Soft, flexible strings ease the creation of passing and additional notes.

Vietnamese songs may be grouped into two major musical systems: the central and southern areas are unified in their definition of modes, whereas the northern area has a system in which individual songs define a mode. These systems share common ground, but do not agree in terminology. Figure 7*c* shows the pentatonic scales most commonly used in both folkloric and especially artistic music, with the tone D treated as the fundamental tone.

Transmigration of scales

The transmigration of scalar units within a song or instrumental piece creates sentiments appreciated by both singers and listeners. This transmigration, involving a change from one scale to another, with or without a return to the original, conforms closely to what Constantin Brăiloiu termed metabole (1955:63–75). In Vietnam, this transmigration occurs unevenly. Pitches are commonly added to the initial scale, as in the old folk songs of the Red River delta; this use is much rarer in theatrical and chamber music.

After a scale (pentatonic or not) has been established in a piece, its gravitational center may shift to a tone a fifth higher, establishing the new scale on this tone before returning to the original scale. In other instances, a new scale may be superimposed on the original, using the same fundamental tone. The number of tones in a given song can be classified as main, additional, and passing degrees (figure 8).

When viewing Vietnamese musical culture, one must focus on two essential elements: the nontempered character of the scales and the transmigration of scalar units. Tones used in folk songs are more localized than those of art music, the latter mostly having been codified nationwide. Finely adjusted intervals, even microtones, are typical of folk songs. Two to twelve tones may be selected from the twelve-tone system of tuning available in Vietnamese music.

The scales of many folk songs, often more complex than those of art music, can easily shift tonal centers. The phenomenon of metabole merits additional comment: groups of three to five tones shift emphasis and move back and forth, centering on differently emphasized degrees of the scale. For example, the song "*Con Nhện Giăng Mùng*" ('The Spider Spins Its Silk Web') (figure 9) features two principal scales: E–↑G–A–↓B–D and A–B–D–E–F♯–A–↓B (the upper octave has a different B), plus smaller scale units. The tonal material for the song thus includes a total of ten tones. The court piece "*Long Ngâm*" has six (figure 10). The tonal material for both songs is shown in figure 11.

Each scalar unit has a value in common with a type of scale traditionally used in other kinds of music. This connection relates to musical moods or metaphorical meanings. For example, "*Con Nhện Giăng Mùng*" moves from the subordinate mode to the main mode, and gradually from the higher part of the range to the lower. A song of farewell, it expresses desperation, a call or cry to friends leaving the singing party, and then a soft, near-silent, self-absorbed statement of sadness:

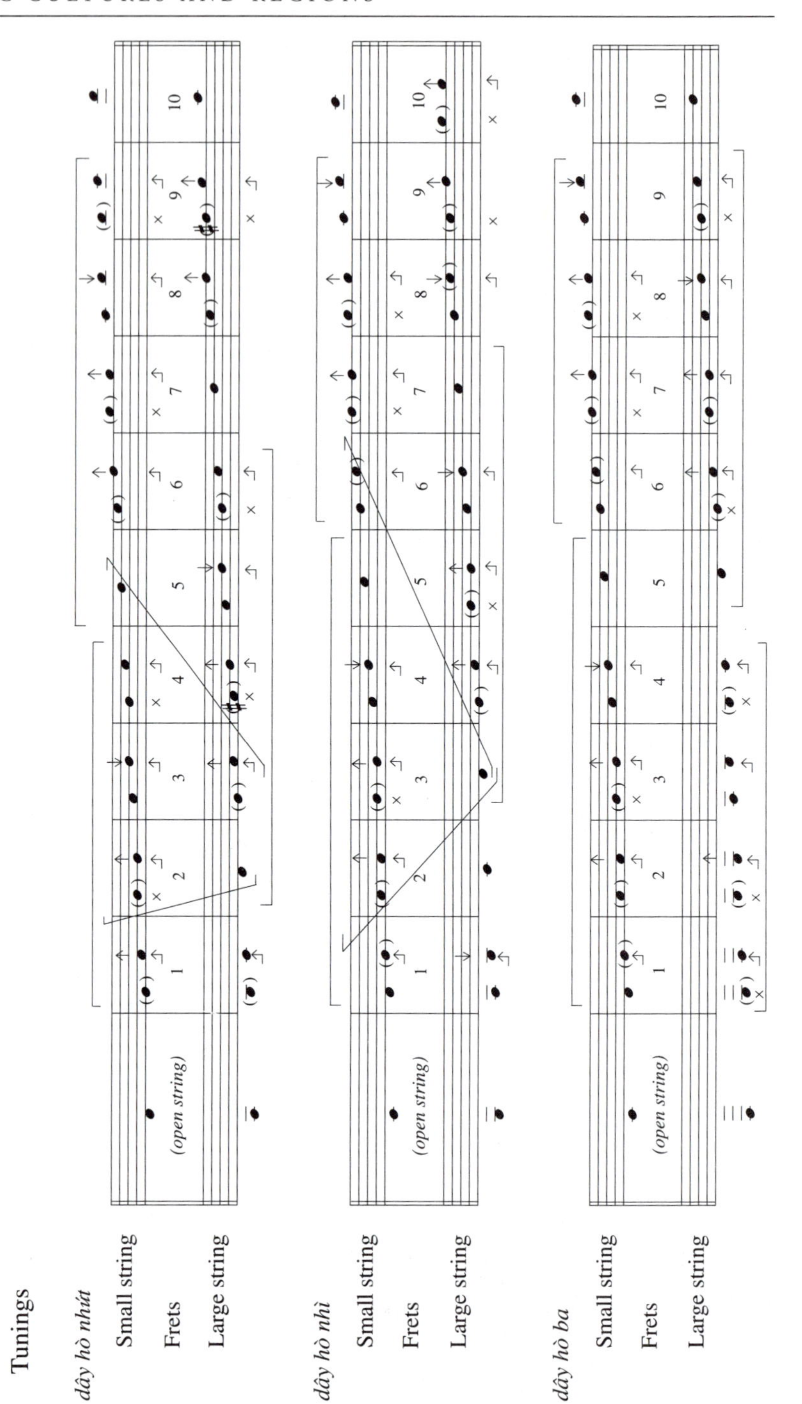

FIGURE 7a The modification of tones on Vietnamese stringed instruments.

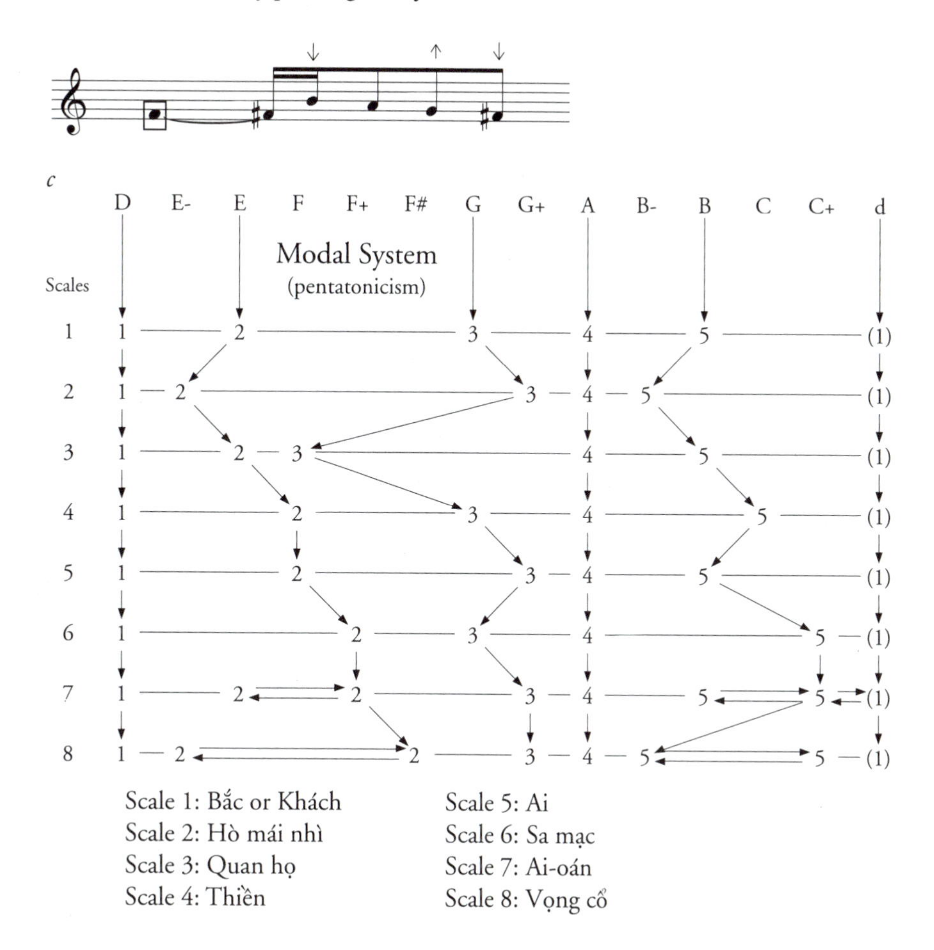

FIGURE 7 *(continued)* (*b*) Notes obtained on a single fret by pressing the string. (*c*) Chart of scales used in the artistic tradition.

> I'll be lonely all through the night.
> Do you know that?
> But there's no other way than accepting it.

According to the meaning of the words, a certain kind of musical line must be used.

Although combinations of units add more tones to the total or principal scale, equating tonal levels (for example, between ↓E and E, B♭ and ↑B♭, B and C, G and ↑G) may reduce the number of scalar tones from ten to seven, six, or five. Thus, if the song is only partially heard, one can easily get the impression of simple pentatonicism.

The *nam* modal system

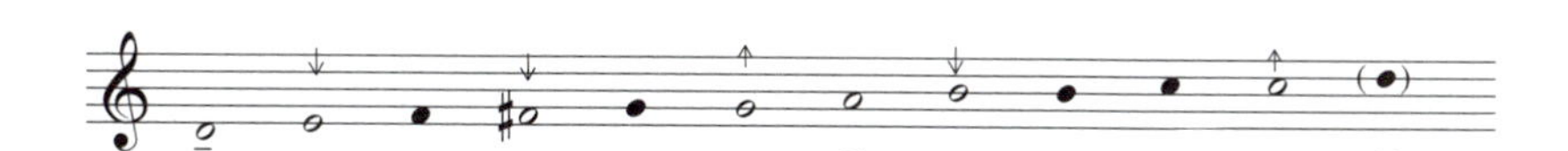

FIGURE 8 Constituent, modified, and decorative pitches in the *nam* modal system.

o = modified pitch for modal scale
● = decorative tone
o̲ = constituent degree of modal scale

rao Metrically free, improvisatory introduction to Vietnamese instrumental music

nói lối Metrically free, introductory phrases for Vietnamese songs

vọng cổ Southern Vietnamese song type, a skeletal framework for improvisation

điệu Vietnamese term meaning scale or mode

metabole Greek derived term for a change of mode or modal pitch level

FIGURE 9 The *quan họ* song of farewell, "*Con Nhện Giăng Mùng*" ('The Spider Spins Its Silk Web'). Scale numbers refer to figure 11*a*.

FIGURE 9
(continued)

Ornamentation

The elaboration of tones occurs frequently in many folk traditions, but ornamentation is far more prevalent in art music and depends on the musical context. That some ornamentations are associated, though not required, with particular scalar tones is a striking aspect of Vietnamese music. The complexity of the ornamentation allows each singer and musician to individualize expression. In vocal music, language naturally plays a major role in this individualization; the three prevalent accents (north, central, south) also influence ornamentation.

Specific terms for ornamental figures, clearly defined in each geographical area, differ greatly from one vocal or instrumental genre to another. It is far more difficult to deal with vocal than instrumental music, because of the myriad linguistic subtleties inherent in the former.

Conceivably, about a dozen types of ornamentation are applicable to each musical genre. But in general, three major types—for voice, *luyến láy* and *láy*; for instruments, *nhấn vuốt*—are noted: vibrato (*rung* for instruments, *ngân* for voice), reversed *pince* (*mổ* for instruments, *bắt chợt* for voice), and gliding (*nhấn* for instruments; *lướt giọng, buông chữ,* and *bắt tròn* for voice). As a rule in a modal scale, each degree may have a different ornamentation. Because of the expressivity and melismatic character of each ornament, its contour may extend so far in an ascending or descending direction that it reaches a neighboring degree and slides into the ornamental motif characteristic of that degree. In this circumstance, one hears a combined ornament—a frequent occurrence in chamber music and theatrical songs.

Vibrato can be either sustained or brief, according to the degree of the mode. Besides using conventional patterns, a musician can individualize vibrato to a level of

FIGURE 10 *"Long Ngâm"* ('Song of the Dragon'), a version for the zither (*đàn tranh*), based on the court melody composed by Trịnh Trọng Tử, a dignitary of the Tràn court, in 1310. This is perhaps the oldest composition surviving in Huế, the former imperial city of Vietnam. Scale numbers refer to figure 11*b*.

expertise appreciated by the most sensitive of connoisseurs. Figure 12 shows visualized motifs based on performances in Vietnamese music.

Ornamentation is complex. In *hát bội,* artists can apply any of the following vocal melismatic ornaments (*láy*) to express different sentiments: *láy ậm ừ* 'closed mouth', *láy âm dương* 'male and female', *láy hột* 'grains', *láy rúc* 'shortening', *láy rãy* 'extending', *láy nhún* 'jumping', *láy chuyền* 'passing', *láy viền* 'bordering', *láy ngắt* 'cutting', *láy giằng xay* 'back and forth', *láy đắp bờ* 'stopping', *láy búng* 'upward curve', and others.

A listener new to Vietnamese music may use melodic patterns from one song as a point of reference in another. Such a use is, in fact, characteristic not only of songs, but also of styles and modes. Musics from different Vietnamese regions have distinctive patterns, centered on degrees of the scale, whether they are the fundamental, underlying, pivotal, or additional notes. Emphasis on a degree varies from one scalar type to another. In terms of mode, one or several melodic patterns can provide some idea of a particular mode. The importance of melodic patterns, however, should not be overstated as primary determinants of a Vietnamese mode; given the priority of ornamentation, melodic patterns merely constitute one of many elements necessary to the process of realizing a mode.

Sentiments

Ingrained in Vietnamese musicians' and singers' minds are the types of sentiment

FIGURE 10 (*continued*)

through which a performer can establish a presence in the music world and communicate with the audience. An artfully ornamented note or a melodious motive can move listeners. Performers must prepare their minds before playing or singing; only by doing so can they correctly express the desired mode. Conversely, poorly wrought ornamentation may expose the weakness in a musician's talent. The improvised introduction (*rao* or *dạo*) thus becomes necessary for any adjustment, as does the exposition of sentiments through musical notes. Thus, Vietnamese music is a modally created music.

Modal sentiments are felt and described according to generally accepted definitions, which include classification into the modal systems *nam* and *bắc*. These are

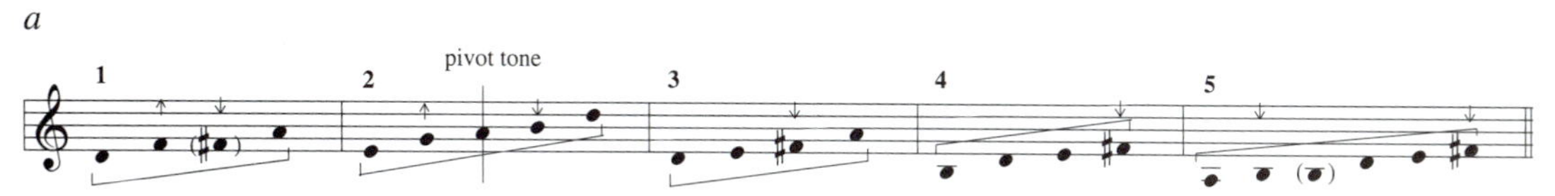

FIGURE 11 Successions of scalar units: *a*, in "*Con Nhện Giăng Mùng*"; *b*, "*Long Ngâm*."

FIGURE 12 The signs and names of ornaments.

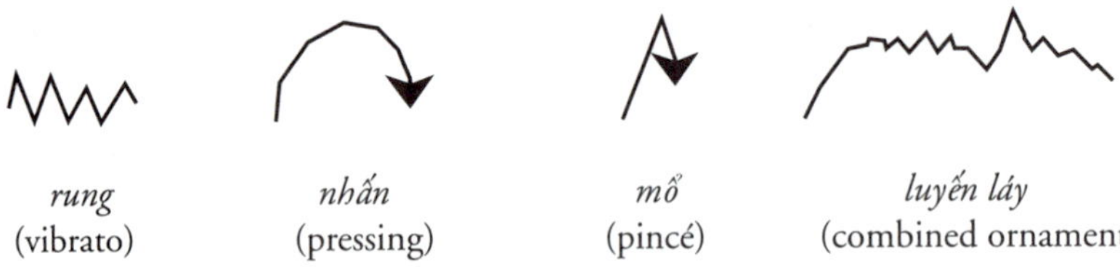

rung (vibrato)	*nhấn* (pressing)	*mổ* (pincé)	*luyến láy* (combined ornaments)

commonly defined by all genres and traditions in Vietnam: *nam* is sad, and *bắc* is happy; however, regional traditions use and define other terms:

ca trù (north)	*huỳnh*	rhapsodic
	pha	mixture of sad and happy feelings
	nao	bright, delightful, overjoyed
ca huế (central)	*ai*	sorrowful
	thiền	religiously solemn
nhạc tài tử (south)	*xuân*	serene and lively
	ai	lamentable
	đảo	serene but straight
	oán	plaintive

Though the question of modes in Vietnamese folk songs is not much discussed—or more correctly, not much agreed on—by Vietnamese ethnomusicologists, complex systems of scales and specific ornamentations exist in many folk songs. These features also conform to related theory in art music, in several ways. The folkloric and artistic traditions within larger geographical areas share traits easily recognized by outsiders. Differences among scales are readily recognized by folk singers, since a mistakenly perceived note greatly affects their singing. Scales of two to seven tones are common in Vietnamese folk songs. Three-tone scales are often found in children's songs and child-related songs, including lullabies, though many lullabies of the southern areas utilize up to a seven-tone scale. Some adult songs, such as *hát đúm,* however, usually consist of only two tones.

Rhythm and meter

Rhythm in Vietnamese music is complex. Syncopation gives the music a spiciness that distinguishes it from Chinese music, superficially the most closely related music style. In addition to metrical organization, some Vietnamese music is unmeasured or nonmetrical. Instrumental ensembles are not only heterophonic in melody but heterorhythmic, creating an interplay that gives Vietnamese music added drive.

Nonmetrical organization

Nonmetrical rhythms play an important role in Vietnamese music, particularly in sung poetry and Buddhist hymns. Sung poetry can last for hours without establishing a musical meter. Buddhist hymns may be preceded or followed by metrical cantillation. In songs, sections of free rhythm may occur as a modal preparation in the beginning or as a transition to another section. In ritual music, these sections are marked by the sounding of a bell; in chamber music, they are marked with a clapper (*song lang*).

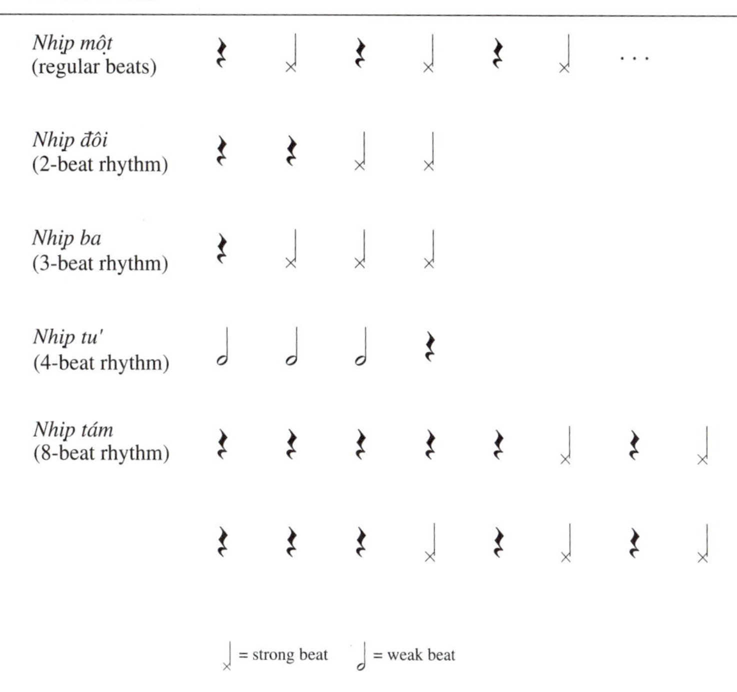

FIGURE 13 Rhythmic patterns: *nhịp đôi* (two-beat rhythm), *nhịp ba* (three-beat rhythm), *nhịp tu* (four-beat rhythm), *nhịp tám* (eight-beat rhythm).

Metrical organization

Nhịp denotes metrical rhythm. Most Vietnamese music is organized metrically according to cycles of beats, with patterns having one, two, three, four, and eight beats. The final beat of each unit is the most emphasized. Three-beat units or ternary meter is rare in Vietnam. What is traditionally called a three-beat measure (*nhịp ba*) is, in fact, a cycle of four beats, of which three are emphasized (figure 13). Cyclical music is most clearly heard in the percussion-dominated ensembles of ritual, festival music (*nhạc lễ*), and theatrical music. A basic pattern can be elaborated and improvised on in various ways. On a more intricate level, "rounding" a musical phrase with a special pattern is also characteristic of many genres: a shorter pattern is added at the end of the phrase.

Theatrical and ceremonial musics emphasize multiple rhythmic patterns by superimposing patterns played on percussion instruments. In theatrical and ritual music, a wooden drum (*mõ*), a clapper (*phách*), and a water-buffalo-horn drum (*mõ sừng trâu*) play interlocking patterns, while other drums and clappers serve as the rhythmic foundation. They assist stage movement and signal on-stage sectional changes. Musicians are trained in standard patterns (*chân phương* 'square'), and then they advance to elaborations (*hoa lá* 'flourishing, flowers and leaves'). A good musician would use the *hoa lá* pattern for most of a performance.

Melodic improvisation is characteristic of Vietnamese music as a whole, but free-metered improvisation by the drummer in introductions and interludes is probably the most appreciated part of any performance. The drummer, as leader of the ensemble, uses special rhythmic formulas to start and end pieces (figure 14).

In the string ensemble, the *đàn nguyệt* or another lute plays in a syncopated manner. This syncopation is realized by emphasizing a weak beat or playing a note preceding a structural note (*nhịp nội*) or following it (*nhịp ngoại*). Playing the note directly on the strong beat is called *nhịp chính diện,* and of course is not a syncopation. These distinctions are recognized in central Vietnamese music, particularly around Huế; in general, however, *nhịp ngoại* is considered syncopated, and *nhịp nội* is not.

FIGURE 14 Drum patterns with the names of strokes: *a*, introductory patterns; *b*, ending patterns. *Key:* any plain note (*toong*) shows a drumstick strike in the center of the skin; with the notehead circled (*tà-roong*), a pair of drumsticks rolls in the center of the skin; with a slash through the stem (*táng*), a drumstick strikes on the margin of the skin; with an X through the stem (*tà-ráng*), a pair of drumsticks rolls on the margins of the skin; with an X for a notehead (*cắc*), a drumstick strikes the wooden body of the drum; with a double slash through the stem (*rụp*), a pair of drumsticks stops rolling in the center of the skin.

a introductory patterns:

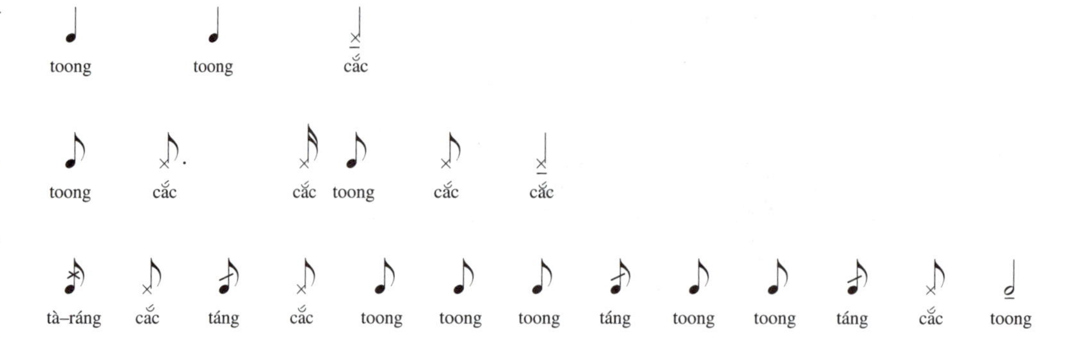

b ending patterns:

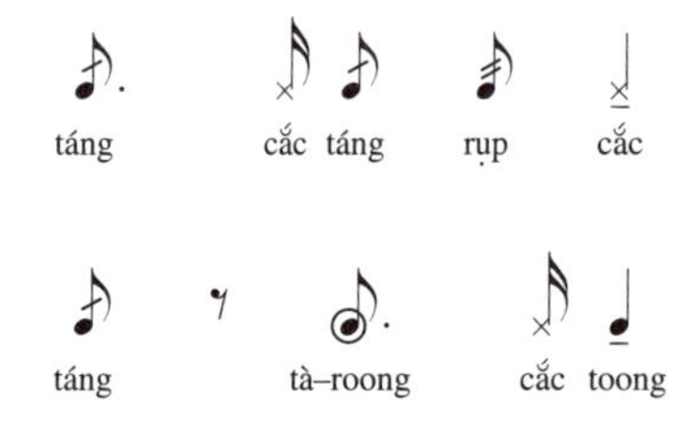

toong = drum stick strike in the center of the skin.

tà-roong = pair of drum sticks rolling in the center of the skin.

táng = drum stick strike on the margin of the skin.

tà-ráng = pair of drum sticks rolling on the margins of the skin.

cắc = drum stick strike on the wooden body of the drum.

rụp = pair of drum sticks stops rolling in the center of the skin.

MUSICAL INSTRUMENTS

Vietnamese musical instruments have a wide variety of origins. Besides indigenous creations, many traditional stringed and wind instruments migrated from Central Asia via China. Since colonization (1884–1954), many Western instruments have been assimilated into Vietnamese music. In all, more than fifty instruments are played by the lowland Vietnamese and nearly two hundred by highlanders. Although there is some overlap, each group plays some distinct instruments.

Because the voice is prominent in Vietnamese chamber music and theatrical music, instruments tend to play an accompanying role in those genres; however, since the voice cannot replace instrumental music in certain aspects of rituals, instruments play an essential role in ceremonial musics, such as those of the imperial court and in temples. From the tenth century or before, instrumental music in Vietnam has served as a homogenizing medium, with instruments from both low and high classes freely exchanged and accepted. For example, the monochord, an instrument invented by peasants, became an integral part of artistic ensembles and was not discriminated against as a low-class instrument, even by the imperial court, until the 1400s, when it fell under Ming influence.

Except for court music, no orchestral ensembles in Vietnam have more than five stringed instruments. For instance, ceremonial ensembles (*nhạc lễ*) of southern Vietnam use twelve to twenty instruments, but most are percussive. The northern chamber-music genres *ca trù* and *hát ả đào* have only three instruments, of which *đàn đáy* is the only stringed one. Where several instruments play together, the texture is heterophonic. In ceremonial ensembles, both strings (*văn*) and percussion (*võ*) combine for an entire piece or for a section. *Tam tấu,* the three-instrument chamber-music genre of central and southern Vietnam, includes a fiddle, a lute, and a zither or a flute. *Ngũ tuyệt* 'combination of five excellent instruments' of central Vietnam includes a board zither, a two-stringed fiddle, a moon-shaped lute, a pear-shaped lute, and a three-stringed lute.

Idiophones

Idiophones may be the earliest and are the most numerous instruments in Vietnam. In many respects, they mark the rhythms of Vietnamese life, announcing, governing, and developing ritual ceremonies and changes in theatrical performances, thus becoming an integral part of them. They are capable of both braying and delicate sonorities. The materials used to make them are wood, bamboo, horn, bronze, and stone. Vietnamese idiophones include prehistoric bronze drums and lithophones, bamboo xylophones, gongs, cymbals, wooden slit drums, bells, and clappers.

The bronze drum (*trống đồng*) is among the oldest of Vietnamese idiophones. It first appeared in the Đong-Sơn period. The Mường still use it for festivals. Since the 1970s, it has been revived for concert performances, but its modern use likely bears little relationship to its earlier musical contexts.

A *đại hồng chung* (figure 15), a large bronze bell, is played in Buddhist ceremonies. It is the largest Vietnamese bell still played. As a type, it is descended from a bell dated in the Lý Dynasty (eleventh to twelfth centuries) and housed in the National Historical Museum, Hanoi. About 1.25 meters high, it hangs inside a tower usually located at the front right corner of the main chapel hall. Another tower, on the left side of the hall, holds the drum of wisdom (*trống bát nhã*), which, when struck with a wooden club covered with tissues, produces a long-resounding, low sound.

FIGURE 15 *Đại hồng chung,* a Buddhist bell of the Lý Dynasty (eleventh to thirteenth centuries). Photo by Phong T. Nguyễn.

The small bell (*tiểu chung*) is a smaller version of the *đại hồng chung.* It is also called *chuông báo chúng* because it calls the monks to assemble. It is hung under the roof of the meeting hall of the museum.

The bell of religious perseverance (*chuông gia trì*), a hemispheric bowl chime, is used in Buddhist ceremonies. It ranges from 20 to 75 centimeters in diameter and reposes on a cushioned ring. It is played to punctuate musical sections of Buddhist chant.

Gongs come in three sizes: a large (*chiêng,* also *cồng*), a middle-sized (*thanh la,* also *tum*), and a small and hand-held (*đẩu,* also *tang*) instrument. The *cồng* is probably the original term for gong; *chiêng* is an onomatopoeic form for the sound made by flat gongs. A set of three small gongs hung on a frame by threads and fixed to a handle is called *tam âm la* 'three-sound gongs.' Vietnamese gongs date to the Bronze Age. They gradually lost most of their ensemble duties and are presently incorporated into ceremonial and theatrical ensembles with many other instruments. Their use in ensembles is preserved only by the Mường, an ethnic group closely linked to the Việt (or Vietnamese) in the Hòa Bình area, and by many minority peoples in the central highlands of southern and central Vietnam.

mõ Slit drums, actually hollowed out of solid material such as wood or bamboo

phách Piece of wood or bamboo struck by two beaters

song lang Foot-operated slit drum struck with a wooden beater on a piece of buffalo horn

sinh tiền Hinged, two-piece clapper with coins on the upper piece and scraped saw teeth on the lower

trống Generic term for Vietnamese drums, most with nailed head(s)

Mõ is a generic Vietnamese term for slit drums not made from hide or metal. Materials used to craft *mõ* include wood, bamboo, and water-buffalo horn. A *mõ* accompanies Buddhist chanting. It has a rounded shape, and bears decorations suggesting features of a fish, as with the Chinese *muyu* and the Japanese *mokkugyo,* both of which mean 'wooden fish.' *Mõ đình,* the *mõ* employed for rituals in village shrines (*đình*), is shaped like the trunk of a tree, and is placed horizontally on a wooden stand. A slit along its body is a bit distended in the middle. A bamboo slit drum called *mõ làng* 'village slit drum' summons people to meetings and signals when there is a thief, fire, or any other local emergency. The *mõ sừng trâu* 'water-buffalo horn', 15 to 20 centimeters long, is played in ceremonial ensembles.

Chimes (*khánh*) are made of bronze (*khánh đồng*) and stone (*khánh đá*). Considered by Vietnamese to have the shape of the petal of a flower, *khánh* have a rounded base and a scalloped top resembling a hat. *Khánh* vary from 37 to 125 centimeters long. They are commonly found in temples.

The *chập chỏa* is a pair of cymbals; a smaller version is called *chập bạt, não bạt,* and *chùm chọe.* The *chập chỏa* (about 50 centimeters in diameter) and *chập bạt* (about 15 to 20 centimeters in diameter) differ in size and musical function: the smaller pair elaborates on the rhythm of the larger. Both instruments are played in theatrical, festival, and ritual music.

The *mộc bảng,* a rectangular wooden plate about 50 centimeters wide, may be played alone or with a small bell in Buddhist temples.

The *phách* may be among the oldest types of clappers used in religious ceremonies, dances, chamber music, and theater. A small piece of bamboo or a wooden block is selected for its sound. Two or three beaters may be used to beat measures on it and to vary the tempo and rhythmic patterns. The *phách* used in northern chamber songs has three beaters, one held in the player's left hand and two in the right. A pair of beaters consists of two halves of a round stick. The singer plays a *phách* to accompany herself. Probably because of the importance of clappers in singing, the term *phách* also means 'rhythm' and 'tempo' in northern Vietnam.

The *song lang,* like the *phách,* is a clapper, used only in southern chamber music. Invented early in the twentieth century, it consists of a flat round piece of wood with a slit in the curved side about 30 centimeters in circumference. A small rounded piece of wood is attached to a thin, flat, U-shaped buffalo-horn "spring," which in turn is attached to the main piece. The musician plays it with his or her foot by pressing the small piece against the larger one, creating a sharp, high-pitched sound to articulate important beats while playing a melodic instrument. Though a small and simple instrument, it has both cultural and musical values in *nhạc tài tử* and *cải lương.* The singer of a *vọng cổ,* a thirty-two-beat song, must hear clicks of a *song lang* on the twenty-fourth and thirty-second beats.

Sinh tiền (figure 16) is another kind of clapper. Two long, flat pieces of wood are connected at one end by a leather hinge. The lower side of the lower piece has teeth,

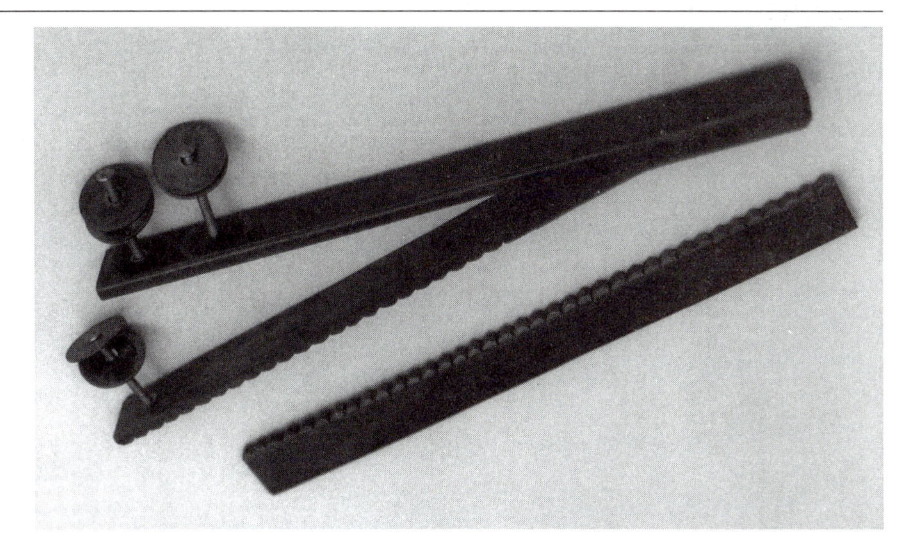

FIGURE 16 *Sinh tiền,* coin clapper. Photo by Phong T. Nguyễn.

along which the player scrapes a third piece of wood, also notched, to produce a rasping sound. A few old coins, loosely secured to the topmost piece of wood on a nail, add a jingling sound. The Lao *mai ngop ngep* is similar, but has no jingling coins. In festivals in and around Hanoi, people perform the *sinh tiền* and *mõ* crossing dance (*sinh tiền mõ lộn*). The *sinh tiền* is rarely used in the south.

The *sanh* or *phệch* is a pair of hard bamboo concussion sticks about 20 centimeters long. Each is flat and identical to the other. It is widely used in the countryside. In Bình Định, in the south-central area, it accompanies folk songs (*bài chòi*). A colotomic instrument, it can guide dance movements and maintain a regular tempo.

Membranophones

Trống is a generic term for membranophones that have one or two skin-covered heads and a wooden body. Depending on their use, these drums have different names, sizes, and shapes. More than twenty drums bear different names, and their sizes range from about 20 to 200 centimeters. Each has a unique set of rhythms and a unique teaching method, indigenous to its regional birthplace.

The *bồng,* unusual because its name does not include *trống,* is a southern Vietnamese drum whose name is likely onomatopoeic. It is a small, one-headed drum used in *nhạc lễ* ensembles. With an hourglass-shaped baked-clay body, it has boa-skin heads. Its pitch depends on the tension of the lacing. Both heads are beaten by hand. The *bồng* probably derived from an ancient, obsolete, hourglass-shaped drum, the *phong yêu cổ.*

The drum of wisdom (*trống bát nhã*), a small drum, announces the beginning and ending of important Buddhist ceremonies. It is placed on a carved wooden stand.

The carrying drum (*trống bung,* also *trống khẩu* 'mouth drum') is a small, two-headed drum with a strap affixed to one side, enabling the player to hold it with one hand while using a wooden stick to beat the drumheads with the other. This drum is played both by Buddhist monks and, in northern villages, to accompany wrestling matches.

Trống cái is the southern term for a small, single-headed drum of the *nhạc lễ* ensemble; in northern Vietnam, it is called *trống bộc.*

The drum of honor (*trống chầu,* also called *trống sấm* 'thunder drum', *trống cái, trống đại lược,* and *trống đại cổ* 'large drum'), the largest of all Vietnamese drums, is used in court music, village temples, traditional theater, *hát bội,* and *chèo.*

The *trống chầu ca trù* 'drum for the *ca trù*' (song with danced accompaniment)

FIGURE 17 The drum and clapper used in *ca trù* or *hát ả đào* chamber song. Photo by Phong T. Nguyễn.

or 'drum for *hát ả đào*' (song of Lady Đào), is played in northern chamber-music genres (figure 17).

The battle drum (*trống chiến*) is used primarily in on-stage battle scenes in theater.

The rice drum (*trống cơm*) is a portable two-headed drum often tuned (in fifths) by the application of rice paste to the center of each head (figure 18). It is related to similar South and Southeast Asian drums, including the Indian *mridàngam,* the Cambodian *sampho,* and the Javanese *kendhang.*

The *trống đạo,* much smaller than the *trống bát nhã,* is used to accompany Buddhist chants of praise (*tán*).

The *trống ngũ bộ* 'drum of the five-instrument ensemble' is a medium-sized drum. It hangs at the player's side and is beaten with a stick during processions in festivals.

The *trống nhạc* or *trống bản* is a pair of drums, each having a different tone, the higher-pitched called female drum (*trống cái*) or civil drum (*trống văn*) and the lower-pitched called male drum (*trống đục*) or military drum (*trống võ*). They are the main instruments of the *nhạc lễ* ensemble.

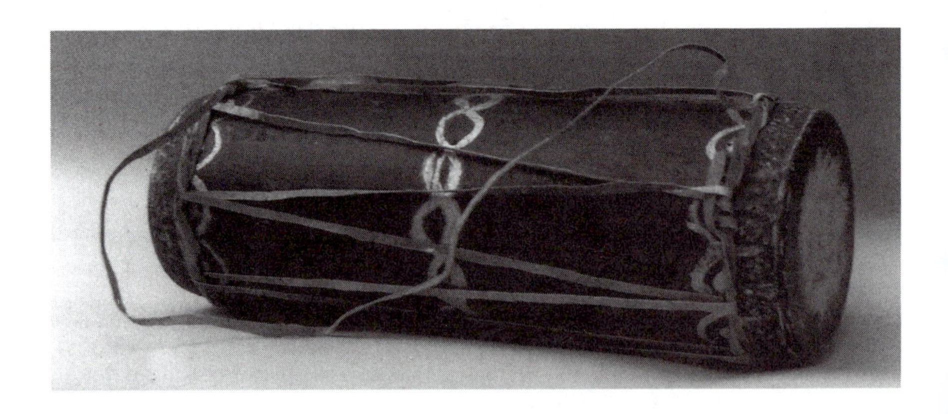

FIGURE 18 A Vietnamese drum (*trống cơm*) tuned with rice paste. Photo by Phong T. Nguyễn.

Chordophones

Vietnamese chordophones include plucked, bowed, and struck instruments, played both solo and in ensembles. About fifteen stringed instruments are used today, and several others have become obsolete. All of these are identified by the classifying word *đàn.* The vibrations of their strings are intended to mimic vocal nuances, both the typical intonations of Vietnamese language and the idiosyncracies of local dialects. A Vietnamese *đàn* usually has an alternate name, indicating its local or linguistic background.

Zithers

The Vietnamese monochord (*đàn bầu* 'gourd instrument,' also *đàn độc huyền* 'single-stringed instrument') (figure 19) has a wood box resonator, with a flexible vertical stick ("neck"), to which one end of its string is tied. Because it originally had a resonator made of a dried gourd, it was called a gourd (*bầu*)—the name retained in the north and central regions. The vertical stick is made of a thin, flexible piece of water-buffalo horn or bamboo. This monochord is the only Vietnamese instrument that produces harmonics, made with a light pluck and touch of the musician's right hand on any of the five nodes of the string. If the string is tuned to D, its tones are D, A, d, f♯, a, and d′, all of which may be produced at any of four octaves. The first octave of the string is located in the middle. In addition, the left-hand bending of the stick changes pitches or ornaments them in accordance with the chosen mode. The *đàn bầu* is played solo or to accompany folk songs, tales, and epics. It has had a remarkable history. Discriminated against at times, it has been an instrument of blind street beggars, yet it was also an instrument of choice at the Trần imperial court (1225–1400).

Trống quân, a single-stringed earth zither, is perhaps the oldest stringed instrument in Vietnam. It is called an earth zither because one end of its string, made of metal or rattan, is set into the ground. The resonator is a hole dug into the ground between the ends of the string, covered by a metal sheet or steel barrel. A wooden stick between the resonator and the string acts as a bridge. Players beat the string rhythmically with a stick. Because the instrument produces a sound thought to be drumlike, it was called *trống quân* 'military drum.' Its primary use is to accompany antiphonal songs (*hát trống quân* 'songs of the military drum').

The Vietnamese board zither (*đàn tranh,* also *đàn thập lục*), has sixteen (sometimes seventeen) strings running along a semitubular body of paulownia wood (figure 20). It is thus distantly related to other East Asian board zithers, especially the Chinese *zheng,* the Korean *kayagum,* and the Japanese *koto.* Indeed, the word *tranh* derives from *zheng,* and *đàn thập lục* means 'sixteen-stringed zither'. Neither the

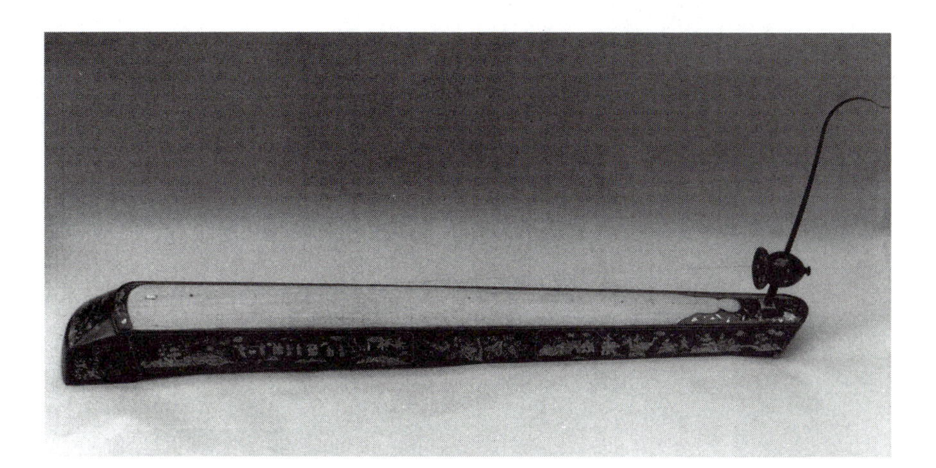

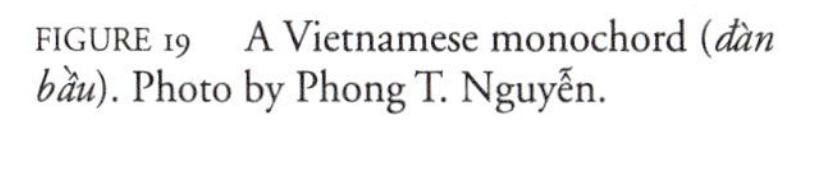

FIGURE 19 A Vietnamese monochord (*đàn bầu*). Photo by Phong T. Nguyễn.

FIGURE 20 A Vietnamese zither (*đàn tranh* or *đàn thập lục*). Photo by Phong T. Nguyễn.

repertoire nor the theory of this zither, however, resembles those of the East Asian zithers. Since its history is largely unknown, several hypotheses have been offered for its origin. An instrument resembling it appears in a bas-relief in Bắc Ninh (northern Vietnam) at Phật Tích Temple, built in the ninth century and renovated during the eleventh. With other zithers, this zither was used in Thăng Long court music before the 1800s, and later became a favorite chamber-music instrument in the central and southern areas. Its strings are tuned pentatonically. They allow deep left-hand pressing to produce additional pitches and ornaments, resulting in hexatonic and heptatonic scales. This zither is a member of two southern ensembles: *nhạc tài tử* (also including a *cò* or a *nhị* and a *kìm* or a *nguyệt*) and a quintet that includes these three instruments plus a pear-shaped lute (*tỳbà*) and a bamboo flute (*sáo*). A three-stringed lute and a monochord can replace the pear-shaped lute and the flute, respectively.

Đàn tam thập lục 'thirty-six-stringed instrument' is a dulcimer of Chinese origin. It is uncertain whether this dulcimer was known in Vietnam before it was introduced by Matteo Ricci, an Italian traveler who in the 1600s had journeyed to China's Guangdong Province, where the instrument was a simple dulcimer with thirty-six strings. As in China, the number of strings has increased to more than eighty, and its shape has changed.

FIGURE 21 A Vietnamese long lute (*đàn đáy*). Photo by Phong T. Nguyễn.

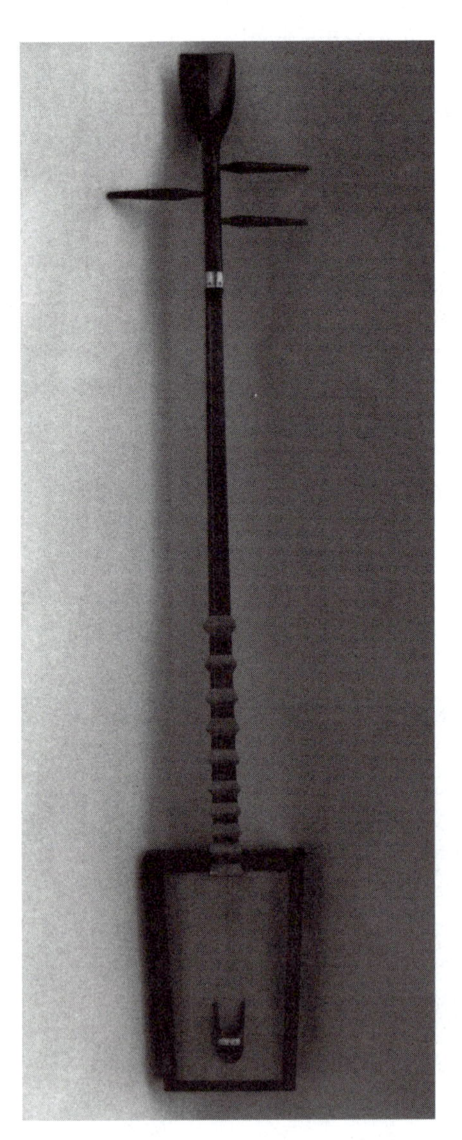

Plucked lutes

The *đàn đáy* is a long-necked, three-stringed lute with a trapezoidal-shaped, backless body (figure 21). Its name probably derives from *đới cầm* (from *đới* 'to be held in standing position', Sino-Vietnamese *cầm* 'stringed instrument', Vietnamese *đàn*). Though its neck is 1.2 meters long, the nine frets cover only the lower half, with an additional one fixed to the soundboard. Thick and high, these frets produce seven equidistant notes, but the open strings provide additional, exceptionally low tones. This lute is the only stringed instrument used to accompany *ca trù*. It attained its greatest popularity in the earlier Lê Dynasty (1428–1789). Because it is not used apart from *ca trù*, some scholars believe it to have been invented as early as the eleventh century, when that genre was created.

The *đàn nguyệt* or *đàn kìm* is a moon-shaped, long-necked lute with two silk strings (figure 22). Though literary sources suggest that this instrument has an East Asian heritage akin to the *yueqin* (China), *woolkum* (Korea), and *gekkin* (Japan), it may be functionally closer to Southeast Asian lutes. Its frets are high and fixed on the neck to provide a pentatonic scale. If the fundamental tone is D, the open string and frets produce successively D, E, G, A, B and their octaves. The *đàn nguyệt*, like the *yueqin*, once had four strings, but their number was reduced to two in the twentieth century. Its strings, the upper one thicker than the lower, are tuned in fourths, fifths, or sevenths. Any of these can serve as the fundamental tone for a song and the pivot point for changing the tonal center, enabling the player to produce a wide range of

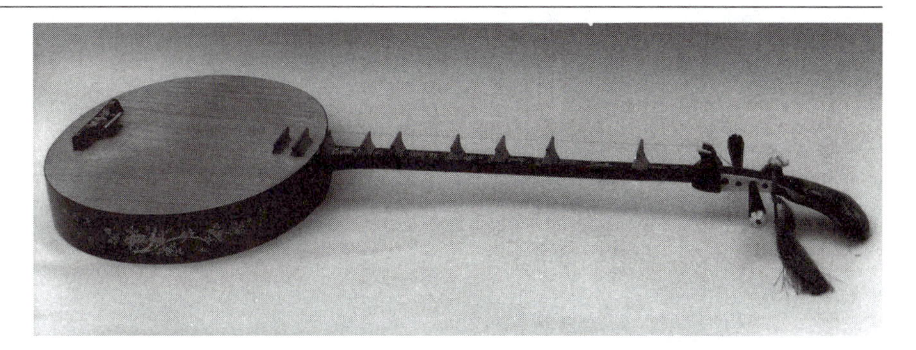

FIGURE 22 A Vietnamese moon-shaped lute (*đàn nguyệt* or *đàn kìm*). Photo by Phong T. Nguyễn.

tones in several Vietnamese scales. This lute is one of the most frequently played traditional instruments in Vietnam.

The *tỳbà,* a pear-shaped lute, first appeared in Vietnam in the early 600s, a few centuries after it had been introduced into China, from Kucha in Xinjiang (Central Asia) during the Six Dynasties, specifically the North and South dynasties (386–534). Its shape and four strings resemble those of the early Chinese *pipa* more than those of the Korean *bip'a* or the Japanese *biwa.* Unlike the *đàn nguyệt* and the *đàn nhị,* this lute remained obscure in the countryside, where it achieved little popularity.

The *đàn tam* or *tam huyền,* a fretless, long-necked lute, derives from the Yuan Chinese *sanxian* and resembles the Japanese *shamisen.* Its resonator, covered with boa skin, produces a sound resembling that of the American banjo. Three strings of graduated sizes are tuned in fourths and fifths. This lute, which occupies only a secondary role in Vietnam, is seldom heard as a solo instrument. The *đàn tứ* resembles the *đàn tam,* but has four strings.

The *đàn xến* is the Vietnamese version of a southern Chinese octagonal lute (*qinqin*), whose rounded sound box has scallops around the edge. It was introduced into southern Vietnam in the early twentieth century. As with other such instruments, the process of Vietnamization included raising the frets, making adaptations to accommodate a heptatonic scale, and changing the strings to a soft, flexible material.

Lục huyền cầm 'six-stringed instrument' and *đàn ghi-ta* are Vietnamese terms for the Western guitar, used in traditional ensembles (figure 23). Originating in the so-called *guitare espagnole* (Spanish *guitarra española*), this instrument was adopted by Giáo Tiên, an elementary schoolteacher and *nhac tài tù* musician in Rạch Gía, a remote province of south Vietnam, in 1920. Later, it became a favorite instrument in *tài tử* and *cải lương.* The physical changes it has undergone in Vietnam are notewor-

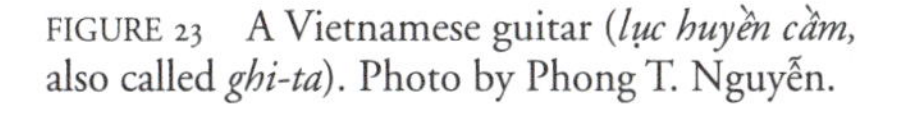

FIGURE 23 A Vietnamese guitar (*lục huyền cầm,* also called *ghi-ta*). Photo by Phong T. Nguyễn.

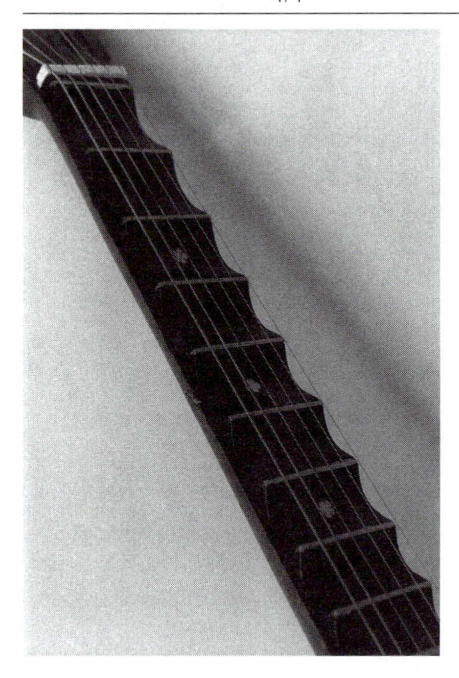

FIGURE 24 The fingerboard of the Vietnamese guitar, showing scooping. Photo by Phong T. Nguyễn.

thy: its strings, though of metal, are softer than strings used in the West, and the wood between the frets has been cut away to allow for the deep string bending required to produce typical Vietnamese ornaments (figure 24). There are three octave-based tunings (*dây*): G–d–g–d′–a′–e″ (*dây Rạch-Gía* 'Rạch Gía tuning'), G–d–g–d′–g′–d″ (*dây Sài-Gòn* 'Saigon tuning'), and G–d–g–d′–a′–d″ (*dây lai* 'acculturated tuning'). Rạch-Gía and Sài-Gòn are places in the areas where those tunings were created. Because the last of these tunings has an interval of a fourth (used for the two smallest strings), identical to a Western tuning, it is dubbed acculturated or borrowed. In the 1970s and 1980s, it came to be seen as a symbol of change and development in southern music. Many new tunings have been created to satisfy a new generation of players and to accommodate male and female singers' tonal ranges.

The *hạ uy cầm* is a steel guitar imported from Hawaii (from *hạ uy* 'Hawaii'). The electric *hạ uy cầm* joined southern music in 1927 in *nhạc tài tử* ensembles and commercial recordings. Its tuning is G'–D–G–B–d.

Đại hồ cầm or *viô-lông xen* (in French, *violoncelle*; in English, violoncello) joined the group of newly assimilated Western instruments in 1927, but it did not last long, probably because of controversy over its size in comparison with traditional instruments.

Bowed lutes (fiddles)

The *đàn nhị* or *đàn cò* (figure 25) is a two-stringed fiddle resembling the Chinese *erhu* and related to Southeast Asian fiddles like the Thai *saw duang*. It is one of the primary instruments in court, theatrical, and ritual music. Thought to have been derived from Turkic or Mongol culture, it has a cylindrical wooden sound box, covered at one end with boa skin. At the center of this skin is a tiny bridge supporting two parallel silk strings, one thinner than the other. These strings are wound around pegs piercing a thin neck about 75 centimeters long near its upper curve. A horse-tail-hair bow passes over the resonator and between the strings. Three other bowed lutes have different resonators: *đàn cò phụ* 'subordinate fiddle', with its slightly larger resonator; *đàn gáo* or *đàn hồ* 'coconut-shell fiddle'; and *đàn cò chỉ* 'little fiddle'. For a *nhạc lễ* ritual performance, these instruments are tuned in fifths, from the lowest to the highest instruments as D–A, F–C, G–d, and A–e (using d as the fundamental tone). The G–d tuning is employed for the principal *đàn nhị*.

The *vĩ cầm* 'horse-tail instrument' or *viô-lông* is a Western violin, tuned d–g–d′–a′. Since 1925, it has often replaced the *đàn nhị* in various kinds of southern music.

In the twentieth century, efforts have been made to add other Western chordophones, including the piano and the mandolin, to traditional Vietnamese music.

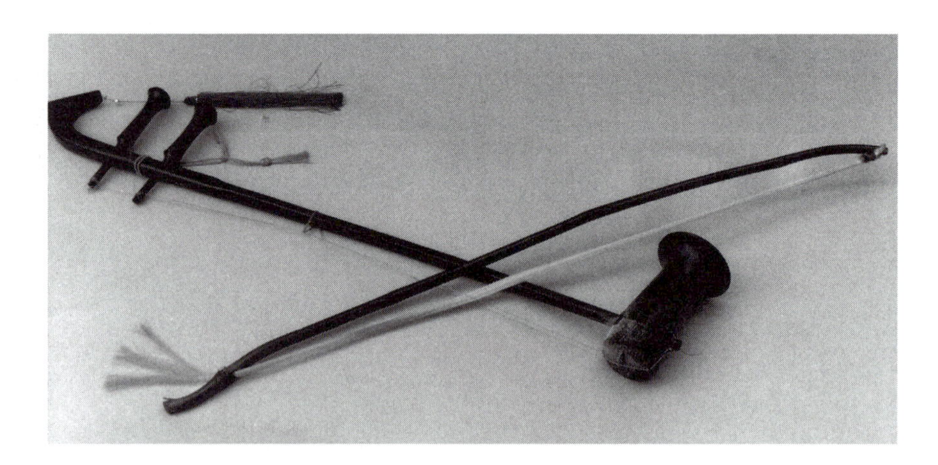

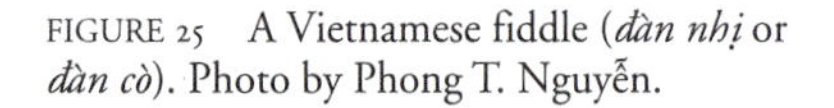

FIGURE 25 A Vietnamese fiddle (*đàn nhị* or *đàn cò*). Photo by Phong T. Nguyễn.

These efforts have failed, primarily because of the physical impossibility of altering the instruments to accommodate Vietnamese aesthetics. This failure parallels the case of the Chinese zithers *qin* and *se,* which achieved only limited use many years earlier.

Aerophones

The *sáo,* a horizontal bamboo flute, is a favorite wind instrument in Vietnam. Unlike the Chinese *dizi,* it does not have a membrane-covered hole, so its timbre does not include the buzz characteristic of the *di.* The *sáo* has six holes, producing the tones C, D, E, F, G, A, and B. If overblown, it produces octaves. A standard *sáo* is about 50 centimeters long and 1.5 centimeters in diameter.

The *tiêu* is a vertical end-blown notch flute. The bamboo chosen for it must be larger and older than that for a *sáo,* to produce lower tones. The *tiêu* has five holes on top and one underneath.

Kèn is a Vietnamese generic term for all kinds of double-reed aerophones. There is reason to believe that this term originated from terms for free-reed mouth organs known among Tai-speakers, *khèn* and *khaen.* Such instruments may have been used by the Việt during the bronze-drum age, as suggested by engravings on these drums. But the Vietnamese *kèn* is a wooden oboe with a flared bell, resembling many such instruments distributed widely in East, South, West, and Southeast Asia, and even in Africa. It comes in various sizes, differentiated by name. The presto oboe (*kèn bóp*) is the smallest; the gourd oboe (*kèn bầu*) or wooden oboe (*kèn mộc*) is largest. The *kèn thau* has a copper outer ring. The presto oboe and the gourd oboe were used in court, theatrical, and ceremonial music in central Vietnam. The wooden oboe, an equivalent of the gourd oboe, is played in *nhạc lễ* ensembles in southern Vietnam, for weddings, funerals, and village festivals. The *kèn thau* (also called *kèn song hỉ* 'double happiness oboe') is a leading instrument of *hát bội* theater.

A conch trumpet (*ốc,* also called *hải loa* 'maritime conch' and *pháp loa* 'Buddhist conch') is still used in Buddhist music. It resembles the Thai *sang,* the Japanese *horogai,* and the Tibetan *dung kar.* It was formerly played in the Vietnamese court orchestra and at shrines to local deities. Water-buffalo tenders play a water-buffalo horn (*tù và*) as a trumpet.

The *kèn lá* is made from a leaf (usually a coconut leaf) rolled into a conical tube by rural children. To play it, they flatten the small end and blow it like a double reed.

Antiquated wind instruments include the *sinh* (Chinese *sheng,* Japanese *shō*), a free-reed circular mouth organ, and the *kèn đôi,* a double-bamboo oboe. The *sinh* was part of the Vietnamese court orchestra, and the *kèn đôi* was a peasant instrument.

FOLK SONGS

The Vietnamese term usually glossed 'folk songs' denotes songs of common people, especially farmers of rice, living in villages. Because of their isolation, their music developed distinctive characters according to their individual demographic, historical, and cultural circumstances. Therefore, regional character is a component of Vietnamese folk songs; it is also manifested in regional dialects, tonal systems, metaphors, legends, and poetry. Folk songs include lullabies, work songs, and entertainment songs. Regional accents are a major factor in localizing singing customs. There are five primary linguistic areas among the Việt: North (or northern delta of the Hồng [Red] River), North-Central (Thanh-Nghệ-Tĩnh area), Central (Bình-Trị-Thiên area), South-Central (Quảng-Nam and Bình-Định area), and South. Consequently, no single type of folk song represents all of Vietnam. The distinctiveness of these areas results from patterns of migration for several thousand years. After Vietnamese civilization had been established in the Red River delta, immigration proceeded, especially after the 1500s, to the central and southern regions. In time,

> Folk songs occur not inside a temple but in its yard or surrounding grounds, because those areas are thought more appropriate for songs that involve games and amorous themes.

the original songs were transformed by the developing linguistic distinctness of the central and southern areas, and the songs of each area became more and more individualized.

Folk songs are sung at seasonal festivals, at work, and at private gatherings. The term *lễ hội* denotes festivals involving not only music, songs, and dances, but also ceremonial and ritual activities. Folk songs occur during *lễ hội*, not inside a temple but in its yard or surrounding grounds, because those areas are thought more appropriate for songs that involve games and amorous themes. Occupational songs mirror the work of people sharing the same job who need either encouragement or entertainment; in these cases, rhythm plays an important role, as diversion or competition. At private gatherings, songs are sung for fun, whether as diversion or competition.

Though there are different singing styles in different places in Vietnam, one rule governs all sung performances (*cuộc hát,* or *canh hát* if it lasts all night). The rule is that the singing should occur in three distinct stages: greeting songs, main or contesting songs, and farewell songs. Several minority ethnic groups also follow this pattern, which serves to socialize by assuring that people get acquainted, encourages the alternation of songs between males and females, and provides a plan by which songs can be developed. As tunes are introduced, they become more complex in linguistic intonation and modal idiom. Most Vietnamese folk songs are performed in an alternating or antiphonal pattern (*hát đối*).

A rich terminology differentiates songs by thematic, melodic, rhythmic, functional, and geographical usages. Accordingly, any Vietnamese province usually has more than one specific kind of folk song. Indeed, with folk songs, no term equivalent to "to sing" is usable for all occasions or all styles; rather, there are myriad, clearly defined terms for each kind or style of singing. The following terms are essential.

Hát

1. *Hát* is a general term for 'singing' and 'acting'. In the northern and north-central regions, the first definition commonly applies. Hence genres there are called *hát xoan, hát ghẹo, hát trống quân* (Vĩnh Phú Province), *hát quan họ* (Hà Bắc Province, figure 26), *hát ví, hát dặm, hát phường vải* (Nghệ Tĩnh Province), and *hát đúm* (Hải Dương Province). Some are sung during special seasons of the lunar year, others at work or on social occasions. *Hát xoan* (the term *xoan* derives from *xuân* 'spring') are sung during spring festivals in Vĩnh Phú Province, the heartland of the Việt people. Like many other kinds of folk songs, *xoan* (a shortened form of *hát xoan*) are associated with specific customs and ceremonies. *Xoan* are not solely a singing activity; rather, their performance includes a mix of chanted poetry, drumming, acting, and dancing. Performers, in groups of ten to fifteen, perform songs and dances with themes relating to love, ritual (showing respect to local deities), riddles, and occupations.

FIGURE 26 Two men and two women sing *quan họ* on a boat in Bắc Ninh Province. Photo by Phong T. Nguyễn.

Quan họ

Quan họ (a shortened form of *hát quan họ*), an antiphonal song, is heard during the spring and fall, when pairs of men and women sing in alternation. The Lim Village Festival, which begins on the thirteenth day of the first lunar month and lasts for several days, is the most popular time for singing *quan họ*. This festival boasts music, wrestling, cockfighting, rituals, and processions. But *quan họ* are not included in the ceremonies; they are performed in the yard of the temple, in houses, on hills, or on boats. Competitive songs of love are sung all night between teams from paired villages: usually the women must reply, repartee fashion, to songs sung by the men; the winning team is the one that devises more ideas or tunes.

Quan họ culture involves not only songs of courtship but also songs devoted to social customs practiced in paired villages: friendship (*quan họ nghiã*), the paired village (*quan họ kết chạ*), worship (*quan họ cầu đảo*), and funerals (*quan họ hiếu*). The most curious of these may be the Diềm Village's *quan họ trùm đầu,* in which singers cover their heads with pieces of cloth or shirts so as not to see each other. Presently, the *quan họ* is the most pervasive type of folk song in Vietnam.

Hát phường vải

In Nghệ Tĩnh Province, work songs are exemplified by *hát phường vải* 'songs of the fabric guild'. Making fabric is a second occupation for farmers who have completed the planting of rice and are awaiting the growth of their crops—a process that takes several months. For their literary value, *hát phường vải* are also of interest to lovers of poetry and folklore. It is believed that *phường vải* singers were only women in the beginning, but as the lyrics became more elaborate, men joined in, permitting male-female alternation. Performances are hosted, at night, by a family whose head is a singer or who simply enjoys listening to songs. Though the assemblages are called guilds (*phường*), no director organizes the work and plans the songs. The members vary from five to twenty or more. Unlike *xoan* and *quan họ, phường vải* are sung by male and female groups with no set number of members.

FIGURE 27 Singers of a *hò* folk song in Bến Tre Province. Photo by Phong T. Nguyễn.

Hò

From Thanh Hóa, Nghệ An, and Hà Tĩnh provinces in the north-central area, the *hò* (pronounced *haw*) is the most popular type of song (figure 27). The term *hò* apparently designates an exhalation, similar to *hô* (pronounced *ho*) and *hố* (also pronounced *ho,* yet with a rising tone). Mainly sung on the water, *hò* are usually heard during work in the rice fields or on rivers, and only occasionally during work on land. Songs of this kind must include the word *hò,* suggesting coordination between singing and rowing, pulling or pushing a boat, bailing out water, or pounding on the ground. Some are unique to boating: "*Hò Kéo Thuyền*" ('Pulling the Boat'), "*Hò Xuôi Dòng*" ('Following the Current'), and "*Hò Qua Sông Hái Củi*" ('Crossing the River to Collect Firewood') of Nghệ Tĩnh Province; "*Hò Mái Xắp*" ('Speedily Rowing the Boat') of Quảng Bình Province; "*Hò Mái Đẩy*" ('Boat Song') of Thừa Thiên Province; and "*Hò Đồng Tháp*" ('Song of the Đồng Tháp'), "*Hò Bến Tre*" ('Song of Bến Tre Province'), "*Hò Bạc Liêu*" ('Song of Bạc Liêu Province'), and others of southern Vietnam. Most *hò* are sung in unmetered rhythms, but some exhibit a rhythmic pulsation. The latter is particularly felt when a song is sung in responsorial style (*xướng xô*): a soloist (*cái kế*) is followed by a chorus (*con xô*).

Lý

Lý are rhythmic songs. Distributed over a wide geographical area in both the central and southern regions of Vietnam, they embrace every aspect of Vietnamese life. Using many metaphors, they compare thoughts and sentiments regarding nature to the human condition. Flowers, birds, butterflies, fish, spiders, dragonflies, horses, and many other natural phenomena provide indirect, abstract descriptions of human love, including missing a loved one, waiting, loyalty, and longing for a reunion. Unlike many other kinds of folk songs, the lyrics of *lý* are not restricted to any particular age, gender, or period.

Ru

Ru, a term used nationwide, is a regionally typical lullaby. In nonmetered rhythms or with a slight pulsation, *ru* are sung by mothers, grandfathers, grandmothers, or sisters, who sit beside the infant's hammock and move it gently back and forth in time to the music. The lullaby is called *ru con* when sung by the mother, grandfather, or grandmother, and *hát đưa em* or *hát ru em* when sung by a sister. Usually, fathers and brothers are too busy with their tasks in the fields to spare time for singing lullabies.

Miscellaneous songs

The forms and styles of rural traditions are clearly reflected in Vietnamese folk songs. Most lyrics exist independently of instrumentation, most of which developed later, and they are little influenced by cultural exchanges with foreigners. Thus, folk songs faithfully preserve forms and musical thoughts that are originally Vietnamese.

Many songs are performed in antiphonal, responsorial, or repartee forms. Singers learned these songs directly from their families, mostly without written texts. These songs help socialize people, encourage them, and challenge them by requiring responses to each other. In *quan họ, hát phường vải,* and certain other types of song, tradition demands that people of both sexes participate in a performance. That a *quan họ* may be sung by a pair of men or women makes it unique in Vietnam: one of the singers leads the singing with a leading voice (*giọng dẫn*), and the other sings with an undervoice (*giọng luồn*), though they are otherwise singing in unison. *Hò,* however, are performed in a leader-group format, with the group including members of both sexes.

Folk songs are now the most collected and researched genre in Vietnam, probably because of governmental encouragement. Some studies have been extremely extensive. Even so, research on folk songs can never be considered complete because new songs are being created and performed every day.

Satirical

Vè are songs that convert various themes into metered humorous or satirical songs. They criticize people who display bad manners and behavior, especially local officials. Stories sung in the *vè* style usually consist of hundreds of four-syllable lines.

Wishing

Wishing songs (*hát sắc bùa*) make wishes on behalf of families on New Year's (Tết). Groups of professional musicians and singers, especially in Nghệ Tĩnh Province and Phú Lễ Village, Bến Tre Province, go from house to house singing *sắc bùa.* In exchange, the performers receive good-luck money from the welcoming families. Such groups in Nghệ Tĩnh accompany themselves with a gong ensemble, but those in Bến Tre use a *sinh tiền* and a drum.

Card game

Card-game songs (*hô bài chòi*) are specific to Bình Định Province. Early in the 1900s, songs developed from the singing of the names of playing cards in the context of actual card games and developed into an independent genre. Though this genre later developed into a theatrical genre (*ca kịch bài chòi*), card-game songs remain popular.

Narratives

The longest folk songs are *kể truyện,* narratives in poetry and prose. A poetic story (*truyện*) usually extends a legend to several thousand verses, often in six- and eight-syllable couplets (*lục bát*). In some places, *kể truyện* (also called *nói thơ* 'speaking the poetry') are chanted unaccompanied; in others, they are accompanied by rhythmic instruments such as a clapper or a drum.

Children's songs

Đồng dao are children's songs. Few children's songs consist only of singing; usually they involve a game or an educational activity. Children's games are musically rich. There are simple game songs like counting chopsticks, bouncing a ball, or throwing sticks, and more complicated games like hide and seek, drop the handkerchief, competitive swinging, and others. Owing to the tonal inflections of the language, many school lessons use singing to ease learning; memorizing a lesson by singing remains a common practice in Vietnam. These songs, in the form of six- and eight-syllable poems, use three tones.

CHAMBER MUSIC

The dissemination of chamber songs and instrumental pieces in written form, including a skeletal musical notation, is common. Special vocal and instrumental training is required for chamber music. These are but two factors that distinguish this genre from folk singing. The most significant distinction, however, is that chamber music requires the existence of literati who appreciate the role of poetry. The performance of poetry brings together musicians, singers, scholars, and connoisseurs.

A chamber-music performance is aimed at a select group. Dating only from the early twentieth century, these genres have attracted large audiences, particularly in the south. They are characterized by the use of narrative poetry, a specific order of songs or composed pieces, a predetermined combination of instruments, and a music theory unique to chamber music. Further, the roles of instrumental music and solo performance are especially important in chamber music.

Early forms of singing and dancing at temples, at the royal court, and at private gatherings were precursors of the present chamber-music genres. Traditional festivals and court presentations thrived in Vietnam from the tenth century under the earlier Lê and Đinh dynasties. The first music guild was created by King Lý Thái Tổ at Thăng Long in 1025. Soon these guilds spread to and flowered in some ten provincial areas, where musical training and nightly performances came to be organized on a regular basis. Originally these performances included dances and rituals.

Today, chamber music is performed primarily in private homes. In northern Vietnam on the anniversaries of the birth and death of a famous singer—one nominated as the patriarch of a music guild—chamber-music singing continues to be associated with ritual ceremonies at certain temples or shrines. Each type of chamber music discussed below possesses an individual repertoire and a particular manner of presentation.

Ca trù

The oldest surviving form of chamber music is *ca trù,* found in the north. Depending on its function, it can be called *hát cửa đình* 'songs at the temple', *hát cuả đền* 'songs at the shrine', *hát cuả quyền* 'songs at the houses of lords and mandarins', *hát ả đào* 'songs of Lady Đào', *hát cô đầu* 'songs of the elder sister', *hát nhà trò* 'songs at the performance house', *hát nhà tơ* 'songs at the governmental house', or *hát thẻ* 'songs of token'. These names bespeak the complexity of this genre's origins.

Vietnam suffered the mass destruction of its books at the hands of Ming invaders in the 1400s, but in one area, a few documents survived: the historical books (*thần phả*) of Lỗ Khê Village, north of Hanoi, provide a detailed history of the founding and early development of *ca trù* (figure 28). These books had been secreted in a temple used as the military headquarters of Đinh Lễ, a general under the heir to the throne, Lê Lợi. They were authored by the fifteenth-century scholars Đào Cử, Nguyễn Bính, and Nguyễn Hiền, all doctors of letters.

Many esteemed poet-scholars have made contributions to *ca trù,* whose texts are the most refined examples studied in Vietnam's high schools and colleges. The oldest

FIGURE 28 A *ca trù* singer playing a *phách* idiophone and a lutenist playing a *đàn đáy*. Photo by Phong T. Nguyễn.

extant text of this kind is a poem by Lê Đức Mao (1462–1529) of the later Lê Dynasty.

Traditionally, *ca trù* poetry, delivered more as chant than song, was performed in a sumptuous manner, which, aside from the main part's having a distinct chamber-music character, involved many instruments, singers, dancers, and ceremonial officiants. A complete performance had to include the following selections, presented in order:

1. *Giáo trống* 'drumming prologue'
2. *Giáo hương* 'introductory song for offering incense'
3. *Dâng hương* 'offering of incense'
4. *Thét nhạc* 'presentation of music'
5. *Hát giai* 'repartee songs by the singer and musician'
6. *Đọc phú* 'reading texts in prose-poetry style'
7. *Đọc thơ* 'reading poems'
8. *Hát tỳ-bà* 'singing the song "*Tỳ-bà*" ('Lute').
9. *Hát đại thục* 'song of Đại Thục'
10. *Múa bỏ bộ* 'dance of gestures'
11. *Múa bài bông* 'dance of flowers'
12. *Tầu nhạc* and *múa tứ linh* 'instrumental music and dance of four sacred animals'

The forms of presentation of *ca trù* are therefore extensive and complex.

From the 1700s on, a new style of presentation emerged: *hát nói* included vocal songs (as shown by the term *nói* 'speaking or voice related'). Nowadays, the *ca trù* repertoire consists mainly of *hát nói* performed by one female singer, one male lutenist, and a drummer, usually a connoisseur of the genre. *Ca trù* music is highly improvisatory, with few restrictions as to the encouraged number of beats and the encouraged kind of melodic variations. The singer (*cô đầu*) plays a clapper. Thus, the instrumental ensemble consists of three instruments: a trapezoidal lute (*đàn đáy*), a drum (*trống chầu*), and an idiophone (*phách*).

FIGURE 29 *Ca huế* chamber songs sung on a boat in the Perfume River, near Huế. Photo by Terry E. Miller.

Ca trù music uses five main modes (*cung*), called *nam, bắc, huỳnh, pha,* and *nao.* Performances feature a variety of styles, which include not only *ca trù* but other genres. There are forty-six separate styles of song (*điệu*). About eighty old songs are still extant, and lyrics continue to be written in *hát nói* style. The singing maintains principles of poetic, aesthetic, and musical performance by adhering to a complicated scheme of dos and don'ts—at least eight dos and six don'ts.

Ca huế

In the 1500s, Huế (then called Thuận Hóa) became the second cultural center after Thăng Long. It was settled by the Nguyễn Lords, a political faction that defected southward to what is now central Vietnam. During the later Lê Dynasty, opposition by the Lords Trịnh (north) and Nguyễn (south) led to remarkable changes in Vietnamese society. Cultural activities were particularly encouraged by the Nguyễns, and Huế therefore attracted artists from the north, including musicians, singers, and literary men, who supported music. Huế became a haven for cultured men fleeing the north. These men in the south thus created a culture, politically independent, in opposition to the north, which had imposed restrictions on the arts.

The genesis of Huế's chamber songs remains uncertain. Based on both social and musical analysis, they were likely a blend of both peasant and aristocratic elements. Consequently, *ca huế* performance (figure 29) may include both folk songs and songs with lyrics composed by scholars, mandarins, lords, and even kings. This music became a refined entertainment for the intellectual elite.

Because of natural and historical conditions, the music of contemporary Huế remains distinct from that of *ca trù.* Most striking is the linguistic difference. Like local folk songs, *ca huế* and to some extent its instrumental music exhibit a character peculiar to the Huế area and immediately recognized by Vietnamese elsewhere.

Ca huế is a composed music in which the number of phrases is fixed. The important songs of *ca huế* include a series of ten royal pieces (*mười bài ngự*). Among them are "*Nam Ai*" ('Lamentation in the *Nam* Mode'), "*Nam Bình*" ('Moderated Mood in the *Nam* Mode'), "*Tứ Đại Cảnh*" ('Four Grandiose Landscapes'), "*Cổ Bản*" ('Old Piece'), "*Lưu Thủy*" ('Stream of Water')," and "*Phú Lục*" ('Prose-Poetry Piece'). New lyrics are written with variations and elaborations based on about twenty original songs, which serve as melodic schemata. Some songs are preceded by a nonmetric, improvised poem in *hò* style. The songs are differentiated into three modal expressions: south (*nam*), north (*bắc*) or guest (*khách*), and Buddhist (*thiền*), which musicians and singers distinguish in performance. The equal-measure character of each phrase results in cyclical meter. Songs are organized into two- or four-measure phrases. Syncopation frequently occurs.

The ensemble accompanying *ca huế* is that of the five excellent instruments (*ngũ tuyệt*): a board zither, a two-stringed fiddle, a moon-shaped lute, a pear-shaped lute, and a three-stringed lute; a transverse flute can replace a lute. This ensemble plays alone at the beginning of or between songs. *Ca huế* singers, like *ca trù* singers, play a clapper (*phách*), but the clapper used in *ca huế* is smaller than the usual *phách*, consisting of a pair of hardwood pieces or pairs of handleless teacups.

As we trace this genre's journey to south-central and southern Vietnam, we see a pattern of change. Although the music of the south-central is region is somewhat similar to *ca huế*, chamber music in the southern areas shows a variety of twentieth-century changes.

Nhạc tài tử

Nhạc tài tử (also called *đờn ca tài tử*) may be translated in two ways, both requiring explanation: 'music and songs of talented persons' or 'amateurs' music'. Both terms express something of the nature of this music: it is chamber music performed by artists of great talent (first meaning) and not for profit (second meaning). It was born in southern Vietnam at the beginning of the twentieth century. Its relation to the music of Huế can be heard in some *ca huế* songs and *nhạc tài tử* instrumental pieces. Some of these songs were adapted from *ca huế*; others borrowed only the titles.

Before *nhạc tài tử* became an established genre, *nhạc lễ*, a southern instrumental ensemble for ceremonies and celebrations, had been created, based on the music of central and south-central Vietnam. *Nhạc lễ* likely began in the 1600s, when the region's temple festivals were founded, and the genre became the foundation of southern music, especially in musical theory and instrumentation.

TRACK 8

In *nhạc tài tử*, the role of instrumentalists equals that of singers. *Nhạc tài tử* has a larger instrumental ensemble than *ca trù* and *ca huế*. Instrumental pieces can be played either in ensemble or solo; therefore, singers and instrumentalists sometimes compete for dominance. *Ca trù* and *ca huế* singers are normally women, but in *nhạc tài tử*, both men and women sing as social equals. *Nhạc tài tử* has been transmitted through the publication of songs and instrumental pieces in books since 1909. The French phonographic companies Béka, Marconi, Odéon, and Pathé released recordings of traditional songs in the late 1930s and later.

The repertoire of *nhạc tài tử* includes both long and short songs. Some were adapted from *nhạc lễ*, *ca huế*, and other southern folk songs, but many new compositions exist. Eventually there were about eighty types of songs for which new lyrics could be provided.

A complex system of modes (*điệu*, also *hơi*) serves as the foundation for melodic development. These modes are *bắc*, *nhạc*, *ai*, *xuân*, *đảo*, *oán*, *quảng*, and *vọng cổ*. Consistent with the fact that improvised variations and elaborations are central to Vietnamese music, a *nhạc tài tử* song accordingly uses a melodic type as a skeletal framework. Each song has a fixed number of equal-measure (or nearly so) phrases. Variations and elaborations are left to individual singers and musicians. Full improvisation lies in the introduction of a song or instrumental piece. This part is called *nói lối* 'introductory declamation' or *ngâm* 'poetic chant' for song, and *rao* 'announcing' for instrumental music. When an instrument accompanies singers, both parts may improvise, though the vocalist takes a leading role.

The *nhạc tài tử* ensemble (figure 30) is thought a light and flavorful form of music, having clear precedents but changed from them. In contrast to *nhạc lễ*, whose sound is dominated by percussion instruments, *nhạc tài tử* consists only of chordo-

ca trù Chamber song of northern Vietnam, accompanied by trapezoidal lute and drum

ca huế Chamber song of central Vietnam, accompanied by string and flute ensemble

nhạc tài tử Chamber song of southern Vietnam, accompanied by string ensemble

xuân phả Ancient genre of masked theater from Thanh Hóa province

múa rối nước Water-puppet theater, found in northern Vietnam

FIGURE 30 A performance of *nhạc tài tử* chamber music in Hồ Chí Minh City, 1993. Photo by Terry E. Miller, 1993.

phones and one small idiophone, the *song lang.* The ensemble normally uses the same instruments as *ca huế.* Some, however, have different names (in the south, the classifier *đàn* is *đờn,* producing *đờn cò* for *đàn nhị, đờn kìm* for *đàn nguyệt, đờn độc huyền* for *đàn bầu.* Others may be added: a coconut-box fiddle (*đờn gáo*); a subordinate fiddle (*đờn cò phụ*) or a lower-tone fiddle (*đờn cò lòn*), a version of the *đờn cò* or *đàn nhị,* but having a larger resonator; and an octagonal lute (*đờn xến*). The *tranh,* the *cò,* and the *kìm* are the main instruments of the ensemble.

With continuity of tradition comes the phenomenon of adoption and adaptation. Since 1920, Western instruments have been adopted and successfully modified for use in *nhạc tài tử*: the *lục huyền cầm* derives from the acoustic guitar, *vĩ cầm* from the violin, *đại hồ cầm* from the cello, and *hạ uy cầm* from the steel guitar. More recently, *đại hồ cầm* disappeared; musicians thought its bulk and sonorities did not meet their needs.

Early *nhạc lễ* musicians set off a smaller section of strings and called it *đờn ca tài tử* or *nhạc tài tử.* The playing of music in the *nhạc tài tử* manner, according to elder musicians, was an addition to the nightlong performance of *nhạc lễ* in festivals and funerals. Intellectuals and governmental officials had a special interest in contributing to this genre. They were the amateur connoisseurs who wrote lyrics for songs or simply supported this art financially. Together they formed circles in Saigon and other cities in the south. The most reputed singers and musicians, coming from the Mekong Delta, contributed to the formation of *cải lương,* a southern Vietnamese musical theater that developed soon after *nhạc tâi tử.*

THEATER

Vietnam is particularly rich in the theatrical arts. It is an expressive culture with considerable contributions in literature (both oral and written), singing, dance, mime, music, and the visual arts (painted faces, costumes, props, decorations). The history of the theater parallels the history of the Vietnamese, if the earliest form of the bronze gong drums is considered. Vietnam's recorded history documents theater for at least a thousand years. There are six major theatrical genres and twenty-plus local folk-drama types. Though more may not have been described yet by researchers in Vietnam, currently available materials show that, within a period of thirty years, their efforts at collection have answered the most intriguing questions of these musical arts.

All traditional theater in Vietnam is musical. It is the most popular of musical genres. Its earliest form was probably peasants' dramas associated with traditional rural festivals. Formal theatrical genres such as *hát chèo, hát tuồng* (also called *hát bội*), and *cải lương* are the most famous elaborate forms that sprang up in the royal court or urban areas.

Like many other theatrical traditions, Vietnamese theater is associated with rites, dances, and folk songs. In Vietnam, this association may go back thousands of years, according to available evidence. The birth of theater in Vietnam is likely revealed in the form of theater called *trò* 'play' or *trò diễn* 'play on stage', still practiced locally and little known to urban people, whose attention is claimed by more extravagant kinds of theater. Important ancient customs involved *tro* as the main festival activity in two areas: Đông Sơn District and Gối Village.

Folk drama

Đông Sơn (pop. 170,000), a 7,500-hectare district of Thanh Hóa Province, is widely known for the discovery of bronze gong drum idiophones. These instruments are important as cultural objects to local people whose ancestors may have lived there more than three thousand years ago. The most ancient customs of Vietnamese life are found in this area, which provides data with regard to dramatic genres. Certain types of plays—some short, some long—occur there several times a year, once a year, once in three years, or once in twelve years. Performances occur in such sites as village roads, open grassy areas, boats on a river, and formal stages at temples of local deities (*đình*). Some villages have retained a reputation for executing complicated plays.

In Đông Sơn, traditional culture retains a great variety of famous plays and variants, including *Tiên Cuội* (*The Fairy and the Moon-Man*), *Lăng Ba Khúc* (*The Melody of Lăng Ba*), *Thủy* (*Irrigation*), *Tình Hú* (*Wow . . . Wow, Animal Cries*), *Trống Mõ* (*Skin and Wooden Drums*), *Chạy Gậy* (*Escape with Sticks*), *Tú Huần* (also called *Lục Hồn Nhung*, an unidentified country), *Hoa Lang* (*Holland*), and *Ngô Quốc* (*A Tribute from China*). In Thọ Xuân, a neighboring town, the masked-dance-theater tradition *xuân phả* 'spring town' survives (figure 31). It consists of five plays: three mentioned above—*Tú Huần, Hoa Lang,* and *Ngô Quốc*—and two others, *Ải Lao* (*Laos*) and *Chiêm Thành* (*Champa*). These plays, which originated during the Đinh Dynasty (tenth century) mostly show stories of the presentation of tribute from neighboring countries (Champa, China, Holland, and Laos). The Holland play is probably from the 1500s and was added to the earlier repertoire.

Dramas may involve up to forty actors and actresses (*Trò Hà Lan*), or even an unlimited number of participants (*Trò Chạy Gậy*), including, in Đông Sơn, children (*Trò Tình Hú*). The lyrics are mostly in poetic lines having four syllables or seven syllables, or in couplets having six- and eight-syllable lines. The plays have no melodic instrumental accompaniment, but a drum dominates them, with a gong and a clapper as subordinate instruments. Rhythmic accompaniment is of absolute importance in guiding developments in the play.

The birthplace of one of the oldest forms of drama, *hát chèo tầu* 'boat drama', is

FIGURE 31 *Xuân phả* masked dance-drama in Thọ Xuân, Thanh Hóa Province. Photo by Phong T. Nguyễn.

Gối Village 10 kilometers north of Hanoi. A performance commemorates the heroine sisters Trưng Trắc and Trưng Nhị, who led the Vietnamese to defeat the Chinese in A.D. 43. The festival lasts for seven days on a several-hectare field. Nine buildings are built for various rituals and music performances held in mornings, afternoons, and nights.

The main stage, measuring four by two meters, is made of wood in the shape of a boat with four wheels under it, allowing it to move. A wood-and-bamboo figure of an elephant mounted on four wheels constitutes a second stage, large enough for only four performers, two of whom play the roles of Trưng Trắc and Trưng Nhị. The boat follows the elephant in a processional performance.

The performers of *hát chèo tầu* are women. The central characters, played by women about fifty years of age, include the Captain (*chúa tầu*) and the General-in-Chief of the Army Recruits (*mẹ chiêu quân*), dressed in elaborately decorated costumes and hats. The Captain also plays a gong, and her two assistants (*cái tầu*) play clappers. The chorus consists of ten girls from thirteen to sixteen years old, playing the roles of rowers (*con tầu*). Like the dramatic forms of Đông Sơn, *hát chèo tầu* consists of dance, mime, and acting, but songs are especially prominent. Typically, a professional and respected singer playing the role of the Captain alternates with the chorus, accompanied by the rhythm of the gongs and clappers. The musical role of the main actress, the solo-chorus responsorial relationship, and historical links to traditional culture are important. Though the festival has music with functions embracing both religious and social values, concluding that the music has no value by itself should be avoided. Songs express pride in the Trưng Sisters' victory.

Hát chèo tầu is strictly associated with the cult of these heroines, who once encamped their army in Gối Village. A shrine was built after they died, and memorial festivals then began, as documented in rare historical writings preserved there. It is difficult to pinpoint the exact date of the beginning of this dramatic genre, but the heroines' acquaintance with the people in the village goes back nearly two thousand years. Music and ceremonies thus relate to the life and culture of the village. It may also be possible to connect this performance to much older forms of dance on boats, seen in engravings on the bronze gong drums of the Văn Lang period (2879–256

B.C.). Boat dramas, or to some extent, dancing with oars on the stage, are common in the Vietnamese performing arts. These considerations reinforce the Vietnamese view that the use of boats is representative of Vietnamese culture.

Most scholars agree that folk drama provided the fundamental elements in the gestation of dramatic genres. These elements include mime and dance, vocal forms and instrumental techniques, speech, and plots. Props such as a walking cane, a stick, oars, masks, a painted face, and costumes not only decorate the stage, but materially and abstractly guide all related dance movements. *Hát chèo tầu,* one of the important events of the musical calendar, occurs not yearly, but sometimes only once in thirty years. The number of years between performances carries a meaning. Some fifty other genres are now known in local areas throughout Vietnam.

Water-puppet theater

Water has been closely associated with the lives of the Việt since antiquity, as recounted in legends and narratives. Farmers of rice, used to working in water, bathe in the ponds in front of their houses, and children play with water and sing while bathing. Water buffalo fight in the fields, keepers of ducks herd their flocks home at dusk, a fisherman catches a large fish, a woman mills rice—these and other scenes are captured in local minds, and figure in the stories of water puppetry.

Water-puppet theater (*rối nuớc,* also *múa rối nuớc*) is probably unique to Vietnam. Its cradle was the Red River delta. It was, in the beginning, an art of peasants. Living persons no longer recall its birth, an event engraved in their minds as "from an old time." As recounted in rare historical books of saints (*thần tích*) or legends heard in Bò Dương, Gia Lộc, and Phú Đa (villages of Thái Bình Province), water-puppet theater came into existence sometime before the sixth century.

This art did not remain within village boundaries. In content, it has always been inclined to innovation: new stories and techniques have been added. Not only ponds but rivers could serve for performances. From the tenth century, the genre became a royal entertainment for kings' birthdays.

The puppets (*con rối*) are carved from a light wood, ranging from 30 to 60 centimeters high. Depending on the story, puppets are painted with an assortment of colors in the forms of a man, a woman, a child, a fairy, an animal, and many other stock types. Puppeteers standing in water behind a screen manipulate them using an intricate mechanism of underwater rods. One stick may control one or more puppets. A stick can move a simple puppet in and out of the water, but it requires both movable parts of the puppet and a complicated mechanism on the stick to manipulate a swimming fish, a dancing dragon, a phoenix, a lion, or a fairy. Sometimes the puppet is fixed onto a turnable disc with additional mechanisms—smaller rods, ropes, or wheels (figure 32).

Puppeteers remain behind a backdrop, a thin bamboo frame and curtain that prevents the audience from seeing them. Looking through the curtain, they coordinate all movements to make the story come alive. The puppets' dancing, acting, and acrobatics occur with music and songs. The show is not simple. The concept requires considerable training. The puppeteers in several villages of Hà Nam Province (including Đông Ngư, Nam Chấn, Nguyên Xá, Phú Đa, and Tràng Sơn) have become specialized, organized troupes (*phường*) possessing distinct skills and plays. Most of them keep their techniques and plays secret among their families, reserving transmission from father to son. They design the puppets used for particular plays. Therefore, some presentations are the exclusive properties of each troupe.

Researchers have collected more than two hundred water-puppet plays in Vietnam. A troupe realizes a literary work through a long, musical structure, a codified form of aesthetics in performance, the highly skilled coordination between music

In water-puppet theater, the audience faces the stage from around the lake. As many as fifteen puppets may interact on stage at once, making wonderful scenes of battles, fairy dances, boat races, or agriculture.

FIGURE 32 A water-puppet-theater play: *King Lê Lợi Returns His Sword to the Turtle.* Photo by Phong T. Nguyễn.

and puppeteers, the articulation of meanings, and reflections on contemporary society, be it village, city, or royal palace.

Singers and musicians present the melodies and styles of *chèo* in the context of *rối nuớc* stories. A small temple on water (*thủy dình*) is built at the side of the pond. The backdrop, representing the front of the temple, has one or two openings, through which the puppets enter and exit as actors and actresses do on a regular stage. The water surface in front of the backdrop serves as a stage. The audience faces the stage from around the lake. Singers and musicians sit inside the temple or on stage right, performing their songs and music, strictly following the movements of the puppets. As many as fifteen puppets may interact on stage at once, making wonderful scenes of battles, fairy dances, boat races, or agriculture. Usually, a performance begins with a flag hoisting and a greeting sung by the happy *tễu*, a smiling little-boy puppet.

Today, the art of water puppetry is included in the curriculum of the School of Dramatic Arts in Hanoi. Professional water-puppet troupes present this art in cities throughout Vietnam and abroad. For foreign visitors to Hanoi, a permanent theater near the Lake of the Restored Sword gives performances nightly; in Hồ Chí Minh City, the Historical Museum within the zoo offers performances daily.

Chèo

The term *hát* also pertains to theater in Vietnam. It has broad meanings: 'singing', 'singing and dance', and 'singing, dance, mime, acting, and music', depending on specific applications. Though the human voice is central to Vietnamese music, *hát* links singing with performative aspects that illustrate the song. In other words, *hát* may mean only 'singing' or some or all of the above aspects. This is illustrated by the fact that in other performing arts (such as *hát chầu văn* 'possession ritual', *hát chèo*

FIGURE 33 *Chèo* musical theater, *Quan Âm Thị Kính* (*Thị Kinh Becomes a Bodhisattva Avalokitesvara*), performed by Thúy Ngần and Vân Quyền. Photo by Phong T. Nguyễn.

tầu 'theater on a boat', *hát bá trạo* 'paddle dance', *hát ả đào* 'chamber songs', and many others), singing is not the only act. Probably because of its religious origin, singing has been conceptually central in *hát* from time immemorial. Therefore, many compound terms all beginning with *hát* designate theatrical forms.

Hát chèo, or, as commonly abbreviated, *chèo,* is a form or art born in northern Vietnam. It survives as a remnant of the culture of the ancient Đai Việt (a former name of Vietnam). Originating in tradition, *chèo* and *tuồng* were probably the theatrical genres held in highest regard by the Lý and Trần dynasties (eleventh to fourteenth centuries). A form related to *chèo* probably appeared even earlier, during the Đinh and earlier Lê dynasties, when the famous actress Phạm Thị Trân was nominated by the king as the National Heritage Lady Artist (*ưu bà*) (Trần and Hoàng 1964). Because satire was a prominent trait, this genre possibly underwent discrimination and was ousted from the Le court in the 1400s. The term *chèo,* besides its literal meaning as 'oar theater', may derive from *trạo* 'satire'.

In the 1700s, with the decadence of the Lê Dynasty, *chèo* regained its influence. Now a new generation of actors and actresses who had mingled with the peasants—even peasants themselves—saw social injustices happening in their villages. They created folklore-based plays that explored social conflict and humor. However, the long-term aim of *chèo* is social education. Most *chèo* plays depict successful persons who have patience, perseverance, studiousness, honesty, or rightness. *Quan Âm Thị Kính* (*Thị Kính Becoming a Boddhisattva Avalokitesvara*) is a typical example of this aim (figure 33).

Chèo is traditionally performed on a mat in the courtyard of a village temple, forming a stage having three sides open to the audience. The front wall of the temple serves as the background. This sort of structure allows the audience and musicians to interact with the actors and actresses. The role of each character, whether good or evil, is judged according to its social value, not according to the artistic skill of the actor or actress. The audience directs comments, exclamations, and answers directly to the characters: "Yes," "Can you behave better than that?" "No, you cannot do that!" or just "O!" Such responses are still heard in city theaters. They create a playful ambience and encourage the performers.

Makeup, costumes, and props are also necessary. Since *chèo* is an abstract theater, no scenic decoration is needed. The task of the actor or actress is to give the appearance of reality through acting, dancing, miming, and singing.

There are more than sixty *làn điệu* (melodic types) in *chèo.* New words are composed for each story. The playwright selects the songs, but the artistic director (*bác hai* 'the elder uncle') is in charge of creating the staged version of the play. Below are the main categories expressing specific sentiments. Other songs are classified as "various":

sắp	delight, happiness, or satire
sử	metric (*hát sử*) and nonmetric (*nói sử*) style for various sentiments
hề mồi	buffoonery
vãn	sadness, chagrin
hát cách	stylistic form, subtlety
lão say	drunk old person
sa lệch	love, sentimentality
đường trường	peace, remembrance, melancholy

Most of these songs consist of four parts: introduction, body, repetition, and conclusion. The introduction is often nonmetrical.

Dance in *chèo* is elaborate. It is associated with songs that include movements used to embellish, feature, and symbolize a character. A fan is the central prop for *chèo* dance, but walking canes, oars, and swords may also be used.

The *chèo* instrumental ensemble includes a small fiddle (*nhị*), a large fiddle (*hồ*), a transverse flute (*sáo*), a moon-shaped lute (*nguyệt*), a zither (*thập lục*), a vertical flute (*tiêu*), a three-stringed lute (*tam*), a dulcimer (*tam thập lục*), gongs, drums of various sizes, and cymbals. The drummer coordinates the music with the actors and actresses and leads the ensemble.

Hát bội, or *tuồng*

The "classical" theater of Vietnam is called *tuồng* in the north and *hát bội* in the center and the south. Spectators can easily see that the differences between *tuồng* and *chèo* involve costumes, makeup, props, and instrumentation. The songs and music of *tuồng* are based on principles different from those of *chèo. Tuồng* has often been compared with Peking opera (*jingxi*), especially for the painted faces, costumes, and gestures, but there are important differences between the genres.

New research has questioned the theory that a Chinese-Mongolian actor named Li Yuan Ki introduced Chinese theater to Vietnam in the 1200s. A soldier captured by the Vietnamese army during an invasion by Mongols of the Yuan Dynasty, he used to be considered the founder of *tuồng.* Newer studies of language, music, dance, and the principles of the genre show that no originally Chinese theatrical texts and music were used in Vietnam (Mịch Quang 1963). Rather, old Chinese stories have been adapted. They constituted a part of the *tuồng,* and required painted faces, costumes, and other conventions of Chinese theater that could not be replaced. It is especially in the use of colors, painted faces, and shoes that reveals the concepts that differentiate *tuồng* and *jingxi. Tuồng*'s use of Chinese materials resembles how Western operatic composers approached Oriental subjects (for example, Puccini's *Madama Butterfly*), in that changes express the culture of the borrower (figure 34).

Tuồng has three categories of vocalization: recitative (*nói lối*), modal songs (*điệu hát*), and melodic types (*bài hát, bài bản*). Recitative is a nonmetrical, declamatory style, used as an introduction or passage from one song to another. Aria is a metrical, narrative style describing characters' actions. The main style expressing *tuồng* traits is the modal songs.

FIGURE 34 Vietnamese classical theater (*tuồng, hát bội*) performed in Nha Trang. Photo by Terry E. Miller.

Tuồng vocal music involves instrumental music functioning both as an independent element and as an accompaniment. Instead of being based on melody types (as in *chèo*), songs in *tuồng* are modal, and the instrumental ensemble realizes a musical mode in an asymmetrical form with the vocal element as two independent units. The point of union is the mode, which contrasts *tuồng* from *chèo* and many other Asian theatrical genres.

The modal category consists of eight modes, representing eight modal sentiments (*điệu*):

ngâm 'declamation'	leisure
oán 'complaint'	chagrin
vịnh 'declamation'	solemnity
bạch 'exposition'	straightforwardness
thán 'lamentation'	regret
xướng 'announcement'	invitation, announcing an event
nam 'south'	sadness
khách 'guest (opposed to host)'	happiness, heroic character

Each of these modes has submodes, which focus general feelings into specific moods. The music expresses these elements of particular mental states through specific scales and subtle ornaments. For instance, *khách* may express the heroic, proud feelings of a general in *khách phú* (a song of half prose, half poetry), a military march in *khách hành binh,* or the soul of a dead general marching in *khách hồn.* The instrumental ensemble plays an instrumental piece in the same mode to articulate the sung poem,

nói lối A nonmetrical introductory recitative preceding the sung poetry of Vietnamese theater

láy Patterned documentation characteristic of *tuồng* theater

trống chầu In *tuồng* theater, a large drum played by an audience member offering praise or criticism

cải lương Genre of popular southern Vietnamese theater that developed around 1920

ca ra bộ Southern Vietnamese chamber music (*nhạc tài tũ*) performed with gestures; predecessor of *cải lương* theater

blending in the exact ornaments required. Both voice and instruments thus work together: the mode deals not only with conventions but also with individuals.

Modes in Vietnamese music usually involve several elements, including scale, a hierarchy of pitches, ornaments, melodic motives, and even rhythms. The *tuồng* artist must know how and when to combine conventional melodic traits with his or her vocal skill. Therefore, stylistic ornaments (*láy*) and vocal types (*hơi*) usually demonstrate correctly and effectively the meaning of words, the role, and the story. *Tuồng* is considered the highest level of the vocal arts in Vietnam because of the sophistication of the vocal ornaments, vocal timbres, and melismas for particular roles. In singing the main songs, actors and actresses must improvise according to the modal character. Few besides artists, musicians, and connoisseurs understand this art fully.

There are seven types of Vietnamese voice: intestine voice (*hơi ruột*), liver voice (*hơi gan*), cheek voice (*hơi má*), jaw voice (*hơi hòm*), head voice (*hơi óc*), chest voice (*hơi ngực*), and throat voice (*hơi cổ*). To visualize the abstract contents of a story, the actor or actress sometimes uses more than one type of voice.

Though singing occurs in a nonmetrical, pulsating, and improvisatory style, instrumental music is realized in a metrical, repetitive manner. The *tuồng* ensemble is composed of idiophones, membranophones, chordophones, and aerophones, but the primary instruments are an oboe with a wooden or copper outer ring (called *kèn bóp* 'urging oboe', *kèn song hỉ* 'double happiness oboe', or *kèn thau* 'copper oboe') and a drum (*trống chiến* 'battle drum'), which leads the ensemble with specific rhythmic patterns at the beginnings and endings of pieces. It coordinates the ensemble with the actors and actresses by supporting their dance movements. There is also a set of drums played by different drummers. The largest one (*trống chầu*) is played by an expert, representing the audience. He praises the artist by playing on the drumhead and he makes unfavorable comments by striking the side of the drum. Originally, this task was assumed by the chief of the village.

Because of its relationship with music for ceremonies and festivals, the history of the *tuồng* ensemble is lengthy. The *tuồng* repertoire consists of instrumental pieces, in four categories: overtures, interludes, accompaniments to dancing, and depictions of characters' emotions.

As with most Vietnamese songs, *tuồng* songs are based on poetry; therefore, *tuồng* is a type of sung poetry. The texts vary from four, five, seven, and pairs of six- and eight-syllable lines. However, the singing is not confined to the scansion of the poetic verse. The lines are stylized by the artists' improvisation. Figurative words (*huóng, kể*) are sometimes added to better connect poetic ideas, to rephrase, or to prolong the musical line.

Tuồng pho and *tuồng thầy* are long masterpieces, and *tuồng đồ* are short plays. Among the latter, comic plays (*tuồng hài*) were favorites of the Nguyễn Dynasty and were performed every night in the center of the royal court. A few court masterpieces continue for one hundred nights. A long story performed during temple festivals in provincial areas usually lasts seven to fourteen nights. This art was appreciated by aristocrats and commoners throughout Vietnam who share love for and excel in literature and music. It suffered a precipitous decline in the twentieth century. In the southern region, *cải lương*, originally an extension of *tuồng*, became an acclaimed modern genre in its own right.

Cải lương

Cải lương developed from *hát bội* and *nhạc tài tử*. Until the beginning of the twentieth century, *hát bội* had been the only major form of theater known to people in south, south-central, and central Vietnam. The genre underwent reform by urban artists and cognoscenti around 1900. Because of the adaptability of *nhạc tài tử*, musicians and actors of *hát bội* embraced this reform, which, they believed, could respond to the needs of the new social order.

As with other traditional forms of chamber music, *nhạc tài tử* singers had performed sitting on a wooden platform; but in the reformed theater, actors and actresses stood to coordinate their actions with the meanings of the songs, creating songs with gestures (*ca ra bộ*). In 1916, the first performance of this kind occurred during an informal meeting at the home of a vice chairman of Vũng Liêm District, Vĩnh Long Province. The first public performance, in 1917, was presented in Sa Đéc Province by André Nguyễn Văn Thận's *Cirque jeune Annam et ca ra bộ Sadec amis* ('Young Annamese Circus and the Friends of *Ca Ra Bộ* of Sadec' [Sa Đéc]). This genre then became popular throughout the prosperous cities of Mỹ Tho, Vĩnh Long, Cần Thơ, and Sa Đéc provinces. Three plays were acted by three performers each.

The landmark of the reform movement was the 1920 presentation of Trương Duy Toản's *Kim Vân Kiều* ('The Story of Kim Trọng, Thúy Vân, and Thúy Kiều'), part I, a long theatrical piece, by the actors and actresses of Châu Văn Tú's troupe. Châu Văn Tú pieced together songs he had composed earlier in Cần Thơ and crafted them into an organized composition based on the famous poetic story of the same title by Nguyễn Du, an eminent eighteenth-century poet. Also in 1920, the term *reform* (*cải lương*) was first applied to this genre.

FIGURE 35 Quốc Thanh *cải lương* theater in Saigon during its heyday, 1970. Photo by Terry Miller.

With repertoire derived from chamber music, *cải lương* was presented as a new form of expression, involving not only singing, but also acting and dancing. Only four years after the birth of *ca ra bộ,* more than twenty *cải lương* troupes were active in major cities of the southern region, supported by wealthy businessmen. Adopting modern techniques of staging and using new songs, this form of theater influenced many aspects of other national performances. Several *cải lương* troupes successfully toured the country. The French phonographic company Pathé began documenting them in 1920. After Pathé, other companies, including Asia, Béka, and Odeon, produced *cải lương* plays, and these recordings helped to popularize the genre and create a star system of *cải lương* singers earning high incomes. This movement coincided with a boom in local business: new factories and industrial investments appeared, particularly in the south. Between 1930 and 1945, many businessmen invested their money in *cải lương* troupes. In that period, at least sixty-seven major troupes were performing new theatrical pieces in the south, and three theaters in Hanoi and the northern provinces offered nightly performances (figure 35).

Unlike *chèo* and *hát bội* (*tuồng*), which use primarily Vietnamese and Chinese stories, *cải lương* adapted legends, epics, romances, satires, and histories, both of Vietnam and of many other countries—China, Egypt, France, India, Japan, ancient Rome, and so on. Its sets require decoration, scenery, and other techniques, as in Western opera. A performance features both singing and spoken dialogue, and though it has acting, dancing, speaking, and mime, the foremost interest in it is singing (figure 36).

FIGURE 36 *Cải lương* performance of a domestic, modern story, *Làm Trai Hai Vợ* ('A Husband with Two Wives'), 1970. Photo by Terry E. Miller.

Songs are based on the *nhạc tài tử* tunes, classified into modes and submodes (the latter called *nuances* by Vietnamese scholars). Special songs are composed for *cải lương* at the climax. These are not complete songs, but sections of songs, performed during specific moments as the story develops. With a basic melody and prescribed phrases, new words express the moods of songs. Much as in the doctrine of the affections (in vogue during the Baroque period of European history), emotional states are represented by the music.

The intrinsic value of *cải lương* lies in how within a song there is a seamless flow between speech and song. Dialogue may be inserted during a rest, or between the vocal sections. The most important type of this genre is *vọng cổ* 'longing for the past', a phenomenon that developed from ordinary Vietnamese music. The first song of this type, "*Dạ Cổ Hoài Lang*" ('Thinking of My Husband on Hearing the Sounds of the Night Drum'), was composed by a *nhạc lễ* musician in 1918. It became popular in traditional private and public performances. The original version consisted of twenty two-measure phrases, each of which eventually increased to four measures. The song was used as a basis for multiple versions and variations. In some cases, each phrase was extended from four to eight measures with a section containing sixteen, thirty-two, or sixty-four measures. Later, though rare, *vọng cổ* has been performed with doubled measures; therefore, each section comprises 128 measures, providing a challenge for musicians and singers to create new ways of performing it—creating new texts, inventing new melodic phrases and tunings, and inventing elaborate techniques (figure 37).

Besides *vọng cổ,* about sixty-seven melodies are available for use in theatrical pieces. As in much Vietnamese theatrical music, a recitative, nonmetric style also exists. The best known are introductory recitative (*nói lối*) and sung poetry (*ngâm*). These terms, used in many regional genres, represent various concepts and definitions. The *nói lối,* most frequently applied in *cải lương* and *nhạc tài tử,* is half spoken, half sung, and precedes the *vọng cổ* song; however, singing in *ngâm* style, as a short song, may also occur here. The melodic types, either derived from folk songs and chamber songs or newly composed, are classified according to the modes found in *nhạc tài tử.* These modes are *bắc, ai, ai-oán, oán, đảo, xuân, nhạc,* and *vọng cổ.*

Cải lương emphasizes singing, and the instrumental accompaniment consists predominantly of stringed instruments. A few percussion instruments are used occasionally in a play. Unlike other traditional theatrical forms, *cải lương* also employs a Western band (guitar, electric bass, saxophone, trumpet, synthesizer, drums), played during the introduction, interludes, intermissions, and/or conclusions of a performance. This band, which does not accompany the traditional songs, plays popular

FIGURE 37 The song "*Dạ Cổ Hoài Lang*" ('Thinking of My Husband on Hearing the Sounds of the Night Drum'). Recorded by Stephen Addiss; transcribed by Phong T. Nguyễn.

tunes, improvises collectively, or plays loud chords to enhance the drama's climax, taking the place of traditional percussion instruments, rarely used today. A foot clapper (*song lang*) is still used with the strings.

Cải lương came to permeate the country as *tuồng* once did. In the far north, it proved a success into the 1930s. Nevertheless, a Vietnamese proverb states: "prosperity engenders decadence"; therefore, despite its success, *cải lương* appears to have illustrated this maxim. In the 1970s, a saturation of randomly selected topics and themes, with an abuse of modern technology, led to a swift decline for this art; in addition, the war and its consequences played a role in its destruction. Today's *cải lương*, as seen in Hồ Chí Minh City, consists of newly written, fantasylike plays, performed for small audiences in rundown theaters by young and lightly skilled performers.

Apart from theatrical stage performances, most dances are performed as part of the yearly cycle of festivals—Buddhist, folk, ritual—and take place in temple yards.

Hát bài chòi

The origin and development of *hát bài chòi* (or *bài chòi*) followed a pattern common to several kinds of Vietnamese theater. The type most similar is *ca ra bộ*, derived from a folk-riddle game (*hô thai*) in which pairs of verses were sung during the spring festival. An elaboration was made with longer poems (*bài chòi câu*), and then a poetic story (*bài chòi truyện*) was created. In 1933 and 1934, this evolved into *hát bài chòi* in Bình Định Province.

Originally *bài chòi* meant 'card game in huts'. The game is played in nine huts built in a circle. The player in each hut has three cards, each containing different two-word names. Eventually the person who calls the names written on these cards (*anh hiệu*) began to sing them. This game continues, but the singing evolved into a form of theater. The development of *hát bài chòi* likely proceeded in four steps, emerging from performances on the ground to a raised stage (*từ đất lên dàn*): one performer sang and played a pair of wooden sticks to the beat; one performer sang and acted, accompanied by musicians playing one to three fiddles, a drummer, and a player of claves; a small troupe of actors and musicians performed; a professional troupe used stage decoration and lighting, accompanied by an instrumental ensemble. During the fourth stage, *hát bài chòi* was widely performed in Bình Định Province. After the Geneva conference of 1954, many artists in one revolutionary *hát bài chòi* troupe fled to the north. Thereafter, audiences in Hanoi and northern provincial cities had opportunities to watch *hát bài chòi* with stories used for political propaganda.

The general traits of this theatrical form are a linguistic accent of the Bình Định area; local narratives with thematic stories borrowed from other areas, including some from the Chinese; a repertoire consisting of four modes (*cổ bản, xuân nữ, xàng xê,* and *hồ quảng*); and an ensemble utilizing instruments of both *hát bội* and *cải lương*. Performers of *hát bài chòi* acquired many of their theatrical techniques—acting, singing, playing musical instruments—from *hát bội* and *cải lương*.

Ca kịch huế *and other theatrical genres*

A genre of musical theater originated in Huế at the same time as *cải lương*. Singers and musicians of *ca huế* chamber music formed troupes (*gánh*), groups (*đoàn*), and teams (*nhóm*), and in addition to their chamber songs, their performances included new versions of folk tunes, composed as elaborations of new pieces. By 1945, thirteen troupes were active in the central and south-central areas; they sometimes toured the north and the south.

In Hanoi and Saigon, French-educated students and literary men created *kịch nói* or *thoại kịch*, a genre derived from Western spoken drama. *Chén Thuốc Độc* (*A Bowl of Poison*), the first piece of spoken theater performed for the public, premiered in 1921 at the French Opera House (Nhà Hát Tây). Other stories, written as poetry meant to be declaimed, were known as *kịch thơ*. Most actors and actresses of this genre had been trained in traditional theatrical genres, which have large repertoires of songs. The performers found *kịch thơ* too restrictive musically and the acting too simplistic. As a result, they soon abandoned it. *Kịch thơ* was thus short-lived; however, *kịch nói* still exists, with a repertoire of several hundred plays.

Love of the theater has continued to stimulate the creation of local genres, which developed as earlier ones had. Following the example of *bài chòi,* some of these genres took root in provincial cities. During the early 1970s, a movement supported in the cultural policies of the former northern government (Democratic Republic of Vietnam) promoted the research and performance of folk songs, originally called peasants' songs because peasants had supported the government during periods of guerrilla warfare. Named according to the places where there have been traditions of folk songs—Nghệ Tĩnh, Hà Bắc, Vĩnh Phú, Hòa Bình, and so on—folk-song theater (*kịch hát dân ca*) was born. New words are written for folk tunes and to match their original moods, to make sense within the story. Troupes of *kịch hát dân ca* perform outside their provincial boundaries. Folk songs were not intended to be theatrical, and difficulties cannot be avoided when contexts change. This is one reason that this theatrical genre remains experimental.

DANCE

Dance is not usually a part of most public performances in cities today. Consequently, it does not stand out as an independent performance genre. For many centuries, a great number of its techniques, costumes, and metaphoric meanings have been integrated into theater. It is typically associated with instrumental music, songs, storytelling, plays, and rituals. Apart from theatrical stage performances, most dances are performed as part of the yearly cycle of festivals—Buddhist, folk, ritual—and take place in temple yards. Dance is believed to be one of the earliest traditions of the Vietnamese. Unlike instrumental music and songs, it has left a strong mark on the visual arts. This section surveys historical aspects and representative types of dancing, extracted from ceremonial and festival contexts.

In the first millennium B.C., dancing was represented in engravings on Đông Sơn bronze gong drums and other archaeological artifacts. Dance gestures of peasant and military derivation reflect the life of the Lạc Việt. A communal dance in which dancers move forward and back with arms outstretched to the sides is found on similar bronze gong drums in Laos and Yunnan (China). Agrarian work and martial arts were depicted in stylized forms in the arts of sculpting and bronze molding during that period. Occupational dances, sword dances, shield dances, musicians' dances (accompanied by mouth organ, drum, and bells), rowing dances, and dances in a circle were prevalent. The latter two remain in practice today in the region of the delta of the Red River and appear to resemble the original forms. As pictured on bronze gong drums, dancers wearing feather headdresses making a circle around the sun suggest both a circular type of dance and a cult of the sun. The most typical kind of dance is the rowing dance, still preserved in most ritual and theatrical performances.

Court dances

For political reasons, dance probably continued to be a martial art, as pictured on the bronze gong drums. The Sisters Trưng in the fourth decade of the first century used dance and martial arts to train their revolutionary army. In fact, dance was practiced by officials in the Việt government annexed by China. The historical annals known as *Việt Sử Thông Giám Cương Mục* described dances at banquets (1959:102): only the Vietnamese officials danced; the Chinese officials evidently did not.

Because of the destruction caused by the war for independence from China, the period between the fourth and tenth centuries left no trace of dance in the visual arts. From the eleventh century, however, craftspeople began to portray dance movements on stone and wood. Bas-reliefs in old temples in the delta of the Red River depict dancers as fairies and musicians (symbolized in Buddhist art). Dance evolved extensively in contexts among both peasants and courtiers from the tenth century. A masked-dance tradition, *xuân phả,* considered a folk dance, was named after a town (Xuân Phố, Spring Town) near the home of King Đinh Tiên Hoàng and was thus related to his court, in what is now Thanh Hóa Province. To these dances were added the roles of foreigners (ambassadors and soldiers) from five countries: Champa, China, Holland, Laos, and *Lục Hồn Nhung* (also called Tú Huần). The last name is unidentified today. The painted masks used in three of the dances are made of cowhide or wood.

Some kings of the Lý and Trần dynasties themselves performed dances at banquets. After the Vietnamese victory, these kings brought to Thăng Long hundreds of female dancers from Champa, a country south of Đại Việt (old Vietnam). King Lý Thánh Tông performed a shield dance at the Chăm royal palace in 1068, when his battling army arrived there. To celebrate the victory over the Yuan Chinese invasion in 1288, Trần Quang Khải and Trần Nhật Duật, generals of the Vietnamese court created the dance of flowers (*múa bài bông*) for a major three-day festival in Thăng Long. This dance has been handed down to the present and is still performed at local festivals in the northern region, albeit in a modified version. Vietnamese scholars believe dance in the Lý–Trần period resembled many genres of folk dance. The gap between the imperial court and the common people was narrow. This situation is often attributed to the prevalence of Buddhism, with its classless character.

From the 1400s, the imperial court elaborated on the distinctiveness of its dances by creating theatrical dances that eventually became famous. These dances included *bình ngô phá trận* 'victory over the Chinese invasion' and *chư hầu lai triều* 'foreign ambassadors visiting our court', created in 1456 under King Lê Nhân Tông. Đào Duy Từ, in the 1600s, choreographed new dances for theater, and today is honored as a founder of *hát bội* (or *tuồng*) in the Bình Định area. Upholding this tradition, the Nguyễn Dynasty (1802–1945) commissioned works for ceremonial dances at court. Unlike in previous periods, the kings of the later Lê and Nguyễn dynasties replicated the convention of the Chinese emperors, who did not dance.

The Đàn Nam Giao, Vietnam's 'Heaven-and-Earth Copulation Esplanade' at Viên Khâu (Round Hill, near Huế), built during King Lý Anh Tông's sovereignty (1138–1175), served for rituals and dances for peace once every three years. After being interrupted for about a century during the Trần Dynasty, this ceremony resumed from about 1403 to 1407. During the Nguyễn Dynasty, 128 dances were performed for it and other important events. They were divided into two groups: civil (*văn*) and military (*võ*).

The eleven prominent dances created for national holidays during the Nguyễn Dynasty are *trình tường tập khánh* 'prosperity wishes', *bát dật* 'eight sages', *lục cúng* 'six offerings', *tứ linh* 'four sacred animals', *lục triệt hoa mã đăng* 'horse-and-flower dance', *tam tinh chúc thọ* 'three stars' dancers wish for longevity', *bát tiên hiến thọ* 'eight fairies wish for longevity', *chiến đấu thắng phật* 'Buddhist dance' (also called *song quang* 'double light'), *nữ tướng xuất quân* 'lady general going to battle', *phiến vũ* 'fan dance', *tam quốc–tây du* 'three kingdoms–western journey'.

The number of dancers varied. Songs were sung in Sino-Vietnamese, accompanied by an instrumental ensemble. Other dances with folk origins were also used in some thirty court ceremonies; they include the boat dance, the unicorn dance, and the male and female phoenix dances.

FIGURE 38 A rowing dance (*múa bá trạo*) in Vạn Ninh Village, Khánh Hòa Province, north of Nha Trang. Photo by Phong T. Nguyễn.

Folk dances

Among the rural populace, agricultural arts and handicrafts stimulated the creation of several kinds of descriptive dances related to planting rice, plowing, fishing, rowing, sewing, making baskets, weaving, raising silkworms, and other activities. These dances are presented in traditional festivals. In the oldest region of the Red River delta, the basic techniques are holding hands in a circle, stretching and waving the arms, lowering the body by bending the legs, and tapping the feet. Other dances show agricultural work and other livelihoods: *mo* and *tùng rí,* which involve animal sounds, have a long history rooted in ancient times.

Because Vietnamese life is traditionally associated with the sea and rivers, many work songs and ritual songs and dances feature the gesture of rowing a boat while traveling or fishing. The most famous dance, the rowing dance, is widespread in Vietnam and is found in various contexts: folk dance, rituals, theatrical genres, and annual ceremonies for gods of the sea at coastal village temples.

Rowing a boat in daily work became stylized into rowing dances, like the *múa chèo tầu,* a dance even introduced to mountain areas. In an artistic realization, dancers in the *xoan* and *dậm* festivals can use fans to symbolize the oars. In the latter festival, the rhythm of the dance is less forceful than that in the original dance. The *bá trạo* is a dance related to the worship of gods of the sea. When a whale dies, fishermen move it to the shore for a funeral near a temple, where they perform a rowing dance meant to carry the whale's soul to the other world. Each year afterward, a ceremony is danced to commemorate this event. The dance is composed of thirty-two to thirty-six dancers, led by a captain (*tổng mũi*), who sings alone and plays a small single-headed drum while rowing dancers arranged in two lines respond to him. To entertain the oarsmen, a buffoon (*tổng lái*) plays the role of steersman and cook. This dance, widely known in Bình Định and Khánh Hòa provinces, has a variety of movements, including opposing, circular, and crossing lines of dancers. The main props are red and white oars, which the performers move up, down, and in circles. This dance is often preceded by two other dances: *múa dâng bông* 'flower-offering dance' and *múa siêu* 'broadsword dance'. The *bá trạo* is accompanied by an oboe, a two-stringed fiddle, an optional lute, and drums (figure 38).

Oars became a central element for the worship dance, which takes place every thirty years in the ritual festival of Gối Village, Hà Tây Province. A seven-day event,

Sisters Trưng Two celebrated sisters who led a rebellion against the Chinese about A.D. 40

múa bá trạo The "oar dance," associated with rituals of the sacred whale

chầu văn Spirit possession ritual of central Vietnam

rỗi bóng Spirit possession ritual of southern Vietnam

múa đăng bông The "flower dance," associated with religious occasions

FIGURE 39 A light dance (*múa đèn*) in Đông Sơn, Thanh Hóa Province. Photo by Phong T. Nguyễn.

it commemorates the Sisters Trưng. Many of its ceremonies include dancing, singing, and playing instrumental music. On the principal day of the festival, a boat placed in the yard of the temple becomes the stage for the dance. To the captain's songs, the oarsmen respond *hò khoan khoan hởi hò khoan.* A mime dance (*múa bỏ bộ*) with archery, weaving, and other actions, also occurs.

Many aspects of work are represented in other dances. Farming and handicraft skills are presented in the twelve sequences of the light dance in Đông Anh District, Thanh Hóa Province. Dancers carry candles in their hands or on their heads, dancing in twelve sections, eleven of which are accompanied by songs: lighting a lamp, planting flowers and beans, sowing seeds of rice (two sections), making baskets, uprooting young rice, planting rice, weaving, making clothes, sewing, and harvesting rice. After each dance section, the dancers and the audience interact in a question-and-answer process (figure 39).

The following dances pertain to the peasants' tradition: *múa chèo tàu* 'rowing dance'; *múa gậy, múa côn,* and *múa hèo* 'stick dances'; *múa săn* 'hunting dance'; *múa quạt* 'fan dance'; *múa đèn* or *múa đội đèn* 'light dance'; *múa đăng bông (hoa)* 'flower-offering dance'; *múa dâng hương* 'incense dance'; *múa siêu* 'broadsword dance'; *múa mo* 'areca-tree-sheath dance'; *múa xuân phả* 'masked dance'; *múa xuân ngưu* 'water-buffalo dance'; *múa chạy cày* 'plow dance'; *múa đầu rối* 'puppet-mask dance'; *múa xoan* 'spring dance'; *múa sinh tiền* 'coin-clapper dance'; *múa rồng rắn* 'dragon-and-snake dance'; *múa tùng rí* 'pole-carrying dance'; *múa bá trạo* 'rowing dance for the sacred whale'.

Religious dances

The rowing dance is also practiced in the boat dance (*múa chèo đò*) and within the possession ritual (*chầu văn,* also *hầu văn*). A pair of oars is used by a dancer-medium representing the Lady of the Water Kingdom (Cô Bo Thoải), the Third Goddess. In a possession ritual, several dances are associated with different spirits. Each dance is appropriate to the character of that spirit. Apart from the rowing dance are the sword dance, the broadsword dance, the torch dance, the stick dance, the flower dance, and other dances specific to this ritual.

In the southern region, the golden-plate dance (*múa mâm vàng*) is performed in trance by a medium (*rỗi bóng*), who sings and dances during a healing session. While performing, she carries on her head a plate decorated with a golden votive tower made of paper. Her skill includes keeping the plate from falling during the fast movements of her body and hands, performed to the rhythm of a drum and other percussion instruments.

The flower dance (*múa đăng bông*), presented almost exclusively in religious ceremonies, is an offering during possession rituals, Buddhist ceremonies, and even Roman Catholic masses. In Buddhist temples in the northern region, it is one of the six courses of offering called *lục cúng.* The court *lục cúng* was developed from this dance, performed by two monks leading the court performers. It is accompanied by a traditional ensemble, *bát âm* 'eight sounds'. Each dance is followed by a song sung by a group of monks and a circular walk around the Buddha's altars. It is essential that the dancers' feet and hands make complex movements (mudras), drawing the strokes for the Chinese character for "flower."

In the southern Vietnamese Buddhist tradition, the sutra-ritual ceremony (*kinh đàn*) is formulated on a similar basis, but its dance does not include offerings. The dance features up to twelve monks dancing while singing long sutra texts. Their lines crisscross among the altars, and their speed of walking is coordinated with the acceleration of the tempo.

In the same area are two other dances, *phá quàn* and *học trò lễ.* The first, a funeral dance, is performed by members of a funeral company before a burial, marked by a Buddhist ceremony. The dance centers on the theme of the difficult journey the funeral procession must make. The lead dancer uses a torch to clear the way around the coffin. He fights with a spirit portrayed by a face-painted dancer. The scene includes jumping, rolling on the floor, and hitting sticks. When this part ends, the moving of the coffin begins. Percussion instruments of the *nhạc lễ* ensemble support the dance. The same ensemble accompanies *học trò lễ* dancers in temple festivals in which offerings are made to local gods or goddesses. A line of dancers carries presents to the main altar, moving in slow steps. Each step consists of lowering the body and bending the legs, touching the floor with the right foot behind the left foot, and moving the right foot forward in a reverse L-shape pattern (forward, then to the right).

Theatrical dances

Dance is a part of all musical theater in Vietnam. Accompanied by instrumental music and songs, dances are symbolic, metaphoric, and expressive of the content of the texts. Two characteristic schools are those of *chèo* and *tuồng.*

Chèo dancers use upper-body movement (trunk, arms, hands, eyes), but *tuồng* dancers emphasize steps and balance their limbs in conformity with the martial arts. In each gesture, dancers express the meanings of the texts. *Chèo* dance is believed to imitate everyday actions, to contain certain rudimentary techniques, and to express in pantomime. During the past three centuries, *chèo* dance was formalized into three kinds of movement: presentational, illustrative, and symbolic. Because of an absence of scenery and props, a performer must dance a typical role: a student (*thu sinh*), a sincere, good woman (*nữ chính*), a bad, immoral, or sinful woman (*nữ lệch*), an old woman (*mụ*), and so on. He or she uses multiple gestures to illustrate songs.

Dancers' props include torches, walking canes, sticks, swords, oars, and fans. The fan, central to most *chèo,* symbolizes aspects of the character, such as shyness, subtlety, dignity, flirtatiousness, and lasciviousness. Holding a fan in her hand, an actress moves toward the center of the stage. The audience cannot see the character until the middle of her introductory song, when she shows her face and begins to dance. This procedure has a great deal to do with the artistic planning and socioaesthetic meaning of the art of *chèo.* It includes three traits: avoiding sharp contrasts, which might go against the social and behavorial nature of the traditional audience; having a song begin to tell the story because of the prominent role of voices; and later illustrating with a fan dance more about the traits and function of the role in the plot.

Tuồng dance adds to Vietnamese theatrical arts a rich terminology. Favored at the imperial court, this art is rooted in folk resources, and boasts the greatest repertoire of the danced arts of Vietnam. It was supported by scholars and senior artists, who devised complex training with specific terms and conventions. Numerous terms define dance movements. The main categories of dance are called movements (*bộ*). There are seventeen basic movements for the hands, ten for the legs. Some dances are performed in bare feet, others in shoes.

Dancing in *tuồng* is an expression of human feelings. Movements of the trunk, arms, head (including a hat), legs, and especially the hands and feet, in stationary and moving positions, convey the meanings of the plot. Many kinds of emotions can be expressed using the head and hat, feet and shoes. Anger is represented by the shaking of ornate items on the actor's hat, or by trembling shoes. The shoes are soled with wood and curved up at the toes to ease the making of back-to-front and left-to-right rocking movements.

Hands and feet are coordinated in a choreographic articulation that balances the structural design of the dancer's bodily movements. Therefore, professional instruction in *tuồng* prohibits performers from breaking lines of arm movement toward the left or right. The soft motion of the arms contrasts with the stiff motions made by the legs.

Dance is also associated with instrumental music and songs. Most songs are in poetic (*thơ*) or prose-poetic (*phú*) form. Speaking is also accompanied by strict techniques of acting. Solo pantomime assisted by the ensemble displays the talents of an actor or actress portraying a military man or a madwoman who, for reasons of extreme anxiety, cannot express himself or herself in words (songs).

About seventy nontheatrical dances exist among the Việt population. Some court and Buddhist dances have been revived. Other dances survive with difficulty, especially in urban areas.

RELIGIOUS MUSIC

Among the most interesting of musics in Vietnam are those associated with religious beliefs. Buddhism, Confucianism, and Taoism are traditionally considered the religions that have long influenced the philosophical life of the Vietnamese. However, the earliest rituals probably derived from animism, a system of beliefs later integrated into the present adoration of saints, gods and goddesses, and heroes and heroines who successfully defended the country from foreign invasions. Religions from India, the West, and the Middle East occur to a lesser degree, but Buddhism, with the most organized system of music, is found in more than one thousand temples nationwide.

The Buddhist liturgy

Through contacts with Indian and Central Asian merchants during the first century, those living in what is now northern Vietnam had an acquaintance with Buddhism, an Indian religion founded by Gautama Siddharta, or Buddha. Though Buddhism elsewhere in Mainland Southeast Asia derives from the Theravada tradition, Buddhism in Vietnam is part of the Mahayana tradition. The term *Bụt* (rhymes with English *boot*), derived from the word *Buddha* (the Enlightened One), denotes the most ancient legends of Vietnam. Buddhist religion, the Way of the *Bụt,* is associated with Vietnamese culture and music at all levels of society. Later, an equivalent term, *phật,* based on the Chinese pronunciation of the Indian name, was used. Formerly, this religion was considered the national religion.

In the second century, the first Buddhist community was founded in Vietnam with five hundred Vietnamese monks (Nguyễn 1982:3). Historical books provide accounts of the founding of Buddhist temples and translation of Sanskrit liturgical texts at the same time. Chant, a kind of heightened speech used to articulate the scriptures, developed early and has continued to evolve. Because Vietnam's Buddhism is Mahayana, its chant shares many traits with those of East Asia.

The basis of ceremonies is the collections of various texts: sutras (*kinh*), the main liturgical texts, translated from Sanskrit to Sino-Vietnamese and Vietnamese; poems

FIGURE 40 A Buddhist ceremony at Từ Hiếu Temple in Huế. Photo by Phong T. Nguyễn.

of praise (*kệ, tán*); mantras (*chú*), a secret language transliterated from Sanskrit; and short phrases and texts used in particular ceremonies. Sutras and mantras are texts commonly found in China, Korea, and Japan. The arrangement of texts for a service varies from country to country and from region to region, but the presence of similar texts does not necessarily indicate the same music. More than thirty services and ceremonies are held in Buddhist temples, public places, and private homes. Any of more than three hundred texts may be selected for use on these occasions (figure 40).

Chanting and singing reveal the same organizational trends found in traditional Vietnamese performing arts. Buddhist music uses three vocal styles: cantillating sutras and mantras, singing poetic hymns, and mixing speech and song. In the first category, a soloist or chorus cantillates, with tempos regulated by the equal beats of a wooden slit drum. The term *tụng* denotes the chanting of sutras; the term *trì,* of mantras. The texts of the hymns may be sung in various styles, depending on the type of poem used in the service or ceremony. This category is probably the most elaborate in the Vietnamese Buddhist tradition. It has styles known as *tán* for songs of praise, *kệ* for daily hymns, and *xướng* for announcing the purpose of the ceremony. The last is responsorial. In other parts of a ceremony, *sám pháp* are chants for reciting the names of saints (buddhas and bodhisattvas) before one prostrates or bows, *đọc* is a reading of a ritual announcement, *bạch* is a statement of the reason for a ceremony honoring a deceased patriarch or a superior monk, *niệm* is a song for the offering of incense, and *thỉnh* uses solemn words to invite the chief of the ceremony. *Tán* is considered the most sublime style, in music and text. Many texts are poems composed by respected monks. Further musical subdivisions are based on the modes and rhythms used; an abundance of terms and definitions distinguish more than ten substyles (Nguyễn Thuyết Phong 1982) (figure 41).

FIGURE 41 A Buddhist chant, "*Niệm Hương*" ('The Offering of Incense').

Music may serve as an intermediary between the living and the dead during ceremonies and rites in which one pays respect and offers thanks to gods and historical figures honored for their good deeds.

FIGURE 42 A *nhạc lễ* ceremonial ensemble in Bến Tre Province. Photo by Phong T. Nguyễn.

Music, as generally understood, is prohibited in Buddhism. One religious precept forbids monks from listening to music made by those outside the religious community. To a degree, however, one can find a common thread of musical meanings and concepts shared by nonreligious lay people and Buddhist monks. In particular, monks understand the concept of mode. Music in everyday monastic life emphasizes the voice and allows only a limited use of Buddhist instruments, yet the *nhạc lễ,* the *đại nhạc,* and the *nhạc bát âm* ensembles are involved in the great ceremonies. These ensembles play during introductory or conclusive parts and accompany the monks' *tán* (figure 42).

Numerous percussion instruments are used in Buddhist temples. These include a slit drum, a bowl bell (*chuông gia trì*), a large bell (*đại hồng chung*), a small bell (*chuông báo chúng*), a large drum (*trống bát nhã*), a small drum (*trống đạo*), a bronze or stone plaque (*khánh*), a wooden plaque (*mộc bảng*), a gong, a hand bell (*linh*), and a pair of conchs (*pháp loa* 'the voice of Buddha's teaching'). Teaching these instruments is part of musical training in the temples, and it is more specialized in the temples of the *ứng phú,* the Vietnamese Buddhist school of chants. The concepts taught in this school were established during the Trần Dynasty (1200s and 1300s). The other two schools were *du phuong* 'school of preaching' and *tọa thiền* 'school of meditation'. All three schools still exist, though in some areas their methods have changed.

Like traditional music, Buddhist chanting varies regionally. No orthodox manner of chanting and singing is consistent throughout the country, though the methods of teaching and the styles of chanting are quite similar. Thus, performances of the

Buddhist liturgy conform to the regional and traditional traits of Vietnamese music. Buddhist influence is not limited to the boundaries of temple compounds and to communities of monks and laymen: it has spread to other religious systems, such as local cults and newer sects; however, in these contexts, there are differences from mainstream philosophy.

Other religious music

Though certain other religious traditions in Vietnam may be wealthier, none has as many followers or as long a history as Buddhism. Chinese Confucianism and Taoism have influenced Vietnamese morality and spirituality more than its music. Their rituals in Vietnam appear more as an amalgamation of traditional rituals than as a reflection of Chinese culture. Ancient religious beliefs native to the Vietnamese constitute a collection of ideas around the commonality that human souls survive death. Music may be used in healing rituals, ceremonies in which one asks for prosperity, or in paying one's respects to the dead during the funeral and at the tomb. Sacred chants are performed in myriad ways that have long been noted in oral folklore and royal documents.

The chầu văn *ritual*

Music may serve as an intermediary between the living and the dead during ceremonies and rites in which one pays respect and offers thanks to gods and historical figures honored for their good deeds. There is neither one god, nor one kind of music. Music and chant are made up of the essence of regional concepts and use materials available in a given region or village. They are entwined with local customs and rules. The *chầu văn* in the northern and central regions and the *rỗi bóng* in the southern areas of Vietnam are two of these practices. Since these beliefs consist of difficult and elaborate systems of myths and rites, there is no easy way to explain their music; however, it is certain that the music is strictly associated with rituals.

The *chầu văn,* one of the most typical religious sects in Vietnam, has many religious and musical practices. The most important instrument of this ritual is the moon-shaped lute; others are gongs and drums. In this ritual, a medium (*đồng*) is possessed by one or more of twenty-four deities. According to this belief, there is a hidden—but real—world of saints, gods, and spirits living in mountains, highlands, jungles, and elsewhere. Mystical, powerful, miraculous, and always helpful, they are worthy of admiration and honor. Though their bodies are dead, their souls are permanently alive. A child who died at a sacred hour might become a saint of this kind. He or she may come to help villagers when invited through a ritual ceremony. *Chầu văn* has two supreme personalities: Trần Hưng Đạo, a thirteenth-century general of the Trần Dynasty, and Liễu Hạnh, a sixteenth-century figure of the later Lê Dynasty.

Chầu văn temples are dedicated to these gods and goddesses, and to others. The temples are lavishly decorated, inside and out. The world of the gods and saints, centered in the praying hall, is much adorned. A possession ritual is organized on the anniversary days of important gods or on private occasions. A medium may be a female or male, who, when in trance, performs dances in front of the altar. A singer and some musicians, sitting on one side, begin to sing and play songs corresponding to the god in possession. Famous, standard texts are used in the rituals: twenty-four texts in temples for the goddess Liễu Hạnh and nine in temples for the god Trần. Texts of praise continue to be composed.

Chầu văn songs are sung in ten modes. Each is associated with a specific mood, scale, rhythmic structure, tempo, and ornamentation. The following is a general outline:

FIGURE 43 A *chầu văn* possession ritual singer and male accompanist playing the *đàn nguyệt* lute. Photo by Phong T. Nguyễn.

hát dọc	singing in free rhythm
phú bình	sung poetry: happy mood, metric
phú dựng	sung poetry: accent, rising tones
phú chênh	sung poetry: a moderately sad mood
phú rầu	sung poetry: sad mood
thỏng	additional, short poem: moderate tempo
còn	energetic: acceleration of tempo
sơn trang	clear, happy mood
thánh thượng ngàn	celebrating: fantasy
xá	Cantonese music style (of the Xá minority)

Because a ritual may last for several hours, the cycle of modes is performed consecutively, and a reprise customarily occurs. The last four modes tend to be expressed as fixed melodies, while the rest are improvised, by both voice and instruments (figure 43).

Vietnam has remarkable religious diversity. Traveling from north to south, one finds distinct faiths active in particular areas. Cao Đài, a newer religion, is peculiar to the southern area. Its liturgical songs, associated with traditional music, have not yet been studied in depth. Roman Catholic and Protestant churches reflect musical traditions derived from the West. Roman Catholic rituals were introduced to Vietnam during the 1500s by missionaries, and the church prospered under French colonization. Though its Latin and French texts were translated into Vietnamese, the foundation of its music was European—with tempered scales, harmony, and instrumental accompaniments. Culturally and musically, this church remains apart from traditional Vietnamese music.

MODERN TRENDS IN VIETNAMESE MUSIC

The twentieth century has presented the Vietnamese with new challenges. During its first decades, music came under heavy pressure from the cultural, economic, and political changes that had begun in late nineteenth-century Vietnam. Colonization and the contacts with Western culture that resulted from it were prominent in driving these changes.

Settings

Before 1900, Vietnam had experienced four centuries of exposure to European culture, first from Roman Catholic missionaries and then through French colonialism. The first attempt to introduce Roman Catholicism into Vietnam began about 1533, with visits by Dominican missionaries (Phan 1961:32). Their efforts were unsuccessful until 1625, when their activities became systematically intensified through their connection with an established base in the Portuguese enclave of Macau. Italian, Portuguese, Spanish, French, and Japanese Jesuit priests visited Vietnam during the north-south division (1500s to 1700s) under the Trịnh and Nguyễn lords, respectively. Parallel to their task of evangelization, these priests studied Vietnamese language, geography, history, and customs. The results of their studies appeared in journals and books published in romanized Vietnamese, Latin, and Portuguese in Rome. In collaboration with Vietnamese Roman Catholics, they created the system of romanization still used for Vietnamese.

Soon after Lord Trịnh Tráng (reigned 1623–1657) sent a letter to Pope Urban VIII praising the cooperation of the Roman Catholic Church, political incidents and cultural misunderstandings disrupted Vietnam's relationship with the church. Persecutions began in the 1800s. Some high-ranking Roman Catholic missionaries with a good knowledge of Vietnam collaborated with French colonial forces as intermediaries or political advisers in planning an invasion. The pretext for this act was to be the protection of their religious men. After decades of bloody fighting, during which the Vietnamese goal of independence failed, the treaties of 25 August 1883 and 6 June 1884 were signed, and France forced the Nguyễn Dynasty to accept the status of protectorate of France. This arrangement led to broad social changes that affected all aspects of Vietnamese life, including the country's cultural, educational, and political affairs.

Early European musical influence

In the 1500s, Latin masses were likely sung by European priests, and possibly by Vietnamese followers. There is, however, reason to believe that no Roman Catholic chant in the Vietnamese language was performed until about 1648, the year in which a baptismal text was created and approved. The first manuscript had been drafted in 1645. Fourteen Vietnamese Catholics whose names appeared in the final text showed their agreement on the application of this service (Đỗ 1972:73–75). The musical rules remained European. From the 1700s, as church-state relations improved, this music expanded among Vietnamese Roman Catholic communities, and more than three hundred thousand Vietnamese converted to Roman Catholicism. In the southern part of the country, there were about three hundred churches (Phan 1961:41–43).

During the colonial period, Western music was taught only in Roman Catholic churches and French schools. This training was offered only for religious usage and to schoolchildren. The general public also heard Western music in military bands, nightclubs, classical-music concerts, and other forms of entertainment for French colonial administrators and their army. The Vietnamese, including those who served the colonial government, remained a passive audience until the 1910s, when a group of them became involved in the movement for reform and modernization, which strove for social and economic changes resembling those sought in other Asian countries at the time. These changes massively and deeply affected Vietnamese music and culture.

Reform

Early in the twentieth century, some Vietnamese worried that their traditional music

bài ta theo điệu tây French-style songs with Vietnamese lyrics, popular in the 1930s

nhạc cải cách Early form of Vietnamese popular music from the late 1930s

nhạc tiền chiến Romantic songs of the 1940s, inspired by German lieder

nhạc cải biên Modernize traditional music, inspired by foreign socialist needs

was becoming extinct. With colonial music pervading society, some sought a remedy in reform. From their efforts sprang musically innovative movements.

In the beginning *reform, renovation,* and *innovation* became the key terms for change in traditional music and theater. During this period appeared three terms that require our attention in surveying music in twentieth-century Vietnam: *cải lương* 'reform, renovation', *cải cách* 'modernization', and *cải biên* 'revision, rearrangement'. There was also a more radical expression, *văn minh* 'civilized, progressed'.

In Haiphong and Hanoi in 1914, *chèo* gave rise to progressive *chèo* (*chèo văn minh*). In the south in 1918, a new musical theatrical genre, *cải lương,* grew from the roots of chamber music (*nhạc tài tử*), while classical theater (*hát bội, tuồng*) was also affected by the obsession for reform. These were followed by reformed *chèo* (*chèo cải lương*) in 1923 in the north. Other changes in *hát bội* (*tuồng*) also occurred from 1917 to 1940. These included the adaption of Pierre Corneille's *Le Cid,* transformed into *Lộ Địch* or *Rodrige* (the name of the principal character in the play) by the celebrated playwright-scholar-official Ưng Bình Thúc Gịa in 1936.

Because musical theater was the most popular form of public entertainment in Vietnam, changes stimulated by the reform movement during the first quarter of the twentieth century most affected the abovementioned theatrical types. Reform affected theater in complex ways, including how songs were composed and rearranged, gaining control over the traditional spontaneity of spoken response by scripting it, adding instruments, adding newly adapted stories, and modifying stage techniques (such as curtains, scenery, lighting, sound amplification, and costumes) in the direction of Western opera or operetta. These changes did not occur in all forms of theater.

The invention of new instruments and modifications to traditional instruments occurred not only in musical theater, but also in traditional ensembles. Ten new instruments, including zithers, lutes, and fiddles, were derived from extant traditional or Western instruments. Three Western instruments, the acoustic guitar, the violin, and the steel guitar, were adopted into the *nhạc tài tử* ensemble. Southern musicians during the 1930s briefly used mandolins to play *vọng cổ* style with the tunings *bạc liêu* (C–F–c–g) and *rạch gía* (C–G–d–a), named after the southernmost provinces (Trần 1962:180). The guitar, however, remains a favorite instrument in *nhạc tài tử* and *cải lương.* It shows how a foreign instrument can be adapted to play Vietnamese music. The wood of the neck between the frets is scooped out to ease the deep pressing on the strings necessary for Vietnamese music. The strings are more pliable than regular ones, and they are tuned differently from Western standards in any of several tunings (Bamman 1991). Currently, an electric version of this guitar has become prevalent. Like the mandolin, the cello enjoyed only a brief vogue.

In the early 1930s, Thái Thị Lang, a close friend of the French composer Henri Tomasi (1901–1971), studied and performed music in Paris, and thus became the first known female Vietnamese pianist and composer. In 1936, after returning to

Vietnam, she developed esteem for Vietnamese traditional music and pursued the idea that the piano was capable of playing its repertoires. Her attempts to realize these goals met with little success.

Innovations to traditional instruments—lutes (*đại ba tiêu* and *tiểu ba tiêu*), a fiddle (*song thương*), and a two-stringed zither (*trùng đồng*)—were credited to Trần Quang Quờn in southern Vietnam. The Khai Trí Tiến Đức Association of northern Vietnam contributed zithers (*thận đức cầm* and *dương tranh cầm*), a fiddle (*luyến chúa cầm*), a three-stringed fretted fiddle (*phụng minh cầm*), other three-stringed fiddles (*bách thinh cầm, bắng minh cầm*), and a six-stringed lute (*lục ý cầm*) (Thụy Loan 1993:112–113). These instruments remained little known and became obsolete a few years after their creation.

As opposed to the skeletal melodies indicated by Chinese character notation, a new musical notation, based on romanized Vietnamese, was invented to help students memorize completely detailed melodies. Teachers of traditional music created new tablatures and notations of pitches, some of which are still used privately or in music schools. One of the most widely known was designed for *đàn tranh,* combining both tablature and the names of tones, by Dr. Nguyễn Văn Bửu and Bùi Văn Hai in 1956.

Modernization

The process of modernization began modestly. After only two decades, it was a powerful force. French songs sung in Vietnamese were first heard during the intermission on the *cải lương* stage in 1923. Considerably popular in the cities for about a decade afterward, this type of entertainment gave rise to other urban fads after 1934. People in Hanoi, Saigon, and some provincial cities enjoyed playing Western instruments, listening to the songs of Tino Rossi and Josephine Baker, and singing French songs with Vietnamese lyrics (*bài ta theo điệu tây* 'songs in Vietnamese language with a French melody'), including "*La Marseillaise,*" "*Madelon,*" "*J'ai Deux Amours,*" the "*Chant du Marin,*" and others. Accompanying these songs were traditional instruments, though undoubtedly some Western instruments were also used.

A kind of popular music called modernized music (*nhạc cải cách*) formed in Hanoi in 1937 and 1938 with the creation of two groups of amateur musician-composers: Myosotis and Tricéa. A campaign to modernize music was triggered by Nguyễn Văn Thuyên, a famous singer in Saigon, whose 1938 nationwide lecturing tour was sponsored by the French Governor of Cochin China (southern Vietnam). Though Nguyễn's lectures were not fully convincing, this event, together with the advent of independent bands, signaled the beginning of the movement. Though the general public embraced modernization hesitantly, francophile Vietnamese viewed it positively, as a new expression of Vietnamese culture. Most of the latter, who represented the learned class, had been students at the École Française d'Extrême-Orient in Hanoi. They were confident of being able to create a new kind of music, blending European compositional techniques and Vietnamese lyrics and, where applicable, traditional melodic idioms. This music, however, completely adopted Western instruments, including mandolin, banjo, harmonica, guitar, violin, piano, saxophone, clarinet, flute, double bass, and steel guitar, and it constituted the first body of popular songs.

These songs do not depend on the traditional system of scales, modes, and contexts. Traditional music, according to the creators of *nhạc cải cách,* was "dissonant, monotonous, unchanged" and "if the listener does not understand the lyrics, the music alone would cause an incompleteness and boredom" (*Việt Nhạc* 1948:1:2).

The creators of this genre of song expended much energy on finding a way to "compose" such music based on their knowledge of Western compositional techniques. During the first two years (1937–1938) about ten songs were published, of which three were in French; about ten more appeared in the next year. From 1940 to 1954, more than one hundred new modern songs were composed. These songs were of many types: romantic songs, poetic theater songs, songs adopted from poems, Boy Scout songs, children's songs, revolutionary songs, and religious songs. Meanwhile, the government supported both research into, and the performance of, Western classical music.

Composers tended to follow one of two tendencies: romantic or activist-revolutionary. Romantic songs that flourished between 1938 and 1945, later called prewar music (*nhạc tiền chiến*), are still sung, both in Vietnam and by overseas Vietnamese. They were inspired by Schubert's and Schumann's lieder, the melodic style of Chopin, and other sources. Their composers had little appreciation for Vietnamese traditional instruments and melodies. The acoustic guitar, both portable and inexpensive, became a favorite instrument in many social gatherings and concerts where a piano was unaffordable. A few dozen professional bands were formed in Hanoi, Saigon, and elsewhere. Alongside these activities occurred the publication of the first music magazines specializing in modern music and intended to promote the movement for popular music.

Activist-composers belonging to various political persuasions began interjecting patriotic themes into their songs. Gradually they divided into opposing factions. First, the youth movement of the Pétain government in France generated excitement in the colonies. From 1941, many young Vietnamese men joined the Boy Scouts as a reaction against the perceived moral corruption in the cities (nightclubs, drugs, and other matters). They advocated a better and healthier life, and gradually invoked in their songs a sense of patriotism aimed at the youth. Finally, revolutionary songs appeared.

Several of the nation's anthems were composed during this period. The "*Marche des Étudiants*" ('Students' March'), composed in late 1941, which later became "*Tiếng Gọi Sinh Viên*" ('Call for the Patriotic Students') and later "*Tiếng Gọi Thanh Niên*" ('Call for the Patriotic Youth'), was eventually used by the former Republic of Vietnam after the time when B*ảo* Đại became head of the nationalist state. At the same time, "*Tiến Quân Ca*" ('March to the Front') was, as it remains, the national anthem of the Democratic Republic of Vietnam (1945–1975) and its successor, the Socialist Republic of Vietnam. Both national anthems were composed by revolutionists: Lưu Hữu Phước ("*Tiếng Gọi Thanh Niên*") and Văn Cao ("*Tiến Quân Ca*").

Before the Vietnamese victory over the French at Điện Biên Phủ in 1954, patriotic music in the revolutionary zone (the countryside) had been under the leadership of the Việt Minh (or Alliance for the Independence of Vietnam), in which the Communist Party was prominent. The first Communist song of this kind, "*Cùng Nhau Đi Hồng Binh*" ('March of the Red Army'), was composed in 1930 by Đinh Nhu. More political songs, mainly marches, were secretly infused into the cities to establish a beachhead. These were revolutionary songs, as opposed to those of the nationalist government of the French Union. After 1954, the latter government moved to the south and continued as the Republic of Vietnam, with support from the United States. Meanwhile, revolutionary songs flourished in the north and in rural areas of the south controlled by the National Liberation Front.

Western classical music

In 1927, the French administration in Vietnam created the Conservatoire Française d'Extrême-Orient, but this institution could not function and after a short period was forced to close. In the 1940s, a strong interest in classical and modern Western music developed. The first formal music school was founded in 1943 by the

Association for Music Studies (Hội Khuyến Nhạc). This school was closed after the reestablishment of the French colonial administration in 1946. During its three years of operation, some three thousand students were enrolled. A thirty-musician brass band was formed, followed in 1945 by an orchestra. During the most heavily attended semesters, there were 320 solfège students, forty-eight violin students, and forty-five piano students (Nguyễn Văn Giệp 1949:8–9). During this period, Western-trained pianist Thái Thị Lang performed regularly on Vietnam's radio system and in concerts with European musicians. Some of her compositions explored elements of traditional music; others were entirely new creations (Ngọc Phách 1948:9).

Interest in Western music intensified with the import of instruments and the study of theory, history, musical practice, and the lives of European and American composers. Concerts of modern music and songs were performed on stage and radio. News of music in Europe and the United States was spread by major musical magazines. A government-supported magazine, *Việt Nhạc* (*Music of Vietnam*), an official organ of the Ministry of Information, promoted the modernization of Vietnamese music in every issue after its inception, in 1948. Thẩm Oánh, an advocate of this movement and editor of the magazine, composed a wide range of modern songs. The first modern children's songbook was also published by composers trained in Roman Catholic institutions and based on works found in Larousse's *Collection Livre Rose,* by Janie Rice Bigelow, Rouart Lerolle, and others.

During the 1940s, an attempt was made to found the first National Conservatory of Music (Nhạc Viện). The founders strove to develop a broad curriculum that included the study of three kinds of music: Western classical, Vietnamese traditional, and popular. They wanted to emphasize Vietnamese traditional music over the other two and asserted that a student must know the basics of traditional music before choosing Western classical or Vietnamese popular music—an idea not followed by later music institutions. Despite nearly a year of planning, social and political problems prevented this conservatory from being established.

Music schools similar to the Association for Music Studies were established in 1956 in Hanoi and Saigon, after the division of the country. An extension of the one in Saigon was founded in Hue in 1962. As it grew, the Trường Âm Nhạc Việt Nam (School of Music of Vietnam) in Hanoi changed its name to Nhạc Viện Hà Nội (Hanoi Conservatory of Music); the Trường Quốc Gia Âm Nhạc (National School of Music) in Saigon changed its name to Trường Quốc Gia Âm Nhạc Và Kịch Nghệ (National School of Music and Theatrical Art) and after 1975, to Nhạc Viện Thành Phố Hồ Chí Minh (Hồ Chí Minh City Conservatory of Music). In the north, the School of Theatrical and Cinematographic Arts was founded in 1959 to teach traditional musical theater. The northern institutions offered thorough training to musicians, composers, and traditional theatrical artists, many of whom gained national recognition at two levels: Artists of Merit and National Artists.

Both composition and Western classical music performance were strongly encouraged in the conservatories. In the north, the composition of popular and revolutionary songs served the government's goals of supporting the war and building a socialist régime. Until 1975, the music school in Saigon was not ostensibly required to serve political purposes.

The Hanoi government received generous support from the former socialist countries of eastern Europe (the Union of Soviet Socialist Republics, Hungary, Bulgaria, Romania), China, and North Korea, allowing it to send many students to study Western music, including conducting, theory, and instrumental and vocal performance. Foreign instructors regularly taught Western music at the Hanoi Conservatory. Today, the current administrators and most instructors in Vietnam's conservatories were trained in these countries, especially in Russia. A smaller number

Cải biên is played mostly by young musicians and is distinguishable by their nontraditional stage manner, which includes costumes and starlike behavior. The music is amplified, and the instrumentation somewhat resembles that of rock bands.

of instructors at the former Saigon National Conservatory of Music and Theatrical Art studied in France and elsewhere in western Europe.

Since 1956 in Hanoi, there have been a large number of instrumental compositions for symphony and chamber orchestras and for solo performance. Composers Nguyễn Đình Tấn, Hoàng Việt, Nguyễn Xuân Khoát, Nguyễn Văn Thương, Châu Minh, and others have heard their symphonic compositions performed on the stage, on radio, and on television in Vietnam and/or in Europe. Đàm Linh, Đỗ Nhuận, Nhật Lai, and others have composed operas. Some of these works are purely Western; others combine Western compositional techniques with Vietnamese lyrics or melodic motifs, or use traditional instruments. Some compositions feature a traditional instrument as a solo instrument and attract the interest of traditional musicians and their audiences. Operatic works use Vietnamese historical or political stories. Combining different kinds of music on the same stage probably began early in the twentieth century in *cải lương*. Otherwise, concerts in the 1940s more likely involved three kinds of music, kept separate: traditional music and theater, Western classical music, and popular music. This mode of presentation persists.

Modern pedagogical methods and curricula are customarily used by all departments of conservatories, including the Traditional Music Department. Students at the Hanoi and Hồ Chí Minh Conservatories are expected to study the basic elements of Western music before further study, whether they specialize in Vietnamese or Western music. All portions of the traditional repertoire known to the teachers have been transcribed into staff notation and are consequently studied by Western methods.

The term *modern music* has various meanings in modern Vietnam. First, there are three musical tendencies in Vietnam: traditional Vietnamese music, popular music, and Western classical music. All involve Vietnamese musicians and composers. Western music encompasses both the classical European repertoire and new—primarily instrumental—compositions by Vietnamese composers. Among these categories, the boundaries between *Western* and *popular* are not clearly defined, and the categories share common ground. Symphonies, concertos, sonatas, and operas are understood as *Western classical,* even though new compositions exist, and some of them involve traditional Vietnamese instruments, but without the traditional conceptual and modal structures.

New "traditional" music

For several decades, the general governmental directive called "traditional but modern" (*dân tộc hiện đại*) has deeply influenced traditional music performances and transmission. Some genres of traditional chamber music and folk song survive in urban areas, but more common are hybrid compositions, mainly created by conservatory composers with training in Western music. The most prominent response to the directive has been the creation of revised traditional music (*nhạc dân tộc cải biên,* or

FIGURE 44 An ensemble plays the modernized instrumental music called *nhạc cải biên*. Photo by Phong T. Nguyễn.

simply *cải biên*), a new traditional music, which, unlike older types, uses traditional Vietnamese, "ethnic" (minority), and modern instruments. The former two have undergone physical and functional modifications to allow for virtuosity and the use of Western scales. The main purposes of the changes are to provide contrasting timbres and ranges within an ensemble (loud against soft, low against high); to combine instruments of different cultural and regional backgrounds; to explore new instruments previously unknown to the Việt (instruments of the minorities and Western instruments); to create a music that better expresses modern society (fast tempos, loud volume); and to perform new compositions that respond to current social and political demands.

Though *cải biên* is actually a modern genre, many official representatives of the cultural establishment represent it as traditional. Numerous foreign recording companies have sent recording teams to Vietnam seeking traditional music, and they have returned with virtually nothing but *cải biên*; consequently, many recordings of this music have appeared in the West labeled traditional. *Cải biên* is played mostly by young musicians and is distinguishable by their nontraditional stage manner, which includes costumes and starlike behavior. Furthermore, the music is amplified, and the instrumentation somewhat resembles that of rock bands, with drums in the back center and melodic instruments in the front. A bass guitar disguised as a long lute (*đàn đáy*) provides the roots of harmonically functional chords. Most musicians stand to play, unless the instrument requires them to sit. A variety of modified ethnic instruments are featured in new compositions. The music confines itself to dominant-tonic chordal patterns, is usually constructed in an ABA form, is metrical throughout, and allows little or no improvisation (figure 44).

Popular songs

Another kind of modern music is new music (*nhạc mới*), also called modern music (*tân nhạc*), formerly called modernized music (*nhạc cải cách*). This is today's popular music. With roots to the 1940s, it is primarily disseminated in commercial settings (clubs and restaurants), on radio and television, in Christian churches (both Roman Catholic and Protestant), and in Buddhist temples where this music is encouraged by the Gia Đình Phật Tử (Buddhist Families, a kind of Buddhist Boy Scouts). In both form and cultural context, this music defines a rather clear boundary between it and traditional music. Consider its musical instruments, entirely of Western origin: to accompany their songs, *nhạc mới* musicians use piano, electric keyboard, guitar, drums, and harmonica whenever financial circumstances allow. Solo and instrumental performances are rare in a country where vocal traditions predominate. The traditional and ethnic instruments of Vietnam are rarely used except to create a folklike

dân ca Popularized folk songs

quan họ Northern Vietnamese antiphonal songs for men and women, performed in boats

character in songs having indigenous traits. Western harmony and vibrato are commonly used. Gliding tones and ornamented notes may be used to realize linguistic patterns by composers who insert fragments of folk melodies into their popular songs. But usually this kind of popular music is rigidly fixed and almost always metric, rarely syncopated or otherwise rhythmically complex.

Its cultural message, as most makers of popular music put it, is not only "to be like people in advanced Western countries," but also, in this musical and cultural mix, "to bridge the differences between East and West." It closes the gap among the linguistic tonal systems of the various regions by using one linguistic accent, that of the north. With its use of ballroom (tango, waltz, slow, or bolero) rhythms, it can transport listeners' imaginations to the ambience of Europe or North America. With the expression of marchlike rhythms, it links people politically, in powerful revolutionary songs. To accomplish individual, social, and political purposes, it reaches everywhere in the country, affecting all social classes. The so-called progressive class listens to and plays this music, which they consider up to date.

The modern folk song

The modern folk song (*dân ca*)—a genre that no longer belongs only to workers, rural or urban—is one of Vietnam's popular musics. It is featured in concerts and is heard on radio and television throughout the country. Both traditional and newly composed but Vietnamese-style melodies have been forced into tempered scales and Western harmony. The potential of improvisation, ornamentation, and syncopation have been greatly reduced. New words have replaced the old. Popular folk singers are considered equal to other singers (including traditional ones) and are nominated as Artists of Merit and National Artists.

Dân ca is roughly the Vietnamese equivalent to the Thai *phleng luk thung* and the Japanese *enka,* newly composed popular songs derived from traditional styles but accompanied by modern instruments playing functional harmonies. In some songs, the instrumentalists accommodate singers by imitating traditional instruments and their way of following the contours of the vocal melody. In Hà Bắc Province (the birthplace of *quan họ*), a troupe of singers calling themselves Đoàn Dân Ca Quan Họ Hà Bắc sings *quan họ* on stage accompanied by modern electric instruments. While they recreate scenes of singing in male-female alternation heard in villages, they have changed the vocal techniques and have eliminated much of the competition to feature individual singers in the manner of popular songs. These genres—the Westernized *nhạc mới* and the Vietnamese-influenced *dân ca*—differ in text and style, but they dominate today's market for live stage performances, audiocassettes, and videocassettes.

In Hồ Chí Minh City and Hanoi, concerts of popular music take place nightly at major modern theaters and in artists' cafes (*quán nghệ sĩ*). These are often integrated into comic skits. A basic instrumental combo must include an electric keyboard, a guitar, a bass guitar, and drums. The acoustic guitar, used as a symbol of modernization, has been replaced by the electric version or by keyboard synthesizer. Electric-organ festivals take place annually in the country's major cities. Children participate in these, attracted by prizes. The Ministry of Culture holds an annual children's concert at the National Theater in Hanoi. About one of ten selections is performed on traditional instruments by teenagers. The rest are popular songs, Western classical music, and dance.

Dancing to popular music began in the mid-1970s in Vietnamese communities in the United States and Europe and spread back to Vietnam. During the 1980s, with the new government's policy of reform *(đổi mới)*, private businesses, including dance clubs and artists' cafés grew, and both are as popular now as they were before 1975 in the south. Karaoke is also widespread, from Hanoi to Hồ Chí Minh City and beyond.

As new technology has allowed the production of audiocassettes and videocassettes, the music business in Vietnam has grown, but compact discs remain too expensive for most Vietnamese. Audiocassettes and videocassettes feature popular music, *cải lương,* spoken theater, and traditional music. Much rarer is Western classical music, which, despite its honored place in the conservatories, is popular mainly among faculty, students, and their friends. Western classical cassettes, CDs, musical instruments, and scores are imported in small quantities. Popular music from the West, especially that of Vietnamese overseas, is mostly censored by the government, but copies are smuggled into the country.

The dynamics of change and the future of Vietnamese music

Regardless of the success of *nhạc mới* since the late 1940s, it remains controversial. Calling it modernized Vietnamese national music and universalism at the beginning of the movement, its creators were trained only in Western music, were associated with the Roman Catholic Church, expressed little respect for indigenous traditions, and had not been trained in traditional music. In the 1940s, their abandonment of traditional instruments and adoption of Western instruments sparked resistance, and even rejection, from many musically skilled people, especially traditional musicians, who refused to participate in the movement. A sharp demarcation was thus drawn, and this situation continues.

Despite myriad efforts to make *nhạc mới* a national music, its composers continue to have little knowledge of traditional music—knowledge of the sort that must be gained through experience rather than systematic training in essentials. In contrast, though traditional musicians were interested in some popular and Western-derived compositions, they have maintained reserved attitudes. Though they might be impressed by large Western instrumental ensembles, many traditional musicians—and perhaps many ordinary Vietnamese—have not seen the Western values expressed there as being equivalent with their own. To trained traditional musicians, the incompatibility of these systems is obvious. To them, the style of the modern folk song (*dân ca*) is of limited interest and provides little satisfaction.

It is difficult to define Vietnamese music in the twentieth century. Music has become a complex of types that can be viewed from different social, historical, and musical perspectives, and their contents and numerous conflicting conceptions symbolize the difficulties of interfacing tradition and modernity, leaving artists in a dilemma.

The intensity of musical change during the twentieth century easily surpasses that of the previous centuries. The adoption of Western music, the revival of traditional music, and the resulting rivalries are themes that run through the entire period. The Western impact on the world seems irreversible in many societies, and for

In the twentieth century, the processes of change in Vietnamese music have had to react to the challenge of modernization. Consequently, a battle rages between the old and the new, between tradition and modernism, between Westernizers and preservationists.

the Vietnamese, traditional music is facing the challenge of alien concepts and behaviors. To cope with changes in the rest of society, it has had to change.

Unlike some traditions in the world, Vietnamese music carries in itself the genes for its evolution—through improvisation, rhythmic vitality, individual creation, and social adaptation. In the twentieth century, however, the processes of change in Vietnamese music have had to react to the challenge of modernization brought about by contact with the West. Consequently, a battle rages between the old and the new, between tradition and modernism, between Westernizers and preservationists.

Comparing the current situation with earlier times, when foreign influences had less impact, reveals striking differences. Foreign scholars have often viewed Vietnamese music as a satellite or dialect of Chinese music. Seeing that many musical instruments and theatrical genres resemble those of China, they have argued for the preeminence of Chinese influence, ignoring the body of indigenous instruments, theories, stories, and concepts. Chinese influence was so pervasive because China's military superiority could keep Vietnam in subjugation, and the Vietnamese adopted musical models from the Ming court in the 1400s. Arguments were raised at the court, but the history inscribed in the royal annals reflected Chinese dominance by ignoring noncourt musics. But the annals include no evidence that Vietnamese music students studied in China or adopted Chinese theory wholesale. In contrast, twentieth-century Vietnamese students of music have studied Western music systematically in China, North Korea, and Europe, and have returned with attitudes that fundamentally change music in Vietnam.

Technology does not exist independent of the humans who create and use it. The same traditional musicians who reject Western musical culture embrace Western technology. The crucial issue today is how Vietnam can modernize without losing its identity. Vietnamese musicians and scholars disagree more about methods and rates than on needs for change and modernization, yet no one is willing to abandon the culture's traditions.

REFERENCES

Bamman, Richard Jones. 1991. "The *Đàn Tranh* and the *Lục Huyền Cầm*." In *New Perspectives on Vietnamese Music,* ed. Phong T. Nguyễn, 67–78. New Haven, Conn.: Yale Council on Southeast Asia Studies.

Brăiloiu, Constantin. 1955. "Un problème de tonalité." In *Mélanges d'histoire et d'esthétique musicales offerts à Paul-Marie Masson*, I: 63–75. Paris: Richard Masse.

Đỗ Quang Chính. 1972. *Lịch sử chữ quốc ngữ 1620–1659* (History of the romanization of Vietnamese). Saigon: Ra Khơi.

Ngọc Phách. 1948. "Một buổi hòa nhạc tưng bừng." *Việt Nhạc* 4:9, 15.

Nguyễn Thuyết Phong. 1982. "La musique bouddhique du Vietnam." Ph.D. dissertation, University of Paris (Sorbonne).

Nguyễn Văn Bửu. 1956. *Bản đờn tranh* (Music for *đờn tranh*). Saigon.

Nguyễn Văn Giệp. 1949. "Su hoat dong cua Hoi Khuyen Nhac" (The activities of the Association for Music Studies). *Viet Nhac* (Hanoi) 29:8–9.

Phan Huy Lê, Hà Văn Tấn, and Hoàng Xuân Chinh. 1989. "Những bước đi của lịch sử Việt Nam." In *Văn Hóa Việt Nam*, pp. 34–40. Hà nội: Ban Văn Nghệ Trung Ương.

Phan Khoang. 1961. *Việt Nam pháp thuộc sử* (History of colonialism in Vietnam). Saigon: Sống Mới.

Thụy Loan. 1993. *Lược sử âm nhạc Việt Nam* (A brief history of Vietnamese music). Hanoi: Âm Nhạc.

Trần Văn Khê. 1962. *La musique Vietnamienne traditionelle.* Paris: Presses Universitaires de France.

Việt Nhạc. 1948. Number 1, 16 August.

Singapore

Lee Tong Soon

Musics of Specific Communities
Musical Genres

Founded in 1819 by Sir Stamford Raffles, Singapore served as an important port of call for the British Empire in Southeast Asia. From 1826 to 1946, with Penang and Melaka, it was part of the Straits Settlements. In 1963, Singapore, Malaya, Sabah, and Sarawak formed what is now known as Malaysia. Two years later, on 9 August 1965, Singapore separated from Malaysia and became a sovereign nation.

Singapore is situated just above the equator, between peninsular Malaysia and the islands of Indonesia. Most of its early immigrants, indigenous to Malaysia and Indonesia, included Malay, Javanese, Boyanese, Bugis, and Balinese. The earliest Chinese immigrants came mainly from Malacca and Riau, and later generations migrated primarily from Guangdong and Fujian provinces, southeast China. The first Indian immigrants arrived from Penang and later from India. Other nationalities among immigrant peoples in Singapore include Arabs and Europeans.

In the late 1990s, with a total population of about three million, the ethnic makeup of Singapore consists mainly of Chinese (77.5 percent), Malays (14.2 percent), and Indians (7.1 percent), with other peoples (such as Eurasians, Armenians, and Jews) making up the remainder. The population in Singapore accounts for the diversity of music in the country, which, through the fusion of traditional and modern aspects, has created a distinctly Singaporean life-style.

MUSICS OF SPECIFIC COMMUNITIES

Singapore has four distinct cultures: Chinese, Malay, Indian, and Eurasian. Among the Chinese population is a group known as Peranakans, with a distinctive mixture of Chinese and Malay cultural traits.

The Chinese

The Chinese population in Singapore speaks various dialects, including Fujian, Chaozhou, Guangdong, Hainan, and Kejia. Dialect groups formed clan associations to support their respective forms of opera (wayang), making these genres locally prominent. Hand-puppet and string-puppet theaters, traditions popular during the first half of the twentieth century, are now mainly engaged during Taoist ceremonies.

A minstrel-like tradition, *zouchang* 'walk-sing', is performed during festive seasons (such as the Chinese Lunar New Year), celebrations of deities' birthdays, and private birthday parties. Walking performers, mostly members of operatic troupes, form ensembles ranging from six to fifteen musicians, accompanied by instruments from the theater (Perris 1978).

During the seventh month of the lunar calendar, the month of hungry ghosts (usually in August), various traditional theatrical genres appear on makeshift stages along the streets. Contemporary urban performances are known as *getai* 'song-stage'. During these performances, popular Mandarin, Fujian, and occasionally English songs are performed to the accompaniment of electric guitars, keyboards, and drum set. Performances by famous local comedians are also part of *getai,* which often highlight current social and political issues.

A contemporary Mandarin vocal genre, *xinyao* 'Singapore ballad', is being revived through the mass media and the openings of cafés and pubs that cater specially to lovers of ballads. *Xinyao* began in the early 1980s among teenage students who sang about unforgettable love affairs, broken dreams, school life, cherished longings, and local topics, usually accompanied by a guitar. The mid-1980s witnessed the rise to fame of several *xinyao* artists, both in Singapore and abroad. The *xinyao* movement suffered a decline in the late 1980s and early 1990s, only to be rejuvenated in the mid-1990s. Though it began under the influence of similar vocal traditions in Taiwan and Hong Kong, performers overseas now look to *xinyao* performers and songwriters for alternative Mandarin hits.

Besides theatrical and vocal performances, the Chinese performing arts scene in Singapore is also marked by orchestral, chamber, and vocal performances, such as *nanguan,* a chamber-music genre from Xiamen in China's Fujian Province. Drumming for the lion dance, a tradition that has always been prevalent in Chinese festive celebrations, is fast becoming a popular musical genre in Singapore. It involves the beating of drums, embellished with the drummer's complex acrobatic movements. Through national competitions and educational activities in schools and clubs, the National Wushu (Pugilistic) Federation is largely responsible for the promotion of this tradition.

The Malays

Vocal genres accompanied by the frame drums *kompang* and *hadrah* are among the most popular kinds of Malay music in Singapore. They involve single-sided, handheld frame drums, said to be of Arabic origin. The *hadrah,* like the tambourine, has cymbal-like discs around its circumference. The frame drums engage in interlocking rhythmic patterns in different rhythmic strains, consistently maintained throughout a performance. Songs accompanied by *kompang* and *hadrah* usually contain religious connotations, sung in praise of God. Necessary in traditional Malay weddings and official functions, both *kompang* and *hadrah* ensembles are recognized as musical symbols of Malay culture in Singapore.

Ensembles including Pehaks, the Persatuan Hadrah dan Kompang Singapura (Singapore Hadrah and Kompang Association), and various clubs have largely been responsible for maintaining these traditions in Singapore. Pehaks, led by percussionist-composer Ahmad Azmi, has promoted *kompang* and *hadrah* through frequent local and overseas performances and has conducted workshops on the art of playing them.

Dikir barat, a traditional Malay vocal genre, is said to have originated in Kelantan, a state on the east coast of peninsular Malaysia. A usual performance

FIGURE 1 A performance of *dikir barat.* Photo by Low Eng Teong, 1995.

involves two leaders (*juara* and *tukang karat*) and a chorus (*awok*). The vocal ensemble sings catchy lyrics with engaging rhythms, enhanced by lively movements of the hands and upper body (figure 1). The lyrics of *dikir barat* are secular, and often suggest patriotism and other themes concerning one's own culture. Often, they are newly composed, tailored to suit the situation, and are attached to stock melodies in a verse-refrain form. The *juara* delivers solo renditions of the verses, the *tukang karat* interjects comical remarks, and the *awok* joins in the refrains. The upper-body movements are choreographed to provide visual representations of the words. The ensemble is usually accompanied by Malay instruments such as *kompang,* gong, and *bonang.*

Ghazal is a vocal tradition said to have been introduced to Singapore via peninsular Malaysia by Arab, Persian, and Indian traders. A popular form of Malay music in the 1950s in Singapore, it preserved some of the most famous pantuns (Malay poetical forms) and Malay folk songs. Accompanying the voices are instruments such as a lute (*gambus*), a drum (*tabla*), a frame drum, an accordion, and a violin. One of the earliest ghazal competitions in Singapore occurred in 1986, with the aim of reviving and encouraging the genre because it was diminishing in popularity.

FIGURE 2 Young players of *angklung* in Singapore. Photo by Low Eng Teong, 1995.

Kuda kepang 'horse-trance dance' and various traditional *joget* dances may still be seen in Singapore during special events, such as cultural shows. *Bangsawan,* a Malay operatic genre that began in the late 1800s, is performed in Singapore mainly during festivals and for tourists. In 1995, a special exhibit, *Curtains Up! The Heritage of Singapore's Performing Arts,* opened at the National Museum. It featured *bangsawan,* with genres of Chinese, Indian, Peranakan, Eurasian, and Malay origin—genres such as *wayang kulit, dikir barat,* and traditional dances.

The troupe Sriwana and the ensemble Rentak Melayu have played central roles in promoting Malay performing arts in Singapore. Formed in 1955, Sriwana began as a *keroncong*-singing group, and have since expanded their repertory to include dance (such as *zapin*) and drama. Rentak Melayu specializes in performing traditional Malay percussive instruments, such as *angklung* (figure 2), *talempong,* and *gendang.* Clubs in Singapore also play important roles in the preservation of Malay traditional arts. The Kampong Kembangan Community Club Pachitan Gamelan Orchestra, formed in 1990 and named after an old Javanese village in Kampong Kembangan, is the first full-fledged Javanese gamelan in Singapore. In addition, the Marine Parade

FIGURE 3 A performance of *bhangra.* Photo by Low Eng Teong, 1995.

Community Club Angklung Orchestra, formed in 1993, has been promoting the art of playing *angklung* through performances at National Day celebrations and other events.

The Indians

The two main styles of Indian classical music, Hindustani and Karnatic, inform the Indian artistic scene in Singapore. The Singapore Indian Fine Arts Society, founded in 1949, locally promotes Indian fine arts. With its philosophy (Art Characterizes Civilization), it is apt to say that the society is foremost in preserving Indian culture in Singapore through the performing arts. Its Academy of Fine Arts supports the Singapore Indian Orchestra and Choir and conducts graded courses on instruments such as flute, *mridangam, sarod, sitar, tabla,* and *veena,* with classes on vocal techniques and classical dances such as *bharata natyam.*

Other forms of Indian music prevalent among the Indian population include *bhajanai* (known as *bhajan* in North India), film music, and temple music that features the *nadhaswaran* oboe and the *thavil* drum as its main instruments. Indian temples in Singapore are patrons of Indian performing arts, and by sponsoring concerts have played a crucial role in promoting Indian music. The Apsaras Arts troupe (specializing in classical Indian dance) and the Kala Mandhir "The Temple of Fine Arts" (specializing in both music and dance) are other associations that have made major contributions to the performing arts in Singapore.

Indian music and dance are prevalent in the Indian festivals celebrated in Singapore, including Pongal (Harvest Festival), Navarathiri (Festivals of Nine Lights), Theemithi (Firewalking), Vaisakhi, and Thaipusam.

The *bhangra* (figure 3), a popular Indian dance that originated in the Punjab, is usually associated with the Punjabi Sikhs. It is usually performed during harvest, Sikh weddings, and other joyous occasions. The Singapore Khalsa Association Bhangra Group, founded in 1986, has been promoting this dance and the music associated with it. Traditional *bhangra* uses such Indian instruments as the *tundhi* and the *dhol;* disco *bhangra,* held frequently in several discothèques in Singapore, uses modern instruments—electric keyboards, drums, and guitars.

bhajanai Lay-sung Hindu devotional songs

bhangra Popular Indian-derived dance-song

dondang sayang Popular song genre said to have originated in Malacca

singapop Popular song of the 1980s and 1990s

The Eurasians

The Eurasian community makes up only about 0.4 percent of the population of Singapore. The term *Eurasian,* believed to have been coined by the British, refers to the descendants of European settlers who married Asian women during the colonial period. Recognized as one of the four distinct ethnic groups of Singapore, Eurasians were among the earliest residents in Singapore soon after its founding. Most of them, especially those of Portuguese descent, trace their roots to Malacca in peninsular Malaysia. The other predominant ancestors of the Eurasian community in Singapore are the British and the Dutch.

The Eurasian Association, founded in 1919, is responsible for the preservation of the Eurasian heritage in Singapore. The association organizes classes to revive the *Kristang* language, a Malaccan-Portuguese creole used in many Eurasian stories, poems, and songs. The Eurasian Association troupe specializes in European folk dances (especially English, Dutch, and Portuguese forms), and has performed widely in National Day celebrations and local cultural events. A type of traditional dance known as *branyo,* said to be exclusive to Eurasians in the Malaysia-Singapore region, is usually performed during Eurasian weddings and social events.

The Peranakans

Singapore is one of the three areas where most Peranakans live; the other two are Malacca and Penang, in peninsular Malaysia. Peranakans, otherwise known as *baba* 'male' and *nonya* 'female', are usually Chinese who speak Malay and adopt certain aspects of the Malay culture but practice Chinese religions and festivals. Peranakans are said to be descendants of early Chinese immigrants from Fujian Province (southern China) to Malacca, who married local Malay women and produced a community that straddles Malay and Chinese cultures.

The Gunong Sayang Association, founded in 1910, has been responsible for ensuring the preservation of the Peranakan heritage in Singapore. One of its most important contributions to the Peranakan performing arts scene is the staging of plays in Peranakan style. These plays, often criticized for being formulaic, vividly portray the life-styles of Peranakan families. Every year since 1985, the association has staged Peranakan plays, and has been a frequent participant in the annual Festival of Asian Performing Arts in Singapore.

Among other musical genres performed by Peranakans is the *dondang sayang,* a vocal genre, said to have originated in Malacca and eventually to have spread to Indonesia, Kuching, Penang, and Singapore. Accompanied by an ensemble made up of the Malay drum, a violin, and a gong, sometimes supplemented by guitar, accordion, and flute, the singers employ the pantun, combined with lighthearted descriptions of salient features of Peranakan culture.

MUSICAL GENRES

Western classical and popular music

The Singapore Symphony Orchestra (SSO), formed in 1979 under the baton of Choo Huey, has been the premier performing group in introducing Western classical music in Singapore. With the aim of educating young Singaporeans in Western classical music, the Singapore Youth Orchestra (SYO), under the directorship of Lim Yau, and the Singapore Youth Choir were formed to provide performing opportunities for aspiring musicians. Local composers, such as Leong Yoon Pin, Bernard Tan, and Phoon Yew Tien, have ventured into Western twentieth-century compositional styles and have had their works performed by the SSO and SYO in the New Music Forum series, launched in 1987 by the Performing Rights Society.

Leong Yoon Pin is one of several local composers who have assimilated local musical idioms with Western classical genres. He was the first Singaporean composer whose composition (*Dayong Sampan,* an overture based on a local tune of the same title) was performed by the SSO—in 1980, under the baton of Israeli conductor Shalom Ronli-Riklis. In 1982, Leong was awarded the Cultural Medallion, the nation's highest award for the arts. In 1993, he became the first Singaporean composer to have his compositions recorded on compact disc, as part of a project organized by the National Arts Council to document works of Singaporean artists.

The Singapore Lyric Theatre, formed in 1990, is Singapore's leading opera-production company. After its inaugural production of Mozart's *The Magic Flute* in 1991, it has performed frequently during the Singapore Festival of Arts. Its repertoire includes *The Merry Widow, The Barber of Seville, Rigoletto,* and *Tosca.*

Since the latter half of the 1980s, popular music by local bands began to proliferate in Singapore. Performing music that includes blues, soul, rock and roll, hard rock, and punk, these bands are succeeding in their attempts to achieve a breakthrough in a scene otherwise dominated by American and British bands. Numerous sponsored concerts provide opportunities for bands to perform original compositions and be recognized by local recording companies.

The year 1991 was said to be a watershed for Singapore pop, also known as *singapop.* Many new local bands emerged through competitions during the year, demo recordings were produced and distributed, and recording companies were willing to sign more local groups. Besides the production of popular music, the local consumption of locally produced popular music is an important determinant in the success of *singapop.* Critics in *BigO* and other local popular-music magazines have argued that an increased consciousness of local products, with an independent infrastructure that supports local popular music, are key factors in the promotion of *singapop.* The featuring of several Singapore bands on the British Broadcasting Corporation World Service program in December 1993 reflects the recognition of *singapop* within the popular-music industry.

Musicals and plays

After the production of the first major local musical, *Beauty World* (1988), a series of original Singapore musicals have been produced and performed, with resounding successes. Some of these musicals revolve around the cultural and social settings of Singapore; others focus on the question of Asian identity. Dick Lee, who composed the music for *Beauty World* (1988), *Fried Rice Paradise* (1991), and *Kampong Amber* (1994), is known for his advocacy of the Asian heritage through his songs and musicals. These musicals are centered on Singaporean themes and settings, while his two other, *Nagraland* (1992) and *Fantasia* (1994), which he conceptualized, wrote, and performed, were concerned with the search for the meaning of Asia and being Asian. *Fantasia*—the title a compound of *fantastic* and *Asia*—was Asian in theme, featuring several traditional song-and-dance items from seven Asian countries (Hong Kong, India, Indonesia, Malaysia, Mongolia, the Philippines, and Singapore), performed by a multinational cast of Asian performers.

Other theatrical companies—Theatre Works, Singapore Repertory Theatre, Pacific Theatricals—have been active in promoting plays and musicals in Singapore. Supported by an infrastructure of private and corporate sponsors and backed by the National Arts Council, Singapore's theatrical scene is a fertile ground for understanding Singaporean culture. Many locally produced musicals, such as Pacific Theatricals' *Bugis Street* (1994), have been warmly received overseas—a response that has encouraged further experiments in local theatrical productions.

Music for the community

In 1986, to foster communal spirit and identity, the Ministry of Education launched a musical project in local schools. With the help of the Singapore Armed Forces Music and Drama Company, this project was well received by schools, which participated by having interclass singing competitions and group singing during school assemblies.

The communal singing project was followed by Sing Singapore, a biennial national program that began in 1988. This program aims not only to promote communal spirit through singing, but to widen the repertoire of Singapore songs. A series of national songs that had been sung in schools since the late 1960s was compiled, and nationwide competitions that featured original Singapore songs were organized as part of the program. These songs, written in English, Malay, Mandarin, and Tamil, focus on themes that range from the history of Singapore, its progress, people, aspirations, to descriptions of the national flower, popular places, and local life-styles.

In 1994, open-air concerts were organized for the first time as part of Sing Singapore, with the additional title *Festival of Songs* to encourage public participation. Nationalistic messages in the songs of Singapore are propagated through recordings and publication of songbooks and further disseminated through music lessons in schools.

The educational system in Singapore provides ample opportunities for people interested in music to gain musical knowledge. Courses in Chinese, Indian, and Malay music are available from institutions and clubs. Western classical music is the most popular form of music currently taught in Singapore. Children get early exposure to music through commercial schools (such as the Yamaha Music School), and more advanced musicians are guided through examinations conducted by foreign music institutions (such as the Associated Board of the Royal Schools of Music, London).

The *chingay* parade (held on the Chinese New Year) and the annual national day celebrations provide opportunities for observing the arts in Singapore. With music and dances from all local ethnic communities, these events show the mixture of cultures within the nation.

The abundance of music in Singapore provides fertile ground for research. However, to define the music of Singapore is a formidable task. Are the Singapore songs featured during Sing Singapore programs representative of Singaporean music? Does *xinyao* fit the description? Can the productions of musicals based on local themes, using local English (known as Singlish), be labeled unique to Singapore?

Music performances as varied as jazz, bagpipes, *karaoke,* professional brass bands, school military bands, and religious music coexist with multitudinous forms of traditional and modern music. Cultural coexistence, and therefore musical variety, is Singapore's strength and identity, reflecting the national goal—unity in diversity.

REFERENCE

Perris, Arnold. 1978. "Chinese Wayang: The Survival of Chinese Opera in the Streets of Singapore." *Ethnomusicology* 22(2):297–306.

Upland and Minority Peoples of Mainland Southeast Asia

The mountainous areas of mainland Southeast Asia are home to some one hundred named minority ethnic groups. But they remain remote, and their musics have barely been explored. Mostly animists who practice swidden agriculture on the steep hillsides, these peoples preserve—with their distinctive rituals, costumes, and social patterns—a collection of musical instruments that includes nose flutes, mouth organs, Jew's harps, and gong ensembles. Our current knowledge of their music only scratches the surface.

Members of the Black Tai minority play rhythms in a wooden trough with hanging bossed gongs and drum, west of Thanh Hóa, Vietnam. Photo by Terry E. Miller, 1994.

Upland and Minority Peoples of Mainland Southeast Asia: An Introduction

Terry E. Miller

Demographically, mainland Southeast Asia can be divided into lowland and upland peoples. In each nation-state (excepting the Republic of Singapore), a significant portion of the population consists of minority groups, most of whom live in the higher elevations. Some groups, like the Karen of Burma and Thailand and the Chăm of Vietnam, have lowland counterparts who have largely adopted lowland, majority life styles. Frank M. Lebar's 1964 publication *Ethnic Groups of Mainland Southeast Asia* names 151 ethnic groups, including the majority peoples. In variety, minority groups vastly outnumber the majority groups, but in population, power, and organization, they remain marginal in most countries.

LANGUAGE FAMILIES OF MAINLAND SOUTHEAST ASIA

It is customary to organize the upland and minority peoples of mainland Southeast Asia according to language family, though the exact classification of some languages remains conjectural. There are four principal language families in mainland Southeast Asia.

The Sino-Tibetan family

Speakers of Sino-Tibetan languages range from northeastern India to Vietnam and include many groups that straddle national borders. Most are minorities, except those of the Sinitic subclass, which includes more than a billion people in the People's Republic of China and ethnic Chinese in Southeast Asia. The Tibeto-Burman subclass includes twenty groups, all minorities except the Burmese. Most live primarily in China, which classifies them as National Minorities. Most such groups living in Southeast Asia migrated there from China. Among them are such groups as the Nagas, who straddle the border of Burma into India and Bangladesh. There are two other major subclasses, the Karen and the so-called Miao-Yao (so-called because both terms were given by outsiders and are pejorative); the people themselves prefer the terms Hmong and Mian, respectively. The Hmong are most widely distributed—in China, Thailand, Laos, Vietnam, and, as a result of the Vietnam War, in Switzerland, the United States, Australia, and elsewhere.

The Austroasiatic family

The Austroasiatic family includes three subclasses: Mon-Khmer, Việt-Mường, and Senoi-Semang. Mon-Khmer includes the majority Khmer of Cambodia and the formerly powerful Mon, but the remaining seventy-four named groups, found mainly in the mountains of Cambodia, Laos, and Vietnam, include mostly little-known peoples. A few, however, including the Bahnar of Vietnam, are somewhat better known. The Việt-Mường subclass includes the majority Vietnamese and the Mường (people usually considered to be the ancestors of the Vietnamese, who continue to live in the uplands). The Senoi-Semang group includes only peoples who live in the mountains of Malaysia.

The Tai-Kadai family

The Tai-Kadai classification embraces mainly the Tai family of languages. Kadai, a created term, embracing only four small groups on China's Hainan Island, is outside the scope of this volume. The Tai include all mainstream, majority people in Thailand and Laos, plus the Shan of Burma, but also upland and nonmainstream groups, like the Black Tai, the White Tai, the Red Tai, the Phuan, and minority Tai-speakers in parts of northern Vietnam and southern China.

The Austronesian (Malayo-Polynesian) family

This language family is extremely widespread. It extends from the mainland into Indonesia and the Philippines and reaches out through Oceania as far east as Rapanui (Easter Island) and into the Indian Ocean as far west as Madagascar. Mainland speakers of Austronesian languages live mainly in Malaysia and Vietnam. There are two subclasses, Chăm and Malay, the latter primarily the language of the majority lowland Malay. Chăm includes lowland Chăm in Vietnam and Cambodia, plus nine upland groups, among which the Jarai and the Rhade are fairly well known.

THE HISTORY OF RESEARCH ON UPLAND CULTURES

Ethnomusicologists have studied the musics of few mainland Southeast Asian upland groups. The most thoroughly documented include groups that fled the wars in Vietnam, Laos, and Cambodia to become refugees abroad. The reasons that studies within the original context are rare is easy to discover: the war in Vietnam put most groups in southern Vietnam (the former Republic of Vietnam) off limits (except to Special Forces troops), and Vietnamese government restrictions on research persisted until 1992 for non-American researchers and until 1994 for Americans because of a U.S.-imposed embargo on trade, lifted during that year. Though the minorities in northern Vietnam have been documented by Vietnamese scholars, and there is even a music school for minorities in Hoà Bình City (west of Hanoi), they have remained largely unknown to outsiders. Research in Laos was nearly impossible until about 1990, and continued to be severely restricted until 1994. The logistics of conducting fieldwork in remote areas of Laos remain difficult. Since 1975, because of security concerns, it has been impossible to study most minorities in Cambodia. Until 1994, access to minorities (called National Brethren) in Burma was severely limited by visa. Since 1994, one-month visas have been permitted; nevertheless, most of Burma's states where minorities live include large areas that have been in rebellion against the central government virtually since independence. The most thorough studies of upland groups has taken place in Malaysia, where neither access nor security has been problematic: several fine recordings and one major book have been published on these musics.

The lack of scholars to do research in upland areas, assuming they could overcome logistical and security problems, remains a major problem. Few scholars from

Few scholars from outside mainland Southeast Asia have done sustained or in-depth research in these musics. Indigenous scholars—if they exist at all—are hampered by lack of funds, recording equipment, and training.

outside mainland Southeast Asia have done sustained or in-depth research in these musics. Indigenous scholars—if they exist at all—are hampered by lack of funds, recording equipment, and training. National archives either do not exist, or exist in only rudimentary forms—though this statement is becoming less and less true for Thailand and Malaysia.

Obviously, the challenges to doing fieldwork in this area are numerous. Researchers face serious problems with security, transportation, language, health, climate, and terrain. The people tend to live in isolated villages at high elevations that can be reached only on foot, or at best in a four-wheel-drive vehicle. Since isolation produces variety, drawing generalizations about these musics is risky, and there are too many villages to visit. Therefore, the articles covering this topic remain incomplete and tentative.

Two of the major figures who did fieldwork in this subject—Hans Oesch of Germany (who worked in upland Malaysia) and Ruriko Uchida of Japan (who worked in upland Thailand and Laos)—died between the time they wrote articles for this encyclopedia and its publication. The scarcity of younger scholars working in this area suggests the situation is not likely to change any time soon.

REFERENCE

Lebar, Frank M. 1964. *Ethnic Groups of Mainland Southeast Asia.* New Haven, Conn.: Human Relations Area Files.

Minority Musics of Vietnam

Phong T. Nguyễn

The musics of the minority peoples of Vietnam have remained obscure to outsiders. Except for some French recordings published in the 1960s and 1970s and covering a limited area of Vietnam, little information is available, even today. The minorities of the central area of Vietnam were difficult to study during the war years, and the area remained off limits to most foreign researchers until 1994. The minorities in the north remain almost unknown to outsiders. Virtually no ethnomusicologists have been doing work in these areas, but this situation is changing. Consequently, this article must be considered tentative and general, based on isolated fieldwork.

Two groups of minority peoples live in Vietnam, one in the uplands and the other in the lowlands. The uplanders live in the cool, mountainous areas bordering Cambodia, Laos, and China, where sources of water are few; the lowlanders live alongside the majority Viet and have easy access to rivers and the sea. Each group has created particular musical expressions.

Lowlanders are mainly the Khmer, the Chăm, and the Hoa (Chinese). A small number of Hoa live in the areas bordering China, but larger groups of them settled as businesspeople in the south during the 1800s. Vietnamese cities have small enclaves of other immigrants (including Arabs, Indians, Indonesians, Pakistanis, and Filipinos).

It is convenient to divide upland culture and music according to two geographical regions: the Trường Son Ranges in the central region (often called the central highlands), and the mountains and plateaus of the north (more exactly, the northeast and the northwest). The peoples living in the central highlands belong to an older layer of population and are probably descended from peoples who settled there about two thousand to four thousand years ago. In the north (except for the Tày, the Mường, and the Thái), most uplanders migrated from southern China between the 1300s and the 1800s.

Living along the Trường Sơn Ranges in the central highlands (called Tây Nguyên, which stretch along the borders with Cambodia and Laos), some twenty ethnic groups speak languages belonging to either the Mon-Khmer or Austronesian language families. Although both vocal and instrumental musics exist in the upland areas, the most representative types are bronze gong ensembles and a rich collection

Trường Sơn Ranges Mountain range running through southern Vietnam, home to minorities

khắp Upland Thai term for repartee song

m'buôt Free-reed mouth organ with gourd wind chest, found in Trường Son Ranges

klông pút Group of seven sounding bamboo tubes, activated by clapping

goong Jarai tube zither with eleven separate strings

of instruments, mostly of bamboo. In contrast, the northern uplanders emphasize vocal music sung in Thái-Lào, Việt-Mường, and Sino-Tibetan languages.

Because the uplanders are largely isolated from the lowland Việt and international influences, their musics have been little affected by the social changes that have disturbed the lives of lowlanders in Vietnam. In general, these musics exhibit a feature that makes them part of another, larger world: the musical instruments and songs of the uplanders in the central highlands relate to phenomena elsewhere in Southeast Asia and Oceania, while those of the northern uplanders relate to the minorities of southern China.

MUSICAL CONTEXTS AND GENRES

Songs of courtship and friendship

Many minority-group songs are sung in alternation by male and female singers of all ages. This pattern, which may alternate young boys and girls, married men and women, or widows and widowers, is not limited to a specific population in Vietnam. During calendrical festivals, especially the New Year and other spring festivals, the Hmong in Ha Giang and elsewhere sing antiphonal courtship songs (*gầu plềnh,* also *phià phá*). Young men and women sing while courting on the side of a mountain or hill. These love songs are sung in styles called *rang* and *thường* by the Mường, *lượn* by the Tày, *sli* by the Nùng, *khắp tua* by the Thái in the north, *avơng* by the Bahnar of the central highlands, and *ayai* by the lowland Khmer in the Mekong Delta.

In Thai, *khắp* means 'to sing'. In a fixed order from the opening of a singing session to the farewell, the Thai sing songs of love (*khắp tua*), including traveling songs, gate-opening songs, introductory songs, greetings, wishing songs, and farewells. The San Diu sing *soọng cô* in a format comparable to that of the *quan họ* of the lowland Việt. Pairs of men and women sing alternately around a campfire (formerly the site of cooking) and thereby invoke an age-old concept of prosperity through its association with cooking, warmth, and community. When singing occurs inside a house, participants give consideration to the relationship between host and guests. If the guests are young men, the host's family must present the young women, led by an experienced female singer from within the family, who sings with them at first. The beginning of the courtship is marked by the serving of betel leaves. These singing sessions may last up to three nights during the spring or fall.

TRACK 9

Courtship and friendship songs reinforce social relationships, but they also exhibit high levels of poetic creativity, conveying intense expressions of love. The exchange of verses requires the singers to formulate responses quickly, combining musical ideas with a sophisticated language of double meanings.

Narratives

Stories, both short and long, are preserved in the minds of many minorities. Storytelling traditions that include rhythm and melody include the Ede *khan,* the

Jarai *hơ ri,* the Bahnar *h'amon,* the Hmong *khâu xià,* and the Khmer *chùm riêng chàpây.* Lying comfortably in a darkened house while listeners sit around a fire nearby, Bahnar storytellers recite *h'amon.* Among the lowland Chăm of central Vietnam, epics have more than a thousand verses.

The most famous stories among the minorities are epics named after heroes. The Jarai and the Ede tell stories of Dam San, Dam Di, and Xinh Nha, while the Mường story *Tẻ Tàt Tẻ Nát* ('The Birth of Life') lasts several nights—a story consisting of more than four thousand lines. The songs of the Lô Lô (also called the Yi and the Mun-gi) are shorter and can be sung or spoken in sections. The tale called *Love Song* consists of fourteen hundred verses.

Ritual songs

Perhaps the most prevalent types of song practiced by minorities concern rituals—for healing, commemorations, weddings, funerals, and other purposes. Among the Tày and the Nùng, the singer-ritualist (usually female) is called *then,* and among the Mường and the Thái in the north, he or she is called *mo.* Specifically, a *then* should be a handsome and skillful performer who can sing, play instruments, and dance. Whether in trance or not, the *then* performs to heal sick people, to attract rain, and to ensure good crops, successful conceptions, and long lives. People believe the *then* has the power to create a friendship between the god of the sun and the god of rain. The healing songs of the Thai *mo* can have up to 450 verses.

In the central highlands, Ede singer-ritualists (*khoa kam*) conduct a ceremony for the god of winds, including songs wishing for the avoidance of storms and for fertility in farming. Some central highlanders conduct rituals that include songs and dances with processions of wooden statues of gods and spirits. The greatest festival in the central highlands is the Sedang water-buffalo sacrifice (*ting ka kpo*), which includes many gong ensembles and songs.

Lullabies and other songs

Most minority peoples have lullabies (Xtiêng *niên con,* Khmer *bompê kôn,* Chăm *ru anuk,* Việt *ru con*). These are often forgotten in urban areas, but they continue to flourish in rural areas, among both the Việt and minorities. Terms for lullabies can be translated as 'rocking babies', 'rocking little sisters', or 'rocking little grandson or granddaughter'.

MUSICAL INSTRUMENTS

With fifty-three minority groups in Vietnam, a complete survey of musical instruments would require much space. Since research among these groups was prohibited or restricted until the mid-1990s, and Vietnamese scholars continue to be hampered by lack of money and recording equipment, a complete inventory is not yet possible. Many groups live in scattered and remote mountainous villages, making generalizations risky. At this point, we can roughly estimate that minorities in both lowlands and uplands have about two hundred kinds of instruments, belonging to all four standard organological categories. Since the names of a given type of instrument vary by language, we will use the terms that are best known in Vietnam.

The Trường Sơn Ranges in the central region offer the most extensive concentration of instruments; in other areas, the variety of instruments is more modest. Among both Mon-Khmer and Austronesians of the central highlands, the gong ensemble is central, though both wooden and bamboo instruments are widely used by individuals. Gong ensembles of some sort are also found among the Mường and the Thái in the north, while the lowland Khmer, living in southern Vietnam, use a set of tuned bossed gongs on a circular rattan rack (*kong thum*) as part of their standard ensemble (*pinn peat*).

The central highlands

In the central highlands, gongs play an important role in the villagers' lives. Each ensemble consists of from three to thirteen flat and bossed gongs, some of which may be doubled or tripled, making a full ensemble large and impressive. The Jarai call an ensemble of three gongs a *trum*; the Bahnar call one with thirteen gongs an *avơng.* The gongs, varying from 30 to 86 centimeters in diameter, are named by size, musical role, and hierarchical function. Gongs may be identified as mother, father, older sister, or younger sister. Each set of gongs has a specific use. The *trum* is associated with the planting of the pole to which the buffalo about to be sacrificed is tied; the *m'nhum,* with festivals; the *arap,* with the abandonment of a tomb (*pothi*); the *avơng,* with gong competitions; the *ho duc,* with a victory celebration; and the *khah,* with a healing ritual. Gongs are held in the players' hands unless they are too heavy, in which case they are supported by a shoulder strap. Drums, having two heads and made in three sizes, are also members of the gong ensembles. The ensembles can play alone or to accompany dance (figure 1).

TRACK 10

Other central-highland idiophones include xylophones and bamboo xylophones (*t'rung, khinh khung*), wooden slit drums and bamboo slit drums (*tơl mo*), bamboo tubes beaten with a stick (*goong teng leng*), bamboo tubes beaten by hand (*t'pol*), and Jew's harps. Among the most remarkable of instruments is a hydraulic bamboo xylophone, the Sedang *koangtác,* complex in both construction and musical function. A frame is built over a stream, especially in rapids or a small waterfall, and bamboo tubes are hung from the frame into the water, resting against a lower frame. The currents fill, tilt, and then empty the tubes, letting them fall back against the frame, sounding a pitch. The biggest of these frames are 60 meters wide and have 120 tubes. Lithophones from prehistoric times have been unearthed in Vietnam, but whether they originated among the ancestors of the present-day minorities is uncertain.

Many aerophones are conceived of as being voices of nature. These include bamboo flutes, single- and double-reed pipes, and free-reed instruments. Among the simplest is the animal horn (*t'diep*), and among the more complex is the polyphonic gourd free-reed mouth organ (*m'buôt*). Seven vertical, open-ended bamboo tubes set in a frame (*klông pút*) are sounded when the player claps his or her hands over the

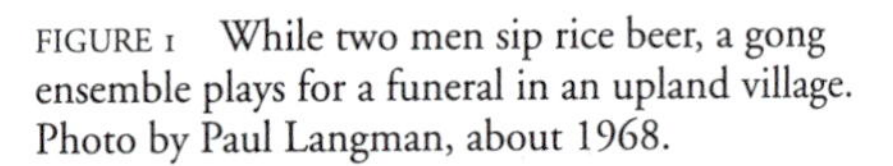

FIGURE 1 While two men sip rice beer, a gong ensemble plays for a funeral in an upland village. Photo by Paul Langman, about 1968.

FIGURE 2 A Xtiêng musician plays a bamboo tube zither (*goong*). Phước Long, Vietnam. Photo by Phong T. Nguyễn, 1994.

openings. Some believe that this instrument originated with farmers who stored grain in bamboo tubes and clapped their hands over the openings to make the last grains fall out when sowing the fields. In the process, they discovered that sounds were resonated by the tubes, and they later added more tubes until the set was standardized as seven. Single- and double-reed instruments are little known, but the Thái and Yao, among others, have such instruments, which they call *pí pặp* and *pí đôi* respectively.

Though less numerous than idiophones and aerophones, chordophones exhibit complex tunings and playing techniques. The most important of these are idiochord tube zithers. The sophisticated Jarai version (*goong*) is played polyphonically to imitate the gong ensembles. Likely the original version is still played by the Xtiêng, who cut the bamboo skin in strips and raise them on tiny pieces of bamboo; the player plucks these strips (figure 2). Others amplify the instrument's sounds with an empty, dried gourd. The Jarai *goong* has eleven metal strings, stretched along the outside of a thick bamboo tube to wooden tuning pegs at the top end. Its tuning is based on that of the gongs. Similar tube zithers are also found in Indonesia (*kteng kteng*) and beyond. Another Jarai tube zither is called *goong đe*.

The Jarai also have a plucked bamboo tube zither (*tol alao*), one of whose strings are beaten with two sticks. Especially unusual is the Jarai one-stringed spike fiddle (*k'ni*). The bowed string, attached to the lower part of the instrument's body, passes over six frets to a tuning peg. A second, resonating string stretches from the bowed string to a piece of wood held in the player's mouth, which serves as a resonator. The main string is set into vibration when bowed with a thin piece of bamboo, 40 centimeters long.

The north

Among the cultural groups of northern Vietnam, musical instruments are fewer, though all four categories exist. In Mường villages, bronze instruments are likely among the oldest. Both the Thái and the Mường, particularly in Hoà Bình and Thanh Hóa provinces, retain bronze drum gongs and gongs. A Mường gong ensemble, consisting of both flat and bossed gongs, has from three to twelve gongs. The Mường have a custom of distinguishing gong sizes by giving them ages: the smallest gong, about 20 centimeters in diameter, is "age one," the next larger one "age two," and so forth. The most important ensemble (*xéc pùa*) is played for making wishes during the lunar New Year's celebrations. Players of the *xéc pùa,* holding their gongs in their hands, go from house to house, playing wishing songs as interludes. According to Mường custom, only the lower-pitched gongs may be played at funerals.

In Thanh Hóa Province, both the Thái and the Mường have an unusual idiophone—a large log, carved into a boat-shaped wooden trough (Thái *loỏng,* Mường *đuống*), played by ten or twelve young women, who on both sides of the trough beat sticks rhythmically against the bottom and the inside. This instrument originated as a rice-pestling trough. It is played with a set of four or five hanging bossed gongs and a hanging drum (figure 3).

The Lô Lô still count the rarely used bronze gong drum as their favorite instrument. They store a pair of drums (male and female) in the ground and unearth them for ceremonies. Accompanying the gong drum is a two-stringed fiddle, whose player dances while playing.

Chordophones, both plucked and bowed, are found commonly among northern groups. These instruments include the Thái-Tày gourd lute (*tính tẩu*) (figure 4) and the Hà Nhì three-stringed lute (*ta in*). The Hmong use one fiddle (*lụ phù*) and the Mường use another (*kò ke*). The Thái-Tày *tính tẩu* has various uses, including solo

The Lô Lô still count the rarely used bronze gong drum as their favorite instrument. They store a pair of drums (male and female) in the ground and unearth them for ceremonies.

FIGURE 3 A Black Tai ensemble plays the rice-pestling trough (*quánh loỏng*) with hanging gongs and a drum. Photo by Terry E. Miller, 1994.

FIGURE 4 A Tày minority woman plays the *tính tẩu* lute in northeastern Vietnam. From *Vietnam: A Multicultural Mosaic.* 1991. Hanoi: Vietnam Foreign Languages Publishing House, fig. 65.

for courting and in ensembles to accompany dances and for rituals involving the *then.*

The Hmong of Vietnam appear to have the most extensive collection of instruments. These include the following: a musical leaf (*blùng*), a water-buffalo-horn oboe (*cu tu*), a Jew's harp (*u cha*), an end-blown flute (*trà pua*), a side-blown flute (*trà pùn tử*), a wooden oboe (*xi u*), a copper oboe (*pua*), a two-stringed fiddle (*lụ phù*), a jingling hollow metal ring (*chia nếnh*), a rattle (*trù nếnh*), small cymbals (*u siế*), a two-headed drum (*chua*), a moon-shaped lute (*điền xin,* also *thà chinh*), and a free-reed mouth organ (*kềnh*). The *kềnh* has six bamboo pipes, fixed into a long wooden wind chest. Each pipe has one metal free reed, except the shortest and longest pipes, which have two reeds in each; this arrangement allows the playing of an interval—a second or third—on a single pipe, but a single note can be obtained by opening or covering the respective holes for fingering. The White Hmong distinguish two types of *kềnh* by scale: the *kềnh là* plays D–F–G–A–C, and the *kềnh xinh* plays D–E–G–A–B.

Music of Upland Minorities in Burma, Laos, and Thailand

Ruriko Uchida
Amy Catlin

The peoples who inhabit the high plateaus of the Golden Triangle of Burma, Laos, and Thailand live in villages consisting of about twenty households each. As isolated minorities, they have few indigenous social or political groupings larger than villages. Some have accepted the central government of the state in which they live, but most have only a tenuous relationship to it. There are more than a hundred such groups, including the Karen of Thailand and Burma; the Kachin in Burma; the Akha, the Lahu, and the Lisu in Thailand; the Hmong, the Kmhmu, and the Yao in Laos; and the Nùng and the Lati in Vietnam. All practice slash-and-burn agriculture and subsist mainly on rice. Some grow opium poppies. Most are illiterate and animistic, and have no formal system of education. Their indigenous dress is highly colorful, often indicative of their subgroup.

Their method of agriculture follows a pattern that affects other aspects of their lives. At the beginning of the dry season, from January to mid-February, the people choose new areas for planting dry rice. In March, they go to the forest and clear a block of land. In April, they burn the cut trees and undergrowth, and spread the ashes over the land as fertilizer. After the paddy has been prepared, each family builds a simple bamboo hut in the corner of its field, so members of the family can guard against animals during the growing season. Just before the rainy season (in May and June), the villagers sow the rice: with sticks, the men dig shallow holes into which the women and children place the seeds. During the months of July and August, they weed the paddy. At the beginning of the dry season (November), they harvest the crops. In December, they thresh. While sowing and harvesting, they conduct collective rituals.

At the foot of the mountains, lowland minorities live agricultural lives influenced by social modernization. They have more complex cultures, combining elements from both the mountains and the plains. Most are integrated into their central governments. They include the Mon and the Shan in Burma; the Lawa, the Plains Karen, and the Tai-lue in Thailand; and the Black Tai and the Red Tai in Laos and Vietnam.

The distinction between lowland peoples and upland peoples is audible in their musics. In the lowlands, music has developed in association with courts, rituals, and

During the New Year celebrations (the most important and joyful time for the Lahu), ancestral spirits return to the village to witness the festivities. Villagers gather in their most colorful attire to drink, eat, sing New Year's songs, and dance.

the aristocracy. It includes professional musicians, as in the *hsaìñwaìñ* of Burma and the *piphat* of Thailand. In this type of music, melodic idiophones (gongs and xylophones) predominate. The texture is heterophonic (or polyphonically stratified), with five- and seven-tone scales the norm. Improvisation occurs within a structured framework. The lowland peoples have not only artistic music, but also artistic dance and drama, like the *lakhawn* in Thailand. For entertainment, they also perform simpler kinds of music.

In contrast, the upland minorities prefer simple traditional songs. Life and music are closely related for them, and they have no professional musicians. The structure of the music is mostly monophonic. Five-tone scales predominate, with a nucleus of a fourth. Improvisation appears in the variations of repeated phrases. The upland peoples enjoy dancing to a simple instrumental accompaniment.

Minority populations cannot be differentiated by country. Since they practice shifting cultivation, they often cross national boundaries. It is more meaningful to group them according to their linguistic affiliations—the language families to which they belong.

THE SINO-TIBETAN (TIBETO-BURMAN) LANGUAGE FAMILY

The Lahu (Mussur)

The Lahu are among the Lolo branch of the Tibeto-Burman family. They divide into at least four groups: Lahu-Hpu (White Lahu), Lahu-Na (Black Lahu), Lahu-Nyi (Red Lahu), and Lahu-Shi (Yellow Lahu), appellations deriving from the colors of the women's dresses. The Lahu of northern Thailand are called Lahu-Shehleh.

The Lahu live in villages spread over a wide area: China's Yunnan Province; the Kengtung area of Burma's Shan State; the northern Thai provinces of Chiangmai, Chiengrai, Lampang, Mae Hongson, and Tak; Nam Tha Province in northern Laos; and parts of northwestern Vietnam. Villages are usually located above 1,300 meters, and houses are built on pilings.

In 1990, the estimated Lahu population was roughly six hundred thousand, divided by country as follows: China, 411,000; Burma, 150,000; Thailand, 68,000; Laos, 10,000; and Vietnam, 4,000. The Lahu in Thailand and Laos have immigrated within the last century or so. New arrivals continue to slip across the Burma-Thai border as the political and economic situation in the Shan State deteriorates.

The Lahu engage in slash-and-burn agriculture on steep mountainsides. Hill rice is their staple. Since they live by shifting cultivation, the land in any given area is soon exhausted, and the village must move. The chief cash crop is opium; tea and chili peppers have secondary importance. As population pressure from the lowlands intensifies, the Lahu and the other upland peoples find their traditional way of life increasingly threatened; fresh, unclaimed land is no longer easy to obtain.

Most Lahu are animistic, believing in good, neutral, and evil spirits, above which is a supreme creator (*G'ui-Sha Er* 'Sky Ghost'). American missionaries, who have been preaching to the Lahu since the beginning of the twentieth century, reinterpret this deity as the Christian God. The most eager proselytizers are from the American Baptist Mission, which by 1950 had claimed twenty-eight thousand converts in Thailand and Burma. Christian Lahu villages do not grow opium.

For the Lahu in Thailand, the annual celebration of the lunar New Year affords traditional opportunities for courtship. Young men visit young women's villages, and boys and girls sing amatory songs to each other. Once a pair chooses to marry, a go-between makes the necessary arrangements. A period of premarital sexual activity invariably precedes the marriage.

The musical life of the Lahu

During the New Year celebrations (the most important and joyful time for the Lahu), ancestral spirits return to the village to witness the festivities. An altar is decorated with white paper streamers attached to bamboo sticks. To please the supreme creator, male and female human figures representing human souls are cut from paper. The senior village priest, headman, and elders offer prayers at a rice-cake altar, a symbolic New Year's tree, and an ancestral shrine. Each head of a household prays to the spirits for the prosperity and health of his household during the coming year. Then villagers gather in their most colorful attire to drink, eat, sing New Year's songs, and dance.

The Lahu perform a dance in which men stamp their feet collectively, and women form a closely swaying circle around them. The men continuously play a free-reed mouth organ with a gourd wind chest (*naw*) (figure 1). This is also a period of courtship for young people, who camp out some distance from the village around two big fires, one for the girls and one for the boys. All through the night, songs of love are sung back and forth, as are ballads and improvised prose. In the morning, the boys playfully rush the girls, and each boy tries to take the turban from the head of a girl who appeals to him. Returning this turban initiates negotiation and more serious contacts. Individual courting-song and love-song singing occurs throughout the year, encouraging sexual play.

FIGURE 1 The free-reed gourd mouth organ (*naw*) used in a Lahu-Shehleh bridge (soul-calling) ceremony. Photo by Paul and Elaine Lewis; used with permission.

The harvest celebration is also important to the Lahu. This ceremony is similar to New Year's. Beating a gong, the senior village priest chants prayers at his house, where a decorated altar has been set up. He gives thanks to the spirit guardian for that year's harvest and asks for a good harvest in the coming year. Then, dressed in their finery, the villagers gather to sing harvest songs and dance passionately, accompanied by a *naw,* a cymbal (*shae*), a gong (*bluck*), and a drum (*chack*).

While sawing, planting, cutting, harvesting, and pounding rice, the Lahu sing, play the *naw,* and dance. Beyond this, they have songs for weddings, funerals, shamanistic activities, curing, narration, and lullabies. At a wedding, the bride and bridegroom sing alternately about their expectations for their future; then guests sing congratulatory songs.

The Lahu have many narrative songs, including a myth of creation. Many Lahu-Na Christians sing Christian songs in church, with gospel songbooks written in the Lahu-Na language and staff notation. Other Christian Lahu also use these songbooks. The Lahu-Shehleh play their own variety of mouth organs (*nokuma, tolem*); their singing differs from that of other Lahu groups.

The structure of Lahu music

Lahu songs use melodies constructed on variations of a five-tone scale conceivable as C–D–E–G–A. They consist of three-tone melodies (C–G–A), four-tone melodies (G–C–D–E, C–E–G–A, G–A–C–E, A–D–F–G), and five-tone melodies (D–E–G–A–B, C–G–A–B–D, C–E–G–A–D, C–G–A–D–E). The vocal range is great, and melodies frequently have large intervals.

Lahu musical instruments

The most characteristic Lahu instruments are free-reed mouth organs, the *naw* and the *nokuma* (also *tolem*). The *naw* is widespread in Yunnan, northern Thailand, Laos, and Vietnam. About 35 centimeters long, it usually has five pipes; in some Lahu regions, it has three, six, or seven. The pipes are of bamboo, with a free reed of metal embedded in each. In bundle form, the pipes pierce a gourd, which serves as a wind chest. The *naw* is known to the Akha as *lachi* and to the Lisu as *fulu.* All Lahu use it for prayer, dancing, and entertainment.

The *nokuma* and the *tolem* have basically the same structure as the *naw.* They use a free reed in each of five pipes gathered into a gourd, but the pipes can be up to 1.5 meters long. The *tolem* is shorter and has a bamboo wind chamber. The Lahu also have a Jew's harp (*ata*). Other Lahu instruments include a three-stringed lute, a gong, and a goblet-shaped drum.

The Akha (Kaw, Ekaw, Hani)

The Akha language belongs to the southern Lolo branch of Tibeto-Burman. Not having their own writing, they use both Roman-based and Thai-based orthographies, devised for them by Christian missionaries.

The Akha believe their original homeland was southern Yunnan, and many still live in that area, where they are grouped with the Woni (Hani and Aini), Lolo-speakers of southern Yunnan. From there they migrated into eastern Kengtung State (Burma), to northern Laos, and to northern Thailand. Akha villages are above 2,000 meters. The houses are built on pilings, the chief's house in the center. On the path entering the village, a sacred gate is constructed, flanked by figures of male and female fertility. Since many Akha live far from administrative centers, their population is difficult to gauge. The most recent estimated figures are Burma, 180,000; China, 150,000; Laos, 59,000; and Thailand, 34,541.

The economic life of the Akha is based primarily on shifting agriculture and the cultivation of opium poppies. Other crops include rice, maize, millet, sugarcane, peppers, vegetables, tobacco, and tea. Hunting and fishing are subsidiary activities, and the Akha have retained their skills as gatherers. Pigs and chickens serve as food and sacrifices. Other livestock include cattle, buffaloes, and horses; the Akha in Thailand also eat dogs.

The Akha are animists. They respect ancestral spirits (*ne*), some of which are malevolent and cause illness; others, including the guardian spirits of houses and villages, are associated with familiar but benign objects. Sometimes, the functions of village priest and village shaman are handled by one person. The shaman (*tumo*) can communicate with good and evil spirits alike. He conducts ceremonies and cures sick people. The Akha wear traditional clothing: the women wear short skirts; to ward off evil spirits, they wear headdresses, even when they sleep.

The musical life of the Akha

The Akha sing with good voices and breath control. Conscientious about maintaining their traditional festivals, they have many annual ceremonies during which music is performed. The relationship of ceremonial music to farming plays an important role in Akha society. There are nine annual ceremonies, each with special songs about the cultivation of rice: before planting, during planting, while weeding the paddy, before the harvest, while driving away evil spirits, for newly ripened rice plants, for cutting the rice plants, for gathering the cut rice plants, and for threshing.

The Akha are tolerant in raising their children. After coming of age, boys (at fifteen) and girls (at thirteen) can marry at will. Young people of these ages sing courtship songs every evening, often at the holy grounds at the edge of a village, where they set up special swings. Annual festivals and New Year's celebrations are prime occasions for courting: young women and men dress up and strut about, showing off their finery and singing songs to one another.

When someone becomes ill, villagers summon a healer. They offer two chickens, a pig, and three eggs in the patient's house, and outside the house they prepare a dog, a pig, five chickens, and a cup of rice wine as sacrifices. The healer sings magically curative songs and offers up prayers. Elders sing admonitory songs to young people, both to keep village life orderly and to instill tribal identity.

Akha funerals are accompanied by animal sacrifices. The corpse is left for a week in the house. Attaching considerable importance to the souls of the dead, the Akha often offer food to the ancestral spirits who attend the funeral. The ritualist sings a funeral song over and over, including a biography of the deceased and instructions on how to serve the ancestral spirits.

The structure of Akha music

Minorities in upland Southeast Asia, considering improvisation a sign of vocal ability, tend to improvise both texts and melodies. However, the Akha seldom improvise. The texts and melodies of their songs are fixed because they wish to maintain their traditional festivals without change.

Akha songs have two types of rhythmic organization: songs of love and the cultivation of rice are unmetrical, but funeral, shamanistic, and admonitory songs are metrical. The former have flowing melodic lines; the latter are repetitions of short and simple recitations. Akha scales are as follows: three-tone (D–E–G), four-tone (D–F–G–A, A–D–F–G), and five-tone (C–D–E–G–A, D–F–G–A–C, A–C–D–F–G).

Akha musical instruments

The Akha play a three-stringed lute (*döm*), a free-reed mouth organ (*lachi*), and a Jew's harp (*chau*), both during festivals and at leisure. They use the *chau* as a disguiser

Akha Tibeto-Burman-speaking people living in north Thailand, Burma, and China

Lisu Biteto-Burman-speaking people living in Thailand, Burma, and China

fulu Lisu free-reed mouth organ with bamboo pipes and gourd wind chest

subü Lisu three-stringed, fretted lute

Karen Tibeto-Burman-speaking people living primarily in upland Burma and northwest Thailand

FIGURE 2 Akha women and girls rhythmically pound bamboo sections on an overturned pig trough to honor village leaders during the swing ceremony. Photo by Paul and Elaine Lewis; used with permission.

of the voice to speak songs of love. They also dance. Young girls often sing while dancing in various styles, including skipping or jumping in lines or circles. The Akha have a dance in which men stamp around in a circle and women form a line to shuffle back and forth in quick, short skips. During some ceremonies Akha women and girls beat bamboo tubes rhythmically into an overturned pig-feeding trough accompanied by a drum and a gong (figure 2).

The Lisu (Lisaw, Lu-tzu)

The Lisu language belongs to the southern Lolo branch of Tibeto-Burman. The Chinese classify Lisu-speakers according to differences in dress and dialect: Bai Lisu (White Lisu), He Lisu (Black Lisu), and Hua Lisu (Flowery Lisu). The Black Lisu of the Upper Salween River have been independent since the early twentieth century. Their original homeland was likely in the north, toward Tibet. Today they are concentrated in Yunnan, China; scattered communities live in Shan State (Burma) and northern Thailand. In 1989, the estimated population of Lisu-speakers was 481,000 in China, 250,000 in Burma, and 18,000 in Thailand.

Villages are located on ridges and mountaintops, at elevations ranging from 1,300 to 3,000 meters. Houses are built on piles or directly on the ground. Swidden agriculture and hunting are the most important economic activities. Rice and maize are the staples. Additional crops include beans, yams, peppers, tobacco, and cotton. Opium poppies are raised by most Lisu, who rank second only to the Hmong as producers of opium. Animals hunted include bears, deer, panthers, foxes, and birds. Domestic animals include goats, pigs, ponies, and chickens.

The Lisu are animists who practice both the worship of ancestors and exorcism. They believe in a variety of spirits, including spirits of the jungle, the earth, the wind, the field, the crops, and heaven; village guardian spirits; and a lightning demon. Malevolent spirits cause illnesses. In shamanistic rituals (*ne pha*), performers treat illnesses by going into trance, singing, and shaking.

The annual spring festival is the high point of the Lisu year. One day during this period is reserved for honoring ancestors with sacrifices of pigs and with visits to graves—a time of drinking and merrymaking, the prime occasion for boys to go courting in neighboring villages.

The musical life of the Lisu

All Lisu instrumentalists are men. Young, unmarried men are the most active instrumentalists, and in every village a few are recognized as the most gifted. This reputation depends not so much on technical skill (as long as the musician upholds the community-wide standards of performance) as on the extent of repertoire and ability to play for hours, or even days, during festivals.

Instrumental music has a strict meter and sung music is freely metered. The two repertoires do not mix, though they are sometimes performed side by side at the same functions. Songs are sung by both sexes. Boys and girls sing songs of courtship, not only during New Year's celebrations, but also in everyday life. On these occasions, someone usually plays an instrument nearby.

During nuptial and New Year's celebrations, festival songs can be heard emanating from Lisu houses while dancing goes on around the spirits' tree, close by. Singers and instrumentalists do not seem disturbed by each other's music. During New Year's celebrations, dancing and music continue for days.

Both dance and music have a religious function to the Lisu. They say that the sounds of instruments and vocalizations please good spirits and prevent disaster. The New Year's performance stimulates a sense of Lisu identity: soul-calling songs and shaman's songs fulfill a religious function, and the texts of many songs stress the values and rules of Lisu society and praise Lisu identity.

FIGURE 3 A Lisu lute (*subü*) hangs on the wall of a house. Photo by Terry E. Miller.

The structure of Lisu music

In Lisu song, the melodic line is typically descending in contour. There are six- and seven-tone scales. Melodies are not fixed: no two singers sing a song exactly the same way. Instead, a song exists in the singer's mind as a basic melodic structure—intervals and relative durations that must be utilized in the melodic flow.

Within these limits, each singer uses the melodic form as he or she likes. The interval of a perfect fourth, formed by sustained tones, is structurally important. Songs are in free meter, regulated by a slow, unstable, organic pulse, which varies from singer to singer. The tempo is about ninety beats per minute. The vocal technique is breathy and unarticulated, and the resultant vocal sound is soft and flowing.

Lisu musical instruments

Lisu instruments include a free-reed mouth organ (*fulu*), a flute (*julü*), and a three-stringed long lute (*subü*) (figure 3). The three may play together as an ensemble.

The Karen

Widely distributed throughout the northern parts of Burma, Laos, and Thailand, the Karen number about 3.4 million. They are usually divided into four subgroups, according to their dialectal differences: the Sgaw, the P'wo, the Thaungthu (or Pa-o), and the Kayah (Karenni). The Sgaw are the most numerous, followed by the P'wo, the Thaungthu, and the Kayah. Racial and linguistic affiliations for these subgroups are not definitely established, but linguists accept that the Karen language belongs to the Tibeto-Burman family.

Formerly the Karen led a typical tribal life, living in longhouses, cultivating hill rice, and practicing animism. Today, the Karen who live in mountainous districts preserve their traditional customs, but those in the plains engage in paddy-rice cultivation and have changed their life-style from tribal to agricultural. In many areas, the lives of the plains Karen are indistinguishable from those of the Thai peasants with whom they share the plains.

Traditionally the Karen were animists. They believed in a variety of spirits, both good and malevolent. These included spirits of water, earth, rocks, trees, paddies, and swidden fields. Ceremonies of prayer in the paddies and swidden fields were performed several times a year to request spiritual aid in growing rice. The most important spirit was Bgha, the matrilineal guardian spirit of households. Some village leaders acted as shamans, conducting worship and medical treatment and administering the village.

Toward the end of the 1800s, missionaries—primarily American Baptists—came from Burma to Karen villages. After the introduction of Christianity, a group calling itself Christian Karen was organized, and they have renounced animistic worship and the use of opium and alcohol. The missionaries also devised a Karen alphabet, based on Burmese.

Buddhism was introduced to the upland Karen from both lowland Karen and the lowland mainstream population. Buddhist Karen are quite devout: they often visit temples and making offerings. On the traditional New Year's festival (*songklan*), they gather at temples and vigorously sing merit-making songs while wearing their best red (adults, boys) or white (girls) clothes.

The musical life of the Karen

The Karen have long had a distinctive traditional music, which has played important roles in their lives. At weddings, the elders, invited as guests, sing to newlyweds about how to earn a living and how to preserve Karen traditional culture.

During funerals, elders sing laments and walk around the coffin for three days and nights. After that, young boys and girls alternately sing courtship songs—a cus-

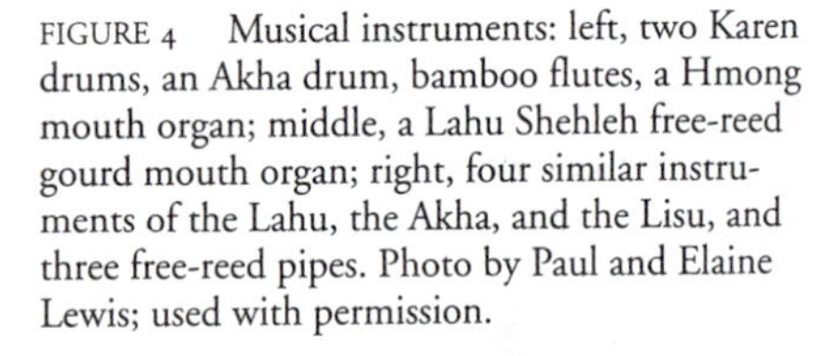

FIGURE 4 Musical instruments: left, two Karen drums, an Akha drum, bamboo flutes, a Hmong mouth organ; middle, a Lahu Shehleh free-reed gourd mouth organ; right, four similar instruments of the Lahu, the Akha, and the Lisu, and three free-reed pipes. Photo by Paul and Elaine Lewis; used with permission.

FIGURE 5 Chordophones: top, used by the Karen; bottom, used by the Lisu, the Lahu, and sometimes the Akha. Photo by Paul and Elaine Lewis; used with permission.

tom that may have arisen from a wish to regenerate the soul of the deceased. The Karen have an abundance of amatory songs: a young boy sings in the evening underneath his sweetheart's window, or each sings to the other while working in a rice field.

The Karen have an especially large collection of legends, whose performance is accompanied by the traditional harp (*tünak*). These include the myth of the Karen's origin, the story of their ancestor Thaw Meh Pah, and tales of their supernatural dreamland, LaLa. Other traditional songs include New Year's songs, cradle songs, children's songs, admonitory songs, house-building songs, and drinking songs.

After 1945, American popular music, including jazz and rock, entered Karen villages through Thailand. Young Karen prefer these kinds of music to their traditional music. Using texts from traditional Karen legends, they play and compose new music in popular styles.

The structure of Karen music

Karen traditional songs have many remarkable musical traits, closely related to their language, which is tonal. This relationship restricts songs to narrow intervals, so melodies are conceived as vehicles for poems. The Sgaw Karen language has six tones in three registers.

The most common Karen scale is based on a perfect fourth, which forms the nucleus of melodies, so one can consider it a trait of melodic motion. Karen scales are as follows: two-tone (D–E), three-tone (D–E–G, D–F–G, E–A–C, D–G–B, D–G–C, C–E–F), four-tone (D–F–G–C, D–E–G–A, E–G–A–C, D–E–G–C, C–E–G–B), and five-tone (D–F–G–A–C, C–E–F–G–B, E–A–C–[E]–G). The last is considered a continuation of a three-tone scale.

Karen music has few accents and tends to be unmetrical. There is some improvisation on musical phrases, but the Karen improvise primarily on the words of songs; they slightly vary repeated melodic phrases to accommodate textual changes. The Karen have good disciplined breath control and sing with a narrow throat. The P'wo Karen sing nasally.

Karen musical instruments

Besides the harp (mentioned above), the Karen play a buffalo horn (*kui*), a bronze drum (*mahoratuk*), a bamboo tube zither (*pap law*), and a three-stringed lute (*tha*). They play the buffalo horn and the bronze drum for religious occasions. Other

When the Kmhmu entertain guests, they gather in their houses, drink homemade grain alcohol from jars, sing welcoming songs, and play musical instruments.

instruments include a goblet-shaped drum, a gong, and cymbals, all of Thai origin (figures 4 and 5). Around 1900, Christian missionaries from Burma set up schools in Karen villages and taught gospel songs and other Western religious music (which they call chant). The Karen succeeded in playing gospel songs and composing new ones.

THE AUSTROASIATIC (MON-KHMER) LANGUAGE FAMILY

The Kmhmu (Kammu, Khmu, Khamu)

The Kmhmu are the largest of the Mon-Khmer groups in northern Laos; they also dwell in northern Thailand and northern Vietnam. The Kmhmu language belongs to the Kmhmuic branch of the northern Mon-Khmer family. Estimates of Kmhmu population in northern Laos are around 400,000, in Thailand between 5,000 and 50,000, and in Vietnam, 32,000. Most Kmhmu living in Thailand have become assimilated into the prevailing national culture. Since Mon-Khmer-speakers preceded the Lao in Laos, the ethnic Lao call the Kmhmu their older brothers.

Kmhmu houses are often built on pilings on mountainsides, at elevations of around 1 kilometer. The Kmhmu engage in slash-and-burn agriculture, and their staple is rice. Other crops include maize, sugarcane, tobacco, and occasionally cotton and opium. For rotating their fields, the Kmhmu use a system that permits their villages not to be moved over wide areas. Permanent wet-rice cultivation techniques, where they are used, are borrowed from the Lao, because many Kmhmu work for Lao farmers as hired laborers. Fishing, hunting, and gathering are supplementary jobs. The Kmhmu gather leaves, roots, bamboo shoots, and mushrooms in the wild. Domestic animals include chickens, ducks, pigs, and dogs. Buffaloes are highly valued both for food and for sacrifices, but few Kmhmu can afford them. The Kmhmu are skilled weavers of baskets and trays, which they trade through Lao merchants.

The traditional Kmhmu system of beliefs is animistic. It deals with spirits of the village, the jungle, mountains, rocks, the sun, and water. When there is an illness, a shaman determines which spirit is causing it, and prescribes the necessary sacrifices; he also takes part in other village ceremonies. The Kmhmu have totems, and the penalty for touching the totemic animal or plant is burning by torch.

The musical life of the Kmhmu

Music has an important role in Kmhmu ceremonies. Shamans ritually call on ancestral spirits and spirits of water, rice, and other items. By chanting and playing the gong, they send off the spirit of a dead person. They sing songs and play musical instruments in ceremonies for weddings, building new houses, harvests, and the New Year.

When the Kmhmu entertain guests, they gather in their houses, drink homemade grain alcohol from jars, sing welcoming songs, and play musical instruments. During such times of amusement, young men and women sing long amatory songs in alternation; they usually express affection indirectly, but on such occasions choose their life partners. The Kmhmu also sing lowland-derived popular songs.

The structure of Kmhmu music

There are structurally two different types of songs in the Kmhmu culture. In one type, each song has a unique melody, consisting of a short musical phrase repeated for each new line of words. These lines are often built of five, six, or seven syllables, with the last syllable in each line rhyming with the first of the following line. Many children's songs and cradle songs are of this type, as are the songs of shamanistic ceremonies, such as sending the soul to heaven and telling fortunes at funerals. The melodic range is narrow, and emphasis is on rhythmic activity. The most commonly used meter is duple.

The other type of Kmhmu song consists of verbally transmitted poems, sung to a limited number of melodic formulas, principally only one melodic formula per village. These melodies can be grouped into several types, which, though structurally similar, are superficially distinct. The distribution of types approximates dialect areas. Each song begins with a long, high-pitched shout, and gradually descends to a pitch one octave lower. This is a kind of recitation tone, usually sung at the end of the song. The metrical structure is free. Poems, such as those for welcoming and songs of love, are often improvised within fixed melodies. This type of song is sung on festive occasions, including weddings, New Year celebrations, and harvests.

Kmhmu songs have two-tone scales (C–G, C–D), three-tone scales (C–D–G, C–E–G), four-tone scales (A–C–E–G, C–E–F–G, A–D–E–G), and five-tone scales (D–E–G–A–C, D–E–G–A–B, C–D–E–G–A).

Kmhmu musical instruments

Kmhmu musical instruments are two bamboo flutes (*pii, tot*), a free-reed raft mouth organ (*khen*), a lute (*saw*), a Jew's harp, a pair of bamboo beaters (*klt*), a clapper (*taaw taaw*), a gong, and a bronze drum. The flutes are of Kmhmu origin, but the *khen* was adapted from the lowland Lao people. The bronze drum is used in ceremonies, especially for summoning rain.

THE TAI-KADAI LANGUAGE FAMILY

The Shan (Taiyai, Dai [China])

The term *Shan* is Burmese for Tai-speakers in eastern Burma, but related people live in northern Thailand and southern China, where they are called Taiyai and Dai, respectively. The Shan are primarily concentrated in Burma's Shan State, where they are strongly Burmanized, though Tai speech, Buddhist religion, and a unique musical style make the Shan distinctive. The number of Tai-speakers in Burma is unknown at present but was estimated at 1.3 million in 1931, and in 1982 China counted 839,000 Dai.

Shan settlements tend to be permanent. Villages are located in valleys or on pockets of level land in the hills. The houses, built almost entirely of bamboo, are raised as high as three meters off the ground. At one end of the village, pagodas, monasteries, shrines, and rest houses, all of which are essential to the religious life of the community, are clustered together.

The Shan engage primarily in wet-rice cultivation. Other crops include tobacco, cotton, sugarcane, maize, vegetables, and fruit. The Shan use opium only as medicine. Domestic animals include horses, water buffaloes, pigs, and chickens. Localized cottage industries include pottery making, lacquerware crafting, and silver working.

The Shan are predominantly Theravada Buddhists. Between the ages of ten and twelve, boys enter a monastery for a short time, serving the monks and learning from them the precepts of Buddhism. Monks are not hierarchically organized, but are divided into sects, according to the strictness of their religious vows. With Buddhism, the Shan believe in the existence of spirits, supernatural forces, omens, and the significance of dreams. Buddhist monks are sometimes credited with occult powers.

At about age fourteen, boys are decorated by a specialist in tattooing. This is regarded as a sign of manhood. Girls ignore as potential spouses any boys who have not been tattooed.

Under independent Burma, some thirty-three substates make up the Shan State, which theoretically has autonomy in matters of internal administration. The heads of substates (*sawbwa*) enjoy the loyalty of most Shan, though they have lost much of their old autonomy. Land-reform programs and compulsory-education plans are now advocated by the Union Government.

The musical life of the Shan

Among the minorities of upland Southeast Asia, the Shan are the most integrated into the cultural modes of mainstream urban society. When the Shan had their own system of education in the Shan State of Burma, they instructed students in their own language and culture. Today, Shan students receive most of their education in the temples or schools of the country in which they reside, whether it be Thailand or Burma, in the majority language.

Shan ensemble music is nearly as complex as that of lowland Southeast Asian peoples. There are three major Shan ensembles—for Buddhist ceremonies, dramas, and entertainment.

The Shan perform Buddhist music in Buddhist ceremonies, especially on the traditional New Year (*songklan*). Villagers in the temple often perform Buddhist music. The contents of these songs include praise of, and prayers for, the Buddha and the philosophy of Buddhism. The Shan often sing Buddhist songs accompanied by the ceremonial ensemble, consisting of a large two-headed drum (*khong*), three sizes of pitched gongs (*mong*), and cymbals (*chap*).

The Shan also have a repertoire of artistic dramas (*yikay*), which resemble the Thai *lakhawn* more than they do its namesake, the Thai *li-ke*. These dramas combine dancing, singing, and instrumental music. Sometimes a performance continues throughout a day and a night. The ensemble for the drama consists of a four-stringed lute, a three-stringed lute, a violin, a flute, a two-headed drum, and cymbals.

The ensemble for leisure music performs the most refined music of the Shan. This ensemble consists of a xylophone (*ranat thum*), a violin, a drum (*taphon*), a tuned drum set (*patt waìñ*), cymbals (*chap*), a fiddle (*toro*), and a small, stick-beaten wooden block (*sengkok*). This ensemble has been influenced by the Burmese *hsaìñwaìñ* and the *piphat* and *mahori* of the central Thai.

The Shan also have songs for social occasions, including amatory songs, New Year's songs, rice-planting songs, harvest songs, fishing songs, visiting songs, drinking songs, and cradle songs. There are, however, no customary songs for funerals. An especially large number of songs of love are available, some for singing by young men and women alternately for courtship.

The structure of Shan music

Shan songs are closely related to their language, which is tonal. They are sung roughly following the tones of their language. There are three vocal styles: *kwamlong khong*, *kwamse khong*, and *kwamcha thai*. Outsiders have difficulty drawing sharp distinctions among these. The Shan associate *kwamcha thai* with their drama.

The Shan use five-tone scales (C–D–E–G–A, D–F–G–A–C) and six-tone scales

(C–E–F–G–A–B, C–D–E–G–A–B). The scale C–E–F–G–A–B has the same tuning used in the Burmese *hsaìñwaìñ*.

THE MIAO-YAO LANGUAGE FAMILY

The Yao (Mian, Man)

The widely used linguistic term *Miao-Yao* is problematic, since both designations are pejorative terms assigned by outsiders. Though officially known as *Yao,* a Chinese term (meaning 'dog' or 'savage'), these people refer to themselves as Mian or Iu Mian (People). In Laos and Vietnam, they are called Man, also meaning 'people'.

According to ancient written records in China, the Yao's ancestors lived in Nanjing, China, where they suffered from drought. Twelve Yao households left for Guangdong and lived there peacefully for eighteen generations, until oppression drove them to Guizhou, then Vietnam and Laos; and from there, they migrated to Thailand.

The Yao language belongs to the Miao-Yao family. They have no indigenous script, but some Yao use Chinese characters. Their estimated population is in Vietnam, 12,000; in Laos, 5,000 (in 1961); and in Thailand, 36,140 (in 1988). The Yao prefer to locate along streams, at heights of about 1 kilometer. Their houses are large, built directly on the ground. They engage in slash-and-burn agriculture and plant mainly rice, opium poppies, and maize. Garden crops include cotton, tobacco, and vegetables; domestic animals are pigs, chickens, horses, and buffaloes. They also engage in commercial crafts such as embroidery and silversmithing. Their earning ability is higher than that of other hill tribes because of their talents as traders.

The Yao are animists, who place great importance on reverence for ancestors. A priest (*mo kung*), conducts spirit-related ceremonies. His power lies in his knowledge of incantations taken from books written in adaptations of Chinese characters. The coming-of-age ceremony (*gua deng*), ancestral worship (*on tsau, ho nian*), and the rite of prayer for everlasting life and immortality (*zuddan*) are important Yao rites, some of which have been influenced by Chinese Taoism.

The musical life of the Yao

The Yao sometimes play music for entertainment, but most of their music is closely related to important events of human life. Ceremonial music, performed for weddings, funerals, and worship of ancestors, has a particularly important role.

During a wedding, young guest musicians play congratulatory music on an ensemble of drums, cymbals, gongs, and an oboe (*yat*), and other guests sing nuptial songs. At a funeral, the ritualist plays a free-reed buffalo-horn aerophone before the coffin is carried from the house; then he continues the service by reciting funeral songs and Buddhist sutras.

At harvest ceremonies, ritualists hold shamanistic services. They call ancestral spirits, go into trance, and dance while holding live chickens with both hands, accompanied by drums, gongs, and cymbals. They groan a descending melody. The pace of their dancing accelerates; they become possessed and begin shouting. After sacrificing chickens and offering the blood to spirits, they dance again, carrying the dead chickens and communicating with the spirits. This kind of shamanistic worship appears in many kinds of ancestral ceremonies.

At New Year's festivals, villagers dress up, drink liquor, sing, and dance, and the most important event is the singing of the narrative song "Banko," about the Yao ancestral dog—a story that helps keep the identity of the Yao alive.

The Yao encourage premarital sex. A girl sings amatory songs beside her lover's house at night. When the boy comes out, they go to a hidden place, sing alternately, and if both agree, sleep in the same bed.

Yao Upland Sino-Tibetan group living in Thailand, Vietnam, and Laos

Hmong Formerly called Miao, a Sino-Tibetan group living in Thailand, Laos, Vietnam, and China

swidden Shifting cultivated field on land cleared of forest

qeej Hmong free-reed mouth organ with six bamboo pipes and elongated wind chest

ncas Hmong Jew's harp, made of metal

The Yao also have collective social songs: work songs in the rice fields, narrative songs of the "seven starts," harvest songs, and lullabies. Owing to the influence of Chinese culture, some Yao use Chinese characters and communicate Chinese images in their literature. Therefore, the poetic texts of Yao songs have become more complex than those of other upland minorities. The Yao also compose poems and improvise the texts of songs.

The structure of Yao music

There are two styles of Yao songs: a narrative style and a vocal style. Songs of the narrative style are metrical (in 2/4 time) and have a melodic nucleus of perfect fourths. Sometimes, the first tone of a song is prolonged. Songs of the vocal style are in free meter. High tones, located at the beginning and middle of the melody, are prolonged, and the melody slowly descends to its end. The structure of these songs consists of the repetition of similar short musical phrases, which have slight variations based on the singer's improvisational abilities.

The scales are classified as two-tone (D–G), four-tone (D–E–G–A, C–E–G–A, D–G–A–B), and five-tone (C–D–E–G–A, D–E–G–A–B, E–F–G–B–C). The musical instruments are an oboe (*yat*), a wooden drum with ox-hide heads, a gong, and cymbals.

—Ruriko Uchida

The Hmong

Hmong words are spelled here in the Roman Popular Alphabet (RPA). Final consonants indicate the tone of the word and are thus not pronounced the way they look to most readers. Double vowels indicate nasalization. Hence, *qeej* is pronounced something like /kaeŋ/, with a falling tone. A *b* denotes a high-level tone; a *j,* high-falling; a *v,* mid-rising; an N-dash (–), mid-level; an *s,* lower-mid-level; a *g,* low-breathy; an *m,* low-glottalized; a *d,* low-rising.

Hmong (*Mong, Hmoob, Moob*) is the name of certain swidden agriculturalists in the higher elevations (900 to 1,500 meters) of northern Vietnam, Laos, and Thailand. They are also known in Western literature as Meo and Miao, an adaptation from *miao* 'sprouts,' the pejorative Chinese name for non-Chinese peoples of southern and southwestern China, numbering about 6 million. Other Hmongic groups in south and southwest China call themselves Mhu (also Hmu), Qo Hsiong, Mong, and Hmao.

—Amy Catlin

The Chinese distinguish the Hmong-Miao according to the predominant color of their dress: Bai Miao (White), Hei Miao (Black), Hong Miao (Red), Hua Miao (Flowery), and Qing Miao (Blue). The ancestors of these Hmong may have migrated to central China and the Yellow River from Siberia before 2000 B.C. Today's Hmong may be descendants of the "three Miao" mentioned in the Chinese *Book of Documents* (third century B.C.), which purports to cover a period as early as 2255 B.C. One theory (Quincy 1988) proposes that early Hmong were Caucasians who originated in southern Russia or the Iranian plateau, speaking a language unrelated to any language other than Yao-Mien, another non-Chinese minority tongue found in China and highland Southeast Asia.

Some Hmong became more or less sinicized, adopting lowland-rice agriculture and other elements of Chinese civilization. The Chinese called them cooked; others, who resisted sinicization, they called raw. From the surrounding linguistic environment, their language acquired tonality, and they absorbed other cultural traits. According to this theory, their racial makeup became mixed with that of the Chinese, mostly through force, so that blond, blue-eyed Hmong have become a rarity; most, however, do not have the epicanthic fold. Whatever their origins may be, and despite various accretions, the Hmong retain a distinctive language and culture, long noted for the richness of its lore.

The Hmong of Southeast Asia first came from Guizhou to Vietnam in the mid-1700s, when, in successive waves, they fled Chinese persecution. By 1900, between forty thousand and sixty thousand had emigrated, mainly from Guizhou, Sichuan, Guangxi, and Yunnan provinces, settling in the highlands of Vietnam and Laos, with a few thousand reaching Thailand. In the mid-twentieth century, about a third of the Lao Hmong population joined with noncommunist forces; after the Pathet Lao victory in 1975, many thousands of these fled to refugee camps along the Thai-Lao border. About one hundred thousand have since resettled in Australia, Canada, France, and the United States, with a nearly equal number remaining in Thai camps or returning to Laos.

The Hmong build their houses on the ground and practice shifting cultivation; some have begun cultivating irrigated paddies. Their staples are rice and maize, and opium poppies are an important cash crop. Other crops include sugarcane, yams, beans, tobacco, and cotton. The Hmong are skilled hunters and fishermen, and they keep ponies, goats, buffaloes, and chickens as domestic animals. Women are proficient in embroidery and other techniques, and men in silversmithing, especially in the making of women's jewelry from old silver coins. As a result, the women are richly dressed at festivals.

—RURIKO UCHIDA

Hmong musical instruments

The *qeej* consists of a wooden wind chest (*taub* 'gourd') with a long tapering neck (*kav* 'stem'), ending in a mouth hole (*ncauj* 'mouth'). The wooden section is made from two identical pieces of mahogany, bound together with straps. The six bamboo tubes (*ntiv* 'finger') are variously curving or straight; they vary in length from the smallest for a child's instrument to about two meters. Each has a single hole for fingering above the wind chest and a metal free reed (*nplaim* 'tongue') over a hole in the pipe enclosed within the wind chest. For extra volume, the lowest tube, the thickest and shortest one, often contains two or three reeds. The tubes are inserted vertically through the wind chest. When the player exhales or inhales and covers one or more holes for fingering, eddies at the edge of the vibrating reed create a standing wave in the tube, and a musical tone is heard (figures 6, 7).

There are two genres of *qeej* compositions: texted (*zaj qeej*), and textless (*ntiv qeej*). Both genres are played successively in rituals, including funerals, ancestral rites, offerings to vital spirits, sacrifices to the drum, and marriages. Texted *qeej* divide into *zaj kab ke* (central to the ritual, directly addressing the soul) and *zaj ua ke* (more

FIGURE 6 During a New Year's celebration, two men play Hmong mouth organs (*qeej*). The White Hmong village of Long Lan, Luang Prabang District, Laos. Photo by Amy Catlin, 1989.

numerous, interspersed between the central points as optional entertainment in the recounting of stories).

The ritual melodies of *zaj kab ke* are usually tripartite in structure. Each of the strophes (*nges,* also *nqais*) is repeated three times, forming a unit (*tshooj*). The end of each unit is marked by a tone played on a specific pipe. When playing around or under the framework for the drum, the player makes three turns counterclockwise to represent the voyage in search of the vital spirit, three turns in place to disorient the spirit so it does not invade the material world, three turns clockwise for the return voyage, and three turns in place again.

The Hmong maintain a close relationship between speech and music. The instrument most capable of conveying the vowels and consonants of Hmong speech is the Jew's harp (*ncas*) (figure 8). It is also quiet, so the player and any listeners must be close together, and others cannot easily eavesdrop. Perhaps the most elegant and sonorous of any Jew's harp in the world, the *ncas* is made of brass, often protected in a scrimshaw case adorned with beads, coins, and colorful threads. Made of a single sheet of brass, whose thickness varies from handle to tip, the blade often thins to less

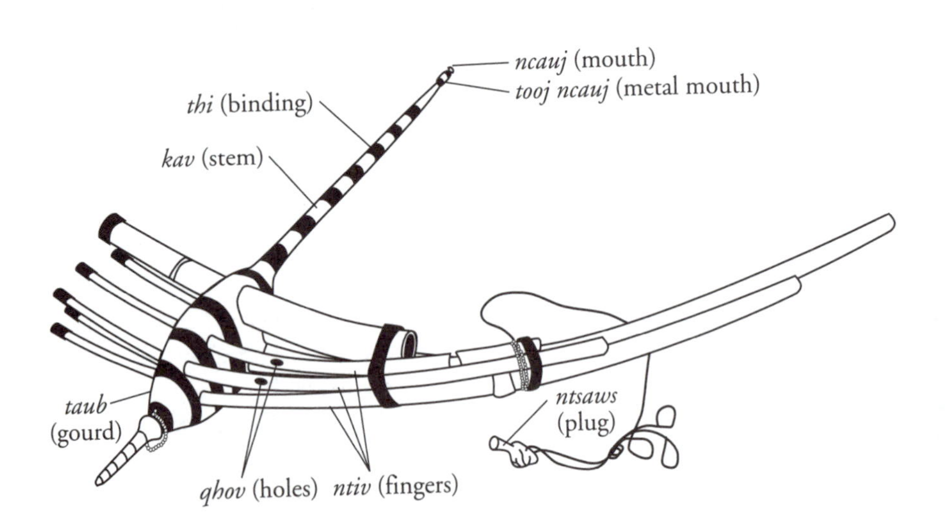

FIGURE 7 The named parts of the Hmong mouth organ (*qeej*). Courtesy of John Michael Kohler Arts Center.

FIGURE 8 May Seha, a Blue Hmong singer, holds a Jew's harp (*ncas*). Chiangmai, Thailand. Photo by Amy Catlin, 1980.

than a millimeter. The tongue and the frame are separated by a hairline incision, which typically outlines three points. The central point is the longest, ending near the handle, and the base of the tongue is closest to the tip, which is strummed (figure 9).

The free-reed pipe (*raj nplaim*) may also be used as an instrument of courting. It is not capable of conveying vowels and consonants, but the player always uses sung poetry for the source of the melody, and frequently both player and listener believe that the text has been understood from the melody alone. The pipe resembles a single *qeej* pipe, but with additional holes for fingering (figure 10).

Other secular instruments include a fipple flute (*raj pus li*) and a two-stringed bowed fiddle (*xi xov*), both played for courting. A funeral horn is mentioned in *qeej* texts, but it has disappeared. Formerly, a free-reed buffalo horn was used, as was a bamboo trumpet.

—AMY CATLIN

Hmong ritual music

Most Hmong are animists. They revere ancestors and believe that spirits (looking and behaving like human beings) inhabit trees, rocks, and fields. Both male and female shamans cure illnesses, practice divining, and conduct exorcisms. Chinese culture has strongly influenced Hmong material culture and religious beliefs. Consequently, some Hmong ceremonies (such as the Quest of the Souls) mix an archaic Hmong character with elements of Chinese Taoism. Some Hmong have converted to Christianity.

—RURIKO UCHIDA

A cultural feature that supports the theory of Hmong origins in Central Asia or beyond is the rite *ua neeb* (*ua* 'to do'; *neeb* 'friendly spirits'), conducted as if the shaman were on horseback, riding through the cosmos, accompanied by the sounds of a gong, a sistrum, and a rattle. The shaman sits facing the altar on a flexible four-legged bench, which serves as his horse, like the Bouriat Siberian shaman's horse baton; his face is covered with a black veil, like the Yakut Siberian mask or handkerchief covering the eyes; his recited liturgy refers to helmet and breastplate of copper and iron, also like the Siberian's. The shaman's journey in trance is conducted to cure sickness by fighting with a sword the evil spirits the shaman hunts down in the cosmos. While he shakes his sistrum (held in his right hand like the horse's reins, and sounding the cadence of a gallop), his helper strikes the gong. The ring rattle held on the shaman's left index finger serves as the horse's bell. The rings hanging from the circular sistrum function as divinatory tools, whose configuration when tossed to the ground tells whether the vital spirits have been captured. A blade protruding from the sistrum cuts invisible connections between spirits and pathways to death. All

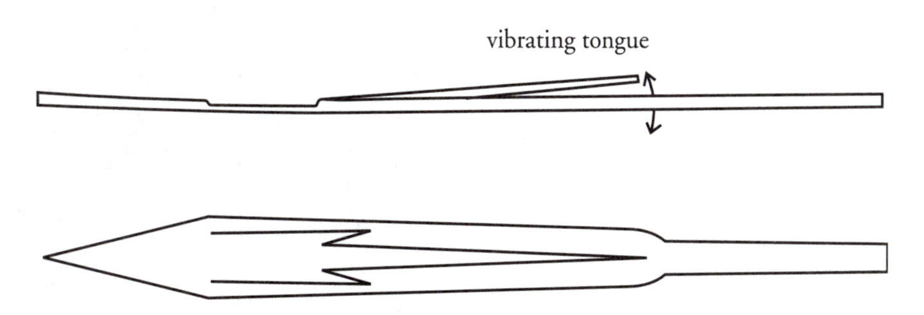

FIGURE 9 Front and side views of the Hmong Jew's harp (*ncas*). Courtesy of John Michael Kohler Arts Center.

At Hmong festivals, musicians entertain the soul of the deceased to keep it from wandering away. After guiding the soul for three days and nights, the musicians release it to find its way to heaven.

FIGURE 10 A Hmong player of the free-reed pipe with finger holes. Photo by Terry E. Miller.

three musical instruments are festooned with strips of red cloth to frighten evil spirits (figure 11).

The shaman liberally punctuates his chants with sounds like *brrr-brrr-brrr,* with tongue trilling in imitation of a horse's whinny. Sung syllabically to melodies in which the eight speech tones are coordinated with four pitches, the texts recount the adventures of the flying horseman as he chases and vanquishes the offending spirits. Ritual texts are also chanted at the annual New Year's festival and for life-cycle events, including marriages and funerals.

—Amy Catlin

Funerals

At Hmong funerals, the corpse lies on a bier. Facing the body, one musician plays the *qeej* and another beats a drum. A lamenter stands to one side of the body, and the spouse of the dead person (if living) to the other; the singer sings loudly, with a descending melody, while the spouse sobs. A priest prays to the dead soul. After the ceremony, the guests form a procession and, accompanied by solemn music, carry the corpse to a nearby mountain.

Throughout the funeral, the six-tubed free-reed mouth organ portrays liturgical texts in a speech-surrogate system. Vowels and consonants cannot be produced on this instrument, but four of the pipes represent the eight word tones in a simplified

FIGURE 11 While an assistant holds a gong (*doua neeb*), the shaman Ka Pao Her plays a sistrum (*txia neeb*) and a rattle (*tsu neeb*). Khek Noy, Thailand. Photo by Amy Catlin, 1984.

manner. The other two pipes add drones and harmony, sometimes joined with one or more melodic pipes that are not being used at that moment. The texts, played and danced by the musician-liturgist using circular and spiral movements to confuse evil spirits, instruct the soul in its ascent through the stages of heaven and back again to the body before burial. These texts are sung first by a singer and then reproduced by the player of the *qeej,* who, during some periods, must, with items of pure music and dance, entertain the soul of the deceased to keep it from wandering away. After guiding the soul for three days and nights, the musicians release it to find its way to heaven.

A drum is also used for the funeral and other ritual occasions. One type, destroyed after the ceremony, is also used when a cow is sacrificed. It is placed either at the central column of the house or according to other clan directives. It must be placed high enough for people to pass under; the player uses two drumsticks while standing on a bench. The other, a permanent drum to protect the house, must be nourished every morning. This drum, found only in a few families and clans, is hung to the left of the principal door, and touching it is forbidden. When it is hung or its skin changed, a pig or a cow must be sacrificed to the domestic spirit that will inhabit it. This drum is also used for ancestral rites. At New Year's, a chicken must be sacrificed to it. Its spirit is usually considered to be masculine, and that of the *qeej,* feminine. One origin myth states that the first *qeej* was made by a Hmong woman; the first drum, by her husband. They produced the instruments when the Hmong first encountered sickness and death, to provide funeral music. In northern Vietnam, however, the mouth organ is considered masculine, and the *qeej* is animated by a feminine spirit.

—Ruriko Uchida

Hmong secular music

Ritual music is designed to communicate with the world of the spirits, but secular music seeks to express thoughts and feelings that transcend the bounds of normal discourse among the living. Like sacred music, Hmong secular music derives largely from speech and conceptual thought, whether sung or played on instruments. Most of its subjects concern love and its manifestations, both individualized romantic love and social forms of love, as among kin and people of an entire community. These thoughts and feelings, considered too emotion laden for ordinary speech, often draw tears from listeners and performers when sung.

The seat of the emotions is considered to be the liver (*siab*). The expression of emotions in song, *hais kwv txhiaj* (*hais* 'to speak', *kwv* denotes the archaic, *txhiaj* 'lyric or narrative song, a riddle'), is to serenade with sung poetry, using occasional long notes. Other types of song include a syllabic male-female song without lengthy notes (*khawv chab*), nuptial songs (*zaj tshoob*), didactic songs sung by older people (*lus taum*), puzzle songs (*lus rov*), and funeral songs (*xiv xaiv*). These songs address the mind, the soul, society, or spirits. *Kwv txhiaj,* sung to the heart, concern emotions, especially love (*hlub*)—romantic love, love of nature, love of the homeland, family love, the loss of love, separation from the beloved, the loneliness of orphanhood, and the loss of the homeland.

Courtship and nuptials

The most important context for singing *kwv txhiaj* is during the courtship games of the New Year's festival. This begins as early as 13 December or as late as 11 January, according to the lunar calendar, but may be modified according to weather and other environmental factors. During the festival (*noj peb caug* 'feast thirty', referring to the thirtieth day of the last month of the year; also *noj tsiab*), rows of unmarried boys and girls throw courtship balls while singing the *kwv txhiaj.* The seventeenth-century writer Lu-Ci-Yun described a Miao festival in Yunnan in which boys danced and played mouth organs in a line, facing a line of singing girls from another village; gradually the two lines merged and formed into couples. Each boy carried off a girl to a secluded spot, returning later to discuss wedding arrangements with the parents.

—AMY CATLIN

Such customs seem related to customs of other ancient Chinese peasants. To avoid intermarriage within a village of relatives, youths of one sex would once a year travel to another village to marry. In China and Laos today, these customs have changed, but the line of boys and girls remains central. The tossing of the courtship ball while singing dialogue songs may be related to the rural Chinese battle of flowers in which participants, while singing improvised courtship songs, throw ferns, flowers, or sachets of scented grains.

At the wedding, the bride wears a dazzling display of silver, finely embroidered clothes, and an enormous headdress. The guests sing long, unaccompanied nuptial songs.

Hmong songs of courtship have a distinct vocal timbre, style of vocalization, and expression. Syllables may be delivered in a either a nonlegato style or a legato one, sometimes with wide intervals (of the fifth to the octave). Notes tend to be of equal duration. Scales may have three, four, five, or more tones.

—RURIKO UCHIDA

Expressions of emotion in song (kwv txhiaj)

Hmong *kwv txhiaj* are repositories of old and valued poetic and musical materials. The poetry relies on the repetition of each verse, replacing two rhymed words in the original verse with another pair of rhymed words in the repetition. The listener is thus engaged by a series of puzzles, solved only with the final word of each pair of verses.

The melodies of *kwv txhiaj* originate in the eight Hmong speech tones, represented in a nonintuitive system of correspondence, not always grasped by Hmong listeners. Thus, listeners often do not understand the verbal message of a song, and many who wish to sing are unable to do so. For this reason, the ability to sing *kwv txhiaj* is highly prized, especially as a courtship tool. Singers use numerous tonal spectra with varying sizes of intervals, sometimes denoting a regional or class affiliation. The minimum number of notes for depicting speech tones is four, as in *qeej* melodies. As the number of notes increases, the potential for misunderstanding decreases; it never completely disappears, because of peculiarities of the tone-note relationship.

The eight Hmong speech tones and their corresponding levels of pitch in a four-tone musical system are: high-level, 3 and 4 (highest); high-falling, 1 (lowest, greatest consistency); mid-rising, 4 (of second-greatest consistency); mid-level, 3; low-level, 1 and 2; low-breathy, 2; low-glottalized, 2; low-rising (alternate), 1. The most significant departures from speech levels are the use of the lowest sung pitch for the high-falling tone and the lack of melodic movement for moving tones. The duplication of level for several tones also contributes to the difficulty of understanding poetry when sung.

These correspondences have been taken from a single performance, but similar ones have been theorized by Eric Mareschal (1976), who notes that the rate of adherence to any system varies from singer to singer. The Hmong do not seem to have a verbal theory to articulate the system. White Hmong (Hmoob Dawb or Bai Miao) musicians have been found to follow a system more consistently than those of the Blue Hmong (Moob Njua or Qing Miao), who take more melodic liberties and have more complicated rules. (For example, the former do not allow repeated notes.) For

FIGURE 12 "*Niaj yais*" ('Oh'), a Hmong song of love, sung by Xia Muas, Fountain Valley, California, 31 December 1984. Transcription by Amy Catlin. After Catlin 1992:49; used with permission.

identifying speech tones in either system, understanding the meaning of the text is more important than the melody. Poetic conventions, especially repetition and parallelisms, help indicate such tones.

This process can be seen in the following example, the first pair of verses in a performance of the most prevalent form of sung poetry, amatory songs (*kwv txhiaj plees*). Rhymed replacement words are shown after each virgule (figure 12).

Niaj yais. . . .
Taj no ntshai luag leej tub ntaus plees nkauj
Nraum twb hais zoo ua luaj no es.
Koj tsis muaj siab tiag,
Tsis txhob daj dee me ntxhais nkauj xwb no es.
Yog muaj siab tiag ces,
Wb li tuav tes zuj zawv mus nce tag lub niag toj *do* / tsoob *rua.*
Plees nkauj nraum hais zoo luaj no es,
Cia wb mus tab wb lub teej cuab es.
Saib wb leej niam leej txiv puas *nco* / *tshuas* yuas,
Txiv leej tub om.

Oh. . . .
Now I fear this young man will strike at this shameless young woman
Out here in the clear and open.
But if you don't really have the heart [*siab* 'liver'],
Don't become involved with this unmarried girl.
But if you really do,
Holding hands, let us go up the big round *empty* hill / *to open* the sexual act.
Like this shameless young woman says,
Let us both see and take care of each other.
We will both see if our mother and father *miss us* / *like us,*
My dear boy.

raj nplaim Hmong free-reed pipe with finger holes

animism Indigenous religion based on belief in spirits

ua neeb Hmong shaman ceremony accompanied by gong, sistrum, and rattle

kwv txhiaj Hmong vocal music closely coordinated with speech tones

lus rov Hmong vocal genre with disguised text

This item was sung in the presence of onlookers who offered their comments to the singer and to each other. Young couples who are not brave enough to withstand so many eyes and tongues may perform under cover of darkness or play on a musical instrument.

Other genres

The other genres of secular sung poetry are too numerous to list, as the types are seemingly infinite. The most common are the laments of an orphan's plight (*kwv txhiaj ntsuag*), homesickness (*tsiv teb tsaws chaw*), loss of the homeland (*pooj teb*), and problems of a daughter-in-law (*ua nyab*). Some forms of sung poetry narrate legends or stories, or are moralistic or didactic. Occasionally, these are played on a mouth organ—in which case the musician first sings the song as a demonstration and then encodes it on the instrument.

In one vocal genre, turning words (*lus rov*), the verbal message is disguised by one or more methods, some of which resemble pig Latin. When set to music, the extra syllable may be sung to a half note on the consistent pitch after each word, using the initial consonant of the word plus the vowel *eev* (a rising tone). An English adaptation of the technique would be: "To teng be beng or eng not neng to teng be eng: that theng is eng the theng ques queng tion cheng." Each *eng* syllable would be sung to a note twice as long as the others. An excerpt from the text of figure 13, a *lus rov,* shows this pattern.

Kuv keev	hais heev	kuv keev
yog yeev	nej neev	niam neev
kuv keev	tsis	pub peeb
nej neev	mus meev	nrog nreev
kuv keev	nej neev	nyob nyeev
ywb yeev	hauv heev	tsev tseev . . .

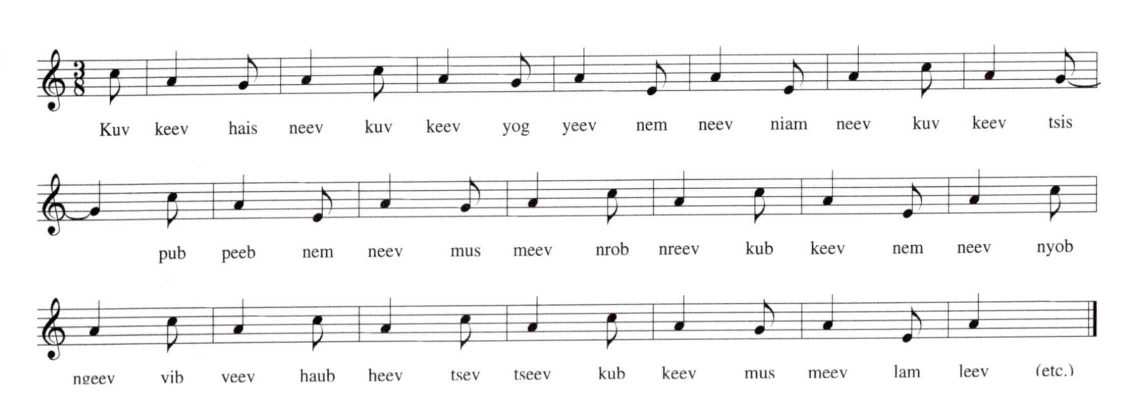

FIGURE 13 A Hmong *lus rov* 'turning words' song as sung by Choualy Yang. Transcription by Amy Catlin.

Without the interpolated syllables, a translation reads: "I am saying that I am your mother, and I won't let you all go with me. You all stay home. I'll bring . . ."

—Amy Catlin

REFERENCES

Catlin, Amy. 1992. "Homo Cantens: Why Hmong Sing during Interactive Courtship Rituals." In *Selected Reports in Ethnomusicology*, vol. 9, ed. Amy Catlin, 43–60. Los Angeles: University of California Press.

Lewis, Paul, and Elaine Lewis. 1984. *Peoples of the Golden Triangle: Six Tribes in Thailand.* London: Thames and Hudson.

Mareschal, Eric. 1976. *La musique des Hmong.* Paris: Musée Guimet.

Quincy, Keith. 1988. *Hmong: History of a People.* Cheney: Eastern Washington University Press.

The Indigenous Peoples (Orang Asli) of the Malay Peninsula

Marina Roseman, partly based on a manuscript by Hans Oesch as translated by J. O'Connell

Three tribal groupings on the Malay Peninsula—the Semang, the Senoi, and the Orang Melayu Asli—are known collectively by the generic term Orang Asli (Original People). They live in the tropical forest, on the mangrove coast, and in other hinterland and urban areas of the Malayan Peninsula, in western Malaysia.

One way the Orang Asli can be differentiated from one another is by their traditional life-styles. The Semang are mostly hunters who live in impermanent constructions. The Senoi, as shifting cultivators, are semisedentary and practice some cultivation in addition to gathering fruits, hunting, and fishing. The Orang Melayu Asli intermarried to a greater degree with Austronesian-speaking maritime peoples now known as Malays, who arrived on the peninsula about 2000 B.C. They live in permanent housing and are cultivators who fish, raise livestock, and sell their products and labor—as do many Semang and Senoi—in Malaysian markets. Representatives of all groups also live in contemporary village and urban settings, particularly in the Orang Asli settlement of Gombak, 16 kilometers from the Malaysian capital, Kuala Lumpur. Gombak developed around the Orang Asli Hospital, founded during the 1940s.

The *Orang Melayu Asli* are also known as Proto-Malays or Aboriginal Malays, including Southern Aslian Semelai and Temoq, and Semaq Beri; and Austronesian Temuan, Jakun (Orang Hulu), Orang Kanaq, and Orang Selatar linguistic groups. All these peoples share a close linguistic affiliation with Malays. The Austroasiatic languages of the *Semang* (including the Northern Aslian Kensiu, the Kentaq Bong, the Jehai, the Mendriq, the Batek, the Mintil and Central Aslian Lanoh, the Semnam, and the Sabum linguistic groups) and the *Senoi* (including the Northern Aslian Chewong, the Central Aslian Temiar, Semai, and Jah Hut; and the Southern Aslian Mah Meri [Besisi] and the Semaq Beri) are incomprehensible to most Malay-speakers. Indeed, their (approximately twenty-one) languages vary considerably from one another, though all the Aslian languages are members of the Mon-Khmer linguistic subfamily of the Austroasiatic family. Most Orang Asli are bilingual and often trilingual, with knowledge of other Orang Asli languages and of Malay and often Chinese dialects.

Another way the Orang Asli groups have been distinguished from one another is

Orang Asli ethnic divisions

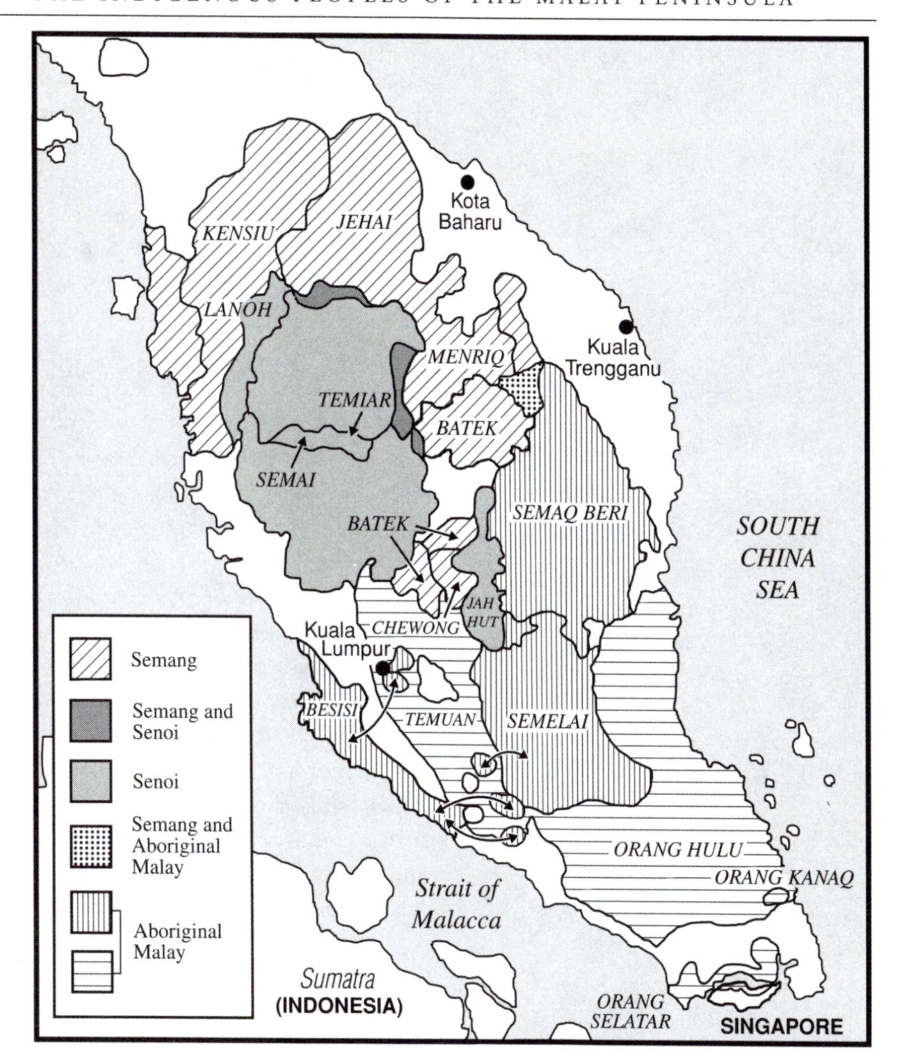

by their physical attributes. The Semang (also known as Negritos, derived from the word for "small dark person"—a legacy from the Spanish colonial presence in Southeast Asia's Philippine Islands) are often darker-skinned and smaller in stature (less than 152 centimeters tall), with thick, curly hair. The Senoi are typified by both curly-haired and straight-haired individuals with darker or lighter brown-toned skin and small stature. The Orang Melayu Asli share more biological attributes with the Malays, given the greater degree of intermarriage among them.

Within the context of the contemporary Malaysian nation, the more than 84,000 Orang Asli make up less than 1 percent of the current national population of about 20 million (1992). The Temiar and the Semai, both of the Senoi ethnic division, constitute the two largest Orang Asli linguistic groups; their languages, with Malay, serve as linguas francas among the aboriginal groups in intercultural communications and in the daily news and musical radio broadcasts of the Orang Asli Broadcast Unit from Radio-TV Malaysia, initiated in 1959.

Orang Asli status within the nation of Malaysia, like that of many indigenous minorities in amalgamated nations, lies suspended amid Malaysia's national goals, which often conflict. On the one hand, these goals embrace Malaysia's competition in the international economy, with demands on land, timber, and hydraulic power, and the increasingly intense religious activities of the Islamic Malay majority in such states as Kelantan. On the other hand lies Malaysia's celebratory approach toward cultural difference in its expressive, performative dimensions, including music and dance; but it takes an ambivalent posture toward cultural difference when this implicates the rights to resources. These goals are subsumed in a governmental rhetoric of Orang Asli integration, sedentarization, and development, often overlaying an agenda of land and resource appropriation. The musical culture of the Orang Asli is affected by these processes, by life-style (including subsistence technology, economic exchange, physical environment, social organization, and demographics), and by an animistic religious orientation and the associated practice of shamanism.

LIFE-STYLE AND ITS IMPLICATIONS FOR MUSICAL CULTURE

All three Original Peoples have used tools dating from the Mesolithic era—tools of stone, bamboo, vines, bone, and animal skins. These materials have been used to construct musical instruments: stone axes were used to cut the wood, and stone blades to chisel musical instruments, such as the Jew's harp. These are augmented, in contemporary times, by metal tools or materials such as metal drum frames stretched with membranes made from commercially produced gunnysacks.

Each group's technology and life-style has implications in the dimensions of musical form, performance practice, and instrument manufacture. Among the Semang, who traditionally had no stable dwellings (and interacted more sporadically with the market economy), musical instruments are always disposable. When the impulse or necessity for the instrumental making of music arises, a Semang may seek out available bamboo from which she or he fashions an instrument, plays it, and then discards it; instruments are thus designed to be both easily made and expendable. The tube zither (*kərantuŋ*) cannot be played after a short period of use. Its three strings easily become worn and extracted. Cut out of the bamboo's epiderm, the strings pass over a bridge and continue to the tube's end, where they split and pass underneath. These production techniques produce a distinctive, richly overtoned and "noisy" timbre.

Bamboo tube stampers, melodic and percussive instruments played in pairs, serve as markers of time in Semang and Senoi rituals. Their lengths, with implications for pitch, are unequal. Semang tube stampers, unlike those of the Senoi, are swiftly constructed for temporary use, their upper open ends roughly finished.

The Senoi are semisedentary settlers. They live in raised wood, bamboo, and thatch homes, in which they make and store their musical instruments. Every two to five years (before postcolonial Malaysian government efforts suggesting, and often compelling, Orang Asli to move into permanent dwellings), Senoi would move their settlements of twenty-five to one hundred people nearer to fertile areas, leaving fallow fields to regenerate from surrounding forest seed and growth.

The Senoi *kərəb* is a two-stringed chordophone (figure 1). Its strings are made of gut threads or jungle vines, not (as with Semang idiophones) bamboo bark. The strings are threaded through drilled holes and knotted underneath. On the upper side, they are tied in a loop around a plank that allows the possibility of individual and precise tuning, often in fourths.

Temiar mediums carefully execute the technical design of the Senoi tube zither *kərantuŋ* (figure 2). The cavities at the ends of the bamboo tube contain seven idiochordal strings, held in place by two nodes at each end and further fastened with rattan vines. This instrument, used for shamanistic purposes, may last for longer than a month, on account of its sturdy construction and infrequent use. In the middle of the tube are two rectangular holes, 10 centimeters wide, gouged out of its side. Two parallel strings lie over these, wedged in place by iron (visible in figure 2 by the left side of the first finger of the player's left hand). The lower of the tube's two nodes is closed, and four gaps are bored in the upper portion. The seated shaman, keeping the tube stable between his left palm and knees, plucks three of the free strings with the thumb and first finger of his left hand. He hits the upper extremity of the tube in a

FIGURE 1 Senoi tube zithers: *left,* five instruments of the *kərantuŋ,* an idiophone; *right,* the *kərəb,* a chordophone. Photo by Hans Oesch, 1963.

quick, regular pattern with a cupped right hand. This action causes vibrations in the body of the *kərantuŋ* and the strings, and displaces the column of air within the tubes. The energy of hitting the tube is transmitted through iron wedges holding the strings, resulting in complexly textured, "noisy" vibrations of the four unplucked strings.

FIGURE 2 Technique of playing a Temiar Senoi *kərantuŋ,* an idiochord tube zither. Photo by Hans Oesch, 1963.

The musical instruments of the Orang Melayu Asli, who have maintained consistently closer contact with the Malay and Chinese inhabitants of the Malayan Peninsula, cover a wide variety, from the simpler thigh xylophone (*kongkong*) to the modern violin. The Orang Melayu Asli use both iron and clay products, but are not acquainted with the arts of smithing or the potter's wheel. Their tube zithers, strung with iron wires, are probably copied from models derived from Sumatra. Like their life-style, their musical culture and instrument construction are products of a great degree of acculturation.

Orang Melayu Asli musical culture includes performance roles and the organization and symbolic weighting of musical sounds, including parameters such as timbre, relative pitch, attack and decay, the interaction of voices, and genre. This musical culture is both influenced by, and actively contributes to, ongoing intracultural and intercultural negotiations entailed in such practices as subsistence technology, social relations, economic exchange, and the gendered division of labor. For example, among the Senoi Temiar, social and sexual stratification is minimalized, though it is not nonexistent. The Temiar trace descent ambilineally (they are neither patrilineal nor matrilineal); they practice marriage by choice; and postmarital residence alternates between the male and the female spouses' natal villages.

More men than women play the ceremonial role of initial singer (medium) in the singing and trance-dancing ceremonies (*gənabag, pɛhnɔɔh*) that form the core of the Temiar musical repertoire. The meanings this bias holds for the construction, expression, and negotiation of Temiar gender roles are found in the social, musical, and cosmological theories that underlie Temiar performance roles.

Through magical practices, Temiar try to influence, soothe, and engage the spirits to render them serviceable to humankind. Performing on musical instruments plays an important role in calling spirits from their natural habitat.

FIGURE 3 During a singing and trance-dancing ceremony, Senoi Temiar women and girls play pairs of short (female) and long (male) bamboo stamping tubes and sing choral responses in interactive overlap with a male shaman, who sings his spirit guide's dream song. Photo by Marina Roseman, 1981.

Initial singers play this performance role primarily by virtue of having received a song during their dreams from the animated spirits of the Temiar social or physical environment—from trees, birds, riverine rapids, and other human beings of their forest environment, and from more recently arriving peoples and commodities from outside the forest: airplanes, wristwatches, canned sardines. Temiar explain that men receive songs more often than women because of their differential relationship to the environment; this difference, in turn, is based on minimal, yet nonetheless marked, differences in the gendered division of labor. As hunters, men have access to the blowpipe. They traverse long distances in smaller, quieter groups, and are thus more inclined to have daily experiences with the forest environment that might lead later to dream encounters with the spirits of that environment. Women, as gatherers working in larger, noisier groups with children in tow, have a smaller geographical range and a less intimate relationship with the forest; they are thus less likely, though not unable, to receive songs from the animated environment. Women, more often engaged in cooking, are also considered less likely to conduct the cool, spiritual liquid (*kahyɛk*) that Temiars say flows concurrently with song from their muses, the animated spirits of the physical and social world.

The gendered division of labor and ecological range is symbolically encoded in instrument construction, pitch, and methods of attack and decay. The pairs of tube stampers accompanying sessions of singing each have a longer and shorter member: the longer tube, with a lower pitch, and played with a technique allowing the sound to resonate, metaphorically replicates the more extensive geographic range of Temiar males, and is indeed termed male; the shorter, with a higher pitch, damped in its playing technique and thus dynamically more constrained, is gendered female (figure 3). Drumstrokes follow suit.

Though a tendency toward gender bias is thus at work in the realms of musical composition, performance roles, and organology, other elements of Temiar performance practice and musical theory work to undo the inequities arising from the gendered division of labor. While recognizing the incipient thrust toward gender inequity embodied in their singing sessions, Temiars labor to undermine that inequity, thereby reinforcing social and sexual egalitarianism (Roseman 1984, 1989). First, the (usually male) initial singer and dream-song composer is answered interactively by a female chorus. Their vocal lines intersect and replicate his so that the differences, while stated, are simultaneously juxtaposed and obscured. Second, both male and female tubes are played in alternation to construct the duple rhythm that underlies the singing—with a consistency, Temiars note, that symbolically joins the pulsing of a human heart with the pulsing of the ambient sounds of the forest. Third, male initial singers and dream-song composers report receiving most of their songs from female spirits: "We may go long distances in our everyday forest activities," men comment, "but during ceremonies, we're stuck on the ground—and it is our female spirit guides who fly above the forest canopy, leap across mountain crests, and have the extended long-range vision that constitutes true knowledge." The cosmological potency of the spirit's animated presence that flows in the medium's song, in both liquid and sound, is thus the product of the dynamic confluence of male and female energy—in which neither valence is dominant or dominated.

ANIMIST RELIGIOUS PHILOSOPHY AND SHAMANISTIC PRACTICE

As indicated in the discussion of the Senoi Temiar dream-song ceremony above, Orang Asli traditionally practice animistic religions based on belief in the potential for animated soul or personhood, not only in humans, but also in animals, plants, and all other entities. Through magical practices, they try to influence, soothe, and engage the spirits of these entities to render them serviceable to humankind. Performing on musical instruments plays an important role in calling spiritual substances from their natural habitat.

A prerequisite for instrumental invocation and entreaty of these spiritual substances among some Orang Asli groups is the perceived existence of living tonalities, with an array of distinct timbral consistencies: the souls of each wild animal, plant, rock, or the earth contain a sound characterized by distinct timbres, tonal rows, melodic contours, vocal ornamentations, rhythms, and other formal musical parameters.

Among some Orang Asli groups, particular musical instruments must be sounded during the summoning of that object; other groups employ vocal music accompanied by tube stampers for this purpose. Players can reach the appropriate experiential realm through performances on musical instruments alone, including the mouth organ, the nose flute, the transverse flute, or the tube zither. They blow or pluck their instruments, improvising upon predetermined parameters and tempering their sound with thickly timbred interludes, thereby contacting the spiritual essence of seemingly inanimate entities such as rocks or trees by way of their imaginal (in Corbin's [1966] sense of the realist and imaginary) sonic character. Only those who can divine and reiterate the appropriate sounds can influence nature through this spiritual medium.

The appropriate musical parameters can be generated only by competent musicians; competence, here, encompasses musical performance and sufficient cosmological knowledge and sociological positioning. Hans Oesch's musical analyses suggest a correlation between chromatic passages and magical efficacy: the greater the tension caused by chromaticism, the stronger the invocation. Roseman's research on Senoi Temiar instrumental and vocal genres (1991, 1995, 1996), however, show that inclusion of chromaticism varies not according to spiritual intensity, but according to variation in the historically specific spirit guide source from which a song or musical genre has been received. Figure 4, for example, shows tonal rows of vocal and instru-

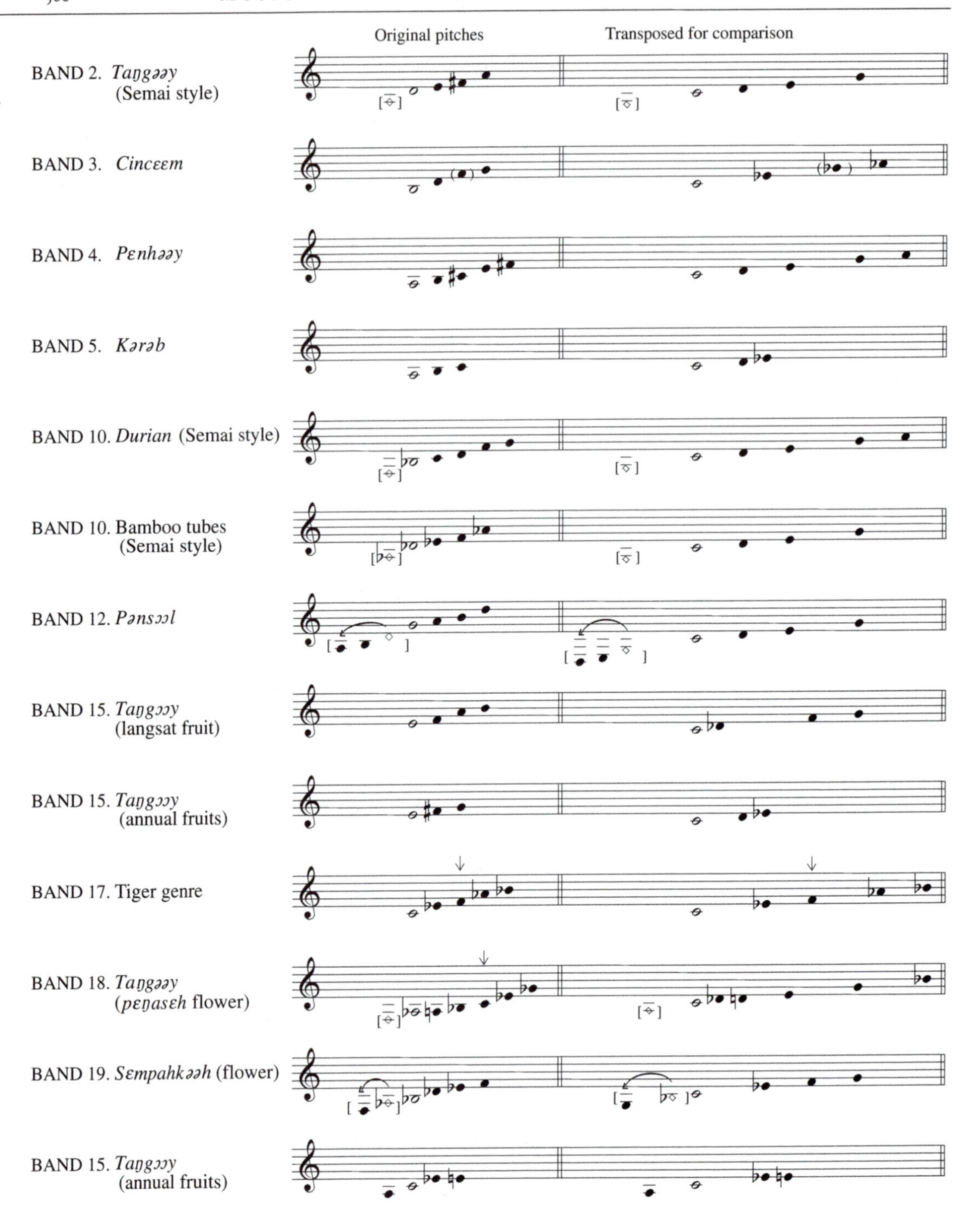

FIGURE 4 Tone rows of Senoi Temiar vocal and instrumental songs and genres. After Roseman 1995.

mental genres originating from various spirit guides. Some tone rows contain semitones; others do not.

Figure 5 compares chromaticism in the tonal rows of one medium's vocal repertoire. Songs associated with his forest spirit guides exhibit semitones. In a recently received song, the spirit of the State of Kelantan announces itself with the musical signature of an anhemitonic pentatonic tonal row.

Many recordings (Noone 1955; Oesch 1977a, 1977b, 1977c; Roseman 1995) contain instrumental invocations of the Orang Asli, all of which are characterized by specific timbral qualities, tonal rows, melodic contours, and rhythmic configurations corresponding to the multiple, detachable "souls" of distinct entities (Roseman 1990). The choice of tones derived from the existing pentatonic scale (sometimes

FIGURE 5 Examples 1 through 6 are tone rows of the vocal genre *taŋgɔɔy* (the *rambutan* fruit tree, and other associated fruiting-season trees, birds, mammals, and insects), received by Abilem Lum, a Temiar Senoi medium of Kampung Bawik, on the lower Nenggiri River in Kelantan from the 1950s through the 1990s. Example 7 illustrates the tone row of "*Sri Kəlantan Kəramaad Rajaʔ Nagaaʔ*" ('The Princess of the State of Kelantan, Holy Place of the Water Dragon'), the song Abilem Lum received in 1991 from the Spirit of the State of Kelantan. After Roseman 1996:261.

three to four notes, and occasionally seven) and the rhythmic form are often left to the performer's interpretation.

Oesch's research indicates that the function of the instrumental playing differs for Semang and Senoi. Among some Semang groups, the nose flute (*salet, nabad*), usually of three holes, but sometimes of two to seven, is played for its utility in magical invocation (figure 6). In the performance of this flute, the nose emits air derived directly from the human soul and uncontaminated by contact with the mouth. The Senoi Temiar say they obtained their nose flutes (*pənsɔɔl,* also termed *siʔɔɔy*) from the neighboring Senoi Semai, and use the instrument in courtship (Roseman 1995, recorded examples 11–13). Built on an anhemitonic scale, Temiar nose-flute melodies emphasize the octave, sixth, fourth, and third above the tonic, and the third and fourth below; this is the same scale the Temiar use in vocal genres they term "Semai style," including the genre *gamok* (derived from souls of the trunks and sap of trees).

FIGURE 6 A Senoi Temiar woman living on the upper Nenggiri River in Kelantan plays a nose flute. Photo by Hans Oesch, 1963.

The mouth-blown transverse flute (Semang *pennig'n yog'n* [*yau*], Senoi *siʔɔɔy*) may be played when a traveler has to wade through a river or slash through underbrush. Motifs played on the jaw's harp (Lanoh *rangoyd,* Jahai-Semang *rangun,* Senoi *juring rangguin* or *gɛngon*) may also influence those entities. Besides the general noise spectrum, the row of four to eight partials is activated several times when the mouth is held as a resonant space around the instrument. Senoi construct melodic motifs on jaw's harp and tube zither that iconically replicate the human and forest soundscape—birdsongs and the sounds of walking in the forest or clearing fields.

The tube zither (Semang *keranteg'n,* Senoi Temiar *kərəb* and *kərantuŋ*) is usually played by women (figure 7). Its sounds invoke all kinds of actions, environments, and beings, including those that might endanger the forest traveler: if a man works during the day in the jungle or operates fish traps in the rivers, a Senoi woman back home in the village may play it to protect him in his travels. Before some Senoi healers administer medicinal substances, such as roots, leaves, or bark, they may use its sound to invoke and activate the spirit of that vegetation. One such melody, played on *kərantuŋ,* can be heard on Oesch's recording 1977a (example 6, played by a

medium Tranced ritualist who is possessed by visiting spirits

shaman Ritualist who, in trance, travels to the land of the spirits to obtain knowledge

hala? The Semang shaman, called halaa? by the Temiar

cenoi Temiar term or rays of light that bear spiritual substances throughout the universe

pano' Temiar ceremonial genre in which spirits are contacted

FIGURE 7 A Senoi Temiar woman living upriver on the Berok River in Kelantan plays a tube zither. The song she is playing can be heard on *Dream Songs and Healing Sounds: In the Rainforest of Malaysia* (Roseman 1995, band 5). Photo by Marina Roseman, 1982.

Temiar from Jeram Kenarap, Kelantan); Oesch finds that the appropriate timbre must be replicated to enable the medication to work. Because quality of timbre, melodic and rhythmic form, methods of attack and decay, and other sonic parameters are significant in these musics, a transcription on five-line staffs is clear only in correspondence with recorded music.

Shamanism or mediumship, a linchpin of Orang Asli life, is a ritual technique fostering participatory relationships between humans and other entities. Singing and trance-dancing ceremonies directed toward such purposes are led by a medium (Semang *hala?,* Senoi Temiar *halaa?*) and require musical and choreographic participation by community members of both genders.

Southeast Asian shamanism joins religious, magical, musical, ecological, and medical components. Trance is differentially experienced by members of various Orang Asli groups and can take shape either as the soul's journey to the spiritual world, the spirit's visitation to the human realm, or a dialectical conjunction of the two. During such a ritual, the shaman gains supernatural knowledge, exorcises malevolent spiritual substances, asks for compassion, and requests assistance for the community and others.

Music is essential to shamanistic activities of all Orang Asli. Imbued with knowledge and power transmitted through a spirit guide's musical gifts, the medium sucks malevolent spiritual substances out of a sick person's body, or returns lost soul components to the patient during rituals of healing (Roseman 1990, 1991, 1996). The medical function of the medium may also involve administering to patients outside the context of singing and trance-dancing rituals. Healing rituals also contain preventive therapeutic functions, as participants join in harmonious, yet paradoxically dangerous, relations with their social and spiritual universe.

Semang animism and musical shamanism

Oesch, drawing on Paul Schebesta (1928a, 1928b) and Ivor H. N. Evans (1923, 1937) in conjunction with his own research (among the Jahai, the Kensiu, and the Lanoh Semang), suggests that the dual foundations of Jahai musico-shamanistic rituals, which last about four hours, are belief in *cenoi* and the cosmic tree. *Cenoi* shamanism (or mediumship) seems to have been most developed among the Jahai, the Kentaq, and the Kensiu. Kirk Endicott (1979) speculates that ideas and practices surrounding the *cenoi* developed among the Kensiu, and observes that the philosophy regarding the cosmic tree is most highly developed among the westernmost Semang.

Oesch visited Semang groups in May of 1963, and his recording 1977b contains eighteen selections, including those recorded among the Jahai (15 May 1963), the Lanoh (two selections, 18 May 1963), and the Kensiu (a flute selection recorded in 1963). The recording also reproduces a Lanoh song recorded on wax cylinder by Paul Schebesta, who worked among the Negrito in the 1920s. Oesch's descriptive notes acknowledge help from Iskandar Carey (1961, 1976), whose scholarly orientation within his role in the British colonial administration of the Orang Asli has benefited subsequent researchers.

Oesch's writings (1973, 1974a, 1974b, 1987a, 1987b), although sensitive and musically detailed, show an overdependence on the research of Schebesta and that of Evans, who arrived even earlier. Oesch would have been thoroughly familiar with Schebesta's work in the German originals. The ceremonies performed during Schebesta's time—before British and Malay influence on Orang Asli traditions had advanced to contemporary levels—differed substantially from what Oesch himself would have observed in the 1960s, or from what is practiced today. In numerous and important writings, Oesch tends to generalize from Schebesta's discussions of Jahai shamanism, allowing them to stand for all Semang, indeed all Orang Asli. Yet Jahai shamanism is, and probably was, quite different from that of Kensiu and other Semang groups. Schebesta's observations were heavily influenced by Christian theology, whose orientation Oesch uncritically absorbed. For later writing on the Semang, see Endicott (1979) and Shuichi Nagata (1995).

Schebesta and Oesch tell us that *cenoi* are small, colorful rays of light—often personified in male or female form—that bear spiritual substances throughout the universe. They connect earth and the human realm with the spiritual world. The shaman initiates ritual contact through contact with personified *cenoi* spirit guides; with their friendly assistance, a Jahai shaman traces the route for the human soul's journey to the spiritual world. The singing medium's soul leaves his body, which lies quivering on the ground, goes on its journeys, and returns to him well after fifteen minutes. By then, the spirit guide will have contacted the upper earthly powers, enabling the shaman to relay to his community the transcendental knowledge gained during the ritual journey. While in a trance, the shaman is a conduit for the *cenoi,* and the force of his religious activities stems from them. Without the *cenoi,* his dialogue with the spiritual realm during the evening ritual would not be possible, for they aid in his ceremonial transformation. In this space of transformation, he can answer questions, heal, and foretell.

Nagata and Endicott observe that though their shamanistic practices differ widely, the Jahai, the Kensiu, the Kentaq, and the Lanoh Semang participate most fully in a cosmology centered upon the cosmic tree, located in the middle of the earthly domain, which connects the upper realms with the lower worlds. On his ritualistic soul journey, the Semang shaman travels to branches—in the skies, on earth, and the underworld. It is possible to speculate that the musical and mythical complex vertically aligning sky and earth, spirit and humans, expressed in the concept of the cosmic tree in Semang cosmology may be influenced by (or may have contributed to the influences converging upon) the stone pillars of the Southeast Asian Megalithic culture. While most research on megaliths has focused on their Austronesian and Indic connections (Bellwood 1985, Kamarul 1992), megaliths are also found in the arc inhabited by early Austroasiatic speakers, reaching from island Southeast Asia through Indochina to east and southern India, and including contemporary groups such as the Austroasiatic Munda-speakers in central eastern India (Babiracki 1991).

A musical spirit ceremony among the Semang Jahai

Semang shamans are known for the *pano',* a ceremonial genre in which they contact supernatural forces during a festivity not bound to any particular time or place (Oesch 1979:79, Schebesta 1957:136–145). Schebesta rightly dubbed this infrequent festivity religious play. A *pano',* such as the one Oesch observed in 1963 while visiting the Jahai of Bandig'n in the Belum River area of Ulu Perak, is distinguished by the sugarcone-shaped hut erected on the edge of the community's camp. The hut (or *pano'*), from which the ceremonial genre may have received its name, was constructed exclusively by women using three-meter-long fronds of the bertam palm (*Eugeissona tristis*). Dense leaves are tied with vines so that they form a cone, with a little entrance left open at the bottom, through which the shaman slips inside. A description of the ceremony observed by Oesch, which he interpolated with interpretive and ethnographic material from his readings of Schebesta, follows.

> After nightfall, before the festivity begins, women and children decorate themselves with flowers, grasses, and leaves. They adorn their hair with bamboo combs etched with protective designs, put on headbands made of rattan fibers, secure scented leaves under their belts, and place orange and red flowers behind their ears. As a special mark of ceremonial costuming, they wear sashes (*tenwag*) made of flowers and *palas* leaves, intertwined with beads made from seeds and tubers; two sashes are hung diagonally across their chests. In a mood of festive anticipation and devotion, they sit by the campfire to await the start of the *pano'.*
>
> The festivities commence with the entrance into the hut of the shaman and an attendant, both equally decorated and carrying incense, probably from indigenous roots and resins. The smoke rising from the hut throughout the ceremony will help carry the shaman to a higher plane toward the latter portion of the celebration. Singing starts as soon as the two men disappear into the hut: the shaman answers the attendant's questions in falsetto, disguising his voice. He sings, mostly in a sacred language, about all the animals and plants into which he has transformed himself during the *pano'.* The choir of spectators answer the invisible shaman's oracle-like voice in verse fashion as they clap their hands. Subsequent questioning reveals that community participants felt the shaman changed not only his voice during this period, but also his physical appearance.
>
> The shaman in the *pano'* is considered to have become the *cenoi* entering him at that moment, and the songs and speech with which he answers his attendant are the spirit guide's voice. After the celebration, the shaman does not remember what he sang or said in the hut. The predominant *cenoi* among the Semang is the tiger *cenoi,* envisioned as an old man (*bidog*). This spirit protects the shaman; other *cenoi* may alight momentarily. Community members exhibit anxiety when the *bidog* announces his arrival by the shivering and shuddering of the shaman's body,

which shakes the hut and rustles its leaves. Once the tiger *cenoi* has entered the hut, the shaman's songs become livelier.

Semang indicate that the awesomeness of the *bidog* arises from his position as a sort of alter ego of a more benevolent deity, Ta Ped'n, son of Kare'i, the personification of thunder. The text of the spirit of the tiger's first song in the ceremony observed by Oesch among the Jahai of Bandig'n tells how the *bidog,* a tiger with "flashing eyes and glowing stripes," journeys from Lanka (possibly a reference to Sri Lanka) with enormous steps, and stealthily enters the hut. He gets into fights with other tigers on the banks of small rivers, including the neighboring tributaries and streams Sengoh, Belaweṅ, Belaṅa, Temeg'n, and Tadoh.

Oesch transcribed and translated the following text from the song for the arrival of the spirit of the tiger (*peningloiṅ bidog*):

Lanka bidog	Old man Lanka Tiger *cenoi*
Kou hnu kou.	*Steps far outward.*
Beredelöd	Flashing eyes
Kou hnu kou.	*Steps far outward.*
Tenteg'n lapis	Glowing stripes
Kou hnu kou.	*Steps far outward.*
Lanka bitul	Straight from Lanka (he comes),
Kou hnu kou.	*Steps far outward.*
Alor Seyinga',	(Onto) the banks of the Sengoh,
Kou hnu kou.	*Steps far outward.*
Belaweṅ,	And the Belaweṅ,
Kou hnu kou.	*Steps far outward.*
Belaṅa,	(Fighting) on the Belaṅa,
Kou hnu kou.	*Steps far outward.*
Alor Temeg'n,	On the banks of the Temeg'n,
Kou hnu kou.	*Steps far outward.*
Alor Tadoh,	On the banks of the Tadoh,
Kou hnu kou.	*Steps far outward.*

In the course of one hour during the *pano'* Oesch witnessed, the shaman transformed himself into various *cenoi* in turn, singing answers to questions asked of him. Of all the *bidog* that appeared in that *pano',* four were especially memorable: the *bidog mantei* (the scaly anteater), the *bidog ta'a* (an animal that dwells near the mild durian tree), the *bidog pas* (a *kejang* deer), and the *bidog bab* (an animal that lives close to the bertam palm). Other *cenoi* visiting the community through the musical mediumship of shamans included the *cenoi cemnoi* (who lives in the *mácam* flower), *cenoi batu'* (a female *cenoi* who emerges from the *rambutan* flower), and *cenoi pelai* (the spirit of the *ramei* flower).

Senoi musical mediumship

The predominant *cenoi* among the Semang is the tiger, who arrives in the specially built hut during Semang musical spirit séances. Cross-influences among Orang Asli groups are apparent in the importance the Senoi Temiar, as well, place on the tiger spirit guide and his musico-ceremonial genre, termed *panoh* or *mamug.* The awe in which tiger shamanism is held is exhibited in the practice of extinguishing all sources of light (including fires in hearths, cigarettes, and kerosene lanterns) when a tiger spirit guide sings through Temiar mediums. A small hut (*panoh, paleey*) similar to those constructed by the Semang Jahai may be constructed in the ceremonial space using bertam fronds.

Temiars are open to both gifts of song and attacks of illness from spirits of fruits. The annual blossoming and fruiting is a time of joy and desire, music and courtship.

Mediums, given the leeway of individual revelation in this relatively egalitarian society, dream-compose their songs in response to personal and historical experiences. Operating within larger stylistic constraints, mediums innovate musically, choreographically, and in the construction of leaf and flower ornaments associated with particular genres according to the instructions received during dreams from their spirit guides (Roseman 1994). Temiar musico-choreographic genres may thus be associated with specific geographical locations, historical periods, and individual dream-song composers (see figures 4 and 5).

This section focuses on the Senoi Temiar, with whom Roseman has conducted extensive research in Kelantan and Perak. Temiar musical genres include those received from tigers (*mamug, panoh*); mountains, rivers, and flowers (*taŋgəəy*); blossoming fruit trees (*pɛnhəəy, nɔŋ tahun, taŋgɔɔy*); spirits of deceased humans (*cincɛm*), the sap of the *ipoh* tree (*gamok*), lightning (*ʔɛŋkuuʔ*), and other forest sources. The genres *səlombaŋ* (dragon of the water) and *pɛhnɔɔh gɔb* (Malay-style trance ceremony) are associated with Malays and Chinese; other songs and genres have been received from "outforester" peoples and things.

Songs received from spirits during dreams are sung by Senoi Temiar mediums during nighttime, housebound ceremonial events termed *gənabag* 'singing' if the session is not intended to invoke the spirits' presence, and *gənabag pɛhnɔɔh* 'singing and trance-dancing ceremony with leaf and flower ornaments' if it is. Singing and trance-dancing ceremonies may be held to celebrate visitors' arrival or impending departure; to punctuate the agricultural cycle of clearing, planting, and harvesting rice swiddens; to effect healing or prevent illness; for the joy of gathering community members and spirits; to end a period of mourning; or to mark points within the fruiting season (end of rains, onset of new foliage, blossoms, fruiting, harvest).

Mediums, who may be male or female, are joined by an interactive choral response usually performed by women, though both genders join in the chorus that initiates the ceremony to conclude a mourning period. Members of the chorus beat pairs of tube stampers against a log (figure 3); their duple rhythms of alternating high and low pitches are accentuated and subdivided by the rhythms of single-headed drums (*batak, bərɑnoʔ*) played by men and/or women.

Fruit-season genres

The annually fruiting trees, flowering after the rains and fruiting before the dry season, mark seasonal changes. The fruit season is a time of plenty, of pleasant outings to scattered orchards marking past settlement sites, of group efforts in gathering and consuming the fruits. The musical genres associated with fruiting trees are quintessential forest genres for the Senoi Temiar of Kelantan and Perak.

Fruit-season genres include *pɛnhəəy*, originating in Perak and associated with the *perah* tree (*Elateriospermum tapos*) (Roseman 1995, band 4). Genres associated with the spirits of the fruits are generally known as the way of the annual fruits (*nɔŋ tahon;*

nɔŋ bərək) in Kelantan. The female spirit of the *rambutan* tree (*taŋgɔɔy*) is the paramount spirit of another genre originating in Kelantan (Roseman 1995, band 15). This genre was first received by the Temiar medium Abilem Lum while working for the Department of Orang Asli Affairs in the mid-1970s, during his posting along the Aring River among Semang Batek and Mendriq peoples, who also sing fruit-season songs associated with the *rambutan* tree.

Fruit-song texts celebrate the weighty boughs of fruit in the trees and the swaying of leaves in the wind. Dancers' bodies bend and sway like the weighted boughs and shivering leaves. Ornaments made from the leaves of fruit trees and bright orange flowers fill the ceremonial arena with their color and fragrance; dancers shaking leaf whisks add to the ceremonial soundscape.

Temiars are open to both gifts of song and attacks of illness from spirits of fruits. The annual blossoming and fruiting is a time of joy and desire, music and courtship. But it is also a time of danger and illness, caused by the capricious desires of spirits of fruit trees, whose awakening interest may result in soul loss for their human consorts. Songs of the annual fruits are powerful in healing ceremonies held to counteract the soul loss that occurs when a stricken Temiar's head soul prefers the fruiting-forest abode of a fruit-tree spirit to his or her body. The actual and metaphorical presence of the tiger, drawn by birds and fruit-eating rodents, adds to the physical and spiritual danger of the season.

Senoi Temiar genres associated with Malays

In the musical genres *səlombaŋ* (or *daŋah*) 'the water dragon', with etymological, mythological, and sociohistorical connections to the *naga* of India and the *selum-von* of Hakka Chinese, and in *pɛhnɔɔh gɔb* 'Malay-style ceremonies', Temiars reflect on their ongoing interactions with the now dominant Malay population. A musico-medical ritual variant of *səlombaŋ* practiced by Senoi Temiar inhabitants of Jeram Kenerap, a settlement on the Upper Nenggiri in Kelantan, was observed and musically transcribed by Oesch, whose description of the contemporary performance of *sɛlombaŋ* conforms with descriptions of its original performances during its emergence around 1926 in the Perias-Yai River Valley of Kelantan.

At dusk, young and old alike gather in the longhouse. In contemporary villages, the government has ordered and subsidized the building of dwellings for smaller nuclear families to replace longhouses; here, ceremonies may be held in one of several places: in the largest such dwelling in a settlement; in the home of a medium or a person seeking musico-medical healing; or in a specially built structure, the *deek dewan*. The dwelling, if made in traditional Temiar style, is constructed of wood, bamboo, and thatch, with a pliant floor of lashed bamboo slats suspended about 2.5 meters off the ground. Women and girls, seated on the floor along the room's perimeter, begin to strike (Temiar *cɛntɔk*, Semang *cantug'n*) bamboo tubes (*gɔh, ʔawɛn*) alternately on a horizontally laid log, producing a higher and lower pattern of tones that introduces the ritual and continues without interruption for hours (figure 8).

Soon afterward, the single-headed *bəranɔʔ* drum and the *batak* drum, smaller in diameter but with a longer body and playing at twice the rate, begin to play together. The drums elaborate on the rhythms of the bamboo tubes as they accentuate and subdivide its beats. A gong may enter, struck alternately on either the high beats or the low beats of the high-low duple rhythm of the tube stampers. The choice varies individually but will remain consistent throughout a selection.

The medium positions himself toward the center of the room, but nearer to the players of bamboo tubes. He sits on the ground, draws a deep breath, and rotates his head in a circle for less than a minute (Senoi Temiar *bə-salɛh* 'swirling', from Malay *saleh* 'to come and go, return'). This movement, drawn from the Malay spirit séance

FIGURE 8 Excerpt from the beginning of a Temiar shaman song, "*Səlombaŋ,*" from Jeram Kenerap, a settlement on the upper Nenggiri river in Kelantan State. After Oesch 1973:240.

main peteri (Laderman 1991), is incorporated into Temiar musico-choreographic genres associated with Malays, which include *səlombaŋ* and *pɛhnɔɔh gɔb.*

The intensification of bodily movement, the percussive dynamics, and the increase in tempo aid the medium's entry into trance. Orang Asli trance rituals are noted for their lack of alcohol or other mind-altering substances; rather, entry into trance is supported by the cultural demarcation of ritual space and time as it is musically, kinetically, and proxemically configured. Pulsing rhythms periodically intensify: the tempo of the tube stampers quickens, and players further subdivide their beats; at such moments, the medium (or, in other Temiar genres, the male and/or female dancers who accompany the medium's performance) are likely to experience the transformation (Senoi Temiar *lɛslāās*) and forgetting (Senoi Temiar *wɛlwəəl*) of trance. This experiential state finds a cognate of sorts in the Malay *lupa* 'to forget', of the Malay séance trance.

The Temiar trance experience is heightened through the manipulation of other musical and performance parameters constructing the dramatic texture. These parameters include what Temiars term sinuous (*bərwɛɛj-wɛɛj*) melodies, a darkened performance area with few points of light emanating from fires in hearths or kerosene lanterns, resinous incense and fragrant leaves, and the participants' intent. The practice of twirling the head to initiate trance is specific to the genres the Temiar associate with the Malay, but all other Temiar musico-ceremonial genres may involve the trance experience; the method of initiating trance in these genres is through intensification, over time, of the bending, swaying, and strolling movements characteristic of the genre.

The medium then rises and begins to dance, holding a leaf whisk of fragrant *calɨn* leaves in his right hand. In the musico-choreographic spiritual genre of *səlombaŋ,* two or three Temiar men often dance alongside the medium. Soon, the medium begins to sing, while a chorus responds in a heterophonic responsorial pattern or echo polyphony (Feld 1988, Roseman 1984). The women and girls playing tube stampers provide the core of this interactive chorus, though dancers and other female, and less often male, participants may also repeat the medium's melody and/or text at the end of each melodic line.

The introductory shamanistic song, Oesch notes, serves as both religious and secular instruction for the Senoi Temiar. If one of them becomes ill (often from malaria), she or he is brought before the entranced medium clothed minimally, with the skin surface covered in rice powder, and laid on the ground beside the fire. The shaman interrupts his dance-song to bend over the patient; then to suck, with noisy smacks through fingers or a lightly closed fist placed on or near the patient's skin surface, the spirit of the sickness out of the body; and finally, to release it out and away from the patient and the settlement by clapping his hands in the direction of the doorway. This is continued, Oesch observes, until no more rice powder can be seen on the patient's skin.

The use of rice powder in this musical genre is another indication of its reference to Malay culture. The Temiar mythologically impute to the Malays their knowledge of the technology of growing rice. Malay spiritual practices also rely heavily on such props as rice powder, popped rice, and eggs, which Temiars incorporate into their Malay-related genres. Dances and songs are often interrupted by the medium, who sometimes puts rice powder on himself, and at other times drinks strongly scented essences derived from roots and leaves.

At the climactic point of the trance, the medium begins to shudder (*kɛnrɔɔk*) and tumbles to the floor, where he lies trembling. At this moment, his soul detaches from his body and commences its travels, while the choruses' song and percussive accompaniment continues. He visits and dances with similarly detached soul components of other entities, and invites the spirits to return with him to the longhouse. The spirits materialize, flowing through participants' bodies in three forms: as song, as movement, and as a cool spiritual liquid, *kahyɛk.*

After the twitching of his body has stopped and the shaman has begun to dance again, he sings with the spirit's voice about its visions; he tells his people how the spirits have answered his questions. He relays what he sees from their perspective as his spirit, dialectically conjoined with that of the spirit guide, soars above the forest canopy and sees long distances to the horizon. Long-range perspective is a Temiar metaphor for wisdom. At this point, the medium may certify—through his verbal interactions with or reports on the spirits—their presence in the ritual space. His words are, in part, in a poetic ceremonial language received by him during dreams, which are then transmitted during performance to the adherents of particular musico-choreographic spirit genres such as *səlombaŋ* or *taŋgɔɔy.*

Entertainment for the spirit guests begins. In ceremonies conforming to the original pattern of *səlombaŋ* and other genres current among the Temiar in the 1930s, the medium and those dancing with him tumble on the burning fire, seize burning sticks, lift them to their mouths, and nibble on them. The pitch-black hut becomes illuminated when, while dancing energetically, they blow on the firebrands they hold in their mouths for a few minutes; the smoke communicates with the spirits. Near the fire, hot water stands ready in a bamboo tube. The men drink some of

Temiar rituals cannot be explained musically by simply analyzing a transcription. One must first examine the issues underpinning Temiar philosophy before making sense of the meaning of the words and their musical setting.

this and disperse the rest in bunches of leaves cradled in their hands: this is drink for the spirits. After stoking the fire, the dancers lie down with the medium in the midst of the flames and extinguish the blaze. Despite all this, Oesch reports that no wounding is evident on the men's skin: a few traces of soot clinging to their sweating bodies are the only reminders of the strains of the evening.

The ritual ends in quiet singing. Temiar participants return to their respective houses, have a bite to eat, and sleep late the next day; their nighttime hunting forays and intensive periods of gathering resources more than compensate for these late awakenings, which contrast with typical daily stirrings around sunrise.

Temiar rituals cannot be explained musically by simply analyzing a transcription. One must first examine the issues underpinning Temiar philosophy before expecting to make sense of the meaning of the words and their musical setting. The textual prose, dreamed by the shaman and sung extemporaneously, is rich in metaphoric allusion.

To translate the texts of Orang Asli songs accurately, one must appreciate the relationship of cosmological events to natural objects. The greatest difficulty of translating lies in the multiplicity of symbols ascribed to the same entity. For instance, if one wants to describe the physical appearance and behavior of a snake in song, one must know that, among Senoi Temiar, the snake lives in a rainbow (which is itself the mother of the earth), yet the snake also belongs to an underworld lake, where the blood sacrifices of the Senoi gather. Thus, the snake represents a tangible wild animal and a mother of the earth, a rainbow, or a blood sacrifice; but it never means only one of these.

In the context of ritual song, music coordinates these multiple meanings. Bamboo tube stampers, drums, and an optional gong serve as timekeepers for the interactively overlapping song phrases of medium and chorus. Low and high tones (about a fourth apart) are alternated on the tubes, with an accented element corresponding to the iambic character of the Senoi language. The percussion instruments establish the rhythms before the singing begins; singers must adjust themselves to the rhythms, but can wordlessly (through tempo manipulation) or jovially (through verbal joking) influence the chorus, drummers, and players of gongs.

Similarly, players of tubes watch the dancers, and when they see a dancer begin to shudder or lose his or her balance, signaling the intensification of the trance experience, they musically encourage the transformative experience, intensifying the dynamics, accents, and tempo of the percussion, further subdividing the rhythms, and pushing the pitch of their choral response into a higher range. Cycles of intensification and dénouement alternate through the night, until finally, softer, slower, lower singing and percussion signal an approaching conclusion—often somewhat informal, at other times marked by specified ritual practices, depending on the spirit guide, the medium, community members, and the purposes for which the ritual was held.

ANALYSES OF MUSICAL STYLE AND STRUCTURE

The authors' observations about musical form consider both the scales used in singing and the way of constructing melodies. In the vocal musics of the Orang Asli, an anhemitonic pentatonic scale occurs mostly in the form of four tones, transcribed approximately as e–f♯–a–b. This pattern may be a short form of (d)–e–f♯–a–b or e–f♯–a–b–(c♯). In many areas, the *səlombaŋ* melody of the Senoi Temiar is only tritonic, and some of the shamanistic dance-songs of the Jahai have only two tones.

Figure 9 shows the melodic line generated as a Temiar medium (*halaaʔ*) sings a song of the genre *səlombaŋ*; the transcription omits choral responses and rhythmic accompaniment, and vertically aligns analogous melodic points. It illustrates the sectionality of melodies and how melodies are elaborated in performance. Numbers 1 through 43 along the bottom of the score mark the repetition of the quarter notes under staffs 1 through 18. This representation demonstrates melodic construction following the principle of formal variation. Oesch analyzed the melody accordingly: the two parentheses over system one point to the two parts of a core element, which sounds in a slightly transformed way in almost all the repetitions. They belong, he suggests, to a basic form, itself never sounded, from which the medium forms variations linked according to the pool of extemporized words and vocables.

Roseman's analyses of this example indicate that Temiar recognize two core phrases in this melody: the first extends, in its successive variations, from the marker numbers of quarter notes 17 through 29; the second, from numbers 31 to 61. These phrases, which correspond roughly with Oesch's "two parts of a core element," share deeper structural principles of construction. Together, Temiar say, these two phrases (*ɲag* 'mouthful') constitute a verse (also termed *ɲag* 'mouthful', but contextually used to refer to a higher taxonomic level of sectionality).

The phrase occurring in systems 6, 8, 12, 13, and 18, and extending in its successive variations from the markers of quarter notes 1 through 20, is a *jɛnhook* phrase (Oesch terms these performance breaks), inserted at will by the singer for various reasons. Among these reasons are to elaborate on the form; to inspire the dancers with additional energy; to give the singer time to rest; and to accompany textual material that will not fit within the melodic, rhythmic, and rhyming scheme of the two song phrases.

Roseman's analyses indicate that Temiar songs have from two to four phrases, sung successively in order, as Temiars describe, "like travelers following one another, backside to frontside, along the trail"; though adhering to the order of succession, singers may omit phrases. The description *backside to frontside* metaphorically describes the rhymes; the last word of phrase 1, for example, usually exhibits assonance, alliteration, or rhyming the end of words with the first word of phrase 2, and so forth. This pattern is common in other Mon Khmer and Tai poetry and lyrics (see, for example, Compton 1979). Temiar mediums dream the basic melodic structure. Spirit guides often give them key textual phrases and poetic ceremonial vocabulary (*dɛhneeh pɛhnɔɔh*), upon which they improvise melodic and textual variations. These range from a few minutes to several hours and are situated within ceremonies that may last several hours, or even from dusk to dawn.

In the example transcribed in figure 8 and analyzed in figure 9, Oesch notes that the first phrase ("woman—I sleep with her—not unhappy am I") is directed at the dragon living in the water of the area of the upper Nenggiri. The narrative takes place at a time when high waters wash the dragon down toward the sea. Roseman's research indicates that Temiar associate the dragon with Malay rulers dwelling at the headwaters of the Kelantan River, and in this genre they contend with the trauma associated with increased Malay domination of Temiar lands, from the river's headwaters to its source, deep in the forest. The genre emerged in 1926, during a historic period of

FIGURE 9 A collective transcription of melodic phrases from the Temiar shaman song "*Səlombaŋ*" of figure 8. After Oesch 1973:245.

flooding, and at a time when Malay and British colonial influence on the forest peoples of peninsular Malaysia was reaching new heights (Roseman in press).

SENOI TEMIAR SINGERS AND HEALERS IN A MODERN WORLD

In dream-song compositions and performances, Temiar situate themselves in relation to the forest around them and increasingly with concepts, commodities, and persons from outside the forest. Orang Asli have long engaged with peoples and things from beyond the forest: Temiar call themselves the people of the forest (*sɛnʔɔɔy sərɔk*), distinguishing themselves from more recently arriving foreign out-foresters (*gɔb*). Temiar dream songs record their interactions with outsiders, among whom are Malays (Austronesian-speaking maritime peoples, first arriving about two thousand years ago and mixing in varying degrees with Temiar and other local aboriginal Austroasiatic speakers), British colonials, Chinese and Tamil workers brought to work British mines and plantations, Japanese occupying Malaya during World War II, anthropologists of varied descent, and Malays in their postindependence roles as members of the mainstream Islamic population and as governmental administrators.

As Orang Asli grapple with their marginalization and political disempowerment as citizens of Malaysia, they express their responses within the realm of mediumship and musical performance. The Temiar medium Abilem Lum of Bawik settlement in Kelantan State gathers the multiple voices of the contenders—people of the forest, Malays, Chinese—within a musico-ceremonial genre received in 1991. This genre was not given to him by the spirit of a particular riverine rapid or deep pool of the forest-river system that drains into the Kelantan River, as might once have occurred. Rather, he received it from the Spirit of the State of Kelantan (Sri Kəlantan Kəramaad Rajaʔ Nagaaʔ 'Princess of the State of Kelantan, Holy Place of the Royal Water Dragon') (see Roseman 1996). During a healing ceremony recorded by Roseman in 1992 and transcribed in figure 10, Abilem sang this song to heal an infant suffering from constipation. Directed toward a particular infant, the performance displays Temiar concepts of the etiology and treatment of disease, and enacts preventive and therapeutic social healing (figure 10).

The State of Kelantan overarches in its political purview culturally diverse and economically competitive populations of Chinese Buddhists, Hindu Tamils, Malay Muslims, Christians of various ethnic identities and religious sects, and predominantly animistic Orang Asli (J. Nagata 1979). Singing this song and employing ritual paraphernalia stipulated by his new spirit guide, Abilem draws on the Spirit of the State of Kelantan to counteract the effects of living in an increasingly multicultural, indeed a transnational world. Like the spirit guide *səlombaŋ* (discussed in figures 8 and 9), Princess Kelantan of the Holy Place of the Royal Water Dragon incorporates the imagery of the *naga,* the mythological snake of the water dragon fundamental to Indic mythology (Bosch 1960), and conjoins this with referents implicating the mythical dragons of Chinese mythology.

In the above-mentioned ceremony, Abilem held singing and trance-dancing ceremonies on several consecutive nights in a large, traditional structure built by villagers from bamboo and leaf thatch, and situated between Abilem's government-issue house, made of wood and zinc, and the logging road. His healing ministrations occurred two or three hours after each ceremony's commencement, when his singing had brought a collection of spirit guides into the ritual realm. The songs included those from the annual fruits genre (*taŋgɔɔy,* discussed above), a genre associated with the spirits of dead humans (*cincɛm*), and Sri Kelantan. By then, the evening's ceremony had already reached several climactic moments, as male and female dancers progressed from strolling, swaying dance movements to the shudders and double-paced jumping in place that mark the deeper transformations of trance. Toward the

Singing this song and employing ritual paraphernalia stipulated by his new spirit guide, Abilem draws on the Spirit of the State of Kelantan to counteract the effects of living in an increasingly multicultural, indeed a transnational world.

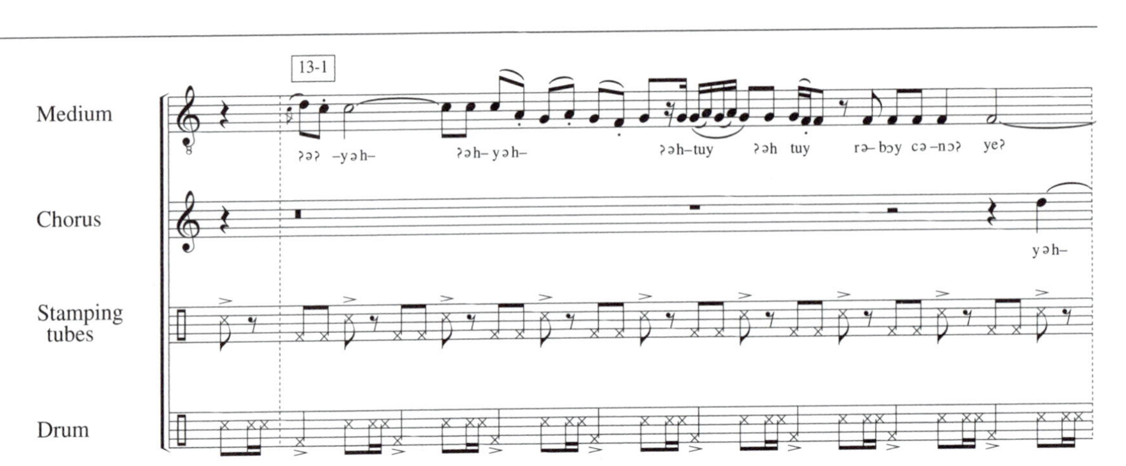

FIGURE 10 Transcription of Abilem Lum's 1991 dream-song composition received from the Princess of the State of Kelantan, Holy Place of the Water Dragon (Sri Kelantan Keramaad Rajaʔ Nagaaʔ). After Roseman 1996:248–251.

FIGURE 10 (*continued*)

(*continued*)

end of each evening's ceremony, after the trancers had returned to the sidelines, the mother of the constipated infant brought the child forward, cuddled in her lap. Abilem sang over the child, while a chorus of women beating bamboo tubes responded interactively. In his song, he invoked Sri Kelantan, asking her to shine out clearly and open the obstruction in the child's bowels.

Abilem employs a variety of ritual vocalizations as his spirit guides move through him. For Temiars, the soul of the heart is the locus of stored memory, thought, and emotion. The head soul is associated with vocalizations; the spirit guide's head soul moves through Abilem as he vocalizes. The most predominant form of ceremonial vocalization is singing (*gənabag*).

Sri Kelantan's song has three cyclically recurring melodic phrases, which form

FIGURE 10 *(continued)* Transcription of Abilem Lum's 1991 dream-song composition received from the Princess of the State of Kelantan, Holy Place of the Water Dragon (Sri Kelantan Keramaad Rajaʔ Nagaaʔ). After Roseman 1996:248–251.

repetitive strophes or verses; the fourteenth strophe is transcribed in figure 10. The three melodic phrases are identified by a dash followed by a numeral: -1, -2, and -3. Strophes are numbered before the dash, as they occur consecutively within the overall song; *14-1* thus refers to the first melodic phrase of the fourteenth strophe.

Just as songs are termed paths that knowledgeable spirit guides chart through the dense jungle, so too, melodic contour is discussed in terms of landscape and river contours. Melodies rise, fall, cut straight across, or wind sinuously; a good song, like a good hike, alternates types of terrain. What the Temiar describe as the disorientation of illness is counterbalanced by the sense of being "located" on the paths inscribed in song.

Abilem also engages in conversational speech (*tɛhnuh*) with other participants, and in formally "spoken" invocations (*bacaaʔ*). In both texts and spoken invocations, he describes or directs the spirit guide's actions, or requests its assistance. Sometimes, directing his speech toward the agent of illness, he speaks harshly (*ʔɛ-ʔa:l*) to frighten it away.

Some of Abilem's vocalizations are directed internally: one vocalization, a sharp, sudden "*ʔah,*" reopens his ears, for in his entranced relationship with the spirit singing through him, he sometimes feels as if his ears are stuffed, and he can no longer hear the bamboo-tube percussion. When he wipes the sweat off his face, clearing and renewing his energy, he often exclaims, "*Swam!*" A soft, momentary whistling on the outbreath helps him "catch his breath" while inhaling.

Other vocalizations embody sonic action: blowing cools the patient; sucking helps extract the agent of illness, bringing it to the patient's body surface, so it can be drawn out into the medium's hand, or swept away with a leaf whisk. Toward the end of the session, his hand successively strikes the bamboo floor while increasing in distance from the patient as he draws the illness out and away. The sounds of the whisk sweep across the infant to clear it of illness—waving in the air to spread the liquid, which flows, like sap, from the spirit guides, or slapping in a direction away from the patient as the agent of illness is released back into the cosmos—adding to the drama of the musical interaction between medium and guide, agent of illness and patient.

As in the performance of all Temiar genres except *pɛhnɔɔh gɔb*, each phrase vocalized by Abilem is interactively answered by the female chorus, whose members beat pairs of bamboo tubes in a duple, high-low rhythm. The rhythms, continuous and familiarized in their repetition, give trancers a sense of constancy throughout their travels. Pulsing like the sounds of the tropical forest and human heartbeats (Temiars say), the rhythms metaphorically conjoin forest and body. When Temiars musically position the "spirits" of foreign commodities within these rhythms, the disconcerting strangeness of new items becomes, at least momentarily, more manageable.

In the text translated below, Sri Kelantan speaks and sings, through Abilem, over the constipated child. Sri Kelantan's first phrase (see line 13–1, below) is marked by the beginning words *tuy ʔəh tuy* 'over there, on the other side'. Mediums entered by their spirit guides speak of a double consciousness, as if their own souls of the heart were moved slightly to the side while the spirit guide sings through them. This phrase is also characterized by the beginning vocable *yəh* (no semantic translation), and the closing vocable *yeʔ* (the first person singular pronoun). In Temiar, verbs are unmarked for tense, number, or gender; and subjects (especially pronouns) can typically be omitted. The resulting ambiguity is exploited by mediums to represent their dialogical conjunction with their spirit guides.

Flower and water imagery refer to the moistening, refreshing liquid (*kahyɛk*) that flows, like sap, from the spiritual world into the human realm during song ceremonies. The spirit's detachable head soul is mobilized through the medium's vocalizations; the moisture thus flows into the patient through the medium's singing and blowing. The liquid also flows through the leaf ornaments and the medium's leaf whisk (lines 14-1, 14-2). Imagery featuring plants extends the metaphors of softening and opening the patient's constricted intestines, as Sri Kelantan describes the opening, blooming, and blossoming of flowers (line 13-2):

[Whistles]
13-1 *Yəh, tuy ʔəh tuy,* my grandchild is so weak;
[Sucks, blows]
13-2 Feel your spirit blossom as my water sprays, my grandchild;
[Blows]
13-3 As I, Sri Kelantan, do dance truly!

In the subsequent song text, Abilem adroitly entangles associated images: the twisting intestines of the patient, the turning of the dancers, and the swirling (*lɛŋwiŋ*) sensibility of trance. The swaying, side-to-side motion of picking flowers (line 15-1), like the soft sway of the motion of leaf whisks worn in dancers' waistbands (line 14-1) intensifies in the twirling, whirling motions associated with the experience of deeper trance (line 14-2). This twisting and turning, when kept within the proper ritual bounds, is the dangerous pleasure described as the experience of the state of trance. In this dizzying space, which Temiars describe as the transformation (*lɛslāās*) of trance, differences and distinctions cease to be problematic. In treatment, invoking this space is said to counteract and soften the hard knot of the illness of constipation. If carried to excess, however, it becomes a crazed swirl, tying up the intestines, or leading a trancer into the illness of soul loss.

kərantuŋ Temiar term for tube zither

rambutan Red, podlike fruit with a "hairy" appearance

gɔh Temiar tube stampers, used in healing rituals

timbre The quality or character of a musical sound

[Whistles]
14-1 *Yəh, tuy ʔəh tuy*, waving and softening *yeʔ*
Vocalization: *ʔah*!
[Sucks]
14-2 It enters, swirling, from my leaf whisk
[Blows]
14-3 Spreading, arriving, in the moisture of my shaking leaves.
15-1 *Yəh, tuy ʔəh tuy*, the buds are soft and weak *yeʔ*;
Spoken: Welcome, you all!
[Blows, sucks]
15-2 My flowers open, spreading afar;
[Blows]
15-3 I dance gracefully.

Voices of the initial singer and chorus intertwine, Temiar say, when the initial singer's phrase ends, descending "from the sky," while the chorus's phrase ascends "from the earth," as in figure 10, from marker 13-3, end of measure 1. Their positions reverse when the choral phrase ends, descending "from the sky," while the initial singer's next phrase ascends. This occurs in figure 10, from marker 13-3, at the end of the second measure, into the beginning of 14-1. In such interactive musical moments, traditional Temiar reciprocal relations of self and society, male and female, human and cosmos, are restated, despite the changing life-styles and value systems that increasingly impinge on Temiar life.

The Spirit of the State of Kelantan is musically defined (in contradistinction to the spirits of the annual fruits) through the structure of the tonal row or steps (*laŋkah* 'the space from one footstep to the next') from which her melody is constructed. The Spirit of Kelantan sings in an anhemitonic pentatonic mode. Her melodies emphasize intervals of a tone (or major second) and, in particular, use stepwise motion within the range of a major third (figure 5, example 7). In contrast, melodies of the annual fruits employ chromaticism, using a preponderance of semitones and minor thirds (figure 5, examples 1 through 6). Sri Kelantan's song does not contain the semitone found in tonal rows of the more than twenty songs of the genre of annual fruits that Abilem has composed (or "interposed") since receiving his first from the *rambutan* fruit tree in a dream in the mid-1970s. The tonal row used to construct the melody of Sri Kelantan's song thus musically indexes her difference from that which has gone before, just as her altar materially indexes Abilem's response to the experience of citizenship in the political framework of the nation-state.

TIMBRE AS A SIGNIFICANT MUSICAL PARAMETER

The musical traits discussed above are primarily melodic and rhythmic, but in the magical effectiveness of Orang Asli music, others are also decisive. In particular, timbre is a significant parameter, both in the stylistic definition of genres, and in the effectiveness of music upon the world as the Temiar configure it.

According to the Temiar *halaaʔ* Terhin of Jeram Kenerap in Kelantan (interviewed by Oesch), tone color is one of the most important parameters manipulated when Terhin plays the tube zither (*kərantuŋ*) as an instrument of animistic conjuration. For healing, he plays it to address the soul substances of the medicines and agents of illness and to give voice to his spirit guides. While plucking its strings, he beats its body, creating a sound that contains an especially high amount of noise. Spectral analysis shows almost no audible partials in the beaten tone, which sounds at approximately 50 decibels; in the plucked tone, the enharmonic noise is lessened, and the first partial (the fundamental of the overtone series) reaches considerably beyond the scope of the noise. A three-dimensional representation of the beaten and plucked tones illustrates this: in the plucked tone, the peak vibration of fundamental on attack stands out clearly; in the beaten tone, a sustained decay is visible. These analyses suggest that especially powerful magical conjurations require a high spectrum of noise (Oesch 1987b:286).

In the role of healer, a shaman plays his *kərantuŋ* for varying amounts of time, knowing how long he has to perform to interact with agents of illness and spiritual helpers. Orang Asli shamans believe they do not play their instruments so much as they enable the instruments to speak; when they manipulate their instruments, they activate spirits' voices.

Spectral analyses of vocal production show the significance of timbre in stylistic differentiation of Temiar spirit-song genres (Roseman in press). For example, compositions in the genre *cincɛm,* received in dreams from the spirits of people who have died, are noted for their vocal icons of crying—sob breaks, vibrato—incorporated into the vocal delivery and melodic structure. As with shamans' instrumental techniques, a spirit song when performed ceases to be considered the shaman's voice, but becomes the voice of the spirit who bestowed it. Calling up that spirit by envoicing its musical gift to the accompaniment of one-headed wooden drums (*bəranɔʔ, batak*) and bamboo tube stampers (*gɔh*), a shaman becomes endowed with the spirit's long-range vision, extensive knowledge, and powers of healing.

ACCULTURATED MUSIC OF THE ORANG MELAYU ASLI

Before the 1940s, the Semang and Senoi lived in relative isolation from the lowland court, colonial, and national cultures. Traders and missionaries operated at the headwaters of major rivers, but rarely entered the mountainous regions at the source of the Nenggiri and Perak rivers. The Orang Melayu Asli, dwelling in villages at the edge of the forest or in mangrove swamps along the coast, historically maintained a greater degree of interactive relations with the village-dwelling and city-dwelling Malays and Chinese. Some, such as the Semelai, whom Oesch visited on the Bera, Jeram, Keratong, and Tembeling rivers, believe they emigrated hundreds of years ago from regions such as Pagar Ruyong in Sumatra or the Minangkabau area of the western highlands of Sumatra, arriving on the Malayan peninsula in the 1200s.

Sumatran elements occur in the music of Orang Melayu Asli; other elements point to a diverse acculturation. The western Malaysian Aboriginal Malays have carefully preserved their indigenous culture, and they give varied rationalizations for the cultural differences between Aboriginal Malays and Malays. For example, a tale of the Jakun (collected by Oesch in Bukit Serok, Ulu Keratong) explains why the Orang Melayu Asli do not know writing:

> At the time of the great flood (*masa dunia karam*), the Malays and the Aboriginal Malays fled into a boat. After painful months of waiting, the floodwaters began to

> drop, and one could see dry land far away. The passengers were so impatient to have solid ground under their feet, that several jumped overboard. While they did so, they were holding their books and writing utensils on their heads with one hand. They tried to swim with the other arm. The Malays were good swimmers and reached the land safely, but the Jakun had to swim with both arms. This is why their books and writing utensils were lost.

This feeling of inferiority among the Orang Melayu Asli persists and is stronger than ever, especially since World War II, when police stations and military forts were built in the regions of their settlements. The government in Kuala Lumpur regularly sends administrators from the Jabatan Hal Ehwal Orang Asli (Department of Orang Asli Affairs), schoolteachers, agricultural specialists, medical doctors, veterinary personnel, and Islamic religious specialists into the country. Although some developmental strategies take Orang Asli interests into account, many governmental projects are rhetorical screens for the appropriation of the forest and for religious evangelism. Clearly, indigenous Orang Asli culture and property rights are threatened, and in some places the authority of village leaders and shamans has been weakened by Malay governmental administration. Pan-aboriginal grassroots political organizations such as POASM (Persatuan Orang Asli Semenanjung Malaysia, 'Orang Asli Association of Peninsular Malaysia') and an Orang Asli daily broadcast of news, interviews, and music by the Orang-Asli–staffed Yunit Siaran Orang Asli (Orang Asli Broadcast Unit) at Radio-TV Malaysia, have helped forge a growing pantribal consciousness and pride among the linguistic and ethnic divisions.

Many Orang Melayu Asli are still dedicated to shamanism and animism, but others have largely been Islamized. The clash of indigenous cultural traditions with those of Malays and Chinese, and the clash between rural and urban cultures generally, have had serious repercussions, even to the extent of having negative effects on the morality and health of the Aboriginal Malay population, among whom in 1963 Oesch reported several cases of murder (see also Dentan 1992).

In some regions, Orang Asli musical culture has lost its traditional basis, but in more isolated areas, animism and shamanism (and their accompanying musics) continue to be practiced. Among the Temuan, the medium is called by the Malayanized title *tok puyang*. Musical rituals held in the evening are often directed toward evicting negative spirits and magically healing illnesses. On band 11 of Oesch 1977c (recorded in 1963), the women of the Temuan settlement of Kampong Guntor, northwest of Batu Kikir in the state of Negri Sembilan, follow the medium's melody heterophonically, their tonal range an octave higher. The melody is based on the triad B♭–d–f, with recitation primarily alternating between the tonic and the major third. The B-flat is also approached from the F below and held for some length, and then a downward octave, from b-flat above to the tonic, is traversed.

Semelai ceremonies are sometimes performed without a specific ritual officiant: on band 13 of Oesch 1977c, recorded in the settlement of Kampong Ba'apa in the upper reaches of the Bera River in Pahang State (Temerloh District), Semelai men sing in honor of the tree that mythologically connects lower and upper realms, and from which ceremonial drums are fashioned. Each singer addresses the tree spontaneously and individually; more or less precisely, the singers hold onto a tonal center, saving the seemingly cacophonous proceedings from tonal chaos (see Hood 1979, Gianno 1990 on Semelai).

Many songs of past rituals are but dimly remembered. Among the Temuan, Oesch recorded a song of the *palong* genre, traditionally a shamanistic call-and-response song ceremonially performed for the growing of fruit during the fruit-harvest season. In 1963, however, it was performed by one male singer and two female

FIGURE 11 The conjuring song "*Dodoi,*" used by a Semelai woman to lull a child to sleep. Transcription by Hans Oesch.

singers in a social context—as a song of love (Oesch 1977c, band 9). That song's transformation from a religious function to the context of courtship illustrates the depth of change in Orang Asli musical culture.

In isolated regions, the Aboriginal Malays still summon spirits using instruments, including the large tube zither *kərantuŋ* strung with metal strings (among the Jakun); the jaw's harp; the horizontal flute *buhbut* (among the Temuan), and the thigh xylophone *kongkong* (among the Temuan). To play the *kongkong,* each of two seated women lays two pieces of hardwood about 61 centimeters long on her thighs so the points of contact correspond to the nodal points of vibration in the wood. The four pieces of wood are cut ideally to produce four tones of the anhemitonic scale when struck with two coarse mallets (*penengkoh*). The *kongkong* can be heard on band 1 of the recording Oesch 1977c: the interval of a fifth, tones b′ and f♯″, are produced on one woman's woods; the major second d″ and e″, on the other's; both combine in melodies that Oesch suggests represent a pentatonic scale of D–E–F♯–[A]–B.

The *kongkong* also sometimes accompanies dance-songs performed to encourage abundance while the Temuan plant and harvest rice; this usage may be the result of acculturation, with the *kongkong* replacing tube stampers. In its construction and manner of playing, the *kongkong* harks back to wooden xylophones commonly found in Sumatra and elsewhere in insular and mainland Southeast Asia. An adoption influenced by northern Sumatran musical culture is the small, conical aerophones, the *serunai* (oboe) of the Semelai, which instrumentally performs sorrowful songs (*menangis* 'to cry'). Orang Melayu Asli also integrate violins into musical performances, following Malay adaptations of the violin within instrumental ensembles to accompany vocal music and dance in social contexts.

Lullabies are another musical genre. In 1963, Oesch recorded a Semelai woman singing her infant to sleep (figure 11). She had placed the baby in a hanging crib, a basket hung on bamboo posts and tied solidly with rope so it could not move, and sang to the infant without rocking it. The anhemitonic *dodoi* was sung continuously in different melodic and timbral variations designed to lull the child to sleep. The woman chose the color of her voice according to the sounds the soul of an infant is thought to have, and she sang variations of the melody until the child fell asleep.

REFERENCES

Babiracki, Carol M. 1991. "Musical and Cultural Interaction in Tribal India: The 'Karam' Repertory of the Mundas of Chotanagpur." Ph.D. dissertation, University of Illinois.

Bellwood, Peter. 1985. *Prehistory of the Indo-Malaysian Archipelago.* New York: Bellwood.

Bosch, Frederik David Van. 1960. *The Golden Germ: An Introduction to Indian Symbolism.* The Hague: Mouton.

Carey, Iskandar. 1961. *Tenglek Kui Serok: A Study*

of the Temiar Language, with an Ethnographical Summary. Kuala Lumpur: Dewan Bahasa dan Pustaka.

———. 1976. *Orang Asli.* Kuala Lumpur: Oxford University Press.

Compton, Carol J. 1979. *Courting Poetry in Laos: A Textual and Linguistic Analysis.* De Kalb: Center for Southeast Asian Studies, Northern Illinois University.

Corbin, Henry. 1966. "The Visionary Dream in Islamic Spirituality." In *The Dream and Human Societies,* ed. G. E. von Grunebaum and Roger Caillois. Berkeley and Los Angeles: University of California Press.

Dentan, Robert Knox. 1992. "The Rise, Maintenance, and Destruction of a Peaceable Polity: A Preliminary Essay in Political Ecology." In *Aggression and Peacefulness in Humans and Other Primates,* ed. J. Silverberg and J. P. Gray, 214–269. New York, London: Oxford University Press.

Endicott, Kirk. 1979. *Batek Negrito Religion: The World-View and Rituals of a Hunting and Gathering People of Peninsular Malaysia.* Oxford: Clarendon Press.

Evans, Ivor H. N. 1923. *Studies in Religion, Folk-Lore and Custom in British North Borneo, and the Malay Peninsula.* Cambridge: Cambridge University Press.

———. 1937. *The Negritos of Malaya.* Cambridge: Cambridge University Press.

Feld, Steven. 1988. "Aesthetics as Iconicity of Style, or 'Lift-up-over-Sounding': Getting into the Kaluli Groove." *Yearbook of Traditional Music* 20:75–113.

Gianno, Rosemary. 1990. *Semelai Culture and Resin Technology.* New Haven: Connecticut Academy of Arts and Sciences.

Hood Mohamad Salleh. 1979. "The Cultural Context of Semelai Trance." *Federation Museums Journal* (new series) 24:107–121.

Kamarul Baharuddin Buyong. 1992. "Archaeological and Ethnological Survey of Megalithic Culture in Kuala Pilah, West Malaysia." Ph.D. dissertation, University of Pennsylvania.

Laderman, Carol. 1991. *Taming the Wind of Desire: Medicine, Psychology, and Aesthetics in Malay Shamanistic Performance.* Berkeley, Los Angeles: University of California Press.

Nagata, Judith. 1979. *Malaysian Mosaic: Perspectives from a Poly-Ethnic Society.* Vancouver: University of British Columbia Press.

Nagata, Shuichi. 1995. "Education and Socialisation in a Semang Resettlement Community of Kedah, Malaysia: The Case of the Kensiu, the Kintak Bogn and the Kintak Nakil." In *Indigenous Minorities of Peninsular Malaysia: Selected Issues and Ethnographies,* ed. Razha Rashid, 86–108. Kuala Lumpur: Intersocietal and Scientific Sdn. Bhd.

Noone, H. D. 1955. *Temiar Dream Music of Malaya.* Smithsonian / Folkways FE 4460. LP disk.

Oesch, Hans. 1973. "Musikalische Kontinuität bei Naturvölkern: Dargestellt an der Musik der Senoi auf Malakka." In *Studien zur Tradition in der Musik: Kurt von Fischer am 60. Geburtstag,* ed. H. H. Eggebrecht and M. Lotolf, 227–246. Munich.

———. 1974a. "Musikalische Gattungen bei Naturvölkern: Untersuchungen am vokalen und instrumentalen Repertoire des Schamanen Terhin und seiner Senoi-Leute von Stammer der Temiar am oberen Nenggiri auf Malakka." In *Festschrift für Arno Volk,* ed. Carl Dahlhaus and Hans Oesch, 7–30. Cologne: Gerig.

———. 1974b. "Oekonomie und Musik: Zur Bedeutung der Produktionsverhältnisse für die Herausbildung einer Musikkultur, dargestellt am Beispiel der Inlandstamme auf Malakka und der Balier." In *Convivium Musicorum: Festschrift Wolfgang Boetticher zum sechzigsten Geburtstag am 19. August 1974,* ed. H. Hoschen and D. P. Moser, 246–253. Berlin: Verlag Merseburger.

———. 1977a. *The Senoi of Malacca.* Bärenreiter Musicaphon BM 30 L 2561. LP disk.

———. 1977b. *The Negrito of Malacca.* Bärenreiter Musicaphon BM 30 L 2562. LP disk.

———. 1977c. *The Protomalayans of Malacca.* Bärenreiter Musicaphon BM 30 L 2563. LP disk.

———. 1979. "Malaysia." In *Südostasien,* ed. Paul Collaer, 74–85. Musikgeschichte in Bildern, 1, 3. Leipzig: Deutscher Verlag für Musik, VEB.

———. 1987a. Musik als Vehikel der Jenseitsreise in schamanischen Kulturen Südostatsiens. In *Entgrenzungen in der Musik,* ed. Otto Koleritsch, 29–36. Studien zur Weltunsforschung, 18. Wien und Graz.

———. 1987. "Die Orang Asli Westmalaysias als Paradigma." In *Aussereuropäische Musik,* ed. Hans Oesch, 2:267–288. Neues Handbuch der Musikwissenschaft, 9. Laaber: Laaber-Verlag.

Roseman, Marina. 1984. "The Social Structuring of Sound: The Temiar of Peninsular Malaysia." *Ethnomusicology* 28(3):411–445.

———. 1989. "Inversion and Conjuncture: Male and Female in Temiar Performance." In *Women and Music in Cross-Cultural Perspective,* ed. Ellen Koskoff, 131–150. Urbana: University of Illinois Press.

———. 1990. "Head, Heart, Odor and Shadow: The Structure of the Self, Ritual Performance and the Emotional World." *Ethos* 18(3):227–250.

———. 1991. *Healing Sounds from the Malaysian Rainforest.* Berkeley: University of California Press.

———. 1994. "Les chants de rêve: des frontières mouvantes dans le monde temiar." *Anthropologie et Sociétés* 18(2):121–144.

———. 1995. *Dream Songs and Healing Sounds in the Rainforests of Malaysia.* Smithsonian Folkways SF CD 40417. Compact disc.

———. 1996. "'Pure Products Go Crazy': Rainforest Healing in a Nation-State." In *The Performance of Healing,* ed. Carol Laderman and Marina Roseman, 233–269. New York: Routledge.

———. In press. *Colonizing the Imagination: Dreams, Songs, and Other Encounters of a Rainforest People.* Berkeley: University of California Press.

Schebesta, Paul. 1928a. *Among the Forest Dwarfs of Malaya,* trans. Arthur Chambers. London: Hutchinson.

———. 1928b. *Orang-Utan: Bei den Urwaldmenschen Malayas und Sumatras.* Leipzig: F. A. Brockhaus.

———. 1957. "Die Negrito Asiens." In *Die Pygmäenvölker der Erde,* 2:2. Studia Instituti Anthropos, 13. Vienna-Mödling: St.-Gabriel.

The Lowland Chăm

Phong T. Nguyễn

The Kingdom of Champa once ruled much of the coast of Vietnam from Dà Nẳng south. The Chăm (or Chàm) are a Malay people who likely came to coastal Vietnam from Java around A.D. 200, bringing Hinduism (in the form called Shaioita Brahmanism) and Mahayana Buddhism. Over time, the Vietnamese kingdom expanded southward, gradually conquering Champa until its demise in 1471. All that remains of the former glory of Champa are the ruins of great temples. Today, the Chăm constitute distinct lowland minorities along the Tonle Sap in Cambodia and in the Châu Đốc area of Vietnam. Their total population in 1988 was estimated to be 155,000, including about 80,000 in Vietnam. Most Chăm in Vietnam remain Hindu, whereas those in Cambodia are largely Shiite Muslim.

FIGURE 1 Chăm musicians play an oboe (*saranai*) and a drum (*baranung*) near Phan Rang, Vietnam. Photo by Phong T. Nguyễn, 1993.

Little is known of Chăm music. Most documentation has been done in Phan Rang, where a troupe of musicians and dancers performs for tourists and visiting delegations. A double-reed oboe and various drums predominate, but the Chăm retain an unusual turtleshell fiddle. A full ensemble includes a two-headed drum (*kinang*), a one-headed drum (*baranung*), an oboe (*saranai*), a turtleshell-body fiddle (*kanhi*), a gong (*chieng*), and bells (*grung*) (figure 1). Other instruments accompany dancing in which the instrumental styles—including *pidenh, patra,* and *chava*—take their names from the dances. Strokes on the leading drum (*kinang*) have names and can be notated with four special signs:

1. *gleng*, the right head is beaten with a stick;
2. *ti*, the right head is struck with a dampened stroke;
3. *to*, the player's left hand strikes the left head near the rim;
4. *ting*, the player's left hand strikes the left head near the middle.

Less commonly seen are the spike fiddle (*koke*), which vaguely resembles spike fiddles of the Thai (*saw sam sai*), the Khmer (*tror Khmer*), and the Arabs; the gourd mouth organ (*rakle*); the bamboo tube zither (*kopin*); the monochord (*kopil*); and cluster bells (*karong*).

The Chăm adopted the culture of India early in their history and were later influenced by Islam, so it is not surprising that some Chăm instruments resemble those of India and Western Asia. Similarly, Chăm melodic style is continuously active, based on small intervals within a narrow range, using unarticulated phrases to build longer melodies. The oboist uses circular breathing to maintain a continuous sound, while the drummer plays cyclic patterns of beats. Superficially, the resulting combination is more like music from the Arabic world than from Southeast Asia, but it also resembles Batak music from Sumatra in Indonesia. The music of the upland Chăm living in the mountains of southern Vietnam is quite different, both in style and in organology.

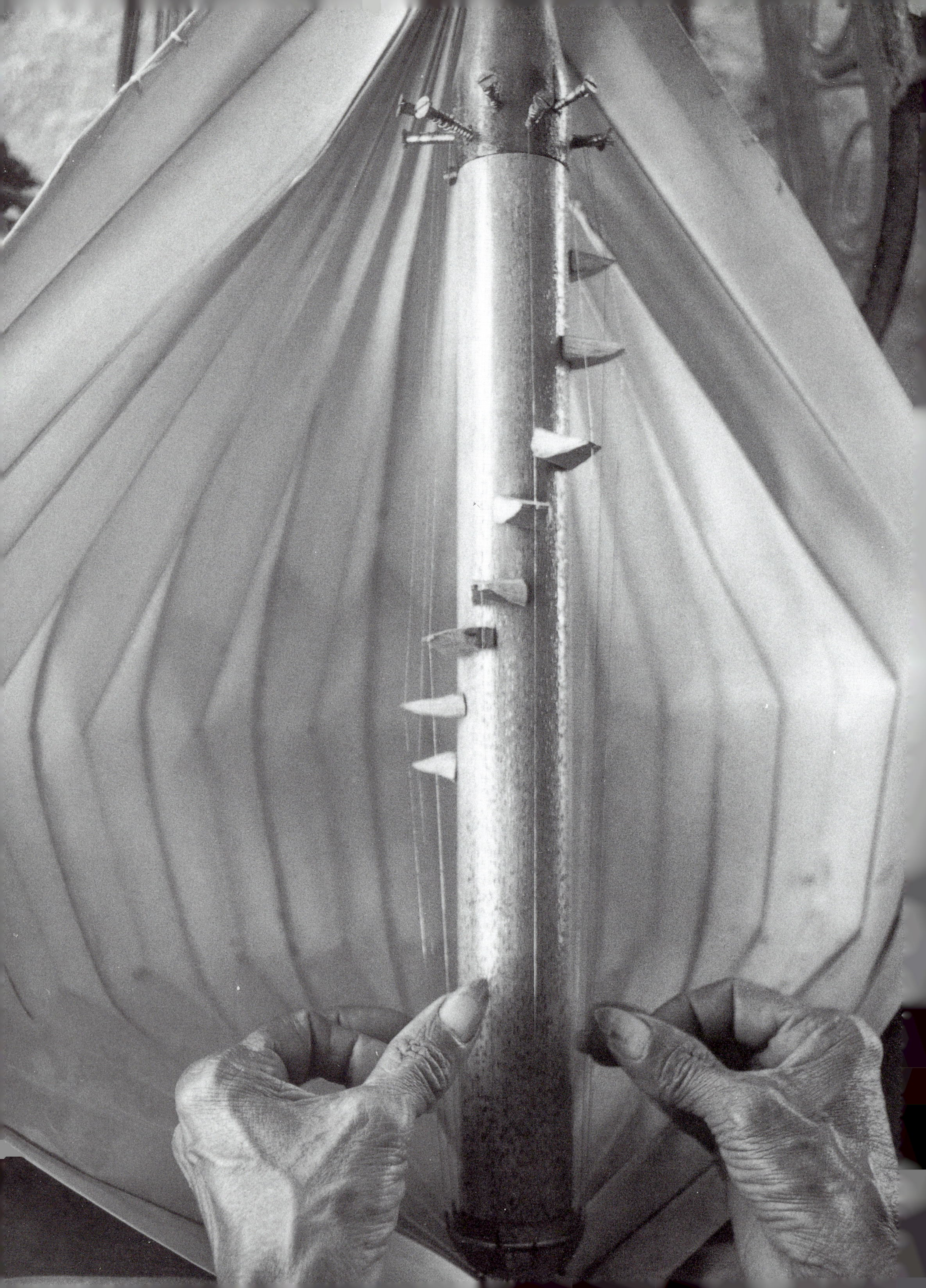

Island Southeast Asia

The islands of Southeast Asia are peopled by hundreds of ethnic groups, of which none entirely dominates the cultural landscape. With national boundaries established only in the last two centuries by European colonizers, it comes as no surprise that the lines dividing Indonesia, Malaysia, and the Philippines are more political than musical. The sounds of bamboo flutes, bronze gongs, and electric guitars permeate the entire area, from the beaches of Bali to the tropical forests of Borneo and the terraced rice fields of the Philippine uplands.

The outer islands of Indonesia are home to a variety of music cultures far different from their more well-known counterparts in Java and Bali. From the island of Roti, the unusual *sasandu* is a zither played by plucking raised strips cut out of a tube of bamboo. The large palm leaf behind the instrument acts as a resonator to make the sound louder. Photo by Christopher Basile.

Island Southeast Asia: An Introduction

Patricia Matusky

The archipelago that extends southward and eastward from the Indochinese mainland stretches more than 5,000 kilometers in an arc encompassing the island of Borneo and all the islands of Indonesia and the Philippines. A constellation of islands large and small, the region has been home to related peoples since prehistoric times.

Four nations currently recognized among these islands are Malaysia, Brunei, Indonesia, and the Philippines. Malay-Indonesian culture, in its broadest sense, predominates in all but the Philippines, where only the peoples of the extreme southern islands and some interior uplands have retained strong links to cultures farther south [see UPLAND PEOPLES OF THE PHILIPPINES]. A fifth nation of the archipelago is Singapore, where Malay culture is a part of the minority.

Most of the islands in this archipelago are geophysically characterized by chains of mountains, active volcanoes, plains, riverine valleys, and coastal swamplands. The mountains, the plains, and the coasts have provided regions for the habitation of peoples who may be broadly distinguished as upland, interior-plains, and lowland groups, each with a distinct kind of sociocultural expression. Most of these peoples are of Malay stock and speak a language of the Austronesian (Malayo-Polynesian) family. A tiny minority living in the extreme highlands of the Malay Peninsula and the Philippines are Negritos, an aboriginal people who live in small communities and maintain traditions separate from those of Malay ancestry [see UPLAND PEOPLES OF THE PHILIPPINES].

Most highlanders belong to tribes, some of which include nomadic hunters and gatherers; most are sedentary dwellers, who practice swidden agriculture, fish, and hunt. In contrast, people of the plains and coasts practice the cultivation of wet rice, often supplemented by farming, fishing, and hunting. The coastal peoples, particularly in western Indonesia, are predominantly Muslim Malays, who claim a great trading and seafaring tradition. They have long been colonizers throughout the islands, and their language (Malay) is the lingua franca of the region. The coastal urban and suburban areas have become home to immigrant minorities, including Arabs, Chinese, Eurasians, Europeans, and Indians.

The great empires of Srivijaya (600s–800s) and Majapahit (1200s–1500s), centered in south Sumatra and central Java, respectively, brought the Hindu and

Island Southeast Asia

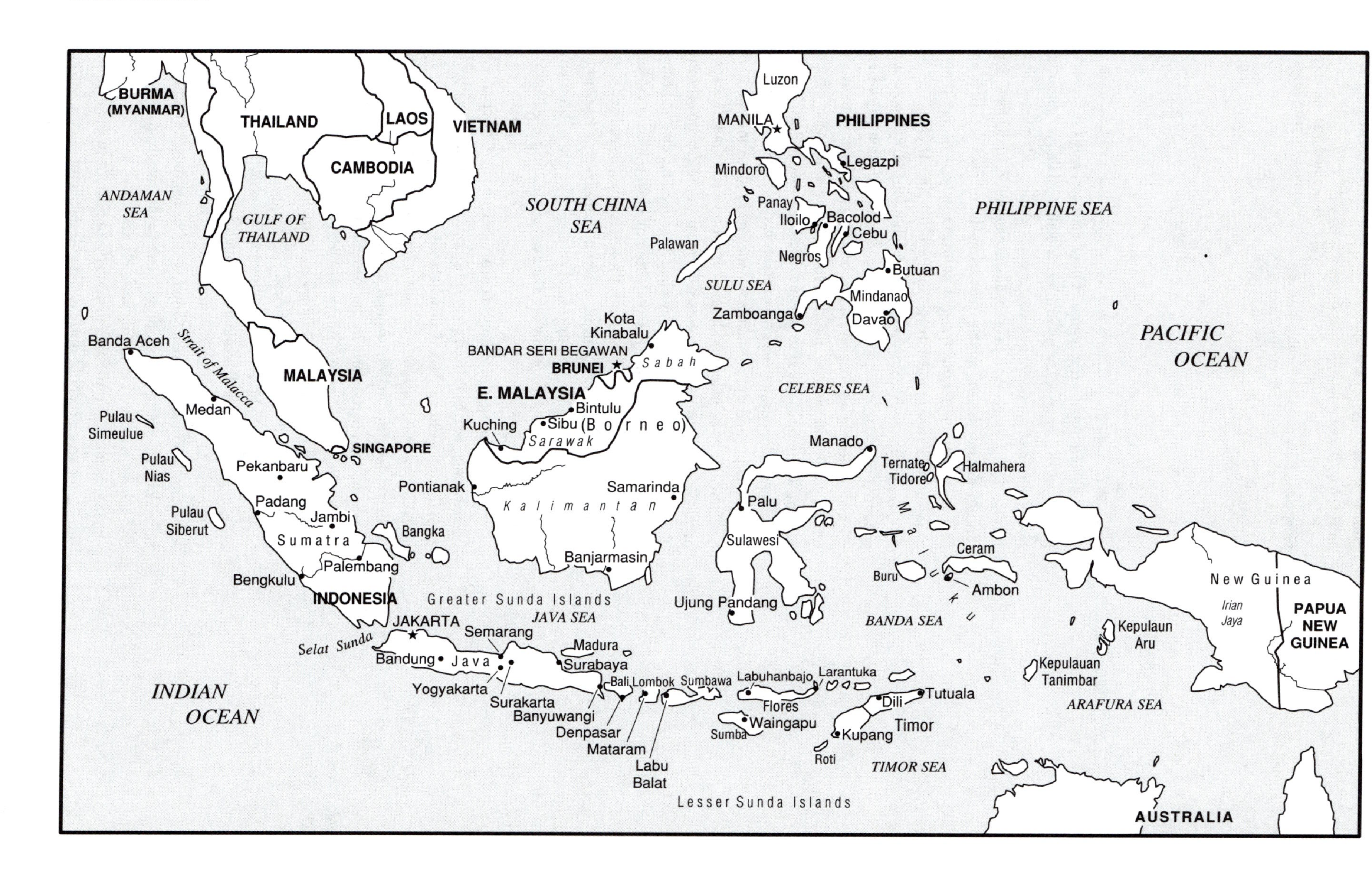

gamelan Stratified gong-chime ensemble

bossed gong Tuned gong with a raised center for striking

Đông Sơn Early period in Southeast Asian history, characterized by bronze drum casting, spreading as far as the Philippines and Borneo

colotomic structure The organization of music by periodic punctuation

Buddhist religions to the region. These empires, however, eventually gave way to Islam and the supremacy of Brunei, Melaka (Malacca), Sulu, and other Muslim Malay sultanates, established throughout the islands of the archipelago from the 1400s onward. In general, peoples of the plains and coasts have embraced Buddhism, Hinduism, and Islam, mixed in varying degrees with earlier animistic practices. Many highlanders retain traces of animism with their acceptance of Christianity, brought by European missionaries in the 1700s and 1800s.

Among the indigenous peoples of island Southeast Asia, music has traditionally enhanced religious and customary practices, and it often reflects aspects of the natural environment. The flora and fauna of a tropical environment, and a mountainous terrain covered with dense rain forests on many islands, have been important determinants of materials used to produce musical instruments. Traditional agricultural, social, and religious practices have established contexts for the use of particular kinds of instruments and the production of specific kinds of musical sounds.

The use of bronze, wood, and bamboo in the manufacture of musical instruments has made musical sounds somewhat homogeneous throughout the islands. The making of bronze was known and practiced on the mainland of Southeast Asia as early as about 3000 B.C., as evidenced at Hoabinhian sites, in present-day north Vietnam and northeaast Thailand. Bronze is thought to have been introduced from the mainland in about the third or second century B.C. (the time of Đông Sơn culture); its making and use burgeoned in Java. The use of bronze led to the development of a type of Đông Sơn bronze kettledrum or gong [see SOUTHEAST ASIA IN PREHISTORY].

During the first or second century before the Christian era, the first bronze bossed gongs may have been created in Java. From there they may have spread to other parts of Southeast Asia. In the islands, bossed gongs, gong chimes, and bronze metallophones consistently exhibit a high level of sophistication in gamelans (the orchestras of Indonesia), though gongs are found throughout most regions of Southeast Asia, particularly in the form of gong chimes. Other aggregations of large, hanging bossed gongs, including the gong-chime ensembles of Borneo, Malaysia, Sumatra, and the southern Philippines, further attest to the importance of the bronze bossed gong in island Southeast Asia.

In addition to bronze, many different woods and bamboo are important materials in making musical instruments throughout the islands. Xylophones—tuned slabs of wood or bamboo—are ubiquitous. They turn up in a variety of forms, including leg, frame, and trough types. Other wood or bamboo instruments include tube and board zithers, mouth organs, flutes, Jew's harps, slit drums, struck and stamped poles and tubes, and several kinds of plucked lutes.

Some musical traits are particularly important in the archipelago. Among cultures using ensembles of bronze gongs and metallophones, musical texture emerges as layer upon layer of distinctive parts. The stratification of sound usually appears as a fixed and repeated melodic-temporal unit, a slow-moving and repetitive colotomic part (often played on hanging bossed gongs), and one or more densely ornamenting parts (played between the tones of the fixed melody). Gongs, metallophones, xylophones, zithers, lutes, flutes, and vocal parts combine to form the elaborate ensembles of Java and Bali. The phenomenon of interlocking parts (or shared parts) is equally important in other ensembles, including large gong orchestras, the stamped-pole or -tube ensembles of north Borneo, and the *gendèr wayang* of Bali.

In these ensembles, each player contributes specific sounds at specific times, producing composite rhythms and melodies. The rhythmic patterns (or rhythmic modes), most often in duple meters, are focal elements in the playing of gong chimes in Borneo and the southern Philippines, and a melody accompanied by a drone or an ostinato figure is an important feature of many instrumental and vocal musics heard throughout island Southeast Asia. Vocal music is a rich tradition throughout the region, with many genres. Among these are long narratives of many kinds; songs of love and courting; children's songs; work songs; laments; and sung genealogies and historical accounts. In many regions, vocal pieces have a melodic line accompanied by a drone, or solo lines interspersed with choral passages in a contrapuntal texture.

The geophysical layout of the islands of Southeast Asia and regular contact among islanders have led to the development of musical features that cross provincial and national boundaries. These features include the use of bronze, bamboo, and wood in the construction of instruments; the prevalence of bossed gongs and gong chimes; and the occurrence of layered and interlocking textures. Though twentieth-century international boundaries separate the island peoples of Southeast Asia, ancient musical culture reveals ties among them—ties that transcend political allegiances.

Sumatra

Margaret J. Kartomi

One of the largest of the Indonesian islands (almost 2,000 kilometers long), Sumatra lies at the westernmost edge of the archipelago, running parallel to the Malay peninsula. Its ecosystems are as diverse as its peoples; from barren, rocky peaks to extensive lowland swamps, the countryside supports a rich variety of flora and fauna. Its natural resources, including oil and rubber, are crucial to the national economy, and it is one of the few remaining areas where Indonesian tigers, elephants, and orangutans live in the wild.

Having attracted foreign traders, religious leaders, conquerors, musicians, and artists for more than two millennia, Sumatra contains many distinct ethnic groups and musical cultures. Moving along the coastal areas and east-west riverine routes, they introduced diverse cultural traditions. The political borders of Sumatra's seven political provinces and the Special Region of Aceh mark approximate borders of some major ethnic groups, but they rarely coincide exactly with cultural areas.

The coastal Malay peoples are distinguishable from the inland peoples as a whole (Kartomi 1980). Each coastal area practices a unique mix of pan-Malay coastal musical styles and repertoires, predominantly vocal, accompanied by frame drums (*rebana*) and pear-shaped lutes of probable West Asian origin (*gambus*) or violins of European origin (*biola*).

Both the inland peoples and the western offshore islanders (on Nias, Mentawai, Enggano, and other islands) have self-contained musical cultures. Even more inward looking and isolated are nomadic or seminomadic gatherers living in the forests, including the Orang Dalem (Kubu) and the Sakai. Inland cultivators typically use gong-and-drum ensembles dating from Buddhist-Hindu times, but isolated forest dwellers favor vocal music accompanied by easily portable instruments, such as flutes and small drums.

CULTURAL HISTORY

The prehistoric musical remains of Sumatra include only iconographical depictions and remnants of bronze kettledrums (*nakara*) of the Đông Sơn culture, which arose in Tonkin about 500 B.C. to A.D. 100 [see SOUTHEAST ASIA IN PREHISTORY]. At Basemah, South Sumatra, a megalith in Đông Sơn style (now housed in the

Sumatra

Palembang State Museum) depicts an elephant-riding man carrying on his back a Đông Sơn drum, apparently a symbol of power and prestige. Remains of two such drums provisionally dated about 1600 B.C. and A.D. 600 (found at Padang Peri and near Curup, respectively) are housed in the Bengkulu State Museum. The frog, the sun, and other designs on their flat circular tympana suggest that they may have been played in rituals to venerate the spirits of nature.

A strong infusion of Buddhist and Hindu elements enriched Sumatra's music, dance, and ritual from the first to the fifteenth centuries, as witnessed by Sanskrit-derived names of instruments and titles of musical pieces throughout the island. The names of the boat-shaped lutes which the Batak subgroups variously call *kucapi, kul-capi,* and *hasapi* derive from ancient Indian lutes called in Sanskrit *kāsyapī* or *kaccha-*

pī-vīnā; the name of the bronze ankle bells (*genta*) worn by Riau-Malay shamans is also of Sanskrit origin.

Music was performed in and around the Buddhist temple complexes built in the great Srivijaya Era, which by the 600s was in full flower, and later included the Malayu Kingdom at Muara Jambi (1050–1250); the kingdom at Muara Takus, on the upper reaches of the river Kampar Kanan (eleventh and twelfth centuries); and the kingdom at Portibi, in Padang Lawas (from the early eleventh century). Srivijaya's capital may have shifted among Palembang, Muara Jambi, and Muara Takus. Only the temples at Padang Lawas have iconographical depictions of scenes of music and dance. These temples belonged to the kingdom of Panei, which in 1024 made obeisance to the South Indian ruler Rajendra-Coladewa and in the 1300s acknowledged the supremacy of the East Javanese Kingdom of Majapahit. As Chinese, Arab, and Old Malay records and the iconographical evidence show, Saivite-Mahayana Tantric Buddhist cults were centered at Malayu, Srivijaya, Padang Lawas, and later at Jambi, Muara Takus, and Pagaruyung. A relief of a man sitting on his right leg, holding a drum on his lap and beating it on both ends, is chiseled at a Wajrayanistic temple at Si Joreng Belangah, Portibi. A flower-holding figure moving to the left is a dancing woman. Another relief shows a man with a set of small bossed gongs fastened to the ends of a wooden frame suspended on a belt from his left shoulder; he is apparently striking a gong with his right hand. The Bahal II temple complex in Padang Lawas shows dancing figures and small bells (Schnitger 1937).

Sets of tuned horizontal gongs with drums are still widely played to accompany ritual and dance throughout Sumatra, and bells are still used in Petalangan, Sakai Malay, and Orang Dalem healing rituals. Ancient music, dance, and ritual based on ancestral and nature-spirit worship tinged with Saivite-Mahayana Tantric beliefs survive in many parts of Sumatra, as do the remains of Buddhist-Hindu inscriptions and statues giving evidence of contact among various parts of Sumatra, Java, India, China, and elsewhere.

Bronze or brass ensembles found throughout Sumatra typically comprise a set of four to twelve small horizontal gongs, a suspended gong or pair of gongs, a set of two to nine drums, and optional wind instrument, vocal part, and cymbals. Flat gongs were once used in Simalungun, but Sumatran gongs normally have a boss, beaten with a soft hammer. Other musical instruments associated with ancient beliefs are (1) solo flutes, oboes, Jew's harps, and bamboo idiochord zithers, used for courting, intimate self-expression, calling a friend in the fields or forest, and magic animal-capturing or honey-collecting rituals and (2) bowed spiked stringed instruments, usually with covered half-coconut-shell bodies, used to accompany storytelling, rituals of healing, or love magic.

Islam was introduced into Sumatra from India from the end of the 1200s, when two Muslim kingdoms were founded at Pasai and Perlak. A rich array of Sunni and some Shi'a music, dance, and ritual developed around Sumatra's coast, either combined with elements of pre-Muslim belief and ritual or sharply distinguished from it. Shi'a influences were reinforced in the 1700s by sepoys brought to man the British fort at Bengkulu, thereby introducing the Shi'a ceremony *tabut* into Sumatran ports.

With the rise of Muslim harbor kingdoms on both sides of the Malacca Strait in the 1400s, Malay courts were established. Several of them survived into the twentieth century, each a patron of a specific style of music and dance. Palaces at Asahan, Deli-Serdang, Palembang, and elsewhere developed ensembles. Coronations (*penobatan*) and royal weddings, funerals, and the breaking of the Muslim fast in the palaces at Bintan, Daik, Indragiri, Melaka, Pagaruyung, Pelalawan, and Siak were marked by music played on the royal *nobat,* an ensemble that originated in Muslim India but developed local styles and became part of the sacred regalia. The first known Malay source to mention the *nobat* was the *Sejarah Melayu* (*Malay Annals*), written during the reign of Sultan Muhammad Shah (1424–1441). Basically, *nobat* consist of a pair of two-headed drums and an oboe. Pre-Muslim court dances were accompanied by bronze ensembles. Muslim-influenced songs and dances, such as the male group dance *zapin* (*bedana*), performed in both court and village, were accompanied by two pairs of small two-headed drums (*marwas,* also *rebana*) and by lutes or guitars. Many have survived.

In the 1500s, the coastal sultanate of Aceh succeeded Pasai as the leading harbor kingdom. It carried on extensive trade with Muslim India. Though unable initially to impose its faith on the Gayo and Alas highlanders of the interior, the Acehnese had converted many coastal areas of Aceh and Minangkabau to Islam by the 1600s, partly by introducing arts such as *dabus* (a Sufi self-mortification ritual with vocal music and frame-drum beating). Minangkabau traders and farmers developed their own Islamic musical culture, some forms of which they combined with pre-Islamic expressions. The Padri War (1820–1832) led to the collapse of royal power at Pagaruyung, and its bronze *talempong* ensembles and dance were replaced partly by Muslim arts, which spread throughout West Sumatra and the southern Batak areas (Mandailing and Angkola). The Dutch eventually put an end to the fighting and continued their colonial rule until after World War II.

Through migration and extensive maritime contact around Sumatra's coast, many forms of music and dance that had developed in certain areas, such as the inland Minangkabau plate dances and Barus-Sibolga's umbrella dances, were transplanted around Sumatra's coastal areas. Arab-influenced dances such as the *zapin* and song-dances such as *indang* (Minangkabau) and *saman* (Aceh) spread widely.

The European conquest of Sumatra began with the fall of Malacca to the Portuguese in 1511, followed by its capture by the Dutch in 1641. A century of direct Portuguese musical influence on Malay-Sumatran courts and villages resulted in the development of syncretized musical genres accompanied by solo violins and in some cases plucked stringed instruments, with drums or frame drums and optional gongs. In these genres, the cyclic drumming, the playing of gongs, and the texts were Malay components, and the vocal and *biola* melodies were Portuguese components. Each area of coastal Sumatra developed its styles of band music and couple dancing.

In the 1800s and early 1900s, as the Dutch colonial government gained control of parts of Sumatra, Dutch-influenced staged theater (*komedi stambul* and *bangsawan*) accompanied by Portuguese-Malay band music spread along Sumatra's east coast, and brass bands (*tanjidor*) became popular in the Kayu Agung area of South Sumatra, where at weddings such bands still play pre-1939 Malay and international popular songs. As Dutch and German missionaries proselytized in parts of South Sumatra, northern and central Bataklands, Nias, and elsewhere, they introduced the singing of harmonic hymns and the use of Western instruments, notably accordions, which local peoples adapted to accompany traditional pre-Muslim and post-Portuguese Malay songs. The regional musical tradition that developed in Batak coffee shops and wine shops of North Sumatra also adopted Western tonal and harmonic material, producing such popular songs as "*Sing-Sing So,*" with solo and choral response sections.

After 1945, when Indonesia gained independence, and especially after 1965, Sumatran and Indonesian band music for electronic and acoustic instruments became popular and largely replaced traditional bronze orchestral music and associated dances in Sumatra's towns and cities, and even in some villages. *Dangdut,* a music that combines elements of Indian film music with Sumatran, Indonesian, and international popular styles, is one of the most widespread forms of entertainment music; however, *orkes gamat* and other Malay bands still perform local Malay songs, often

Access to popular music has led to a change of attitude to Sumatran traditional art, which has become somewhat secularized and commercialized at the demand of sponsors, tourists, and the media.

using electronically amplified instruments, and the old bronze music and associated dances are still performed in many villages.

CURRENT MUSICAL RESOURCES

Music education in the primary and secondary schools of Sumatra includes choral singing of regional and national songs, and in areas where teachers and facilities are available, performing arts of both Muslim and pre-Muslim origin. The government encourages students to perform for visiting dignitaries and election campaigns. Postsecondary instruction in Sumatran music and dance is given in the departments of ethnomusicology at the North Sumatra and Nommensen Universities (Medan) and the Academy of Music in Padang Panjang, West Sumatra. Private troupes perform for local and foreign tourists in the Toba and Maninjau lake areas as they do in such towns as Pariaman and Bengkulu, which attract tourists to see spectacular annual *tabut. Dabus* troupes perform for Mobil and other firms operating in Lhok Seumawe, Aceh. Sumatran troupes have performed in Europe, the United States, Hong Kong, and Australia, and many Sumatran groups have performed on national television or on special occasions in Jakarta. Traditional dances are continually being modernized in provincial cities, often accompanied by popular music or Malay bands. Though bronze and other ensembles of pre-Muslim origin survive in most parts of Sumatra, they are in short supply and sometimes in disrepair. Many are said to have been lost or melted down in times of hardship. Because of the lack of powerful royal or other standardizing influences, diverse types of ensembles and systems of tuning occur throughout Sumatra, even in neighboring villages. When new bronze instruments are ordered from foundries in Java, they often arrive with Javanese or Western diatonic tunings, rather than appropriate local ones, though attempts are sometimes made beforehand (by drawings and measurements of pitch) to make them look and sound authentic to the specific area. In Minangkabau and areas with access to tin, sets of gongs are usually made of brass (copper and tin alloy) rather than bronze (copper and zinc alloy), as in Java. Their lesser resonance or ringing quality allows Minangkabau musicians to play much faster interlocking parts than the Javanese. Given the diversity of local Sumatran tunings and artistic forms and the prestige gained by copying Javanese styles, Sumatran artists sometimes find themselves in a quandary when the government asks them to modernize and standardize their traditional music and dance for national and international consumption.

Indonesian rule since 1950 has intensified the Sumatrans' access to international Malay and Indonesian popular music. With this access came a change of attitude to Sumatran traditional art, which has become somewhat secularized and commercialized at the demand of sponsors, tourists, and the media. Symptoms of these trends include choreographing traditional dances to electrified instrumental and vocal sounds, encouraging virtuoso performance, and promoting glamorous stars. New music is being created in the postsecondary schools, but few Sumatran composers have emerged. Composers such as Simanjuntak of the Batak area and Jusuf Rahman and Mahdi Bahar in West Sumatra have created or arranged regional or national songs, but experimental composers are yet to emerge.

Partly because of a lack of roads and opportunities for fieldwork, sustained research into Sumatran music began only in the early 1970s. Early contributions include Snouck Hurgronje's references to Acehnese music in 1893–1894 (1906 [1893–1894?]), Hornbostel's armchair account of Kubu music (near Palembang) in 1908, Heinze's account of Batak music in 1909, Brandts Buys and Brandts Buys's survey of the vocal and instrumental music of Nias in 1929, Kunst's 1930 survey of the same in 1938, Kunst's article on South Sumatran music in 1950, and Claire Holt and de Maré's filmed dances in Nias and Batakland in 1939 with Holt's posthumous notes (1971a, 1971b). Musicological publications since the 1970s include Liberty Manik's article on Toba (1973–1974); Artur Simon's records and articles on Karo, Toba, and other Batak groups (1982, 1984, 1984–1985, 1985, 1987); Margaret Kartomi's records and articles on Mandailing and Angkolan music (1981a, 1981b, 1983a, 1983b, 1990a), articles on west coast Malay (1981c, 1986a, 1986b, 1991b), Minangkabau (1972, 1979, 1990b), Acehnese (1991a), South Sumatran music (1986c, 1993, 1996), and articles on musical instruments of all Sumatra's provinces; David Goldsworthy's article on North Sumatran east-coast Malay music (1978); and Ashley M. Turner's article on Riau music (1991). Philip Yampolsky's series of compact discs on Smithsonian / Folkways includes releases of music (and extensive liner notes) of the areas of Toba Batak, Karo Batak, and Nias (vol. 4), Minangkabau (vols. 6 and 12), Riau and Mentawai (vol. 7), and Gayo and Lampung (vol. 12). In addition, Rainer Carle published on Batak opera (1981, 1982) and Nigel Phillips on Minangkabau *sijobang* singing (1980). Theses were written on music of the east-coast Malays (Goldsworthy 1979), the Toba Batak (Okazaki 1994), Simalungun (Jansen 1980), Pakpak (Moore 1985), and Nias (Turner 1982).

Archival holdings of Sumatran music and instruments from all provinces of Sumatra, held at Monash University's Department of Music, were collected between 1970 and 1996 by Kartomi, Goldsworthy, Moore, Turner, and Mauly Purba. Berlin's Museum of Ethnography holds Batak archival materials collected in the 1970s and early 1980s by Simon. The University of Amsterdam's Ethnomusicological Archive contains materials collected by Kunst and others. Various museums in Amsterdam, Leiden, Leipzig, and Wuppertal contain Sumatran musical instruments.

REGIONAL MUSICS OF SUMATRA

Sumatra's diversity precludes a universal discussion of its music, so, for clarity, this article divides the island into its major regions. Though certain ensembles and genres are shared among regions, differences in ethnicity (and therefore, musical meaning and context) require separate discussions. The following section starts at Sumatra's northernmost tip and continues along the body of the island, incorporating the small islands within their respective provinces.

The special region of Aceh

Aceh, which became a fully Muslim state in the 1500s, is rich in Muslim devotional arts based on solo and choral singing and collective body movement, which developed as missionaries spread Islam throughout the province; however, most of the music, dance, and ritual of Aceh are amalgams of Muslim and pre-Muslim practices. Aceh divides into the coastal Acehnese and the inland Gayo and Alas cultures. Historically, it was one of the most powerful regions in the area. The Acehnese developed elaborate weaponry; they continue to be renowned for their skills in making gold and silver jewelry and for their embroidery using metallic threads. Deeply conservative in their religion, they are recognized across the archipelago for their commitment to Islam, though their cultural practices include harvest rituals and other ceremonies dating from pre-Islamic times.

The frame drum (*rapa'i*) is by far the most important instrument. It occurs in three sizes: the *rapa'i peulot* (also *geurimphang*), about 25 centimeters in diameter, which accompanies a devotional dance in Pidie; the medium-sized *rapa'i daboih,* common all over Aceh; and the *rapa'i Pase* (also *rapa'i urok*), about 70 to 100 centimeters in diameter by about 2 meters long, in North Aceh. Pase (also Pasai) was the site of the first Acehnese sultanate in the 1200s. Good *rapa'i* made by religiously gifted shamans are highly valued as heirlooms because they represent the owner's soul. After an evening of devotional singing (*zikir*), a set of five *rapa'i Pase* may be played until morning in praise of God, and in times of war, in praise of heroism. Competitions are held between two villages, with the judges sitting midway between and judging the music according to its clarity and beauty.

Another devotional form is *daboih* (Indonesian *dabus*), in which scores of cross-legged men sing texts about the prophets to their own *rapa'i daboih* accompaniment, rising at times to a pitch of excitement, especially when singing the name of the Prophet Muhammad. On entering a state of religious concentration, its leaders (*syek*) perform spectacular acts of self-mortification, seemingly without damage or pain. *Daboih* has often been performed to raise martial spirits before battle. In competitions, one troupe aims to defeat the other by disrupting its musical beat and thereby the religious concentration and invulnerability of its *syek* while he is mutilating himself.

The other main instrument is the human body. Choral music is often accompanied by rhythmic stamping, choreographed body movements, slapping, clapping, and finger clicking, as in the *seudati* (also *sadati,* from Arabic *sahadati* 'remember God'). The *seudati* features male dancers standing in a row or a circle; they perform extremely vigorous movements accompanied by fast interlocking bodily sounds while two male singers (*aneuk seudati*) stand apart and sing texts about religion or other topics, ancient or modern. Their *syek* and his helper (*apit*) sing mainly six-tone melodies in slow (*meulek*) and fast (*tajam*) tempos between choral responses by the dancers. *Seudati* probably developed in Aceh's golden age, the reign of Sultan Iskandar Muda, who ruled over large areas of northern coastal Sumatra and Malaya in the 1600s. Like *daboih,* it was performed to raise martial spirits before battle or to celebrate a victory. It was therefore subject to the magic power of the enemy's shaman, who sometimes made his foes too sick to dance.

In West Aceh, female versions of *seudati* include female *seudati* (*seudati inong*), *laweut* (from Arabic *salawat* 'greetings'), and *pho* (originally a sad dance at the death of a child, hailing from South Aceh). Girls sing religious or secular texts in response to phrases sung by a solo singer (*sahi*), led by their *syek,* beating the upper part of their chests and performing other body-striking or body-slapping sounds.

Aceh proper—around the capital, Banda Aceh—is the home of an ensemble that accompanies former royal welcoming dances, consisting of an oboe (*seurune kalëe*), a medium-sized *rapa'i,* optional solo vocal and choral parts, and a pair of two-headed cylindrical drums (*geundrang*).

Pidie, in east Aceh, is known for its virtuoso violin playing, which accompanies storytelling or humorous exchanges of *pantun* by a mixed couple performing Portuguese-Malay–style hops and steps. Another Malay-influenced area in east Aceh is Tamiang, where dances such as *japin* (*zapin*), *ula-ula lembing* 'cobra dance', *inai* 'red-fingernail dance' (where the *inai* symbolizes female virginity at a wedding), and *sirih* 'betel dance' are performed by young girls to the accompaniment of violin (*piol*) and two-headed drums (*gandang*). They may also be accompanied by an *orkes sinan-*

FIGURE 1 Single-reed pipe (*bebeulen*), Takengon (Gayo), Aceh Province. Photo by H. Kartomi, 1982.

dung timur (Malay orchestra), which adds to the violin and drums a *jokelele* (ukulele), guitars, and accordion, or an *orkes gambus,* which adds a lute (*gambus*) to the ensemble. Dancers also include *zapin* (*japin gambus*), a genre of West-Asian-derived dance-songs performed by groups of men, women, or (since the 1980s) both, accompanied by a lute, several *marwas,* and optional instruments such as a harmonium or an accordion (*akordeon*).

The Gayo people of central and southeast Aceh play ensembles of horizontal gongs (*canang*), idiochord bamboo zithers (*taganing*), and bamboo idiochord zithers (*kacapi*). Their typical Muslim devotional forms are *saman* and *daboih.* The *canang-* or *saman*-accompanied *guwel* 'to sound' dance, the basis of all local dances, is performed at weddings and chief's-installation ceremonies by two virtuoso dancer-singers depicting a bird and a white elephant. Their singing is periodically interspersed with a male choral refrain. After a solo drum introduction, a gong sounds, and the horizontal gongs, a medium horizontal gong (*momong*), two vertical gongs (*agung*), an oboe (*serune*) or a flute (*bensi*), and a frame drum (*guwel*) enter. In *saman* performances, a group of men sit or stand close together singing religious texts to body percussion and frame-drum playing. A highly popular male choral-singing form is *didong Gayo,* which groups perform competitively. In the *taganing* ensemble, women beat three-stringed zithers in interlocking fashion. An alternative to the *serune* is a single-reed pipe (*bebeulen*) (figure 1), played with the circular-breathing technique. A rice-stalk pipe or bamboo pipe, it has an idioglot reed cut near the top, with a horn-shaped flare made of wound pandanus strips.

In the Blangkejeren area, the *canang situ* 'seven *canang*', an ensemble that contains a wind instrument and gong pair, accompanies bridal processions, dances, and art-of-self-defense displays. Up to five *kacapi* and a ring flute (*bangsi*) form the *canang kacapi* ensemble. The *bines* is danced outdoors by a row of unmarried women, who punctuate their ornamented choral singing (*redep*) with clapped rhythmic motives. In the *didong* dance, girls sing *pantun* to welcome an elder or guests before a wedding, accompanied by their own body-percussion sounds.

In addition to *canang* ensembles, the Alas people at celebrations play a five-key xylophone (*canang kayu* 'wooden gong'). Their main Muslim form is *maseukat,* in which a row of boys in alternate kneeling and sitting positions beat their chests and perform other body percussion and movements in fast rhythmic patterns.

North Sumatra Province

The province divides into the Malay coastal areas (east and west), the Batak interior, and the offshore island of Nias. Three main strata of coastal Malay arts coexist: those associated with animist or syncretic animist-Hindu beliefs; those associated with Muslim culture; and the syncretic, Portuguese-influenced Malay. Batak groups include both Christians and Muslims in the northern and southern interior of the province. The island of Nias has developed musical genres unique to the island.

Malay coastal culture

The animist stratum includes narrative and children's songs, which have a narrow melodic range; rice-threshing, honey-collecting, fishing, and fish-trap-invocation songs, which are heptatonic and have a range of an octave or more; xylophone (*gambang*) music, with two women playing interlocking pentatonic structures; spirit-invocation healing songs (*puaka*); instrumental dance music; and art-of-self-defense, plate, candle, and *inai*-leaf dances, which often combine heptatonic melody with a pentatonic accompaniment on a horizontal five-gong ensemble (*tilempong*). The Muslim stratum consists of the call to prayer, Qur'ānic cantillations, and devotional songs by frame-drum-playing men at Muslim festivals. Baby-thanksgiving cere-

rebana Frame- and bowl-shaped drums
joget Social dance
ronggeng Professional female singer-dancer
sinandung North Sumatra wistful dance-song for a single female dancer
gondang Toba Batak tuned drum ensemble

monies (for the birth of a healthy baby), weddings, and circumcisions are marked by *hadrah* (choral, frame-drum-accompanied, solo-and-choral singing of Muslim texts with rhythmic body movement by a line of male singer-dancers), *marhaban* (female solo and choral singing), *qasidah* (female solo or choral religious singing), or *dabus.* The only instruments the religious leaders allow are the frame drum (*rebana*), the lute (*gambus*), and drums (*marwas*). Most songs are heptatonic with a range of about an octave, combining metrically free solo introductions with unison main sections in quadruple meter (Goldsworthy 1979).

The Portuguese-Malay stratum combines European, Latin American, and secular West Asian or Indian popular music elements including the *biola;* major and minor scales; melodies focusing on a tonic, a dominant, a subdominant, and a leading note; a tonic triad; harmony; and modulation. The Portuguese-Malay repertoire includes courting dance-songs, such as *joget, ronggeng, ma'inang,* and *sinandung.* Modern forms include Malay pop (*pop Melayu*), in which a Western band and one or two optional Malay instruments accompany a solo singer. As in east Aceh, *zapin* is popular. In *ronggeng,* couples dance and exchange *pantun* to the accompaniment of a violin, one or two frame drums, and a gong. Formerly, professional female entertainers (*ronggeng*) traveled in troupes of dancers and musicians, performing with paying male partners. *Joget* is a fast triple- or compound-duple-meter dance-song or a modern female dance performed in a hall with paying male partners (*joget moderen*). *Ma'inang* are fast quadruple, triple, or compound-duple dance-songs, formerly danced by ladies-in-waiting at the Malay courts. *Ronggeng* and other Malay dances were included in 'nobility' theatrical shows (*bangsawan*) popular in the 1920s and 1930s that combined Malay, Arabic, Indian, and modern Western theatrical and musical qualities. *Lagu dua* 'two songs' are dance-songs in triple or 6/8 meter; *serampang duabelas* 'twelve variations' is a type of fast *lagu dua*; and *sinandung* 'song' is a wistful dance-song in slow quadruple meter for a single female dancer. *Inang* is a slower but graceful and lively dance. *Lagu dua, serampang duabelas,* and *inang* songs have one-bar repeated drum patterns; *sinandung* songs have four-bar patterns (Goldsworthy 1979).

Ronggeng and *joget* music, in which couples dance and exchange sung *pantun* verses to the accompaniment of a violin and latterly a Western drum kit, are the clearest and most popular examples of Portuguese-Malay music. Since the 1970s, Malay pop *pantun* accompanied by pop and jazz instruments and West Asian–influenced coastal Malay songs (*irama padang pasir*) became popular, combining east-coast Malay, West Asian, and Western features. For a fee, bands play them at celebrations, and they are widely disseminated by cassette.

Pre-1945 Malay courts at Serdang and Deli promoted royal ensemble music (*nobat nafir*). Narrative songs (*hikayat*), the art of self-defense (*pencak silat*), classical Malay songs (like *dedeng* and *sinandung*) and dances, and social dances (*ronggeng* and *joget*) entertained the sultans and their entourages at court. Theatrical forms played at court and in the villages included (in the Riau islands) *mendu* (K. S. Kartomi 1986), *bangsawan* (Tan 1993), and (at Serdang) *ma'yong*. The latter was accompanied by *biola, gedubang* (drum), two gongs, and two struck wooden keys.

West coast pre-Muslim forms, especially at Barus and Sibolga, include ceremonial cradle songs (*buai*) at baby thanksgivings; versions of the *sikambang*, a song that tells a legend about an ancestral mermaid; *dampeng*, songs performed in a bridegroom's procession to his bride's home; unaccompanied *talibun*, epic story-songs or songs of advice; and the drum-accompanied art of self-defense. Portuguese-Malay dances and music (*kapri*) are performed at weddings and baby thanksgivings. A vocalist sings a loud, ornamented melody with violin and frame drums to accompany umbrella, kerchief, and plate dances, in which men take male and female roles.

Batak culture

The Batak people, consisting of the predominantly Christian Toba, Simalungun, Karo, and Pakpak or Dairi subgroups in the north and the Muslim Angkola or Mandailing in the south, have an array of animist-Hindu mortuary ceremonies and a varied music-and-dance repertoire for raising warlike spirits before a battle or celebrating a victory. Each group has entire repertoires for honoring ancestors, representing clan relationships, ritually propitiating gods and spirits, curing, and entertainment. The Batak concentrated in the interior of the province for centuries, keeping themselves in isolation until the mid-1800s. Batak houses are raised on stilts; the two roof ends rise higher than the center, somewhat like buffalo horns. Various ceremonies take place in or near the house.

At Toba ceremonies, musicians play on a balcony in the roof of a traditional house, with dancing in a square below. In Mandailing, the musicians play a set of nine single-headed drums attached to the wall of a ceremonial pavilion and a gong set suspended from the roof; they hold the gongs, cymbals, and oboes (*sarunei*) by hand as they play.

All Batak subgroups accompany their dances at official ceremonies with sets of drums, gongs, a solo wind instrument, and optional solo voice. In Toba, the *gondang* ensembles have five graded drums (*taganing*) and a bass drum (*gordang*), four gongs, and an oboe. In Mandailing, the royal ensembles of *gordang sembilan* have nine drums, the shamans' *gordang lima* have five, and commoners' *gondang* have a pair of two-headed drums. They each include a pair of gongs, two to six small gongs (*mongmong*), a single-reed or double-reed wind instrument, and a pair of cymbals. Simalungun *gonrang* ensembles have six or seven drums or in the *gonrang dagang* two two-headed drums, an oboe, and four gongs. Karo *gendang sarunei* ensembles have a small two-headed drum, to which a tiny, two-headed drum (*gendang anakna* 'child drum') is attached, plus a larger two-headed drum (*gendang indungna* 'mother drum'); they also use two gongs and an oboe. The Karo Batak use tube zithers (*keteng-keteng*) in place of drums for small-scale indoor ceremonies but otherwise use drums for outdoor ceremonies and rituals. Other instrumentation includes a percussion idiophone and a flute (*beluwat*) or a lute (*kulcapi*). The Pakpak *genderang* contains five to nine drums, and its *gendang* contains two two-headed drums; the *genderang* also has three gongs, a split gong or percussion plaque, an oboe, and an optional pair of cymbals.

In all subgroups except the Karo, the gongs are normally called *ogung* and the oboes *sarunei*. In Mandailing, however, *sarunei* are mostly single-reed instruments. Pieces played by the ensembles are distinguished by their drum rhythms, often named after a spiritual phenomenon, such as Mandailing's *gondang alap-alap tondi* 'ancestral-souls-come-down rhythm'. Each instrument has a precisely defined musical role. In some cases (such as the Mandailing *gordang sembilan*) drum sets are played in virtuoso interlocking fashion. In Toba, playing is further complicated by the tuning of the drums. The oboist weaves an intricately ornamented, relatively free-rhythmic melody. The gongs play damped and undamped sounds in cyclic punctuating patterns.

Toba theater includes *opera Batak,* performed by actors who also sing and dance to the accompaniment of two short-necked lutes (*hasapi*), flute, and xylophone (*garantung*), with an optional drum (*odap*); and marionette theater (*sigale-gale*), accompanied by the same five-key xylophone (*garantung*). A related ensemble, the Toba *gondang hasapi,* has a boat-shaped lute (*hasapi*) and plays at relatively quiet indoor rituals and entertainment.

Nias Island

Nias has a self-contained musical culture. In the north, traditional arts have largely been replaced by those of Christian missionaries since the mid-1800s, but people in the south still perform male war dances, slow female-homage dances, choral dances, sung epics with drums and gongs, mass choral songs, and intimate music played on bamboo instruments. Ritual music associated with the former nobility and maintenance of cosmic order is mainly choral, or solo vocal plus choral.

Until the 1970s, the people of Nias had a stratified martial society, steeped in small-scale internecine warfare. Dramatic mass dances to honor the nobility or prepare for war were performed without music, except for mass choral effects or spirited cries by individual dancers. During war dances, performed by troops wearing heavy iron coats over bark-derived cloth and carrying spears and shields, a general may formally address his troops in song, informing them of strategies, to which they sing loud responses of agreement. At formal meetings, such as the trial of a thief, all present sing stylized choral responses to formal questions posed by the chief (or today, his descendant). Such solo and mass choral singing (*hoho*) is performed in unison or two to three parts with or without dancing at weddings, funerals, and victory celebrations.

Specific to Nias is a pair of tuning-fork-shaped bamboo-tube buzzers (*duri dana*), played for self-entertainment or to express sadness at the death of a loved one, sometimes with a flute (*zigu*). In each hand, the player holds a tube cut to form two lamellas, and strikes it on opposite sides of his right knee, producing a buzzing tone (containing up to four pitches) and varying the prominence of its partials by opening and closing holes cut near the grasping end of each tube, usually producing two pairs of thirds a tone or a semitone apart.

West Sumatra Province

The three musical areas of the province are the highlands or heartland of Minangkabau (*darek*), the coastal areas (*pasisir*), and the Mentawai Islands.

Highland Minangkabau

The Minangkabau are famous throughout the archipelago for their architecture of many-peaked roofs in imitation of curved water-buffalo horns. They are also famous for the spiciness of their food, and Minangkabau restaurants are found in areas outside the heartland. Minangkabau society is matrilineal—one of the few such societies in Indonesia. The stunning scenery of the highlands has made it a target area for tourism, which has in turn led to the packaging of certain forms of the Minangkabau performing arts for tourists. As in other areas within Sumatra, ancient and modern genres exist side by side and may even overlap.

Pre-Muslim highland genres include brass or bronze gong ensembles (figure 2); vocal music with flute (and optional fiddle accompaniment); choral singing by

FIGURE 2 Gong-chime and frame-drum ensemble (*talempong* and *rabano*), Desa Nan XII and Desa Delimo, Padang Lawas, West Sumatra Province. Photo by H. Kartomi, 1985.

dancers as they welcome guests; the art of self-defense; and a theatrical form with circular dances sometimes introduced by or interspersed with gong-chime or flute music between scenes. The royal *nobat,* an ensemble of the Pagaruyung court, has disappeared, as have the gongs that were once played only in the presence of royalty; however, gongs are still played in the gong-chime ensembles of some areas, including Payakumbuh.

The brass or bronze gong-chime ensembles of the highlands are known as *talempong, calempong,* or *canang.* The ensembles may be either processional or stationary, depending on the purpose of the performance. *Talempong* normally contain three or four pairs of horizontal gongs or two pairs and a single gong, a pair of two-headed drums (*gandang*), a single-headed drum or frame drum, and in the Sawahlunto-Sijunjung areas, a medium-sized suspended gong or pair of gongs (*aguang*). Sometimes an oboe (*sarune*), a paddy oboe (*sarune batang padi*), or, in the Pariaman area, a rice-stamping trough (*gandang lasuang*) and large cylindrical drum (*dol*) are included.

In three highland areas (Sawahlunto-Sijunjung, Payakumbuh, inland Pariaman), the ensembles are normally played by women, unlike in most other areas of Indonesia, where bronze ensembles are usually played only by men. In processional *talempong* (*talempong pacik*), each player beats one or two *talempong* held on her left hand and arm. Processional *talempong* are played to raise everyone's spirits as they join in a cooperative-work procession to the rice field, and to accompany forms of the plate dance (with *sarunai, adok,* and *gandang*) at a wedding or a ceremony to appoint an elder (*datuak*). In seated *talempong* (*talempong duduak*) or Javanese *talempong* (*talem-

The end-blown bamboo flute (*saluang*) is prominent throughout the Minangkabau heartland. Longer than arm's length, it must be held aslant, and continuous sound is produced by circular breathing.

FIGURE 3 Lithophone (*alu bakatentang*), Desa Nan XII and Desa Delimo, Padang Lawas, West Sumatra Province. Photo by H. Kartomi, 1985.

pong Jao), used for indoor ceremonies, five or six small gongs rest in a frame on soft material to improve their resonance. Players of pairs of *talempong* are designated according to their order of entry, which varies from village to village; in Sisawah, *paningkah* designates the first player, *pamalun* the second, and *pambaon* the third. Tunings, combinations of instruments, and indigenous classifications of bronze ensembles vary from village to village. Since the 1970s, diatonic *orkes talempong* have been played in the Music Academy in Padang Panjang. In Padang Lawas, *talempong* musicians also play a remarkable lithophone, *alu bakatentong*. Women beating long wooden poles against a stone base produce interlocking rhythms (figure 3).

The end-blown bamboo flute (*saluang*) is prominent throughout the Minangkabau heartland, especially in Agam and Solok. Since it is longer than arm's length, the player holds it aslant; continuous sound is produced by circular breathing. It usually accompanies classical songs (*dendang*) with a melody that deviates slightly from the vocal line and fills in pauses between vocal phrases. Sometimes the *saluang* produces a countermelody with a high degree of melodic ornamentation and variation in dynamic level, with at least five primary tones in the octave, depending on the area and the genre for which it is used. It accompanies songs about love and nature, or songs with a magic purpose, including, in the Solok area, shamans' tiger-capturing songs. The typical long end-blown bamboo flute of the Payakumbuh area is the *simpelong* (*sempelong*), on which sad instrumental music or vocal accompaniments are played.

Minang vocal music consists mainly of slow songs (*sadiah* 'sad'), the texts of which deal with loneliness, unrequited love, and other such topics, especially the traditional practice of young men leaving home to win their fortune in a faraway place; laments (*ratok*) cried by a professional mourner; and songs (*ratok*) by a sugar-palm-sap collector, who believes that more sap will flow from the tree if he or she cries. Though *ratok* are banned by religious leaders, who say one should feel happy when a soul goes to heaven, they are still known to some singers. Cheerful songs (*bagurau*) also exist, as does a Portuguese-Malay repertoire for young people's social mixing, played on the coastal *orkes gamat.* Long stories (*kaba,* in Payakumbuh *sijobang*) are sung by upland storytellers to their own two-stringed fiddles (*rabab darek*) or matchbox-percussion accompaniment.

Using four-, five- or six-tone palettes close to diatonic tuning, *indang* singer-dancers sing symmetrical musical phrases with varied repeats in strict quadruple meter to Muslim, moral-didactic, or political texts, commencing with a Muslim injunction. The male and, since the 1980s, cross-legged female *indang* singer-dancers sit in a row, moving their bodies, heads, or arms in identical or alternately identical formations, sideways, diagonally, and back and forth. They also play interlocking rhythms on a frame drum (*indang,* Pariaman *rapa'i*).

Randai, theater performed by the light of a full moon after a harvest, a wedding, or other ceremony, combines circular dancing using rising and falling motions (*galombang* 'wave'), singing, dramatic scenes, and instrumental music. Audiences are often called together by a coconut-leaf horn (*pupuik gadang*), followed by *talempong* music. An introductory dance to greet the audience and a poetic prologue sung by the leader precede the dancing of *galombang,* the main sound effects for which are produced by dancers clapping their hands in front of their bodies or between their legs. Within the circle of dancers, actors perform scenes from a selected traditional or modern story. Between scenes, a pair of singers alternate to comment on the story.

Though the Minangkabau preserve tenets and expressions of pre-Muslim beliefs, they distinguish clearly between instruments and genres of foreign Muslim origin and those of the "authentic" (*asli*) pre-Muslim stratum. The former include religious singing (*diki Mauluk*), brass-tray percussion (*salawek dulang*) (figure 4), a plucked lute (*gambus*), frame drums (*rabano* and *rapa'i*), and Pariaman drums (*dol* and *tasa*). People widely believe these instruments and the devotional musical forms they accompany were used by missionaries to disseminate Islam throughout Minangkabau from the late 1500s.

In Payakumbuh, *diki Mauluk* (*zikir Maulud*) focuses on Muhammad's birth in the month of Maulud. All-night performances, sometimes for several nights, celebrate such events as a local man's successful completion of a Qur'ān-reading examination or a local pilgrim's departure for Mecca. Cross-legged men sing religious songs to their own frame-drum accompaniment. Choosing a text from the Qur'ān in front of him, the leader sings two lines for all to join in, repeating it many times, followed by a *pantun* in the vernacular praising Muhammad. *Salawek dulang* (from Arabic *sholawat* 'to sing'), in which two male singers accompany their singing by rhythmical-

FIGURE 4 Bronze trays (*salawek dulang*), Sisawah, Sijunjung, West Sumatra Province. Photo by H. Kartomi, 1985.

ly beating brass trays (*dulang*), are performed at weddings, circumcisions, on the hundredth day after a death, and on national or religious holidays, sometimes in the form of competitions. Teenage girls in religious schools sing religious songs (*kasidah*), the poetic texts of which deal with divine and human devotion, and since the 1980s also song-dances (*nasit*), accompanying themselves on frame drums.

Gambus lutenists are almost always male, though a female vocalist or vocal group is sometimes allowed. Handmade lutes vary in size and shape; they usually have four or six pairs of strings. Minangkabau and other Sumatran groups take part in regional, national, and international competitions. At weddings, baby-thanksgiving celebrations, and circumcisions, one or more lutes, an optional violin, an accordion, and frame drums play religious songs or love songs.

Minangkabau styles of *dabus* (Minangkabau *dabuih*) are noncompetitive and may combine Muslim devotions with pre-Muslim burning of incense and male or female shamanic activity. Groups of men meet in each other's houses to rehearse devotional exercises and perform at ceremonies on request.

The most spectacular Muslim ceremony in West Sumatra is *tabut* (Minangkabau *tabuik*), practiced only in the town of Pariaman. It and its offshoot, *dol-tasa* (a repertoire played on several large two-headed *dol* and a small single-headed, earthenware *tasa,* a drum of Indian origin), derive from the late 1600s and early 1700s, when Shi'a sepoys were transported by British colonizers to help maintain the fort at Bengkulu. After the fort was disbanded, the sepoys' families settled in Pariaman and other coastal towns and spread the practice of *tabut.* Each year from the first to the tenth day of Muharram, sepoy descendants in Pariaman reenact the story of the martyrdom of Ḥusain, Muhammad's grandson, at the battle of Karbalā. Each Shi'a family constructs an elaborate model of the heavenly bird (*burak*) which they believe transported Ḥusain's coffin to heaven. Sorrowful chanting and loud mass drumming accompany the rituals, and after a mock battle between participating villages, the main *burak* and the model coffin above it are thrown into the sea to commemorate the ascent of Ḥusain and his brother Ḥasan to heaven. *Dol-tasa* drumming performances and contests are still held in the hinterland, where the *dol* has replaced the traditional drum (*gandang*) in *talempong* ensembles.

Minangkabau's most creative and popular contribution to Islamic art is the religious and political song-dance known as *indang,* texts of which are adapted to express contemporary messages. *Tabut* has also become adapted to the requirements of tourism, thereby becoming somewhat secularized.

Coastal Minangkabau

As coastal Minangkabau is not a major rice-growing area, *talempong*-playing processions to the rice fields are not widespread along the coast except in Ranah Pasisir, where four players each play a pair of *talempong* with a *gandang* and another plays a wooden oboe (*sarunai kayu*), and in Painan-Salido, where performers play six *talempong,* a frame drum (*adok*), and a *sarunai* in processions to clear irrigation channels. Seated ensembles are rare on the coast.

Along the northern coast, three-stringed coastal fiddles (*rabab pasisir*) have coconut-shell (and, in the south, wooden) bodies shaped somewhat like those of Western violins, with one string that may serve as a drone. Storytellers (*tukang kaba*) are employed by hosts to sing long tales (*cerito,* also *kaba*), either unaccompanied (except for the storytellers' own *rabab* accompaniment, with extensive double stopping at the octave or fifth) or with an *adok* or a *dulang.*

Rantak kudo (*rantak* 'to move in time', *kudo* 'horse') is a popular ceremonial dance in Painan-Salido. Four male dancers imitate the movements of a vigorous horse while a singer, accompanied by a *gandang* and an *adok,* advises a bridal couple or comments at a baby's haircutting ceremony, a housewarming, or a ceremony to appoint an elder. In *gilo lukah* 'crazy fish trap', dancers dressed in women's clothes hold a fish trap. As the shaman's chanting and the atmosphere become more intense, the trap seems to move of its own accord, symbolizing a love-crazed man desiring a reluctant girl.

The coastal Minangkabau area has many other styles of dancing. The *tari kain* (scarf dance), in which a pair of male dancers brandish dance-scarf ends at each other, is an art-of-self-defense performance to violin and drum accompaniment. *Sikambang* are dances like those of Barus in that they serve to mourn the death of a baby. *Gelombang duobale* 'twelve waves' is a dance in a circle by twelve dancers to their own body-percussion accompaniment while *bando kanduang* (representative of female ancestors) and servants offer betel to guests. In the extreme south, the *nenet* and the *gandai* are danced by unmarried girls to flute accompaniment, primarily for ceremonial purposes.

The plate (*piring*), the umbrella (*payung*), and the handkerchief (*saputangan*) dances are popularly performed to the accompaniment of either *talempong* or *gamat* music. In *gamat,* a *ronggeng*-like genre, two men (one of whom plays a female role) sing and dance in Portuguese-Malay style to the accompaniment of a violin, guitars, double bass, frame drums, and an optional lute, or in *gamat moderen,* a Western drum kit, electric guitars, an electronic organ, and a solo singer. *Langgam Melayu,* songs about love or homesickness, are sung in a moderate to slow *langgam* tempo to *gamat* accompaniment.

Mentawai Islands

Hunters, gatherers, and fishermen in the Mentawai Islands have a unique non-Muslim culture. Their ensemble of three or four slit drums (Siberut *tuddukat,* Sipora *tuddukan*) serves for making music and signaling. The drums, cut from tree trunks, rest on crossed sticks on the floorboards. Players produce a rhythmic pulse by beating the upper middle edge of the slit with a hammer and create complex improvisatory rhythms by beating the drum with one or two wooden rods. There is no standard tuning. The hammer is used on three drums for signaling; each rhythm and sound has a semantic meaning such as "an old man has died," or "a house is on fire."

Three or four skin drums (*kateobak*) plus bamboo or metal concussion bars (*sin-*

Mainland arts linked to animist beliefs include the unaccompanied ritual songs sung by shamans as they perform a dangerous task, such as collecting honey from a hive high in a tree.

na) accompany dancers at ceremonies of healing and sacrifice. The *kateobak*, a long, single-headed cylindrical drum, is made from a hollowed-out tree trunk, with a snake skin, deer skin, or lizard-skin head. In south Siberut, the largest *kateobak* (*inania* 'mother') plays the downbeats while the middle ones (*katalaga*) play the upbeats and the back one (*kateitei*) plays syncopated rhythms. Other instruments used by priests in healing and other ceremonies are flutes, imported gongs, and small hand bells.

To while away the time in the forest and to practice signaling, one or two players of either sex, each holding two wooden rods, beat a xylophone (Siberut *tudduglag*, Pagai *lelega*) of three or four keys resting on crossed sticks. Mentawai singing tends to use heavy vibrato and make abrupt shifts to and from falsetto voice; performance contexts include both quiet, private moments within the home and shamanic rituals for curing or appeasing spirits. Songs may also accompany ritual dancing.

Riau Province

Many people of Riau believe they are the original Malays from whom sprang the Malay coastal populations of Indonesia and Malaysia. The province divides into halves: the mainland, crossed by four major rivers; and insular Riau, containing more than three thousand offshore islands. Island Riau people practice more Portuguese-Malay and Islamic forms of music and dance than the people of the mainland area. The most remarkable aspect of mainland performing arts is the rich tradition of pre-Islamic healing ceremonies, practiced to a lesser extent on some of the islands. Mainland Riau and the islands are united by remnants of a village-linked Malay court culture, developed at the palaces of Siak Sri Indrapura on the Siak River, Pelalawan on the Kampar River, and Rengat on the Indragiri River, and on Penyengat and Lingga (Daik) islands. Living among islanders and mainlanders are seminomadic, isolated groups known as Suku Asli (Original Peoples), including the Akit, the Sakai, the Talang Mamak, and the Suku Laut (Sea People), who prefer to live in a mainly pre-Islamic way. Muslim villagers include Petalangan Malay (shifting cultivators living around the Kampar riverbanks and islands near its mouth); Malays of the upper and middle reaches of the Indragiri, Siak, and Rokan rivers, coastal Malays; and Riau Islanders.

FIGURE 5 Open end-blown flute (*sempelong*), Kampung Talau, Riau Province. Photo by H. Kartomi, 1984.

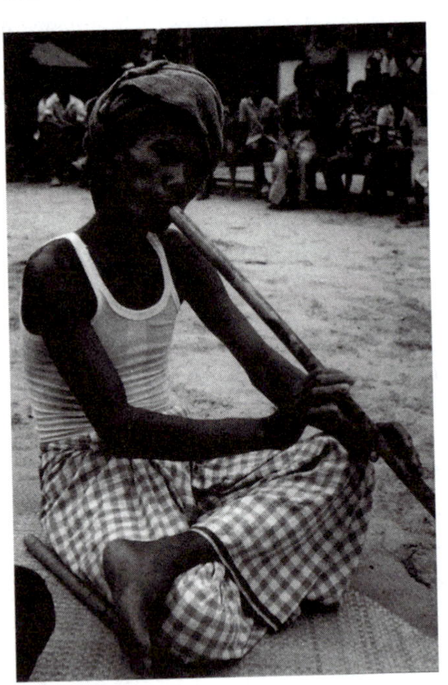

Mainland Riau

Mainland arts linked to animist beliefs include the unaccompanied ritual songs sung by shamans as they perform a dangerous task, such as collecting honey from a hive high in a tree, and music played on the end-blown flute (*sempelong*), which has four or five holes for fingering, each of which is said to have been burned out on the death of a child. The flute is associated with love magic, lullabies, and children (figure 5).

Notable remains of Buddhist-Hindu culture include the string of small bronze bells played by shamans in mainland healing ceremonies, the five- or six-key xylophone (*gambang*) ensembles, which occur in three sizes, and the *celempong* ensembles, which have a five- or six-gong *celempong;* a pair of suspended thick-rimmed gongs *(tetawak, tawak-tawak, agung*); and a pair of long, two-headed drums (*gandang panjang*), one of which plays the leading rhythmic part (*peningkah*), and the other the continuous filling-in part (*penyelalu*). These ensembles, sometimes with an added rice-stalk oboe (*sounai batang padi*), accompany plate dances and art-of-self-defense performances.

The bells shaken in Petalangan healing ceremonies (*belian*) to protect all present are but one sign of the antiquity and symbolic meaning of the seven main healing-ritual types in Riau. Prayers containing Hindu terms are combined with Islamic chants. To symbolize the seven stages of the shaman's spiritual journey after reaching a state of trance, two drummers on a single two-headed drum (*ketobung*) play a minimum of seven named rhythms without a break. The healer (*kemantan*) sings long streams of mainly descending free-metered melodies, independent of the drummed rhythm (Turner 1991).

Sakai healers also sound a set of bells. The bird dance (*tari olang*), in which dancers move like flying birds, is unique to Sakai healing rituals, as is the *tari kuda lambung,* with its horselike movements, and Sakai solo flute music. To accompany the healer's spiritual journey, two drummers play large frame drums (*bebano*).

Coastal Malay healing ceremonies (*bedukun, bedikie*) resemble their Petalangan counterparts, but contain more Muslim prayers, substitute Muslim-associated frame drums for the *ketobung,* and sing Muslim songs of praise. Singing in healing ceremonies around the upper Indragiri River is accompanied by the fish-skin-resonated, half-coconut-shell bowed lute (*robab*), and in the Talang Mamak area by a large two-headed drum (*katabung*).

The Talang Mamak, who live in the forest near the upper Indragiri River, practice many art-of-self-defense forms, including *silat pangian,* accompanied by a pair of two-headed drums (*gendang*), one for leading and one for following, and a gong (*tetawak*). Players of the Jew's harp (*begenggong*), flute (*puput*), and *canang* ensemble (a set of five horizontal gongs called *canang,* a gong, and a pair of drums) draw on a large repertoire of named pieces.

The most important royal object at Riau's five former courts was the *nobat,* believed to be the magic root of the sultan's power, and played only to mark his presence at occasions such as coronations and royal births, weddings, and funerals. Since the Sumatran courts no longer exist, *nobat* are no longer played. At Indragiri, the ensemble consisted of a pair of heavy, roughly hewn, oval-shaped, two-headed drums (*gendang nobat*), one of which produces the lead rhythm (*peningkah*), and the other the continuous rhythm (*penyelalu*), and a wooden oboe (*nafiri*). At the Siak palace, the *gendang nobat,* played only by Akit Malays, comprises a pair of drums, a silver oboe (*nafiri*), and a gong (*tetawak*). A similar ensemble at the Pelalawan palace was allowed to be played only by the Suku Bono people, who live at the mouth of the Kampar and know how to sail safely through the tidal waves there. The *nobat* from the former island kingdom of Daik on Lingga Island consists of two two-headed drums (*gendang panjang*), two small copper drums (*gendang penganak*), two frame drums (*kencane*), two small hand-held gongs (*mong*), a small suspended gong (*tawak*), a silver oboe (*nafiri*), and two ivory oboes (*serunai*).

Riau's major guest-welcoming dance is *tari inai* (*inai*-leaf dance), the most refined and elaborate forms of which were developed in the courts, usually accompanied by an ensemble of *biola,* frame drums, and optional gong.

Malays in Riau and elsewhere in the province are noted for their enjoyment of storytelling (*hikayat*), improvised poetry (*syair* and *pantun*), lullabies, and sad songs, sung at funerals. Mainland Riau stories, called long songs (*nyanyi panjang*), are sung by a storyteller with or without accompaniment.

Another old Malay art in Riau is erotic dancing and exchange of *pantun* with paying male dancers by semiprofessional female dancer-singers (*ronggeng*) accompanied by male musicians, who formerly traveled by boat in itinerant troupes. The slight hops, occasional use of triple meter in a mainly quadruple-meter genre, and the harmonic implications and double stopping of the *biola* part in *ronggeng* are examples of Portuguese influence, though *ronggeng* probably preceded the Portuguese. Partly because of governmental prohibition, a Muslim ban on mixed-sex dancing, and an association of *ronggeng* with love magic, prostitution, and alcohol, traditional Malay *ronggeng* have died out, replaced by modern *ronggeng* performances, in which a singer in a modern band sings popular songs in *pantun* form. The band usually consists of a violin, a flute, a piano-accordion, a double bass, bongos, maracas, and a Western drum kit, or some combination of these. After buying a ticket, men dance with hostesses (*joget*), facing but not touching them.

Island Riau

Bintan, Penyengat, Lingga, and other islands are famous not only for their *tari inai* and other Malay court dances (such as the modern *serampang duabelas* 'twelve-step dance'), but also for the virtuoso West Asian–derived *zapin,* danced by groups of men or (nowadays) women, accompanied by a lute, a violin, a singer, a gong, and frame drums or sets of four or six drums (*marwas*) playing *joget* rhythms. Male Muslim-associated music includes *zikir, ghazal* (solo singing with harmonium, tabla, and Malay drums), *kompang* (small to medium-sized frame-drum beating with unison singing in fast or medium tempo), *bebana* (large frame-drum beating with unison singing), *berdah* (brass-tray beating with slow unison singing at a wedding), *hadrah* (*rebana* playing by cross-legged boys or girls, with body movements), *rodat* (collective *rebana* playing and body movement), *lagu rebana* (female unison singing of religious songs and love songs with fast frame-drum beating), *Maulud Nabi* (unison songs about Muhammad's birth), and *dabus.*

The islands' forms of musical theater, presented on makeshift stages with backdrop, props, and orchestra, are a match for the long story-songs on the mainland. Masked theater (*ma'yong, ma'inang*), preserved on Mantang and in Kijang (on Bintan Island), is accompanied by two goblet-shaped drums (*gedombak*), two gongs, an oboe (*serunai*), a small suspended gong (*mong*), an iron percussion bar (*breng*), and singers and a chorus. In the Pulau Tujuh archipelago to the northeast, the main theatrical form, *mendu,* is accompanied by a violin, a suspended gong, a pair of cylindrical drums, and an empty biscuit tin struck with sticks.

Jambi Province

The major groups of people in Jambi are the Jambi Malay lowlanders, living around the Batang Hari River and its tributaries in the Tanjung Jabung, Batang Hari, Muarabungo Tebo, and Sarolangun Bangko areas; Kerinci Malays in the highland basin to the west; and nomadic Orang Dalem (Kubu Malays) in the forests of the Sarolangun Bangko, Muarabungo Tebo, and Batang Hari areas. Many other ethnic groups—Chinese, Javanese, Arabs, Malaysians, Japanese—populate the province, especially its capital city, Jambi.

The pre-Islamic genres of all three groups include ceremonies of healing, other shamanic songs, art-of-self-defense performances, and vocal or instrumental music for intimate emotional expression, courting, and self-entertainment. Brass (*kelintang, kromong*) and xylophone (*kelintang kayu, gambang*) ensembles, with their dances and songs, occur only among the Jambi-Malay lowlanders, whose Muslim genres include

FIGURE 6 *Sike* (*zikir*) ensemble for Muslim devotional singing with frame-drum accompaniment, Kampung Bunga Tanjung, Gunung Kerinci, Jambi Province. Photo by H. Kartomi, 1987.

hazrah (with *rebana* accompaniment) and *sike* (*marhaban,* male, female, or mixed singing about Muhammad's life). Kerinci Muslim genres include *bertale* (*sike,* Muslim male devotional singing with frame-drum accompaniment; figure 6), *rangguk* (girls' dancing and singing of religious texts, in the Sungei Penuh area), and *tale naik haji* (pilgrimage songs, in which male pilgrims link arms, cry, and sing sad songs as they depart for Mecca).

Post-Portuguese musical genres in Jambi and among Kerinci Malays include the *orkes Melayu* (violin, gong, *tetawak* 'small gong', and pair of *gendang*) and the songs and dances it accompanies. Along the lower Batang Hari, a Malay orchestra of a violin, a gong (*ketawak-tawakan*), and a *jidur* (medium-sized drum) accompanies nighttime performances of Abdul Muluk (*Dul Muluk*) theater. The gong-and-xylophone ensembles are played by women; the *orkes Melayu,* by men. Vocal and *biola* melodies are punctuated by a gong and *tetawak,* and cyclic rhythms are played on the two-headed drums. This ensemble, with optional Western popular or Latin American instruments added, accompanies dances all over Jambi, including *tari piring* (in which mixed couples exchange *pantun* verses and dance with *joget*-style movements while rotating a plate in each hand), *tari dana* (*japin,* accompanied by a lute, a violin, an accordion, a *rebana,* and Western percussion), and *tari joget* (in which boys and girls exchange *pantun* and dance in couples).

Jambi-Malay Lowlanders

At Jambi-Malay weddings and circumcision ceremonies, the *kelintang* (set of three to six horizontal gongs) or *kromong* (set of five to twelve gongs) are played by one or two women. Others play a suspended large gong and a small *ketawak* and a pair of *gendang* while a soloist sings. Single or two-part, their interlocking melodic lines accompany art-of-self-defense displays. Sometimes the *kelintang* are played in procession to the fields. Before 1945, when the Sultan of Jambi or his family would sail in state to attend a royal wedding or other important functions, *kelintang* ensembles were traditionally played on a royal barge to accompany the yellow-barge ceremony (*lancang kuning*) and dances. Pieces from this repertoire are still played in the Tanjung Jabung area. *Gambang* xylophone ensembles in the Batang Hari area and the similar wooden gong ensembles (*kelintang kayu*) in Muarabungo Tebo, including a five- or six-key xylophone, a gong, a *ketawak,* and a pair of drums, are played by women to accom-

The most remarkable form of pre-Muslim music and dance in Kerinci is the week-long healing ceremony (*asiek*), in which entranced dancers perform such feats as walking on cups and plates without breaking them.

pany pieces of a similar repertory of songs and dances, and xylophones are played to scare away birds in the fields.

Villagers use aged sets of five to twelve horizontal gongs, no two sets tuned alike. Frequent changes of tempo, interlocking and two-part melodic structures, cyclic rhythms, melodies and formulas, and gong and alternating gong or *ketawak* punctuation (mostly every two or four beats) are the operative musical principles. Large and small brass ensembles accompany Malay song-dances, including *sekapur sirih* 'betel offering', danced by nine girls (in the lowlands) or thirteen girls (in Kerinci), one of whom carries a betel-nut-filled bowl under a royal umbrella borne by one or three male assistants; *tari piring duabelas* (twelve-plate dance), in which dancers holding two plates walk on twelve plates on the ground (in the Batang Hari area); and *tari inai,* the *inai*-leaf welcoming dance.

Kerinci-Malay Highlanders

The most remarkable form of pre-Muslim music and dance in Kerinci (except in the strictly Muslim south) is the week-long healing ceremony (*asiek*), led by the trance leader (*belian salih tua*), his female assistant (*salih gadis*), and musicians (a singer and the players of a *rabaneo* and a *dap,* a medium and a large frame drum). Once a spirit has been called, the sound of the drums becomes quite penetrating (Kerinci *nyaheng,* Indonesian *nyaring*). The *salih gadis* believes that in her final spiritual journey she is entering the house of a spirit healer who can help cure the patient. Entranced dancers perform such feats as walking on cups and plates without breaking them. Similar ceremonies, held to celebrate the erection of a new house, to put a man-eating tiger into a trance so it can be caught more easily, to request blessings at planting time and harvesttime, and to clean gongs and other heirlooms, also feature unaccompanied songs (*tale*).

Female choral and solo singers performing the yes dance (*tari iyo-iyo*) at ceremonies to appoint a chief (*depati*) are accompanied by a gong pair (*geong*) and drums (*gendeang*), with the women exclaiming in song, "Yes, yes, we agree you become *depati!*" A pair of gongs, drums, a flute, and a tube zither (*gendeang bambu*) accompany Kerinci's main form of the art of self-defense (*silat gabangan*). In *rangguk,* a dance intended to raise cooperative spirits, female dancers sing appropriate texts accompanied by a *rebana* and a gong; such songs for a common task include *tale gotong royong* 'cooperative songs', in which two pairs of women sing responsorial *pantun* and other women play a frame drum and a gong or clap. Songs (*matap*) by a professional mourner at a funeral, or when extracting sugar-palm sap from a tree, are sung in the north.

The Orang Dalem

The more nomadic of the Orang Dalem, living in Jambi's and Palembang's swampy lowlands, play only portable instruments such as flutes and drums. They sing ornamented descending songs to mourn, to attract and trap a dangerous tiger, and to soothe a child to sleep. The melodic style of their end-blown ring flute (*damuk*) and its longer version (*tampoi*) resemble their vocal style. Unlike the Kerinci, but like the Riau Malays, their healing shamans (*belian salek, malim*) play sets of bells (*genta*). They may address their requests to ancestral spirits, Hindu deities, or Muhammad. Betel-and-incense dances (*sirih layang*) and bird dances (*burung andam*) are accompanied by singing, frame drums (*redap*), and a gong.

Bengkulu Province

Bengkulu divides into mideastern uplands, coastal areas, and Enggano Island. The Rejang inhabit the uplands; the Kaur, the Mana, the Serawai, the coastal Rejang, the Lais, the Ketahun, and the Muko-muko populate the coastal areas. The province was once a part of South Sumatra, but separated in 1968; it is famous for its megalithic monuments and large national park.

Ceremonies based on homage to ancestors and natural spirits are rare except among the Suku Dalem, including the Serawai (around Pino and Mana in the south) and the Rejang (in the mideastern uplands and mid-northern coastal area), who accompany these ceremonies on brass or bronze ensembles, or on oboe and drums. Vestiges of these rituals survive among the Muko-muko and the Kaur, who also play love songs on end-blown flutes (*bengsi* or *serdam*) at weddings. Lovers still follow the tradition of mouthing responsorial *pantun* (*andai-andai*) into a Jew's harp (*ginggong*) in the dead of night at the girl's house. Rituals based on paying homage to natural spirits are also found among the Suku Terasing (Isolated Peoples), who include the Suban, living in the Rejang uplands, and the forest-dwelling Enggano, whose music, primarily vocal, serves for making love magic, capturing tigers, and performing other mystical rites.

Many traditional Serawai dances are performed around a wooden pole. At Serawai weddings, daytime ritual dances by the bridal chaperone and men or women are performed for the bridal couple around a pole to which a buffalo has been tied, later to be slaughtered for feasting. In the evenings, the pole serves the function of separating males from female dancers, who perform supervised courting dances (*tari lelalawan* 'opposition-of-the-sexes dances') to the accompaniment of a bronze ensemble (*kelintang*; figure 7) comprising a set of six horizontal gongs (*kelintang*) and one or several frame drums (*redap*). The melodic leader (*kelintang pangkal*) is responsible for beginning and ending the piece and playing interlocking rhythmic patterns; the melodic follower (*kelintang panimbal*) and the lead drummer (*redap pangkal*) are responsible for establishing and changing tempo. Each dance is based on a specific rhythm. The Serawai also play flutes and oboes (*serunai*), and have a large repertoire of self-defense dances. Young men and women sing responsorial *pantun* to each other, accompanied by violin (*biola*) and frame drums (*rebana*).

At both upland and coastal Rejang weddings, ritual dancers also dance around a pole to which a sacrificial buffalo has been tied. The nights are occupied by mixed-sex dancing under a chaperone's control. Ancestor-honoring and life-crisis ceremonies are accompanied by the *kromong* (*kelintang*) ensemble consisting of a set of five, seven, nine, or twelve horizontal gongs (*kromong, kelintang*), a suspended gong (*gung*), and a long, two-headed drum (*gandang panjang*) or a large frame drum (*dep*). *Kromong*-accompanied ritual dances associated with the goddess of rice include the plate dance (*tari piring*), in which dancers walk on twelve plates arranged on the sides of a square to symbolize a path around a rice field, and the rice-seed-swaying dance (*tari dundang benih*), performed before planting and after harvesting.

At funerals, professional Rejang mourners sing sad songs (*ratap*). The coastal Rejang and the Muko-muko also specialize in slow, female ceremonial dances such as

FIGURE 7 *Kelintang* ensemble (gong chime and frame drums), Kampung Gelumbang, Bengkulu Province. Photo by H. Kartomi, 1983.

the *tari nenet,* danced by four girls to the accompaniment of an oboe (*sarunai nenet*) and a heavy frame drum (*dep*), at circumcisions, weddings, baby-haircutting rituals, and guest-welcoming ceremonies. Girls also perform seven slow *nenet* accompanied by seven songs based on a legend about the ancestral hero Malim Deman, who found a bird that turned into the girl he married, but was murdered by a jealous rival. The seven songs are accompanied by *sarunai gandai* and a *redap* (*dep*).

In the south, the Kaur, for ceremonial dances, also play *kelintang* ensembles of seven horizontal gongs and two frame drums or a *gamulan* of five horizontal gongs.

Common to all areas of Bengkulu but especially the coastal areas is the unaccompanied Malay or accompanied Portuguese-Malay vocal genre *dendang,* designated the official music of Bengkulu in the Dutch colonial period. Songs to call the wind by fishermen at sea are unaccompanied. Sad songs (*dendang*) contrast with happy songs (*dendang riang*), but most songs deal with unrequited love or unfortunate fate. Accompanied songs include the responsorial singing of *pantun* between men and women (*ma'inang*), and the widely known Portuguese-Malay song "*Kaparinyo,*" which accompanies the umbrella (*payung*) dance. Songs are usually accompanied by a violin (*biola, biol*) and one or several large, heavy frame drums (*redap*). In the Kaur districts, *dendang* ensembles may also include an Indian harmonium. During an introduction by the violinist, the drummers enter to establish the meter. By a low-pitched drummed sound (*tum*) they mark the end of each rhythmic cycle, which usually measures eight or sixteen beats. After the first verse is sung, a choral refrain and instrumental interlude follow. The heptatonic, vocal and violin melodies are usually in minor or major keys, with modulations to closely related keys.

As along most parts of Sumatra's west coast, especially the Barus-Sibolga area, the vocal style ranges from the loud, high-pitched, small love-song style (*dendang sayang gecik*), with its wealth of melismas, glides, and glottal stops, to the soft, low-pitched, retiring love-song style (*dendang sayang mundur*). Like the styles of singing, the styles of drumming are divided into the loud (*degam*) and the soft (*ketira*), each of which has several standard rhythms—loud rhythm one (*degam satu*), loud rhythm two (*degam dua*), and so on. The loud style is noted for the variability of its rhythms and dynamics (loud to moderately loud), and the soft style for the repetitiousness of its rhythms and the constancy of its dynamics. The player of the *biola* is the leader (*pangkal*); the drummers are the followers (*panimbal*).

Talibun, a vocal genre found along Bengkulu's west coast, is based on strict four-, eight-, or twelve-line poetic forms. Bengkulu *talibun* is usually sung after the *rendai* dance at a wedding or other celebration, to the response of another singer. Like *pantun* verse, it may contain lines of allusion and lines of real meaning, offering advice or religious knowledge. All *talibun* poetry is sung to one basic melody, often performed in relatively free rhythm.

Either *kelintang* or *dendang* music may accompany coastal Bengkulu's common repertoire of dances, which includes the fan (*kipas*) dance, the scarf (*slendang*) dance, the long-cloth (*kain panjang*) dance, the plate (*piring*) dance, and the sword (*pedang*) dance, most of which are based on Malay *joget*-style steps and movements of the art of self-defense. The acrobatic round (*rendai*) dance, performed by a pair or several pairs of art-of-self-defense dancers, is accompanied by a fast, cyclic rhythm played only on the *redap.*

The main form of devotional Muslim music in Bengkulu's coastal areas is the *hadrah.* A circle of elders (*majlis*) meet in each other's houses or at a ceremony to sing devotional songs to their own frame-drum accompaniment, led by a religious leader. Members of a *majlis,* which often contains several violinists, also frequently perform *dendang.*

The most important ceremony in Bengkulu town is *tabot,* which resembles *tabuik* in Pariaman. As in West Sumatra, it celebrates the ascent of Muhammad's grandsons to heaven, and the main musical instruments are the large cylindrical drum (*dol*) and the earthenware drum (*tasa*). Bengkulu's unique contribution to *tabot* is the game *ikan-ikan* 'fish' and its offshoot, *gajah-gajah* 'elephants', accompanied by *gamat* music (violin, drums, accordion) played in the streets for contributions. After parading their floats, the celebrants carry the most important one to the nearby grave of Syek Burhanuddin, believed to have brought Islam and *tabot* to Bengkulu.

Enggano Island, named after the Portuguese verb *enganar* 'to deceive', lies about 100 kilometers off the coast. The Enggano Islanders were formerly a forest-dwelling people living in virtual isolation. Their main musical instrument is the conch (*keneo*), which when blown produces one loud note. Only one *keneo* is used in the ritual *tari semut* (ant dance), played by the first of a long row of male and female dancers, each holding the person in front by the waist. Up to forty conchs are played in the war dance, however, producing many pitches; men wearing traditional bark-and-leaf clothes stand upright and raise their spears in the air, or hold them while standing in a slightly crouched position. These dances are now being developed for tourism.

South Sumatra Province

South Sumatra, especially Palembang, is an important area for the Indonesian economy. Because it has major reserves of oil, it generates a large percentage of the country's export revenue. Palembang, the provincial capital, was once the location of Srivijaya, an important Buddhist-Hindu kingdom that flourished for four centuries from before the 700s. As with Lampung, its proximity to Java and Jakarta, the nation's capital, has made South Sumatra more subject to Javanese and international influences.

The main musical areas of South Sumatra are the western uplands and the Musi, Ogan, and Komering river basins. South Sumatra's musical identity is primarily Muslim and Malay, as exemplified by the *dana,* a Muslim dance popular throughout the province. Many choreographers and dancers feel that even traditional bronze-ensemble-accompanied dances should be accompanied by Malay orchestras (*orkes Melayu, orkes gambus*) despite their pride in Srivijaya. Local people believe the bronze orchestras and the *randai* and other guest-welcoming dances performed by the

Groups of up to four women in the Tanjung Sakti area play ritual music while stamping the husks off the grain in a round wooden trough, producing interlocking rhythms and sometimes adding a melody on a guitar.

Basemah and the Rejang of the western uplands are survivals of South Sumatra's Buddhist-Hindu period. They think the bronze orchestras in the Ogan-Komering area south of Palembang were transplanted by Abung migrants from Lampung and elsewhere. The orchestra and shadow-puppet theater of the former Palembang court are of Javanese origin.

Music that predates the Buddhist-Hindu era is still performed, especially in the uplands of Basemah (as Tanjung Sakti) and Rejang and among the Anak Dalem who inhabit the forest, along the riverbanks and swamps of Musi Banyuasin (the Jani area), Musi Rawas, and Lahat (the Ringgan area). Honey-collecting singing and other shamanic singing, the music of mourning, courting music played on a Jew's harp, introspective solo or ceremonial singing or playing of flutes after a death or on other sad topics, music for stamping rice, art-of-self-defense displays, and male-female responsorial singing and other vocal music are all based on reverence for natural spirits and ancestors. A Buddhist-Hindu or Muslim attribute may be added to these musical forms in performance, but they primarily express animist beliefs.

Basemah uplands

In the Basemah uplands, mystical songs to calm the bees while a shaman (*piawang*) carries a burning torch up a tall tree and throws it down for the bees to follow while he collects the honey are called songs to defeat the honeybees (*lagu ngalaka medu*). Spells sung to praise or censure a tiger are sung by a shaman who has befriended tigers. The Anak Dalem play frame drums and flutes, having healing-dance and vocal-music repertoires. During spiritual journeys, healers dance and shake sets of bronze bells (*genta*) inherited from Buddhist-Hindu times. Rejang shamans (*dukuen*) express their belief in ancestral spirits' power through singing and ceremonies of divination and healing. The same applies in the Ogan-Komering area, where crocodile-, snake- and tiger-capturing shamans (*pawang*) and birth-facilitating mystics (*pawang pontianak*) sing their mantras. Sad music in the highlands is sung by professional mourners and accompanied by a player on the *serdam,* an end-blown ring flute with three front holes and a back hole, which produces elaborate microtonal ornamented passages by circular breathing. When players of *serdam* are called to the home of a deceased person on the first, third, seventh, and fortieth days after a death, they may play all night for several nights on end, stimulating the open expression of grief by those present.

Like most people in Sumatra, the Basemah believe that Jew's harps (*ginggung*), played by lovers to each other, are an ancient kind of instrument. A *ginggung* is a thin, rectangular bamboo strip that has been split to produce a long vibrating tongue. The player holds it with the left hand in his or her half-open mouth; a right-hand finger vibrates the other end by tugging a small cord attached to it. As the player changes the size of the oral cavity, the harmonics change, and a melody is produced.

FIGURE 8 *Harmonika* (chromatic button accordion) accompanies the vocalist Tanjung Sakti, South Sumatra Province. Photo by H. Kartomi, 1971.

Since the early twentieth century, when German missionaries converted part of the population of upland Tanjung Sakti to Christianity, musicians adopted the *harmonika* (chromatic button accordion; figure 8), adapting to it the happy and sad anhemitonic pentatonic melodies that they formerly sang or played on the Jew's harp or the *serdam.*

Music played for ancient agricultural rites is rare; however, groups of up to four women in the Tanjung Sakti area play ritual *cintuk* ('pole-beating' music) or *lisung* ('trough-stamping' music) while stamping the husks off the grain in a round wooden trough, producing interlocking rhythms and sometimes adding a melody on a guitar. In the Ogan-Komering area, rice-stamping troughs have two main holes, beaten rhythmically by a maximum of four women.

Martial displays of the art of self-defense in Burai are performed by two men with knives and daggers, accompanied by a small gong played on the lap and a two-headed drum or by a large gong and a set of three drums.

Vocal music of ancient origins in Basemah includes loud, responsorial jungle-call singing (*rejong*) with improvised exchanges of quatrain verses (*cang-incang*) by a mixed couple singing about social issues, such as the good deeds of an elder at his induction ceremony, and sad *ringit* songs at the loss of a spouse or valuable possessions. Lullabies (*ngayun buai* 'sway and sing to sleep') in Burai have a six-tone palette, with slight melodic ornamentation and frequent changes of tonal center, and sleep- or religion-oriented texts.

In Basemah, the Ogan-Komering River basins, and elsewhere, hosts employ semiprofessional storytellers to sing long stories (*guritan*) all night at weddings and other ceremonies. After singing prayers to ancestors, a storyteller begins by performing chantlike melodies, which alternate with melodically ornamented or melismatic sections.

The heritage of the golden age of Srivijaya is maintained in South Sumatra by the long-golden-fingernail dances (symbolizing virginity) and other female-welcoming dances, accompanied by a variety of bronze gong-and-drum ensembles, which lend luster to formal occasions in regions—throughout the province and other areas, extending north as far as Thailand—that were once part of greater Srivijaya. These ensembles are called *keromongan* in Kayuagung (figure 9) and *tabuhan* in the nearby area of Burai Lama. Their main instrument is a set of horizontal bronze gongs, called *keromongan* (*ngeromong*) in Kayuagung, *canang* in Burai Lama, and *kelitang* (also *kulitang, kalintang, keromong, tabuhan*) in the Menggala area. In Kayuagung, the *keromongan* ensemble consists of a *keromongan* (seven to sixteen small gongs resting on soft cloth in a wooden frame), a suspended medium-sized gong (*tawak-tawak*), a small gong (*canang*), a large suspended gong (*gong*), a small high-pitched gong (*rujih*), and a two-headed drum (*gendang*). In Burai Lama, the *canang* ensemble comprises a *canang* (eight or nine horizontal gongs), played with a single large gong; in the Menggala area, the *kelitang* ensemble consists of a *kelitang* (nine to twelve gongs), two large suspended gongs (*talo balak* and *talo tanggung*), a small suspended gong (*bende*), a pair of cymbals (*gujih*), a cylindrical drum (*ketipung*), and a frame drum (*terbang*).

Other mainland areas

In the Rejang area, *kelintang* ensembles contain a *kelintang* (four, five, six, seven, or nine horizontal bronze or iron gongs), a cylindrical drum (*gendang panjang*), a frame drum (*redap*), and a suspended gong. Sometimes an oboe (*serunai*) or a violin substitutes for the horizontal gongs. Around Pagaralam (Basemah), sets of four gongs (*tale, gelintang*) combine with a frame drum. The combination of gongs with violin and

FIGURE 9 *Keromongan* ensemble (gong chime, gong, and drum), Kayuagung, South Sumatra Province. Photo by H. Kartomi, 1988.

frame drums unites elements of Buddhist-Hindu, Portuguese-Malay, and West Asian origin, sometimes accompanying an animist agricultural or other rite.

In the Ogan-Komering area (especially Burai), bronze ensembles accompany the Malay *tari piring,* with female dancers walking on plates while rotating a saucer containing a lighted candle in each hand. At Kayuagung weddings and other celebrations, *tabuhan* ensembles accompany the weaving dance (*tari benang setukal*), in which five dancers in bridal costumes are accompanied by the *rapdorap* rhythm (*rapdorap* being the onomatopoeic sound of a moving loom), played in interlocking fashion on the fourteen-gong *tale.*

In the Lahat district, the main courting dance (*gegerit*) is based on an eaglelike shoulder-raising movement. Both music and dance combine Muslim elements with pre-Muslim ones. The ensemble consists of the horizontal *tabuhan,* a large suspended bronze *gung* playing a cyclic rhythmic pattern, a two-headed *gendang,* a set of *marwas,* and a lute.

If bronze, brass, or iron gongs typify the Buddhist-Hindu stratum, the frame drums (*terbangan, rebana, tamburin, tamurin*) and small two-headed drums (*marawis, marwas, ketipung*) identify the Muslim stratum. Strict Muslims disassociate themselves from gong ensembles and female or mixed-sex dancing; however, in most areas, Muslim or pre-Muslim conflict has been resolved by the local religious leaders, who respect and allow both traditional and Muslim arts to be practiced.

West Asian music influenced South Sumatra from the early 1500s, when a Muslim sultanate of mixed Javanese and Arabic blood sprang up in Palembang. Many pre-Muslim rural dances are now accompanied by Arabic-influenced instrumental ensembles, and local and transplanted Malay songs by an *orkes Melayu.*

The most widespread devotional musical form, *zikir,* is performed regularly by male or female groups accompanying themselves on large and small *rebana* and frames with jingles (*kerincingan*). Devotees repeat the names of God and the prophets to reach an ecstatic state of union with God. In a secular form of this practice (*rodat,* from Arabic *roddat*), men or women sit, kneel, or stand close together, performing identical or alternating body movements to their own vocal and frame-drum accompaniment. A special form of *zikir* with a solo singer and chorus, or two groups of solo singer and chorus, is *serapal anam* 'holy prophet'. Besides singing praises of Muhammad, each group (of which there are more than one hundred in Palembang) takes turns singing texts that pose religious questions to be answered by the other group. Because no instruments are used, *serapal anam* may be performed in mosques. Other popular forms of *zikir* are *kasidah, hadrah,* and *dabus.* The main Arabic-influenced form of dance is *zapin* (*japin*), accompanied by jingles (*tambrin*), jingle-bearing tambourines (*zap*), three drums (*marawis*), and a bass drum (*hajir*), with a lute, a flute (*seruling*), and a violin playing leading melodic roles. Bongos, guitars, and a pair of two-headed drums (*gendang dua*) may be added. The tempo and rhythm are led by the player of the main *marawis,* with his two followers on the other pair of *marawis.* To the accompaniment of solo and choral songs, a group of girls dance fast, vigorous *zapin,* alternately singing in loud chorus and clapping their hands, sitting and moving close together, and walking in fast-moving formations while performing exquisite movements with their hands.

Traditional courting dances that combine *serapal-anam*-type and traditional movements and music in the Lahat and Pagaralam uplands include the lemon-grass dance (*tari erai-erai*) and the donation dance (*tari dana*). In the lemon-grass dance, unmarried boys and girls, or girls taking the roles of both sexes, dance in couples and sing verses about love, poverty, wealth, or homelessness, accompanied by a three-stringed violin played with double stopping, a flute (*suling*), a frame drum (*terbangan*), a two-headed drum (*kendang*), and a chorus singing Malay songs in diatonic or Arabic scales. The donation dance is danced by boys, girls, or mixed groups, kneeling or standing in separate rows, moving rhythmically and singing in unison about Islamic laws and precepts to their own frame drum (*redep*) and frame jingle (*kicikan*) accompaniment. The main singer draws from a repertoire of ten *dana* songs, singing an Arabic-style melody with a two-tetrachord scale, accompanied by a violin, a *redep* (*rebana*), a set of *marwas,* and a lute. Taught in the religious schools (*madrasah*), it is also performed in *dul muluk.*

Another form of West Asian–influenced music is the *orkes gambus,* in which musicians accompany Malay songs with a lute, a *gung, gendang,* and a pair of two-headed drums (*ketipung*). *Orkes Melayu* in this area consist of a violin, a harmonica (*harmonika*), a guitar (*gitar*), a large bass (*strengbas*), a tambourine (*tamrin*), a flute (*suling*), and a solo singer performing Malay songs.

Dul muluk, theater popular to the east and south of Palembang, consists of dialogue, dance, and singing, with a cast of about twenty-five actors, who traditionally take at least two days and nights to complete a performance at a celebration. Male actors take the female roles, but do not try to imitate the female voice. A basic repertoire of twenty-five songs having Malay, Indian-, or Arabic-influenced melodies is accompanied only by male musicians, who between and within scenes play three violins, a bass drum (*jidur*), and a small gong (*ketawa*). Plots usually follow the adventures of the hero, Dul Muluk, or are taken from *A Thousand and One Nights.* Like *bangsawan,* a nearly obsolete and more expensive form of staged theater, *Dul Muluk* had its heyday in the 1920s and 1930s. It was probably introduced in the late 1700s from India.

wayang kulit Leather shadow puppetry
kromongan South Sumatran gong-chime and ensemble
bangsawan Malay nobility theater shows
kelittang Abung gong-chime and ensemble

Bangka and Belitung

The main musical forms on the islands of Bangka and Belitung are of Arab or Malay origin. Bangka's most popular dances include its specific form of the Malay *serampang duabelas* 'twelve-step dance' and *selendang* 'scarf dance', couple dances in which men play both male and female roles. These dances are accompanied by a syncretic ensemble comprising a coconut-shell rebab, an optional violin, a lute, a small gong, a *gendang,* and a frame drum (*terbangan*). Other popular Muslim forms are *bedabus* and *zikir.* In South Bangka, music and dance are performed at mass weddings during which as many as twenty-four couples are married, each with its own diviner. Besides the *nugal* (rice-planting dance) and *cakter* (round dance), the *tuber* is danced by a shaman in trance to exorcise evil spirits. Traditional art is not strong in the towns because most of the inhabitants are migrants or their descendants (from Sulawesi, Kalimantan, and the Malay Peninsula). Bangka and Belitung were subject to various royal centers in past centuries, including Johore, Minangkabau, Bantam, and Palembang.

Musical responses to external influences

Unlike other Malay palaces in Sumatra, the culture of the Palembang palace (*kraton*), built from 1737, was Javanese-Muslim. One royal Malay practice that it borrowed, however, was the royal barge-rowing competition. Unlike other Malay palaces, the strictly Muslim *kraton* forbade all dancing in the palace. Its unique artistic contribution was its *wayang kulit purwa* (ancient shadow-puppet theater) or *wayang kulit Palembang,* accompanied by a bronze *kromongan* (*tabuan, gamelan*) orchestra. The original puppets were a gift from the Sultan of Demak when Islam was in the process of spreading to South Sumatra during the seventeenth century. The *kromongan* consists of a *gambang* and a *saron* (metal-slab instrument) as main melodic instruments, a pair of gongs (*gong panimbul* and *gong penuntun,* main and follower gongs), a *kenong* and a *kempur* (horizontal gongs, each resting on crossed cords in its own box), a *kromongan* (two rows of six small gongs), and a pair of truncated conical two-headed drums (*gendang*). Three rebabs, a Chinese oboe (*terompet Cina*), a two-stringed zither (*kecapi*), and a male singer (*sintren*) complete the ensemble. The *saron,* playing the lead melody (*kepala lagu*), is played fast and loudly, somewhat like a Balinese metallophone. *Wayang* was performed in the former palace to lend luster to celebrations, but it never became a people's art.

The main Dutch influences on South Sumatran music were found in the now obsolete *bangsawan* theater and the brass band (*tanjidor*), still prominent in Ogan-Komering, with four ensembles in Kayuagung alone. *Bangsawan* dates from the late 1800s, and brass bands from the early twentieth century. Male brass-band musicians in Kayuagung play trombone (*trombon*), saxophone (*saxofon*), French horn (*altohorn*), clarinet (*klarinet*), trumpet (*trompet*), kettledrum (*snar,* also *tambur*), bass drum (*dram*), and a pair of cymbals (*simbal*). Besides playing popular Malay and international songs from the 1920s, such as "*L'Amor*" ('Love'), "*Bintang Hatiku*" ('Star of My Heart'), and "*Seribu Tahun Berjanji*" ('Promise for a Thousand Years') at weddings, the band takes part in a remarkable procession of finely dressed unmarried men and women parading from the bride's home to the groom's for one of the many parties at an Abung-style wedding.

Lampung Province

Lampung consists of the Abung (Pepadon) interior, the mainly Javanese transmigrant area around Metro Town, and the Malay coastal areas. The impact of Javanese migration to Lampung cannot be underestimated; the Javanese have had a profound effect on urban and rural social relations, language, and the performing arts.

Bronze ensembles of pre-Muslim origin are still played in the interior and along the coast. Although the Abung people call these ensembles *kelittang, kelenongan,* or *tabuhan,* the coastal people call them *kulitang, kulintang, keromong,* or *tabuhan.* However, bronze-ensemble music and other pre-Muslim forms of art are better preserved among the inland people than along the coast.

The Abung, who believe they originated in megalithic times around Lake Ranau, spread since the 1700s throughout the north and northeast plains of Lampung. Their royal center at Menggala remains their cultural center. Bronze ensembles around Menggala and the district capital, Kotabumi, usually include nine or twelve horizontal gongs (*kelittang*), a pair of large suspended gongs (*talo balak* and *talo tanggung*), a small suspended gong (*bende*), a pair of cymbals (*gujih*), a cylindrical drum (*ketipung*), and a frame drum (*terbang*). Similarly, the *kelenongan* ensemble contains a gong (*betuk*) and a pair of small gongs (*canang*). In Menggala, two musicians play the *kelittang,* but in Kotabumi only one musician plays. In contrast to the vigor of the music, the dances are slow, with intricate hand-and-finger movements. The *canget,* dating from Buddhist-Hindu times and danced by girls wearing long golden fingernails and boys wearing royal costumes, welcomes guests at a wedding, a baby's birth celebration, or a ceremony to confer a title on a local leader or a royal bridal couple. Other male ceremonial dances (*nyambai*) were performed at major ceremonies, as when a chief (*raja*) was appointed (*dipepadonkan* 'raised on a throne') or a royal couple was married.

Surviving remnants of ancient Abung culture include music for the Jew's harp (*ginggung* or *juring*), played by courting couples, and a large repertoire of ring-flute (*sadam*) music to express love or lament a child's death, with ornamented melodies normally moving within the range of up to a fifth. Shamans also sing magic songs to help them capture human-eating tigers and to call for rain in times of drought. Gifted storytellers sing stories (*warahan*) for nights on end, interspersing their tales with moral teachings. From the 1940s, *warahan* were converted into theatrical performances by traveling troupes. Since the 1980s, the Lampung government has encouraged their development. They are now known in Jakarta and elsewhere as the specific form of Lampung theater, accompanied by *kelittang* music.

In the 1990s, employees of the Department of Education and Culture in Lampung's capital, Tanjung Karang, tried to establish a standard tuning for a new *kelittang,* being made in Java. Measuring the tunings of the oldest twelve-gong *kelittangan* in the former royal household at Terbunggi Besar, south of Menggala, they found that the nine gongs in good condition were tuned approximately to g_1–b_1–d–e–g(+)–a–b^1–g^1–f^1, and concluded that the tuning was basically slendroid—like the anhemitonic, pentatonic Javanese sléndro. Nevertheless, there is a great diversity of tunings and a high degree of tolerance of gong-pitch variation among gong-ensemble musicians in Lampung.

In Liwa, a mountainous area to the east of Krui, *kelintang* are made of either bronze or bamboo. At celebrations, eight-key bamboo xylophones called *gamolan* are played with a pair of gongs (*tala*), a pair of two-headed drums (*gindang*), and brass cymbals (*rujih*) in four main tempos to accompany the betel dance (*sekapur sirih*), performed by girls wearing bridal costumes and long fingernails.

Muslim performing arts are less popular inland than along the coast, whose inhabitants speak variants of Malay. In Kalianda, *hadrah* and *berzanzi* songs and the *bedana* (*zapin*) and other dances of West Asian origin are popular, having been transplanted via Riau. These dances are accompanied by (1) the Lampung orchestra (*orkes Lampung*) of a vocalist, a violin, a *suling*, an *akordeon*, a two-headed *gendang*, and a set of *ketipung*; (2) a lute and a set of *marwas*; or (3) a bronze *kelittang* with a vocalist singing a heptatonic melody to an Arabic text, including a drum pair (*ketipung* or *marwas*) playing loud sections (*takto*) alternating with soft ones, and two *gung* sounding every four beats. The long-fingernail dance (*tari sembah*), however, is accompanied by a twelve-gong *kulintang*, a two-headed *terbang*, and a pair of suspended gongs (*tetawak*). Malay dances such as *joget*, *kipas* 'fan', and *serampang duabelas* and songs of the *ma'inang* repertoire have been transplanted into this area from Riau and Deli, accompanied by a lute and four *ketipung* (*marwas*).

At Krui, an important cultural center on the west coast, visiting traders transplanted many Malay and Arabic music and dance forms, including classical Malay *budindang* songs, sung solo in free meter or accompanied by a violin and a *gendang*, and *gambus Arab* songs, accompanied by a violin and *rebana*. At celebrations in the Krui area, bronze *canang* (*kelintang*) ensembles accompany slow, elegant dances such as the fan-shaped leaf (*pampang kapas*) dance by girls in bridal costumes. The ensembles consist of nine horizontal gongs (*canang*), with one musician playing the main rhythm (*tabuh rantauan*) on six of the gongs and the other playing interlocking pattering rhythms (*tabuh peputuk*) on the remaining three, with the large suspended *gung* and a small horizontal gong (*talo*) punctuating the *canang* melody, and a pair of frame drums (*tabuh rebana*) providing a rhythmic base. Traditional weddings, which formerly lasted three days, also have Muslim components, including *badikier* (*zikir*), sung by scores of men to their own *terbang* accompaniment.

REFERENCES

Brandts Buys, J. S., and A. Brandts Buys. 1929. "Inlandsche dans en muziek." *Timboel* 3(2):13–18.

Carle, Rainer. 1981, 1982. *Die Opera Batak: Das Wandertheater der Toba-Batak in Nord Sumatra.* 2 vols. Berlin: Dietrich Reimer Verlag.

Goldsworthy, David. 1978. "Honey-Collecting Ceremonies on the East Coast of North Sumatra." In *Studies in Indonesian Music,* ed. Margaret J. Kartomi, 1–44. Clayton: Centre of Southeast Asian Studies, Monash University.

———. 1979. "Melayu Music of North Sumatra." Ph.D. dissertation, Monash University.

Heinze, R. von. 1909. "Über Batak-Musik." In *Die Bataklânder,* ed. Wilhelm Volz, 373–381. Nord-Sumatra, 1. Berlin: D. Reimer.

Holt, Claire. 1971a. "Dances of Sumatra and Nias: Notes." *Indonesia* 11:1–20.

———. 1971b. "Batak Dances: Notes." *Indonesia* 12:65–84.

Hornbostel, Erich M. von. 1908. "Über die Musik der Kubu." In *Die Orang-Kubu auf Sumatra,* ed. B. Hagen, 245–256. Frankfurt: Baer.

Jansen, Arlin D. 1980. "Gonrang Music: Its Structure and Functions in Simalungun Batak Society in Sumatra." Ph.D. dissertation, University of Washington, Seattle.

Kartomi, Karen S. 1986. "Mendu Theatre on the Island of Bunguran, Sumatra." Honors thesis, Monash University.

Kartomi, Margaret J. 1972. "Tiger-Capturing Music in Minangkabau, West Sumatra." *Sumatra Research Bulletin* 2(1):24–41. Reprinted as "Tigers into Kittens." *Hemisphere* 20 (5):9–15, 20(6):7–13.

———. 1979. "Minangkabau Musical Culture: The Contemporary Scene and Recent Attempts at its Modernization." In *What Is Modern Indonesian Culture?* ed. G. Davis, 19–36. Athens: Ohio University Press.

———. 1980. "Musical Strata in Sumatra, Java, and Bali." In *Musics of Many Cultures,* ed. Elizabeth May, 111–133. Berkeley, Los Angeles, London: University of California Press.

———. 1981a. "Dualism in Unity: The Ceremonial Music of the Mandailing Raja Tradition." *Asian Music* 12(2):74–108.

———. 1981b. "Lovely When Heard from Afar: Mandailing Ideas of Musical Beauty." In *Five Essays on the Indonesian Arts,* ed. Margaret J. Kartomi, 1–16. Clayton: Centre of Southeast Asian Studies, Monash University.

———. 1981c. "Randai Theatre in West Sumatra: Components, Music, Origins, and Recent Change." *Review of Indonesian and Malayan Affairs* 15(1):1–44.

———. 1983a. *The Angkola People of Sumatra: An Anthology of Southeast Asian Music.* Bärenreiter Musicaphon BM30 SL2568. LP disk and booklet.

———. 1983b. *The Mandailing People of Sumatra: An Anthology of Southeast Asian Music.* Bärenreiter Musicaphon BM30 SL2567. LP disk and booklet.

———. 1986a. "Kapri: A Synthesis of Malay and Portuguese Music on the West Coast of North Sumatra." In *Cultures and Societies of North Sumatra,* ed. Rainer Carle, 351–393. Berlin and Hamburg: Dietrich Reimer Verlag.

———. 1986b. "Muslim Music in West Sumatran Culture." *The World of Music* 3:13–32.

———. 1986c. "Tabut—A Shi'a Ritual Transplanted from India to Sumatra." In *Nineteenth and Twentieth Century Indonesia: Essays in Honour of Professor J. D. Legge,* ed. David P. Chandler and M. C. Ricklefs, 141–162. Monash: Monash University Centre of Southeast Asian Studies.

———. 1990a. "Parallels between Social Structure and Ensemble Classification in Mandailing." In *On Concepts and Classifications of Musical Instruments,* ed. Margaret J. Kartomi, 215–224. Chicago: University of Chicago Press.

———. 1990b. "Taxonomical Models of the Instrumentarium and Regional Ensembles in Minangkabau." In *On Concepts and Classifications of Musical Instruments,* ed. Margaret J. Kartomi, 225–234. Chicago: University of Chicago Press.

———. 1991a. "Experience-Near and Experience-Distant Perceptions of the Daboih Ritual in Aceh, Sumatra." In *Von der Vielfalt musikalischer Kultur: Festschrift für Josef Kuckertz, zur Vollendung des 60 Lebensjahres,* ed. Rüdiger Schumacher, 247–260. Berlin: Free University.

———. 1991b. "Dabuih in West Sumatra: A Synthesis of Muslim and Pre-Muslim Ceremony and Musical Style." *Archipel* 41:33–52.

———. 1993. "The Paradoxical and Nostalgic History of 'Gending Sriwijaya' in South Sumatra." *Archipel* 44:37–50.

———. 1996. "Contact and Synthesis in the Development of the Music of South Sumatra." In *Festschrift for Andrew McCredie,* ed. David Swale. Adelaide: University of Adelaide.

Kunst, Jaap. 1938. *Music in Nias.* Leiden: Internationales Archiv für Ethnographie. Supplement 38.

———. 1950. "Die 2000-jährige Geschichte Süd-Sumatras gespiegelt in ihrer Musik." *Kongress-Bericht Lüneburg,* 160–167.

Manik, Liberty. 1973–1974. "Eine Studienreise zur Erforschung der rituellen Gondang-Musik der Batak auf Sumatra." *Mitteilungen der Deutschen Gesellschaft für Musik des Orients* 12:134-137.

Moore, Lynette M. 1985. "Songs of the Pakpak of North Sumatra." Ph.D. dissertation, Monash University.

Okazaki, Yoshiko. 1994. "Music Identity and Religious Change among the Toba Batak People of North Sumatra." Ph.D. dissertation, University of California at Los Angeles.

Phillips, Nigel. 1980. *Sijobang.* Cambridge: Cambridge University Press.

Schnitger, F. M. 1937. *The Archaeology of Hindoo Sumatra.* Leiden: E. J. Brill.

Simon, Artur. 1982. "Altreligiöse und soziale Zeremonien der Batak." *Zeitschrift für Ethnologie* 107(2):177–206.

———. 1984. "Functional Changes in Batak Traditional Music and its Role in Modern Indonesian Society." *Asian Music* 15(2):58–66.

———. 1984–1985. *Gondang Toba / Northern Sumatra.* Museum Collection Berlin (West), 12. 2 LP disks.

———. 1985. "The Terminology of Batak Instrumental Music in Northern Sumatra." *Yearbook for Traditional Music* 113–145.

———. 1987. *Gendang Karo / Northern Sumatra, Indonesia—Trance and Dance Music of the Karo Batak.* Museum Collection, Berlin (West), 13. LP disk.

Snouck Hurgronje, C. 1906 [1893–1894?]. *The Acehnese,* trans. A. W. S. O'Sullivan. 2 vols. Leyden: E. J. Brill.

Tan, Sooi Beng. 1993. *Bangsawan: A Social and Stylistic History of Popular Malay Opera.* Singapore: Oxford University Press.

Turner, Ashley M. 1982. "Duri-Dana Music and Hoho Songs in South Nias." B.A. thesis, Monash University.

———. 1991. "*Belian* as a Symbol of Cosmic Reunification." In *Metaphor and Analogy: A Musical Dimension,* ed. Margaret Kartomi, 121–145. Sydney: Currency Press.

Java

R. Anderson Sutton
Endo Suanda
Sean Williams

Java is part of the chain of active volcanoes that encircles the Pacific Ocean and extends along the Indonesian Archipelago. A long, narrow island, it has steep, terraced mountains and broad plains. Its urban centers resemble dense villages, as the cities have spread out and enveloped their suburbs. An intensely fertile rice-growing area, it supports millions of inhabitants.

Java is home to two main ethnic groups: the Javanese (the largest proportion of the Indonesian population), and the Sundanese, who occupy large parts of the western portion of the island. In addition, Java has the nation's capital, Jakarta, on the northwest coast. Jakarta is the national melting pot, where hundreds of thousands of migrants from other areas of Indonesia and outside the country have established a base. Indonesians of Chinese descent, a large minority in each of Java's urban areas, maintain cultural traditions separate from those of the Sundanese and the Javanese.

CULTURAL GEOGRAPHY

The island has three provinces (West Java, Central Java, East Java) and two special regions (Yogyakarta and Jakarta), distinguished from the others because of their function as cultural and political centers. Each province is locally perceived as different from the others, and within each province, certain localities maintain separate cultural identities. Close to the border between West and Central Java are two culturally distinct areas: Cirebon (on the north coast of West Java) and Banyumas (close to the south coast of West Central Java). Each exhibits a Sundanese-Javanese blend of language and musical culture. East Java includes both the eastern portion of Java and Madura, a linguistically and culturally distinct island. The culture of East Java shows influence from the Hindu island of Bali and its minority population, descended from Indian immigrants.

The coastal and central traditions of Java differ in many ways; because coastal culture inherently looks outward, it has absorbed many more off-island influences. Java is now a primarily Muslim island, but Islam entered via the coastal cities. Crucial aspects of regional divisions within Java are (1) that centers are more important than

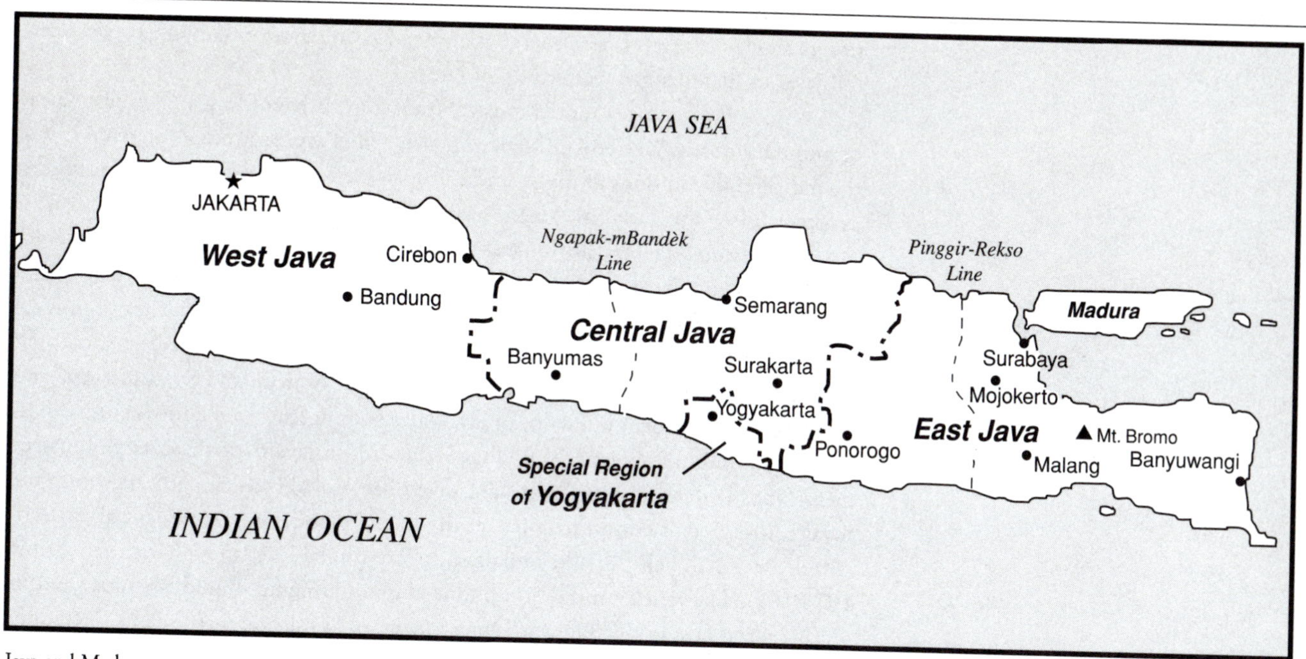

Java and Madura

peripheries, and (2) that spheres of influence overlap and intersect with others. These aspects make the delineation of Java's internal musical boundaries a difficult enterprise.

The primary vehicle for musical expression in Java is the gamelan, a gong-chime ensemble that includes large hanging gongs, rows of small kettle-gongs and gong chimes, metallophones, barrel-shaped drums, and sometimes a bamboo flute, a plucked zither, or a bowed spike lute. The ensemble performs for a variety of events, including instrumental music or the instrumental accompaniment of voice, dance, or theater. These performances may occur as part of a ritual or sacred calendrical event, or as part of a governmental function or commercial venture. Each performance reflects features of a particular genre or trait. In the following sections, the authors highlight musical features important to each area.

CENTRAL AND EAST JAVA

The island of Java has an exceedingly rich musical heritage, representing several major cultural groups and regional traditions. With roughly 100 million people on an island of less than about 130,000 square kilometers, Java is also one of the most densely populated areas of the world. The urban sprawl that characterizes some of Java's largest cities is rapidly encroaching on the countryside, but large portions of Java include expansive areas of rice fields, and the island is home to numerous active volcanoes. Though the term *Java* denotes the entire island, the eastern two-thirds of the island is the culturally Javanese region. The western third, Sunda, is the home of the Sundanese, whose language, music, and culture differ from those of the Javanese (see "Cirebon" and "Sunda," below).

The Javanese language has multiple honorific levels for many items of vocabulary: vernacular "Low Javanese," used by persons of higher status speaking to those of lower status, and by intimate friends; and one or several levels of "High Javanese," used by persons of lower status speaking to those of higher status, and by those of more or less equal status who are not on intimate terms. Use of the higher honorific levels is most characteristic of areas near the central Javanese courts, but manipulation of linguistic levels is essential to dialects of Javanese from Banyumas (west-central Java) to Blambangan (eastern tip of Java).

Various indigenously rooted musical traditions thrive in Java alongside an array of popular, mostly Western-influenced genres. This article presents an overview of the indigenous traditions of the Javanese, focusing on the music of ensembles known as gamelan [see also POPULAR MUSIC AND CULTURAL POLITICS].

The Javanese have the longest recorded history of any of the peoples of Indonesia, dating back nearly two thousand years. Major influences have come from India, China, West Asia, Europe, and the Americas. The earliest evidence of musical activity in Java consists of the remnants of several large bronze kettledrums, thought to have been introduced from the Đông Sơn culture of mainland Southeast Asia and southern China. Indian influence in Java dates back at least to the fifth century. Bas-reliefs on Hindu temples and Buddhist structures in Java depict a variety of instruments, mostly derived from India, that were once probably in use, at least within the royal courts. Small Hindu temples on the Dieng plateau in central Java about A.D. 750 depict small bells, small cymbals, a three-stringed lute, and a bar zither (Kunst 1973:107). The reliefs on the Borobudur, the monumental Buddhist stupa built in south-central Java in the 800s, present a vast array of musical instruments, including shell and straight trumpets, side-blown flutes, end-blown flutes (or double-reed aerophones), mouth organs, lutes, bar zithers, arched harps, double-headed drums, a xylophone, bells, and a knobbed kettle-gong (Kunst 1973:107). Similar instruments are also represented in the reliefs of the tenth-century Hindu temple complex Laro Jonggrang, at Prambanan.

During the early Hindu-Javanese period (fifth through eleventh centuries), courtly centers of power were located in central Java, especially in the area of Mataram, south-central Java, near the present-day city of Yogyakarta. Rule then shifted to east Java, with courts located near the present-day cities of Kediri and Singosari. The Hindu-Javanese period culminated with the Majapahit Empire, centered near present-day Mojokerto in east Java, and lasted from about the 1200s until the end of the 1400s. East Javanese temple reliefs give evidence of additional kinds of instruments, including the banana-shaped *kemanak,* a dumbbell-shaped *réyong* (still occasionally used in Balinese *gamelan angklung*), and a multistringed zither (like the present-day *siter* or *celempung*; see below).

Evidence of musical and theatrical activity in Hindu-Javanese times is found not only in the temple reliefs, but also in literature written in Kawi (Old Javanese), a language whose script and vocabulary are closely related to Sanskrit. From this literature we learn of noisy percussive ensembles used in battles, wind and stringed instruments accompanying female dancers at court, and the existence of masked dance and shadow puppetry—all of which were to undergo substantial transformation, but not eradication, with the rise of Islam and the coming of Western colonials.

Muslim traders introduced Islam to Java over the course of several centuries, primarily along the north coast. By about 1500, the strength of Islam in Java had apparently forced the Hindu courtiers to disperse, mostly to the island of Bali, or to remote areas of east Java: Mount Bromo (east of Malang, home of the present-day Tengger Javanese) and Blambangan (the eastern tip of Java, home of the present-day Osing Javanese). A series of Muslim courts rose and fell, first in areas near the north coast east of Semarang (Demak, Kudus) and then in the south-central Javanese region of Mataram. The immediate musical ramifications are not clear; the instrument most closely associated with Islam in Java today—*terbang,* a frame drum—had already been mentioned in *Smaradhana,* a twelfth-century literary work. The adoption of Islam does not seem to have radically altered musical practices. The rendering of poetry in song (*tembang*), the playing of ensembles of predominantly percussive instruments (*tetabuhan*), and various combinations of these two seem to have been practiced at all levels, from court to remote hamlet, for many centuries down to the present.

In the early 1500s, visitors from Europe first made their appearance in Java. A century later, they had established what was the beginning of three centuries of colonial rule. Before reaching eastern Indonesia, Portuguese seafarers had arrived, introducing plucked lutes and a vocal style whose influence can still be heard in Indonesian *kroncong* [see POPULAR MUSIC AND CULTURAL POLITICS]. From the first arrival of the Dutch East-India Company (1596) until the government of the Netherlands took over the company (1800), this private company, with substantial military force at its disposal, took ever greater control of the island of Java. Pitting rival Javanese rulers against one another, it radically transformed the political and cultural map. A dispute over succession between members of the central Javanese royal family, manipulated by the Dutch, resulted in 1755 in the division of Javanese royal power into two rival courts in south-central Java, only 60 kilometers from one another: Surakarta (also called Solo) and Yogyakarta (also called Yogya). Further rivalries a few years later (1757) and again during the period of British rule (1811–1816) produced further divisions with the addition of two lesser courts, the Mangkunegaran in Surakarta and the Pakualaman in Yogyakarta.

Despite the growing presence of European music, from military marching bands to various kinds of entertainment music (see Notosudirdjo 1990), indigenous musical practice appears to have had little European influence, at least with regard to musical instruments, scales, or style of performance. Rather, conceptions about music—even the idea of music as an art, separate from other categories of human expression—seem to have been the most substantial form of Western influence until the 1980s. Nevertheless Javanese rulers came to value Western music with indigenous ensemble music as part of their regalia. And during the twentieth century, particularly with the advent of mass media (radio and recordings), various forms of Western and Western-influenced music have become widely known by the Javanese, from urban elite to peasant farmers.

The occupation of Java by Japanese troops (1942–1945) was followed by the Indonesian revolution (1945–1949) and the final expulsion of the Dutch. Throughout these upheavals and the subsequent era of independence, indigenous musical traditions of Java have persisted, undergoing varying degrees of change in function, substance, and meaning.

Cultural geography

Though one can speak of Javanese music in reference to instruments, genres, repertoire, and performance style, many aspects of it are widely acknowledged to have originated in one region or at one court, and to represent the aesthetic sensibilities of one subcultural or social group.

The predominant tradition of gamelan music throughout all of Java is the court-derived tradition of Surakarta (or Solonese style), in the province of Central Java. (In the present article, *Central Java,* with uppercase *C,* refers to the province, and *central Java* to the broad cultural region, including Yogyakarta, Surakarta, and other areas culturally central Javanese.) Through radio, recordings on cassette, and live performance, this music is now heard frequently in areas as remote from Surakarta as Banyuwangi (at the eastern tip of Java), and elsewhere in the Indonesian archipelago where Javanese have migrated. It is sometimes simply called Javanese or central Javanese, but musicians and informed listeners continue to identify it as Solonese style (*gaya Solo*). It consists of a vast repertoire of pieces, most of which emphasize

In Central Java, the Yogyanese argue that their tradition is more legitimate, whereas the Solonese argue that Yogyanese music is more archaic and Solonese more progressive.

intricate and florid vocal and instrumental lines. It is quintessentially *alus*—a term implying refinement, subtlety, and smoothness.

Within the heartland of south central Java, the Yogyanese cultural tradition contrasts with that of Surakarta. Music in Yogyanese style can be heard throughout much of the Daerah Istimewa Yogyakarta (Special Region of Yogyakarta), a small area with the status of a province within the Republic of Indonesia and governed by the sultan of Yogyakarta. However, this music is nurtured most consistently by the musicians of the Yogyakarta court (*kraton*) and among the elite. Other musicians in the Special Region of Yogyakarta tend to prefer Solonese style or to mix styles and repertoires.

Though based on many of the same principles and drawing on similar repertoire, Yogyanese music tends to be more *gagah* 'strong, robust' and *prasaja* 'forthright, austere'. Yogyanese and Solonese agree that for the most part Yogyanese style represents older practice associated with the Mataram court before the division of Java. Yet whereas Yogyanese argue that their tradition is therefore more legitimate, Solonese argue that Yogyanese music is more archaic and Solonese more progressive. Indeed, certain stylistic elements in Yogyanese practice suggest it is an older tradition; but because the two courts have sought to define themselves in opposition to one another, both traditions have undergone substantial change.

Moving away from these two central Javanese courts, one encounters differing degrees of regional variation. Many names can be found for particular genres—combinations of voices, instruments, dance, or theater—that may be known in only one small town. Some of these are described by Kunst (1973 [1934]) and by Pigeaud (1938), others by Javanese students in their undergraduate and graduate theses at the schools and colleges of performing arts. It would be inappropriate even to try to list all of these in this context, but Javanese identify substantial regional subcultural areas whose local traditions of music and performance are readily distinguishable from those of the court centers.

The north-coastal region of Central Java, known as *pasisir,* is the site of a stronger Muslim tradition than found elsewhere in Java. There, ensembles combining voices with the accompaniment of *terbang* are prominent, with popular genres, such as *qasidah,* that draw heavily on Arabic musical style. In addition, a few gamelan pieces and a unique local style in Semarang suggest a distinctive Semarang gamelan tradition may once have thrived, though Solonese influence has been strong there since the 1920s. Several vocal pieces from this area employ a unique scale, closer to a Western diatonic scale than to Javanese scalar systems. These are sometimes heard accompanied by gamelan instruments—in which case the vocal part stands out by its maintenance of the nongamelan scale.

In the southwestern region of the province of Central Java, inhabitants of the former residency (a Dutch administrative unit) of Banyumas support a variety of local genres that make up a thriving local tradition. These include not only gamelan music, but several small bamboo ensembles (*calung, angklung*), vocal music (*macap-*

at), trance-dance (*èbèg*) music, and vocal imitation of gamelan (*jemblung*) (see Lysloff 1990b; Sutton 1985b, 1986a, 1986b). Banyumas lies west of the *Ngapak-mBandhèk* line, a cultural boundary that runs from east of Tegal on the north coast of Java, south through Banjarnegara to the south coast. The boundary is defined by many traits, including artistic practice, food, dress, and dialect. Banyumas dialect is distinguished from other forms of Javanese, not only by words and phrases unique to the region, but also by pronunciation of words it shares in common with other Javanese dialects. Banyumas music tends to be lively and spirited, often with a strong element of humor. During the 1970s and 1980s, the gamelan music of Banyumas gained popularity among musicians in other parts of Java.

The province of East Java is culturally more complex than either Central Java or the Special Region of Yogyakarta. In cultural orientation, the portion west of the Brantas River—the cultural boundary often called *pinggir-rekso* 'guarded edge, guarded border', a line dating back to the eleventh-century rule of King Airlangga—is mostly central Javanese. East of it, in the middle portion of the province (areas around Surabaya, Malang, and Mojokerto) are the east Javanese (*arèk* Javanese), including the Tengger. (In the present article this area is called eastern Java, in contrast to the province of East Java.) The island of Madura, part of East Java, is home to the Madurese. Extensive contact with the Javanese over many centuries notwithstanding, the Madurese speak a separate language and maintain arts and culture that differ substantially from any of the Javanese subgroups. Over the past several centuries, Madurese have migrated in large numbers to the eastern portion of the island of Java, where they have maintained a distinctive identity. At the easternmost tip of the island are Osing Javanese of Banyuwangi and rural Blambangan, who speak a dialect of Javanese and practice a range of characteristic performing arts bearing resemblances to several Balinese genres.

Residents of East Java tend to see themselves, and to be judged by others, as more *kasar* 'coarse, rough, opposite of *alus*' than central Javanese; musical traditions throughout the province reflect this contrast. The drumming, for example, in various ensembles among the *arèk* Javanese, the Madurese, and the Osing Javanese, can be loud and syncopated—often complex, seldom subtle. Especially among the *arèk* Javanese (and the central Javanese of this province), the music of the mainstream Solonese tradition has gained increasing prominence, providing a refined alternative to local practice without eradicating it. Nevertheless, strong central Javanese influence has caused concern among some musicians and local officials. To define this province culturally, official governmental directives have encouraged the support of certain genres and practices that contrast most clearly with the Solonese tradition of Central Java, giving greater legitimacy to arts indigenous to East Java and inspiring new combinations of repertoire and style from diverse groups within the province.

Through the mass media, in particular among the several star individuals and performing groups most frequently represented on commercial cassettes, borrowing and blending across subcultural boundaries has become increasingly popular. But even as this blending produces a measure of homogenization, it highlights regional differences. Java's cultural geography is in flux but remains diverse, making it necessary to avoid broad generalizations about Javanese music.

Review of the scholarly literature

References to music appear in Old Javanese literature dating back a thousand years and in early accounts by Chinese and Western visitors. Musical scholarship by Javanese and Western writers began during the 1800s and has intensified through the 1900s. The encyclopedic poem *Serat Centhini,* documented in its most often cited recension during the early 1800s at the court of Surakarta, contains lists of pieces and descriptions of music, dancing, and theatrical performances witnessed during the wanderings of several young men (Paku Buwana V 1986–1991; Soeradipura et al. 1912–1915). In a two-volume compendium on Javanese culture, Thomas Stamford Raffles (1817) offers descriptions of musical instruments and practices in a manner more thorough than any offered by Dutch writers previously. Several decades later, writings by Cornets de Groot, Dutch administrator of Gresik, East Java, were published; he described musical ensembles, including an eastern Javanese *gamelan surabayan,* and listed repertoire and performance context (Cornets de Groot 1852). The Yogyanese *Pakem Wirama,* a prose manuscript begun in 1889, with accretions probably through the 1920s, contains not only lists of instruments and extensive description of musical practice but represents in notation several instrumental parts for more than seven hundred pieces in the Yogyanese repertoire (Kertanegara et al. 1889–?). Portions of this work, translated by Hardja Susilo, appear in Hood 1984. The Dutch scholar Groneman (1890) contributed the first published book on Javanese music, describing musical practice at the Yogyakarta and Pakualaman courts and providing examples of indigenous notation, with a score in Western notation.

During the early 1900s, Djakoeb and Wignjaroemeksa published two volumes: one a description of gamelan music and its contexts of performance (1913), the other containing the main instrumental part for 128 Solonese *gendhing* (gamelan pieces) in cipher notation (1919). Other books of notation were published (Komisi Pasinaon Nabuh Gamelan 1924, 1925), with articles pertaining to gamelan. During the 1920s, with the establishment of the Java Instituut and its journal *Djawa* (that is, Java), scholarly publications grew substantially. J. S. Brandts Buys (often with his wife, A. Brandts Buys–Van Zijp) wrote extensively, not only about gamelan (1921, 1929) but also about musical instruments and practices away from the courts—in rural areas of central Java (1925), and in Banyuwangi (1926) and Madura (1928).

The most prolific scholar on Javanese music between 1900 and 1950 was Jaap Kunst. His study of musical instruments during the Hindu-Javanese period (1968 [1927]) is the most authoritative source on early Javanese music, based on extensive reference to temple reliefs, archaeological evidence, and literary citations. His monumental work *De Toonkunst van Java,* translated and revised as *Music in Java: Its History, Its Theory, and Its Technique* (1973 [1934]), is a comprehensive scholarly study that remains the major resource on Javanese music, emphasizing the major court traditions of Yogya and Solo, but covering many varieties of Javanese music. Careful and detailed description and copious illustrations represent exemplary ethnographic work, now of great historical value. Kunst's attempt in it to fit Javanese instrumental tunings with Hornbostel's theory of overblown fifths was inconclusive and has long since been dismissed, but his other theoretical inquiries into such Javanese concepts as *pathet* (modal classification) have proven insightful, often serving as a springboard of inspiration for future scholars.

Among other Dutch works, Pigeaud's *Javaanse Volksvertoningen* (1938) stands out as an encyclopedic source devoted primarily to dance and drama, but with valuable data on musical accompaniment for many genres throughout Java. Complementing the Dutch sources is Warsadiningrat's history, rich in anecdotes, of the Solonese musical tradition (completed in 1944, published in 1972 and in English in 1987).

Following the Indonesian Revolution, scholarly studies of Javanese music have proliferated. Two substantial studies by Javanese scholars teaching at formal music schools in Surakarta—formerly KONSER and ASKI, now SMKI and STSI (Indonesian University of the Arts), respectively—have provided a widely cited canon. Sindoesawarno's *Ilmu Karawitan* (1987 [1955]) presents systematic discussion of basic Javanese musical concepts including tunings, formal structure of gamelan pieces, tempo and subdivision levels (*irama*), modal classifications (*pathet*), and instrumental variations (*cèngkok / garapan*). In a more comprehensive, two-volume study, *Catatan-catatan Pengetahuan Karawitan* (1984 [1969, 1972a]), Martopangrawit offers a general explanation of formal structures, melodic phrasing, and the techniques and aesthetics of variation; a complex theory of *pathet* (based primarily on performances on the multi-octave metallophone *gendèr*); a detailed discussion of the various pentatonic orientations within the seven-tone *pélog* scale; and remarks on singing. Martopangrawit also wrote and edited numerous books of musical notation (notably 1972b, 1973, 1975, 1976), used as standard references by students in Solo and elsewhere.

Western scholars and some younger Javanese scholars in recent decades have tended to focus on particular Javanese musico-theoretical questions, or on cultural contextual issues. Foremost among these has been the issue of the nature and determinants of *pathet.* Mantle Hood's dissertation (1954) argues that *pathet* classification is based on the main melodic theme, especially its cadential patterns, played on single-octave metallophones (*saron*). To address this question, Judith Becker's dissertation (1980 [1972]), though primarily concerned with musical change, draws on a larger corpus of pieces than Hood, and on the theoretical writings of Sindoesawarno and Martopangrawit. Though limiting her inquiry to the part played by the *saron,* she bases her theory on a multi-octave conception of melodic contour, proposing that contours, levels of pitch, and positions within the rhythmic framework of a piece combine to determine its *pathet.*

Drawing on the work of Martopangrawit and on Sumarsam's knowledge of performance practice, a brief study by McDermott and Sumarsam (1975) goes beyond the *saron* part, in either its single-octave form or multi-octave conception, to identify *pathet* in *gendèr* patterns (*cèngkok*) and to show *pathet* change (or modulation) within certain pieces. In a master's thesis (1987 [1973]), Susan Walton proposes two systems of *pathet,* one relating to instrumental pieces, the other to vocal and vocally oriented parts within pieces that combine instruments and song. Referring to these and other sources, Harold Powers (1980) offers a neat summary of the complexities of the *pathet* question. In a comprehensive analysis of *pathet* in the *pélog* system, Sri Hastanto (1985) goes beyond previous theorists.

The absence of an absolute standard for determining intervals in the tuning of Javanese instruments has intrigued scholars since Alexander J. Ellis (1884) studied the issue. Trying to support Hornbostel's theory of overblown fifths, Kunst (1973 [1934]) measured intervals on many gamelans, but he limited his measurements to one octave. With tone-measurement data from several Javanese gamelans in California, Hood (1966) proposed a new understanding of Javanese scalar systems, demonstrating patterns of stretched and compressed octaves over the seven-octave range of a full gamelan. A team of researchers at Gadjah Mada University, Yogyakarta, conducted a statistical study (Surjodiningrat et al. 1972) measuring intervals in fifty-eight gamelans in the royal courts of Yogyakarta and Surakarta, arriving at a more complex view than that proposed by Hood. In a dissertation, Martin Hatch (1980) analyzed interval structure and tuning from the perspective of vocal music, suggesting relationships between the size of intervals and *pathet.* Roger Vetter (1989) offers a retrospective on these and other studies on tunings, including early works.

Another topic attracting scholarly interest has been Javanese performance. Heins has written on tempo and subdivision in performance (1969), on music in the context of courtly dances (1967), and on cueing in shadow-puppet performances (1970). Susilo (1984) and Sumarsam (1984a) have described musical practice in dance-drama (*wayang wong*) and shadow puppetry, respectively.

A large central Javanese gamelan consists mostly of knobbed gongs and metal-slab percussive instruments augmented by several drums and other instruments. Instruments are tuned either to a version of the *sléndro* scale or to a version of the *pélog* scale.

Numerous works have addressed variation and improvisation in instrumental and vocal performance (*garapan* 'treatment', 'working out'). Hood (1971, 1988) writes of "group improvisation" constrained by a list of identifiable factors, including *pathet,* formal structure, and context. In a dissertation, R. Anderson Sutton (1982, revision published 1993) argues that Javanese musical practice should be understood as variation—in the relation between parts heard simultaneously (heterophony), in the repetition of parts over time, and even in the process of composition. Javanese studies of *garapan* include not only various books of notation, but Rahayu Supanggah's dissertation (1985) on performance in the Solonese gamelan tradition. Relating to *garapan* is the multi-octave, vocally oriented melodic construct that Sumarsam (1975a, 1984b) and others have called inner melody (*lagu batin*). A similar concept, more instrumentally oriented, is discussed by Sutton (1979).

The issue of formal structure in gamelan pieces—patterns of cyclic repetition and rhythmic coincidence—is mentioned at least briefly in many studies but has been covered most insightfully by Hoffman (1978), J. Becker (1979a), and Becker and Becker (1981), each of whom relates Javanese musical structures to Javanese concepts of time and history. Other studies devoted to analysis of musical structures include linguistic approaches applied to *garapan* (Sutton 1978) and to the genre *srepegan* and related pieces (Becker and Becker 1983 [1979], critiqued in Perlman 1983; and Hughes 1988).

Several important studies have been devoted to vocal music. Margaret Kartomi's dissertation (1973a [1968]) applies extant theories, including Hood's identification of *pathet*-based cadential formulas, to repertoires of Javanese song (*tembang macapat*). Rüdiger Schumacher (1980) notates, translates, and analyzes the songs of the Javanese puppeteer-narrator (*dhalang*). Hatch (1980) offers a wide-ranging study of Javanese singing in relation to literature, history, and Javanese aesthetics, including a lengthy chapter on a famous singer, Nyi Bei Mardusari. Walton's study (1987 [1973]) also emphasizes vocal music, analyzing female singers' melodic formulas. Sutton (1984a, revised version 1989) focuses on female singers' social roles in present and historical contexts.

Major scholars have addressed questions of ancient history and recent change. In 1970, Hood, drawing on Javanese legends and photographic evidence of bronze drum-chime performances in southern China, theorized that Javanese gongs and gong-chime ensembles originated in bronze drums. The first of his trilogy on Javanese gamelan music is largely a historical novel elaborating this theory (1980). With focus on two twentieth-century composers (Ki Wasitodiningrat and Ki Nartosabdho), Judith Becker (1980) shows how gamelan music, in response to political and social upheaval, has undergone substantial changes, particularly since national independence. Becker's concern with historical change is also reflected in her work on cyclic structure and rhythmic coincidence (1979a; Becker and Becker 1981), her study of music of the 1970s (1979b), and her interpretive article on gamelan, metal-working, and the Javanese worldview (1988). Hatch proposes greater attention by scholars to Javanese musical history (1979) and addresses changes in vocal music and its contexts (1976). In a richly detailed study, Jennifer Lindsay (1985, Indonesian translation published in 1991) offers considerable historical depth and analysis of musical and cultural change in Yogyakarta.

Lindsay's work is also one of several studies devoted to music within a particular regional or local tradition. Others focusing on Yogyakarta are Vetter (1986) on court music and Sutton (1984b) on the tension between court and regional culture. Margaret Kartomi has written important articles on music in rural Java: on ceremonies involving trance in the Banyumas and Semarang areas of Central Java (1973b), and on the processional genre *réyog* of Ponorogo, East Java (1976). Sutton (1985a, 1991a) has addressed issues of regionalism in musical traditions throughout the central and eastern Javanese areas. Philip Yampolsky's discography of the national recording company (1987) identifies many genres and trends by region. Works by René Lysloff (1990a, 1990b) and other works by Sutton (1985b, 1986a, 1986b) cover Banyumas in detail. Crawford (1980) provides a brief but valuable overview of traditions in East Java Province. Paul Arthur Wolbers offers historical background and description of several genres in Banyuwangi (1986, 1987, 1989).

Most of the works mentioned above contribute to an understanding of Javanese musical aesthetics. The works of J. Becker (1979a, 1980), Becker and Becker (1981), Hatch (1980), and Sutton (1982, 1993) in particular propose interpretations relating music to other realms of Javanese experience. Ward Keeler also presents compelling interpretive work on aesthetics in several studies (1975, 1987).

Since colonial times, not much work has been done on rural traditions, particularly those showing little relationship to gamelan. Nor has attention been given to the growing presence of Western music in Java, with the exception of Notosudirdjo's master's thesis (1990) on Western music in nineteenth-century Java.

Musical instruments

Javanese culture emphasizes percussive ensembles, usually incorporating one or more knobbed gongs and drums. The larger of these ensembles are usually called gamelans, sets of instruments unified by shared tuning, and often by decorative carvings and paintings. Gamelans exist in multiple configurations at the courts and throughout Java. This section offers, first, a description of the instruments that make up the large, court-derived gamelans of central Java, with comments on differences between Yogyanese and Solonese variants. Coverage of regional variants, instrumental construction, symbolic significance, special ritual ensembles, and other instruments follows.

A large central Javanese gamelan consists mostly of knobbed gongs and metal-slab percussive instruments augmented by several drums and other instruments (figures 1 and 2). Instruments are tuned either to a version of the *sléndro* scale (five tones with nearly equidistant intervals, usually notated 1–2–3–5–6) or to a version of the *pélog* scale (seven tones with large and small intervals, usually notated 1–2–3–4–5–6–7). Large gamelans (*gamelan seprangkat* or *gamelan sléndro-pélog*) include a complete set of instruments in both scalar systems, but a gamelan can be considered complete with sufficient instruments of one or the other system. Gamelan pieces (*gendhing*) are either in *sléndro* or in *pélog*; the two systems are used together only rarely—in one ritual piece, and in some late-twentieth-century experimental works.

The Javanese categorize instruments in several ways—by shape and construction of the sounding part of the instrument, by shape and construction of the resonator or suspending device, by placement in relation to other instruments (front and back),

FIGURE 1 The knobbed-gong and metal-slab instruments of a central Javanese court gamelan (Surakarta style). Photo by R. Anderson Sutton.

by association with instrumental or vocal music (loud and soft), by performance technique (one-handed or two-handed), and by musical function (melodic, rhythmic, and so on). The definitions below are grouped by the first of these systems. On the classification of Javanese instruments, see also Kartomi (1990).

Knobbed gongs (pencon)

Gong ageng, largest hanging gong, suspended vertically by rope from a wooden rack (*gayor*); usually one or two per gamelan; in low Javanese *gong gedhé,* often called simply gong.

Siyem, medium hanging gong, suspended vertically by rope from a wooden rack; usually one to four per gamelan; also called *gong suwukan.*

Kempul, small hanging gong, suspended vertically by rope from a wooden rack; usually from three to five in *sléndro* and three to six in *pélog.*

FIGURE 2 Female singers (*pesindhèn*) and hanging gongs of a central Javanese gamelan (Yogyakarta style). The writing inside the hanging gongs indicates the degree of pitch and the name of the gamelan (the *pélog* ensemble Kyahi Sirat Madu and the *sléndro* ensemble Kyahi Madu Kéntir). Photo by R. Anderson Sutton.

Kenong, large, deep-rimmed kettle-gong, resting horizontally on rope or string in a wooden frame (*rancakan*); usually five in *sléndro* and six in *pélog* (omitting pitch 4).

Kethuk, small kettle-gong, resting horizontally on string in wooden frame; one for each scale.

Kempyang, pair of small kettle-gongs, resting horizontally on string in wooden frame; for *pélog* only.

Bonang barung, set of ten, twelve, or fourteen kettle-gongs resting horizontally on strings in a wooden frame in two parallel rows; one for each scale; often called simply *bonang,* in eastern Java known as *bonang babok.*

Bonang panerus, like *bonang barung,* but an octave higher; one for each scale.

Of the knobbed gong instruments, the *gong ageng, siyem,* and *kempul* are struck with a rounded, padded beater; the others with stick beaters padded with wound string.

***Keyed instruments* (wilahan)**

Saron demung, largest and lowest-register member of the *saron* family; six or seven thick metal keys resting over a trough resonator (*rancakan*) or, in some areas, a box resonator (*kijingan*); usually one or two in each scalar system; usually called *demung.*

Saron barung, middle-sized member of the *saron* family, like *demung,* but one octave higher; usually two to four in each scale; also called *saron ricik,* or simply *saron.*

Saron peking, smallest-sized member of the *saron* family, like *saron barung,* but one octave higher; one, or occasionally two, for each scale; also called *saron panerus,* or simply *peking.*

Gendèr slenthem, six or seven broad, thin metal keys, each suspended by string over individual bamboo or metal tuned resonators (*bumbung*) in a wooden frame (*rancakan*); one for each scale; also called *gendèr panembung,* more often simply *slenthem.*

Gendèr barung, like *gendèr slenthem,* but with twelve to fourteen narrow, thin metal keys; one for *sléndro,* two for *pélog*: one in pentatonic *bem* scale (tones 1, 2, 3, 5, 6); and one in pentatonic *barang* scale (2, 3, 5, 6, 7); often referred to simply as *gendèr,* in eastern Java known as *gendèr babok.*

Gendèr panerus, like *gendèr barung,* but one octave higher: one for *sléndro,* two for *pélog*; one in *bem,* one in *barang.*

Gambang kayu, xylophone with seventeen to twenty-three wooden keys resting over a wooden box resonator (*grobogan*); one for *sléndro,* one or two for *pélog*: if two, one in *bem,* one in *barang,* like *gendèr*; if only one, keys tuned to tone 1 (for *bem*) and tone 7 (for *barang*) are used interchangeably (and called *sorogan* 'exchange'), depending on the piece; usually referred to simply as *gambang.*

Of the keyed instruments, the *saron* instruments are struck with bare wooden mallets, the *gendèr* instruments and *gambang* with softly padded disc beaters.

Other melodic instruments

Celempung 'zither', supported at about a thirty-degree angle on four legs, with twenty to twenty-six metal strings arranged in ten to thirteen double courses; plucked with the thumbnails of both hands and damped with the fingers; one for *sléndro,* one or two for *pélog*: if two, one tuned to *bem,* the other to *barang* (compare *gendèr*); otherwise, tuned to one or the other, depending on the piece (compare *gambang*).

Siter, small zither, resting on the floor or in a wooden frame, with ten to twenty-six metal strings in single or double courses; same technique of playing as *celempung*; one for *sléndro,* one or two for *pélog.*

gong ageng Large hanging gong
bonang barung Larger of two gong-chimes
saron demung Large metallophone with trough resonator
gendèr barung Lower metallophone with tube-resonated keys
gambang kayu Wooden xylophone
suling End-blown bamboo ringstop flute
rebab Two-stringed bowed spike lute
kendhang Double-headed drum, in several sizes

Suling, end-blown bamboo notched ring flute; one for *sléndro,* one or two for *pélog.*

Rebab, spike fiddle, with one string wrapped around a peg at the lower end, providing two playing filaments, tuned about a fifth apart, and with a small wooden resonator covered by a membrane; one or two per gamelan.

Percussion instruments

Kendhang gendhing, largest hand-played drum, with two heads laced onto a barrel-shaped shell; one per gamelan; also called *kendhang bem* and *kendhang gedhé.*

Kendhang ciblon, middle-sized hand-played drum, same construction as *kendhang gendhing,* but smaller; also called *kendhang batangan,* or simply *ciblon* and *batangan.*

Kendhang ketipung, smallest hand-played drum, same construction as *kendhang ciblon,* but smaller; also called *kendhang penunthung,* or simply *ketipung.*

Bedhug, large stick-beaten barrel drum, with two heads tacked onto a cylindrical shell, suspended in a wooden rack; one per gamelan.

Other instruments frequently encountered in gamelan performance are the *keprak,* a wooden box used to accompany dancing, and the instruments played by the puppeteer-narrator (*dhalang*) in shadow-puppet performances: metal plaques (*kecrèk*) and the large wooden chest in which puppets are stored, both struck by a wooden knocker (*cempala*). (The puppeteer-narrator also strikes the *kecrèk* with his toes when both hands are occupied.) Rarer, but essential for certain pieces, is the pair of banana-shaped metal idiophones known as *kemanak.*

In performance, no ensemble is complete without female solo singers (*pesindhèn*) and a male chorus (*gérong*); however, some pieces or sections of pieces are strictly instrumental, employing only the instruments of the loud-playing (*soran*) ensemble: *gong ageng, siyem, kempul, kenong, kethuk, kempyang, engkuk-kemong, bonang* family, *saron* family, *gendèr slenthem, kendhang* family, *bedhug.*

Pieces or sections with vocalists feature the soft-playing (*lirihan*) ensemble, though usually with all or most of the loud-playing ensemble being played softly: *gendèr barung, gendèr panerus, gambang kayu, celempung* and/or *siter, suling,* rebab, vocalists (*pesindhèn* and *gérong*).

Soft-playing instruments are usually in the front of the ensemble, nearest to the audience, with the largest gong instruments in the back and the *saron* family in the middle. Instruments are usually arranged either parallel or at right angles to one another, suggesting coordination with cardinal directions; otherwise, the precise arrangement is not standardized.

Regional variation in instrumentation

Though gamelans throughout Java are quite similar to one another in many respects, slight differences in instrumentation, range, appearance, and timbre distinguish them by region. Many of the finest ensembles of Yogyakarta use an additional set of *bonang,* known as *bonang panembung* and tuned an octave lower than *bonang barung.* Solonese gamelans often include *engkuk-kemong,* a pair of kettle-gongs either suspended vertically or resting horizontally in a frame, used only for *sléndro.* Solonese gamelans accompanying *wayang kulit* usually contain one, or occasionally two, nine-keyed *saron,* in addition to or instead of the *saron barung*; these are called either *saron sanga* (from *sanga* 'nine') or *saron wayang.* Solonese wayang accompaniment is likely to use in place of the *ciblon* a slightly larger drum, the *kendhang wayang.*

In the region of Banyumas, large gamelans contain all or most of the instruments listed above (except *bedhug*) and with a small *ketipung* set up on its end, rather than resting in a stand or lying on the floor (compare Sundanese *kulanter*). Eastern Javanese gamelans are characterized by the presence of a heavy-shelled, thick-skinned drum known as *gambyak,* capable of producing a loud, crackling sound, one of the most outstanding features of eastern Javanese ensemble music. Another gamelan instrument typical of eastern Java is the *ponggang,* a set of medium-sized kettle-gongs somewhat smaller than *kenong* and tuned an octave lower. The instrument known as *slenthem* in east Java is often not a *gendèr* type (with keys suspended over tube resonators), but essentially a low-pitched *saron* with knobbed keys, struck with a padded beater rather than a bare wooden mallet (found in some older central Javanese ensembles with the name *slentho*).

Yogyanese instruments tend to be larger and louder, especially the *bonang* and *saron* families, than those of other regions. Solonese carving and ornamentation of instrument cases tends toward the most filigree and greatest use of motifs of a mythical snake (*naga*). The curls at each end of the wooden resonator on Yogyanese *saron* tilt upward, in contrast to those of the Solonese, which curl downward. Eastern Javanese *saron* resonators, in contrast to either, are often made in *kijingan* style (planks of wood, rather than carved from a single log).

The construction of gamelan instruments

The metal gamelan instruments are manufactured from bronze (*gangsa*), brass (*kuningan*), or iron (*wesi*), with strong preference for bronze, the most sonorous, the most durable, and the most expensive. Bronze instruments are mostly forged, or sometimes cast in rough form and then forged. The varieties of knobbed-gong instruments are usually entirely forged in a lengthy and difficult process that may take as long as one month in the case of the *gong ageng.* Gongsmiths shape the molten bronze through repeated hammering and heating, forming first the flat face of the gong, then the shoulders, and finally the knob (Jacobson and van Hasselt 1975 [1907]).

Bronze gongs and keys take twenty to thirty years before their pitch is completely settled. New instruments may undergo radical change in pitch—a minor third, or even more—during the first several years after their manufacture. They require frequent retuning, a demanding process: keys are filed (in the center to lower pitch, at the edges to raise it). Gongs may be filed for fine adjustments, but must be hammered into a slightly different shape to change the pitch markedly. Javanese often express a preference for older instruments, partly because of the impracticality and expense of retuning. It is also said that the mixture of copper and tin in the older bronze was better than in the bronze used currently, and the sound of the older instruments is sweeter, richer, less harsh.

Metalworkers in some societies occupy a low social rank, but in Java those who make bronze gamelan instruments and the fine laminated daggers (*kris*) for which Java is also famous are honored. The process of transforming molten metal into sonorous objects or weapons is believed to be fraught with danger from the spiritual world, and the resulting gongs or krises are often imbued with magical power. Smiths undergo ritual preparation, fasting, and abstinence from sexual intercourse, and may assume mythical identities during the actual forging of these objects, with the head smith becoming the Javanese mythical prince Panji and the others becoming Panji's family and servants (Kunst 1973[1934]:138). Not all gamelan instruments are believed to be spiritually powerful, but many sets and even individual instruments are venerated with honorific names, and are periodically given offerings of incense and food. The names range from those suggesting stately power, such as Kyahi "Harja Negara" (Venerable "Prosperous Realm") to more whimsical titles, such as Kyahi "Kanyut Mèsem" (Venerable "Tempted to Smile"). The name, with the carving, the painting, and the tuning, make each gamelan a unique entity whose instruments belong together as a set, altogether different in ethos from a Western ensemble (orchestra, quartet, and so on).

Ceremonial gamelans

In addition to large gamelans (*gamelan gedhé, gamelan lengkap*) are several varieties of ceremonial gamelan, old ensembles whose use has been restricted to rituals among royalty and nobility. Considered the most ancient is the type known as *gamelan munggang,* still used to accompany solemn processions and formerly accompanying a range of courtly activities and public tournaments. A three-toned ensemble, it consists mostly of large kettle-gongs: large three-kettled *bonang,* several *penontong* (like *kenong,* usually suspended), and one *kethuk.* Two *gong ageng,* a large *kendhang gendhing* and *ketipung,* and a pair of cymbals (*rojèh*) complete the ensemble.

Another three-toned ensemble, often played with a *gendèr* (Solonese) or several *saron* (Yogyanese), is *gamelan kodhok ngorèk* 'croaking frog'. It is similar to the *gamelan munggang,* but with smaller *bonang* kettles (six or eight per instrument) and, in some versions, bell trees (known variously as *gentha, klinthing, byong,* or *kembang delima*) and/or small cymbals (*kecicèr*). This ensemble accompanies rites of passage, such as weddings and circumcisions, and formerly accompanied public spectacles in which a tiger was speared or matched to fight a water buffalo.

Also used for festive occasions and associated primarily with royalty and high-ranking officials is the *gamelan cara balèn* (*cara* 'way', 'manner'; *balèn* can mean 'return', 'repeat', but also 'as in Bali'), which, like the *munggang* and the *kodhok ngorèk,* consists predominantly of large knobbed-gong instruments, but tuned to either four or six tones in *pélog.* These include large single-rowed *bonang* (the lower-pitched female set called *gambyong,* the higher male set called *klènang*), *gong ageng,* one or two large *kenong,* one or two large *penontong,* and two *kendhang.* The name of the ensemble is believed to derive either from its resemblance to Balinese gamelans, or to its short, repeating ostinatos. For certain pieces, these ensembles were formerly played with larger *pélog* ensembles.

Most imposing of the ceremonial gamelans are several *gamelan sekati,* which play during much of the Muslim holy week (sixth through twelfth of the Javanese month of Mulud, corresponding with the Islamic month of Rabi 1). These are *pélog* ensembles, consisting of large *saron,* two *gong ageng, kempyang,* a *bedhug* (no *kendhang*), and one double-rowed *bonang,* played by two players, one of whom is flanked by two additional kettles. (The high, male row serves as *kenong.*) Both the Solo and Yogya courts house two *gamelan sekati.* Carried out of the palace through the large north square (*alun-alun*) to special pavilions on the grounds of the large mosque (located in both Solo and Yogya just west of the *alun-alun*), they play in alternation throughout much of the day and well into the night, drawing spectators from the city and surrounding villages (Kunst 1973; Sumarsam 1981; Toth 1970).

FIGURE 3 Singer-dancers accompanied by the Banyumas *calung*; on the right, the audience is partly visible. Photo by R. Anderson Sutton.

Other ensembles and instruments

The number of combinations of instruments in central and eastern Java is extraordinarily large. Many are described briefly by Kunst (1973) and Pigeaud (1938). Here it will suffice to mention several ensembles prominent within a particular region, with several types of ensembles widespread throughout Java.

In central Java, one finds small gamelans. Those consisting mostly of soft-playing instruments, without *bonang* or *saron,* are called *gamelan klenèngan* or *gamelan gadhon.* In place of the *gong ageng,* these often substitute a *gong kemodhong,* consisting of two large keys tuned slightly apart and producing a sound resembling that of the gong. For other knobbed-gong instruments (*kempul, kenong, kethuk, bonang*), some itinerant gamelans (*gamelan thuk-brul, gamelan mondrèng, gamelan ringgeng,* and others) substitute metal-keyed instruments, usually of iron.

In the region of Banyumas, the bamboo-xylophone ensemble *calung* is quite popular. It usually consists of two multi-octave bamboo xylophones (one known variously as *gambang penodhos, gambang penggedhé, gambang pengarep,* or *gambang barung,* the other as *gambang panerus*), two single-octave bamboo xylophones (known as *slenthem* and *kethuk-kenong*), a blown bamboo gong, and two small *kendhang.* This ensemble accompanies one or more singer-dancers known as *lènggèr* (or sometimes *ronggèng*) (figure 3). Closely related but less common are *angklung* ensembles, in which the two multi-octave *gambang* and the *slenthem* are replaced by a single set of fifteen or so shaken bamboo idiophones (*angklung*), played by three musicians.

In Banyuwangi, East Java, one finds two distinctive ensembles: one known as *gandrung* (after the female singer-dancer it accompanies), the other as *angklung* (after one of its main instruments, though markedly different from the Banyumas *angklung*). The *gandrung* consists of two Western violins (*biola*), two *kethuk,* a *kempul,* a small gong, a triangle (*kluncing*), and two *kendhang.* It is played mainly at social occasions at which men in the audience are enticed to dance with one or more *gandrung* (female singer-dancers), the centers of attention. Larger, the *angklung* of Banyuwangi incorporates some of the *gandrung* instruments, with others—mostly percussion idiophones. It takes its name from the *angklung,* which here refers not to a shaken bamboo idiophone, but to a multi-octave bamboo xylophone set in a high frame. The ensemble contains a pair of Banyuwangi *angklung,* with three registers of nine-keyed metallophones (*slenthem, saron barung, saron panerus,* all usually of iron), and occasionally adds a bamboo flute (*suling*) or a double-reed aerophone (*tètèt*). In addi-

It is not unusual for the musicians at one of these events to perform through most of a night, beginning shortly after dusk and ending only at three or four in the morning.

tion to accompanying dance and song, Banyuwangi *angklung* ensembles are now used in remarkable and often fiercely competitive musical contests (*angklung caruk*) (Wolbers 1987).

Throughout central and eastern Java, under various local names (*kuda képang, èbèg, jaranan, jathilan,* and others), one finds hobbyhorse-trance dance troupes, usually accompanied by *kendhang* or several single-headed conical drums (*dhog-dhog*), two small gongs, and one or more other melodic instruments: *saron,* double-reed aerophone, *angklung* (the shaken variety), and even *bonang.* Similar ensembles, featuring a double-reed (*slomprèt*), accompany *réyog Ponorogo,* the best-known variant of the processional genres of dance known as *réyog.* And people in certain parts of East Java, especially the Madurese, use small percussion ensembles (*sronèn*) that feature a similar double reed. More purely drum ensembles also exist, such as the *réyog kendhang* of Tulungagung, East Java, with many *dhog-dhog* and just one small kettle gong. Also widespread, particularly in more devout Muslim circles in rural areas, are *terbangan,* ensembles consisting mostly or sometimes entirely of single-headed frame drums. These accompany groups singing in Javanese or Arabic for numerous genres of music (*genjringan, slawatan, jani-janèn*) related to Islamic themes. In central Java, *terbang* sometimes accompany vocal music in *gérongan* (male-chorus) style, mostly from the standard gamelan repertoire, in a performance genre known as *laras madya* (or *santiswaran*).

Western instruments that now abound in Java, from saxophones to synthesizers, are discussed briefly in the section on popular music below. Despite incongruities in tuning, Western wind instruments and field drums have been used in combination with some of the *pélog* gamelan pieces in the Yogyakarta courtly repertoire. And instruments inspired by Western military music (fifes and drums) have long been used for Javanese soldiers' music (*prajuritan*), with indigenous gongs (*bendé*) and cymbals (*kecèr*).

Solo instruments are rare in Java. The main one is the slit drum *kenthongan,* primarily a village signaling device. A large rice-pounding block (*lesung*) may serve as such an instrument, played by several players, each pounding a separate rhythm with a large pole, resulting in interlocking timbres.

Music, dance, theater

Musical activity in Java is usually intended in part to entertain its listeners, but this entertainment is often an integral component of ritual ceremony. Other than Western or Western-influenced popular music, the music one is most likely to hear in Java today is that which accompanies dance or theater—many genres of which are themselves most frequently performed for rituals, such as weddings, circumcisions, anniversaries, business openings, and so forth. So-called concerts of music, with an audience intended to listen attentively to a series of musical pieces in the manner of an audience for Western art music, have only recently been staged. One hears gamelan music without dance or drama broadcast on radio and television, on commercial cassette recordings, and live only at events called *uyon-uyon* (Yogya) or *klenèngan* (Solo and eastern Java). Some of the repertoire for these events can be heard also in the accompaniment of dance and theater, and even the patterns of drumming often follow the traditional choreographies of an imagined female dancer, the flirtatious *gambyong.*

Relaxed and informal, an *uyon-uyon* or *klenèngan* permits extensive social interaction among the parties present: the host family, the musicians, the invited guests, and the uninvited guests (neighbors and passers-by who wish to stop by to listen). These performances are usually sponsored as part of a rite of passage (a wedding, a circumcision) or an anniversary, and are intended both to entertain and to contribute to the maintenance of balance between the supernatural realm and the human realm. Performing the music is therefore important in its own right, independent from the attention and appreciation by any audience, who may be busy conversing and hearing the performance only as background music.

It is not unusual for the musicians at one of these events to perform through most of a night, beginning shortly after dusk and ending only at three or four in the morning. The hosts normally give the musicians several full meals during the performance, and keep them well supplied with snacks, tea, coffee, and, in some cases, liquor. The invited guests are also served meals and beverages (though liquor is rarely offered to guests) and provided with places to sit—either on mats or in chairs. The uninvited guests, though welcome to listen, are not provided with seats, nor are they served food and beverages. (They might purchase refreshments from stalls set up by people selling drinks, snacks, and cigarettes.) Most of those who attend, whether invited or uninvited, leave long before the event is over. And while they are present, some pay greater attention to the music than do others. Those most interested in the music might offer their praise of a particular player or singer and request a favorite piece. The musicians vary the types of pieces they perform, starting with more subdued and austere pieces and choosing increasingly lively pieces as the evening progresses.

Musicians almost always wear traditional Javanese clothing: batik wraparound skirts for both women and men, patterned blouses (*kebaya*) for women, and long-sleeved jackets (*surjan* or *beskap*) and turban (*blangkon* or *iket*) for men. Invited guests are likely to dress somewhat more formally than they do in daily life, either in modified Western clothing or in traditional dress.

Ceremonial gamelans (*munggang, kodhok ngorèk, cara balèn, sekati*) are exceptional in their use exclusively for the portions of ritual ceremonies that do not involve either dance or drama. Yet the *munggang* and the *kodhok ngorèk* both may accompany some kind of action (procession, meeting of bride and bridegroom). In recent years, the special styles and repertoires of all these gamelans have inspired dance and theatrical accompaniment in which ceremonial pieces and techniques are transferred to the larger, "standard" gamelans.

For some Javanese, various kinds of chanting and choral singing to the accompaniment of *terbang* serve in a ritual capacity similar to that of gamelan music. *Terbang* music is preferred by those who identify most closely with Islam of a more or less orthodox variety (the *santri* Javanese), rather than its blend with indigenous Javanese and Hindu-Buddhist elements (the *abangan* Javanese); on this distinction, see Geertz (1960). In some genres, *terbang* musicians dance as they play or sing, often in a sitting position, recalling styles of Islamic performance in the Muslim areas of other islands, such as the *saman* of the Gayo in Sumatra.

Itinerant troupes of musicians and dancer-actors are not so numerous today as they were a generation or two ago. Nevertheless, in the 1970s and 1980s one still encountered small troupes who would either perform for a particular ritual occasion (hired by a family hosting a wedding or a circumcision ceremony, for example) or simply set up in a public place and request remuneration from those who watch. Several varieties of such troupes have been most prominent. Hobbyhorse trance-dance performers and musicians seem now to be the most common. Some varieties (*barongan*) add the figure of a mythical lion (*barong*), danced usually by two persons. The activity of the entranced dancers, usually accompanied by short interlocking ostinatos in fast tempo, fascinates onlookers and can range from moving like an animal to eating glass. Other related genres—such as *réyog Ponorogo,* which includes masked dancers, one with an extraordinarily large peacock-feather headdress (Kartomi 1976)—may not involve trance.

Singer-dancers

Also widespread until the 1960s were small troupes consisting of several musicians with a reduced set of gamelan instruments (a *saron,* a gong, a *gendèr,* a *kendhang*) and one or more singer-dancers (either female or male in female attire for dancing). The singer-dancers were known variously as *talèdhèk* (central Java), *lènggèr* (Banyumas, also Lumajang area of eastern Java), *ronggèng* (western central Java), *tandhak* (eastern Java, especially Surabaya-Mojokerto), and *andhong* (Malang area of eastern Java). Men would pay the singers for the opportunity of joining them in an erotic social dance.

Nowadays, the practice of men paying to dance with a singer-dancer survives in hosted *tayuban,* parties in which a group of gamelan musicians and several singer-dancers are hired to perform for a village ceremony, such as the annual village cleansing (*bersih désa*) or a family rite of passage (figure 4). Though casual consumption of alcohol is not typical in Java, the *tayuban* is an occasion at which men are expected to consume generous quantities of it. *Tayuban* often begin in the middle of the day, when children and women flock to watch; they usually last until the early hours before dawn, by which time only the male participants and the professional performers remain. Both the drinking and the erotic social dancing have led many strongly Muslim communities and local and regional governmental officials to frown on *tayuban,* though the government does not ban them (Hefner 1987). Formerly wide-

FIGURE 4 Two singer-dancers at the beginning of a *tayuban,* surrounded by women and children. Photo by R. Anderson Sutton.

spread throughout Java, *tayuban* are now found mostly in eastern Java and certain rural areas of central Java (Gunung Kidul, near Yogyakarta; Sragen, near Surakarta; see Hughes-Freeland 1990).

From the singer-dancer tradition evolved *gambyong,* a more urbane and respectable dance. It stands apart from most other kinds of Javanese dance in the absence of any narrative component; the dancer simply performs a variety of sensuous movements. Many of these occur in other Javanese dances, but usually as the actions of a particular character. Somewhat comparable in its essentially non-narrative quality is *ngrémo,* a popular dance of eastern Java. In its female version, it can be related to the *gambyong*; in its more popular male style, to male bravura and an eastern Javanese stance against colonial oppression during the last years of the Dutch presence in Java.

Court and classical dance

A Javanese dancer usually represents a particular mythological character—either in a dance-drama or in an excerpt presented as a piece (*pethilan, beksan*). Though in the dances most closely related to martial arts (*wirèng* and some *beksan*) the individual dancers may not have the names of characters, they present in their dance some kind of martial event (a drill, a challenge, a fight, and so on), and may include dialogue. Highly refined, the female ensemble dances of the Javanese courts—*bedhaya* (normally with nine dancers) and *srimpi* (normally with four)— appear rather abstract; but these, too, may present particular Indian-derived or indigenous Javanese stories, albeit by stylized means (Brakel-Papenhuijzen 1992). The Yogyanese repertoire of *bedhaya* and *srimpi* are more consistently narrative than the Solonese (Murgiyanto 1991:3–4).

Javanese dance movements represent types of characters that can be grouped under three broad headings: female (*putri*), refined male (*alusan*), and strong male (*gagahan*). Many of the named kinetic patterns are used by all three categories of dancer, but with the female version being the most contained and intricate, the refined male version smooth and more open, and the strong male version the most bold and angular. Javanese have developed unique kinetic patterns for numerous major characters representative of these categories, plus certain ogres (*buta*), clown-servants (*punakawan*), and disciples (*cantrik*), yielding a rich variety of movements. Javanese audiences widely recognize these movements, with particulars of costuming and style of speaking, as essential markers of a character's identity.

The gamelan accompaniment for Javanese dance, though flexible enough to allow individual interpretation, is highly constrained in several respects. Many dances are set to one piece or a medley of pieces, others to one of several with identical formal structure (see below). Yet new choreographies abound, often drawing on extant pieces that have not formerly been designated for the character or characters being depicted in the dance. The drumming often specifically relates to the dancers' movements, especially when the *ciblon* (*batangan*) or, in eastern Java, *gambyak* is used.

Puppetry

Because much of Javanese dance is narrative, it is scarcely possible to mention dance without mentioning theater. Among Java's theatrical genres, the one that Javanese and outsiders consistently single out as the supreme aesthetic achievement of the Javanese is leather-shadow puppetry (*wayang kulit* 'leather shadow'), in which two-dimensional leather puppets cast shadows on a screen (figure 5).

Wayang kulit

TRACK 11

Wayang kulit is accompanied by a gamelan, formerly somewhat reduced in size from the full gamelan described above (without *bonang, saron demung,* or *saron peking*).

wayang kulit Leather shadow puppetry

wayang golèk Three-dimensional rod puppetry

wayang klithik Flat wooden puppetry

wayang wong Human dance-drama

wayang topèng Human dance-drama in which the performers are masked

FIGURE 5 *Dhalang* Ki Sugino Siswocarito reaches for a shadow puppet; the puppets at the screen are fixed in a banana trunk. Photo by R. Anderson Sutton.

This is an ancient tradition in Java, one that has developed over the course of more than one thousand years. Several genres of *wayang kulit* are distinguished by name, based on the source of the stories and characters depicted. By far the most popular is *wayang purwa,* whose stories are episodes based on Javanese versions of the Indian epics *Mahabharata* and *Ramayana*, or interpolated episodes involving the characters from these epics (see further Anderson 1965; Brandon 1970; Clara van Groenendael 1985; and Sears 1991). The repertoire used for the accompaniment of *wayang purwa* is mostly in the *sléndro* system, though since the 1950s pieces in *pélog* have often been used for variety if the ensemble is *sléndro-pélog.*

Other genres of *wayang kulit,* now rarely seen, include *wayang gedhog,* depicting stories of the east Javanese prince Panji to the accompaniment of music in pélog, and recently invented genres on themes of the revolution, Christianity, and so forth. People in certain parts of central Java, such as Kedhu, prefer w*ayang golèk,* a genre employing three-dimensional doll puppets with sléndro gamelan accompaniment. Another obsolescent genre of puppetry is *wayang klithik* (also known as *wayang krucil*), which uses flat wooden puppets to present stories of the eastern Javanese hero Damar Wulan and the Javanese kingdom of Majapahit, with music in *sléndro.* A Chinese puppet theater (*wayang potèhi*) is popular in some Chinese communities, where it is accompanied by Chinese instruments (Clara van Groenendael 1990).

Performances of *wayang kulit* are nearly always associated with a ritual celebration. They last from early evening (seven-thirty to nine) until around dawn (five to six). Almost as lengthy, but usually performed during daylight hours, is *ruwatan,* intended to protect against spiritual dangers believed to be unleashed by certain circumstances of life, such as combinations of siblings (for example, the birth of twins or of five boys).

Wayang kulit, whether *ruwatan* or not, is a powerful art. It holds strong symbolic significance for many Javanese, young and old, urban and rural. Many see in its stories (*lakon*) a microcosmic representation of divine order, a revelation of archetypal characters and situations lying behind the seeming unpredictability of daily human existence. Javanese frequently interpret current events and everyday human interaction with reference to the plots and characters of the famous wayang stories, and they tend to revere accomplished *dhalang* as spiritually powerful individuals, not merely entertainers. Though cultivated at the royal courts and patronized by wealthy urbanites, *wayang kulit* is widely performed in villages, appreciated by members of all social strata—peasant farmers of rice, urban drivers of pedicabs, and rich businessmen alike.

Though each performance is in some ways unique and new stories are constantly being created, basing most performances on the two main Indian epics means that audiences are familiar with the characters, and in many cases, with the plot. Audiences therefore do not need to pay rapt attention to every portion of the performance. Indeed, much of their behavior at a performance is similar to that described above for audiences at *uyon-uyon* and *klenèngan*—guests eat and drink, converse among themselves, and often leave well before the end of a performance. Uninvited guests are welcome; they may stand or squat, usually on the same side of the screen as the puppeteer and musicians (away from the host's house). Invited guests are provided with seats; more often than not, they view the performance from the side of the shadow.

The performance divides into three or four main sections determined by the modal category (*pathet*) of the music. The following table gives the *pathet* sequence in several traditions (Mojokerto after Crawford 1980:202; Gempol after Timoer 1988:1:139):

Central Java: Surakarta (and elsewhere)
nem, 9:00 P.M.–1:00 A.M.
sanga, 1:00–3:30 A.M.
manyura, 3:30–5:30 A.M.

Central Java: Yogyakarta
nem, 9:00 P.M.–1:00 A.M.
sanga, 1:00–3:30 A.M.
manyura, 3:30–5:00 A.M.
galong, 5:00–5:30 A.M.

East Java: Mojokerto
sepuluh, 7:30–10:00 P.M.
wolu, 10:00 P.M.–1:00 A.M.
sanga, 1:00–3:30 A.M.
serang, 3:30–5:00 A.M.

East Java: Gempol
wolu, then *sepuluh,* 8:00–9:00 P.M.
sepuluh, then *wolu,* 9:00 P.M.–2:00 A.M.
sanga, 2:00–4:00 A.M.
serang, 4:00–6:00 A.M.

With few exceptions, one can expect during the first *pathet* section a slow introduction to the story, mixed with philosophical reflections, and rather little action. As the night progresses, extemporaneous humor and entertaining music alternate with more lively dramatic action (during the second *pathet* section). The last several hours (the final one or two *pathet* sections) involve the most highly charged encounters, punctuated by battles, with some form of resolution just before dawn, though often only a temporary resolution within the larger compass of the epic, of which one night's *lakon* is merely an episode.

In *wayang kulit,* all narration (*janturan, cariyos*), dialogue (*antawacana*), manipulation of puppets (*sabetan*), singing of mood songs (*sulukan*), and direction of the musicians is carried out by one individual, the *dhalang.* Though most *dhalang* are male, the profession is not restricted to men. Whether male or female, the *dhalang* must be able to speak in many voices, not only differentiating male and female characters, but between many characters and character types of either sex. So skilled can *dhalang* be at this that *wayang kulit* is widely enjoyed over the radio and on cassette, with audiences able to follow the story and know the characters without even seeing the puppets. Aside from some late-twentieth-century experiments, the *dhalang* does not work from a fixed text. He or she is the consummate oral performer, neither reading lines nor at least after the first scene reciting them from memory. Even if the episode to be presented is a famous one, it will be the *dhalang*'s own version, with ample opportunity for interpolation of topical issues, up-to-date humor, and musical choices.

In performance, the *dhalang* sits close to the screen (*kelir*), to the right of a large wooden chest for puppets (*kothak*). By knocking with a wooden beater (*cempala*) against the chest, and by knocking, usually with his foot, against metal plaques (*kecrèk, kepyak*) suspended on its side, the *dhalang* signals the musicians, and accentuates certain movements of the puppets. Most of the puppets needed for a performance will be within reach; many of those not to be used will be arrayed on the left and right sides of the screen, implanted in the extremities of soft banana logs, which also hold the on-stage puppets. The shadows are cast by a single source of illumination just over the *dhalang*'s head: an oil lamp (*bléncong,* now rare in Java), a compressed-fuel lantern, or, most common since the early 1970s, an electric light. Purists complain that electric lights do not give the shadows the lifelike flickering of the oil lamps; but others, including many *dhalang,* complain of the soot and smoke from the oil lamps (and the hazards from occasional spillage) and the heat from the compressed-fuel lanterns.

Music for *wayang kulit* draws on several repertoires. Matters of choice and sequence are partially constrained by tradition, but allow the *dhalang* considerable flexibility to make spontaneous choices to which the musicians must be prepared to respond. Heard frequently throughout every performance are the theatrical pieces for entrances, exits, journeys, and fights: in central Java, *ayak-ayakan, srepegan, sampak* (in Yogya, also *playon*)—sometimes collectively called *gendhing lampah* 'moving pieces'; in east Java, *ayak, srempeg, krucilan, gedhog* (terms whose use overlaps). These pieces are characterized by dense gong punctuation, short melodic phrases, and special endings, which can be signaled at the end of any phrase, enabling the *dhalang* to tailor the music to dramatic needs. These the *dhalang* requests by a particular combination of knocks (*dhodhogan*) (Heins 1970; Sumarsam 1984a). In fact, several different melodies exist for each of these pieces, one or more for each *pathet.* Thus, for example, in Solonese *wayang kulit,* when the *dhalang* gives a signal for *sampak* during the second main portion of the evening, the musicians know to play *sampak pathet sanga.* Within a given *pathet,* an alternative to the standard version would be chosen to fit a particular character or mood (*srepegan "tlutur"* for sad scenes).

Gamelan pieces other than these are also used. The pieces played for the opening scene in any *wayang kulit* performance in central or east Java are multi-sectional, some quite lengthy, with sparse gong punctuation. During the scene dominated by clown-servants, the musicians often perform light, humorous pieces (*lagu dolanan*) often of recent vintage. When tradition does not prescribe the piece, the *dhalang* either requests it by naming its title outright, or by hinting at it (*sasminta*) through a set phrase or a keyword before the end of his narration or dialogue. At many points during a performance, the *dhalang* sings mood songs that establish a particular emotional atmosphere (calmness, sadness, distress, tension, rage, and so on).

The styles of performance used in *wayang kulit* do not differ in fundamental ways from gamelan performance in other contexts. Nevertheless, the music has a distinctive sound to listeners familiar with the range of Javanese music. The tempos tend to be fast, and the drumming is often a highly syncopated and, in Solonese tradition, subtle style (*kosèkan*).

Wayang wong

Much of the music associated fundamentally with *wayang kulit* is heard also in the accompaniment of the various dance-drama traditions that portray episodes based on the same mythological sources. Most closely related is the dance-drama form known as *wayang wong* 'human wayang', in which dancers wear costumes closely imitating the look of the puppets, and often even dance in a quasi-two-dimensional manner resembling the motions of the puppets. With rare exceptions, *wayang wong* presents stories from the repertoire of *purwa.*

Two distinct varieties of *wayang wong* have been known from the late 1800s: an elaborate royal version practiced in the large pavilions (*pendhapa*) at the main court of Yogyakarta, with related development at the Mangkunegaran in Solo; and a commercial version (*wayang wong panggung*), performed in proscenium theaters in Solo and throughout much of central Java (see further Soedarsono 1984 and Susilo 1984). Earlier in the twentieth century, royal *wayang wong* performances in Yogyakarta's main court sometimes lasted as long as three days, with hundreds of dancers for just one episode. Today, Yogyanese troupes perform shorter versions, lasting from half an hour to several hours. Until the 1970s or 1980s, commercial *wayang wong panggung* companies performed one episode per evening, lasting four hours or longer. They were popular through the 1960s, but have since fallen on hard times, despite efforts to modernize and appeal to trend-conscious young Javanese—efforts that have included shortening the time of performance to about two-and-a-half to three hours. In the 1990s, large companies still perform, albeit to small crowds, and often with governmental subsidies.

Wayang wong, whether court or commercial, uses many of the musical conventions of *wayang kulit*: the same adjustable theatrical pieces (*gendhing lampah*), other *gendhing,* and mood songs; the same sequence of *pathet* (though adjusted for the different span of time involved); and similar drumming and tempo treatment. But instead of a *dhalang* operating puppets and knocking signals on a chest in which they are stored, a narrator (often called *dhalang*) sings mood songs, gives narration, and cues the musicians by knocking on a small wooden slit drum (*keprak*) and, in Solonese style, on metal plaques (though smaller than those used by the *wayang kulit dhalang*).

Wayang topèng

Aside from a few roles in the Yogyanese version, *wayang wong* dancer-actors do not wear masks. In the genre known as *wayang topèng* 'masked wayang', however, all dancers are masked. Though masked dances from this dance-drama are still popular

Ludruk employs an all-male cast to present stories on contemporary issues or local history, interspersed with comic interludes and songs sung by transvestite singers.

as individual items in a dance concert, full-length presentation of narrative episodes through masked dance-drama are rather rare.

Yet in certain areas of rural Java (like Klaten, Central Java; and Malang, East Java) and on the island of Madura, *wayang topèng* troupes remain active. They usually present episodes from the Panji stories, accompanied by pélog gamelan music and mood songs (Onghokham 1972). As with *wayang wong,* a narrator (usually called *dhalang*) sings mood songs, provides narration, and signals musicians. In addition, in some areas (like Madura and Malang), he also speaks the parts of all characters but the clown-servants, whose masks cover their eyes but not their mouths, so they may be heard clearly by the audience as they joke with each other.

Other indigenous theater

During the late 1800s, two genres of dance-drama with sung dialogue arose among the nobility and lesser courts in central Java: *langen driyan* (formerly *langen driya*) and *langen mandra wanara.* Both are thought to have been developed and polished by one highly talented individual, R. M. A. Tandhakusuma, a Solonese master of dance who spent time in Yogyakarta in the late 1800s. In contrast to other genres of drama in Java, these rely on written texts, requiring the singer-dancers to memorize their lines.

Langen driyan (from *langen* 'entertainment' and *driya* 'heart', 'sense') presents episodes from the story of the mythical eastern Javanese hero Damar Wulan. Though known in a musical-narrative version in Yogyakarta (as *langen driya*), it has become the quintessential performance genre at the Mangkunegaran court, where it is normally performed by an all-female cast of dancers singing their lines. In the late twentieth century, men began taking roles in it, and the singing is now often performed by singers sitting with the musicians rather than by the dancers, as was formerly the norm.

Even in this genre, some of the conventions of *wayang kulit* persist: the use of a mix of *gendhing lampah* and other *gendhing,* and a *dhalang* signaling musicians (as in *wayang wong panggung*) and singing an occasional mood song. But each episode does not proceed through all *pathet.* One of the main kinds of pieces used is *gendhing sekar*—gamelan pieces whose main melodies are based on vocal pieces (*sekar, tembang*) performed with full instrumentation and with singing by the dancers. The other kind is a predominantly vocal genre (*palaran*), in which the dancer sings *macapat,* accompanied by most of the soft instruments (excluding rebab), the *kendhang ciblon,* and the steady punctuation of the *kempul,* the *kenong,* and the *kethuk,* with *siyem* (or occasionally *gong ageng*) marking the ends of major phrases. *Saron, slenthem, bonang,* and rebab are tacit. *Palaran* are essentially *srepegan* pieces, but with the main melody performed by the vocalist, rather than by *saron* and *slenthem.*

A similar genre, utilizing essentially the same types of music, developed in Yogyakarta. Known as *langen mandra wanara* (from *mandra* 'many' and *wanara* 'monkey'), it presents episodes from the Ramayana (in which monkeys play an essential role), with dancers who sing and dance while kneeling (Suharto 1979; Vetter 1984). In recent decades, women have taken the few female roles in it. As in *langen driyan,* most of the dialogue is delivered through either *gendhing sekar* or *rambangan,* the Yogyanese versions of *palaran.*

Neither *langen driyan* nor *langen mandra wanara* is performed often, but the music associated with both, particularly the *palaran* and the *rambangan,* is now an essential element in gamelan concerts (*uyon-uyon, klenèngan*), recordings, and many forms of indigenous theater: *wayang kulit, wayang wong panggung,* and *kethoprak.*

Kethoprak *and* ludruk

Kethoprak is one of the most enduringly popular types of indigenous theater in Java (Hatley 1980). It is primarily a genre of spoken drama, drawing on Javanese legendary history for its stories. It involves little dance in some variants, none in others; but music is essential to it. The musical instrumentation has undergone considerable change since its supposed beginnings with rice-block accompaniment. It is now always accompanied by a gamelan, with rhythmic signals to musicians by *keprak.* Variants of the *gendhing lampah* predominate, especially for entrances and exits, *srepegan* or *playon. Gendhing sekar* and *palaran* (or *rambangan*) serve to express emotions and sometimes to advance the plot. They are delivered with less restraint than in *langen driyan* or *langen mandrawanara*—often in fast tempos, with loud drumming and explosive bursts from *saron.* Mood songs do not occur in *kethoprak.*

The most famous theatrical genre of eastern Java is *ludruk* (also spelled *ludrug* in Javanese); see Peacock 1968 and Hatley 1971. While *kethoprak* has gained a strong following throughout both central and eastern Java, even in Banyuwangi, *ludruk* is rarely performed outside the province of East Java, and mainly in the *arèk* Javanese area (Surabaya-Mojokerto-Malang and environs). *Ludruk* employs an all-male cast to present stories on contemporary issues or local history, interspersed with comic interludes and songs sung by transvestite singers. As with *kethoprak,* the musical accompaniment is now a gamelan, though *ludruk* employed other instrumentation in the past. Wongsosewojo lists an aerophone ("*trompet,*" probably a double-reed instrument), a single-headed drum (*jidhor*), a double-headed drum (*kendhang*), an *angklung,* and sometimes a group of small *terbang* (1930:204). During the 1960s, the gamelan sometimes used central Javanese *gendhing lampah* (especially *srepegan*) for entrances and exits, but the norm, at least since the early 1970s, has been a piece sometimes called *Lancaran "Surabayan"* and sometimes *Jula-juli.*

Ludruk is a distinctively eastern Javanese item, performed with eastern Javanese instrumental techniques, including the loud and syncopated *gambyakan* drumming unique to eastern Java. The vocal interludes are also accompanied by gamelan, though the songs are often chosen from the repertoire of popular songs employing Western tuning.

Like *wayang wong panggung,* both *kethoprak* and *ludruk* are often commercial ventures, set up with a proscenium stage and an audience purchasing tickets to enter. Still, *kethoprak* and *ludruk* troupes may also be hired to perform as part of a wedding or circumcision ceremony, when they are more likely to perform late into the night but not until dawn, as is the norm for *wayang kulit.*

Music in other contexts

In the twentieth century, and particularly in the decades since Indonesian independence, several important developments have provided new contexts for hearing Javanese music in isolation from other performing arts. Most profound has been the widespread use of radio for gamelan-music broadcasts. Since the dawn of the commercial-cassette industry (around 1970), recording also has become a significant factor in creating star performers and groups. Government-sponsored contests (*lomba*) have brought performers of numerous kinds of music into competition. Gamelan music is the predominant variety, but the singing of *macapat, calung, gandrung,* and *angklung Banyuwangi,* and rice-block-stamping music, among others, have all been featured in contests.

Most recent are the concerts of new music (unorthodox and experimental pieces) for gamelan and other ensembles of indigenous instruments, with many Western conventions: tickets for admission, short duration (several hours), recognition of the composer, who (like most composers of Western art music) has worked out the details of each part. These are confined to academic institutions, mostly the university-level Sekolah Tinggi Seni Indonesia (STSI) in Surakarta, where the director, Dr. Sri Hastanto, and senior members of his staff (Dr. Rahayu Supanggah Al. Suwardi, and others) compose new works and require experimental composition from their students.

Tunings, scalar systems, modes

Javanese music employs two scalar systems (*sléndro* and *pélog*), neither of which is standardized with respect to tonal intervals or absolute pitches. The resulting variety is not an accident due to carelessness, but a reflection of keen interest on the part of the Javanese in nuance and subtle variation. Javanese tuners seek not to replicate preexisting tunings, but to create for each ensemble a unique tuning that remains recognizably *sléndro* or *pélog*—and pleasing (*kepénak*). Indeed, *laras,* the Javanese term for scale and for tuning, can also mean 'harmonious' and 'in agreement'. Rather than matching the pitch of keys and gongs to those of other ensembles or to some independent standard, tuners work intuitively, often tuning one multi-octave instrument (*gendèr* or *bonang*) first in a painstaking process in which the instrument is played, tuned somewhat, played again, and tuned until a desirable scale is obtained. In former times, it was even forbidden to try to copy the tuning of a royal gamelan.

Javanese gamelan music is essentially pentatonic. *Sléndro* consists of five tones per octave, spaced at nearly equidistant intervals. Though one or two intervals are slightly larger than the others, their sizes (as measured in cents) and their placements within the octave vary from one gamelan to another. Music in *sléndro* may avoid or deemphasize one of these (see the discussion of *pathet* below). The tones are still known by the following names, though reference by numeral is most common now: pitch 1 = *barang* 'thing'; pitch 2 = *gulu* (High Javanese *jangga*) 'neck'; pitch 3 = *dhadha* (High Javanese *jaja*) 'chest'; pitch 5 = *lima* (High Javanese *gangsal*) 'five'; pitch 6 = *nem* 'six'.

Pélog is usually described as a seven-tone scalar system with large and small intervals. The names of pitches and the corresponding numerals are: pitch 1 = *penunggul* 'first' or *bem* (no other meaning); pitch 2 = *gulu* (compare *sléndro*); pitch 3 = *dhadha* (compare *sléndro*); pitch 4 = *pélog* (possibly from *pélo* 'unclear pronunciation'); pitch 5 = *lima* (compare *sléndro*); pitch 6 = *nem* (compare *sléndro*); pitch 7 = *barang* (compare *sléndro,* pitch 1)

Though *pélog* is a seven-tone system, no piece of *pélog* music, instrumental or vocal, uses all seven tones in equal or near-equal distribution. Instead, many *pélog* pieces are entirely pentatonic, and the others, using six or even seven tones, are limited within most phrases to five tones at most. The seven-tone *pélog* scale, then, is best understood as an overlay of several pentatonic scales, each of which consists of a pattern of small (S) and large (L) intervals (figure 6). Though pitches 1 and 7 sometimes both appear within the same piece, they are in complementary distribution and do

FIGURE 6 Pentatonic orientation in *pélog* system.

pélog scale	1	2	3	4	5	6	7	$\dot{1}$	$\dot{2}$	$\dot{3}$	etc.

Five-tone scales:

bem (1)	1	2	3		5	6		$\dot{1}$	$\dot{2}$	$\dot{3}$	etc.
	S	S	L		S	L		S	S		
bem (2)	1	2		4	5	6		$\dot{1}$	$\dot{2}$		etc.
	S	L		S	S	L		S			
barang (1)		2	3		5	6	7		$\dot{2}$	$\dot{3}$	etc.
		S	L		S	S	L		S		
barang (2)		2	3	4		6	7		$\dot{2}$	$\dot{3}$	etc.
		S	S	L		S	L		S		

S = small interval
L = large interval
Numerals refer to pitch degrees
Superscript dots indicate upper register

not occur within the same phrase. Similarly, pitch 4 can replace pitch 3 in *bem* and pitch 5 in *barang.*

Closely related to the concept of *laras* is the Javanese modal concept *pathet.* Neither the intuitive understandings of Javanese musicians, nor the writings of Javanese and other scholars concur completely on a comprehensive definition of this concept. It combines elements of tonal hierarchy, range, and intervallic structure with extramusical associations of mood and time of day or night. In each scalar system, Central Javanese identify three main *pathet* (figure 7), which variably emphasize and avoid (or deemphasize by allowing only on weak beats) certain tones.

Hood (1954) demonstrates the prominence of certain cadential formulas in the *saron* melody of each *pathet.* J. Becker argues that listeners recognize *pathet* on the basis of three "factors": the identity of a "melodic pattern, formula, or contour," its level of pitch, and its position within a compositional structure (1980:81). Many melodic patterns occur in all *pathet,* but their level of pitch and distribution within a given piece directly correlate with the designation of *pathet.*

Both Becker's and Hood's studies provide valuable but incomplete analyses. Studies of multi-octave instruments (Martopangrawit 1984 [1972a]; McDermott and Sumarsam 1975) and of vocal music (Hatch 1980; Walton 1987) suggest that *pathet* can be understood as something akin to the Western notion of key, with transpositions between *pathet* (and even modulations between *pathet* in some pieces). For example, melodic patterns (*cèngkok*) that end on pitch 6 in *sléndro pathet manyura* can be transposed down one tone to end on pitch 5 in *sléndro pathet sanga.* Many

FIGURE 7 Tonal hierarchy and range in central Javanese *pathet.*

	pathet	Tones emphasized	Tone avoided
sléndro	*nem* 'six'	2, 6, 5	1
	sanga 'nine'	5, 1, (2)	3
	manyura 'peacock'	6, 2, (3)	5
pélog	*lima* 'five'	1, 5	7
	nem 'six'	5, 6	7
	barang 'thing'	6, 2, (3, 5)	1

sléndro Nearly equidistant tuning system
pathet Modal classification system
pélog Gapped-scale pentatonic tuning system
karawitan Gamelan-based court music
gendhing Gamelan-based musical composition

pieces are performed in both these *pathet,* choice being determined by musical context or, occasionally, a singer's whim. The *manyura* version is simply one tone higher than the *sanga* version. *Sléndro pathet nem* is generally considered to be the lowest of the three *sléndro pathet,* but pieces are only rarely transposed into *pathet nem* from other *pathet.* Instead, some musicians interpret *pathet nem* as consisting largely of an ambiguous mix of *sanga* and *manyura,* with only a few distinctive, low-range patterns in *pathet nem.*

Determining *pathet* in *pélog* is a different matter. *Pathet barang* is easily recognized by the presence of pitch 7 and the absence or near-absence of pitch 1. *Pathet lima* and *pathet nem* are less easily distinguished from one another, as both utilize pitch 1 and avoid pitch 7, and pieces in both may emphasize pitch 5. Within *pathet nem,* musicians often distinguish passages or whole pieces with a seeming *sanga* orientation (emphasizing pitch 5 and avoiding pitch 3) from those with a seeming *manyura* orientation (emphasizing pitch 6 and avoiding pitch 5). Whole pieces of the latter orientation are sometimes labeled as *pélog pathet nyamat mas,* or even as *pélog pathet manyura.* This dual orientation within *pélog pathet nem* suggests something of a parallel with the ambiguity in *sléndro pathet nem.* Yet in *sléndro,* the *pathet nem* pieces are said to represent the calmest and most subdued moods, comparable to the *pélog* pieces in *pathet lima,* rather than *pathet nem.* In fact, in the cases of ambiguity in *pélog,* it is often the criterion of calmness, rather than melodic contour or tonal hierarchy, that musicians cite as determining that a piece is in *pathet lima* rather than *pathet nem.* Nevertheless, some musicians obviate the confusion by grouping these two together as *pathet bem.*

Pathet categories vary slightly within central Java, and extensively between central and eastern Java. Yogyanese recognize a fourth *pathet* (*galong*) as a kind of subcategory of *manyura,* heard only during the last part of the *manyura* period in *wayang kulit* performances. In Banyumas, most of the older pieces are classified as *pathet sanga* or *pathet manyura,* but some rethinking has introduced *pathet nem* as an acceptable category for pieces outside the wayang repertoire (though the pieces in question are more spirited and lighthearted than would be normal for *pathet nem* in the Yogyanese or the Solonese traditions). Semarang once knew a *pathet sepuluh* (High Javanese *sedasa* 'ten') used for pieces in the opening of a wayang.

The category *sléndro pathet sepuluh* survives in eastern Java, where it is comparable to central Javanese *sléndro pathet nem,* not only in its tonal emphasis, but in its association with calm moods and the first part of the wayang. *Pathet wolu* 'eight' is the eastern Javanese equivalent to central Javanese *pathet sanga.* And eastern Javanese *pathet sanga* is equivalent to central Javanese *pathet manyura.* Primarily for wayang music, eastern Javanese also recognize a fourth *pathet—serang* 'attack', which, like Yogyanese *galong,* resembles *pathet manyura,* though strongly emphasizing tone 3. Terminology for *pélog pathet* in east Java is not uniform, but usually derives from *sléndro.* Musicians in the Malang area, where *pélog* is prominent, treat *pélog* as two systems, each with three *pathet*: *pélog bem* (also called *pélog sorog*), with *pathet sepuluh, wolu,* and *sanga*; and *pélog barang* (also called *pélog miring*), with *pathet wolu, sanga,* and *serang.*

Only since the 1970s have *pathet* categories in eastern Java been widely applied to pieces outside the wayang repertoire—apparently in an effort to provide greater legitimacy for local music through emulation of central Javanese theoretical standards. Sometimes musicians use central Javanese terminology instead of eastern Javanese, or even mixed with it—in which case the designation *pathet sanga* can be confusing.

Repertoires and formal structures

No single term in Javanese covers the range of expression identified in English as 'music'. The term *musik* (from Dutch *muziek*) may sometimes be used in this way among the educated elite, but most Javanese reserve that term for Western or Western-inspired music as distinct from indigenous music. The term used most widely for the latter is *karawitan,* currently applied in official circles to indigenous music throughout Indonesia, but understood by most Javanese as a Javanese term referring to Javanese music. In the latter usage, *karawitan* includes the instrumental music of gamelans and other ensembles employing Javanese scales, the sung poetry known as *tembang* (High Javanese *sekar*), and various combinations of instrumental and vocal music. The root *rawit* means 'intricate', 'complicated', and the word *karawitan* was applied in former times to "intricate" performing arts of all kinds, not just the musical arts, distinguishing certain supposedly crude, village arts from refined, courtly arts. Even today, one would feel more comfortable including the interweaving textures of gamelan music under the heading *karawitan* than the simpler patterns of rice-block-stamping music. As the coverage of all genres of music in Java is beyond both my abilities and the space available, the following section is concerned primarily with gamelan music and *tembang.*

Gendhing formal structures

The mainstay of gamelan music is the repertoire of *gendhing,* gamelan pieces with cyclic structures and whose phrases, punctuated by the sound of gongs, repeat until a signal is given to end. The patterns of punctuation are characterized by combinations of interlocking alternation and simultaneities or "coincidences."

Each *gendhing* consists of one or more repeatable *gongan*—phrases marked off by large gongs, *gong ageng* or *siyem.* After a short solo introduction, each *gendhing* begins with the stroke of a gong; each *gendhing* also ends with the stroke of a gong. Each *gongan* is subdivided into shorter phrases (usually two or four, of equal length) known as *kenongan,* marked off by one of the *kenong,* sounding with the gong stroke and at regular temporal intervals in between. Each *kenongan* is further punctuated by *kethuk,* and longer *kenongan* by *engkuk-kemong* or *kempyang.*

In central Java, *kempul* is omitted from large *gendhing* (those with *kenongan* longer than eight beats), apparently because its use would detract from the subdued, meditative feeling of these pieces. In small *gendhing* (two, four, or eight beats per *kenongan*) and in small and large *gendhing* in eastern Java, the *kempul* alternates with the *kenong,* sounding at the midpoint of the *kenongan.* In Solonese and most Yogyanese small *gendhing,* the *kempul* is not played in the *kenongan* immediately after the gong stroke. (This *kempul* rest is called *wela*). In wayang pieces (*gendhing lampah*), a *kempul* sounds with every other stroke of a *kenong,* occasionally replaced by *siyem* or *gong ageng.* In some eastern Javanese wayang pieces, a *kempul* sounds a steady rapid pulse, with *kenong* played less frequently. In archaic ceremonial ensembles, other instruments may serve as markers, but in these, as in contemporary *gendhing* of all

FIGURE 8 The formal structure of a *ketawang*, in circular and linear presentations.

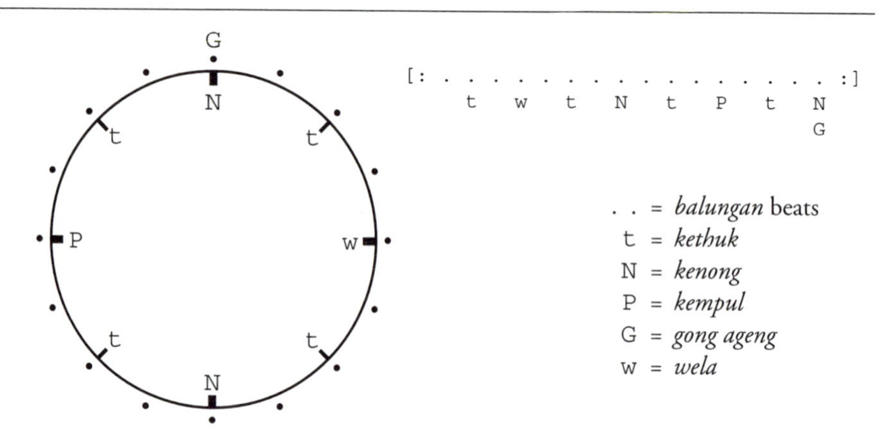

regional traditions, the principles of cyclic repetition, interlocking punctuation, and coincidence prevail.

The Javanese differentiate many formal structures by the particular interlocking and coinciding patterns of the gong instruments and their rhythmic fit with the steady beat of the main instrumental melody. This melody (*balungan* 'skeleton', 'outline') is usually played on the *saron* and the *slenthem.* By Javanese convention, notation of the *balungan* places the strongest beat at the end of a grouping rather than at the beginning. Thus, the even-numbered beats have the greater rhythmic weight. Where Westerners counting four beats would give primary stress to beat one, secondary stress to beat three, and tertiary stress to beats two and four, Javanese would give primary stress to beat four, secondary stress to beat two, and tertiary stress to beats one and three. As a result, the heaviest of all beats, the one coinciding with the gong stroke, is notated at the end of a line, not the beginning. The names of formal structures differ somewhat from one tradition to another. What is presented below is a discussion of formal structures in Solonese *karawitan,* with comments on significant differences in other traditions.

Javanese normally represent the schemata for formal structures in linear fashion, as this is the most practical to reproduce. The circular approach developed by J. Becker (1979a) and Hoffman (1978), showing the *gongan* as the face of a clock, is a neat visual analog to the cyclic structure of *gendhing.* Figure 8 shows the structure of a *gongan* in the form known as *ketawang,* a small form with two *kenongan* per *gongan.*

Small gendhing

In performance, a solo introduction (*buka*) leads into the entrance of a full ensemble and the simultaneous sounding of *kenong* and gong, leading without pause into the first *gongan* of a *gendhing.* In some cases, small *gendhing* (such as *ketawang* pieces) are joined directly to other pieces in a medley—in which case no solo introduction would be played.

Ketawang is distinguished from most other small forms by the presence of only two *kenongan* per *gongan.* Three other small forms have four *kenongan* per *gongan* and are distinguished from one another by the number of *balungan* beats per phrase. *Lancaran* form consists of only two beats per *kenongan*; *lancaran mlaku* (in Yogya, *bubaran*), of four per *kenongan*; and *ladrang,* of eight. Otherwise, the pattern of interlocking among the gong instruments is identical. The spacing of the dots representing the *balungan* is varied in figure 9 merely to fit the necessary information for each form onto one line, and does not reflect the tempo of performance (see the explanation of *irama* on next page).

FIGURE 9 Three formal structures with four *kenongan* per *gongan*. In *lancaran*, instead of *gong ageng*, *siyem* often marks the *gongan*.

lancaran form

```
[:  .  .  .  .  .  .  .  .  :]
  t w t N t P t N t P t N t P t N
                                G*
```

*In *lancaran*, *gongan* often marked by *siyem* (instead of *gong ageng*).

lancaran mlaku/bubaran form

```
[: . . . . . . . . . . . . . . . . :]
  t w t N t P t N t P t N t P t N
                                G
```

ladrang form

```
[: . . . . . . . . . . . . . . . . . . . . . . . . . . . . . . . . :]
   t   w   t   N   t   P   t   N   t   P   t   N   t   P   t   N
                                                               G
```

In *pélog*, a piece in *ladrang* form would normally be played with *kempyang* sounding between the other punctuating gongs—on all the odd-numbered (weak) beats. In some *sléndro* pieces in *ladrang* form, the *engkuk* would sound on the odd-numbered beats, and the *kemong* would sound with the *kethuk* on every other even-numbered beat (that is, second, sixth, tenth, and others).

Large gendhing

After a solo introduction, a large *gendhing* proceeds through a calm section (*mérong*), consisting of one or more *gongan* with the same formal structure. This section repeats until a signal, usually a change of tempo, cues musicians to make a transition (*umpak minggah*) to a second main section (*inggah*, also called *minggah*), which repeats until a cue is given to end or proceed to a different piece. For some large *gendhing*, musicians customarily perform the *mérong* and then proceed either to the *inggah* of a different piece or to a small *gendhing* (most often in *ladrang* form).

The category of large *gendhing* incorporates a variety of forms distinguished by the number of *kenongan*, the length of *kenongan* phrases (at least sixteen beats), the number of *kethuk* per *kenongan*, and (in the *mérong* section) the density of the playing of the *kethuk*. For example, a *gendhing kethuk 2 kerep, minggah 4* has four *kenongan* per *gongan*, with two *kethuk* strokes per *kenongan* in the *mérong*, occurring "frequently" (*kerep*)—that is, on the fourth of each group of eight *balungan* beats. In the *inggah* section, the *kethuk* always falls on the second of each group of four *balungan* beats (just as it does in *ladrang* form)—hence, with greater frequency than in the *mérong* (figure 10).

Gendhing lampah

The *gendhing lampah*, or wayang pieces, are characterized by much denser playing of the form-determining instruments. In each of them, the *kenong* plays twice per *kempul* stroke, with *kethuk* strokes between *balungan* beats. The *gong ageng* or *siyem* (both represented below as *G*) replace the *kempul* at the end of melodic phrases that are not uniform in length. The pattern of replacement in some cases, primarily in accompaniment of dancing, is determined only at the moment of performance by a signal from the drummer or the player of the *keprak*. In *ayak-ayakan*, the *kempul* unit consists of four *balungan* beats; in *srepegan*, two beats; in *sampak*, only one (figure 11).

With the exception of *srepegan* and *sampak*, drummed with great variation by *ciblon* (or its slightly larger version, the *kendhang wayang*), each formal structure has one or several associated drum patterns. The patterns for the large *gendhing* are the sparse and calm *kendhang siji* (High Javanese *kendhang setunggal* 'one drum'), patterns played on the *kendhang gendhing*. If a second drummer is present, he will play

One of the most important criteria in distinguishing repertorial items in a single regional tradition is the kind of interaction between vocal or vocally oriented melody and instrumental playing.

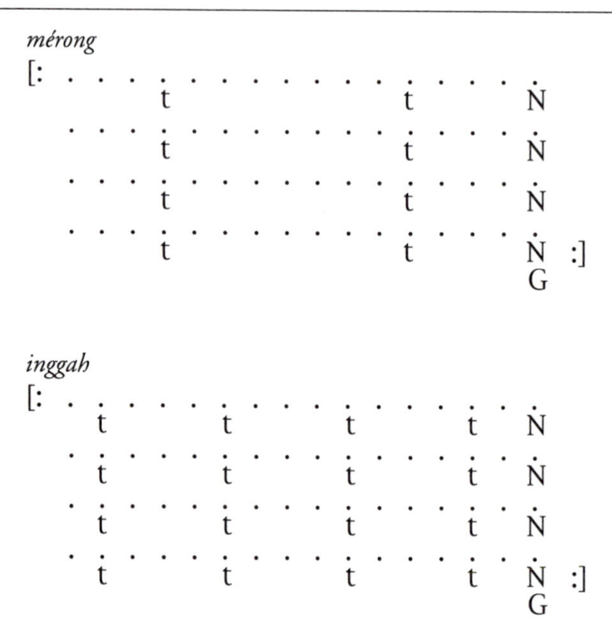

FIGURE 10 *Mèrong* and *inggah* sections, *gendhing kethuk 2 kerep, minggah 4.*

an optional ostinato on the *ketipung.* Some *ladrang* and *ketawang* pieces may be accompanied by *kendhang siji,* but the small *gendhing* more often involve the somewhat livelier *kendhang loro* (High Javanese *kendhang kalih* 'two drums'), patterns that combine *kendhang gendhing* and *ketipung.*

Shown in figure 12 is the *kendhang loro* for a *gongan* in *ladrang* form, at slow tempo (about thirty *balungan* beats per minute). The precise sequence of strokes may vary slightly from one player to another, but this is representative of Solonese tradition. So important is the drum pattern that in Yogyanese tradition, musicians refer not to the *kethuk* structure (*Gendhing "Lambangsari," kethuk 4 kerep, minggah 8*), but to the drum pattern (*Gendhing "Lambangsari," kendhangan jangga*).

Other than by gong structure or *kendhang* pattern, Javanese classifications of *gendhing* draw on several factors, including style and context, predominant instrumentation, and regional association. For instance, the repertoire of *gendhing Banyumas* (a region in west-central Java) is distinguished from *gendhing Jawa timuran* (eastern Javanese). *Gendhing tayub,* pieces associated with *tayuban,* feature spirited playing and short *gongan. Gendhing bonang* (or *gendhing bonangan*) are pieces featuring *bonang* and other loud-playing instruments. The Yogyanese term, in fact, is *gendhing soran* 'pieces in loud style'. The Solonese sometimes distinguish pieces by the instrument that performs the introduction: *gendhing gendèr* or *gendhing rebab.*

FIGURE 11 Formal structure in *gendhing lampah,* with examples from *sléndro pathet nem.* It is customary in notation to leave a little extra space between groups of four *balungan* tones (called *gatra*), a grouping comparable to a measure in Western music.

Schematic formula for structure of *gendhing lampah*:

ayak-ayakan:

```
[:   .   .   .   .  :]                              .   .   .   .
  t   t N t   t N     (repeat × ?)          t   t N t   t N
                P                                          G
```

srepegan:

```
[:   .   .  :]                      .   .
  t N t N      (repeat × ?)       t N t N
      P                               G
```

sampak:

```
[:   .  :]                 .
  N N     (repeat × ?)   N N
  t P                    t G
```

Examples of phrases from *gendhing lampah* in *sléndro pathet nem*:

ayak-ayakan:

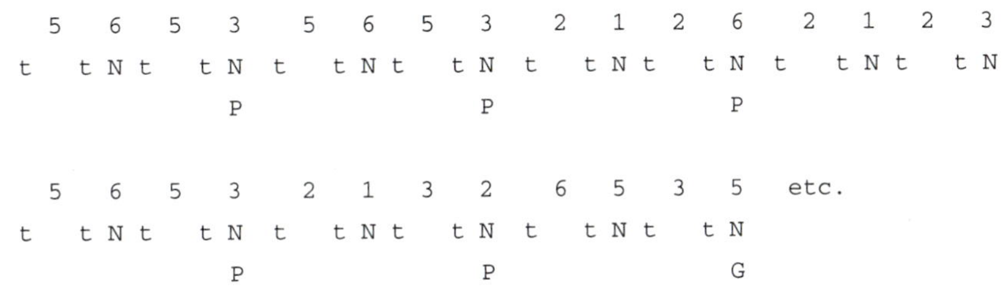

srepegan:

```
    6   5   6   5    2   3   5   3
  t N t N t N t N  t N t N t N t N
      P       P        P       G

 5   3   5   3    5   2   3   5    1   6   5   3    6   5   3   2     etc.
t N t N t N t N  t N t N t N t N  t N t N t N t N  t N t N t N t N
    P       P        P       P        P       P         P       G
```

sampak:

```
  5   5   5   5     3   3   3   3
N N N N N N N N   N N N N N N N N
t P t P t P t P   t P t P t P t G

  3   3   3   3     5   5   5   5     2   2   2   2    etc.
N N N N N N N N   N N N N N N N N   N N N N N N N N
t P t P t P t P   t P t P t P t P   t P t P t P t G
```

Vocal music

The Javanese maintain several vocal genres, many of which are combined with instrumental playing. One of the most important criteria in distinguishing among repertorial items within a single regional tradition is the kind of interaction between vocal or vocally oriented melody and instrumental playing. The resulting dichotomy is sometimes expressed as *tembang* (High Javanese *sekar* 'sung poetry', 'vocal') and *gendhing* ('cyclic pieces', 'instrumental'). The term *tembang* is also used to denote a subset of songs within the larger category of vocal music.

Musicians usually distinguish three major classes of *tembang: tembang gedhé* (High Javanese *sekar ageng*) 'large', 'great', *tembang tengahan* 'medium', and *tembang*

FIGURE 12 *Kendhang* pattern for *ladrang* (*kendhang loro*).

```
  .   .   .   .    .   .   .   .N
kokokokokokokod d  kTd D koo o o

  .   .   .   .    .   .   .   .N
okd okd odDd.Dd o  o o d D kod D

  .   .   .   .    .   .   .   .N
d D o d odD o Tdd  d d D d .dD d

  .   .   .   .    .   .   .   .N/G
 dD dD dD dD dD  kokokodokdD d D
```

T = slap on small head of *ketipung*
D = "Dhang"—deep sound on large head of *kendhang gendhing*, with soft "Tak"
d = "dhung"—high sound from large head of *ketipung*
k = "ket"—soft sound from either head of *ketipung*
o = "tok"—rim stroke from small head of *ketipung*

macapat (etymology unclear, but debated; *maca* 'to read', *pat* 'four'). In stanzaic patterns, *tembang gedhé* are closely related to patterns of Indian prosody and are distinguishable by number of syllables per line and per segment (*pedhotan*) within a line. All have four lines per stanza. In contrast, *tembang tengahan* and *macapat*—categories that sometimes overlap—are distinguishable by number of lines, number of syllables per line (*guru wilangan*), and ending vowel of each line (*guru lagu*) (figure 13).

Each *macapat* meter is associated with a limited range of emotions or appropriate subject. *Dhandhanggula* often serves as the opening meter in a long poem consisting of stanzas in several or many meters. *Sinom* is considered appropriate for didactic poetry, *pucung* for riddles. *Asmarandana, kinanthi,* and *mijil* are used for poetry relating to matters of love; *maskumambang* serves for longing or loneliness. *Pangkur* and *durma* are favored for the more violent emotions and for poetry describing conflict. Yet these associations are not strictly adhered to; didactic passages occur in all these meters.

For each meter, one or more basic melodies are known (*sinom wènikenya, sinom grandèl, sinom parijatha, sinom logondhang,* and so on). These melodies have great variability, even among central Javanese (Hatch 1980:413–472)—much greater than the occasional variation in number of syllables or final vowel. *Tembang* was once quite common in Java, from mothers singing their young ones to sleep, to formal

FIGURE 13 Metrical forms of *tembang macapat* and some *tembang tengahan*.

	Number of lines	Number of syllables and final vowels for each line
asmarandana	7	8i, 8a, 8o (or 8é), 8a, 7a, 8u, 8u
*balabal**	6	12a, 3é, 12a, 3é, 12a, 3é
dhandhanggula	10	10i, 10a, 8é (or 8o), 7u, 9i, 7a, 6u, 8a, 12i, 7a
durma	7	12a, 7i, 6a, 7a, 8i, 5a, 7i
*gambuh**	5	12u, 8i, 8u, 8i, 8o
*jurudemung**	7	8a, 8u, 8u, 8a, 8u, 8a, 8u
kinanthi	6	8u, 8i, 8a, 8i, 8a, 8i
maskumambang	4	12i, 6a, 8i, 8a
*megatruh***	5	12u, 8i, 8u, 8i, 8o
mijil	6	10i, 6o, 10é, 10i, 6i, 6u
pangkur	7	8a, 11i, 8u, 7a, 12u, 8a, 8i
pucung	4	12u, 6a, 8i, 12a
sinom	9	8a, 8i, 8a, 8i, 7i, 8u, 7a, 8i, 12a
*wirangrong**	6	8i, 8o, 10u, 6i, 7a, 8a

*tembang tengahan (others are tembang macapat)

**classified as macapat by some, tengahan by others (see Kunst 1973: 125)

gatherings where readers would take turns reading and singing verses from lengthier works interspersed with discussion of textual meanings and implications (Arps 1992). Since the 1970s, however, the purely vocal rendering of *tembang* has been most evident in occasional government-sponsored *macapat* contests.

Vocal-instrumental interrelationships

The greatest legacy of *tembang* songs in Central and East Java is their interaction with the playing of gamelans—in which they serve as introductions to *gendhing,* as predominant melodies in *palaran* (in Yogya, *rambangan,* a vocal-instrumental genre), as bases for the instrumental melodies of some *gendhing,* and as texts for existing *gendhing.* The *tembang gedhé* are most often heard as *bawa,* sung by one singer (usually male) accompanied by only a few tones played on the *gendèr.* As an introduction, a *bawa* leads directly into a *gendhing.* Florid variations of *tembang,* sung by a soloist (male or female), serve as the main melody in *palaran.*

The degree to which vocal music has inspired instrumental composition cannot be fully known, but evidence of vocal models is turning up for more and more pieces (Sumarsam 1992:318–406; Susilo 1989). Widely acknowledged is the basis of *sekar gendhing*—gamelan pieces whose *balungan* follow the basic contour of a *tembang,* and are named after the *tembang* melody (*Ketawang "Kinanthi Sandhung," Ladrang "Pucung"*). When *tembang* meters are sung with *gendhing* that have not been modeled on a known *tembang,* the metrical form is maintained, while the vocal melody is determined by the main instrumental melody (*balungan*) of the *gendhing.* By far the most common choice is *kinanthi,* with its six lines of uniform length.

Mood songs (sulukan)

Mood songs, sung by *dhalang* in various genres, constitute another major category of vocal repertoire. Usually known as *pathetan* (in Yogya as *lagon,* in eastern Java as *sendhon*), these set or underscore a calm atmosphere. They are accompanied by soft-playing instruments (rebab, *gendèr, gambang, suling*), with occasional punctuation by hanging gongs and *kenong* (Brinner 1995). In eastern Javanese *wayang kulit,* the *gendèr panerus* joins this ensemble for *sendhon* accompaniment. As their name suggests, *pathetan* also serve to establish *pathet* at the beginning of each period of a wayang performance. In purely instrumental renditions, with a rebab serving as the melodic leader, *pathetan* are almost always played before and after a major piece or sequence of pieces in *klenèngan* concerts.

Agitated-mood songs (*ada-ada,* in eastern Java *greget saut*) indicate anger, danger, impending battle, and other heightened emotions or situations. These are accompanied by *gendèr,* rapid knocking by the *dhalang* on metal plaques and on the chest in which puppets are stored, and occasional punctuation by hanging gongs and *kenong.* Similar to *pathetan* but often omitting the rebab are the Solonese *sendhon,* which also suggest a calm mood. Sadness of a calm variety is suggested by *Sendhon "Tlutur,"* great pathos or anger mixed with sadness by *Ada-ada "Tlutur."* In both kinds of *tlutur,* the *dhalang* sings a melody in *barang miring,* a scale that veers from the fixed *sléndro* instrumental scale on several tonal degrees, depending on the *pathet.*

The sources of text and melody for *sulukan* are diverse; many are difficult to trace (Probohardjono 1984 [1966]). Some draw on the *tembang gedhé* repertoire, and others, particularly those recently created by *dhalang* since the 1960s, draw on *tembang macapat.* The most famous *sulukan* are those in *sléndro* for *wayang purwa* and related dances. A separate set of *sulukan* exist in *pélog* for *wayang gedhog* plays and their derivatives (Probohardjono 1954). Though not named explicitly (as are the *tembang* models for *sekar gendhing*), *sulukan* appear to underlie some *gendhing.* At

Ranging from erotic to didactic, *wangsalan* present their message in the form of a puzzle. The first line does not usually convey the intended message, but suggests the meaning or sound of words or phrases in the second line.

least some *gendhing lampah* have melodic contours similar to certain *sulukan;* they may have served as models for the instrumental melodies of these *gendhing* (Susilo 1989).

Other genres of vocal music

Many Javanese children's games involve the singing of songs known as *lagu dolanan.* These are now rare as game-accompanying songs, but are sung to the accompaniment of a gamelan as part of the active vocal-instrumental repertoire known as *lagu dolanan,* mostly with *lancaran* or *srepegan* forms. Inspired by the style of these *lagu dolanan* are numerous compositions by Javanese composers of the postcolonial period. Hardjo Soebroto, Ki Wasitodiningrat, and Ki Nartosabdho are the three most famous composers of such pieces, but others have composed at least a few. Musicians sometimes identify these pieces as new creations (Indonesian *kreasi baru*). This term is not limited to such vocally based works, but most recent compositional activity has been vocally inspired.

Other vocally oriented genres range from *jineman,* which lightheartedly feature a solo *pesindhèn* with gamelan (without rebab), to *gendhing kemanak,* with austere and sacred singing by a female chorus accompanied by gong instruments (*kethuk, kenong, gong ageng*), *kendhang,* and a pair of banana-shaped idiophones (*kemanak,* whose pitches are outside the singers' scale). And much of the vocal music heard in the context of gamelan performance consists of solo *sindhènan* (the singing of the *pesindhèn*) within a *gendhing* for which tradition has not explicitly established a text or a vocal melody. Instead, the singer chooses a text from a large repertoire of poems, most often in the form known as *wangsalan,* consisting usually of two lines of twelve syllables each, divided into two parts (four plus eight syllables). These lines she renders in a series of melodic phrases (*cèngkok*), most of which exist as independent entities that constitute part of her repertoire, rather than as phrases unique to or prescribed for a particular *gendhing.* The realization of each *cèngkok* will differ at least slightly from one individual *pesindhèn* to another, but the repertoire of *cèngkok* is shared, for the most part, at least within a given regional tradition.

Ranging from erotic to didactic, *wangsalan* present their message in the form of a puzzle. The first line does not usually convey the intended message, but suggests the meaning or sound of words or phrases in the second line. Often the first part of the first line relates in this way to the first part of the second line, and likewise for the second parts of the two lines.

> Ujung jari, | balung rondhoning kalapa,
> Kawengkuwa, | sayekti dadi usada.

> Fingertip [= *wengku*], | palm-leaf spine [= *sada*],
> To be cared for, | truly causes healing.

The *pesindhèn* also uses other poetic forms, usually less subtle ones (such as *parikan*), which for coherence rely on rhyme rather than suggested meaning. *Parikan* are often light, humorous, or even risqué in mood.

Regional perspectives on repertoire

While the kinds of instrumental, vocal, and vocal-instrumental pieces described above are found throughout Java, certain regions emphasize certain genres, forms, or scalar systems. In Banyumas, the repertoire is mostly *sléndro*, though some Banyumas *macapat* (*asmarandana* and *pangkur*) use a deviating scale similar to Sundanese *madenda*, and new *lagu dolanan* are often composed in *pélog*. In the area of Malang, *pélog* gamelans, and thus *pélog* music, are predominant, even for *wayang purwa* in some rural districts. The ensemble music of Banyuwangi (*angklung* and *gandrung*) is mostly in a five-tone scale some would identify as *sléndro*.

For Yogyanese and Solonese traditions, because written records date back more than a century, we can identify hundreds of *gendhing*—well over one thousand for Solo, and nearly that many for Yogya. These include not only a great number of *gendhing* in each of the smaller formal structures, but literally hundreds of large *gendhing*. Yet gamelan repertoires, like all active repertoires around the world, frequently change. Many large *gendhing*, associated primarily with the grandeur of the courts, are rarely performed. Instead, new pieces, especially *lagu dolanan* and other pieces in smaller forms, are taking their place.

The gamelan and *calung* repertoire of Banyumas, an area that prides itself on the outgoing nature and humor of its people and music, consists almost entirely of vocally oriented pieces in *lancaran* form. Semarang maintains a distinctive repertoire of *gendhing bonang*, utilizing only loud-playing instruments played in a uniquely Semarang style; it once had a local wayang repertoire, separate from that of other regions. Elsewhere in central Java more obscure local repertoires persist, such as the unique *gendhing lampah* that accompany *wayang golèk* of the Kedhu area, between Yogyakarta and Banyumas.

The eastern Javanese heartland, despite intensive borrowing from central Java, has maintained more than three hundred eastern Javanese *gendhing*. These include some large *gendhing* (with two major sections and *kenongan* of sixteen or more beats) and many pieces whose formal structures are comparable to those of the central Javanese small *gendhing*. Eastern Javanese equivalents to *ketawang, lancaran,* and *ladrang* are in eastern Javanese academic circles now called *cakranegara, giro*, and *luwung*, respectively, with other terms for other formal structures. However, the eastern Javanese more generally classify their repertoire by context and style, as in *gendhing tayub, gendhing wayang,* and so on. For eastern Javanese loud-playing pieces, musicians usually distinguish between *giro* (shorter-phrased, ceremonial pieces, structurally comparable to central Javanese *lancaran*) and *gendhing gagahan* (longer-phrased 'strong pieces'). The eastern Javanese wayang repertoire is quite separate from that of any central Javanese tradition, with uniquely eastern Javanese melodies, techniques, and forms (Sutton 1991a); nevertheless, like central Javanese pieces, these feature melodic phrases of unequal length, with dense playing of the gong instruments.

Banyuwangi *gandrung* music is essentially vocal, with the violins following the singer-dancer's vocal melody in heterophonic fashion (Brandts Buys 1926; Wolbers 1992). The gong-punctuation patterns differ from those elsewhere in Java, but the phrases between strokes on the largest gong are mostly quite short (comparable to four or eight beats in central Javanese music). To outwit opponents in *angklung caruk* contests, musicians create many *angklung* pieces, at least in part; yet they maintain a repertoire of older pieces, many of which consist of several clearly demarcated sections, some in free rhythm. Some of these are based on songs; others, especially the more recent ones, show the influence of Balinese music, particularly the style of *gamelan gong kebyar.*

In Madura, ensembles maintain a variety of uniquely Madurese pieces, with Madurese versions of Solonese pieces apparently introduced into the court of Sumenep because of a series of marriages between members of the Sumenep and Solonese royal families (1800s and early 1900s). More widespread are *sronèn,* ensembles consisting of a double-reed aerophone, drums, gongs, and sometimes other metallophones. From information available, it appears that *sronèn* can both accompany vocal music (often sung in falsetto by a male transvestite) and perform purely instrumental music, though often with the double-reed playing variations based on a song.

Performance practice

Rhythm and tempo

The rhythmic orientation of Javanese music ranges from steady, even beats in a hierarchy of subdivisions in purely instrumental music to a free-rhythmic, parlando delivery in purely vocal lines. Most of the music combines elements of the two. Binary subdivision characterizes the formal structures discussed above, with the number of beats in full cycles and subsections almost always representing an even multiple of two.

One of the essential elements in the performance of most gamelan pieces, not found in other genres, is the play of *irama,* the level of subdivision of the basic pulse (*thuthukan balungan* '*balungan* beat'). Javanese currently recognize five levels of subdivision, determined by the ratio between this beat (often represented by the melody played on the *saron barung* and the *saron demung*) and the parts that evenly subdivide it (played most consistently on the *saron peking,* the *bonang panerus,* the *gambang,* and the *celempung*). Figure 14 portrays the rhythmic relationship between this beat and the fastest pulse, played on the *gambang.*

The term *irama,* sometimes glossed 'tempo', is better understood as the temporal 'space' between beats, measured by the subdividing instruments. The *irama* level, then, is a result of the *balungan* tempo. As the beat slows down, the tempo reaches a

FIGURE 14 Five levels of *irama.*

irama lancar 'swift', 'fluent' = *irama seseg* 'tight', 'dense': 1:2
balungan beats: . . . . etc.
gambang beats . . . .

irama tanggung 'in between' = *irama* I: 1:4
bal. beats: . . . . . etc.
gmb. beats . . . .

irama dadi 'settled' = *irama* II: 1:8
bal. beats: . . . . etc.
gmb. beats . . . .

irama wilet 'intricate' = *irama* III': 1:16
bal. beats: . . .
gmb. beats . . . .

irama rangkep 'double density' = *irama* IV: 1:32
bal. beats: . .
gmb. beats . . . .

point at which the subdividing instruments can double. At this point, the Javanese speak of a change of *irama* level. Within each level, the tempo can vary without bringing about an *irama* change; but in the performance of many pieces, the tempo of the *balungan* gradually slows to one half, and then to one quarter of its initial rate, yielding a change of *irama* during each transition, as the subdividing instruments double their ratio with the *balungan.* As a result, the tempo of the subdividers remains relatively constant from one settled *irama* level to another. The only exception is *irama rangkep,* normally performed with a fast tempo for the subdividing instruments. Keeler (1987:225) aptly compares the process of *irama* change to the shifting of gears by the driver of an automobile. In response to changes of tempo, executing smooth changes in *irama* level is one of the skills Javanese musicians must master. Playing with the expansion and compression of time is fundamental to the aesthetics of gamelan music throughout central and eastern Java.

The regions of Java share similar practices with respect to *irama* levels, binary or parlando rhythmic orientation, and general flow in performance. In each region, pieces tend to start fast and then slow down, with additional changes of tempo likely—either slowing or speeding up. For the most part, tempo (and thus *irama* level) remains constant for substantial periods, sometimes for many minutes at a stretch. Except in especially agitated circumstances in dramatic accompaniments, pieces end with a ritardando and a brief pause before the final gong. In nearly all traditions, the drummer leads the tempo, though a melodic leader (rebab or *bonang barung*) may hint at a tempo change.

Beyond traits shared throughout Java, however, the approaches to tempo represent one important stylistic element that sets one regional tradition off from another. For example, Yogyanese tempos are usually slower than Solonese, especially in the case of dance accompaniment. Gamelan and *calung* performances in Banyumas are sometimes dazzling in their breakneck tempos for the subdividing instruments. In *calung,* these instruments are actually interlocking bamboo xylophones, played in perfect synchronization to reach composite tempos as high as six hundred beats per minute. The small repertoire of Semarang *gendhing* are usually played with a distinctive sequence of ritardandos that suggest an ending, only to spring back at double tempo for one or more additional statements of the final section. In this case, the subdividing instruments do not change their ratio with the *balungan,* but slow down and speed up with it (in contrast to comparable tempo changes elsewhere in Java). And in the gamelan music of the Surabaya-Mojokerto-Malang area of eastern Java, tempo fluctuates widely within a single *irama* level, particularly in the accompaniment of dance.

Melodic instrumental conventions

Under this heading, rather than attempting a description of the techniques employed in playing Javanese instruments, I offer a description of instrumental conventions in the contemporary performance of central Javanese gamelans, noting some of the most significant divergences among regional traditions.

The loud-playing ensemble

Fundamental to an understanding of instrumental practice is the relationship between the melodic outline (*balungan*) and the treatment (*garapan*) of this outline in the strands of variations that elaborate or abstract it. The *balungan* is almost always realized explicitly on the single-octave *saron barung, saron demung,* and *slenthem.* In Yogyanese tradition, the term formerly referred to a more sparse (and hence more "skeletal") part, played on the large *bonang panembung* in octaves (second and fourth beats of each *gatra* or four-beat *balungan* phrase); nowadays, however, most

Some musicians refer to a multi-octave implicit melody (*lagu batin* 'inner melody'), not sounding on any one instrument but serving as a guide to variations played on other instruments.

Yogyanese use the term as other Javanese do, referring to the more rhythmically dense *saron* part, with multi-octave melodic implications.

The *balungan* is the only instrumental part usually played by more than one person simultaneously; it is memorized, though versions of the *balungan* for the same piece vary from region to region, and even from one individual to another within a single locale. Players of the non-*balungan*-carrying instruments are expected to know the *balungan* and to construct their parts in relation to it. Some musicians refer to a multi-octave implicit melody (*lagu batin* 'inner melody'; Sumarsam 1975a and 1984b, Sutton 1979), not sounding on any one instrument but serving as a guide to variations played on other instruments.

The *balungan* part is often a steady progression of tones, one per *balungan* (four per *gatra*, as 2353 2121). Passages are often interspersed with *balungan gantungan* 'hanging *balungan*', in which the same tone is reiterated, often with rests (actually sustaining the previous beat, as 5 5 . . 5 5 . 6). Some pieces or sections are characterized by a sparser *balungan* part, with only two tones per *gatra* (as . 2 . 3 . 2 . 1) in the style known as *nibani* 'to fall intentionally'. Found in many Yogyanese *gendhing* and other traditions are passages with eight tones per *gatra*, known as *balungan ngracik* (23532121 35321635). Irregular and syncopated patterns also occur, but are rare enough to stand out as clear departures from the widely used patterns.

The instruments that play the *balungan* within their single-octave ranges also perform variations of the *balungan* in certain contexts. In most regional traditions, players insert a single tone between each tone of the *balungan*—a technique known as *pancer*. For example, the *balungan* for *Ladrang "Liwung"* (Yogyanese tradition) normally adds a *pancer* tone as soon as the tempo settles. Often this tone for *sléndro gendhing* is high 1; otherwise, as in *Ladrang "Liwung,"* it is either absent or not prominent in the *balungan*. In Yogyanese tradition, only the *saron barung* play *pancer*. When they do, the *slenthem* anticipates the *balungan* tones, emphasizing the offbeats in a technique known as *gemakan* 'like [the sound of] a quail'. And the *saron demung* vary the *balungan* in this context with paired interlocking tones (*imbal, pinjalan*), one part anticipating and playing in between the beats (*nggawé* 'to do', 'to make'), the other following and playing adjacent tones on and between the *saron* beats (*nginthil* 'to tail', 'to drop like sheep dung') (figure 15).

FIGURE 15 Yogyanese techniques of variation on *balungan*, in *Ladrang "Liwung."*

balungan : . 2 . 1 . 2 . 6
saron pancer : 3 2 3 1 3 2 3 6
slenthem gemakan : 2 2 2 . 1 1 1 . 2 2 2 . 6 6 6 .
demung nggawé : 2 2 5 2 1 3 1 1 2 5 2 2 3 6 6 6

demung nginthil : 3 3 3 2 2 2 2 1 3 3 3 2 5 $\dot{1}$ $\dot{1}$ 6

(The two *demung* combined : 2323532212321211 2353232235$6\dot{1}6\dot{1}66$)

FIGURE 16 Solonese *banyakan* technique of variation, in *Ladrang "Sembawa."*

balungan : . 3 5 6 7 6 5 3
saron barung : 3 3 6 6 6 6 3 3
saron demung : 5 3 5 3 5 6 5 6 7 6 7 6 5 3 5 3
slenthem : 5 3 5 3 5 6 5 6 7 6 7 6 5 3 5 3

(*demung* and *slenthem* combined : 5533553355665566 7766776655335533)

Other techniques of *balungan* variations in Solonese tradition include the playing of *saron barung, saron demung,* and *slenthem* in the combination known as *banyakan* 'like [the sound of] a goose' (figure 16).

In other contexts, particularly in pieces that accompany *wayang kulit* and other dramatic forms, a pair of *saron barung* may perform interlocking variations. And one or two *saron barung* or nine-keyed *saron wayang* may perform wandering variations at twice or four times the tempo of the *balungan.*

The remaining member of the *saron* family, the *saron peking,* plays simple variations of the *balungan* melody, anticipating or echoing the *saron* melody, either tone by tone (*nacah*), or in a simple alternation between two successive tones (*nacah selang-seling*) (figure 17).

In most current practice, the *saron peking* participates in *irama* changes by doubling or halving the ratio of its subdivision with the *saron barung* part, though in some Yogyanese and Semarang practice it does not. Some gamelans have two *saron peking*—in which case two players play interlocking parts, one consistently playing between the beats of the other, and the two parts combining to produce a melody that usually resembles that of Solonese practice illustrated in figure 16. In eastern Javanese traditions, lively pieces or sections of pieces involve an interlocking between the *saron peking* (playing on and between beats) and the *bonang panerus* (playing between the beats of the *saron peking*).

The principal *garapan* instruments of the loud-playing ensemble are the pair of *bonang: barung* and *panerus.* Three basic techniques of variation characterize these instruments. Convention and context determine which of the three is appropriate. The simplest is *gembyangan nyegat* 'cutting in octaves', the anticipation of prominent *balungan* tones with regular offbeat octaves on the *barung,* with something close to triplet subdivision on the *panerus.* This technique is reserved for pieces with short *gongan* phrases, either light or swift in mood. It contrasts to a more contemplative and subdued technique, *mipil* 'to pick off one by one' or *mlaku* 'to walk', in which both *bonang barung* and *panerus* vary the *saron* melody, primarily by alternating successive tones, with the *panerus* playing at twice the speed of the *barung.* Passages of *mipil* are often interspersed with the repetition of a tonal degree in groups of three, usually in octaves (*gembyangan* or *duduk*), but in Solonese tradition sometimes only a single low-register tone (*duduk tunggal*). This repetition serves to emphasize a prominent *balungan* tone, often itself reiterated or sustained (*balungan gantungan*). The third technique, called *imbal* or *pinjalan,* is a lively interlocking between *bonang barung* (playing on and between *saron* beats) and *panerus* (playing between *bonang barung* beats). The interlocking on *bonang*—often interspersed with rapid flourishes (*kembangan*), leading to prominent tones of the *saron* melody—is the flashiest, most playful, and most lighthearted of the three *bonang* techniques.

With rare exceptions, the *bonang* participate in the process of change in *irama*

FIGURE 17 Techniques of *saron peking* variation, in *Ladrang "Wilujeng."*

balungan (on saron) : **5 6 5 3 2 1 2 6**
anticipating *nacah* (Yogya and Semarang) : 5 5 6 6 5 5 3 3 2 2 1 1 2 2 6 6
echoing *nacah* (Solo, *irama tanggung*) : 5 5 6 6 5 5 3 3 2 2 1 1 2 2 6 6
nacah selang-seling (Solo, *irama dadi*): 5566556655335533 2211221122662266

FIGURE 18 Techniques of *bonang* variation, excerpt from a *srepegan.*

gembyangan nyegat

balungan : 3 5 6 5 3 2 1 2

bonang barung : 5 . 5 . 5 . 5 . 2 . 2 . 2 . 2 .

(in octaves)

bonang panerus : .5.5..5..5.5..5 ..2.2..2..2.2..2

(in octaves)

mipil (with *gembyangan/duduk*)

balungan : 3 5 6 5 3 2 1 2

2 2

bonang barung : 3 5 3 5 6 5 6 5 3 2 2 . 2 2 . .

2 2 2 2 2

bonang panerus : 353.353.656.6565 322.22.22.22.22.

(*gembyang an/duduk*)

imbal (with *kembangan*)

balungan : 3 5 6 5 3 2 1 2

bonang barung : 2 5 2 5 2 5 2 5 6 2 6 22.235612

bonang panerus : 3.6.3.6.6.3.6.3. 3.1.3.1.21636162

(*kembangan*)

level. The parts given in figure 18 would be played for *irama tanggung.* Were the tempo slowed and *irama* changed to *irama dadi,* the *bonang* parts would double, with some variation, and what now fills one *gatra* would fill half a *gatra.* The *bonang barung* would essentially play the *panerus* part in figure 18, and the *panerus* would play at twice that density: 353.3535 would become 353.353.353.3535.

The *bonang* is often identified as the melodic leader of the loud ensemble. The *bonang*'s anticipation of the tones of the melody played on the *saron,* particularly in the *mipil* technique, can actually spell out the melody well enough that an adept player, with no reference to notation, can perform a piece he has not memorized.

The soft-playing ensemble

From steady, rapid beats on the *gambang,* to florid melodies of *pesindhèn,* to subtle but commanding strains of a rebab, the soft-playing ensemble is the heart of contemporary *garapan.* The soft-playing percussion instruments—*gambang, celempung* (and *siter*), *gendèr panerus, gendèr barung*—resemble those of the loud-playing ensemble in their adherence to a subdividing rhythmic paradigm, some more strictly than others. Of these, the *gendèr barung* part is rhythmically and melodically the most complex. Playing mostly in a two-part counterpoint, it is the most revered of the soft-playing subdividers. Rhythmically more subtle are the rebab (which may contribute to the subdivision, but often plays in syncopation with the main beat) and the *suling,* many of whose melodic patterns are independent of the predominant instrumental beat.

Players of the soft-playing instruments build their parts mostly by drawing on a vocabulary of melodic elaborations (*cèngkok*), whose precise realizations (called *wiletan* by some) are closely related, though in small ways distinguishable from those of other players. A flexible but limited relationship exists between the *cèngkok* and the melodic contexts that comprise the *gendhing* in various repertories. A single *cèngkok* can serve appropriately for a variety of musical contexts, but for some *gatra,* more than one *cèngkok* can be played. A player makes choices based on response to those he or she hears other players using as they perform together, and on his or her own preferences at the moment, including a desire for variation for its own sake.

For an example of soft-playing *garapan,* we can consider a transcription of rebab, *gendèr barung, gambang,* and vocal parts for a passage from *Gendhing "Gambir Sawit"* (figure 19). A more detailed survey of soft-playing instrumental techniques is given in Sutton 1993. See also Hood 1988; Perlman 1993; Sumarsam 1975b, 1984b; and Sutton 1975.

As is typical in most central Javanese practice, the *gérong* (male chorus) part adheres both to the regular pulse of the percussion instruments and to the melody of the *balungan,* whereas the *pesindhèn* part floats freely over this pulse, exhibiting considerable rhythmic and melodic independence from the *balungan* and other percussive parts. Like the soft-playing instrumental parts, both these vocal parts are built from *cèngkok,* independent of any particular piece. The *gérong* melody is in unison with the *balungan* at the end of most *gatra,* while the *pesindhèn* melody usually lags behind, arriving at the *gatra* final tone well after the next *gatra* has begun. In eastern Javanese tradition, solo vocal lines comparable to those of the *pesindhèn* here typically reach the goal tone either simultaneously with, or even ahead of, the instruments.

Many *gendhing* performed in soft-playing style will be stopped in mid-phrase by a signal from the drum, at which point the *pesindhèn* (or more rarely a solo male vocalist) is expected to perform a florid solo, accompanied only by occasional referential tones supplied by the *gendèr barung.* At the appropriate moment, the drummer signals the reentry of the other instrumentalists, and the *gendhing* resumes, ending eventually at the sounding of a gong, or proceeding on to another *gendhing.* This stop, known as *andhegan* (*pedhotan* in Banyumas, *pos* in eastern Java), provides an opportunity for focus on the skills of the vocalist.

The rebab part characteristically elaborates and anticipates the *balungan* and other melodic parts. In the first system, the rebab moves to pitch 5 at the end of the first *gatra,* well before the *balungan* or other instruments arrive at this pitch. The *gambang* and the *gendèr,* like other soft-ensemble instruments (*celempung, gendèr panerus*), provide melodic elaboration around the *balungan* melody, coinciding with the *balungan* at the end of most *gatra* and coordinating with the other parts in heterophonic texture.

Some Javanese musicians refer to the practice of *nunggal-misah* 'to join–to separate' underlying good soft-ensemble playing of *garapan,* in which each part joins (in unison) with other parts at moments during the performance of passage, but also exhibits significant independence, particularly between standard points of convergence, such as the final tones of a *gatra.* For the *gendèr,* the left hand's part is heard as fundamental, with the right hand providing a kind of obbligato, such that the dyad 6 (right hand) and 2 (left hand) is a settled conclusion for a passage of *balungan* ending on pitch 2. The *gambang* plays mostly in octaves, and covers a wide range, elaborating on the multi-octave flow of melody in soft-ensemble gamelan music.

Rhythmic instrumental conventions

The instruments providing rhythmic direction in gamelan performance are the *kendhang* (drums) and, in dance and dramatic performances, the *keprak* (slit drum) and the *kecrèk* (metal plaques). The *bedhug,* found in some gamelans, serves primarily to accentuate the *dhang* in certain two-drum (*kendhang loro*) patterns; in *gamelan sekati,* it is the only drum, but serves more as a subdivider of phrases (like *kempul*) than as a leader of rhythms.

The playing of *kendhang* in Solonese and Yogyanese traditions ranges from the sparse sounding of large *kendhang gendhing* in the *mérong* of large *gendhing* (and often the *inggah* sections of these *gendhing*) to the rapid and syncopated drumming on *ciblon* typical of the accompaniment of lively male and female dance. *Kendhang*

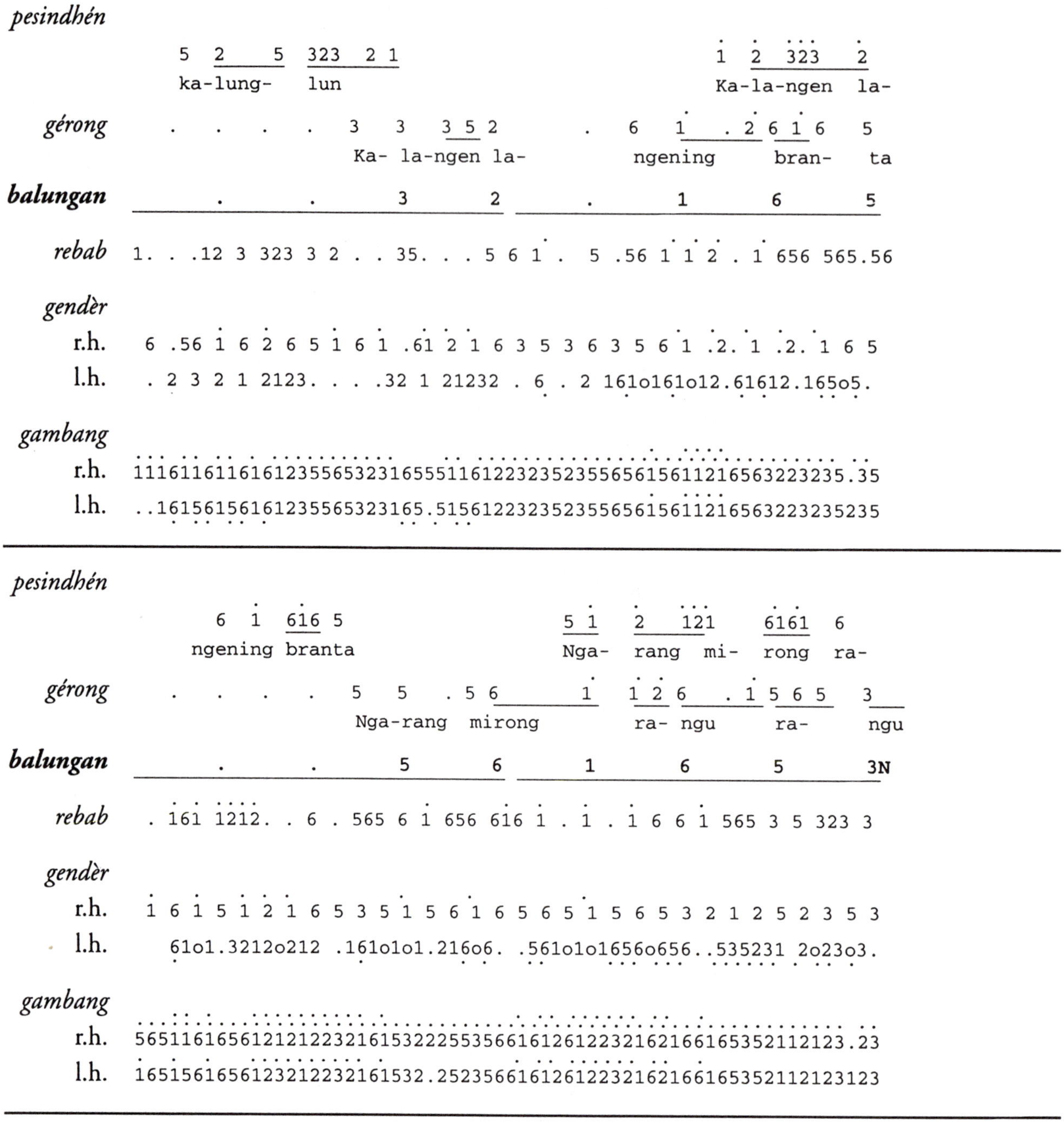

pesindhén

5 2 5 323 2 1 1 2 323 2
ka-lung- lun Ka-la-ngen la-

gérong . . . . 3 3 3 5 2 . 6 1 . 2 6 1 6 5
Ka- la-ngen la- ngening bran- ta

balungan . . 3 2 . 1 6 5

rebab 1. . .12 3 323 3 2 . . 35. . . 5 6 1 . 5 .56 1 1 2 . 1 656 565.56

gendèr
r.h. 6 .56 1 6 2 6 5 1 6 1 .61 2 1 6 3 5 3 6 3 5 6 1 .2. 1 .2. 1 6 5
l.h. . 2 3 2 1 2123. . . .32 1 21232 . 6 . 2 161o161o12.61612.165o5.

gambang
r.h. 1116116116161235565323165551161223235235565615611216563223235.35
l.h. ..1615615616123556532316 5.5156122323523556561561121656322323523 5

pesindhén

6 1 616 5 5 1 2 121 6161 6
ngening branta Nga- rang mi- rong ra-

gérong . . . . 5 5 . 5 6 1 1 2 6 . 1 5 6 5 3
Nga-rang mirong ra- ngu ra- ngu

balungan . . 5 6 1 6 5 3N

rebab . 161 1212. . 6 . 565 6 1 656 616 1 . 1 . 1 6 6 1 565 3 5 323 3

gendèr
r.h. 1 6 1 5 1 2 1 6 5 3 5 1 5 6 1 6 5 6 5 1 5 6 5 3 2 1 2 5 2 3 5 3
l.h. 61o1.3212o212 .161o1o1.216o6. .561o1o1656o656..535231 2o23o3.

gambang
r.h. 565111616561212122321615322255356616126122321621661653521121 23.23
l.h. 165156165612321223216153 2.2523566161261223216216616535211212 3123

two *gatra* per system
o = damping key on *gendèr* before striking next key in the part of the same hand (damping following striking of next key is assumed)
subscript dots = one octave below middle tessitura
superscript dots = one octave above middle tessitura
double superscript dots = two octaves higher than middle tessitura

FIGURE 19 Soft-ensemble *garapan*, excerpt from a *Gendhing* "*Gambir Sawit.*"

loro, patterns for shorter pieces, though livelier than one-drum patterns (*kendhang siji*), nevertheless fall toward the calm end of the continuum (figure 12).

Solonese tradition also includes *kosèk,* a subtle but animated set of drum patterns (Martopangrawit 1972b). Performed on one drum (*kendhang gendhing, ciblon,* or *kendhang wayang*), these patterns are heard most often in *wayang kulit* accompaniment (especially *kosèk wayangan*). Though reminiscent of drumming on *ciblon* in their syncopation and constant activity, they are usually played more quietly—and most important, they do not constitute accompanying patterns for specific dance or dramatic movements. *Ciblon* patterns relate to specific movements; even with no dancer or puppet present, knowledgeable listeners can follow the choreography of movements implied by drumming on *ciblon. Kosèk* may have had its inspiration in the accompaniment of specific movements, but is now a more purely aural form.

Drumming on *ciblon* consists of patterns named for particular movements. These patterns are used in a variety of *gendhing,* large and small. In addition to accompanying dancing, the *ciblon* frequently plays in gamelan concerts (*klenèngan, uyon-uyon*)—in which case it usually plays patterns derived from the accompaniment for *gambyong,* the flirtatious solo female dance (Martopangrawit 1972b; Sumarsam 1987). The patterns are coordinated with the formal structure of the *gendhing,* with certain patterns repeating *gongan* after *gongan* and others changing from one to the next—usually in an alternation between moving patterns (*mlaku*) in one passage and standing patterns (*mandeg* 'stop') in the next.

As drumming directs the performative tempo and flow, the drummer's responsibility is usually to signal the ending of a *gendhing,* with a change from the normally repeating pattern (or, in the case of the playing of *ciblon,* repeating paradigm) to a special ending (*suwuk*). Usually the drummer does this by gradually slowing the tempo, but on hearing the change in drumstrokes, experienced musicians know to end, even with no change of tempo (as occurs in some *gendhing lampah*).

Styles of drumming vary widely from one region to another. In Banyumas, one drummer often plays a small *ciblon* in combination with one or more *ketipung,* each standing vertically on one of its heads. Comparable to the playing of *ciblon* in Solonese traditions, the drumming is usually lively, but with greater abandon and more syncopation. The drumming for the small body of Semarang *gendhing bonang* employs *kendhang gendhing* and *ketipung,* but often with a beater used on the *kendhang gendhing.* The patterns alternate long pauses with lively syncopations and the extensive use of the *dhung* sound of the *ketipung* (Sutton 1991a:113). More subdued loud-playing *gendhing* of the eastern Javanese tradition use a similar combination of two drums, often with a beater, but the hallmark of eastern Javanese drumming is the playing of the *gambyak* drum, which can be animated, even in the *gedhugan* style employed in the calmer section of a large *gendhing* only to let loose with crackling pyrotechnics (*gambyakan*) in the second section.

With a limited vocabulary of rhythms, the percussive knocks on the *keprak,* the *kecrèk,* and the chest in which puppets are stored accentuate dancers' or puppets' movements, signal musicians to begin a *gendhing,* change tempos, or end. Initiated by the master of the dance or the *dhalang,* the signals to the gamelan musicians are confirmed by the *kendhang.* The styles of knocking (*dhodhogan*) for accompanying puppetry vary from one regional tradition to another, both in the configuration of specific signals and in the basic sound. For example, the knocking in Yogyanese *wayang kulit* is typically more rapid than that in Solonese.

Of indigenous instruments other than those heard in gamelans, the most prominent are *terbang* (frame drums), used in various genres throughout central and eastern Java and Madura. Most of these employ several smaller *terbang* playing interlocking polyrhythms, with punctuation provided by one or more large *terbang.* Double-reed instruments (*sronèn*), heard in a variety of ensembles in eastern Java and Madura, perform intricate melodies, alternating sustained tones with rapid figuration, often outside the intervallic structures of either *sléndro* or *pélog* (Kartomi 1976). Rice-block-pounding music, enjoying something of a revival because of government-sponsored contests, involves interlocking patterns of contrasting timbres (and sometimes contrasting pitches), with each of five or six players holding one large pole, pounding one or more surfaces of a large, partially hollowed-out log.

Pedagogy and transmission

Before the 1900s, music in Java was learned exclusively through informal transmission, and almost entirely without the use of musical notation. According to accounts by older Javanese, aspiring musicians would simply observe performances as carefully and as often as possible, hoping for a chance to show what they had learned. Mistakes were met with scorn, and verbal explanations were minimal until an aspiring musician had succeeded in demonstrating substantial understanding of the music and its technical demands. Once one had convinced one's elders of seriousness of musical purpose and sufficient level of skill, only then might one gain the privilege of occasional advice and individual teaching, though seldom regularized into a series of lessons. This kind of informal learning continues in Java, but it has mostly been replaced by a system of formal education whose influence has led to explicit instruction, use of notation, and a far less intimidating relationship between expert and learner.

Musical notation

Essential to this change in pedagogy was the development of musical notation for Java's gamelan music. In the latter part of the 1800s, with impetus from Dutch intellectuals interested in preserving Javanese arts, several systems of notation developed. Early use was made of Western notation, particularly for Javanese vocal music, albeit with staves modified to accommodate Javanese tonal systems.

The first known notation of *gendhing* (developed in the 1860s and attributed to Adiwinata, a Yogyanese prince) was a cumbersome writing out in Javanese script of the names of each successive tone of the *saron* melody in vertical columns, with indications of gong punctuation (*kenong, kethuk, kempul,* gong) to the side of the corresponding *saron* tone.

A second notation, *nut ranté* or *titilaras ranté* 'chain notation', came into use around 1870 or shortly thereafter (Perlman 1991). It was an adaptation of Western notation on staffs, with parallel (though not equidistantly spaced) horizontal lines, one line for each scalar degree. The melody was represented by single or double dots placed on the lines (but not spaces between them), joined with a wavy line (or "chain"); its higher-pitched tones often appeared on the lower lines, and its lower-pitched tones on the higher—the reverse of the Western arrangement. In some versions, no horizontal lines appear; instead, melodic tones are represented by Javanese letters placed in relationship to one another on a two-dimensional field, with rhythm represented on the horizontal axis and pitch on the vertical.

A more comprehensive graphic notation, *titilaras andha* 'ladder notation', developed among Yogyanese nobility in the last quarter of the 1800s. With parallel lines representing each tone on the *saron,* each staff ran vertically from top to bottom, with black dots representing the *saron* tones. Horizontal lines marked the *balungan* beat. Appended to this core were signs for gong punctuation, for multi-octave melodic register of *garapan* parts, for drumstrokes (*kendhang gendhing* and *ketipung,* but not *ciblon*), and sometimes for the melodic abstraction known as *balungan,* played by the *bonang panembung* and the *slenthem.*

In the late 1890s, at the *kepatihan* (prime minister's residence) in Surakarta, Javanese musicians developed a cipher notation known as *titilaras angka* 'numerical notation', or simply *titilaras kepatihan.* Now the preferred notation for gamelan and vocal music, it is in common use throughout central and eastern Java, and the other forms of notation are all but forgotten. In contrast to the related cipher system, developed in the era just before independence by the great Javanese educator Ki Hadjar Dewantara (using numerals 1–5 in transposition depending on *pathet*), the *kepatihan* system assigned numerals to each pitch degree with superscript and subscript dots to indicate higher and lower registers. It indicates gong punctuation either by a set of diacritical marks placed under, over, or around the numerals (downward arc for *kenong* tone, upward arc for *kempul,* circle for gong tone, and so on), or by appended letters (the version used throughout this article, with *N* for *kenong, P* for *kempul, G* for gong, and so on). Illustrations of these systems can be seen in J. Becker 1980:15–18, Dewantara 1964, Groneman 1890 (plaat I and plaat II), and Kunst 1973:2:491–499.

When notation first appeared, it was considered primarily a means to fix a source for reference; should anyone forget a *gendhing,* he or she could check the *saron* part, and sometimes other parts, in notation. Through the end of the colonial era, the only performers who might use notation in performance were the player of the *bonang barung* (the melodic leader) and the drummer (the rhythmic leader). Today, even for long and rarely played pieces, the better musicians still play entirely without the aid of notation, though to refresh their memories they may well consult notation before performance. The use of notation has gained a foothold in teaching and performing, but the music is still fundamentally an oral tradition—formulaic but variable, resistant to complete standardization.

Javanese teachers of music expanded the *kepatihan* system to develop notation for all *garapan* parts (*bonang, gendèr,* rebab, and so on) and vocal parts. As a teaching device, such notation provides a clear example, usually of a simple or simplified version of a *gendhing* or a *cèngkok,* but it is intended only as a beginner's aid, to provide a basis on which aspiring musicians learn through intensive aural exposure to the music. *Gendhing* are almost never written out in score. If players of *garapan* instruments use notation in performance, as they often do in the late twentieth century, they use the *balungan* part to help construct their own parts through a combination of recall and generation based on an aural understanding of the music.

For playing *kendhang,* various notational systems have developed. After *titilaras andha* with modified Javanese letters indicating the sounds of drums, the Solonese experimented with systems utilizing Latin letters, read from left to right across the page. Most *kendhang* notation has been for one-drum and two-drum patterns, and has probably contributed to the near standardization of these patterns. Musicians have also notated the drumming of the *ciblon* in central Java and the *gambyak* in eastern Java, but few musicians rely on notation at any stage in learning to play these drums.

Music education

One of the driving forces in spreading the use of notation and in standardizing theoretical understanding of gamelan music in general has been the growth of formal music education. Court-style gamelan music and dance began to be taught as an adjunct to courtly dance at the Kridha Beksa Wirama school in Yogyakarta in 1918. At about the same time in Surakarta, gamelan instruction began to be offered at several institutions, including the court-sponsored museum, Radya Pustaka, and by private organizations such as Pananta Dibya (founded in 1914). Until the end of the colonial era, formal schooling in Javanese music was limited to institutions and clubs outside the main school system.

In 1950, less than a year after the Dutch had been driven out of the country, the Indonesian government established in Surakarta the Konservatori Karawitan Indonesia (Indonesian Conservatory of Traditional Arts), a high school for performing arts. Intended as a locus for combining regional traditions and creating new national arts, this institution has focused almost exclusively on traditional Javanese performing arts, with a faculty mostly of accomplished Solonese musicians, dancers, and puppeteers. In later years, comparable institutions were founded in Yogyakarta

Phonograph recordings have been made in Indonesia since the first decade of the twentieth century, but it was radio, introduced in the 1920s, that had the greater impact on indigenous music until the rise of commercial recordings on cassettes in the 1970s.

FIGURE 20 Javanese gamelan music as it is taught in schools: Pak Rasito leads a class at SMKI Banyumas, 1986. Photo by R. Anderson Sutton.

(Konservatori Tari Indonesia, Indonesian Conservatory of Dance, 1961), in Surabaya (Konservatori Karawitan Indonesia, 1973), and in Banyumas (Sekolah Menengah Karawitan Indonesia, Secondary School of Traditional Arts, 1978) (figure 20). Now known officially as Sekolah Menengah Karawitan Indonesia, these are designated individually by locale (Solo, Surabaya, and so on).

Postsecondary institutions were founded during the 1960s and 1970s: Akademi Seni Karawitan Indonesia (Indonesian Academy of Traditional Arts, ASKI) in Surakarta, 1964; Akademi Seni Tari Indonesia (Indonesian Academy of Dance, ASTI) in Yogyakarta, 1964; and Sekolah Tinggi Kesenian Wilwatikta (Wilwatikta University of the Arts, STKW) in Surabaya, in the mid-1970s. In the late 1980s, ASKI was renamed Sekolah Tinggi Seni Indonesia (Indonesian University of the Arts, STSI); and ASTI combined with other arts colleges in Yogyakarta under the umbrella of Institut Seni Indonesia (Indonesian Arts Institute, ISI). Each of these institutions has emphasized gamelan music inherited from previous generations, but creative innovations have been strongly encouraged at the postsecondary level, particularly since 1978.

Each institution emphasizes the tradition of the immediate region. For example, SMKI Surabaya offers courses in eastern Javanese gamelan, dance, and wayang; and ISI offers courses in Yogyanese arts. Solonese tradition is well represented at all these institutions, but other cross-regional offerings are less regular. The central Javanese institutions offer no regular instruction in eastern Javanese arts. Banyumas tradition is taught at STSI, but otherwise only at SMKI Banyumas. However, classes in music and dance of the major traditions from neighboring cultural areas, Sunda and Bali, form part of the regular curriculum at most of these institutions. The result has been both a heightened awareness of cultural boundaries and a growth in experimental artistic cross-fertilization.

Many amateur groups study gamelan music with teachers either trained at these institutions or directly influenced by their methods. Local, provincial, and national levels of government sponsor contests and festivals in which these groups compete. Musical contests (*lomba*) abound in contemporary Java, contributing to a degree of standardization as groups are required to perform particular pieces conforming to certain guidelines determined by contest committees. In addition to gamelan contests, contests cover a variety of folkloristic arts (*kesenian rakyat*) that involve music, including various forms of dance-drama, *calung-lènggèr,* rice-block-pounding music, *terbang* music, *réyog,* and other processional genres. In a conscious effort by government officials to revive "endangered" artistic forms, contests may even feature obscure genres. In Banyuwangi, in addition to contests of local genres such as *gandrung,* a musical competition between rival *angklung Banyuwangi* known as *angklung caruk* may be so spirited as to erupt into a brawl (Wolbers 1987).

Music and the mass media

The mass media, particularly radio and commercial recordings, have played a central role in the dissemination of music in Java. Phonograph recordings have been made in Indonesia since the first decade of the twentieth century, but it was radio, introduced in the 1920s, that had the greater impact on indigenous music until the rise of commercial recordings on cassettes in the 1970s. Cheaper than phonographs, radios could provide aural access to a changing variety of performances.

In the Java of the late 1990s, mass-media technology is widespread. Most urban households have radios and cassette players, many have television sets, and a rapidly increasing minority have VCRs and satellite dishes. Even before villages had lines for electric power, it was not uncommon to find radios, cassette players, and televisions powered by car batteries. Now most Javanese villages have electricity, making such items easier and cheaper to use. Although individuals may tune in to a particular show on radio or television, it is not unusual to find either (or both) turned on and serving as background for socializing, eating, or doing housework. Musicians often listen to the radio to hear new pieces and new renditions of older pieces. For many musicians, radio serves as the primary source for learning new repertoire, as well as current norms and variants in the treatment or interpretation of older pieces. Musicians also learn from cassettes that they purchase themselves or borrow from friends or neighbors.

Some radio broadcasts are live, but there has been a trend toward the use of commercially produced recordings on cassettes or recordings of sessions by professional or amateur musicians in a radio studio, with multiple takes if necessary. At public institutions and in private lessons, recordings on cassettes (commercially available or privately recorded) routinely serve as standard accompaniments for instruction in dancing. In some contexts, public performances of dance are accompanied by cassette rather than live musicians, but this situation is still unusual.

Radio

The first radio station in Indonesia was BRV (Batavia Radio Vereniging), founded in the early 1920s. It was followed in the late 1920s by NIROM (Nederlands-Indische Radio Omroep Maatschappij) and VADERA, both of which were operated directly by the Dutch colonial government and broadcast some Javanese music. Early stations devoting extensive airtime to indigenous music were MAVRO in Yogyakarta and

SRV and SRI in Surakarta. These stations routinely broadcast directly from the courts, providing a relatively limited number of radio owners with unprecedented access to the repertoires and styles regarded as the supreme achievements of Javanese music. In addition, MAVRO maintained its own group of gamelan musicians, many of whom were court musicians—from the sultan's court, the *kepatihan* (the prime minister's residence), and the *pura Pakualaman* (lesser court of Prince Paku Alam). The lack of competition on the airwaves enabled listeners to receive clear radio signals from distant stations. Musicians far from the court cities, then, could listen frequently to the court music of both Solo and Yogya, modifying their own performances in response.

In eastern Java, music associated with the Surabaya area was broadcast during the 1930s by CIRVO (Centraal Indonesische Radio Vereniging Omroep) and NIROM stations in Surabaya. These broadcasts helped spread knowledge of Surabaya gamelan traditions, including the use of Surabaya *gendhing* for *klenèngan* as pioneered by Wongsokadi (see below).

During the Japanese occupation (1942–1945), much musical activity was curtailed, but live gamelan music continued to be broadcast on Japanese-controlled Radio Hosokyoku, with studios in central and eastern Java. The national radio station (Radio Republik Indonesia, RRI) was established in September 1945, only a month after the declaration of independence. It currently maintains studios throughout the archipelago, including the following cities in central and eastern Java: Malang, Purwokerto, Semarang, Surabaya, Surakarta, and Yogyakarta. Each of the Javanese branches of RRI devotes considerable time to broadcasting gamelan music and related dramatic genres (including *wayang kulit, wayang wong, kethoprak,* and in eastern Java, *ludruk*). With the exception of RRI Malang, each supports a group of studio gamelan musicians who perform for live broadcasts (or sessions prerecorded for later broadcast) at least once a week. Since the early 1980s these musicians have held formal status as civil servants.

The airwaves in Java are crowded with many private radio stations broadcasting a dizzying variety of music, drama, news, and information. Although Indonesian and Javanese pop music predominate, many stations devote at least some of their schedule to gamelan music and traditional drama. On almost any night, one can choose among Javanese *klenèngan, kethoprak,* and a complete *wayang kulit* (broadcast from about 9:00 P.M. until dawn); most of these are broadcasts not of live performances but of commercial recordings.

Television

Since the introduction of television (1962), the government-controlled television stations in Indonesia have devoted little attention to traditional performing arts. Nevertheless, *kethoprak* performances are broadcast regularly, with other indigenous dramatic genres, such as *wayang kulit* and *wayang wong,* presented occasionally.

Gamelan performances are broadcast occasionally, but are usually of amateur groups, rather than the skilled professionals of the radio stations, courts, or puppeteer troupes. Musicians may be entertained by some of these broadcasts, but the forum for important new repertoire and innovative treatment of traditional *gendhing* is widely acknowledged to be radio—and since the early 1970s, the commercial cassette industry.

Recording

Javanese were introduced to the technology of recording in the late 1800s, when gramophones were first imported. Foreign recording companies recorded varieties of Javanese music from the beginning of the twentieth century—before and during the

FIGURE 21 A variety of recorded genres, from classical to pop, is sold at local cassette stores. Photo by R. Anderson Sutton.

early days of radio. As late as the 1950s, one could still encounter itinerant disk jockeys toting a phonograph and a collection of disks, which customers could commission to be played for a small fee. Few Javanese were wealthy enough to purchase the disks and the equipment with which to play them.

Commercial disks of Javanese music were produced from the 1950s through the early 1970s by several Indonesian companies, including Aneka Record, Elshinta, Indah Record, Serimpi, and the national recording company Lokananta (formerly Indravox). Among these, Lokananta, based in Surakarta, stood out as exemplary, both in the quality of recording and in the skill and stature of the musicians it recorded (mostly the studio musicians of RRI stations). Though not widely distributed through sales, the recorded music and dramatic arts, particularly on Lokananta, became widely known and highly influential through repeated broadcasts on RRI and other stations. Choice and grouping of repertoire, arrangements, and even details of vocal and instrumental styles on these recordings became authoritative standards, emulated by musicians throughout central and eastern Java.

In 1973, Lokananta ceased producing disks and began devoting its efforts to the medium of cassettes, which several years earlier they and other private companies had begun to produce. In addition to a rapidly evolving, primarily Jakarta-based industry, many companies were established with a focus primarily or exclusively on gamelan music and indigenous theatrical forms, especially *wayang kulit* and *kethoprak* (figure 21). Prominent among these—rivaling Lokananta in breadth of coverage, quality of performance, and sometimes quality of recording—are Ira-Record (Jakarta and Semarang, formerly Wisanda), Fajar (Semarang), Borobudur (Semarang), and Kusuma (Klaten). Most of these offer a range of indigenous musical and dramatic genres from central and eastern Java. Smaller companies have concentrated on particular regional traditions—Hidup Baru and Nusa Indah in Banyumas, CHGB and Nirwana in Surabaya, Bumi Putra / Jayabaya in Malang, Ria in Banyuwangi, and Semar Record in Sumenep.

Having made recorded music accessible to a wide sector of society, the cassette industry has sometimes been regarded as a threat to the continuation of live musical performance. Indeed, Javanese not uncommonly purchase or even rent a recording of an eight-hour *wayang kulit* for playing at a family ritual event (wedding or circumcision). And although live performance does continue, the Javanese strongly prefer to hire star performers (famous puppeteers, gamelan groups, *pesindhèn*) whose fame has been gained largely through their representation on commercial cassettes. The cassette industry has produced a sharp division between performers chosen for recordings, who may earn a substantial living as musicians, and competent but nameless performers, who secure only occasional engagements.

The sheer number of cassette releases—thousands of gamelan music cassettes, hundreds of seven- or eight-hour sets of complete *wayang kulit,* and even close to one hundred cassettes of *calung Banyumas*—is staggering. Because the technology is inexpensive, local genres once thought to be near extinction have enjoyed a resurgence of popularity, as their image has been refurbished by the legitimizing powers of representation on cassettes. The potential for homogenization has been largely blunted by the variety of versions available on cassettes.

Performers and composers

Until the late twentieth century, making music in Java was fundamentally communal, with little public acclaim for players or composers. In villages, many musicians are farmers or petty tradespeople by day and perform music (*gamelan, slawatan, réyog,* and so on) on an occasional basis. In towns and cities, members of the old nobility and new élites may participate as amateurs in gamelan performances. Yet

Musicians still serve the courts, partly out of reverence for royalty, partly for the stature a courtly rank brings to themselves and their families, and partly for the contacts and exposure it provides for other professional musical activities.

most gamelan music one encounters, whether in live performances or on radiobroadcasts or cassettes, is performed by professional who earn a substantial portion of their income from their activities as musicians.

The profession of music goes back many centuries in Java, with large groups of court musicians fully supported by the royal courts, and itinerant rural musicians hiring themselves out for performances, or even begging from one locale to the next. The status of musician is low in Java, lower than that of dancer or puppeteer. Nevertheless, many musicians earn a meager living from their art, and a few have gained fame and wealth, thanks in large measure to modern mass media.

The division of labor in musical performance remains largely segmented by gender. Professional instrumentalists are nearly always male. In the past, the main exception was the player of the *gendèr* for *wayang kulit,* often the puppeteer's wife. Otherwise, the only professional female musicians were the singers (*pesindhèn*), who before the twentieth century were usually singer-dancers (*talèdhèk, tandhak,* and others), often associated with prostitution. Since the 1960s, with the profession of *pesindhèn* not only gaining in respectability but becoming lucrative, interest in studying singing has grown significantly, particularly among rural girls. Professional female players of *gendèr* are now a rarity, but amateur women's gamelan groups (*ibu-ibu*) have sprung up in great numbers, primarily in the larger towns and cities of central and eastern Java, where they probably outnumber amateur men's.

Musical patronage takes several forms in contemporary Java. Each of the four central Javanese courts maintains a corps of musicians with the official status of court musician (*abdidalem niyaga*) or court singer (*abdidalem pesindhèn*) at various individual ranks; but none of the courts has the financial means to pay even the musical directors a living wage. Musicians still serve the courts, partly out of reverence for royalty, partly for the stature a courtly rank brings to themselves and their families, and partly for the contacts and exposure it provides for other professional musical activities.

Aside from a few famous gamelan music directors and composers (discussed below), those seeking to make a living as gamelan musicians may accompany popular puppeteers (some of whom work nearly every night during certain months of the year), or they may join the ranks of the Indonesian civil service—as musicians affiliated with particular national radio stations (RRI), or as teachers at one of the educational institutions devoted to Java's performing arts. Though the salary is low, the affiliation with one of the RRI stations can win important prestige and invitations for far more remunerative engagements at private events, such as weddings and circumcisions.

Teaching is increasingly the position of choice for Java's young musicians able to secure the necessary formal credentials. Competition for jobs teaching at the arts institutions mentioned above is especially keen. In addition, Javanese gamelan music is taught formally at other institutions offering a broader or differently focused curriculum. It is also taught at institutions outside the central and eastern Javanese region, such as SMKI and ASTI in Bandung, and Institut Kesenian Jakarta (IKJ) in the national capital. Another means of support, usually insufficient by itself, is the offering of private and group instruction outside the formal educational system. Most often, professional musicians combine the activities mentioned above in an effort to patch together a livelihood.

Recordings have contributed substantially to the creation of stars among certain gamelan musicians and composers. In former times as well, some musicians won fame for their skills, at least among fellow musicians and musical enthusiasts. Well known in Surakarta during much of the twentieth century were the court musician K. R. T. Warsadiningrat (1882–1975, formerly known as Prajapangrawit) and others. In Yogyakarta, many residents were familiar with the musicianship of court drummer and occasional composer Ki Laras Sumbaga, and the all-round performer and prolific composer Ki Wasitodiningrat (formerly known as Wasitodipuro and Cokrowasito).

Wasitodiningrat gained fame far beyond his native Yogyakarta, however, mostly from recordings of his compositions and arrangements of traditional *gendhing*. He has now retired from teaching at several American universities; before his work in the United States, he dominated gamelan musical life in Yogyakarta for decades, serving as director of the court musicians at the *pura Pakualaman* and as director of gamelan music at the Yogya studio of RRI. He composed many light, vocally oriented pieces (*lagu dolanan*), some of which entered the standard repertoire and are heard widely throughout central and eastern Java.

Hardjosoebroto (Yogya) and Martopangrawit (Solo) were also famous as innovative composers of light and at times experimental *gendhing*. Martopangrawit, for decades until his death (in 1986), was the supreme authority on Solonese gamelan music. In addition to a large corpus of original compositions and a multitude of talented students, he has to his credit a sizable outpouring of scholarly theoretical works (such as Martopangrawit 1984 [1972a]) and exhaustive books of notation (such as Martopangrawit 1972b, 1973, 1975, 1976). He served as court musician at the main court (*kasunanan*) in Surakarta and as senior teacher at ASKI (now STSI).

The most famous gamelan musician was unquestionably Ki Nartosabdho (1925–1985), who earned a reputation not only as a superb drummer but also as an innovative and sometimes controversial composer and as one of the two or three most sought-after puppeteers in Java. He was born in Wedhi, a town between Yogya and Solo. In 1945, he moved to Semarang as permanent drummer for the Ngesthi Pandhawa *wayang wong* troupe. By the time of his death, he had composed hundreds of new *gendhing*, had reworked vocal parts and arrangements for scores of traditional *gendhing*, had directed music for hundreds of *gamelan* cassettes, and had recorded close to one hundred full-length (eight-hour) performances of *wayang kulit*. During the last years of his life, he maintained a busy schedule of live performances of *wayang kulit*, often receiving the equivalent of thousands of dollars for one evening's performance.

Musicians in other regions have not gained nearly the recognition of Ki Nartosabdho or Ki Wasitodiningrat. Nevertheless, the drummer and composer Rasito and the singer and composer S. Bono are famous in the Banyumas region. Wongsokadi (1869–1954) was widely acclaimed as an innovator in eastern Javanese music, responsible for introducing *sindhènan* into the local repertory and for presenting these *gendhing* for listening pleasure (*klenèngan*), expanding beyond the limits of *tayuban* and *wayang kulit*. He worked for various radio stations: CIRVO and NIROM in the 1930s, Hosokyoku during the Japanese occupation, and RRI Surabaya in the early 1950s (Proyek Penelitian den Pencatatan Kebudayaan Daerah 1976). Today, because of extensive exposure through radio and commercial cassettes, the puppeteer, composer, and gamelan director Suleiman and the former RRI Surabaya gamelan director Diyat Sariredjo are also famous throughout much of eastern Java. In general, however, the top puppeteers enjoy the greatest fame, earning fees that far surpass those of any of the musicians.

Among musicians, despite the greater responsibility of the musical director (usually the drummer), it is the top *pesindhèn* who often command the largest fees. In a world in which men make decisions on hiring, potentially alluring female performers serve as a stronger draw to performances than any but the top male musicians. A sponsor can gain prestige in the local community by hiring one or more famous *pesindhèn*. Many of the famous ones reside in or near Solo and are called to perform throughout Java. Because of their RRI broadcasts, countless cassette releases, and appearances with top puppeteers, *pesindhèn* such as Prenjak, Sunarti, Supadmi, and Tukinem are known to many. So, too, are Ngatirah (who often sang at RRI Semarang and with Ki Nartosabdho's group, Condhong Raos) and Suryati (who lives in Banyumas, sang with Condhong Raos, and continues to sing with other central Javanese groups and the top local Banyumas puppeteer Ki Sugino). Well known to many Javanese was the legendary Nyi Bei Mardusari, who as a young villager was chosen to become a vocalist and dancer at the Mangkunegaran court. Featured on early recordings, she taught at Konservatori Karawitan Indonesia during the 1950s and early 1960s.

New developments

Javanese music has never been static. Like many primarily oral traditions, it has been based on internal dynamism and variability. During the colonial era, the size of the ensemble grew, many new pieces entered the repertoire, and some new styles of playing and vocal-instrumental combinations came into vogue.

In the era of Indonesian independence, particularly from the late 1950s onward, accomplished musicians composed many new pieces, many of them based on the style of Javanese children's game songs called *lagu dolanan*. These pieces, with more experimental and unusual pieces by Ki Wasitodiningrat and young composers, are usually called *kreasi baru* 'new creations'. Many of them emphasize the vocal line, often delivered by male and female singers in unison. In a few instances, two vocal lines move in counterpoint—almost certainly a response to Western musical influence, without precedent in the *karawitan* tradition.

Several composers have written pieces employing triple meter, which presents considerable challenge to musicians accustomed to using standard four- and eight-beat patterns (*cèngkok*) to create their parts.

Since the early 1980s, the composition of *kreasi baru* has grown tremendously, with an enormous increase in both the number of pieces composed and the number of musicians composing them. Many of these imitate or adopt Indonesian popular tunes in *dangdut* style [see POPULAR MUSIC AND CULTURAL POLITICS]; others employ the infectious rhythms of the popular Sundanese *jaipongan*.

Outside the realm of pop styles, the focal point for the most innovative work in recent years has been the postsecondary institution STSI in Surakarta. Before the early 1980s, students were required to demonstrate mastery of the *karawitan* tradition by composing a *gendhing* in traditional style. Since that time, however, due in large measure to the directives of Gendon Humardani, head of ASKI until his death (1983), students have been required to compose a modern piece demonstrating creativity and originality. The resulting pieces usually employ standard gamelan instruments, though they may use nongamelan instruments, even newly invented ones.

Al. Suwardi, a faculty member at STSI and widely recognized as one of the most innovative composers, has used a gigantic log xylophone and an electrically operated vibraphone, both of which he constructed himself. He and others have applied unusual techniques to playing standard gamelan instruments. In one piece by Suwardi, kettle-gongs (*bonang*) are turned upside down and partially filled with water. Each of several players holds an inverted kettle in one hand and rotates it in the air as he strikes the knob with a beater. The shifting water alters the pitch, rendering each kettle the source of a wide spread of pitches, sounded with eerie glissandi caused by the changing angle of the water inside the kettle. Less radical techniques involve the playing of *saron* with several beaters simultaneously, performing rapid glissandi on *saron* and metallophones, and the simultaneous playing of *sléndro* and *pélog* instruments or rapid alternation between them.

Some of the experimental compositions incorporate substantial passages from extant traditional pieces and employ standard techniques. Others draw on performance styles from the neighboring traditions of Sunda and Bali, but apply them to Javanese instruments in unusual juxtapositions. Nontraditional uses of extant traditional passages and techniques can be just as surprising as the radical techniques mentioned above. They give the compositions a high degree of unpredictability, requiring different attitudes and responses from an audience than do older pieces. They are presented in concerts lasting only a few hours, with small audiences sitting quietly and listening attentively.

The new compositions by faculty and students at STSI, with comparable works being produced at other institutions, have been largely experimental, conceived as artistic and intellectually challenging, rather than as accessible and entertaining. As a result, one finds little awareness of these pieces outside the confines of STSI and other similar institutions. Few are available on commercial recordings or broadcast on the radio. Most professional gamelan groups, such as those in the employ of popular puppeteers and those affiliated with RRI stations, do not learn this repertoire. Nevertheless, pieces once thought too radical—the *kreasi baru* of the 1950s and 1960s, with more recent pieces in this style—are now standard fare in gamelan performances throughout Java.

It is too early to predict what wider effects experimental compositions will have in Java, but they are bound to influence the history of *karawitan,* which has always evolved in response to changing social conditions and aesthetic sensibilities. The continued vitality of Javanese music is due not only to its basic internal dynamism and tolerance for individual creativity but also to Javanese openness to change.

CIREBON

The region of Cirebon, located at the approximate cultural boundary between the Sundanese and the Javanese, encompasses aspects of both cultures. Whether culturally it is more similar to the Sundanese of West Java or to the central and east Javanese (hereafter, Javanese) is uncertain, but its location has deeply affected the mixture of cultures that produce Cirebonese music.

Besides the locally dominant ethnic groups (Javanese, Sundanese, Madurese), other ethnically distinct marginal groups (*suku sisipan*) have occupied Cirebon and surrounding regions. The 1400s and 1500s saw large migrations from different places, such as Sunda, Java, China, and mainland Southeast Asia. Today, Cirebon has evolved its own unique culture. Linguistically and in some forms of art (such as shadow plays and woodcarving) it is closer to the Javanese than to the Sundanese; in other cultural aspects (such as music and dance) it is closer to the Sundanese.

Cirebonese culture is supposedly a mixture of the two more dominant cultures: Sundanese to the west, and central Javanese to the east. Indeed, Caruban, an early

Shadow plays, gamelans, and other forms of art are traditionally believed to be the creation of the nine Islamic saints, who invented them to help spread Islam.

name for Cirebon, is often glossed 'mixed' (Carbon 1972). In reality, however, the situation is more complicated. Cirebonese influences on the Sundanese in music and dance are actually greater than vice versa. In the 1500s, Cirebon developed into an Islamic kingdom. Before then, its area had been part of both Galuh and Pajajaran, Sundanese Hindu kingdoms. Central Javanese cultural influences during the Mataram Period (in the 1600s and the 1700s) are great, but some Cirebonese cultural aspects are older. Architecture, woodcarving, and musical expression are similar to fourteenth-century east Javanese Hindu culture, as well as to Balinese cultures of today (Wagner 1959; Wright 1978). Even now, the musical practices and terminologies in Cirebonese gamelans have more similarities to those of the east Javanese than to those of the central Javanese.

The development of Cirebonese culture is linked closely to the emergence of the so-called northern coastal culture (*kebudayaan pasisir*) during the rise of the Javanese-Islamic period, which superseded the existing Java-Hindu culture. The Cirebonese kingdom, one of the largest Islamic kingdoms in Java, was founded by Sunan Gunung Jati, one of nine famous Islamic saints (*Wali Sanga*) and the only one to become a king (Siddique 1977). As the northern coastal culture adopted most aspects of the Java-Hindu culture (with modifications to suit their indigenous philosophy), some of the fourteenth-century Majapahit culture survives in Cirebon.

This link is strengthened by the belief that traditional arts are the saints' creation, especially Sunan Kalijaga, and therefore, have symbolic Islamic significance. Further, Cirebonese professional artists believe they are descendants of one of the saints, either Pangeran Panggung or Sunan Kalijaga. Most artists, besides priding themselves on their blood, strongly believe that, as descendants of Pangeran Panggung, only they can perform the traditional arts correctly. Many keep oral and written records of their genealogies, and they tend to marry endogamously so that they will have genetically pure artistic descendants. Though Cirebonese artists are not usually members of the upper social strata, they are proud of being born with a guaranteed profession (Suanda 1981).

Since 1677, the Cirebonese kingdom has been divided into two kingdoms, Kasepuhan ("The Old") and Kanoman ("The Young"), each with its court (*kraton*). A third court, that of the Kacirebonan principality, was established in 1807 (Sunardjo 1983). An even smaller court, Kaprabonan, was established before World War II. These divisions were initially the result of political tension, but the courts also function as religious centers. Even now, when none of the courts has political power, they retain strong religious functions. The kings and their descendants are believed to have spiritual power. Villagers, farmers, merchants and artists come individually or communally to the king (*sultan, pangéran*) or princes (*élang*) to ask for blessings or to be cured of spiritual and physical illnesses.

The city of Cirebon is now one of Indonesia's medium-sized cities. Almost everything is available in the city, from pedicabs to airplanes, from inexpensive lodgings to international hotels, from *sintren* groups (see below) to bands that play rock. The population of municipal Cirebon (37 square kilometers) was about 255,000 in 1990–1991, but the Cirebon cultural area includes the regencies (*kabupaten*) of Cirebon (988 square kilometers, 1.6 million people) and Indramayu (2,000 square kilometers, 1.4 million people), parts of the regencies of Majaléngka, Kuningan, Subang, Karawang, Tangerang, and Sérang, and even some areas in the Brebes and Tegal (central Java) regencies. Roughly, it involves the Cirebonese-speaking areas, which include no fewer than 5 million people (about 2.75 percent of Indonesia's population).

The Cirebonese language may be said to be a dialect of Javanese. About 80 to 90 percent of its words can be easily understood by Javanese listeners, whereas only about 10 to 20 percent can be understood by Sundanese. The Cirebonese script is exactly like the Javanese, but the Sundanese script, which also came from central Java, has some modifications, and not all letters are compatible. The pronunciation, however, is similar to that of the Sundanese. The open syllable, written *a,* is pronounced /a'/ in Cirebonese and Sundanese, though it is pronounced /o/ in Javanese. The word *rama* (in Javanese and Sundanese script), for example, is pronounced /rama'/ in Cirebonese and Sundanese, and /romo/ in Javanese. Though Cirebonese people call themselves Javanese (*wong Jawa*) and call Javanese the eastern people (*wong wetan*), some of their cultural expressions are similar to those of the Sundanese.

Islam and music

Most Cirebonese are Muslims. Consequently, their culture has strong Islamic elements. As in most parts of Java, however, there is little Arabic musical influence. The scalar, modal, and musical influences reflect the regional culture, rather than West Asian musical culture just as Javanese-Hindu music contains few Indian music elements. In the past, the melody of the call to prayer (*adzan*) and the reciting of the Qur'ān in many villages were in *sléndro* or *pélog* scale, rather than in a West Asian scale, as heard today.

Some Cirebonese musical instruments—like frame drums, variously called *trebang* (or *terbang*), *genjring* (with metal jingles) *gembyung,* and *brai*—are believed to have come from West Asia. Drums, the only musical instruments found in mosques, include a slit drum, a large double-headed drum used to signal the time of prayer, and the possible addition of one or more kinds of frame drums. Few musical ensembles with these frame drums, however, are still associated with the mosque. The acrobatic performance of *sidapurna,* which often includes magical elements and has nothing to do with Islam, is accompanied by an ensemble of *genjring.* The *randu kentir,* a folk-dance group in Indramayu, uses these frame drums to function as *ketuk* and *gong.*

Because Islam came to Indonesia through Sufism, it blended easily with the local religion and culture. Indigenous Javanese (Hindu) artistic traditions were adopted by Islam, and were transformed to include Islamic symbolic teaching. Shadow plays, gamelans, and other forms of art are traditionally believed to be the creation of the nine Islamic saints, who invented them to help spread Islam (Ricklefs 1981). The *gamelan sekati,* which does not sound at all like West Asian music, is considered the most Islamic (see the discussion of *gamelan sekati* in "Central and East Java," above). This type of gamelan is still played in the court compounds only for the celebration of Muhammad's birthday (at Kanoman) and major Islamic holidays, Idul-fitri and Idul-'adha (at Kasepuhan). Even though the shadow-puppet theater (*wayang kulit*) is forbidden by fundamentalist Muslims, some people still believe that by understanding the philosophical symbols found in a box of puppets, one can learn as much of

Islam as by reading the Qur'ān. Even the monster play (*berokan*) and the *ronggeng* (professional female dancer-singer, often associated with prostitution) are believed to embody elements of Islamic philosophy (Sutton 1989) [see WAVES OF CULTURAL INFLUENCE: Islam].

Islamic fundamentalism, however, has grown since the 1800s, as direct contact with West Asia has become more accessible through pilgrimages, Islamic universities (which include the study of Arabic), publications, and other mass media, such as radio, television, and especially the cassette industry. In most parts of Java, every neighborhood has several mosques, whence, through raised loudspeakers, one can hear Qur'ānic recitation and the call to prayer five times daily—all in a West Asian melodic style.

Contexts involving musical performance

Traditional Cirebonese music is rarely performed in concert halls. Indonesia does, however, support several concert halls, which are concentrated in the large cities (for example, Jakarta and Surabaya), and are normally reserved for Western or classical music. Though in the late twentieth century some regional music schools have arisen, the most common setting for learning music is still in the actual performances (Suanda 1986). Performances are associated with one or more kinds of individual or communal ceremonies. Except ceremonies in villages and courts, performances occur on a temporary stage built in the yard or on the street in front of the house of the person who commissioned them.

The function of the arts is still closely connected to village rituals involving initiation, rice, the sea, and ancestors. Though most artists are not farmers, they not only know much about farming, but in many ways are responsible for its ritual process. Farming rice, the primary and most spiritualized crop, and initiations are the best examples of how traditional performing arts are intrinsic to the entire cultural, spiritual, and ecological setting. Annual village rituals vary from one village to another, but most villages have five annual ceremonies: *sidekah bumi, ngunjung, kasinoman, mapag tamba,* and *mapag Sri.* Another ceremony, *nadran,* is for fishermen in the coastal villages.

The *sidekah bumi* 'earth blessing' is held before the farmers start working in the fields, usually in the months of September through December, as a blessing or offering to the earth, appealing for good luck in the next rice planting. The *ngunjung,* a ceremony of thanksgiving, is offered to the ancestral spirits and performed at the graveyard of the village founder or a powerful religious figure, to thank God for a good harvest, and to hope for better ones. *Ngunjung* is often held at the same time as *sidekah bumi. Kasinoman* 'youth', in some areas called *ngarot,* is a ritual party for the young people, for their work contributes to the success of their parents' rice fields; it may also be a ceremony for boys to court girls.

Mapag tamba 'picking up the remedy' is the ceremony after the planting and weeding of the rice field, around January and February. In it, celebrants pick up holy water from a sacred place (usually one of the palaces in Cirebon, or from the graveyard of the king, Sunan Gunung Jati) to be spread out in people's rice fields as a treatment against rice-specific disease. The *mapag Sri* 'welcoming Sri' is held before harvesttime, around March and April, to celebrate the coming of the goddess of rice, Dewi Sri. In the *nadran* or *pesta laut* (sea ceremony), celebrating or honoring the god of the sea or the god of fish, fishermen thank God and pray for better luck. Another ceremony that is performed less and less is the communal exorcism (*baritan* or *barikan*), held at a crossroads, in a graveyard, or in the middle of a rice field.

For all these ceremonies, all kinds of groups perform predominantly theatrical genres, such as *wayang kulit* 'shadow-puppet theater', *wayang golèk* 'rod-puppet the-

FIGURE 22 Masked dance is an important part of the *kasinoman* ceremony. Photo by Endo Suanda.

ater', and *wayang topèng* 'masked-dance theater' (Foley 1984, 1986, 1990; Rogers-Aguiniga 1986; Suanda 1986, 1988). For *sidekah bumi, mapag Sri,* and *nadran,* special shadow-puppet stories must be performed: Bumi Loka, Sri-Sadana, and Budug Basu, respectively. For *kasinoman* (figure 22), groups perform the masked dance *tayuban* or the social dance *ketuk telu* or *dangdut,* Indonesia's pop of the late twentieth century (Hatch 1985; Yampolsky 1989). *Ngunjung,* usually the most exciting event, involves a great parade by most of the villagers and performances by several groups. The biggest ceremonies are held in the villages of Trusmi and Astana, which have the graves of the founders of the city and kingdom of Cirebon. In these villages, tens of thousands of people from all over the Cirebon and Indramayu regions may be involved in the parade, with all kinds of artistic, allegorical, or symbolic performances. Dozens of artistic groups perform for several nights in the graveyards. Their performances are offerings to their ancestors, with the hope of good luck and the maintenance or increase of their social popularity.

The most frequent events involving music, however, are weddings and circumcisions, making up about 60 percent of all such events. The remainder are for other types of life-cycle ceremonies, such as the seventh month of pregnancy (as in several other areas of Indonesia), exorcism (*ruwatan*), execution of a vow or oath when one recovers from illness or has good luck (often held with weddings and circumcisions), the artists' *buka panggung* (opening of the stage), *atur-atur* ('esteem' from the artists to ancestors), independence-day celebrations, street performances (*babarang,* for *sintren* and *topèng* groups), and festivals. Therefore, the villages, not the courts or the cities, are the center of traditional Cirebonese performances.

Musical systems

Like other parts of Java, Cirebon has musical forms that can be categorized into gamelans and other ensembles.

Gamelans

Cirebon has several types of gamelan, more in the tradition of the folk than that of the courts. Like shadow-puppet theater, the gamelans' refinement and sophistication have less to do with patronage than with professionalism and the family system. Cirebonese artists are exclusively professionals.

gamelan prawa A *sléndro* ensemble used to accompany wayang (puppet theater) and *topèng* (masked dance)

gamelan pélog A *pélog* ensemble used to accompany *tayuban* dance

FIGURE 23 Several musicians perform on the *gamelan rénténg*, a Cirebonese (and Sundanese) village ensemble. Photo by Endo Suanda.

Court gamelans

All the court gamelans are similar in that all have a one-row gong chime (*bonang*) like the Balinese *réyong* and *trompong*, as opposed to the two-row *bonang* of the modern Javanese gamelan. Furthermore, they are all in *pélog*-like tuning, and musically refrain from developing or changing to suit modern tastes. The exclusive court gamelan are the *gamelan sekati* (also *gamelan sukati*) and the *gamelan denggung*. The former is found in both the Kasepuhan and Kanoman courts. In Kanoman, as in other Javanese courts, this gamelan is played only for Mulud, Muhammad's birthday; but in Kasepuhan it is played on Idul-fitri (the holiday following Ramadan) and Idul-'adha (the traditional pilgrims' holiday).

The older *gamelan denggung*—perhaps three centuries old or older, and found in the Kasepuhan court but no longer played—resembles the Sundanese *gamelan degung* of today (see below). This means that it could be originally from Sunda (North 1988), or conversely, that the Sundanese *degung* ensemble originated in Cirebon. Regarding the one at the court of Kacirebonan, now rarely played, only one piece (*lagu*) is known, entitled "*Lagu Denggung*" and performed to make rain. The other court gamelan is the *gamelan balé bandung*, basically the same as the *gamelan rénténg*, a village ensemble also found in parts of Sunda (figure 23).

FIGURE 24 Ibu Sawitri, an elderly dancer from Cirebon, performs the premasking section of a *wayang topèng* dance. Photo by Sean Williams, 1988.

Modern gamelans

Most widely used, the modern gamelan clearly exhibits not only musical theory, tuning, modal, and compositional systems, but also the relationship between music and cultural settings, both traditional and modern. As in most parts of Java and Bali, music is rooted in two systems of tuning, *pélog* and *sléndro*. Hood (1972) calls these systems the deep structure of Javanese and Balinese music.

Cirebon has two kinds of modern gamelan: *gamelan prawa* and *gamelan pélog*. *Prawa* is basically a high-pitched *sléndro*. Compared with Sundanese *saléndro* and Javanese *sléndro*, it may be one or two keys (150 to 400 cents) higher. The two are never combined to create one set having both *pélog* and *prawa*, as in Javanese gamelan. Those that have both sets, as in the courts, are kept separate, and their functions differ. The *gamelan prawa* accompanies *wayang topèng* (figure 24), and *gamelan pélog* accompanies *tayuban*; however, the *gamelan pélog* is now more and more widely used for both *wayang* and *topeng*, especially in the southern part of Cirebon.

The composition of instruments in either ensemble is similar. A complete set of *gamelan prawa* for *wayang* accompaniment consists of these:

Two sets of *saron*, medium-pitched metallophones, seven to nine keys each
Titil, high-pitched metallophones, eight to eleven keys
Gendèr, metallophones with individual resonator tubes, ten or eleven keys
Bonang, gong-chimes, twelve keys or pots, usually played by two people facing each other
Kenong, large horizontal kettle-gongs, five pots
Jenglong, five pots, one octave lower than *kenong*
Ketuk and *kebluk*, small and large kettle-gongs
Klènang, a pair of *bonang*-size kettles
Kemanak, buffalo-ear-shaped concussion idiophones
Bèri, round metal rattles; *gambang*, xylophones, sixteen to eighteen keys

The *genjring* ensemble includes four or more frame drums, which play interlocking rhythms. The vocal parts are mostly in Arabic, especially when the *genjring* accompanies the *rudat,* a devotional dance performed in a mosque.

FIGURE 25 The *gamelan prawa* ensemble is played as dozens of children look on. Photo by Endo Suanda.

Suling, end-blown bamboo flute
A set of *kendang,* large *kendang ged* and two small drums, *ketipung*; *bedug,* large double-headed barrel drum
A set of three hanging gongs, *kiwul* (smallest), *gong sabet* (midsized), and *gong ageng* (largest) (figure 25).

The *pélog* set has nearly the same instruments, except that most *gamelan pélog* have an additional, high-pitched set of *bonang* (called *kemyang*), while few *gamelan prawa* have it (figure 26). *Gamelan pélog* also includes the *suling miring,* a side-blown bamboo flute with a vibrating membrane. The melodic instruments use more keys than those in the *prawa* set. A unique feature of *pélog* tuning is that for some of the metallophones and the *gambang,* not all the keys are arranged in their cases. In *patut sepuluh* mode, for example, the *bungur* and *barang* keys are placed at the side of the rack, or even on the floor. When the *patut* changes, the key arrangement changes. No *gamelan pélog* ensemble has *gendér* because a *gendér* does not have easily removable keys.

The individual pitches of *prawa* and *pélog* are indicated in figure 27, with comparison to Sundanese and Javanese. None of these systems is compatible with those of Western diatonic scales, but the diatonic tones are included for a rough comparison. The Sundanese and Javanese pitches vary considerably. Their names are important because gamelan music has clear modal systems, *patut.* Understanding *patut*

FIGURE 26 The extra set of high-pitched *bonang* is one of the features that distinguish *gamelan pélog* from *gamelan prawa;* the difference in tuning is another. Photo by Endo Suanda.

(Javanese *pathet)* can be one of the most complicated issues in gamelan musical systems, but several studies by Javanese gamelan scholars (Hastanto 1985; Hood 1954) have shown that, in principle, *patut* can translate into 'mode' or 'key' in Western music. The change of *patut* can mean the change of the level and hierarchical relationship of pitches and the change of mode or scale—that is, intervallic structure.

In *prawa*, where intervals are more or less equidistant, the scales of all five *patut* are virtually identical, but in *pélog*, the *patut* is much more complicated. Though *pélog* has seven tones, in each *patut* there are only five main tones. If in *prawa* there are only five *patut,* since there are only five keys, in *pélog* there are many more than seven *patut,* as shown in figure 27, where IV in each *patut* is the gong, or strongest tone, and becomes the name of the *patut*; I, its fifth; II, the second "gong" tone; III and V, the "weakest" tones.

A piece named "*Barlen,*" for example, can be performed in all the *patut* above by changing the pitch hierarchy without changing the name of the piece (as happens in Sunda). Unlike in Java or Sunda, in Cirebon there are *prawa*-like scales in the *pélog*

FIGURE 27 Tunings of Cirebonese *prawa* and pélog, Sundanese *saléndro* and *pélog*, and Javanese *sléndro* and *pélog*, with tempered tones for comparison.

Cirebonese	*Western*	*Sundanese*	*Javanese*
prawa:	(approximate)	*saléndro:*	*sléndro:*
laras 'tone'	(A)	*barang*	*nem* 'six'
miring 'tilted'	(B)	*loloran*	*lima* 'five'
sanga 'nine'	(F#)	*panelu* 'third'	*dada* 'chest'
sepuluh 'ten'	(E)	*bem/galimer*	*gulu* 'neck'
panjang 'long'	(D)	*singgul*	*penunggul*
pélog:	[Western]	*pélog:*	*pélog:*
laras 'tone'	(A#)	*barang*	*nem* 'six'
miring 'tilted'	(A)	*loloran*	*lima* 'five'
bungur	(G)	*liwung/bungur*	*pélog*
sanga 'nine'	(F)	*panelu* 'third'	*dada* 'chest'
sepuluh 'ten'	(D#)	*bem/galimer*	*gulu* 'neck'
blong	(D)	*singgul*	*penunggul*
barang 'thing'	(C)	*sorog*	*barang*

FIGURE 28 *Patut* in *prawa* and *pélog.*

Patut* in *prawa:

laras	*miring*	*sanga*	*sepuluh*	*panjang*	*Patut* name
I	II	III	IV	V	*sepuluh*
V	I	II	III	IV	*panjang*
II	III	IV	V	I	*sanga*
IV	V	I	II	III	*laras*
III	IV	V	I	II	*miring*

Patut* in *pélog:

barang	*laras*	*miring*	*bungur*	*sanga*	*sepuluh*	*blong*	*Patut* name
	I	II		III	IV	V	*sepuluh*
	V	I		II	III	IV	*blong*
	V	I	II		III	IV	*blong-bungur*
	I	II	III		IV	V	*sepuluh-bungur*
	IV	V		I	II	III	*laras*
III	IV		V	I	II		*laras-prawa*
I	II		III	IV		V	*sanga-prawa*
I		II	III	IV		V	*san-pra/miring*
IV	V		I	II		III	*barang* (with *blong*)
II	III		IV	V		I	*bungur*
IV		V	I	II	III		*barang*
II		III	IV	V		I	*bungur/Nylendro*
	III	IV		V	I	II	*miring*

set (see the *patut* "*Laras-Prawa*" and "*Sanga-Prawa*" in the *pélog* chart of figure 28). The singing would be in a "true" *prawa* scale, but the instruments would be in *pélog prawa,* a *pélog* scale that resembles *prawa,* causing slight differences between the two.

Gamelan pieces are cyclic. A large gong marks the ending of each cycle, and other gongs and kettle pots outline the form in a colotomic or punctuating manner. Form is determined by the colotomic instruments and the drums, and the piece adheres to the form. However, one piece may include one or more gong cycles, and one cycle may be subdivided in a variety of ways. In gamelan, a piece is almost always performed repetitively, though it is never repeated in exactly the same way. The composition might also be a suite consisting of several pieces (*lagu*). The piece is divided into smaller units or phrases by *kenong* strokes. The most common piece is in the *renggong* form, which has four *kenong* and five *kiwul* strokes in one cycle, precisely as in the Sundanese gamelan tradition.

Figure 29 shows this structure with other colotomic instruments (nonmelodic ones or those that mark time). In performance, this piece can be played in many different tempos. Doubling in density when slower, and halving in density when faster, are common practices, not only in almost all Indonesian gamelan playing, but also in the mainland Southeast Asian gong ensembles (J. Becker 1980). Therefore, one *kenong* phrase above, for example, could be expanded from two to four, or eight, or sixteen, or thirty-two beats of the *saron.* Changes in density and tempo are among the important aesthetic elements in the playing of gamelans.

Other compositional forms include some irregular *kenong* structures. One stroke of a gong may cover two, three, four, six, eight, ten, twelve, sixteen, or thirty-two *kenong.* Those with fewer than eight in one gong are categorized as small pieces (*lagu alit* or *lagu cilik*); others are categorized as large pieces (*lagu ageng* or *lagu gedé*). A unique piece, *lagu Tratagan,* has three or four gong notes, with two, three, and four *kenong* in one gong cycle (see examples in Wright 1978).

FIGURE 29 The *renggong* form and its colotomic patterns.

kenong (N) :	. . . N . . . N . . . N . . . N
kiwul (W), *gong* (G) :	. W . . . W . . . W . W . W . G
ketuk (t), *kabluk* (b) :	tbt.tbt.tbt.tbt.tbt.tbt.tbt.tbt.
kemanak, low/L, high/H :	L H L H L H L H L H L H L H L H
klénang, low/l, high/h :	lhlhlhlhlhlhlhlhlhlhlhlhlhlhlhlh
béri (x) :	. x . x . x . x . x . x . x . x

Other ensembles

Other ensembles of Cirebon are small groups of six or fewer instruments. The frame-drum ensemble, under a variety of names, is widespread. The *genjring* ensemble includes four or more frame drums, which play interlocking rhythms ornamented by strong strokes on a *bedug. Genjring* drums (figure 30) have three pairs of metal rattles attached to them (*genjring* is onomatopoeic, *jring* being the sound of drum and the rattle), and play loud, exciting music. The vocal parts are mostly in Arabic, especially when the *genjring* accompanies the *rudat,* a devotional dance performed in a mosque. But in the *sidapurna,* an acrobatic show, the text is mixed with local poems in the Cirebonese dialect.

The other frame drums (*gembyung* and *brai*) are usually larger than the *genjring,* and they lack metal attachments, so they sound softer and lower, and utilize less variation in rhythm. Responsorial singing—a solo leader and a chorus (*jawab* 'answer')—is more prominent than the playing drums. Until the 1950s, most mosques had some kind of ensemble. Now only a few retain any instruments, and few of them are playable. The mosque in Astana (next to the graveyard of Sunan Gunung Jati) has an ensemble that is played at least once a year during the *sidekah bumi* (and *nadran*) ceremony by a group from Bayalangu Village. Another common performance setting for this ensemble is in the mosque, at Mulud, and also around rituals relating to birth, such as the seventh month of pregnancy and name-giving ceremonies. The text is from Arabic, but most of the melodies are in *sléndro.* Even so, the melody would easily be recognized as an Islamic one by people all over Java.

The music of *brai* (from *birai, birahi* 'love') from Bayalangu, though not associated with ensembles in mosques, mostly consists of the responsorial or antiphonal singing of prayers (*dikir*) using the Qur'ānic phrase of *la illaha ilallah Muhammad* [*u*]

FIGURE 30 The onomatopoeic *genjring* frame drums (background) provide a ringing accompaniment to the *bedug.* Photo by Endo Suanda.

ketuk tilu Cirebonese small village ensemble
dangdut Hindi film-influenced popular music
angklung Tuned, shaken bamboo rattles
sintren Cirebonese ensemble of stamping tubes and pots

rasulullah, mixed with the Cirebonese language. The group is more a devotional sect than a performing ensemble. They still regularly perform about fifteen times altogether for their own annual rituals, which mostly occur in cemeteries. The group consists more of women than men; there are two solo leaders, one male and one female. These traits all reflect the strong Sufistic root in Cirebonese musical traditions.

Trebang randu kentir is unique to the Indramayu region. Though it has two *trebang* (the smaller functioning as *ketuk,* and the larger as a gong), and though artists believe it was created by one of the nine famous Islamic saints, it is not associated with mosque music. Instead, it is more like *topèng* but without melodic instruments, and is also used to accompany nonmasked dance resembling *topèng.*

Ketuk telu 'three *ketuk*', another small ensemble, resembles Sundanese *ketuk tilu* (see below), but it incorporates Cirebonese songs. The *ketuk* is a horizontal kettle-gong in a wooden frame; three of them form the centerpiece of a *ketuk tilu* ensemble. In Sunda, the *ketuk tilu* in its traditional setting is practically obsolete; in Cirebon, there are still a few ensembles, often performing at the *kasinoman* or *ngarot* ceremony in Indramayu. Today, however, the ensemble also presents traditional pop (*pop Sunda* or *pop Cirebonan*), including *dangdut* and modern music resembling *tarling,* a light form of pop using guitar and *suling.* The current ensemble includes an electric guitar, violin, a pair of gongs, a pair of *klènang,* three *ketuk,* and a set of *kendang,* all of which accompany dancing female vocalists and male instrumentalist-singers (figure 31).

FIGURE 31 Dancing vocalists perform with male audience members. Photo by Endo Suanda.

Bamboo musical instruments (*angklung* and *calung*), single-headed drums (*dog-dog*), zither (*kacapi*), and bowed lutes (rebab or *tarawangsa*), though widespread in Sunda, are seldom found in Cirebon. The *angklung* ensemble of shaken bamboo rattles is found only in the village of Bungko, where it still performs in village rituals. The *dog-dog* is found only in a few areas, and the *kacapi* and *tarawangsa* or rebab are not found at all. The rebab, sometimes played in court gamelans, is usually imported from Kuningan, a Sundanese-speaking region, as is its player.

Sintren, another small ensemble, is popular in Cirebon and Indramayu. Its special feature is to use earthenware and bamboo musical instruments. Two ceramic pots, each covered by a rubber membrane made from the inner tube of a tire, are tuned differently (with different tension or sizes) and played as drums. Two other small bamboo tubes for stamping, tuned about a minor third apart and called *ting-tung,* are played as keepers of the beat, like *ketuk,* and a big tube for stamping or large ceramic pot serves as a gong. This ensemble accompanies choral singing in a semi-magical performance, the *sintren* calling the goddess Dewi Sri to enable a bound girl to untie and dress herself inside a covered cage for roosters (Ardiwijaya 1978; Foley 1985).

New developments

The city of Cirebon has no significant Western-style musical bands (such as Indonesian bands that play rock or jazz), for most such groups prefer to live in bigger cities, like Bandung or Jakarta. However, many *dangdut* bands throughout the Cirebon regions often combine with modern *tarling* (Wright 1988). Indeed, they are often named *tarling dangdut,* and are found even in small towns.

The large groups, popular and therefore wealthy, may also have electric guitars (playing melody and bass), synthesizer, set of drums, tambourine, flute, and violin, along with the traditional *suling, kendang,* gongs, *ketuk-kebluk,* and *kecrèk.* Many have powerful outdoor sound systems, with dozens of microphones and two large walls of speakers. Abdul Ajib's *tarling,* one of the top groups, often comes to the stage with a truck-mounted satellite antenna. The group presents foreign television programs to attract people's attention before the performance, instead of the traditional instrumental introductory section (*talu*).

The influence of urban (and Western) musical culture on the average Cirebonese village, therefore, comes, not from the city of Cirebon, but from Jakarta and Bandung, both for live performances and especially for radio and television broadcasting and cassettes. *Pop Sunda,* heavily broadcast on Bandung television stations, deeply influences young village artists and results in Cirebonese pop music. The arrangement of Bandung's *gamelan wanda anyar* 'fresh-breeze gamelan', pioneered by the late Mang Koko Koswara and further developed by Nano Suratno and other Bandung Conservatory graduates, is now being adopted by Cirebonese gamelans.

The most significant Sundanese musical influence on Cirebon is the *jaipongan* style of drumming. Because the old drummers have neither the energy nor the dexterity to perform in its style, they have all now retired from drumming to play other instruments. Therefore, if in earlier times the *wayang kulit* drummers were always the more senior musicians, now all of the groups have young drummers (in their teens or early twenties). The drums themselves have changed in shape from conical to barrel-shaped drums, complete with loops for toes to manipulate the lower pitch of the biggest drumhead, as in Sundanese drumming. These drummers maintain Cirebonese traits of drumming generally, but the overall sound of the drums differs from that of the early 1980s.

Another recent phenomenon is that the older, extended gamelan pieces are beginning to disappear. One reason for this is shrinking time for performance; anoth-

FIGURE 32 Local drums, a blown bamboo "gong" (right), and *bonang* (lower left) blend with a Chinese *sona* (left) to create a unique outdoor sound. Photo by Endo Suanda.

er is the growing tendency among Cirebonese audiences to pay attention only to the voice of the female singer (*sindén*). Finally, most young drummers are unable to lead the ensemble in the performance of complicated pieces.

Nevertheless, the influences between modern and traditional music seem to go both ways: traditional groups are adopting urban styles (including Westernization), while urban groups are adopting local and village repertoires. In addition, some musical blending between Chinese and local styles occurs (figure 32). Gamelan groups are incorporating diatonic melodies, notably from *dangdut* (when melodic instruments cannot follow the vocal melodies, they become nonmelodic instruments or simply cease playing), and a few gamelans have started using violin (*biola*). However, it is popular for modern Indonesian bands that play rock to adopt traditional repertoires and instruments. Even the *sintren* melodies have been discotized and dangdutized, and several volumes of cassettes have been released.

The impact of the Akademi Seni Tari Indonesia, or ASTI (the music, dance, and theater academy) of Bandung is becoming obvious, especially in elite, urban society. Pring Gading, a troupe led by Handoyo, who trained at ASTI in Bandung and at Bagong Kusudiardjo's school in Yogyakarta, has produced colossal new dance-dramas (involving up to three hundred artists), performed at a new open-air stage in Cirebon, on stage in Jakarta, and on the national television station in Jakarta. These productions, and several other neotraditional art performances, were sponsored by a new social association—Yayasan Sunyaragi, formed by wealthy élite Cirebonese living in the cities of Cirebon, Bandung, and Jakarta—eager to revive Cirebon's cultural identity.

Graduates of national performing arts academies in Bandung and Surakarta are increasing. Some come from the families of professional artists, who formerly seldom went beyond elementary school. In fact, the Sekolah Menengah Karawitan Indonesia (SMKI), a high school for the performing arts, was founded in 1991 at the Kasepuhan court center. Systems of notation, other musical traditions, and new compositional approaches are taught by outsider (mostly ASTI graduates from Sundanese regions). This will unquestionably contribute to narrowing the gap between village and urban music, and among Cirebonese, Sundanese, and other styles of Indonesian music. In terms of the regeneration of traditional arts, however, so far there does not appear to be a problem, since there are still many young musicians and puppeteers throughout Cirebon. Among traditional artist families, more than 80 percent of their descendants become artists who realize more than 90 percent of the village performances.

SUNDA

The Sundanese, numbering approximately 30 million people, are Indonesia's second largest ethnic group. They live in the province of West Java (often called Sunda by foreigners), encompassing the interior highlands, the coastal areas, and Cirebon, a culturally distinct region. The boundary between West and Central Java lies at the eastern foothills of the Priangan Highlands, and a wide band of west-central Java from north to south incorporates cultural elements from both West and Central Java.

Until the late 1800s, West Java was sparsely populated. Bandung, the provincial capital, one of the largest cities in Indonesia and a major industrial center, is the home of several important educational institutions. Most Sundanese live within the provincial boundaries; some commute to Jakarta for work. Rural areas of West Java are intensively cultivated with rice, coffee, tea, and other crops. The presence of active volcanoes contributes to the fertility of local soil.

Those who consider themselves ethnically and politically Sundanese speak Basa Sunda, which incorporates words from English, Dutch, Javanese, Betawi (Jakarta's dialect), and other languages. Related to both Javanese and Balinese, Sundanese uses five levels of speech, depending on the status of the speaker(s) and auditor(s). Most Sundanese music includes vocalists, and the language used for songs falls within specific levels, affecting the relative status of the genre.

Most Sundanese are Muslims. Though considered conservative in their faith, they have a broad definition of what constitutes being a Muslim, and they often combine their concepts of Islam with traditional animist beliefs. The Hindu-Buddhist tradition, prevalent in the culture of Central and East Java, is less apparent in Sunda. Sunda has its own history of Hindu-Buddhist influence, but what has remained since the entry of Islam is limited to certain mystic practices, isolated religious sites or statues, and aspects of Sundanese status divisions (Wessing 1978). When Hindu-Buddhist elements appear in the Sundanese performing arts, their presence is often acknowledged as being the result of influence from Central Java.

Though several small kingdoms rose and fell before the 1300s, none was significant in relation to political powers outside of Sunda. In 1333, the kingdom of Pajajaran was founded at Pakuan, near what is now the city of Bogor. The era of Pajajaran represents the Sundanese at their most politically powerful in relation to other Javanese kingdoms. It is considered their most important historical and cultural period. Pajajaran was a pre-Islamic trading kingdom in competition with the East Javanese kingdom of Majapahit (A.D. 1293–1530). The area under the control of Pajajaran did not include the Islamized coastal areas of North Java, and its weakness was that it did not fully control the ports through which its commerce passed. In 1579, when the Sultan of Banten had the royal family killed, Pajajaran disappeared. As an important symbol of Sundanese identity, it features frequently in songs and stories.

After the fall of Pajajaran, the entire area of Sunda was subject to annexation by Mataram, an Islamic Central Javanese kingdom. By the mid-1600s, Sunda was under the administration of Central Javanese regents, responsible for the importation of Central Javanese cultural traits that continue to influence the upper levels of Sundanese culture: batik, gamelan music, dance, sung poetry, and wayang (Heins

The Sundanese use the term *khas Sunda*—that which is characteristically Sundanese—to refer to important regional traits in music, dance, cuisine, clothing, and other aspects of Sundanese culture.

1977). Because of the dispersal of the local population, however, the cultural influence from Central Java among villagers was minimal, and Sundanese musical traditions continued largely unchanged.

In 1677, Mataram relinquished its Sundanese territorial claim to the Dutch East India Company, which then profited from Sundanese cash crops, including coffee and tea. The colonialists expelled the Central Javanese regents from Sunda and replaced them with Sundanese nobles, who, though they answered to Dutch administrators, grew wealthy, and their patronage of the performing arts reached its height during this period. After 1864, the Dutch developed the city of Bandung as the colonial administrative center, and it remains the administrative heart of Sunda.

Sunda is divided into regencies (*kabupaten*), further subdivided into multiple *kacamatan, kalurahan,* and villages (*desa*), the smallest political units. A large bureaucratic structure supports these subdivisions, and the entire province is overseen by the provincial government. The Sundanese are the main ethnic group in West Java, but many Javanese, Chinese, Batak, Minang, Balinese, Ambonese, and other Indonesian peoples live there too, particularly in Bandung and in "Jabotabek" (Jakarta-Bogor-Tangerang-Bekasi), the area surrounding the capital. Foreign nationals in West Java number in the thousands, particularly in the larger cities, including Bandung and Bogor.

When the Sundanese refer to their performing arts, they are careful to describe what they call *khas Sunda* 'that which is characteristically Sundanese'—a designation that bears a sense of regional identity. A musical genre may be performed all over West Java, but regional variations in style, context, and instrumentation may inspire the localized terms *Garutan, Cirebonan,* or *Sumedangan* (referring to performance in the styles of Garut, Cirebon, or Sumedang, respectively). This continually shifting concept extends beyond the performing arts to many features of Sundanese culture, including cuisine, plants, clothing, architecture, human physical traits, geographical features, and literature.

The variety of Sundanese performing arts precludes a detailed examination of clothing; however, generalizations may be made. In traditional genres not associated with village life (such as court-derived gamelans), performers wear clothing that duplicates what is worn by the aristocracy. Women wear a tightly fitted, long-sleeved, front-closing blouse (*kabaya*) and a wrapped batik *kain* (a single piece of cloth, pulled tightly around the hips and extending to the floor). Men wear a front-pleated batik *sarung* (a vertical tube of cloth, tied around the waist) and a type of morning coat (*takwah*) with a tied batik cap (*bendo*). Both male and female outfits, originally derived from Central Javanese formal wear, are considered appropriate Sundanese formal wear. Village performances are considerably less formal: though women may still wear *kabaya* and *kain,* the latter are usually shorter and looser. Men may wear loose black pants and shirts, or a basic plaid *sarung,* a T-shirt, and a black cap (*peci*), usually worn by devout male Muslims. Costumes are specific to each dance.

The state of musical research

The literature available in English on Sundanese music was sparse until the 1970s and 1980s. Before then, the bulk of musicological attention had been focused on the music of Central Java and Bali. Sundanese scholars have researched many aspects of modern and early Sundanese music and published their findings in both Indonesian and Sundanese. These works have been a boon to foreign researchers with a grasp of either language. Of works in English, Jaap Kunst's *Music in Java* (1973 [1934]) is the most widely known early publication that includes a section on Sundanese music; however, much of its information is out of date, and is not set in context. Though many Japanese researchers have conducted fieldwork in Sunda, few have published in English.

Recent research has resulted in the production of English-language sources on Sundanese music and culture. Among them are Baier 1986 (*angklung*), Falk 1982 (*tarawangsa*), Foley 1979 (*wayang golèk*), Harrell 1974 (*gamelan degung*), Heins 1977 (gamelans), Kartomi 1973a (*macapat*), Van Zanten 1989 (*tembang Sunda*), Weintraub 1990 and 1997 (*pantun* and *wayang golek*), and Williams 1990 (*tembang Sunda*). Useful articles have appeared in *Asian Music, Balungan, Ethnomusicology, The New Grove,* and *Selected Reports in Ethnomusicology.*

Sundanese and other Indonesian researchers have developed a body of information on the Sundanese performing arts, but these works are limited to those who read the language. Research in progress includes doctoral dissertations on Sundanese and Cirebonese wayang and Sundanese mainstream gamelan traditions, but foreign researchers have ignored large areas of the Sundanese performing arts. Rapid change in the organization of ensembles and the emphasis on creative adaptation in Sunda call for more research on composition.

Little village music has been studied by outsiders. Lively genres, such as traditions using the ocarina (*taleot*), Jew's harp (*karinding*), and side-blown bamboo flute (*bangsing*), have yet to be examined; and unaccompanied vocal musics, such as Islamic verses (*cigawiran*), ritual choral singing (*beluk*), and folk songs (*lagu rakyat*), are rarely studied by academics. Important areas of musical accompaniment—for hobbyhorse trance-dance performance (*kuda renggong*), circumcision-associated lion dance (*sisinggaan*), exhibitional trance-related performance (*seni debus*), and Islamic Sundanese music (including *terbang* and *bedug* traditions)—have yet to be studied in depth. Any of the area-specific genres would yield rich resources for future study.

The structures of Sundanese music

A large proportion of Sundanese music is performed on gamelans, sets of bronze or iron instruments supported by carved wooden racks. A Sundanese gamelan usually consists of a core group of metallophones (*saron*), horizontal gong-chime sets (*bonang*), vertically suspended gongs (*go'ong*), and a set of barrel drums (*kendang*). Other features, including xylophones, aerophones (flutes or oboes), a bowed lute, and vocalists, are included according to the type of ensemble.

Pieces for gamelan are normally organized in cycles, with the ending of each cycle marked by the low pitch of the *go'ong.* These cycles may be played many times in a single piece. The drummer demarcates the cycle by outlining specific patterns; he also acts as the timekeeper, coordinator, and controller of dynamics. With specific patterns, he outlines dancers' movements. Most cycles include some type of periodic punctuation, performed by the large and small gongs. Each piece derives from a primary structural outline of tones (*patokan*), which determines which pitch of the colotomic instruments is played and the duration of each cycle. A single *patokan* may serve as the structural outline for a large number of melodies; therefore, Sundanese melodies outnumber Sundanese *patokan.* The melodic repertoire in Sundanese music may be shared by a variety of genres; it is not limited to specific types of instruments.

The relative density of a cyclic piece (*wilet*) resembles the Javanese concept of *irama.* It occurs in measurements of half, single, double or quadruple, and is a means of determining the overall structure of a piece. The *wilet* indicates how frequently the *go'ong* stroke occurs and how densely the piece is ornamented. In general, the smaller the *wilet,* the lesser the ornamental density. A piece in half *wilet* (*satengah wilet*) will include a compact structural outline with little room for expansive melodic improvisation, whereas a piece in double *wilet* (*dua wilet*) may be four times as dense in ornamentation. Pieces in double or quadruple *wilet* usually sound slow because the colotomic instruments are spaced further apart; these densities are believed to be more musically challenging because of the degree of improvisation they require.

Sundanese music uses three main systems of tuning (*surupan*), called *pélog, sorog* (in gamelan, *madenda*), and *saléndro. Pélog,* in turn, appears in two forms: the five-tone *pélog degung* (used for *gamelan degung* and *kacapi*-based genres) and *pélog jawar,* a seven-tone *surupan,* based on Javanese *pélog.* Sundanese musical theory shares some terms with Javanese theory, but Sundanese *pélog* does not correspond at all to Javanese *pélog*; it refers to a special pentatonic *surupan,* played on *gamelan degung* and several other ensembles. Each Sundanese system of tuning uses five tones, numbered and named in relation to each other. Each system has a unique set of tonal hierarchies that differ from piece to piece.

In figure 33, the original names of the tones of each scale are listed left to right in order from lowest to highest. These older names are used by most traditional musicians. The second line lists the Sundanese tonal numbers, often used by conservatory students. The third line lists the tonal pitches in the system of solfège developed early in the twentieth century by the Sundanese theorist Machyar Kusumadinata. The final three lines of the chart detail the approximate diatonic equivalents of the *pélog, sorog-madenda,* and *saléndro* scales, respectively (Van Zanten 1989).

Because each ensemble differs slightly from the others in tuning, these tunings are always relative. Performers of vocal parts, bowed lutes, and wind instruments commonly select tones from outside the system being used by the rest of the ensemble. For example, a vocalist performing in *sorog* may sing a tone from *saléndro* at an appropriate moment in the song. In addition, many songs in *sorog* tuning may be accompanied by an ensemble fixed in *saléndro* tuning. Certain compositions also deliberately use outside tones. Most ensembles are limited to a single system of tuning (most frequently, *saléndro*) because the pitches of the instruments are fixed, but a few, such as *tembang Sunda,* may change tunings during the course of a performance.

The Sundanese use a system of numerical notation that applies to tones in any tuning. This system is the reverse of the one used by the Javanese: from lowest to highest, the tones of Javanese *sléndro* are notated by the Javanese as 12356 (the numbering of some Javanese scales is nonsequential), whereas they are called 54321 by the Sundanese. This notation permeates Sundanese musical practice in that pitches of instruments of the lowest frequency are called high, and vocal ornaments that include a leap to a pitch of a higher frequency are indicated visually by a downward-moving

FIGURE 33 Sundanese systems of tuning. The caret (^) in *saléndro* indicates that the pitches are raised slightly.

barang	*kenon*	*panelu*	*galimer*	*singgul*	
hiji (1)	*dua* (2)	*tilu* (3)	*opat* (4)	*lima* (5)	
da	*mi*	*na*	*ti*	*la*	
F	E	C	B flat	A	[*pélog*]
F	E	D	B flat	A	[*sorog/madenda*]
F	D(^)	C	B flat	G(^)	[*saléndro*]

gesture of the hand or figure on the printed page. This usage dates from the development of modern Sundanese musical theory by Jaap Kunst and Kusumadinata (Kusumadinata 1969 and Kunst 1973 [1934]). The structure of written musical theory established by them is still followed in Sundanese music institutions, though Sundanese written theory now contrasts sharply with Sundanese practice (Weintraub 1993).

Genres and ensembles

More than two hundred types of performing arts exist in Sunda, but not many are performed more than a few times a year or beyond seasonal or ritual limitations. The Sundanese are strongly bound to the agricultural cycles and local conditions of where they live or were born—a tendency that has led to the development of dozens of area-specific genres. Some musical genres have spread from an original point of creation to other parts of Sunda, becoming part of the general Sundanese musical legacy. Many are labeled according to their instrumentation: for example, *kacapi-suling,* a combination of a boat-shaped zither (*kacapi*) and an end-blown bamboo flute (*suling*).

The genres and ensembles selected for discussion here have outlasted popular trends or have had a significant historical impact on the development of modern Sundanese music. The selected groups include gamelans, *ketuk tilu / jaipongan, kendang penca / rampak kendang,* bamboo ensembles, *pantun, tembang Sunda, kacapi-suling, kacapian,* music of the Baduy, and popular music. This selection describes a large percentage of the music regularly performed or recorded in Sunda. Vocal music is so pervasive in Sunda that a vocal category would include most of the common ensembles.

Gamelans

Gamelans in Sunda encompass a variety of types, from the ubiquitous five-tone *gamelan saléndro* to the rare seven-tone *gamelan pélog, gamelan ajeng,* and others. The history of gamelans in Sunda begins with their entry from the courts of Cirebon in the 1500s (Wright 1978). It continues with the importation of gamelans on the arrival of Javanese regents in the Priangan area in the 1600s. Gamelans were important to aristocratic households as symbols of power and prestige. The two most common types of gamelans in Sunda today are *gamelan saléndro* and *gamelan degung.* Both are named after their tunings, which in the case of *gamelan degung* refers to *pélog degung,* a special five-tone tuning.

Gamelan saléndro

Gamelan saléndro is used in several different musical contexts: instrumental performance, and as accompaniment for a solo female vocalist (*kliningan*), a dance, or the Sundanese three-dimensional rod-puppet theater (*wayang golek*). It sometimes accompanies drama (*sandiwara*), dance-drama (*sendratari*), and martial arts (*penca silat*).

Gamelan saléndro includes metallophones, gong chimes, gongs, drums, a bowed spiked lute, and a vocalist (figure 34). The basic rhythmic cycle is demarcated by the gongs—a large gong (*go'ong*), small gongs (*kempul*), and a row of large kettle-gongs (*kenong*). These instruments all play colotomic or punctuating patterns, determined by the *patokan.* This musical structure is tied together with a set of barrel-shaped, double-headed drums (*kendang*). Depending on the style, the drummer is responsible for tempo and dynamic changes, dance accompaniment, and special effects (such as explosive strokes to accompany martial-arts kicks).

The metallophones of *gamelan saléndro* are played in three octaves: two *saron* in the central octave play patterns based on the *patokan* (sometimes in interlocking pat-

Gamelan saléndro is likely to be heard at important social events—weddings, circumcisions, military or government occasions, store openings, ritual feasts, neighborhood celebrations, and musical rehearsals.

FIGURE 34 The *gamelan saléndro* ensemble of the Festival of Indonesia group from Bandung, West Java; Rina Oesman, Euis Komariah, and Dheniarsah Suratno, vocalists. Photo by Marc Perlman.

terns), a *panerus* plays selected pitches of the *patokan* an octave below the *saron,* and a *peking* plays a denser elaboration of the *saron* melody an octave above. A xylophone (*gambang*) densely elaborates the *saron* part. A pair of gong chimes (the low-pitched *bonang* and the high-pitched *rincik*) further elaborate the melody. The vocalist (*pasindén*) and the player of the bowed lute (rebab) are central to performances in that each carries a version of the melody (*lagu*).

The versatility of *gamelan saléndro* has led to its use in many areas of Sunda as the ensemble to be played in nearly any context. Because of the Sundanese belief that *saléndro* is a "parent" (an all-encompassing Sundanese tuning), *gamelan saléndro* may accompany songs in any of the other systems of tuning. It is likely to be heard at important social events—weddings, circumcisions, military or government occasions, store openings, ritual feasts (*hajat*), neighborhood celebrations, and musical rehearsals (*latihan*). A typical performance might include a mixture of songs accompanied by the ensemble (*kliningan*), instrumental music, and accompaniment of a variety of dances from classical (*klasik*) to modern (*moderèn*) and social dance (*jaipongan*).

When *gamelan saléndro* accompanies dancing, the relationship between the drummer and the rest of the ensemble changes. In the performance of instrumental pieces or vocal *kliningan,* the role of the drummer is that of timekeeper, density referent, and follower of the piece's structural outline, but in the accompaniment of dance, the drummer takes a more active role. The connection between the drummer and the dancer may supersede the relationship between the melody and the dancer. Though most Sundanese dances are performed to specific pieces, some dances may be performed to a variety of pieces. In general, the drummer is responsible for mirroring the character of the dance by matching the patterns of the drumming to the steps of the dancing.

Sundanese dance (Indonesian *tari*; high Sundanese *ibing*) appears in a variety of forms and at various social levels. Many classical dances once performed by the aristocracy originated among the Javanese and were brought to Sunda during the Javanese-regency period (1600s and 1700s). *Tari kursus* (from the Dutch, 'course' dance) is a refined social dance. It divides into four basic types of characters, said to represent different human traits. It was lifted from *tayuban* (another form of social dance) and taught in private courses to members of the aristocracy by Radén Sambas Wirakusumah—hence the name, *tari kursus.* Like most other dances, it is accompanied by *gamelan saléndro.*

Sundanese dance has also absorbed elements from Cirebon. Some Sundanese dancers maintain that most classical Sundanese dances derive from Central Java, but it is widely acknowledged that Sundanese masked dance (*tari topèng*) evolved in the last one hundred years as a result of influence from Cirebonese masked-dance traditions (North 1988). The famous mid-twentieth-century choreographer Cece Somantri created popular stage dances in classical style (for example, *tari merak,* the peacock dance) that have spread throughout Sunda, in both performing-arts groups and schools. Several of Sunda's most active choreographers in the twentieth century (including Cece Somantri, Nugraha Sudiredja, and Irawati Durban) have reworked some older dances and created entirely new ones based on older models. In Bandung, the presence of ASTI (Akademi Seni Tari Indonesia, the Indonesian Dance Academy) has led to the development and acceptance of many new dances.

Performances of rod-puppet theater are accompanied by a small, portable *gamelan saléndro.* This theater is not usually performed with dance; however, the puppets sometimes dance, and the ensemble's repertoire often includes pieces for dance. Puppetry is done at night, usually all night, and if it occurs on the same stage as a (human) dance, the performances are temporally separated. A puppet group is frequently hired to perform all night after the formal daytime celebration of a life-cycle ritual. When a performance occurs, loudspeakers, food stalls, and infectious joviality may attract an entire neighborhood or village. Puppets are created in small workshops that may or may not be connected to the compound of a famous puppeteer (figure 35). Many more puppets are created by nonspecialists for the tourist trade.

FIGURE 35 Apprentices work on creating and finishing new *wayang golèk* puppet heads at the studio of Aming Sutrisna in Bandung. Photo by Cary Black.

FIGURE 36 Cepot, a *wayang golek* puppet, represents the Sundanese Everyman. Photo by Cary Black.

Performances of rod-puppet theater occur in both urban and rural settings. Its stories mostly derive from the *Mahabharata* and the *Ramayana,* Hindu epics (in which case the performance is called *wayang golek purwa*), with occasional Islamic stories (*wayang golek cepak*). These stories may be supplemented with local tales, anecdotes, songs, comic interludes, and political and social commentary. The puppetmaster (*dalang*), as leader of the group, is responsible for telling the story, manipulating the puppets, working with the drummer to control the tempo, and determining the overall structure of the performance. Performances are often sponsored in gratitude for good fortune, or simply as one aspect of the ritual celebration of a circumcision or other festive occasion (figure 36).

Gamelan degung

Gamelan degung is the other primary Sundanese gamelan, formerly an all-male instrumental ensemble, which, in its "classic" version, performs a repertoire of about thirty instrumental pieces. It began as an instrumental ensemble closely associated with the Sundanese aristocracy and was originally performed to welcome visitors to the regents' homes. Its current form developed during the early twentieth century. In the last several decades, these instrumental pieces have been largely supplanted by simple cyclic patterns (*patokan*), which may support any number of melodies. Female vocalists (*juru kawih*) have become a standard feature of *degung* performances. The instrumentalists are now usually young women, who dress identically and perform easy pieces to provide visual and aural entertainment for wedding guests (figure 37). Though the classic repertoire is limited, hundreds of new pieces are now performed regularly on modern *gamelan degung.*

Gamelan degung has far fewer instruments and players than *gamelan saléndro* and is tuned to a type of *pélog* known as *pélog degung.* It performs in a colotomic structure, established by the suspended gong (*go'ong*) and six medium-sized suspended gongs (*jenglong*). The *go'ong* marks the ends of phrases, and the *jenglong* plays the *patokan. Kendang* are played with a small beater in the right hand and a bare left hand.

The main melody in a classic *gamelan degung* is carried by the *bonang,* a single-row gong-chime set placed in a V or U shape. The *bonang* of *gamelan degung* physically resembles the double-row gong chime *bonang* and *rincik* of *gamelan saléndro,*

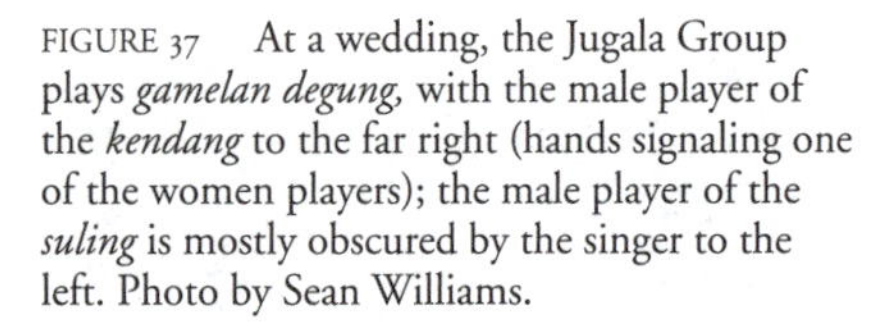

FIGURE 37 At a wedding, the Jugala Group plays *gamelan degung,* with the male player of the *kendang* to the far right (hands signaling one of the women players); the male player of the *suling* is mostly obscured by the singer to the left. Photo by Sean Williams.

but its function and tuning differ markedly. A small, four-hole, end-blown bamboo flute (*suling degung*) plays embellishments of the *bonang* melody. Two metallophones (*saron*) play abstractions of the *suling* and *bonang* melody. In modern *gamelan degung* performances, the *suling* and *kendang* are still played by men, but the rest of the instruments are often played by women. The melody is performed by the vocalist and still embellished by the *suling,* but is now only rarely played on the *bonang.*

Gamelan degung is most likely to be heard at neighborhood celebrations in Bandung and other towns. Because of its connection to the aristocracy, it is not considered a village ensemble. Competitions among urban districts have led to its local sponsorship. Performers come from the neighborhood, or from among the spouses of men who have similar occupations. Rehearsals (*latihan*) are lively affairs that usually attract neighbors, who drop in to listen, enjoy refreshments, and gossip. Sundanese perceptions of the ensemble have evolved from the concept of a restricted, difficult, male-only ensemble to a popular, easy, mostly female-oriented one. This change makes many more potential female performers eager to join a group, either as instrumentalists or as vocalists. *Gamelan degung* frequently accompanies large numbers of female vocalists (*rampak sekar*) and individuals performing *pop Sunda* songs (Williams 1989).

Other village gamelans thrive in Sunda, and local scholars have been active in investigating them. Many village gamelans are named with an older designation, putting the word *go'ong* before the type of ensemble, as in *go'ong renteng, go'ong ajeng,* and *go'ong kromong,* as opposed to *gamelan renteng, gamelan ajeng,* and *gamelan kromong.*

Ketuk tilu *and* jaipongan

Ketuk tilu performance is firmly rooted in the villages of Sunda. The ensemble includes three kettle-gongs (*ketuk*) in a single rack; hence the name, *ketuk tilu* 'three kettle-gongs'. It accompanies traditional Sundanese social dancing. Variants of its performance occur in many areas of Sunda, known by different names depending on the area. In the vicinity of Sumedang, it is known as *bangreng*; in Ciamis, it is called *ronggeng gunung* (Tirasonjaya 1979). In these variants, the instrumentation, drum strokes, and dances are essentially similar to those of *ketuk tilu.*

Ketuk tilu is performed in the evenings at village celebrations of various types, including harvests and life-cycle ceremonies. In a typical performance, the player of the *ketuk* strikes the instrument in the melodic pattern of low–medium–high–medium, or high–low–medium–low. This pattern is supported by the *go'ong,* struck every eight or sixteen beats; the *kendang,* which outline the rhythmic cycle; and a set of *kecrek,* small percussive metal plates that make a clashing sound. The primary melody is carried by a solo female singer-dancer (*ronggeng*) and a rebab. These instruments are portable, so the ensemble can be taken to whichever village is having a celebration (Manuel and Baier 1986). The overall texture of a performance is filled in with the interlocking shouts (*senggak*) of male instrumentalists, audience members, and dancers.

Ketuk tilu pieces consist of an introduction in free rhythm and short, fixed-rhythm sections of varying duration. The drummer pays close attention to the dancer (as in every Sundanese form of dance) and is responsible for building tension, keeping the tempo steady, halving or doubling the density (*wilet*), and introducing transitions between sections. *Ketuk tilu* drumming features rapid shifts in density and texture. The combination of flashy drumming with the performance of a sexy singer-dancer is an important aspect of Sundanese music for social dancing in the villages. The style of dance incorporates elements of humor, eroticism, and pantomime.

The *ronggeng* of the past (and sometimes of the present) would stand in front of

ronggeng Professional female singer-dancer

jaipongan Sundanese indigenous popular dance form

gamelan degung Sundanese pélog gong-chime ensemble

FIGURE 38 A solo female dancer of *jaipongan* (Nani) in a typically bold, confident stance. Her costume has leggings rather than a skirt to allow her feet to be far apart. Photo by Cary Black.

the ensemble of musicians, dancing solo and dancing with various male partners. She was assumed to be a prostitute (Manuel and Baier 1986; Sutton 1989), and her partners in dancing could have the option of becoming her sexual customers. Female singer-dancer-prostitutes are found in many areas of Java. In Sunda, *ronggeng* have developed into regionally important figures because of the popularity of sexy female vocalists in the offshoot of *ketuk tilu* known as *jaipongan.*

In the 1970s, Gugum Gumbira Tirasonjaya created *jaipongan* from what he believed to be the most interesting and compelling elements of *ketuk tilu,* gamelan saléndro, and dynamic, village-style drumming. It includes the free-rhythm introduction and drumming of *ketuk tilu,* the female *ronggeng,* and much of the *ketuk tilu* repertoire. However, it is most often performed on *gamelan saléndro,* rather than on *ketuk tilu.* The *kempul* takes an extremely active role, being played in rapid, syncopated strokes, which often correspond with those of the drum. The patterns of the drumming correspond exactly to a repertoire of movements of the dancing, and a good performance usually includes an elegant sequence of improvisational interplay between the drummer and the dancer. The style of the dancing combines Sundanese martial arts (*penca silat*), dancing of *ronggeng,* classical Sundanese dance, *tari kursus,* aspects from masked social dance (*topèng banjet*), and elements from American break dancing, the imitation of Sundanese people and animals, and the choreography of Martha Graham (figure 38).

FIGURE 39 A *kendang penca* ensemble performs at the darkened edge of a stage, watching the dancers. Photo by Sean Williams.

Kendang penca *and* rampak kendang

Kendang penca (Indonesian *pencak*) is the percussive ensemble that accompanies the Sundanese version of the ubiquitous Indonesian martial-arts dance, *penca silat.* It can be heard at any of the Sundanese *penca silat* schools (*perguruan*), often centers of social activity for young men (and, less frequently, young women). The ensemble consists of two *kendang,* a small suspended gong (*bende*), and one or two *tarompet,* double-reed wind instruments, played using circular breathing (figure 39). The *kendang* are divided in terms of parent (*kendang indung*) and child (*kendang anak*). For each rhythmic cycle, the parent usually plays an ostinato, and the child mirrors the movements of the dancer(s).

The performance begins with the players of *kendang* and *tarompet* improvising briefly in free rhythm. Several well-defined rhythmic cycles (*tepak*) then follow. The fixed-rhythm section begins in a medium tempo (*tepak dua* or *paleredan*) as the dancer—dressed in loose-fitting black pants and shirt, with a belt around the waist and a strip of cloth wrapped around the head—begins to circle in rhythmic steps. *Tepak dua* uses the longest gong cycle, and is the least dense. Drummers signal the next rhythmic cycle (*tepak tilu*), and the density increases. In both *tepak dua* and *tepak tilu,* the player of the *tarompet* improvises on various popular Sundanese folk songs (*lagu rakyat*), trading off with another player of a *tarompet* when one is available.

At a drummer's signal, the tempo increases dramatically, and the density of the strokes of the gong doubles as the fighting begins. In this section, onomatopoeically called *padungdung,* new drum strokes coincide with the kicks and punches of the fighters or solo performer. The instrumentalists and spectators shout *Mati!* 'Dead!' and other inflammatory words. The *tarompet* pitch rises rapidly into the highest register in improvisational figures, using vibrato and other dramatic techniques. Weapons are sometimes used in addition to hands and feet. Injuries and deaths sometimes occur, but performers have studied a philosophy and specific protective tactics, and they distinguish between basic sparring competitions and solo dance in *penca,* which incorporates *penca* philosophy and laws governing behavior and belief.

A development that appears to be specific to Bandung is *rampak kendang* 'drum

FIGURE 40 Six sets of *kendang* alternate between solo and group playing, accompanied by *gamelan saléndro* to the right (Jugala Group). Photo by Sean Williams.

group', a large ensemble of drums. Created by Gugum Gumbira Tirasonjaya in the 1980s, it uses multiple sets of *kendang,* accompanied by *gamelan saléndro* (figure 40). *Kendang* solos alternate among several leaders, and the other players of *kendang* provide a thunderous accompaniment. Other percussive instruments, such as the Islamic frame drum (*terbang*), may add visual and sonic effects. A single *rampak kendang* piece may last up to thirty minutes. For almost every performance, advanced groups alter the drumming arrangements. Many performances include acrobatic movements, including the throwing of drums, elaborate gestures of the hand and the body, and choreographed clowning.

Bamboo ensembles

The three main types of Sundanese bamboo ensembles are *angklung, calung,* and *arumba.* The exact features of each ensemble vary in contexts, related instruments, and relative popularity. Except for *calung* (regularly recorded by one Sundanese group), bamboo instruments do not have a strong market in the cassette industry. When searching for a cassette of bamboo instruments, one is most likely to find one in a diatonic tuning, recorded in Jakarta, containing Indonesia's top ten patriotic songs.

Angklung

Angklung is a generic term for sets of tuned, shaken bamboo rattles. It is found in many other places in Indonesia, but its greatest variety occurs in Sunda. A description from 1704 (Baier 1986), its first known mention in writing, calls it a large processional ensemble, used to welcome visitors at regents' homes. Each instrument has two to four bamboo tubes, tuned from one to three octaves apart and suspended loosely from the top of a frame. When the instruments are shaken, two small extensions of each tube strike each side of a slot within the lower part of the frame, creating sounds. *Angklung* are played in interlocking patterns, usually with only one or two instruments played per person (figure 41).

The combination of instruments depends on the type of *angklung* being performed. The most common traditional Sundanese one, *angklung buncis,* is tuned to *saléndro.* It uses up to a dozen players of *angklung,* a player of a *tarompet,* four drummers (playing *dog-dog,* conical single-headed drums), vocalists, and others, including players of gongs, clowns, and people designated to stimulate audience interaction. The vocalists perform songs in call-and-response, popular styles, interlocking

FIGURE 41 College students play bamboo *angklung* in a procession far removed from its ritual origins. Photo by Sean Williams.

senggak, spontaneous rhymes, and high-pitched melismatic singing (*beluk*) in Javanese poetic meters (*pupuh*). The drummers have polyrhythmic competitions with one another, dodging in and out of the procession and trying to trick one another into making mistakes.

Angklung is used in Sundanese processions, sometimes with trance or acrobatics. As the performers go forward, they arrange themselves into patterns, including figure-eights, circles, and double lines. Performed at life-cycle rituals and feasts (*hajat*), *angklung* is believed to maintain balance and harmony in the village. It is most closely associated with the Sundanese goddess of rice, Nyi Pohaci Sanghyang Sri, popularly known as Dewi Sri. The connection between rice and bamboo—grasses essential to Sundanese survival—is strong [see BAMBOO, RICE, AND WATER].

Through the performance of *angklung,* the goddess of rice is enticed to the fields to ensure a good harvest. The performance of *angklung* in accordance with the seasonal agricultural calendar ensures the continuity of the cycle of planting, growth, and harvesting. By perpetuating this cycle through joyous, chaotic processions, the performers keep the village in tune with nature.

In its most modern incarnation, *angklung* is performed in schools as an aid to learning about music. Tuned diatonically, sets of one hundred or more instruments are played by children. The ease with which these instruments are made (compared with forging a gamelan) and the low cost of purchasing a set make *angklung* an Indonesian alternative to pianos or other diatonic instruments. The melodies most commonly studied by students are the dozens of Indonesian patriotic songs they must memorize. In typical performances of this music, a teacher conducts the students by standing in front of the class with the numbers of the pitches written on a board. The lively and humorous processional aspect of the performance is omitted, as is any connection with agricultural ritual.

Calung

Related ensembles, *calung,* fall into several categories of which the most common is modern *calung* (*calung moderèn*). Like those in *angklung,* its instruments are of bamboo, but each consists of several differently tuned tubes that are fixed onto a piece of bamboo instead of being loosely suspended. *Calung* are usually tuned to *saléndro.* The player, usually a man, holds the instrument in his left hand and strikes it with a beater held in his right. The highest-pitched *calung* has the greatest number of tubes and the densest musical activity; the lowest-pitched, with two tubes, has the least.

As in puppetry, the resolution of conflict is one of the most important aspects of the *pantun* story, because it provides a cathartic release for the audience.

Calung is nearly always associated with earthy humor. The performers sing and move while they play, sometimes using their beaters or instruments to represent other objects. Topics are often bawdy and involve extensive puns, satire, and in-jokes. The butt of many jokes is usually the player of the lowest-pitched *calung.* He plays the least, stands at the end of the ensemble, uses the most exaggerated gestures of the arms, and has the largest beater. He rarely has the chance to sing or verbally defend himself, so his role may be taken by the best mime of the group.

Arumba

The most modern of the three ensembles is named for the *arumba,* a diatonically tuned set of bamboo xylophones on stands, often played by women—in particular, members of Dharma Wanita, the organization of government officials' wives. An *arumba* is frequently joined by modern instruments, including a drum set, an electric guitar, a bass, and keyboard instruments. Recent recordings of *arumba* include the reggae hit "Rivers of Babylon," the pop song "Spanish Harlem," Indonesian patriotic tunes, and a few *pop Sunda* hits.

Zither ensembles

The Sundanese zither (*kacapi*) often serves to represent Sundanese culture. It plays as either a solo or an ensemble instrument, associated with both villagers and aristocrats. It may take the form of a boat in *tembang Sunda,* or the form of a board zither in *kacapian.* It is sometimes drastically modified to include more strings, electric and electronic devices, and various styles of playing. *Pantun, tembang Sunda, kacapi-suling,* and *kacapian* are its most common uses.

Pantun

Pantun is a genre of Sundanese epic narrative. It is most often performed by a blind male vocalist (*juru pantun* 'performer of *pantun*'), who usually accompanies himself on a *kacapi,* an eighteen-stringed boat-shaped or board zither (figure 42). The performance of *pantun* dates from before the 1500s—before influences from Central Java or Islam. It was mentioned in the *Sanghyang Siksa Kandang Karesian,* a Sundanese manuscript written in 1518. As a vital performing tradition, it is the source of a variety of modern Sundanese performing arts, including *kacapian* and *tembang Sunda.* Furthermore, other Sundanese arts, such as puppetry, are a continual influence on *pantun* performers.

The performance of *pantun* usually occurs as part of a ritual Sundanese feast (*hajat*). As with most Sundanese performing arts, the performance is often tailored to the situation after consultation with the patron or sponsor. Because certain stories carry specific ideological, religious, or cultural meanings, stories are selected or rejected according to the type of ceremony being performed.

The zither used for *pantun* is usually tuned to *pélog* or *saléndro* and except dur-

FIGURE 42 The blind singer of *pantun* Ki Subarma of Ciwidey in West Java plays a *kacapi*, accompanied by a rebab. Photo by Andrew Weintraub.

ing periods of intense recitation is performed in a relatively fixed meter. It accompanies songs (*lagu*), but may also play stereotypical melodic patterns, which advance the action, giving the performer a break from recitation, or heightening the dramatic tension. When accompanying *lagu,* the zither is played in two styles: the first is a variety of repeating patterns (*kemprang*) specific to each song; the second, any of several types of ostinatos that accompany recitatives. Melodic flourishes on the zither serve as aural indicators of specific characters or moods.

After the proper types of offerings are made and the appropriate time of night has arrived, the performance may begin. The performer recites Sundanese mythological tales, interspersed with songs, comments, jokes, and allegories. He is believed to have a strong connection to the world of spirits and is respected for his knowledge. His presence is as much a symbolic blessing on the ceremony as the actual blessing he requests from the gods during the performance.

The typical narrative tells of a Sundanese hero who must undergo a series of conflicts (contests, battles, ordeals) before finding a resolution. As in puppetry, the resolution of conflict is one of the most important aspects of the story, because it provides a cathartic release for the audience. Most *pantun* stories are indigenously Sundanese, but Islamic and non-Sundanese stories have also been documented (Weintraub 1990).

Performers of *pantun* use the basic storyline to carry the tale, embellishing freely and filling in details. They build the text on standard patterns and poetic devices, including rhymes and allusions. Songs often add details and elaborate on the story, fulfilling a variety of functions: invocations, blessings, representations of any aspect of the story, and entertainment. Their primary function is to enhance the storyline, yet they are not essential to the development of each character.

During the 1980s, *pantun* developed into several different styles. It continues to be appreciated by villagers, but as the broadcast media gained influence, some performers had to shorten their performances from the traditional all-night *pantun* to ones lasting just a few hours. Some performances since the 1980s have included female vocalists, other instruments, and additional songs, designed more for entertainment than for ritual. In Sundanese villages, *pantun* is still performed in its original contexts.

FIGURE 43 A *tembang Sunda* ensemble. *Left to right:* the *kacapi,* the *suling,* and the *rincik* are played behind the singers Euis Komariah (holding the microphone) and Neneng Dinar. Photo by Sean Williams.

Tembang Sunda

Tembang Sunda, known in Cianjur as *cianjuran,* is a type of sung poetry developed in the regency of Cianjur in the late 1800s. It began as an entertainment in which aristocrats would sing in poetic meters derived from Central Java (*pupuh*) or perform songs derived from Sundanese epics (*lagu pantun*), accompanied by local instruments. Its topics include Sundanese history, aspects of nature, mythology, romance, heroic figures, and tragedies. It is currently centered in Bandung, where many descendants of the Sundanese aristocracy and most of the current performers live.

In performance, one or more singers are accompanied by an eighteen-stringed zither (*kacapi*), a smaller, fifteen-stringed zither (*rincik*), and a six-hole end-blown bamboo flute (*suling*) (figure 43). A typical performance includes sets of about fifteen minutes each, consisting of several heavily ornamented free-meter songs (*mamaos*) followed by a fixed-meter song (*panambih*). This genre may be performed in the *pélog, sorog,* or *saléndro* tuning, and it is occasionally performed in the *mataram-mandalungan* tuning, a rare, high-pitched type of *pélog.* Most performances, however, are in *pélog* and *sorog.* The *kacapi* and the flute freely accompany the vocal melody during the free-meter songs, following and imitating the vocal ornamentation. When the set ends with a fixed-meter song, the *rincik* musically elaborates on the *kacapi* patterns at a density twice that of the *kacapi.* When performances occur in *saléndro* tuning, the flute is replaced by a two-stringed bowed lute (rebab), normally played for fixed-meter songs.

Tembang Sunda is traditionally performed in the evenings by musicians and singers, who receive no pay for their performances. In an ideal performance (reminiscent of the genre's original setting), the only members of the audience are other musicians and singers, attentively listening while awaiting their turns to participate. Other venues that now often involve monetary reimbursement include weddings, circumcisions, dinners for members of the military or foreign guests, hotel lobbies, and restaurant pavilions. These performances are tied less to the appropriate time of day (evening), the normal progression of songs (serious to light, historical to romantic), or systems of tuning (*pélog* to *sorog* to *saléndro*) than traditional performance dictates. Instead, they are directed almost entirely by the needs of the setting and the employer.

For the descendants of the Sundanese aristocracy, *tembang Sunda* functions as a sonic link to the past, not only to the era just before independence (when aristocrats enjoyed certain privileges), but also to precolonial Pajajaran (Williams 1990). Because the sound of the *suling* is strongly associated with village life, and because bamboo flutes may be found nearly everywhere in Sunda, an aural connection is also made to the rural areas. Most of the people who listen to and perform *tembang Sunda* were raised outside Bandung, often in semirural areas.

Kacapi-suling

Kacapi-suling as a separate ensemble is a recent urban offshoot of *tembang Sunda.* It developed during the 1970s as a recorded genre, pioneered by the musicians Uking Sukri (*kacapi*) and Burhan Sukarma (*suling*), and supported by the Hidayat Recording Company of Bandung. It is still only rarely performed live. *Kacapi-suling* is the instrumental performance of the fixed-meter songs (*panambih*) of *tembang Sunda,* and includes the usual *tembang Sunda* instrumentation of *kacapi, rincik,* and *suling.* The essential structure of a fixed-meter song resembles the cyclic structure of a *gamelan degung* piece in that a "gong" (bass string) sounds at the end of each cycle, and the internal phrases are separated by colotomic markers of phrases (*jenglong*) or connective transitional tones (*pancer*), which are also played on the bass strings of the *kacapi.*

In a typical *kacapi-suling* performance, the player of the *kacapi* outlines the cyclic structure (*patokan*), alternating octaves with the right hand and performing syncopated bass patterns with the left. The player of the *rincik* performs elaborate variations of the structural pattern at twice the density of the *kacapi,* roughly conforming to the register of the melody played on the flute, which often begins at a low pitch, ascends in register through the progression of the song, and descends during the final cycles.

The flute's function in *kacapi-suling* is to improvise along the contours of the cyclic structure. Sometimes the flutist plays sections of tunes normally sung by a *tembang Sunda* vocalist; this practice derives from sections in the songs when the vocalist rests and the flutist carries the melody briefly. Other players may use the established song as a point of improvisational departure, returning only occasionally to the song's melody. Still others use only the cyclic structure and leave out the precomposed melody, creating an entirely new one.

Each cycle may be as short as twenty seconds or as long as ten minutes, depending on the song normally sung to the ensemble's accompaniment. The complete performance of the tune depends entirely on the players' whim, because it is not limited by lyric content. Many fixed-meter songs have the same cyclic structure, so the performers can lead from one piece directly into another with no transition, or they can string together suites of songs with related structures.

Sometime in the early twentieth century, *kacapi-suling* was used to play fixed-meter songs within the context of performances of *tembang Sunda*; later, it played versions of classical *gamelan degung* melodies (now known as *dedegungan*). Most current performances are of instrumental fixed-meter songs, because the *dedegungan* are considered technically too difficult for average players. *Panambih patokan* are easy to perform. *Kacapi-suling* is sometimes performed at normal *tembang Sunda* events when the vocalists need a break (figure 44), or to warm up the audience. It can also be heard at hotels and restaurants where tourists gather, but its current function appears to be recorded background music.

Kacapian

Kacapian, another genre using a zither (*kacapi*) as its primary instrument, is one of the sources of Sundanese popular music. Its main proponent, Koko Koswara (1915–1985), developed a flashy style of playing a flat board zither (*kacapi siter*) that made it attractive to young people; he created some of the first modern melodic and

The *kacapi siter* is one of the few instruments that women may play; its origins in the Sundanese villages, which are less affected by sex roles in music, have given rise to particularly talented female performers of *kacapian.*

FIGURE 44 During a break in an all-night gathering of performers of *tembang Sunda,* the *kacapi-suling* instrumentalists keep the music going. The *rincik* (left, played by Nana Suhana) and the *kacapi* (right, played by Gan-gan Garmana) flank the player of the *suling* (Iwan). Photo by Sean Williams, 1989.

rhythmic hooks used in Sundanese music; and he spurred the popularity of a type of fixed-meter vocal music not restricted to women. Until the development and popularization of *kacapian,* most fixed-meter songs in *tembang Sunda* could be sung by women only. Because of the casualness that roadside singers accorded to fixed-meter songs, singing in this style was considered undignified for men. Some *kacapian,* however, were specifically created for men to sing—which afforded them a new avenue of performance.

Kacapian is flexible in its tunings. The most likely tuning a Sundanese person will hear *kacapian* in is *saléndro,* which often accompanies village songs and comic performers (*jenaka Sunda*). However, the *kacapi siter* used for *kacapian* is easy to retune, and songs in *pélog, sorog,* or even Western diatonic tunings are regularly performed. Some performers will bring several *kacapi siter* to a performance to switch from a village song to a patriotic song to a *pop Sunda* song in various tunings.

An important aspect of *kacapian* is its variety of instrumentation. The *kacapi* remains the central instrument, but it may be accompanied by a *rincik,* a *go'ong,* a rebab, a box-shaped bowed lute (*tarawangsa*), a violin (*biola*), a guitar (*gitar*), or even an entire gamelan (Van Zanten 1989). The *kacapi siter* is one of the few instruments that women may play; its origins in the Sundanese villages, which are less affected by sex roles in music, have given rise to particularly talented female performers of *kacapian,* such as Yoyoh Supriatin and Nyai Sumiati.

The role of the *kacapi* in *kacapian* remains at the forefront, no matter what other instruments are played. Its participation in the overall song has increased dramatically. Though it usually accompanies a vocalist, it is used in *kacapian* as an elaborate melodic accompanist, rather than as an outliner of structure (as in *kacapi-suling*). Through the use of dramatic techniques (such as plucked tremolos, damping, and syncopated patterns in both hands), the player of the *kacapi* functions nearly independently in an ensemble, providing more than enough musical activity to support a vocalist as an active and nearly equal partner.

The vocal music accompanied by this style of playing *kacapi,* known as *kawih,* serves in a variety of contexts, including gamelan. One of the definitions of *kawih* is 'light vocal music', distinguishing it from *tembang Sunda.* It is considered much easier to perform than *tembang Sunda,* not only in vocal ornamentation, but also in memorization and feeling (*pangjiwaan*). It extends beyond *kacapian* into the *pop Sunda* repertoire, and is associated with fixed-meter songs in *tembang Sunda.*

Kawih lyrics use complicated rhymes, often in the form of rhyming couplets (*sisindiran*)—either a single couplet (*wawangsalan*) or a pair of couplets (*paparikan*). The first section of a couplet usually describes an aspect of nature, and the second describes the topic of the verse—love, a political situation, religion, or a dispute. Many lyrics are up to date in criticizing current events, and the Sundanese predilection for musical humor allows for subtle plays on words.

Music of the Baduy

Some Sundanese live outside the mainstream culture. About six thousand Baduy, believed to be descendants of the original inhabitants of the Sundanese region, have resisted cultural and religious influences from outside their territory. They live in an isolated area of South Banten. Unlike most Sundanese, they consider outside influences or any aspect of change to be unacceptable. They divide into two groups, the inner Baduy and the outer Baduy, determined by their location in the Baduy area and by their beliefs. The inner Baduy are the more conservative; they do not use transportation, do not read or write, do not use money, and have little or no contact with outsiders (Van Zanten 1994; Wessing 1977). Since the Indonesian government restricts researchers from dealing with them, almost no research by outsiders has been done on their performing arts.

Having successfully resisted Islam, Hindu Buddhism, and Christianity, the Baduy are considered by many non-Baduy Sundanese to be living repositories of aboriginal Sundanese culture. The instruments deemed acceptable to the inner Baduy are a small boat-shaped zither (*kacapi*), a wooden bowed lute resembling the *tarawangsa* (*rendo*), several types of bamboo flutes (*suling* and *élèt*), and a type of *angklung* (Van Zanten 1989). The Baduy use these instruments to accompany song in performances of agricultural rituals and epic narratives (*pantun*). The *suling* serve a variety of purposes, including entertainment, courtship, and vocal accompaniment (figure 45). In addition, several small solo instruments, such as the *karinding* (Jew's harp), are used for entertainment (figure 46). All these instruments are considered inherently and indigenously Sundanese by modern Sundanese society, and are also found in many types of non-Baduy village music.

Sundanese popular music

For decades, the Sundanese have enjoyed performances of locally created popular music. In addition to nationally popular genres (such as *dangdut* and *kroncong*), the Sundanese have developed a unique regional style, *pop Sunda.* It began as a Sundanese musical imitation of American and European popular music played on Western band instruments (electric guitar, organ, bass, and so on). Performances were always in a diatonic tuning and 4/4 meter on a drum set, and used a heavy, consistent vocal vibrato, in contrast to the Sundanese variable vibrato. The language, Sundanese, was almost the only factor indigenous to the area.

In the mid-1980s, composer Nano Suratno (generally known as Nano S.) reshaped *pop Sunda* to conform more closely to Sundanese musical idioms. Through

FIGURE 45 Mang Pe'i tries an *élèt* he has just made. Photo by Wim Van Zanten.

the creation of several hits in *pélog*, which could be accompanied by either a diatonic pop-style band or traditional ensembles, he broke through the barrier separating popular from traditional Sundanese music. The new songs always had strong melodic or rhythmic hooks—a compositional technique borrowed from Western popular music, but previously pioneered in Sunda by Koko Koswara in the *kacapian* genre. Their success created a demand for more songs in *pélog* performable by any ensemble.

Nano Suratno's songs were covered by various ensembles in several different tunings, and the genre of *pop Sunda* expanded. Vocal competitions, sponsored by large corporations, spurred the solidification of a true *pop Sunda* vocal style, which generally includes traditional ornamentation (including the variable-speed vibrato). Based on the success of the first band recording of the revitalized genre ("*Kalangkang,*" recorded by Nining Meida and Getek's Band), most *pop Sunda* recordings since the mid-1980s have included the standard Sundanese *kendang* (which has variable pitches) and a bamboo flute or a keyboard imitation of it. These two aural cues, plus the sound of the system of tuning and the use of the Sundanese language, are essential in identifying the genre (Williams 1989).

FIGURE 46 For entertainment, the Baduy play bamboo Jew's harps (*karinding*). Photo by Wim Van Zanten.

Once the new-style *pop Sunda* had become firmly established in the Sundanese ear, the previously popular diatonic *pop Sunda* tunes abruptly fell under the category of nostalgic songs (*lagu-lagu nostalgia*), and are currently revived only at weddings when a band that plays rock is present and people request old songs. Attempts were made in the early 1990s to bring diatonic tuning back into *pop Sunda* (particularly by composers in strong competition with Nano Suratno), but these attempts showed little promise of gaining popularity, except as novelties.

Pop Sunda is heard primarily on cassettes, and secondarily at weddings, circumcisions, and business and governmental events. Most musicians buy the cassettes as much for their own enjoyment as to learn the latest tunes. By knowing the latest repertoire, musicians are likelier to be hired, even for traditional events. Most traditional female singers of the *tembang* and gamelan repertoires include in the back of their songbooks the lyrics to the ten most requested *pop Sunda* songs. The ensemble provided for an event such as a wedding depends entirely on the hosts, but it is likelier to be an ensemble in a traditional system of tuning than a keyboard-based pop band. The performance of a diatonic song accompanied by an ensemble in *pélog* is considered too challenging to be tried by many—which limits the potential market for *pop Sunda* tunes in diatonic tuning.

In the face of Sundanese young people's exposure to international popular music, *pop Sunda* is the strongest local contender for their attention. Many older people approve of and enjoy *pop Sunda* because of its hooks and its conformity to local systems of tuning and vocal styles; others feel it has wrested attention from traditional Sundanese music. Musically, it is the only link between popular international music and traditional Sundanese music.

Music and musicians in Sundanese society

Music is performed in a variety of contexts in Sunda, from department-store openings to late-night gatherings among friends. Musical performance does not always involve pay, and performers may be selected as much on the basis of their connection to a patron or their family ties to the primary performers as on their ability to play. Performance is normally a participatory activity; people from the audience are expected to join in (*kaul*) at least once during a performance by singing, playing, or dancing. The concept of *kaul* derives from the sense of fulfilling a vow of participation with one's teacher. When one agrees to *kaul,* the teacher is honored. Guests and government officials are particularly targeted for this type of participation, generally in an atmosphere of gaiety and laughter.

The Sundanese regard music specialists with ambivalence. Strong adherents to Islam often look down on instrumental music. Furthermore, traditional music is sometimes considered ancient and outdated, and performers are sometimes accused of preventing the country from moving forward by persisting in playing music no longer relevant to the needs of a developed society. Musicians are also acknowledged to have a special kind of charismatic power that may be respected and even feared.

Most musicians who perform on weekends, at monthly meetings, or at seasonal rituals do not consider themselves professionals. They rarely call themselves musicians. Nonmusicians usually claim to enjoy music, and almost always claim a specific genre of music as their favorite, whether it be traditional, a type of local or national Indonesian popular music (like *dangdut* or *kroncong*), or American, European, or Chinese pop. Claiming a genre of music usually places the speaker in a specific social class, because musical genres are often bounded by class.

Class, gender, age

One of the strongest Hindu-Buddhist influences in Sunda is a sense of class and hierarchy. Distinctions of class still shape interpersonal relationships in Sunda, from determining who may cultivate romantic ties to dictating which music is most appropriate for a specific setting. Despite official pronouncements claiming that divisions of class no longer exist, they appear throughout the Sundanese performing arts and in society in general.

The Sundanese accept a general division between refined (*alus*) and coarse (*kasar*). In musical terms, this continuum has fluid boundaries, which change according to the setting, the lyrics, the performers, the instrumentation, and other variables. Until the 1980s, the relative status of a type of music was determined primarily by its audience; *tembang Sunda* was aristocratic because its intended audience was the nobility, and *angklung* was low class because its audience consisted of farmers and villagers. If the audience consisted of middle-class urbanites, the status of the music fell somewhere in between.

These distinctions are no longer nearly so strong, because almost every major genre of Sundanese music has undergone a series of transformations that have entailed crossing class boundaries. The cassette industry has had a strong impact on

Many of the most respected female musicians in Sundanese society are excellent players of gamelan or other instruments, but they rarely perform publicly as instrumentalists or for money.

the mixing of musical genres with intended audiences, as music that was once the province of the few has become readily available to the many. Furthermore, the emergence of a Sundanese middle class and the ability of middle-class families to afford musical entertainment at life-cycle events have brought a variety of genres into the neighborhoods and homes of anyone who can afford to hire a group.

Historically, vocal music (especially *tembang Sunda*) has been at the top of the musical hierarchy. Its association with aristocratic performance in the 1800s and its ties to major Sundanese ensembles have tended to keep it at the forefront. *Gamelan degung,* also associated with the aristocracy and performed instrumentally, is still regarded as a high-status ensemble, though its repertoire includes popular songs. At the other end of the scale is music performed in villages. Both villagers and aristocrats assume that setting determines status. Despite these distinctions, however, Sundanese are free to enjoy any type of music they like.

Sundanese music is strongly divided along gender lines. Specific genders are required for the proper performance of each type of music, and crossing the gender boundary is far less appropriate, even for modern performances, than crossing a class boundary. In general, men are the instrumentalists, though women have in the last few decades begun to play *angklung, gamelan degung,* and some other instruments. The instruments most strongly tied to men are drums and winds. In all-female ensembles (*gamelan ibu-ibu* 'women's gamelan'), the drum and flute parts are still always performed by men.

Male musicians sometimes hold daytime jobs, but may spend all night performing at musical jobs. Musicians who belong to popular groups may depend entirely on their relationship to the group's patron and their musical income to support themselves and their families. Female musicians rarely consider themselves professionals. Many are young mothers with children, and the money they receive for their performances supplements their husbands' incomes. Some women cease to perform when they marry, and husbands may forbid their new wives to perform for money because of the association of pay with prostitution.

Male musicians, in contrast to their female counterparts, are not severely limited to specific musical activities, and may freely switch instruments and genres. Though it is unusual for a male instrumentalist of a low-status genre to perform in a high-status ensemble (or vice versa), it is not at all unusual for the same instrumentalist to play most of the instruments within a specific genre. Men may act as vocalists, within limits; in *tembang Sunda,* they sing only free-meter songs. In gamelan performances, their vocal role is as the *alok,* or male counterpart to the featured female vocalist.

Female performers function in Sundanese musical culture primarily as vocalists or dancers. When women play as a group in a performance of *gamelan degung,* they play in a simpler style than do the men who play the same ensemble; they sometimes pay closer attention to the match of their clothing, hair, and makeup than to what they play. Female players of typically male-oriented instruments exist, but their performances are rarely taken seriously. Many of the most respected female musicians in Sundanese society (both historically and currently) are excellent players of gamelan or highly talented players of *kacapi* or other instruments, but they rarely perform publicly as instrumentalists or for money.

As dancers, women tread a thin line of respectability. In traditional Sundanese society, female dancers sometimes functioned as social and/or sexual partners for their patrons (Manuel and Baier 1986). Social dance is still considered a risky activity for young women of good family because of its origins in *ronggeng*. Women who choose to perform as dancers of *jaipongan,* for example, often select the solo staged version of the dance rather than the version for couples in villages, streets, or Sundanese nightclubs. By performing as a soloist, the dancer is brought closer to the setting of modern dance with respected, established choreography and further away from its improvised form in a traditional setting.

Being a dancer of classical Sundanese or certain types of modern semiclassical choreography, such as the peacock dance (*tari merak*) or the butterfly dance (*tari kupu-kupu*), is considered acceptable for young women and children. Classical dance is still associated with both Sundanese and Javanese aristocratic society, particularly because many of the finest early classical Sundanese male dancers were members of the aristocracy. Furthermore, the origin of Sundanese classical dance in the Central Javanese courts, and the Sundanese respect for established Central Javanese traditions, help gain classical dance social acceptance. Modern choreography, associated with postindependence Indonesia and trained dancers, is also respectable because it is not associated with villages.

The strongest exception to the general rule of separation of the genders is in music schools and general-music classes in regular schools. Young men and women participate almost equally in all major Sundanese instrumental ensembles, including drumming groups, and they learn to compose new pieces together. Women and men teach music as equals at these institutions, but because students usually fall back into gender-based social distinctions outside the school environment, few female students specialize in the traditionally male-dominated instruments or ensembles. Many opt for a general-music education or a specialty in voice or dance.

Economic factors may help determine the decision by female graduates of music schools to restrict themselves to socially acceptable musical roles. Few are likely to be hired as part of an instrumental ensemble, because musical directors—scheduling late-evening or all-night performances—hesitate to ask a woman to perform as an instrumentalist in an otherwise all-male ensemble. An exceptionally good female vocalist or dancer, however, could easily be hired by one of the famous regional performing groups (*lingkung seni*) and maintain her good name.

The respect accorded performers of Sundanese music from young musicians and members of Sundanese society usually increases as they get older. Young musicians listen attentively to their musical elders, learning the old ways of performing while adapting and changing the genres to keep up with the latest developments. Musicians speak reverently of musicians who have died and spend hours discussing the expertise of musical specialists in their respective genres.

In sharp contrast to the tendency of respecting older musicians, performers aged forty and up are hired less frequently for musical jobs than young performers. Musical directors cite the young performers' flexibility in time and musical skills as the reasons for the discrepancy between ideology and reality. In musical situations that do not require pay, people from a much broader age spectrum may freely participate. Children are actively encouraged to join in almost any musical activity when appropriate, and precocious youngsters compete from preschool through high school for awards and the prestige of winning a competition in music or dance.

Musical patronage

The patronage of music in Sundanese society has undergone a dramatic change as a result of social upheavals in postindependence Indonesia. Before independence, musicians were often part of a patron's household, or were attached to a wealthy family through blood ties or historical links. The wealth given the patrons by the Dutch in turn enabled them to support musicians and dancers. Keeping a musical group on one's grounds was an important aspect of maintaining prestige.

Immediately following independence, when Dutch funds no longer flowed through the patrons, musicians were forced to rely on other means for support. Some turned to other activities (such as farming), which enabled them to stay in the area. Others migrated to Jakarta or Bandung. Stripped of the old ties of family and patronage, musicians had to rely on service jobs, private lessons, or connections made during trips with their patrons. For some, the then-new radio station, Radio Republik Indonesia (RRI), provided work.

Since the 1960s, musicians have been sponsored by new types of patrons—not always members of the Sundanese aristocracy, but successful businessmen, highly ranked military or government officials, foreign ethnomusicologists, and wealthy Chinese-Indonesians—who wish to strengthen their ties to the community by demonstrating their support of traditional Sundanese performing arts. Chinese-Indonesians control most of the Sundanese cassette industry and retail cassette distribution, so their ties to the performing arts community are quite strong. The performing-arts groups (*lingkung seni*) formed under new patronage are now the standard ensembles hired for performances.

In large Sundanese towns and cities, the *lingkung seni* is the most common arrangement between groups and their patrons. These groups are typically centered around the home of a leader or patron, who may or may not be a performer. Personnel fluctuate according to who is available on the day of a performance and who is in good standing with the leader. Despite any personnel changes, the name of the group stays the same. Core group members are usually included in most performances, and outsiders are brought in to fill the remaining positions. Ideally, musicians belonging to any *lingkung seni* should be flexible enough to fulfill any request, even if it includes pop or dance-band music. Group leaders are expected to rely on every connection they have to accede to the whims of the person hiring the group.

Training Sundanese musicians

The Sundanese have a variety of ways to learn music. In traditional settings, a young musician attends a regular rehearsal (*latihan*) over a long period of time, simply to watch and listen to someone whose playing is considered worth emulating. After a friendship or understanding has developed between the student and the more experienced musician, the student might be asked to participate musically by playing one of the simpler instruments or one of the easier pieces. Eventually, the student assumes the right to request hints, ornaments, or songs from the experienced musician. Formal paid lessons are rarely given, but single requests are almost always honored.

Requesting something from an experienced musician immediately places the student in debt, and he or she may then be expected to help the musician in a variety of menial ways. Complex relationships involving debt are built during the course of a musician's lifetime, and students rarely switch from one experienced musician to another because of the ill feelings such a switch would create. Similarly, by coming to a rehearsal, potential students align themselves with that group or the group's leader, often in hopes of being asked to participate in paid performances when they have developed the skills and experience.

In Sundanese villages, young children commonly begin their musical education in a parent's lap. By closely watching their parents perform, many Sundanese village musicians absorb almost their entire musical repertoire long before they ever pick up an instrument. By trying the pieces themselves, children may grow into adult musicians or dancers.

Students may study directly from the cassette recordings of experienced musicians. Within a single genre, the availability of recordings on cassette allows students a broad spectrum of examples on which to base their personal styles of playing. Some students emulate their favorite musician; others select ones whose ornamentation or improvisations will showcase their own musical abilities. Most students develop a repertoire that reflects that of their teacher and are careful not to perform their teacher's rivals' pieces.

Many students gain musical experience through attendance at a regional conservatory in Bandung, such as the Sekolah Menengah Karawitan Indonesia (SMKI) or the Akademi Seni Tari Indonesia (ASTI). Both have programs that encourage diverse playing and dancing in addition to a grasp of Western and several Indonesian music theories. Students are not expected to specialize in any one instrument or genre, yet most choose one they prefer. These institutions attract village-raised musicians who demonstrate promise; they also attract Bandung-raised musicians who plan to be professional musicians but lack degrees in music.

Many of the teachers at these institutions and the music teachers at regular institutions come from the ranks of former music students, and some are not specialists in the instruments, genres, or forms they teach. Teachers must have a degree in music to get a job at an institution, and many musicians in Sunda do not have degrees in music. As a result, there is competition and stylistic discrepancy between students who gain experience through the institutions and those who gain it by playing and studying with the masters.

Composition and experimentation

The Sundanese pride themselves on their willingness to accept new musical ideas and incorporate changes into existing genres. Many of the region's strongest composers are those whose musical training is rooted firmly in traditional performance practice, who feel a compelling interest in maintaining a sense of Sundanese autonomy, but who are most interested in expanding the boundaries of existing ensembles, genres, and forms. Composers and performers continue to speak respectfully of the older generation of musicians. Composers who earlier in the century promoted change—for example, Koko Koswara, who pioneered developments in *kacapian* and popularized this style outside Bandung— are highly venerated by modern musicians.

Genres once played frequently but no longer performed regularly are honored by a retroactive shift of their dates of creation. The instrumental *gamelan degung* is often spoken of as if it were several hundred years old; it developed during the early part of the twentieth century, though some say its roots may extend to the Pajajaran era. Similarly, *tembang Sunda,* which might date from the mid-1800s, is sometimes claimed to be thousands of years old. Such antedating is a form of respect offered to now-venerable genres, and not necessarily reflective of musicians' actual knowledge. Instead, an expanded tenure for the performance of a specific type of music may describe its appropriate setting, which could indeed go back several hundred years.

The issue of experimentation and change is important to Sundanese composers, in part as a matter of regional pride. Some composers refer to their ability to be flexible and work with new creations (*kreasi baru*) as a feature that sets them apart from their counterparts in Central Java and Bali, though the Javanese and Balinese are rich in new creations of their own.

The success or failure of new compositions and genres depends on the

Frequently, musicians learn new pieces from cassettes, and an effective way for a composer to sell cassettes of his compositions is to produce modern melodies in a favored traditional style.

Sundanese cassette industry, the primary medium through which music is disseminated. Though videos of Sundanese performers appear regularly on local television, they are less representative of local artists and genres than of groups that have the money or connections to get onto the broadcast. Musicians take the production of a cassette seriously, because a good performance on a well-marketed cassette can bring them higher status among their peers, plus a greater likelihood of participation in an international tour.

Frequently, musicians learn new pieces from cassettes, and an effective way for a composer to sell cassettes of his compositions is to produce modern melodies in a favored traditional style. Preferably, the original performer should already have a major reputation. Some performers solicit compositions from the more famous composers so that buyers will be as tempted by the composer as by the performer. The Sundanese are as quick as anyone to spot a hook in a composition, and a piece with a strong hook may catch on in a matter of weeks, making the cassette a bestseller.

If a new composition is commercially successful, other musicians will cover it, possibly in a different genre. A song originally recorded with *gamelan degung* accompaniment may be recorded with *kacapi-suling, gamelan saléndro, kendang penca,* or *calung* accompaniment (for examples in popular Indonesian music, see Yampolsky 1989 and Williams 1989). The more cassettes that sell as a result of these recordings, the stronger the composer's reputation for creating hits. The stronger the reputation, the greater the freedom for exploring new genres, combinations of instruments, and experimental systems of tuning.

Ethnographic troupes and tourism

Sundanese performing groups have begun to enter the field of international touring and entertainment for tourists. The creation of an ethnographic troupe suitable for touring requires a performer who can cope with unfamiliar surroundings and food, versatility in playing a variety of instruments or being able to dance and play, and the ability to get a passport and visas. A potential member's close relationship to the leader (blood relative, student, neighbor) is yet another variable determining troupe membership.

Performers who have had experience traveling abroad and already have a passport are far more likely to be recruited than those who do not. The logistics and expense of acquiring a passport are so complicated that leaders take its presence or absence into account when considering a candidate for membership. The more versatile a performer, the more likely he will be selected. The result of this process is that, in some cases, the ethnographic show presented to foreigners can be a low-level representation of everything a troupe can present, rather than a sample of several high-quality genres. Troupes frequently travel to Singapore, Hong Kong, Malaysia, Thailand, Saudi Arabia, Japan, the United States, France, Germany, and Holland—but not so far as South America or Africa.

An ethnographic troupe may be an offshoot of the standard Sundanese performing arts group (*lingkung seni*). The initial contract is usually made through the leader, who hires his core group and some outsiders to fulfill all the requests for specific genres. In a touring situation, the stakes are much higher than in an average performance because of the prestige of having successfully completed an international tour. A single trip abroad may gain a performer entrance into a better group, a recording contract, a teaching position, or other marks of higher status.

In a performance for foreigners (usually meaning an international tour or large-scale performance in Jakarta or Bandung), the Sundanese try to present visually exciting genres that best represent their diversity. Most leaders that have toured acknowledge competing with Javanese and Balinese troupes who have preceded them, and part of the competition is to be more diverse in their presentation than the other two ethnic groups.

A typical ethnographic show will include rod-puppet theater, *kliningan, tari klasik, tari topèng, tari jaipongan,* and one or more of the heavily costumed modern dances (such as the peacock dance), all accompanied by a *gamelan saléndro*. It may also include a performance of diatonic *angklung, tembang Sunda,* or *gamelan degung*. These options depend on the sponsors, who may or may not be willing to pay for the extra cost of shipping the other instruments. The *gamelan saléndro* is considered practical because it accompanies multiple genres.

When a sponsor makes a specific request, the group does all it can to fulfill that request. If an Islamic leader arrives for a performance, the group may try to incorporate Arabic verses or add Islamic frame drums to honor him. Special verses in Arabic, Dutch, English, and Japanese are learned and brought out when the situation requires. If the group can play *angklung,* it will more likely tour with a diatonic set than a traditional *saléndro* set, because leaders, members, and some sponsors believe the ensemble should be able to play the national anthem of the majority of the members of the audience, in addition to melodies the audience will recognize, such as the "Blue Danube" waltz.

In actual practice, the performance presented by an ethnographic troupe from Sunda is rarely representative of a traditional Sundanese performance. Under normal circumstances in Sunda, the audience talks almost continuously during a performance, except in the rare situation of musical gatherings in which the listeners are performers themselves. Children are a constant presence at performances, and the musicians and dancers are quite relaxed about their performances. Sundanese audiences rarely applaud for more than a few seconds, and in some cases not at all. Appreciation for a performer's expertise is more often expressed through the sudden sucking in of air through the teeth or other quiet sounds, which can be heard only by people in the immediate surroundings.

REFERENCES

Anderson, Benedict. 1965. *Mythology and the Tolerance of the Javanese.* Monograph Series, Modern Indonesia Project. Ithaca, N.Y.: Cornell University Press.

Ardiwijaya, Raden. 1978. "Sintren Seni Tradisi." *Kawit* 16(4):16–23.

Arps, Bernard. 1992. *Tembang in Two Traditions: Performance and Interpretation of Javanese Literature.* London: School of Oriental and African Studies.

Baier, Randal E. 1986. "Si Duriat Keueung: The Sundanese Angklung Ensemble of West Java, Indonesia." M.A. thesis, Wesleyan University.

Becker, A. L. 1979. "Text Building, Epistemology, and Aesthetics in Javanese Shadow Theater." In *The Imagination of Reality: Essays in Southeast Asian Coherence Systems,* ed. A. L. Becker and Aram Yengoyan, 211–243. Norwood, N.J.: Ablex.

Becker, A. L., and Judith Becker. 1981. "A Musical Icon: Power and Meaning in Javanese Gamelan Music." In *The Sign in Music and Literature,* ed. Wendy Steiner, 203–215. Austin: University of Texas Press.

Becker, A. L., and Judith Becker. 1983 [1979]. "A Grammar of the Musical Genre *Srepegan.*" *Asian Music* 14(1):30–72.

Becker, A. L., and Aram Yengoyan, eds. 1979. *The Imagination of Reality: Essays in Southeast Asian Coherence Systems.* Norwood, N.J.: Ablex.

Becker, Judith. 1979a. "Time and Tune in Java." In *The Imagination of Reality: Essays in Southeast Asian Coherence Systems,* ed. A. L. Becker and Aram Yengoyan, 197–210. Norwood, N.J.: Ablex.

———. 1979b. "People Who Sing; People Who Dance." In *What Is Modern Indonesian Culture?* ed. Gloria Davis, 3–10. Athens: Ohio University Center for International Studies.

———. 1980 [1972]. *Traditional Music in Modern Java: Gamelan in a Changing Society.* Honolulu: University of Hawaii Press.

———. 1988. "Earth, Fire, *Sakti,* and the Javanese Gamelan." *Ethnomusicology* 32(3):385–391.

Becker, Judith, and Alan Feinstein, eds. 1984, 1987, 1988. *Karawitan: Source Readings in Javanese Gamelan and Vocal Music.* 3 vols. Ann Arbor: Center for South and Southeast Asian Studies, University of Michigan.

Brakel-Papenhuijzen, Clara. 1992. *The Bedhaya Court Dances of Central Java.* Leiden: E. J. Brill.

Brandon, James R. 1967. *Theatre in Southeast Asia.* Cambridge, Mass.: Harvard University Press.

———. 1970. *On Thrones of Gold: Three Javanese Shadow Plays.* Cambridge, Mass.: Harvard University Press.

Brandts Buys, J. S. 1921. "Over de ontwikkelingsmogelijkheden van de muziek op Java" (On the developmental possibilities of music in Java). *Djawa* 1, Praeadvies 2, 1–90.

———. 1926 "Over muziek in het Banjoewangische" (On music in Banyuwangi). *Djawa* 6:205–228.

———. 1928. "De Toonkunst bij de Madoereezen" (The music of the Madurese). *Djawa* 8:1–290.

———. 1929. "Een en ander over Javaansche muziek" (This and that about Javanese music). *Programma van het Vijfde-Congres ter gelegenheid van het tienjarig bestaan van het Java Instituut,* 45–63.

Brandts Buys, J. S., and A. Brandts Buys–Van Zijp. 1925. "Oude Klanken" (Old sounds). *Djawa* 5(1):16–56.

Brinner, Benjamin E. 1995. *Knowing Music, Making Music: Javanese Gamelan and the Theory of Musical Competence and Interaction.* Chicago: University of Chicago Press.

Carbon, P. A. 1972. *1720 Purwaka Tjaruban Nagari,* trans. the Penanggung Jawab Sejarah Cirebon dan staf Kaprabonan. Jakarta: Bharata.

Clara van Groenendael, Victoria. 1985. *The Dalang behind the Wayang.* Verhandelingen van de Koninklijk Instituut voor Taal-, Land- en Volkenkunde, 114. Dordrecht, Holland, and Providence, R. I.: Foris Publications.

———. 1990. "Po-te-hi: The Chinese glove-puppet theatre in East Java." Paper presented at the International Symposium on Indonesian Performing Arts, School of Oriental and African Studies, University of London, July–August, 1990.

Cornets de Groot, A. D. 1852. "Bijdrage tot de kennis van de zeden en gewoonten der Javanen" (Contribution to the knowledge of the manners and customs of the Javanese). *Tijdschrift voor Nederlandsch Indie* 14(2):257–280, 346–367, 393–424.

Crawford, Michael. 1980. "Indonesia: East Java." *The New Grove Dictionary of Music and Musicians,* ed. Stanley Sadie. London: Macmillan.

Dewantara, Ki Hadjar. 1964. *Serat Sari Swara* (Essence of sound / voice), 2nd ed. Jakarta: P. N. Pradnjaparamita.

Djakoeb [Jakub] and Wignjaroemeksa [Wignyarumeksa]. 1913. *Lajang anjoeroepaké Pratikelé bab Sinaoe Naboeh sarto Panggawéné Gamelan* (Writings on methods for studying the playing and making of gamelan). Volkslectuur, 94. Batawi [Jakarta]: Pirma Papirus.

———. 1919. *Serat Enoet Gending Sléndro* (Book of *gendhing* in sléndro). Volkslectuur, 94. Batavia [Jakarta]: Landsdrukkerij.

Ellis, Alexander J. 1884. "Tonometrical Observations on Some Existing Nonharmonic Musical Scales." *Proceedings of the Royal Society* 37:368–385.

Falk, Catherine A. 1982. "The Tarawangsa Tradition in West Java." Ph.D. dissertation, Monash University.

Foley, M. Kathleen. 1979. "The Sundanese 'Wayang Golek': The Rod Puppet Theatre of West Java." Ph.D. dissertation, University of Hawai'i.

———. 1984. "Of Dalang and Dukun-Spirit and Men: Curing and Performance in the Wayang of West Java." *Asian Theatre Journal* 1(1):52–75.

———. 1985. "The Dancer and the Danced: Trance Dance and Theatrical Performance in West Java." *Asian Theatre Journal* 2(1):28–49.

———. 1986. "At the Graves of the Ancestors: Chronicle Plays in the Wayang Cepak Puppet Theatre of Cirebon, Indonesia." In *Historical Drama,* ed. James Redmond, 31–49. Themes in Drama, 8. Cambridge: Cambridge University Press.

———. 1990. "My Bodies:The Performer in West Java." *The Drama Review* 34(2):62–80.

Geertz, Clifford. 1960. *The Religion of Java.* New York: Free Press.

Groneman, J. 1890. *De Gamelan te Jogjakarta.* Amsterdam: Johannes Müller.

Harrell, Max Leigh. 1974. "The Music of the Gamelan Degung of West Java." Ph.D. dissertation, University of California, Los Angeles.

Hastanto, Sri. 1985. "The Concept of Pathet in Javanese Gamelan Music." Ph.D. dissertation, University of Durham, England.

Hatch, Martin. 1976. "The Song Is Ended: Changes in the Use of Macapat in Central Java." *Asian Music* 7(2):59–71.

———. 1979. "Towards a More Open Approach to the History of Javanese Music." *Indonesia* 27:129–154.

———. 1980. "Lagu, Laras, Layang: Rethinking Melody in Javanese Music." Ph.D. dissertation, Cornell University.

———. 1985. "Popular Music in Indonesia." In *Popular Music Perspectives,* vol. 2, ed. D. Horn, 210–227. Goteborg: The International Association for the Study of Popular Music.

Hatley, Barbara. 1971. "Wayang and Ludruk: Polarities in Java." *The Drama Review* 15(3):88–101.

———. 1980. *Ketoprak Theatre and the Wayang Tradition.* Melbourne: Monash University Press.

Hefner, Robert. 1987. "The Politics of Popular Art: *Tayuban* Dance and Culture Change in East Java." *Indonesia* 43:75–94.

Heins, Ernst L. 1967. "Music of the Serimpi 'Anglir Mendung'." *Indonesia* 3:135–151.

———. 1969. "Tempo (Irama) in de M.-Javaanse gamelanmuziek." *Kultuurpatronen* 10–11:31–57.

———. 1970. "Cueing the Gamelan in Javanese Wayang Performance." *Indonesia* 9(April):101–127.

———. 1977. "Goong Renteng: Aspects of Orchestral Music in a Sundanese Village." Ph.D. dissertation, University of Amsterdam.

Hoffman, Stanley B. 1978. "Epistemology and Music: A Javanese Example." *Ethnomusicology* 22(1):69–88.

Hood, Mantle. 1954. *The Nuclear Theme as a Determinant of Paṭet in Javanese Music.* Groningen: J. B. Wolters.

———. 1966. "Sléndro and Pélog Redefined." *Selected Reports* 1(1):28– 48.

———. 1970. "The Effect of Medieval Technology on Musical Styles in the Orient." *Selected Reports* 1(3):148–170.

———. 1971. "Aspects of Group Improvisation in the Javanese Gamelan." In *Musics of Asia.* Manila: National Music Council.

———. 1972. "Music of Indonesia." In *Music,* ed. Mantle Hood and José Maceda, 1–27. Leiden and Cologne: E. J. Brill.

———. 1980. *The Evolution of Javanese Gamelan, Book I: Music of the Roaring Sea.* Wilhelmshaven: Edition Heinrichshofen.

———. 1984. *The Evolution of Javanese Gamelan, Book II: Legacy of the Roaring Sea.* Wilhelmshaven: Edition Heinrichshofen.

———. 1988. *The Evolution of Javanese Gamelan, Book III: Paragon of the Roaring Sea.* Wilhelmshaven: Edition Heinrichshofen.

Hughes, David. 1988. "Deep Structure and Surface Structure in Javanese Music: A Grammar of *Gendhing Lampah.*" *Ethnomusicology* 32(1):23–74.

Hughes-Freeland, Felicia. 1990. "*Tayuban:* Culture on the Edge." *Indonesia Circle* 52:36–44.

Jacobson, Edward, and J. H. van Hasselt. 1975 [1907]. "The Manufacture of Gongs in Semarang," trans. Andrew Toth. *Indonesia* 19:127–152, plates.

Kartomi, Margaret. 1973a [1968]. *Matjapat Songs in Central and West Java.* Canberra: Australia National University Press.

———. 1973b. "Music and Trance in Java." *Ethnomusicology* 17(2):163– 208.

———. 1976. "Performance, Music and Meaning in Réyog Ponorogo." *Indonesia* 22:85–130.

———. 1990. *On Concepts and Classifications of Musical Instruments.* Chicago Studies in Ethnomusicology. Chicago: University of Chicago Press.

Keeler, Ward. 1975. "Musical Encounter in Java and Bali." *Indonesia* 19:85–126.

———. 1987. *Javanese Shadow Plays, Javanese Selves.* Princeton, N. J.: Princeton University Press.

Kertanegara, et al. 1889–? "Pakem Wirama: wileting gendhing berdangga." Manuscript in several versions, housed at Krida Mardawa library, Yogyakarta *kraton,* and National Museum, Jakarta; romanized typescript in Sono Budoyo Museum, Yogyakarta.

Komisi Pasinaon Nabuh Gamelan. 1924. *Buku Piwulangan Nabuh Gamelan* (Book of lessons for playing gamelan), vol. 1. Surakarta: Pangecapan Swastika.

———. 1925. *Buku Piwulangan Nabuh Gamelan* (Book of lessons for playing gamelan), vol. 2. Surakarta: Budi Utama.

Kunst, Jaap. 1968 [1927]. *Hindu-Javanese Musical Instruments.* The Hague: Martinus Nijhoff.

———. 1973 [1934]. *Music in Java: Its History, Its Theory, and Its Technique,* 3rd ed., rev. and enlarged by Ernst Heins. 2 vols. The Hague: Martinus Nijhoff.

Kusumadinata, R. Machyar. 1969. *Ilmu Seni Raras.* Jakarta: Pradnya Paramita.

Lindsay, Jennifer. 1985. "Klasik, Kitsch or Contemporary: A Study of the Javanese Performing Arts." Ph.D. dissertation, University of Sydney.

———. 1991. *Klasik, Kitsch, Kontemporer: Sebuah Studi Tentang Seni Pertunjukan Jawa,* trans. Nin Bakdi Sumanto. Yogyakarta: Gadjah Mada University Press [translation of Lindsay 1985].

Lysloff, René. 1990a. "Srikandhi Dances Lènggèr: A Performance of Music and Shadow Theater in Banyumas (West Central Java)." 2 vols. Ph.D. dissertation, University of Michigan.

———. 1990b. "Non-Puppets and Non-Gamelan: Wayang Parody in Banyumas." *Ethnomusicology* 34(1):19–36.

Manuel, Peter, and Randal E. Baier. 1986. "Jaipongan: Indigenous Popular Music of West Java." *Asian Music* 18(1):91–110.

Martopangrawit, R. L. 1972b. *Titilaras Kendangan* (Drum notation). Surakarta: Akademi Seni Karawitan Indonesia.

———. 1973. *Titilaras Cengkok-cengkok Genderan dengan Wiletannya* (Notation of melodic patterns for *gendèr* with their variations), vol. 1. Surakarta: Akademi Seni Karawitan Indonesia.

———. 1975. *Titilaras Gendhing dan Sindenan Bedaya-Srimpi Kraton Surakarta* (Notation of *gendhing* and vocal parts for *bedhaya* and *srimpi* of the court of Surakarta). Surakarta: Akademi Seni Karawitan Indonesia.

———. 1976. *Titilaras Cengkok-cengkok Genderan dengan Wiletannya* (Notation of melodic patterns for *gendèr* with their variations), vol. 2. Surakarta: Akademi Seni Karawitan Indonesia.

———. 1984 [1969, 1972a]. *Catatan-Catatan Pengetahuan Karawitan* (Notes on knowledge of gamelan music), trans. Martin Hatch. In *Karawitan: Source Readings in Javanese and Vocal Music,* ed. Judith Becker and Alan Feinstein, 1–244. Ann Arbor: Center for South and Southeast Asian Studies, University of Michigan.

McDermott, Vincent, and Sumarsam. 1975. "Central Javanese Music: The Pa*t*et of Laras Sléndro and the Gendèr Barung." *Ethnomusicology* 19:233–244.

Morgan, Stephanie, and Laurie Jo Sears, eds. 1984. *Aesthetic Tradition and Cultural Transition in Java and Bali.* Madison: University of Wisconsin Center for Southeast Asian Studies.

Murgiyanto, Sal. 1991. *Dance of Indonesia.* New York: Festival of Indonesia Foundation.

North, Richard. 1988. "An Introduction to the Musical Traditions of Cirebon." *Balungan* 3(3):2–6.

Notosudirdjo, R. Franki S. 1990. "European Music in Colonial Life in Nineteenth-Century Java: A Preliminary Study." M.A. thesis, University of Wisconsin–Madison.

Onghokham. 1972. "The Wayang Topèng World of Malang." *Indonesia* 14:111–124.

Paku Buwana V. 1986–1991. *Serat Centhini (Suluk Tambanglaras),* romanized by Kamajaya. 12 vols. Yogyakarta: Yayasan Centhini Yogyakarta.

Peacock, James. 1968. *Rites of Modernization: Symbolic and Social Aspects of Indonesian Proletarian Drama.* Chicago: University of Chicago Press.

Perlman, Marc. 1983. "Notes on 'A Grammar of the Musical Genre *Srepegan*'." *Asian Music* 14(1):17–29.

———. 1991. "Asal-usul notasi gendhing Jawa di Surakarta: suatu rumusan rejarah nut ranté." *Seni Pertunjukan Indonesia* 2(2):36–68.

———. 1993. "Unplayed Melodies: Music Theory in Post-Colonial Java." Ph.D. dissertation, Wesleyan University.

Pigeaud, T. 1938. *Javaanse Volksvertoningen: Bijdrage tot de Beschrijving van Land en Volk.* Batavia: Volkslectuur.

Powers, Harold. 1980. "Mode." *The New Grove Dictionary of Music and Musicians,* ed. Stanley Sadie. London: Macmillan.

Probohardjono, R. Ng. S. 1954. *Sulukan Pélog: Buku Kanggé Njuluki Padalangan Wajang Gedog.* Surakarta: Budhi Laksana.

———. 1984 [1966]. *Sléndro Songs of the Dhalang,* trans. Susan Pratt Walton. In *Karawitan: Source Readings in Javanese Gamelan and Vocal Music,* ed. Judith Becker and Alan Feinstein, 439–523. Ann Arbor: Center for South and Southeast Asian Studies, University of Michigan.

Proyek Penelitian dan Pencatatan Kebudayaan Daerah. 1976. *Ensiklopedi Seni Musik dan Seni Tari Daerah Jawa Timur* (Encyclopedia of music and dance in the region of Eastern Java). Surabaya: Departemen Pendidikan dan Kebudayaan.

Raffles, Thomas Stamford. 1978 [1817]. *The History of Java.* 2 vols. Kuala Lumpur: Oxford University Press.

Ricklefs, M. C. 1981. *A History of Modern Indonesia: c.1300 to the Present.* Bloomington: Indiana University Press.

Rogers-Aguiniga, Pamela. 1986. "Topeng Cirebon: The Masked Dance of West Java as Performed in the Village of Slangit." M.A. thesis, University of California, Los Angeles.

Schumacher, Rüdiger. 1980. *Die Suluk-Gesang des Dalang im Schattenspiel Zentraljavas.* 2 vols. Munich and Salzburg: Musikverlag Emil Katsbichler.

Sears, Laurie Jo. 1991. "Javanese Mahabharata Stories: Oral Performances and Written Texts." In *Boundaries of the Text,* ed. Joyce B. Flueckiger and Laurie J. Sears. Ann Arbor: University of Michigan, Center for South and Southeast Asian Studies.

Siddique, Sharon. 1977. "Relics of the Past: A Sociological Study of the Sultanates of Cirebon, West Java." Ph.D. dissertation, Universität Bielefeld, Germany.

Sindoesawarno, Ki. 1987 [1955]. *The Science of Gamelan,* trans. Martin Hatch. In *Karawitan: Source Readings in Javanese Gamelan and Vocal Music,* ed. Judith Becker and Alan Feinstein, 389–407. Ann Arbor: Center for South and Southeast Asian Studies, University of Michigan.

Soedarsono. 1984. *Wayang Wong: The State Ritual Dance Drama in the Court of Yogyakarta.* Yogyakarta: Gadjah Mada University Press.

Soeradipura, R. Ng., et al., eds. 1912–1915. *Serat Tjenthini: Babon Asli Saking Kita Leiden ing Negari Nederland* (The book of Centhini: from an original manuscript in Leiden, The Netherlands). 8 vols., bound as 4. Betawi [Jakarta]: Ruygrok.

Suanda, Endo. 1981. "The Social Context of Cirebonese Performing Artists." *Asian Music* 13(1):27–42.

———. 1986. "Cirebonese Topeng and Wayang of the Present Day." *Asian Music* 16(2):84–120.

———. 1988. "Dancing in Cirebonese Topeng." *Balungan* 3(3):7–15.

Suharto, Ben. 1979. *Langen Mandra Wanara di Daerah Istimewa Yogyakarta.* Yogyakarta: Proyek Pengembangan Institut Kesenian Indonesia, Departemen Pendidikan dan Kebudayaan.

Sulendraningrat, P. S. 1975. *Sejarah Cirebon.* Cirebon: Lembaga Kebudayaan Wilayah III.

Sumarsam. 1975a. "Inner Melody in Javanese Gamelan Music." *Asian Music* 7(1):3–13.

———. 1975b. "Gendèr Barung, Its Technique and Function in the Context of Javanese Gamelan." *Indonesia* 20:161–172.

———. 1981. "The Musical Practice of the Gamelan Sekatèn." *Asian Music* 12(2):54–73.

———. 1984a. "Gamelan Music and the Javanese Wayang Kulit." In Morgan and Sears 1984:105–116.

———. 1984b. "Inner Melody in Javanese Gamelan." M.A. thesis, Wesleyan University. In *Karawitan: Source Readings in Javanese and Vocal Music*, ed. Judith Becker and Alan Feinstein, 245–304. Ann Arbor: Center for South and Southeast Asian Studies, University of Michigan.

———. 1987. "Introduction to Ciblon Drumming in Javanese Gamelan." In *Karawitan: Source Readings in Javanese and Vocal Music*, ed. Judith Becker and Alan Feinstein, 171–203. Ann Arbor: Center for South and Southeast Asian Studies, University of Michigan.

———. 1992. "Historical Contexts and Theories of Javanese Music." Ph.D. dissertation, Cornell University.

———. 1995. *Gamelan: Cultural Interaction and Musical Development in Central Java.* Chicago: University of Chicago Press.

Sunardjo, R. H. Unang. 1983. *Meninjau Sepintas Panggung Sejarah Pemerintahan Kerajaan Cerbon 1479–1809.* Bandung: Tarsito.

Supanggah, Rahayu. 1985. "Introduction aux styles d'interpretation dans la musique javanaise." Ph.D. dissertation, University of Paris.

Surjodiningrat, R. M. Wasisto, P. J. Sudarjana, and Adhi Susanto. 1972. *Tone Measurements of Outstanding Javanese Gamelans in Jogjakarta and Surakarta.* Yogyakarta: Gadjah Mada University Press.

Susilo, Hardja. 1984. "Wayang Wong Panggung: Its Social Context, Technique, and Music." In *Aesthetic Tradition and Cultural Transition in Java and Bali*, ed. Stephanie Morgan and Laurie Jo Sears, 117–161. Madison: University of Wisconsin Center for Southeast Asian Studies.

———. 1989. "The Logogenesis of Gendhing Lampah." *Progress Reports in Ethnomusicology* 2(5).

Sutton, R. Anderson. 1975. "The Javanese Gambang and its Music." M.A. thesis, University of Hawaii.

———. 1978. "Notes Toward a Grammar of Variation in Javanese *Gendèr* Playing." *Ethnomusicology* (22)2: 275–96.

———. 1979. "Concept and Treatment in Javanese Gamelan Music, with Reference to the Gambang." *Asian Music* 9(2):59–79.

———. 1982. "Variation in Javanese Gamelan Music: Dynamics of a Steady State." Ph.D. dissertation, University of Michigan.

———. 1984a. "Who Is the Pesindhèn? Notes on the Female Singing Tradition in Java." *Indonesia* 37:118–131.

———. 1984b. "Change and Ambiguity: Gamelan Style and Regional Identity in Yogyakarta." In *Aesthetic Tradition and Cultural Transition in Java and Bali*, ed. Stephanie Morgan and Laurie Jo Sears, 221–245. Madison: University of Wisconsin Center for Southeast Asian Studies.

———. 1985a. "Musical Pluralism in Java: Three Local Traditions." *Ethnomusicology* 29(1):56–85.

———. 1985b. "Commercial Cassette Recordings of Traditional Music in Java: Implications for Performers and Scholars." *World of Music* 27(3):23–45.

———. 1986a. "The Crystallization of a Marginal Tradition: Music in Banyumas, West Central Java." *Yearbook for Traditional Music* 18:115–132.

———. 1986b. "New Theory for Traditional Music in Banyumas, West Central Java." *Pacific Review of Ethnomusicology* 3:79–101.

———. 1989. "Identity and Individuality in an Ensemble Tradition: The Female Vocalist in Java." In *Women and Music in Cross-Cultural Perspective*, ed. Ellen Koskoff, 111–130. Urbana and Chicago: University of Illinois Press.

———. 1991a. *Traditions of Gamelan Music in Java: Musical Pluralism and Regional Identity.* Cambridge Studies in Ethnomusicology. Cambridge: Cambridge University Press.

———. 1993. *Variation in Central Javanese Gamelan Music: Dynamics of a Steady State.* Special report 28. DeKalb: Center for Southeast Asian Studies, Northern Illinois University.

Timoer, Soenarto. 1988. *Serat Wewaton Pedhalangan Jawi Wetanan* (Standards of east Javanese shadow puppetry). 2 vols. Jakarta: P. N. Balai Pustaka.

Tirasonjaya, Gugum Gumbira. 1979. "Ketuk Tilu Merupakan Tari Rakyat Khas Jawa Barat" (*Ketuk tilu* is an original West Javanese folk dance). *Kawit* 23(1):19–27.

Toth, Andrew F. 1970. "Music of the Gamelan Sekati." B.A. honors thesis, Wesleyan University.

Van Zanten, Wim. 1989. *Sundanese Music in the Cianjuran Style: Anthropological and Musicological Aspects of Tembang Sunda.* Providence, R.I.: Foris Publications.

———. 1994. "Aspects of Baduy Singing." Paper presented at the workshop "Performing Arts in South-East Asia" at the Koninklijk Instituut voor Taal-, Land- en Volkenkunde (KITLV), Leiden University, Netherlands. Available from the KITLV.

Vetter, Roger R. 1984. "Poetic, Musical and Dramatic Structures in a Langen Mandra Wanara Performance." In *Aesthetic Tradition and Cultural Transition in Java and Bali*, ed. Stephanie Morgan and Laurie Jo Sears, 163–208. Madison: University of Wisconsin Center for Southeast Asian Studies.

———. 1986. "Music for 'The Lap of the World': Gamelan Performance, Performers, and Repertoire in the Kraton Yogyakarta." Ph.D. dissertation, University of Wisconsin at Madison.

———. 1989. "A Retrospect on a Century of Gamelan Tone Measurements." *Ethnomusicology* 33(2):217–227.

Wagner, Frits A. 1959. *Indonesia: The Art of an Island Group.* New York: Crown.

Walton, Susan Pratt. 1987 [1973]. *Mode in Javanese Music.* Athens, Ohio: Ohio University Center for International Studies.

Warsadiningrat. 1987 [1972]. *Sacred Knowledge about Gamelan Music,* trans. Susan P. Walton. In *Karawitan: Source Readings in Javanese Gamelan and Vocal Music*, ed. Judith Becker and Alan Feinstein, 1–170. Ann Arbor: Center for South and Southeast Asian Studies, University of Michigan.

Weintraub, Andrew. 1990. "The Music of Pantun Sunda: An Epic Narrative Tradition of West Java, Indonesia." M.A. thesis, University of Hawai'i.

———. 1993. "Theory as Institutionalized Pedagogy and 'Theory in Practice' for Sundanese Gamelan Music." *Ethnomusicology* 37(1):29–40.

———. 1997. "Constructing the Popular: Superstars, Performance, and Cultural Authority in Sundanese *Wayang Golek Purwa* of West Java, Indonesia." Ph.D. dissertation, University of California, Berkeley.

Wessing, Robert. 1977. "The Position of the Baduy in the Larger West Javanese Society." *Man* 12(2):293–303.

———. 1978. *Cosmology and Social Behavior in a West Javanese Settlement.* Athens, Ohio: Ohio University Center for International Studies, SEA Program.

Williams, Sean. 1989. "Current Developments in Sundanese Popular Music." *Asian Music* 21(1):105–136.

———. 1990. "The Urbanization of Tembang Sunda, an Aristocratic Musical Genre of West Java, Indonesia." Ph.D. dissertation, University of Washington.

Wolbers, Paul Arthur. 1986. "Gandrung and Angklung from Banyuwangi: Remnants of a Past Shared with Bali." *Asian Music* 18(1):71–90.

———. 1987. "Account of an Angklung Caruk, July 28, 1985." *Indonesia* 43:66–74.

———. 1989. "Transvestism, Eroticism, and Religion: In Search of a Contextual Background for the Gandrung and Seblang Traditions of Banyuwangi, East Java." *Progress Reports in Ethnomusicology* 2(6).

———. 1992. "Maintaining Using Identity through Musical Performance: *Seblang* and *Gandrung* of Banyuwangi, East Java (Indonesia)." Ph.D. dissertation, University of Illinois at Urbana-Champaign.

Wongsosewojo, R. Ahmad. 1930. "Loedroek." *Djawa* 10:204–207.

Wright, Michael R. 1978. "The Music Culture of Cirebon." Ph.D. dissertation, University of California, Los Angeles.

———. 1988. "Tarling: Modern Music from Cirebon." *Balungan* 3(3):21– 25.

Yampolsky, Philip. 1987. *Lokananta: A Discography of the National Recording Company of Indonesia, 1957–1985.* Madison: University of Wisconsin Center for Southeast Asian Studies.

———. 1989. "Hati Yang Luka: An Indonesian Hit." *Indonesia* 47:1–17.

Bali

David Harnish

Bali, perhaps Indonesia's most famous island, is known worldwide for its art, music, and dance. Visiting writers and scholars have frequently commented on artistic activity in Balinese society since the early 1800s, observing that everyone is both artist and farmer (or nobleman). Though twentieth-century Balinese society has undergone many changes, this perception remains fairly valid. The local religion, a form of Saivite Hinduism with an integrated pre-Hindu ancestor cult, demands artistic work as a form of religious practice. All Balinese traditional music has roots in religious belief. Music and art are so ingrained into religion and into daily life that until recently they had no equivalent terms in the Balinese language except as components of ritual work (*karya*). Learning and performing the arts are a normal experience of life. Music and dance, like harvesting rice, are believed to be beneficial for the village. They are necessary components of major celebrations, and the performing arts have long functioned as a traditional form of education and enculturation.

The arts, and particularly music, accompany the stages of the human cycle of life. Balinese are greeted with music at birth, and at death are accompanied to the cremation grounds with it. The temples of Bali have a cycle of their own; they must be purified and revived through annual festivals that reconnect the past with the present through prescribed rites, offerings, and performing arts. Among the performing arts of Bali, music has the greatest ritual function.

Most Balinese music is orchestral and is performed on ensembles known as gamelans (usually bronze, but sometimes made of other materials), comprising gongs, metallophones, kettle gongs, and drums, unified by their musical structure. Most Balinese orchestral music consists of traditional and ceremonial pieces, theater and dance accompaniment, and a genre developed in the twentieth century, *kebyar* 'to flare up', which includes newer recreational compositions based primarily upon traditional forms and styles. The ceremonial pieces are handed down from the ancestors; the newer compositions are credited to named composers, acknowledged as great artists.

The *gamelan gong kebyar,* a gamelan developed from a ceremonial model, emerged in 1915, and has performed the vast majority of modern compositions. The *kebyar* success led to the later movement *kreasi baru* 'new creation', virtuoso *kebyar*

There are more than twenty-five different varieties of gamelan in Bali, distinguished by size, musical instruments, tuning, repertoire, context, and function.

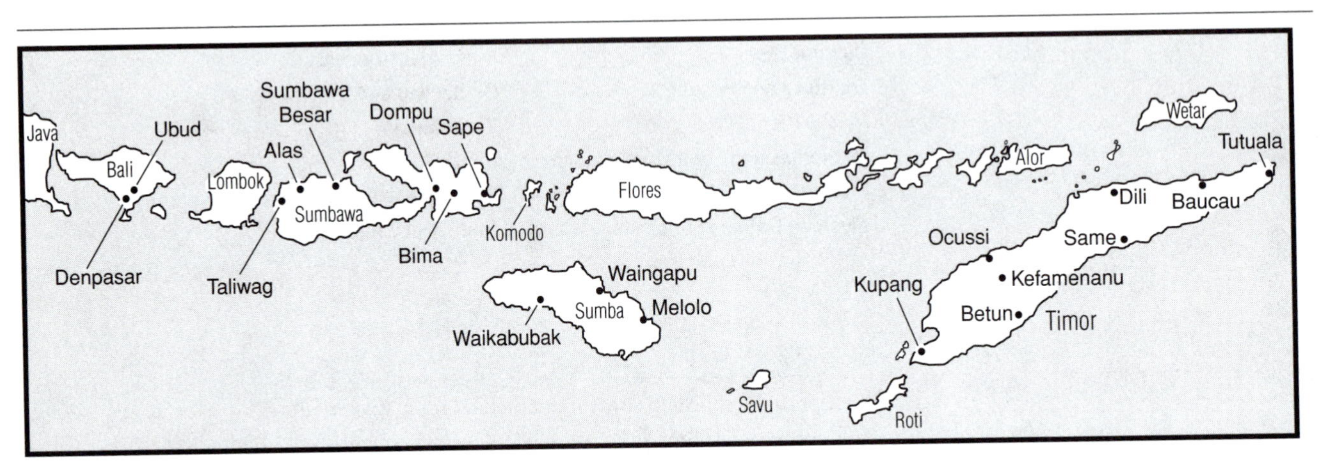

Bali, Nusa Tenggara Barat (Lombok and Sumbawa), and Nusa Tenggara Timur

pieces, still based on traditional forms and structures, but expanding into new musical territory. Two genres initiated in the 1970s reflect globalization but have yet to find general acceptance. They are *musik kontemporer* 'contemporary music' (developed primarily in conservatories), which often deviates radically from traditional forms and structures, and *Bali pop* 'popular music of Bali', youth-directed songs based on Western popular music with occasional Balinese elements and sung in Balinese and Indonesian languages. In 1986, a *kebyar*-style repertoire, *kreasi baleganjur* '*baleganjur* creation', developed for the processional *gamelan baleganjur,* and has found success. Performed by male youth, *kreasi baleganjur* demonstrates how successive generations of musicians develop new styles from indigenous material in response to social and aesthetic changes.

Traditional music constantly undergoes renewal, change, transformation, and variation, both in the villages and towns and in the influential conservatories. The treatment of traditional material—tempos, figuration, elaboration, dynamics—is repeatedly altered to suit a particular group, or to reflect an emerging aesthetic. Some compositions are known all over the island, and each area has its own preferred style of performance. However, many compositions are known only within certain regions or even within single villages. Bali, an island roughly half the size of Delaware, supports a striking diversity of musical styles, pieces, and orchestral configurations.

There are more than twenty-five different varieties of gamelan in Bali, distinguished by size, musical instruments, tuning, repertoire, context, and function. Among these, six or seven are common throughout the island, whereas others are found in only a few villages. Though some villages own only a single gamelan, others own several of the standard ensembles, with perhaps two or more of certain types. The other gamelans are usually found in remote villages. Each gamelan in a village has its own context, meaning, and function.

The older the ensemble, the greater the closeness to the ancestors and the greater its accumulation of spiritual power; therefore, most older ensembles are considered sacred. These gamelans are thought to possess magical properties, and their performances are believed capable, for example, of creating rainfall or protecting the village. Some of the sacred ensembles are believed to have originated in the East Javanese empire of Majapahit, or to have been bestowed on the village directly by deities. Most gamelans, however, are not held sacred, though they are greatly respected and thought to harbor a spirit presence which normally inhabits the gong(s) of the ensemble. The imagery of Majapahit and other kingdoms in East Java still provides models of refinement and behavior for many Balinese and is the basis for many types of music, theater, and poetry.

Bali is located just to the east of Java. Historically, its culture has experienced several waves of influence from Java, and this has contributed to the development of Balinese ensemble music, as evidenced by a similar music terminology and inventory of instruments. The Javanese also influenced different types of poetry. Poetry in Bali is always sung, and each different type of Balinese poetry has prescribed contexts. The development of context-specific poetry has helped preserve the various poetic forms, and scribes have loyally transcribed the texts for centuries. Bali has retained Javanese poetic forms that have been mostly abandoned by the Javanese. The Balinese rarely adapted Javanese musical traditions, however, but used Javanese concepts to inspire artistic development uniquely their own. Internal innovations have also revolutionized the role of the arts, leading to new creations.

CULTURAL HISTORY

It is difficult to establish the roots of early Balinese society. The island, like much of Southeast Asia, was inhabited by an Australoid people about forty thousand years ago. About five thousand years ago, the first peoples of Malayo-Polynesian stock began settling along the coasts, and this settlement intensified from two thousand to three thousand years ago. Some direct Indian influence on Bali began in the 700s or 800s, and perhaps earlier; Javanese Hindu-Buddhist influence first occurred in the 800s. Agriculture focusing on wet rice, which governs much of the organization of Balinese society and first developed in the 600s and 700s, was greatly expanded, and small kingdoms evolved on Indic and Javanese concepts.

Writings and bas-reliefs on temples and monuments show that certain aerophones and chordophones once existed, but this evidence may have been fashioned to accommodate Indic cultural models. Although bamboo aerophones probably were used, chordophones probably were not, and it is likely that wood and bamboo idiophones played an important role in the music. Though large bronze kettle-shaped drums were forged in Bali more than a thousand years ago, they served, not for making music, but for rituals in a manner unknown today. In time, bronze idiophones emerged, perhaps because of increased levels of Javanese influence.

Balinese culture received varying degrees of Javanese influence from the 900s to the 1200s, and was heavily influenced by the East Javanese kingdom of Majapahit during the 1300s and 1400s. In the 1500s, with the encroachment of Islam in Java, artisans, priests, and nobles of this empire fled to Bali, where aspects of Javanese and Balinese culture continued to develop, particularly in the court centers of Gelgel and Klungkung. From this period until Dutch colonization (1908–1942), the courts set the standards for music, dance, and theater, as kings, who invited and supported the finest artists from the villages, commissioned the development of several types of performing arts, many of which still exist.

Bali appears to have been relatively isolated from the Javanese between 1650 and 1945, and Balinese hegemony, deliberately invoking the imagery of Majapahit, spread to colonize Lombok, the neighbor island to the east, in the 1600s and 1700s. Balinese aristocrats fought among themselves throughout the centuries, eventually dividing Bali into eight districts, all of which were threatened by expanding Dutch military interests. While the districts of Buleleng and Jembrana accepted subordinate relationships with the Dutch colonial powers in the 1800s, most of the other districts fell to Dutch imperialism following fierce warfare and mass suicides in 1906 and 1908. The Dutch quickly consolidated their power and colonized the island.

Colonization immediately limited court revenues in most districts, which resulted in a sharp decline of patronage for the arts, particularly for the court gamelans and theater genres. Gamelans, like theater, demonstrated the spiritual power of the courts. Following colonization, the court ensembles were sold, pawned, or given outright to the villages. With the decline of the court gamelans, the spiritual power of the courts declined as well. Some ensembles fell into disuse, later to be melted and reforged either into new ensembles or into bullets for the Japanese during their World War II occupation of Indonesia. The courtly theater forms declined and almost vanished after Dutch colonization. The situation worsened during the early period of independence.

The transference of gamelans from the courts to the villages caused greater musical activity in the villages, which in turn led to changes in musical styles and practices, the most important being the development of the *kebyar* instrumental style. This style, which emerged from traditional repertoire and compositional form, resulted in changes of instrumentation, dynamics, and the role of music in general. Derived from the word *byar* 'flare', it developed in north Bali in 1915 and quickly spread to south Bali, then more gradually throughout the rest of Bali. A new form of dance was created which expressed the tension and excitement of the music, and the *kebyar* movement gave new recognition to composers and choreographers. *Kebyar* paralleled the new political and social orders emerging in Bali and provided a new outlet for the substantial artistic energy of Balinese villagers. Except for sacred forms, this style influenced all forms of music, dance, theater, and even the plastic arts. The *kebyar* movement has since progressed through several phases, and can be seen as an indicator of change within Balinese society.

Some writers have tried to distinguish between court or classic music and folk music, but such distinctions are arbitrary in contemporary Bali. Genres of music are not associated with particular classes, and performers come from all levels of Balinese society. The performing arts are communal efforts, whether they be the remaining court forms, such as the refined *gambuh* theater, or village *gong kebyar* ensembles.

Following independence, Bali was first grouped politically with the Lesser Sunda islands. Because it was the last Hindu area and the main tourist attraction, Bali was established as its own province in the Republic of Indonesia in 1958. With a population now approaching 3 million and receiving well over 1 million visitors per year, Bali is facing many challenging problems. The use of land on the island—of only about 5,620 square kilometers—has intensified, and Bali's natural resources are starting to erode. Developing new roads through rice fields and irrigation channels, centralizing authority, and expanding systems of communication throughout the island are immense and sensitive problems. The Balinese have also had to confront modernization, urbanization, mass media, public education, and becoming part of Indonesia, all of which have caused a number of changes in the modified system of castes, in etiquette, in divisions of labor, in the agricultural cycle, and in the process of rituals. However, Balinese leaders and local government have taken steps to help ensure the culture's preservation.

Bali first became a tourist attraction in the 1920s. Tourism increased dramatically in the 1930s, fell off during World War II, reopened in the 1950s, and increased again during the late 1960s. The most significant event for tourism was the opening of an international airport in Bali in 1969. This caused the number of tourists to double immediately, and some merchants and artists began exploiting the visitors. In the area of music, groups began presenting secularized forms of sacred theater. The government gradually responded by disallowing any new performances of sacred arts, though they let established performances continue, and officials initiated other steps to help preserve the culture. Balinese language and religion are now taught in school; conservatories have helped maintain all of the performing arts; and radio and commercial recordings have indirectly helped maintain religious identity in the face of tourism.

TREATISES AND RESEARCH

Two primary court manuscripts describe the origins of music, music theory, and the general relationship of music and musical instruments with cosmology. These are the *Prakempa* and the *Aji Gurnita* manuscripts, both written between 1850 and 1900 (Bandem 1986). Much of the information contained in them is the same, with the *Prakempa* emphasizing the more esoteric aspects of music and the *Aji Gurnita* emphasizing the more erotic aspects. Both manuscripts display the nineteenth-century courtly conception of the arts as written by scribes of the priestly caste, who were concerned with linking music to the gods and cosmos for the greater glory of the courts.

Apart from observations of early Dutch officials and other nationals trading with Bali, and an important contribution by Jaap Kunst and C. J. A. Kunst–Van Wely (1924), the only significant music research by a foreigner was Colin McPhee's work in the 1930s (McPhee 1966). His writings are still an important resource for Balinese music studies. Other scholars, travelers, and adventurers who researched Balinese music include Jane Belo, Miguel Covarrubias, Ernst Schlager, and Walter Spies. During and since the 1950s and 1960s, research by foreign scholars, composers, and musicians has increased and intensified. Noteworthy scholars include Lisa Gold, Mantle Hood, Ruby Ornstein, Urs Ramseyer, Danker Schaareman, Tilman Seebass, Michael Tenzer, Andrew Toth, Adrian Vickers, Wayne Vitale, and Richard Wallis.

Balinese and other Indonesians have also become important scholars of Balinese culture and music. I Made Bandem, I Wayan Dibia, I Wayan Rai, and a number of the faculty at the Balinese conservatories have received advanced degrees in Java and abroad, and these scholar-performers are making new discoveries in Balinese music studies and writing in international publications (Bandem 1979; Bandem and deBoer 1981; DeVale and Dibia 1991). Other renowned scholars, such as I Nyoman Rembang and I W. M. Aryasa, have published excellent studies only in Indonesian. These scholars' publications are among the most authoritative available on Balinese music. Two new organizations—the Society for Balinese Studies and the Indonesian Society for the Performing Arts—are of interest to both Indonesian and foreign researchers of Balinese music.

MUSIC THEORY

Form and structure

Balinese ensemble music is often characterized by the term *stratified polyphony,* though the various melodic lines are usually rooted in the same melodic flow. Certain musical parts and instruments are more important to the music than others, but all are necessary. Musical pieces are normally termed *tabuh* 'accent, beat' or *gending* 'composition' (referring equally to instrumental and vocal music). The music basically consists of a nuclear melody, the *pokok* 'trunk', within a cyclic metric structure. Some instruments perform the *pokok*; some punctuate it; some play an expansion or elaboration of this melody; some perform metrical punctuation; and one or two

pokok Central melody and basis for figuration

kotekan Rapid, interlocking figuration characteristic of Balinese music

angsel Dramatic rhythmic break

pengawak "Body" section of fixed-meter piece

saih pitu Seven-tone tuning system

groups of instruments normally play figurations (*kotekan*) to create multiple layers of musical sound. The higher-pitched instruments, considered the least important to a given composition, usually perform in figuration. These interlocking figurations, in which two musicians play parts of a single line, are found in nearly every type of orchestral music and constitute one of the distinguishing characteristics of Balinese music. Unlike in Java, vocal lines are rare in ensemble music, and there is no concept of an independent vocal melodic line. Similar to Java, however, the drummers set the tempo and signal changes of dynamics, musical sections, and endings.

Because interlocking parts must maintain consistency and many instruments serve metrical functions, little individual improvisation occurs. The term *group improvisation,* sometimes applied to Indonesian ensemble music, may be apt for Balinese music in which a group is led by cues from the drums or from the leaders of particular music sections. The ensemble members as a group treat the material as they see fit, and group precision is the goal. However, the lead drummer has some flexibility in his part as does the melodic leader, who plays a metallophone (*pengugal*) or a gong chime (*trompong*), and both practice limited improvisation. Particularly when accompanying theater or narrative dance, where music must follow dance, the group—and especially the drummers—must watch the dancers closely. Pieces may be expanded or contracted to follow the dance or flow of the theater, and transitions may be necessary at any time. Dramatic rhythmic breaks, *angsel,* normally performed by the entire ensemble except for the punctuating instruments and *pokok,* are signaled by the drum to accompany dance movements of particular emphasis. *Angsel* occur in both dance accompaniment and purely orchestral pieces.

Balinese musical form normally includes introductions, one or more sections forming the body of a piece (which may repeat a number of times), and an ending or concluding section. Many pieces have three parts, a configuration which in Bali has extramusical, anthropomorphic, and cosmological significance. The music is cyclic, with large gongs marking the endings of the largest melodic phrases, and other families of instruments punctuating the metric cycle or coinciding at predetermined points within the cycle; the contrasting patterns of punctuation or colotomy define specific forms.

Many scholars argue that the cyclic structure of the music is linked to the conception of the passage of time as cyclic. The ceremonial repertoire of the *gamelan gong,* the orchestra most frequently engaged for ritual events, features compositions with three main sections having anthropomorphic associations—head, body, foot—and constitutes a metaphorical journey from mountain to sea. The head (*pengawit* 'source') is usually not metered, but the body (*pengawak*) uses metric gong cycles of from sixty-four to 128 beats for the nuclear melody, and the foot (*pengecet* 'additional') contracts to a form of eight or sixteen beats, and gradually increases in tempo until the final stroke of the gong concludes the piece. One purpose of these pieces, which often require thirty minutes or more for complete realization, is to suspend the

FIGURE 1 A *pengawak* section of the *tabuh pat* form of sixty-four beats.

```
g/k . . . . . . . p . . . . . . .
k   . . . . . . . p . . . . . . .
k   . . . . . . . p . . . . . . .
k   . . . . . . . p . . . . . . .   (return to g/k)
```

FIGURE 2 The *gilak* form of eight beats.

```
g . . . g p . p
```

FIGURE 3 The *gegaboran* form of sixteen beats.

```
g . . . p . . . m . . . p . . .
```

g = gong
p = kempur (smaller hanging gong)
m = kemong (much smaller hanging gong)
k = kempli (horizontally mounted gong)

normal passage of time. The form known as *tabuh pat* 'four strikings' covers sixty-four beats of the nuclear melody, and serves for most of compositions in this repertoire (figure 1). Larger forms are augmentations of this form.

Melody, colotomic pattern, and number of beats combine to create individual compositions (also called *tabuh*) associated with particular moods, emotions, or characters in dance and theater. This is particularly true in *gambuh* and other genres of theater, where characters are introduced with their associated *tabuh*. Many traditional compositions derive from a single *tabuh* associated with a context or character. The *tabuh* for each theatrical genre, however, tend to be unique; but *kebyar* compositions may borrow *tabuh* from various traditions and put them together in succession to form a single movement following an opening tutti section. In addition, there are short ostinato forms, including *gilak* or *gilakan* (figure 2), a martial or active pattern often associated with strong male dances; *gegaboran* (figure 3), associated with female dances; *bapang*, which often accompanies dances of mythic or demonic animals; and *batel*, a repetitive pattern, commonly used to accompany fight scenes or turmoil.

Modes and systems of tuning

Most Balinese music is pentatonic. Both instrumental music and vocal music adhere to one of the two tonal systems, known as *pélog* and *sléndro*. *Sléndro* consists of five tones to the octave, spaced at nearly equidistant intervals. *Pélog* is a seven-tone system with large and small intervals (including two intervals close to semitones), from which various pentatonic modes are formed. Most gamelans in Bali, however, are uniquely tuned, with neither a standard beginning pitch nor precise interval distances for the different tunings. Metalsmiths (*pande*) use their own collections of bars for tuning, after which the smiths or professional tuners (*penglaras*) adjust the tuning to suit the musicians or owner. Therefore, there are often major differences between one *sléndro* (or *pélog*) tuning and another. The pitches seem to be placed more within tonal zones than in accordance with a precise intervallic structure.

Not all Balinese musicians use the general terms *sléndro* and *pélog*, which are Javanese in origin [see JAVA]. The indigenous concepts of Balinese tonality exist, instead, within the context of the modal system (*patutan*) and scalar system (*saih*) of particular ensembles. *Sléndro*, for example, exists as *saih gendèr wayang* 'row of *gendèr wayang* tones' (on the instrument used for the shadow-play theater), *pélog* exists as the *saih pitu* 'row of seven' tuning used for such ensembles as *gamelan gambuh* and *gamelan gambang*.

The complete seven-tone *saih pitu* system of *gamelan gambuh* incorporates five theorized modal scales, each consisting of five primary and two auxiliary tones; most groups use four or three of these modes. There is some evidence that *saih gendèr*

FIGURE 4 Tunings of various ensembles. The numbers specify the intervals in cents.

Heptatonic *pelog saih pitu (gambuh),* Batuan

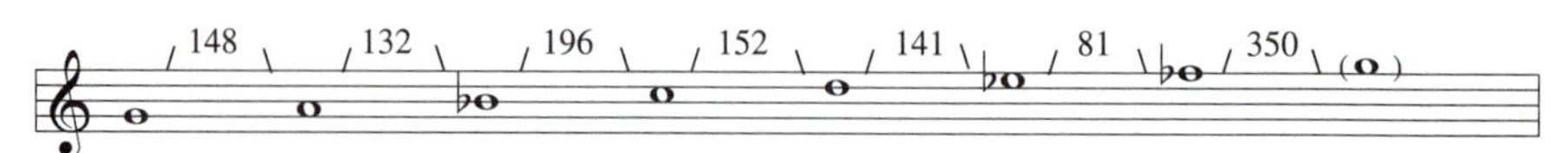

Heptatonic *pelog saih pitu (gambang),* Sukawati

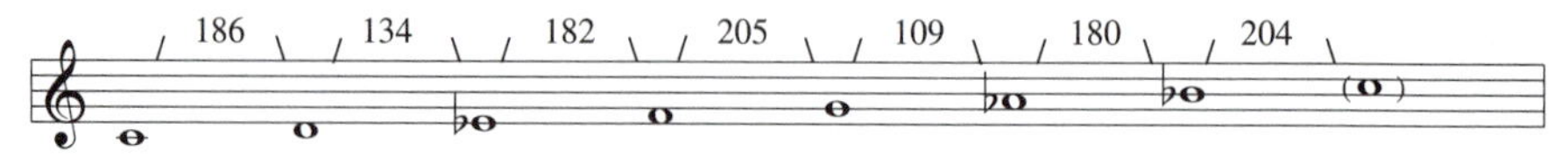

Pentatonic *pelog saih gong,* Peliatan

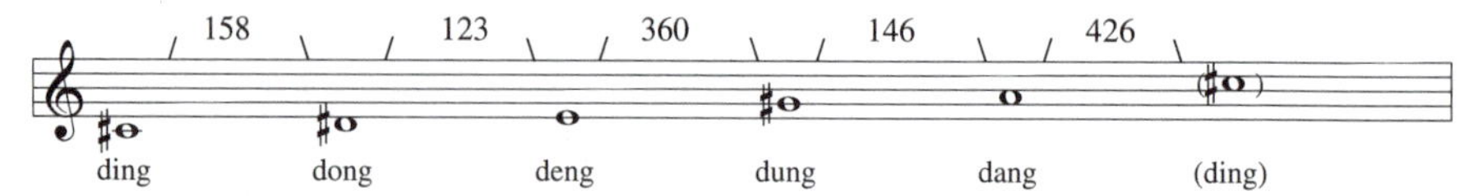

Pentatonic *slendro saih gender wayang,* Tabanan

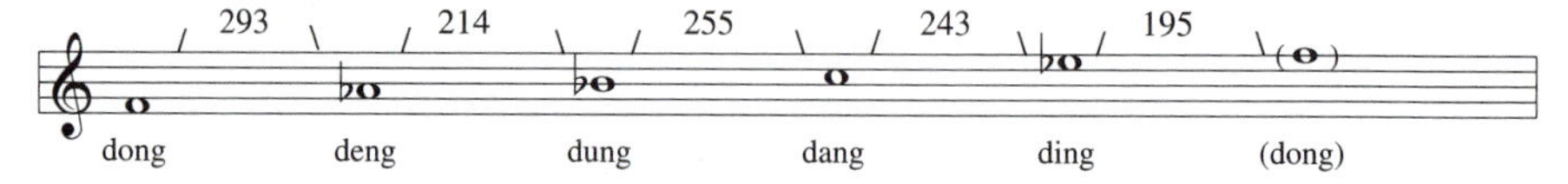

Tetratonic *saih angklung,* Kesiman

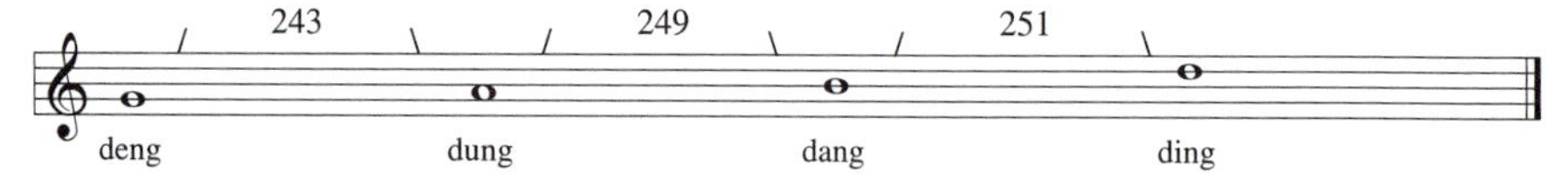

wayang incorporates modal scales, but not all musicians believe as much. The best known *saih pitu* system consists of pitches named *ding, dong, deng, penyorog, dung, dang, pemero*; and then starts over with *ding* through successive octaves. The terms *penyorog* 'inserted tone' and *pemero* 'false tone' indicate auxiliary pitches. When these tones are removed, the remaining five tones create the pentatonic modal scales. The pentatonic *saih gendèr wayang* pitches are normally named (from lowest to highest) *dong, deng, dung, dang,* and *ding* (figure 4).

The *saih pitu* scale is not popular but is revered as a mystical scale associated with refined courts and sacred music. The most popular mode derived from it—and the most famous of the Balinese tonal system—is the pentatonic *selisir,* also called *saih gong* 'row of gong tones' or *saih lima* 'row of five'. This scale, the primary realization of *pélog* tuning, is considered an independent system and is used in the *gamelan gong* orchestras; a higher-pitched *selisir* scale is used in the former court *gamelan pelégongan*; and *selisir* is one of the core *gamelan gambuh* and *gamelan Semar pegulingan* modes. This scale has been so influential within Balinese music culture that some bronze heptatonic court orchestras were retuned accordingly. These terms concerning systems of tuning and ensembles are also used in certain types of Balinese vocal music.

There are several theories about the relationship of *pélog* and *sléndro* in Bali. Most musicians believe that the two are separate systems, with *pélog* comprising *saih pitu* and *saih gong* scales; and *sléndro,* the pentatonic *saih gendèr wayang* and the tetratonic *saih angklung* of the *gamelan angklung.* For practical purposes, *saih gong* is the most common realization of *pélog,* and *saih gendèr wayang* the most common realization of *sléndro.*

The *Prakempa* manuscript states that both *pélog* and *sléndro* form part of a ten-tone system related to cosmology, with each tone relating to a deity of the four cardinal directions, their subdivisions, and two in the center for the gods Siwa and Buddha. It states that *pélog* has a masculine quality, its primary tones related to the god Semara, white sperm, and the five waters; and that *sléndro* has a feminine quality, its main tones associated with the goddess Ratih, red sperm, and the five fires. According to the manuscript, when the spirit of two systems unify, their ten tones merge into seven—which forms *genta pinara pitu,* from which pentatonic *pélog*, and pentatonic and tetratonic (*saih angklung*) *sléndro* scales can derive. Some evidence suggests that this system may be in practice within the *gambuh* theater (see "Theater ensembles," below) tradition of Batuan village; otherwise the theory represents the cosmological ideal.

The *Prakempa* indicates that music, through these different scales, balances binary relations and unifies humankind with the elements of life and the three worlds within the macrocosm and the microcosm. There is thus an isomorphic mapping of musical sound with the structure of the cosmos and the elements of life, and music is given affective and efficacious qualities. Though the *Prakempa* is concerned with esoteric aspects of music not necessarily shared or even understood by musicians, these concepts, which often have no bearing on actual music practice, are consistent with theories within the plastic arts and architecture.

Tonality may prescribe function among the ensembles. Gamelans in *saih pitu* tuning have vital ritual functions. However, those in *saih gong, saih gendèr wayang,* and *saih angklung* tunings also have important uses at rituals, and each has its own special qualities. The *saih gong* tonality is considered powerful, able to signal together divine and human worlds and evoke the imagery of the past appropriate for temple festivals and other rituals; the *saih gendèr wayang* tonality is associated with the night, the shadow play, and ancestor spirits to contextualize a rite within the imagery of epic stories; and the *saih angklung* is normally considered to have a sweet but sad quality, appropriate for cremations, other life-cycle rites, and sometimes temple festivals. However, if a village owns only a single gamelan, it will use that ensemble for all vital rituals, regardless of tonality.

Notation

Music in Bali is transmitted orally, without the use of notation. A rare instance of notation is found in palm-leaf manuscripts (*lontar*) containing nuclear melodies from ceremonial pieces, using the Sanskrit-based written alphabet to represent the Balinese solmization syllables (*ding, dong, deng,* and so on). Similar linear notations are used at conservatories. While the former use of notation preserves important ceremonial pieces, the latter expedites learning and performance. Though simple in format, the notation adds symbols for the gong patterns from which the drumming patterns are derived, and the other parts can be deduced from general practice. Rhythm is unimportant, since *pokok* tones are of equal duration, and precise intervals are governed by the ensemble used.

Pokok and colotomy are the cornerstones of Balinese gamelan music. Concepts of expanded melody, abstraction, and figuration in an ensemble are determined by the group or its leaders. Districts, and sometimes even neighboring villages, treat musical material in contrasting ways.

MUSICIANS AND THEIR ORGANIZATION

Musicians organize themselves into collective groups (*seka* or *sekaha*) to perform for particular occasions or to maintain a performing group for village or tourist performances. A *sekaha* generally comprises people who come from a subvillage unit or who are related, though occasionally groups consist of members from different villages. Members include both musicians (*penabuh*) and dancers (*pregina*), if dance is

> The main contexts for making music are the web of rituals that has sustained Balinese culture over the centuries. Major rituals often include one or more gamelans playing at different times or simultaneously in one or more locations.

part of performance, and the *sekaha* does not acknowledge the modified caste distinctions of Balinese society.

The musicians of the *sekaha* are traditionally males from ten to seventy or more years old, with the exception of the growing number of all-female groups (*ibu-ibu*) and some groups in government-sponsored conservatories. Members' ages are sometimes parallel to the ages of repertoires and instruments. Older men usually prefer and are associated with the older and more ceremonial repertoire and ensembles; younger men usually prefer and are associated with faster and more intricate music and *kebyar.* Extensive rehearsals and vigorous musicianship are necessary for a performance of *kebyar,* but are not normally needed for the more static ceremonial repertoire. Though their music is less demanding technically, the maturity of the older musicians is sometimes thought important to the proper realization of the stately or refined ceremonial music, in which lengthy pieces performed only once a year must be recalled.

Music is transferred informally, and young boys usually learn by sitting on their fathers' laps during rehearsals and performances, and by going through the motions of playing or actually playing the instruments. Children are encouraged to watch and participate in most of the arts, and are usually in the front row at theatrical presentations.

More constraints are attached to the learning and performance of sacred ensembles, however. In some cases, none but the musicians and priests may approach the instruments. Normally, though, children are allowed to play instruments of sacred ensembles during breaks in performance at rituals, but never during a performance. Learning to play these instruments is difficult because some ensembles, due to supernatural sanction, are played only for one or two rituals a year, if that. At all other times, the instruments are placed in hallowed space, often in a priest's home, a special storehouse, or a temple; and no one may play or even observe the instruments. In general, the knowledge of music is considered a supernatural science, and great care is taken in handling the instruments and positioning them for performance.

MUSICAL CONTEXTS AND FUNCTIONS

The main contexts for making music are the web of rituals that has sustained Balinese culture over the centuries. These primarily include life-cycle rituals (birthdays, rites of giving names, marriages, the filing of teeth, cremations), and temple festivals, which form parts of the Hindu Balinese theological taxonomy of rituals known as Panca Yadnya (Five Sacrificial Offerings). Other contexts include political affairs, national holidays, village fund-raisers, and performances for tourists.

Temples, numbering more than twenty thousand, are at the center of Balinese ritual activity. Three basic temples, together called *kahyangan tiga,* often complete a village: the *pura puseh* 'temple of origins', the *pura desa* or *pura bale agung* 'central village temple', and the *pura dalem* 'temple of the dead'. Villagers are obligated to attend festivals normally held once every 210 days at these temples, and most individuals participate in festivals at other kinds of temples including ward temples, home temples, clan temples, "navel" temples, hill temples, sea temples, rice temples, and so forth. Festivals, normally called *odalan*, are held at each of these temples and usually include performances of gamelans and dances. Every Balinese should undergo the life-cycle rites mentioned above, and these usually include music and sometimes dance and theater, if the family involved can afford the expenditure.

Scholars have often noted the complex system of languages in Bali, with five acknowledged levels of Balinese language (three in common use), plus archaic Javanese, classical Javanese, and Sanskrit—all existing simultaneously. Each language has its own function and references its own meaningful codes; each constitutes its own discourse within Balinese culture. In addition, virtually all Balinese speak Indonesian (the national language); because of the tourist trade, many speak English, and a few speak Japanese. The various gamelans can be seen as similarly addressing a complex of functions, with each constituting its own discourse in fulfilling part of a social or religious context.

Major rituals often include one or more gamelans playing at different times or simultaneously in one or more locations. There are distinctive spatial and temporal orientations to Balinese performing arts, and these orientations relate to the function of the performance and the meaning of the context. Gamelans are held to be able to reference the past or particular imagery, such as evoking the grandeur of the mythic courts or reenacting a local legendary event. The *gamelan gambuh,* for instance, with its combination of flute and bowed lute, is thought to evoke the quality of the fifteenth-century East Javanese Majapahit court. The gamelan is a symbol of that period and can reference it through performance. This type of referencing is beneficial for the successful completion of a ritual context, in which representations of folklore and cosmology are efficacious agents.

All gamelan performances are essentially active ritual offerings. Both the sound structure of the music and the decorated cases of the musical instruments embody codes parallel to those within ritual formulae, food offerings, and cosmology. Gamelan performance in general is believed to embody the second of three elements considered essential to a ritual: thought (*idep*); sound, word, voice (*sabda*); and action (*bayu*). Prayer and meditation fulfill the thought element; gamelan, the sound; and dance, the action: all can be viewed as extensions of the rites of the high priest. The priests recite mantra invocations (realized as prayer), ring their *genta* bell (whose sound is realized by the gamelan) to reinforce the mantra, and perform hand gestures (*mudra,* realized as dance) to complete the invocations. This establishes the performing arts as elaborate offerings with efficacious qualities necessary to complete a ritual.

Frequently, several ensembles perform simultaneously at major rituals. This creates the lively and bustling atmosphere (*rame*) that helps generate an experience of community and collective spirituality. Each gamelan represents a particular spiritual value and references a particular past, and when many gamelans perform simultaneously, there is a comprehensive representation of the cosmos and the legendary past. It is not uncommon at a major temple festival to witness two or three different gamelans, two or three dances, theater, or shadow puppetry, and a choir all performing at once. This brings the past into the present and creates the communal spiritual experience intended by the festival.

MUSIC IN BALINESE COSMOLOGY

The Balinese view of the world is based on threes. The modified system of castes includes three acknowledged levels and a fourth, outer level; the system of naming children includes three children and a fourth, other child; there are three different levels of requirements within life-cycle rituals; three main village temples with three divisions in their structures and altars; three gods within the Hindu Trinity; and a tripartite structure to both the macrocosm and microcosm. In addition, musical compositions usually include three main sections, the cases of musical instruments have three sections, dance characterization acknowledges three divisions within the body, and most types of painting, statues, dance costumes, and ritual offerings also have three divisions. This links the arts directly to cosmology and worldview.

Balinese gamelan have tripartite dimensions with anthropomorphic and macrocosmic qualities, and reflect the village social organization. Gongs, kettle-gongs, and bars of metallophones, plus instrument cases, stands, and resonators, all acknowledge three horizontal divisions of head, body, and foot, mirrored in the three divisions (*utama, madya, nista*) of the macrocosm, which in turn are parallel to the geographic configuration (mountain, midworld, sea) related to the layout of temples, home compounds, and whole villages. The instruments also have three vertical divisions, and the resulting three-by-three configuration represents a nine-part mandala, a pictorial display of the cosmos, which is related to the construction of home compounds, pavilions, temples, and the sequence of planting seedlings in the fields. Some scholars have asserted that gamelan music is an aural mandala organized on these same concepts, with metric cycles representing structured mandala and the three-part compositional form representing the tripartite structures of head–body–foot and mountain–midworld–sea. Esoteric treatises support this hypothesis and indicate that musical tones are associated with deities, directions, colors, days of the week, and weapons to create a mandala structure.

A gamelan can also be seen to reflect the village order, with the gongs representing the respected elders, low-pitched metallophones as older adults, mid-range metallophones as adults, the drums as political leaders, and the high-pitched metallophones, gong chimes and cymbals as youngsters. A gamelan is thus a self-portrait of the villagers. The instruments appear to have additional extramusical associations. For example, the *Prakempa* treatise states that *gong ageng* (largest hanging gong) represent the divine mountain and the Hindu god Siwa, while the *trompong* (gong chime) represents the lotus, the *kempur* (small hanging gong) all that is pure, and so forth.

In 1971, a concept emerged from a seminar among Balinese intellectuals and leaders that divided dance and theater in terms of their level of sacredness into (expectedly) three main categories, based on their spatial dimensions at temple festivals: *wali, bebali,* and *bali-balihan.* The performances called *wali* take place in the inner sanctum of temples; *bebali* performances in the middle or second courtyard; and *balih-balihan* performances in a third courtyard, creating a continuum from most to least sacred. This follows the heaven-earth-underworld and mountain-midworld-sea macrocosm framework and the head-body-foot microcosm framework, all of which proceed from most to least sacred. The basis of the concept is the mountain-sea axis (*kaja-kelod*), which governs the positioning of a temple and extends to the arts related to the respective spaces within the axis. Though the concept of relative sacredness is too general for a research tool and is limited to spatial dimensions of the performing arts, it demonstrates the significance of tripartite configurations among Balinese and represents an internal development within the arts as educated Balinese seek to understand and describe in modern terms the meanings of their arts.

The concepts underlying Balinese music theory and musical instruments thus have parallels to those that form cosmology and worldview. There is an isomorphic mapping of musical system with cosmology; a similar mapping evident in the plastic arts, dance characterization, temples, home compounds, village positioning, ritual formulae, food offerings, macrocosm and microcosm, and so forth. Music is therefore strongly interrelated with other cultural systems that are fed by similar underlying concepts.

MUSICAL INSTRUMENTS

The Javanese-Indonesian term *gamelan* 'things struck together' is applied to every ensemble, and refers to a group of instruments played, or specifically struck, together. Because of variations of tuning, instruments are particular to their ensembles and cannot be played with other gamelans. Gamelans consist primarily of bronze instruments, with a few ensembles featuring bamboo or wood instruments. The original Balinese equivalent for *ensemble* is *gambelan,* from *megambel* 'to strike', and the word *gong* is sometimes used to denote entire ensembles. The different types of gamelan are commonly known simply by their name without the word *gamelan* preceding; thus, the ensembles *gamelan gong kebyar* or *gamelan angklung* are usually called *gong kebyar* and *angklung.*

The primary type of instrument in Bali is the bronze idiophone. These include gongs, metallophones, gong chimes, cymbals (made of bronze or iron), rare bell trees, and assorted small percussion instruments. Other idiophones include wooden and bamboo xylophones, bamboo tube stampers, bamboo and hollowed-out wooden log idiophones, bamboo or brass cattle bells, palm-rib Jew's harps, bamboo shakers, and several rarer instruments. There is one standard type of membranophone, a double-headed cylindrical drum, which comes in many sizes. Aerophones consist of bamboo, or the rare wooden, straw, and even conch instruments. Chordophones are few, but include one standard bowed lute with limited use; an idiochord one-stringed bamboo tube zither; and only a few rare plucked chordophones. There is no established organological system that separates instruments in terms of the production of sounds. Instruments are regarded in terms of the gamelan to which they belong, and are classified into families of instruments that perform related musical functions within gamelans. Instruments and whole gamelans are highly respected creations and are ritually purified every thirty weeks.

Idiophones

There are clear priorities among the various bronze instruments. Gongs are distinguished from metallophones, which are distinguished from gong chimes. The large hanging gongs are clearly the most important instruments in any ensemble that includes gongs. In fact, the name given to the gong(s) of a gamelan through a name-giving ritual is meant to include the entire ensemble. Gongs also receive offerings and incense before performance on behalf of the ensemble, and the spirit of the gamelan is believed to reside within the gongs. All gongs except the *gong beri,* a rare and sacred instrument, have bosses.

The largest hanging gongs are the pair of *gong ageng*: the *gong lanang* 'male gong' (smaller and pitched slightly higher), and the *gong wadon* 'female gong' (larger and pitched slightly lower). These gongs, normally about sixty-five to eighty-five centimeters in diameter, define the colotomic structure as they conclude the largest melodic phrasal lengths and the metric cycles of the music. They are struck in alternation by a large padded mallet. Each produces an acoustical beat (*ombak* 'wave'), an amplitude modulation heard as a pulsation. This beat is created by cold hammering the gong at specific points to the left and right of the boss. Four or five different beat levels, all given names, are available to makers of gongs. Unlike other bronze instruments, *gong ageng* are normally made in Java.

Other colotomic instruments are the *kempur* and the *kemong.* The former is a much smaller and higher-pitched hanging gong than the *gong ageng,* and it supplies secondary structural punctuation. Some ensembles, such as the *gamelan angklung,*

gamelan gong kebyar The most prevalent type of Balinese instrumental ensemble, developed in the early twentieth century to play the dynamic, modern kebyar style

gong lanang Smaller "male" hanging gong

gong wadon Larger "female" hanging gong

gangsa Metallophone

réong Gong-chime played by several performers

trompong Gong-chime played by soloist

ceng-ceng Cymbals

have no large gong and use *kempur* as the main colotomic marker. The smaller hanging gong, the *kemong* (sometimes called *klentong*), alternates punctuation with *kempur,* except in some ceremonial ensembles where it is replaced by the *kempli,* a horizontally mounted kettle-gong. At other times, the *kempli* (also called *kajar* or *tawa-tawa,* depending on the type of gamelan) acts primarily as a timekeeper, though the *kajar,* a kettle-gong suspended horizontally with a sunken boss, plays syncopated figurations in most ensembles, while the *tawa-tawa* is often a *klentong*-sized gong held on the lap. The *bende* (or *bebende*) is an optional hanging gong with a sunken boss, whose musical role is more related to the cymbals than to the metric cycle.

Metallophones constitute the majority of instruments in most gamelans, and together may cover a range of three to five octaves. Single-octave metallophones normally play the nuclear melody or a reduced abstraction of it, while double-octave metallophones perform figurations or ornamentation. Metallophones, generally called *gangsa,* are of two types: *gangsa jongkok* and *gangsa gantung.* The former are resting-bar instruments of five bronze bars lying over a shallow trough resonator. The latter (also called *gendèr*) are suspended-bar instruments of from four to fifteen bevel-edged bars suspended over individual bamboo resonators in a wooden case. Both are played with hammers of wood or horn in the right hand, but the largest and deepest *gendèr* (*jegogan*) are played with padded mallets. The players damp previously struck bars of the *gangsa* with the left thumb and forefinger as the next bar is struck, so that two sounds are not heard simultaneously. This is particularly important for the double-octave *gendèr* (*pemade* and *kantilan*), which often perform rapid interlocking figurations.

The *gangsa* are made in identical pairs tuned slightly apart to create an acoustical beat. The closer the tuning, the faster the beat. Different groups have their own preferences, but usually the tunings between the pairs of *gangsa* stay within a range of 25 to 60 cents, with the higher-pitched bars having the smallest intervals and creating beats vibrating at more than seven times per second. This beat, along with those produced on the *gong ageng,* is what gives Balinese gamelan its shimmering effect.

Gong chimes are sets of from four to twelve tuned kettle-gongs resting or suspended in a single row over a long wooden case. The best known are the *trompong,* of ten kettles; and the *réong* (or *reyong*), usually of twelve kettles, but also known with four, six, and eight. The additional kettles of the *réong* were added in the 1930s. All gong chimes are played with cord-bound sticks, and are damped by returning the sticks to the knobs of the kettles after they have been struck. The *trompong* is played melodically by a soloist, whereas the *réong* is played by two to (more normally) four players in interlocking figuration.

Cymbals consist primarily of *ceng-ceng* and *rincik* (or *ricik*). *Ceng-ceng* refers generally to cymbals and specifically to a group of held cymbals used in large gamelan and in procession. *Rincik* denotes a smaller pair or set of three or five upturned cymbals mounted on a base struck with a pair held by the player. Sometimes the base is tortoise-shaped, with an upturned cymbal or cymbals mounted on the back, but otherwise it is a block of wood. While the *ceng-ceng* are played in interlocking figurations, the *rincik* play at the fastest pulse, punctuate the rhythmic breaks, and often reinforce the interlocking patterns and syncopation of the two membranophones.

Membranophones

Most ensembles include two double-headed cylindrical membranophones played together: the *kendang lanang* 'male drum' and the *kendang wadon* 'female drum'. These drums are tuned and come in many different sizes, from the large ones used in *kebyar* to the small ones used in the *gamelan angklung.* In some gamelan traditions, the *kendang wadon* drummer leads; in others, the *kendang lanang* drummer is the leader. For some types of ceremonial music and for accompanying strong male dances, players use a drumstick in the right hand; otherwise, they create a number of open and muted sounds forming an interlocking figuration with the hands alone.

A second type of membranophone is the rare *terbana,* a bowl-shaped drum normally associated with Islam, sometimes used in the *janger* form of dance and in an experimental form of the *gamelan arja* when accompanying so-called Malaysian folk songs (*pantun*). Other membranophones include the *tambur,* a rare, sacred, barrel-shaped, double-headed drum, which forms an ensemble with a single gong in a few areas of East Bali; the *bedug,* which forms part of the *gamelan gong beri*; and the *kendang mabarung,* the largest Balinese membranophone, found only in West Bali and used in processional ensembles.

Aerophones

Suling, end-blown bamboo flutes of various sizes, are used in several gamelans. They most frequently perform an expanded version of the nuclear melody. Other aerophones are rare, and include free-reed *padi* pipes (usually called *serunai*), wooden oboes (*preret*), and conchs (*serungu* or *sungu*). The functions of the *serunai* and *preret* are flexible. The latter has been known to accompany the martial-art dance, *pencak silat,* with a small ensemble, and to perform with vocalists at temple festivals—a tradition that may have originated on Lombok. The *serungu* forms part of a rare ensemble of three instruments which calls forth underworld spirits (*butakala*) to receive offerings in ritual settings.

Chordophones

Among the chordophones, the rebab is a two-stringed, bowed spike lute, used in a few gamelans, particularly *gamelan gambuh.* With its horsehair bow, it is used to paraphrase or expand the nuclear melody. The *guntang* is a bamboo idiochord zither struck with a small stick. Two of these, a larger one for the main punctuation and a smaller one as timekeeper, are sometimes used in the *gamelan arja.* A rare chordophone is the *manolin* (or *mandolin*), a plucked lute with keys found in a few areas in East Bali, which plays melodies in both *pélog* and *sléndro* in small ensembles. A plucked lute (*gambus*), new to Bali, has been introduced by Muslims in the Klungkung area. Pianos, guitars, and electronic instruments are still rare in Balinese homes, but are becoming more popular.

ORCHESTRAS AND ENSEMBLES

Bali has a variety of ensembles: large bronze orchestras consisting of from twenty-five to forty instruments; specific ensembles to accompany theater; processional ensembles; bamboo or palm-rib ensembles; and sacred ensembles. Each has its own orchestration, function, and context.

Gamelan gong

The Balinese call their largest, most ubiquitous ensembles *gamelan gong* (or, often, simply *gong*). The most common of these is the *gong kebyar,* which developed early in the twentieth century out of the older *gong gedé* and quickly eclipsed it in popularity.

The *gamelan gong* in its ceremonial form can perform at virtually any type of ritual, though it is most associated with temple festivals. The orchestra and its repertoire signify ceremony. This gamelan, the loudest of Balinese ensembles, will normally be positioned in a second courtyard at temple festivals, or outside the main home compound at family life-cycle rituals. The positioning is never truly close to the space of the most sacred transformations at such rituals, yet is always a conspicuous spot between the innermost sacred space and the outer temple or village space. This is because the function of the ensemble is to mark the spatial limits of the event, to signify the transition of normal time to the extranormal or sacred time of the event, and to act as a bridge between inner and outer dimensions—both in terms of the village and the inner event, and in terms of the world of deities and the world of humans. Like incense, which is believed to ascend to the deity world and entice deities to descend through the smoke, music is often thought to act as a vehicle through which the deities enter the event.

The ceremonial repertoire of the *gamelan gong,* called *gending gong* (or *pegongan*), consists of *gangsaran* 'speedy pieces' and *lelambatan* 'slow, stately pieces'. The performance begins with *gangsaran,* pieces normally consisting of one or two melodic phrases covering short gong cycles (or *gongan*) of sixteen or eight beats per stroke of a gong, repeated many times. This is the explosive start of the ritual. Later, the orchestra will perform the *lelambatan* pieces, which have greater functional importance. *Lelambatan* pieces contain *gongan* with from sixty-four to 128 beats. As the event unfolds, the orchestra begins with *lelambatan* pieces in the smaller metric cycles, gradually progressing to those in the largest metric cycles as the ritual approaches its climax.

Esoteric treatises state that the *gamelan gong* was created by the priests of the skies and is associated with the heavens, whereas the *gamelan bebonangan* was created by and is associated with the powerful underworld spirits. Temple festivals and life-cycle ceremonies address both the heavens and the underworld through offerings, and these gamelans are the formal ensembles for ritual contexts which together unify these respective spheres into the middle world. The *gamelan bebonangan* (see "Processional ensembles," below) is played to accompany offerings for the underworld spirits and accompanies processions to holy places, where its loud martial pieces using short cycles of gongs are believed to frighten away these spirits and purify the spatial discourse of the procession.

The *gong gedé,* the elder type of *gamelan gong,* is the largest of Bali's gamelans, with forty or more instruments in its original form (figure 5). Only a few sets remain today. Court gamelans before colonization, most were reforged as *gong kebyar* to meet the change of Balinese aesthetics during and following colonialism. The orchestras remaining today generally consist of twenty-five to thirty instruments. *Gong gedé* are characterized by the two *gong ageng*; numerous single- and double-octave metallophones spanning four to five octaves, which play or punctuate the nuclear melody; and a *trompong* soloist, who plays an expanded version of the nuclear melody.

Other instruments of the *gong gedé* include the *kendang lanang* and *kendang wadon,* the leaders of the group performing formal patterns and signaling functions in interlocking figuration; a number of *ceng-ceng* of various sizes, together often

FIGURE 5 A *gamelan gong gedé.* To the front are the *gangsa jongkok*; to the left the *trompong*; in the back, the gongs. McPhee Collection, UCLA, 1930s.

called *kopyak,* also played in interlocking figuration; and the *trompong barangan,* a gong chime pitched an octave higher than the *trompong,* which doubles the *trompong* melody, and/or a *réong* of four to six kettles played in interlocking figuration by two musicians.

Gong kebyar, the more recent type of *gamelan gong,* includes the *gong ageng,* the *kempur,* and the *kendang lanang* and *kendang wadon*; but the *trompong* is replaced by a large ten-bar metallophone (*giying* or *pengugal*), and the *saron* are replaced by four mid-range (*pemade*) and four-octave-higher (*kantilan*) *gendèr* metallophones. A low-octave pair (or two pairs) of single-octave *gendèr* (*calung* or *jublag*) play the nuclear melody, and the lowest-octave pair of *gendèr* (*jegogan*) punctuate the nuclear melody at regular intervals—at an eight-to-one, a four-to-one, or a two-to-one ratio. Other instruments, such as *suling* and rebab, are often included. The *réong* in *gong kebyar* is greatly expanded from that of the *gong gedé,* and consists of twelve kettles played in changing interlocking parts by four musicians, who sometimes strike the rims or bosses of the kettles together to create brassy or strongly syncopated chordlike clusters of sounds. These syncopated parts, reinforced by cymbals (*rincik*), are also played for *angsel,* which bring the ensemble together for powerful rhythmic breaks. *Gong kebyar* music provides a good example of multilayered sound that can be interpreted as stratified polyphony (figure 6). In many pieces, there is so much embellishment that the nuclear melody can hardly be heard.

The *gong kebyar,* consisting of about twenty-five instruments, often performs in secular contexts; however, it regularly assumes a ritual function and performs the ceremonial repertoire of the *gong gedé,* and many groups add a *trompong* for these pieces. The *gong kebyar* repertoire has also incorporated pieces from bronze court orchestras (*Semar pegulingan, pelégongan*) and pieces to accompany masked dances and some types of theater (figure 7). However, the *gong kebyar* is mostly known for its virtuoso *kebyar* repertoire: explosive pieces composed to accentuate the dynamic qualities of the instruments. The term *kebyar,* in fact, refers to the explosive, metrically free unison attack that normally occurs at the beginning of a piece in this style. Because of regular competitions involving the whole island, groups are encouraged to maintain high standards of performance and experiment with new ideas. The repertoire, called

The *gamelan Semar pegulingan* was originally for the private enjoyment of the nobility. It was played when the king was sleeping with the queen in his chambers.

FIGURE 6 Stratification in one complete gong cycle of "*Penyuwud*," a *gilak* form and concluding composition.

kreasi baru, is constantly expanding because composers nearly always use the *gong kebyar* for their new works.

Smaller bronze orchestras

The *gamelan Semar pegulingan* 'gamelan of the god of love of the bedroom', originally a court orchestra, resembles the *gamelan gong,* but omits *gong ageng, réong,* and large cymbals. It is tuned slightly higher than the *gamelan gong* and is played with lighter and more padded hammers; it therefore has a lighter and sweeter sound. The instrumentation includes a fourteen-kettle *trompong* and several pairs of metallophones, often only different sizes of *gendèr,* but sometimes high-pitched *saron*; two *kendang,* a large *kempur,* and a *kajar*; rebab and *suling*; one or more small sets of cymbals and other small percussive instruments, sometimes including a bell tree (*gentorak*).

In its original form, the *Semar pegulingan* was a seven-tone orchestra used to play theater pieces (*gambuh*) instrumentally in the proper modal scales, though the orchestra normally acknowledged only three of the possible five modes. But over the course of the twentieth century, most of these orchestras have been retuned or the bars reforged to accommodate solely the pentatonic *selisir* mode. Today, only four complete seven-toned *Semar pegulingan* remain outside the conservatories. There were also hexatonic orchestras that could be used to play pieces in two main modal scales (*selisir* and *tembung*). Over time, these were similarly adjusted to solely accom-

FIGURE 7 A *gamelan gong kebyar* in rehearsal. McPhee Collection, UCLA, 1930s.

modate pentatonic *selisir* tuning. The colotomy, extra percussion, drumming technique, tonality, and much of the repertoire derive from the *gamelan gambuh* (see below). The *trompong,* however, is given the opportunity to freely elaborate and expand upon the original *suling gambuh* melodies. Without a second *trompong* to accommodate, as in the *gamelan gong,* and with fourteen kettles rather than ten, the *trompong* of the *Semar pegulingan* can more freely interpret the tones of the nuclear melody. This represents one of the highest levels of improvisation in Balinese music.

The *Prakempa* manuscript mentions a number of variants of *Semar pegulingan,* but they were closely related instrumentally, and all functioned in the courts for the private enjoyment of the nobility. The gamelan was to be played when the king was sleeping with the queen in his chambers. It is clear that the gamelan was highly respected in the courts to create a properly powerful yet refined atmosphere, and it even had its own courtyard of performance, the *semarabawa* 'place of Semara, the god of love'. Each king considered it necessary to own at least one *Semar pegulingan,* and lesser nobles throughout Bali sought to own one to enhance their status (figure 8).

With the decline of courts, *Semar pegulingan* has virtually disappeared, but several villages still retain the orchestras, and the conservatories continue to teach the tradition. With the change to pentatonic tuning and the incorporation of new repertoire, *Semar pegulingan* has begun to separate from *gambuh.* Some collective groups (*sekaha)* have adapted *gamelan pelégongan* and *gong kebyar* repertoire and technique to *Semar pegulingan*—which has led to more *kebyar*-like treatment of traditional pieces. Many composers are also writing new compositions for the orchestra.

The *gamelan pelégongan* is an orchestra closely related to the *Semar pegulingan.* It originally accompanied the *légong* dance in the courts; hence its name. The orchestra uses only the five-tone *selisir* tuning and incorporates *gambuh* pieces and some new pieces into its repertoire of *légong.* The gamelans accompanied a large number of dances and dance-dramas in the courts, but since colonization they have mainly accompanied several *légong* dances, particularly the famous *légong kraton,* featuring two or three girls who take different parts in turn. This orchestra replaces the *trompong* of the *Semar pegulingan* with two pairs of thirteen-to-fifteen-bar *gendèr,* but is otherwise almost identical. Sometimes, a reciter will sing narration within the orchestra to accompany the *légong* dances. Originally, the repertoire of *pelégongan*

FIGURE 8 A *gamelan Semar pegulingan:* a *gendèr rawat* and gong. McPhee Collection, UCLA, 1930s.

demanded more rehearsal time than *Semar pegulingan.* It was more musically complex and included more interlocking figuration (*kotekan*). Today, however, these orchestras borrow repertoire and instruments from each other, and the techniques of the *Semar pegulingan* and the *gamelan pelégongan* have become so similar that many earlier distinctions have become blurred. The repertoires of both orchestras are often appropriated by the *gong kebyar.*

An orchestra nearly identical to *pelégongan* accompanies the *calonarang* theater and the dancing of the Barong, a mythical beast. *Calonarang* is a theatrical form that pits the Calonarang, a witch (sometimes called Rangda), against the forces of the tenth-century East Javanese King Erlangga. Performance, which exorcises an area of underworld spirits, is normally conducted during festivals at the temples of the dead near cemeteries and cremation grounds. The Barong may confront the Calonarang, but this meeting is not normally part of the story, and the Barong occasionally appears in other theatrical contexts, accompanied by its own repertoire of pieces.

The *gamelan angklung* is smaller than *gamelan gong* orchestras. It consists of about sixteen instruments, pitched higher and much smaller in size than those of all other gamelans. It has always been a village orchestra, disassociated with the courts. It has a lighter, more intimate sound and carries more emotional associations. It can therefore be placed closer to the inner compound of a home during a family life-cycle ceremony, though the ensemble also performs a repertoire and function similar to the *gamelan gong* when used at temple festivals (figure 9). Today, there are far more *gamelan angklung* than all of the court orchestras mentioned above. With the exception of some orchestras (found primarily in North Bali) that have added a fifth tone, this gamelan is tuned to a four-tone scale which probably derives from *sléndro.*

Gamelan angklung uses a small, nonresonant, and often out-of-tune *kempur* as its only gong, and includes several pairs of single-octave (four-key) *gendèr,* a lower-octave pair of *gendèr* to play the nuclear melody, a timekeeping *tawa-tawa,* a *réong* normally of eight kettles, *rincik,* two small *kendang* played with light drumsticks, and often one or more *suling.* The instruments actually called *angklung* are shaken bamboo rattles tuned to sound a pitch normally in three octaves, but they only rarely appear in the orchestras of their namesake. Some orchestras in areas of East Bali

FIGURE 9 A *gamelan angklung:* metallophones in front; the rare *angklung* rattles in back. McPhee Collection, UCLA, 1930s.

retain the *angklung* instruments played in interlocking technique, but use them only in procession. The *gamelan angklung* has its own traditional repertoire consisting of pieces of irregular length and whimsical titles, a few pieces from the *gendèr wayang* tradition, and sometimes a special ceremonial repertoire (*lelambatan*); and the orchestra can also play modified *kebyar* pieces with the addition of larger drums and gongs.

A few old-style *gamelan angklung* with slightly different instrumentation exist in mountain villages of East Bali. In some areas of Bali, the *gamelan angklung* can form a unique processional ensemble—composed of the smaller metallophones (suspended with a strap around the players' shoulders), *kendang,* gongs, and *suling*—which proceeds around a village to announce the death of a prominent villager.

Theatrical ensembles

The *gamelan gambuh* is the former court orchestra that accompanies *gambuh* theater. It was the most important of the ensembles that functioned within the noble houses, and its purpose was to perform for the life-cycle rituals of the nobility. The repertoire, systems of tuning, and hand-drumming technique of its ensemble are credited as the foundations of Balinese music. *Gambuh* is similarly considered a source of Balinese theater and dance. The theater is based mostly on plays of East Javanese court life, and the music and dance are the most refined and solemn in Bali. The function of performances of *gambuh* is to invoke the presence of Indonesian, rather than Indic, legendary figures and heroes. The tradition almost vanished in the twentieth century, and today there are few active groups.

The ensemble contrasts with other Balinese gamelans in that it does not include metallophones or gong chimes (figure 10). Instead, it normally features four *suling* about a meter long, with a range of over two octaves. They perform in unison or slight heterophony a number of melodic compositions connected with a specific character or dramatic situation. A rebab joins the *suling* melody in unison or paraphrase, occasionally breaking off to freely interpret the melody. Main punctuation is supplied by *kempur* and *kajar,* with a few small bronze percussive instruments pro-

Arja stories derive from varied sources: Indian epic plots, legends from medieval East Javanese courtly life, similar stories set in Bali, and Chinese tales of passion. Young people flock to performances for opportunities to flirt.

FIGURE 10 A *gamelan gambuh:* four *suling* on the left; a rebab on the right; percussion behind. McPhee Collection, UCLA, 1930s.

viding secondary punctuation. Other instruments include the two *kendang, rincik, gentorak* (bell tree), and *gumanak* (a struck metal cylinder similar to the Javanese *kemanak*). The *gumanak* fills in the intervals between the secondary punctuation along with the *kangsi,* two pairs of small cymbals mounted between forked sticks struck against the ground.

The ensemble includes a singer-reciter (the *juru tandak*), and a small group of singers who explain and comment on the dramatic action. The dancer-actors sing in archaic Javanese, with refined characters (nobles) using a high upper voice, and coarse characters (demons, warriors) using a heavy chest voice. The music changes with the entrance of each new character.

The modal scales of *gambuh* derive from the system of fingering the *suling* (*tekep* 'to close the flute's holes'), which essentially transposes a pentatonic system through successive steps in the *saih pitu* scale, always maintaining two auxiliary tones. The pentatonic modal scales in ascending order are *tembung, lebeng, baro, selisir,* and *sunaren.* This system informs the *Semar pegulingan saih pitu* theory, and is the basis for all forms of Balinese *pélog. Gambuh* pieces often begin in one mode and modulate to others, sometimes not to return. Apart from *selisir,* several of these modes have become rare or forgotten in *gambuh* practice around Bali. This indicates both the decline of the court traditions and the constant appeal of *selisir,* which is today the tuning of virtually all *gamelan gong* and *pelégongan* orchestras.

The *gamelan arja* (also called *geguntangan* and *pearjaan*) accompanies the popular and relatively secular *arja,* a theatrical genre using many conventions of *gambuh* but placing greater stress on singing and emphases on romance, comedy, ribaldry, and melodrama, combined with contemporary reflection. Described as an operetta, *arja* features actors who sing in a variety of systems of tuning, which better bring out the emotive qualities of the text. Many musicians feel that *arja* is the pinnacle of Balinese performing arts because it demands technique and creative improvisation in music, dance, and drama. The ensemble features a few *suling,* which together can accommodate scales resembling *saih angklung, saih gendèr wayang,* and *saih gong* (*selisir*). Musicians must be prepared for the change of tuning, as indicated by the dancer-actors' singing, which often includes ornaments beyond the immediate tonality of the *suling.* The melodies are linked to the melodic formulae and contours of poetic forms called *tembang,* in which the libretti are written.

The other instruments include two *kendang, rincik, guntang, kempli,* and *kelentang.* The *guntang,* a bamboo tube with a thin bamboo strip struck with a small stick, is often called *kempur,* and supplies the main end-marking punctuation. Formerly, a second and smaller *guntang* functioned to keep the beat; it has been replaced by *kempli* and *kelenang,* playing on and off the beat respectively. There are three main types of compositions: short instrumental pieces, acting as an overture and as interludes; pieces that accompany dancers' entrances; and song accompaniment. For the latter, only *suling, guntang, kempli,* and *kelenang* are used.

The stories of *arja* derive from varied sources: Indian epic plots, legends from medieval East Javanese courtly life, similar stories set in Bali, and Chinese tales of passion. *Arja* developed first as an all-male dance, but young women assumed the main roles in the late 1920s, when a greater emphasis was placed on singing. *Arja* is a popular genre, so the archaic Javanese it originally used extensively has been replaced by Balinese. Performances follow an established form, usually beginning late at night and lasting until the morning hours. *Arja* is almost as much a social occasion as a musical play, and young people flock to performances for opportunities to flirt. Occasionally, groups of the finest male and female *arja* performers around Bali collect to perform together. The popularity of *arja* was eclipsed in the 1970s by *drama gong* (see below), a newer form currently in decline, but *arja* nevertheless remains a fairly popular theater form.

The *gendèr wayang* ensemble is used to accompany shadow-puppet plays (*wayang kulit*). It usually consists of a quartet of ten-bar, double-octave *gendèr* metallophones in the five-tone *sléndro* tuning (*saih gendèr wayang*). Stories used in the play are typically derived from the Hindu epic *Mahabharata.* There is a larger pair of instruments (*gedé* or *pemade*), with a second pair (*barangan*) pitched an octave higher. The instruments are played with a padded disk-shaped mallet in each hand, occasionally with unified motions, but usually in a contrapuntal fashion, and the bars must be struck and damped by the same hand (figure 11). In most of the repertoire, the players' left-hand parts create a nuclear melody in unison in the lower octave, while their right-hand parts normally interlock in figurations in the upper octave (figure 12). The players also frequently perform passages in unison or parallel motion (figure 13).

To accompany shadow plays, there are categories of pieces that are performed differently throughout Bali. Certain pieces (*petegak* 'sitting down') are played while the puppeteer (*dalang*) takes his place; some are grouped together into an overture (*pemungkah* 'opening') as he readies his puppets; others are reserved for specific parts of the play. There are both refined pieces (often metrically free, normally accompanying the puppeteer's singing) and strong pieces (using ostinatos to accompany action). A few of the pieces are associated with specific characters, especially clowns, and other pieces accompany the drama or specific scenes. For example, "*Tetangisan*" ('Weeping') accompanies sadness, and *batel* pieces, as in other Balinese music, accompany anger or fighting. The performance follows a typical form, but musicians are never quite sure how long particular scenes will last, because the puppeteer determines the length of each scene. There are, therefore, a number of standard ways to lengthen and shorten or end pieces, restate or transpose material, and so forth. The group is normally led by the senior player on one of the large *gendèr.*

FIGURE 11 A *gendèr wayang* quartet: a *gendèr gedé* or *pemade* on the left; a *gendèr barangan* on the right. McPhee Collection, UCLA, 1930s.

Gendèr wayang can also be played outside of *wayang* to accompany life-cycle rites, such as tooth-filing rites and especially cremations. The pieces are normally derived from *wayang*, and the complex theatricality is transmitted through musical association. *Gendèr wayang* are sometimes considered to belong to a family of ensembles associated with cremation ceremonies, which also includes the gamelans *gambang* and *angklung*. Two *gendèr* are sometimes hoisted up on the cremation tower to play as the tower is carried toward the cremation grounds. If a performance of *wayang kulit* is part of the program of a cremation ritual, the story performed will often be "*Bima Swarga*," in which the man-god Bima, searching for his father's soul, bravely descends to the underworld and then ascends to heaven. This story symbolizes dedication to parents and the release of the soul.

The *gendèr wayang* ensemble is considered to be delicate and quite intimate, and may be played in close proximity to the priests as they ritually wash a corpse before a cremation, or placed beside the pavilion used for the filing of teeth. This ensemble also accompanies *wayang lemah*, the ritual daytime play of puppets held within the courtyard of the inner temple during a festival, placed next to the high priest as the priest blesses the offerings and ritually creates holy water. The daytime performance is mainly for deities, has its own efficacious qualities, and sanctifies and solemnizes the rites of the priests. The ordinary evening shadow play maintains ritual impor-

FIGURE 12 Two *gendèr wayang* with right-hand figuration.

FIGURE 13 Two *gendèr wayang* in unison style.

tance, but has greater entertainment value, and is performed frequently at life-cycle ceremonies and occasionally at temple festivals.

There is not always a quartet of *gendèr* for *gendèr wayang*. In some areas of North Bali, only the larger pair of *gendèr* are used for performance. The basic quartet can also be expanded to form the *gamelan batel*, the ensemble that accompanies the shadow play for stories from the *Ramayana*. The *gamelan batel* also accompanies *wayang wong*, the masked human theater of *Ramayana* stories, and *parwa*, the human theater of *Mahabharata* stories developed after *wayang wong*.

The *gamelan gong kebyar* can accompany a number of theater genres: *topeng*, traditional masked theater; *prembon*, a popular combination of theater styles; *drama gong*, popular, new theater, based on traditional forms and emphasizing comedy; *sendratari*, *kebyar*-style theater, first created at the conservatories; sometimes *janger*, flexible youth theater of various styles; and even *arja*. When the *gong kebyar* accompanies *arja*, the actors sing mostly in the *saih gong* (*selisir*) system of tuning, and this restriction reduces the melodic and emotional complexity of their performance. Further, *gong kebyar* is much louder than *gamelan arja*, and therefore the actors must sing louder and less intimately. Despite these changes in performance, many people prefer the *gong kebyar* for *arja*.

Processional ensembles

The main processional gamelans are the *bebonangan* or *baleganjur*, ensembles consisting of two *gong ageng*, a *kempur*, a number of *ceng-ceng kopyak* played in interlocking figuration, a number of kettle-gongs (*réong*) individually held and played in interlocking figuration, a timekeeping *kajar*, and two *kendang*. These ensembles are usually assembled from the instruments of a *gamelan gong* (usually omitting the *ding*-toned kettle-gongs, creating a four-tone *pélog* scale), and only in rare cases are made and kept as independent ensembles. Occasionally, the term *baleganjur* 'walking army' is used to denote a larger, more complete ensemble or processional ensembles without kettle-gongs. Sometimes, processional ensembles are assembled from *gamelan angklung* and can therefore use the *saih angklung* tuning and omit *gong ageng*.

The pieces played by these processional ensembles, normally called *gilakan* or *baleganjuran*, consist of an eight-beat metric cycle which is repeated, with the *ceng-ceng* and *réong* providing figuration and often dropping out in alternation. The music has a pronounced martial quality, and often accompanies dancers carrying weapons and ritual objects in procession.

A new style of *baleganjur* music, *kreasi baleganjur*, emerged from the STSI conservatory in 1986 and spread rapidly to urban centers and villages. It features *ceng-ceng kopyak* (usually eight sets), kettle-gongs (*réong*, usually four), a timekeeper (*kempli*), two *kendang*, and gongs, and is virtuosic. Interlocking parts and drum patterns frequently change, and are more complicated than those in traditional pieces. *Kreasi baleganjur* has inspired a whole new repertoire, and has added showmanship and choreography to performance. Heated competitions are common among the growing numbers of groups. Similar to *kreasi baru*, which emerged from traditional *gamelan gong* repertoire, *kreasi baleganjur* arose from traditional *baleganjur* pieces, and has

Some of the pieces are so sacred that their names are secret, and recordings are not permitted. In some villages, nonvillagers, considered impure and polluting, are restricted from even seeing the instruments.

captured the imagination of a new generation of male youth. It has also led to the manufacture and maintenance of *gamelan baleganjur* as complete ensembles disassociated from *gong kebyar.*

Another type of processional ensemble is sometimes called *gamelan barong,* a flexible combination of instruments played by children in procession. They accompany a Barong mask, and go throughout a town requesting donations. Still another processional gamelan is the rare *kendang mabarung* from West Bali, which features *bebonangan* instrumentation (along with metallophones) and includes large *kendang* more than two meters long.

Bamboo and wood ensembles

The bamboo and wood ensembles include *pejogedan bumbung, genggong, gamelan jegog,* and *gong suling.* The *pejogedan bumbung,* also called *gamelan joged,* accompanies the social dance in which a female dancer (*joged*) selects partners from an audience for short, improvised duets. Originally, bamboo tube stampers accompanied the dance, but today the accompaniment consists of *tingklik* or *rindik* (bamboo xylophones in *sléndro* tuning, occasionally in *pélog*), with *kendang, rincik, suling,* and *kempur.* The *tingklik* are played with two long mallets in a technique similar to *gendèr wayang,* though the split bamboo bars need not be damped. Frequently, four *tingklik* and one *suling* are invited to play in hotel lobbies, providing atmospheric background music. Other types of *joged* normally use *rindik* in *pélog* tuning and often borrow repertoire from *legong,* a dance for little girls. A new ensemble, *joged kebyar,* combines *tingklik* with several *gong kebyar* instruments.

Genggong are palm-rib Jew's harps played in an ensemble, often called *gegenggongan,* which includes *guntang* (a one-stringed bamboo tube zither functioning as a gong), *kendang, suling,* and *rincik.* The ensemble occasionally accompanies small theatrical plays. The *gamelan jegog* is an ensemble of various sizes of bamboo xylophones, the smallest of which include 30.5-centimeter-long split-bamboo bars, and the largest of which have bars up to 4 meters long. Modern villagers state that the xylophones are tuned to a four-tone *pélog* scale, while others feel the tuning is derived from *sléndro.* When entered in regional competitions, there may be twenty or more xylophones, producing a thunderous bamboo sound, and often two groups play at once trying to drown each other out. For accompanying dances and theater, *kendang, ceng-ceng,* and other basic percussion are added. *Gamelan jegog* exist only in West Bali. The *gong suling* is a flexible ensemble found throughout much of Bali, consisting of several bamboo flutes at four different sizes, with various percussion and two *kendang.* The *suling* replicate different *gamelan* parts, the repertoire is derived from the *gamelan gong,* and there is no fixed context for performance.

Sacred ensembles

There are a variety of sacred ensembles, most of which have seven tones. The *gamelan gambang,* normally consisting of four xylophones of cut bamboo bars and one, two, or four *saron* (*gangsa jongkok*), and the *gamelan selundeng,* consisting of iron metallophones of different sizes, are the best known. The *gambang* instruments are the xylophones with fourteen bars arranged so the player can use a forked mallet in each hand to play octaves in alternation and form a figuration with the other players, while the seven-bar *saron* provides the nuclear melody, nearly always played in a unique, eight-beat rhythm called *gambangan,* which can be understood as a meter of 5+3. This gamelan has a different *saih pitu* tonality than that used for *gambuh,* and an inherent theory of its own that informs the practices of other sacred gamelan. At one time, *kidung* singing (sung poetry in Middle Javanese) was included in *gambang* performance, but it is now obsolete. The ensemble performs primarily at cremation rituals (*ngaben*), and it also performs at temple festivals in some old villages of East Bali.

The *gamelan selundeng* (also *selunding, selonding*), one of the oldest of all Balinese ensembles, consists solely of six to eight iron bar metallophones, some of which replicate the musical functions of colotomic and agogic instruments, while others perform nuclear melody and figuration. This gamelan is especially associated with the Bali Aga, early Balinese who received little or no Javanese influence and are considered descendants of the original inhabitants of Bali. Ensembles exist only within a few villages in East Bali and mountainous Central Bali. The serene and light music of the ensemble includes orchestral pieces and dance accompaniment, which adds a *ceng-ceng.* Though many ensembles claim a unique repertoire, some pieces for dancing appear to be borrowed from *gamelan gambang.* Some of the pieces are so sacred that their names are secret, and recordings are not permitted. In some villages, nonvillagers, considered impure and polluting, are restricted from even seeing the instruments. New pieces are now composed for the ensemble at the conservatories, nonsacred pieces on specially made nonsacred *gamelan selundeng.* Unfortunately, the ceremonial *selundeng* tradition is currently in decline and may soon disappear in some villages.

The iron bars are of divine origin, have magic power, and must be kept in a constant state of purity. Most ensembles include metallophones of eight bars each, sometimes with four bars in two separate resonant boxes carved from wooden blocks. For performance, the ensemble is often taken up to its own pavilion within the row of pavilions reserved for the men of the village.

The *gamelan luang* consists of two *saron,* two *gendèr* (which stress the *saron* melody at regular intervals), a bamboo xylophone, a *trompong* of sixteen kettles in two rows, a single *kendang,* a single *gong ageng,* and *ceng-ceng.* Found primarily in a few villages in south-central Bali, this ensemble is used for cremation and mortuary rites, though it also functions within temple festivals and accompanies dance with the addition of a second *kendang* and some added colotomic instruments (*kempur, kelenang*) and the omission of the bamboo xylophone. The theory and tuning are apparently related to *gambuh.* The *trompong* is often performed in doubled figuration by two players on either side of the instrument, and the kettles are arranged like a Javanese *bonang.* Because of restrictions on use and secret repertoires, conducting research on any of these ensembles is extremely difficult for nonvillagers.

VOCAL MUSIC

Unlike Java, Bali has no traditions of vocal music as an integral part of gamelan practice. Vocal music in Bali is sung by individuals, by study groups, and by choirs. The music is normally determined by the length of stanzas, the number of syllables per line, the arrangement of long and short vowels, and the ending vowel of each line. The poetic meter determines the rhythm, number of pitches, melodic patterns, and overall melodic contour. The context of performance, however, governs the musical elements; the same text will be given different musical treatment in different settings. The emotional quality of the poem may inform the selected scalar system, and each type of poetry expresses distinctive historical and cultural values.

There are three broad types of sung Balinese poetry: *kekawin, kidung,* and *tembang.* While the structures of these forms originated in Java, most *kidung* and *tembang* and a large portion of *kekawin* were composed in Bali, and the melodies and performance practices of these poetic traditions are purely Balinese today. *Kekawin* are poems in the Old Javanese language based on Indic meters. Parts of major *kekawin* literature, such as the *Ramayana* and the *Bharatayuddha* (the latter derived from the *Mahabharata*), are often "performed" by study groups at life-cycle rites and temple festivals with each line first being sung and then translated and interpreted. These groups, called *sekaha pepaosan* 'reading clubs', consist of a group of men who generally select passages appropriate to the ritual context. *Kekawin* and *kidung* are also performed by individuals at life-cycle rites of prominent villagers and nobility.

Kidung are often romantic, quasi-historical poems mostly in the Middle Javanese language, developed in Bali as a result of Javanese influences, using Indonesian poetic meters and often forming the basis of *gambuh* drama. At temple festivals, *kidung* are usually sung by groups, sometimes organized into *sekaha* and comprising mostly elderly women. The performance accompanies the rites within the inner sanctum of the temple, with one or more leaders singing the text and the others following along, using long sustained tones with little ornamentation. Solo *kidung* performances, however, include extensive ornamentation, embellishment, and melisma and are improvised according to the taste and skill of the singer who usually reads from a palm-leaf manuscript. *Tembang* is the most lyrical form of poetry, derived from the Javanese *macapat* tradition but mostly composed in Balinese. More dramatic and emotional in content, *tembang* are the main vocal idiom in *arja.*

The most famous vocal music is the *kecak* chorus, the group of seventy-five to two hundred men who represent the monkey army from the *Ramayana* and imitate the various instruments of the gamelan with onomatopoeic sounds. *Kecak* (sometimes called *gamelan swara* 'voice gamelan'), originally accompanied trance dances and contained sections of interlocking singing of syllables such as *cak.* Around 1931, during experimentation and after a suggestion by Walter Spies, the noted specialist in Balinese arts, the trance group was expanded, and more elaborate parts were added to create a dramatic, quasi-theatrical performance of short story excerpts (normally the "Kidnapping of Sita") from the *Ramayana.* The members of the chorus (clad only in sarongs, and usually wearing a large hibiscus flower behind one ear) follow a leader chanting *cak* and *cok* with a wide range of dynamics. They occasionally sing passages in unison as they perform several choreographed movements while seated. Dancers sing, and a narrator explains the drama. Despite its fame, *kecak* has no ritual and only limited recreational functions within Balinese society, and is primarily a performance designed for foreign audiences, though artists enjoy composing and choreographing new performances. Nevertheless, one can still hear *kecak* in its original trance-accompaniment role in several villages during ritual events.

A similar vocal performance is *cakepung,* in which a much smaller group of men onomatopoeically imitate gamelan instruments in a tradition originating on the neighboring island of Lombok. A reciter first sings from the *Monyeh* ("Monkey") manuscript, and another translates as in a reading group, with all men sitting in a circle drinking palm wine (*tuak*). Then a group member begins joking, and the men begin singing and eventually start dancing and acting wildly, before settling down to let the reciter begin singing again. As the evening wears on and the men get more drunk, the performance gets wilder and wilder. A *suling* and a rebab accompany the

TRACK 12

nonmetric singing, and play an expanded nuclear melody during the sections of gamelan imitation. The tonality varies: some pieces use a pentatonic *pélog* scale, and others use *sléndro*. *Cakapung* is found only in East Bali, and related vocal traditions exist in remote villages. A similar tradition, *wayang jemblung*, is found in the Banyumas area of Java [see JAVA].

DANCE

In addition to the purely orchestral pieces of the sacred, ceremonial, and *kebyar* repertoires, a wealth of compositions cannot be separated from dance. Dance ranges from the dynamic expressions of *kebyar*, to the animated faces of stock theater characters, to the serene composure of temple dancers during festivals. There are both narrative and nonnarrative dances, described in an abbreviated fashion here to indicate the relationship of music and dance. The narrative dances include *gambuh, arja, topeng, wayang wong,* and *parwa*. These dances include many stock characters—good kings, princes, bad kings, prime ministers, queens, princesses, clowns, ladies-in-waiting—introduced by the performance of their representative *tabuh*. These *tabuh*, however, are specific to the ensemble; for example, the *tabuh* for a king in *arja* is different from that in *topeng*.

The characters within theater and dance dramas are of two types: *alus* or *manis* 'refined, sweet', and *keras* or *kasar* 'strong, coarse'. Dance characterization acknowledges three components—head and upper body, middle body, and foot and lower body—which mirror the tripartite divisions of compositional form and the macrocosm. The *keras* characters emphasize movements in the lower body, and the *alus* characters in the upper body. Movement vocabulary for the *keras* characters, such as a demon warrior, will stress strong, lower-body movements with legs spread apart and large steps, but *alus* characters, such as a refined prince, move more slowly with limbs closer to the body and more concentrated upper-body movements. Performance contexts are varied: *gambuh* may be performed at life-cycle ceremonies of the nobility; *wayang wong, parwa,* and *arja* are normally attached to performance programs as *tontonan* 'things to watch' at temple festivals; and *topeng* may occur at both. *Wayang wong, parwa,* and especially *topeng* and *gambuh* have vital ritual functions, while *arja* is less ritualistic and unattached to religious proceedings, but has a greater social function and serves to gather participants to enjoy theater together.

The nonnarrative dances include *kebyar*, social, and temple dances— genres that are totally unrelated. The *kebyar* dances emerged from the technique of *légong* dancing, the narrative dances of girls portraying figures from epic and romantic tales accompanied by the *gamelan pelégongan*. The early *kebyar* dances, made famous by the choreographer and dancer I Mario, mimicked musical expressions and were normally danced in a sitting or squatting position, sometimes with a dancer playing an instrument, such as the spectacular *kebyar trompong* in which the dancer sits or squats in front of the *trompong*, spinning and flourishing his beaters as he plays and dances. *Tari lepas, kebyar* dances invented after World War II, expanded choreographic possibilities and allowed dancers to portray characters with works that embody themes. "*Oleg Tamulilingan* 'Flirtation of Two Bumblebees'" and "*Taruna Jaya*" 'Victorious Young Man'" are examples of this style still performed.

The social dances primarily consist of *joged*, a term denoting the female dancer, who selects partners in turn from the audience for spontaneous duets, which are flirtatious or even erotic. Originating in the courts and apparently deriving from *légong*, *joged* dancers were retained by kings for their own and their guests' entertainment, and an introductory dance would mimic *légong*. An alternate form of this dance was *gandrung*, performed by female impersonators, who would select partners from the audience just as in *joged*. [For more on singer-dancers, see JAVA.] Today, *gandrung* has

joged Social dance

rejang Temple dance for unmarried girls or postmenopausal women

baris Temple dance for men

sendratari Modern Indonesian dance drama with music, created in the mid-twentieth century

all but vanished, and what groups remain feature young women. The most common *joged* form is *joged bumbung,* accompanied by an ensemble of bamboo xylophones, usually in the *sléndro* tuning. Neither *kebyar* nor social dances have contexts of fixed performances.

Among the temple dances are the *rejang,* a dance of either unmarried girls or postmenopausal women of the village, and *baris,* in which male dancers carry either a particular type of weapon or offerings. The *rejang* dances symbolize beauty and humility as offering, while the *baris* dances seek to protect the deities and the temple space. These dances often have their own repertoire; pieces accompanying *rejang* and other dances with offerings are normally lyrical or stately in nature, while those accompanying *baris* dances are martial. A variety of gamelans can supply the accompaniment. Generally, the most refined gamelans accompany offering dances, while *gamelan gong* or processional gamelans accompany *baris* dances. These temple dances, which have the least choreography and demand minimal skill, are among the most sacred dances in Bali. In contrast, the *kebyar* dances, which demand the most skill, are among the most secular dances.

Apart from the *Calonarang* and a few other dance dramas in which dancers may fall into trance, most trance dancing is nonnarrative and performed at temple festivals to allow deities to "enter" or "sit upon" the dancers and either simply dance or impart to the priests information about problematic situations in the village. Many of these dances, most frequently found in East Bali and often called *onying* or *daratan* (also applying to the dancers), involve *kris,* daggers that the dancers thrust against their chests during trance. The uninjured dancers demonstrate the power of the possessing deity, and priests intervene in the rare cases of injury. Accompaniment is supplied by a variety of different ensembles around Bali, though *gamelan gong* and processional ensembles are the most frequently used, and the music is normally loud and up-tempo. In addition to *kris* dances, performed on a regular basis, *sanghyang* are trance dances normally performed to address severe crises. There are four main *sanghyang,* with nearly two dozen lesser-known kinds found in remote villages. The most famous is the *sanghyang dedari,* in which girls ten to twelve years old, possessed by divinities, dance on male participants' shoulders. These dances, which probably precede Hindu Javanese influence, are accompanied by a specific group of songs sung by women, called *gending sanghyang,* and the chanting of the *kecak* chorus.

GOVERNMENT-SPONSORED CONSERVATORIES

The national government of Indonesia has established conservatories and art schools in the urban areas of Bali: at the secondary school level, and at the level of universities and graduate schools. KOKAR, an acronym for Konservatori Karawitan Indonesia (Conservatory of Gamelan Practice at the secondary school level, meant to include all performing arts), was founded in 1959 and came under national government administration in 1962, eventually changing its name to SMKI, Sekolah Menengah

Karawitan Indonesia (Secondary School for Indonesian Gamelan Practice). The regional government established the university, ASTI, Akademi Seni Tari Indonesia (Indonesian College of Dance) in 1967, which was nationalized in 1969 and has since been subsumed under STSI, Sekolah Tinggi Seni Indonesia (Indonesian Arts University). The intent of the schools is to preserve the traditional performing arts and allow students to study and gain an appreciation of the various music and dance styles around the island, and even around the nation of Indonesia; for some, study is a step toward becoming a professional. The schools bring in music masters from various areas of Bali to teach students, who are also sent back into villages to teach villagers. Several new trends and theatrical forms, such as the *kebyar*-style *sendratari* theater, have been initiated and sustained through the conservatories. The schools have also produced a large number of *kreasi baru* compositions, and have initiated the *kreasi baleganjur* style, which is currently popular among male youth.

Though the conservatory efforts have led to increased artistic activity and to the greater understanding of the performing arts around Bali, they have also resulted in less regional diversity. The conservatory groups are well rehearsed and maintain the highest performance standards; they are engaged for all high-profile events. When they perform around Bali, impressed local groups seek to emulate their sound and their dance technique. Graduates return to their villages and lead their village performing groups in the conservatory style, continuing to erode the local styles. The conservatories have released a large number of audiocassettes that have caused some uniformity in performance style among the village groups. Groups have also retuned their gamelans to pitches approximating the conservatory gamelan. Many Balinese feel that musical leadership is being centralized within the government, when traditionally this leadership lay with the musicians and groups within the villages and regions. The development and sponsorship of annual gamelan competitions and especially the Bali Arts Festival (held each June) bring together village and conservatory and men's and women's groups, and are the forums for the latest trends in composition and arrangement of new and traditional material.

Several of the staff members at STSI have studied with contemporary composers abroad or been influenced by such composers and their works. These musicians, as well as other local composers, have created new, almost radical pieces that deviate entirely from traditional forms of composition and phrase structure, and contain elements of atonality. These compositions (*musik kontemporer* 'contemporary music') may involve traditional instruments played differently, use new instruments or ordinary items as musical instruments, combine instruments from different ensembles, involve the musicians frantically moving between instruments and wearing unorthodox or Western dress, include extended passages in free rhythm, or include yells, screams, and other vocal techniques unrelated to any traditional music.

All the above elements are outside the Balinese music aesthetic, and are totally foreign to the listening audiences. The music challenges the order of traditional and *kreasi baru* music, and introduces an element of heterogeneity into the music culture oriented toward gong cycles, a culture where even *kebyar* compositions have a common root in traditional Balinese music. Yet these innovations reflect Bali's greater assimilation into the larger world, and the internal evolutions of musical practice and understanding. Composers feel compelled to create such pieces for a variety of reasons, one being a desire to expand themselves artistically. Thus far, performances of *musik kontemporer* have been restricted to concert programs at the conservatories, and at festivals in Jakarta. Audience reaction is mixed: audiences tend to jeer at moments of silence or experimental passages, and applaud during sections using more traditional Balinese musical elements. There are reports that the music will be recorded and marketed, but it is hard to imagine its receiving broad acceptance in Bali. It cannot function in ceremonial settings the way traditional music does, cannot be considered recreational music like *kebyar,* and may have limited meaning as art music. Nevertheless, some Balinese composers have received international recognition for their works, and the music has become part of the scholastic curriculum. Six semesters of composition are now required of music students at the STSI conservatory; the sixth concerns exclusively *musik kontemporer.*

Music and other arts were always amateur activities, undertaken for the betterment of the individual and the village in general, or simply to fulfill a needed temporary ritual service for the village. However, the combination of tourism, the conservatories, and researchers studying music, coupled with the normal indigenous demand for particular artists or theater or music forms, has created an emerging class of professional musicians.

Professionalism first occurred within the plastic arts in the 1970s, when tourists began to buy almost anything produced. Within music, this trend developed more slowly. Currently, there are many musicians whose sole activities, apart from participation in some village events, are to teach and perform music and perhaps make or sell musical instruments. Most of these professionals have trained within the conservatories. During precolonial times, courts often engaged talented individuals as permanent court musicians, and they were generally housed in the courts. Their counterparts today often live in nontraditional urban settings, teach in conservatories, perform with groups of their choice, and are frequently paid in cash.

TOURISM AND RECENT TRENDS

Tourism has had a powerful impact on the arts. Tourists tend to descend on Bali with one of three destinations in mind: the beaches and shops of the coastal areas; the expensive hotel complexes at the southern tip of the island (with their all-inclusive entertainment packages); and the "cultural tourism" village destination of Ubud and its environs, where tourist-oriented performances occur nightly. The success of tourist performances has encouraged the formation of performing groups, supplied much-needed revenues to many villages, and given artists the motivation to seek new material. Artists have frequently sought past material and revived almost obsolete dances and orchestral pieces to present to tourists. Some tourists and foreign scholars have also assisted in preserving threatened performing arts, such as *gambuh,* and supported a revival of these forms. This has led some observers to suggest that tourism has replaced the courts as the primary source of patronage for the arts.

Yet tourism has also encouraged performers to restrict the length of orchestral pieces, pieces for dancing, and theater excerpts to adjust the material to the tastes and limited attention span of tourists. These restrictions have become so standard that the artists themselves are beginning to forget the complete versions of the pieces. Many of the groups performing for tourists are also not well rehearsed and are not doing justice to the material. Tourism has thus encouraged a quantity but not a quality of arts, and has spawned misunderstandings and misinterpretations of material. But what is most threatening about tourism is that farmers are encouraged to sell their fields of rice to businessmen or major corporations who have government support to set up art shops or hotels. If this trend of selling lands continues, it may have an impact on the rice-cultivation practices that are still the backbone of the rituals that sustain the whole culture. This could erode the meaning of both the rituals and the performing arts functioning at those rituals.

While the educated composers are creating new works deviating from traditional music, many Balinese youth are turning more and more to American and Indonesian popular music. The ready availability of inexpensive cassettes has created a rapid influx of Western and Jakarta-based popular music. What is now called *musik pop* or *pop Indonesia* (pop in Western styles, sung in Indonesian) is well known to most young Balinese, particularly to those living in urban areas. The Indonesian popular form *kroncong* never achieved popularity among the Balinese, and Indian-influenced *dangdut* has made only minor inroads into Balinese culture, reportedly due to the Islamic nature of much *dangdut.* Many restaurants, hotels, and Balinese themselves have been playing recorded *kacapi-suling* and *degung* music from West Java for atmosphere and relaxation. In the late 1970s, a new style of popular music, now called *Bali pop,* emerged. These songs are sung in a mixture of Balinese and Indonesian, address the sentiments of Balinese, often include Balinese musical elements, and mention place names in Bali. Like *pop Indonesia,* this genre uses Western instruments. It may evolve further and become a normal part of youth culture in the urban centers of Bali.

REFERENCES

Bakan, Michael B. 1993. "Balinese *Kreasi Baleganjur*: An Ethnography of Musical Experience." Ph.D. dissertation, University of California, Los Angeles.

Bandem, I Made. 1979. "Bali: Music." *The New Grove Dictionary of Music and Musicians,* ed. Stanley Sadie. London: Macmillan.

———. 1986. *Prakempa: Sebuah Lontar Gambelan Bali.* Denpasar: Akademi Seni Tari Indonesia Denpasar.

Bandem, I Made, and Fredrik Eugene deBoer. 1995. *Kaja and Kelod: Balinese Dance in Transition,* 2nd ed. Kuala Lumpur: Oxford University Press.

Belo, Jane, ed. 1970. *Traditional Balinese Culture.* New York: Columbia University Press.

DeVale, Sue Carole, and I Wayan Dibia. 1991. "Sekar Anjar: An Exploration of Meaning in Balinese Gamelan." *The World of Music* 33(1):5–51.

de Zoete, Beryl, and Walter Spies. 1973 [1938]. *Dance and Drama in Bali.* Selangor, Malaysia: Oxford University Press.

Dibia, I Wayan. 1992. "Arja: A Sung Dance-Drama of Bali." Ph.D. dissertation, University of California, Los Angeles.

Gold, Lisa. 1992. "Musical Expression in the *Wayang* Repertoire: A Bridge between Narrative and Ritual." In *Balinese Music in Context: A Sixty-Fifth Birthday Tribute to Hans Oesch*, ed. Danker Shaareman, pp. 245–77. Winterthur: Amadeus-Verlag.

Hood, Mantle. 1975. "Improvisation in the Stratified Ensembles of Southeast Asia." *Selected Reports in Ethnomusicology* 2(2):25–34.

Kunst, Jaap, and C. J. A. Kunst–Van Wely. 1924. *De Toonkunst van Bali.* Weltevreden: G. Kolff.

McPhee, Colin. 1966. *Music in Bali: A Study in Form and Instrumental Organization in Balinese Orchestral Music.* New Haven and London: Yale University Press.

Ornstein, Ruby Sue. 1971. "Gamelan Gong Kebjar: The Development of a Balinese Musical Tradition." Ph.D. dissertation, University of California, Los Angeles.

Rai, I Wayan. 1996. "Balinese *Gamelan Semar Pagulingan Saih Pitu*: The Modal System." Ph.D. dissertation, University of California, Los Angeles.

Ramseyer, Urs. 1977. *The Art and Culture of Bali.* Singapore: Oxford Press.

Schaareman, Danker, ed. 1992. *Balinese Music in Context: A Sixty-Fifth Birthday Tribute to Hans Oesch.* Winterthur: Amadeus-Verlag.

Schlager, Ernst. 1976. *Rituelle Siebenton-Musik auf Bali.* Bern: Franck.

Seebass, Tilman. 1990. "Theory (English), Lehre (German), versus Teori (Indonesian)." *Report of the XIVth International Congress of the International Musicological Society held at Bologna 1987,* 200–211.

Seebass, Tilman, I Gusti Bagus Nyoman Panji, I Nyoman Rembang, and I Poedijono. 1976. *The Music of Lombok: A First Survey.* Bern: Franke.

Tenzer, Michael. 1991. *Balinese Music.* Singapore: Periplus Editions.

Toth, Andrew. 1975. "The Gamelan Luang of Tangkas, Bali." *Selected Reports in Ethnomusicology* 2(2):65–80.

Vickers, Adrian. 1985. "The Realm of the Senses: Images of the Court Music of Pre-Colonial Bali." *Imago Musicae* 2:43–77.

Wallis, Richard Herman. 1979. "The Voice as a Mode of Cultural Expression in Bali." Ph.D. dissertation, University of Michigan.

Nusa Tenggara Barat

David Harnish

Nusa Tenggara Barat (NTB), comprising the islands of Lombok and Sumbawa, lies east of Bali and west of Nusa Tenggara Timur. Formed in 1958 (originally including Bali), NTB is one of Indonesia's twenty-seven provinces. Sumbawa is far larger than Lombok (15,600 to 4,700 square kilometers, respectively), but Lombok has far more people. Long dry seasons make wet-rice agriculture, the staple food farther west, difficult in most areas.

NTB has six districts, administered by a governor in Mataram, West Lombok. The three main ethnic groups are the Sasak of Lombok and the Samawa and Mbojo of Sumbawa. The Sasak and Samawa are culturally and ethnically related to the Balinese and Javanese; the Mbojo are related to peoples of Flores. Each group has a distinct language and history, but all share Islam, to which 95 percent of the population adheres, practicing a reformed Sunni version.

Social contexts for making music in NTB include life-cycle rites (marriages and circumcisions, but not mortuary ceremonies), holidays, harvests, and social celebrations. An Islamic reform movement swept over Lombok and Sumbawa in the twentieth century, changing most rituals and their musical traditions; but in Lombok, some musical traditions still function within the contexts of unreformed Islamic rituals. Through competitions and presentations, local culture-and-education departments have preserved and revived some of these traditions.

Lombok is enjoying an increase in tourism, and ensembles often play for tourists. Sumbawa is expecting to develop tourism further in the early twenty-first century. The performing arts are encouraged throughout NTB to assert regional and national identities.

MUSICAL TRAITS WITHIN THE PROVINCE

Before Dutch colonization (1893–1942), Lombok had been colonized by the Balinese, whose influence still marks many Sasak cultural expressions. Music is frequently performed on a variety of gamelans, some consisting primarily of bronze instruments, as in Bali and Java. The instrumentation of this music features a central ("nuclear") melody, played on a metallophone, a wind instrument, or a gong chime (or any combination of them), punctuated by gongs within specific metrical cycles.

Faster-moving ornamentations, often interlocking figurations, are performed on a gong chime or metallophones, and drums have agogic and signaling functions.

The aesthetic changes farther east in Lombok. The tonalities, stratified melodic structures, and gong cycles are gradually replaced by quasi-diatonic tunings and heterophonic melodies, accompanied by drumming. Ensembles are smaller. Vocals are more important, and often include Arabic inflections. Instrumentation relies more on winds (double reeds especially) and strings (plucked and bowed lutes), with fewer bronze instruments than in the west of the island.

These tendencies continue throughout Sumbawa, though the diversity of instruments decreases, and scalar material often covers only four or five tones. Several Samawa and Mbojo court traditions remain from sultanate periods; courtly ensembles and dances are occasionally revived through private and government efforts. Many martial dances are performed across Sumbawa, particularly by the Mbojo. Songs are often topical and romantic, and individuals or groups sometimes improvise sung poetry.

Samawa and Mbojo musical elements and instruments are similar. Double and single reeds are the primary melodic instruments, accompanied by drums and occasionally by a xylophone, cymbals, and a gong. Gong chimes and metallophones are not used.

LOMBOK

Lombok, roughly 70 kilometers east of Bali, has always been within the shadows of Java and Bali. It absorbed extensive cultural influences from these islands, and was colonized and controlled by them. However, other cultural and religious influences—from West Sumatra, and even from West Asia—also inspired the development of several performing-arts traditions on Lombok. These traditions, coupled with those developed internally and others based on Javanese and Balinese models, form a unique and diverse cultural matrix. Lombok probably has a greater variety of music, dance, and theatrical forms than any other area of comparable size in Indonesia; and though some scholars consider it culturally impoverished compared with Java and Bali, it is rich in arts compared to the islands farther east.

The music of Lombok has two main cultural strata: one reflects Javanese-Balinese values, and the other reflects Sumatran, pan-Islamic, and Arab-Persian values. The cultural identity of the Sasak, the dominant ethnic group, constituting nearly 95 percent of Lombok's 2 million people, has gradually changed orientation from the former to the latter. Consequently, many Sasak musical forms associated with Javanese-Balinese values have declined, while those associated with Islam have prospered. This change in orientation was a result of several historical developments.

Before the 1900s, Sasak culture encouraged broad participation in music and other arts. The community considered these efforts beneficial. The performing arts were the medium for enculturation, considered to have efficacious qualities, such as causing rainfall or invoking the divine. In the twentieth century, however, Sasak leaders have scrutinized their traditions, and have discouraged most participation in the arts. They have insisted that music be subordinate to religion, that Islamic literature be the basis of education, and that only God can control nature. In the latter half of the 1900s, musical performances of any kind were infrequent until the 1980s, but there is now renewed interest in music and broad government support for performance genres.

Cultural history and geography

The Sasak are of Malay-Polynesian origin. The interior of the island was settled about two thousand years ago, but the coastal areas were settled perhaps as much as four thousand years ago. Hindu and Buddhist Javanese influence came in varying stages from the 800s until the 1400s, and several small kingdoms were established by Javanese nobles. In the 1500s and 1600s, Islamic influences came from Java, Sumatra, Makassar, and neighboring Sumbawa, and most of the people gradually accepted a syncretic Islamic faith.

In the 1600s and 1700s, Balinese from Karangasem invaded and colonized Lombok, establishing seven competing noble houses and settling much of West Lombok. They restricted the Sasak aristocracy's rights over land, and the Sasak then used Islam as a rallying point for rebellion. Several revolts broke out in the 1800s, and a few enjoyed marginal success. In the early 1890s, Sasak leaders approached the Dutch colonial leaders, asking for assistance; the Dutch, who mistakenly believed Lombok rich in minerals and disliked its (Balinese) king, agreed to intervene. They tried a combination of intimidation and diplomacy, but the Balinese rebelled and attacked. After suffering a major defeat in which a general and two colonels were killed, the Dutch returned to crush the Balinese colonialists, then colonized the island themselves. The Japanese supplanted the Dutch in 1941, and the national independence of Indonesia was proclaimed after 1945. To many Sasak nobles, independence meant a new form of colonization—by Java.

Sasak nobles had initiated the cause of Islam against the Balinese—a cause immediately taken up by religious leaders, and even used against the Dutch. The ensuing movement empowered commoner religious leaders, *tuan guru,* whose influence in the twentieth century gradually surpassed that of the nobles. The *tuan guru* have tried to eliminate all non-Islamic elements from Sasak society, including pre-Islamic and syncretic Islamic rites and the music and performing arts associated with them. Their efforts have diminished the frequency and importance of music, leading to a loss of many traditions. In the early 1900s, most of East and Central Lombok, the areas of the greatest Islamic and least Balinese exposure, underwent a swift conversion to a reformed, modernist model of Islam, understood to be orthodox Sunni Islam. West and North Lombok have changed more slowly; less orthodox religious leaders and more deeply embedded syncretic beliefs persist. Several communities in these areas still practice syncretic beliefs and traditions in the transition to a more orthodox Islamic worldview.

Sasak syncretic faith combines Islamic elements with Hindu and Buddhist elements, embedded within a strong cult of ancestors, similar in many respects to early-1800s syncretic forms of Islam in Java and Hinduism in Bali. The small and shrinking portion of the populace that follows these practices is called Waktu Telu or Wetu Telu (Three Times, Three Stages)—which refers to the three annual periods during which individuals or their representatives should pray and the number of types of obligatory ceremonies. Because of persecution and the changing identity of Sasak Muslims, however, there are no longer any true Waktu Telu villages, and virtually no one calls himself or herself Waktu Telu. Today, villagers who maintain old Sasak beliefs also fulfill orthodox Islamic obligations, such as attending the mosque on Fridays. The vast Sasak majority are the Waktu Lima (Five Times), who accept the tenets and obligations of Islam, including the five daily prayers. Sasak Muslim artists, faced with bans on traditional music by religious leaders throughout the twentieth century, have created new musical ensembles based on combinations of pan-Islamic and pre-Islamic models, so that much of the music associated with syncretic Islam has been replaced by more "acceptable" music still essentially Sasak.

In addition to these two sociocultural groups are the Boda, a small minority of Sasak Buddhists, plus a larger minority of Hindu Balinese remaining from the Balinese colonial period. The history of the Boda is vague, though ancient Javanese manuscripts mention that legendary figures encountered Sasak Buddhists. The Boda, numbering more than twelve thousand, have retained early Sasak beliefs and traditions once shared throughout Sasak society, but their worldview is changing as they gradually become more Buddhist and adopt an Indonesian cultural identity. The Balinese, whose ancestors held power over the Sasak during colonization, have had to adjust to the status of political and religious minority since the Dutch military victory (1894). They have limited their ritual traditions so as to not impose upon their Muslim neighbors. They have strongly preserved some traditions (as most minorities do) while adapting Sasak cultural elements into other traditions. They now number about eighty-five thousand, and their culture is enjoying a renewal, partly from increased communication with Bali and partly from an increased level of tolerance as legislated by the five national Indonesian principles, collectively called Pancasila.

Lombok has long been considered akin to Bali and part of the Javanese cultural continuum, and Balinese colonization strengthened this link. The islands are similar geographically, despite the famous Wallace Line, which runs between Bali and Lombok, marking climatic and botanical differences. Lombok is only slightly smaller (4,700 square kilometers compared to Bali's 5,620), and both have a range of peaks culminating in high volcanic mountains, which dominate the landscape and traditional cosmology. Thus, the culture of Lombok was sometimes considered a mere extension of Bali, and after Indonesian independence, the islands were grouped together politically. It eventually became clear, however, that Lombok and Bali have separate identities. In 1958, Lombok joined its eastern neighbor-island, Sumbawa, to form the province of Nusa Tenggara Barat. Sasak Muslim identification has grown so dramatically in the later twentieth century that Lombok has the greatest ratio of Muslims undertaking the hajj in all of Indonesia. Hajji, because of their pilgrimage, achieve a high social status in Lombok society. Commoners who become hajji receive the social status and title of lower nobility.

Foreign research in Lombok has been limited to early Dutch observations, later visits by a few Dutch scholars, a small number of postindependence ethnographies by scholars and doctoral students, and a few musical studies. Lombok has attracted neither the international scholarship of Balinese and Javanese studies, nor the national government resources necessary for serious and authoritative Indonesian research in Lombok. The regional government in Lombok has conducted studies from which it has produced some informative works. The Culture and Education Department has published reports on history, folklore, ritual traditions, economy, and the performing arts. Unlike Bali and Java, Lombok has few indigenous manuscripts on old local culture, and only a few Javanese and Balinese manuscripts mention Lombok.

Organization of music and musicians

The Sasak have a wealth of musical ensembles and vocal music practices; different districts and villages around the island maintain unique traditions. The musical traditions reflect either Javanese and Balinese or Sumatran and West Asian cultural antecedents, reconstituted into Sasak expressions. Music, directly related to cultural orientation, is believed to embody religious values associated with one or the other antecedent. Religious orientation and musical traditions have thus become intertwined. The elements of musical form and the composition of instruments have become parts of the arguments over what is acceptable music and what is authentic Sasak music.

Musical organizations are informal groups drawn from a community. In villages that retain some Waktu Telu traditions, most villagers perform artistically at some time during their lives. Within orthodox Sasak villages, musical activity is markedly lower, and few villagers are involved in the performing arts. Performing ensembles in general are rare in Lombok, and solo performers almost unknown. Groups are nor-

There are many other forms of idiophones, both of metal and of wood, some with specific sociomusical uses. The *rantok* is a rice-pounding trough on which four women using wooden poles perform rhythms in an interlocking technique.

mally restricted to males, except for a few dances and theatrical forms that include women. Women who involve themselves in the performing arts are usually ascribed a low social standing.

Learning music generally occurs on an informal basis, with instrumentalists receiving limited teaching and then being left alone to refine their parts or develop their own style. Few musicians are considered great masters or great teachers. Learning and performing, though discouraged in some villages, is normally open to all strata of society, and no musical forms are related to any specific class. As in Bali, organizations are frequently called *seka,* particularly in West Lombok. Organizations growing in popularity are Islamic youth brotherhoods, attached to mosques. These groups gather on Thursday evenings to sing from Islamic texts, especially the *Barzanji,* a book in Arabic tracing Muhammad's life.

Musical instruments and ideology

Some Sasak musical instruments reflect cultural practices associated with Waktu Telu traditions, and some instruments reflect Islamization and contemporary values associated with Waktu Lima traditions. Most musical traditions involve ensembles usually called gamelans, meaning simply a collection of instruments meant to be played together. As in Bali and Java, most instruments belong to a particular gamelan and are not played with other ensembles. There is no islandwide organological system in Lombok, but instruments have ideological associations that classify them as nonbronze and bronze. Nonbronze instruments are mostly free of ideological concern, but bronze instruments are associated with Javanese and Balinese cultural traditions, traditions deemed non-Islamic.

Some religious leaders have tried to forbid the use of bronze instruments, calling them Balinese and pagan. Bronze instruments, sometimes called the voice of the ancestors, have been targeted because they have always been used in traditional, syncretic Islamic ritual contexts. The main intentions of these leaders have been to disallow such ritual contexts and preclude the aural experience of the performance of bronze gamelans. In the 1990s, however, leaders have only rarely scrutinized music, and they may accept the remaining traditions from the pre-Orthodox era as essential to Sasak cultural identity.

Among the idiophones, bronze instruments include gongs, gong chimes, and metallophones. The terminology for most of these instruments reflects Balinese influence, and many instruments were made in Bali. Some of the large gongs were reportedly made in Java, though most of these gongs are not so big as those of Javanese or Balinese ensembles. Most gongs are simply called gong, with the largest being the *gong ageng* or *gong beleq,* and the others *col, cil,* or other onomatopoeic names. In a few ensembles, a pair of large gongs, the *gong lanang* and *gong wadon* (male and female gongs, respectively), or the *col cil* (lower and higher gongs), are included in the instrumentation. The hanging gongs have bosses and are about 50 to 75 centimeters in diameter. These have a colotomic function, marking the end of the longest melodic phrases. A few gamelans include smaller hanging gongs, *kempul* or *gong kodeq,* which provide secondary punctuation to the metric rhythmic cycle. Some different large, single, horizontally suspended kettle-gongs punctuate phrasal structures at given points in the cycle, provide a timekeeping function (*petuk*), or provide an agogic function in interlocking figuration (including the *kenat* and *kajar*).

With few exceptions, gong chimes are called *réong.* They contain from four to twelve kettle-gongs. They are always used to provide interlocking figuration and to outline the primary melody through this figuration. It is a vitally important instrument, since there are several Sasak ensembles without other melodic instruments in which the *réong* is the sole pitched instrument. The gong-chime tradition is apparently taken from Balinese ensemble music yet has developed in distinct ways. The figurations are different from those in Bali, and there is evidence that small gong-chime traditions existed in Lombok before Balinese colonization. Some ensembles—for instance, the ancient and sacred *gamelan jerujeng*—feature gong chimes called *kemong* or *klentang,* consisting of either two or four kettle-gongs.

Metallophones, normally called *gangsa,* appear to be derived from Balinese gamelan practice, but are not included in many gamelans. As in Bali, ten-bar *gangsa* are often made in pairs and tuned slightly apart to produce an acoustical beat. Nearly all Sasak metallophones are *gendèr*-type instruments with bevel-edged bars suspended over individual bamboo resonators contained within a wooden instrument case. In the few Sasak gamelans that do include metallophones, there are normally fewer than in Balinese gamelans. The metallophones within the largest Balinese-influenced gamelans, the *gamelan gong Sasak,* include two large five-bar instruments usually called *jegogan,* which punctuate the melodic phrases; a large ten-bar metallophone which performs melodic leadership and ornamentation called *giying, beleq,* or *gedé*; and several pairs of two sizes of smaller ten-bar metallophones (*pemade* and *kantilan*) which play figuration. Occasionally, a pair of mid-range five-bar metallophones are added to play the nuclear melody. A few other ensembles, however, include only two or four metallophones, called by a variety of names.

There are many other forms of idiophones, both of metal and of wood, some with specific sociomusical uses. Cymbals, called *ceng-ceng* and *rincik,* are usually made of iron and appear in a number of ensembles, where they perform an agogic function. Other nonbronze idiophones include the wooden *rantok,* the bamboo *grantang,* the iron *klentang,* and the tin *gula gending.* The *rantok* is a rice-pounding trough on which four women using wooden poles perform rhythms in an interlocking technique. One unique tradition in Bayan, occurring on Maulid (Muhammad's birthday), combines *rantok* with the sacred *gamelan Maulid* in a performance to help guarantee fertility. The rare *gamelan grantang* consists primarily of bamboo xylophones, and is mostly used to accompany the *gandrung,* a social dance. This ensemble was kept by several noble houses until the mid-twentieth century, and was used either to accompany dancers retained for noble entertainment or to perform a courtly repertoire now lost. The *klentang* is an instrument usually realized as a single bar pegged onto a single small box, played by a musician in interlocking technique with other musicians while in procession. *Klentang* of different sizes are played together to create the five-tone *gamelan klentang* or *klentangan. Gula gending* refers to the music pounded by peddlers on tin containers for sugar, whose sound resembles that of the steel drum. The peddlers use their hands and fingers to play on containers to attract buyers, and the instrument normally produces five tones. The music is considered a unique type of street music, and is sometimes staged for local performances. Other idiophones include jaw's harps (*slober* and *genggong*), used in small ensembles.

Aerophones include double-reed oboes (*preret*), end-blown bamboo flutes (*sul-*

ing), and single rice-stalk cylinders (*serune* or *gendola*). The *preret* assumes two different forms: a wooden cone with attached wooden bell or a wooden cone with an attached wooden cylindrical piece extending the bore. The instrument with attached bell is found most often in North and West Lombok, and the other mostly in Central and East Lombok. The *preret* nearly always has one ventral and seven dorsal holes for fingering, occasionally having six dorsal holes. It performs the main melody in many different ensembles, some associated with Waktu Telu traditions, and others with Islam. There are also rare traditions in West Lombok of solo and duo *preret* versions of sacred poetry, and of accompaniment to sung poetry at ritual events. *Suling* come in many sizes, and are tuned in several different ways. The largest is the meter-long *suling pewayangan* or *selisir,* used in the ensemble that accompanies Sasak shadow plays (*wayang Sasak*). A separate *suling* tradition is that of the three-hole *suling* (*suling loang telu*), which plays solo, melancholy melodies to charm women. This flute, which used to have ritual formulas written within it to increase its efficacy, has been forbidden in a number of villages because of the success of the players' intentions. The rice-stalk *serune* pipe is played for recreation; however, a few wooden oboes, also called *serune,* fulfill specific ritual functions in remote villages.

Sasak chordophones are of two types: bowed and plucked. One of the bowed instruments is the *redeb* (or rebab), a two-stringed spike lute, played primarily to accompany a men's choral and dance form, *cepung.* As in Bali and Java, this instrument is associated with vocal melodies. To accompany sung poetry in other contexts, it is played in the sacred *gamelan baris* at Lingsar, and it has reportedly been used to accompany Sasak shadow plays. Violins (*biola*) are other bowed instruments used in a number of small ensembles. There are also two plucked lutes: the *manolin* and the *gambus.* The former, usually positioned horizontally when played, has a varying number of strings and is used on few occasions, usually with an ensemble to accompany the theatrical form *kemidi rudat.* The latter (sometimes called *penting*) usually has four strings (sometimes in double courses), and is included in a few ensembles, such as *kecimol* and *cilokaq* (see below). All these chordophones may have been introduced from Sumatra with Islamic literature or may have had Portuguese Christian antecedents.

Membranophones are of four types: double-headed cylindrical drums (*gendang* or *kendang*), similar to those in Java and Bali; double-headed barrel drums; bowl-shaped drums; and frame drums. Two *gendang* are used in many genres of traditional ensemble music, one of them slightly smaller and higher-pitched (*lanang*) and the other slightly larger and lower-pitched (*wadon*), as in Bali. The two drums generally play in figuration, marking musical beginnings, tempos, transitions, and conclusions. The *cilokaq* ensemble is unique, and may feature either of two sets of drums: the *gendang rebana,* which consists of three bowl-shaped drums; or the *kempol,* two drums that lightly punctuate the musical structure. Excepting *gendang beleq* (a powerful dance, in which drummers use mallets in their right hands), drummers use open and muted strokes of their hands to create a variety of sounds.

The *gendang* is a traditional instrument associated with Java and Bali, but the *rebana,* the *jidur,* and the *bedug* are membranophones associated with Islamic values and West Asia. The term *rebana* is used for single-headed membranophones of several sizes and shapes: small and large frame drums; and large bowl-shaped drums, sometimes called *terbana* or *terbang.* In addition to the bowl-shaped *rebana* used for *cilokaq* and other genres, there are frame-drum-shaped *rebana* with attached cymbals, often called *tar.* A large barrel-shaped drum similar to the large *rebana* is the *jidur,* used in a variety of ensembles, usually as a musical timekeeper. The *bedug* (or *bedhug*), used in mosques, is a large and often double-headed barrel drum whose heads are tacked. A player or cleric uses a large wooden mallet to sound combinations of beats, signaling a variety of messages, for example, calling people to prayer or announcing a villager's death. Since the 1970s, however, tapes of the call to prayer (*azan, adhan*) are blasted over loudspeakers, and the *bedug* are rarely played, though many mosques maintain them as a symbol of earlier religious practice.

Sasak music: theory and practice

Theory and orchestration

There is no codified theory for Sasak music, and the music and musical ensembles around the island often differ greatly in tuning and practice. However, a number of musical elements in ensemble and vocal music create an outline of a theory. The twentieth-century religious movement, which restricted musical performance, no doubt contributed to the limited notion of theory and practice—a situation made worse because musicians do not customarily talk about their traditions, and their terminology varies. Unlike in Java and Bali, there is no clear theoretical modal system, though practice implies that there may be a system. Music is transferred orally, there being no known system of musical notation.

Few Lombok terms define musical form. Most traditional gamelan pieces use gong cycles consisting of two, four, eight, or, more rarely, sixteen beats; a few theater pieces have irregular forms of up to and beyond eighty beats per gong cycle. There are several types of pieces consistently found in a variety of ensembles, particularly those accompanying the shadow play and traditional theater. For example, *lederang* (a rhythm, related etymologically to the Javanese *ladrang*) is usually an eight-beat gong cycle; *rangsangan* 'fast, stimulating' is a two-beat gong-cycle form that accompanies action; and *janggel* 'walk' is a four- or eight-beat form used to depict travel. Melodies often extend over several cycles, and solo wind and string instrumentalists are allowed a degree of improvisation. In many smaller ensembles, drums and cymbals double their intensity at regular intervals to increase musical tension, then return to their normal level of activity to resolve at the stroke of a gong.

Many music forms use tonality related to the Javanese *pélog* and *sléndro* tonal systems. This is particularly true in West Lombok, where Balinese influence seems to have strengthened the use and standardization of these systems. The farther one gets from West Lombok, however, the greater the systems of tuning ensembles deviate from *pélog* and *sléndro*. Musicians in general do not know Javanese terms, and there are no standard terms defining the systems of tuning. The complete *pélog* system in Java and Bali is a series of seven tones with two semitones, from which modal scales can be derived. The practice of deriving modal scales from a heptatonic system of tuning is rare in Lombok. It occurs only within the declining song tradition known as *tembang Sasak*. The predominantly *pélog*-derived tonality found within many ensembles is related to the pentatonic *selisir, saih lima,* or *saih gong,* a scale found in Balinese gamelans (figure 1). The *sléndro* tonality is a pentatonic anhemitonic scale of nearly equidistant intervals, found primarily within vocal music (figure 2). There are several ensembles using tetratonic scales: some appear related to the *pélog* tonality;

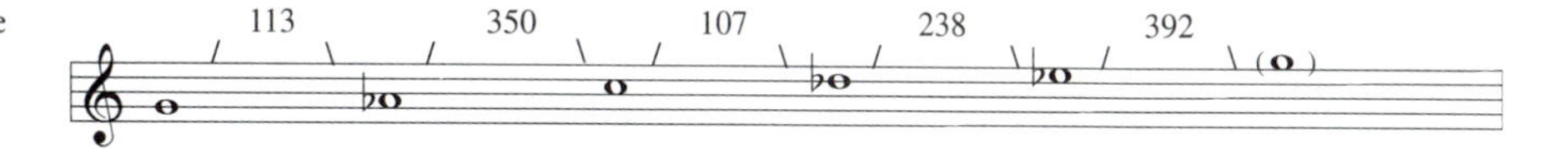

FIGURE 1 Pentatonic *pélog, gong Sasak,* a scale found in gamelans. Lenek Village. The numbers indicate intervals in cents.

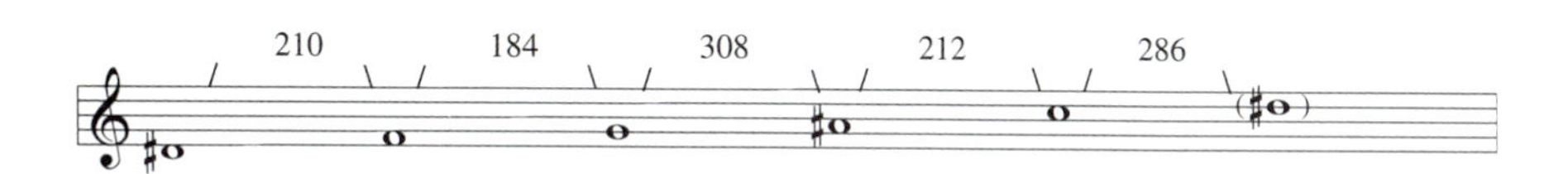

FIGURE 2 Pentatonic *sléndro, tandak geroh.* Lenek Village.

Bronze instruments in Lombok are associated with traditional pre-Islamic, Javanese, and Balinese cultural values. Nonbronze instruments are associated with contemporary Sasak identity and Islamic values.

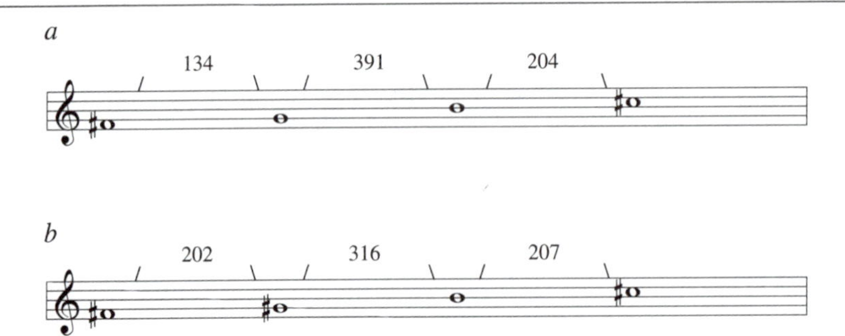

FIGURE 3 Lombok scales: *a*, Tetratonic *pélog*-like scale, *preret*, Mataram; *b*, tetratonic *sléndro*-like scale, *tandang mendet*, Sembalun Bumbung Village.

others to *sléndro*; and others still to neither tonal system (figure 3). There is also a separate tonal concept used in music associated with Islam and the Waktu Lima, featured in many vocal practices and nonbronze gamelans. This music often uses a heptatonic and quasi-diatonic system (figure 4). As with other Sasak music, no terminology defines this system.

Ensembles can mostly be divided into those that consist primarily of bronze instruments and those that do not. The former group is associated with traditional identity, pre-Islamic, Javanese, and Balinese cultural values; the latter is associated with contemporary Sasak identity and Islamic values. The orchestration of the more traditional bronze gamelans is similar to Balinese orchestration: nuclear melodies or expanded nuclear melodies are played on metallophones or aerophones or both; gong chimes or other metallophones or a combination of them provide figurations; cymbals and drums provide agogic functions; and the gong(s) provide(s) the colotomy (figure 5). A composite melody often emerges from the interlocking figurations within the music, frequently approaching *pélog* or *sléndro* in tonality, and there are several layers of musical sound.

Orchestration is quite different within the more contemporary ensembles, associated with Islam. There is a greater emphasis on a single melodic texture with melodic instruments playing lines in heterophony, a greater use of voices following the same melodies, and few if any instruments playing figurations. There is neither a sense of nuclear melody nor its abstraction or stratification, and the agogic membranophone functions support heterophonic melodies.

Concepts of Sasak tonality and composition forms are also distinctive. Traditional gamelans often employ tonality related to *sléndro* or *pélog*, and use colotomic cyclic forms that are regular and expand in a consistent manner; the tonality of

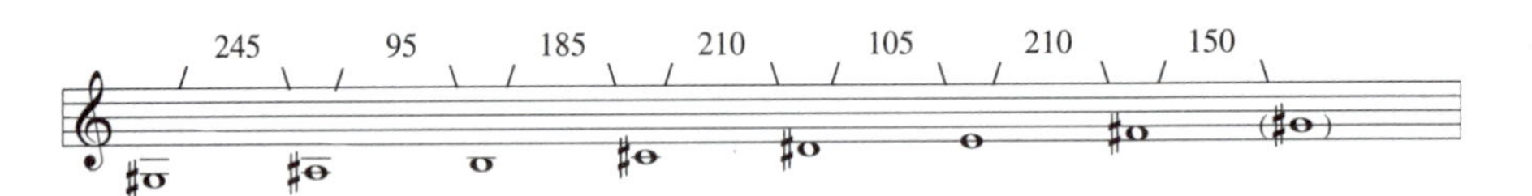

FIGURE 4 Quasi-diatonic (but nontempered) scale, *zikrzamman*, Sayang-Sayang Village.

FIGURE 5 "*Pejarakan*," melody and colotomy, *gamelan baris*, Lingsar Village. Derived from the shadow-play repertoire, the piece resembles that of other theatrical repertoires. *M*, melody, played by *redeb* and *suling*; *T*, *tambur*, the timekeeping drum; *G*, gong, played once every four *tambur* beats.

contemporary ensembles is usually diatonic, and the compositional forms are varied, more linear, and still developing, as composers create new music. The contrasting instruments of these two types of ensembles strongly affects the listening experience. Although traditional gamelans primarily feature the sound of bronze, the more contemporary ensembles feature chordophones, aerophones, and voices in heterophony. The two types of ensembles therefore embody greatly differing aesthetic systems, thought to arise from two distinct religious orientations.

Ensembles and their contexts

The basic, traditional Sasak ensemble is the *gamelan gendang beleq* or *oncer*, also called by regional names (figure 6). The main instruments are the *réong* (normally with four kettle-gongs) and the aerophones (one or two *suling* and sometimes *preret*), with accompaniment by cymbals (*rincik*), a single horizontal gong (*petuk*), a hanging gong, and sometimes one or two small gongs (one being the *oncer*). The ensemble can perform at different occasions such as life-cycle rites (especially marriages and cir-

FIGURE 6 The *gamelan beleq*; a variation of the *gamelan oncer*, the basic Sasak bronze gamelan. Note the size of the drums. Photo by David Harnish, 1988.

cumcisions), ceremonies to invoke rainfall, and national holidays. It can accompany a number of dances, such as *gendang beleq*, and theatrical forms, such as *kayaq*. The *gendang beleq* dance features two drummers who dramatically confront one another and play interlocking figurations on their large (*beleq*) drums. *Kayaq* is a theater of folk plays in which several characters use masks or half masks. Its songs and melodies are considered sad and melancholy, typical of Sasak musical expression.

As in Bali and Java, the few remaining sacred gamelans, found mostly in North and West Lombok, are considered heirlooms. The *gamelan beleq*, similar to the above-mentioned *gamelan gendang beleq* but without the aerophones, is considered sacred in some communities. A few *gamelan beleq* found in high mountain villages accompany sacred ritual dances. Other sacred gamelans using similar instrumentation include the *gamelan jerujeng* (found primarily among the Boda) and the *gamelan Maulid* (performed only on and around Muhammad's birthday). A unique heirloom ensemble is the *gamelan tambur*, which consists of only a *tambur* membranophone and a gong. It represents warlike power, as it accompanies the *batek baris*, a martial dance. The *gamelan baris* adds *redeb, suling,* two *gendang, rincik, kenat,* and *kajar* to this basic instrumentation, evoking the atmosphere of East Javanese courtly life, as it accompanies the *telek* (or *batek*) dance at the Lingsar temple festival in West Lombok.

There are several processional ensembles. The *gamelan barong tengkok* is famous for accompanying riders in hoisted wooden horses at marriages, especially in Central Lombok. Its most striking visual feature is its two *réong*, carried by two Barong masks doubling as instrument cases. Other instruments in the ensemble include two *gendang*, cymbals, *kempul, petuk,* and *suling* or *preret*. The *gamelan tawak-tawak*, which can function in any type of procession, is named after its small gong (*tawak-tawak*). The ensemble consists additionally of a larger gong, six individually carried kettle-gongs played in figuration, two timekeeping kettle-gongs, two *gendang*, and eight sets of cymbals attached to large tasseled lances.

The *gamelan gong Sasak*, an ensemble developed in the early twentieth century, reflects Balinese influence. It adds a large number of metallophones and an expanded *réong* to the instrumental inventory of the *gamelan tawak-tawak*. The tuning is the *saih gong* or *selisir* pentatonic tonality, and the repertoire includes traditional gamelan

FIGURE 7 Different sizes of drums in the *gamelan rebana*. Photo by David Harnish, 1989.

pieces, newly created compositions, and Balinese *gong kebyar* compositions. The ensemble generally performs for recreational purposes, and may accompany certain dances such as the social-flirtation dance, *gandrung*. The *kamput* ensemble belongs to a small class of ensembles that feature *preret* with gong, *rincik, gendang,* the timekeeping *petuk,* and usually one or two *suling*. This ensemble, now becoming rare, performs for life-cycle rites and holidays.

The *gamelan rebana* was reportedly formed in the late 1800s to be a substitute for banned ensembles of bronze. There are normally ten to fifteen *rebana* in the ensemble, with the various drums tuned to perform the parts of bronze gamelan instruments (figure 7). The drums in this ensemble all have goatskin drumheads ranging from about 20 to 60 centimeters in diameter, and the ensemble also includes a timekeeping *petuk* and one or more *rincik*. The large drums, *beleq* and *kodeq*, serve gonglike functions in the ensemble. Their membranes are laced through metal hoops at the bottom of the drums to stretch and support the membranes further. The drums are usually tuned to a pentatonic, *pélog*-related scale, and are sometimes tuned diatonically. The ensemble is played primarily for life-cycle rites, especially marriages, and performs both in stationary position and in procession. The repertoire is fairly flexible. Its core is adapted from traditional gamelan pieces, but even popular songs and Balinese gamelan pieces are sometimes performed. Several pieces are considered to have efficacious qualities, such as aiding the fertility of the soil, and performers generally place small offerings around the ensemble to prevent misfortunes during performance. Thus, though the ensemble was developed to replace bronze gamelans in accordance with new religious ideology, it has retained much of the function and

wayang Sasak Shadow puppetry concerning Amir Hamza, uncle of Muhammad

lontar Palm-leaf manuscript used in areas of Indonesia to record literary and religious works and music notation

cepung Lombok men's choral and dance form

pantun Sung poetry in the form of rhymed couplets

repertoire of traditional gamelans. In a smaller form, it also accompanies the *rudat,* a dance of supposedly Arabic or Persian soldiers.

The ensemble that accompanies the theater form *kemidi rudat* is sometimes called *musik rudat,* and is distinct from the *gamelan rebana.* This ensemble consists of violin, *jidur, rincik,* gong, and sometimes *manolin* and *suling.* The stories of *kemidi rudat,* a form apparently related to *stambul* theater (popular in Java in the early 1900s), are taken from the story of the thousand and one nights, told in the Malay language; most of the actors dance and sing. Similar ensembles often accompany other theatrical forms ("Cupak Grantang" and "Amaq Abir," for example), though bronze gamelans may also be used.

The most important ensemble in a theater context is the *gamelan wayang Sasak,* which accompanies the local shadow play. This ensemble features the *suling pewayangan* as the sole melodic instrument (figure 8), with gong, two *gendang, rincik, kenat,* and *kajar.* The repertoire of Sasak shadow plays consists of six or seven standard pieces, various sustaining patterns to accompany battles, and special introductory pieces. The plays are drawn from the seven volumes of *Serat Menak,* stories concerning Amir Hamza, Muhammad's uncle, usually in his identity as Jayaprana, sent to prepare the world for Islam. *Wayang Sasak* is performed in a mixture of Sasak, Classical Javanese, and Balinese languages; the clowns, who reflect and comment upon the story as it progresses, often speak in Sasak (figure 9). Shadow plays were used for proselytizing Islam earlier in the 1900s, but they have often been forbidden by religious leaders because they depict human forms and retain pre-Islamic ritual processes. Rumored to have been introduced from Java in the 1600s, the puppets most closely resemble those of Cirebon, but the theatrical conventions most closely resemble those of Bali. The tradition, with performances once held regularly at various rituals, is becoming secularized and is often performed for Sasak youth in recreational settings.

TRACK 13

FIGURE 8 *Suling pewayangan* or *selisir,* the flute of *wayang Sasak.* Photo by David Harnish, 1989.

Two closely related ensembles that reportedly developed after 1945 are *cilokaq* and *kecimol.* These ensembles do not accompany theater, but play for life-cycle rites, holidays, and simply for recreation. They usually consist of one or two *gambus,* one or two violins, three *gendang rebana* (each with a different function) played by a single musician, *rincik,* one or two vocalists, and sometimes *preret.* The vocalists perform in the Sasak language. The music may have been influenced by the Javanese popular music *kroncong* (once associated with *stambul* theater), or perhaps from music of the theatrical *kemidi rudat.* The songs, developed from Sasak poetry, use varied tonalities. The term *kecimol* is now also applied to a street band of various instruments, which performs for weddings and accompanies reveling and often drunk attendants dancing in a large circle.

Sasak vocal traditions

There are a number of Sasak vocal traditions: some are related to Javanese and

FIGURE 9 A puppeteer recreates the world at the beginning of a performance of *wayang Sasak*. Photo by David Harnish, 1989.

Balinese traditions, and some are associated with Islam. The primary vocal music related to Java and Bali is *tembang Sasak* 'Sasak songs', songs in the Sasak language using Javanese meters (derived from *macapat* tradition) performed in scales related to *pélog* and *sléndro*, and often written on palm-leaf strips (*lontar*). Individuals or groups (*pepaosan*) are frequently invited to perform, in sung recitation, literature at life-cycle rites related to the particular context. The performances use many techniques, such as slow glissandi, typical of other Sasak songs, which distinguish the Sasak style from those of Bali and Java. Some individuals use inflections apparently derived from Islamic-associated music practice. A counterpart to *tembang Sasak* is *hikayat,* Islamic literature written with Arabic letters on palm-leaf manuscripts in Malay. A group of men reads and translates the literature into Sasak, with appropriate chapters chosen to be sung at the given occasion (figure 10).

FIGURE 10 A man sings from *hikayat,* Islamic literature written with Arabic letters on palm-leaf manuscripts in Malay. Photo by David Harnish, 1989.

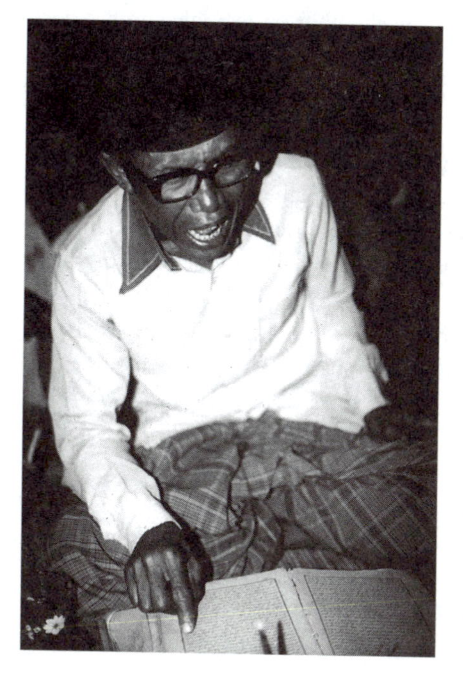

Cepung, a two-part recreational form involving six or more men, was developed by both Sasak and Balinese in Lombok. The first part features solo recitation in free meter, followed by individual sung translation from the *Monyeh* (*Monkey*) manuscript; the second part adds a fixed-meter chorus that onomatopoeically imitates the parts of gamelan instruments. A *redeb* and a *suling* accompany the recitation in rubato, and then perform an expanded heterophonic melody in the metered choral section. The men drink palm wine (*tuak*), and eventually the performance gets wild. Islamic religious leaders have never approved of *cepung.*

There are several local types of sung poetry, some of which use the rhyming form *pantun,* found throughout Indonesia and other parts of Southeast Asia. *Pantun* are sung in the Sasak language in an improvised manner back-and-forth among thousands of girls and boys engaged in ritualized courtship at the annual *bau nyale,* a festival in southern Lombok.

Two types of indigenous poetry are *tandak geroh* and *badede*. The *tandak geroh* (also called *dendang geroh*) is sung poetry, usually in the form of couplets, accompanied by one or two *suling,* in which the text is acted out through spontaneous dance or sung response, usually in light social contexts. The *badede* are in the form of couplets or duplets, and include four separate subtypes of poetry relating to function: to lull children to sleep, to honor deities, to appease spirits and chase away sickness, and to make friends happy. A duplet poetic form related to *badede* is *kayaq,* melancholy songs. The tonality of these forms is usually tetratonic or pentatonic, related to *pélog* or *sléndro.* Glissandi are common in Sasak vocal music, and they add a melancholy element to the music: one singer stated that the use of a glissando at a particular point in a text is saddening because it is "like the sudden shadow of the mountain."

Several vocal traditions are directly associated with Islam. *Burdah,* the singing of devotional songs, involves a group of men (usually only hajji) playing large *rebana* (also called *terbana* or *terbang*) drums while singing. *Qasidah rebana* is musically similar to it, but is a song of praise usually sung by a soloist. *Hadrah,* a Malay-Islamic tradition perhaps introduced from Sumbawa, is a sung poetic form that accompanies choreographed movement within Islamic brotherhoods and can lead to trancelike states. *Zikrzamman,* featuring a group of men (including clergy) who sing from the *Barzanji,* other Islamic literature, and the teachings of local religious leaders, is perhaps the most intriguing of the Islamic vocal traditions. It is performed almost exclusively within mosques, often on Thursday nights, and includes movements and concentration that can lead to trancelike states (figure 11). The music consists of nine distinct sections, which modulate among different scales as in Arabic *maqamat.*

All these genres are performed primarily on Islamic holidays, and the scale is usually diatonic. Singing these genres, all of which are in Arabic, is thought to be spiritually meritorious, especially during holidays.

Balinese traditions in Lombok

Balinese music in Lombok is distinct from music in Bali in many ways. Both the ensembles and the music differ slightly, and there are some Sasak influences. Balinese gamelan music occurs primarily at the many temple festivals and life-cycle rites (birthdays, tooth-filing ceremonies, marriages, cremations) held in Balinese communities, which are found almost exclusively in West Lombok. In the 1970s and 1980s, Balinese performing arts were systematically excluded from regional competitions and government-sponsored performances. Now, however, tolerance appears to be greater, and the local government is becoming aware of the unique nature of Balinese arts in Lombok.

There are not so many different types of Balinese music in Lombok as in Bali, and the music culture is not nearly so vibrant, but the Balinese have preserved some traditions and maintain a number of other unique expressions. The main ceremonial gamelan is the five-tone *gamelan gong kuna,* closely related to the *gamelan gong* and *gong gedé* of Bali—a tradition possibly better maintained in Lombok than in Bali.

The *gamelan angklung* is a smaller ensemble of four tones. Unlike *gamelan angklung* in Bali, most metallophones are of the resting-bar variety, rather than the suspended-bar kind. There is also a distinction within the processional *gamelan baleganjur* tradition. The Lombok ensemble omits *réong,* considered in Bali the most important instrument of the ensemble. The wooden oboe (*preret*) is occasionally used within the *gamelan baleganjur,* and some of the repertoire derives from Sasak gamelans, further distinguishing this ensemble. The wooden oboe is also played solo at temple festivals—a tradition that may originate in Sasak practice. The singing of *kidung* poetry at temple festivals, as in Bali, is rare in Lombok, and is often replaced by wooden-oboe performance.

FIGURE 11 A *zikrzamman* performance by a brotherhood at a mosque. Photo by David Harnish, 1989.

New developments

There are neither secondary schools nor universities devoted to the performing arts. A single university (ASRI, Akademi Seni Rupa Indonesia) is dedicated to plastic arts and offers occasional classes on dance and music. One or more performing-arts schools, however, will possibly be established within the next decade. Students from Mataram University originating from the six districts of Nusa Tenggara Barat (comprising Lombok and Sumbawa) have been organized by the government to present performing arts from their particular districts for others within the province. The Culture and Education Department has established its own ensemble, which performs a variety of Sasak dances and new compositions.

These groups are often sent through the districts to perform for and educate the people about both their own performing arts and those of other districts. Because of

In Lombok, new performing groups of all sorts are registering with the government, and regional competitions in music and dance have seen entries rise dramatically in the last few years.

historical and religious developments that curtailed the arts, people know little about the music and dances within their own district, and virtually nothing about the traditions of other districts. The local government, through these performances, intends to inform the people about their district, provincial, and Indonesian cultural identity. The government is also encouraging participation in the arts as a way to preserve tradition and identity in the face of modernization and Western influence introduced through tourism. These efforts are counteracting those of religious leaders who have sought to ban most of the performing arts.

Government-sponsored ensembles, and other Sasak and Balinese artists, have begun to create new music and dance compositions for dancing and to develop new plots within various theatrical forms. New dance movements, theatrical conventions, and compositional forms, drawing upon traditional forms and Balinese and Javanese influences, and new supposedly Islamic-inspired musical forms, emerge annually. New performing groups of all sorts are registering with the government, and regional competitions in music and dance have seen entries rise dramatically in the last few years. These developments demonstrate that the arts and artistic activity are gaining a renewed popularity.

The Indonesian popular musics known as *dangdut* and *musik pop* (or *pop Indonesia*) have become well known in Lombok. What has emerged in response is a growing style of Sasak popular music based on Indian-influenced *dangdut,* called *dangdut Sasak, orkes Melayu* (a term shared throughout Indonesia), and *qasidah Sasak*, which uses mostly Western instruments and rhythms derived from Malaysian and Indian film music. These terms define the same style: a *dangdut* style of music and instrumentation produced locally, which features Sasak and Islamic imagery and often uses the Sasak language. *Musik pop,* which exclusively uses Western popular music instruments and form with Indonesian lyrics, has also grown in popularity in the urban centers, and there are annual pop-singing competitions. A growing audiocassette industry is supporting these styles.

SUMBAWA

Sumbawa, one of the Lesser Sunda Islands of Indonesia, joins its neighbor-island to the west, Lombok, to form the province of Nusa Tenggara Barat. The Australian climatic influence is evident in local plants and the meager annual rainfall. Because of this and the roughness of the topography, wet-rice agriculture, the common model in much of Indonesia, is difficult in parts of Sumbawa.

The southern coast is lined with extinct volcanic peaks that plunge into the Indian Ocean, while the north coast consists of plains, river basins, and a mountain range culminating with Mt. Tambora at 2,820 meters. The island is just over 270 by 90 kilometers, and has about fifty people per square kilometer. A population of 850,000 is sparsely spread over three districts: Sumbawa (West Sumbawa), Dompu, and Bima-Raba in the east.

Two main ethnic groups, the Sumbawanese and the Bimanese (known locally as Samawa and Mbojo), inhabit the island; the former live in West Sumbawa, the latter in Dompu and Bima. The Sumbawanese and their language (Bahasa Samawa) are ethnically related to the Sasak, the Balinese, and the Javanese. The Bimanese are darker in features and a racial mix of Malay and Australoid; their language (Bahasa Bima) is related to that of Flores. The dividing line between the two culture areas lies close to Dompu.

Islam, shared by both groups, is the dominant socioreligious force in Sumbawa; in fact, Sumbawa is one of the most rigorously Islamic islands in Indonesia. Remote peoples in the mountains follow Islamic or Christian practices combined with elements of animism and Buddhism.

Cultural history

Sumbawa was a feudal island consisting of small animist kingdoms with minimal Hindu-Buddhist elements before the 1500s, then two centuries of Islamic influence followed contact with the trading culture of Makassar in southern Sulawesi. Islam, perhaps introduced in West Sumbawa a bit earlier by an expedition from Java, was embraced by the Sultan of Bima and his followers in the 1630s, and later the Sultan of Makassar placed a family member on the throne. Makassar politically dominated the island in the early 1600s. The ethnic Sasak of Lombok's Selaparang Kingdom governed Sumbawa until Balinese forces drove out both Makassarese and Sasak in 1740. Throughout this period, the royal sultanate families of the palaces in Sumbawa Besar and Bima sustained contacts with the Sultanate of Goa in South Sulawesi and with Islamic cultures in Sumatra and West Java. Though some of the remaining royalty claim descent from the rulers of Goa, many of the old court manuscripts are written with Arabic letters in the Malay language, and indicate a close connection with the Banten Kingdom of West Java.

The local royalty signed treaties recognizing Dutch hegemony from the 1600s to the 1800s, but Dutch officials never bothered to colonize Sumbawa and only sent an administrative and military staff in the early 1900s. A local catastrophe was the eruption of Mt. Tambora in 1815, believed to have killed more than half the island's population. West Sumbawa was partially repopulated with peoples from other islands (Javanese, Sasak, and others), adding a level of diversity to that area. More recently, small groups of Balinese have migrated to West Sumbawa and the other districts. Because of the sparseness of its population, Sumbawa has been deemed by the national government in Java an area in which to resettle Indonesian migrants from more densely populated islands.

Since Indonesian independence from the Dutch (1945), local royalty have lost their titles, and most have abandoned their palaces. The courts (Sumbawa Besar, Bima) had supported musicians and encouraged the development of fine arts. These arts included small ensembles of double-reed oboe (or flute), drums, and gongs; male and female dances; and sung poetry. Several of these have disappeared with the decline of the courts. Occasionally, efforts are made to recreate these arts to preserve cultural identity and attract tourists. Some genres of music and dance appear related to those of Lombok, probably due to the extensive contact of these islands over the centuries. In the early twentieth century, pan-Indonesian-Islamic reforms swept over Sumbawa, resulting in the loss of many indigenous and traditional arts. A few new musical forms associated with Islam have emerged in substitution, but the arts in general are not so vibrant nor as valued as in islands to the west (Lombok, Bali, Java).

Musical instruments, traditions, and contexts

The contexts for making music are varied in Sumbawa. A number of musical forms are associated with Islam, some with the nobility, a few with romance and courtship, and many with work and recreation. Two primarily musical life-cycle contexts are circumcisions and marriages. Male circumcisions are held between the ages of seven and eleven, depending upon village custom, and are occasions of great celebration. Marriage ceremonies are complicated, last several days, and differ significantly in Sumbawa and Dompu-Bima. An indigenous ceremony waning in Sumbawa is the first hair-clipping rite, held after three or four months of a baby's life.

Several traditions were restricted to life-cycle rites and coronations of nobility; many of these have disappeared or assimilated new functions to survive. A unique ceremony, now perhaps obsolete, was that celebrating a noblewoman's seventh month of pregnancy. Music is often associated with religious events and holidays. The primary religious holiday is Maulid (Muhammad's birthday), celebrated for a week; another is Lebaran, a feast held after Ramadan, the month of fasting. There are also a number of local Islamic observances. National holidays and harvest festivals are two other contexts for making music.

Sumbawa is well known for its horses, and there are frequent horse races in which music is sometimes presented; in addition, buffalo races in West Sumbawa are held before the rice-planting season. There are also dances of mock battles—for example, the Sumbawanese *parise*, in which two men strike at each other with rattan staves, and the Bimanese *lanca*, in which two men use their knees to strike at each other. Dances derived from the martial art *pencak silat* are also found throughout Sumbawa. Formerly associated with festivals of the sultanate, these dances are frequently performed for national holidays and for tourists. No theatrical forms of Sumbawa appear to predate the twentieth century, many of the dances are nonnarrative, and there are no masked-dance traditions.

Musical instruments and elements

Strings, winds, drums, and other percussion are all found in Sumbawa. The most important stringed instrument is the bowed *biola*, similar to the Western violin but slightly lower in pitch. It is especially used in Bima and Dompu, and may have been adapted from Portuguese models. Portuguese traders frequently visited Sumbawa in the 1500s and 1600s. The *gambo*, an eight-stringed (double course) plucked lute, is sometimes used for songs and dances in various parts of the island and occasionally called *gitar*. It is thought to have originated not with the Portuguese, but with the Bugis of Sulawesi. Winds consist primarily of double-reed oboes (*silu* in Dompu and Bima), single reeds (*serune* in West Sumbawa, *serone* in Bima) and bamboo flutes (*suling*, found only occasionally but throughout the island). The *silu* is a unique metal double-reed oboe (mostly nickel) with attached metal bell and one ventral and seven dorsal holes for fingering; *silu* produced since the late 1980s have been made of wood. *Serune* are made of a combination of bamboo and palm leaf, with one ventral and six dorsal holes for fingering. Reed pipes from rice-paddy stalks (*kendola*) are sometimes found in small ensembles. Wind instruments are played with a circular-breathing technique.

There is a wide variety of drums including the *kendang*, found everywhere but more concentrated in West Sumbawa (double-headed, slightly conical drum similar to Sasak and Balinese models); the *rebana*, found all over the island (various sizes of frame and bowl-shaped drums, some with attached cymbals); the *jidur*, found only rarely but throughout Sumbawa (large barrel drum); and the *tambur* or *tambu*, found in Dompu and Bima (large drums with bodies of metal, possibly with Portuguese antecedents). Single bronze hanging gongs (normally called gong) are common in ensemble, especially in West Sumbawa. Gongs mark melodic cycles of two, four, eight, and (rarely) three beats. On rare occasions, a kettle-gong is added to keep the pulse. Two other idiophones are *rantok* and *palompong:* the former, used occasionally in small ensembles, is a rice trough into which women stamp bamboo tubes; the latter is a small, three- or four-key wooden xylophone, played by soloists for their own recreation and sometimes in Sumbawanese ensembles.

Ensembles are small when compared to those of islands west and there are far fewer bronze instruments. Several ensembles consist simply of a single- or double-reed aerophone, a drum, and a gong. The musical forms are usually short and utilize repetition and variation. There sometimes emerges an aesthetic reminiscence of West Asia, because of the rigor of the drumming (often with cross-rhythms), florid string and double-reed melodies, monophonic or heterophonic texture, and the occasional use of Arabic. There is little sense of the Javanese tonal systems that extend from Java into Bali and Lombok. Scalar systems are diverse; some are quasi-diatonic, while others contain as few as four tones. The discussion below includes both dance and music, and divides West Sumbawa (Samawa culture) from Dompu and Bima (Mbojo culture).

West Sumbawa

Ensemble music and dance

The standard ensemble of West Sumbawa consists of single-reed *serune* (or oboe or flute), gong, and drum, and is sometimes called *ansambel musik Sumbawa* 'Sumbawanese music ensemble'. Occasionally cymbals, kettle-gong, *palompong* xylophone, or a second or third drum may be added. These ensembles accompany a range of ceremonial and recreational settings, and a large number of dances. Among the ceremonial dances are *kosok kancing* and *nguri*, both of which have been recreated from their earlier obsolete forms. *Kosok kancing* features six dancers combining men and women, and is still occasionally used for circumcisions and marriages of nobility. The *nguri* dance was held for ceremonies entertaining the sultan (particularly when he was sick and required a cure) and is now frequently performed to receive honored dignitaries, guests, and tourists. It features four women performing slow and refined movements contrasting with rapid single-reed melody and powerful drumming. *Dadara nesek* is a traditional dance (not courtly) featuring four women performing movements of weaving cloth, and *berampakan* is a dance of joy for a bountiful harvest; both use the accompaniment as above. A unique and nearly obsolete tradition (not yet revived) is *tanak*, a dance for happy occasions performed before the sultan by a group of men and women singing a combination of text and nonsense syllables coordinated with the *serune* melody.

The *gong genang,* an ensemble similar to the typical Sumbawanese one above, consists of a small gong, small *kendang* drum, *serune* single-reed, and occasionally the *palompong* xylophone. This ensemble, the only one occasionally called a gamelan, accompanies the martial-art dance, *pencak silat*, using two different rhythmic patterns to accompany the blows, kicks, and dance movements. The *gong genang* also accompanies the *joge bungin* women's dance formerly associated with palace festivals and recreation and now in danger of disappearing.

An entirely different type of ensemble is the *rebana rea*, which consists of one or two large *rebana* drums to keep the pulse, and one or two smaller ones to fill in the rhythms. It is used to accompany Islamic prayers and songs in Arabic. *Rebana rea* often functioned at marriage ceremonies, but couples today prefer more modern music, and its use has become restricted to events around mosques and religious holidays. Regional songs and folk songs are often accompanied by the *gambo,* sometimes in small ensembles. Another small ensemble consisting of *serune* and *rantok* accompanies a topical sung poetry, *gandang*, occasionally performed after communal work in the village or in the fields.

sakeco Samawan semi-improvisatory topical, humorous sung poetry

langko Samawan romantic repartee songs between men and women

badéde Functional couplets, generally sung by older women

Barzanji Biographical or praise songs about Muhammad

genda Mbojo Bimanese court ensemble

Vocal music

The most popular and virtuosic tradition is *sakeco*, topical and sometimes humorous poetry sung in Sumbawanese. Two men must sing as one, overlapping at precisely the right moment, while one (or both) taps out rhythms on a medium-sized *rebana*. Some passages are in unison while others feature one singer performing a line and stopping to breathe as the second singer continues on to a second line of poetry. After a while, the tempo increases into a section called *racik,* and the singers overlap more quickly, singing only half lines of poetry and alternating between overlapping and unison or heterophonic texture. Performances, held in conjunction with life-cycle ceremonies and recreational events, must emotionally involve the audience in creating an intimate atmosphere, and there is an element of improvisation as performers strive to strike a responsive chord within the audience. The poetry also contains valued educational elements, and *sakeco* attracts both young and old audiences. In West Sumbawa, some vocal forms include this phenomenon of singers overlapping lines to create a continuous melody. The aesthetic of continuous melody may derive from Sumbawanese aerophones, played with a circular-breathing technique, which provides constant melodies.

Another major vocal tradition is *langko*, romantic poetry (*lawas*) lyrically sung in Sumbawanese between groups of males and females. The pieces form part of the Sumbawanese body of traditional songs, *temung*, considered more complicated than the poetry of *sakeco. Langko* is performed during rest periods while harvesting rice, and there is an element of competition. Two or more men will sing poetry using a given song, which must be sung back precisely but with different text by two or more women. Whichever group fails to render the melody properly loses.

Three other forms of sung poetry are *badéde*, *balawas*, and *saketa*. There are a number of different types of unaccompanied *badéde*, generally sung by older women: one type for noblewomen who are seven months pregnant, another for babies receiving their first hairclipping, another for lulling babies. *Badéde* are also known in Lombok. *Balawas* is a term for the arrangement of poetry in Sumbawanese for other vocal forms, and also for a recreational performance in which two or three individuals take turns singing poetry of the same meter. *Saketa* are spontaneous call and response work songs (leader-chorus, with the chorus responding in vocables), accompanied by *serune* and performed for communal projects, such as building a house, planting and harvesting rice, and buffalo races. Nearly all of the above vocal forms are performed with stylistic distinctions in the western and eastern areas of West Sumbawa.

Songs associated with Islam are nearly always in Arabic. One such tradition is *Barzanji*, a collection of biographical and praise songs about Muhammad, said to have been compiled many centuries ago by the Persian saint Barzan and brought to Sumbawa via Sumatra in the late 1600s. These songs are performed to bless a harvest or a home, for a baby's hairclipping ceremonies, for religious holidays and the fasting month, and often for religious education on Thursday evenings in mosques. Men sing together, often breaking into two groups and performing choreographed movements with the songs. Occasionally *ratip*, a small *rebana* drum, will be used in a form known as *ratip barzanji*. This latter form is not performed in mosques because *ratip* and other instruments are not allowed there. *Rebana rea* (briefly described above) and *ratip rebana rea* use two sizes of *rebana* frame drums (large and small) which accompany Islamic prayers, hymns, and other songs sung in Arabic. These latter forms occasionally appear at marriages or circumcisions and on religious holidays, where they would perform outside the mosque. Another tradition, *hadra*, consists of songs of praise, and also is never performed in mosques; it is better known in Dompu and Bima, and is discussed further below.

Dompu and Bima

Ensemble music and dance

The court ensemble *genda Mbojo* consists of a large drum (*tambu* or *tambur*), two smaller *kendang*, and a double-reed *silu*. This ensemble performs some instrumental pieces and accompanies dances. The *silu* is the most important instrument and in past decades and centuries required special ceremonies before the production and the playing of the instrument. The Bimanese ruling house apparently still owns a few fourteenth-century *silu* from the palace of Goa in southern Sulawesi, and *genda Mbojo* occasionally uses these; otherwise the more common Bimanese model is utilized. The musicians of this ensemble are determined by descent; they have performed instrumental pieces and accompanied court dances in the Bimanese sultanate for centuries.

One of the court dances accompanied by *genda Mbojo* is *kanja*, a male martial dance thought to have been created by a sultan in the eleventh century. Another reportedly dating from the same time is *lenggo*, a nonnarrative dance by four men or women (of the proper descent, like the musicians) with small and refined movements to welcome guests and celebrate events within the sultanate. In past centuries, this dance was performed atop a houselike structure, carried in processions greeting the sultan and his guests. A third, *sere*, features two noble male warriors with spears and shields, who perform ritual formulas to make themselves invulnerable in battle; a variation of this dance involves two long rows of male dancers who clear the path of royal processions. These traditions of music and dance will not pass to the next generation, and will likely disappear in the near future, though there are reports that efforts are underway to revive these traditions and transfer them from the sultan to wealthy individuals and the Culture and Education Department of the provincial government.

A second ensemble, sometimes called *ansambel musik Bima*, consists of *silu*, *kendang*, and gong, and accompanies a number of martial and heroic dances featuring two male dancers carrying spears, cudgels, daggers, or shields. The most popular and demanding dance is *mpaa kantao*, which sometimes adds a *serone*. The dances are used for recreation, or are staged for government-sponsored performing-arts events. There are an unusually large number of martial dances in Dompu and Bima. Two others are *fatininu* and *baleba*, which both utilize *pencak silat* movements and are accompanied by the same type of ensemble. Still more are *naka* and *dahalira*. *Dahalira* is a women's martial dance, and *naka* is a male dance with daggers accompanied only by *tambur* and *kendang*.

Another ensemble is the *kareku kandei*, rice pounder and mortar, respectively. At least six women pound out a minimum of five patterns (a sixth part is improvised) forming a polyrhythmic texture, and this pounding often accompanies regional songs. Performance contexts for *kareku kandei* are weddings, circumcisions, and recreation.

Vocal music

Perhaps the most widely known of all Bimanese music is *rawa Mbojo*, which features a vocalist (usually female) singing a variety of Bimanese songs (romantic, heroic, advice, laments) accompanied by *biola*, or occasionally by *gambo*. It requires a more demanding technique than many other traditions, includes ornate passages in free and set meter, and is performed during harvest festivals, marriage ceremonies, and just about anywhere people congregate. Singers sometimes dance. Another tradition is *nua,* in which males and females sit in a circle and sing *pantun* (rhyming couplets, found throughout the archipelago) accompanied by bowls used for betel. Each participant must spontaneously sing *pantun* relating to a particular topic while tapping out a rhythm on the betelnut bowl and passing it to the person on the right. The songs, performed in the local language, are those of advice, suggestion, allusion, and satire. Performed for recreation, *nua* is apparently in decline because few people can perform it properly today.

Hadra is probably the best known form associated with Islam. The term refers to a body of Arabic poetry and songs of praise about the life of Muhammad. Men sing these songs in four-line stanzas with *rebana* accompaniment. *Hadra* may include choreographed movements, and is performed for religious holidays, national holidays, and circumcisions. There is also *lomba hadra*, a competition in which men spontaneously sing and follow each other in a question-and-answer format. Losers are those who fail to follow the proper form. Other forms associated with Islam are songs apparently deriving from the *Barzanji* and other songs of praise and other songs performed around religious holidays.

New arts and genres

Though there are no institutions of higher learning in Sumbawa to inspire composers and choreographers, a number of new pieces are created almost annually by Sumbawanese and Bimanese artists. The local and regional Department of Culture and Education offices have been encouraging artists to create, assisting with staging and promoting their works. These offices sponsor music and dance competitions, and winners represent the different districts at provincial competitions in Lombok.

The new arts are based largely on traditional models; only rarely have artists borrowed forms or material from other Indonesian cultures. The Sumbawanese basic ensemble—*serune*, gong, *kendang*—is used for new pieces in West Sumbawa, sometimes augmented with a second gong or drum or both, cymbals, and *palompong*. One of the best known new creations (*kreasi baru,* a term used throughout Indonesia) is *barapan kebo*, a dance based on water-buffalo movements during races. The dance involves two men who become buffalo and four other male dancers. A second example is *dadara bagandang*, featuring women singing while performing nine movements associated with harvesting rice. Artists have also been interested in combining music forms in ensemble. One example of this is *gendang dan langko*, in which two *rebana*, *serune*, and *gambo* (or *gitar*) accompany several women singing *langko*-style poetry.

Perhaps inspired by theater forms in Lombok, three new plays have been created by different artists in the same area of West Sumbawa. *Lalu dia lala jince*, *mirata*, and *batu nganga* are these musical plays. The first concerns romantic plays of happiness, and is performed by six men and six women; the second is based on heroic stories and performed by six men; the third, based on traditional tales, is performed by four women. These plays are performed for holidays and recreation and are accompanied by the standard Sumbawanese ensemble. One musical play developed early in the twentieth century, *tanjung menangis*, comes from the northern region, and involves seven performers (men and women mixed) enacting local legends of nobles. This play is also accompanied by the standard Sumbawanese ensemble.

There are not so many new creations among the Bimanese. Most dances are accompanied by a standard Bimanese ensemble (*silu*, *kendang*, gong), occasionally augmented with a second drum or stringed instrument. Two new dances for women are the *rebana* dance (*tari rebana*) and the candle dance (*tari lilin*). The former involves six or more women playing small *rebana* (*ratip*) while they dance, and the latter has women carrying lit candles on a plate. *Tari lilin* are also known in other parts of Indonesia. A musical play probably developed earlier in this century is *toja*, a form based on the mystical legends in old sultanate chronicles, performed by four to six women and accompanied by a *genda Mbojo* ensemble.

REFERENCES

Harnish, David D. 1985. "Musical Traditions of the Lombok Balinese: Antecedents from Bali and Lombok." M.A. thesis, University of Hawaii.

———. 1986. "Sasak Music in Lombok." *Balungan* 2(3):17–22.

———. 1988. "Religion and Music: Syncretism, Orthodox Islam, and Musical Change in Lombok." *Selected Reports in Ethnomusicology* 7:123–138.

———. 1990. "The *Preret* of the Lombok Balinese: Transformation and Continuity within a Sacred Tradition." *Selected Reports in Ethnomusicology* 8:201–220.

———. 1991. "Music at the Lingsar Temple Festival: The Encapsulation of Meaning in the Balinese / Sasak Interface in Lombok, Indonesia." Ph.D. dissertation, University of California, Los Angeles.

———. 1992. "The Performance, Context, and Meaning of Balinese Music in Lombok." In *Balinese Music in Context: A Sixty-Fifth Birthday Tribute to Hans Oesch*, ed. Danker Schaareman, 29–58. Winterthur: Amadeus.

Muller, Karl. 1991. *East of Bali: From Lombok to Timor*. Singapore: Periplus Editions.

Proyek Penelitian dan Pencatatan Kebudayaan Daerah. 1979. *Ensiklopedi Musik dan Tari Daerah Nusa Tenggara Barat (Lanjutan)*. Mataram: Departemen Pendidikan dan Kebu dayaan.

Yaningsih, Dra. Sri, Umar Siradz, and I Gusti Bagus Mahartha. 1988. *Peralatan Hiburan dan Kesenian Tradisional Daerah Nusa Tenggara Barat*. Mataram: Departemen Pendidikan dan Kebudayaan.

Nusa Tenggara Timur

Christopher Basile
Janet Hoskins

The Indonesian province of Nusa Tenggara Timur (NTT, the Eastern Lesser Sundas) includes the islands of Sumba, Savu and Rai Jua, Roti and Ndao, Timor with the offshore island of Semau, and Flores with the islands of Komodo and Rincah to the west and Solor, Adonara, Lembata, Pantar, and Alor to the east. The province divides into twelve administrative districts (*kabupaten*), which roughly correspond with the major ethnic divisions of the area. The provincial capital is Kupang, located at the western end of Timor. NTT has poor natural resources, a semiarid tropical climate with low rainfall and a long dry season, and a population of more than 3 million people pressing heavily on available land. With a per-capita income of less than half the national average, it is one of the poorest regions in Indonesia (Barlow 1991).

The peoples of NTT are exceptionally diverse. Distinct subgroups migrated to the region in the distant past, and local origin tales reflect this migration. By a conservative estimate, at least thirty distinct Austronesian languages are spoken in NTT, as are a number of non-Austronesian languages on Timor, Alor, and Pantar. Linguistic subgroupings and dialects make the linguistic picture even more complex, with most islands characterized by continuous linguistic variation. For example, the small island of Roti possesses eighteen different dialects forming a chain across the island, with dialects at either end of the chain almost unintelligible to one another. The people of the islet of Ndao, just off the west coast of Roti, speak another language altogether.

Geographic and historical factors have also contributed to the region's cultural diversity. With mountainous hinterlands dividing the larger islands, transportation has always been difficult and communications limited. Hostility and warfare between neighboring peoples, and even villages, were endemic until the early decades of the twentieth century. In addition, the lack of political hegemony by any one people, the historical division of the region among two colonial powers (the Dutch and the Portuguese), and internal pressures to accentuate differences between neighboring communities, have contributed to making NTT culturally diverse; nevertheless, within this context of diversity, some common cultural motifs occur (Fox 1988).

Hand-woven textiles (*tenun ikat*) play a central role in the lives of most of the peoples in NTT. Textiles serve as clothing, especially during ceremonial occasions,

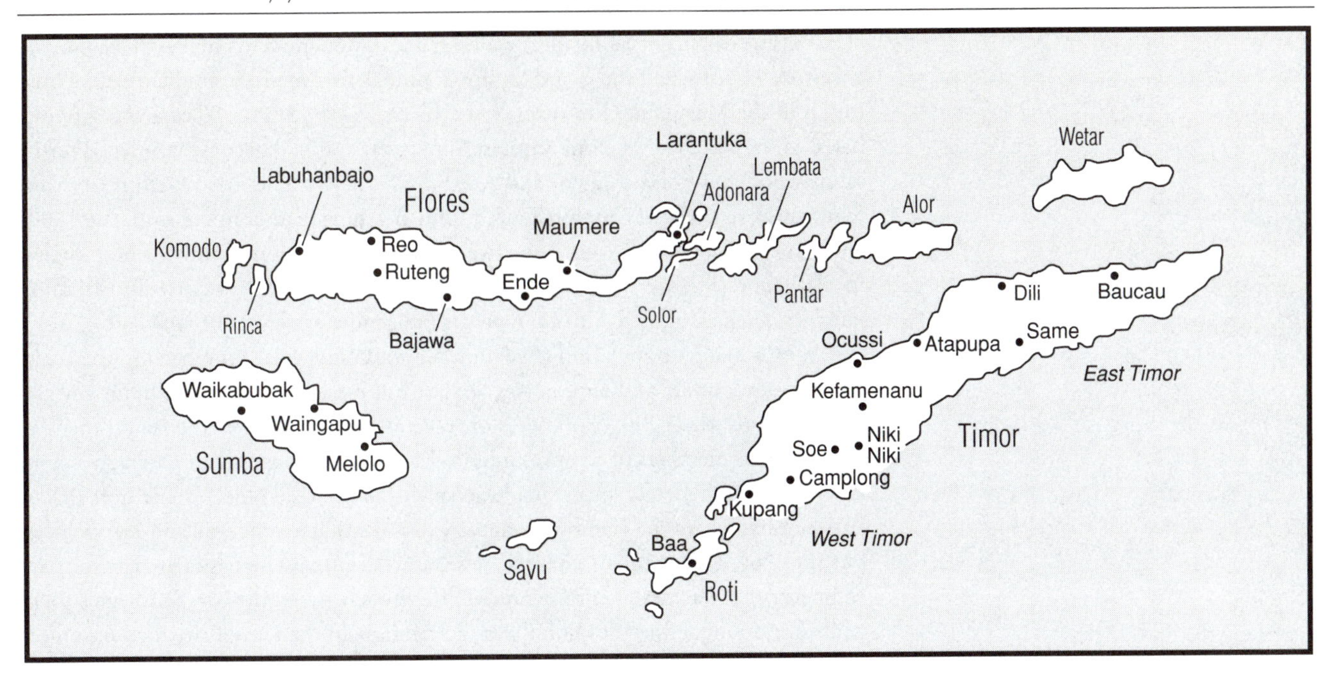

Nusa Tenggara Timur

and are a key ingredient in a complex web of traditional social and economic transactions. The remarkable wealth of ethnic variety in the region is clearly displayed through the medium of *tenun ikat* cloth, with its colorful and symbolically significant patterning and myriad details of manufacture and use. Arguably the leading focus of artistic expression in NTT, textiles throughout the area are designed and produced mainly by village women.

Throughout NTT, directed marriage has traditionally been a means of forming alliances between social groups. In many areas, there is a preference for cross-cousin marriage: a man's preferred mate is his mother's brother's daughter; a woman's, her father's sister's son. Connubium and alliance—like the composition of textile designs, the organization of space, and the structure of the local state or community—reflect a perception of reality as fundamentally dualistic. The sociocosmic dualism that underlies NTT society receives possibly its most eloquent expression in a variety of local, lively, and ongoing traditions of ritual oration that employ parallelism. Found throughout the region, these traditions encode and express social wisdom and significant ritual knowledge in a form that is itself pervasively dyadic.

Though NTT is in many respects isolated, located in the far corner of the Southeast Asian cultural world, its sandalwood forests, particularly in Timor and Sumba, have attracted international traders since the early centuries of the Christian era. By the 1500s, the sandalwood trade had drawn Europeans to the region and resulted in NTT's becoming one of the first areas in Asia to experience sustained European contact. Thus, although NTT's relative isolation has contributed to the conservative maintenance of local traditions, these traditions have incorporated influence from the diverse trading peoples drawn to the region. Over the course of many centuries, Arab, Indian, Chinese, Javanese and European peoples have each left their marks on every aspect of culture in NTT, including music.

SUMBA

Sumba lies southwest of Flores, at the western end of the outer arc of the Lesser Sunda Islands. Its climate is hot and dry, particularly in the east. Most of the population lives on inland plateaus, where grasslands support herding and small-scale agriculture. The origins of Sumbanese clans are recounted in sacred myths of semidivine ancestors who reached the island by ship. Sumba's first mention in documented history is in the Majapahit chronicles of the 1300s. By the 1600s, Sumba was subordinated to the sultanate of Bima (in East Sumbawa) and had become renowned for its sandalwood and horses (Taylor and Aragon 1991:210). The first Dutch treaty with Sumba was signed in 1756, but Dutch influence remained nominal until the 1800s and was not consolidated until the twentieth century. Today, Sumba is best known for its elaborate and distinctive textiles (*ikat*) and for the dramatic rituals, including jousts (*pasola*), associated with Marapu, its indigenous system of beliefs.

Sumba and its population (five hundred thousand) have long been in the backwaters of Indonesia, and Sumba was the last Indonesian island to maintain a pagan majority until the 1990s. Followers of traditional ways all over the island identify themselves as members of a community of Marapu worshippers and pray and sing to an invisible audience of ancestors, local spirits, and sacred objects. The domains of East Sumba (where the Kambera language is spoken) are autocratic and hierarchical, but those of West Sumba (where nine separate regional languages are spoken) are competitive and achievement oriented. Differences between these societies are strong, while important similarities link them, particularly in the area of ritual communication.

Because of religious conservatism, music on Sumba is still primarily sacred, and musical instruments are among the most important objects of the Marapu. Singing and dancing occur most often in the feasting months after the rice harvest (July through September), when people gather in their ancestral villages. As the rainy season approaches (in October and November), the high priest of the calendar enforces a period of ritual silence (East Sumbanese *wulla tua* 'respected months', West Sumbanese *wulla padu* 'bitter months'), when striking drums and gongs, bowing fiddles, and blowing into flutes are forbidden. The making of music is taboo until the ceremonies to welcome the new agricultural year are held in February or March. The only exception permitted—and only if a special rite is performed with sacrifices to request it—is a funeral, which would be inconceivable without the sounds of a mournful gong beating to announce the death.

Bronze gongs first came to Sumba as trade items from Java, brought by Muslim merchants in exchange for horses, sandalwood, and slaves. Gongs (East Sumbanese *anamongu,* Anakalangu *mamongu,* Weyewa *tala*) are played with padded sticks (*patundungu,* also *patumbungu*). The number of gongs varies between five and seven, depending on the piece and whether the ceremony is one of mourning or rejoicing. In East Sumba, gongs are played with a standing drum (*lamba*); in West Sumba, a similar drum (*bendu*) is used with a hanging drum (*bamba*) and sometimes a handheld drum (*deliro*). Whether played in mourning or in rejoicing, the sound of the gong ensemble is always augmented by men's cries (*kayaka*) and women's piercing, sustained ululations (*kakalaku*). These call-and-response cries are also performed with only drum accompaniment during formal occasions to signal the beginning of an important ritual prayer or sacrifice.

Gongs are among the most valuable forms of imported wealth on Sumba. Each gong has a name and is said to have a voice and to be inhabited by a spirit (not a local one, but one that has migrated from a splendid kingdom to the west). The spirits of the gongs must be notified whenever they are moved. Since all other Sumbanese musical instruments are locally manufactured, gongs occupy a position of prominence, in both legend and daily life. Only noble houses may own them, and they mark high aristocratic status. When a particularly sacred gong is played in East Sumba as the body of a noble person is carried to the tomb, all the dead person's possessions (horse, dog, rooster, human slaves) are said to fall into trance and slump convulsively to the ground. Gongs are also sometimes given as a part of nuptial negotiations (for more information about Sumbanese marriage and exchange goods, see Geirnaert 1989:456 and Hoskins 1988:131).

Gong pieces come from a traditional, circumscribed repertoire and are made up of repeated, interlocking patterns. Special gong pieces, which may not be played at any other time, are performed at royal funerals to announce the arrival of each party of guests [see SULAWESI]. Twice each day in the week before the burial, the gongs play a special piece, signaling the guardians of the dead to enter trance and accompany the deceased on visits to his ancestors. In East Sumba, gong pieces usually begin with two large gongs (*katala*), which are hung next to each other, with the larger gong on the player's right. Then two medium-sized gongs (*nggaha*) enter, suspended with the larger gong above the smaller. Two small gongs (*kabolulu, paranjangu*) and the *lamba* drum complete the ensemble.

Many ancestral villages have a specific house named as the home of the gongs and upright drum, and sometimes only descendants of this ancestral house have the right to play the instruments. A cracked or damaged gong is said to have lost its soul, and a special rite, including sacrifices of pigs and buffaloes, must be conducted to placate the offended soul and return its voice to the gong.

Musical instruments intermediate between human beings and the Marapu, who are both protectors and punishers. The first ritual act in any feasting sequence is to plant the gong stand (*kadanga landa tala*) and set up the post for the drums (*katuku ndende bendu*), marking the central location of the instruments and linking them in a chain of communication with the world of spirits. The Sumbanese say they cannot speak to their ancestors without the rhythms of the drums and the gongs, and they cannot persuade the ancestors to do anything without a good performer's coaxing song.

In the Kodi District of West Sumba, each major category of ritual performance is defined by the set of musical instruments used in its performance. The first offering made before the rite starts is an offering to the spirits of these instruments. The upright drum (*bendu*) is the primary ritual actor in an all-night singing ceremony (*yaigho*), held in response to some form of affliction (most often illness, but also a fire, a poor harvest, an accidental fall). The drum is the one told to travel "like a butterfly sent flying, like a bird set singing" to the world of spirits, piercing through seven layers of the heavens to catch the ear of the deities who control health and fertility. An offering of betel leaf and dried areca nut is placed on top of the drum, and a song is sung to the spirit inside the drum. The song tells of the origins of the drum, how it was carved from a piece of driftwood and given the shapeliness of a young woman ("You with the slender waist, the curved breasts"), whose cavity is pierced by the voice of the male singer. The first drum was covered with the skin of a sacrificed slave girl, so her spirit continues to live there, though these days the human skin has been replaced with the hide of a young buffalo calf. The song of the drum transposes her story of suffering to provide a model for the origins of the shamanistic power to cure. In effect, the drum, rather than the singer, acts as the shaman (Hoskins 1988).

The upright drum is played with sticks by a seated singer, accompanied by an assistant who beats a horizontal drum (*deliro*) with his hands. Inside the house, gongs are hung from roof rafters near the front veranda and are beaten rhythmically to accompany the singer's words. A narrative of the affliction is recited by one or several orators (*touta liyo*), who engage in a dialogue with the singer. Each of them provides a series of accounts of which angry spirits might have caused the trouble, phrased in the paired couplets of ritual language. The singer then sets their words to the rhythms of the drums and gongs, so they can travel up to the Marapu deities. The human audience hears an extended process of negotiation between the human per-

The vigorous, warlike dances popular in West Sumba contrast strongly with the slower, more dignified style found in the east, where people dance in a circle at funerals and noble weddings.

formers to determine the correct version of the cause of affliction, but the Marapu deities are said to hear only the music and songs.

A more elaborate ceremony is a *woleko,* defined by the fact that a stand of five gongs is erected outside the house to thank the spirits for their assistance. Buffalo are sacrificed to feed them. The singing includes a series of long pieces "sung to the dance ground" (*lodo nataro*), in which male and female dancers face each other, the men charging forward with spears, shields, and bush knives toward the women, who tremble and flutter their hands. In a series of invasions and retreats, new dancers and occasional solo performers repeat this formation all through the night. Sometimes the dancing heats up to such an extent that some male dancers lose control, waving their swords carelessly or falling convulsively to the ground, so spectators move them out of the dance ground. Gender-specific dancing alternates with a spoken dialogue between orators who tell the story of the origins of the feast and name each of the Marapu who will receive a share of the sacrificial meat the next day.

The vigorous, warlike dances popular in West Sumba contrast strongly with the slower, more dignified style found in the east, where people dance in a circle at funerals and noble weddings. A line of women moves forward slowly to the mournful tones of a long song about ancestral origins. Holding onto the top edge of an imported Indian *patola* cloth, they begin to move in a circle, first spiraling inward, then turning out again. Each movement is highly controlled and deliberate: the winding and unwinding of the spiral may take almost an hour to complete. The people of Wanokaka, West Sumba, perform a different dance: both men and women wield bush knives and move threateningly in a spiral formation.

Music performed in the central dance grounds of the ancestral villages is the most prestigious and sacred form of Sumbanese music, but more modest genres are performed in other locations. Music is a required accompaniment to any form of large-scale collective work, so a singer must be invited (and paid) to perform at gatherings where people drag the wooden pillars that will become posts for houses and thatch the roofs of ancestral cult houses. Singers are also hired to encourage the several hundred people who drag large stones to the villages, where the stones are made into megalithic graves. Stone-dragging songs (*bengo*) are the longest and most elaborate of the work songs (*lodo paghili*). They use a courtship idiom to speak of the stone as a lovely, light-skinned bride, who travels across the water to meet her intended husband in the ancestral village.

As part of the preparations for the yearly calendrical ceremonies and *pasola,* teasing courtship songs (*kawoking*) are sung along the beaches of the west coast of Sumba. Verses exchanged between giggling groups of boys and girls deride the others' sexual prowess. They are performed during a period of license, when young people enjoy unusual freedom; other activities during that time may include participation in boxing matches (*patukengo*) or traditional games with spinning tops or a discus.

Songs of love and other more personal matters (*lavitti*) are a less stringent form of verse than the formally paired couplets of ritual language. Repetitive and plaintive, they are composed in response to real-life incidents, using natural metaphors to evoke images of a lost sweetheart or an absent lover. Many romantic *lavitti* are sung without musical accompaniment (young men like to practice them as they herd horses and water buffalo), but they can also be sung to the accompaniment of a one-stringed fiddle (*dungga roro*) or a two-stringed plucked lute (*jungga*). The tunes may also be played on a nose flute (*poghi*). Recreational songs, shared during long evenings when guests come to visit in the gardens, are sometimes accompanied by a bamboo jaw harp (*nggunggi*), or a four-holed bamboo flute (*kapika,* also *taleli*).

One form of traditional narrative is stories with songs, which usually recount the founding of a village and the acquisition of heirlooms. The stories are told by a single narrator, a descendant of the ancestral house in which they are recited, and must be preceded by a chicken sacrifice and divination to request ancestral permission. The storytelling lasts all night. Long periods of simulated dialogue and narrative alternate with songs. Each song marks a journey, for instance the crossing of one of the seas the hero must pass in his search for a bride, the piercing of a level of the sky to travel to the upper world, or the traversing of various landscapes while dragging a tombstone.

The songs are in the paired couplets of ritual language and must be repeated without errors, or the singer may endanger himself. The songs must be repeated at least seven times at different points in the story, and sometimes two or three sets of repeated songs may occur as part of the same narrative. Most tellers of long traditional narratives are male, but women also excel in the style. In East Sumba, these long narratives with songs are associated with the period after the rice harvest. In Kodi, they may be told at the yearly calendrical rites to welcome the swarming of sea-living worms (*nale*). Sumbanese chanting style is bold and rhythmic, and the chanter's voice must be strong to be heard clearly by the assembled audience of humans and spirits.

Another musical genre performed without instrumental accompaniment is the funeral dirge (*hoyo*), sung only by women as they attend the corpse during the period preceding the burial. The words express grief and suffering through an array of traditional formulas, commenting not only on the dead person's life, but also on the shock of bereavement that living people experience. Some long funeral dirges may be repeated at rites to commemorate a dead person or to consecrate his or her tombstone. Each dirge recalls a narrative about the origins of mortality, in which Mbora Poka died under a banyan tree, and human death became inevitable.

FLORES

Flores is located in the Lesser Sunda islands, northwest of Timor. A rugged, mountainous island, it is home to about one and half a million people, of several distinct ethnic groups, each with its own language and customs. The eastern area of the island was named Cabo das Flores (Cape of Flowers) by sixteenth-century explorers from Portugal, and Flores eventually became the name for the entire island. In order across the island from west to east, the five major languages are Manggarai, Ngada, Ende-Lio, Sikka, and Lamaholot, but within these major divisions there are numerous subdivisions. Ngada Regency, for example, is home not only to the Ngada people, but to the Nage and the Keo, and to several other, smaller, but still distinct, ethnic groups. The influence of both Roman Catholic and Protestant Christianity and Islam is pervasive. Some areas such as the coastal regions of Manggarai were dominated by Muslim kingdoms for centuries, and Flores's main city of Ende is NTT's major Muslim port. However, indigenous practices continue in many areas. Sikka, for example, is one of the few places in NTT where it is not unusual to still see handwoven *tenun ikat* cloth worn in daily life (figures 1 and 2). Ancient Đông Sơn gong-

FIGURE 1 Tied and dyed *ikat* threads dry in the sun before being woven into cloth. Photo by Cary Black, 1988.

drums (*moko*) are still presented as part of elaborate traditional marriage-exchange arrangements there and in Lamaholot-speaking areas. Music and dance continue to play a central role in the cultural life of the peoples of Flores; each ethnic group has a distinctive style and repertoire (Kunst 1942). Though instrumental music occurs in most places in Flores, the areal variation of the island's vocal music is one of its strongest and most distinctive musical features (Yampolsky 1995a:5).

Certain types of instruments occur across the island, differing generally in name, construction, number of strings or keys, and methods of playing. Bamboo idiochord tube zithers are found all over Flores. Eastern Flores has a three- or four-stringed version (*klong-klong*) and a five-stringed one (*gong tondu*). The Sikka version (*santo*) may have from six to nine strings; the Ende-Lio version (*gobato*), three; the Ngada version (*beko fui*), five; and the Manggarai version (*nggri-nggo*), five or six. The people of the Lamaholot area use a one-stringed, struck bamboo idiochord (*baba*). The Ngada ver-

FIGURE 2 Finished *ikat* cloths for sale at a local market. Photo by Cary Black, 1988.

FIGURE 3 Duelers with whips in Rajong, Manggarai, 1927. Koninklijk Instituut voor Taal-, Land- en Volkenkunde. Courtesy of the Royal Institute of Linguistics and Anthropology, Leiden, The Netherlands.

sion is *goweto* or *sowito*, and the Manggarai version is *bemu nggri-nggo* (also *tinding*).

Also found throughout Flores is a simple xylophone (Lamaholot *preson*, Sikka and Lio *letor,* Ende *geko,* and Ngada *ridu*), made of wooden keys placed across two parallel supports. The Manggarai *do'u da* differs slightly: the keys are connected to one another with string. Everywhere in Flores people play xylophones with drums during healing ceremonies, and their tuning and arrangement of keys is variable.

Ensembles of gongs and drums occur throughout Flores. Metal gongs, originally from Java, are known in Flores by a variety of cognates with the Javanese gong (Ende-Lio *nggo,* Ngada *go,* Sikka *gong*). Gongs are played in a variety of ceremonial contexts, usually to accompany dancing. Only in Manggarai do they accompany competitive dueling (*parise,* also *main caci*), in which opponents take turns trying to lash one another with a long rawhide whip, or defending themselves with a round shield (*nggiling*) and a length of rattan (*agang*) (figure 3). Contestants switch sides when the whip finally draws blood. After these duels, a lengthy vocal performance (*mbata*), sometimes lasting all night, may occur as part of a ritual for predicting the coming agricultural cycle (Yampolsky 1995b:17).

In *mbata* songs a male soloist is the lead singer, accompanied responsorially by a male, female, or mixed chorus, with men and women singing in octaves or parallel intervals. Lyrics deal with local traditions and may only be sung in ritual contexts. Some *mbata* may be accompanied by drums and gongs. The style of songs in some areas of Manggarai can incorporate yodeling, and stories abound of singers sitting on opposite hillsides, competing with one another across ravines.

The style of songs in some parts of the Ngada area features multipart songs with drones (not just in the low register, but also in the middle register), differing greatly from the melismatic, solo style of Manggarai (Kunst 1942). People of Ngada have a variety of end-blown flutes, played solo or in ensembles, sometimes accompanied by bamboo stamping tubes (*thobo*). The *foi doa* is a double flute with a single mouthpiece; the *foi dogo* is a triple flute, with the middle pipe acting as a drone. An indirectly blown bass flute (*foi mere,* also *foi pai*) is unique to the Ngada area. Flutes of all types are played only while the rice is ripening; after the harvest, they may not be played until the next season's planting.

Drum-and-gong ensembles (*laba go*) contain five gongs, plus a Florinese version of a European side drum (*laba,* also *tambur*). The *todagu* ensemble plays rhythmically

In some areas of the Sikka Regency, gongs may be presented as part of elaborate marriage-exchange arrangements, with elephant tusks, special textiles, and other important goods.

FIGURE 4 In this Boawae boxing match, referees (*right and center*) try to restrain the contestants. Photo by Roy W. Hamilton, 1991.

complex and exciting music for bamboo slit drums (*toda*), usually four instruments divided among three players, plus two high, narrow standing drums (*laba toda*). Other drums played in Ngada include a squat, single-headed, handheld drum (*laba dera*), and a standing, single-headed drum, played with sticks (*laba wai*). Because drumming has magical potency in Ngada, it is prohibited there outside of feast days.

In keeping with the popular Florinese custom of competitive fighting, the Soa and Boawae districts of Ngada are known for their boxing matches (*etu*), which last several days (figure 4) and include a full night of dancing to the accompaniment of reverent songs before matches. During the fights, long lines of men from each side perform chants (*dioe*) while using bamboo stamping tubes to mock and discourage the other side.

In Ende-Lio Regency, the most important expressive event is the *gawi* dance, led by male dancers either forming a closed circle while female singers in a semicircle perform canonic singing, or leading a long, mixed-sex spiral around a public square (figure 5). *Gawi* occur at a variety of rituals (usually concerning agricultural cycles), celebrations (as for victory in war or headhunting and making peace), and other traditional festivals. In one Lio village, the *gawi keu* is a *gawi* performed as part of a post-harvest festival of thanksgiving and fertility. In it, villagers crowd into lineage houses and beat coconut half-shell idiophones on the floor, singing a responsorial chorus to the oration and solo singing of an older male leader. The performance lasts most of the night and accompanies individual dancers, who display cherished *ikat* textiles as they dance. Because every village has its own agricultural calendar, *gawi* are village-specific events.

For weddings, people of the Ende-Lio area have a nuptial duet (*feko genda*), consisting of a side-blown flute (*feko*) and a frame drum (*genda*). This duet performs for events surrounding the wedding: to entertain during the bride-wealth negotiation, to escort and entertain guests, to accompany dancing afterward (when individual dancers display a cloth), and to accompany the newlyweds as they walk through the village, greeting the inhabitants of each house (figure 6). Playing the *feko genda* ensemble on the village ceremonial plaza (*kanga*) is forbidden. *Nggo lamba,* a gong-and-barrel-drum ensemble, accompanies warriors' dances and major community ceremonies and celebrations. The gong may not be played with a frame drum: it must be played with a barrel drum. Because of the prohibition against playing a side-blown flute in the plaza, the *nggo lamba* is the appropriate ceremonial ensemble there. Singing in Ende-Lio is mostly in diatonic unison and canonic.

In some areas of the Sikka Regency, gongs may be presented as part of elaborate marriage-exchange arrangements, with elephant tusks, special textiles, and other important goods. The balance between "male" goods (durable, such as tusks, gold, and gongs) and "female" goods (used by being cut and sewn, therefore require being remade or reciprocated; durable goods can be traded back later; female goods are

FIGURE 5 *Gawi,* a dance in a circle, in the village of Pu'utuga, Ende-Lio regency. Photo by Cary Black, 1988.

nondurable and therefore have to be created for each trade) is maintained throughout the exchange (Lewis 1994).

Vocal music in Sikka includes solo and choral singing. A male soloist sometimes participates in a responsorial performance, accompanied in harmony by a mixed chorus. Choral singing in the regency varies from what appears to be church-based harmony (using major and minor thirds) to unison responses, to interlocking vocables. Most of the local choral music is sung unaccompanied, or is accompanied only by clapsticks or other small percussion instruments. Even if third-based harmony in Sikka has arisen through the influence from the Roman Catholic Church, its sound differs from that of standard Indonesian church music (Yampolsky 1995a:7).

FIGURE 6 The *feko genda* ensemble accompanies a variety of events relating to engagements and weddings. Photo by Cary Black, 1988.

The Lamaholot-speaking area of East Flores Regency includes the islands of Solor, Adonara, and parts of Lembata. As in Sikka, gongs or elephant tusks (from mainland Southeast Asia, India, or Sri Lanka) may be presented in exchange for textiles as an important part of nuptial negotiations. In the Lamaholot-speaking area, a common vocal genre is a communal agricultural work song (*berasi*), in which two singers sustain intervals that approximate minor and major seconds. Other Lamaholot genres in this style include songs for building and dedicating a new house, giving thanks for an abundant harvest, and recounting historical clan epics. Because of the similarity in the vocal styles between the Eastern Flores and the Balkans, the pioneering ethnomusicologist Jaap Kunst suggested that people from the Balkans had migrated to Southeast Asia in about 800 (Kunst 1960 [1954]); despite the unlikelihood of such an occurrence, the aural similarities between Balkan and East Flores styles are remarkable. Lamaholot song genres often accompany dance, as in *hama,* a dance featuring sung genealogies and local history.

WEST TIMOR

The largest of the Lesser Sunda islands, Timor lies southeast of Flores. Before the arrival of the Portuguese (in the 1500s) and the Dutch (in the 1600s), Timor was ruled by petty chieftains who controlled the cutting of the island's white sandalwood for trade with China, India, and Java. After a protracted struggle for supremacy, Timor was divided politically in 1851: the Portuguese took the east and Oecussi (a district in West Timor), and the Dutch took the west. When Indonesia achieved independence, West Timor became part of the Republic of Indonesia. In 1975, with the Portuguese withdrawal, Indonesia invaded and annexed the eastern part of the island, which it claims as its twenty-seventh province, though the United Nations has not recognized the claim.

As in Flores, the plastic arts receive greater international attention than the performing arts. Weaving is a primary activity for Timorese women, and wood or buffalo-horn carving is done everywhere on the island. Traditional homes in Timor are deeply symbolic, expressing important local spiritual, temporal, and sexual values (Hicks 1988:146). All the Timorese people, and most of the inhabitants of the neighboring islands, follow the basic principle of dualism, balancing contrasting elements, like life and death, light and dark, male and female. Gender-specific symbols are frequently built into homes in various areas throughout Timor (Taylor and Aragon 1991:203).

Important cultural differences divide West and East Timor. The latter is home to a dozen or so languages (known collectively as Belu), which share certain dominant cultural traits. In West Timor, the Atoni are the predominant group, particularly in the central highlands. West Timor is also inhabited by Tetum (Belu) people in the north and east, the Helong of the island of Semau, and Rotinese and Savunese migrants in and around Kupang, the provincial capital.

The Atoni

The Atoni call themselves Atoin Meto (People of the Dry Land). They are regarded as the autochthonous population of Timor, forced west and into the interior mountains by waves of Belunese and Rotinese migrants. Striking features of Atoni traditional life include beehive-shaped houses (*uma lopo*), and boldly colored and intricately patterned textiles.

Though most Atoni are now Protestant Christians, traditional ceremonial life continues in most hamlets and villages, with music and dance playing an important role in propitiating ancestral spirits (*nitu*). Atoni society is arranged patrilineally, but only female members of the community may perform in the ritually significant drum-and-gong ensemble (*sene tufu*). *Sene tufu* is usually played to accompany dancing. To augment the sound of the drum and the gongs, dancers sometimes attach *bano* (bracelets with metal jangles) or *te oh* (bracelets with leaf baskets, containing a handful of sand) to their ankles. A *sene tufu* consists of six gongs (*sene*) and one standing, single-headed drum (*tufu*), played with sticks. The gongs are divided among three players: one woman plays the two largest (*kbolo*), one plays the two medium-sized gongs (*ote*), and one plays the two small gongs (*tetun*). The gongs repeat short, interlocking patterns, which are repeated at great length, accompanied by a *tufu,* which has greater latitude for variation and improvisation.

Atoni songs sung in informal gatherings are often improvised and narrate actual events, both ancient and contemporary. Unlike the performers of *sene tufu,* singers are usually male. *Koa* is a genre of song in which the singer rhythmically speaks a text to musical accompaniment—a style that younger Atoni jokingly liken to rap. The main instrument for accompanying singing or for playing instrumental music is a four-stringed fretless plucked lute (*leku,* also *pisu* and *bijol*) that is strummed in a strong, rhythmic style. In a typical Atoni ensemble, one or more *leku* provide the chordal accompaniment for heterophonic playing by a viola (*heo*), a wooden ocarina (*feku*), and an end-blown bamboo flute (*bobi*) (figure 7). Instruments borrowed from the Portuguese may join the Atoni ensemble. These include a side-blown flute (*simaku*), a comb-and-tissue kazoo (*kili*), and a guitar (*gitar*). Other Atoni instruments include a trough xylophone (*sene hauh*) and a six-stringed bamboo idiochord (*sene kaka*).

West Timor is also rich in jaw harps, usually played by a solitary person for personal enjoyment. The *knobe besi,* an Atoni version of the metal jaw harp, was most likely borrowed from the Portuguese. The *knobe oh* is a wooden jaw harp found throughout the Indonesian archipelago. A tongue is cut from a thin piece of wood, to which a string is attached. Yanking the string sets the tongue in vibration, and the player's oral cavity serves as a resonating chamber. The local musical bow (*knobe kbetas*) is played by plucking the string with the end of the bow, held in the mouth. The

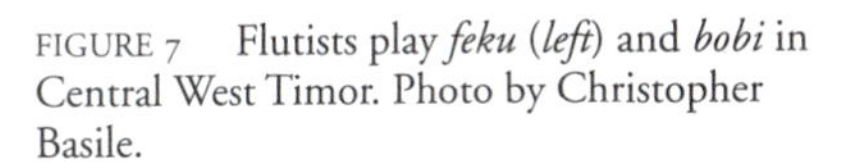

FIGURE 7 Flutists play *feku* (*left*) and *bobi* in Central West Timor. Photo by Christopher Basile.

sasandu Multistringed tube zither with palm leaf resonator

bini Rotinese ritual language form, using parallelisms, reserved for proverbs, poetry, and song

manahelo Chanter fluent in poetic language

meko Rotinese bronze or iron gong

Atoni think it their oldest musical instrument, claiming they have played it since time immemorial.

ROTI

The southernmost island in Indonesia, Roti is in the outer arc of the Lesser Sundas, just southwest of Timor. Rotinese origin myths describe the migration of separate groups from the north via Timor and attribute the foundations of Rotinese culture to the intermarriage of these "people come from the seas" with the aboriginal inhabitants. Each domain in Roti has traditional narratives and genealogies associated with its ruling dynasty, and the accuracy of these oral histories is corroborated by Dutch written records (Fox 1971). Portuguese Dominicans established a mission on the island in the late 1500s, but by 1662 the Dutch had signed treaties of contract with the island's rulers. Under the Dutch, the Rotinese were able to establish one of the first self-supporting school systems in Southeast Asia, and to achieve a syncretism of Protestant Christianity with Rotinese tradition. During the 1800s, the Dutch authorities transplanted sizable communities of Rotinese to the Kupang area of Timor to aid in the struggle against the Portuguese, and about fifty thousand Rotinese now live in West Timor, in addition to the approximately ninety thousand inhabitants of Roti.

FIGURE 8 The *sasandu* tube zither with palm-leaf resonator (*haik*). Photo by Christopher Basile.

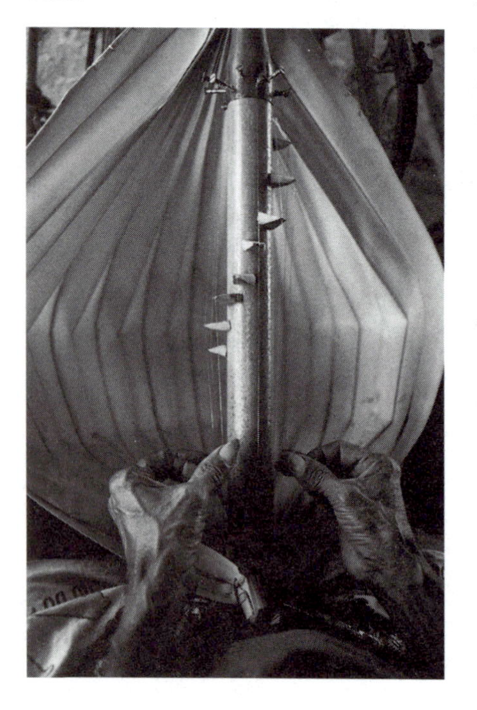

Rotinese culture is primarily mediated through rituals of oration. Cultural symbols such as the distinctively Rotinese hat (*ti'ilangga*) and *patola*- (Indian double-*ikat*) derived textiles, whose patterns and motifs determine the wearer's clan and status, are also important. Perhaps the most prominent medium and physical symbol of musical culture in Roti is the *sasandu,* a tube zither with a palm leaf resonator. Other important musical forms include a gong ensemble (*meko*), a song-accompanied circle dance (*e'ea*), chanted invocations (*bapa*), and a diatonic tube zither (*sasando biola*).

The *sasandu* consists of a section of bamboo with ten or eleven metal strings running its length, fixed in a resonator made of the fan-shaped leaf of a *lontar* palm (*Borassus sundaicus* Beccari). The strings are usually strands of motorcycle coupling wire, their pitch adjusted with movable bridges and tuning pegs. The resonator is a palm leaf shaped into a pleated hemisphere (*haik*) (figure 8). The Rotinese put the *haik* to countless other uses, and like the *lontar* palm itself, it is an important cultural symbol. The Rotinese derive vital sustenance by tapping the juice of the *lontar,* collected in *haik* hung in the tree's branches. Rotinese commonly call the *lontar* palm their tree of life (for more information about the *lontar* palm, see Fox 1977). The central role it plays in Rotinese society is echoed in the incorporation of the *haik* into the structure of the *sasandu.*

Rotinese myths and oral traditions show the importance of the *sasandu* in the Rotinese structuring of reality, placing the origin of the instrument alongside the origins of marriage, exogamy, mourning, and death. *Sasandu* music is portrayed as having magical power and as a means of separating the human world from the animal. Tradition claims that the use of magic strings (*taliliti*) will make the player of a *sasandu* irresistible to any woman who hears his playing, and these strings are traditionally outlawed on the island. Thus, the *sasandu,* and by extension music in general, are associated with the polar forces of life and death, the natural and the supernatural, and rejoicing and mourning (Basile 1996).

The *sasandu* is tuned to a pentatonic scale approximating G–B-half-flat–C–E-half-flat–F over two octaves, with a high G added on the eleven-stringed version of the instrument (actual starting pitch varies from player to player). While *sasandu* tuning usually falls close to this model, most players stretch and compress intervals at will, and adjust octaves to produce noticeable beats. This is especially true among musicians more isolated from outside musical influences. Conversely, players who live in and around the provincial capital, Kupang—where greater exposure to television, radio, and cassettes is the norm—tend more toward tempered tuning, even eliminating half-flat notes, creating the impression of distinctly major and minor sonorities.

Though the *sasandu* has a solo repertoire, it is almost always played as an accompanying instrument for song. As a society, the Rotinese highly value the skillful manipulation of language, and the song texts exemplify this. Though Roti is a small island, it was formerly subdivided into eighteen autonomous states, each of which possesses its own version of the Rotinese language. Song texts creatively exploit these dialect differences, incorporating loan words from nearby Ndao, Semau, and Kupang. Most importantly, a ritual form of language, *bini,* is reserved for proverbs, poetry, and song, also called *bini. Bini* is the salient feature of *sasandu*-accompanied song, and it is primarily by his knowledge of *bini* and his ability to creatively use it that a singer is judged.

Bini form requires the parallel poetic phrasing of virtually all of the text's semantic elements (Fox 1974). According to standard Rotinese poetic syntax, the verse *Ana ma ndule dae, ina falu ndule oe* 'Orphans cover the earth, widows cover the water' is based on the parallel relationship of orphans (*ana ma*) with widows (*ina falu*), and earth (*dae*) with water (*oe*). There are thousands of such dyadic pairs for the student of *bini* to master, and their proper use in parallel phrases is the basis of ritual language. Though a poet can theoretically construct formally correct but meaningless *bini,* poets never do. In the example cited, the idea that orphans and widows are everywhere expresses a pervasive Rotinese metaphor for existence, comparing the human condition in general with the unfortunate state of orphans and widows. The theme underlying most *bini* used in Rotinese song is that the world is ruled by ineluctable fate, and that life is often disappointing, and ultimately ephemeral.

Most *sasandu*-accompanied songs alternate verses in poetic language with a refrain in standard Rotinese. Each song is identifiable by its distinctive refrain, *sasandu* part, and melody, but the verses are variable, and singers will often use the same *bini* in many different songs. An older song style with texts consisting entirely of *bini* is performed by chanters (*manahelo*) fluent in poetic language, but is becoming rare. Today, some musicians are composing new versions of traditional songs, incorporating puns and social commentary in reflection of changing conditions in contemporary Rotinese life (Basile 1995).

As an instrumental form, the *sasandu* has much in common with the *meko* gong ensemble. Because the relationship between the two is close, some Rotinese claim the *sasandu* was invented so that one musician could achieve the same results as the six or more players required for a *meko* group, while others argue that the *meko* developed from the *sasandu.* The two instruments share a common repertoire, with the tuning of the nine *meko* corresponding to the nine lowest strings of the *sasandu.* In addition, the *sasandu* is always accompanied by a small drum, or by tapping the instrument's *haik* with a stick, to produce rhythmic patterns like those played on the large *labu* drum that accompanies the *meko.* The qualified answer as to which came first, the *sasandu* or the *meko,* would have to be the *meko.* Though the *sasandu* almost certainly predates the *meko* ensemble as it is known today, an earlier form, the *meko ai,* can be said with equal certainty to predate the *sasandu.*

The Rotinese term *meko* originally denoted the indigenous idiophones of the island. It was adopted for metal gongs when they arrived from Java, in the early 1800s. The earliest *meko* are said to have been made from resonant flat rocks or the coconut-sized fruit of the *lontar,* collected and played as percussion instruments. The wooden gong (*meko ai*) was a type of xylophone consisting of nine keys of tuned, split bamboo or wood, set over a trough resonator. Older Rotinese recall the *meko ai* being played at family gatherings during their childhood, whereas the metal *meko* were reserved for more formal occasions. Now virtually extinct, the *meko ai* was typically played by two persons, each using two lengths of wood or bamboo as mallets, with the keys arranged in ascending pitch from the player's right to left. This spatial relationship is maintained on the *sasandu,* where the right hand plays the bass notes, and the left the treble, and the *meko ai*'s system for naming and classifying pitches is still used by both the *sasandu* and the *meko* gong ensemble.

The *meko ai* gave way to *meko* ensembles as they are known today, comprising nine (or sometimes ten) either locally made iron or imported bronze, bossed gongs, and a *labu* drum. The *labu* drum is made from the trunk of a coconut or *lontar* palm, with a water-buffalo skin, cowskin, or deerskin membrane about 30 centimeters in diameter. Standing about 70 centimeters high, it is played with two sticks. The *meko* are each played with one stick, and range in size from about 50 to 10 centimeters in diameter. Compositions are made up of short, interlocking parts, which may repeat indefinitely, played at uniform tempo and maximum volume. With its brash and bold style, the ensemble provides a sharp contrast to the quiet and introspective *sasandu.*

The nine *meko* are divided into four groups; from largest to smallest in size they are three *ina,* two *nggasa,* two *leko,* and two *ana.* A tenth *meko,* if added, extends the upper range of the ensemble, and becomes the third *ana.* Typically, one player each will play the *ina,* the *nggasa,* and the *leko* parts, while the *ana* are divided among two players. A piece begins with the players of the *meko* entering one at a time, normally starting with the *leko,* and when the parts are sufficiently stable, the *labu* drum joins in. The single *labu* achieves timbral variation by alternating muted (*li mukuk*) and ringing (*li naruk*) strokes. Among the *meko,* the largest *ina* and the smaller *nggasa, leko,* and *ana* are played muted, and the remaining five *meko* are played unmuted.

Meko groups perform at weddings, wakes, house-dedication ceremonies, and other gatherings, often accompanying dance. Warfare was common between the domains that formerly divided the island, and traditional dances reflect this situation. *Mudipapa* is a women's dance to bid farewell to warriors departing for battle, and *tae beno* is danced by a warrior's family to celebrate his safe return. Men learned *kaka musu* as a preparation for war, and it is said that they entered the battlefield dancing it and singing its *meko* accompaniment, because proper ritual warfare imitated the dance. *Foti,* a men's martial dance, combines rapid and aggressive footwork with graceful upper-body movement to demonstrate the dancer's mettle. *Meko* also accompany the dancelike martial-arts drills (*basili*), and the *nafepa e'ik,* a ritual in which a woven *ikat* cloth protects its wearer from savage blows from a length of wood.

Unlike other Rotinese dances, the *e'ea* features no *meko* or other instrumental accompaniment, but is led by a *manahelo* singing verses in *bini,* answered by the oth-

FIGURE 9 The electric *sasando biola* is played by its inventor, Edu Pah. Photo by Christopher Basile.

er dancers in chorus. The *manahelo* chooses his text to suit the occasion of the dance, which may be performed to invoke rain, or as part of the ceremonies connected with marriage, death, or the completion of a house. The participants, including men, women, and children, form a circle by holding one another's elbows, and perform steps that cause the circle to turn counterclockwise, slowly to their right. *E'ea* may last for hours, with the choral response and the dance's tempo and steps determined by the *manahelo*'s song.

All the traditional Rotinese performing arts are related, either to a greater or lesser degree, to Songo (Offering), the indigenous Rotinese religion. Songo involved offerings to the spirits (*songo nitu*) and continues to play an important role in society, despite the conversion of most Rotinese to Protestant Christianity. Its major celebration is Hus, a festival that includes feasting, horse racing, music, dance, and *bapa. Bapa* consists of invocations and tales, chanted in strict ritual language by a *manahelo.* He is joined by a group who, using their right hands only, all beat a single *labu* drum in unison. The tempo is slow, and a performance can continue for hours, until it accelerates for the ending section. More than ninety major Hus festivals were formerly held throughout the year in Roti, but now only one is.

The *sasando biola,* unlike the *sasandu,* the *meko,* the *e'ea,* or the *bapa,* is the only Rotinese musical form not actually associated with traditional Rotinese music. *Sasando biola,* a diatonic and expanded version of the *sasandu,* is used to play hymns and non-Rotinese folk and popular songs. Its tuning and arrangement of pitches vary, but most instruments have between twenty-four and thirty-nine strings and can play in two diatonic keys over a range of about three octaves. Some players of *sasando biola* use a wooden box as a resonator, rather than the traditional *haik,* and there is even an electric version with a pickup or internal microphone (*sasando biola listrik*), played through an electric amplifier (figure 9).

SAVU

The Savu islands (Rai Hawu and Rai Jua) are located in the outer arc of the Lesser Sundas, about midway between the larger islands of Flores and Timor. Though Savu is isolated, hot, and dry, with virtually no forest and little water, the Savunese (who

A complete Savunese gong ensemble has seven gongs, a set of cymbals, and a drum. The ensemble's style of playing is lively and loud, and compositions consist of repeating, interlocking parts.

call themselves Dou Hawu) maintain a high population density through their skillful exploitation of the *lontar* palm, which is tapped for its juice. Linguistically, Savunese is closely related to Ndaoese and the languages of Sumba, with some Rotinese and Timorese borrowings. Savunese have migrated in large numbers to East Sumba, and in lesser numbers to West Timor.

A Savunese legend about an early folk ancestor named Madja-Pahi may indicate a link between the Savunese and the fifteenth-century Javanese Majapahit Empire. The Dutch signed a treaty with the five domains of Savu and Rai Jua in 1756, and united Savu under a single raja in 1918. During the colonial period, the Savunese developed a reputation as excellent soldiers, and the Dutch impact on Savu was limited. Today, though most Savunese are at least nominally Christian, important collective rituals associated with the indigenous religion are still maintained, and Savunese traditional law (*adat*) remains influential.

Traditional life in Savu is governed by a lunar calendar, which prohibits ceremonial music and dance during part of the year. This period of ritual silence ends with the harvest, when the lively sound of the *padoa* marks the beginning of the high ceremonial season. As in other forms of eastern Indonesian circle dancing, male and female dancers of *padoa* join arms and sing and dance, sometimes continuing until dawn. Savunese *padoa* is unique, however, in that the participants attach small baskets filled with mung beans to their ankles to augment their singing with the sound of the rhythmic shuffling of the beans in time with their steps. When the season of ritual dancing of *padoa* ends, these baskets of beans are stored until the following year, when their contents are planted as seed.

For several weeks, the singing and bean-basket percussion of the dancers of *padoa* is the only ritual music allowed in the high ceremonial season. Then, at the time appointed by the ceremonial calendar, immediately following a day of ritual cockfighting and a night of dancing *padoa* under a full moon, the *namangngu* gongs and the *dere* drum are played for the first time in more than five months. Later that day, they are played again as riders continuously circle a large tree in a kind of equestrian dance, likened to the *padoa*. *Namangngu* and *dere* music is then permitted until the planting season that begins the next Savunese year (Fox 1979).

A complete Savunese gong ensemble has seven gongs, a set of cymbals (*wo paheli*), and a drum (*dere*). Pieces typically begin with the two small gongs (*leko*), followed by the two medium gongs (*wo peibho abho*), and finally, the three largest gongs (*didala ae, didala iki, gaha*). The *namangngu* ensemble's style of playing is lively and loud, and compositions consist of repeating, interlocking parts drawn from a small traditional repertoire.

Other Savunese musical instruments include the wooden jaw harp (*tebe*), a four-holed, ring-stop bamboo flute (*hekido*), and the *ketadu* 'that which satisfies' family of instruments. Unlike the *namangngu,* these instruments are usually played by soloists in relatively informal contexts. The *ketadu haba,* a tube zither with *lontar*-leaf resonator, resembles the Rotinese *sasandu,* but with eight metal strings (rather than the ten or eleven found in Roti), and with a different style of playing and repertoire. The distinguishing feature of both tube zithers is their *lontar*-leaf resonator, which reflects the central place of the *lontar* palm in the lives of these two eastern Indonesian peoples. The *ketadu haba* most likely developed as a Savunese version of the Rotinese *sasandu,* though some Savunese claim that the opposite borrowing occurred. The *ketadu mara* is a trough xylophone of the type found throughout the Indonesian archipelago, with nine wooden keys, played with sticks made from *lontar* branches. Finally, the instrument called simply *ketadu* is a two-stringed, plucked, boat-shaped lute resembling the Sumbanese *jungga.*

REFERENCES

Basile, Christopher. 1995. "Mythological Narratives, Standing Tales and Talk: Rotinese Perspectives on the Origin and Development of the Sasandu." Paper presented at the thirty-third world conference of the International Council for Traditional Music, Canberra.

———. 1996. "The Troubled Grass and the Bamboo's Cry: The Significance of the Rotinese Sasandu." In *The Asian Arts Society of Australia Review* 5(1):5.

Fox, James J. 1971. "A Rotinese Dynastic Genealogy: Structure and Event." In *The Translation of Culture: Essays to E. E. Evans-Pritchard,* ed. T. O. Beidelman, 37–77. London: Tavistock.

———. 1974. "Our Ancestors Spoke in Pairs: Rotinese Views of Language, Dialect and Code." In *Explorations in the Ethnography of Speaking,* ed. R. Bauman and J. Scherzer. London: Cambridge University Press.

———. 1977. *Harvest of the Palm: Ecological Change in Eastern Indonesia.* Cambridge, Mass., and London: Harvard University Press.

———. 1979. "The Ceremonial System of Savu." In *The Imagination of Reality: Essays in Southeast Asian Coherence Systems,* ed. A. L. Becker and Aram A. Yengoyan. Norwood: Ablex Publishing.

———. 1988. "Introduction." In *To Speak in Pairs: Essays on the Ritual Languages of Eastern Indonesia,* ed. James J. Fox, 1–28. Cambridge: Cambridge University Press.

Geirnaert, Danielle C. 1989. "The *Pogo Nauta* Ritual in Laboya (West Sumba): Of Tubers and *Mamuli.*" *Bijdragen tot de Taal-, Land- en Volkenkunde* 145(4):445–463.

Hicks, David. 1988. "Art and Religion on Timor." In *Islands and Ancestors: Indigenous Styles of Southeast Asia,* ed. Jean-Paul Barbier and Douglas Newton, 138–151. Munich: Prestel-Verlag.

Hoskins, Janet. 1988. "Arts and Cultures of Sumba." *Islands and Ancestors: Indigenous Styles of Southeast Asia,* ed. Jean Paul Barbier and Donald Newton, 120–138. Munich: Prestel-Verlag.

Kunst, Jaap. 1942. *Music in Flores: A Study of the Vocal and Instrumental Music among the Tribes Living in Flores.* Leiden: E. J. Brill.

———. 1960 [1954]. *Cultural Relations between the Balkans and Indonesia,* 2nd ed. Amsterdam: Koninklijk Instituut voor de Tropen (Royal Tropical Institute). Mededeling 107, Afdeling Culturele en Physische Anthropologie, 47.

Lewis, E. D. 1994. "Sikka Regency." In *Gift of the Cotton Maiden: Textiles of Flores and the Solor Islands,* ed. Roy W. Hamilton, 149–169. Los Angeles: University of California Press.

Taylor, Paul Michael, and Lorraine V. Aragon. 1991. *Beyond the Java Sea: Art of Indonesia's Outer Islands.* Washington, D.C.: National Museum of Natural History.

Yampolsky, Philip. 1995a. *Vocal and Instrumental Music from East and Central Flores.* Music of Indonesia, 8. Smithsonian / Folkways Recordings SFCD 40424. Compact disc.

———. 1995b. *Vocal Music from Central and West Flores.* Compact disc. Music of Indonesia, 9. Smithsonian / Folkways Recordings SFCD 40425. Compact disc.

Sulawesi

Margaret J. Kartomi

Sulawesi is an island of peninsulas. Portuguese seafarers called it Pontos dos Celebres (Cape of the Infamous), because its cape north of Minahasa saw frequent shipwrecks. From this term came both the English name for the island (Celebes) and the official name, used since Indonesia achieved independence. The island divides into four provinces: North Sulawesi, with the main towns of Manado and Gorontalo; Central Sulawesi, whose main towns are Palu and Tolitoli; Southeast Sulawesi, with its center in Kendari; and South Sulawesi, with the main towns of Watampone and Ujung Pandang.

Most of the population lives in the southern and northern peninsulas, where plains permit large settlements. Four major ethnic groups inhabit Sulawesi: the Makassarese, the Buginese, the Torajans, and the Minahasans. The Makassarese and Buginese, inhabiting the southern peninsula, have related but distinct languages, and are mainly Muslim traders and seafarers, renowned for their schooners. The Torajans are mostly Christian animists, and inhabit the highlands of South and Central Sulawesi; once feared as headhunters, they are known for the elaborateness of their funerals. The Minahasans, mainly Christians, have been more influenced by Dutch culture and education than any other group in Sulawesi. Some key resources for more in-depth study of this island's musical culture include Abidin 1974, Crystal and Crystal 1973, Holt 1939, Kartomi 1981 and 1988, and Kaudern 1927. Cultural information not specific to music can be found in Nooey-Palm 1988 and Taylor and Aragon 1991.

THE BUGINESE AND THE MAKASSARESE

The Buginese live throughout lowland South Sulawesi; the Makassarese, mostly in and around Ujung Pandang and the southern coast. As both peoples were always extraordinary shipbuilders, sailors, merchants, traders in slaves, adventurers, and warriors, lowland South Sulawesi people were known for their skills as seafarers.

The Buginese and Makassarese have much in common. Both have seen centuries of foreign trading, and some of their dances and music show Portuguese, Persian-Arabic, and other influences. For both, the most representative musical instruments are a two-stringed spike fiddle (*gesó-gesó*), a boat-shaped two-stringed

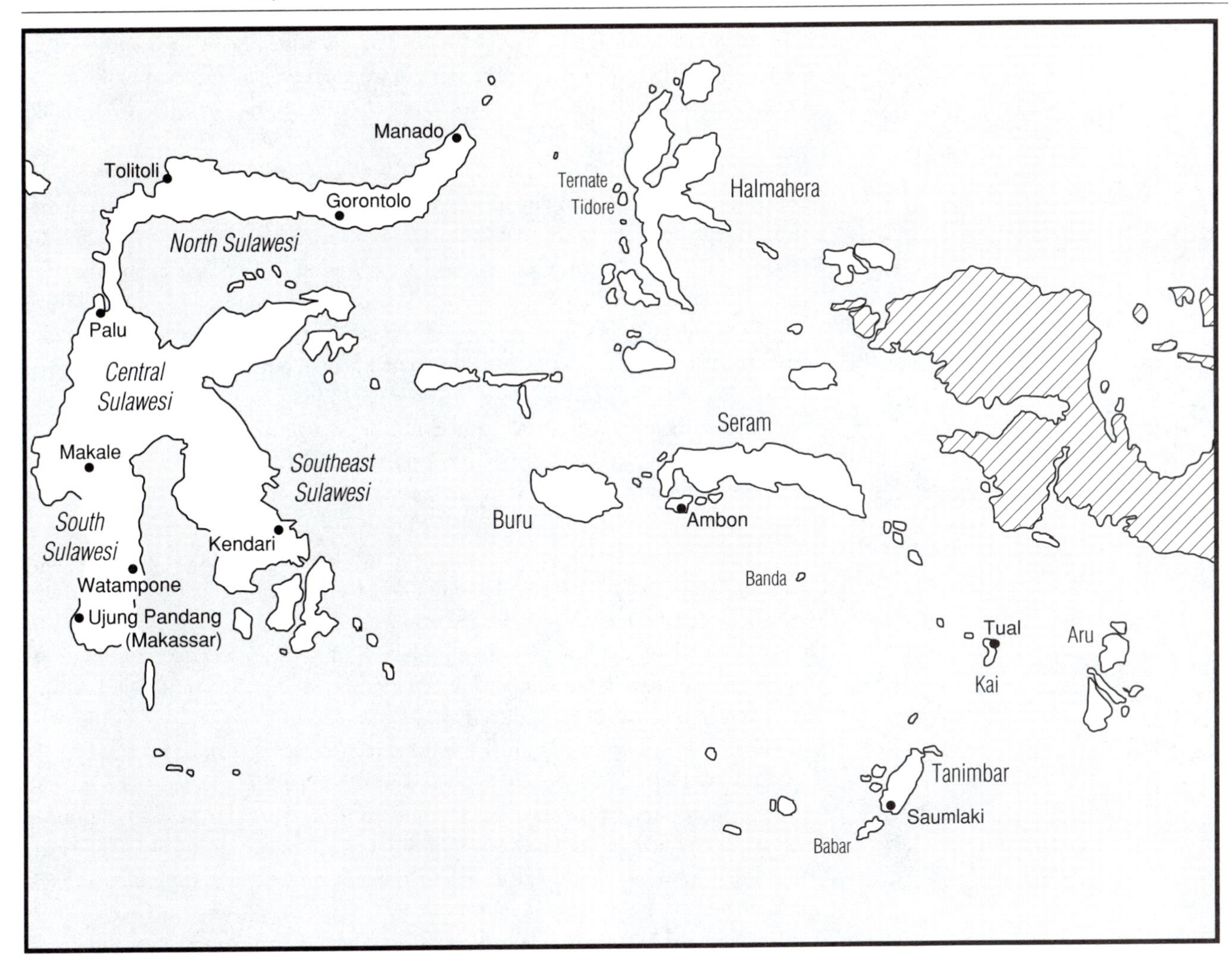

Sulawesi and Maluku

lute (Makassarese *kacapi,* Buginese *kacaping*), a reed pipe (*puwi-puwi*), and pairs of two-headed cylindrical drums (*ganrang*).

A typical traditional Makassarese dance is a court dance (*pakarena*), performed by girls, in any of several forms. This dance survives alongside dances associated with agricultural rites and the welcoming of guests at important rituals. In the *bosara,* a dance created in the 1980s, girls in costume welcome guests. Another notable dance, *pakurru sumangga,* is also performed to welcome guests; one of its offshoots is the *mikki* (*ammikki*), a dance that features small steps and shrugs.

Some Buginese and Makassarese music and dance evoke the sea, as does processional music played on drums (*tunrung ganrang*), intended to celebrate Makassarese sailors' courage. Both coastal and inland villagers enjoy listening to storytellers who sing epics or other traditional stories (*sinrili*) for nights on end, accompanying themselves on a spike fiddle.

Ancient literary works, including those written on palm-leaf manuscripts (*lontará*), give clues about the history of local music. The *Lontará Bugis* mentions that the ruler's music was played on three *ganrang* and a gong; Muslim frame drums (*rebana, tambur*) were used for war. The epic *I La Galigo,* which dates from before the 1300s, mentions a *tamboro,* but no reference to this instrument appears in later literature (Abidin 1974:161–169). A pair of *ganrang* and a gong still form the ensemble that accompanies performances of such traditional dances as the old Buginese court dance *pajaga* (Holt 1939:79–86). Sometimes, as when it accompanies a *pakare-*

na, this ensemble includes a reed pipe (*puwí-puwí*), which flares slightly toward its bell and is usually made of several sections of wood and metal; mention of the *puwí-puwí* in one of the historical chronicles (*Lontará Makassar*) suggests that it was an old court instrument.

After working at sea or in the fields, some Buginese and the Makassarese like to spend their evenings singing quatrains (*pantun*), sometimes improvising humorously in reply to each other's contributions. These performances are accompanied by a local zither (*kacapi*), which resembles related forms on nearby islands, including the southern Philippines. This zither is often elaborately carved; its handle, soundboard, foot, and bridge are all cut from one piece of wood; a lid perforated by several holes closes the back of its resonator. Men or women play it, either to accompany singing or with a bamboo tube zither (*lea-lea*), a *ganrang,* and a gong. Though popular, the *kacapi* is not mentioned in the *Lontará* chronicles—suggesting that it never served as a court instrument. Images of bar zithers (northeast Sulawesi *kalindo,* Central Sulawesi *dunde* and *suntu,* west Toraja *suntang*) on the Borobudur temple in Java prove this kind of zither is an ancient instrument in Indonesia.

Buginese and Makassarese conversion to Islam (in the 1600s) brought about the adoption of some Persian-Arabic musical instruments, including the frame drum (*rebana*) and the *gambus,* a pear-shaped wooden lute with decorated sound holes and a tapering neck, ending in a receding pegbox. Both peoples practice Muslim devotional arts, including (at certain birth celebrations, weddings, and other Muslim rituals) *kasidah,* songs in Arabic, which may be accompanied by *gambus* and drums. The art of self-defense (*pencak silat*) is also widely practiced, accompanied by drums.

In the latter half of the twentieth century, some Buginese and Makassarese styles of dance and music have become more polished and virtuosic. Drumming tends to be more vigorous and varied in its dynamic level.Traditionally solo instruments may now be combined into a forty-piece orchestra (*orkes kacapi suling*), including one or more *kacapi, suling, ganrang, lea-lea,* gong(s), and *anak becing* (metal percussion bars). In South Sulawesi, music and dance still retain ritual functions, but the meanings of ritual contexts have often changed as performance serves to portray regional identity, benefit party politics, and further the commercial entertainment industry.

THE TORAJANS

Parts of South and Central Sulawesi are the home of about half a million Torajans (Highlanders). Legend claims that their ancestors arrived in a storm from the northern seas, whereupon they pulled their boats ashore and used them as roofs for their houses. Large and spectacular, these houses point skyward, adorned with the horns of water-buffalo, important totemic animals.

The Torajan cultures have produced a diverse musical scene. Their music may be divided into two categories: music associated with happy events and that for sad events or feelings. Happy music occurs in a variety of contexts. Harvest and other thanksgiving dances are accompanied by one to four players performing on a large drum (*gendang*). Early risers entertain themselves and their families with music played on flutes (*tulali*). Old men traditionally greet the day with songs (*kambori*). At harvesttime, a sugarpalm-leaf horn (*pábarrung*) sounds from the hilltops and may be played during certain rituals. A one-stringed fiddle (*gesok-gesok*) is played in some ceremonies. In the 1980s, a *pompang* (or *bas*), an ensemble of bamboo flutes, became popular in schools and for celebrations (figure 1).

Sad music is played primarily at funerals, which are the main musical occasions and the most important artistic, social, religious, and even political events in Toraja. These rituals enact the local religion (Aluk To Dolo, animist and based on the

FIGURE 1 A Toraja flute ensemble (*bas*). Photo by H. Kartomi.

worship of ancestors), practiced by about 30 percent of Torajans. Local belief divides the universe and the world of ritual into two halves, marking life and death. When a person dies, a preliminary burial occurs; the family of the deceased then accumulates resources for the funeral. Years can elapse between the preliminary burial and the funeral.

Elaborate ceremonies for the dead have been present in various parts of Indonesia throughout history. In Hindu Java during the first millennium, great royal mausoleums were built; they are still revered as ancestral temples. Artistic ceremonies are held in rural Java and elsewhere to contact ancestral spirits. Spectacular funerary ceremonies are also important in Bali, where the aim of cremation is to free the soul from earthly constraints. In funerary and other ceremonies of the Mandailing people (of North Sumatra), tuned drums call ancestral spirits, and buffaloes are traditionally sacrificed to aid the soul of the deceased. The sacrificial cult of the buffalo has also been practiced by various Dayak peoples of Kalimantan and several other ethnic groups.

FIGURE 2 A circular men's dance at a Toraja funeral. A photograph of the deceased is visible at the funeral house. Photo by H. Kartomi.

Performances at Torajan funerals

Poetry sung collectively at a Sa'dan Toraja funeral may compare the ancestors of the deceased with the sun, the moon, or another natural entity, like a rainbow. A massive choir of mourning men, singing intricately embellished, long-held notes, dance near the house holding the corpse, in a slow-moving circle. Each dancer (*to mábadong*) puts his right hand on the left shoulder of the next, and all take identical steps in rhythm with the singing. Sometimes they cup both hands in a downward movement, expressive of mourning (figure 2).

As guests arrive, the master of ceremonies announces them over a loudspeaker in a tower house, built near the house containing the corpse. The arrival of each party of guests is marked by distinct patterns played on a gong. A pair of flutists and a singer perform almost continuously in the tower house, their laments sounding through loudspeakers over the valley. The bamboo flute, the most common Torajan instrument, is decorated with carvings, and sometimes with a buffalo-horn cone attached to its end (see also figure 4).

It is not unusual for hundreds of guests to attend a Torajan funeral, which may last a week. The guests are housed in temporary bamboo dwellings, arranged in

At a Torajan funeral, the lamenting of the male chorus merges with the music of the vocal-flute ensemble, broken up now and then by insistent gong rhythms, while dancers' drumming and whistling contribute an element of gaiety.

FIGURE 3 The setting of a Toraja funeral. Drawing by the Department of Geography, Monash University, from a sketch by M. Kartomi.

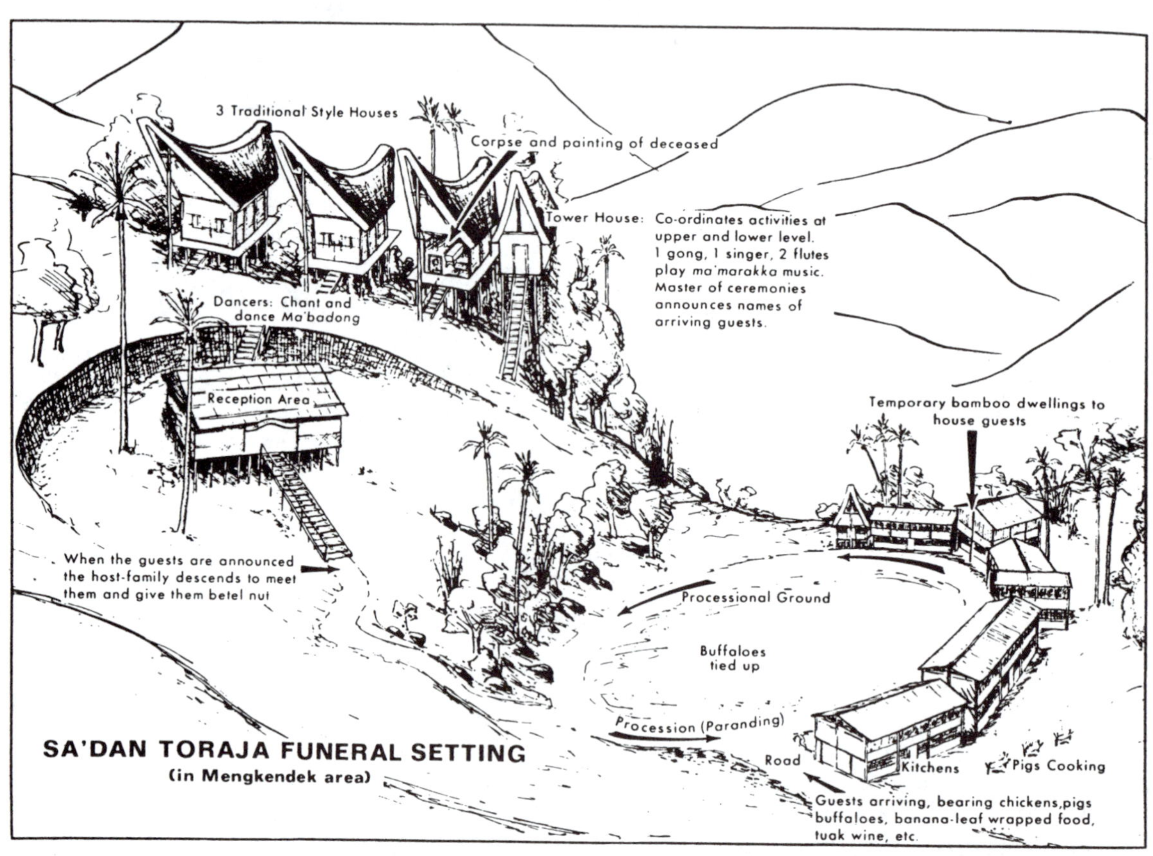

a semicircle around a processional ground. These dwellings are the result of elaborate preparations by the organizers of the funeral, who pay for the construction and decoration of some traditional Torajan houses in a clearing on, for example, the most impressive of the hillsides around a valley. After the funeral, people burn these dwellings down (figure 3).

A complicated system of indebtedness operates between hosts and guests. Guests who can afford to do so present buffaloes as gifts. Men ceremonially slaughter the buffaloes, which the crowd eats. If a guest owes the host a buffalo because that host has given the guest one at a previous funeral, that guest will be too ashamed to attend the funeral if he cannot repay the debt; however, a host does not automatically accept all gifts, lest he himself become overly indebted.

Guests arrive bringing pigs, wine, and other gifts. The host family welcomes them with a ceremonial presentation of betel and leads them to the corpse, for formal

FIGURE 4 A *mámarakka* ensemble: a vocalist and end-blown flutes (*suling lembang*) with a buffalo-horn flare and six holes for fingering perform in the tower house at a Toraja funeral, Mengkendele, South Sulawesi Province. Photo by H. Kartomi, 1974.

sobbing (*bating*). Then these guests join the others in dancing and chanting poetry, frequently continuing all night and a large part of the next day. Through this lamenting, with its unison vocal gasps and its dynamic surges and abatements, the participants express their grief and venerate the deceased.

Meanwhile, professional musicians perform *mámarakka* music. Long bamboo flutes with a carved buffalo-horn flare (*suling lembang*) accompany a female vocalist (figure 4). Unlike the male choral music, with mainly semitone and stepwise intervals and a limited range (a maximum of a third for any one period), the vocal-flute ensemble covers a range of about three octaves (with overblown tones) in a basically pentatonic palette. The flute parts vary from each other only in attack and degree of melodic embellishment; the flutes usually play almost in unison.

Aleatoric musical effects result from the arbitrary combination of sounds produced at different parts of the ceremonial site. The lamenting of the male chorus merges with the music of the vocal-flute ensemble, broken up now and then by insistent gong rhythms, while dancers' drumming and whistling contribute an element of gaiety.

Music also plays a role in the procession on the day of the burial. Warrior-dancers and drummers head the procession, and wailing women accompany the coffin, which men eventually haul up the face of a cliff and place in a cavity hewn in the cliff. On the exterior of the cliff is placed an effigy (*tau-tau*) of the deceased. These effigies are sometimes grouped by the dozens, standing with arms outstretched (palms upward) and open eyes, surveying the panorama and guarding the deceased.

Other ensembles

The *rere,* an ensemble of the Bare-e Toraja area of Central Sulawesi, takes its name from a bamboo instrument that combines elements of an idiophone and an aerophone. A hollow bamboo tube, it has a node at the bottom end, and can be played singly or in pairs. The upper two-thirds of its length is cut away, forming two lamellae. Two triangular holes for fingering face each other on each side of the distal part of this tube, each with a slit running up to the space between the lamellae. The player holds the tube in his right hand and strikes one lamella on his left wrist. The instrument produces one fundamental tone, but the prominence of its partials varies according to whether the holes are closed or not. It resembles the *duri dana* of Nias,

FIGURE 5 A Minahasan gong ensemble (*kolintang*) from earlier times, as accompaniment for a war dance (Kaudern 1925–1944, vol. 4, Fig. 120, p. 455).

but its sound has a longer decay period than that of the Nias instrument. The ensemble may include bull roarers, Jew's harps, bamboo zithers, nose flutes, and gongs.

Gorontalo ensembles

In Gorontalo, male dancers carrying swords often present the *tari tidi* (dance with swords) in nuptial processions. Music is provided on conch and flute orchestras (*orkes bea*) and *kacapi* ensembles, while male elders playing frame drums (*rebana*) sing Muslim songs of advice to the couple.

THE MINAHASANS

North Sulawesi (also called Manado) is the most heavily Protestant province in Indonesia; 95 percent of the population is Christian, of which 80 percent are Protestant and the rest Roman Catholic. Minahasan culture has long been affected by outside influences. In the 1500s, Spanish missionaries began colonizing North Sulawesi from their base in the Philippines. After the departure of the Spanish (in the late 1500s), the spice sultanates of Ternate exerted their influence over northern and eastern Sulawesi. In the 1600s, the Dutch gained control over the Minahasans. Present-day Minahasan culture shows traces of all of these influences.

At harvesttime, thanksgiving celebrations are held all over Minahasa, featuring indigenous dancing, conch bands, and *kolintang* performances. *Kolintang* is the main musical ensemble of the Minahasans. The modern *kolintang* is a xylophone—not to be confused with the set of bossed kettle-gongs formerly known in Minahasa as *kolintang* and in the southern Philippines as *kulintang* (figure 5). References to the old gongs are scattered through local ethnographic and missionary literature. Eventually, this instrument fell into disuse, and its name was appropriated for the modern xylophone.

REFERENCES

Abidin, Andi Zainal. 1974. "The I La Galigo Epic Cycle of South Celebes and Its Diffusion," trans. C. C. Macknight. *Indonesia* 17:161–169.

Crystal, Eric, and Catherine Crystal. 1973. *Music of Sulawesi*. Ethnic Folkways FE 4351. Notes to LP disk.

Holt, C. 1939. *Dance Quest in Celebes*. Paris: Les Archives Internationales de la Danse.

Kartomi, Margaret J. 1981. "His Skyward Path the Rainbow Is: Funeral Music of the Sa'dan Toraja." In *Hemisphere* 25(5):303–309.

———. 1988. "Ritual Music and Dance: Contact and Change in the Lowlands of South Sulawesi." In *The Twelfth Festival of Asian Arts,* ed. J. Thompson, 26–35. Hong Kong: Urban Council.

Kaudern, Walter A. 1925–1944. *Games and Dances in Celebes.* Ethnographical Studies in Celebes, IV, ed. B. Hagen. Götenborg: Elanders Boktryckeri.

———. 1927. *Musical Instruments in Celebes.* Ethnographical Studies in Celebes, III, ed. B. Hagen. Göteborg: Elanders Boktryckeri.

Nooey-Palm, Clémentine H. M. 1988. "The Mamasa and Sa'dan Toraja of Sulawesi." In *Islands and Ancestors: Indigenous Styles of Southeast Asia,* ed. Jean-Paul Barbier and Douglas Newton, 86–105. New York: Metropolitan Museum of Art.

Taylor, Paul Michael, and Lorraine V. Aragon. 1991. "Sulawesi." In *Beyond the Java Sea: Art of Indonesia's Outer Islands,* 173–200. Washington, D.C.: Smithsonian Institution.

Maluku

Margaret J. Kartomi

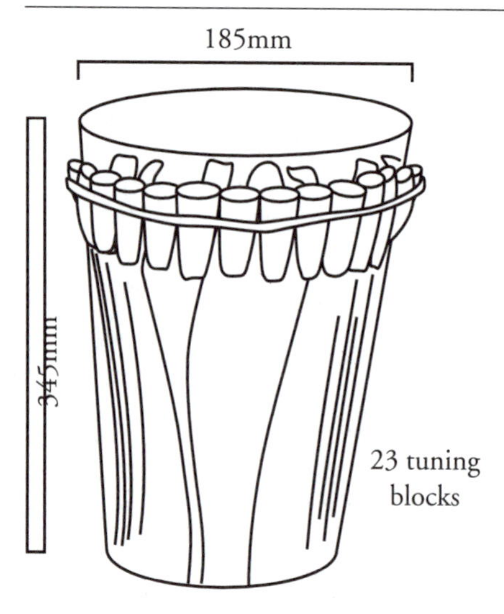

FIGURE 1 A pan-Maluku *tifa* drum, Ternate, North Maluku.

Maluku Province (sometimes called the Moluccas) includes the spice islands and hundreds of other islands, large and small, stretching between Timor, Sulawesi, and Irian Jaya. Though off the beaten path, they were once at the center of intense international disputes among Portuguese, Dutch, and other European powers.

The musics of Maluku share many elements with those of Sulawesi. Some of the music of the Minahasa (of North Sulawesi) is closely related to that of northern Maluku, especially with the former spice sultanates of Ternate and Tidore, and with other islands in the Halmahera group. In the Tanimbar Archipelago (South Maluku), round dances with choral singing of the type found in Southeast Sulawesi are common, as are war dances resembling those of North Sulawesi. Ambon (central Maluku) shares cultural attributes with North Sulawesi, partly because of Dutch impact on both places, and partly because of interisland trade.

The culture of Maluku is a synthesis of local tradition and outside influences. Most of the population is Christian. Exceptions are the northern part of the province and Kai Dullah Island (Kai Archipelago), predominantly Muslim areas. The traditional performing arts of Maluku reflect indigenous beliefs, which predated the arrival of Christianity and Islam.

Ceremonies include processions of boats in the central and southern parts of the province. Ensembles of bronze gong chimes and drums occur in central and southern Maluku, and imported court ensembles exist in Ternate and Tidore. The Maluku drum (*tifa*) is ubiquitous (figure 1); a frame drum (*rebana*) is prominent, especially in Muslim areas.

RESOURCES

The earliest written source referring to the music cultures of northern and central Maluku was a set of volumes about the Indonesian archipelago by the Dutch traveler François Valentijn (1724–26). Thereafter, the most useful sources include descriptions of the indigenous and European-influenced music and dance in Ambon by the English naturalist Alfred Russel Wallace (1869). A Dutch study of Malay songs and dances in Ambon and the Uliase Archipelago was published by W. Joest (1892:1–3, 4). An encyclopedia entry on music and musical instruments of Maluku was published in 1918 (Snelleman 1918:24–26). A preliminary study of music and dance in the Kai Archipelago by the Dutch ethnomusicologist Jaap Kunst appeared in 1945.

In 1984, an introductory book on music and dance in central and southeast Maluku appeared (Gieben et al. 1984). Siwalima, the museum in Ambon, contains valuable collections of musical instruments from Maluku. The provincial department of education and culture has collated data on the performing arts, but they are incomplete and unpublished. Ethnomusicological studies of music in the Muslim north—historical and new music and dance on the twin islands of Ternate and Tidore—have been published (Kartomi 1992, 1993), as has an ethnomusicological overview of the whole of Maluku (Kartomi 1994).

NORTHERN MALUKU: TERNATE AND TIDORE

From the 1400s, the sultans of the spice islands, with palaces at Bacan, Jailolo (Halmahera), Ternate, and Tidore, became wealthy from the spice trade and supervised the development of a rich repertoire of music, dance, and ritual. These artistic expressions, based mainly on village arts and rituals, included dancing and singing in couples (*ronggeng*), healing rituals (*salai jin*), and adapted Muslim forms such as *dabus, samroh,* and *salewat* (devotional singing and/or ritual).

The cultural identity of the sultanates of Ternate and Tidore was determined largely by the people's beliefs, based on the veneration of ancestors and natural spirits, and by the acceptance of Islam starting in the 1400s. Local identity was also colored by trading and cultural contact with Chinese and Arabs from the 1600s or earlier, trade with Javanese from the late 1400s, and conflicts with each other and the sultanates of Jailolo and Bacan from about the 1400s. The primary male dances in the courts are martial, and the performing arts are a synthesis of local and foreign cultural expressions, especially those from Java, West Asia, and Europe.

Traditionally, when guests visited the palace, the sultan received them with dancers and musicians in the front pavilion (*pendopo*) of the palace. On state occasions, holy days, and celebrations, hundreds of the sultan's subjects came to the palace to perform music and dance. Traveling *ronggeng* troupes performed, and the sultan himself sometimes danced with female dancers of *ronggeng.*

In the courts, a local dance (*tari lala* 'mixing dance', also *tari yon*), derived from *ronggeng* and performed at traditional ceremonies (*kedaton*), was more popular than *ronggeng.* Its melodies had a West Asian and Malay character. Typically, an introduction by a bamboo duct flute (*filutu*) was followed by a pair of drums and a female vocalist, who sang a version of the flute's melody to a quatrain (*pantun*). A male singer from the audience would then sing a response. Mixed couples or single-sex groups performed fast, elegant movements of the hands, stepping forward or backward on every fourth drumbeat. Arab-influenced Malay dances in Ternate and Tidore, including *samroh, dana-dana,* and *japin,* resemble dances of Riau and other Malay coastal areas of Indonesia.

Other village entertainments brought to court on special occasions included stories, related by gifted storytellers (*saihu, pawang*), who, especially at moving moments, interpolated the illustrative singing of quatrains with the legends and ancestral histories they told or the axioms (*dahlil*) they sang. The bamboo idiochord tube zither (*tifa tui* 'bamboo drum', now rare) was played in the palaces to accompany singing or dancing. The tube of this zither has a node at each end, with a hole cut in one node. Five bamboo strings are prized lengthways from the tube's surface, and the two pairs plus the single string are linked and tautened with two bamboo bridges each. A bamboo tongue attached over a hole cut in the middle of the tube vibrates when the string is beaten, giving a low-pitched sound. All strings are beaten with a pair of hammers to produce interlocking sounds.

Kolokie (combining *kololo* 'circumnavigate' and *likie* 'mountain'), a spectacular royal ceremony, has been revived whenever the Ternate volcano threatens to erupt, as it did in 1984 and 1987. Under the previous sultan, it was held every year after Lebaran, the feast celebrating the end of Ramadan. As tradition demands, the sultan encircles the island, sitting on a throne in his flagship (*prahu juanga*), attended by a fleet of drum-carrying boats (*tifa oti*). At sea while Ternate people pray in the mosque next to the palace, the musicians in the boats play two or three drums and a gong to accompany a male dancer and ladies-in-waiting (*dayang-dayang*). The fleet formerly included longboats (*kora-kora*), which also contained drums.

Some of the dances performed at court have been rechoreographed by government-organized troupes in Ternate and Tidore. The main group of male dances (*cakalele,* combining *caka* 'spirit that can cause harm, inner power' and *melele* 'jump here and there') feature vigorous hops and jumps. More refined, serious dances (*hasa, soya-soya*) are performed by one or two military men, accompanied in Ternate by a long drum (*tifa gila*), or a short drum (*tifa podo*). Holding a small wooden shield and a sword (*peda*) and wearing a long black coat, trousers, and headdress, the musician accompanying the dance strikes a *tifa gila* with a pair of beaters. The body of the drum, 3 meters long, is cut from the trunk of a coconut palm. It is normally stored suspended from the roof of a pavilion on the grounds of the palace. Its head, of goatskin or deerskin (about 40 centimeters in diameter), is pulled taut by twenty-four tuning wedges (*sidiahi, suro*), held in place by rattan chains and knots. The *hasa bunga* (martial dance with variations) features lively movements and drumming, with the drummer's left hand providing abrupt or varied rhythms to counter the regular rhythm played with his right (figure 2).

Seven martial dances are traditionally performed in the pavilion, either before or after battle. One of the dances (*badansa*) is performed at the foot of the front stairs of the palace as the sultan descends to receive guests. All seven dances are performed by a consort of ten soldiers with a commander in front, wearing yellow and red costumes and carrying swords. The commander calls out war cries (*maulili*). The dance is accompanied by an ensemble that combines local instruments (*tifa* and *rebana*) and European ones (*biola* 'violin', *besi tiga hoek* 'triangle', and *dabi-dabi* 'cymbals'). Additional instruments are used for some dances. Melodies played on the violin feature European traits, including dotted rhythms and near-diatonic tuning. Melodies often use only a five-tone palette, such as G–F–E–D–C. Cyclic rhythms, played on the *tifa* and the *rebana,* are indigenous in style.

Another musical genre specific to the courts is a bronze ensemble (Ternate *kulintang* or *kolintang,* Tidore *jalanpong*). According to the present sultan, the Ternate set was given to the twentieth sultan of Ternate, Zainan Abidin Syah, by one of the nine Javanese Muslim holy men (*wali sanga*) [see JAVA: Cirebon]. The ensemble is played only during the sultan's processions to the mosque during the festivals of Idul fitri and Idul'adha.

The *kulintang* comprises a set of eight horizontal gongs (*momo,* collectively called *kulintang* and *remoi sahi-sahi,* where *remoi* means 'one voice' or 'melody' and *sahi-sahi* means 'many voices'), a vertical gong (*saragi*), a double-headed drum (*baka-baka*), a set of four vase-shaped short drums (*tifa podo*), a triangle, and a pair of local-

FIGURE 2 A martial dance (*hasa bunga*) of Maluku Province. Photo by H. Kartomi.

FIGURE 3 Excerpt from a *kulintang* ensemble piece of Maluku Province.

ly made cymbals (*dabi-dabi,* also known by their onomatopoeic name, *cik*), with wooden handles attached to each disk. The sound the ensemble produces is known by the onomatopoeic expression *cikamomo bum,* where *cik* refers to the sound of the cymbals, *momo* to the horizontal gongs, and *bum* to the vertical gong. The short drums, the most widespread and commonly used drums throughout northern Maluku, are either held horizontally on the player's left knee or rested on the floor; in procession, they are held vertically under left arms. Players beat them with both hands. The *kulintang* is played in interlocking fashion by four musicians playing a pair of *momo* each, led by a leader (*dopdo*). After a short introduction on the cymbals, all the instruments enter, with the gong playing on every eighth beat. The texture includes dotted rhythms of European origin played on the triangle, local-style interlocking patterns on the horizontal gongs, and local-style cyclical patterns played on the vertical gong and drums (figure 3).

Valentijn's account of northern Maluku verifies that *kulintang* comprising sets of small gongs, suspended gongs, and a drum have existed there for centuries. He mentioned copper bowls (*tatabuang*), a set of differently pitched gongs, played with two hammers or sticks in Ternate; the term *tatabuang,* denoting a set of small gongs, is still used in central Maluku, but not in the north. Valentijn added that *tatabuang* were played with gongs and a big drum on local longboats (whose name he spelled *cora-cora*). Elsewhere, he mentions "a big *tifa* or drum" (1724– 26:22–23).

Several dances for women are performed or led by the sultan's ladies-in-waiting (*jojaru ici* 'small unmarried ladies') or girls from a village whose inhabitants are close to the court. In the most remarkable female court dance (*lego-lego*), up to twenty ladies-in-waiting are accompanied by a woman playing a small frame drum (*tampiang*) and a female vocalist, who sings advice to—and even criticism of—the sultan. Traditionally, the singing and dancing lasted for hours; the sultan sometimes danced with the girls. Such dances may be centuries old. Valentijn mentioned that four or more twelve-year-old girls danced and sang at Ternate to the accompaniment of a *rabana,* which he described as a "round, not very thick drum," played with a small gong (1724–26:19).

In most respects, the Ternate palace culture bears an uncanny resemblance to that of Tidore though the inhabitants of these islands were mortal enemies for centuries, and are still archrivals. Each side emphasizes supposed cultural differences with its counterpart. Both sides traditionally used bronze ensembles for royal processions to the mosque, and both used a bowed spike lute (*rababu*) and flutes as the

Performances of *dabus* may be presented by as many as twenty-five men, whose religious joy inspires them to perform spectacular acts of self-mortification, such as stabbing themselves with metal awls, without feeling any pain.

main melodic instruments in ensembles accompanying singing and dancing. Members of the Tidore royal family say their *jalanpong* were played every night during Ramadan to awaken the sultan and family to eat their early morning (predawn) meal and to accompany the sultan's processions to the mosque on the holy days Idul fitri and Idul'adha; in Ternate, the *kulintang* is used only for the last purpose. The *rababu* have three strings in Ternate and one in Tidore, yet both peoples describe parts of the instrument in similarly anthropomorphic fashions. The construction of the flute on each island is similar, but the repertoires differ.

One of the most popular forms of entertainment in Ternate and Tidore is *ronggeng*. To the accompaniment of a frame drum and a gong, or of a flute, two or three *tifa podo,* and a gong, or of a *gambus* and four drums (*marwas*), a male and female singer take turns singing responses to each other (*pantun saut*). At weddings, girls and women dance in Malay-Portuguese style on a makeshift stage. In commercial or government-organized shows, male partners press money into the *ronggeng* girls' hands for the privilege of dancing with them.

Musical accompaniment for *ronggeng* features heptatonic or hexatonic Portuguese-Malay melodies, played on the flute and doubled by the vocalist, punctuated in cycles on the drums and gong. In the gong cycle *mote-mote mobaku,* the gong is struck on every first, fifth, and thirteenth beat of a sixteen-beat cycle. The flutist plays a short introduction (*maku nonako* 'getting to know each other'), followed by entries on the drums, the gong, and the voice, with the leading and following drums playing in unison, or with the following drum interlocking (*siduniru*) with the lead drum. At the end, the flutist usually trails off with a short melodic postlude. Sometimes a *gambus,* two pairs of *marwas* (small, two-headed drums), and a male and/or female singer substitute for the ensemble. Electric guitars, *rebana,* and a Western set of drums are often used.

One form of pre-Muslim ritual still frequently performed is the healing ceremony (*salai jin*). After burning incense in front of the gong, preparing offerings, and singing and dancing to the accompaniment of *rababu, tifa, rebana,* and gong, the shaman (*sousou*) goes into trance and contacts ancestral spirits. After a melodic introduction on the *rababu,* the drummers play loud, high-pitched rhythms, and the *sousou* begins to sing, using a restricted range.

At most celebrations, Muslim music and dance are dominant. At a wedding, the groom proceeds from his parents' house to that of his wife's parents, preceded by girls bearing plates of flowers. Dancers performing the art of self-defense follow, accompanied by players of *rebana,* who, while playing, sing the Muslim confession of faith. On arrival, the groom joins a roomful of men playing *rebana* and singing songs of praise (*hadrat nabi*). The imam then performs the marriage rites. Other Muslim arts seen at ceremonies include *salewat* (songs asking Allah to bless the Prophet), *dabus* (ritual self-mortification), and girls' devotional dances (*samroh, tari dana*), in which a descending Arabic-style melody is repeated many times with accompaniment from a

FIGURE 4 *Dabus* drums of Maluku Province. Photo by H. Kartomi.

gambus, a *tifa,* and a *rebana* accompaniment, while *ronggeng*-like movements are performed.

In the villages, *dabus* performances are often presented by as many as twenty-five men. Sitting cross-legged, with open copies of the Qur'ān resting on cushions in front of them, they sing praises of Allah and the prophets [see SUMATRA: Aceh; West Sumatra]. Two religious leaders (*imam syek*) lead the singing and collective playing of frame drums, while a third presides. His role is to care for the main performers (*ngufa-ngufa*), whose religious joy inspires them to perform spectacular acts of self-mortification, such as stabbing themselves with metal awls, without feeling any pain. When the assembly names Muhammad, the singing and drumming reaches the height of excitement: the small frame drums (*tampiang*) produce fast, loud, high-pitched sounds over lower-pitched cyclic rhythms, played on large frame drums (*aluan*) (figure 4).

CENTRAL MALUKU

Banda Islands

The present-day Bandanese are of mixed descent, including people claiming European, Chinese, and Arabic ancestry and descent from Maluku and Sulawesi groups. The Bandanese language differs from Indonesian in only a handful of words. The Bandanese are thus a group based not on heritage, but on place of birth.

The chief local ceremony is a centuries-old dance-drama, *cakalele* (a term familiar in neighboring islands). Through secret symbolism, this genre contains the names of slaughtered original Bandanese nobles (Tsuchiya 1990:64).

Ambon and the Uliase Archipelago

In Ambon and the Uliase Archipelago, where Protestant Christianity is strongest in the province, the performing arts are strongly influenced by European models, including church music and local versions of dances and dance-related music popular in Holland in the 1800s. Orchestras of various-sized side-blown bamboo flutes (*suling,* figure 5), optional drums, and a clarinet, plus wind bands of locally made clarinets and brasses, are played in near-diatonic tuning.

FIGURE 5 *Suling* flutes used in a church flute ensemble, Ambon Museum, Maluku Province. Photo by H. Kartomi, 1989.

Remnants of the pre-Muslim, pre-Christian culture of the original inhabitants of the area—the *orang Alifuru*—also remain. Double-row gong chimes (*totobuang*), comprising nine or twelve small, near-diatonic bronze gongs on a wooden underframe, and portable near-diatonic xylophones (*tatabuhan kayu*) are still played (Heins and van Wengen 1977:142), usually with a *tifa,* a *rebana,* and a gong. Formerly, they were owned only by members of royal families and their descendants, who valued them as heirlooms (Gieben et al. 1984:22). Valentijn reported having heard an instrument he called *totobuang,* consisting of five or six small gongs in a frame, beaten by a pair of sticks.

The main Alifuru dance was the martial *cakalele,* originally performed by men holding shields before they went on a hunt or to battle (van Hoëvell 1875:23) and accompanied by drums (*tifa*) and a gong. These instruments, suspended at the door of a house or in a mosque, were beaten with specific rhythms, like *tifa orang mati* (to announce a death) and *tifa marinyo* (to call people together). Suspended bronze gongs (*ahuu*) of various pitches were beaten with a soft hammer; greatly valued, they were included in a bride price and were the expression of status and power [compare with similar exchanges of gongs in NUSA TENGGARA TIMUR]. A blown bamboo wind instrument, consisting of a narrow tube inside a wider tube (*gumbang*), is known in Saparua.

After 1512, when the Portuguese assumed power, the non-Muslim population of northern and central Maluku converted to Roman Catholicism and performed Portuguese Catholic music, which remained influential long after 1605, when the Dutch took over and converted many Maluku people to Protestantism. In the mid-1800s, Wallace described indigenous music and dancing in Protestant Ambon as still being mixed with music of the formerly dominant Roman Catholic church for its feasts and processions (Wallace 1869:300). In general, the colonial literature depicts the people of Maluku as being likely to perform music and dance at any opportunity—for celebrations, life-cycle ceremonies, and at work, as when rowing boats or producing sago, the staple (Gieben et al. 1984:19).

Another autochthonous dance extant in Ambon is the magic bamboo dance (*bambu gila*), in which male dancers bounce long bamboo poles up and down to the accompaniment of *tifa.* They go into trance, and the poles seem to bounce of their own accord. A performance of this dance in the Muslim area of Hitu, a town on Ambon's north coast, was described by van Hoëvell in 1875, and was recorded on videotape by the author in the same place in 1991.

Seram

The main ritual of the Huaulu of northern Seram in central Maluku is the *kahua,* a feast whose most important element is a nighttime dance, in which men and unmarried women participate. It was formerly connected with headhunting, and was held every time one or more heads was captured. Today, it celebrates any major event that enhances the society's self-esteem or confirms its vitality, such as the initiation of boys, the installation of someone in office, or the rebuilding of a community house. It has a counterpart in a *cakalele*-style diurnal war dance (*usali*). Throughout the duration of the *kahua,* daytime dances alternate with nighttime dances.

The *usali* begins with the elders ritually taking the drums that hang in the community house and placing them on the veranda with gongs. As musicians play the music, other men dance in front of the house. When darkness is complete, the singers and drummers sit at the center of the veranda, and the *kahua* dance begins. It must not be interrupted until well after dawn, when the slow beat suddenly turns into a frenzied one, and the men, mustering all the energy left to them, rush out and break into a spirited war dance. They rest until the afternoon, when they dance the *usali* again, and again after sunset, they dance the *kahua* until dawn. This process continues for at least five days, and more often for ten; then the feast may slacken. But for several months (and sometimes, as in 1987–1988, for more than one year), dances will now and then be held for a few nights in a row. The dancing is not continuous, but the taboos that mark the ritual period are. It is taboo to perform any other ritual that involves the use of drums, though curing rituals may be performed in an incomplete form—without drumming and dancing. At the completion of the feast, people spend from one to five nights in competitive singing (*sewaa*), required at funerals to send away the shadows of the dead (Valeri 1990:62). Settled village communities, including Soahuku and Amahai (near Maroki), maintain this musical culture, in modified forms.

Buru

The aboriginal *orang Alifuru* still live inland and along part of the coastal areas of the island of Buru. At ceremonies, while men play small conical *tifa* (of which the largest is 38 centimeters long), men and women sing and dance the *lego* in circular formations. Valentijn described *lego* as being a round dance accompanied by the slow singing of responsorial songs (*assoy,* now spelled *asoi*). These and *tutohato* are forms of responsorial singing in slow tempo to honor someone, as opposed to *hasuha-a,* ceremonial singing in fast tempo (Valentijn 1724–26:164). The dance is begun by the head of a group of families, after which the guests and others present join in, with male dancers carrying a shield and sword. The *cakalele* is danced on Buru, accompanied by a large *tifa* and a gong. A meter-long bamboo zither (*totobuan kawat*) is also played there. It consists of five bamboo strings, raised on two bridges, and has a bamboo tongue that resonates over an opening in the tube. It produces an interlocking melodic pattern. Homemade three-stringed bowed chordophones (*viol*) are common. Formerly, ensembles of one large gong and five small gongs (*totobuang*) were exchanged as part of the bride price.

SOUTHEAST MALUKU

FIGURE 6 *Nekara* drum of the Đông Sơn period, Desa Faan, Kei Kecil, Maluku Province. Photo by H. Kartomi, 1989.

Kai Archipelago

A Đông Sơn drum (*nekara*) in Kai Kecil, though broken and treated nowadays as a sacred object rather than a musical instrument, suggests that Kai's musical culture is of great age (figure 6). The inhabitants of the Kai Archipelago are believed to have originally migrated from islands to the west. This origin contrasts with that of the populace of the Aru Archipelago (just east of Kai), who are predominantly Melanesian. The local nobility are believed to have migrated from Seram.

Traditional performing arts appear to be better maintained in Kai's Roman Catholic communities than in the Protestant or Muslim ones. Roman Catholic services feature ensembles of bamboo flutes (*suling bambu*) and traditional songs. The indigenous religion, based on worship of ancestors and natural spirits, includes the veneration of ancient bronze kettle-gongs as ancestral objects.

A typical musical ensemble in Kai uses two gongs of medium and small size (*dada*), a drum (*tifa*), and a bamboo flute (*savarngil*) (figure 7); it accompanies all dances. There are fifty-two known types of traditional dance in Kai. Formerly, the snake dance (*tari ular*) was the ceremony by which a new king was selected. *Tari kibas* is a fan dance. To symbolize the termination of warfare in peace and victory, male martial dancing may be merged with Malay- or Portuguese-influenced female dancing.

The unaccompanied singing of refrains is the basis of song in Kai, with allusive texts, rather than poetic ones. Types of songs include magical songs to aid in the col-

Types of Kai vocal music include magical songs to aid in the collection of honey, songs to bring safety at sea, and laments for orphaned children.

FIGURE 7 Ensemble of drums and gongs: big drums (*tifa laai*), small drums (*tifa kot*), and a gong (*dada*); a flute (*savarngil*) is absent from this photo. Letwuan, Kai, Maluku Province. Photo by H. Kartomi, 1989.

lection of honey, songs to bring safety at sea, and laments for orphaned children. *Ngel-ngel* are traditional songs, sung all night long at weddings and other ceremonies. They are in free meter, in a highly melismatic style. Their texts may consist of advice on male-female love or family relations, or relate historical tales or genealogies. When whales wash ashore, special songs are sung for a whole night. An identical ceremony of songs is held once a year to cleanse the villagers of misdeeds (Barraud 1990:44). A special genre of songs of advice (*snehet-snehet*) is also sung in Kai, as are *baut-baut,* epic songs sung in processions of boats, marking occasions when the raja collected important guests. *Tifa* ensembles and dancers performed on a platform at the front of the boat during the journey, while the raja sat on another platform in the middle.

In Kai, Muslim music is typified by art-of-self-defense performances accompanied by one *gambus* and five to six small double-headed drums (*mewas*). *Tari sawat* is a popular Muslim-based mixing dance, and *tari sasoi* is a special dance to honor the raja. *Tiwa nam* is a *ronggeng*-like Malay fan dance, performed by adolescent girls.

Aru Islands

Because of the former lack of communications in the Aru Islands, virtually every village has developed a unique repertoire of songs (*didi*), including songs sung on boats when at sea (*mararei, bela, jer lavlavi*). The main instruments are a drum (*tifa,* also *titir*), a gong (*daldala*), a Jew's harp (*berimbak*), and a conch trumpet (*tapur*). Gongs come in various sizes, under several names: *bumbong, daldala sermin, jawa, jawa tapuran, sepelpel, sigila, sigkodar, talakoka,* and *wangur gural.* At feasts, the Aru people perform *dalair,* dances accompanied by singing and drumming (Gieben et al. 1984:78–79).

Tanimbar

The population of the Tanimbar Archipelago (southern Maluku) is predominantly syncretic Christian-animist. Like their neighbors in the Babar and Kai islands, their beliefs incorporate the ceremonial use of intricately carved ancestral statues. Migration myths describe the ancestors' arrival from Sumatra and Java by way of Flores and Timor, and continuing on to Seram, but none describes migration to Tanimbar from central Maluku. Three villages in Tanimbar feature a large stone in the shape of a boat as their traditional meeting place, and one village has an ancient bronze kettle-gong in a place of honor at its center.

Ceremonies are held for births, funerals, new houses, to request rain, for successful fishing, and to celebrate the opening and harvest of a new garden. *Nabar panas pela* is a ceremony in which the heads of two villages drink one another's heated blood to show that they are friendly and cannot go to war. Mixing dances symbolize the cooperation of the villagers working together in the fields. The name of the war dance (*t'nabar mpuk-ulu* 'happy-head dance') refers to the warrior's display of the enemy's head. As part of the *angkosi* dance, men and women sing and respond to quatrains as a way of teasing and getting to know one another. The competitive singing of quatrains is an important feature of the New Year celebration. In a round dance (*badendang*), girls sing and dance together.

Men accompany many ceremonies with the playing of a large drum (*empa-empal*). Women seem to be the exclusive players of *tifa* (locally called *tibal*). Gongs (*titir*) are also played. Formerly, the people would begin their day with dancing. They would garden or hunt until the afternoon, and then dance again. But today, this sort of life style is locally obsolete. Church services incorporate indigenous songs and ceremonial dances (*t'nabar*), with the participants wearing traditional costume, including bird-of-paradise feathers. Though there are no birds of paradise in Tanimbar, the feathers grace the headdresses worn during ceremonial dancing because people believe their ancestors wore them. As in most other parts of the country, traditional performing arts are often adapted to suit the political ends of post-1965 Indonesia.

Babar Archipelago

In the Babar Islands (west of Tanimbar), fertility rituals play a central part in village communities. There is a striking similarity between the central theme of the fertility ritual and the main theme of the myths of creation. During the New Year fertility ritual (which lasts nearly a month), the *lulya* dances are performed. These include a men's round dance accompanied by a long song with fixed lyrics, a women's round dance accompanied by a song with improvised lyrics that refer to fishing, and a mixed-sex line dance accompanied by a song asking for rain (Van Dijk and de Jonge 1990:5–6).

REFERENCES

Barraud, Cecile. 1990. "A Turtle Turned on the Sand in the Kei Islands; Society's Shares and Values." *Bijdragen tot de Taal-, Land- en Volkenkunde* 1:146:35–55.

Gieben, Claartje, Renée Heijnen, and Anneke Sapuletej. 1984. *Muziek en dans, Spelletjes en Kinderliedjes van de Molukken.* Hoevelaken, The Netherlands: Christelijk Pedagogisch Studiecentrum.

Heins, Ernst, and G. van Wengen. 1979. "Maluku (Molukken)." In *Musikgeschichte in Bildern: Südostasien,* ed. Paul Collaer, 142–143. Leipzig: VEB Deutschen Verlag.

Joest, W. 1892. "Malayische Lieder und Tänze aus Ambon und den Uliase (Molukken)." *Internationales Archiv für Ethnographie* 5:1– 34.

Kartomi, Margaret J. 1992. "Appropriation of Music and Dance in Contemporary Ternate and Tidore." *Studies in Music* 26:85–95.

———. 1993. "Revival of Feudal Music, Dance and Ritual in the Former 'Spice Islands' of Ternate and Tidore." In *Culture and Society in New Order Indonesia,* ed. Virginia Hooker, 185–220. New York, Oxford: Oxford University Press.

———. 1994. "Is Maluku Still Musicological Terra Incognita? An Overview of the Music-Cultures of the Province of Maluku." *Journal of Southeast Asian Studies* 25(1).

Kunst, Jaap. 1945. *Een en Ander Over de Muziek en den dans Op de Keieilanden.* Amsterdam: Koninklijke Vereeniging Indisch Instituut. Mededeling 64.

Snelleman, J. F. 1918. "Muziek en Muziekinstrumentum in Niederlandsch Oost-Indië." *Encyclopedie van Nederlandsch-Indië,* 24–26.

Tsuchiya Kenji and James Siegel. 1990. "Invincible Kitsch or as Tourists in the Age of Des Alwi." *Indonesia* 50:61–76.

Valentijn, François. 1724–26. *Oud en Nieuw Oost-Indien, Vervattende een Naauwkeurige en Uitvoerige Verhandelinge van Nederlands Mogentheyd in die Gewesten, Benevens eene Wydlustige Beschryvinge der Moluccos, Amboine, Banda, Timor, en Solor, Java, etc.* 5 vols. Dordrecht: Joannes van Braam. Amsterdam: Gerard onder de Linden.

Valeri, Valerio. 1990. "Autonomy and Heteronomy in the Kahua Ritual: A Short Meditation on Huaulu Society." *Bijdragen tot de Taal-, Land- en Volkenkunde* 1:146:56–73.

van Dijk, Toos, and Nico de Jonge. 1990. "After Sunshine Comes Rain: A Comparative Analysis of Fertility Rituals in Marsela and Luang, South-East Moluccas." *Bijdragen tot de Taal-, Land- en Volkenkunde* 1:146:3–20.

van Hoëvell, G. W. W. C., Baron. 1875. *Ambon en Meer Bepaaldelijk de Oeliasers, Geografisch, Ethnographisch, Politisch en Historisch.* Dordrecht: Joannes van Braam. Amsterdam: Gerard onder de Linden.

Wallace, Alfred Russel. 1869. *The Malay Archipelago.* London, Macmillan.

Borneo: Sabah, Sarawak, Brunei, Kalimantan

Patricia Matusky

The Southeast Asian island commonly known as Borneo is divided into three twentieth-century nations. The Malaysian states of Sarawak and Sabah (formerly British North Borneo) are located in the north and far northeast of the island, respectively. These states joined the Federation of Malaysia in 1963, and are sometimes called East Malaysia. The sultanate of Brunei Darussalam (Brunei, Abode of Peace) occupies a small area on the northwest coast between the two Malaysian states, and the three Indonesian provinces of Kalimantan make up the remaining (and largest) part of the island.

The geology of Borneo features mountain ranges and high plateaus. Several navigable rivers drain the island in nearly all directions from its center. Many of the upper reaches of the rivers are interlaced with dangerous, sometimes impassable rapids. Much of the year, the forest covering much of Borneo receives heavy rainfall. In most areas, especially the interior, accessibility and travel are difficult, even in the best of times. The dwellings of most central Borneo peoples are built along waterways, but the difficulty of travel isolates many communities. The distribution of the population is sparse in the interior, but increases toward the coast. Except in the far north, Borneo's coastal areas are swampy, but they remain the sites of its greatest urban development and population density.

CULTURAL GEOGRAPHY

The ethnic groups of Sabah, Sarawak, and Kalimantan are distinguished by culture and language (Leach 1950; Rousseau 1988, 1989). Many terms, like Pari, Klemantan, or Kalamantan were coined by early writers on Borneo to refer collectively to the peoples of the interior, but such terminology is obsolete and meaningless. A long-used term, *Dayak,* once served as an all-encompassing designation for many of the indigenous peoples of the island (excluding Malays and Javanese). It still commonly denotes a much broader group of people in Kalimantan than in Sarawak. In Kalimantan, it is recognized as a designation that encompasses smaller groups, like the Kenyah and the Kayan; in Sarawak, it applies to the Iban (formerly Sea Dayak) and the Bidayuh (formerly Land Dayak).

The central region of Borneo, encompassing parts of East and West Kalimantan

The vocal music of the indigenous peoples of Borneo includes epics and other narratives, plus songs for life-cycle events and rituals associated with religion, healing, growing rice, hunting game, and waging war.

The island of Borneo

and the interior parts of Sarawak, is inhabited by peoples who have stratified societies and practice swidden agriculture. The main ethnic groups in this region are the Kayan, the Kenyah, and the Kajang (who live in longhouse structures on riverine sites), and the Kelabit peoples (who live on the interior highland plateau); each of these ethnicities has many subgroups. The nomadic (or recently settled) hunters and gatherers of this area are known as Punan and Penan peoples. Local people often conflate distinct groups into these categories, misapplying the term Penan to Punan or vice versa.

Along the major rivers, the main groups in the northwest (Sarawak) are the Iban, the Bidayuh, the Melanau, and the Malay. To the northeast (Sabah), the predominant ethnolinguistic groups are the Kadazan (also called Dusun), the Bajau, the Orang Sungei, and the Murut. Many minorities also live in these areas. West

Kalimantan is home to some of the central Borneo groups, plus the Maloh and the Iban; the eastern section finds mainly the Kayan, the Kenyah, and related peoples, and a substantial Javanese group. As a result of immigration that began around the 1500s, many Javanese live in South Kalimantan. Many Ngaju and Barito groups live in Central Kalimantan. The Malay population, in varying numbers, lives mainly in towns and cities throughout the coastal areas of Borneo, and occasionally in market towns along the major rivers. The coastal towns and cities are the centers of commerce and communication, linking Borneo to other parts of Southeast Asia, and in them, most other immigrant groups (including Chinese, Indians, and Eurasians), live.

Generations ago, the immigrant peoples brought their own music cultures to Borneo, and their traditions have been perpetuated by their descendants. In the twentieth century, the Malays still use the frame drum (*rebana*) in making music, and perform musics similar to those of the Peninsular and other Malays. Significant examples include musical genres associated with religious practice (*agama*)—the call to prayer (*azan*) and devotional singing (*zikir*)—and the social dances *zapin* and *joget,* still popular among many young Malays of inland market towns. The early Javanese immigrants brought a form of the gamelan (orchestra of bronze gongs and metallophones), which survives in East and South Kalimantan. The Chinese, who live in great numbers in north and west Borneo (especially in Sarawak and Sabah), excel in Western music. They also continue to perform their traditional instrumental and vocal musics. Their prominence in Sarawak has led to the development of public displays of Chinese culture, including festivals for the deities of various temples, opera troupes in the streets, processions for the Chinese New Year with dragons accompanied by drums and gongs, and clubs for youths. Among the indigenous groups in Sarawak, Sabah, and Kalimantan, the variety of music is a dynamic aspect of traditional life. These indigenous musics appear in both vocal and instrumental forms.

VOCAL MUSIC

The vocal music of the indigenous peoples of Borneo includes epics and other narratives, plus songs for life-cycle events and rituals associated with religion, healing, growing rice, hunting game, and waging war. Songs to welcome visitors to the longhouse or to accompany dancing, and sung narratives to relate genealogies are usually collective endeavors, with both skilled and semiskilled singers taking part. Some vocal genres feature exclusively male or female solo singers; other forms require the effort of an ensemble of either single or mixed genders. No professionalism in musical performance is recognized in traditional Borneo societies, though communities acknowledge expertise in singing a particular genre or playing a given instrument.

The singing voice tends to be small, with moderate resonance and volume. Nasalization varies in intensity from one group to another; most vocalists, exercising the muscles and resonant cavities of the nasal pharynx, use a high proportion of upper partials at all levels of pitch. Consequently, they obtain a strident vocal quality, especially at higher tonal levels; female voices sometimes achieve a shouting quality. In some central Borneo societies, each female singer covers her mouth with one hand as she sings—a phenomenon found most notably among the Kajang groups of interior Sarawak.

In Sabah, Sarawak, and Kalimantan, vocal forms reflect various aspects of life (for translation of, and commentary on, many types of Dayak songs, see Rubenstein 1985 and 1990). Vocal music—including funeral dirges, epics, and songs of love and courting, war, and general entertainment—remains one of the principal means of preserving and disseminating the oral literature and customary practices of Borneo.

Singing for dances

Among the indigenous groups in Sabah, Sarawak, and the interior of Kalimantan, vocal music is a major form of dance accompaniment. Collective line dances (or long dances), performed in a row or a circle, are accompanied by the dancers' singing, with percussive rhythms created by the dancers' stamping and other footfalls. To celebrate an engagement, a wedding, a birthday, or any other social event, the Bajau peoples of Sabah perform a lengthy instrumental form called *batitik,* followed by the dance *berunsai* (Frame 1976:159–160). The musical accompaniment of the *berunsai* consists of a sung text, with stamping feet on the floorboards by the male dancers, creating a steadily repeated rhythmic pattern. The dancers sing in question-and-answer style, with the male dancers vocalizing a line of text in response to that sung by the females. A set number of textual lines makes up a verse, sung using the same narrow-ranged tetrachordal melody for each line of text.

Kajang groups of Sarawak also use song and repetitive rhythmic patterns stamped by dancers' feet. Kajang line dances for the ceremony of headhunting (*ngayau,* common among many Borneo groups until the mid-1800s, when it was outlawed) are accompanied by songs consisting of texts sung in a syllabic style by men and women as they dance in rows or circles. Either the male or female dancers periodically punctuate the sung text using a refrainlike descending melodic line, much in the style of the *wa,* a Kajang vocal narrative.

The Murut peoples of the interior regions of Sabah still perform the *lansaran,* formerly sung to celebrate the taking of heads, but now a form of general community entertainment. It features poetic verses sung by male and female dancers as they dance in circular formations on a specially sprung floor. In community centers, this floor (*lansaran*) is built of elastic planks and logs, which, whenever the dancers shift their weight in tandem with shuffling footsteps, enable the floor to bounce and hit against beams beneath it. As the steps set up a regular, percussive beat and a resulting crash of the floor against the beams beneath it, the male and female dancers alternately sing the poetic verses, each group in unison. A given tune, within the melodic range of a fourth, is repeated for each verse, as the singers focus on a reciting pitch, and finally descend to a lower tone in each line of text. The melodies use many slides and microtones (Frame 1976).

In Kenyah longhouses of central Borneo and Sarawak, adults perform line dances and a traditional dance of war (*lekupa*). In the latter dances of Kenyah-Badang, one male dancer is a solo singer, and everyone else sings in chorus. The style, predominantly unison, contrasts with some passages in rudimentary singing in parts, stressing the harmonic intervals of octave, unison, and third (figure 1).

The style of singing the *lekupa* (characterized by two-line verses) is syllabic, with little or no melodic ornamentation. The soloist begins a short opening line of text, and is joined by the chorus. The entire group then sings a longer line, so the complete melody of the verse is structured in two main phrases of unequal length, as five plus seven bars. The melodic range may be as wide as an octave, using a pentatonic scale. Essentially strophic, this form is accompanied by a repeated percussive rhythm,

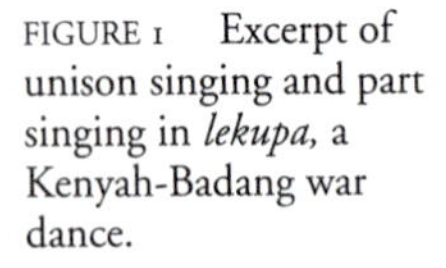
FIGURE 1 Excerpt of unison singing and part singing in *lekupa,* a Kenyah-Badang war dance.

FIGURE 2 The melody and drone of a *kui,* a song sung at the *kui* ceremony of the Kenyah.

stamped by the dancers. Kenyah song lyrics tend to outline some of the most fundamental social codes and appropriate standards of behavior (Gorlinski 1995).

Singing for rituals

As practitioners of swidden rice cultivation, the Kenyah also use vocal music in rituals related to growing rice on hillsides. An important ceremony (*kui,* also *kue*) is held before the seed is planted each season. It is sung by a solo male participant, who with all others involved in the planting and singing, holds onto a long horizontal bamboo pole, in effect linking everyone in a communal effort for planting rice. As participants execute a slow shuffle to the side, the soloist sings a given melodic and textual line, and all others sing in chorus. The soloist's melodic line is in free rhythm, with occasional long melismas on a single syllable (figure 2).

The soloist's melody encompasses an octave, but individual melodic phrases are built on the lower or upper tetrachord of that octave. Throughout the *kui,* the chorus intones a movable drone, moving up or down a perfect fourth, according to the solo singer's melodic focus. Among the Kenyah, and also among their neighbors, the Kajang peoples of Sarawak, a male soloist sings many long poems (*pantun*) in a similar style, accompanied by an all-male chorus intoning the drone, which may or may not be movable.

Singing for narration

A notable vocal genre mainly of several Kajang groups of the interior of Sarawak is the sung narrative known as *wa* and *mu'a* 'the singing of the *wa*' (Strickland 1988:67). It is usually a lengthy work, performed to welcome a guest to the longhouse, to open or close a specific event, or to relate a genealogy. It is usually sung by several female singers: each in turn serves as a soloist, while the others sing a choral refrain. The narrative is structured in stanzas consisting of lines of text governed by set rhymes and bounded by certain textual markers. A soloist sings the textlines in a strictly syllabic style, and the chorus punctuates the narrative at periodic intervals with a refrainlike, descending melodic line (sung on the vocable *é*), sometimes in unison, but usually in heterophony.

In a typical rendition of the *wa* sung by the Kajang-Sekapan, the soloist sings a given line of text within the melodic range of a fourth or a fifth above or below the tonal center. At periodic intervals, one of the other singers begins the refrain on the tonal center (but in the upper octave), and sings a descending line, at whose midpoint the entire chorus joins in. The seemingly independent contrapuntal lines established by the soloist and the chorus during the *é* are related—possibly by textual reference, and certainly by tonal material. A hexatonic scale is the tonal basis for the melodic material in both parts. The musical rhythm of some *wa* is free, but in other renditions (notably those of the Punan Bah, in the same geographical area), it is strictly duple, with much use of dotted rhythms in the soloist's part (Matusky 1986:221–223).

timang Iban ritual chanting

magaggong Kadazan music in which large drums are beaten in interlocking rhythms

gendang rayah Iban gong ensemble

tawak Large, deep-rimmed gongs

gendang panjai Iban gong-chime ensemble

Singing for religion

In the traditional religions of Borneo, the spiritual world is an important and powerful force, which always requires attention, and sometimes requires communication and propitiation. Iban peoples of Sarawak and West Kalimantan know a form of ritual chanting to communicate with the spiritual world as *timang* (also *pengap*). The chanting is performed by a bard (*lemambang*), who intones texts to invite spirits to join in a given feast (*gawai*). He is assisted by another bard, who sings or chants in alternation with him. The genre has four types: to ensure the community's general welfare (*timang beintu-intu*), to ensure good fortune (*timang tuah*), to request fruitful seed and bountiful harvests (*timang beneh*), and to request the spirits' presence at any ritual of high significance in the longhouse community (*timang gawai amat*).

The *timang* is usually structured in the form of a stanza (sung by the bard), followed by a short refrain (sung by an all-male chorus). The assistant bard responds with a complementary stanza, followed by the refrain. The pattern of statement and response, with the interjected choral refrain, may continue all night, until the intended objective is achieved (Masing 1981). Since many of the indigenous peoples of Sabah, Sarawak, and Kalimantan have accepted Christianity, another type of communication with the spiritual world takes the form of hymns. Robust hymn singing occurs in unison or sometimes in parts, with the accompaniment of a piano or a guitar, using diatonic scales in major and minor modes.

INSTRUMENTAL MUSIC

A rich variety of instruments characterizes the instrumental music of Borneo, including gongs, flutes, zithers, and Jew's harps. Some are used to accompany dance (Hudson 1971), and others are played for personal enjoyment. The following discussion includes some representative instruments and their contexts, but a complete survey of instrumental music on Borneo has yet to be completed (for more information, see Frame 1982 and Ongkili 1974)

Gongs and gong chimes

People of Malaysian Borneo and Kalimantan consider the bronze bossed gong an object of high value, in both musical and nonmusical contexts. As an item of economic wealth, the gong carries a high price in barter and trade, and its use in rituals and in communication with the spiritual world is important. In musical contexts, it is found in small ensembles that play music to welcome visitors, accompany dances, and enhance rituals. Formerly, gongs were used to transmit messages from one longhouse to another as players beat out rhythmic patterns.

In Sabah, Sarawak, and parts of Kalimantan, large bossed gongs—in diameters ranging from 30 centimeters to more than 70 centimeters—are heard in ensembles that have from five to nine or more hanging gongs. In Sabah, large gongs are beaten in interlocking rhythms in the music known as *magagung,* which accompanies the

FIGURE 3 A typical ensemble of large gongs: one small *canang* (or *gan,* left), one *bandai* (background), two deep-rimmed *tawak,* and one *agung* (middle right). Photo by Patricia Matusky.

sumazau, a traditional dance of the Kadazan. Other musical forms played by orchestras of large gongs occur throughout the northwest and central parts of Borneo, and accompany dances and ceremonies. These ensembles provide the repetitive interlocking rhythmic patterns at thunderous levels of intensity, which signal and welcome the arrival of special guests to longhouses and villages. The Bidayuh of northwest Sarawak typically use nine hanging gongs in their orchestras of large gongs. The Iban of Sarawak and West Kalimantan, and the Kajang and Kayan groups of central Borneo, use five or fewer gongs (Sandin 1974). Among central Borneo peoples, the large gongs are usually beaten by men; the smaller ones, by women. The Iban of Sarawak and West Kalimantan often call this ensemble *gendang raya* (or *kandang rayah*) 'celebration drums'; other groups use the phrase *main gong* 'playing the gongs.' Kenyah gongs tend to be "untuned," relying on overall contrast of pitch rather than the creation of specific tonal contours (Gorlinski 1994).

In these ensembles, players beat repeated rhythmic patterns on the gongs, using either sustained, resonant tones (the boss is not damped) or short, staccato tones (the boss is damped immediately after being hit with a padded beater). Just as in the interlocking styles of drumming *gendang silat, wayang kulit,* and *gendang tarinai* of Peninsular Malaysia, the practice of playing interlocking or shared parts is important in the ensembles of large gongs of Borneo. In a typical ensemble, one or more large, deep-rimmed gongs (*tawak, tawag*) are struck with padded beaters (one player per gong) in a set rhythmic pattern, the player beating on the central boss, the secondary boss (the raised portion of the face immediately around the central boss), or a combination of the two (figure 3). One or more large, shallow-rimmed gongs are struck on the boss with a wooden stick in a repeated rhythmic pattern complementing that of large *tawak.* Finally, medium- and small-sized hanging gongs of various names are struck on the boss or the rim with wooden sticks. These gongs play a distinctly interlocking rhythmic pattern. Last, an ostinato of two pitches that alternately signify the downbeat (low pitch or timbre) and the upbeat (high pitch or timbre) of each main pulse is played on a pair of small bossed gongs (figure 4). The rhythmic patterns played by these ensembles are structured in duple meter in repetitive four-beat or eight-beat units.

In addition to hanging gongs, most orchestras of this type include one or more drums, usually hit with a pair of wooden sticks. In Sarawak, the Bidayuh orchestras use both large and small double-headed drums, called *gendang* (*kandang*) and *dumbak,* respectively. Iban orchestras include a long drum (*ketebong*) or cylindrical drums (*dumbak*). Drummed rhythmic patterns support those of the deep-voiced gongs

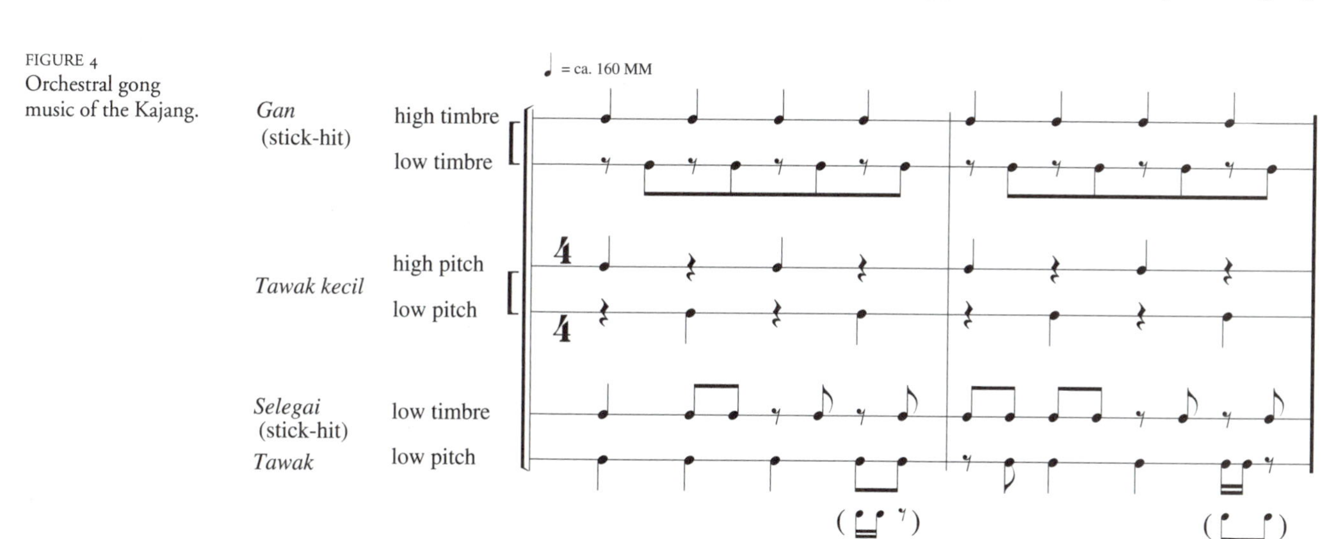

FIGURE 4 Orchestral gong music of the Kajang.

(*tawak*). In these orchestras, timbre is as important as pitch, and specific pitches themselves are insignificant. With the use of the stick-hit drums and the striking of wooden sticks or padded beaters on the gongs, the totality of sound emerges as a multipart interlocking of distinct timbres, with staccato and resonant pitches, producing composite and repetitive rhythms.

The gong chime ensembles of the Iban peoples of west and northwest Borneo are related to the *gulintangan, kulintangan,* and *kulintang* traditions of Brunei, Sabah, and the southern Philippines, respectively [see ISLAMIC COMMUNITIES OF THE SOUTHERN PHILIPPINES). The Iban often call this ensemble long drum (*gendang panjai*) or *engkeromung*, for it consists of one gong chime (*engkeromung,* eight or more small bossed gongs, suspended in a long wooden rack), two or more large-sized and medium-sized hanging bossed gongs (*tawak, bandai*), and one or more long, single-headed, cylindrical drums (*gendang panjai,* also *kandang panjai*). Iban women traditionally play the gong chime and the hanging gongs; the men play the hand-hit drums. The drum begins, and the gong chime and then the hanging gongs enter at staggered temporal intervals.

In a typical piece, the long drum sets up a rhythmic pattern (usually four beats long), played and varied by both the gong chime and the low-pitched hanging gong. The basic pattern is sustained throughout a given piece, every other beat punctuated by the player of the smaller hanging gong in unison with another player beating out a drone on the highest-pitched gong of the gong chime. Rhythms are usually in duple meter; the tempo begins at a medium pace and gradually increases in speed.

This ensemble provides music to accompany the dance (*ngajat*) formerly danced by Iban warriors, but today performed as entertainment by a solo male. For celebrations, to entertain guests visiting the longhouse, or for any other festive occasion, the *gendang panjai* is a popular form of music. Similarly, the *kulintangan* of Sabah usually features a gong chime of eight to twelve gongs, one or more drums, two medium-sized hanging gongs (*bandil*), and two *tawag.* This orchestra also provides music for dance-and-entertainment music for weddings and other celebrations.

The bossed gongs and other bronze instruments are reportedly found in East and South Kalimantan, where, in the south province, orchestras resemble gamelans, brought to the region by Javanese colonists. In East Kalimantan, an old form of gamelan is still extant. It consists of several large, bossed, hanging gongs, other metallophones, a xylophone, a rebab, a double-reed pipe, and drums (Hood 1980).

Bamboo, wooden poles, and xylophones

Throughout Malaysian Borneo and Kalimantan, large hardwood poles and a wooden mortar are used to pound new rice to separate the chaff from the grain, and bamboo tubes are sometimes used to cook the rice. Wooden poles and bamboo tubes are examples of the basic materials and tools used in many different occupations, especially work involving the cultivation of rice. As an extension of work, the implements used for the physical motions of sowing, harvesting, and pounding the grains of rice and the wooden and bamboo implements used in these events have become music-making instruments in daily activities and ritual contexts.

Several groups living in the central Borneo region stamp poles made of bamboo or wood. Players stamp the poles to chase away unwanted or undesirable elements, originating in both the seen and unseen worlds. In an event called *huduk apa* 'chasing away whatever', some Kayan male groups use wooden poles (about 1.4 meters long), one to a player. The players don frightening masks. With poles, they stamp out the pulse of their footsteps as they parade, in single file, around the veranda of their longhouse. Accompanying them are gongs (*tawak*), which provide an interlocking rhythmic pattern in duple meter. Eventually, in a climactic fury of shouts and hisses, the

FIGURE 5 The bamboo tube stampers (*kesut*) play resultant rhythms, used in procession by Kajang women of Sarawak. Photo by Patricia Matusky.

participants gather around a central place on the veranda, waving their poles in the air in a symbolic gesture.

Other groups in central Borneo stamp poles to chase away bad or evil elements. Kajang women of Sarawak stamp sets of six or more decorated bamboo poles (1.4 to 1.8 meters long) in precisely interlocking rhythms as they walk in procession in the ancient *ngayau* ceremony, formerly performed to greet the warriors upon their return from battle and headhunting. Though battles and headhunting no longer occur, women still stamp the poles on festive occasions. The poles and the stamping are locally called *kesut* (figure 5). The leader of the procession normally carries two poles and stamps out a distinct rhythmic pattern; all other players stamp one pole each, the downbeat and the upbeat of each main pulse being marked by alternate players in the procession. The rhythmic patterns may be additive or divisive, and sometimes syncopation distinguishes the leader's pattern from that of the others.

The poles used to pound rice in the traditional method utilizing the mortar (*lesung*) and pestle (*antan,* also *alu*) also serve as stampers in musical contexts [see MALAYSIA (PENINSULAR)]. In many parts of Borneo, teams of three to four women pound rice. With precise timing and rhythm, they lift the pestle and pound or stamp the grains of rice in the well of the mortar. This activity finds its musical parallel as entertainment after work, when women, usually in teams of three, stamp the pestles at select locations on the top surface of the mortar. Typically among the Kayan of central Borneo, two women, each holding a single pestle, alternately stamp their poles near the center of the mortar, achieving a low timbre. Each stroke marks the upbeat and the downbeat of the recurring pulse in the rhythm. Simultaneously, the third player stamps her pestle near the edge of the mortar, obtaining a higher timbre, which distinguishes her rhythmic pattern. The rhythms played by these trios are invariably in duple meter at a fast tempo, and the lead player's pattern features syncopated rhythms (figure 6).

The hardwood poles used to pound rice also serve as concussion idiophones in musical performances associated with growing rice among the Kayan and Kenyah of Sarawak and East Kalimantan. A similar tradition of music and dance, at one time performed during planting rice by certain Kenyah groups of East Kalimantan, is *pangpagaq* (Gorlinski 1989). Among some Kayan groups of central Borneo, women's

The tradition in Sarawak of striking tuned bamboo tubes in interlocking patterns strongly resembles some of the music traditions of the Sulu Archipelago and the southern Philippines.

FIGURE 6 Pestles, mortar, and bamboo poles as used by the Kayan of central Borneo.

striking of wooden pestles (*alu*) and men's or women's striking of bamboo tubes (*tangbut*) require three pairs of wooden poles, laid crosswise on top of two parallel logs: people strike each pair of poles together in a rhythmic pattern (figure 7).

As in other percussive musics using poles in Malaysian Borneo and Kalimantan, the steady running beat in the music is played by two pairs of pestles, while a specific rhythmic pattern is beaten out on the third pair. Duple or triple meters, a fast tempo, and some syncopation characterize this music. In the Kayan tradition, two stick-hit bamboo tubes join the ensemble. The shorter bamboo beats out a continuous, high-pitched drone (a single note per beat), while the larger, low-pitched bamboo provides a short, reiterated pattern. In Kayan communities, women play the *alu,* and either male or female players strike the *tangbut.* Some Kenyah men of Sarawak, who play

FIGURE 7 Musical activities related to the cultivation of rice include *alu* and *tangbut,* played among the Kayan peoples of Sarawak; three pairs of concussion poles (*alu* 'rice-pounding pestles') and two struck bamboo tubes (*tangbut*) play resultant rhythms. Photo by Patricia Matusky.

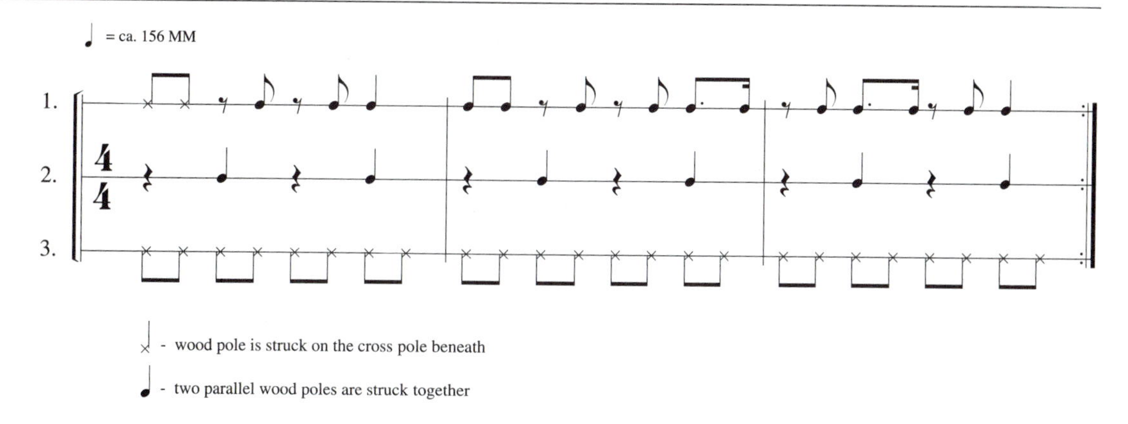

FIGURE 8 Kenyah concussive poles: *tatip kamang* 'chasing away pests'.

these pestles as part of growing rice activities, call the tradition *tatip kamang* 'routing out pests.' They strike pairs of pestles together in much the same style as that of their Kayan neighbors, but use a faster tempo (figure 8).

Sets of tuned bamboo tubes in various sizes and tunings serve as musical instruments among some Borneo peoples. Sets of bamboo tubes called *togunggak* or *togunggu* are carried, one tube to a player, and are struck with a wooden stick to beat out interlocking rhythmic patterns, resulting in repeated composite melodic and rhythmic phrases. The *togunggak* were formerly played in headhunting ceremonies of the Murut peoples of north Borneo. Imitating music for gong orchestras, the Bidayuh peoples of northwest Sarawak play similar sets of tuned, stick-hit bamboo tubes (*peruncung,* also *keruncung*) while walking back to the longhouses after work in the paddies. In these ensembles, the two highest-pitched tubes play an ostinato, while the low-pitched tubes play rhythmic patterns imitating those of the *tawak* and other large gongs. This tradition, including the names and styles of instrumental playing, strongly resembles some of the musical traditions of the Sulu Archipelago and the southern Philippines [see ISLAMIC COMMUNITIES OF THE SOUTHERN PHILIPPINES].

The music played on the xylophones of Borneo usually accompanies dancing, but it may also be heard in the performance of sung epics in Sabah, and perhaps in parts of Kalimantan. The xylophone of Sarawak and East Kalimantan is a small raft of slats suspended over a wooden, boxlike frame, or separate, tuned slats laid across the top of the frame. In both cases, the slats are struck with a pair of short wooden beaters as the player sits on the floor before the instrument. The Kenyah of Sarawak and East Kalimantan call this instrument *jatung utang,* and among some groups, its tuning is a pentatonic scale.

The xylophone in East Kalimantan was formerly a large raft of beams, suspended and played in fields of rice (Gorlinski 1989:286). Among the Kenyah peoples of central Borneo, the *jatung utang* is usually found in ensemble with a plucked lute (*sampi',* Kayan *sapeh* and *sapi'*), or with a mouth organ and a guitar, to perform music that accompanies dance. The dances of war (Iban *ngajat,* Kenyah *kanjet, kancet, tu'ut*) performed today by both male and female dancers are typically accompanied by two plucked lutes and the *jatung utang* (figure 9). The melodies of music for dancing are played heterophonically on a lute and a xylophone while a second lute provides an ostinato. The xylophonist provides a movable drone in the form of a repeated pitch, changing as required to support the central tone of melodic phrases as they shift from one range of the scale to another.

Alternately, in Sabah, the small raft xylophone (*gambang*) may be made of wood or bamboo with a boxlike frame. The slats are struck with a pair of padded beaters. Another xylophone, *gabbang,* played by the Suluk peoples along the eastern coast of Sabah, consists of tuned slats, laid crosswise on top of a wooden box resonator.

Finally, a simple version of the xylophone, consisting of slats laid across two short planks (positioned obliquely), is called the *kulintangan*—a term usually applied to the gong chime of Sabah. Rural peoples in the far north of Sabah say this *kulintangan* is used mostly by children to learn the melodic and rhythmic parts of pieces and techniques of playing before performing on the *kulintangan.* In north Borneo and possibly other parts of the island, a *gambang* or a *gabbang* accompanies dancing and the singing of epics. A typical ensemble consists of a *gabbang,* a pair of wooden or bamboo concussion idiophones, and a singer.

Notable wooden and bamboo idiophones in Borneo are a slit drum (*tengkuang*) and an idioglottic Jew's harp. The use of the slit drum today is uncertain, but the Jew's harp is found throughout the island, known by local names, including *ruding, geruding, bungkau, junggotan,* and *tong.* The player taps its base or pulls a string to create short rhythms. It usually played solo, but in parts of central Borneo, it is played with a tube zither (*satong*). In the *tong* and *satong* ensemble of the Kajang, a short, iterative melody on the *satong* is played simultaneously with a dronelike short rhythmic figure plucked on the Jew's harp (*tong*). A *tong* is sometimes played solo during courting; as a solo instrument and in ensembles, it provides music for general entertainment.

Chordophones

Lutes

A famous plucked lute in Sarawak and East Kalimantan is the *sapeh* (also known as *sape, sambe, sampi', sapi, sampeh,* and *sampeq*) of the Kayan, the Kenyah, and more recently the Kajang of the interior of Sarawak. It is usually made in pairs, ideally carved from the same tree trunk (Koizumi 1976:39–47). The body is a meter or more long, in a narrow rectangular shape (about 25 centimeters wide, tapering some 10 centimeters to the base end), with a hollow, open backside and a short homogeneous neck. Usually three or four wire strings, attached near the base of the body, run over small bridges and movable frets to lateral pegs at the top of the neck. The lowermost string, using the greatest number of frets, plays the melody, and the other strings play a dronelike ostinato.

Sapeh tunes may be played for general entertainment, but more frequently they accompany dancing. Line dances, the *ngajat lasan* (a solo dance of war performed by

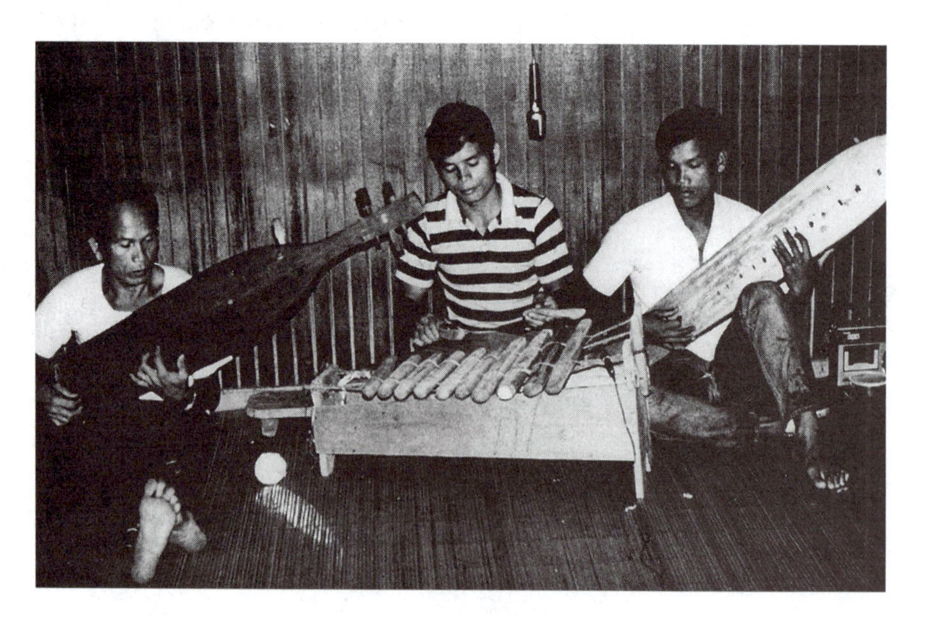

FIGURE 9 The ensemble of plucked lute (*sapeh*) and xylophone (*jatung utang*) plays music for dance among the Kayan and Kenyah peoples in Borneo. Photo by Patricia Matusky.

a dancer of either sex), the *musuh* (a battle dance, by two male dancers with shields and swords), and the *datun julud* (a collective female line dance) all require *sapeh* music accompaniment (for commentary on the *mandau* dance and musical accompaniment of the Dayaks of East Kalimantan, see Soedarsono 1968:219). The melody of a *sapeh* is usually sectionalized, with variations and specific ornaments featured in successive repetitions (Gorlinski 1988). An integral part of *sapeh* pieces is a melodic and rhythmic drone or ostinato, played every four beats throughout a piece by the player of the melody or a second player. Traits of *sapeh* pieces include an abundance of ornaments, the shifting of melodic phrases to and from the high register of the instrument, strict duple meter, and a continuous ostinato.

A lute still played in Sabah is the *sundatang,* a two- or three-stringed plucked lute with a long, rectangular body and long neck. Like the *sapeh* pieces, the tunes played on the *sundatang* have a repeated melody with an accompanying drone. Other lutes used at one time include the one- and two-stringed bowed lutes (*enserunai, merebab, rabup*) and the plucked *balikan* (also *blikan*) and *tinten* of the Iban and Bidayuh of Sarawak.

Tube zithers

Another important stringed instrument in Borneo is the bamboo idiochord tube zither called *satong* or *lutong* (in Sarawak and Kalimantan) and *tongkungon* (in Sabah). It consists of a section of bamboo, closed at each end by the natural node, but opened along its length by a carved slit. It has four to eight strings (depending on where it is found) cut from the cortex of the bamboo and tightened and tuned by wooden bridges inserted beneath the strings. The strings are plucked by the fingers as the tube is cradled in the hands and supported against the player's body. Solo, repeated melodies played on the *satong* may be three, four, or five beats in length. Some feature triplet or dotted rhythms, and the harmonic intervals frequently heard are thirds and fifths.

The *satong* is usually played alone for personal entertainment, though it may also be heard in ensemble with a Jew's harp (*tong*). In contrast, the tube zither of Sabah (*tongkungon*) plays music in imitation of orchestral music for hanging gongs. It has eight strings, tuned to match those of the hanging gong ensemble in a given village, and plucked to imitate the parts of the particular gongs. A similar use of the tube zither (*kecapi*) is found in the northeast region of Peninsular Malaysia, as players imitate the gong parts and drum parts of *wayang kulit.*

Other chordophones

Early writers on the peoples of Borneo mention two additional stringed instruments, a musical bow (*basoi,* also *busoi*) and a plucked harp (*engkeratung*) (Roth 1980 [1896]). The *basoi* is a single string attached to a bow, placed over a hollow pot or gourd resonator and struck with a wooden stick. The *engkeratung* is a small, angular harp using three to five strings, formerly played by the Maloh peoples of Sarawak (and perhaps West Kalimantan). The use and continued existence of these instruments are uncertain.

Aerophones

Flutes

The end-blown bamboo flute, ubiquitous in Malaysian Borneo and Kalimantan, is known by many terms, including *suling, seruling, kesuling, ensuling,* and *nabat.* Most local flutes have four or more equidistant holes near the distal end of the instrument, and are blown by positioning the tube vertically or somewhat obliquely to the

The Bidayuh of west Sarawak play large flutes in rituals to summon spirits and ordinarily use the small ones for courting.

FIGURE 10 Excerpt from a flute (*seruling*) melody of Borneo, in free rhythm.

mouth. In most mouth-blown flutes of Borneo, the blowhole is designed by shaving one end of the bamboo tube to obtain a sharp edge. Some *suling* are capable of playing an octave or more, and their soft melodic phrases are spun out in an improvisatory style, sometimes with little repetition, and descend the interval of a fourth or fifth at the end of each phrase. The rhythm is usually free (figure 10).

Flute music is sometimes heard at funerals, but is more commonly played for entertainment in intimate settings. The Bidayuh of west Sarawak call their mouth-blown flutes large-sized (*banci*) and small-sized (*encio*). They may play large flutes in rituals to summon spirits and ordinarily use the small ones for courting. Both in Bidayuh communities and among some groups in Sabah, these flutes are also played in ensembles. Similarly, the nose flute repertoire consists of soft, through-composed melodies, focusing on a given tonal area for several beats at the end of each phrase. Just as in music for mouth-blown flutes, the interval of a fifth is emphasized in many pieces for nose flutes, especially at the end of improvisatory melodic phrases. In the northern regions of Borneo, the nose flute (*selingut, selengut, turali, sangui*) is usually a solo instrument, played for events associated with religion or for individual entertainment.

Mouth organs

Mouth organs of Borneo are known by a variety of names, including *engkerurai* (among the Iban of Sarawak), *sumpotan, sumbiling, buah padas, tabarau,* and *kelulut* (in Sabah), and *keledi* or *keluri* (in central Borneo and other parts of Kalimantan). The number of pipes and the size of the wind chamber varies from one region to another. Most mouth organs of Borneo consist of six to eight single-reed bamboo pipes, tied in a bundle or a raft, with the section of the pipe containing the reed secured by beeswax (or a similar material) in a dried, hollowed gourd. The natural stem of the gourd serves as the mouthpiece, into which a player blows air, while covering the holes (at the base of the pipes) or the ends of the pipes themselves, producing specific pitches. One of the pipes always sounds as a drone.

The music played on a mouth organ may serve for general entertainment, but also accompanies dance. An archaic and rarely performed dance, performed by the neighboring Kajang and Kenyah of the interior regions of Sarawak, is a line dance by

FIGURE 11 In a typical performance on a bull roarer (*kidiu*) of Borneo, distinct pitches of short duration follow a regularly recurring pattern in duple meter.

both men and women, in which the lead dancer (a male) is the player of the mouth organ, whose melody, accompanying the steps of the dance, is structured in an eight-beat repeated phrase, with the drone pitch reiterated nearly every other beat. Its predominant harmonic intervals are the octave, third, fourth, and fifth, within the tonal context of a pentatonic scale.

Other winds

An aerophone associated with growing rice is the bull roarer, played by the Kenyah of Sarawak and central Borneo. Some Kenyah groups call it and its music *kidiu,* and play it to chase away pests as the stalks of rice are being harvested. It has a small, flat, rectangular piece of wood (barely half a centimeter thick) attached to a string attached to a meter-long stick. It comes in pairs (in both large and small sizes). As an individual player holds the stick of one *kidiu* and swings it through the air, the wood at the end of the string produces two pitches, depending on its direction and airspeed. In fields where rice is growing, two players of *kidiu* swing their instruments alternately, producing four different pitches in an interlocking rhythmic pattern. A typical performance produces distinct pitches of short duration in a regularly recurring pattern in duple meter (figure 11).

Other wind musics are played on simply made instruments, required or desired for a particular occasion. The reed instrument (*kungkuvak,* also *pumpuak*) of north Borneo is made from the leaf of the mature rice plant. Sustained tones or simple, short melodic phrases played on it can be heard as entertainment during the rice harvest.

REFERENCES

Frame, Edward. 1976. "Major Musical Forms in Sabah." *Journal of the Royal Asiatic Society, Malaysian Branch* 49(2):156–163.

———.1982. "The Musical Instruments of Sabah, Malaysia." *Ethnomusicology* 26(2):247–274.

Gorlinski, Virginia K. 1988. "Some Insights into the Art of *Sape* Playing." *Sarawak Museum Journal* 39, 60 (new series):77–104.

———. 1989. "*Pangpagaq:* Religious and Social Significance of a Traditional Kenyah Music-Dance Form." *Sarawak Museum Journal* 40, 61 (new series), part 3:280–301.

———. 1994 "Gongs among the Kenyah Uma' Jalan: Past and Present Position of an Instrumental Tradition." *Yearbook for Traditional Music* 26:81–99.

———. 1995. "Songs of Honor, Words of Respect: Social Contours of Kenyah Lepo' Tau Versification, Sarawak, Malaysia." Ph.D. dissertation, University of Wisconsin.

Hood, Mantle. 1980. "Outer Islands: Borneo (Kalimantan)." *The New Grove Dictionary of Music and Musicians,* ed. Stanley Sadie. London: Macmillan.

Hudson, Judith M. 1971. "Some Observations on Dance in Kalimantan." *Indonesia* 12:133–150.

Koizumi, Fumio, ed. 1976. *Asian Musics in an Asian Perspective, Report of Asian Traditional Performing Arts.* Tokyo: Heibonsha.

Leach, Edmund. 1950. *Social Science Research in Sarawak.* London: Her Majesty's Stationery Office.

Masing, James Jemut. 1981. "The Coming of The Gods: A Study of the Invocatory Chant (Timang Gawai Amat) of the Iban of the Baleh Region of Sarawak." Ph.D. dissertation, Australian National University.

Matusky, Patricia. 1986 and 1990. "Aspects of Musical Style among the Kajang, Kayan and Kenyah-Badang of the Upper Rejang River: A Preliminary Survey." *Sarawak Museum Journal* 36:185–229, 40: 115–49.

Ongkili, James P. 1974. "The Traditional Musical

Instruments of Sabah." In *Traditional Music and Drama of Southeast Asia,* ed. Mohd. Taib Osman, 327–335. Kuala Lumpur: Dewan Bahasa dan Pustaka.

Roth, Henry Ling. 1980 [1896]. *The Natives of Sarawak and British North Borneo.* 2 vols. London and Kuala Lumpur: Truslove and Hanson, and University of Malaya Press.

Rousseau, Jérôme. 1988. "Central Borneo: A Bibliography." *Sarawak Museum Journal* 38, 59 (new series). Special monograph 5

———. 1989. "The People of Central Borneo." *Sarawak Museum Journal* 40, 61 (new series), part 3:7–17.

Rubenstein, Carol. 1985. *The Honey Tree Song, Poems and Chants of Sarawak Dayaks.* Athens, Ohio, and London: Ohio University Press.

———. 1990. *The Nightbird Sings: Chants and Songs of Sarawak Dayaks.* Dumfriesshire, Scotland: Tynron Press.

Sandin, Benedict. 1974. "The Iban Music." In *Traditional Music and Drama of Southeast Asia,* ed. Mohd. Taib Osman, 320–326. Kuala Lumpur: Dewan Bahasa dan Pustaka.

Soedarsono. 1968. *Dances in Indonesia.* Jakarta: P. T. Gunung Agung.

Strickland, S. S. 1988. "Preliminary Notes on a Kejaman-Sekapan Oral Narrative Form." *Sarawak Museum Journal* 39, 60 (new series):67–75.

The Lowland Christian Philippines

Corazon Canave-Dioquino

The Philippines is an archipelago of 7,100 islands, bounded in the west by the South China Sea, in the south by the Celebes Sea, in the east by the Philippine Sea (which opens into the Pacific Ocean), and in the north by the East China Sea. It consists of seventy-seven provinces grouped in fifteen regions, including the Cordillera Autonomous Region (CAR) in the north, the Autonomous Region of Muslim Mindanao (ARMM) in the south, and the National Capital Region (NCR), which covers the metropolitan Manila area.

By religion, the population divides into three broad categories: Christians, Muslims, and followers of indigenous religions. Christians, the most numerous, are concentrated in the lowlands of Luzon and the Visayan Islands. Muslims are concentrated in Mindanao, the Sulu Islands, and southern Palawan. Followers of indigenous religions mostly inhabit upland northern Luzon, Mindanao, and Palawan.

This article focuses on the musical roots of the lowland Christians of Luzon and the Visayan Islands (the central islands of Panay, Negros, Cebu, Bohol, Leyte, and Samar). In southern Luzon, the provinces of Sorsogon, Albay, Camarines Sur, and Camarines Norte are collectively called the Bicol Region; the provinces of Quezon, Batangas, Laguna, Cavite, and Rizal, and the islands of Marinduque and Mindoro are collectively called the Tagalog Region.

PRE-CHRISTIAN MUSICAL TRADITIONS

When the Spaniards landed on Philippine soil, the indigenous Filipinos had a thriving musical culture of their own—a fact shown by numerous chroniclers, beginning with Antonio Pigafetta in 1521. Reports made by friars, civil servants, and travelers describe instrumental and vocal music, sometimes mentioned in passing, sometimes in detail. These reports cite various types of vocal genres, including epics relating genealogies and exploits of heroes and gods; work songs related to planting, harvesting, and fishing; ritual songs to drive away evil spirits, or to invoke blessings from good spirits; songs to celebrate festive occasions, particularly marriage, birth, victory at war, and the settling of tribal disputes; songs for mourning the dead; songs of courting; and children's game-playing songs. Musical instruments included those of bronze, wood, or bamboo—gongs, drums, flutes, zithers, lutes, clappers, and buzzers.

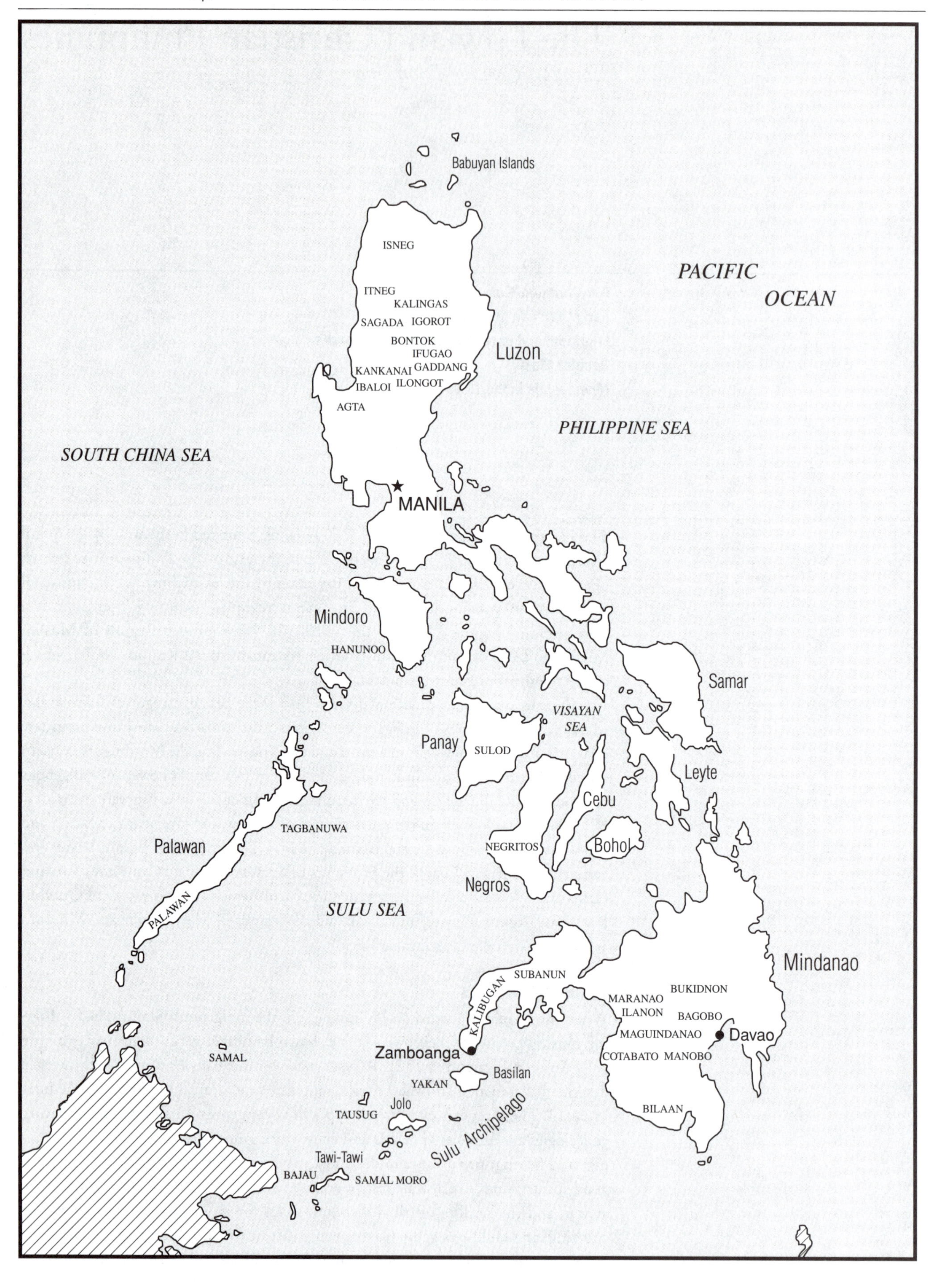
Babuyan Islands
ISNEG
ITNEG
KALINGAS
SAGADA
IGOROT
BONTOK
IFUGAO
KANKANAI
GADDANG
IBALOI
ILONGOT
AGTA
Luzon
PACIFIC OCEAN
PHILIPPINE SEA
SOUTH CHINA SEA
MANILA
Mindoro
HANUNOO
Samar
VISAYAN SEA
Panay
SULOD
Leyte
Cebu
TAGBANUWA
Palawan
NEGRITOS
Bohol
Negros
PALAWAN
SULU SEA
Mindanao
SUBANUN
KALIBUGAN
BUKIDNON
MARANAO
ILANON
BAGOBO
MAGUINDANAO
Davao
Zamboanga
COTABATO
MANOBO
SAMAL
Basilan
YAKAN
Jolo
TAUSUG
Sulu Archipelago
BILAAN
Tawi-Tawi
BAJAU
SAMAL MORO

(opposite) Cultural groups of the Philippines

Traditional musics still exist among indigenous tribes scattered throughout the archipelago, but the bulk of Filipino music was changed with the influx of Western influences, particularly Spanish-European culture, prevalent from the 1500s to the 1800s. During the period of Spanish colonization, a transformation of the people's musical thinking occurred, and a hybrid form of musical expression, heavily tinged with a Hispanic taste, sprouted and took root.

Hispanization was inextricably linked to religious conversion. The Spanish regime made the Filipinos construct parish churches, and missionaries taught the people to live in towns surrounding the churches. To attract the populace, the missionaries enhanced their liturgical rituals—the Mass and offices—with pomp and grandeur. Roman Catholic holy days and civil fiestas were celebrated with elaborate prayers and processions, accompanied by feasting and games, not unlike celebrations in Seville and Andalucía, in Spain.

EARLY CHRISTIAN INFLUENCES

Friars in religious orders were directly responsible for introducing a new musical language when they taught the *indios* (a term the Spaniards used for the natives) to perform Gregorian chant (*canto llano*) and polyphony (*canto de órgano*). The dispersal of religious orders all over the islands resulted in the widespread establishment of schools, where boys were taught the liturgy and its accompanying music.

The Franciscan order

A mandate issued by the Franciscan Order stipulated the establishment of primary schools for boys (*primeras escuelas de niños*) in all towns. In these schools, boys were to be taught to pray, read, write, count, and help at Mass and the administration of the sacraments. In addition, they were to be taught singing and how to play the organ, flutes, and the other musical instruments used in churches.

In 1606, the Franciscan Father Juan de Santa Marta (b. 1578), a tenor who had served in the cathedral of Zaragoza, Spain, was put in charge of a seminary in Lumbang, Laguna. Four hundred boys from nearby towns were subsequently trained in singing and the playing of musical instruments. Once the training was over, these boys returned to their respective towns to pass on to others what they had learned.

Other notable Franciscans were Father San Pedro Bautista (1542–1597), the first to teach Western music to the Tagalogs (of Pagsanjan, Lumbang, and Los Baños in Laguna province); Father Gerónimo Aguilar (d. 1591), who as guardian of the convent of Naga ordered the teaching of Gregorian chant, polyphony, and instruments in the towns of Camarines province; Father Antonio de Maqueda, who taught in Mahayhay, Laguna province; and Father José de la Virgen, assigned from 1717 to 1767 to the Bicol Region, where in Bicolano he wrote a book on Gregorian chant.

The Jesuit order

Father Pedro Chirino, Jesuit procurator in the Philippines, wrote in 1604 about the Jesuit work throughout the country before 1597. He cited the presence of choirs and music for organ, flutes, and clarinets, which performed for masses and vespers, and at rites celebrating solemn feasts, particularly during Holy Week and Easter. The congregation sang litanies, *salves* (hymns of praise to a saint), and *misereres* (hymns with texts similar to litanies, seeking forgiveness) In all the places he visited, he saw converts singing the doctrine (*cantando la doctrina*) in the chapels, at home, in the fields while working, and even in boats while fishing. This doctrine was *Doctrina Christiana* (1593), the first book printed in the Philippines. It contained texts of the Lord's Prayer, the Ave Maria, and two other prayers, with lists of the fourteen articles of faith, the seven sacraments, the seven capital sins, the fourteen acts of mercy, the Ten Commandments, and the act of general confession.

In Carigara, Leyte, ecclesiastical music was sung to Bisayan texts. Padre Antonio Masvesi, writing in 1748 about the life of Padre Pedro de Estrada, Jesuit provincial, mentioned Estrada's Bisayan *Historia de la Pasión de nuestro Señor Jesú Christo* (*Story of the Passion of our Lord Jesus Christ*) and various prayers and hymns to the Virgin Mary and other saints, and to the holy cross. The faithful were encouraged to sing these instead of indigenous music.

The Augustinian order

The Augustinians arrived on Philippine soil in 1565. An orchestra was organized in 1601 at the convent of Nuestra Señora de Guadalupe. Additional instruments for the orchestra were brought by Father Juan Torres in 1643. A teacher at the convent, Fray Marcelo de San Agustín (d. 1697), organist and composer, taught the choir.

Elsewhere in the Philippines, Father Lorenzo Castillo (1686–1743), composer of masses, *villancicos,* airs, and vespers, taught more than two thousand Tagalog, Ilocano, and Visayan (Panay and Cebu) boys. Other noted Augustinian friar-musicians included Father Juan Bolívar (arrived 1739) in Manila and Panay, Father Ignacio de Jesús (arrived 1737), choirmaster of Guadalupe Church, and Father José Calleja (arrived 1750).

Other friars' schools

The friars also established more formal schools, intended for the sons of native ruling families to be groomed as future leaders (*cabezas de barangay* 'heads of small towns', or *gobernadorcillos* 'little governors'). Aside from Roman Catholic doctrine and basic reading, writing, and arithmetic, the curriculum included vocal and instrumental music.

Some of the early schools were the Jesuits' Colegio de Manila (1595) and its annex, Colegio de Niños (1596). It was at the Colegio de Niños de la Santa Iglesia Catedral (Cathedral Boys' College), where many future Filipino musicians received their training. The school was founded in the early 1740s at the behest of the Archbishop of Manila, Juan Ángel Rodríguez, (d. 1742).

The impact of the friars' musical indoctrination of indigenous Filipinos was immeasurable. It gave rise to a new form of Spanish-influenced paraliturgical and secular folkloric music. It also created a new breed of Filipino musicians.

LITURGICAL AND PARALITURGICAL MUSICAL GENRES

As Filipinos embraced the new religion, they grafted indigenous traditions and practices onto Roman Catholic rituals and celebrations, many of which are still alive. Alongside liturgical music (including the Mass, hymns, psalm verses) many extraliturgical musical genres arose, in conformity with opportunities presented in the Christian liturgical calendar.

Christmas music

Carols

During Advent, which marks the beginning of the Christian ritual year, it became customary for carolers to roam through streets serenading households with their shepherds' songs (*pastores*). In Bicol, the *pastores sa belén,* also called *villancicos* (after seventeenth- and eighteenth-century Christmas songs cultivated in Mexico), are sung and danced. In Catanduanes after each Mass of the *misa de aguinaldo* (a novena of dawn masses, starting on 16 December), twelve young girls seek monetary contributions by going caroling dressed as angels in long robes and wide hats.

The Cuyunon sing the *tambora* or the *pastores,* the latter accompanied by a drum and a flute (*tambora kag tipanu*) or a larger band of chordophones and dancing. The Visayans call their Christmas songs *daigon* (also *dayegon* and *daygon*). In some areas of Cebu, specific *daigon* are sung on particular days; these include "*Rico, rico,*" for 23 and 24 December; "*Ato karong saulugon*" ('Let us celebrate'), for 15–31 December; "*Año Nuevo*" ('New Year'), for 1–5 January; "*Tulo ka mga hari*" ('Three Kings'), for 6–14 January; and "*Señor santo Niño*" ('Mister holy child'), for 15–31 January.

Panunuluyan

An elaborate outdoor drama, variously called *panunuluyan, pananawagan, pananapatan, o kagharong,* and *solomon* in different provinces, occurs on Christmas eve. Performed in the streets, this tradition reenacts Mary and Joseph's search for lodging. The Virgin and St. Joseph stop at designated houses, seeking shelter in song. The owner of the house turns them away, also in song. Eventually the holy couple end their search at the courtyard of the church, or inside the church, where a simulated stable has been erected.

The pageant ends with the birth of Jesus at midnight, climaxing with the midnight mass, replete with sung alleluias and Christmas carols. The pageant must have been patterned after Mexican *posadas,* but in Mexico the dramatic enactment occupies nine consecutive days before Christmas.

Lenten music

Pabasa *or* pasyon

The Lenten season is the occasion for many extraliturgical ceremonies. Foremost is the *pabasa,* the intoning of a passion (*pasyon*), a versified story of Jesus's death on the cross. Sponsored as part of a vow of thanksgiving for special favors received (*panata*), the *pasyon* is sung in homes, in makeshift sheds built along streets, or in barrio chapels. Its singing became nationwide during the Spanish period, but the date of its first public performance is unknown.

The Tagalog have five known versions of the *pasyon*; the Ilocano, the Pampango, the Bicolano, the Bisayan, and other groups have their own versions. Father Gaspar Aquino de Belén, the first known Filipino to write a *pasyon* text, in 1703 printed his Tagalog version, *Mahal na Passion ni Jesu Cristong Panginoon natin na Tola* (*Holy Passion of Jesus Christ Our Lord*).

The most popular Tagalog text is the *Kasaysayan ng Pasiong Mahal ni Hesukristong Panginoon Natin Sukat Ipag-alab ng Puso ng Sinumang Babasa* (*Story of the Holy Passion of Jesus Christ Designed to Inspire the Reader*), author unknown. It is also called the *Pasyon Henesis* or *Pasyon Pilapil* after Father Mariano Pilapil, who edited the text for publication in 1814. The extent of its use is attributed to its having been officially approved by the Roman Catholic hierarchy. Another text, *Pasyon Kandaba* (*Kandaba Passion*), printed in 1852, was *El libro de la vida: historia sagrada con santas reflexiones y doctrinas morales para la vida cristiana en verso tagalo* (*The Book of Life: Sacred History with Pious Reflections and Moral Teachings for the Christian Life Written in Tagalog Verse*) by Father Aniceto de la Merced, parish priest of Kandaba, Pampanga Province.

The text of the *Kasaysayan ng Pasyon Mahal* as edited by Mariano Pilapil consists of 2,660 stanzas, each consisting of five eight-syllable lines. It begins with the creation of the world, covers the life of Jesus, and ends with Empress Helena's finding

pasyon Versified story of Jesus' death on the cross, a "passion"

pabasa Another term for the Passion story, or *pasyon*

punto Skeletal melodic formula used in singing the *pasyon*

flores de Mayo Unofficial ritual of presenting flowers to the Virgin each day in May

tibag Outdoor drama reenacting the discovery of the cross on which Jesus was crucified

FIGURE 1 *Pasyon* melodic formula, *puntong taal.* The text—partly Latin, partly Tagalog—recounts Jesus' prayer in the Garden of Gethsemane: "My Father, if it is possible, let this cup pass away from me" (Luke 22:42).

the holy cross. It contains sixty-eight intervening episodes, which insert twenty moral lessons or sermons (*aral*). The stanzas of each episode may be performed in narrative (*salaysay*) or as dialogues.

The *pasyon* text is sung to basic or skeletal melodic formulas (*punto*), based on widely different tunes, ranging from old, traditional, chantlike melodies to those based on Westernized folk songs, operatic airs, and (more recently) popular hits. Older *punto* are of various types, known by local names, including *tres caídas, kinalamyas, biniyulin, taru, binangonan, sinauna, tabat,* and *inosana.* These tunes have specific styles, some of which refer to their area of origin. In the Tagalog Region, *tabat* is reserved for Good Friday, and *inosana* for Palm Sunday.

The *puntong taal* (a melodic formula of the Taal area) prevalent in southern Batangas has a range of a perfect fourth occasionally extending to a fifth. The text is set syllabically, but the ends of musical phrases have melismatic ornamentations, hovering above and below a resting tone. Though the skeletal shape of the *punto* is set, the chanter is free to ornament it.

Figure 1 is an example of the *puntong taal* as sung by a female chanter (Mirano 1991). It is a setting of one stanza from the *Kasaysayan ng Pasyon Mahal,* or *Pasyon Henesis.* Lines 1, 3, and 4 similarly move in an ascending pattern; lines 2 and 5 begin similarly, in a descending pattern. The ABAAB structure for each stanza is fairly consistent throughout this *punto.*

Chanting the entire *pasyon* takes from sixteen to twenty hours. The manner of chanting varies from region to region. Stanzas are sometimes sung by chanters (*mambabasa*) in round-robin style, and sometimes alternately by two chanters. Elaborate rituals may involve eight to twenty chanters divided into two groups: women chanters (*tiple* 'soprano') and men chanters (*baho* 'bass'). The chanters are seated around a long, low table, women on one side, men on the other, as the sides sing the stanzas alternately. A variation followed in Cuyo, Palawan, is responsorial, with an alternation between a leader and a chorus singing in harmony. Since the early 1990s, the *pabasa* has been aired over the radio, starting on Wednesday of Holy Week and ending on Good Friday.

The practice of the *pabasa* gave rise to related forms, which reflected cultural practices of pre-Spanish Filipinos at wakes and during the singing of epics. On such occasions, games of wit and riddles were chanted to keep the participants awake. The *sabalan, tumbukan,* and *tanungan* are *pasyon* debates, which take place after the chanting of the passion, while the chanters and invited guests receive food and refreshments. The *sabalan* is a game of wit, intended to show off one's mastery of the *pasyon* text. Two participants or two groups of participants engage in a display of poetic skill. The protagonist poses a question or a riddle, which the rival must answer by quoting a portion from the *pasyon* text. The exchange, performed in song using the *pasyon* melodic formulas, may go on until the early hours of the next day. It ends when one party cannot answer the other.

Variations of this poetic game are practiced in various areas, where they are known by other names. Quezon Province has a complicated version, called *tapatan,* which proceeds in several stages: *tapatan* (in front of the house), *sagutan* (in the doorway), *pagtanggap* (inside the house), *bugtungan* (the main body, consisting of riddles and answers, done in the house), and *pamamaalam* (leave-taking). At each stage, a lively exchange occurs, showing off the protagonists' mastery of the *pasyon* text. The exchange is intoned on a *pasyon punto* (melodic formula) (Yraola 1977).

Pananapat

In Rizal Province, *pananapat* takes the form of caroling. Singers intoning portions of the *pasyon* text go from house to house, where they receive coins, which they use to purchase items and services necessary for the processions that take place during Holy Week. These expenses include decorations for the carriages that carry the saints' images, fees for the bands hired to accompany the procession, and possibly food for the participants.

Outdoor rituals and dramas

Salubong

The elaborate Christian rituals of Holy Week gave rise to enacted playlets, like *Salubong sa Linggo ng Pagkabuhay* (*Easter Sunday Meeting*) and *Humenta. Salubong,* which occurs early on Easter Day, is a local creation based on the concept of the Virgin Mother meeting her newly risen son. Two processions, following different routes, leave the church. One procession, headed by the parish priest, carries the figure of the risen Jesus; the other procession is joined by the community, and bears the statue of the grieving Mary (Latin *Mater Dolorosa*), her face covered by a veil of mourning. Depending on availability, other figures—St. Peter, St. John, Mary Magdalene, Mary Salome, Mary Jacobe—may join the entourage.

At an appointed time, under an arch in the courtyard in front of the church, the processions meet. One, two, or more children dressed as angels are lowered from positions atop the arch, and they lift away Mary's veil—at which point the people sing a modern-style hymn based on the text of *Regina caeli laetare,* an antiphon sung at compline from Easter Sunday to Friday after Pentecost. Originally, the standard Gregorian chant may have been sung, but by the 1990s, the text had been set to hymns composed in a twentieth-century style of Western hymnody. More elaborate versions of the *salubong* use a band that plays a lovely *pasodoble* (march in double time) while church bells ring. The Easter Mass follows the ritual.

Humenta

This ritual takes its name from the figure of Christ on a donkey (*humenta*), which participates in a procession on the evening of Palm Sunday, accompanied by a band playing a funeral march (*punebre*). The procession stops at four points, where makeshift altars, decorated with palms and red banners, have been erected. At each stop, the hymn *Osana* is sung, in a different version at each station (Tiongson 1975). These versions are in a twentieth-century Western idiom, set to the Latin text of the first antiphon sung on Palm Sunday during the blessing of the palms: *Hosanna filio David.*

Moriones

More extended festivals and dramas emerged, though these no longer had any connection with liturgical services. The *moriones* in Marinduque (south of Luzon) is celebrated yearly from Wednesday of Holy Week to Easter Sunday. The name *morion* derives from a local term coined to refer to the centurions of Jesus's time, and the participants are called *moriones.* Colorful and grotesque masks made of wood cover their faces, and the typical costume is a bamboo helmet decorated with coconut bristles and colored paper, a long cape, a vest, and leggings.

The *moriones* prance around the streets, chasing children, playing pranks on onlookers, and creating chaos. As part of their performance, they carry the *kalutang,* an instrument made of two wooden sticks about 2.5 centimeters in diameter and 30 centimeters long, struck against each other, on which they incessantly produce vigorous rhythms.

The climax of the festival occurs on Easter Sunday, when the open-air drama *Pugutan* is reenacted. Principal characters include a legendary blind centurion, Longinus (whose sight was supposedly restored when a drop of Jesus's blood fell on him), scribes, Pharisees (played by prominent local citizens), Pontius Pilate, and some high priests. The drama starts when Longinus, wearing a frightful one-eyed mask, is appointed to guard the tomb of Jesus. He witnesses the Resurrection, runs to report it to Pilate, and proclaims the news to the town. The *moriones* give chase and catch him, but he escapes. This happens seven times, until Longinus surrenders. Pilate orders his beheading (the mask is removed), and the headless Longinus is paraded around town by the jubilant *moriones.* Longinus is finally laid to rest at high noon of Easter Sunday.

Senaculo

A more widespread drama staged during the Lenten season, particularly during Holy Week, is the *senaculo* 'cenacle' (the room in which the Last Supper occurred). This play portrays the life of Jesus, beginning with the events leading to his birth and ending with the assumption of Mary into heaven and her coronation there. Its texts come from the *Pasyon Henesis,* the *Pasyon Kandaba,* and three other volumes: *Martir sa Golgota* (*Martyrs of Golgotha*), the *Quince Misterios* (*Fifteen Mysteries*), and the *Tronco del Mundo* (*Origin of the World*).

Presentations of *senaculo* began around the first decade of the 1800s and had reached full flowering by the 1890s. Versions of this play exist in Bicolano, Bisaya, Ilocano, Pampango, Tagalog, and other major languages of the islands. The *senaculo* involves a cast of thirty or more characters. Presentations of *senaculo* lasted several nights. It was staged in the town plaza, or in the courtyard of the church, and from neighboring and outlying *barrios* attracted thousands of onlookers, who came on foot or by water-buffalo cart.

Lines are either spoken (*ablada*) or sung (*cantada*). Sung lines are delivered syllabically on melodic formulas (*punto*), resembling inflected monotones. Simple turns occasionally break the reciting tone, particularly at the ends of lines. The melodic range of the *punto* usually does not exceed a sixth. These *punto* are delivered in specific styles, each of which corresponds to one kind of character. The *tagulaylay* style, for example, is reserved for Jesus, the Virgin Mary, and other holy characters.

The instruments that make up the accompanying band depend on what is available or affordable. Instruments typically used are clarinet, cornet, trombone, string bass, large drum (*bombo*), smaller drums, and cymbals. The band accompanies the main characters' entrances and exits. A march in *pasodoble* time underscores the pride and arrogance of the Kings, their soldiers, Judas, and the devil. Solemn and slow, the funeral march (*punebre*) accompanies Jesus, the Virgin Mary, and the other holy (*banal*) characters. These marches, in simple four-measure phrases of varying structures (such as ABAC and ABAB) may be originally composed. Some performances feature a famous march such as Chopin's Funeral March or the "Colonel Bogey March" when the latter was at the height of its popularity, occasioned by its use in the film *The Bridge over the River Kwai* in the 1950s.

Maytime festivities with music

May is the month in the Christian calendar dedicated to Mary, and the month when feasts of patron saints are celebrated.

Flores de Mayo

Devotion to Mary took the form of several rituals, which (though not part of official texts) are celebrated inside the church. During the whole month of May, it became customary to offer flowers to Mary every afternoon. The offering is called *flores de Mayo* (also *floresan* and *bulaklakan*). The practice is said to have started around 1865. The rosary is recited, and between the mysteries, hymns in a nineteenth-century Western idiom, known to adults and children, are sung.

This practice has many variations. In southern Luzon, it is called Offering to Mary (*Alay kay Maria*). Set hymns are sung first by the offerers of garlands, and then by the carriers of bouquets. Then the entire participating community sings a forty-five-stanza *dalit,* with a refrain intervening between stanzas. The text of each stanza and the refrain are each made up of four eight-syllable lines. The music to these hymns is composed by local musicians.

Tibag

An outdoor drama reenacting the search for and supposed discovery of the cross on which Jesus was crucified used to be performed in the streets during the months of April and May. Main characters included the Empress Helena, her son Prince Constantine, and a retinue of ministers, generals, and soldiers. Several mounds of earth were set up in the town near the plaza. They represented the hills and mountains that had to be leveled so the cross could be found; hence the name *tibag* 'to dig'. When found, the cross was carried into the church. The text of the *tibag* was in verse, and may have been intoned or sung (Tiongson 1975).

Santacrusan

The *tibag,* no longer performed, gave rise to *santacrusan,* a widespread folkloric tradition. Processions honoring the holy cross, these are held in the town streets during May. Participants holding lighted candles sing "*Dios te salve, Maria*" ('God save you,

May is the month of fiestas honoring local patron saints with feasts and merriment, invariably including band music, singing, and dancing.

Mary') and "*Kruz na Mahal*" ('Beloved Holy Cross'). Sometimes flowers are strewn along the way. Sometimes the procession is held only for nine consecutive days instead of each day of the month. Usually on the last Sunday of May, a large celebration, *patapos,* is held. The procession is more elaborate and is often accompanied by a band; expenses are borne by a sponsor, called brother (*hermano*) or sister (*hermana*). Participants wearing elaborate gowns represent different personages.

The procession follows black-painted children, who represent the pagans before the Spaniards' arrival. At the head of the procession are the holy cross and bearers of candles (*siryales*), followed by a flag bearer (*abanderada*) carrying the Philippine flag and St. Macarius representing the monks. The principal personages are the Empress Helena with her escort Prince Constantine and the Queen of the Flowers. More elaborate processions include imagery taken from the Old Testament and the Litany of the Virgin, such as Judith, Esther, Tower of David, Faith, Hope, Charity, Stella Matutina (Morning Star), and others.

Subli

Another devotion to the holy cross, called *subli,* is practiced in southern Batangas. This practice venerates an icon called Mahal na Poong Santa Krus (Holy Christ Crucified). An account dated about 1595 (de Castro 1790) tells of the miraculous powers of this cross, but the earliest written description of the *subli* appeared in 1888 (Retana 1888). The *subli,* then and today, is performed in honor of the Mahal na Poon as part of a vow (*panata*) in thanksgiving for blessings received. It consists of *laro,* a series of musical items, dances, and poems.

Subli songs are strophic. Each is sung to a melodic formula (*punto*), ornamented by the performer. The songs are sung solo or responsorially by two groups of female singers. The text is heptasyllabic, with four lines per stanza; some stanzas have five to seven lines. When the dancing begins, the drum (*tugtugan*) and bamboo percussion tube (*kalatong*) play an ostinato-like rhythm, often drowning out the singing. In the *awitan* section, the solo singer, accompanied by a guitar or by the drum, sings twelve-syllable verses while the dancers continue. The dancers, separate groups of men and women, execute intricate patterns of steps, moving in circles and squares, intersecting while turning, and exchanging places using basic steps and gestures underscored by the drum and bamboo castanets held in their hands. *Subli* performances abound in May, particularly on the Feast of the Finding of the Holy Cross celebrated on the third of the month (Mirano 1989).

Other celebrations

Town fiestas

May is the month of fiestas honoring local patron saints with feasts and merriment, invariably including band music, singing, and dancing. A popular patron saint is Saint Isidore the Farm-Laborer, whose feast is celebrated on 15 May. He is the patron of hundreds of towns in Pampanga, Nueva Ecija, Tarlac, Laguna, Ilocos Sur, Pangasinan, and Batangas.

Saint Isidore the Farm-Laborer is the patron of an abundant harvest. In San Isidro Nueva Ecija, the fiesta includes a parade of male water buffaloes, farmers carrying samples of their harvest, and fishermen carrying nets and baskets. Young and old dance in the streets to the music of the town band. Others sing to the accompaniment of a guitar or a *bandurria,* an instrument of the lute family. In Lucban, Quezon, the townspeople decorate their homes with multicolored and many-shaped *kipping,* made of finely ground rice flattened into thin sheets resembling onionskin paper. Vegetables, fruits, and native cakes are likewise displayed, hung in windows and doorways. Every house along the route of the afternoon procession is elaborately decorated. The procession starts in the church and winds its way along the streets. After it has passed, visitors and spectators customarily grab the decorations.

Pangangaluluwa

All Saints Day and All Souls Day (1 and 2 November) are important dates in the Filipino Christian calendar. On these days, ordinary business comes to a halt, and households assemble in cemeteries to pay homage to their dead. They clean the graves and decorate them with flowers. They light candles and string electric bulbs, and spend most of the day and night keeping vigil while feasting on packed meals. In the Tagalog Region, groups of singers roam the streets in the evening, serenading households with *pangangaluluwa* (also *palimos*). In sixteen-syllable quatrains, each song greets the owner of the house, narrates a miraculous event in the Bible, and ends with a plea for alms.

SECULAR MUSIC

Lowland rural Christian Filipinos continue to celebrate life-cycle, occupational, and social events with the making of music. The music exhibits a blend of Asian and western styles. Life-cycle songs include lullabies, songs of love, nuptial songs, songs of death, and burial songs.

Lullabies

Lullabies have improvised texts addressed to the child, explaining why the mother is away, exhorting him to be good, or promising a reward on waking up. Among the Tagalog, the lullaby is called *huluna* or *oyayi.* The melodies have a narrow range—three neighboring notes, ornamented with turns (figure 2). Other terms for lullaby are *yekyek* (Bikol), *duruyanon* (Ilongo), and *duaya* (Pangasinan). In the following text of a *huluna* (after Mirano 1991:63, trans. C. C. Dioquino), the mother gives a reassuring reason for being away. Leng is a name by which young girls are called; Biyanggo is a person's nickname.

Ay Leng, tulog ka na.	Leng, go to sleep.
Ay kung tutulog di'y,	When you sleep,
Ang ina mo'y nasa malayo.	Your mother will be far away.
Nasa kabila ng pinto	She will be outside the door
At nananahi ng iyong baro	Sewing your dress
Na dadala kay Biyanggo.	To take to Biyanggo.

Songs of love, courtship, and marriage

Harana

Comprising a large repertoire, *harana* (Spanish *jarana* 'serenade') is the umbrella term for serenades among the Tagalog, the Pampango, the Bikolano, the Ilocano, and the Pangasinan. Among the Tagalog, the serenade consists of a series of songs.

FIGURE 2 Lullaby (*huluna*), as sung by Francisco Caringal. Note the narrow range and long passages of ornamentation on single syllables.

*Leng is a name by which young gilrs are called.

**Biyanggo is a nickname of a person.

The *pananapatan* (also *pagtawag* or *pagpapakilala*) is sung beside a young lady's window. The lady usually waits until after a second song has been sung before opening the window. She then invites the serenaders into the house, and they sing a *pasasalamat* to thank her for the invitation. This they follow with a *pagtumbok*, which requests the young lady to sing a song. A second request-song, called *paghiling,* follows. What ensues is an exchange of songs between the young lady and the serenaders. When the serenaders leave, they sing a *pamamaalam* (Yraola 1977).

The texts of these songs follow the structure of traditional Tagalog poetry (*plosa*), consisting of quatrains of twelve-syllable lines. The music, in the Western idiom, uses I–IV–V progressions, often accompanied by a guitar.

Kumintang

Various nineteenth-century accounts—de Mas 1843, Mallat 1846, Walls y Merino 1892, Martínez de Zúñiga 1893, Paterno 1893—mention the *kumintang,* a term that denotes several related things: a song, a style, a dance, and a combination of these. It may serve as a term for songs whose text, though about love, may express other feelings, like anger and resentment. Some songs are narrative; others make social commentaries.

The name *kumintang* was given to a large area in southern Luzon, covering what is now Batangas, Mindoro, and part of Laguna. The prevalence of this genre in this area accounts for the use of the term *kumintang* to denote the melodic style peculiar to the region. The *kumintang* was also danced, depicting love between a man and a woman. The friars frowned on the sensuousness of this display.

Musical debates

Musical debates are common. These debates originated from pre-Spanish games of wit called *duplo* and *karagatan,* and were verbal battles between two people or two camps, based on any topic. Among the Ilongo, the *bensiranay* (also *banggi*) is a debate sung by serenaders after they have been invited into a house. The Sebuano sing the *balitaw,* a debate-dance between a man and woman. In Pangasinan, such debates are called *turba*; in Ilocos, similar songs are called *inarem.*

Pamanhikan

A tradition among lowland Christian Filipinos is *pamanhikan,* asking for a prospective bride's hand. Its attendant ceremonies vary from simple to elaborate. An extended version consists of three stages: proposal (*bulong*), agreement (*kayari*), and offering (*dulog*). In the proposal, the suitor's representatives visit the young lady's parents, subtly expressing their purpose with sung verses. After the proposal, the suitor must render service (cutting firewood, fetching water, helping plant and harvest) to his loved one's family.

The agreement takes place after weeks of service. The suitor's representatives visit the girl's family, and if the suitor has been deemed acceptable, they are invited to return. Several visits by these representatives ensue, when gifts of food, wine, and cigarettes are brought. Singers of *kumintang* accompany the representatives. At the actual agreement, a representative of the bridegroom-to-be offers a toast in verse, using *plosa* structure. Another spokesman recites more verses. Then the singers perform didactic verses concerning good assets and noble customs. The girl's spokesman responds in verse, and a long exchange of verses by both parties, interspersed with more verses by the singers, follows until the girl's father seals the covenant by lighting some candles.

During the last stage of the *pamanhikan,* the date and time for the wedding is set. This stage is accompanied by feasting, merrymaking, singing, and dancing. Although this type of *pamanhikan* prevailed during the Spanish regime, it no longer takes place. A simpler version occurs in rural Tagalog areas. The boy's and the girl's parties merely exchange verses and sing songs. Often professional singers are hired for the occasion. Ilocanos sing *insiglot* or *inikamen* like a debate while making arrangements for the marriage.

Music for death

The Filipinos show love and respect for the dead in different rituals. A three-day wake, *patatlo,* is accorded to a young person; a nine-day wake, *pasiyam,* to adults. Wakes are the occasion for friends and relatives to join the grieving family in prayer. Visitors stay up all night, keeping awake by guessing riddles (*bugtungan*) and playing games of pledges (*juego de prenda*). They intone improvised verses called *dalit, duplo,* and *karagatan,* all of which the archbishop of Manila pronounced illegal and irreligious in 1741.

The *dalit* is always sung after opening prayers, which include the Lord's Prayer and the Hail Mary. It is based on a text of four- to eight-syllable verses and sets the tone for the ensuing activities. The *duplo* is a poetical contest delivered extemporaneously in *plosa* form. The topics are limitless, stressing exaggerated rhetoric, mixed with humor and sarcasm, allegories, and witticisms. The contest between two protagonists can last all night. Similar to the *duplo* is the *karagatan,* a game in which participants try to recover a ring. The finder of the ring is given the right to claim its owner's affection. The joust in verse takes place between men and women. Other songs for the dead include the Ilocano *dung-aw,* the Ilongo *belasyon* and *bensidoray,* the Cuyunin *pulao,* and the Bicolano *dotok.*

Music for birthdays and anniversaries

A unique tradition in the island of Marinduque, southwest of Luzon, is the *putong* (also *panubong*), which honors a birthday celebrant or an important visitor. Serenaders sing a series of songs in three parts: first at the gate of the house, second

pandanggo Work song from Batangas accompanied by a guitar

sanghiyang Thanksgiving ritual for good fortune or other matters, from Cavite

kagong Curing ritual from Bataan performed by twelve priests and priestesses

awit Metrical romances of Christians and Muslims, recited on melodic formulas

corrido Story about Christians and Muslims, recited on melodic formulas

while entering the house, and finally in front of the honoree. They give the honoree, seated in the middle of the drawing room between two children dressed as angels, a floral crown (*putong*). Some dance before the celebrant, while others strew flowers and coins on the floor.

Occupational songs

Farmers in rural areas sing different types of work songs. In Batangas, the *pandanggo* is a song-dance accompanied by a guitar. Male participants are called *pandanggeros*; females, *pandanggeras.* They sing while dancing with stamping steps accentuated by clapping hands. The text of their songs may be based on passages from the Bible or a passion. Sometimes the text is based on metrical romances, whose text is said to be *orihinal* (from Spanish *original*). When the text is on the subject of love, courtship, or marriage, it is called *pabula* (also *palipad*). Singing may be done as in a debate between two participants, or like a narration by one singer.

In Cavite, a song called *karansa* is accompanied by a split bamboo clapper (*katupi*). A similar song in Batangas is called *talalay,* and the bamboo clapper is called *talampi.* These songs are sung by musicians in the fields, while planting or weeding.

Fishermen sing the *malahiya* while out at sea. It may be sung as a solo song or as in a debate between two singers. The text is improvised to a basic melodic formula.

Ritual music

As most lowland Filipinos converted to Roman Catholicism, pagan rites gave way to folkloric Christianity. Practices involving offerings of food and sacrifices to spirits became intertwined with invocations to Jesus as God, and to his mother and other saints. In Cavite, the *sanghiyang* ritual is done in thanksgiving for good fortune, in supplication for a better future, to cure a sick person, and to inaugurate a new home. It begins with a recitation of the rosary and a litany of saints. Offerings of cakes made of rice, fried bananas, boiled eggs, chicken, and boiled meat are arranged in a particular pattern on a low table, with lighted candles, medals, a rosary, cigarettes, and old coins. Reciting prayers in a half-spoken, half-sung manner, the medium (*magsasanghiyang*) invokes spirits and gods, and goes into a trance.

Kagong, a similar curing ritual in Bataan, is performed by twelve priests and priestesses. Softly intoning a prayer, they arrange their medals, amulets, stones, and dried leaves on a plate before the sick person, whom they dance around, to the accompaniment of two guitars and a *bandurria,* shouting occasionally. In a trancelike state, they catch the evil spirit with a red handkerchief.

Epics, metrical romances, ballads

Among the Christian communities, the most famous epics are the Ilocano *Lam-ang* and the Bicolano *Ibalon.* In the 1800s, the popularity of these epics waned, and in their place metrical romances, introduced by Spanish colonizers, took over. These were stories of dashing knights, of princes and princesses, of biblical heroes, of Greek and Roman gods. A favorite topic was conflicts between Christians and Muslims. Known as *awit* and *corrido,* the stories were recited on set melodic formulas. The two forms differ in poetic structure and style of rendition. The most famous *awits* in Philippine literature are *Florante at Laura, Don Juan Tiñoso,* and *Siete Infantes de Lara*; the most popular *corrido* is *Ibong Adarna.*

The *awit* as cited in several travelogues bears different connotations. *Awit* is an umbrella term for song; however, it may refer more specifically to the intonation of metrical romances, and to melodic formulas used to improvise texts in accompaniment to dancing, as in the *pandanggo.* In some hispanized areas, ballads about heroes or historical events, or commentaries on social and political events, are still sung. The Visayan *composo* is one such ballad. It is sung to set melodies in the Western diatonic idiom, often with a guitar strumming I–IV–V harmonies.

Florante at Laura, by Francisco Baltazar (also known as Balagtas), is one of the best known of the metrical romances. It is an *awit,* written in dodecasyllabic quatrains and couplets. Frequently quoted excerpts include the couplet on the rearing of children (Tiongson 1994:340):

Ang laki sa layaw, karaniwa'y hubad
Sa bait at munit, sa hatol ay salat.

Reared in ease, one is deficient
In good sense, and in judgment.

The quatrain on the power of love is likewise cited often.

O pagsintang labis na makapangyarihan,
Sampung mag-aama'y iyong nasasaklaw.
Pag ikaw ang nasok sa puso pinuman,
Hahamaking lahat masunod ka lamang.

Love, your allure is overpowering,
And you rule over both fathers and sons.
When you enter the heart of anyone,
He would defy all to follow your bidding.

The story of this text is encapsulated in its title: *Florante and Laura in the Kingdom of Albania—Based on Various Historical Scenes or Portraits Relating to Events in Olden Times in the Greek Empire—and Written in Verse by One Who Delights in Tagalog Verse.* It was first published in 1853 and has since undergone numerous editions in Tagalog and translations in Pampango, Bicol, Pangasinan, English, Spanish, and German.

The *corrido Ibong Adarna,* by an anonymous author, is about the search for a magic bird by three princes: Don Pedro, Don Diego, and Don Juan. It was first published in 1900. As in most metrical romances, *Ibong Adarna* opens with a religious invocation (Damiana 1987:166, trans. C. C. Dioquino).

O Virgen Inang marikit,
Emperadora ng Langit,
tulungan po yaring isip
matutong makapagsulit.

Oh, beautiful Virgin Mother,
Empress of Heaven,
Help this mind
Learn what to say.

Sa awa mo po't talaga,
Virgeng walang makapara,
akong hamak na oveja
hulugan nang iyong gracia.

In your mercy,
Virgin without compare,
On me, this humble lamb,
Pour forth your grace.

MUSICAL LIFE IN THE 1800s

In the mid-1800s, exposure to more forms of Western music occurred in urban areas. There was an increased interest in music other than that used in the church or to accompany daily activities. Piano lessons were given to young girls at the Beaterio de

Santa Catalina (established in 1696). At the Colegio Español de Educación de Señoritas, music was part of a curriculum that included French, drawing, and sewing. In boys' schools, vocal and instrumental music was taught alongside physics, metaphysics, and philosophy. Eventually the products of such an education formed an elite group that cultivated Western arts, facilitating the further dissemination of Western concepts.

The members of this educated elite, called *ilustrados,* patronized concerts and operas, or hosted informal gatherings (*tertulias*), evening entertainments that included renditions of music and poetry. Favorite compositions included light classical works, and piano transcriptions of operatic airs by Rossini and Verdi.

Dances

Dances from Mexico, Spain, and other European cities were performed at balls or soirées. Before long, foreign dances like the habanera, the tango, the fandango, the *seguidilla,* the *jota,* the *curacha,* the polka, the mazurka, the *danza,* and the rigadoon were adopted. Today, they form the bulk of popular dances of lowland Christians. The Castilian and Andalusian fandango became the local *pandanggo.* It retained the triple time and the moderately fast tempo of its model (the waltz), but as it spread, each locality developed its own typical movements and accessories. The hat used in the Visayan and Ilocano *pandanggo* is replaced by lighted lamps in Mindoro.

Variations of the Spanish *jota* from Aragon became indispensable at provincial fiestas, and thus there arose the *jota paloana* of Palo, Leyte; the *jota vintarina* of Vintar, Ilocos Norte; the *jota batangueña* of Batangas, and many more.

The rhythms of the Cuban habanera in slow or moderate duple time and its later outgrowths, the *danza* and the tango, were incorporated into many dances. Examples are the *mascota* of Isabela, the *sainita* of Nueva Viscaya, and the *annafunan* of Cagayan. In the 1900s, many composers wrote music in the *danza* habanera style.

European ballroom dances, including the polka, the mazurka, and the waltz (*valse*), were popular at soirées and balls in the 1800s. In time, they faded from the ballroom scene, but variants appeared in regional lowland dances and folk songs. The quick duple rhythms of the polka are present in the Ilocano *pamulinawen* and the Tagalog *leron-leron sinta.* The rigadoon, once a French courtly dance, became the *rigodón,* which opens a prestigious state, national, provincial, or community function, participated in by people of high social standing.

The music for all these dances is homophonic, harmonized in the major-minor tonal system. The melodies are cast in strictly phrased eight-measure periods or sixteen-measure double periods. The music is divided into sections ranging from two to more than eight. Each section is variously repeated, to form structures such as ABAB, ABACAB, and so on. Occasionally there is a metric or tonal change in the sections.

The dances were accompanied by whatever instruments were available. Walls y Merino (1892) cites the guitar and bass guitar (*bajo de unas*) as the usual combination in towns, though he also saw an ensemble of one clarinet and two trombones. In the later period of the Spanish regime, a favorite accompanying ensemble was the *cumparsa* (also *comparsa*), said to have been an adaptation of similar instrumental groups, the *murza* (also *murga*) in Mexico and Spain and the *estudiantina,* popular in Spanish universities. During the early years of the American regime, the *cumparsa* was superseded by the *rondalla.*

Rondalla

The *rondalla* is an ensemble consisting of plucked instruments: the *bandurria,* the *laud,* the *octavina,* the six-stringed *gitara,* and the bass guitar. The *bandurria* is pear-shaped lute with a flat back, a round hole, and a fretted neck. It has fourteen strings, tuned in fourths: f♯–b–e_1–a_1–d_2–g_2. It serves as the melodic instrument of the ensemble. The *laud* and the *octavina* are tuned like the *bandurria,* but pitched an octave lower. They supply the inner harmonies of the ensemble, but may furnish contrapuntal elaborations to the *bandurria*'s melodic lines. The *laud* is shaped like the *bandurria,* but has a longer neck and two f-holes. The *octavina* is shaped like a small guitar. The *gitara* may be six-stringed or five-stringed, the former being more common. The six strings are tuned to e–a–d_1–g_1–b_1–e_2. Its main function is to supply the arpeggiated or chordal underpinnings of the melody. The four-stringed bass guitar is tuned like the contrabass. Before 1910, it was slightly bigger than the ordinary guitar, and was played on the performer's lap. When it was enlarged, it was supplied with a tailpiece, and hence was played upright, like the contrabass.

The size of a *rondalla* ensemble ranges from about eight to thirty or more instruments. A small *cumparsa* could consist of one *bandurria,* one *gitara,* and one bass guitar, but the usual *rondalla* ensemble consists of four *bandurrias,* one *laud,* one *octavina,* one *gitara* and one bass guitar. Larger formations include more than sixteen *bandurrias* and three each of the other instruments.

Today, such groups play in concert performances. Lately, a *piccolo bandurria* has been introduced, as have a variety of percussion instruments, whose number varies, depending on the demands of the music. The percussion group may include a bass drum, a snare drum, cymbals, a marimba, tambourines, castanets, triangles, and a tom-tom.

The repertoire of these ensembles ranges from simple folk songs to arrangements of Baroque music for lute and guitar, classical overtures and operatic arias. *Rondallas* were in vogue at the beginning of the 1900s. Resurgences of *rondalla* groups occurred in the 1940s, the 1950s, and again in the 1970s. Many schools and companies have their own *rondallas.*

Kundiman

Kundiman, lyrical songs of love popular in the 1800s, were composed in the Western idiom. They usually began in a minor key, and in their second half shifted to a major one. The lyrics are on romantic love, and usually portray the faithful but forlorn pleadings of a lover willing to sacrifice all on behalf of his beloved. *Kundiman* also served as a vehicle to express patriotic sentiments.

Folkloric dramas

In rural areas, a favorite form of entertainment, particularly during fiestas, was dramas. Outdoor presentations, they resembled religious reenactments like the *pananawagan* and the *senaculo.*

Carillo

One such type of outdoor presentation was the *carillo,* a shadow play that used cardboard figures held before a lighted lamp, projecting their shadows onto a white sheet. Themes of the plays were medieval tales and legends. Spoken parts were drawn from *corridos* or *awits,* with native songs interspersed between scenes. In Tagalog areas, the play was called *carillo,* but it was called *titre* in Bataan, Ilocos, Pangasinan, and the Visayas; *gaglo* or *kikimut* in Pampanga; and *aliala* in La Union.

It is not known exactly when the *carillo* began, though it was pre-Spanish, and may have been introduced by Malay immigrants. Early presentations used themes derived from the Indonesian *wayang.* During Spanish times, these gave way to themes taken from the metrical romances. The *carillo* was brought to Manila in the later 1800s. An area in Quiapo, Manila, was called *karilyuhan* 'place where *carillos* are performed'. The form died out during the early twentieth century.

Themes of *sarswelas* revolved around idealized Filipino characters and situations in a romantic love story. A prevailing theme was the Filipino family—the love of a poor boy and a rich girl, the quarrel between a jealous wife and a tired husband.

Moro-moro

The *moro-moro* is an old form of drama with music accompanying entrances, exits, duels, and fights. It is a type of *comedia,* the melodrama brought to the islands by the Spaniards, featured in celebrations for important persons or during feasts of saints. It depicts conflicts between Christians and Muslims. In rural areas, it was performed in open spaces. The missionaries used it for religious purposes, for they found in it a means of gathering crowds and projecting Roman Catholicism. Eventually it made its way to the stages of more formal theaters.

In Manila, several theaters catered to the *moro-moro.* The earliest was Teatro Cómico, built in 1790. By 1850, several theaters—Teatro Lírico de Tondo, Teatro Arroceros, Teatro Binondo, Primitivo Theater, and Teatro Rizal were presenting these plays to an audience that included foreigners.

Music is an essential part of the *moro-moro.* The traditional guitar and percussion accompaniments were augmented by brass instruments borrowed from town bands. As in the *senaculo,* the *marcha* (in a slow tempo) and the *pasodoble* (in a fast tempo) accompany the entrances and exits of the actors. Usually the *marcha* is reserved for Christians—kings, queens, princes, and princesses, and the *pasodoble* is used for the Muslims (*moros*). Fights, performed in set movements (which vary by region), are accompanied by the *pasodoble.* The *punebre,* a funeral march, accompanies lamentations. Snare drums and cymbals are used for lightning and thunder effects. Personages of high rank are announced by trumpet calls.

Moro-moro texts are written in twelve-syllable quatrains (though some have two, five, or six lines) with a caesura after the sixth syllable. Originally, verses were chanted on melodic formulas resembling those used in *pasyon,* but later, lines were declaimed on a pitch higher than that of the normal speaking voice. The *moro-moro* was known as *curalda* or *kumidya* in Pampanga, *linambay* in Cebu, *colloquio* in Bikol, and *bakal-bakal* in Pangasinan.

Sarswela

A theatrical form that had a tremendous impact on native drama was the Spanish zarzuela, a play with music and dance. It was introduced to the Philippines in 1879 with the performance of *Jugar con Fuego* (*To Play with Fire*) by a troupe led by Dario Céspedes. It was, however, Alejandro Cubero (with his wife Elisea Raguer) who organized a zarzuela troupe using local talents. Famous local zarzuela actors were Ignacio Ramos, Alfredo Ratia, Juan Reyes Bautista, Joaquin Gavino, Patrocinio Tagorama, Antonina Bautista, Candelaria Punzalán Patrocinio Carvajal, Titay Molina, Venancia Suzara, María Cárpena Práxedes, Julia Fernández, and Juana Ángeles. Eventually, Filipino playwrights began writing zarzuelas in Spanish for theatrical groups. By 1900, native *sarswelas* in the vernacular had emerged in Pampanga, Cebu, Bohol, Pangasinan, Ilocos, Iloilo, and the Tagalog areas.

Sarswelas, the native adaptation of the Spanish zarzuelas, were dramas with music, consisting of instrumental numbers, solo songs, ensembles, and choruses. Short, one-act dramas had about five musical entrées; larger works had proportionally more. Most *sarswelas* opened with an instrumental overture, variously called *sinfonia, introducción,* or *preludio.* Succeeding acts opened with an intermezzo or an entr'acte. Solo songs were light airs with lyrical melodies, often cast in *danza, balitaw,* or *valse* rhythms, in vogue at the time. Cadenzas frequently adorned these songs. When called for by the dramatic situation, some solos were rendered in *hablado* (spoken) style, similar to *parlando* recitative. Ensembles were duets, trios, or quartets performed by the main characters of the play. Occasionally, instrumental dances were interspersed. Each act ended with a grand tableau, called *concertante final* or *escena final.*

Much of the music written for the *sarswelas* has been lost. It was customary at the time for the composer to sell his rights to the dramatist, who then kept the scores. Thus, though texts of *sarswelas* were published, the music seldom was. Though *sarswelas* are primarily identified with their respective playwrights, some notable Filipino composers provided the music for the dramas. These composers will be discussed later.

Themes of *sarswelas* revolved around idealized Filipino characters and situations in a romantic love story. A prevailing theme was the Filipino family—the love of a poor boy and a rich girl, the quarrel between a jealous wife and a tired husband, parental opposition to marriage—or similar variants. In the early years of the 1900s, the *sarswela* served as a vehicle to express nationalist sentiments. Political *sarswelas* flourished in Manila. The dramas featured encounters between Filipinos and Spaniards, or Filipinos and Americans, with the Filipinos always emerging victorious. *Walang Sugat,* by Severino Reyes (music by Fulgencio Tolentino), was a bitter diatribe against Spanish imperialism.

Operas

Public theaters were the venues of plays, operas, and concerts. Opera companies from Europe performed at these theaters with increasing frequency. The 13 April 1905 issue of the journal *El Renacimiento* cites sixty-six operatic presentations by various visiting and local opera groups. These included *La Traviata, Lucia di Lamermoor, Il Trovatore, Aïda, Rigoletto, Faust, La Bohème, La Sonnambula,* and *La Gioconda.*

The first Filipino opera company was organized in 1886–1887 by Ladislao Bonus. Members of the company included Teodora San Luis, Josefa Tiongson, sopranos; Victoria Medina, mezzo-soprano; Andrés Ciría Cruz, Pedro Alcántara, Alejo Natividad, tenors; Domingo Guazón, baritone; and Eduardo Ciría-Cruz and José Canseco, basses. The company presented *Lucrezia Borgia, Linda de Chaminoux, Lucia di Lamermoor, La Traviata,* and *Fra Diavolo.* The same group presented the first Filipino opera, *Sandugong Panaginip* (*Dreamed Alliance*) by Ladislao Bonus at the Zorilla Theater on 2 August 1902. The libretto, in Spanish, was written by Pedro A. Paterno, and was translated into Tagalog by Roman Reyes. Paterno wrote the libretto of two more operas: *Magdapio* (1902) and *Gayuma* (*Mysterious Charm*), both with music by Alejo Carluén.

Public concerts and recitals

The same theaters presented recitals featuring visiting artists. The Theatro Filipino featured Eduard Reményi, violinist (1886), Albert Friedenthal, pianist (1892), and local artists José Silos (1900) and José Estella (1901).

Many recital programs included musical numbers by various performers (singers, instrumental soloists, chamber groups). A typical recital was described in the

28 March 1892 issue of *La Ilustración Filipina*. The performance took place in Malacáñang Palace, and included the following numbers:

Gran Sexteto .... Barbedette
Villamer (violin), Marzano (violin), Valdez (viola),
Garcia (violoncello), Gonzales (contrabass), Marquez (piano)
"Pace Mio Dio," *Forza del Destino* .... Verdi
Sra. Zobel, soprano; Sr. Coppa, piano
Cuarteto I, Canzoneta, ob. 12 .... Mendelssohn
Villamer (violin), Marzano (violin), Solís (viola), Garcia (violoncello)
"O mio Fernando," *La Favorita* .... Donizetti
Srta. Canellas, soprano; Sr. Coppa, piano
Adagio, Sonata Pathética .... Beethoven
Marzano (violin), Garcia (violoncello), Stulz (piano), Solin (harmonium)
"Linsana [sic] Parola," *Aïda* .... Verdi
Sr. Iglesias; Sr. Coppa, piano
Romance sans paroles .... Duport
Les Moutons .... Martini
Villamer (violin), Garcia (violoncello), Stulz (piano)

Publications and music clubs

The audience that patronized concerts, operas, and other stage presentations kept abreast with the latest news from abroad through foreign publications. Philippine publications on music, literature and the sciences appeared. Among these periodicals were *La Ilustración Filipina* (1859); *La Lira Filipina* (1877) and *Los Miércoles* (1892). These and similar periodicals were short-lived, however. They were published by music societies and clubs composed of professional musicians, amateurs, and dilettantes.

Aside from publications, these clubs presented private recitals, conducted musical and literary contests, instituted short-term courses in vocal and instrumental music, drawing, sculpture, and declamation, and promoted fund-raising benefits. Some of these associations were *Sociedad de Recreo, Sociedad Anónima, Sociedad Musical Filipina de Santa Cecilia, Círculo Musical, Unión Artístico Musical,* and *Asociación Musical de Filipinas.*

Instrumental music

As early as 1788, Juan de la Concepción, an Augustinian friar assigned to the archbishopric of Manila, wrote in his *Historia General de las Islas Filipinas* "the Filipinos were inclined to play instruments and performed rather well, especially the violin" (1788–92:313). The same sentiment was echoed in other reports. In 1838, Adolfo Puya y Ruiz noted that it was rare to run across moderately educated women who did not know how to play the piano, the harp, or the guitar. In 1856, Henry T. Ellis, an English naval officer, marveled at "how quickly they (the musicians) pick up tunes by ear. . . . They go through most of the airs of any opera they have once heard with great taste and spirit, without being able to read a note of music" (1856:233).

From these and similar accounts, it can be gathered that in the 1800s, the homes of most wealthy families in Manila and other urban areas had a piano or a harp. Young ladies were taught to play these instruments, and the head of the household customarily asked his daughter to perform for visitors. The guitar, the violin, the accordion, and the flute were also favored instruments.

Bands

Every town had its band or orchestra; some towns had two or more. These bands participated in civic festal celebrations. A major function was to play at religious processions in which statues of saints in elaborately decorated carriages were drawn through the major streets.

In Manila, the most famous venues for performances by bands were the Plaza Mayor, the Calzada, and later the Luneta, where bands played from six to eight in the evening. Manilans gathered at the park to feel the sea breezes, listen to the music, and see their neighbors. Writing in 1831, A. M. Stewart attested that nowhere had he heard finer music; in 1846, Jean Baptiste Mallat claimed he had not heard any band as good in Spain.

It was the same tradition that the Philippine Constabulary Band displayed under the baton of American Colonel Walter H. Loving. Organized in 1902, it started with a group of thirty musicians, which soon increased to eighty. In 1904, it took part in the Grand Exposition in St. Louis, Missouri, where it received the grand prize and a gold medal. At a Luneta performance held on 7 September 1903, the following program was announced in the *Manila Times*:

March, Hands across the Sea.......Sousa
Overture from *Norma*.......Bellini
Grand Jota, La Dolores.......Breton
Danza delle Ore, *La Gioconda*.......Ponchielli
Beautiful Danube.......Strauss
Selections from *Floradora*.......Stuart

To this day, the band tradition continues in the Philippines.

Orchestras

Between 1850 and 1900, several orchestras were organized in Manila. These played for zarzuelas, performed overtures and intermezzi between short plays, and played for visiting opera companies. Sometimes they presented programs of purely orchestral music; more often, the programs explored a varied repertoire, with solo songs or other solo instrumental numbers. Favorites were popular airs by Auber, Rossini, Thomas, and Waldteufel.

These orchestras bore different names, but the same musicians played in them, each with a different conductor. Some early orchestras were the Gruet Orchestra, Ramón Vales, first director; the San Juan del Monte Orchestra, Joaquín Aragon, first director; the Rizal Orchestra, José Estella, first director; the Oriental Orchestra, Bonifacio Abdón, first director; and the Marikina Orchestra, Ladislao Bonus, first director. Notable was an all-woman orchestra, the Orquesta Feminina de Pandacan, established in 1890, and directed by Ladislao Bonus. It had one flute, one saxophone, one cornet, one trombone, four first violins, two second violins, one viola, one cello, and one contrabass.

Of the early orchestras, the Molina Orchestra, founded in 1896, lasted the longest—until 1935. It was said to have been, until 1910, the only orchestra "devoting its time to the interpretation of classical music." It played for visiting Italian opera companies, sometimes under the baton of an Italian conductor. It also assisted at high masses held at the Santo Domingo Church in Intramuros. Filipino conductors of the orchestra included Alejo Carluén, Gavino Carluén, José Estella, Bruno Santana, Bibiano Morales, Fulgencio Tolentino, Juan Hernandez, Mariano Baja, and Bonifacio Abdón.

After 1900, during the American regime, other orchestras were formed. The

rondalla Ensemble of plucked, guitarlike instruments

carillo Outdoor shadow play using cardboard figures

moro-moro Of Spanish origin, a drama with music depicting conflicts between Christians and Muslims

sarswela Philippine form of light opera derived from the Spanish zarzuela

musikong bumbong Early form of "brass band" using homemade bamboo instruments

Monday Musical Club founded the Manila Symphony Orchestra, which existed from 1911 to 1914. The Asociación Musical de Filipinas organized the Philippine Constabulary Symphony Orchestra in the mid-1920s. The same group was reorganized as the Manila Symphony Orchestra, which continued until the 1980s. Other orchestras were the Philippine Cultural Concerts Symphony Orchestra under Ramón Tapales, and the University of the Philippines Philharmonic Orchestra under Francisco Santiago. During the Japanese regime, the New Philippine Symphony Orchestra was convened.

In 1946, the Filipino Youth Symphony Orchestra under Luis Valencia was organized; when it disbanded, its members joined the Manila Symphony Orchestra and the Philippine Philharmonic Orchestra. As members of the resident orchestra of the Cultural Center of the Philippines, members of the Philippine Philharmonic Orchestra are assured of a regular salary. In 1985, a chamber orchestra was organized and subsidized by the Philippine Commercial and Industrial Bank (PCIB); called the Manila Chamber Orchestra, it has had a successful concert series through the present.

Training programs for future professional orchestral members are undertaken by the Philippine Youth Orchestra, based at the University of the Philippines, and the Pasaknungan Orchestra for young children, funded by the Cultural Center of the Philippines.

Musikong bumbong

Brass bands were the model for an indigenous group of instruments made of bamboo. Called *musikong bumbong,* this band was first organized by a group of nationalist revolutionaries (*katipuneros*) in 1896. Similar bamboo bands still exist. In Malabon, Rizal, musicians called the St. Anthony Original Bamboo Band claim to be fourth-generation descendants of the 1896 group.

Musical training

During the last five decades of the Spanish period and the early years of the American regime, Philippine composers of serious music were products of schools that had been set up by friars during the early years of colonization and carried on by lovers of music and musical organizations.

It was only during the American period that formal schools of music were established in the Philippines. Early chroniclers' records tell of decent instrumental music and choirs in towns all over the islands, and say these musicians performed in various church functions, but these performers received most of their training in locally established ecclesiastical schools, not in conservatories.

Music education in religious schools

The most influential of the friars' schools was the Colegio de Niños de la Santa Iglesia Catedral (The Boys' Choir of the Holy Cathedral Church), established in

Manila in the mid-1700s. It grew into a full-fledged conservatory of music, where music classes were offered in solfège, vocalization, composition, organ, and stringed instruments. By 1800, a more solid curriculum had evolved, patterned after that used in music conservatories in Madrid. The products of this school became leaders of music in Manila and its environs.

In Santo Domingo, the Dominican church maintained a choir. Boys were given a rudimentary music education, which included singing and playing the organ and the piano. Another influential force was the orchestra and church choir of Saint Augustine Cathedral. A long line of Augustinian monks who had received musical training in Spain shared their musical expertise at the cathedral, training the choir and orchestra. Many were composers, contributing religious works (masses, hymns, carols) to the church choir books.

Music was included in the curriculum of the Jesuit-run Ateneo Municipal of Manila and the Dominican-run San Juan de Letrán. These were the only official institutions for secondary education in the city. Convent schools for girls (Santa Isabel, established in 1632; and Santa Rosa, established in 1750) offered a curriculum that covered music, embroidery, and good manners.

Music education through music clubs and societies

The Liceo Científico Artístico Literario, founded in 1877, aimed to propagate literature and the fine arts. This it achieved by sponsoring public concerts and contests in poetry, the sciences, painting, and music. Its plans to establish a conservatory of music and declamation were abruptly ended by the revolution (1898).

Three different groups, the Centro Artístico (inaugurated in 1901), the Centro de Bellas Artes (1902), and the Centro de Artistas (1904), had similar objectives. The Centro Artístico offered classes in solfège, violin, piano, *bandurria,* mandolin, guitar, harmonium, and musical composition. The Centro de Bellas Artes offered courses in music, painting, and architecture. Its faculty included professors in solfège, singing, piano, harmony, composition, violin, viola, cello, bass, clarinet, oboe, flute, and brasses. The Centro de Artistas offered courses in music, painting, architecture, sculpture, poetry, and literature.

Composers, conductors, performers

Graduates, students, and members of the above-mentioned institutions and schools were the musicians, composers, and performers whose activities made up the musical life in Manila and other urban centers in the latter half of the 1800s. These musicians were connected either with the church or with the theater. Those involved in the theater participated in the performances of zarzuelas and operas.

Ecclesiastical musicians

Musicians served the Roman Catholic Church in various capacities: as members of the choir, principal or assisting organists, choral directors or cantors, and orchestral conductors. The earliest written record of a Filipino ecclesiastical musician concerns the lay Augustinian brother Marcelo de San Agustín. A native of Malate, Manila, he took his vows on 5 September 1652 and died in 1697. Of him it was written "he can be the crowning glory of the *Indios Tagálogos* because of his rare virtue, his services, so efficiently and willingly rendered to the Manila convent in various capacities or offices for which God gave him skill and ability. He was a dexterous organist, skillful in playing other instruments . . . , composer and teacher of singers at the convent. He made and wrote many books for the service of the choir" (quoted in Gaspar de San Agustín 1890:238).

A long line of ecclesiastical musicians followed. Notable among them was

Natalio Mata (1833–1896), from a family of musicians. A graduate of the Colegio de Niños, he became organist at the Quiapo Church in Manila. When his son Manuel took over as organist (at the age of fourteen), the elder Mata directed the choir, who with one exception were amateur musicians. Natalio Mata, a tenor, played the flute and occasionally conducted the Gruet Orchestra. He was on the faculty of the Colegio de Niños Tiples, where he taught vocal and instrumental music. He composed religious works (masses, *gozos,* rosaries, hymns) and arranged Spanish compositions for his choir.

Like his father, Manuel Mata (1861–1901) wrote religious music for the Quiapo Church Choir. His *Misa Pastorela* is the first known setting of the ordinary of the Mass that utilized native musical motives. An accomplished pianist, Manuel also composed light works, mostly waltzes and polkas, for the piano.

Balbino Carrión (1840–1919) was the principal cantor of Natalio Mata's choir at Quiapo Church. Because his voice was beautiful, he was invited to sing in other churches. Eventually he joined Chananay, a dramatic troupe, and appeared in plays, zarzuelas, and operas; he once essayed the role of Manrico in *Il Trovatore.* During the troupe's provincial tours, he would sing in churches. When in Manila, he continued to sing at Quiapo Church.

Contemporary with Balbino Carrión was another ecclesiastical musician, Marcelo Adonay (1848–1928), who came from a family of musicians. His father was a member of the town band in Pakil, Laguna, and all his brothers could play one or more instruments. At the age of eight, he was taken to Manila, where he entered the service of Saint Augustine Church as an altar boy. The organ and orchestra at the church inspired him to teach himself how to play, first the organ and then the piano and the violin; years later, he became a member of the church orchestra, and in 1870, its director. He remained at this post until 1914. At the church in 1887, he conducted the first performance of Beethoven's *Missa Solemnis* in Manila.

Though principally an ecclesiastical musician, Adonay participated in the musical life in Manila. He appeared in public performances of chamber music, and gave recitals of instrumental and vocal music. He taught music in several girls' schools (Santa Catalina, Santa Rosa) and at the Centro de Bellas Artes (1902). His works, though unpublished, include compositions for ecclesiastical use—offertories, *salves, gozos, despedidas,* hymns, and masses. Notable was his *Misa Solemne* for chorus and orchestra (1903), based on Gregorian chants. He also wrote secular music: marches, quartets, quintets, and solo pieces. *Rizal Glorified* is a symphonic program work of his, written in seven movements.

Band musicians

Another kind of musical ensemble was the band. Bands proliferated in towns and barrios all over the country. Filipino musicians also became members of regimental bands of the Spanish army. Simplicio Solís (1826–1910) spent some forty years as director of Regimental Band No. 5, stationed in Manila and traveling to Jolo, Zamboanga, Cavite, and Cotabato. On his retirement in 1887 he directed the Pasig Band and gave lessons in guitar, mandolin, *bandurria,* and *laud.*

His four sons—José, Rosalio, Urbano, Juan—were also musicians. Rosalio and Juan, like their father, were members of regimental bands. Rosalio (1862–1896) became director of Regimental Band No. 74, stationed in Manila, Jolo, and Cotabato. He then was assigned as director of Regimental Band No. 72, but while in Iligan, Mindanao, was implicated in the revolutionary movement and executed in 1896.

José Canseco (1839–1902) spent his early years as a boy soprano (*tiple*) at Saint Augustine Church, and was later appointed to the choir of the Manila Cathedral. In

1863, he was among the choristers who survived the earthquake that destroyed the church while services were in progress. Between 1882 and 1889, he became active in orchestral and stage performances. He conducted the Gruet Orchestra (1882), and helped organize the all-female orchestra in Pandacan in 1886. With Ladislao Bonus, he was instrumental in the formation of the all-Filipino opera company. He left the opera company in 1889, and turned his talents to band music, directing a band in Narvacan, Ilocos Sur (1889). In 1891, he was appointed bandmaster of Regimental Band No. 71, assigned to Zamboanga. In Iligan in 1896, he was imprisoned for alleged involvement in the revolutionary movement. After his release from prison, he spent the remaining years teaching piano, solfège, harmony, and composition. His works are unpublished; they include religious hymns, light songs, instrumental dances, and marches. He scored a zarzuela, *La Muerte de Lucrezia* (*The Death of Lucrezia*), with libretto by Ronderos.

José Sabas Libornio (1858–1915) was a bandsman who emigrated to Peru, where he became general director of Las Bandas de Música del Ejército in 1896. As a boy, Libornio was a *tiple* at the Manila Cathedral. Subsequently he joined Infantry Band No. 7, and traveled to Jolo, Zamboanga, and Cotabato. He was also associated with bands in Rizal, Ilocos, and Nueva Ecija. In 1882, he joined the Charino Circus as a musician, and left the country with the troupe in the following year. After various travels, he settled in Peru, where he spent his remaining years directing Peruvian military bands. In 1905, he founded the Conservatorio Libornio in Lima. His works include *danzas,* marches, mazurkas, polkas, quadrilles, and waltzes, plus arrangements of music by classical composers.

Vicente Marifosqui (1866–1936) was known primarily as director of the Pasig Band, the Banda Arévalo, the Banda Dimasalang, and the National Guard Band. He also led bands in Cavite and Nueva Ecija.

Theatrical musicians

The presentations of zarzuelas, plays, and operas in the latter half of the 1800s involved many musicians—composers, instrumentalists, singers, and conductors. In 1886–1887, Ladislao Bonus (1854–1908), a native of Pandacan, organized the first completely Filipino opera company in 1886–1887, with himself as director and conductor. The company's first presentation, Donizetti's *Lucrezia Borgia,* was produced in the town's cockpit. The company was invited to repeat the performance in Manila, where it ran for at least two successive nights. Soon, knowledge of Bonus's expertise as conductor and instrumentalist (he played violin, viola, cello, and bass) became widespread, and he was engaged by the Manila Cathedral Orchestra (1888–1896), the all-woman Orkestang Babae (also Orquesta Feminina, 1890), the Marikina Orchestra, and the Pasig Band. He conducted the Arévalo Band, which performed at the Regional Exposition in Hanoi (1902), winning first prize. His singular achievement, however, was his composition of the first opera in Tagalog, *Sandugong Panaginip* (*Dreamed Alliance*). He also wrote the music for several Tagalog *sarswelas*: *Unang Pag-ibig* (*First Love*), with libretto by Eliseo Mendoza, and *Ang Buhay* (*Life*), with libretto by Miguel Mansilungan.

Florencio Lerma (1861–1897) directed orchestras that provided the music in local theaters. He worked with several troupes engaged in performing zarzuelas touring the Philippines. In 1897, implicated with the revolutionary movement, he was executed with ten others, collectively known as the Bicol martyrs. When the zarzuela turned native, vernacular texts appeared in Pampango, Cebuano, Bikolano, Pangasinan, Ilocano, Ilongo, and Tagalog. The most famous of the vernacular *sarswelas* originate from the Tagalog region.

José Estella (1870–1943), known as the king of Filipino waltzes, trained in conservatories in Madrid and Brussels. His *Filipinas para los Filipinos* was a satire on an American congressional bill prohibiting American women from marrying Filipino men.

Other composers who worked closely with playwrights include Bonifacio Abdón (1876–1944), Alejo Carluén (1872–1941) and his brother Gavino Carluén (active from 1890 to 1930), José Estella (1870–1943), Fulgencio Tolentino (active from 1890 to 1920), Juan Hernandez (1882–1945), Ramón Corpus (1893–1952), Francisco Buencamino (1883–1952), Leon Ignacio (1882–1967), and Francisco Santiago (1889-1947).

Bonifacio Abdón (1876–1944), a violinist and conductor, worked with the dramatist Patricio Mariano writing the music for the *sarswelas Ang Sampaguita* (*The Sampaguita*), *Deni, Ang Tulisan* (*The Bandit*), *Luha't Dugo* (*Tears and Blood*), *Declaración de Amor* (*Declaration of Love*), *Carnaval No. 1, Huwag Lang Lugi sa Puhunan* (*Just to Break Even*), *Ang Anak ng Dagat* (*Child of the Sea*), and *Lihim at Pag-Ibig* (*Secrecy and Love*). He also furnished the music for Aurelio Tolentino's *sarswelas La Rosa* (*The Rose*), *La Boda Maldita* (*The Accursed Wedding*), *Manila Cinematográfica* (*Cinematographic Manila*) and *Crimen Sobre Crimen* (*Crime on Crime*). Other *sarswelas* he wrote include Pantaleón López' *Delingkente* (*The Delinquent*) and *Muling Pagsasampalataya* (also known as *Dancing School,* jointly composed with Leon Ignacio), *Masamang Kaugalian* (*Bad Habits,* jointly composed with Remigio Agustín). For Maximino de los Reyes, Abdón composed the music of *Ang Mag-Anak* (*The Family*) and *Kandungan* (*The Lap*), and for José N. Sevilla's *Si Rizal at ang mga Diwata* (*Rizal and the Spirits*), *Saan Kayo Naroroon* (*Wherever You Might Be*) and *Plaridel.*

Alejo Carluén (1872–1941) composed music for some thirty-one *sarswelas,* including six to librettos by Felipe Paguía, six by B. Buenaventura, and two by Severino Reyes. The last is considered a major Filipino dramatist. For Reyes, Carluén composed the music of *Ang Mga Pusong Dakila* (*Great Hearts*) and *Mga Pinag-Pala* (*The Blessed Ones,* 1903). It was Carluén who wrote the music for two early Tagalog operas, *Magdapio* and *Gayuma* (*Mysterious Attraction*), both on librettos by Pedro Paterno. His brother, Gavino Carluén, composed the music for three of Severino Reyes's works: *La Boda de San Pedro* (*St. Peter's Wedding,* 1902), *Huling Pati* (*The Last Will,* 1904), and *May Sugat* (*There Is a Wound,* 1912).

José Estella (1870–1943), known as the king of Filipino waltzes, trained in conservatories in Madrid and Brussels. He wrote the music to *Ligaya* (*Joy,* 1904), a zarzuela in Spanish by the famous actor José Carvajal (1862–1928). Collaborating with Severino Reyes, Estella supplied the music for two two-act *sarswelas: Filipinas para los Filipinos* (*Filipino Women for Filipino Men,* 1905), *La Venta de Filipinas al Japón* (*The Sale of the Philippines to Japan,* 1906), and *Ang Opera Italiana* (*The Italian Opera,* 1906). *Filipinas para los Filipinos* was a satire on an American congressional bill prohibiting American women from marrying Filipino men. Music for *Ang Opera Italiana* consisted of arrangements of famous operatic arias. Estella also composed the music for two one-act *sarswelas* in the Pampango dialect by Juan Crisóstomo Soto (1867–1918), *Ing Loro ning Gobernadora* (*The Governor's Parrot*), and *Ing Dalaga*

(*The Maiden*). He directed the Rizal Orchestra (established in 1898), which played for many presentations of *sarswelas.* In 1933, a three-act opera in Tagalog, *Lakambini* (*The Muse*), on a libretto by Patricio Mariano, was performed at the Metropolitan Theater in Manila, with music by Estella.

Fulgencio Tolentino (active from 1890 to 1930) directed the Molina Orchestra when it was attached to the Gran Zarzuela Tagala (established in 1902), managed by Severino Reyes (1861–1942), the dean of Filipino dramatists. The company staged Reyes's works in Manila, and toured the provinces of Cavite, Laguna, Batangas, Tayabas, and Marinduque. Tolentino composed the music for Reyes's *sarswelas Ang Kalupi* (*The Pocketbook,* 1902), and *Walang Sugat* (*There is a Wound,* 1902) and his lyric drama *Los Mártires de la Patria* (*Martyrs of the Country,* 1903) (Samson 1972). *Walang Sugat* had its premiere at the *Zorilla Theater* on 14 June 1902. It was a bitter diatribe against Spanish imperialism. Reyes's *Pilotea,* also known as *La Boda de San Pedro* (*St. Peter's Wedding,* 1902), with music by Gavino Carluén and Tolentino, focused on religious fanaticism and its detrimental effect on the country's progress.

Juan Hernandez (1882–1945) joined the faculty of the University of the Philippines Conservatory of Music when it was founded in 1916, and conducted the Molina Orchestra. This brought him in contact with Severino Reyes, for whom he supplied the music of three three-act *sarswelas: Minda Mora* (*Minda, the Moro Woman,* 1904); *Lukso ng Dugo* (*Call of Blood,* 1906); and *Puso ng Isang Pilipina* (*The Heart of a Filipino Woman*).

Other composers who collaborated with Severino Reyes were the violinist Ramón Corpus (*Liham ng Hilahil* 'Letter of Tribulation', n.d.; *Ang Tatlong Babae* 'The Three Women', 1914; and *Ang Dalagang Masaya* 'The Happy Maiden', n.d.), Teodoro Araullo (*Gloria o Habeas Corpus* 1907), Crispino Reyes (*A San Lázaro* 'To St. Lazarus', 1907), Antonio J. Molina (*Ana María,* n.d.), and Francisco Santiago (*Si Margaritang Mananahi* 'Margarita the Seamstress', 1913).

Other playwrights

Contemporary with Severino Reyes were the playwrights Aurelio Tolentino (1867–1915), Hermógenes Ilagán (1875–1943), Pantaleón López (1872–1912), and Patricio Mariano (1877–1935). Francisco Buencamino (1883–1952) composed the music to two Tolentino *sarswelas* (*Germinal Liceo de Manila* 'Lyceum of Manila', 1908; and *La Paz y Buenviaje* 'Peace and Safe Voyage', 1911), and four Mariano works (*Marcela,* 1904; *Si Tio Selo* 'Uncle Selo', 1905; *Yayang,* 1905; and *Pangakong Hindi Natupad* 'Unfulfilled Promise', 1905).

Other composers who worked with Tolentino were Fortunato Pineda (*Sinukuan* 'Vanquished', 1902; *Venus,* and *La Parla Maecena* in Spanish, 1909); Camilo Dizon (*Pilipinas at España* 'The Philippines and Spain', 1901; *Ang Makata* 'The Poet'; *Ing Sundang ning Meangubie* 'The Sword of the Dead'; and *Ding Kambal* 'The Twins'); Teodoro Araullo (*Sumpaan* 'Promises', 1904); and Crispino Reyes (*Aray* 'Ouch', 1911). Tolentino wrote *Rizal y los Dioses* (*Rizal and the Gods*), music by Simplicio Solís, which some consider the first Tagalog opera, preceding Paterno-Bonus' *Sandugong Pangaginip*; however, since the manuscript is unavailable, its exact date is difficult to establish. Judging from its title, it may have been written in Spanish.

Tagalog dramatist Pantaleón López (1872–1912) authored some twenty *sarswelas,* in which he himself was actor or director, having formed his own dramatic company. Leon Ignacio (1882–1967) directed the orchestra of López's troupe and supplied the music to several of López's plays, including *Ang Infierno* (*Hell,* 1902); *Muling Pagsampalataya* (*Dancing School,* with Bonifacio Abdón); and *Rosa* (1903). *Rosa* enjoyed more than a hundred performances in Manila and the Tagalog provinces.

After the troupe splintered, with one group joining dramatist Hermógenes Ilagán. López turned to composers Bonifacio Abdón, Hipolito Rivera, and Alejo Carluén for his music. Leon Ignacio, collaborating with Ilagan, supplied the music to *Dalagang Bukid* (*Country Maiden*), *Lucha Electoral* (*Electoral Struggle*), *Ilaw ng Katotohanan* (*Light of Truth*), *Kagalingan ng Bayan* (*Greatness of the Country*), *Puñal de Rosa* (*Rosa's Dagger*), *Después de Dios* (*After God*), and *El Dinero* (*Money*). In all, Ignacio composed the music for some seventy *sarswelas. Ang Kiri* (*The Coquette*) and *Alamat ng Nayon* (*The Country Legend*), written by Servando de los Ángeles, and *Paglipas ng Dilim* (*The Passing of Darkness*), written by Precioso Palma, were revived and performed in the 1980s.

During the first three decades of the 1900s, the city of Iloilo was called Queen City of the South. As a commercial center, it had an elite class of landowners and middle-class merchants who supported the theater; soon there emerged a flowering of the Iloilo *sarswela,* whose most notable writers were Valente Cristobal (1875–1945), Jimeno Damaso (1885–1936), Ángel Magahum (1867–1935), Serapio Torre (1892–1942), José María Ingalla (1888–1914), José María Nava (1891–1954), Miguela Montelibano (1874–1969), and Eriberto Gumbán (1861–c. 1926). Music for these works was composed by Juan Paterno, Teodoro Gallego, Leocadio Calero, Roman Brillantes, Bibiano Calero, Gerardo Chávez, Rufo de la Rama, Felipe Prado, Antonino Ledesma, and José Mijares (Fernández 1978). As in the Tagalog regions, Manila included, not much of the music has survived.

As a rule, composers of *sarswela* functioned as conductors of the orchestra. Often they were instrumental performers in their own right. Many taught in schools or gave private lessons in homes. They appeared in large musical concerts and in smaller gatherings, where music programs formed the main attraction of informal or semi-formal occasions.

Other performers

Among the virtuosos of the late 1800s was violinist Manuel Luna (1856–1883). He came from an illustrious family that included a celebrated painter, a revolutionary general, and a surgeon. He received his musical training at the Real Conservatorio de Madrid. He concertized in Spain, France, and Italy, and returned to the Philippines at the end of 1879. He participated in many concerts and private recitals under the auspices of the Liceo Científico Artístico Literares. He was a competent orchestral and choral conductor.

Cayetano Jacobe (1876–1940) was a homegrown violin virtuoso whose concerts were warmly received. While touring the United States with the Philippine Constabulary Band, he gave solo recitals. In 1916, he was appointed violin professor at the University of the Philippines Conservatory of Music.

Other performers of note during the last decades of Spanish rule were pianists Ramón Valdez, Antonio García, José Muezo, Hipolito Rivera, Diego Pérez, Dolores Paterno, Julian Felipe, Francisco Roxas, Gavino Carluén, Fulgencio Tolentino, and Crispin Reyes; violinists Andrés Dancel, Ignacio Morales, Felix Resurrección Hidalgo, Gonzalo Marzano, Florencio Lerma, Bibiano Morales; flutists Juan de Dios Morales, Alejandro Francisco, Juan Silos; organist Manuel Mata; and singers Balbino Carrión, Andrés Ciría Cruz, and Andrés Ortiz.

REFERENCES

Castro y Amadeo, Pedro de. 1790. "Historia de la Provincia de Batangas por Don Pedro Andrés de Castro y Amadeo en sus viajes y contraviajes en toda esta Provincia año de 1790." Madrid: MS Archivo Nacional, Códice 931, 7.

de la Concepción, Juan. 1788–92. *Historia general de las islas Filipinas.* Manila: Agustín de la Rosa y Balagtas.

Ellis, Henry T. 1856. *Hongkong to Manila and the Lakes of Luzon in the Philippine Islands in the Year 1856.* London: Smith, Elder.

Eugenio, Damiana. 1987. *Awit and Corrido: Philippine Metrical Romances.* Quezon City: University of the Philippines Press.

Fernández, Doreen G. 1978. *The Iloilo Zarzuela 1903–1930.* Quezon City: Ateneo de Manila University Press.

Mallat, Jean Baptiste. 1846. *Les Philippines: Histoire, Géographie, Mœurs, Agriculture, Industrie et Commerce des Colonies Espagnoles dans l'Oceanie.* 2 vols. Paris: Imprimerie de Madame Veuve Bouchard-Hazard.

Martínez de Zúñiga, Joaquín. 1893. *Estadismo de las Islas Filipinas y mis Viajes por este País.* Madrid: Imprenta de la Viuda de M. Minuesa de los Rios.

Mas, Sinibaldo de. 1843. *Informe Sobre el Estado de las Islas Filipinas en 1842.* Madrid.

de la Merced, Aniceto. 1852. *El libro de la vida: historia sagrado con santas reflexiones y doctrinas morales para la vida cristiana en verso tagalo* (The book of life: sacred history with pious reflections and moral teachings for the Christian life written in Tagalog verse). Manila: Librería y Papelaría de J. Martínez.

Mirano, Elena Rivera. 1989. *Subli, Isang Sayaw sa Apat na Tinig.* Manila: Museo ng Kalinangang Pilipino, Cultural Center of the Philippines.

———. 1991. "Ang Mga Tradisyonal na Musikang Pantinig sa Lumang Bauan, Batangas." Ph.D. dissertation, University of the Philippines, Diliman, Quezon City.

Paterno, Pedro. 1893. *El Individuo Tagalo y su Arte.* Madrid: Imprenta de los Sucesores de Cuesta.

Pilapil, Mariano, ed. 1976 [1814]. *Kasaysayan ng Pasiong Mahal ni Hesukristong Panginoon Natin Sukat Ipag-alab ng Puso ng Sinomang Babasa (Pasiong Henesis).* Manila: Aklatang Lunas.

Puya y Ruiz, Adolfo. 1838. *Filipinas: Descripción General de la Provincia de Bulacan.* Manila: R. Mercantil de Diaz Puertas.

Retana, Wenceslao Emilio. 1888. *El Indio Batnagueno,* 3rd ed. Manila: Tipo Litografía de Chofre y Cia.

———. 1895–1905. *Archivo del Bibliófile Filipino. Recopilación de documentos históricos, científicos, literarios y políticos, y estudios bibliográficos.* 4 vols. Madrid: Imprenta de la Viuda de M. Minuesa de los Rios.

Samson, Helen. 1972. "Extant Music in the Zarzuelas of Severino Reyes." M.Mus. thesis, University of the Philippines.

San Agustín, Gaspar de. 1890. *Conquistas de las Islas Filipinas.* Valladolid: Luis N. de Gavira.

Stewart, A. M. 1831. *A Visit to the South Seas in the U.S. Ship Vincennes, during the Years 1829 and 1830 with Scenes in Brazil, Peru, Manilla, the Cape of Good Hope, and St. Helena,* vol. 2. New York: John P. Haven.

Tiongson, Nicanor G. 1975. *Kasaysayan at Estetika ng Sinakulo at Ibang Dulang Panrelihiyon sa Malolos.* Quezon City: Ateneo de Manila University Press.

———, ed. 1994. *Philippine Literature.* Manila: Cultural Center of the Philippines. CCP Encyclopedia of Philippine Art, 9.

Walls y Merino, Manuel. 1892. *La Música Popular de Filipinas.* Madrid: Libreto de Fernando Fe.

Yraola, Marialita T. 1977. "Ang Mga Awiting Tagalog." *Musika Jornal* 1:42–78.

Art Music of the Philippines in the Twentieth Century

Ramón P. Santos

Since initial missionary contact in the 1500s and subsequent widespread Christianization, the Philippines has been profoundly influenced by composers, compositions, and trends imported from Europe and the Americas. These influences have occurred on two major fronts: artistic traditions of the classical, romantic, and modern eras, and popular traditions. On both fronts, the Philippines has produced composers whose creations span all the major genres of the twentieth century.

PHILIPPINE MUSIC AROUND 1900

By 1900, European musical traditions had already taken root in most Christianized Filipino communities. In rural areas, the proliferation of Western music and dances, like the *cachucha,* the fandango, and the *zapateado,* had reached remarkable proportions, despite the stylistic retention of pre-Christian musical traits and functions. Western instruments, like the *vihuela,* violins, guitars, flutes, and other instruments had long been assimilated or adopted in the local making of music (Blair and Robertson 1973 [1903]:45:271–278).

Musical life in urban centers and capitals, however, was dominated by a Western repertoire consisting of ecclesiastical choral music, *sarswelas* (from the Spanish zarzuela), operas, and performances by various orchestras, bands, and plucked string ensembles called *rondallas.* The training of Filipino natives in singing European vocal music and playing Western instruments started in convents (San Nicolás 1973 [1605]:21:152) and military regiments as early as the 1500s (De León 1977:2213).

By the twentieth century, practically every church had a Filipino maestro and a choir of trained singers. In prominent churches and cathedrals, religious orders, including Recollects (a religious order affiliated with the Augustinians), Franciscans, and Jesuits, conducted semiformal instruction in singing and playing. One such place is the Colegio de Niños de la Santa Iglesia Catedral, which produced some of the early famous musicians, including the pianists Antonio García and Máximo Nazario, the violinist Salvador Piñón, and the composers Simplicio Solís and Fulgencio Tolentino (Bañas 1975:111).

Toward the end of the 1800s, individual musicians became known countrywide for their talents, either as performers or as composers. These included José Canseco and Marcelo Adonay, whose versatility as a church musician gained him the sobriquet "Palestrina of the Philippines." A pianist-composer, Diego C. Pérez, was one of the first Filipinos to compose a large-scale work based on native tunes—*Recuerdo de Filipinas y Sus Cantares* (*Memories of the Philippines and Its Songs*). A gifted student of his, Dolores Paterno, composed the song "*Flor de Manila*" ('Flower of Manila'), which became part of the early popular repertoire.

Musical societies consisted mainly of orchestras and chamber groups, organized by prominent musicians, performing in concerts and assisting opera and *sarswela* productions. Some of these ensembles included the Orquesta Feminina de Pandacan (Women's Orchestra of Pandacán) and the Marikina Orchestra, both conducted by Ladislao Bonus. In 1902, Bonus made history by writing the first Filipino opera: *Sandugong Panaginip* (*Dream of Sandugo*). Another was the Rizal Orchestra, founded in 1898 by Martín Ocampo and conducted by José Estella, a famous composer of *sarswelas*. The violinist-composer Bonifacio Abdón directed the Oriental Orchestra. In 1896, Juan Molina organized the Molina Orchestra, one of the most active ensembles, which not only presented its own concerts, but also performed in church services and provided instrumentalists for visiting opera companies.

Each major city and town had at least one band, usually owned and managed by prominent musicians and their families. Some of the outstanding groups included the Banda Zabat (founded in 1820 by Lorenzo Zabat y Chico) and the Peñaranda Band, initiated by Pedro Mercado in 1876. The bands performed in processions, parades, and concerts in connection with important feasts and holy days. They also accompanied local theatrical presentations like the *comedia* and the *senaculo*, the Lenten reenactment of the passion of Jesus Christ (Tiongson 1991:238, 250). Another band function was, and still is, playing for funerals and other civic gatherings. Standard pieces in the band repertoire included the *Marcha Real* (the Spanish national anthem), usually played outside the church during high masses, at the time of the transubstantiation of the bread and wine into the body and blood of Jesus Christ; the *Himno de Riego* (named after Emiliano Riego de Diós, a leader of the Philippine revolutionary government), a march in 6/8 time, which accompanied scenes of battle in the *comedia* or *moro-moro*; and marches and *pasodobles*, fast virtuosic pieces in duple time.

Another popular ensemble was the *rondalla,* an ensemble of plucked strings, played mostly by young adults, of either sex. Earlier introduced as *comparsas* and *estudiantinas* 'student orchestras' (Patricio 1955), *rondallas* played popular tunes and accompanied theatrical presentations in lieu of brass bands. Others, like the famous Yellow Taxi String Band and Manila Symphonic Rondalla, played a more sophisticated repertoire of arrangements of orchestral works (Bañas 1975:109). In rural communities, brasses and *rondalya* instruments would combine to form hybrid musical ensembles.

THE ANGLO-AMERICAN PERIOD: INSTITUTIONS AND ENSEMBLES

In the Treaty of Paris (1898), Spain ceded the Philippines to the United States. A significant change that then occurred was the establishment of a system of public education in which music was part of the curriculum. On the tertiary level, music academies and conservatories replaced centers for training young musicians, which religious orders had previously run. These institutions produced professional musicians who not only were trained in performance, but also were taught theory, music history, and even composition. The faculties consisted of foreign artists and local musicians (Bañas 1975:111–130).

One of the earliest music schools founded in the twentieth century is the music department of St. Scholastica's College, run by Benedictine nuns. Starting as an informal program of instruction in music for the all-girl school in 1906 under the direction of Sister Winfrieda Muller, the music school was formally established in 1907 by Sister M. Baptista Battig, formerly Helene Battig, a concert pianist and pupil of the famous European pedagogue Ludwig Deppe (1828–1890). Sister Baptista guided the school to its development as a full-blown conservatory of music; she died on 26 January 1942 (St. Scholastica's College 1992).

The Conservatory of Music of the University of the Philippines opened in 1916, in accordance with a bill passed by the Philippine Assembly. Its first director was Wallace George, a choral-music expert from the New England Conservatory of Music. He was succeeded in the position by other foreign teachers, including Guy F. Harrison, Robert Schofield, and Alexander Lippay, until the appointment of the first Filipino director in 1930, Dr. Francisco Santiago, a famous pianist and composer. The faculty of the U.P. Conservatory of Music was a mix of foreign and local musicians—Wilma Hillberg, Vladimir Elin, Carlyle Smith, Julio Esteban Anguita, Fernando Canon, Jeno von Takacs, Vassily Prihodko, and composers Nicanor Abelardo and Juan Hernandez, the pianists Lucia Francisco and Elisa Maffei, and the violinists Ramón L. Corpus and Bonifacio Abdón (*Conservatory of Music, University of the Philippines: 1916–1960* 1960).

Another school that produced outstanding graduates was the Academy of Music of Manila, founded in 1930. Directed by Alexander Lippay of Austria, it offered courses in piano, strings, voice, composition, conducting, choral singing, Italian, German, English, and elocution (Bañas 1975:125). Other notable institutions for professional musical training include the Centro Escolar University Conservatory of Music, the Music Department of Santa Isabel College, the Lyric Music Academy, and the Schola Cantorum, founded in 1921 by Esperanza de la Rosa, specializing in the development of young musicians. All these institutions are in greater Manila.

Music instruction in the public schools and the postsecondary institutions produced a large number of musicians, some of whom were able to further their studies abroad and even gain international renown. They included the composers Nicanor Abelardo and Francisco Santiago, the conductor Federico Elizalde, the pianist José Maceda, and the singers Isang Tapales and Jovita Fuentes, who was acclaimed in the role of Cio-Cio San in *Madama Butterfly* in leading European opera houses, including La Scala and the German State Opera Theaters (Chung 1979).

During the early twentieth century, interest in Western classical music was sustained, not only by local recitals and concerts in the music schools, but also through regular presentations by musical organizations, like the Centro de Artistas (founded in 1904), the Asociación Musical de Filipinas (1919), the Manila Chamber Music Society (inaugurated in 1921), the Choral Art Association (1930), and the Manila Music Lovers' Society (1935) (Bañas 1975: 154–59). The cultural scene was complemented by performances of renowned visiting artists, including Eduard Reményi (1830–1898), Jan Kubelik (1880–1940), Mischa Elman (1891–1967), Andrés Segovia (1893–1987), Jascha Heifetz (1900–1987), Pierre Fournier (1907–1986), and Yehudi Menuhin (b. 1916) (Bañas 1975:137–147).

After 1945, Filipino musicians continued to gain national and international prominence as concert artists and winners in highly prestigious competitions in Western countries: the soprano Evelyn Mandac, the baritone Aurelio Estanislao, the violinist Oscar Yatco, the pianists José Contreras, Nena del Rosario-Villanueva, Cecile Licad (awarded the Leventritt Prize), and the University of the Philippines Madrigal Singers. In the meantime, regular concerts were presented by various orchestral ensembles, including the Manila Symphony Orchestra, the Filipino Youth Symphony Orchestra, the Quezon City Philharmonic Orchestra, and the University of the Philippines Symphony Orchestra. Though conducted by different music directors, the orchestras shared the majority of their members until 1973, when Luis Valencia founded the Cultural Center of the Philippines Philharmonic Orchestra (now the Philippine Philharmonic Orchestra), which has since operated as a full-time professional ensemble.

In creative music, courses in theory and composition offered at the conservatories and music academies further honed local musicians' skills in the classical forms. During the first three decades of the twentieth century, the first Filipino sonatas, symphonies, concertos, and concert overtures were written. Among these are Nicanor Abelardo's First Quartet in F Major and Piano Sonata (both written in 1921), and Francisco Santiago's String Quartet in G Major and Concerto in B-flat Minor (1924). Bonus's *Sandugong Panaginip* was followed by other operas, including *Magdapio,* by Alejo Carluén, and *Lakambini* (*The Lady*), by José Estella (1933). Most of these works were in highly chromatic harmonic idioms, influenced by the music of Beethoven, Brahms, Chopin, Liszt, Tchaikovsky, and Wagner, and by the operas of Donizetti, Puccini, and Verdi.

Nationalism

After more than three hundred years of Spanish rule, resistance to yet another colonial power was articulated in the works and activities of artists, political and civic leaders, and other members of the local intelligentsia. In music, a big part of the creative output of local composers consisted of patriotic hymns and marches, carryovers from the Philippine Revolution against Spain. Two composers closely associated with early revolutionary music were Julio Nakpil and Julian Felipe. Nakpil composed *Amor Patria* (*Love of Country,* 1893) and the highly dramatic *Salve Patria* (*Hail to the Country,* 1903), an extended piece for chorus and orchestra. Julian Felipe wrote the *Himno Nacional de Filipinas,* which the revolutionary government of General Emilio Aguinaldo adopted; first composed as an instrumental march, then given a Spanish text that was later translated into Tagalog, *Pambansang Awit ng Pilipinas* (Philippine National Anthem) achieved its present form.

Another musical genre used to express turn-of-the-century nationalist sentiments is the *kundiman,* a song of love in moderate 3/4 time, which evolved from pre-Christian courtship songs (*komintang*) of the Tagalog, later developed into cultivated songs (Molina 1977). Revolutionary *kundiman* (*kundiman ng himagsikan*) were first heard during the revolt against Spain in 1896, identified with the popular song "*Jocelynang Baliwag*" ('Jocelyn from Baliwag'). The texts of the revolutionary *kundiman* enshrined the Motherland as the object of affection and devotion (T. Maceda 1993). These pieces retained their popularity throughout the American regime and into the Japanese occupation, when they sustained the morale of local guerrilla units (T. Maceda 1992).

Also during the American occupation, the seditious Filipino musical theater represented by the *sarswela* reached its peak. Modeled on the zarzuela in the late 1800s, the Filipino *sarswela* gained widespread popularity, not only among the Tagalog-speaking population, but also in Christianized regions all over the country. In Manila, the artistic standard of the *sarswela* was enhanced by the collaboration of the leading playwrights, Severino Reyes and Hermógenes Ilagán, and highly trained composers, including Leon Ignacio, José Estella, Fulgencio Tolentino, and Nicanor Abelardo.

What started as a form of musical entertainment whose plots revolved around aspects of everyday community life with allusion to moral teachings became a channel for antigovernmental feelings. The seditious contents of works like Juan Abad's *Mabuhay ang Pilipinas* (*Long Live the Philippines,* premiered March 1900), Pascual Poblete's *Pagibig Sa Tinubuang Lupa* (*Love for the Land of Birth,* May 1900), and

While foreign researchers concentrated on the theory and sociology of the musical cultures, the Filipinos collected traditional music for the purpose of transforming and utilizing it as materials for teaching and composition.

Aurelio Tolentino's *Kahapon, Ngayon at Bukas* (*Yesterday, Today, and Tomorrow,* May 1903) evoked the occupation government's displeasure. Suppression of nationalist *sarswelas* was carried out by fining and imprisoning authors, directors, and producers (Fernandez 1981 [1905]). Partly due to official censorship, the *sarswela* declined in popularity. Its regression was further induced by the introduction of another medium of entertainment, the cinema (Santos 1992:94).

In the meantime, composers who continued to master the techniques of writing in the extended symphonic and operatic forms imbued their works with local themes and folk songs as a gesture of nationalism. Native instruments were incorporated in isolated orchestral works. Francisco Santiago's *Tagailog Symphony* (*River-Dweller Symphony*) is remembered for its quotations of folk tunes and use of a Jew's harp (*barimbao*). Antonino Buenaventura's Rhapsodietta for Piano and Orchestra is based on a Manobo theme, and his celebrated tone poem *By the Hillside* uses a melodic motif derived from nose-flute music of the Cordillera highlands. In 1939, Felipe Padilla de León composed the *Mariang Makiling Overture,* based on the story of the legendary maiden who perished with a broken heart and turned into Mount Makiling, in Laguna Province. Other outstanding works containing local materials include the "Mayon" Piano Concerto of Francisco Buencamino, and Nicanor Abelardo's Piano Concerto in B-flat and String Quartet. The generation of Filipino composers closely identified with musical nationalism also includes Antonio Molina, a cellist who composed chamber music, and Lucio San Pedro, Hilarión Rubio, Rodolfo Cornejo, and Lucino Sacramento.

Musical research and resources

Early-twentieth-century studies of Philippine native musics were made by foreign scholars, mostly anthropologists, ethnographers, and missionaries, including Roy Barton, Laura Benedict, H. Otley Beyer, Fernando Canon, Alphonse Claerhoudt, Fay Cooper Cole, Frances Densmore, Albert Gale, Fletcher Gardner, Otto Sheerer, S. C. Simms, Jeno von Takacs, Morice Vanoverbergh, and Dean Worchester (Dioquino 1982). In 1904, tribal musicians of the Negritos and the Tinggian from the Cordillera highlands were taken to the St. Louis Exposition, where their musics came to foreign scholars' attention; instruments acquired then are part of the collection in the Field Museum of Natural History in Chicago (Manuel 1979:5).

In the 1930s, the Filipino musicians and writers Francisco Santiago, Antonio Molina, and Justice Norberto Romualdez became involved in research on native musics and instruments. In 1934, President Jorge Bocobo of the University of the Philippines created a cultural committee and gave it the task of collecting native musics and dances from all over the country. In the following four summers, the research team of Antonino Buenaventura (composer), Francisca Reyes Tolentino (dancer), and Ramón Tolentino (administrator), gathered a sizeable collection of music and dances from different regions of the country.

While foreign researchers concentrated on the theory and sociology of the musical cultures, the Filipinos collected traditional music for the purpose of transforming and utilizing it as materials for teaching and composition. In the postwar period, a more sophisticated method of studying Philippine native musics characterized the efforts of younger scholars—Harold Conklin, Albert Faurot, John Garvan, the folklorist Arsenio Manuel, the linguist Ernesto Constantino, and José Maceda, a former concert pianist and local pioneer of ethnomusicology.

Today, field collections of native Filipino music are housed in libraries and archives, including the University of the Philippines Ethnomusicology Archive, Xavier University in Cagayan de Oro City, Mindanao State University, and the St. Louis University in Baguio City.

Modernism in Philippine music

During the twentieth century, modern forms, styles, and techniques offered Filipino writers, painters, and musicians new challenges and artistic goals. Early contact with twentieth-century music worldwide was made through local musicians who trained in the West, plus foreign teachers and artists who came to settle or work in the Philippines during the American regime. The music of the Western composers Debussy, de Falla, Khatchaturian, Prokofieff, Ravel, Shostakovitch, and Stravinsky found places in recital and concert programs.

Composer Nicanor Abelardo, on returning from his studies at the Chicago Musical College in the United States in 1931, was the first to break away from traditional musical idioms. He began to apply a new harmonic language in his landmark compositions *"Cinderella" Overture,* Sinfonietta for Strings, *Panoramas,* and Violin Sonata (figure 1), all composed in 1931. His style of composing shows the influence of Viennese Expressionism, characterized by ambiguous tonalities, long-drawn-out and disjunct melodic lines, multimeter, and polyrhythmic structures. His death, in 1934, delayed the spread of modernism in Philippine art music. Being a highly respected pedagogue, he could easily have influenced his peers and pupils with the new musical vocabulary.

In the years immediately after Abelardo's death, several compositions were written with some elements of early-twentieth-century musical idioms. Ambiguous and dissonant tonalities were used by Antonio Molina in his piano pieces *Malikmata* (*Transfiguration*) and *Dancing Fool.* Antonino Buenaventura's symphonic works, like *By The Hillside, "Youth" Symphonic Poem,* and *Rhapsodietta on a Manobo Theme,* feature the tonal language and textural orientation of impressionist music. In these works, modern dissonances and tonal ambiguities served more as coloristic dressing than as part of an acquired language.

One of the few unorthodox works that came out in the post-Abelardo period is Ramón Tapales' *Philippine Suite,* completed in 1937. Though Tapales trained in Europe as a concert violinist, he wrote several pieces with some innovative features. "Mindanao Orchids," the first movement of the *Philippine Suite,* is constructed on a simple four-note motive used as a drone. The third movement, "Savage Dance," uses dissonant tonal combinations and new instrumental techniques (Santos 1991:159).

PHILIPPINE MUSIC DURING THE JAPANESE OCCUPATION

Musical life during the Japanese occupation (1942–1945) veered in a different direction. The Japanese imperial government implemented a nationalist program in Philippine music, basically promoting Filipino performing artists and encouraging the composition of works (mostly short hymns and marches) that extolled the virtues of the "Co-Prosperity Sphere" and "Pan-Asianism." The program also promoted the exchange of artists between Japan and the Philippines, and the learning of Japanese songs in schools.

FIGURE 1 The beginning of Nicanor Abelardo's Violin Sonata, 1931.

Most of the musical products that came out of this period were propagandist. All forms of Anglo-American music, both classical and popular, were banned. Since Hollywood films were also prohibited, many movie houses were available for concerts and staged performances. Some Spanish and local *sarswelas* were revived, and short musical skits (named *gindula*) were composed by Felipe Padilla de León and aired over the radio. No major musical work written during the period may be considered significant to the development of modernism or art music in the country (Santos 1992).

THE POSTWAR PERIOD

In the 1950s, composers fresh from studies abroad espoused the cause of modern music. Eliseo Pájaro developed a neoclassic style based on counterpoint and fugal devices, pandiatonic harmonization, chromatic sequences of melodic fragments, and syncopation. His works include symphonies and tone poems, including *Life of Lam-Ang*; concertos; choral odes; the nationalist operas *Binhi ng Kalayaan* (*Seeds of Freedom*) and *Balagtas at Celia*; quartets; and cycles of songs, embedding folk songs in bitonal harmonies.

Another neoclassicist is Lucrecia R. Kasilag, who studied theory and composition in the United States. In her involvement in the folkloric program of the Philippine Women's University as Music Director of the world-famous Bayanihan Dance Troupe, she collected and studied indigenous and other Asian instruments and music that she encountered during her travels. Her concept of East-West fusion became the underlying principle in her works, where she would combine timbres of Western and non-Western musical instruments and the scales of different musical systems. Her major works include Toccata for Percussion and Winds (1958), *The Legend of Sari-Manok* (1963), *Filiasiana* (1964), and Concert-Divertissement for Piano and Orchestra (1960). In her extended work for theater, *Dularawan* (1969), the main inaugural piece of the Cultural Center of the Philippines, she fused drama, opera, and dance for solo voices, choirs, actors, dancers, and an orchestra of Asian instruments.

Other neoclassicists include Alfredo Buenaventura, Jerry Dadap, Ángel Peña, and Rosendo Santos, a prolific composer who took up residence in the United States. In 1955, Eliseo Pájaro and Lucrecia Kasilag led their colleagues in forming the League of Filipino Composers, committed to the development of a national identity in Philippine music.

NEW MUSIC: THE FINAL DECADES OF THE TWENTIETH CENTURY

The 1960s saw dramatic changes. With the spread of avant-gardism in the West and the discovery of new sources of musical thought through the study of non-Western musics, a new path was opened to modern music in the Philippines. As in other countries, composers in the Philippines realized that extensive exposure to non-Western musics suggested the use of alternative compositional materials and processes.

José Maceda

A leading figure in this development, José Maceda (b. 1917), abandoned a notable career as a concert pianist and piano pedagogue in favor of ethnomusicology and composition. After his studies in anthropology and ethnomusicology at Columbia University, Indiana University, and UCLA (where he earned his Ph.D. in 1954), he engaged in extensive fieldwork on the musics of non-Christian communities and rural villages in Luzon and Mindanao, and in other parts of Southeast Asia [see UPLAND PEOPLES OF THE PHILIPPINES]. From these studies, he gained insights into the philosophies of village cultures. In addition, his familiarity with *musique concrète* while training in France provided a contemporary perspective in translating non-Western concepts of music into modern compositions.

What may be regarded as Maceda's style consists of musical and extramusical concepts, like mass structures of timbres (the sonic colors of non-Western instruments) and durations, drone and melody, slow permutation of events in time, rituals, the use of physical space, and a technology made up of human energies as opposed to machine power. He has given life and shape to these ideas in such works as *Ugma-Ugma* (*Connections,* 1964) and *Agungan* (*Gongs,* 1966), based on sound masses and durations; *Pagsamba* (*Worship,* 1968), with ideas based on village rituals and uses of sonic space; *Ugnayan* (*Relations,*1974) and *Udlot-Udlot* (*Interdictions,* 1975), using an environment of sounds created by hundreds of people; *Ading* (a Kalinga vocal genre, 1978), *Siasid* (*Tiruray Song*), and *Aroding* (*Tagbanwa Jew's Harp,* 1983), projecting the slow permutation of time.

Major festivals and conferences attended by international figures in modern music also contributed to the general awareness for New Music. The most significant event was Musics of Asia, a conference in 1966.

In *Pagsamba,* a monumental work, Maceda set the Filipino mass text as a modern ritual piece for two hundred performers. It formally utilized the acoustical space of a round chapel in which choirs of singers and reciters, gongs, and bamboo instruments created masses of sounds that traveled around the circular space.

Maceda's compositions in the 1960s and 1970s used exclusively native Philippine and Asian instruments, but in the 1980s, he expanded his tonal palette and included Western instruments in his scores. His later works emphasized the aesthetic parameters of non-Western musical systems in opposition to existing tonal and structural functions of the sounds of Western instruments and standard ensembles. In *Siasid,* he used violins for the first time, in combination with percussion drones and low-blown bamboo tubes. His later works include *Distemperament* (1992) for a symphony orchestra whose instruments are distributed in groups of three, and the Piece for Five Pianos (1993).

In addition to the conceptual and technical innovations of Maceda's compositions, the concerts he produced and directed in the 1960s and 1970s presented new concepts in musical programming. Suggesting a more liberal view of music from a multicultural perspective, these concerts featured musics of diverse styles—Chinese *nan guam,* Maguindanao *kulintang* music, Debussy's *Mallarmé Songs,* Edgard Varèse's *Intégrales,* and his own *Ugma-Ugma* in the 1964 Concert of Asian and Avant-Garde Music (Santos 1991:165). Maceda composed *Ugnayan* in 1974 for twenty radio stations to broadcast twenty different tapes of recorded sounds of indigenous instruments simultaneously over Metro-Manila and environs. *Udlot-Udlot*—for eight hundred performers (figure 2)—was first performed in the parking lot of the Cultural Center of the Philippines in 1975.

Festivals and conferences

Major festivals and conferences attended by international figures in modern music also contributed to the general awareness for New Music. The most significant event of the 1960s was Musics of Asia, a conference in 1966 (also organized by Maceda with the assistance of UNESCO), which brought to Manila such personalities as Ton de Leeuw, Yuji Takahashi, Chou Wen Chung, and Iannis Xenakis, with ethnomusicologists Mantle Hood, Trần văn Khê, and William Malm (Maceda 1971).

In 1975, the Third Asian Composers League Conference-Festival, held in Manila, was attended by composers from Australia, Hong Kong, Japan, Korea, Taiwan, Thailand, and the United States. Subsequently, lectures and workshops on New Music were presented by Peter Michael Braun, Daryl Dayton, Erhard Karkoschka, and Gilles Tremblay.

Ramón Pagayon Santos

The first among a younger generation of composers to respond to the challenges of New Music was Ramón Pagayon Santos (b. 1941). During his studies in the United

FIGURE 2 Excerpt from José Maceda's *Udlot-Udlot*, for eight hundred performers, 1975.

Tugtuging na maisasagawa ng 30 o libo-libong mga tao

Likha ni José Maceda Hunyo 1975

I. TULOY TULOY (Drone)

TUNOG Sounds	BALANGKAS (Rhythmic Patterns)	BILIS (Speed)	TAGAL (minutes)
KATAPUSAN	R1a. Unang bariyasyon: (1st var.)	Ang bilis ng lider ang sundin mula 2 hang gang 4 na bilang sa isang segundo.	00' to 01'
	Tugtug: I I · I · (Paulit-ulit)		01' to 02'
	Bilang: 1 2 3 4 5 (Paulit-ulit)		02' to 03'
	I = Magpatunog. Ihataw ang pamalo ng Kanang Kamay sa pamalo ng Kaliwang kamay.		03' to 04'
	· = Walang tunog		04' to 05'
HANGGANG	LAHAT AY SABAY-SABAY		05' to 06'
	R1b. Pangalawang bariyasyon (2nd Var.)		06' to 07'
	1. I I · I ·		07' to 08'
	2. I I · I ·		08' to 09'
KALUTANG	3. I I · I ·		09' to 10'
	4. I I · I ·		10' to 11'
	5. I I · I ·		11' to 12'
LAHAT	A. 5 grupo ang manunugtog. Halimbawa, kung 1000 ang kasama sa Udlot-Udlot, 200 ang tagatugtog ng Tuloy-tuloy. Sa 200 ito, 40 ang tutugtog ng no. 1; 40 ang tutugtog ng no. 2; 40 ang tutugtog ng no. 3, etc. Huli-huli ang pasok ng bawat isa.		12' to 13' … 20' to 21'

II. HALUÁN (Mixed Sounds)

TUNOG (ODDS)	BALANGKAS (Rhythmic Patterns)	BILIS (Speed)	TUNOG (EVENS)	BALANGKAS (Rhythmic Patterns)	BILIS (Speed)	TAGAL (minutes)
WALA			WALA			00' to 01'; 01' to 02'
BA-LING-BING	R2. Bilangin ang 2 numero. Tumugtug sa unang bilang. 5+7; 5+9; 7+9; 7+11; 5+11	3-5 na bilang sa 1 seg.	BA-LING-BING	R2. Bilangin ang 2 numero. Tumugtug sa unang bilang. 6+8; 6+9; 6+10; 6+11; 5+8	3-5 na bilang sa 1 seg.	02' to 03'; 03' to 04'; 04' to 05'
WALA			WALA			05' to 06'; 06' to 07'
BA-LING-BING	R2: 2+3; 2+4; 2+5; 3+4; 3+5.	4-5 bi-lang-1 seg	BA-LING-BING	R2: 7+5; 5+8; 7+9; 7+11; 5+11	3-5 bilang sa 1 seg	07' to 08'; 08' to 09'
WALA			BA-LING-BING	R2. Bilangin ang 2 numero. Tumugtug sa unang bilang. 2+3; 2+4; 2+5; 3+4; 3+5	4-5 bilang sa 1 seg.	09' to 10'
TONG ÁTONG	R2: 5+7; 5+9; 7+9; 7+11; 5+11	3-5 bilang sa 1 seg				10' to 11'; 11' to 12'
TONG ÁTONG	R2. Bilangin ang 2 numero. Tumugtug sa unang bilang. 2+3; 2+4; 2+5; 3+4; 3+5.	4-5 bilang sa 1 seg.	WALA			12' to 13'
			TONG ÁTONG	R2. Bilangin ang 2 numero. Tumugtog sa unang bilang. 6+8; 6+9; 6+11; 6+10; 6+12	3-5 bilang sa 1 seg	13' to 14'; 14' to 15'; 15' to 16'
WALA			WALA			16' to 17'
TONG ÁTONG	R1: Sabaysabay o Isa-isa ang pagpasok. Gr. 1 1 2 3 4 5; Gr. 2 etc. 1 2 3 4 5	2-4 bilang sa 1 seg.	TONG ÁTONG	R1: Sabaysabay o Isa-isa ang pasok. Gr. 1 1 2 3 4 5; Gr. 2 etc. 1 2 3 4 5	2-4 bilang sa 1 seg.	17' to 18'; 18' to 19'; 19' to 20'; 20' to 21'

III. TINIG (Voices)

WALA

10" 5" 15"

o wa - - - - - k

WALA

10" 5" 15"

o wa - - - - - k

WALA

10" 5" 15"

o wa - - - - - k

States, Santos initially composed neoclassic pieces (Suite for Flute, Clarinet, Viola, Cello, and Piano, and Four Movements for Chamber Orchestra), and atonal works (Music for Nine Instruments, *Pied Beauty*). He later focused on improvisational pieces (*Time Improvisations* and Toccata for Piano and Two Performers), and open-ended forms (Five Pieces for Two Pianos).

Returning to the Philippines, Santos expanded his compositional materials and ideas. *Para Sa Intermisyon* (intended for performance during intermission) and *Ritwal ng Pasasalamat* (1976) were influenced by the functional aspect of traditional musical practices; *Likas-An* (*Nature-ing*) was inspired by the dynamic forces of the local natural environment; *Siklo* (*Cycle*), *Awit* (*Song*), *Ta-O* (*Per-Son*), *Awit ni Pulau* (*Song of Pulau*), and *Daragang Magayon* are mixed-media works, related to the concept of integrated arts in non-Western traditions.

Santos's latest works are especially influenced by his study of traditional Philippine and Asian cultures. *Ba-Dw Sa Ka-Poon-An* (*Divinity Badiw*) was derived from the *badiw,* the principal vocal genre of the Ibaloy of the Cordillera highlands. This composition explores the dichotomy between the free style of leader-chorus singing and the synchronized articulation of nonvocal sounds (figure 3). The work is intended to express a concept of time that greatly diminishes distinctions among motion, stasis, change, and recurrence.

Francisco Feliciano, Conrado del Rosario, and others

Tangential to the compositions of Maceda and Santos (derived from abstract elements and broad conceptual frameworks of native musics) are the works of other Filipino composers who have mastered advanced techniques of New Music writing. Though their basic musical ideas are either inspired by or derived from Philippine and Asian musics, they are treated and developed according to formal and organizational logic of Western classical music. Two leading exponents of this style are Francisco Feliciano and his pupil Conrado del Rosario.

Francisco Feliciano (b. 1941) studied with Eliseo Pájaro and Isang Yun in Berlin and Krzysztof Penderecki at Yale. Some of his major works are *Fragments, Verklärung Christi,* and *Voices and Images* for large orchestra, *Transfiguration* for orchestra, chorus, and narrator, and *Isostasie III,* for strings and woodwinds. In his orchestral work *Pagdakila sa Kordilyera* (*To Honor the Cordillera*), Feliciano incorporated Philippine ethnic instruments in the score. He has also contributed significantly to modern musical theater with his ballet *Yerma* (1982), based on the poetry of Federico García Lorca, the full-length opera *La Loba Negra* (*The Black She-Wolf,* 1989), and the music drama *Sikhay Sa Kabila Ng Paalam* (*Striving beyond Farewell*).

In addition to composing and being active as a choral and orchestral conductor, Feliciano established the Asian Institute for Liturgy and Music (now the Asian School of Music, Worship and the Arts), a school devoted to the exploration of traditional musical idioms in Asia for utilization in Christian liturgy and worship. In 1993, the institute produced an experimental musical drama, *Ayyuwan Chi Pita* (*Promise of the Earth*), whose story revolves around contemporary human rights and environmental issues affecting the minority communities in the Cordillera highlands. The music, composed by Feliciano and select composition students, was based on the music of the Kalinga people; it incorporated the tribe's vocal styles and other musical practices.

Conrado del Rosario (b. 1958) likewise studied in Berlin with Isang Yun, and has resided in Germany since 1982. His works are based on tonal intervals and pitch cells derived from native music. He develops them into rich and highly polished textures of sound, as in *Tongali* (Kalinga nose flute) for flute solo, and *Twilight Temples* for flute, saxophone, percussion, cello, and piano.

FIGURE 3 Excerpt from Ramón Santos's *Ba-Dw Sa Ka-Poon-An* for three vocal groups, stones, and wooden percussion, 1987.

FIGURE 3 *(continued)*

Belonging to the generation of Del Rosario is Josefino Toledo (b. 1959), who trained extensively in France and the United States. Though he, too, developed a technical facility in New Music idioms, including electronic music procedures, he bases the overall structural frameworks of his music on theoretical aspects of non-Western musics. In his massive orchestral work *Trenodya Ke Lean* (*Threnody for Lean*) No. 6, he not only used a native mode as thematic material, but also applied the principle of the layering of sound and a heterophonic relationship of somewhat independent melodic lines.

Another notable modern Philippine composer is Bayani de León (b. 1942), a contemporary of Santos and Feliciano. De León started his career as a composer by writing *sarswelas,* including *Handog ng Diyos* (*God's Offering*) and *Hibik Sa Karimlan* (*Cry in the Darkness*), and progressive pieces for the *rondalya.* As a graduate student at the University of California in San Diego, he studied composition with Roger Reynolds and interacted with West Coast composers, including John Cage. He composed pieces on his favorite reading topics (cosmology, metaphysics, Asian philosophy), including *Okir* (*Design*) and *Puso* (*Heart*). His later works show a neoromantic temperament, rooted in the Filipino art song *kundiman* and the generally lyrico-romantic aspect of Philippine music. One example is *Sugatang Perlas* (*Wounded Pearls*) written in 1992, a music-and-dance drama based on the women characters in José Rizal's novel *Noli Me Tangere* (*Touch Me Not*).

Filipino composers familiar with worldwide modernism are still few in number, compared with those in countries such as Japan, Korea, and Taiwan. Nevertheless, their individual efforts have sustained an interest among the young to explore new directions in composition, especially in the context of native cultural traditions. Jonas Baes (b. 1961), a composer-researcher, has initiated the Huntahang Bayan (Community Dialogue), communal making of music based on contemporary issues. His colleague Verne de la Peña (b. 1959) has also produced works derived from Filipino and Asian traditional performing arts, the puppet theater *Si Suan, Si Suan,* and the dance-dramas *Agueda* and *Pagpili ng Ministro* (*The Minister's Choosing*).

NATIVE TRADITIONS IN CONTEMPORARY MUSICAL LIFE

New awareness of the kinship and physical proximity of Filipinos to various forms of music has given rise to the recognition that native musics are an important part of the dynamics of contemporary life. Regional festivals have been either revived or enhanced, partly motivated by governmental tourism programs. Some of the more prominent events are the *dinagyang* in Iloilo, which commemorates the coming of the image of the Child Jesus (*Santo Niño*) to the natives of Panay Island; the *Imbaya,* harvest festival of the Ifugao; the *pahiyas,* harvest festival of the Tagalog of Quezon Province; and the *Kamulaan* in Cotabato, a festival of native performing arts of the various highland communities of Mindanao.

In addition to newly composed works, scholars and other creative artists have collaborated to produce modern replicas—stylized or adapted versions—of native folklore, such as epics and dances. Some of these productions include the modern dance-drama *Tales of the Manuvu* (based on the research of the folklorist Arsenio Manuel); *Rama Hari* (a rock opera by Ryan Cayabyab on the story of the Ramayana); and the *Hinilawod* (a dance-drama based on the anthropologist F. Landa Jocano's collected epics from Antique Province, titled *Labaw Doggon*). A modern theatrical adaptation of the Maranao epic *Ang Paglalakbay ni Radiya Mangandiri* (*The Journeys of Raja Mangandiri*), with a striking resemblance to the characters and episodes of the Ramayana, resulted from the research of Mamitua Saber, Juan R. Francisco, and Nagasura Madale.

Viewed collectively, the musical development in contemporary Philippine society appears to draw resources from older traditions. While it shows various directions and aesthetic orientations, it may be perceived as representing a unique expression of a people seeking alternative musical thought and contributing toward the liberation of music from exclusively Western artistic concepts.

REFERENCES

Bañas, Raymundo C. 1975. *Filipino Music and Theater.* Quezon City: Manlapaz Publishing.

Blair, Emma Helen, and James Alexander Robertson, eds. 1973 [1903]. *The Philippine Islands 1493–1898.* 55 vols. Mandaluyong: Cachos Hermanosted.

Chung, Lilia Hernandez. 1979. *Jovita Fuentes: A Lifetime of Music.* Manila: Jovita Fuentes Musicultural Society.

Conservatory of Music, University of the Philippines: 1916–1960. 1960. Quezon City: University of the Philippines Conservatory of Music.

De León, Felipe Padilla. 1977. "Banda Uno, Banda Dos." *Filipino Heritage* 8.

Dioquino, Corazón C. 1982. "Musicology in the Philippines." *Acta Musicologica* 54:124–147.

Fernández, Doreen. 1981 [1905]. "Introduction." In *The Filipino Drama,* ed. Arthur Stanley Riggs. Manila: Ministry of Human Settlements.

Maceda, Teresita G. 1992. "Pagbigay Tinig Sa Piniping Sa Piniping Kasay-sayan ng Hubalahap: Papel Ng Awit Sa Kilusang Gerilya Sa Panahon Ng Hapon" (Giving voice to the mute history of the Hukbalahap: role of song in the guerilla movement during the Japanese time). In *Panahon ng Hapon* (Japanese Occupation), 107– 126. Manila: Cultural Center of the Philippines.

———. 1993. "Imahen Ng Inang Bayan Sa Kundiman Ng Himag-sikan" (Image of the motherland in *kundiman* of the revolution). Manuscript. University of the Philippines: Department of Filipino, College of Arts and Sciences.

Maceda, José M., ed. 1971. *Musics of Asia.* Manila: National Music Council of the Philippines and UNESCO.

Manuel, E. Arsenio. 1978. "Towards An Inventory of Philippine Musical Instruments." *Asian Studies* 1978:1–72.

Molina, Antonio J. 1977. "The Sentiments of Kundiman." *Filipino Heritage* 8:2026–29.

Patricio, María Cristina. 1955. "The Development of the Rondalla in the Philippines." Research paper. University of the Philippines.

St. Scholastica's College. 1992. *A Harvest in Sprung Rhythm: St. Scholastica's College School of Music 1907–1992.* Anniversary pamphlet.

San Nicolás, Fray Andrés de. 1973 [1605]. "General History of the Discalced Augustinian Fathers." In *The Philippine Islands 1493– 1898,* ed. Emma Helen Blair and James Alexander Robertson, 21:111–317. Mandaluyong: Cachos Hermanos.

Santos, Ramón P. 1992. "Nationalism in Philippine Music during the Japanese Occupation: Art or Propaganda?" *Panahon ng Hapon* (Japanese Time) 2:93–106.

Tiongson, Nicanor, ed. 1991. *The Cultural Traditional Media of the Philippines.* Manila: ASEAN and the Cultural Center of the Philippines.

Popular Music in the Philippines

Ramón P. Santos, with Arnold Cabalza

A local concept of popular music germinated in the Philippines during the Anglo-American period, catering to a mass-based audience in the field of social entertainment. Beginning in the early decades of the twentieth century, Philippine popular music developed into a varied repertoire of folk songs in dance rhythms, songs of love, Broadway-inspired music, ballads, and rock and its offshoots—disco, jazz fusion, rap, and punk. As in other countries, popular music has thrived extensively among young people and has been widely disseminated through the electronic media of radio, cinema, and television. Live performances are presented as fund-raisers during fiestas, and attractions at political rallies and other forms of public demonstrations. In the last decades of the century, piped-in music—consisting mainly of popular tunes—has come into vogue in restaurants and public conveyances.

THE ERA OF BIG BANDS

Before World War II, various genres of popular music were played in dance halls and vaudeville shows. A potpourri of numbers in these shows included slapstick comedy, skits, tap dancing, song medleys, and *kundiman.* The dance halls, however, featured orchestras and bands that played foxtrot, swing, charleston, tango, and waltz. Some of the leading local ensembles included the Abelardo Orchestra, the Ilaya Orchestra of Santiago Cruz, and groups led by Juan Silos, Tito Arévalo, and Serafín Payawal. Early Filipino popular music consisted of folk songs arranged in danceable rhythms, like boogie-woogie versions of the Bikol folk song "*Sarung Banggi*" ('One Starry Night') and *Bahay Kubo*" ('My Nipa Hut' [a *nipa* is a Philippinne palm leaf]). Also performed were themes from local movies, mostly carryover stories from the Filipino *sarswela.*

American jazz and popular music for dancing were banned during the Japanese occupation, but the postwar period saw a resurgence of popular music. In addition to the previous repertoire of dances originating in the United States, new styles of dancing were introduced, mostly of Latin American origin: samba, rumba, guaracha, mambo, and appalachicola (a variant of the mambo, first popular in the 1950s).

In 1953, Xavier Cugat's visit spurred interest in Latin American music for dancing and resulted in the formation of *cumbancheros,* amateur ensembles that usually

In the 1980s, the Filipinization of popular music gained further headway with the emergence of the Manila sound, a composition characterized by a form of urban jargon called Taglish, a contraction of Tagalog and English.

included a harmonica, a guitar, an accordion, a one-stringed bass (with the resonating body of an empty army gasoline tank), and a percussion section of bongos, conga, rattle, güiro, and maracas. The music was mostly dance-oriented arrangements of local songs, both traditional and newly composed. Though *cumbancheros* thrived for no more than a decade, they responded to the mass-entertainment needs of a war-torn society. Fiestas and other communal celebrations, in both urban and rural areas, were enlivened by their performances, and radio stations sponsored competitions among them.

In the meantime, the postwar era witnessed a renewed interest in American jazz, promoted by such experts as saxophonist Exequiel "Lito" Molina, pianists Romy Posadas and Fred Robles, and bassist Angél Peña. By the 1920s, Filipino jazz musicians had developed such a reputation that since then they have been in demand to play on cruise ships and in the entertainment centers of many Asian countries.

THE ERA OF ROCK AND ROLL

In the 1960s, rock and roll made a strong impact on Filipino musicians and the local mass media. The electrifying performances of its exponents, especially Bill Haley, Elvis Presley, Chubby Checker, and Little Richard reached and captivated Filipino audiences via jukebox, radio, cinema, and records. The electronic media also introduced other styles identified with such personalities as Neil Sedaka, Johnny Mathis, Perry Como, Tom Jones, the Platters, and others.

The Filipino popular-music community absorbed the new currents, and responded by finding local counterparts of American musical idols. To discover the best imitators of the American originals, radio and television sponsored amateur contests for singers, such as Student Canteen and Tawag ng Tanghalan (Call of the Stage). The results of extensive media searches included Eddie Mesa for Elvis Presley, Bert Nievera for Johnny Mathis, Diomedes Maturan for Perry Como, and Victor Wood for Tom Jones. The Platters were copied by the local Splatters, as the Moonstrucks, the Hijacks, R. J. and the Riots, and the Deltas popularized even newer styles of dancing, like the twist, the mashed potato, and the watusi.

Despite the widespread appetite for foreign songs and the idolization of foreign artists, original compositions were being written and performed by singers who chose to develop their own styles. Early hits included Clod Delfino's "*Hahabul-habol*" ('Running After'), as sung by Bobby Gonzales and Sylvia La Torre, and Fred Panopio's rendition of "*Pitong Gatang*" ('Seven Gantas') (a *ganta* is a local unit of grain measure, the equivalent of 3 liters) in country style. Songs of love in English, inspired by American ballads, also found their place in the local popular-music repertoire; in the 1960s, these included "A Million Thanks to You" by Alice Doria Gamilla and "Never Say Goodbye" by Willie Cruz.

In the early 1970s, songs of love in the vernacular began to capture the local market, drawing influences from the *kundiman* and Broadway songs. Movie-music composers had tremendous success with such compositions as "*Ngayon at Kaylanman*" ('Now and Forever') and "*Kastilyong Buhangin*" ('Sand Castle') by George Canseco, "*Ang Langit Sa Lupa*" ('Heaven on Earth') and "*Dahil Sa Isang Bulaklak*" ('Because of a Flower') by Leopoldo Silos, "*Gaano Kita Kamahal*" ('How Much Do I Love You') by Ernani Cuenco, and "*Saan Ka Man Naroroon*" ('Wherever You Are') by Restie Umali. This success encouraged a younger generation of composers to contribute to the proliferation of modern songs of love, such as "*Magsimula Ka*" ('Begin') by Gines Tan, "*Ewan*" by Louie Ocampo, and "*Lupa*" ('Earth') by Charo Unite.

Both national and international popular-song competitions—the Metro Manila Popular Music Festival, Himig Awards, the Tokyo Music Festival, the World Popular Song Festival—not only brought fame to winning Filipino songs, but also enhanced the careers of Filipino singers, including Hajji Alejandro, Kuh Ledesma, Celeste Legaspi, Jacqui Magno, Lea Navarro, Rico J. Puno, Basil Valdez, and Leo Valdez. Popular Filipino songs and local artists gained further support from the Broadcast Media Council, which passed Resolution 77–35 requiring the playing of two selections of OPM (original Pilipino music) for every hour of broadcast.

In the meantime, styles popularized by the Rolling Stones, Led Zeppelin, and the Jefferson Airplane inspired the music of the Juan de la Cruz Band, which in response created "*Balong Malalim*" ('Deep Well'), "Project," and "*Laki Sa Layaw*" ('Spoiled Brat'). Mike Hanopol, a former member of the band, later created his own compositions, including "*Buhay Musikero*" ('Musician's Life') and "*Awiting Pilipino*" ('Filipino Song'). Other popular performers of rock of the period include the Maria Cafra Band, Sampaguita, and Frictions, which entertained the growing local discothèque clientele.

Filipino rock operas were also produced: Nonong Pedero's *Tales of the Manuvu* (1977), on a text by Bien Lumbera; *Gomburza* (1982), by Philip Monserrat and Chinggay Lagdameo; and *Nukleyar*, a production of the Philippine Educational Theater Association (PETA). Ryan Cayabyab, one of the most successful composers of pop, contributed *Ramahari* (*Rama the King*, 1980) and *El Filibusterismo* (*The Filibuster*, 1991), based on the second novel of José Rizal. Cayabyab has also experimented with fusing traditional Filipino rhythms and melodic elements with jazz and rock. His output includes the extended compositions *Misa* (1983) and *Kapinangan* (1981), plus songs of lighter character, such as "*Kay Ganda ng Ating Musika*" ('How Beautiful Is Our Music', 1978) and "*Tsismis*" ('Gossip', 1981).

In the 1980s, the Filipinization of popular music gained further headway with the emergence of the Manila sound, a composition characterized by schmaltzy lyrics and the use of a form of urban jargon called Taglish, a contraction of Tagalog and English. Manila-sound songs easily spread among young audiences, mostly composed of students from exclusive sectarian schools.

A leading pioneer of the Manila sound, the Hotdog Band, came out with its initial hits "*Ikaw Ang Miss Universe Ng Buhay Ko*" ('You Are the Miss Universe of My Life'), "Manila," and "*Pers Lab*" ('First Love'). The Cinderella Band contributed "*Superstar Ng Buhay Ko*" ('Superstar of My Life') and "*Boyfriend Kong Baduy*" ('My Nerd Boyfriend'). Another exponent of the Manila sound was the APO Hiking Society, which included in its repertoire satirical songs such as "American Junk," a jab at the supposed colonial mentality of young Filipinos. Other APO Hiking Society songs were directed against the regime of Ferdinand Marcos.

BALLADIC STYLES OF POPULAR MUSIC

The music of Bob Dylan, Joan Baez, and Peter, Paul, and Mary made a strong impact on Filipino folk balladeers, whose poetry covered a broad range of contemporary issues—the tyranny of the Marcos government, corruption, American economic imperialism, gender issues, environmental pollution, and the emulation of Filipino values and patriotism. A sampling of these compositions includes "*Ako'y Pinoy*" ('I am a Filipino') and "*Tayo'y Mga Pinoy*" ('We're Filipinos') by Florante de Leon, Freddie Aguilar's prize-winning "*Anak*" ('Child'), and "*Babae*" ('Woman') and "*Base Militar*" ('Military Bases') by the folk-singing duo of Carina Constantino David and Rebecca Demetillo Abraham. Other prominent names include Susan Fernandez Magno, Gary Granada, and Jess Santiago.

On the lighter side, Yoyoy Villame, a former driver of a jeepney, has been catering to a more plebeian audience with his witty narratives. His subjects include folksy interpretations of such historical events as the Spanish discovery of the Philippines (*Magellan*) and commentaries about everyday experiences such as traffic congestion (*Trapik*). He sings his poetry to medleys of preexisting tunes, some of which include nursery songs.

The folk-ballad style was furthered by such late-1980s groups as Asin ('Salt'), Edru Abraham's Kontra-Gapi (a contraction of *Kontamporaryong Gamelang Pilipino*) ('Contemporary Filipino Gamelan'), and Bagong Lumad ('New Tradition'), led by Joey Ayala. These groups included in their ensembles traditional ethnic instruments such as the Jew's harp (*kubing*), bossed gongs laid in a row (*kulintang*), tube stampers (*tongatong*), deep-rimmed bossed gong (*agung*), and two-stringed lute (*faglong*).

FILIPINO POP IN THE 1990s

The adoption of the latest trends in the world of American pop remains a strong component in the local youth culture. The stage performances of such local singing idols as Joey Valenciano and Martin Nievera bear the imprints of Michael Jackson's artistry. Rap musicians such as M. C. Hammer and Vanilla Ice had their immediate Filipino counterparts in Francis Magalona and Andrew E. Rap artists who have created Filipino lyrics have also covered a gamut of topics from positive Filipino values and a sense of patriotism ("*Mga Kababayan Ko*" ['My Countrymen']) to sex and highly mundane subjects ("*Humanap Ka Nang Panget*" ['Choose an Ugly One']).

Philippine pop has branched out into several directions from its initial function as music for dancing and entertainment. It now appears in a variety of forms that represent the multifaceted and complex needs of a highly acculturated society. In spite of the sustained influence of a global pop-music industry, Filipino songwriters have sought to use the medium to express contemporary views and sentiments regarding their own life as a people with a unique history and culture. At the same time, performers have begun to develop styles and mediums with elements related to native Filipino musics.

Filipino pop music of the late 1990s has developed along two main lines—one in which show bands play covers of international (but especially British and American) hits in bars and hotel lounges and a thriving do-it-yourself scene in which underground bands take an active role in composing, arranging, and recording their own music. The show bands, at least partly an outgrowth of the vestiges of colonialism, cater to upper middle-class Filipinos, tourists, and American military personnel. In style, instrumentation (singer plus rhythm section) and audience, show bands have not changed since the 1960s; their repertoire relies heavily on standard lounge hits—songs by Barry Manilow, Neil Diamond, and other late-twentieth-century crooners.

The strongest new growth in Filipino popular music has been in the alternative-music scene. The typical band's setup may include a singer, a drummer, a guitarist, a bassist, a keyboardist, and any other instruments deemed necessary to the style, or any other instruments that the members happen to play. The alternative-music scene in the Philippines encompasses a variety of styles (some of them blended), including grunge, heavy metal, reggae, ska, folk, and punk, in addition to more standard styles of rock and pop. No matter what the style, however, these bands perform in small clubs for dedicated audiences and are generally not financed by big business; nor do they have the luxury of extended contracts with a hotel or a nightclub.

Most of the significant alternative bands tend to model their style after one or more famous foreign bands, but original compositions are the norm, rather than the exception. In addition, the vocalists may sing in either English or Filipino. The possibility for one of these alternative bands to produce a hit is fairly limited, because the major record labels do not financially support alternative music as much as they support the kind of mainstream pop that will establish a steady income. For any of these groups, the term *hit* is relative, compared with the more prominent bands that have signed with major record labels. The groups under discussion tend to press their own homemade recordings, and they receive limited airplay on alternative radio stations and in clubs.

The alternative-pop sound tends to be upbeat and derivative of the guitar-based American light-rock sound of the late 1970s through the 1980s. Alternative-pop bands of the 1990s include Side-A, who first gained popularity in the 1980s. Influenced by such foreign bands as Toto and the Doobie Brothers, their compositions are generally in English and tend to focus on love. Some of their more popular songs of the early 1990s include "Hold On," "So Many Questions," and "Forevermore." Another pop band, Introvoys, came to the forefront by 1992. Like those of Side-A, Introvoys' songs ("Will I Survive?" and "Line to Heaven") are generally in English and focus on teenage love.

In the independent-rock scene, three of the most important bands offer a choice of blended styles and influences. The Dawn is popularly credited with starting the entire trend of underground Filipino bands; they were influenced by the New York City and London "New Wave" movement in the 1980s (the Talking Heads, Blondie, and other groups), but developed a heavier sound in the early 1990s. They disbanded in 1995, but their contributions to the scene are still valued. Afterimage, which came to the forefront in 1992, falls generally under the rock rubric, but relies heavily on the keyboard synthesizer. The sound of the band appears to reflect influence from such foreign bands as U2, Yes, and Rush. Songs in English and Filipino, such as "Next in Line," "*Pagtawid*" ('Crossing'), and "*Habang May Buhay*" ('Until There Is Life'), have lyrics about personal experiences, introspection, and the exploration of individual values. The Eraserheads have been influenced by folk, pop, and the Beatles, but their sound is grittier in its use of electric guitars and drums. They first became popular in 1993, and two of their biggest hits ("*Pare Ko*" ['My Pal'] and "*Magasin*" ['Magazine']) are sung in Filipino. Most of the Eraserheads' repertoire centers on student and teenage life, delivered with wit and sentimentality.

The styles of grunge, reggae, ska, and punk have each spawned Filipino practitioners since the mid-1990s. Many of the most important hits from these bands are sung in Filipino, though English is also used. The Teeth, a grunge band that became popular in 1995 is modeled roughly after some U.S. bands that came to popularity in the 1980s—bands such as Nirvana, Alice in Chains, and Pearl Jam. The reggae band Tropical Depression, formed in 1992, had gained popularity in the Philippines by 1993. Their songs include "*Kapayapaan*" ('Peace') and "*Bilog Nanaman Ang Buwan*" ('The Moon Is Full Again'), and their closest aural counterpart is Bob Marley and the Wailers. By the mid-1990s, Put3ska—whose name is a pun on *putris-ka* 'you son-of-a-gun'— was rising in fame. Modeled after those of the British band Madness, their English-language hits include "Manila Girl" and "Birthday Song." The punk group

The styles of grunge, reggae, ska, and punk have each spawned Filipino practitioners since the mid-1990s.

Yano is stylistically similar to the Clash and the Sex Pistols, British punk groups of the 1970s and 1980s. Yano began performing extensively in 1994, and two of their strongest songs include "*Tsinelas*" ('Slippers') and "*Banal Na Aso, Santong Kabayo*" ('Sacred Dog, Holy Horse').

As each new wave of musical influence reached the Philippines in the twentieth century, certain styles and bands have caught on with the record-, cassette-, and CD-buying public. However, a foreign band's popularity does not guarantee the creation of an indigenous response. In addition, any local response may not occur for years, sometimes decades. The rich array of Filipino and foreign popular musics, and the varied settings in which they may occur, have contributed to the availability of virtually any type of popular music that an eager listener desires.

Islamic Communities of the Southern Philippines

Ramón P. Santos

Diversity in Islamic Musical Traditions
Instrumental Music
Vocal Music

Musical practices of the Islamic communities in the southern Philippine islands of Mindanao and the Sulu Archipelago reflect separate pre-Islamic cultural traditions. Histories of relations, contacts, and alliances with peoples outside these communities contributed to the distinctiveness of their characters—the Tausug with peoples from North Borneo (Mednick 1957) and the Samal with communities from Johore (Stone 1962). The Maguindanao had a lesser degree of contact with neighboring peoples, and the Maranao were long isolated from the outside world (Cadar 1975), but both eventually became recipients of foreign cultural influences during centuries of dynamic commercial activity.

From the 800s to the 1400s, trade flourished in the region, bringing into close contact peoples from the Middle East, China, the Malay Peninsula, the Philippines, Borneo, the Indonesian Archipelago, and as far south as New Guinea. Participating for centuries in commercial activities, the Philippines not only acquired artifacts (like Chinese ceramics and Javanese and Sumatran pottery and gold ornaments), but also absorbed cultural influences from overseas. The period of the expansion of the Majapahit Empire is cited for the proliferation of musical instruments and the cross-fertilization of myths and epics (Fox 1959).

The Islamic community in the Philippines consists of five major ethnolinguistic groups: the Maguindanao, of Cotabato; the Maranao, of Lanao and Cotabato; the Samal and Jama Mapun, of the Sulu Islands of Sibutu and Cagayan de Sulu (Casiño 1976); the Tausug, of the Sulu islands of Jolo, Siasi, and Tawi Tawi; and the Yakan, of Basilan and Zamboanga, on the westernmost tip of Mindanao. Other smaller groups are the Sama-Bajao, a seafaring people, scattered throughout the Sulu Archipelago; the Sangil, in Cotabato and Davao; and the Melebugnon, of Balabac Island.

Before the first traces of contact with other religious civilizations (at the start of the first millennium), animistic beliefs and forms of worship pervaded the cultural practices of the early Filipinos. Though pre-Islamic faiths drew some influences from Hinduism, they remained essentially characterized by the worship of local divinities and spirits of dead ancestors—worship that called for the services of mediums and shamans. Even today, ritual practices have survived. These include *pagipat,* a curing

Despite the prominence of Islamic institutional precepts in popular social life, local religious interpretations have allowed pre-Islamic artistic practices to flourish.

rite of the Maguindanao, and *magigal jin,* a possession dance of the Sama-Bajao of Sitangkai.

Islam came to the southern Philippines at different stages. Its presence is attributed to the activities of Muslim traders and Sufi missionaries, and the arrival of Muslim political figures (Abubakar 1983). Its initial presence resulted from international trade controlled by Arabs and other Muslims from West Asia. The antiforeign policy of China in the 800s intensified the movement of Arab merchants directly between North Africa and Southeast Asia (Fox 1959). Many Muslim traders, settling in Borneo and the Sulu Islands, married into the local populations, which consisted of sultanates and extended families.

In the 1300s, Islam was formally introduced with the arrival of holy men (*makhdumin*) whose principal mission was to attend to the spiritual needs of the Muslim residents. Genealogical accounts (*tarsilas*) single out the Sufi missionary Makdum Karim for having made headway in Islamizing Jolo (Majul 1974).

In the eastern and northern portions of Mindanao, the proliferation of Muslim traders and teachers eased the founding of Islamic political institutions by Muhamad Kabungsuan, a highly influential Arab-Malay. Marital alliances between foreign Muslims and local converts resulted in the Islamic ancestries of Maguindanao, Buayan, and Butig, and the principle of politics by marriage later spread among the Maranao, who were related to the Ilanon of the Butig lineage.

Through the work of such missionary groups as the Hadramaut Sayyid, Islamic influence spread extensively, and was felt as far north as Luzon. In 1521, with the coming of the Spanish, the Philippines became the final frontier of the missionary odyssey of Islam in Southeast Asia. The imposition of Christianity checked the growth of Islam, and through a series of armed conquests and eventual conversions, diminished its influence. However, the Filipino Muslims in Mindanao, who successfully resisted the Spanish conquest of the islands, preserved both a common religious heritage and their ethnic independence.

It is within a larger historic and cultural perspective that the artistic traditions of the Islamic communities can be perceived: the culture combines indigenous practices related to animist worship, a semicourt tradition (emanating from cultural contacts with other Southeast Asian peoples and civilizations), traditional arts from older Islamic countries, Islamic forms of worship, and views on the social distinction between religious and secular forms of art. Through different levels of adaptation and accommodation, most pre-Islamic practices have become cultural icons of the Filipino Muslim communities.

DIVERSITY IN ISLAMIC MUSICAL TRADITIONS

The distinctiveness of the cultures that make up the larger Islamic society in Mindanao and Sulu precludes the possibility of viewing their musical practices as belonging to one single tradition. Similarities do exist in the musical inventories, as in some vocal styles within the larger society, but theoretical concepts, functions, aesthetics, and repertoires differ from culture to culture, and even from village to village belonging to one language group.

To provide a comprehensive description of the musics of Filipino Muslim communities, the present essay has pieced together basic information from area studies by various scholars: the Maguindanao by José Maceda (1963, 1984, 1988) and Aga Mayo Butocan (1987); the Maranao by Usopay Cadar (1975, 1980) and Steven Otto (1985, 1996); the Tausug by Thomas Kiefer (1970) and Ricardo D. Trimillos (1972); the Yakan by Arsenio Nicolas (1977); and the Sama of Sitangkai by Maceda and Alain Martenot (1976). This writer's research on aspects of Maranao vocal repertoire and instrumental musical forms of the Maguindanao, the Yakan, the Tausug, and the Bajao have also been included.

The musical practices of these societies reflect the fusion of disparate traditional traits. Despite the prominence of Islamic institutional precepts in popular social life, local religious interpretations have allowed pre-Islamic artistic practices to flourish. Ancient rites and beliefs have remained principal sources of communication with a metaphysical world. Instead of setting canonic restrictions on artistic expression, the forms of art of these Islamic cultures have enhanced the stylistic breadth of existing repertoires, especially vocal ones. This kind of artistic freedom may reflect each local society's sense of independence from any one dominant political or religious ideology.

INSTRUMENTAL MUSIC

The bossed-gong cultures with horizontal gongs laid in a row (figure 1) are the most visible and familiar symbols of the musical traditions of Filipinos in western Mindanao and the Sulu Archipelago. They are related to other bossed gongs in Southeast Asia—Borneo, Indonesia, Thailand, and some village peoples in Guangxi, Hubei, and Yunnan provinces of southern China. The principal instrument, called *kulintang* by the Maguindanao and Maranao is a set of graduated gongs laid in a row in a wooden frame. The set usually consists of seven to eight gongs, with as many as eleven or thirteen in some groups (like the Tausug), or as few as five (among the Yakan in Basilan island). Young boys and girls practice on a miniature copy of the *kulintang* called *sarunay*, a set of rectangular metal plates with a protrusion in the center. The plates are held together by strings on both ends and laid on a wooden frame, where they are separated by wooden pegs that join the two sides of the frame (figure 2). Each of the following groups—the Maguindanao and Maranao of western Mindanao, and the Tausug, the Yakan, and the Sama-Bajao of the Sulu Archipelago—uses some form of bossed-gong ensemble; a discussion of other instruments follows.

The Maguindanao

Maguindanao Province is dominated by the Mindanao River, which runs about 300 kilometers before it spills into Illana Bay. The river's floodplain is responsible for the

FIGURE 1 Horizontal bossed gongs. The wooden frame is 160 centimeters long; the gongs are 18–22 centimeters wide. Courtesy University of the Philippines Archive.

FIGURE 2 The *sarunay,* a small type of *kulintang* made of metal plates with rounded protrusions. Photo by Ramón P. Santos.

fertility of the soil. The river serves as an important link among people in the province, and through ease of transport and communication has contributed to a relative consistency in musical ensembles and genres. Most of the Maguindanao people are farmers of rice, and rice is one of the primary exports of the province.

Among the Maguindanao of Datu Piang of the upper Mindanao River, the *kulintang* is the primary musical instrument (figure 3). Other gong instruments of this group include one, two, or three vertically suspended gongs: the *agung* (a large, deep-rimmed gong, with a higher boss), two pairs of *gandingan* (gongs with narrower rim and lower boss), and one *babandil* (smaller than an *agung,* with a narrower, turned-in rim and a low boss). The ensemble is complemented by a drum called *dabakan.*

Kulintang tones are not tuned to a fixed temperament. Researchers have observed a loose sequential pattern of large and small intervals in extant eight-gong sets, but the arrangements of the tones vary from one set to another. In the construction of *kulintang* gongs, the lowest (*pangandungan*) and the highest (*pamantikan*) are the first to be cast. The tones of the other gongs are then adjusted to each other in relation to the two extremes (Maceda 1963).

The *kulintang* is important social property. Being closely identified with individual families, the instruments of the ensemble—especially the old types, called *burunay*—are highly valued, priceless heirlooms that can command a high price as dowries. The ownership of these instruments indicates high social status and cultivated taste (Butocan 1987).

One primary function of *kulintang* music is to entertain guests at public occasions, including weddings, baptisms, and other formal rites, providing a unique medium of interaction within the community. This interaction may be in the form of a competition, in which players pit their musical and creative skills against each other, or in a dialogue between individual men and women, which could later develop into courtship.

The Maguindanao *palabunibunyan,* a Simuay ensemble, consists of five performers playing an eight-gong *kulintang,* two *agung,* two pairs of *gandingan,* a *babandil,* and a goblet-shaped drum (*dabakan*). The *kulintang* is played with two mallets of light wood (*basal*) (figure 4). The two *agung,* facing each other, are played with one rubber-padded mallet. Some playing techniques that produce different tones and durations include muffling the boss with the left hand and alternately striking the boss with the padded end of the mallet, followed by striking the surface with the unpadded part (*kadtinengka*). The two pairs of *gandingan* are played by one musician using two padded mallets, with each hand striking two gongs that face each other. The older *gandingan* are larger in size, with a longer resonance (ringing for a

FIGURE 3 Maguindanao *kulintang* ensemble of Catabato, Mindanao. Photo by Ramón P. Santos.

longer period of time). The smaller *gandingan,* about 40 centimeters in diameter, produce higher tones. The *babandil* is usually struck on the rim with a pair of thin bamboo sticks, producing bright, metallic sounds.

The instruments have different roles in the musical fabric. The *kulintang* serves as a melodic instrument, determining the shape of each piece. The *agung* provides a rhythmic line, while the *gandingan,* with their overlapping sonorities, create a continuum of sound. The *dabakan* maintains the rhythmic motion, while the *babandil* serves as a principal ostinato instrument. In most cases, the *babandil* introduces each piece by playing the appropriate rhythmic mode, followed by the *dabakan.* The function of the *babandil* as an ostinato instrument may be taken by a separate musician

FIGURE 4 Aga Mayo-Butocan, professor of Maguindanao music in the College of Music, University of the Philippines, plays a *kulintang.* Visible in the background are one *babandil,* four *gandingan,* and parts of two *agung.* Photo by Ramón P. Santos.

kulintang Southern Philippine instrument, a row of five to eight bossed gongs

agung Large, deep-rimmed hanging gong used in the *kulintang* ensemble

gandingan Pair of shallow-rimmed gongs used in the *kulintang* ensemble

babandil Small gong with turned-in rim and low boss, used in the *kulintang* ensemble

dabakan *Kulintang* ensemble drum with goblet-shaped coconut wood body and goatskin head

FIGURE 5 Excerpt from a Maguindanao *kulintang* performance. Transcription by Aga Mayo Butocan and Ramón P. Santos.

on the *pamantikan* (the highest gong of the *kulintang*). The transcription in figure 5 illustrates the arrangement of a typical piece.

Though *kulintang* music is usually regarded as a secular social activity, it has been integrated into religion-sanctioned activities such as weddings (*kalilang*) and baptisms (*paigo sa ragat* 'seawater baptism'). In the curing rite called *kapagipat* and its variants *pagipat* and *pagubad*, the *tagunggo* rhythm is played to accompany the dance of exorcism by a medium (*pedtunungan*) in the patient's house. The *tagunggo* is

FIGURE 5 (*continued*)

played by the *kulintang* ensemble to accompany the *sagayan,* a dance of communication with the world of spirits. The dancer-medium is often garbed as a warrior, armed with a kris and a shield.

Most of the instruments of the *palabunibunyan* are played singly for various social and religious functions. Young men can play the *gandingan* to communicate their love to young women. Because the four distinct tones of the *gandingan* duplicate different tones in the Maguindanao language, basic phrases can be communicated to people listening for them. The *agung,* traditionally considered a male instrument, is played to call people to assemble or mark important hours of the day during Ramadan (particularly prior to the beginning and ending of fasting), or to announce the death of a parent (figure 6). The sound of the *agung,* when properly transmitted, is considered to possess supernatural powers. The large drum called *dabu-dabu* is sounded each Friday to mark noontime prayers (Butocan 1987).

FIGURE 6 The *agung,* shown suspended, with mallet. The width of the face is 50 centimeters. Courtesy University of Philippines Archive.

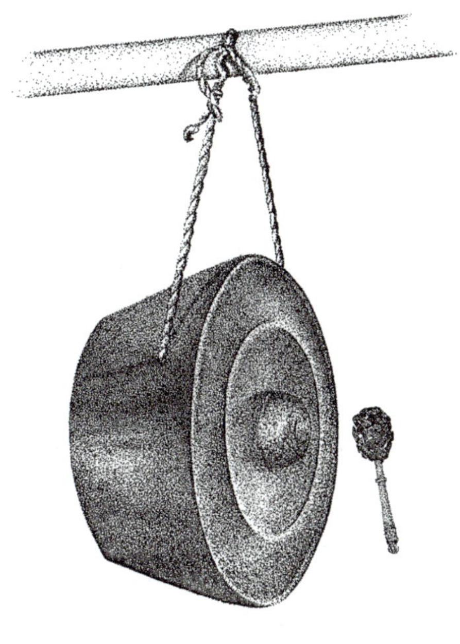

In a work on the Maguindanao *kulintang* tradition in Datu Piang, José Maceda wrote that the repertoire is based on three rhythmic modes, usually played as a suite of pieces: *duyug, sinulug,* and *tidtu.* A fourth mode, *tagunggo,* is usually reserved for rituals and ceremonies. In the village of Simuay, the modes are called *binalig, sinulug,* and *tidtu.* According to Butocan (1987), the modes relate to different shades of moods and emotions: *binalig* expresses strong feelings, such as anger or joy, *sinulug* evokes sentimentality, and *tidtu* creates excitement (figure 7). *Tidtu* is especially well suited to musical jousts, exhibiting the players' virtuosity. A series of pieces based on the modes and their variations could be grouped as a suite and played as an extended descriptive composition related to a common theme. The following set piece was played by a group from Datu Piang, led by Salbanon Beray and Salima Limba, musically relating the phases of courtship and the cycle of life:

Silung (modern *binalig*), portraying two lovers.
Sinulug, in which a woman accepts a man's suit, and they plan to marry.
Tidtu, when the man's parents agree on the dowry.
Binalig, when the dowry and wedding are publicized.
Anun (modern *sinulog*), when the wedding is solemnized.
Tagunggo, for the offspring's baptism.

The individual pieces in the Simuay *kulintang* repertoire usually consist of five sectional types: an introduction, repeated sections, an ascending transition, a descending

FIGURE 7 Four Maguindanao *kulintang* rhythmic modes as played on the goblet-shaped drum (*dabakan*). Transcription by Aga Mayo Butocan.

transition, and a conclusion. The repeated sections can be extended in length at the player's pleasure.

Old and modern styles of playing in Simuay are called *minuna* and *sinaguna,* respectively. The *minuna* style is usually slower and more formal, using the large *gandingan.* An older social etiquette is observed with regard to traditional gender assignments on the instruments and to formalities in the invitation to perform and acceptance. The musical orientation of *sinaguna* appeals to the younger generation of players, who prefer the smaller *gandingan,* a faster rhythmic pace, and highly ornamental renditions. In the latter style, traditional gender propriety is often dispensed with. Creativity is more remarkable, sometimes reaching the fringes of the canonic limits of older tradition, especially in musical competitions. The late virtuoso Mamaluba Guiamalon of Pikit, Cotabato, entertained his audiences by rearranging the sequential position of the gongs, or sometimes putting them in cluster on a native mat and playing blindfolded.

The Maranao

Most Maranao people live in the province of Lanao del Sur, an area dominated by Lake Lanao, partly bordered by mountains. Like the Maguindanao, the Maranao grow rice as a primary crop. One of the most conservative of the Filipino Muslim groups, the Maranao tend to isolate themselves from outside cultural and political influences. As with the Mindanao River, Lake Lanao's presence in the Maranao heartland has led to greater musical consistency than if the population had been widely dispersed.

Another major bossed-gong tradition exists among the Maranao. The Maranao *kulintang* ensemble consists of an eight-piece *kulintang,* a *dubakan,* a *bubundir,* and two deep-rimmed gongs: the *pumalsan* and the *penanggisa-an,* played separately by two musicians. Maranao *kulintang* music has been described as a medium for expressing Maranao traditional culture and etiquette, and as a form of communication, especially among the players. Musicians' formal and artistic conduct during a performance is particularly emphasized, including the manner of approaching and moving away from the instruments, and the appropriate position for handling and playing each instrument. On the way to the *kulintang,* a lady performer walks with deliberate grace, the right hand swaying slowly by her side, and the left hand holding the long wraparound skirt called *malong.* Other ceremonial activities, such as short vocal exhortations, could occur before the actual making of music begins. Seniority and deference to the more seasoned masters are also observed whenever many performers are present on a given occasion. The playing of the *kulintang* usually occurs in private homes or ancestral houses called *torogan* (Cadar 1975).

The two principal instruments of the Maranao *kulintangan* are the *kulintang* (usually played by a young woman) and the *dubakan* (traditionally reserved for men). Their musical renditions are likened to a dialogue, sometimes developing into courtship, moderated by the *bubundir* (Cadar 1975). As the *kulintang* sets the musical idea and elaborates on it, the *dubakan* responds according to the musical nuances and permutations, in the manner of a poetic interlocution between a young man and a woman. The two *agung* lend their support to this interaction, with the *penanggisa-an* providing the basic pulse and the *pumalsan* providing elaboration.

Each *kulintang* piece is made up of melodic segments or phrases consisting of eight strokes, called *tukimug*—a term directly related to poetry, song, or proverb (Cadar 1980). Each *tukimug* may be repeated, varied, or extended by one or two more segments. A *tukimug* usually consists of tones, belonging to either the first four gongs (*kundongan*) or the four upper gongs (*anonan*), with the *kundongan tukimug* centering on gong 3 and the *anonan* on gong 6. A *tukimug* that contains tones 3, 4, 5, and 6 usually functions as a transition between the lower and the upper ranges of the *kulintang* (Otto 1985).

The *kulintang* repertoire consists of pieces about practically all aspects of Maranao life and culture, including "*Kapupanok*" ('Bird'), "*Kasolotan*" ('Sultan'), "*Kapmangurib*" ('Sunset on the Western Horizon'), "*Kaplakitan*" ('Love Proposal [on Behalf of Someone Else]'), "*Kapanon*" ('Sentiment'), "*Kasagoronan*" ('Musical Sounds'), and "*Kaphemabaro*" ('Naughty Lady'). Studies on the Maranao *kakolintang* (art of playing *kulintang*) have come up with classifications based on either thematic content (moral values, nature, abstract concepts), or stylistic orientation (*andung* 'old', *bago* 'new', and compositions of non-Maranao sources).

Among the collection of the Maranao *kulintang* repertoire are signature pieces, which usually provide the high point in important public performances. They are highly regarded, not only for their structural complexity and demands on the artist's skills, but also for the depth of their emotional and intellectual content.

"*Kapaginandung*" ('Things of the Past') and "*Katitik Panday*" ('Creative Beating'), being related to each other, belong to the *andung* category of pieces. "*Kapagonor*" ('High Art') and "*Kapromayas*" ('Piece from the Town of Rumayas') are the leading pieces in the *bago* repertoire. They represent the new style, including the *kapangolilat sa kulintang*, the art of twirling the mallets during the performance of "*Kapagonor.*" The performer ordinarily starts the piece using both mallets, which usually have tassels and are painted with primary colors. As the music progresses with the participation of the other instruments, the player of the *kulintang* continues to delineate the melody with her right mallet while twirling the other mallet. When she feels that the music can be sustained by the supporting instruments, the player stops beating altogether, and twirls both mallets simultaneously, making periodic punctuations on either of the two principal tones (Otto 1985).

The pieces are composed or adapted from existing songs or poetic verses; each piece is identified not only by its melodic (gong) patterns, but also by its tempo and basic rhythmic structure. The complexity of each piece of music, in number and development of *tukimug,* is based on the amount of information being expressed. The piece "*Kasolotan,*" for example, is a satirical narrative song about the fortunes of a young man who traveled to Manila to seek a position in government. The improbability of realizing his ambition, implying a lengthy and almost endless process, lends itself well to a long musical discourse. In Maranao society, the ability to vary, develop, and extend thematic materials is considered an important determinant of artistic maturity and skill.

Some of the instruments can also be played singly. The *agung* is usually sounded to announce the enthronement or crowning of a sultan, or formally greet distin-

Tausug *kulintangan* music is usually heard during weddings and other social functions and serves for general entertainment. The *lubak-lubak* pieces are played to accompany dancing and may be extended as long as the dancers can sustain their movements.

guished guests (*inandang*) in a social gathering. A patriarchal leader (*datu*) can summon his subjects by having the summons (*kaburuburu*) sounded on the *agung,* the same instrument that plays the *kabalok* to announce the death of a member of a family. The large drum called *dabu-dabu* is used to announce the prayers on Friday at noon.

The Sulu Archipelago

The Sulu Archipelago encompasses at least nine hundred islands (including the large islands of Basilan, Jolo, and Tawi-Tawi) in two provinces: Sulu in the northeast, and Tawi-Tawi in the southwest, close to Borneo. Because of its proximity to northeastern Borneo, the Sulu Archipelago is included in the continuum of horizontal gong-chime music cultures extending from Borneo through Mindanao. *Kulintang* and instruments resembling *kulintang* are used by the Tausug, the Yakan, and the Sama-Bajao.

The Tausug

The *kulintangan* ensemble of the Tausug of Jolo includes a *kulintangan* consisting of eight or eleven gongs laid in a row, and a pair of hanging gongs called *duwahan.* This pair of gongs consists of the *pulakan,* a medium-sized, deep-rimmed gong; and the *bua,* a large, narrow-rimmed gong that people in Jolo believe was brought by Chinese traders at the turn of the 1300s. In addition to the *kulintangan* and *duwahan,* the basic rhythmic structure is articulated on a large, deep-rimmed gong called *tunggalan* or *aalakan,* and a pair of two-headed drums, the *gandang.* A sixth musician plays the rhythmic ostinato *tung-tung* on *tutuntungan,* one of the upper gongs of the *kulintang.* Sometimes the *aalakan* is played with one *kulintang* gong and a *gandang* (Kiefer 1970).

Kulintangan music is usually heard during weddings and other social functions and serves for general entertainment. The pieces are categorized in three types: *sinug,* a two-part piece, consisting of a slow introduction and a rhythmic section; *kuriri,* a single-part piece, characterized by a fast tempo; and *lubak-lubak,* also a single-part piece with a characteristic tune. The *lubak-lubak* is played to accompany dancing and may be extended as long as the dancers can sustain their movements. The three types of compositions are played in sequence, though several tunes on the *sinug* and the *kuriri* may be performed before the *lubak-lubak.*

The Yakan

Quite related to the *kulintang* music of the Tausug is the repertoire of the *tagunggu* ensemble of the Yakan of the island of Basilan. The two Yakan types of composition, usually played one after the other, are the preparation (*te-ed*) and the composition proper (*kuriri*). The latter has a faster tempo (figure 8). Each composition may be extended indefinitely. The music is highly improvised, revolving around the *lebad,* a

TRACK 14

FIGURE 8 Excerpt from a *kwintang* performance of a Yakan *kuriri,* as played by Juwing Jamma. Transcription by Ramón P. Santos.

musical unit that represents a shade of emotion or extramusical idea. Each piece contains various *lebad,* which the player of the *kwintangan* expands by repetition, juxtaposition, and permutation. According to the people from Lamitan in Basilan, a musician's artistic skill is measured by the number of *lebad* he or she can recreate in a performance, and on the manner of putting them together in logical sequence. The basic Yakan scale consists of five tones, roughly corresponding to the intervallic sequence of C–E–G–A–C.

A principal instrument of the *tagunggu* ensemble is the horizontal five-gong *kwintang* (figure 9). Other instruments are a cracked bamboo tube (*gandang*) and a set of three hanging *agung* (figure 10). Optional instruments include a five-key xylophone (*gabbang*) and percussion beams (*kwintangan kayu*). A separate player plays the *nulanting,* a rhythmic ostinato, on the highest gong of the *kwintangan.* The number of players varies, because the *agung* may be performed by one, two, or three musicians (*meglebuan*). When a single performer plays them, one foot rests on the inner chamber of the lowest gong (*lerukan*), the left hand holds the side of the boss of the

FIGURE 9 The Yakan *kwintang,* a five-gong melody instrument. Photo by Ramón P. Santos.

FIGURE 10 The Yakan *agung,* a set of three gongs played by a single musician. Photo by Ramón P. Santos.

highest gong (*labuan*), and the middle-pitched gong (*penagungguan*) is left to resonate. The three *agung* may be played independently of the *kwintangan* and the *gandang* (*ngagung*) (Nicolas 1977).

Tagunggu music of the Yakan is heard in wedding celebrations, during a *paggunting* (baptism-initiation) and *pag-tamat* (graduation from training in Qur'ānic reading). Sometimes a dance is performed by a young woman; it has graceful body movements and rhythmic motions of the fingers. In contrast, a man with a lance and a shield dances around her in a frenzy, protecting her from harm.

Sama-Bajao

An even closer association between *kulintang* music and dance is practiced by the Sama, also known as the Bajao, whose main source of livelihood and existence is the seas around the Sulu Archipelago. Most of the available data on the Sama are found in the recordings and notes of Alain Martenot and José Maceda on the people of Sitangkai.

The orchestra (*pangongka'an*) of the Sama from Sitangkai has a *kulintangan* of seven to nine gongs, played by two performers. The *kulintangan* melodies consist of three to eight tones, normally played by the right hand. The left hand sounds the lower gongs at a slower rhythm. The second *kulintang* musician plays an ostinato pattern on one of the highest gongs (*solembat*). The rest of the ensemble includes the *tamuk,* a large hanging gong played by one musician; the *bua,* a narrow-rimmed gong; and the *pulakan,* a smaller *agung.* The drum (*tambul*) is a long bronze cylinder with a goatskin head.

The entire ensemble is closely associated with dance, and performances occur on special occasions, including circumcision (*magislam*), marriage (*magkawin*), and dances of possession (*magigal jin*). The metaphysical aspect of the musical performance is part of its total effect, since it is believed that the spirits and the powers of dead ancestors reside in the instruments, whose sounds channel communications between the world of spirits and the human community.

In the gong music of the Sama, distinctions of gender in instrumental assignment are more strictly observed than in other areas. Women play the *kulintangan,* and men play the hanging gongs. The drum may be handled by either men or women. Wooden castanets (*bola'bola'*) are used exclusively by female dancers in secular pieces (Martenot and Maceda 1976).

In the repertoire of Sama gong music, the *titik tagunggu* is considered the simplest because only three gongs of the *kulintangan* are played. It is usually performed as a ceremonial piece, sometimes aboard a boat, with dancers rhythmically clicking their castanets. The *titik tabawan* and the *titik jin,* however, are possession dances, performed by female and male mediums, respectively. The *lellang,* another piece related to possession by spirits, is performed as a concluding part of a rite, and is reserved to the chief medium. The orchestration of the gong music differs from piece to piece, as in *titik jin,* which uses only two hanging gongs, and in *titik tagunggu,* which dispenses with all the hanging gongs.

Outside the musical repertoire with directly supernatural character are pieces of less religious nature. The *tariray* is usually danced by young women with subtle erotic movements of the hands and body, in contrast with the *titik tabawan,* associated with older women (Maceda and Martenot 1976). Among the Sama-Bajao of Bus-Bus on Jolo island, the *duldang-duldang* 'darling-darling' is a song-dance debate performed by pairs of male and female dancers, who alternate in singing verses of courtship in high, strained timbres. The female dancers, as in other instances, wear long and pointed artificial fingernails, called *djang-gay* (figure 11). The interaction is supported by the playing of a melodic-rhythmic drone on the *kulintangan.* Two other pieces

FIGURE 11 Two Sama-Bajao children performing *duldang-duldang,* a courtship song-dance debate, as a third child plays a *kulintangan.* Photo courtesy NAMCYA Foundation.

are independent of dance. One is the *titik to'ongan,* a variational piece rendered in fast tempo. Another is the *sambulayang,* which virtuosically employs the entire tonal gamut of the *pagongka'an.*

Other instruments

Aside from the bossed-gong traditions, Islamic communities in Mindanao and Sulu have a wide collection of other instruments, ranging from bamboo and wooden idiophones to a variety of strings and winds.

Among the Maguindanao of Dinaig, Maguindanao Province, a wooden version of the *kulintang* is made of hardwood slats cut in graduated sizes, each slat tuned by the removal of a sliced curve in its middle (figure 12). Because the tones on the

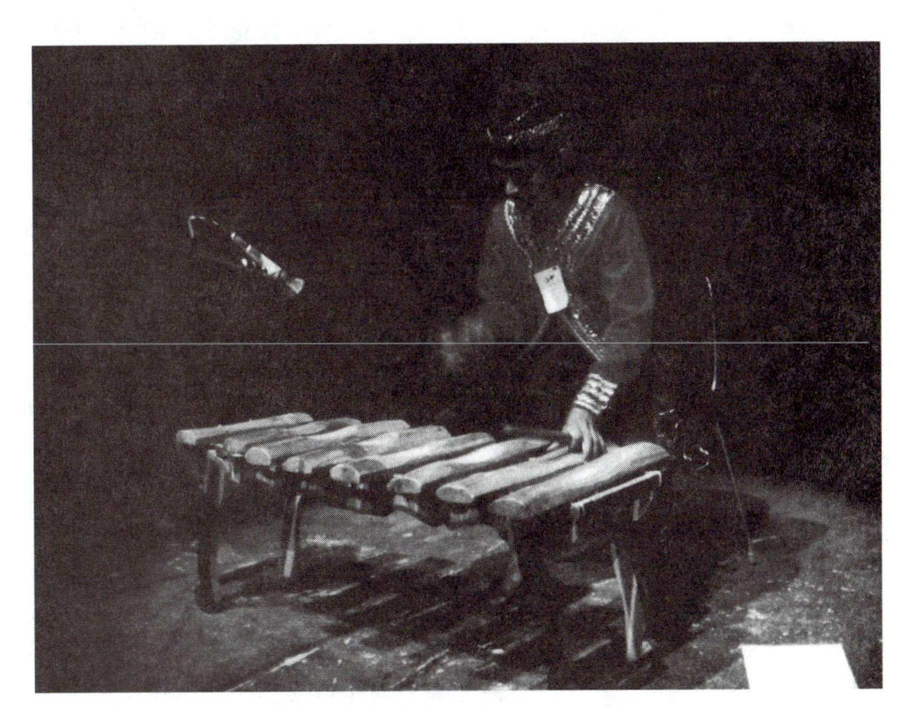

FIGURE 12 Salipada Muhamad, a Maguindanao musician, plays a wooden *kulintang.* Photo courtesy NAMCYA Foundation.

kwintang Yakan instrument having five bossed gongs in a row

gabbang Small, flat xylophone from the Sulu Archipelago

kwintangan kayu Yakan percussion beams made up of five logs

luntang Maguindanao percussion beams made up of five to eight logs

Ramadan Ninth month of the Muslim calendar, a period of fasting

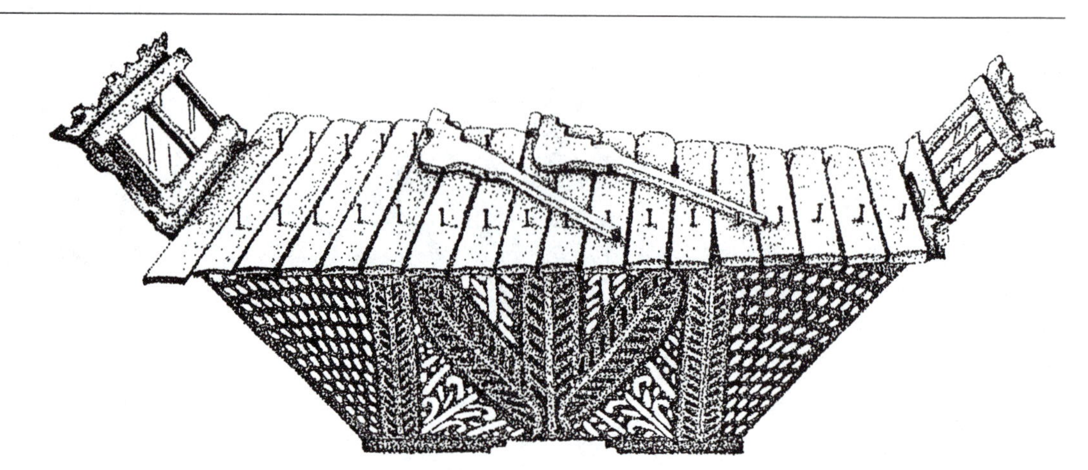

FIGURE 13 The *gabbang,* a bamboo xylophone, with its mallets shown resting on the keys. The longest slat is 50 centimeters long; the shortest, 31 centimeters. Courtesy University of the Philippines Archive.

instrument sound for only a short period of time, the instrument is suited to pieces in the modern (*sinaguna*) or fast (*barikata*) style of playing. The modern music of the *agung* is also played on two to four pieces of small bamboo half tubes of varying sizes, called *tamlang agung.* When two half tubes are played, the musician sits on a stool cross-legged with one tube tucked vertically between the legs. The other is held by the left hand horizontally against the other, forming a cross. The player strikes the outer portions of the tubes alternately with a wooden mallet, producing different patterns of tones. When playing on four pieces, the musician sits on the ground with the legs extended forward, parallel to each other. They serve as the stand on which the pieces of bamboo rest. With two wooden mallets, the musician then plays a rapid succession of melodic patterns. These instruments are usually played for entertainment, especially on occasions that call for the competitive exhibition of musical skills by youths.

The *gabbang,* a bamboo xylophone, is common among several groups, especially in the Sulu communities. This instrument consists of blades graduated by size and resting on a trapezoidal wooden resonator with cloth padding between the blades and the sides of the box (figure 13). The number of blades varies—from five in the Yakan *gabbang* to as many as sixteen among the Tausug. It also has the variable function of either solo or accompanying instrument. The Yakan *gabbang* has the same repertoire as the *kwintang* and other solo instruments. Its playing includes the tapping of a rhythmic ostinato (*nulanting*) on a portion of the resonator box.

Among the Tausug in Luuk and the Sama from Sitangkai, the xylophone is also played to accompany songs and dances—for example, the *le'le',* humorous songs among the old folks, also enjoyed by the young (Maceda and Martenot 1976). The *gabbang* is also a solo instrument, sometimes accompanied by the *biola,* a four-stringed bowed instrument (Kiefer 1970).

During the agricultural season, several instruments are quite prominent. These include percussion beams, bamboo clappers, a scraper, and log drums.

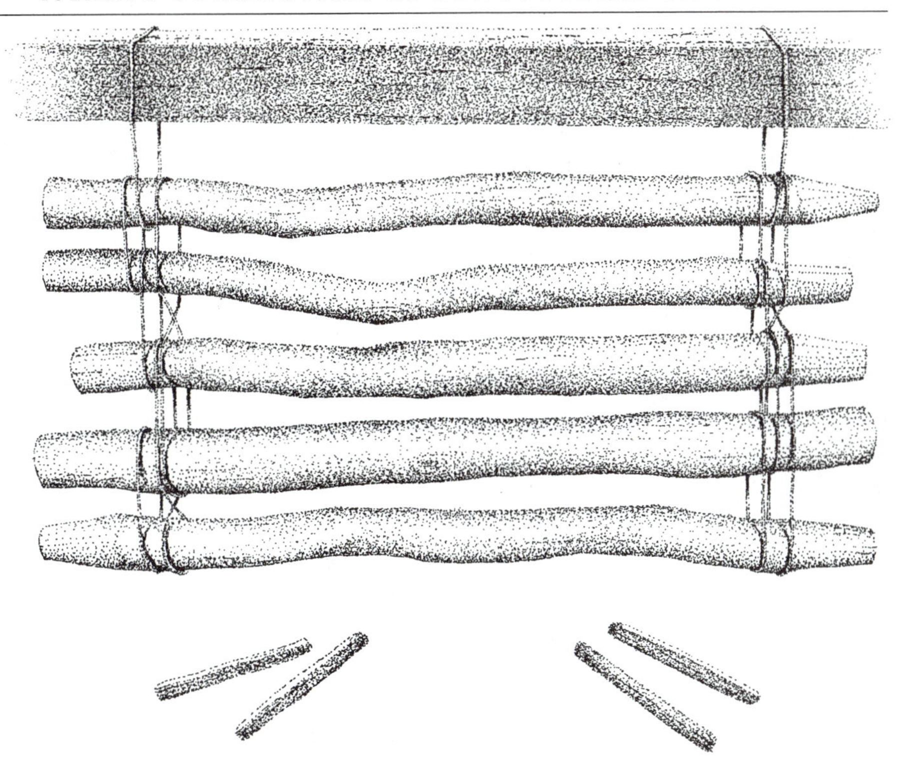

FIGURE 14 A Maguindanao *luntang,* shown with sticks. Each log is about 140 centimeters long. Courtesy University of the Philippines Archive.

The percussion beams (*luntang*) of the Maguindanao is a set of five to eight logs, sharpened on one end and suspended horizontally, one below the other, from a tree or outside a house (figure 14). One musician plays on the sharpened portion while another beats a rhythmic ostinato on the middle part of one log. Farmers play *luntang* to keep birds out of the fields, or simply to while away the time. At the start of the Islamic fasting month of Ramadan, the *luntang* is also sounded to wake up the community so that people can eat their meals before the fast begins (Maceda 1963).

Similar to the *luntang* is the Yakan *kwintangan kayu,* which consists of five hanging logs, topped by bamboo and suspended from the branch of a tree facing the rice fields (figure 15). Each beam is likewise tapered on one end, which the principal player strikes with a wooden mallet (*lisag*). The other *lisag* plays a basic pulse on the bamboo pole. The music of the *kwintangan kayu* may be played by one (*ngwintang*), or two (*kajali*), and even as many as five musicians. The playing is almost continu-

FIGURE 15 Two Yakan play a *kwintangan kayu* at the beginning of the agricultural cycle. Photo courtesy NAMCYA Foundation.

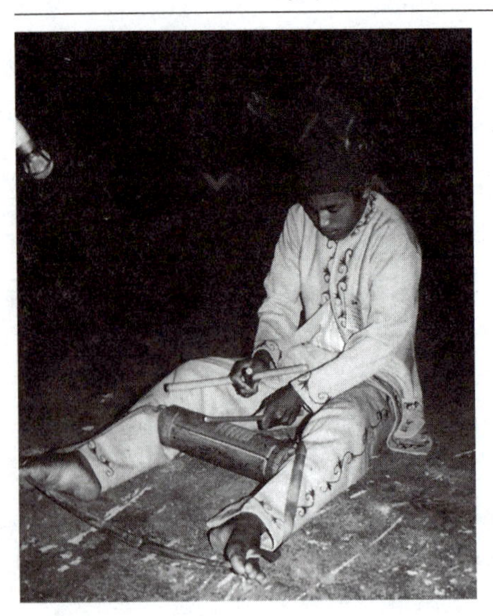

FIGURE 16 A Maranao musician plays a bamboo scraper (*garakot*). Photo courtesy NAMCYA Foundation.

ous, starting immediately after the planting of rice seedlings until the time they break from the ground. The sound of the *kwintangan* is believed to induce productivity from the planting field (Nicolas 1977).

As the flowers sprout, the *kwintangan kayu* is removed, and a pole (*kopak-kopak*) with bamboo clapper (*dalupal*) on top is placed in the middle of the field. A string is attached to the *dalupal* and extended to the farmer's dwelling. From there it can be pulled anytime to create loud rattling sounds to scare the birds and other animals on the ground (Nicolas 1977).

The Maranao scraper (*garakot*) is another instrument used to drive away unwanted scavengers of the field—birds, rats, and insects. Sometimes, however, young men play it to attract the attention of passing women, or to show off their musical skills in friendly competitions.

The scraper is a hard-dried bamboo tube, closed on both ends by the nodes. One portion of the body is etched with notches, and a slit hole runs from one end to the other. The scraper is usually tucked on both ends between the performer's legs (figure 16). The left-hand stick plays a steady rhythm on the chipped surface of the tube, while the right-hand stick taps different parts of the body, producing a variety not only of rhythmic patterns, but also of attacks and timbres. To further demonstrate exceptional concentration, skilled players may gradually shift their positions from sitting to lying on their backs and raising the scrapers in the air with their feet without missing a beat or interrupting the music.

The *kagul* of the Maguindanao in Datu Piang is both a scraper-type instrument and an idiochord half zither with one string lifted from the other side of the tube's body. While one stick scrapes the notches the other stick strikes the string. People play the *kagul* to drive away animals while gathering food (Maceda 1963).

The Yakan celebrate harvests with the music of a log drum (*tuntungan*), a resonated suspended plank made of a flat board with a rounded portion toward one end and suspended from a frame. Suspended upside down and serving as resonators are two differently sized earthen jars whose mouths are two to five centimeters away from the board. Two players with *lisag* play on the rounded portion of the log, while another plays on the flat end with a long wooden shaft (Nicolas 1977).

Small groups of farmers watching over the fields indulge in a more intimate form of entertainment by playing wind instruments. The *oniya-niya* of the Maranao, made of a leaf of a coconut and a stalk of rice, produces a reedy, haunting sound, which can frighten unwanted animals in the fields.

Also popular are two flutes: the ring flute (Maguindanao and Yakan *suling*, Maranao *insi*, Sama *pulao*) and the lip-valley flute (Maguindanao *palendag*). The former, similar to the Javanese *suling*, is identified by a ring made of a rattan strip that is wrapped around the hole for the mouth. The lip-valley flute has an open mouthpiece cut in a curve, supporting the player's lower lip. The flutes vary in length (from 35.5 to 61 centimeters) and in the number of holes. Makers of flutes measure inexactly the distances between the holes, resulting in variable interval relations between tones, but the music is mostly pentatonic, with an addition of one or two auxiliary tones (Maceda 1963).

The flutes in western Mindanao and Sulu have their own solo repertoires, mostly intended for self-entertainment and courtship. One distinct feature of flute technique of playing is circular breathing, which enables the players to create a continuous line of sound without breaks between phrases or melodic units.

The Jew's harp (Maguindanao and Maranao *kubing*, Yakan *kulaing*) is also widespread, not only in the Islamic communities, but also in highland cultures, and even in some rural Christian communities in Luzon and Visayas. Differences in it among the various language communities may lie in make and design (from the simplest to the most elaborately carved, sometimes with tassels) and in their repertoires. A favorite instrument of courtship and recreational repartee, the Jew's harp simulates the sounds of speech, including prosody. A nonspeaker of the local language has difficulty understanding renditions in that language, but can appreciate the sounds from a purely aural point of view. Moreover, in courtship, the phrases are based on metaphorical language and local poetic expressions. Because of its portability, almost every young Yakan has a *kulaing* tucked in his headband everywhere he goes (Nicolas 1977).

Another instrument for intimate and familiar listening is the lute, a two-stringed instrument, whose body is shaped like a boat with a long neck and an intricately curved pegboard. The thin wire strings, tuned a perfect fourth apart, are plucked with a rattan plectrum. Though the lute is not accompanied by any other instrument, the player's thumb taps a rhythmic drone on its body.

The playing of lutes among Muslims in Mindanao and Sulu usually differs stylistically from those of other Mindanao cultures, especially Tagakaolo, Manobo, and T'boli. In the last, the performer usually plays the lute (Manobo *kudlung,* Tiboli *hagelong* or *hagelung*) while dancing or with body movements, sometimes coupled with singing and the complement of a polychordal tube zither (Manobo *saluray*).

The lute (Maguindanao *kutyapi* or *kutyapiq,* Maranao *kotyapi*) is usually played in a sitting position (figure 17). A solo instrument, it never accompanies the voice—a practice prevalent among the Palawan highland people. In the Mindanao lute, the twelve movable pyramid-shaped frets made of beeswax may be arranged according to two pentatonic modes: the anhemitonic *dinaladay* and the *binalig* 'necklace', which has a semitone in its lower octave. The repertoire may be classified by these modes. The first typically has a slower tempo, and pieces in the second are played with sometimes mesmerizing speed. Moreover, the *dinaladay* is used for pieces about the sounds of nature (including human-made objects), and the *binalig* pieces express emotions and sentiments (Maceda 1988). The music has been noted to be highly refined and expressive, sometimes even to the point of generating unusual adulation and erotic attraction for the player on the part of an audience of the opposite sex (Maceda 1963).

Among the Maranao, the *kotyapi,* besides being a solo instrument, can also be part of a serenade ensemble (*kapanirong*). The pieces either express abstract feelings and ideas, or derive from existing songs and ballads (Otto 1985). The Tausug *biola* is believed to have been adapted from the Western family of bowed stringed instru-

FIGURE 17 Surrounded by listeners, Samaon Sulaiman, a Maguindanao, plays a two-stringed boat-shaped lute (*kutyapi*). Photo by Ramón P. Santos.

Epics serve as a repository of oral history containing not only the lives and legendary deeds of hero-ancestors, but also genealogies and the people's relationship to the Prophet Muhammad.

ments by way of the Portuguese influence in Indonesia. The *biola* can be played as a solo instrument, or used to accompany the voice and the *gabbang*. With a relative tuning based on fifths, its music can be made to replicate other forms of musical renditions, including lyrical songs of love, the highly melismatic style of the *luguh* (structural formula of Qur'ānic recitation), and the rhythmic music of the *gabbang* (Kiefer 1970).

Other chordophones include zithers. The *tangkol,* a four-stringed version of the tube zither, is also used by the Manobo, Bagobo, and Cordillera tribes in Northern Luzon. As a recreational instrument, it is played by two women, one plucking the melody and the other playing the drone. The Maranao *sirongaganding,* an idiochord tube zither, has a leather flap on one end and strings lifted from the body. It is played by plucking the strings and tapping a rhythmic accompaniment on the drumlike end.

VOCAL MUSIC

Vocal musical expression in the Islamic communities in Mindanao and Sulu covers a broad spectrum of forms—ancient epics and religious songs, ceremonial exhortations, entertainment ballads, songs of love, lullabies, and songs for various occasions. Stylistic differences exist in rendering these forms, most often indicative of influence from other cultures, like the florid style of singing in West Asia. The vocal styles may well be represented in varying degrees by the two styles of singing among the Tausug from Luuk: *tayil* style, slow, religion-oriented, metrically free, melismatic, with high tessitura and optional accompaniment; and *paggabbang* style, suited to secular songs, in fast tempo, metered, syllabic, and with medium tessitura and instrumental accompaniment.

Locally the most prestigious form of vocal expression is reading the Qur'ān. Occasions such as Maulud (commemoration of the Prophet Muhammad's birthday) and baptisms—usually timed to occur during Maulud and the hundredth day after a person's death—call for this reading. Training in it is usually conducted formally under the tutelage of a master (*gulu*). Among the Yakan, the tutoring and learning (*magsambag*) is often done at night, when everyone else is asleep. The disciple (*mulid*) is required to repeat and commit to memory *luguh* after *luguh,* intoned by the teacher. At a student's oral examination, the *tarasul* is sung, commenting on the verses of the thirtieth chapter of the Qur'ān. The end of training is marked by formal graduation, called *magtam'mat* (Nicolas 1977).

Qur'ān-reading competitions are held annually to select the Philippine representative to the international meet, held in different Islamic countries. Filipino readers have won major prizes in the International Qur'ān Reading Contest; these prizewinners included A'Nisa Saguira Pendaliday in 1974, Noraina Kagubatan in 1993, Abdul Bashit Imam in 1994, and Abdul Latif and Hasna Pendatukan in 1995.

Religious songs

Religious songs are closely related to Qur'ānic recitation. They can be heard during the Friday noon service, before and after Ramadan (*puwasa* 'fast'), during Maulud, and in commemorating the anniversaries of deaths. The Friday noon service (*zubor*) is one of the prayers observed on specific hours of the day, from morning until midnight. It opens with the *adhan* or *bang*, a responsorial invocation sung on melismatic melodies by the imam and the deacon. The *fatiha* is chanted in the middle of the service, and the *lasib* is sung at the end (Maceda 1963).

The start of *puwasa* (which usually falls after harvest) is marked by the sounding of the log drum or large skin drum (*dabu-dabu*). The evening prayers are preceded and capped by the singing of the *talawi*, divided into three parts.

The first is a syllabic invocation, punctuated at the end of each phrase by a chorus of men chanting the word *Muhammad*. The second part is also syllabic, with the chorus closing the prayer with the word *amin*. The third part is a highly melismatic vocal setting between a lead chanter and the chorus.

During Maulud, *dikil* or *dikir* are sung. Available in a wide variety, these are poetic verses containing lessons of the Prophet Muhammad, recounting important events in his life, or praising his works. Among the Maguindanao sources of *dikir* texts are two Arabic books: *Molud sa riful alam* and *Birjanyi naaru* (Maceda 1963). In the Tausug Maulud ceremony, the *luguh Maulud* are sung in mosques in Jolo during the entire month of commemorating the birth of Muhammad. The songs, rendered in the *tayil* style (with high tessitura and free melismatic lines), are taken from the book *Kitab Maulud Shafari-anam* (*The Birth of the Glory of Mankind*). They may be sung alone or in alternation between leader and chorus or between smaller groups of singers (Kiefer 1970).

Epics

Aside from religious musical forms, epics and classical narrative forms have remained an important cultural facet of the vocal repertoires, not only among the Islamic communities, but in almost all major language groups in the Philippines. In most cases, the epics serve as a repository of oral history containing not only the lives and legendary deeds of hero-ancestors, but also genealogies, stories of the origin of the world, and the people's relationship to the major deities, and in the case of the Islamic people, to the Prophet Muhammad. Though some groups might have a collection of epics, one or two of these tales can be considered the primary literary symbols of each group's cultural heritage—the *Kudaman* of the Palawan, the *Ibalong* of the Bikol, the *Biag ni Lam-Ang* of the Ilokano, the *Hudhud* of the Ifugao, the *Ullahingan* of the Manobo, and the *Hinilawod* of the Sulod of Panay (Maranan et al. 1994).

Among the Islamic cultures of Mindanao and Sulu, some representative epics are the *Radya Indara Patra* and the *Diwata Ksalipan* of the Maguindanao, and the *Darangen* of the Maranao. Though the spread of the two great Hindu epics *Ramayana* and *Mahabharata* in Southeast Asia does not appear to have reached the Philippines, recent scholarship has unearthed an epic with striking similarity to the *Ramayana* with the title "*Tutolan ko Radia Mangandiri*" ('Story of Radia Mangandiri'). The epic was first narrated to Dr. Mamitua Saber in 1939 by two women, Ba-I Pamoki and Ba-I Kadiag of Dansalan (now Marawi City) in Lanao. The story follows the search of Mangandiri for Tuwan Potre Malano Tihaia, whom Maharadia Lawana had abducted. Earlier, Lawana had transformed himself into a golden goat. Mangandiri was assisted in his quest by the monkey Laksamana, who later turned out to be his son (Francisco 1993).

Epics are known only to a select few who have either undergone a semiformal process of learning or have been informally trained by an elderly sage. The epic poems (*kata-kata*) of the Sama and Yakan are recited only by mediums and other important persons who have the authority to conduct rituals. Among the Sama, the singing of an epic story is performed in private, sometimes only by the narrator, or in the company of chosen apprentice. The recitation is usually timed during a full moon, and the narrator intones the verses while lying on his back (Maceda and Martenot 1976). The singing of the *kata-kata,* which normally lasts for several nights, serves as the main highlight of an important public gathering (Nicolas 1977).

The Maranao epic, *Darangen,* is also a prominent cultural icon. Since it contains the history of the Maranao people and their important ancestors, knowledge and the ability to perform it are markers of good breeding and exceptional artistic accomplishment. To be able to quote important passages from the epic, especially in connection with moral and social values, likewise marks a cultured person. Outside the epic itself are songs called *kandurangen,* rendered in the style of the *Darangen* (Cadar 1980).

The training of a singer of epics is long and arduous, entailing much sacrifice. The period of apprenticeship is long, and cultivates important social and spiritual values. According to Sindao Banisil, oldest daughter of Sultan Otil Banisil of Calocan, Marawi City, added credentials—such as the ability to recite the Qur'ān, perform ancient rites, and play the *kulintang* or the *kotyapi*—can enhance public respect for one's qualifications as an epic singer.

Epics are rendered with both reciting tones and short melismatic passages. A feature of narrative singing is its rhythmic relationship to the text, sometimes to the point of creating a metric pulse, based on the linear division of the verses.

Other narrative forms

Short narrative songs are also performed during important gatherings. Tausug traditional ballads (*langkit*) are a strong component of contemporary oral literature: they chronicle recent events, ranging from the historic burning of a town in Jolo to humorous accidents in the life of an ordinary person. Singers of *langkit* are often hired to entertain guests, and each narration can run from ten minutes to several hours. The singing is usually accompanied by a *gabbang* or a *biola* (Kiefer 1970). A similar form is the *nahana* of the Yakan, a short narrative song about the life of a famous person or specific events in the community. These songs may be rendered on different tunes, classified as either old (*dehellu*) or new (*dembulli*) (Nicolas 1977).

In Yakan wedding celebrations (*magkawin*), the *jamiluddin* is sung to recount the story of how the couple first met, and of later events that led to the present engagement or marriage. *Jamiluddin* can also be considered an important part of the occasion, when the parents of both parties meet to agree on their children's union. Part of the nuptial ceremony is the singing of the *sa-il* or *lunsey,* mostly containing words of advice to the couple regarding the difficulties and trials of married life.

Songs of love

Expressions of love among the Maguindanao are in either of two styles of song: the *sindil,* replete with vocal devices and requiring subtle changes in vocal timbres, and the *bayok* (also the general term for song), more syllabic, with a limited vocal range and a quality free of special vocal techniques (compare *sindil*). The former is more difficult to execute, and only a few can master its technique. The *bayok* is used in sung debates; despite the simplicity of its musical elements, it can effectively convey the metaphorical and figurative language of the poetry (Maceda 1963).

The songs of love vary in style—from the more archaic *baqat* of the Tausug, which uses ancient language, and is sung in the formal *luguh* style, to the more contemporary *kapranon* of the Maranao, a highly sentimental ballad rendered in a some-

FIGURE 18 Excerpt from a Maranao *bayok* as sung by Noraina Sidic in 1991. Transcription by Ramón P. Santos.

what melismatic, somewhat rhythmic mode of singing. The Tausug *leleng* is a highly modernized version of such ballads of love as the *tenes-tenes* or the *duldang-duldang.* It is much favored by the young and has absorbed considerable influence from popular Western tunes. The traditional accompanying instruments, including the *gabbang* and the *biola,* have been replaced by the guitar and the ukulele.

Songs for entertainment

Other forms of vocal entertainment include the Yakan *meglebulebu seputangan* and the Maranao *kapamelo-malong.* The former genre is a song debate between male and female groups, exchanging proverbs and metaphorical adages and passing a waist-

kutyapi, kutyapiq Long, slender plucked lute of the Maguindanao

bayok General term for song among the Maguindanao, but also for sung debates

datu Prince, a member of the aristocracy in the Islamic community

onor High-caliber artist or musician within an Islamic community

kalangan Occupational songs associated with fishing among the Sama people

FIGURE 18 (*continued*)

band (*seputangan*) from one group member to another. The latter genre is sung by a woman while demonstrating in delicate movements the ways of wearing the *malong.*

Musical exhortations

In public assemblies, such as the enthronement of a *datu* or a graduation (*magtam'-mat*), musical orations greet important personages and extol the importance of the occasion. A highly regarded form of these is the Maranao *bayok* (figure 18). A *bayok*-singer (*pabubayok*) is usually an *onor,* a high-caliber artist, who has undergone extensive training in *kambayok* (art of *bayok* performance) and other artistic, intellectual, and religious activities. The rhetoric of the *bayok* requires the singer to establish through extemporized speech the relationship between the present event and its principal personalities and the entire Maranao cultural heritage. This includes quotations from famous pieces of Maranao literature, including the *Darangen.*

In every *bayok* performance, the *onor* puts forward for public scrutiny his or her own artistic being, including stage presence and the ability to capture the audience's attention and interest. The singing commences with subtle utterances on the lower vocal register, gradually increasing in intensity and range as the exhortation unfolds. The high point is reached when the singer shifts to the singing of portions from the *Darangen* itself, and the music becomes more rhythmic and syllabic. The singer accompanies this portion with the rhythmic tapping (*tintik*) of any object within reach, or the graceful swaying of her hands, each holding a fan. *Bayok*-singing competitions are highly anticipated occasions, especially when *onor* are introduced.

Songs for children

Lullabies and children's songs are an important part of the vocal repertoire. The Tausug *langan bataq-bataq* are songs sung by mothers and older men while rocking the baby's cloth cradle. The subjects of the songs include birds, animals, feelings (of joy or sadness), and thoughts (about portents that will have some bearing on the child's future). The singing is done with high and loud voice. Though the text is in Tausug, the rendition belongs to the melismatic *tayil* vocal tradition (Kiefer 1970). In contrast is the Yakan lullaby called *ya-ya,* sung softly and more slowly (Nicolas 1977). The *magbinua* of the Sama sing of a world of dreams in gentle tones, almost speech-like, within a limited vocal range (Maceda and Martenot 1976). Among the Maguindanao, special lullabies (*sangel*) are sung for either male or female children. Texts of these lullabies are punctuated by nonsense phrases, like *bungbung mang-mang,* and are sung on a melody consisting of two to three principal tones (Maceda 1963). The Sama *aembo-aembo,* however, is an onomatopoeic song of play, sung in rhythm with the rocking of a baby between the mother's raised feet. At the end of each short verse, the feet are straightened, and the baby slides to the mother's lap, usually to its delight (Martenot and Maceda 1976). Sama children's songs usually have short melodic phrases, repeated in connection with specific games. The Sama *puk lara* is sung by children who sit in a circle, playing a game of catch.

Occupational songs

In some communities, occupational songs comprise an important segment of local literature. Among the Sama, whose existence is closely associated with marine life, various strophic songs (*kalangan*) are sung on fishing expeditions. The texts of these songs are usually improvised, alluding to the kinds of fish the mariners intend to catch, and to the manner of catching them. The texts are sung on preexisting musical patterns, representing a vocal range of about an octave. The patterns consist of melismatic phrases and syllabic recitations, which show a strong influence from *luguh.* The term *lugu'kamun* actually refers to a type of song that the young sing while fishing for squill.

In contrast, the *kalangan magsangkalia* is sung during deep-water fishing, especially in a search for sharks. The activity, which requires ritualized behavior, occurs during specific times of the year and during a particular phase of the moon. Its high point is the playing of the *kuluk-kuluk,* a sistrum made of a bamboo frame, holding an odd number of coconut shells cut in half. The sounds produced by the instrument are supposed to attract the sharks.

People sing *kalangan taebba* while fishing above shallow-water reefs. The song texts usually express feelings about the natural landscape and life in the sea. They have a more rhythmic character, loosely synchronized with the alternate plying of poles between one singer and a companion.

Music for the dead

Highly emotional and personalized vocal exhortations can be heard in connection with the death of a loved one. The Tausug *hadis* tradition has a strong religious orientation in that *hadis* songs (accompanied by the *biola*) usually cover sacred topics, and are sung in a melismatic style. The texts usually express general thoughts on life and death, and memories that the dead person has bequeathed to the community. Before the day of burial, the Qur'ān is recited by a group of young women for seven days in the house of the deceased. This portion of the ritual is called *pangadjiq* (Kiefer 1970).

The Sama perform a lamentation (*lu'ui*) to relieve the emotional and psychological stress brought about by a death. The song, which consists of somewhat wailed descending vocal phrases, provides a channel for expressing good memories and reproaches the deceased for having abandoned the living.

REFERENCES

Abubakar, Carmen. 1983. "Islamization of Southern Philippines: An Overview." In *Filipino Muslims: Their Social Institutions and Cultural Achievements,* ed. F. Landa Jocano, 6–13. Diliman: Asian Center, University of the Philippines.

Butocan, Aga Mayo. 1987. *Palabunibunyan: A Repertoire of Musical Pieces for the Maguindanaon Kulintangan.* Manila: Philippine Women's University.

Cadar, Usopay Hamdag. 1975. "The Role of Kulintang Music in Maranao Society." *Selected Reports in Ethnomusicology* 2:2:49–62.

———. 1980. "Context and Style in the Vocal Music of the Muranao in Mindanao, Philippines." Ph.D. dissertation, University of Washington.

Casiño, Eric. 1976. *The Jama Mapun: A Changing Samal Society in Southern Philippines.* Quezon City: Ateneo de Manila University Press.

Fox, Robert. 1959. *The Philippines in Pre-Historic Times.* UNESCO National Commission of the Philippines.

Francisco, Juan R. 1993. "The Ramayana in the Philippines." In *Ang Paglalakbay ni Radiya Mangandiri.* Souvenir Program, Philippine Educational Theater Association Kalinangan Ensemble.

Kiefer, Thomas. 1970. *Music from the Tausug of Sulu.* Bloomington: Indiana University. LP disk.

Maceda, Jose. 1963. "The Music of the Maguindanao in the Philippines." Ph.D. dissertation, University of California at Los Angeles.

———. 1984. "A Cure of the Sick *Bpagipat* in Dulawan, Cotabato (Philippines)." *Acta Musicologica* 56:93–105.

———, ed. 1988. *Kulintang and Kudyapiq: Gong Ensemble and Two-String Lute among the Maguindanaon in Mindanao Philippines.* University of the Philippines. 2 LP disks.

Maceda, Jose, and Alain Martenot. 1976. *Sama de Sitangkai.* Office de la Recherche Scientifique et Technique Outre-Mer, Société de la Recherche Linguistiques et Anthropologiques de France. LP disk.

Majul, Cesar Adib. 1974. "The Muslims in the Philippines: An Historical Perspective." In *The Muslim Filipinos: Their History, Society and Contemporary Problems,* ed. Peter Gowing and Robert McAmis, 1– 12. Manila: La Solidaridad.

Maranan, Edgardo, E. Arsenio Manuel, and Jonathan Chua. 1994. "Epic." In *Philippine Literature,* ed. Nicanor G. Tiongson. Manila: Cultural Center of the Philippines. CCP Encyclopedia of Philippine Art, 9.

Mednick, Melvin. 1957. "Some Problems of Moro History and Political Organization." *Philippine Sociological Review* 5(1):39–52.

Nicolas, Arsenio. 1977. "Ang Musika ng mga Yakan sa Pulo ng Basilan" (The music of the Yakan on the island of Basilan). *Musika Jornal* 1:79–10.

Otto, Steven W. 1985. *The Muranao Kakolintang: An Approach to the Repertoire.* Marawi City: Mindanao State University.

———. 1996. "Repertorial Nomenclature in Muranao Kolintang Music." *Asian Music* 27(2):123–130.

Stone, Richard L. 1962. "Intergroup Relations among the Tausug, Samal and Badjaw of Sulu." *Philippine Sociological Review* 10(3–4):107– 133.

Trimillos, Ricardo D. 1972. "Tradition and Repertory in the Cultivated Music of the Tausug of Sulu, Philippines." Ph.D. dissertation, University of California at Los Angeles.

Upland Peoples of the Philippines

José Maceda

During the last Ice Age, the Philippines were part of the Asian continent, with flora and fauna resembling those of the mainland. The first inhabitants came by foot; later arrivals traveled farther into the Pacific, using long and open sailboats (Beyer 1948).

Excavations on Palawan Island show a practice of jar burial about three thousand years ago, like that of Borneo and Vietnam, suggesting a movement of peoples from the mainland to the Southeast Asian islands (Fox 1977). Archaeological discoveries in northern Mindanao reveal ceramics and Yueh-type wares, indicating trade with China during the Five Dynasties (A.D. 907–960) and large plank-built and edge-pegged boats (*balangay*) about 15 meters long, with radiocarbon dates as early as A.D. 320. Musical instruments, including gongs, bells, and a cymbal, were among the artifacts these excavations unearthed (Ronquillo 1987).

Historical records from the 1300s show first contacts with Islam in western Mindanao and in the Sulu islands. European influence began in the 1600s, when Spain established a presence in the islands. Hinduism and Buddhism, though they influenced Indonesia and continental Southeast Asia, had no lasting impact on Philippine culture.

The languages of the Philippines and the aborigines of Taiwan form the northern group of Austronesian languages of insular Southeast Asia. Philippine languages may be divided into three geographical areas: north, middle, and south (McFarland 1983). Together, they number some 65 million speakers. Musically, what remains of aboriginal traditions is confined to peoples in Northern Luzon, Mindanao, the Sulu archipelago, Palawan, and Mindoro. Accordingly, this article is divided into two segments: the North (covering the traditions of the Cordillera) and the South (dealing mostly with the musics of non-Muslim peoples of Mindanao, Sulu, Palawan, and Mindoro). Filipinos living on Luzon and the Visayan islands created a new music based on a Western idiom but with a genuine Philippine character; in the process, however, it lost most of its Asian identity.

The aborigines of the Philippines are an impopulous Negrito group, living in small communities in parts of Luzon, with some in the South. Their language, culture, and music retain some aboriginal qualities, but are much influenced by their Southeast Asian–type neighbors.

Bamboo is important not only for shelter, food, weapons, traps, and receptacles, but also for musical instruments—flutes, buzzers, clappers, scrapers, reeds, lutes, zithers, Jew's harps, and slit drums.

Two plants, bamboo and rice, have a direct relationship with both lowland and upland Philippine music. Bamboo is important not only for shelter, food, weapons, traps, and receptacles, but also for musical instruments—flutes, buzzers, clappers, scrapers, reeds, lutes, zithers, Jew's harps, and slit drums. Though root crops are a staple of mountain peoples, rice has the greatest cultural and ritual value, and is the focus of agricultural feasts, held during planting and especially after harvest [see BAMBOO, RICE, AND WATER].

THE NORTH

The Cordillera of Northern Luzon is home to more than one million people speaking related languages: Bontok, Ibaloy, Ifugao, Ilonggot, Isneg, Kalinga, Kankanay, Tinggian, and lesser-known ones (McFarland 1983). Each group of languages, with distinct geographical boundaries, has its own political and social structures, divisions of land, agricultural rites, feasts, and music.

A wet-rice system of agriculture prevails. The mountainsides are leveled off to form parcels of land or terraces to hold the water necessary for growing rice. They are constructed in many-shaped tiers, one higher than another, along gorges sometimes 600 meters deep. The terraces cover a wide area, creating spectacular panoramic views.

Gong traditions

Flat gongs, the principal musical instruments in the Cordillera, are played especially in rice-harvesting ceremonies, weddings, and pacts of peace. The playing of gongs is also associated with headhunting, as indicated by the boasting songs, punctuated with screams and shouts, describing headhunting raids, which heroes declaimed in formal ceremonies after a gong performance. Using percussion sticks to play music similar to the gong music honoring a beheaded person's body, and playing gongs to welcome warriors returning from a raid, are other indications that headhunting had religious significance apart from the mere act of war (Nicolas 1987).

The Bontok of Sadanga, Mountain Province

Among the Bontok, several stages in the cultivation of rice involve rituals: preparation of the field, care of seedlings, planting, weeding, and harvesting. A simple but common ritual is abstinence from work (*te-er*), lasting a few days. Its occurrence is loudly proclaimed in the central part of the village by an elderly ritualist, early in the morning; prayers (*kapya*) and the sacrifice of a chicken follow. During the evenings, especially during this abstinence from work, boys court girls in their sleeping quarters (*pangis*). This time is an occasion to play the nose flute (*kalaleng*), whose descending pentatonic melodies sound pleasing in the silence of the night, almost as inaudible as the Jew's harp (*awedeng*) that some boys play instead. The girls sing responsorial

FIGURE 1 With sticks, the Bontok of Sadanga, Luzon, play flat gongs (*gangsa*) as they move in circular formations. Photo by José Maceda, 1970s.

songs (*kudya, tinaroyod*) or choral songs (*salidommay*) in which they prod the boys, hiding in the darkness, to identify themselves.

Unlike women's sleeping quarters, the men's dwelling (*ator*) is a center for recreation and a formal site for meetings to discuss local issues and wedding plans, or to settle disputes. A stone wall marks its importance as a social institution. In preparation for the harvest, elderly members of a men's dwelling may decide to hold a feast (*fegnas*), at which choral songs (*salidommay*) and long solo songs (*dango, ullalim, kalimusta*) are sung, and flat gongs (*gangsa*) are brought out of their hiding places, each contributing to at least one complete ensemble of six gongs, for rarely does one family have all six (Yraola 1979).

Among the Bontok, nuptial rituals are the most elaborate occasions for feasting and making music. The village of Sadanga has three stages of wedding celebrations—*karang, lopis, chuno*—which noble and rich families are bound by duty to complete. *Karang* is the simplest and least expensive, but *lopis* and *chuno* are also enormous celebrations, involving the sacrifice of many water buffaloes (*carabao*), plus pigs and several dozen chickens. These feasts are occasions for collective singing (*ayyeng, sowe-ey*) by older, respected men of the community, followed by the playing of flat gongs (*gangsa*; figure 1).

The Bontok have two styles of performance on gongs, *falliwes* and *takik.* In *falliwes,* two groups of players among the six musicians play with soft wooden sticks (*pattong*), hitting the face or outer surface of the gongs in alternating beats. Only men, principally belonging to the same men's dwelling, play these gongs. They dance around in circles and spirals, vigorously swaying their hips and stepping high. The gongs are suspended from a wooden handle held waist-high by the left hand, but during the dancing, the men may lower them near the ground, and in crouching positions, hit them softly. Then, suddenly springing upright, they may hold the gongs head-high and hit them loudly, creating brilliantly exuberant rings, enjoyed by the audience. During the dancing, women gradually join in, making a group of their own, eventually encircling the men, ending the dance.

During these festivities, women wear colorful costumes—locally woven skirts with linear designs, beautiful blouses, and beads, some with precious stones considered heirlooms and worn as headdress (Reid 1961). Men wear elegant, voluminous, brightly colored loincloths, which shine in the sun, contrasting with the brown of their skin.

In the city of Bontok, *takik* is played and danced by one or two men, or a girl and a boy, in freer, faster rhythms and movements than those of *falliwes.* The dancers move independently of each other, quickly changing postures, turning in pirouettes as they hit the gong up in the air, first on one side, and then on the other. One dancer brings the gong near the ground, and quickly raises it back in the air.

The Kalinga of Kalinga-Apayao Province

The Kalinga live just north of Mountain Province. This area, which includes the Isneg, is one of the more isolated of the mountain provinces, but trade and the influx of settlers are influencing traditional culture.

More than the other Cordillera groups, the Kalinga have preserved a bamboo-and-gong musical tradition, played in everyday life and festivities, showing the preservation of materials belonging to an earlier bamboo age and a later bronze age. They have more types of bamboo instruments and more varied manners of playing gongs than most other upland groups. The Northern Kalinga play gongs similar to those of the Tinggian of Abra Province, who may have received a part of their music culture from the Kalinga.

The Southern Kalinga favor two types of playing gongs: *topayya* and *palook,* both reserved for men. In *topayya,* six players tap and slap the gongs with their hands. First they pick up their favorite instruments, which are lying on the ground with rims up, and walk toward a corner of the arena for dancing, where they form a line. As they hang their gongs from their belts, they kneel and let the gongs lie on their laps, face up and rims down. Each instrumentalist taps his instrument with either his left or his right palm, listens to the sound and reverberation, and if dissatisfied, exchanges it for another.

In *gangsa topayya,* the player of the lead instrument (*balbal*)—the largest in diameter (about 40 centimeters)—starts with the traditional beat, consisting of an alternation of a left-hand slap and a slide by the right palm on the face of his gong. The second instrumentalist (*kadua*) follows with the same motions, one beat behind. Then the third (*katlo*) and fourth (*kapat*) do likewise, each behind the other by one beat. The musical result is a rising melody of four tones. After the four gongs are heard, the fifth gong (*opop*) plays an ostinato, a simple ringing left-hand slap toward the edge of the gong, quickly damped by the right hand. The sixth gong (*anungos*) first plays a more elaborate improvisatory rhythm before settling into a steady beat, with both hands tapping one side of the gong. After a while, the first player abandons his rhythmic pattern and with both hands plays a quicker, changing meter. The repeating melody of four gongs, the ostinato of the fifth gong, and an improvisation on either the sixth or the first gong make up the music (figure 2).

Dance is an integral part of this music. An elderly couple, usually prominent members of the community, move in a circular fashion. In time with the music, the man chases his partner, rushing forward with heavy steps, like a rooster chasing a hen, as she scampers away in small steps to the other side of the circle. She remains in place, dancing light steps with arms held high, bent at the elbows, until she is pursued again to another sector of the circle. This dance excites the audience, which laughs and shouts in good-natured fun until the dance ends with the couple shaking hands.

In the other Kalinga gong music, *pattung,* six or more men perform by striking their gongs with wooden sticks. As they dance in one line, one group beats its rhythmic phrase while the other group alternates the same rhythmic phrase. There ensues an opposition of strong and weak beats as they dance vigorously in circles and spirals with changing movements, stooping, and standing. Suddenly, they stop advancing and continue dancing and playing in place. They then change their style of movement: the man at one end of the line hops with both feet sideways, followed immedi-

FIGURE 2 A Kalinga *gangsa topayya,* about 1910. Courtesy of Father Francisco Billiet.

ately by the others. Next, the man at the other end of the line reverses the process. The men resume the spiral dance, which they end by laying their gongs together in one corner of the arena.

The Ifugao of Ifugao Province

The Ifugao, like the other peoples of the Cordillera, are partly cultivators of a wet system of agriculture. Their old rice terraces, carved out of sharp-edged ridges, are oriented toward the movement of the sun, and their systems of farming are associated with strong religious beliefs. These beliefs are a particularity of their culture, which considers rice a ritual product rather than an essential need of consumption (Concepción 1995). Their social organization and a complex agricultural system, including oral histories and local architectural types, is described in detail in a major work, *Ethnographic Atlas of the Ifugao* (Conklin 1980). A similar terraced agricultural tradition, extending over large areas in Yunnan, China, shows a possible relationship between the two areas. Gong music, songs, and epics are performed within the context of rituals.

The Ifugao use three flat gongs (*gangha*) to produce repeating musical patterns as ostinati. One gong (*tobop*) lies on the lap of a kneeling performer, who plays it with both hands. The left hand taps the face of the gong to produce a brilliant ring, while the right, clenched into a fist, strikes and slides on the gong to dampen the ring. Alternate strokes between right and left hands create alternately ringing and sliding sounds. The other gongs (*ahot, hibat*) are beaten with sticks in distinct rhythms.

The Northern Kalinga-Tinggian of Kalinga-Apayao Province

More varied gong musics are found among the Northern Kalinga-Tinggian. The *inila-ud* ensemble consists of three gongs (*patpat, keb-ang, sapul*) and one drum (*tambul*). Three male performers in a kneeling position lay the gongs on their laps. Each plays his own rhythm, using a stick in the left hand to hit the gong and an open right palm to dampen and tap another beat.

The *pinalaiyan* ensemble consists of four gongs and one drum. The first gong

pinalaiyan Among the Northern Kalinga-Tinggian, an ensemble of four gongs and a drum

sulibao Ibaloy ensemble of drums, gongs, and iron bars

balingbing Kalinga buzzer consisting of a bamboo tube split in two

kolitong Idiochord tube zither with strips of bamboo skin raised on pegs and played as "strings"

nose flute Small, soft-sounding flute activated by air from the player's nostrils

(*talagutok*) and the third (*saliksik*) are laid on the ground, rims facing down, and are each struck with a stick, producing a hollow sound with the earth as resonator. The second gong (*pawwok*), held by the left hand, is made to stand upright on its rim touching the ground, as the player strikes its ventral side, as opposed to its dorsal side, with a stick. The fourth gong (*pattong*) hangs freely from the left hand, as the right hand strikes its side. The drum provides a steady beat, which holds together the rhythms of these gongs.

The Ibaloy of Benguet Province

The Ibaloy have developed the *sulibao* ensemble, combining two slim, conical drums, two flat gongs, and a pair of iron bars. The drums are only about 70 centimeters tall, with faces 10 centimeters wide, and are found nowhere else in the Philippines. They produce a quiet music in which all five instruments can be heard distinctly.

One drum with a slightly higher pitch (*sulibao*) is played with vigorous slaps of both hands; the other drum (*kimbal*) plays contrastingly steady, muted sounds. One gong (*pinsak*), suspended from a handle held by the left hand, is struck with a stick on its ventral side; the second gong (*kalsa*) is also played with a stick, improvising first with loud beats, then with muffled ones. The fifth instrument (*palas*), a pair of clappers, produces a drone of fast, ringing strokes. The Ibaloy also retain the *kulimbet,* an ensemble of two conical drums and a gong, to play exclusively for curing ceremonies.

The Isneg of Kalinga-Apayao Province

The Isneg, living around the Apayao River in the extreme north of the Cordillera, have retained vestiges of flat-gong music and various forms of songs. The Ilonggot, living in the eastern region, retain no gongs but preserve the use of three-stringed bowed lutes, not found in the rest of the Cordillera. Isneg flat-gong music consists of two gongs (*hansa*) played by women, and one long conical drum (*ludag*), reminiscent of long drums in Kalimantan, played with loud sounds by men. Two dances (*tadek, talip*) for this music resemble those of the Kalinga, and may actually have come from that region.

Bamboo and other instrumental traditions

The foregoing examples of flat gongs define a music of colors, indefinite pitches, and repeating musical phrases. Similarly, bamboo percussion instruments express themselves with indefinite pitches. The existence of two such similar musics—the older, bamboo; the newer, bronze—shows how the two musical cultures have interrelated over time, particularly in Northern Luzon.

Among the Kalinga, a popular bamboo musical instrument is the buzzer (*balingbing*), with a split dividing its thin bamboo tube in two. When the tube is struck against the ulnar side of the open palm of the left hand, the halves vibrate. Whether

FIGURE 3 Excerpt from a melody as played on the Kalinga tube zither (*kolitong*). The numbers denote digits, starting with the thumb. Transcription by José Maceda.

right hand	’	3	3	3	1	3	’	1	3				
	c♯	e	e	e	f♯	e	a	f♯	e	c♯	b	b	b
left hand	3						1			3	2	2	2

the buzz is fast or slow depends on whether the halves are held tightly or loosely against each other. A rattan ring around the base of the tube may be adjusted to tighten the halves, thus tuning the rise or descent in pitch or change in color of the instrument's sound. The *balingbing* is now played as an ensemble of six, but the Ibaloy also know it as a solo instrument (*pakkung*). About 80 centimeters long, it produces low sounds of long duration.

Quill-shaped bamboo tubes (*patang-ug*), when struck against a hard object (like a stone or a piece of hardwood), produce indefinite pitches and are played for recreation. Formerly, boys played them to ward off bad spirits that might have been lurking along their paths. Originally, bamboo tubes (*tongatong*) were instruments female mediums used to call spirits to visit the human world and help cure the sick, but now they, too, are used in musical ensembles for recreation. Bamboo Jew's harps (*ulibao, giwong, onnat*), xylophone staves (*patatag*), polychordal zithers (*kolitong, kulibit, kolesing*), paired-string zithers (*dongadong, pasing*), a whistle flute (*olimong*), a notched flute (*paldong*), and a nose flute (*tongali*) are other bamboo musical instruments used at social functions in a manner different from gongs.

Idiochord tube zithers (*kolitong*) have as many as ten strings lifted from the bamboo tube itself, carefully tuned to the tones of a pentatonic scale (B–C♯–E–F♯–A) and their upper octaves. The ten tones of the strings are distributed around the tube to ease plucking. The tube is held at its midsection. The thumb and second and third fingers of both hands pluck strings, successively or alternately (figure 3). Each vertical line is equal to an eighth note read at a metronomic speed of about 200. The thumbs, number 1 of both hands, pluck strings in the front of the tube facing the performer, while the long fingers, numbers 2 and 3 of both hands, pluck strings on the back side of the tube.

The nose flute is played by several groups of people, but among the Kalinga other flutes—a whistle flute (*olimong*) and a lip-valley or notched flute (*paldong*)—are more often played. Panpipes (Bontok *dew-dew-as*) are no longer extant, but the Kalinga version of five separate pipes (*saggeypo*) played by five men still exists. Each performer blows a pipe assigned to him, and together they produce a repeating melody. The repetition appears simple, but occasional deviations, such as one pipe's taking the place of another, produce different melodic turns. This technique demands perfect coordination between the players.

The Ifugao use a bamboo clapper (Ifugao *hangar, palipal*), which chanting priests play in long ritual songs (*lewlewa*) to inaugurate a rice field or a new house. As the priests sing, they mark their chanting with regular strokes of the clapper on the carcass of a sacrificed pig. The *palipal* has kept its ritual function and has not been used in secular sessions.

Another Ifugao instrument, a yoke-shaped wooden bar (*bangibang*), has unique social importance, as it is played jointly by groups of men in villages only on the violent death of one of their members. Several groups of men dance along mountain trails, making their way in slow steps toward the center of town, where discussions about the death follow. The performers hold a rattan handle, tied at the center of the bar. Each strikes one side of the bar as he assumes a pose, his body somewhat stooped, with instruments held at the level of the waist or near the ground. Three simple rhythms, each played by a separate person, make up the musical organization of the *bangibang*. Since dozens of groups of men form lines, all playing these rhythms at different speeds, the parade of separate groups dancing along mountain trails produces a spectacular rhythmic diffusion.

The Ilonggot have a special instrument, a three-stringed fiddle (*litlit*), unknown to all the other Northern groups, and the Negritos of Quezon Province play a musical bow (*gulimmed*) not found elsewhere in the Cordillera. The Ibaloy and the Ifugao both play board zithers (*tadcheng, kaltsang*), equivalent to the tube zithers of the other groups.

Vocal music

Vocal music in the Cordillera is known for its epics, chanted songs in verse (Bontok *ugod,* Ifugao *hudhud,* Kalinga *ullalim*) praising famous heroes. In Northern Kalinga, women singers of the epic *Gasumbi* are also mediums. They use seven-syllable lines describing the courting and headhunting exploits of the hero Gawan, fitting traditional melodies of different musical genres into the epic (Prudente 1986). In Southern Kalinga, the epic *Ullalim* deals similarly with the adventures of three heroes—Dulliyaw, Dullawan, and Banna—belonging to the same family. Kalinga epics usually have seven syllables per line, but they may have more (Billiet and Lambrecht 1970).

Hudhud are sung by Ifugao women at harvesttime in the rice field and at wakes. In *hudhud da Aliguyon ke Bugan* (Dulawan 1970s), the lines vary from six to fourteen syllables, and ends of lines are followed by a choral response.

Bontok responsorial vocal music (*ayyeng, sowe-ey, chaing*) is a powerful means of expression. To emphasize the importance of the song, groups of men and women reiterate the ends of verses. At Bontok wakes, men and women take turns on successive nights sitting before the deceased, who is seated upright and tied to a chair (*sangadil*)—a ritual practice to honor important personalities before their burial. Responsorial songs (*agar, garey, churwassay*) praise the dead person and recall his contributions to the community and his help to his family. At Ibaloy political rallies, a leader honors a candidate for office with short poetic lines, the ends of which are repeated by a whole group of followers (*badiw*). In Kalinga pacts of peace, solo forms of song (*dango, ading*), are a means of polite expression; they are sung by representatives of contracting parties in simple melodic formulas, filled in with improvised texts, to greet and welcome guests. At weddings, the bride's party sings in verse its contribution to the nuptial feast, and the groom's side responds with its contribution in the same spirit of gentility.

THE SOUTH

In the southern Philippines, about 1.5 million people living in the mountains of Mindanao and other islands have kept alive an indigenous music culture related to the music of the Maranao, the Magindanao clustered along the banks of the Mindanao River, and the Tausug, the Sama, the Bajao, and the Yakan of the Sulu islands—all of whom acquired a Muslim culture in the 1300s and 1400s. The mountain folk speak languages of another family, the principal ones being Manobo, Subanun, Bagobo, Bilaan, Tiboli, Tiruray, Mandaya, and Tagakaolo in Mindanao; Palawan, Tagbanwa, and Batak in Palawan; and Hanunoo, Bukid, Pula, and others in Mindoro (McFarland 1983).

These people live in dense forests, in small settlements far apart from each other, and are governed by customary law (*adat*) interpreted by wise, elderly men who adjudicate litigations between households. They cultivate a dry-rice system of agriculture. Especially during harvest, festivities are, as in Palawan, occasions for sipping rice beer from precious jars, followed by gong playing, dancing, and chanting. Mediums (*balian, mambunong, babalyan*) cure the sick and perform ablutions in rivers. The exchange of betel is still a practice between bride and bridegroom; blowguns may still be seen in Palawan.

A dry-rice system of agriculture is accomplished in stages—slashing, burning, planting, tending, and harvesting—accompanied by rituals, prayers, chanting, and playing musical instruments. Rice is planted in holes dug by a line of men equipped with sharpened dibbles. The Subanun use three kinds: a plain wooden stick (*garak*), a stick with a clacker (*taha-taha*), and a bamboo pole (*buhahay*) with rustling leaves on top and pieces of broken glass inside. The clack of the *taha-taha* and the rustling leaves and tinkling of the *buhahay* create rhythmic patterns, enlivening the work. The men are followed closely by women, who drop seeds of rice into the holes, which boys and girls walking behind the women then fill with soil. Singing, joking, and teasing lessen the burden of the work. Men sing, "Women should throw the rice seeds (*palay*) exactly into the holes with just one accurate stroke." Women respond, "Men must bore rice and clear holes with equal spacing between them" (Georsua 1987).

Gong traditions

Several ensembles of hanging gongs distinguish the music of the South, where bossed gongs mark the main differentiation from the flat-gong culture of the North. In turn, bossed gongs are related to hanging gongs in Indonesia and Malaysia. In Mindanao, Palawan, and Mindoro, hanging gongs form a musical culture separate from ensembles which incorporate them with gongs laid horizontally in a row (*kulintang*). Ensembles using the *kulintang* are traditionally associated with peoples of Muslim culture in Mindanao and Sulu [see ISLAMIC COMMUNITIES OF THE SOUTHERN PHILIPPINES].

Suspended gongs are played mostly by mountain people, practitioners of swidden agriculture, in thanksgiving festivals after harvest. These festivals involve consuming vast quantities of rice, sacrificing animals, drinking rice beer, dancing, and singing. Hanging gongs have a wider geographical distribution than the *kulintang*, introduced later in Mindanao along riverine areas and the Sulu Islands through trade and cultural contacts with Indonesia and Malaysia.

The Tiboli of Western Mindanao

The Tiboli live in the Tiruray highlands of South Cotabato Province. One of their major rituals includes a thanksgiving feast (*moqninum*), also a renewal of marriage vows; it is a ritual accomplished in stages lasting several years. Hanging gongs are played during lavish feasts. Tiboli gongs are big, heavy instruments, with a prominent boss and wide turned-in rims.

The Tiboli identify their gongs according to whether they are pounded into shape or made by other methods, such as the lost-wax process. The heaviest gongs (*tembaga*), grayish in color, bear the marks of having been beaten into shape. Though *tembaga* contain more lead or copper, and are valuable as heirlooms, dowries, and items of exchange, they are not used in performance. The *benegulitok* are lighter instruments, similar in appearance to the *tembaga*. The *sembakung* are the least heavy of the pounded type. *Blowon* are distinctly lighter gongs, with a smooth yellowish surface, probably made by the lost-wax process; they are the least precious gongs.

A Tiboli gong-ensemble performance consists of two musical parts: a repeating sound played by one gong and a melody played by three other suspended gongs. The heaviest gong (*tang*) slowly repeats the lowest sound, interspersed with melodic parts played on three smaller gongs (*semagi*): *blowon bong, blowon gebelaq,* and *blowon udiq.* There may be one player for the two musical parts, or two players—one for the *tang,* and another for the three *semagi.* The players may be men, women, or children.

After a while, the performer of the melody gongs stops playing. With small steps, he dances away from the gongs, following the drone beats of the largest gong. Then he winds his way back to the gongs and resumes playing the melodic part.

FIGURE 4 The Bagobo suspended gong ensemble (*tagunggo*) is identical to that of the Kalagan. The largest, lowest-pitched gong plays a steady beat equivalent to a drone, while the other gongs provide improvisatory patterns. Photo by Fokke de Jager.

All gongs are damped by assistants who hold the bosses, rims, or faces of the instruments during performance. The *semagi* (melodic) gongs may so interchange that when they are played, their sequence of tones changes. The melody becomes a permutation of the three tones, identifiable as pieces of music with names: *semagi semfili, semagi tahu, semagi semfifai,* and others.

The Kalagan of Davao Province

The Kalagan, a group of people living near Davao Gulf, use the *tagunggo,* a set of six large gongs, each as heavy as those of the Tiboli. They are suspended from a sturdy branch, with the lighter gongs on top and the larger ones below, their bosses facing two players of either sex. One plays a regular beat on the largest gong (*patawaganan*), and the other plays pentatonic melodies on the five other gongs: *unsaran, babandilanan, tabaganan, litokanan,* and *tulus* (figure 4).

After a while, the performer of the melody gongs stops playing. With small steps, he dances away from the gongs, following the drone beats of the largest gong; his steps take the place of the gong melody. Then he winds his way back to the gongs and resumes playing the melodic part. Some *tagunggo* employ three performers. One plays the lowest-sounding gong; the second plays two or three gongs of higher pitch; and the third plays the other gongs. Bigger gongs occupy such a wide space, the third player must stretch and sometimes leap to strike the farthest ones (figure 5).

FIGURE 5 This Takakaolo *tagunggo* is played like a Bagobo *tagunggo.* The player on the left holds the boss to dampen the sound of the gong; the other player holds the rim of her gong, also to dampen the sound. Courtesy of University of Pennsylvania Ethnomusicology Archives.

The Subanun of Zamboanga del Sur Province

The Subanun are the primary tribal group of the far end of Southwest Mindanao. Subanun ensembles use two hanging gongs and other percussion. The variation in their instrumentation and their use in different social functions demonstrate an interest in colors of sound, rather than in pitch.

The *megayep* ensemble is played exclusively by men for healing rituals (*mekanu*) and to ask the spirits for a good harvest. These rituals are held in the medium's house, where one sacred gong (*gandingan*) is kept. A medium-sized instrument with a narrow rim and a shallow boss, it is played by two performers. One hits the boss with a mallet, producing a long, rhythmic beat (*dlayun*). The other uses two sticks: he holds one in his left hand to strike the back of the boss, and he holds the other in his right hand to strike the rim of the gong. A second gong (*gagung pon*) is a heavier instrument, struck by a mallet on its boss to sound another beat, with a lower sound (*dlabu*); another player hits the rim of this gong with a pair of sticks. The third instrument, a pair of porcelain bowls (*phinggian*), is struck with two sticks, producing two tones.

This instrumentation is preserved in three other ensembles played for wedding ceremonies (*beklog*). One ensemble (*gandingan*)—not to be confused with the sacred hanging gong of the same name—consists of two gongs, *gagong pon* and *babandil,* and a pair of porcelain bowls. The *babandil* replaces the sacred gong, *gandingan,* which does not leave the medium's house. The second ensemble, *thanggunggu,* also employs the *gagong pon* and one of smaller gongs: *gagung thumbaga, burnay, tiyanggi, slabon,* or *galang.* The third ensemble, *gandang-gandang,* uses a *gagung pon* and a pair of small *gagung.*

Another ensemble, *kinilisong,* is played exclusively during harvest rituals to accompany dances. It is made up of a heavy gong (*gagung pon*), a bamboo slit drum (*dlisung*), and a pair of bamboo poles (*pemuli*). A dancer shakes rattan leaves (*kumpas*) in each hand to provide a rustling sound as background (Georsua 1987).

Palawan Island

Palawan was once a part of a land bridge connecting Borneo to parts of the Philippines. Its inhabitants, like those of the Sulu Islands, bear some relationship to the peoples of North Borneo. The Palawan, Tagbanwa, and Batak are the remaining peoples least influenced by Western culture.

The Palawan have another version of a hanging-gong ensemble (*basal*), played in harvest ceremonies (*tambilaw*), held in large houses especially built for festivities. Drinking rice beer, dancing, singing, and storytelling are integral parts of the celebration. The gong ensemble is led by a drum (*gimbal*), which plays ostinati. A pair of small gongs (*sanang*) played by two men produces brightly metallic sounds when struck with a pair of sticks on the rim and boss. As one *sanang* plays a sequence of loud tinkling sounds, the other attenuates its volume. The alternately loud and soft sounds between the two *sanang* ebb and flow in contrast to a steady drumbeat. Another pair of heavy gongs (*agung*) supplies still another layer of low, opaque sounds, playing against each other. If there are three *agung*, the third instrument plays a regular beat, to which the two other *agung* adjust. Sometimes there is only one *agung*, which plays a uniformly booming sound.

The music of the whole ensemble is accompanied by dances (*tarek*) performed by young women lined up on one side of the large house. At certain times in the music, one girl rushes to the center of the floor and jabs her feet in fast, alternating steps, in time with the loud sounds of one *sanang*. Each dance lasts only for a few seconds, as long as the rhythms of the *sanang*. It is quickly followed by that of another girl (Revel 1992). The sequence of jabbing steps, with loud *sanang* beats, so electrifies the audience that they shout and scream with pleasure and excitement.

The Tiruray of southern Mindanao, Maguindanao Province

All the foregoing ensembles use large, heavy gongs with wide, turned-in rims. Among the Tiruray, five smaller and lighter gongs (*agung*) are played by men, women, or girls as entertainment during weddings and festivals (figure 6). They produce a gentle music of repeating melodies.

Each instrument hangs from a string held by the left hand as the right strikes the boss with a padded stick. The musicians line up following the ascending or descending pitches of their gongs, and play standing, walking, or seated. Each gong is assigned a rhythm, and together they produce a melody with approximate tones D–C–B–A–G. Permutations of these tones are identified as pieces of music with assigned names: *serangsang, linggeng, turambes,* and other appellations.

Bamboo and other instrumental traditions

In Mindanao, many musical instruments are not made of bronze. Those made of bamboo include flutes (*palendag, suling, lantoy*), slit drums (*agung a bentong*), scrapers (*tagutok*), paired-string zithers (*takumbo, katimbok*), polychordal zithers (*sluday, tangkol*), and Jew's harps (*kubing, kumbing, aruding*). Those made of other materials are log drums (*edel*), hanging percussion beams (*kagul*), one-stringed fiddles (*duwagey, dayuray*), three-stringed fiddles (*gitgit*), two-stringed lutes (*kudyapiq, kusyapiq, hagelung, faglung*), conch trumpets (*budyung*), and drums (*gimbal*). All these instruments are widely distributed across the South. In some cases, only the term for the instrument and the repertoire differ from place to place.

TRACK 3-15

Lutes come in different sizes and shapes—long, short, narrow, wide, rectangular, bulbous, and with or without designs, decorations, or tassels. Two-stringed plucked

FIGURE 6 Tiruray *agung* are the smallest hanging bossed gongs in Mindanao. Photo by José Maceda.

lutes are played by several groups of people: one string plays the melody, while the other twangs a drone. Such lutes may be played with a bamboo polychordal zither, as among the Palawan and the Ata, or as solo instruments practically embraced while danced with, as among the Tiboli. The melody string has movable frets to allow for tuning to two kinds of scales, each with a separate repertoire applied to distinct social functions. In the Palawan *kusyapiq,* a pentatonic tuning without semitones (*bagit*) creates a music evocative of nature and the environment—the sound of leaves, bird-calls, and caterpillars walking. A much larger lute (about 2.5 meters long) is tuned to a pentatonic scale with semitones (*kulilal*) to play a music of courtship. Verses of seven syllables and in stanzas of two, three, or four lines are sung by a young swain in unison with his instrument. Repeating interludes between verses allow him to compose his text before proceeding with the next lines (Revel 1992).

A bowed monochord (*kutet, duwagey, dayuray*) has for its body the shell of a coconut or a wooden box, with a lid made of bark or the skin of an animal. It plays repeating melodies within a narrow range. Polychordal bamboo zithers (*togo, tangkol, sluday*) have larger tubes than those found in Luzon. Among the Tiruray, two women players share the instrument: one holds the lower end and plays one sound while the other holds the upper end and plucks a choice of tones between several strings. Another instrument, with paired strings and a strip of wood binding its strings at their midpoint, is more of an idiochord (*takumbo, thambobok, kudlung*) than a chordophone. Underneath the strip of wood is a small hole. When the right hand strikes a stick on this strip, the bamboo tube reverberates with a low sound. The open palm of the left hand taps the left end of the open tube, closing and opening it, thus changing the timbre of the vibrating strings.

FIGURE 7 Among the Tiruray and other linguistic groups, the lip-valley or notched flute (*palendag*) is tuned to a pentatonic anhemitonic scale to play music representing nature and the environment.

There are at least four kinds of flutes in the southern Philippines. These are the lip-valley or notched flute, the ring flute, the whistle flute, and the chip-on-tube flute. Lip-valley flutes and ring flutes are longer instruments; in the hands of accomplished musicians, they make long, winding melodies, which can easily change from one octave range to the next by overblowing (figure 7). These flutes are particularly important for their manner of tuning, based on the octave. The middle of the flute is where the first hole is made, and subsequent holes are measured from it. The middle

palendag On Mindanao, a type of bamboo flute

kubing Small, bamboo Jew's harps in Mindanao

gitgit Three-stringed fiddle in Mindanao

kusyapiq Palawan plucked lute

kutet Bowed monochord with coconut or wood body and bark or skin resonator, in Mindanao

FIGURE 8 On Mindanao, suspended logs (*luntang*) are a form of Tiruray and Magindanao xylophone. Here, two players produce a repeating drone while a third plays a melody on the five remaining logs, striking them on their pointed edges. Courtesy of the University of Pennsylvania Ethnomusicology Archives.

hole produces the octave, and descending scales from this octave produce anhemitonic and hemitonic varieties (Maceda 1990). Among the Magindanao of Mindanao, the ring flute (*suling*) is tuned to a hemitonic scale, and the notched flute (*palendag*) is tuned to an anhemitonic scale, each with a separate repertoire for different social functions.

Log drums are a rare musical instrument, unique to Mindanao. Among the Tiboli, they are large, hollowed trunks, on the open hollows of which a plank lies between two pieces of twine encircling the ends of the log; thus, the plank does not touch the log. Two people beat on this plank. One sits before its midsection, with a stick or a rod held upright in each hand, and beats up and down in fast alternating strokes, producing hollow, resounding tones. The other player stands at one end of the plank and beats irregular rhythms with a long pole. After a while, the player with the long pole dances away from the plank, returning to poke out a few irregular rhythms before continuing her dance. The two performers provide contrasting musical elements: ostinato for the first player, improvisation for the player-dancer. Although gongs and other ensembles feature a similar music-and-dance combination, the log drum provides the simplest example of this musical principle.

Xylophones are used by the Tiruray and Magindanao groups in the South. One type of xylophone uses horizontally suspended logs (*luntang*). The musical principle at work in playing the *luntang* resembles that of playing the *tagunggo*: one musician (or sometimes two) plays a dronelike ostinato while another plays a melody on the remaining logs (figure 8).

Vocal music

In the South, epics or stories of famous heroes are sung by soloists at special gatherings, when the audience may spend the night listening to singing, interrupted only by the singer's drinking a glass of water and resting for a while. Epic singers are frequently mediums, respected for their ability to communicate with spirits; through the epics they sing, they are the keepers of their people's cultural and historical traditions.

Some of the known epics of the inland groups in Mindanao are *Guman* of the Subanun, *Agyu* of the Bukidnon, *Tuwaang* of the Manuvu, and *Manggob* of the Mansaka. Among the Palawan, the epic *Kudaman* recounts the hero's exploits and describes feasts honoring the spirit of rice, the playing of gongs, and the drinking of rice beer, a beverage of great symbolic value. *Kudaman* is chanted in free verse, with the constant repetition of a few tones. Personalities in the epic are identified through levels of pitch, colors, changes of tempo, and the use of a melodic center. A Bagobo song, "The Maiden of the Buhong Sky" (Manuel 1958), is an episode of the epic *Tuwaang,* sung in verse usually of eight syllables, recounting Tuwaang's meeting with the maiden and his travels and adventures.

Other songs include songs of love, songs for drinking, and lullabies. Among the Tiruray, *siasid* and *balikata* are parables sung by male leaders during nuptial feasts. The Subanen use *shemba* as a general term for short songs having fourteen syllables per line. Examples of *shemba* are songs of love (*gbayuk*), songs for drinking (*ghanabana*), children's songs (*dienna*), and lullabies (*bombong*) (Georsua 1987).

The Tagbanwa of Palawan make rice-wine-drinking feasts special occasions for alternate singing between men, who drunkenly bellow their verses. The social system brings people together through drinking with partners, making blood-brother pacts, dancing, and singing (Fox 1961).

MUSICAL STYLES

The indigenous music of the Philippines is represented by gongs and bamboo instruments played by people living in the Cordillera of Northern Luzon, the mountains and coastal regions of Mindanao, and other islands of the South. Within each area, certain musical constants can be observed. Counting in units of two or four is the basis of the music of gongs and some bamboo instruments. Repetition, ostinato, or drone—with or without melody—make up the musical structure of most instrumental ensembles in the Philippines (Maceda 1974).

Flat gongs and bossed gongs belong to different geographical areas. In all of Southeast Asia, flat gongs are concentrated in Northern Luzon and the central highlands of Vietnam. Bossed gongs in the southern Philippines are hanging gongs, or gongs laid in a row. Hanging gongs are played by upland peoples for rituals related to a swidden type of agriculture. They are older instruments to which gongs in a row were added and played by riverine peoples in Mindanao and island peoples in Sulu. Cultural groups that use hanging gongs play a music of punctuation and permutation—a musical process different from "melodic" processes, induced by two-handed techniques employed in smaller gongs in a row. The term *gong-chime* does not distinguish between punctuational and melodic gongs, formed by a historical and perhaps an evolutionary process. Neither does it show the difference between flat gongs and bossed gongs belonging to separate cultures and historical periods.

Instruments made of bamboo are varied. They are buzzers, scrapers, slit drums, quill-shaped percussion tubes, tube stampers, xylophone staves, Jew's harps, polychordal zithers, paired-string idiochords, whistle flutes, ring flutes, notched flutes, nose flutes, chip-on tube flutes, and panpipes.

For bamboo flutes, a system of tuning based on octaves is practiced by almost all people in Mindanao, Sulu, Palawan, and Northern Luzon. Hemitonic and anhemitonic scales are byproducts of an octave-based tuning. Two kinds of flutes use these scales in the same language group of people, with separate musics for different social occasions. Similarly, two kinds of lutes use these scales, with separate repertoires for different occasions. Examples of an octave-based tuning in Indonesia are widespread, suggesting a scalar theory different from the Chinese circle-of-fifths theory. Other upland peoples' instruments not made of bamboo or bronze are two-stringed lutes, one-stringed and three-stringed fiddles, guitars, conch trumpets, log drums, and percussion beams.

Songs change in a manner unrelated to musical instruments. In Northern Luzon, songs with a rhythmic pulse and chants with repeating tones and introductory phrases differ from melismatic songs in the South, which reflect a different set of influences. Some syllabic songs in the South display indigenous styles antedating the more florid singing style typical of cultures influenced by Islam.

REFERENCES

Beyer, Henry Otley. 1948. "Philippine and East Asian Archeology." *National Research Council of the Philippines* 29(December):1–82.

Billiet, Francisco, and Francis Lambrecht. 1970. *The Kalinga Ullalim.* Baguio: Catholic School Press.

Concepción, Rogelio N. 1995. "The Ifugao Rice Terraces Today." Paper presented at the Regional Thematic Study Meeting on the Asian Culture and Its Terraced Landscapes, organized by UNESCO Nation Commission of the Philippines, Banaue, Ifugao Province, Philippines, 28–29 March 1995.

Conklin, Harold C. 1980. *Ethnographic Atlas of the Ifugao.* New Haven, Conn.: Yale University Press.

Dulawan, Manuel. 1970s. "Tuwali Oral Folk Literature." Typescript. University of the Philippines, Ethnomusicology Archives.

Fox, Robert. 1961. "Social Aspects of the Rice-Wine Complex among the Tagbanwa of Palawan Island, Philippines." Typescript.

———. 1977. "Manunggul Cave." *Filipino Heritage* 1:169–173.

Georsua, Racquel. 1987. "Traditional Practices among the Subanen in Lapuyan, Zamboanga del Sur, with Special Reference to Music." M.A. thesis, University of the Philippines.

Maceda, José. 1974. "Drone and Melody in Philippine Musical Instruments." In *Traditional Drama and Music of Southeast Asia,* ed. Mohd. Taib Osman, 246–273. Kuala Lumpur: Kementerian Pelajaran Malaysia.

———. 1990. "In Search of a Source of Pentatonic Hemitonic and Anhemitonic Scales in Southeast Asia." *Acta Musicologica* 72(2–3):192–223.

Manuel, E. Arsenio. 1958. *The Maiden of the Buhong Sky: A Complete Song from the Bagobo Epic Tuwaang.* Quezon City: University of the Philippines.

McFarland, Curtis D. 1983. *A Linguistic Atlas of the Philippines.* Manila: Linguistic Society of the Philippines.

Nicolas, Arsenio. 1987. "Ritual Transformations and Musical Parameters, a Study of Selected Headhunting Rites on Southern Cordillera, Northern Luzon." M.A. thesis, University of the Philippines.

Prudente, Fe. 1986. "Musical Process in the Gasumbi Epic of the Buwaya Kalinga People of Northern Philippines." Ph.D. dissertation, University of Michigan.

Reid, Laurence. 1961. "A Guinaang Wedding Ceremony, Dancing and Music." *Philippine Sociological Review* 9(3–4):1–84.

Revel, Nicole. 1992. *Philippines, Musique des Hautes Terres Palawan.* CNRS, Le Chant du Monde LDX 74 865. Compact disc.

Ronquillo, Wilfredo. 1987. "The Butuan Archeological Finds: Profound Implications for Philippines and Southeast Asian History." *Man and Culture in Oceania* 3:71–78.

Yraola, Marialita T. 1979. "Ang Musika ng mga Bontok Igorot sa Sadanga, Ialawigang Bulubundukin." *Musika Jornal* 3:41–112.

Glossary

Page numbers in *italic* indicate pages on which illustrations appear.

See page xvi for a guide to pronunciation.

aalakan Tausug deep-rimmed bossed gong (898)

abangan Syncretic Javanese Muslims (647)

adhan Islamic call to prayer; also *azan* (907)

ading Kalinga solo peacemaking song (920)

adok Minangkabau frame drum (613)

aembo-aembo Sama onomatopoeic play song (911)

agar Bontok women's funeral song (920)

aguang Large vertical gong of Sumatra (609)

agung Suspended bossed gong of Sumatra and the Philippines (605, 615, 886, 892, 893, 895, 897–99, *900*, 924)

agung a bentong Maguindanao bamboo slit drum (924)

ahuu Hanging bronze gongs of Ambon (818)

Akha Tibeto-Burman-speaking people living in northern Thailand, Burma, and China (537, 540–42)

alap Free-meter improvisation of Indian raga (67)

alu Pestle used for pounding rice in Borneo (831, 832)

aluan Large frame drums on Ternate and Tidore (817)

Aluk To Dolo Torajan animist religion (806–807)

alun-alun Town square in Java (644)

alus 'Refined, subtle', applied to Javanese style or to character in Balinese dance (634, 635, 719, 757)

alusan Male refined character type in Javanese dance (649)

anak becing Buginese/Makassarese metal percussion bars (806)

anamongu Bronze or iron gongs from Sumba (788)

andhong Javanese female singer-dancer (648)

andung Maranao old style of playing (897)

angkalung Shaken bamboo idiophone of Thailand, played in pitched sets (232)

angklung Tuned, shaken bamboo rattles from Indonesia (52, 114–15, *138*, 634, 645–46, 710–11, 748–49)

Angkor Vat Temple complex in Cambodia, center of ancient Khmer civilization (9, 153, 157–58)

angkosi Dance with cross-gender responsorial quatrain singing in Tanimbar (821)

angkuoch Khmer Jew's harp of bamboo or iron (166, 205)

angsel Dramatic rhythmic break in Balinese music (734, 745)

animism Religion that personifies natural elements (44, 48–53, 59–61, 558)

anonan Maranao upper gongs of the *kulintang* (897)

antan Pestle used for pounding rice in Borneo (831)

anun Maguindanao modern *binalig* rhythmic mode (895)

anyeiñ Burmese entertainment theater of music, women vocalists, and clowns (374, 377, 385)

apsara Khmer heavenly maiden (64, 157, 187)

arakk Khmer ceremony for worshipping spirits (18, 155, 159, 166, 172, 193–95, 209, 213)

arèk East Javanese heartland (635)

arja Balinese operetta about romance, comedy (750–51, 753, 757)

aruding Palawan Jew's harp (924)

arumba Bamboo xylophone ensemble of Sunda (712)

asli Malay song genre using fixed texts (427, 433–36)

asli langgam Modern Malay song genre with *biola* (violin) (435)

Atoni Predominant ethnic group in West Timor (796–98)

ator Bontok men's sleeping and meeting place (915)

Austroasiatic Language family including Khmer, Vietnamese, and Senoi (529)

awedeng Bontok Jew's harp (914)

awit Metrical romances of Christians and Muslims, recited on melodic formulas (853)

awitan Solo section of *subli* performance in Philippines (848)

ayaye Cambodian village vocal repartee with instrumental ensemble (23, 202, 532)

Ayuthaya Capital of Siam from 1350 to 1767 (11, 55, 70, 153, 187, 219, 222, 229, 238, 366, 378, 382)

ayyeng Bontok men's ritual antiphonal song (915, 920)

azan/adzan Islamic call to prayer, elsewhere *adhan* (431, 687, 769, 825)

baba One-stringed struck bamboo idiochord of Flores (792)

babandil (1) Maguindanao medium-size bossed gong; (2) Subanen suspended gong (892, 893, 923)

babarang Street performance in Cirebon (689)

bắc One of two modal systems in Vietnam (455, 463–64)

badéde Functional sung poetry from Lombok and Sumbawa (775–76, 782)

badiw Ibaloy antiphonal singing (878, 920)

bago Maranao new style of playing (897)

baho Bass voice in Philippines (845)

bai si Spirit ritual common to Thailand, Laos, and Burma (64)

bajo de unas Bass guitar, in Philippines (854)

baka-baka Double-headed drum of the Ternate *kulintang* ensemble (814)

balawas Samawan sung poetry (782)

balikata Tiruray parables (927)

balingbing Kalinga bamboo buzzer (918–19)

balitaw Cebu poetic song debate (851)

bamba Large, single-headed standing drum of Sumba (788)

bambu gila Men's trance dance with bamboo poles on Ambon (818)

banci Bidayuh large-mouth flute (836)

bandurria European pear-shaped plucked lute, found in Philippines (849, 852, 854–55)

bang Islamic call to prayer, Philippines (907)

banggi Iloilo song debate on love (850–51)

bangibang Ifugao wooden percussion bars (919–20)

bangsawan Theater shows of the Malay nobility, derived from Persia (68, 92, 125, 134, 426–27, 601, 606, 607, 626)

bangsi End-blown bamboo flute of Sumatra (605)

bano Ankle bracelets with metal jingles, worn in West Timor (797)

bapa Narratives and genealogies in ritual language of Roti (798, 801)

bapang Ostinato pattern accompanying animal dances in Bali (735)

barang Javanese pitch name (656)

baranung Lowland Chăm single-headed drum (590)

barapan kebo Sumbawan dance based on water buffalo movements (784)

barikata Maguindanao modern style of playing (902)

baris Men's temple dance of Bali (758)

barongan Trance dance, prelude to *kuda kepang* (412–13)

Barzanji Biographical/praise songs about Muhammad (766, 782–83)

basakk Khmer village theater genre of Chinese origin (155, 157, 158, 166, 169, 201)

basal Palawan gong ensemble (924)

basoi Maloh obsolete musical bow with resonator (835)

batel Repetitive pattern accompanying fight scenes in Bali (735)

batik Patterned, waxed, and dyed cloth from Indonesia (700)

batil Malay overturned brass bowl hit with sticks (420)

baut-baut Epic songs sung in processions of boats on Kait (820)

bayok Maguindanao syllabic style of singing (908, 910)

bebonangan Processional ensemble of Bali (744, 753–54)

bedana Muslim-influenced songs and dances in Sumatra (601)

bedhaya Refined women's court dance of Java (649)

bedhug Large double-headed cylindrical drum of Java (642)

bedug Large double-headed barrel drum of Cirebon and Lombok (75, 692, 695, 743, 768–69)

begenggong Jew's harp of the Talang Mamak, Sumatra (615)

beklog Subanen wedding ceremony (923)

beko fui Five-stringed bamboo idiochord tube zither of Flores (792)

Belu Collective term for peoples of East Timor (796)

bem Javanese pitch name (656)

bemu nggri-nggo One-stringed struck bamboo idiochord of Flores (793)

bendu Single-headed standing drum of Sumba (788, 789)

bengo Long songs to accompany stone dragging in Sumba (790)

bensi/bengsi Sumatran end-blown flute (605, 619)

bensiranay Iloilo song debate on love (850–51)

berampakan Samawan post-harvest thanksgiving dance (781)

berasi Vocal duet from East Flores (23)

bèri Cirebonese round metal rattles (691)

berimbak Jew's harp in the Aru islands (820)

berokan Monster play of Cirebon (688)

berunsai Bajau song and dance form (826)

besi tiga hoek European triangle in Ternate (814)

bey choan Long rhythmic cycle, "third level" in Khmer music (181, 182)

bhajanai/bhajan Lay-sung Hindu devotional songs (521)

bhangra Popular Indian-derived dance–song (521)

bijol Four-stringed fretless plucked lute of West Timor (797)

binalig Maguindanao rhythmic mode (895, 905)

bines Acehnese female song and dance form (605)

bini Rotinese ritual language form using parallelisms (799)

biola (1) European violin; (2) Low-pitched violin in Sumbawa (411, 598, 601, 606, 615–17, 619, 620, 645, 698, 716, 768, 780, 784, 814, 902, 905–906, 908, 909, 911)

blowon Tiboli bossed gongs (921)

bobi End-blown bamboo flute of West Timor (797)

boeng mang kawk Thai set of seven tuned drums, of Mon origin (235)

bola'bola' Sama wooden castanets (900)

bombo Large bass drum of Philippines (847)

bonang Gong-chime, found throughout Java (20, 643, 685, 690, 691, 692, 701, 704, 706–707)

bonang barung Larger of two gong-chimes in Java (641)

bonang panerus Smaller of two gong-chimes in Java (641)

bongai Malay repartee singing for weddings, circumcisions, etc. (424)

bonn chaul chhnaim Khmer New Year festival (198)

bonn cheat Khmer festival honoring the nation (199–200)

bonn kathinn Khmer festival of offerings to Buddhist monks (199)

bonn omm touk Khmer water festival with boat races (199)

bonn phka Khmer flower festival to raise money (199)

boria Theatrical genre from Penang area (426)

Borobudur Buddhist temple in Central Java (9, 62, 632)

bossed gong Tuned gong with a raised center for striking (596)

bouñcì Large, double-headed barrel drum of Burma (375)

Brahman Hindu god of creation (64)

brai (1) Cirebonese large frame drum without jingles; (2) Muslim ensemble (687, 695–96)

bua Tausug and Sama large hanging gong (898, 900)

bua loi Thai ensemble for boxing and theatre, same as *klawng khaek* (246)

bubaran Formal arrangement of Javanese gamelan piece (660)

bubundir Maranao medium-size bossed gong (896)

budindang Lampung free-meter song form (628)

budyung Hanunoo shell trumpet (924)

buhahay Subanen bamboo dibbling pole (921)

buka panggung Ritual opening for shadow theater, in Malaysia and Cirebon (403, 428, 689)

burdah Arabic hymn singing with *rebana* (776)

buta Ogre character type in Javanese dance (649)

byau' Burmese struck wooden block with stick (371)

byò Pair of large, stick-beaten drums from Burma (375)

ca huế Vocal chamber music of central Vietnam and Huế area (23, 449, 482–83)

ca kịch huế Recent theatrical genre of Huế area in Vietnam (449, 496–97)

ca ra bộ Southern Vietnamese chamber music performed with gestures (493, 496)

ca trù Northern Vietnamese chamber music (23, 454, 467, 469, 480–82)

cadence Resolution of a harmonic progression (15)

cải lương Genre of popular southern Vietnamese theater that developed around 1920 (70, 88, 449, 454, 493–95, 508, 509)

cakalele (1) Vigorous male dances on Ternate and Tidore; (2) Centuries-old dance drama on the Banda islands; (3) Martial dance accompanied by drums and gong on Ambon (814, 817, 818, 819)

cakapung Male vocal imitation of Balinese gamelan (756–57)

calonarang Nineteenth–century Balinese theatrical form (748)

calung Struck bamboo xylophone ensemble of Java and Sunda (634, 645, 667, 669, 697, 711–12)

canang (1) Pair of small knobbed gongs in rack in Malaysia; (2) Sumatran gong-chime and ensemble (404, 605, 609, 615, 623)

canget Lampung Buddhist-Hindu dance (627)

cantrik Disciple character type in Javanese dance (649)

carillo Tagalog shadow play (855)

celempong Riau gong-chime and ensemble (615)

celempung Four-legged metal-stringed box zither of Java (632, 641, 643, 668, 672–73)

cempala Wooden knocker used by *dhalang* in Javanese *wayang kulit* (642, 652)

ceng-ceng Small hand cymbals of Bali and Lombok (67, 742–43, 744, 767)

cèngkok Formulae for variation and improvisation in Javanese music (637, 672, 673, 684)

cenoi Temiar term for rays of light that bear spiritual substances throughout the universe (569)

cepung Men's choral and dance form of Lombok (768, 775)

cerek Malay pairs of wood/bamboo sticks struck together (408, 411, 412)

chan dio Shortest of three rhythmic cycles in Thai music (265, 279–80)

chant Musical recitation of a sacred text (131)

chap Thai medium-size cymbals connected by a cord, flatter and thinner than the *ching* (228)

chập chỏa Pair of medium-size cymbals, found in Vietnam (468)

chapei/chapey/chapey dang veng Cambodian long-necked lute with two to four strings (23, 66, 155, 171, 194, 196, 197, 202, 238)

charieng chapay Narrative genre from Cambodia (23, 238)

chầu văn Vietnamese spirit possession ritual (60, 89, 500, 505–506)

chèo Traditional theater of northern Vietnam (23, 88, 124, 449, 488–90, 501, 508)

chhap Medium Khmer cymbals, thinner than *chhing* (163)

chhing Cambodian pair of small, thick metal cymbals connected by a cord (67, 157, 162–63)

Chin Ethnic group from Burma (52)

ching Pair of Thai small cymbals connected by cord (16, 17, 46 67, 228)

chordophone Stringed instrument (17)

chrieng chapey Khmer narrative accompanied by long-necked lute (*chapey*) (155, 161, 171, 202, 238)

chuida Outdoor ensemble from China (71)

churwassay Bontok honorary funeral song (920)

cilokaq Wind, string, and drum ensemble of Lombok (768, 774)

ciwaìñ Burmese set of twenty-one graduated bossed gongs mounted horizontally in a circle (367–68, *369*)

colotomic structure The organization of music by periodic punctuation (20–21, 597)

comparsa/comparza Plucked-string ensemble from lowland Philippines (23, 854, 869)

composo Visayas heroic/political ballad (853)

corrido Story about Christians and Muslims, recited on melodic formulas (853, 855)

counterpoint Simultaneous multiple lines of music with different rhythms (131)

cumbanchero Popular music dance ensemble from Philippines (883–84)

cumparsa Plucked-string ensemble of Philippines (854–55)

dabakan Goblet-shaped drum of Philippines (892–93)

dabi-dabi Cymbals in Ternate (814, 815)

daboih Acehnese Sufi ritual of self–mortification (604, 605)

dabu-dabu Maranaon large religious drum (895, 898, 907)

dabus (1) Sufi ritual of self–mortification; (2) Sufi–derived dance with iron awl (414–15, 601, 604, 606, 612, 813, 816–17)

dada Small and medium hanging gongs on Kai (819)

dadara bagandang Women's harvest dance of Sumbawa (784)

dadara nesek Samawan women's weaving dance (781)

dahalira Mbojo women's martial arts dance (783)

đại hồng chung Large bell for Buddhist ceremonies in Vietnam (467)

đại nhạc The oboe-dominated ritual ensemble of Vietnam's court (70, 448, 504)

daigon Cebu Christmas songs (843)

dalair Feast dances performed in the Aru islands (821)

dalang Puppeteer in shadow-puppet theater; also *dhalang* (405, 706, 751)

daldala Hanging gong in the Aru islands (820)

dalit Praise song for the Virgin Mary (847, 851)

daluogu Percussion ensemble from China (71)

dalupal Yakan bamboo clapper (904)

đàn bầu Monochord with box resonator from Vietnam (59, 471)

dân ca Modernized Vietnamese folk song (81, 514–15)

đàn cò Vietnamese two-stringed fiddle with narrow, waisted body (472, 474, 490)

đàn đáy Vietnamese long-necked, trapezoidal lute with three strings (467, 472, 481, 513)

đàn độc huyền Vietnamese monochord with box resonator (471)

đàn gáo Vietnamese two-stringed fiddle with coconut shell body (474, 490)

đàn ghi-ta Modified Spanish guitar, found in Vietnam (473–74, 508)

đàn nguyệt/đàn kìm Vietnamese long-necked, moon-shaped lute (70, 238, 465, 472–73, 490, 505, 506)

đàn nhị Vietnamese two-stringed fiddle with narrow, waisted body (472, 474, 490)

đàn tam Vietnamese long-necked, snakeskin-covered lute, from Chinese *sanxian* (473, 490)

đàn tam thập lục Vietnamese hammered zither with thirty–six strings, of Chinese origin (472, 490)

đàn tranh/đàn thập lục Vietnamese semi–tubular board zither with sixteen or seventeen strings (70, 131, *462*, 471–72, 490, 509)

đàn tỳ-bà Vietnamese pear-shaped lute, from Chinese *pipa* (70, 473)

đàn xến Vietnamese lute with petal-shaped body (473)

dangdut Hindi-film-influenced popular music, common to Malaysia and Indonesia (23, 68, 104–106, 110, 439, 601, 689, 696, 697, 761)

dangdut Sasak *Dangdut* sung in Sasak (778)

dango (1) Kalinga solo peacemaking song; (2) Bontok long solo song (915, 920)

danza Habanera-derived music and dance of Philippines (854)

datu Muslim patriarchal leader (910)

dayegon/daygon Cebu Christmas songs (843)

dayuray Bukidnon one-stringed fiddle (924, 925)

dedegungan Gamelan-based *kacapi-suling* pieces of Sunda (715)

degung Sundanese gong-chime (107)

degung kawih *Gamelan degung* with vocals, from Sunda (706, 717)

dek rap Thai rap music (99–100)

deliro Small hand drum of Sumba (788, 789)

dendang (1) West Sumatra songs with *saluang*; (2) Bengkulu songs with *biola* and *redap* (611, 620, 621)

dep Bengkulu heavy frame drum (619, 620)

dere Single-headed standing drum of Savu (802)

dhadha Javanese pitch name (656)

dhalang Puppeteer in shadow puppet theater; also *dalang* (638, 642, 652)

Dhammayut A sect of Buddhism founded in the 1830s (288)

dhog-dhog Single-headed drum of Java (646)

didi Generic term for songs in the Aru islands (820)

didong Acehnese women's dance with *pantun* (605)

điệu Vietnamese system of modes (15, 67, 455, 482, 483, 491–92)

dikil/dikir Poetic songs about the prophet Muhammad (907)

dikir barat Malay men's choral singing of secular texts (425–26, 519–20)

dinagyang Ilongo religious festival (881)

dinaladay Maguindanao lute mode (905)

dlisung Subanen slit drum (924)

đoàn văn công Vietnamese traveling performance troupes (88)

dondang sayang Improvised-text song genre from Melaka (433–35, 522)

đồng dao Children's songs of Vietnam (479–80)

Đông Sơn Early period in Southeast Asian history, characterized by bronze drum casting, spreading as far as the Philippines and Borneo (10, 40–41, 43, 44–46, 58, 445, 446, 467, 596, 598–99, 632, 791–92, 819)

do'u da Manggarai xylophone connected with string (793)

doùpá Burmese small, double-headed barrel drum (375)

drone Continuous sound (18)

duaya Pangasinan lullaby (849)

dubakan Goblet-shaped drum of Philippines (896, 897)

Dul Muluk South Sumatra heroic theater (625)

duldang-duldang Sama song-dance debate (900, *901*)

dumbak Bidayuh, Iban small double-headed drums (829)

dunde Central Sulawesi bar zither (806)

dungga roro One-stringed fiddle of Sumba (791)

duplo Poetic game of wit, played in Philippines (850, 851)

duri dana Nias bamboo-tube buzzers (608)

Dusun Ethnic group from Kalimantan (51)

duwagey Manobo one-stringed fiddle (924, 925)

duwahan Tausug and Sama pair of hanging gongs (898)

duyug Maguindanao rhythmic mode (895)

edel Tagakaolu log drum (924)

e'ea Roti circle dance with antiphonal singing (798, 800–801)

empa-empal Large drum to accompany ceremonies in Tanimbar (821)

encio Bidayuh small mouth flute (836)

engkeratung Maloh obsolete harp zither (835)

engkeromung Iban gong-chime of *gendang panjai* (830)

engkuk-kemong Pair of kettle gongs in *sléndro* tuning, Java (643)

ensuling Bamboo ring-stop flute of Borneo (835)

equal-tempered tuning Tuning based on harmonic overtone series (129)

er hu Chinese two-stringed fiddle (70, 238, 281)

estudiantina Students' plucked string ensemble, found in Philippines (869)

ethnocentrism Valuing a particular culture over others (12)

faglung Bilaan two-stringed lute (924)

falliwes Bontok dance music with sticks (915)

fandango Rapid, triple-meter Spanish dance (854)

fawn Various kinds of northern Thai dance, e.g., *fawn thian* (313–14)

feko Transverse flute of Flores (794)

feko genda Flute and drum ensemble of Flores (794)

feku Wooden ocarina of West Timor (797)

filmi Popular song from Indian films (62, 68, 101, 104)

filutu Bamboo duct flute on Ternate and Tidore (813)

fixed-pitch instruments Instruments, such as xylophones and gong circles, whose pitch cannot be changed during performance (387)

flores de Mayo May rite with flowers and song, in Philippines (847)

foi doa Ngada double flute (793)

foi dogo Ngada triple flute (793)

foi mere/foi pai Ngada indirectly blown bass flute (793)

free-reed pipe Aerophone with a free-standing reed (11, 58–59)

fulu Upland Thai (Lisu) gourd mouth organ with bamboo pipes and gourd wind chest (540, 543)

gabbang Bamboo xylophone, common to Borneo and Philippines (833, 834, 899, 902, 906, 908)

gagah 'Strong, robust', in Javanese (634)

gagahan Male strong character type in Javanese dance (649)

gagong pon Subanen heavy gong (923–24)

galombang West Sumatra circular dance form (611)

gamat West Sumatra male/male couple dance (613)

gambang/gambang kayu Eighteen-key wooden xylophone of Java (58, 73, 103, 107, 605, 615, 616, 626, 641, 691, 704, 833, 834)

gambang kromong Chinese-oriented Indonesian music (73)

gambo Eight-stringed plucked lute of Sumbawa (780, 781, 784)

gambuh Theatrical genre of Bali (732, 735, 737, 746, 749, 757, 760–61)

gambus Plucked, pear-shaped lute, related to *'ud*, common to Malaysia and Indonesia (432, 437, 438–39, 520, 598, 605, 606, 611–12, 743, 768, 774, 806, 816, 817, 820)

gambus Arab Lampung Arabic song with violin and *rebana* (628)

gambyak Double-headed East Javanese drum (643, 649)

gambyong Javanese nonnarrative women's dance (647, 649)

gamelan Indonesian stratified gong-chime ensemble (11, 13, 20, 28, 102, 596, 639, 689, 702, 703–707, 741, 767, 776, 825)

gamelan angklung Four-tone village ensemble of Bali and Lombok (741–42, 748–49, 776)

gamelan arja Balinese *suling* and percussion ensemble (743, 750–51)

gamelan balé bandung Cirebonese court ensemble similar to *gamelan rénténg* (690)

gamelan baleganjur Processional ensemble of Bali and Lombok (730, 753–54, 776)

gamelan baris Gong-chime ensemble of Lombok (768, 772)

gamelan barong tengkok Wedding ensemble of Lombok (772)

gamelan cara balèn Ceremonial historical ensemble of Java (644, 647)

gamelan degung Sundanese *pélog* gong-chime ensemble (116, 702, 703, 706–707, 715, 720)

gamelan denggung Oldest court ensemble of Cirebon (690)

gamelan gadhon Small, soft-sounding ensemble of Java (645)

gamelan gambang Sacred xylophone and metallophone ensemble of Bali (735, 754–55)

gamelan gambuh *Suling*, rebab and percussion ensemble of Bali (735, 736, 739, 743, 747, 749–50)

gamelan gendang beleq Main traditional Sasak ensemble (771, 772)

gamelan gong Large, older ceremonial ensemble of Bali (734, 736, 744, 753)

gamelan gong kebyar Balinese dynamic modern gamelan style (13, 18, 21, 23, 729–30, 732, 738, 741, 744–45, 753, 759–60)

gamelan gong kuna Main ceremonial ensemble of Lombok (776)

gamelan gong Sasak Modern Sasak ensemble (767, 772)

gamelan grantang Rare ensemble accompanying social dance in Lombok (767)

gamelan jegog West Bali bamboo xylophone ensemble (754)

gamelan jerujeng Sacred ensemble of Boda people (767, 772)

gamelan klenèngan Small, soft-sounding ensemble in Java (645)

gamelan klentang Interlocking *klentang* processional ensemble in Lombok (767)

gamelan kodhok ngorèk Ceremonial historical ensemble in Java (644, 647)

gamelan luang Balinese sacred xylophone and metallophone ensemble (755)

gamelan Maulid Lombok sacred ensemble played during Maulid (767, 772)

gamelan munggang Ceremonial three-toned historical ensemble of Java (644, 647)

gamelan pelégongan Balinese ensemble accompanying *legong* (736, 745, 757)

gamelan pélog A *pélog* ensemble used to accompany *tayuban* dance in Cirebon (691–94)

gamelan prawa A *sléndro* ensemble used to accompany *wayang topèng* in Cirebon (691–94)

gamelan rebana Drums tuned to gamelan pitches in Lombok (773–74)

gamelan saléndro Sundanese *saléndro* gong-chime ensemble (703–706, 708)

gamelan sekati Ceremonial historical ensemble of Java and Cirebon (644, 647, 673, 687, 690)

gamelan selundeng Sacred iron-bar metallophone ensemble of Bali (755)

gamelan Semar pegulingan Small, soft-sounding court ensemble of Bali (736, 745, 746–47)

gamelan tambur Drum and gong ensemble for dance in Lombok (772)

gamelan wayang Sasak Ensemble to accompany wayang puppetry in Lombok (774)

gandang (1) Sumatran two-headed drum; (2) Samawan topical sung poetry; (3) Tausug two-headed drum; (4) Yakan cracked bamboo instrument (604, 609, 613, 781, 898, 899)

gandang lasuang West Sumatra rice-stamping trough (609)

gandingan (1) Maguindanao bossed gong; (2) Subanen sacred medium-size gong (892–93, 896, 923)

gandrung (1) Java female singer-dancer; (2) Banyuwangi percussion ensemble (645, 656, 667)

gangha Ifugao flat gongs (917)

gangsa (1) Kalinga and Bontok flat gongs; (2) Metallophone of Bali and Lombok (23, 742, 767, 915)

gangsaran Balinese up-tempo piece (744)

ganrang Buginese/Makassarese two-headed cylindrical drums (805, 806)

garantung Toba Batak wooden xylophone (608)

garapan Formulae for variation and improvisation in Javanese music (637, 638, 669, 671, 672, 673)

garey Bontok men's funeral song (920)

garokot Maranao bamboo scraper (904)

gata bera Drum from Sri Lanka (66)

gawi Ceremonial circle dance of Flores (794)

geduk Malay double-headed barrel drum hit with stick (404, *405*)

gedumbak Malay single-headed goblet-shaped drum (404)

gegaboran Balinese ostinato pattern accompanying women's dance (735)

geko Ende xylophone (793)

gembyung Cirebonese large frame drum without jingles (687, 695)

genda Frame drum of Flores (794)

genda Mbojo Mbojo court ensemble (783, 785)

gendang Large double-headed drum from Malaysia and Indonesia (66, 404, *405*, *421*, 433, 615, 623, 626, 768, 772, 773, 806, 829)

gendang beleq Lombok dance with two drummers (768, 772)

gendang panjai Iban gong-chime ensemble (830)

gendang raya Iban gong ensemble (23, 829)

gendang sarunei Karo Batak drum and gong ensemble (607)

gendèr Indonesian metallophone with tube-resonated keys (637, 691, 692, 742, 745, 747, 748, 753, 767)

gendèr barung Javanese lower-pitched metallophone with tube-resonated keys (641)

gendèr panerus Javanese higher-pitched metallophone with tube-resonated keys (641)

gendèr slenthem Javanese deepest metallophone with tube-resonated keys (641)

gendèr wayang Balinese metallophone quartet for *wayang kulit* (597, 735, 751–53)

genderang Pakpak Batak drum and gong ensemble (607)

gendhing Gamelan-based musical composition of Java (636, 639, 659–63, 669)

gendhing bonang Formal arrangement of Javanese gamelan piece (667)

gendhing lampah Theatrical pieces used in Javanese wayang (652)

gending Gamelan-based musical composition of Bali (733)

genggong Balinese Jew's harp (754, 767)

genjring (1) Cirebonese frame drum with jingles; (2) Cirebonese ensemble (687, 695)

genta Buddhist-Hindu bronze ankle bells, worn in Sumatra (600, 619, 622)

gérong Javanese male chorus accompanied by gamelan (642, 646, 673)

geruding Jew's harp of Borneo (834)

gesó-gesó Buginese/Makassarese two-stringed spike fiddle (804–805)

gesok-gesok Torajan one-stringed fiddle (806)

getai Contemporary Singaporean stage performance of Chinese origin (519)

geundrang Acehnese two-headed cylindrical drum (604)

ghazal Genre of Malaysian folk music derived from India and Middle East (438–39, 520)

gilak Balinese ostinato pattern for men's strong dances (735)

gilo lukah West Sumatra men's fish-trap dance (613)

gimbal Palawan cylindrical drum (924)

ginggong/ginggung Sumatran Jew's harp (619, 622, 627)

gitara Six-stringed guitar of Philippines (854–55)

gitgit Hanunoo three-stringed fiddle (924)

giying Balinese metallophone used in *gong kebyar* (745)

go'ong Large hanging gong of Sunda (701, 703, 706)

gobato Three-stringed bamboo idiochord tube zither of Flores (792)

gondang Toba Batak tuned drum ensemble (23, 607)

gong ageng Large hanging gong of Indonesia (640, 692, 740, 741, 742, 744, 745, 766)

gong gedé Rare largest ceremonial *gamelan gong* in Bali (744, 745)

gong genang Samawan ensemble to accompany *pencak* (781)

gong kebyar Balinese dynamic modern gamelan style (13, 18, 21, 23, 729–30, 732, 738, 741, 744–45, 753, 759–60)

gong kodeq Small hanging gong of Lombok (767)

gong lanang Smaller "male" hanging gong of Lombok (766)

gong sabet Medium-sized gong of Cirebon (692)

gong suling *Suling* used to replicate gamelan in Bali (754)

gong tondu Five-stringed bamboo idiochord tube zither in Flores (792)

gong wadon Larger "female" hanging gong in Lombok (766)

gongche pu Chinese music notation (451)

gonrang Simalungun Batak drum ensemble (607)

goong Jarai bamboo tube zither of Vietnam (535)

goong teng leng Beaten bamboo tubes, upland Vietnam (534)

gordang (1) Large bass drum in Toba Batak *gondang*; (2) Mandailing Batak drum and gong ensemble (607)

gordang sembilan Mandailing Batak nine-drum ensemble (607)

goweto One-stringed struck bamboo idiochord of Flores (793)

gɔh Temiar tube stampers, used in healing rituals (573, 585)

gula gending Ensemble of tin sugar containers in Lombok (767)

gulintangan Gong-chime ensemble of Brunei (830)

gulu Javanese pitch name (656)

gung Large vertical gong of Sumatra (619)

guntang Balinese one-stringed bamboo tube zither (743, 751, 754)

guritan South Sumatra long narrative form (623)

guru Indian teacher (121)

guwel Acehnese frame drum; basis of all Gayo dances (605)

hạ uy cầm Hawaiian steel guitar, found in Vietnam (474)

habanera Cuban dance of Spanish origin (854)

hablado Quasi-spoken lines in the *sarswela* of Philippines (857)

hadis Tausug songs about death (911)

hadra/hadrah (1) Malaysian theatrical genre derived from Islamic singing; (2) Arabic praise songs about Muhammad; (3) Single-headed frame drum of Arabic origin (409–10, 519, 606, 616, 621, 628, 776, 783, 784)

hadrat nabi Islamic praise songs on Ternate and Tidore (816)

hagelung Tiboli two-stringed lute (924)

haik Palm-leaf resonator for the *sasandu* (798, 800, 801)

hajat Ritual feast or celebration in Sunda (704, 711, 712)

hajji Muslim who has been to Mecca (765, 766)

hala? The Semang shaman, called *halaa?* by the Temiar (568)

hangar Ifugao ritual clapper (919)

harana Serenade in Philippines (849–50)

hasa Refined men's dance in Ternate, accompanied by a *tifa* (814)

hasa bunga Men's martial dance in Ternate (814)

hasuha-a Fast responsorial singing on Buru (819)

hát Vietnamese term for "singing"; prefix for theater genres (476)

hát ả đào Alternate name for *ca trù* chamber song in Vietnam (447, 467, 470)

hát bá trạo Vietnamese "paddle dance" folk theater of central Vietnam (499)

hát bài chòi Traditional theater of central Vietnam (496)

hát bội Central Vietnamese theater (23, 449, 462, 490–93, 508)

hát chầu văn Spirit possession ceremony in Vietnam (500)

hát chèo tầu Ancient folk drama of Gối near Hanoi (485–87)

hát sắc bùa Vietnamese wishing songs for New Year (Tết) (479)

hekido Four-holed bamboo ring-stop flute of Savu (802)

Helong Inhabitants of the island of Semau (796)

heo Viola in Timor (797)

hikayat Sasak Islamic writings on palm leaf (775)

Hmong Sino-Tibetan upland group living in Laos, Thailand, Vietnam, and China (550–59)

hnè Burmese conical aerophone with six-piece reed and detached bell (370–71)

hnyìñ Extinct Burmese free-reed mouth organ (365)

hò Vietnamese work songs in rice fields and on rivers (478)

hô bài chòi Vietnamese songs associated with playing cards (479)

hoho Nias solo and choral singing (608)

hồi quảng Cantonese tune adopted by Vietnamese musicians (70)

hơi Vietnamese ornamentation specific to a mode (455)

homrong Thai ceremonial suites and overtures in classical music (252, 253, 279)

hoyo Pre-burial dirges sung by women in Sumba (791)

hsaìñwaìñ Burmese classical ensemble (13, 15, 18, 22, 128, 366–74, 385)

hudhud Ifugao epic (920)

huduk apa Kayan pest-dispersal ceremony (830–31)

huluna Tagalog lullaby (849)

humenta Palm Sunday procession in Philippines (846)

hun Northeast Thai Jew's harp (318)

hün krabawk Classical-based rod puppet theater of Thailand (250, 257, 279)

husapi Lute from Borneo and Sumatra (66)

Iban Ethnic group from Borneo (51, 823–25, 828–30, 835–36)

iconography The visual representation of a subject (12)

ideograph Graphic depiction of meaning, as in Chinese characters (69)

idiophone An instrument that itself vibrates to produce sound (11)

imam Muslim religious leader (907)

Imbaya Ifugao harvest festival (881)

inang Genre of folk dance in Malaysia (437)

inarem Ilocos song debate (851)

indang (1) West Sumatra religious/political performance; (2) West Sumatra frame drum (601, 611, 612–13)

inila-ud Kalinga-Tinggian ensemble of three gongs (917)

insi Maranao ring-stop flute (904)

irama Tempo and subdivision levels in Javanese music (637, 668–69)

ja-khe Thai three-stringed floor zither in crocodile shape (239, 271, 272, 282–83)

jaipongan Sundanese indigenous popular dance form (93, 107, 111, *138*, 697, 703, 704, 708, 721, 725)

jalanpong Bronze gong-chime ensemble in Tidore (814, 816)

jamiluddin Yakan wedding song (908)

jataka Story of a past life of the Buddha (66, 116)

jatung utang Kenyah wooden xylophone (833)

jemblung Vocal performance of Banyumas gamelan (635)

jenglong (1) Cirebonese low-pitch horizontal kettle gongs; (2) Sundanese set of six hanging gongs (691, 706, 715)

jidur Large barrel drum of Indonesia (625, 768, 780)

jikay Comic theatrical genre of Malaysia and southern Thailand (410–11, 412)

joge bungin Samawan women's dance for palace events (781)

joged/jogett Genre of popular social dance, common to Malaysia and Indonesia (436–37, 520, 606, 616, 621, 628, 754, 757–58, 825)

joget gamelan Dance-drama of Terengganu, accompanied by gamelan (417, 427, 428–29)

joi Northern Thai courtship singing (313)

jota Triple-time Spanish-derived dance (854)

jungga Two-stringed lute of Sumba (791, 803)

ka law Southern Thai Buddhist ritual ensemble (305)

kaba (1) Malay storytelling accompanied by *biola* (violin); (2) West Sumatra narratives with two-stringed fiddles (413, 420, 611, 613)

kabaya Close-fitting, long-sleeved women's blouse of Sunda (700)

kabupaten Regency, administrative district in Sunda and Cirebon (687, 700)

kaca-kaca Sundanese structure symbolizing center of the universe (53)

kacapi (1) Large eighteen-stringed zither from Sunda; (2) Malay tube zither played solo; (3) Makassarese boat-shaped two-stringed lute (66, 425, 605, 703, 712, *713*, 714, 716–17, 805, 806, 810)

kacapi-suling Instrumental version of *tembang Sunda* (703, 712, 715, 724, 761)

kacapian Modern *kacapi*-accompanied vocal music (703, 712, 715–17)

kacaping Buginese boat-shaped two-stringed lute (805)

kagong Bataan curing ritual (852)

kagul (1) Maguindanao scraper-type instrument; (2) Tiruray suspended percussion beams (904, 924)

kahua Main celebratory ritual on Seram (818–19)

kain Length of batik worn as a skirt in Sunda (700)

kajar Horizontal kettle gong of Lombok (767, 772)

kakalaku Ceremonial ululation of women in Sumba (788)

kakolintang Maranao art of playing the *kulintang* (897)

kalaleng Bontok nose flute of *te-er* ritual (914)

kalangan magsangkalia Sama shark-fishing song (911)

kalangan Sama strophic fishing song (911)

kalangan taebba Sama shallow-reef-fishing song (911)

kalatong/kalutang Bamboo or wooden percussion sticks of Philippines (846, 848)

kalimusta (1) Kalinga love song; (2) Bontok long solo song (915)

kalindo Northeast Sulawesi bar zither (806)

kambori Torajan song performed by men to greet the day (806)

Kamulaan Mindanao highlands festival (881)

kandang rayah Iban gong ensemble (829)

kanhi Lowland Chăm turtle-shell-body fiddle (590)

kanja Mbojo women's martial arts dance (783)

kantrüm Khmer village ensemble in northeast Thailand (210–11, 213, 214–15)

kapamelo–malong Maranao song about traditional dress (909–10)

kapanirong Maranao serenade ensemble (905)

kapika Four-holed bamboo ring-stop flute of Sumba (791)

kar Khmer wedding ceremony (18, 155, 195–96)

karagatan Poetic game, played in Philippines (850, 851)

karansa Cavite outdoor working song (852)

karaoke Amateur singing to prerecorded accompaniment (99)

karawitan Javanese gamelan-based court music (659, 684)

kareku kandei Rice pounder and mortar music of Sumbawa (783–84)

Karen Upland ethnic group from northern Thailand and Burma (26, 543–46)

kasar 'Crude, rough', Javanese term (635, 719)

kasidah Muslim devotional songs in Arabic, also *qasidah* (612, 806)

kasinoman Ritual party for youth in Cirebon (688–89)

kata-kata Yakan and Sama epic poems (908)

kateobak Mentawei single-headed cylindrical drum (613–14)

katimbok Tagakaolu paired-string zither (924)

kaul Sundanese casual participation in a musical event (719)

kawih Fixed-meter songs of Sunda (717)

kawoking Teasing courtship songs of Sumba (790)

kayaka Ceremonial men's cries of Sumba (788)

kayaq Lombok theater with melancholic songs (772, 776)

kayari Section of the *pamanhikan* in Philippines (851)

kbach Khmer system of dance gestures (189, 204)

kbolo Two largest *sene* gongs of West Timor (797)

kẽtruyện Narratives of poetry and prose of Vietnam (479)

kebluk Large kettle gong of Cirebon (691)

kebudayaan pasisir Coastal culture of north Java (686)

kecak Balinese male chorus representing monkey army (756)

kecimol Wind, string, and drum ensemble of Lombok (768, 774)

kecrèk Javanese and Sundanese idiophone made of hanging metal plates (107, 642, 652, 673)

kekawin Sung poetry in Old Javanese (756)

keledi Kajang mouth organ (836)

kelenongan Gong-chime and ensemble of Sumatra (627)

kelintang Gong-chime and ensemble of Sumatra (616, 617, 619, 620, 621, 623, 627–28)

kelitang/kelittang Gong-chime and ensemble of Sumatra (623, 627)

keluri Kenyah mouth organ (836)

kemanak Banana-shaped metal idiophone of Java and Cirebon (632, 642, 691)

kemidi rudat Popular theatrical form in Lombok (768, 774)

kemong Balinese small hanging gong (741, 742)

kempli Balinese horizontally mounted gong (742)

kempul Small hanging gong of Indonesia (640, 659, 703, 708, 767, 772)

kempur (1) South Sumatra large horizontal gong; (2) Small hanging gong of Bali (626, 740, 741–42, 745, 748, 749)

kempyang Javanese small kettle gong, *pélog* tuning only (641)

kemyang High-pitched gong-chime of Cirebon (692)

ken Free-reed mouth organ in raft form, found in Cambodia, Laos, and Thailand (172)

kèn Family of double-reed aerophones of Vietnam (475)

kenat Horizontal kettle gong of Lombok (767, 772)

kendang Double-headed drum from Indonesia (66, 692, 701, 703, 709, 710, 743, 744, 745, 748, 780, 781, 783)

kendang penca Percussive ensemble used for *penca silat* (703, 709, 724)

kendhang Double-headed drum of Java (645, 673–75)

kendhang ciblon Medium double-headed barrel drum of Java (103, 642)

kendhang gendhing Large double-headed barrel drum of Java (642)

kendhang ketipung Small double–headed barrel drum of Java (642)

keneo Enggano conch shell (621)

kenong (1) South Sumatra large horizontal gong; (2) Large, deep-rimmed kettle gong of Indonesia (626, 641, 659, 691, 703)

kenthongan Javanese wooden slit gong (646)

keprak Javanese wooden box used to accompany dance (642, 653, 673)

keras 'Strong, coarse'; applied to characters in Balinese dance (757)

keromongan Sumatran gong-chime and ensemble (623, *624*)

keroncong Portuguese-derived folk music from Melakka (439, 520)

kertok kelapa Series of slabs over coconut resonators, found in Malaysia (425, *433*)

keruncung Bidayuh bamboo tubes (833)

kesi Malaysian pair of small cymbals (404)

kesuling Bamboo ring-stop flute of Borneo (835)

kesut Kajang bamboo pole stamping (831)

ketadu Two-stringed boat lute of Savu (802, 803)

ketadu haba Eight-stringed tube zither with resonator, from Savu (802–803)

ketadu mara Nine-keyed wooden trough xylophone of Savu (803)

ketawang Formal arrangement of Javanese gamelan piece (667)

keteng-keteng Karo Batak tube zither (607)

kethoprak Javanese spoken historical theater with music (655)

kethuk Javanese small kettle gong (641)

ketipung Cirebonese small double-headed barrel drum (692)

ketobung Riau two-headed drums (615)

ketuk Small kettle gong of Cirebon (687, 691, 696)

ketuk telu Small village ensemble of Cirebon (689, 696)

ketuk tilu Sundanese small coastal village ensemble (107, 703, 707–708)

khaen Free-reed mouth organ from northeast Thailand and Laos (15, 22, 46, 61, 67, 115–16, 131, 141, *146*, 214, 215, 225, 316, 321–24)

khánh Chimes of stone or bronze, found in Vietnam (468, 504)

khao Northern Thai narrative genre, sometimes accompanied (313)

khap/khắp Vocal genres common to northeast Thailand and central and northern Laos (13, 22, 340, 341, 359, 532)

khap ngeum Repartee song genre of Vientiane area (18, 22, 347)

khap phuan Repartee song genre of Phuan minority, northern Laos (347–48)

khap sam neua Repartee song genre of Houaphanh province (348–49)

khap thai dam Vocal genre of Thai Dam minority, northern Laos (349)

khap thum Repartee song genre of Luang Phrabang (22, 349–51)

khaw law Original name of *pong lang* in northeast Thailand (318–19)

khawng Single, bossed gongs of Thailand (230, 305, 311–12)

khawng khu Southern Thai pair of bossed gongs (305)

khawng mawn Thai vertical, U-shaped set of bossed gongs (231, *232*)

khawng wong lek Smaller circle of eighteen bossed gongs from Thailand (231, 270)

khawng wong yai Larger circle of sixteen bossed gongs from Thailand (121, 231, 270)

khene Lao free-reed mouth organ, also *khaen* (Thailand) (338–40, *342–49*, 351–53, 355, 356, 358, 361)

khim Small hammered zither of Chaozhou, Chinese origin (239–40, 282–83, 312, 350, 355)

khimm Hammered zither of Chinese origin (169, 183, 196)

khloy Khmer end-blown duct flute of bamboo (172, 183, 196, 197, 213, 236)

khlui Thai bamboo or wood fipple flutes, in three sizes (235–36, 256, 257, 271, 272, 312)

Khmer The mainstream culture of Cambodia (11, 151)

Khmer Rouge Communist political organization of Cambodia (81, 90, 118, 119, 123–24, 151–52, 154, 159–60, 187, 205, 208–10)

khon Classical masked theater, based on the *Ramayana*; found in Thailand and Laos (241, 250–52, 279, 357)

khong vong Lao series of bossed gongs on circular rattan frame (354, 355)

khru Thai teacher (121)

khrüang sai Thai court entertainment ensemble of strings and flute (22, 245–46, 331)

khse muoy Half-gourd resonated monochord from Cambodia (18, 169, 194, 196)

khui Lao bamboo fipple flute (338, 345, 350, 355, 358)

khwan Spirit essence of a human being (64)

kịch nói Western-inspired spoken theater of Vietnam (496–97)

kidiu Kenyah bull roarer (837)

kidung Type of metered sung poetry in Bali and Lombok (755, 756)

kili Comb and tissue kazoo from West Timor (797)

kinang Lowland Chăm two-headed drum (590)

kinh The mainstream, lowland Vietnamese population (444)

kinilisong Subanen gong ensemble (923–24)

kiwul Small gong of Cirebon (692)

klang chhnakk Khmer ensemble used for funerals (168, 197)

klawng ae Long Northern Thai single-headed drum (311)

klawng khaek (1) Thai two-headed barrel drums; (2) Ensemble for boxing and theater (66, 234, 246, 266–68)

klawng that Pair of Thai large barrel drums played with sticks (233, 251)

klawng yao Long Central Thai single-headed drum (303–304, 319)

klènang Pair of small kettle gongs from Cirebon (691)

klenèngan Social events accompanying ceremonies in Java (647, 683)

klentang Single key fixed on wooden box, from Lombok (767)

klentong Balinese small hanging gong (742)

kliningan Sundanese vocal music in *gamelan saléndro* (703, 704)

klông pút Vietnamese group of seven sounding bamboo tubes, activated by clapping (534–35)

klong-klong Three-stringed bamboo idiochord tube zither from Flores (792)

k'ni Bowed monochord stick zither of the Jarai, Vietnam (59, 535)

knobe besi Metal jaw harp from West Timor (797)

knobe kbetas Musical bow from West Timor (797–98)

knobe oh Wooden jaw harp from West Timor (797)

koa Rhythmically spoken song to musical accompaniment, from West Timor (797)

koangtac Sedang hydraulic bamboo xylophone, Vietnam (534)

kolintang Minahasan xylophone (810)

kolitong Kalinga polychordal zither (919)

kolokie Volcano-calming ceremony on Ternate (814)

komedi stambul Dutch-influenced stage theater in Sumatra (601)

komintang Tagalog courtship song (871)

kompang Malay single-headed frame drum of Arab origin (424, 431, 519)

kopak-kopak Long bamboo pole to disperse birds in Philippines (904)

korng mong Khmer single, suspended bossed gong (165)

korng vung Khmer gong circle (157, *158*)

korng vung tauch Khmer higher-pitched gong circle, sixteen to eighteen gongs (*164*, 165)

korng vung thomm Khmer lower-pitched gong circle, with sixteen gongs (*164*, 165, 197)

kosok kancing Samawan life-cycle dance for nobility (781)

kotekan Rapid, interlocking figuration characteristic of Balinese music (734)

kotyapi Maranao two-stringed plucked lute (905, 908)

krajappi Central Thai long-necked lute with four strings (66, 237–38)

krap Several kinds of Thai concussion idiophones (228–29, 305)

krapeu Three-stringed floor zither of Cambodia (169, *170*, 183, 196)

krapp Khmer pair of bamboo or wood clappers (163)

kraton One of the Central Javanese courts (626, 634, 686)

kraw Thai slit-bamboo signaling device (232)

kreasi baru New musical composition, pan-Indonesian term (129, 666, 684, 723, 729, 746, 749, 759–60, 773)

kris Fine laminated dagger, made in Java (643, 758)

kroeung damm Khmer classification term for percussion instruments (161)

kroeung khse Khmer classification term for stringed instruments (161)

kroeung phlomm Khmer classification term for wind instruments (161)

kromong/kromongan Sumatran gong-chime and ensemble (616, 617, 619, 623, 626)

kroncong Eurasian colonial-based popular music of Indonesia (102–104, 633, 671, 664)

kroncong asli "Original" *kroncong* music (102–103)

krong Large slit-bamboo signaling device from Thailand (232)

kubing Mindanao Jew's harp (886, 904, 924)

kuda kepang Malay hobby-horse trance dance, preceded by *barongan* (412–13, 520)

kudlung Hanunoo paired-string zither (905, 925)

kudya Bontok love song, antiphonal song (915)

kudyapi/kudyapiq Maguindanao two-stringed lute (66, 924)

kue/kui Kenyah rice-planting ceremony (827)

kugiran Guitar-dominated popular song genre of Malaysia (441–42)

kulaing Yakan Jew's harp (904–905)

kulimbet Ibaloy drum and flat gong ensemble (918)

kulintang/kulintangan Horizontal bronze gong-chime and ensemble of Indonesia and Philippines (20, 23, 29, 627, 628, 794, 814–16, 830, 834, 886, 891–902, 921)

kulitang Horizontal bronze gong-chime and ensemble of Sumatra (623, 627)

kuluk-kuluk Rattle made of coconut and bamboo from Philippines (911)

kumbing Subanen Jew's harp (924)

kumidya Spanish-influenced stage play from Philippines (856, 869)

kumintang Philippine song and dance depicting love (850, 851)

kundiman Lyrical love song of Philippines (855, 871, 881, 883, 884)

kundongan Maranao lower-pitched gongs of the *kulintang* (897)

kungkuvak North Borneo reed pipe (837)

kuriri Tausug and Yakan single-part piece (898)

kusyapiq Palawan two-stringed lute (924, 925)

kutet Subanen one-stringed fiddle (925)

kutyapiq Maguindanao two-stringed plucked lute (905)

kwintangan Yakan set of bossed gongs (899)

kwintangan kayu Yakan hanging log beams (899, 903–904)

kwv txhiaj Hmong courtship game songs (555–58)

kwv txhiaj plees Hmong sung poetry; amatory songs (557)

laba dera Single-headed squat hand drum of Flores (794)

laba go Drum and gong ensemble of Flores (793)

laba toda High, narrow standing drum of Flores (794)

laba wai Single-headed standing drum of Flores (794)

labu Single-headed standing drum of Roti (800, 801)

ladrang Formal arrangement of Javanese gamelan piece (667)

lagu Musical piece from Cirebon and Sunda (690, 694, 704, 713)

lagu cengeng "Weepy" song from Indonesia (93)

lagu dolanan Javanese light, humorous pieces (653, 666, 683, 84)

lagu dua Sumatran dance songs in triple meter (606)

lagu-lagu rakyat Pan-Malaysian contemporary songs (439–40, 442)

lai Modal system used for performance on the Thai *khaen* (15, 67, 323–24)

lakhon/lakhawn Various types of Thai dance-drama (241, 251, 253–57)

lam Vocal performance common to northeast Thailand (13, 18, 320–21, 340, 351)

lam ban xok Repartee song genre of central-southern Laos (341, 345, 351)

lam khon savan Repartee song genre of Savannakhet area, central-south Laos (22, 341, 345–46)

lam klawn Northeast Thai repartee song with *khaen* (22, 115, 325–26, 332, 342)

lam mahaxay Repartee song genre of central-southern Laos (341, 346)

lam mu Theatrical genre in northeast Thailand (115–16, 327–28, 353)

lam phanya yoi Regional type of repartee song with *khaen* in northeast Thailand (327)

lam phi fa Northeast Thai spirit-healing ceremony (329)

lam phlün Local theater from northeast Thailand (115–16)

lam phu thai Vocal genre of the Phu Thai minority of southern Laos (341, 346–47)

lam phün Northeast Thai narrative song accompanied by *khaen* (325)

lam ploen Theatrical genre in northeast Thailand (328–29, 352–53)

lam rueang Adaptation of northeast Thai theater (133)

lam salavane Vocal genre of Salavane province, Laos (18, 22, 344–45)

lam sing Modern form of *lam* in northeast Thailand (18, 142, 320–21, 327, 332–33)

lam sithandone Repartee vocal genre from Champassak area (341, 343)

lam som Nearly extinct vocal genre of southern Laos (341, 343–44)

lam tang vay Repartee song genre of central-southern Laos (18, 345)

lamba Single-headed standing drum of Sumba (788)

lanat Laotian suspended horizontal xylophone (57, 354, 355)

lanca In Bima, fighting style that uses the knees (780)

lancang kuning Malay royal barge rowing competition (617)

lancaran Formal arrangement of Javanese gamelan piece (667)

langan bataq-bataq Tausug lullaby (910–11)

langen driyan Javanese women's dance-drama with sung dialogue (654–55)

langen mandra wanara Javanese men's dance-drama with sung dialogue (654–55)

langgam jawa *Kroncong* music specific to Java (102–103)

langgam kroncong *Kroncong* music from Indonesia (102)

langkit Tausug ballad (908)

langko Samawan competitive sung poetry (782)

lansaran Murut headhunting song and dance form (826)

lantoy Manobo chip-on-ledge flute (924)

laras Tuning, scale, in Javanese (656)

latihan Sundanese public jam session or rehearsal (704, 707, 722)

laud Pear-shaped plucked lute from Philippines (854–55)

lavitti Love songs using informal verse in Sumba (790–91)

láy Patterned ornamentation characteristic of *tuồng* theater, Vietnam (492)

lea-lea Buginese/Makassarese bamboo tube zither (806)

lebad Yakan musical unit in instrumental music (898–99)

Lebaran Feast held after Ramadan (780)

lego Circular men's or women's song and dance of Buru (819)

lego-lego Women's court dance with vocals on Ternate (815)

légong Girls' narrative dances of Bali (747, 757)

leku Four-stringed fretless plucked lute from West Timor (797)

lekupa Kenyah-Badang songs and dances (826–27)

lelambatan Slow, stately piece of Balinese music (744, 749)

le'le' Tausug humorous song (902)

leleng Tausug and Sama love repartee (909)

lellang Sama spirit possession piece (900)

lemambang Iban bard (828)

lènggèr Javanese female singer-dancer (645, 648)

lenggo Mbojo nonnarrative welcoming dance (783)

lesung Rice-pounding block from Java and Borneo (646, 831)

letor Sikku and Lio xylophone (793)

li-ke Thai urban street theater (95, 99, 221, 222, 256, 301–303, 352–53)

lima Javanese pitch name (656)

lingkung seni Performing arts group in Sunda (721, 722, 725)

liriban Javanese soft-playing ensemble (642)

Lisu Tibeto-Burman-speaking people living in Thailand, Burma, and China (537, 542–43)

lithophone Stone xylophone (56–57, 129)

lkhaon Khmer generic term referring primarily to theater or play (155, 200)

lkhaon khaol Masked play of the Khmer court (155, 190)

lodo paghili Work songs of Sumba (790)

lontar Palm-leaf manuscripts used in areas of Indonesia to record literary and religious works and music notation (775, 805, 806)

lontará Buginese palm-leaf manuscripts (805)

lubak-lubak Tausug dance piece (898)

lục huyền cầm Modified Spanish guitar found in Vietnam (473–74)

ludag Isneg large conical drum (918)

ludruk Javanese contemporary or local theater (655)

luguh Formula of Qur'ānic recitation (906, 907, 908, 911)

luk krung Big band jazz from Thailand (96–97, 100)

luk mot A coda affixed to a Thai classical composition (275)

luk thung Thai popular music genre (96–98, 99, 100)

lulya New Year fertility ritual dances in the Babar islands (821)

luntang Maguindanao and Timray suspended xylophone (903, 926)

lus rov Hmong vocal genre with disguised text (558)

lu'ui Sama lamentation to relieve bereavement (911)

ly Class of Vietnamese folk song comparing human actions to nature (478)

macapat Metered sung poetry of Java (634–35, 664, 667)

magagung Kadazan music in which gongs are beaten in interlocking rhythms (828–29)

magbinua Sama song about a dream world (911)

magigal jin Sama dance of possession (890, 900)

Maha Gitá Printed anthology of Burmese classical songs (373, 395)

Mahabharata Indian epic (66)

Mahanikai The older, typical sect of Buddhism (288)

Mahayana Buddhist sect from China (444, 502)

maholi String and flute classical ensemble in Vientiane (356, 358)

mahorathük Bronze "drum" idiophone in Thailand (231)

mahori Court ensemble blending idiophones and chordophones (17, 22, 243–45, 264)

main caci Competitive whip dueling in Flores (793)

main pulau Type of song performed by Malaysian women weeding dry rice fields (423)

main puteri Malay healing ceremony (417, 421, 524)

ma'inang (1) Sumatran fast-meter dance songs; (2) Bengkulu *pantun* singing (606, 620)

mak yong Dance-drama of Kelantan province, Malaysia (406–407, 412, 417, 421, 427)

mak yong laut Malay theater from southern Thailand, similar to *jikay* (411)

makot Chant style of Dhammayut-sect Buddhist temples (291–92)

malahiya Tagalog fishing song (852)

Malayo-Polynesian Language family including Malay, Chăm, and Jarai (529)

mámarakka Torajan funeral music for bamboo flutes and female vocalist (809)

mamongu (1) Bronze or iron gong; (2) Anakalangu language (788)

manahelo Roti chanter fluent in poetic language (799, 800–801)

manolin Instrument similar to European mandolin, found in Bali and Lombok (743, 768, 774)

manora Type of southern Thai theater named for the leading character, also performed in Malaysia (22, 254, 306–307, 404, 411–12)

mapag Sri Cirebonese welcoming ceremony for the goddess Sri (688–89)

mapag tamba Cirebonese post-planting ceremony (688)

Marapu Sumbanese indigenous belief system (788)

marwas Small, two-headed drums of Ternate and Tidore (816)

maseukat Acehnese men's percussive dance form (605)

masjid Building designated for Islamic gatherings (*74*)

masri Genre of Malay dance (437)

Maulid Prophet's birthday, in Sumbawa (780)

maùñ Hanging, bossed gong of Burma (371)

maùñsaìñ Burmese set of eighteen or nineteen bossed gongs on wooden frames in five rows (368–69, *370*)

mawlam Singer from northeast Thailand (61, 96, 320)

ma'yong (1) Malaysian theater; (2) Riau masked theater (19, 23, 92, 125, 134, 607, 616)

m'buôt Free-reed mouth organ with gourd wind chest, found in Trường Sơn Ranges (534)

medium Tranced ritualist who is possessed by visiting spirits (568)

megayep Subanen healing gong ensemble (923)

meglebulebu seputangan Yakan song debate (909–10)

mek mulung Traditional theater of Kedah state, Malaysia (407–408, 412)

meko Bronze or iron gong of Roti (798, 799, 800)

meko ai Nine-keyed trough xylophone (800)

metabole Transmigration of pitches allowing modal modulation (67, *177*, *263*, 456, 457)

metallophone Metal xylophone (20)

mi jaùñ Mon crocodile-shaped floor zither (365)

microtonal Interval less than a semitone (100 cents) (109)

Minangkabau Ethnic group of Sumatra (51)

minuna Maguindanao old *kulintang* playing style (896)

mõ Vietnamese wooden slit drum in fish shape for Buddhist rituals (465, 468)

mode Fundamental guidelines for composition and improvisation (15, 127, 390)

mohlam Lao singer from northeast Thailand (89)

mohori Khmer court ensemble for entertainment music (155, 156, 183–85)

molam Traditional singer of Laos (340, 343)

momong Acehnese medium horizontal gong (605)

mongmong Small gongs of Mandailing Batak ensembles (607)

monochord Chordophone with one string (59)

moriones Mindoro Holy Week masked celebration (846)

moro-moro Christian/Muslim folk drama (854, 856, 869)

mosque Building designated for Islamic gatherings (73)

motive Short melodic phrase (14)

mridanga Barrel-shaped drum from India (66)

múa bá trạo The Vietnamese "oar dance," associated with rituals of the sacred whale (500)

múa đăng bông The Vietnamese "flower dance," associated with religious occasions (499)

múa rối nước Water-puppet theater found in northern Vietnam (487–88)

muezzin Performer of *azan*, Islamic call to prayer (431)

muoy choan Khmer short rhythmic cycle, "first level" (168, 181, 182)

musikong bumbong Bamboo instrument ensemble of Philippines (860)

musiqa Arabic word denoting music as distinct from chant (430–31)

muzik klasik Western classical music in Malaysia (440)

muzik seriosa Western classical music in Malaysia (440)

Myanmar Current official name of Burma (363)

na' Burmese spirit (44, 66)

nabar panas pela Blood-drinking ceremony in Tanimbar (821)

nadran Cirebonese ceremony honoring Allah, the sea, and fish (688–89, 695)

nafiri Straight trumpet of *nobat* ensemble in Malaysia (429)

naga Mythological serpent (52)

nahana Yakan song about a famous person (908)

naka Mbojo men's dance with daggers (783)

nam One of two Vietnamese modal systems (455, 463–64)

namangngu Bronze or iron gong of Savu (802)

nan guan South Fukien music of T'ang dynasty (876)

nang pra mo thai Northeast Thai shadow-puppet theater (252, 307, 325, 329)

nang talung Southern Thai shadow-puppet theater, also found in Malaysia (221, 252, 307–309, 404)

nang yai Large-shadow-puppet theater of Thailand (252–53, 264, 279)

naphat Classical music genre from Thailand (128, 258)

na'pwè Spirit propitiation rite of Burma (61, 372–73, 394)

nathap Thai cycle of drum strokes (265)

nathap propkai Thai longer set of three drum-cycle patterns (265–66)

nathap sawngmai Thai shorter set of three drum-cycle patterns (265)

naw Upland Thai (Lahu) gourd mouth organ (539–40)

ncas Hmong Jew's harp made of metal (552–53)

nehara Kettle drum of *nobat* ensemble, Malaysia (429)

nekara Bronze Đông Sơn drum of Kai Kecil (819)

nem Javanese pitch name (656)

nenet Bengkulu women's ceremonial dances (613)

ngajat Iban men's war/entertainment dance (830, 833, 834)

ngayau Kajang ancient headhunting ceremony (826, 831)

ngel-ngel Melismatic free-meter ceremonial songs on Kai (820)

nggo Ende-Lio gong (793)

nggri-nggo Five-stringed bamboo idiochord tube zither of Flores (792)

nggunggi Bamboo jaw harp of Sumba (791)

ngrémo Nonnarrative men's dance of Java (649)

ngufa-ngufa Main performers of *dabus* on Ternate and Tidore (817)

ngunjung Cirebonese thanksgiving ceremony (688, 689, 691)

nguri Samawan slow women's reception dance (781)

nhạc cải cách Early form of Vietnamese popular music from the late 1930s (449, 509–10, 513)

nhạc dân tộc cải biên Modernized "traditional" Vietnamese music mixing lowland and upland genres (89, 119,129, 134, 512–13)

nhạc huyền Nguyễn-dynasty court ensemble (448)

nhạc lễ Ritual ensemble of southern Vietnam (465, 467)

nhạc mới Modern popular songs of Vietnam (513–14, 515)

nhạc tài tử Vocal/instrumental chamber music of southern Vietnam (23, 70, 472, 483–84, 494, 508)

nhạc tiền chiến Romantic Vietnamese songs of the 1940s, inspired by German lieder (510)

nhịp Metrical organization of rhythm in Vietnamese music (465)

nobat Malay-based Muslim drum and oboe ensemble (23, 427, 429–30, 600–601, 609, 615)

node Vibration-free point (59)

nói lối Metrically free, introductory phrases for Vietnamese songs (454)

nora Alternate name for *manora* theater in Thailand (306–307)

nose flute Small, soft-sounding flute activated by air from the player's nostrils (791, 836, 914)

nua Song tradition of spontaneously trading verses in Sumbawa (784)

ốc Conch shell trumpet of Vietnam (475)

octavina Guitar-shaped plucked lute of Philippines (854–55)

ogung Large vertical gong of Sumatra (607)

olimong Kalinga whistle flute (919)

oniya-niya Maranao reed instrument (904)

onor Maranao *bayok* singer (910)

orang Alifuru Aboriginal inhabitants of Ambon, Buru, and environs (818, 819)

Orang Asli Upland peoples of peninsular Malaysia (401)

organology The study of musical instruments (10, 12, 56)

orkes bea Torajan conch and flute ensemble (810)

orkes gambus South Sumatra Arab-influenced music (605, 621, 625)

orkes Lampung Lampung wind, string, and drum ensemble (628)

orkes Melayu Malay songs with stringed instruments (104, 439, 617, 621, 625)

orkes sinandung timur Acehnese Malay-based string ensemble (604–605)

ostinato Continuously repeated pattern (45)

ote Medium-size *sene* gongs of West Timor (797)

òzi Long, single-headed goblet-shaped drum of Burma (375)

pábarrung Torajan sugar-palm leaf horn (806)

pabasa Chanting of Christ's Passion in Philippines (843–45)

padoa Savunese circle dance with ankle baskets (802)

paggabbang Tausug secular singing style (906)

paghiling Sung by serenaders in *harana* ritual, Philippines (850)

pagtumbok Sung by serenaders in *harana* ritual, Philippines (850)

pahiyas Tagalog harvest festival (881)

pajaga Buginese court dance accompanied by *ganrang* and gong (805)

pakarena Makassarese court dance performed by girls (805–806)

pakhavaj Drum from India (66)

pakkung Ibaloy bamboo buzzer (919)

palabunibunyan Maguindanao traditional ensemble (892–95)

paldong Kalinga notched flute (919)

palendag Maguindanao notched flute (904, 924, *925*, 926)

Pali Sacred language of Theravada Buddhism (65, 206, 290–91)

palipal Ifugao ritual clapper (919)

palwei Bamboo, end-blown fipple flute of Burma (371, 377)

pamamaalam Serenade at end of *harana* ritual, Philippines (850)

pamanhikan Tradition followed during marriage proposal, Philippines (851)

panambih Fixed-meter portion of *tembang Sunda* (714, 715)

pananapat Rizal practice of itinerant chanters (845)

pananapatan (1) First songs of *harana* ritual, Philippines; (2) Tagalog outdoor Christmas drama (843, 850)

pananawagan Tagalog outdoor Christmas drama (843, 855)

pancer Transitional tone within *patokan* in Sundanese music (715)

pandanggo Batangas song-dance (852)

panerus Low-pitched metallophone of Sunda (704)

pangangaluluwa Songs sung from house to house in Philippines (849)

pangongka'an Sama gong ensemble (900)

pangpagaq Kenyah concussion idiophones (831)

pano' Temiar ceremonial genre in which spirits are contacted (570–71)

pantun (1) Malay form of four-line poetry verses; (2) Rhymed couplets, pan-Indonesian; (3) Buginese/Makassarese sung quatrains, also found in Maluku; (4) Sundanese narrative epic performances with *kacapi* (424, 435–36, 604, 605, 606, 611, 616, 619, 620, 712–13, 717, 775, 784, 806, 813, 827)

pantun saut Cross-gender responsorial singing on Ternate and Tidore (816)

panunuluyan Outdoor Christmas drama in Philippines (843)

parise (1) Mock battle dance between men in Sumbawa; (2) Florinese competitive whip dueling (780, 793)

parwa Balinese human theater derived from *wayang wong* (757)

pasasalamat Songs sung during *harana* ritual, Philippines (850)

pasindén Female vocalist for *gamelan saléndro,* Sunda (704)

pasodoble March in double time (846, 847, 856, 869)

pasola Marapu ritual jousting match (788)

pastores Christmas songs in Philippines (842–43)

pasyon Vernacular text about Christ's Passion, sung in Philippines (843–45, 856)

pa'talà Burmese suspended bamboo xylophone with twenty-four keys (22, 57, 378, *379*)

patang-ug Kalinga quill-shaped bamboo percussion tubes (919)

pathet Javanese modal classification system (15, 67–68, 636, 637–38, 651–52, 657–59)

patokan The structural outline of a piece of Sundanese music (701–702, 703–704, 706, 715)

pattong Kalinga wooden sticks for striking gongs (915)

patut Cirebonese modal classification system (692–93)

patutan Balinese modal classification system (735)

pa'waìñ Burmese circle of twenty-one tuned drums in a wood frame (367, *368*)

pedagogy Methods of teaching (119)

pejogedan bumbung Xylophone ensemble for *joged* dance, Bali (754)

peking Sundanese high-pitched metallophone (704)

pélog Gapped-scale pentatonic tuning system, found throughout Indonesia (656–57, 691, 692, 693–94, 702, 718, 735, 769–70)

penanggisa-an Maranao deep-rimmed, bossed gong (896, 897)

penca/pencak silat Indonesian martial arts performance (606, 703, 708, 709, 780, 781, 783, 806)

pendhapa Large pavilions at Javanese courts (653)

pengawak "Body" section of fixed-meter piece of Balinese music (734)

penja duriyang Northern Thai ensemble of free reeds and strings (312)

penunggul Javanese pitch name (656)

peruncung Bidayuh bamboo tubes (833)

pesindhèn Female Javanese vocalist accompanied by gamelan (103, *640*, 642, 666–67, 673, 684)

petuk Timekeeping horizontal kettle gong of Lombok (767, 771, 772, 773)

pey pork Khmer free-reed pipe with finger holes (172, 194, 205)

pey prabauh Khmer cylindrical double-reed aerophone (172–73, 194, 196, 197)

pey-aw Khmer cylindrical, double-reed aerophone (172, 212, 213)

phách Piece of wood or bamboo struck by two beaters, Vietnam (465, 468, 481, 483)

phanya Courtship poetry in northeast Thailand (6, 321)

phin Plucked lute of northeast Thailand (18, 66, 316, 338)

phin hai Northeast Thai ceramic jars with plucked rubber bands (317–18, 320)

phin nam tao Chest-resonated stick zither from northern Thailand (66, 311)

phin phia Multi-stringed stick zither from northern Thailand (66, 311, 315)

phleng dio Solo instrumental classical Thai compositions (281)

phleng hang khrüang Short "coda" pieces attached to longer compositions in Thailand (282)

phleng kar Cambodian village wedding song (23)

phleng khorat Repartee songs of Nakhon Ratchasima (Khorat) city, Thailand (140, 300)

phleng kret Classification term for "miscellaneous" compositions in Thai music (281)

phleng la Thai compositions for ending a concert (281)

phleng laim Class of Khmer court compositions for dance (182)

phleng lamtat Repartee village song of central Thailand (299–300)

phleng luk krung Thai popular song accompanied by Western instruments (96–97, 331–32)

phleng luk thung Popular music genre from Thailand (96–97, 115, 320, 332–33)

phleng naphat Thai instrumental compositions for ceremony and theater (275, 278)

phleng phua chiwit Thai popular music incorporating social criticism (98)

phleng phuang malai Thai village song genre sung in a circle (299)

phleng phün ban Village folk song genres of Thailand (22, 114, 298–99)

phleng phün muang Agricultural song from Thailand (114)

phleng rüa Antiphonal songs for men and women, sung on boats in Thailand (229, 299)

phleng rüang Ceremonial suites and overtures in Thai classical music (278–79)

phleng samai Modern Cambodian music (157)

phleng skor Class of classical compositions for Khmer drumming (182)

phleng tap Short suites of melodious compositions in Thailand (279)

phleng thai düm The classical repertoire of Thailand (223)

phleng thai sakon Thai popular music genre (97)

phleng thao Thai composition in three *chan* tempo levels (128, 269, 275, 279–80)

phleng yai Long, texturally complex classical Thai compositions (280)

phram Leader of a spirit ritual in Thailand, Laos, or Burma (64, 295)

pi Thai family of double or quadruple reeds of various shapes (236, 358, 411, 412)

pi aw Thai short, cylindrical quadruple reed, rare (236–37)

pi chanai Double-reed aerophone from Thailand (66, 237, 249)

pi chawa Thai conical wooden quadruple reed, of Javanese origin (*235,* 237, 264, 307, 308, 309, 312)

pi choan Khmer medium rhythmic cycle, "second level" (168, 181, 182)

pi chum Northern Thai free-reed pipes with finger holes (310)

pi kaeo Quadruple reed with bulbous-shaped body from Laos (355)

pi mawn Large, conical quadruple reed of the Mon ensemble (237)

pi nai Double-reed aerophone from Thailand (17, *242*, 251, 261, 262, 264, 271, 272, 305)

pinalaiyan Kalinga-Tinggian gong and drum ensemble (917–18)

pinn Extinct angular harp from Angkor carvings (*157*, 169)

pinn peat Khmer classical court ensemble (11, 23, 134, 155, 157–58, 168, 183)

pipa Chinese pear-shaped lute (70, 473)

piphat Classical ensemble of Thailand (11, 17, 22, 241–43, 258–62, 272)

piphat mai khaeng Thai *piphat* ensemble with hard mallets (241)

piphat mai nuam Thai *piphat* ensemble with padded mallets (242)

piphat mawn Ensemble of Mon origin for funerals (242–43)

pisu Four-stringed fretless plucked lute of West Timor (797)

plosa Structure of Tagalog poetry (850, 851)

poghi Nose flute of Sumba (791)

pohaci A Sundanese spirit (50)

pokok Central melody and basis for figuration in Balinese music (733, 737)

pompang Torajan ensemble of bamboo flutes (806)

pong lang Northeast Thai vertical xylophone of logs (*57*, 318–19, 338)

pop Indonesia Western-influenced popular music of Indonesia (106–109)

pop Melayu Western pop band with solo singer in Sumatra (606)

pop Sunda Indigenous popular music of Sunda (712, 717–19)

portamento Melodic slide between two pitches (14)

posadas Mexican outdoor Christmas drama, found in Philippines (843)

poy Free-reed mouth organ of upland Cambodia (157, 172)

prajuritan Javanese soldier's music (646)

Prambanan Hindu temple in Central Java (62)

prasaja 'Forthright, austere', in Javanese (634)

prawa Cirebonese five-tone tuning system (691, 692, 693–94)

preret Wooden double-reed aerophone of Bali and Lombok (743, 767–68, 771, 772, 773, 774, 776)

preson Lamaholot xylophone (793)

puaka North Sumatra invocational healing songs (605)

Pugutan Open-air drama, climax of the *moriones* festival in Philippines (846)

pulakan Tausug/Sama deep-rimmed bossed gong (898, 900)

pulao Sama bamboo ring-stop flute (904)

pumalsan Maranao deep-rimmed gong, one of the pair of *agung* (896)

punakawan Clown-servant character type in Javanese dance (649)

punebre Funeral march music in Philippines (846, 847, 856)

punto Standard melodic formula in Philippines (844, 847, 848)

putong Celebratory wreath or crown in Philippines (851–52)

putri Female character type in Javanese dance (649)

puwasa Islamic month of fasting in Philippines (907)

puwi-puwi Buginese/Makassarese reed pipe (805, 806)

qasidah Type of Islamic-based popular music, also *kasidah* (606, 634)

qasidah rebana Arabic solo praise song (776)

qeej Hmong free-reed mouth organ with bamboo pipes and elongated wind chest (*59*, 551–52, 554–55)

quan họ Northern Vietnamese antiphonal song performed in boats (477)

Qur'ān The Islamic canon of Muhammad's writings, intended to be chanted (430)

rababu Bowed spike lute of Ternate and Tidore (815, 816)

raga (rag) Modal system used in India (15, 67)

raj nplaim Hmong free-reed pipe with finger holes (553, *554*)

raj pus li Hmong fipple flute (553)

Rama Character from the Indian epic *Ramayana* (51, 64–65)

Ramadan Islamic holy month of fasting (73)

Ramakian Thai version of the Indian *Ramayana* epic (250–51, 253, 257, 279)

Ramayana Indian epic (65, 66, 189)

rambutan Red, podlike fruit with a "hairy" appearance, native to Malay peninsula (573)

rammana Thai wooden frame drum with single head (233, 268–69)

rampak kendang *Gamelan saléndro* with drummers as soloists (703, 709–10)

ramwong Western-influenced social dance from Thailand (82, 91)

ranat Thai xylophones (57, 163)

ranat ek Lead xylophone in a Thai classical ensemble (17, 22, 229, 270–71)

ranat ek lek Thai higher-pitched metallophone, with twenty-one keys (230, 271)

ranat kaeo Thai crystallophone (struck idiophone with glass keys) (125)

ranat thawng Thai higher-pitched Thai metallophone, same as *ranat ek lek* (230)

ranat thum Thai lower-pitched xylophone, with seventeen or eighteen keys (229, 271)

ranat thum lek Thai lower-pitched metallophone, with sixteen to eighteen keys (229, 230, 271)

randai (1) Type of Minangkabau theater including self-defense (*pencak silat*); (2) West Sumatra danced theatrical form; (3) South Sumatra welcoming dance (413–14, 611, 621)

randu kentir Folk dance of Indramayu (687)

rantak kudo West Sumatra ceremonial hobby-horse dance (613)

rantok Rice-stamping tube and trough in Lombok and Sumbawa (767, 781)

rao Introductory unmetered improvisation in Vietnamese music (15, 67, 454, 463)

rapa'i Acehnese frame drum (604, 611)

ratok West Sumatra lament (611)

rawa Mbojo Music for female singer and *biola*, Sumbawa (784)

Reamker Cambodian version of Indian *Ramayana* (189, 191, 192–93, 216)

rebab (1) Two-stringed bowed spike lute found throughout Southeast Asia; (2) Malay three-stringed, long-necked fiddle (21, 107, 238, 402, 412, 413, 417, 420, *421*, 626, 642, 673, 697, 704, 713, 714, 716, 743, 768)

rebana (1) Malay single-headed, round frame drum, sometimes found with spokes; (2) Frame and bowl-shaped drums of Indonesia (408, 424, 433, 598, 601, 606, 619, 768, 776, 780, 781, 782, 783, 805–806, 810, 812, 814, 816–17, 818, 825)

rebana besar Islamic vocal performance with *rebana ubi* drums (431–32)

rebana rea Samawan drums to accompany Arabic song (781, 783)

rebana ubi Large, single-headed wooden conical drum of Malaysia (424–25, *431*)

redap Bengkulu frame drum (620, 621)

redeb Two-stringed bowed spike lute of Lombok (768, 772, 775)

reggae Popular musical genre from Jamaica (110)

rejang Balinese women's temple dance (758)

rendai Bengkulu acrobatic round dance (621)

renggong Common musical form in Cirebon (694, *695*)

réong Gong-chime with several players in Bali and Lombok (742, 745, 748, 767, 771, 772, 776)

repartee Sung debate pitting men against women; often a courtship ritual (6, 23, 114, 202, 222, 298–99, 313, 321, 325, 327, 340)

rere Torajan bamboo ensemble (809)

réyog Processional dance genre of Ponorogo (639, 646, 648, 679)

ridu Ngada xylophone (793)

rigodón Opening dance in Philippines (854)

rincik (1) Sundanese small fifteen-stringed zither; (2) High-pitched gong-chime of Sunda; (3) Balinese small set of upturned cymbals (704, 714–15, 716, 742–43, 745, 748, 767, 771, 772)

roam vung Khmer popular social dance in circular form (208)

rodat (1) Malaysian theatrical genre of Islamic origin; (2) South Sumatra secularized *zikir* performance (409–10, 625)

rối nước Water-puppet theater found in northern Vietnam (487–88)

rondalla Plucked stringed instrument ensemble of Philippines (854–55, 868, 869)

rondo Musical form based on a recurring phrase (14)

roneat Khmer xylophone (57)

roneat dek Khmer higher-pitched metallophone, with twenty-one keys (164–65)

roneat ek Khmer higher-pitched xylophone, with twenty-one keys (163–64)

roneat thong Khmer lower-pitched metallophone, with sixteen keys, now obsolete (165)

roneat thung Khmer lower-pitched xylophone, with sixteen keys (164)

ronggeng (1) Professional female singer-dancer of Indonesia; (2) Genre of popular social dance in Malaysia; (3) Couple dancing and singing (19, 23, 82, 104, 106, *427*, 436–37, 606, 616, 648, 688, 707–708, 813, 816)

ru Class of Vietnamese lullaby songs (478–79)

ruan Chinese moon-shaped lute (70, 238)

rudat Performance held inside mosques in Cirebon (695)

ruding Jew's harp of Borneo (834)

rujih Cymbals of Sumatra (628)

rumanea Khmer frame drum with single head (169)

ruwatan Type of protective wayang ceremony in Java and Cirebon (651, 689)

sabalan Chanted game of wit, played in Philippines (845)

sadam Lampung ring-stop flute music (627)

sadiah West Sumatra slow, sad songs (611)

safe Lute from Borneo and Sumatra (66)

sagayan Maguindanao spirit communication dance (895)

saggeypo Kalinga set of five pipes (919)

saih Tuning, scale in Balinese music (735)

saih angklung Tuning system for Balinese *gamelan angklung* (736, 737, 753)

saih gendèr wayang Five-tone tuning system in Balinese music (735–37, 751)

saih gong Tuning system for Balinese *gamelan gong* (736–37, 753)

saih pitu Seven-tone tuning system in Balinese music (735, 736–37)

saing Khmer conch shell trumpet (157, 174, 205)

sakeco Samawan topical and humorous sung poetry (782)

saketa Samawan spontaneous antiphonal work songs (782)

salai jin Healing rituals in Ternate and Tidore (813, 816)

salaw Northern Thai bowed lute with two or three strings (98, 310–11)

salawek dulang West Sumatra vocal and brass-tray music (611–12)

salaysay Style of chanting the Passion in Philippines (844)

saléndro Nearly equidistant pentatonic tuning system in Sundanese music (702)

salidommay Bontok popular group songs (915)

saluang West Sumatra end-blown bamboo flute (23, 610–11)

salubong Staged meeting between the Virgin Mary and Christ, in Philippines (845–46)

sam chan Longest of three rhythmic cycles in Thai music (265, 279–80)

saman Acehnese men's percussive religious dance (601, 605, 647)

Samawa West Sumbawan culture area (779)

sampho Khmer horizontal barrel drum with two heads (168, 182)

sampi'/sampeq Kenyah/Kayan plucked lute (833)

sanang Palawan pair of suspended gongs (924)

sang Conch shell horn of Thailand (*235*, 237, 249, 475)

sang yok Chant style of Mahanikai Buddhist temples (291–92)

sangel Maguindanao lullaby (911)

sanghiyang Cavite curing ritual (852)

sanghyang Trance dance of Bali (758)

sangui North Borneo nose flute (836)

Sanskrit Classical language of India (65)

santacrusan Christian Maytime processions in Philippines (847–48)

santo Six-stringed bamboo idiochord tube zither of Flores (792)

santri Orthodox Javanese Muslims (647)

sanu Northeast Thai musical bow attached to kite (317)

sàñdeyà Old Burmese term now applied to piano (365)

sáo Horizontal bamboo flute without membrane (472, 475, 490)

sapeh/sapiʔ Kenyah/Kayan plucked lute (66, 833, 834–35)

saragi Vertical gong of the Ternate *kulintang* ensemble (814)

saranai Lowland Chăm double-reed aerophone (590)

saraphan Tuneful Buddhist chant for lay people (293)

saron Indonesian metallophone with trough resonator (626, 637, 641, 643, 691, 701, 704, 707, 755)

saron barung Javanese medium metallophone with trough resonator (641, 643)

saron demung Javanese large metallophone with trough resonator (641)

saron peking Javanese small metallophone with trough resonator (641)

sarswela Spanish-derived music-drama of Philippines (23, 856–57, 863–65, 866, 868, 869, 871–72, 874)

sarunay Miniature version of a *kulintang*, Philippines (891, *892*)

sarune/sarunei Reed aerophone of Sumatra (607–608, 609)

sasando biola Diatonic *sasandu* used for hymns and folk songs (798, 801)

sasandu Multi-stringed tube zither with resonator from Roti (23, 798–800, 803)

satong Kajang bamboo tube zither (834, 835)

saúñ Burmese arched harp, the last surviving harp in Southeast Asia (15, 22, 132, 377–78)

savarngil Bamboo flute on Kai (819, *820*)

saw Northern Thai repartee song accompanied by *pi chum* ensemble (313)

saw bang Northeastern Thai bowed tube zither (317)

saw duang Two-stringed fiddle from Thailand (11, 17, 71, 238–39, 269, 271, 272, 282–83, 305, 307, 308, 474)

saw lakhawn Northern Thai theater (313)

saw pip Northeast Thai bowed lute with metal can body (18, 317, 320)

saw sam sai Thai three-stringed spike fiddle with coconut body (170, 238, 271, 272, 590)

saw u Thai two-stringed fiddle with coconut body (239, 256, 271, 272, 282–83, 305, 307, 308)

sawng chan Medium-length rhythmic cycle in Thai music (265, 279–80)

sawng na Two-headed cylindrical drum of Thailand (235, 266)

say diev Half-gourd, chest-resonated monochord of Cambodia (169, 205)

sbek tauch Khmer small-size shadow-puppet theater (191)

sbek thomm Khmer large-shadow-puppet theater (191)

seka Communal music-making group in Bali and Lombok (737–38, 766)

selampit Malay narrative genre accompanied by rebab (420–21)

selengut/selingut North Borneo nose flute (836)

selisir Tuning system for Balinese *gamelan pelégongan* (736, 746–47, 750, 753)

semagi Tiboli set of melody gongs (921–22)

semangat "Soul" or "enthusiasm" in Indonesia (51)

sempelong Riau flute for love magic (614–15)

senaculo Outdoor Passion play (846–47, 855, 869)

sendratari Modern Indonesian dance-drama with music, created in the mid-twentieth century (759)

sene Gong of West Timor (797)

sene hauh Trough xylophone of West Timor (797)

sene kaka Six-stringed bamboo idiochord of West Timor (797)

sene tufu Gong and drum ensemble of West Timor (797)

sep noi Laotian string and flute ensemble of Luang Phrabang, called *maholi* in Vientiane (356)

sep nyai Laotian classical ensemble of Luang Phrabang, called *piphat* in Vientiane (356)

sepha Thai narrative genre accompanied by pair of *krap* (241, 258–59, 272, 279)

serampang duabelas Malay twelve-step dance (606, 616, 626, 628)

serdam South Sumatra end-blown ring flute (619, 622–23)

sere Mbojo noble men's warrior dance (783)

serone Single-reed clarinet of East Sumbawa (780, 783)

seruling (1) Malay whistle flute; (2) Bamboo ring-stop flute of Indonesia (424–25, 625, 835)

serunai Malay multiple-reed wooden aerophone (66–67, 404, *405*, 407, 411, 429, 587, 615, 616, 619, 623)

serune (1) Sumatran reed aerophone; (2) Lombok single-rice-stalk aerophone, also double-reed aerophone; (3) Single-reed clarinet of West Sumbawa (605, 768, 780, 781, 782, 784)

seudati Acehnese men's martial group dance (604)

seung pong fai Laotian responsorial singing in the streets during the rocket festival (341)

sewaa Competitive post-feast singing on Seram (819)

shakuhachi Japanese vertical flute (131)

shaman Animistic tranced medium dealing with spirits (543, 568)

shemba Subanen term for short songs (927)

shenai Conical double-reed aerophone from India (66–67)

sheng Free-reed mouth organ from China (46, 475)

Shiva Hindu deity (64)

sì Pair of small, bell-shaped cymbals from Burma (67, 371, 378, 379–80)

Siamese Former name for peoples of Thailand (70)

siang tok Melodic pitch simultaneous with final drum cycle stroke in Thai music (265)

siasid Tiruray parables (927)

sidapurna Acrobatic performance of Cirebon (687, 695)

sidekah bumi Earth blessing ceremony of Cirebon (688–89, 695)

silat Malaysian martial-arts-derived dance with drum accompaniment (422)

silu Double-reed aerophone of Sumbawa (780, 783, 785)

silung Maguindanao form of modern *binalig* (895)

simaku Transverse flute of West Timor (797)

sinaguna Maguindanao modern *kulintang* playing (896, 902)

sinandung North Sumatra women's wistful dance-song (606)

sindil Maguindanaon love songs (908)

sing Pair of Lao small cymbals connected with cord (67, 355)

singapop Singaporean popular songs of the 1980s and 1990s (523)

sinh tiền Vietnamese scraped wooden clapper with jingling coins (468–69, 479)

Sino-Tibetan Language family including Burmese, Hmong, and Yao (528)

sinrilí Buginese/Makassarese epics and traditional stories (805)

sintren Ensemble of stamping tubes and pots in Cirebon (689, 697, 698)

sinug Tausug two-part *kulintang* piece (898)

sinulug Maguindanao rhythmic mode (895)

sirongaganding Maranao tube zither (906)

Sisters Trưng Two celebrated Vietnamese sisters who led a rebellion against the Chinese about A.D. 40 (486, 497, 500)

sitār Long-necked plucked Indian lute (66)

Sita Female lead character from the Indian epic *Ramayana* (51, 52)

siter Small Javanese board zither (66, 632, 641, 643, 672–73)

sito Large, double-headed "royal" drum of Burma (375–76)

siyem Medium hanging gong of Java (640)

sizhu Indoor ensemble from China (71, 73, 272)

skor arakk Khmer single-headed goblet-shaped drum of clay or wood (166)

skor chey Khmer two-headed cylindrical drum (168)

skor chhaiyaim Long, vase-shaped single-headed Khmer drum (167)

skor khek Pair of long drums from Cambodia (66)

skor klang khek Khmer long, cylindrical, two-headed drums (167)

skor thomm Pair of large barrel drums from Cambodia (166–67)

skor yike Large frame drum in *yike* theater, Cambodia (167)

slekk Tree-leaf mirliton of Cambodia (155, 169, 205)

sléndro Nearly equidistant tuning system, found throughout Indonesia; *saléndro* in Sunda (109, 627, 656–58, 667, 735, 769–70)

slomprèt Double-reed aerophone (646)

sluday Bilaan polychordal tube zither (924, 925)

snehet-snehet Songs of advice on Kai (820)

sneng Khmer animal horn with free reed (155, 157, 172, 194, 205)

so i Lao two-stringed fiddle with cylindrical body (338, 350, 355, 358)

so ou Lao two-stringed fiddle with coconut body (350, 355, 358)

song lang Vietnamese foot-operated wooden drum with clapper attached (464, 468, 495)

Songo Rotinese indigenous belief system (801)

soran Loud-playing ensemble of Java (642)

sorog Gapped scale pentatonic tuning system in Sundanese music (702, 714, 716)

sousou Shaman of the pre-Islamic *salai jin* healing ceremony (816)

sowe-ey Bontok ritual song for wedding feasts (915, 920)

sowito One-stringed struck bamboo idiochord of Flores (793)

sralai Khmer multiple-reed aerophone with bulging shape (17, 157, 173–74, 213, 236)

sralai klang khek Khmer small wood or ivory double reed with flared bell (173–74, 197, 202–203)

srimpi Refined women's court dance of Java (649)

sronèn Madurese percussion ensemble (646, 668, 675)

stambul Jakarta-based theatrical form (774)

string Thai rock and roll music (97–98)

suat Ordinary style of chanting Buddhist texts (289, 290–91)

subli Devotional practice in Philippines (848)

subü Lisu three-stringed, fretted lute (543)

sukhwan Spirit ritual common to Thailand, Laos, and Burma (64, 295–96)

sukiyaki Dinner accompanied by Laotian classical music (138)

suku sisipan Ethnically distinct marginal groups of Cirebon (685)

sulibao Ibaloy conical drum and ensemble (918)

suling End-blown bamboo ring-stop flute, found throughout Indonesia and Philippines (73, 642, 645, 692, 703, 707, 714–15, 743, 748–50, 767–68, 771, 772, *774*, 775–76, 780, 835–36, 904, 924, 926)

suling bambu Bamboo flutes used in Catholic services on Kai (819)

suling lembang Torajan bamboo flute with carved buffalo-horn flare (807, 809)

suling miring Transverse bamboo flute with membrane in Java (692)

sulukan Mood song performed by *dhalang* in Java (652, 665–66)

sundatang Two- or three-stringed plucked lute of Borneo (835)

süng Northern Thai plucked lute (310, 313, 316)

suntang Torajan bar zither (806)

suntu Central Sulawesi bar zither (806)

suona Chinese oboe (70, 71)

swidden Agricultural practice in which steep hillside fields are cleared and burned (527)

tabot Bengkulu religious theatrical work (621)

tabuh Individual composition in Balinese music (733, 735, 757)

tabuhan Gong-chime and ensemble of Sumatra (623, 624, 627)

tabut West Sumatra religious theatrical work (600, 602, 612–13)

taganing (1) Acehnese bamboo zither and ensemble; (2) Toba Batak graded drums (605, 607)

tagunggo (1) Rhythmic mode in Philippines; (2) Yakan *kulintang* ensemble; (3) Kalagan set of heavy suspended gongs (894–95, 898–900, 922)

tagutok Maranao scraper (924)

taha-taha Subanen bamboo dibbling pole (921)

Tai Language family common to mainland Southeast Asia (11, 218)

Tai-Kadai Language family including Thai, Lao, and Shan (529)

takik Bontok men's dance (915–16)

taklempong Malay ensemble for *randai*, consisting of three gong chimes (414)

takumbo Mandaya paired-string zither (924, 925)

tala (1) Rhythmic modal system used in Indian classical performance; (2) Bronze or iron gong, Weyewa language (68, 788)

talalay Batangas working song (852)

talam Small Indian cymbals (67)

talawi Three-part Muslim song of Philippines (907)

talèdhèk Javanese female singer-dancer (648, 682–83)

taleli Four-holed bamboo ring-stop flute of Sumba (791)
talempong/tilempong West/North Sumatra gong-chime and ensemble (601, 605, 609–10, 613)
talibun Bengkulu vocal genre similar to *pantun* (621)
tambilaw Palawan harvest ceremony (924)
tambora (1) Cuyo Christmas song; (2) Drum of Philippines (843)
tambul (1) Sama long bronze cylindrical drum; (2) Kalinga-Tinggian cylindrical drum (900, 917)
tambur Metal-bodied Muslim frame drum (772, 805)
tamlang agung Maguindanao small bamboo half-tubes (902)
tampiang Small frame drum on Ternate (815, 817)
tamuk Sama large hanging gong (900)
tân nhạc Modern popular songs of Vietnam (449)
tanak Rare Samawan dance for happy occasions (781)
tandak geroh Sung couplets with *suling*, Lombok (775–76)
tandhak Javanese female singer-dancer (648, 682–83)
tang Tiboli lowest-sounding gong (921)
tangbut Kayan struck bamboo tubes (832)
tangkel Four-stringed tube zither of Philippines (906)
tangkol Bukidnon polychordal zither (924, 925)
tango An Argentine dance in 2/4 meter (854)
tanjidor Brass bands in Sumatra (601, 626–27)
tapatan Chanted game of wit, played in Philippines (845)
taphon Thai asymmetrical, two-headed barrel drum mounted horizontally (233–34, 354, 355)
tapur Conch trumpet in the Aru islands (820)
tar Frame drum with jingles, from Lombok (768)
tarek Palawan dance of young women (924)
tari Dance, pan-Indonesian term (613, 615, 616, 617, 618, 620, 705)
tari asyek Court-derived dance and dance-drama of Malaysia (427, 428)
tari inai Northern Malay dance genre (415–16, 417, 424, 427)
tari kibas Fan dance on Kai (819)
tari kursus Refined social dance of Sunda (705, 708)
tari lala Mixed-couple dancing on Ternate and Tidore (813)
tari lilin Dance with candles on a plate, from Sumbawa (785)
tari rebana Men's dance-drumming form of Sumbawa (785)
tari sasoi Special dance on Kai to honor the raja (820)
tari tidi Torajan dance with swords (810)
tariray Sama women's dance (900)
tarling Guitar-and-flute-based popular music of Cirebon (696, 697)
tarompet Double-reed oboe from Sunda and Java (67, 709, 710)
tarsila Historical record of genealogies in Philippines (890)
tatabuang Set of small gongs in Central Maluku (815)
tatabuhan kayu Wooden xylophones of Ambon (818)
tau-tau Torajan funeral effigy (61, 809)
tavil Drum from India (66)
tawag/tawak Large, deep-rimmed gongs of Borneo (829–30, 833)
tawak-tawak Medium-size suspended gong of Sumatra (615, 623)
tayil Tausug slow singing style (906, 907)
tayò Violin-shaped Mon fiddle, obsolete (365)
tayuban Musical party with singer-dancers, common in Indonesia and Malaysia (106, 648–49, 662, 689, 691, 705)
te oh Ankle bracelets with leaf baskets, from West Timor (797)
te-ed Yakan introductory instrumental piece (898)
te-er Bontok ritual of abstinence from work (914)
tebe Wooden jaw harp of Savu (802)
tehyan Two-stringed bowed lute from Indonesia (73)
tembaga Tiboli heaviest bossed gongs (921)
tembang Type of metered vocal performance in Indonesia (632, 659, 663–65, 714, 751, 756)
tembang Sasak Sasak metered sung poetry (769, 775)
tembang Sunda Aristocratic sung poetry of Sunda (116, 132, 702, 712, 714–15, 720)
Temiar Subgroup of the Senoi people of upland Malaysia (26, 562)
teng thing Northern Thai barrel drum, similar to *taphon* (311)
Tengger Ethnic group from Java (51)
terbana Large bowl-shaped drum of Bali and Lombok (743, 768, 776)
terbang Indonesian single-headed Muslim frame drum (623, 632, 646, 647, 675, 687, 710, 768)
tetawak (1) Single hanging bossed gong of Malaysia; (2) Hanging gong of Sumatra (404, *421*, 615, 617, 628)
tètèt Double-reed aerophone of Java (645)
tetun Smallest *sene* gongs of West Timor (797)
tham khwan Thai ceremony to restore a person's spiritual essence (259–60)
thambobok Subanen paired-string zither (925)
thang (1) Thai melodic idiom of a particular instrument; (2) Thai style of a teacher or "school"; (3) Thai pitch level of a composition, mode (263–64, 270, 339–40)
thanggunggu Subanen gong ensemble (923)
thañ hmañ Tonic pitch based on lowest note of *hnè*, Burma (375)
thaun Goblet-shaped drum with single head, Cambodia (168–69)
Theravada Buddhist sect originating in Sri Lanka (287)
thet Thai Buddhist preaching, in Pali or vernacular (259, 289, 292–93)
thet mahachat Thai preaching/chanting the story of Prince Wetsandon, the Buddha-to-be (259, 293)
thobo Bamboo stamping tubes of Flores (793)
thon Thai wood or clay single-headed, goblet-shaped drum (233, 305)
thượng Upland minority population of Vietnam (444)
tibag Re-enactment of search for Holy Cross, in Philippines (847)
tidtu Maguindanao rhythmic mode (895)
tiêu End-blown notch flute of Vietnam (475, 490)
tiểu nhạc Vietnam's court ensemble of strings (448)
tifa Ubiquitous pan-Maluku drum (812, 814, 818, 819, 820, 821)
tifa gila A long drum in Ternate used to accompany the *hasa* dance (814)
tifa podo Vase-shaped short drums of the Ternate *kulintang* ensemble (814, 816)
tifa tui Bamboo idiochord zither on Ternate and Tidore (813)
ti'ilangga Traditional palm-leaf hat of Roti (798)
timang Iban ritual chanting (828)
timbre The quality or character of a musical sound (14, 584–85)
tinding One-stringed struck bamboo idiochord of Flores (793)
tingkat Unofficial caste system of Bali (65)
tingklik Bamboo xylophone of Bali (754)
tingtung Cirebonese stamping tubes used in *sintren* (697)
tiple Soprano voice or boy soprano, in Philippines (845)
tirtha Balinese holy water (53)
titik jin Sama dance of possession (900)
titik tagunggu Sama piece in *kulintang* repertoire (900)
titil High-pitched metallophone of Cirebon (691)
tiwa nam *Ronggeng*-like fan dance performed by adolescent girls on Kai (820)
t'nabar Ceremonial dances of Tanimbar (821)
t'nabar mpuk-ulu War dance to display captured head in Tanimbar (821)
to mábadong Torajan male funeral dancer (807)
toda Bamboo slit drum of Flores (794)
todagu Bamboo slit drum and drum ensemble of Flores (793–94)
togo Tiruray polychordal zither (925)
togunggak/togunggu Murut interlocking bamboo tubes (833)
toja Musical play based on legends in Sumbawa (785)

tong Kajang Jew's harp (834, 835)

tongatong Kalinga stamping tubes (886, 919)

tongkungon Sabah bamboo tube zither (835)

Tonle Sap The "Great Lake" in western Cambodia (154)

topayya Kalinga gong ensemble of six men (916)

topeng Indonesian mask or masked dance performance (110, 689, 691, 696, 705, 708, 725, 753, 757)

topeng banjet Modern village music from Java (126, 708)

totobuan kawat Idiochord bamboo zither of Buru (819)

totobuang (1) Double-row gong-chimes of Ambon; (2) Set of large and small gongs on Buru (818, 819)

touxian Chinese two-stringed fiddle of Chaozhou province, China (11, 71, 239, 281)

trae Various kinds of Thai trumpets (237)

trebang Frame drum of Cirebon (696)

trebang randu kentir Drumming ensemble of Indramayu (696)

trompong Balinese gong–chime played by soloist (20, 734, 740, 742, 744, 745, 747)

trống Generic term for Vietnamese drums, most with nailed head(s) (469)

trống chầu In *tuồng* theater of Vietnam, a large drum played by an audience member offering praise or criticism (492)

trống cơm Vietnamese two-headed drum with rice paste on heads (470)

trống đồng Bronze drum idiophone of Vietnam (467)

trống quân One-stringed zither played over hole in ground, Vietnam (471)

tror Generic Khmer term for bowed lutes (170)

tror chhe Khmer two-stringed cylindrical fiddle, tuned D–A (170, 183, 184)

tror Khmer Khmer three-stringed spike fiddle with a coconut body (170, 194, 196, 197, 238, 590)

tror ou Khmer two-stringed fiddle with coconut resonator (171, 183, 184, 196)

tror so tauch Khmer two-stringed cylindrical fiddle, tuned G–D (171, 183, 184, 196)

tror so thomm Khmer lower-pitched two–stringed fiddle, tuned D–A (171, 183, 184)

t'rung Upland Vietnamese vertical bamboo xylophone (446, 534)

Trường Sơn Ranges Mountain range running through southern Vietnam (446, 531)

tudukkan/tudukkat Mentawai slit drum ensemble (613)

tufu Single-headed standing drum of West Timor (797)

tukimug Maranao poetic segment in music (897)

tulali Torajan flute (806)

tumbuk kalang Malaysian folk performance derived from rice-pounding songs (423)

tung-tung Tausug rhythmic ostinato in *kulintangan* (898)

tunggalan Tausug large *agung* (898)

tunrung ganrang Makassarese processional drum music for sailors (805)

tuntungan (1) Tausug upper *kulintang* gong; (2) Yakan log drum (898, 904)

tuồng Vietnamese theater genre (23, 88, 448, 490–93, 501–502, 508)

turali North Borneo nose flute (836)

turba Pangasinan song debate (851)

tutohato Slow responsorial singing to honor someone on Buru (819)

ty bā lệnh Nguyễn-dynasty ritual court ensemble (448)

ua neeb Hmong shaman ceremony accompanied by gong, sistrum, and rattle (553)

ugod Bontok epic (920)

ullalim (1) Kalinga epic song; (2) Bontok long solo song (915, 920)

uma lopo Atoni beehive-shaped traditional dwelling (796)

usali Men's daytime war dance of Seram (818–19)

uyon-uyon Social events accompanying ceremonies in Java (647)

valse European-influenced waltz (854)

variable-pitch instruments Instruments, such as fiddles and flutes, whose pitch is infinitely controllable during performance (387)

vè Class of satirical songs of Vietnam (479)

villancico Spanish-derived polyphonic religious composition, found in Philippines (842)

vīṇā Plucked lute from India (66)

viol Three-stringed bowed chordophone of Buru (819)

Vishnu Hindu deity (52)

vọng cổ Expandable song structure used in *cải lương* theater, Vietnam (454, 494, 508)

vung phleng pey keo Khmer court ensemble for ancestral worship (197)

wa Kajang sung narrative form (827)

wà Small clapper of split bamboo, from Burma (378, 379–80)

wai khru Thai ritual ceremony to honor one's teacher (64–65, 120–21, 227, 253, 258, 278, 299, 301)

Waktu Lima Orthodox Muslims in Lombok (764, 770)

Waktu Telu Nominal Muslims in Lombok (764, 765, 766)

wale'hkou' From Burma, large clappers of slit bamboo section (371)

wali Cirebonese term for Islamic saint (686)

warahan Lampung theatrical stories of Sumatra (627)

wat A Buddhist temple complex in Thailand (288)

wayang Shadow puppetry of Indonesia (*76*, 667, 688, 703)

wayang gedek Malay shadow-puppet theater in Thai style (*nang talung*) (404)

wayang gedhog East Javanese wayang based on *Panji* stories (650)

wayang golèk Three-dimensional rod puppetry in Java, Cirebon, and Sunda (650, 667, 688–89, 703, 706, 725)

wayang klithik Javanese flat wooden puppetry (650)

wayang kulit General term for leather shadow-puppet theater, throughout Indonesia and Malaysia (23, 76, 92, 134, 308, 403, 520, 626, 643, 649–53, 688–89, 697, 751, 753, 829, 835)

wayang kulit Jawa Indonesian *wayang purwa* in Malaysia (403–404, 428)

wayang melayu Nearly extinct, formerly royal shadow puppet theater of Malaysia (404–405, 417, 428)

wayang potèhi Chinese puppetry accompanied by Chinese music, found in Java (650)

wayang purwa Shadow puppetry based on Hindu epics, found in Java and Sumatra (626, 650)

wayang Sasak Shadow puppetry about Amir Hamza, found in Lombok (768, 774, *775*)

wayang Siam Indigenous shadow-puppet theater in northern Malaysia (404–406, 412, 417, 425, 428)

wayang topèng Masked dance based on *Panji* stories, Java (653–54)

wayang wong Masked human theater of Bali and Java (637, 653, 753, 757)

widyadhari Nymphlike goddess of Bali (52)

wilet Density referent of a piece of Sundanese music (702, 707)

wo paheli Savunese cymbals (802)

woleko Ceremony of thanksgiving in Sumba (790)

wot Circular bamboo panpipes of northeast Thailand (318)

xi xov Hmong two-stringed fiddle (553)

xinyao Contemporary Singaporean songs in Mandarin Chinese (519)

xuân phả Ancient genre of masked plays from Thanh Hóa province (498)

yaya Yakan lullaby (911)

yak̲wìñ Pair of Burmese large cymbals (371)

yaigho All-night singing ceremony in Sumba (789)

Yao Upland Sino-Tibetan group living in Thailand, Vietnam, and Laos (537, 549–50)

yikay Shan (Burma) dance drama (548)

yike Village theater genre of Chăm origin (155, 158, 200–201)

yòudayà Burmese genre of classical songs said to be derived from the Siamese at Ayuthaya (55, 372, 380, 382, 393, 394–95)

yue qin Chinese moon-shaped lute (70, 472)

yue she Chinese music clubs, found in Vietnam (70)

zapin West Asian–derived songs and dances of Malaysia and Sumatra (437, 601, 605, 606, 616, 625, 628, 825)

za'pwè Burmese classical theater accompanied by *hsaìñ* (373–74, 377, 389, 396, 399)

zarzuela Spanish-language play with music and dance (856)

zheng Chinese sixteen-stringed zither (70, 471)

zikir Chanting of Islamic verse, usually accompanied by drumming; also *dikir* (409, 431–32, 604, 616, 625, 626, 628, 825)

zikrzamman Women's choral music of Lombok (776)

zither Chordophone with parallel strings (20)

zouchang Singaporean narrative tradition of Chinese origin (519)

A Guide to Publications on Southeast Asian Music

GENERAL WORKS ON SOUTHEAST ASIAN MUSIC, DANCE, AND THEATER

Becker, Judith. 1968. "Percussive Patterns in the Music of Mainland Southeast Asia." *Ethnomusicology* 12(2):173–191.

Bernatzik, Hugh Adolf. 1940. "Musikinstrumente der Bergvoelker Hinderindiens." *Atlantis* 12:152–155.

Brandon, James R. 1967. *Theatre in Southeast Asia.* Cambridge, Mass.: Harvard University Press.

Cogniat, Raymond. 1932. *Danses d'Indochine.* Paris: Éditions des chroniques du jour.

Emmert, Richard, and Yuki Minegishi. 1980. *Musical Voices of Asia: Report of Asian Traditional Performing Arts.* Tokyo: Heibonsha.

Ghulam-Sarwar Yousof. 1994. *Dictionary of Traditional South-East Asian Theatre.* Kuala Lumpur: Oxford University Press.

Gironcourt, Georges de. 1943. "Recherches de géographie musicale en Indochine." *Bulletin de la Société des études indochinoises* 17:3–174.

Gronow, Pekka. 1981. "The Record Industry Comes to the Orient." *Ethnomusicology* 25(2):251–284.

Heger, F. 1902. *Alte Metalltrommeln aus Südost-Asien* (Old Metal Drums in Southeast Asia). Leipzig: K. von Hiersemann.

Heinze, Ruth-Inge. 1988. *Trance and Healing in Southeast Asia Today.* Bangkok: White Lotus.

Higham, Charles. *The Archaeology of Mainland Southeast Asia.* Cambridge and New York: Cambridge University Press.

Hood, Mantle. 1975. "Improvisation in the Stratified Ensembles of Southeast Asia." *Selected Reports in Ethnomusicology* 2(2):25–34.

Jones, Arthur M. 1971. *Africa and Indonesia: The Evidence of the Xylophone and Other Musical and Cultural Factors.* 2nd ed. Leiden: E. J. Brill.

Kartomi, Margaret J. 1995. "'Traditional Music Weeps' and Other Themes in the Discourse on Music, Dance and Theatre of Indonesia, Malaysia and Thailand." *Journal of Southeast Asian Studies* 26(2):366–400.

Kempers, A. J. Bernet. 1988. "The Kettledrums of Southeast Asia." *Modern Quaternary Research in Southeast Asia.* Vol. 10. Rotterdam: A. A. Balkema.

Knosp, Gaston. 1907. "La musique Indochinoise." *Mercure Musical* 3:889–956.

———. 1909–1910. "Notes sur la musique Indochinoise." *Revista Musicale Italiana* 16:821–846, 17:415–432.

———. 1911–1912. "Rapport sur une mission officielle d'étude musicale en Indochine." *International Archiv für Ethnographie* 20:121–151, 165–188, 217–248; 21:1–25, 49–77.

———. 1922. "Histoire de la musique dans l'Indochine." *Encyclopédie de la musique*, ed. Albert Lavignac, 3100–3146. Paris: Librarie Delagrave.

Koizumi, Fumio, Yoshihiko Tokumaru, and Osamu Yamaguchi, eds. 1977. *Asian Musics in an Asian Perspective: Report of [Asian Traditional Performing Arts, 1976*]. Tokyo: Heibonsha.

Manuel, Peter. 1988. *Popular Musics of the Non-Western World.* New York: Oxford University Press.

May, Elizabeth, ed. 1980. *Musics of Many Cultures.* Berkeley: University of California Press.

Miettinen, Jukka O. 1992. *Classical Dance and Theatre in South-East Asia.* Singapore: Oxford University Press.

Miller, Terry E. 1982. "Free-Reed Instruments in Asia: A Preliminary Classification." In *Music East and West: Essays in Honor of Walter Kaufmann,* ed. Thomas Noblitt, 63–100. New York: Pendragon Press.

Mohd. Taib Osman, ed. 1974. *Traditional Drama and Music of Southeast Asia.* Kuala Lumpur: Dewan Bahasa dan Pustaka.

Morton, David. 1975. "Instruments and Instrumental Functions in the Ensembles of Southeast Asia: A Cross-Cultural Comparison." *Selected Reports in Ethnomusicology* 2(2):7–16.

The New Grove Dictionary of Music and Musicians. 1980. 20 vols, ed. Stanley Sadie. London: Macmillan. [Articles on Burma, Indonesia, Kampuchea, Laos, Malaysia, the Philippines, Thailand, and Vietnam].

The New Grove Dictionary of Musical Instruments. 1984. 3 vols, ed. Stanley Sadie. London: Macmillan.

Reid, Anthony. 1988. *The Lands below the Winds.* Southeast Asia in the Age of Commerce, 1450–1680, 1. New Haven, Conn.: Yale University Press.

Ryker, Harrison, ed. 1991. *New Music in the*

Orient: Essays on Composition in Asia since World War II. Buren, The Netherlands: Frits Knuf.

Scanlon, Phil, Jr. 1985. *Southeast Asia: A Cultural Study through Celebration.* Monograph series, special report 23. De Kalb: Center for Southeast Asian Studies, Northern Illinois University.

Shadow Images of Asia. 1979. Washington, D.C.: American Museum of Natural History.

Smith, R. B., and W. Watson. 1979. *Early South East Asia: Essays in Archaeology, History and Historical Geography.* New York: Oxford University Press.

Taylor, Eric. 1989. *Musical Instruments of South-East Asia.* Singapore: Oxford University Press.

Zarina, Xenia. 1967. *Classic Dances of the Orient.* New York: Crown Publishers.

MAINLAND SOUTHEAST ASIA

Cambodia

Anak Charanyananda. 1989. "Srei Khmauu and Phliang, the Principal Songs in Rwam Mamuad, a Curing Ritual, in Surin, Thailand." M.A. thesis, University of the Philippines.

Brunet, Jacques. 1969. *Nang Sbek: Théâtre d'ombres: danse du Cambodge.* Berlin: Institut International d'Études Comparatives de la Musique.

———. 1979. "L'Orchestre de mariage Cambodgien et ses instruments." *Bulletin de l'École française d'Extrême-Orient* 66:203–247.

Catlin, Amy. 1987. "Apsaras and Other Goddesses in Khmer Music, Dance, and Ritual." In *Apsara: The Feminine in Cambodian Art,* ed. Amy Catlin, 28–36. Los Angeles: The Woman's Building.

———. 1992. *Khmer Classical Dance Songbook.* Van Nuys, Calif.: Apsara Media for Intercultural Education.

Cravath, Paul. 1985. "Earth in Flower: An Historical and Descriptive Study of the Classical Dance Drama of Cambodia." Ph.D. dissertation, University of Hawaii.

———. 1986. "The Ritual Origins of the Classical Dance Drama of Cambodia." *Asian Theater Journal* 3(2):179–203.

———. 1992. "Khmer Classical Dance: Performance Rites of the Goddess in the Context of a Feminine Mythology." *Selected Reports in Ethnomusicology* 9:81–92.

Daniélou, Alain. 1957. *La Musique du Cambodge et du Laos.* Pondichéry: Publications de l'Institut Français d'Indologie.

de Gironcourt, George. 1941. "Motifs de chants cambodgiens." *Bulletin de la Société des études indochinoises* 16(1):51–105.

———. 1944. "Recherches de géographie musicale au Cambodge et à Java." *Bulletin de la Société des études indochinoises* 19(3):49–83.

Groslier, Bernard-Philippe. 1965. "Danse et Musique sous les Rois d'Angkor." *Felicitation Volumes of Southeast Asian Studies,* 2:283– 292. Bangkok: Siam Society.

Groslier, George. 1929. "Le theatre et la danse au Cambodge." *Journal Asiatique* January–March: 125–143.

Kodish, Debora, ed. 1994. *The Giant Never Wins: Lakhon Bassac (Cambodian Folk Opera) in Philadelphia.* Philadelphia: Philadelphia Folklore Project.

Leclere, Adhemard. 1911. *Le théâtre cambodgien.* Paris: Ernest Leroux.

———. 1912. *Cambodge: Contes, légendes et jatakas.* Niort: Imprimerie Nouvelle G. Clouzot.

Miller, Terry E., and Sam-Ang Sam. 1995. "The Classical Musics of Cambodia and Thailand: A Study of Distinctions." *Ethnomusicology* 39(2):229–243.

Musique Khmère. 1969. Phnom Penh: Imprimerie Sangkum Reastr Niyum.

Phleng phun ban lae ganlalen pun ban jangwat surin (Local music and entertainments of Surin Province). 1984. Surin, Thailand: Surin Teachers College.

Pich, Sal. 1970. *Lumnoam Sangkhep ney Phleng Khmer* (A brief survey of Khmer music). Phnom Penh: Éditions de l'Institut Bouddhique.

Prasidh Silapabanleng. 1975. "Thai Music at the Court of Cambodia." *Selected Reports in Ethnomusicology* 2(2):3–6.

Sam, Chan Moly. 1987. *Khmer Court Dance.* Newington, Conn.: Khmer Studies Institute.

———. 1992. "Muni Mekhala: The Magic Moment in Khmer Court Dance." *Selected Reports in Ethnomusicology* 9:93–114.

Sam, Sam-Ang. 1988. "The Pin Peat Ensemble: Its History, Music, and Context." Ph.D. dissertation, Wesleyan University.

———. 1989. *Khmer Court Dance: A Performance Manual.* Newington, Conn.: Khmer Studies Institute.

———. 1992. "The Gloating Maiden in Khmer Shadow Play: Its Text, Context, and Performance." *Selected Reports in Ethnomusicology* 9:115–130.

Sam, Sam-Ang, and Patricia Shehan Campbell. 1991. *Silent Temples, Songful Hearts: Traditional Music of Cambodia.* Danbury, Conn.: World Music Press.

Sam, Sam-Ang, and Chan Moly Sam. 1987. *Khmer Folk Dance.* Newington, Conn.: Khmer Studies Institute.

Sem, Sara. 1967. "Lakhon Khol au village de Svay Andet, son role dans les rites agraires." *Annales de l'Université des Beaux-Arts* 1:157– 200.

Sheppard, Dato Haji Mubin. 1968. "The Khmer Shadow Play and Its Links with Ancient India: A Possible Source of the Malay Shadow Play of Kelantan and Trengganu." *Royal Asiatic Society, Malaysian Branch, Journal* 41(1):199–204.

Sisowath. N.d. *Musique du Cambodge.* Phnom Penh: Direction du Tourisme Khmer.

Strickland-Anderson, Lily. 1926. "The Cambodian Ballet." *Musical Quarterly* 12:266–274.

Le Théâtre dans la vie khmère. 1973. Phnom Penh: Université des Beaux Arts.

Thierry, Solange. 1963. *Les Danses sacrées.* Paris: Sources Orientales.

Thiounn (Samdech Chaufea). 1930. *Danses cambodgiennes.* Phnom Penh: Bibliothèque Royale du Cambodge.

Thailand

(Phya) Anuman Rajadhon. 1961. *Life and Ritual in Old Siam: Three Studies of Thai Life and Customs.* Edited and translated by William J. Gedney. New Haven, Conn.: HRAF Press.

———. 1968. *Essays on Thai Folklore.* Bangkok: Social Science Association Press of Thailand.

———. 1990. *Thet Maha Chat.* 3rd ed. Thai Culture, new series, 21. Bangkok: Fine Arts Department.

Becker, Judith. 1964. "Music of the Pwo Karen of Northern Thailand." *Ethnomusicology* 8(2):137–153.

———. 1980. "A Southeast Asian Musical Process: Thai Thaw and Javanese Irama." *Ethnomusicology* 24:453–464.

Bidyalankarana, Prince. 1926. "The Pastime of Rhyme-Making and Singing in Rural Siam." *Journal of the Siam Society* 20:101–127.

———. 1941. "Sebha Recitation and the Story of Khun Chang Khun Phan." *Journal of the Thailand Research Society* 33:1–22.

Bowring, John. 1969 [1857]. *The Kingdom and People of Siam.* 2 vols. Kuala Lumpur: Oxford University Press.

Brereton, Bonnie Pacala. 1995. *Thai Tellings of Phra Malai: Texts and Rituals Concerning a Popular Buddhist Saint.* Tempe: Program for Southeast Asian Studies, Arizona State University.

Chaturong Montrisart. 1961. "The Classical Dance." *Journal of the Music Academy Madras* 32:127–143.

(Phra) Chen Duriyanga. 1990a. *Thai Music.* 6th ed. Thai Culture, new series, 15. Bangkok: Fine Arts Department.

———. 1990b. *Thai Music in Western Notation,* 4th ed. Thai Culture, new series, 16. Bangkok: Fine Arts Department.

Coedes, George. 1963. "Origine et evolution des diverses formes du theatre traditionnel en Thailande." *Bulletin de la Société des Études Indochinoises* 38:489–506.

Cooler, Richard. 1986. "The Use of Karen Bronze Drums in the Royal Courts and Buddhist Temples of Burma and Thailand: A Continuing Mon Tradition?" In *Papers from a Conference on Thai Studies in Honor of William J. Gedney,* ed. Robert J. Bickner, Thomas J. Hudak, and Patcharin Peyasantiwong, 107–120. Ann Arbor: Center for South and Southeast Asian Studies, University of Michigan.

His Royal Highness Prince S. A. R. Damrong Rajanubhab. 1928. "L'orchestre siamois." *Extrême Asie–Revue indochinoise,* new series 27:132–142.

———. 1931. *Siamese Musical Instruments.* 2nd ed. Bangkok: The Royal Institute.

His Highness Prince Dhani Nivat Kromamun Bidyalabh Birdhyakorn. 1947. "Pageantry of the Siamese Stage." *National Geographic Magazine* 91:200–212.

———. 1948. "The Shadow-Play as a Possible Origin of the Masked Play." *Journal of the Siam Society* 37(1):27–33.

———. 1952. "Traditional Dress in the Classic Dance of Siam." *Journal of the Siam Society* 40(2):133–146.

———. 1965. "Hide Figures of the Ramakien at the Ledermuseum in Offenbach, Germany." *Journal of the Siam Society* 53(1):61–66.

———. 1988. *Shadow Play (The Nang).* 6th ed. Thai Culture, new series, 3. Bangkok: Fine Arts Department.

Dhanit Yupho. 1952. *Classical Siamese Theatre.* Translated by P. S. Sastri. Bangkok: Hatha Dhip.

———. 1963. *The Khon and Lakon.* Bangkok: Fine Arts Department.

———. 1987 [1971]. *Thai Musical Instruments.* 2nd ed. Translated by David Morton. Bangkok: Fine Arts Department.

———. 1989a. *The Khon.* 6th ed. Thai Culture, new series, 6. Bangkok: Fine Arts Department.

———. 1989b. *Khon Masks.* 6th ed. Thai Culture, new series, 7. Bangkok: Fine Arts Department.

——. 1990a. *The Custom and Rite of Paying Homage to Teachers of Khon, Lakhon and Piphat.* 5th ed. Thai Culture, new series, 11. Bangkok: Fine Arts Department.

———. 1990b. *The Preliminary Course of Training in Thai Theatrical Art.* 8th ed. Thai Culture, new series, 13. Bangkok: Fine Arts Department.

Duangjai Thewtong. 1984. "Village Music in Central Thailand: A Field Study of Mooban Pohuk." M.A. thesis, Kent State University.

Durrenberger, E. P. 1975. "A Soul's Journey: A Lisu Song from Northern Thailand." *Asian Folklore Studies* 34:35–50.

Dyck, Gerald P. 1975a. "Lung Noi Na Kampan Makes a Drumhead for a Northern Thai Long Drum." *Selected Reports in Ethnomusicology* 2(2):183–204.

———. 1975b "They Also Serve." *Selected Reports in Ethnomusicology* 2(2):205-216.

———. 1975c. "The Vanishing Phia: An Ethnomusicological Photo Story." *Selected Reports in Ethnomusicology* 2(2):217–229.

Ellis, Alexander J. 1885a. "On the Musical Scales of Various Nations." *Journal of the Society of Arts* 33:485–527.

———. 1885b. "Appendix to Mr. Alexander J. Ellis's Paper on 'The Musical Scales of Various Nations' read 25th March, 1885." *Journal of the Society of Arts* 33:1102–1111.

Fuller, Paul. 1979. Review of *The Traditional Music of Thailand,* by David Morton. *Ethnomusicology* 23(2):339–343.

———. 1983. "Thai Music, 1968–1981." *Yearbook for Traditional Music* 1983:152–155.

Gaston, Bruce. 1987. "Thai Court Music: Buddhism and Hinduism in Harmony." In *Music of the Royal Courts,* 15–18. Bangkok: The Sound Bank Board.

Gervaise, Nicolas. 1688. *Histoire naturelle et politique du Royaume de Siam.* Paris: Claude Barbin.

Gerini, G. E. 1912. *Siam and Its Productions, Arts, and Manufactures.* N.p.: no publisher.

Ginsberg, Henry D. 1972. "The Mahohra Dance-Drama: An Introduction." *Journal of the Siam Society* 60:169–181.

Guelden, Marlane. 1995. *Thailand: Into the Spirit World.* Singapore: Times Editions.

Hamilton, Annette. 1993. "Video Crackdown, or the Sacrificial Pirate: Censorship and Cultural Consequences in Thailand." *Public Culture* 5(3):515–531.

Hipkins, A. J. 1945 [1888]. *Musical Instruments Historic, Rare, and Unique.* London: A. and C. Black.

Hornbostel, Erich M. von. 1920. "Formanalysen an siamesischen Orchesterstücken." *Archiv für Musikwissenschaft* 2:306–333.

Kobkul Phutharaporn. 1985. "Country Folk Songs and Thai Society." In *Traditional and Changing Thai World View.* Bangkok: Chulalongkorn University Research Institute and Southeast Asian Studies Programme.

Krebs, Stephanie Laird. 1975. "Nonverbal Communication in Khon Dance-Drama: Thai Society Onstage." Ph.D. dissertation, Harvard University.

Kurosawa, T. 1941. *Investigation of Musical Instruments in Thailand.* Bangkok: Nippon-tai Bunka Kenkyusyo.

La Loubere, Simon de. 1691. *Du Royaume de Siam.* Paris: Jean-Baptiste Coignard.

———. 1969 [1693]. *A New Historical Relation of the Kingdom of Siam.* Kuala Lumpur: Oxford University Press.

Larson, Hans Peter. 1976. "The Instrumental Music of the Lisu in Northern Thailand." In *Lampang Reports,* 225–268. Copenhagen: Scandinavian Institute of Asian Studies.

———. 1984. "The Music of the Lisu of Northern Thailand." *Asian Folklore Studies* 43(1):41–62.

Léonowens, Anna Harriette. 1870. *The English Governess at the Siamese Court.* Boston: Fields, Osgood.

Lewis, Paul, and Elaine Lewis. 1984. *Peoples of the Golden Triangle: Six Tribes in Thailand.* London: Thames and Hudson.

List, George. 1961. "Speech Melody and Song Melody in Central Thailand." *Ethnomusicology* 5:16–32.

Mareschal, Eric. 1976. *La musique des Hmong.* Paris: Musée Guimet.

Marre, Jeremy, and Hannah Charlton. 1985. "Two Faces of Thailand." In *Beats of the Heart: Popular Music of the World,* 198–214. New York: Pantheon Books.

Marshall, Harry Ignatius. 1932. "The Use of the Bronze Drum in Siam." *Journal of the Burma Research Society* 22:21–22.

Mattani Rutnin, ed. 1975. *The Siamese Theatre: A Collection of Reprints from the Journals of the Siam Society.* Bangkok: The Siam Society.

———. 1978. "The Modernization of Thai Dance-drama, with Special Reference to the Reign of King Chulalongkorn." Ph.D. dissertation, University of London.

Mendenhall, Stanley T. 1975. "Interaction of Linguistic and Musical Tone in Thai Song." *Selected Reports in Ethnomusicology* 2(2):17–24.

Miller, Terry E. 1979. "The Musical Traditions of Northeast Thailand." *Journal of the Siam Society* 67(1):1–16.

———. 1981. "The *Mawlum Pee Fah* Ceremony of Northeastern Thailand." In *Proceedings of the Saint Thyagaraja Music Festivals: Cleveland, Ohio, 1978–81,* ed. T. Temple Tuttle, 82–93. Cleveland: Greater Cleveland Ethnographic Museum.

———. 1984. "Reconstructing Siamese Musical History from Historical Sources: 1548–1932." *Asian Music* 15(2):32–42.

———. 1985. *Traditional Music of the Lao: Kaen Playing and Mawlum Singing in Northeast Thailand.* Contributions in Intercultural and Comparative Studies, 13. Westport, Conn., and London: Greenwood Press.

———. 1991. *An Introduction to Playing the Kaen.* Rev. ed. Kent, Ohio: Author.

———. 1992a. "Thai Classical Music Comes to America: Cultivating a Rare Species in a Musical Greenhouse." *Journal of the Siam Society* 80(2):143–148.

———. 1992b. "The Theory and Practice of Thai Musical Notations." *Ethnomusicology* 36(2):197–222.

Miller, Terry E., and Jarernchai Chonpairot. 1979. "Shadow Puppet Theatre in Northeast Thailand." *Theatre Journal* 31(3):293–311.

Miller, Terry E., and Jarernchai Chonpairot. 1981. "The Ranat and Bong-Lang: The Question of Origin of the Thai Xylophones." *Journal of the Siam Society* 69:145–163.

Miller, Terry E., and Jarernchai Chonpairot. 1994. "A History of Siamese Music Reconstructed from Western Documents, 1505–1932." *Crossroads: An Interdisciplinary Journal of Southeast Asian Studies* 8(2):1–192.

Miller, Terry E., and Sam Sam-Ang. 1995. "The Classical Musics of Cambodia and Thailand: A Study of Distinctions." *Ethnomusicology* 39(2):229–243.

Mom Dusdi Paribatra Na Ayuthya. 1962. *The Regional Dances of Thailand.* Bangkok: Foundation for Advancement of Educational Materials.

Moore, Sidney. 1969. "Thai Songs in 7/4 Meter." *Ethnomusicology* 13(2):309–312.

Morton, David. 1968. *The Traditional Music of Thailand: Introduction, Commentary, and Analyses.* Los Angeles: Regents of the University of California.

———. 1974. "Vocal Tones in Traditional Thai Music." *Selected Reports in Ethnomusicology* 2(1):88–101.

———. 1975. "Luang Pradit Phairo." *Selected Reports in Ethnomusicology* 2(2):v–viii.

——. 1976. *The Traditional Music of Thailand.* Berkeley: University of California Press.

The Musical Compositions of His Majesty King Bhumibol Adulyadej of Thailand. Bangkok: Chitralada School, 1996.

Myers-Moro, Pamela. 1986. "'Songs for Life': Leftist Thai Popular Music in the 1970s." *Journal of Popular Culture* 20(3):93–113.

———. 1988. "Names and Civil Service Titles of Siamese Musicians." *Asian Music* 19(2):82–92.

———. 1989. "Thai Music and Attitudes towards the Past." *Journal of American Folklore* 102:190–194.

———. 1990. "Musical Notation in Thailand." *Journal of the Siam Society* 78:101–108.

———. 1991. "Teachers on Tape: Innovation and Experimentation in Teaching Thai Music." *Balungan* 5(1):15–20.

———. 1993. *Thai Music and Musicians in Contemporary Bangkok.* Center for Southeast Asian Studies monographs, 34. Berkeley: University of California Press.

Nicolas, René. 1924. "Le lakhon nora ou lakhon chatri et les origines du théâtre classique siamois." *Journal of the Siam Society* 18(2):85–110.

——. 1927. "Le Théâtre d'Ombres au Siam." *Journal of the Siam Society* 21:37–52.

Nitaya Kanchanawan. 1979. "Elvis, Thailand, and I." *Southern Quarterly* 18(1):162–168.

Panya Roongrüang. 1990. *Thai Music in Sound.* Bangkok: author. Book and three cassettes.

Paritta Chalermpow Koanantakool. 1980. "A Popular Drama in Its Social Context: Nang Talung, the Shadow Puppet Theatre of South Thailand." Ph.D. dissertation, Cambridge University.

Picken, Lawrence E. R. 1984. "The Sound-producing Instrumentarium of a Village in North-East Thailand." In *Musica Asiatica* 4:213–244. Cambridge: Cambridge University Press.

Picken, L. E. R., C. J. Adkins, and T. F. Page. 1984. "The Making of a Khāen: The Free-Reed Mouth-Organ of North-East Thailand." *Musica Asiatica* 4:117–154.

Prasidh Silapabanleng. 1975. "Thai Music at the Court of Cambodia: A Personal Souvenir of Luang Pradit Phairoh's Visit in 1930." *Selected Reports in Ethnomusicology* 2(2):3–5.

Pratuan Charoenchitt, ed. N.d. [ca. 1987]. *Folk Music and Traditional Performing Arts of Thailand.* Bangkok: Office of the National Culture Commission, Ministry of Education.

Pringsheim, Klaus. 1944. "Music of Thailand." *Contemporary Japan* 13:745–767.

Schwörer, Gretel. 1982. "Die Mundorgel bei den Lahu in Nord Thailand: Bauweise, Funktion und Musik." *Beiträge zur Ethnomusikologie,* 10.

Seelig, Paul S. 1932. *Siamese Music.* Bandoeng: J. H. Seelig & Zoon.

Smithies, Michael. 1971. "Likay: A Note on the Origin, Form, and Future of Siamese Folk Opera." *Journal of the Siam Society* 59:33–64.

Smithies, Michael, and Euayporn Kerdchouay. 1972. "Nang Talung: The Shadow Theatre of Siam." *Journal of the Siam Society* 60:377–387.

Smithies, Michael, and Euayporn Kerdchouay. 1974. "The Wai Khru Ceremony of the Nang Yai." *Journal of the Siam Society* 62(1):143–147.

Stern, Theodore, and Theodore A. Stern. 1971. "'I Pluck My Harp': Musical Acculturation among the Karen of Western Thailand." *Ethnomusicology* 15:186–219.

Stumpf, Carl. 1901. "Tonsystem und Musik der Siamesen." *Beiträge zur Akustik und Musikwissenschaft* 3:69–138.

Surapone Virulrak. 1980. "Likay: A Popular Theater in Thailand." Ph.D. dissertation, University of Hawai'i.

Tambiah, S. J. 1968. "Literacy in a Buddhist Village in North-East Thailand." In *Literacy in Traditional Societies,* ed. Jack Goody, 86–131. Cambridge: Cambridge University Press.

——. 1970. *Buddhism and the Spirit Cults in North-East Thailand.* Cambridge: Cambridge University Press.

Tanese-Ito, Yoko. 1988a. "The Relationship between Speech-Tones and Vocal Melody in Thai Court Song." *Musica Asiatica* 5:109–139.

———. 1988b. "Taikoku koten kakyoku ni okeru kasi no seichou to uta no senritu tono kankei" (The relationship between speech tones and vocal melody in Thai court song). Ph.D. dissertation, Tokyo National University of Fine Arts and Music.

Terwiel, B. J. 1979. *Monks and Magic: An Analysis of Religious Ceremonies in Central Thailand,* 2nd ed. Bangkok: Curzon Press.

Thai Classical Music. 1971. 2nd ed. Bangkok: Fine Arts Department.

Ubonrat Siriyuvasak. 1990a. "Commercialising the Sound of the People: *Pleng Luktoong* and the Thai Pop Music Industry." *Popular Music* 9(1):61–77.

———. 1990b. *The Dynamics of Audience Media Activities: An Ethnography of Women Textile Workers.* Bangkok: Women's Studies Programme, Chulalongkorn University.

Vajiravudh, Maha. 1967. "Notes on the Siamese Theatre." *Journal of the Siam Society* 55(1):1–30.

Verney, Frederick. 1885. *Notes on Siamese Musical Instruments.* London: William Clowes and Sons.

Walker, Anthony R. 1983. *Lahu Nyi (Red Lahu) New Year Celebrations in North Thailand: Ethnographic and Textual Materials.* Taipei: The Orient Cultural Service.

Wells, Kenneth E. 1975. *Thai Buddhism: Its Rites and Activities.* Bangkok: Suriyabun.

Wong, Deborah Anne. 1991. "The Empowered Teacher: Ritual, Performance, and Epistemology in Contemporary Bangkok." Ph.D. dissertation, University of Michigan.

———. 1990. "Thai Cassettes and Their Covers: Two Case Histories." *Asian Music* 21(1):78–104.

———. 1995. "Thai Cassettes and Their Covers: Two Case Histories." In *Asian Popular Culture,* ed. John Lent, 43–59. Boulder, Colo.: Westview Press.

Wong, Deborah Anne, and René T. A. Lysloff. 1991. "Threshold of the Sacred: The Overture in Thai and Javanese Ritual Performance." *Ethnomusicology* 35:315–348.

Laos

Archaimbault, Charles. 1991. *Le sacrifice du buffle a S'ieng Khwang (Laos).* Paris: École Française d'Extrême-Orient.

Bertrain, Yves. 1986. *Kab Ke Pam Tuag: Cov Zaj: Les funerailles: chants et récitatifs.* Javouhey, Guyana: Hmong Patrimony Series.

———. 1987. *Kab Ke Pam Tuag: Txheej Txheem: Les funerailles: ordonnance de la cérémonie.* Javouhey, Guyana: Hmong Patrimony Series.

Berval, René de, ed. 1959. *Kingdom of Laos: The Land of the Million Elephants and of the White Parasol.* Translated by Mrs. Teissier du Cros et al. Saigon: France-Asie.

Bond, Katherine, and Kingsavanh Pathammavong. 1992. "Contexts of dontrii lao deum: Traditional Lao Music." *Selected Reports in Ethnomusicology* 9:131–148.

Brengues, Jean. 1904. "Les mo lam: la chanson au Laos." *Revue indochinoise,* new series 2:588–592.

Catlin, Amy. 1981. *Music of the Hmong: Singing Voices and Talking Reeds.* Providence: Rhode Island College.

———. 1983. *Music of the Hmong: Singing Voices and Talking Reeds.* Providence, R.I.: Center for Hmong Lore, Museum of Natural History.

———. 1985a. "Harmonizing the Generations in Hmong Musical Performance." *Selected Reports in Ethnomusicology* 6:83–98.

———. 1985b. "Speech Surrogate Systems of the Hmong: From Singing Voices to Talking Reeds." In *The Hmong in the West: Observations and Reports,* ed. Bruce Downey and Douglas Olney, 170–197. Minneapolis: University of Minnesota Press.

———. 1986. "The Hmong and Their Music: A Critique of Pure Speech." In *Hmong Art: Tradition and Change,* ed. Joanne Cubbs, 11–18. Sheboygan, Wisc.: Kohler Arts Center.

———. 1992. "Homo Cantens: Why Hmong Sing during Interactive Courtship Rituals." *Selected Reports in Ethnomusicology* 9:43–60.

Chonpairot, Jarernchai. 1990. "Lam Khon Sawan: A Vocal Genre of Southern Laos." Ph.D. dissertation, Kent State University.

Compton, Carol. 1975. "Lam Khon Savan: A Traditional Form and a Contemporary Theme." In *A Tai Festschrift for William J. Gedney,* ed. Thomas W. Gething, 55–82. Southeast Asian Studies working paper 8. Honolulu: University of Hawaii.

———. 1977. "Linguistic and Cultural Aspects of the Lam: The Song of the Lao Mohlam." Ph.D. dissertation, University of Michigan.

———. 1979. *Courting Poetry in Laos: A Textual and Linguistic Analysis.* Special report 18. De Kalb: Northern Illinois University.

———. 1992. "Traditional Verbal Arts in Laos: Functions, Forms, Continuities, and Changes in Texts, Contexts and Performances." *Selected Reports in Ethnomusicology* 9:149–160.

Conquergood, Dwight. 1989. *I Am a Shaman: A Hmong Life Story with Ethnographic Commentary.* Minneapolis: SARS Project, University of Minnesota.

Daniélou, Alain. 1957. *La Musique du Cambodge et du Laos.* Pondichéry: Publications de l'Institut français d'indologie.

Escoffier, Andre. 1942. *Dans le Laos au chants des khènes, poèmes.* Hanoi: Imprimerie d'Extrême-Orient.

Gagneux, Mme. Anne Marie. 1971. "Le khène et la musique Lao." *Bulletin des amis du royaume lao* 6:175–181.

Guillemet, Mme. Eugène. 1923. *Les chants du khene laotien.* Hanoi: Imprimerie d'Extrême-Orient.

Hang, Ly. 1962. "Musique de danse laotienne." *Musica* 99 (June):13–17.

Hartmann, John F. 1992. "The Context, Text, and Performance of Khap Lue." *Selected Reports in Ethnomusicology* 9:33–42.

Houmphanh Rattanavong. 1992a. "The Lamluang: A Popular Entertainment." *Selected Reports in Ethnomusicology* 9:189–192.

———. 1992b. "Music and Instruments in Laos: Historical Antecedents and the Democratic Revolution." *Selected Reports in Ethnomusicology* 9:193–202.

Humbert-Lavergne, M. 1934. "La musique à travers la vie laotienne." *Zeitschrift für Vergleichende Musikwissenschaft* 2(1):14–19.

Kham-Ouane Ratanavong. 1973. *Learn to Play the Khène / Apprenez le khène.* Vientiane: Bulletin des amis du royaume lao.

Knosp, Gaston. 1922. *Laotian Songs.* Bangkok.

Lefevre-Pontalis, Pierre. 1896. *Chansons et fêtes du Laos.* Paris: Ernest Leroux.

Lindell, Kristina et al. 1982. *The Kammu Year: Its Lore and Music.* London: Curzon Press.

Lundstrom, Hakan. 1984. "A Kammu Song and Its Structure." *Asian Folklore Studies* 43(1):29–39.

Lundstrom, Hakan, and Damrong Tayanin. 1981. "Kammu Gongs and Drums." *Asian Folklore Studies* 40:65–86, 173–189.

Mahoney, Therese Mary. 1995. "The White Parasol and the Red Star: The Laos Classical Music Culture in a Climate of Change." Ph.D. dissertation, University of California at Los Angeles.

Mareschal, Eric. 1976. *La Musique des Hmong.* Paris: Author.

Miller, Terry E. 1985. "The Survival of Lao Traditional Music in America." *Selected Reports in Ethnomusicology* 6:99–110.

———. 1992. "A Melody Not Sung: The Performance of Lao Buddhist Texts in Northeast Thailand." *Selected Reports in Ethnomusicology* 9:161–188.

Miller, Terry E., and Jarernchai Chonpairot. 1979. "Review-Essay: The Problems of Lao Discography." *Asian Music* 11(1):124–139.

Mottin, Jean. 1979. *Contes et légendes Hmong Blanc.* Bangkok: Don Bosco Press.

———. 1980a. *55 Chants d'amour Hmong Blanc.* Bangkok: Siam Society.

———. 1980b. *Fêtes du nouvel an chez les Hmong Blanc de Thailande.* Bangkok: Siam Society.

———. 1982. *Allons faire le tour du ciel et de la terre: le chamanisme des Hmong vu dans les textes.* Bangkok: White Lotus.

———. 1984. "A Hmong Shaman's Séance." *Asian Folklore Studies* 43(1):99–108.

Burma (Myanmar)

Becker, Judith. 1967. "The Migration of the Arched Harp from India to Burma." *Galpin Society Journal* 20:17–23, pl. v–vii.

———. 1969. "Anatomy of a Mode." *Ethnomusicology* 13(2):267–279.

Fraser-Lu, Sylvia. 1983. "Frog Drums and Their Importance in Karen Culture." *Arts in Asia* Sept.–Oct.:50–63.

Frost, Helen, and Lily Strickland. 1927. *Oriental and Character Dances.* New York: A. S. Barnes.

Garfias, Robert. 1975a. "A Musical Visit to Burma." *World of Music* 17(1):3–13.

———. 1975b. "Preliminary Thoughts on Burmese Modes." *Asian Music* 7(1):39–49.

———. 1981. "Speech and Melodic Contour Interdependence in Burmese Music." *College Music Symposium* 21(1):33–39.

———. 1985. "The Development of the Modern Burmese Hsaing Ensemble." *Asian Music* 16:1–28.

Guillon, E. 1971. "Sur 21 Chansons populaires mon." *Homme* 11:58–108.

Halliday, Robert. 1914. "The Kalok Dance of the Talaings." *Journal of the Burma Research Society* 4:93–101.

Juvenis. 1825. "To the Editor: The Harp of Martaban." *The Quarterly Musical Magazine and Review* 7:451–456.

K [U Khin Zaw]. 1981. *Burmese Culture: General and Particular.* Rangoon: Sarpay Beikman.

Khin Zaw, U. 1940. "Burmese Music: A Preliminary Enquiry." *Journal of the Burma Research Society* 30(3):387–460.

———. 1975. "A Folk Song Collector's Letter from Shwebo." *Selected Reports in Ethnomusicology* 2(2):165–170.

Marano, P. A. 1900. "A Note on Burmese Music." In *Burma,* ed. Max Ferrar and Bertha Ferrar, appendix C. London: Sampson Low, Marston.

Marshall, Harry Ignatius. 1929. "Karen Bronze Drums." *Journal of the Burma Research Society* 19:1–14.

Obayashi, T. 1966. "The Wooden Slit Drum of the Wa in the Sino-Burmese Border Area." *Beiträge Japan* 3:72–88.

Okell, John. 1964. "Learning Music from a Burmese Master." *Man* 64:183.

———. 1971. "The Burmese Double-Reed 'Nhai.'" *Asian Music* 2(1):25– 31.

Picken, Lawrence E. R. 1984. "Instruments in an Orchestra from Pyu (Upper Burma) in 802." *Musica Asiatica* 4:245–270.

Rao, H. S. 1928. "Note on a Musical Instrument Common in the Northern Shan States." *Man in India* 8:61–62.

Rodrigue, Yves. 1992. *Nat-Pwe: Burma's Supernatural Sub-Culture.* Kiscadale, Scotland: Paul Strachan.

Sachs, Curt. 1917. *Die Musikinstrumente Birmas und Assams im K. Ethnographischen Museum zu München.* Munich: Verlag der Königlichen Bayerischen Akademie der Wissenschaften.

Shway, Yoe. 1963 [1882]. *The Burman: His Life and Notions.* Reprint of 3rd ed. [1909]. New York: W. W. Norton.

Singer, Noel F. 1992. *Burmese Puppets.* New York: Oxford University Press.

———. 1995. *Burmese Dance and Theatre.* Kuala Lampur: Oxford University Press.

Stewart, J. A. 1932. "A Mon Song of the Seasons with a Translation and Notes." *Journal of the Burma Research Society* 22:135–150.

———. 1937–1939. "The Song of the Three Mons." *Bulletin of the School of Oriental and African Studies* 9:33–39.

Tekkatho Maung Thu Hlaing. 1993. *Myanmar Traditional Orchestra Instruments.* Rangoon [Yangon]: U Tin Ohn.

Williamson, Muriel. 1968. "The Construction and Decoration of One Burmese Harp." *Selected Reports in Ethnomusicology* 1(2):45–72.

———. 1975a. "Aspects of Traditional Style Maintained in Burma's First 13 Kyò Songs." *Selected Reports in Ethnomusicology* 2(2):117–163.

———. 1975b. "A Supplement to the Construction and Decoration of One Burmese Harp." *Selected Reports in Ethnomusicology* 2(2):111–115.

———. 1979a. "The Basic Tune of a Late Eighteenth-Century Burmese Classical Song." *Musica Asiatica* 2:155–195.

———. 1979b. "A Biographical Note on Myáwadi Sá, Burmese Poet and Composer." *Musica Asiatica* 2:151–154.

———. 1981. "The Correlation between Speech-Tones of Text-Syllables and Their Musical Setting in a Burmese Classical Song." *Musica Asiatica* 3:11–28.

Malaysia

Abdullah bin Mohamed (Dato). 1971. "The Ghazal in Arabic Literature and in Malay Music." *Malaya in History* 14(1).

Affan Seljug. 1967. "Some Notes on the Origin and Development of the Naubat." *Journal of the Royal Asiatic Society, Malaysian Branch* 40(1):149–152.

Ahmad Omar. 1984. "Joget Gamelan: The Art of Orchestral Dance." *Performing Arts* 1(1):38–41.

Aishah Ali. 1981. "A Glorious Chapter in the Malay Film Industry." In *New Straits Times Annual,* 36–45. Kuala Lumpur: Straits Times Press.

Balfour, Henry L. 1904. *Report on a Collection of Musical Instruments from the Siamese Malay States and Perak.* Fasciculi Malayanses, Anthropology. London: University Press of Liverpool.

Beamish, Tony. 1954. *The Arts of Malaya.* Singapore: Donald Moore.

Blacking, J. A. R. 1954–1955. "Musical Instruments of the Malayan Aborigines." *Federation Museums Journal* 1(11):35–52.

Brunet, Jacques. 1971. *Wayang Kulit: Schattentheater aus Malaysia.* Berlin: Internationalen Institut für vergleichende Musikstudien und Dokumentation.

Chopyak, James. 1986. "Music in Modern Malaysia: A Survey of the Musics Affecting the Development of Malaysian Popular Music." *Asian Music* 18(1):111–138.

———. 1987. "The Role of Music in Mass Media, Public Education and the Formation of a Malaysian National Culture." *Ethnomusicology* 31(3):431–454.

Couillard, Marie-Andrée, M. Elizabeth Cardosa, and Margaret R. Martinez. 1982. "Jah Hut Musical Culture and Content." *Contributions to Southeast Asian Ethnography* 1:35–55.

D'Cruz, Marion Francena. 1979. "Joget Gamelan, a Study of its Contemporary Practice." M.A. thesis, Universiti Sains Malaysia.

Cuisinier, Jeanne. 1936. *Danses magiques de Kelantan.* Paris: Gallimard.

———. 1957. *Le théâtre d'ombres a Kelantan.* Paris: Gallimard.

Dobbs, Jack Percival Baker. 1972. "Music in the Multiracial Society of West Malaysia." Ph.D. dissertation, University of London.

Endicott, Kirk. 1979. *Batek Negrito Religion: The World-View and Rituals of a Hunting and Gathering People of Peninsular Malaysia.* Oxford: Clarendon Press.

Frame, Edward. 1976. "Several Major Musical Forms of Sabah Malaysia." *Journal of the Royal Asiatic Society, Malaysian Branch* 49(2):154–163.

———. 1982. "The Musical Instruments of Sabah, Malaysia." *Ethnomusicology* 26(2):247–274.

Ghulam-Sarwar Yousof. 1976. "The Kelantan Mak Yong Dance Theater, a Study of Performance Structure." Ph.D. dissertation, University of Hawaii.

———. 1982a. "Mak Yong: The Ancient Malay Dance Theatre." Asian Studies 20:108–121.

———. 1982b. "Nora Chatri in Kedah: A Preliminary Report." *Journal of the Royal Asiatic Society, Malaysian Branch* 55(1):53–61.

———. 1983. "Feasting of the Spirits: The Berjamu Ritual Performance in the Kelantanese Wayang Siam Shadow Play." *Kajian Malaysia* 1(1):95–115.

———. 1987. "Bangsawan: The Malay Opera." *Tenggara* 20:3–20.

———. 1992. *Pangguiig Semar: Essays an Traditional Malay Theatre.* Kuala Lumpur: Tempo Publications.

Ginsberg, Henry D. 1972. "The Manora Dance-Drama: An Introduction." *Journal of the Siam Society* 60:169–181.

Gorlinski, Virginia. 1988. "Some Insights into the Art of Sape' Playing." *Sarawak Museum Journal* 39(60):77–104.

Hamilton, A. W. 1920. "The Boria." *Journal of the Royal Asiatic Society, Straits Branch* 82:139–144.

———. 1982. *Malay Pantuns.* Singapore: Eastern Universities Press.

Hose, Charles, and McDougall, William. 1912. *The Pagan Tribes of Borneo.* 2 vols. London: Macmillan.

Kloss, C. B. 1906. "Malaysian Musical Instruments." *Journal of the Royal Asiatic Society, Straits Branch* 46:285–287.

Ku Zam Zam, Ku Idris. 1983. "Alat-Alat Muzik Dalam Ensembel Wayang Kulit, Mek Mulung dan Gendang Keling di Kedah Utara" (Musical instruments in the shadow play, *mek mulung,* and *gendang keling* ensembles of North Kedah). In

Kajian Budaya dan Masyarakat di Malaysia, ed. Mohd. Taib Osman and Wan Kadir Yusoff, 1–52. Kuala Lumpur: Dewan Bahasa dan Pustaka.

———. 1993a. "Nobat: Music in the Service of the King—The Symbol of Power and Status in Traditional Malay Society." In *Tinta Kenangan,* ed. Nik Safiah Karim, 175–193. Kuala Lumpur: Jabatan Pengajian Melayu, Universiti Malaya.

———. 1993b. "Tumbuk Kalang: Satu Genre Muzik Ke'a Pertanian Padi" (*Tumbuk kalang:* a musical genre related to the cultivation of rice). In *Segemal Padi Sekunca Budi,* ed. Nik Safiah Karim, 207–222. Kuala Lumpur: Akademi Pengajian Melayu, Universiti Malaya.

Ladderman, Carol. 1991. *Taming the Wind of Desire: Psychology, Medicine and Aesthetics in Malay Shamanistic Performance.* Los Angeles: University of California Press.

Linehan, W. 1951. "Nobat and the Orang Kalau of Perak." *Journal of the Royal Asiatic Society, Malayan Branch* 24(3):60–68.

Lockard, Craig A. 1991. "Reflections of Change: Sociopolitical Commentary and Criticism in Malaysian Popular Music Since 1950." *Crossroads: An Interdisciplinary Journal of Southeast Asian Studies* 6(1):1–106.

Malm, William P. 1969. "Music of the Ma'yong." *Tenggara* 5:114–120.

———. 1971. "Malaysian Ma'yong Theater." *The Drama Review* 15(3):108–121.

———. 1974. "Music in Kelantan, Malaysia and Some of Its Cultural Implications." In *Studies in Malaysian Oral and Musical Traditions,* 1–49. Michigan Papers on South and Southeast Asia, 8. Ann Arbor: University of Michigan.

———. 1979. "Music in Malaysia." *World of Music* 21(3):6–18.

Matusky, Patricia. 1980. "Music in the Malay Shadow Puppet Theater." Ph.D. dissertation, University of Michigan.

———. 1982. "Musical Instruments and Musicians of the Malay Shadow Puppet Theater." *Journal of the American Musical Instrument Society* 8:38–68.

———. 1985. "An Introduction to the Major Instruments and Forms of Traditional Malay Music." *Asian Music* 16(2):121–182.

———. 1986. "Aspects of Musical Style among the Kajang, Kayan and Kenyah-Badang of the Upper Rejang River [Sarawak]." *Sarawak Museum Journal* 36(57):185–229.

———. 1989. "Alat-Alat dan Bentuk-Bentuk Muzik Tradisi Masyarakat Melayu" (Instruments and forms of traditional music in Malay society). In *Masyarakat Melayu: Struktur, Organisasi dan Manifestasi,* ed. Mohd. Taib Osman, 248–319. Kuala Lumpur: Dewan Bahasa dan Pustaka.

———. 1990. "Aspects of Musical Style among the Kayan, Kenyah-Badang and Malay Peoples of the Upper Rejang River [Sarawak]." *Sarawak Museum Journal* 41(62):115–149.

———. 1992. "Musical Instruments of the Indigenous Peoples." In *Sarawak—A Cultural Legacy,* ed. Lucas Chin, 217–230. Kuching: Society Atelier Sarawak.

———. 1993. *Malaysian Shadow Plan and Music: Continuity of an Oral Tradition.* Kuala Lumpur: Oxford University Press.

———. 1994. "Music of the Mak Yong Theater of Malaysia: A Fusion of Southeast Asian Malay and Middle Eastern Islamic Elements." In *To the Four Corners,* ed. Ellen Leichtman, 25–53. Warren, Mich.: Harmonie Park Press.

Mohammad Anis Mohammad Nor. 1986. *Randai Dance of Minangkabau Sumatra, with Labanotation Scores.* Kuala Lumpur: University of Malaysia Press.

———. 1993. *Zapin: Folk Dance of the Malay World.* Singapore: Oxford University Press.

Mohammad Ghouse Nasaruddin. 1979. "The Desa Performing Arts of Malaysia." Ph.D. dissertation, Indiana University.

Mohd. Taib Osman, ed. 1974. *Traditional Drama and Music in Southeast Asia.* Kuala Lumpur: Dewan Bahasa dan Pustaka.

Oesch, Hans. 1973. "Musikalische Kontinuität bei Naturvölkern: Dargestellt an der Musik der Senoi auf Malakka." In *Studien zur Tradition in der Musik: Kurt von Fischer am 60. Geburtstag,* ed. H. H. Eggebrecht and M. Lotolf, 227–246. Munich.

———. 1974a. "Musikalische Gattungen bei Naturvölkern: Untersuchungen am vokalen und instrumentalen Repertoire des Schamanen Terhin und seiner Senoi-Leute von Stammer der Temiar am oberen Nenggiri auf Malakka." In *Festschrift für Arno Volk,* ed. Carl Kahlhaus and Hans Oesch, 7–30. Cologne: Musikverlag Hans Gerig.

———. 1974b. "Oekonomie und Musik: Zur Bedeutung der Produktionsverhältnisse für die Herausbildung einer Musikkultur, dargestellt am Beispiel der Inlandstamme auf Malakka und der Balier." In *Convivium Musicorum: Festschrift Wolfgang Boetticher zum sechzigsten Geburtstag am 19. August 1974,* ed. H. Hoschen and D. P. Moser, 246–253. Berlin: Verlag Merseburger.

Rahmah Bujang. 1977. "The Boria: A Study of a Malay Theater in Its Sociocultural Context." Ph.D. dissertation, University of Hull.

———. 1987. *Boria, a Form of Malay Theatre.* Singapore: Institute of Southeast Asian Studies.

Roseman, Marina. 1984. "The Social Structuring of Sound: The Temiar of Peninsular Malaysia." *Ethnomusicology* 28(3):411–445.

———. 1989. "Inversion and Conjuncture: Male and Female in Temiar Performance." In *Women and Music in Cross-Cultural Perspective,* ed. Ellen Koskoff, 131–150. Urbana and Chicago: University of Illinois Press.

———. 1990. "Head, Heart, Odor and Shadow: The Structure of the Self, Ritual Performance and the Emotional World." *Ethos* 18(3):227–250.

———. 1991. *Healing Sounds from the Malaysian Rainforest.* Berkeley: University of California Press.

———. 1994. "Les chants de rêve: des frontières

mouvantes dans le monde temiar." *Anthropologie et Sociétés* 18(2):121–144.

———. 1996. "'Pure Products Go Crazy': Rainforest Healing in a Nation-State." In *The Performance of Healing*, ed. Carol Laderman and Marina Roseman, 233–269. New York: Routledge.

Sarkissian, Margaret. 1993a. "Music, Dance, and the Construction of Identity among Portuguese Eurasians in Melaka, Malaysia: A Preliminary Report." *Tirai Panggung: Jurnal Seni Persembahan* 1(1):1–16.

———. 1993b. "Music, Identity, and the Impact of Tourism on the Portuguese Settlement, Melaka, Malaysia." Ph.D. dissertation, University of Illinois at Urbana-Champaign.

———. 1994. "'Whose Tradition?': Tourism as a Catalyst in the Creation of a Modern Malaysian 'Tradition'." *Nhac Việt* 3:31–46.

———. 1995. "'Sinhalese Girl' Meets 'Aunty Annie': Competing Expressions of Ethnic Identity in the Portuguese Settlement, Melaka, Malaysia." *Asian Music* 27(1):37–62.

Sheppard, Mubin. 1938. "The Trengganu Rodat." *Journal of the Royal Asiatic Society, Malayan Branch* 16(l):109–114.

———. 1967. "Joget Gamelan Trengganu." *Journal of the Royal Asiatic Society, Malaysian Branch* 40(l):149–152.

———. 1972. *Taman Indera: Malay Decorative Arts and Pastimes.* Kuala Lumpur: Oxford University Press.

———. 1973. "Manora in Kelantan." *Journal of the Royal Asiatic Society, Malaysian Branch* 46(l):161–170.

——. 1975. "Traditional Musical Instruments of Malaysia." *Selected Reports in Ethnomusicology* 2(2):171–182.

———. 1983. *Taman Saujana: Dance, Drama, Music and Magic in Malaya Long and Not-so-Long Ago.* Petaling Jaya: International Book Service.

Strickland-Anderson, Lily. 1925. "Music in Malaya." *Musical Quarterly* 11:506–514.

Sweeney, Amin. 1972a. *Malay Shadow Puppets: The Wayang Siam of Kelantan.* London: The British Museum.

———. 1972b. *Ramayana and the Malay Shadow Play.* Kuala Lumpur: National University of Malaysia Press.

———. 1974. "Professional Malay Story-Telling: Some Questions of Style and Presentation." In *Studies in Malaysian Oral and Musical Traditions,* 47–99. Michigan Papers on South and Southeast Asia, 8. Ann Arbor: University of Michigan.

Tan Sooi Beng. 1988. "The Thai Manora in Malaysia: Adapting to the Penang Chinese Community." *Asian Folklore Studies* 47(1):19–34.

———. 1989a. "From Popular to 'Traditional' Theatre: The Dynamics of Change in Bangsawan of Malaysia." *Ethnomusicology* 33(2):229–274.

———. 1989b. "The Performing Arts in Malaysia: State and Society." *Asian Music* 21(l):137–171.

———. 1989c. "A Social and Stylistic History of Bangsawan, c. 1880–1980: Correspondences between Social-Historical and Musical-Theatrical Change." Ph.D. dissertation, Monash University.

———. 1993. *Bangsawan, a Social and Stylistic History of Popular Malay Opera.* Singapore: Oxford University Press.

———. 1994. "Moving Centre Stage: Women in Malay Opera in Early Twentieth Century Malaya." *Kajian Malaysia* 12(1–2):96–118.

Teeuw, A., and Wyatt, D. K. 1970. *Hikayat Patani.* The Hague: Martinus Nijhoff.

Thomas, Phillip Lee. 1986. *Like Tigers around a Piece of Meat: The Baba Style of Dondang Sayang.* Singapore: Institute of Southeast Asian Studies.

Tunku Nong Jiwa, Raja Badri Shah, and Haji Mubin Sheppard. 1962. "The Kedah and Perak Nobat." *Malaya in History* 7(2):7–11.

Ulbricht, H. 1970. *Wayang Purwa: Shadows of the Past.* Kuala Lumpur: Oxford University Press.

Wan Kadir Yusoff. 1983. "Pertumbuhan Budaya Popular Masyarakat Melayu Bandaran Sebelum Perang Dunia Kedua" (The establishment of urban Malay popular culture before the Second World War). In *Kajian Budaya dan Masyarakat di,* ed. Mohd. Taib Osman and Wan Kadir Yusoff, 53–107. Kuala Lumpur: Dewan Bahasa dan Pustaka.

———. 1988. *Budaya Popular Dalam Masyarakat Melayu Bandaran* (Popular cuture in Malay urban society). Kuala Lumpur: Dewan Bahasa dan Pustaka.

Werner, R. 1973. "Nose Flute Blowers of the Malayan Aborigines (Orang Asli)." *Anthropos* 68:181–191.

Wilkinson, R. J. and Windstedt, R. O. 1957. *Pantun Melayu.* Singapore: Malaya Publishing House.

Winstedt, R. O. 1929. "The Perak Royal Musical Instruments." *Journal of the Royal Asiatic Society, Malayan Branch* 12:451.

Wright, Barbara Ann Stein. "Wayang Siam: An Ethnographic Study of the Malay Shadow Play of Kelantan." Ph.D. dissertation, Yale University.

Vietnam

Addiss, Stephen. 1971a. "Music of the Cham Peoples." *Asian Music* 2(1):32–38.

———. 1971b. "Theater Music of Vietnam." *Southeast Asia* 1:129–152.

———. 1973. "*Hat A Dao,* the Sung Poetry of North Vietnam." *Journal of the American Oriental Society* 93(1):18–31.

———. 1992. "Text and Context in Vietnamese Sung Poetry: The Art of Hat A Dao." *Selected Reports in Ethnomusicology* 9:203–224.

Bamman, Richard Jones. 1991. "The *Đàn Tranh* and the *Lục Huyền Cầm*." In *New Perspectives on Vietnamese Music,* ed. Phong T. Nguyễn, 67–78. New Haven, Conn.: Yale Council on Southeast Asia Studies.

Bezacier, L., 1946. "Des découvertes archéologiques au Tonkin" (Archaeological discoveries in Tonkin). *Revue de l'Académie des Inscriptions* 412–428.

Condominas, George. 1951–1952. "Le lithophone préhistorique de Ngut Lieng Krak." *Bulletin de l'École française d'Extrême-Orient* 45(2):359–392.

Dong Son Drums in Viet Nam. 1990. Hanoi: Viet Nam Social Science Publishing House.

Dournes, Jacques. 1965. "La musique chez les Jorai." *Objets et Mondes* 5(4):211–244.

Dumoutier, Georges. 1890. *Les Chants et les traditions populaires des annamites* (Songs and popular traditions of the Annamites). Paris: Ernest Leroux.

Hoàng Yến. 1919. "Le musique à Hué, don-nguyet et don-tranh." *Bulletin des amis du vieux Hué* 6:233–287

———. 1953. *Music at Hué, Don-Nguyet and Don-Tranh.* Translated by Keith Botsford. New Haven, Conn.: HRAF Press (Translation of Hoàng Yến, 1919).

Hùynh Khắc Dụng. 1970. *Hat Boi: Theatre traditionnel du Viet-Nam.* Saigon: Kim Lai Ấn Quán.

Janse, O. R. T. 1962. "On the Origins of Traditional Vietnamese Music." *Asian Perspectives* 6:145–162.

Le Ba Sinh. N.d. *Marionnettes sur eau / Water Puppetry.* Ho Chi Minh City: The History Museum.

Le Bris, E. 1922. "Musique annamite: Airs traditionnels." *Bulletin des Amis du vieux Hué* 9:255–309.

———. 1927. "Musique annamite; les musiciens aveuges de Hue–Le Tu-dai-canh." *Bulletin des amis du vieux Hué* 14:137–148.

Lê Tuấn Hùng. 1991. *The Dynamics of Change in Hue and Tai Tu Music of Vietnam Between c. 1890 and c. 1920.* Working paper 67. Clayton: Centre of Southeast Asian Studies, Monash University.

Nguyễn Đình Lai. 1955. "Étude sur la musique Sino-Vietnamienne et les chants populaires du Viet-Nam." *Bulletin de la Société des Études Indochinoises,* new series, 31(1):1–91.

Nguyễn Huy Hong, and Trần Trung Chính. 1992. *Les marionnettes sur eau traditionnelles du Vietnam.* Hanoi: Éditions en langues étrangères.

Nguyễn Thuyết Phong. 1982. "La musique bouddhique du Vietnam." Ph.D. dissertation, University of Paris (Sorbonne).

———. 1989. "Restructuring the Fixed Pitches of the Vietnamese Dan Nguyet Lute." *Asian Music* 18(1):56–70.

———, ed. 1990a. *New Perspectives in Vietnamese Music.* New Haven, Conn.: Department of International and Area Studies, Yale University.

———. 1990b. *Textes et chants de la liturgie bouddique vietnamienne en France.* Kent, Ohio: Association for Research in Vietnamese Music.

Nguyễn Thuyết Phong and Patricia Shehan Campbell. 1990. *From Rice Paddies and Temple Yards: Traditional Music of Vietnam.* Danbury, Conn.: World Music Press.

Nguyễn Văn Huyen. 1933. *Les chants alternés des garçons et des filles en Annam.* Paris: Paul Geuthier.

Phạm Duy. 1975. *Musics of Vietnam,* ed. Dale R. Whiteside. Carbondale: Southern Illinois University Press.

Pham Huy Thông. 1990. *Dong Son Drums in Viet Nam.* Hanoi: The Viet Nam Social Science Publishing House.

Schaeffner, André. 1951. "Le lithophone préhistorique de Ndut Lieng Krak." *Revue de Musicologie* 97–98:1–19.

Song Bân. 1960. *The Vietnamese Theatre.* Hanoi: Foreign Languages Publishing House.

Trần Văn Khê. 1960. "Instruments de musique revelés par des fouilles archéologiques au Viet Nam." *Arts Asiatiques* 7(2):141–152.

———. 1961. "Aspects de la cantillation: Techniques du Viet Nam." *Revue de musicologie* 47:37–53.

———. 1962. *La musique vietnamienne traditionelle.* Paris: Presses Universitaires de France.

———. 1967. *Viet-Nam: Les traditions musicales.* Paris: Buchet-Chastel.

———. 1969. "La musique dans la société vietnamienne actuelle." In *La musique dans la vie,* 2:121–156. Paris: ORTF.

———. 1975. "Vietnamese Music." *Selected Reports in Ethnomusicology* 2(2):35–48.

Varton, Paul. 1908. "Journal d'une chanteuse annamite." *Bulletin Française, Société International de Musique* 4:165–180.

Weiss, Peter. 1970. *Notes on the Cultural Life of the Democratic Republic of Vietnam.* Translated from the German edition of 1968, Notizen zum Kulturellen Leben in der Demokratischen Republik Viet Nam. New York: Dell.

Singapore

Kong, Lily. 1995. "Popular Music and a 'Sense of Place' in Singapore." *Crossroads: An Interdisciplinary Journal of Southeast Asian Studies* 9(2): 51–77.

Perris, Arnold. 1978. "Chinese Wayang: The Survival of Chinese Opera in the Streets of Singapore." *Ethnomusicology* 22(2):297–306.

ISLAND SOUTHEAST ASIA

Indonesia

Abidin, Andi Zainal. 1974. "The I La Galigo Epic Cycle of South Celebes and Its Diffusion." Translated by C. C. Macknight. *Indonesia* 17:161– 169.

Adams, Marie Jeanne (Monni). 1981. "Instruments and Songs of Sumba, Indonesia: A Preliminary Survey." *Asian Music* 13:73–83.

Anderson, Benedict. 1965. *Mythology and the Tolerance of the Javanese.* Ithaca, N. Y.: Cornell University Press. Monograph Series, Modern Indonesia Project.

Arjo, Irawati Durban. 1989. "Women's Dance among the Sundanese of West Java, Indonesia." *Asian Theatre Journal* 6(2):168–178.

Arps, Bernard. 1992. *Tembang in Two Traditions: Performance and Interpretation of Javanese Literature.* London: School of Oriental and African Studies.

———, ed. 1993. *Performance in Java and Bali: Studies of Narrative, Theatre, Music, and Dance.* London: School of Oriental and African Studies, University of London.

Baier, Randal E. 1985. "The Angklung Ensemble of West Java: Continuity of an Agricultural Tradition." *Balungan* 2:8–16.

———. 1986. "Si Duriat Keueung: The Sundanese Angklung Ensemble of West Java, Indonesia." M.A. thesis, Wesleyan University.

Bandem, I Made. 1980. "Bali: Music." *The New Grove Dictionary of Music and Musicians,* ed. Stanley Sadie. London: Macmillan.

Bandem, I Made, and Fredrik Eugene deBoer. 1981. *Kaja and Kelod: Balinese Dance in Transition.* Selangor, Malaysia: Oxford University Press.

Barraud, Cecile. 1990. "A Turtle Turned on the Sand in the Kei Islands; Society's Shares and Values." *Bijdragen tot de Taal-, Land-en Volkenkunde* 1:146:35–55.

Basile, Christopher. 1996. "The Troubled Grass and the Bamboo's Cry: The Significance of the Rotinese Sasandu." *The Asian Arts Society of Australia Review* 5(1):5.

Becker, A. L. 1979. "Text Building, Epistemology, and Aesthetics in Javanese Shadow Theater." In *The Imagination of Reality: Essays in Southeast Asian Coherence Systems,* ed. A. L. Becker and Aram Yengoyan, 211–243. Norwood, N. J.: Ablex Publishing.

Becker, A. L., and Judith Becker. 1981. "A Musical Icon: Power and Meaning in Javanese Gamelan Music." In *The Sign in Music and Literature,* ed. Wendy Steiner, 203–215. Austin: University of Texas Press.

Becker, A. L., and Judith Becker. 1983 [1979]. "A Grammar of the Musical Genre Srepegan." *Asian Music* 14(1):30–72.

Becker, A. L., and Aram Yengoyan, eds. 1979. *The Imagination of Reality: Essays in Southeast Asian Coherence Systems.* Norwood, N. J.: Ablex Publishing.

Becker, Judith. 1975. "Kroncong, Indonesian Popular Music." *Asian Music* 7(1):14–19.

———. 1979a. "Time and Tune in Java." In *The Imagination of Reality: Essays in Southeast Asian Coherence Systems,* ed. A. L. Becker and Aram Yengoyan, 197–210. Norwood, N. J.: Ablex Publishing.

———. 1979b. "People Who Sing; People Who Dance." In *What Is Modern Indonesian Culture?* ed. Gloria Davis, 3–10. Athens, Ohio: Ohio University Center for International Studies.

———. 1980. *Traditional Music in Modern Java: Gamelan in a Changing Society.* Honolulu: University of Hawaii Press.

———. 1988. "Earth, Fire, Sakti, and the Javanese Gamelan." *Ethnomusicology* 32(3):385–391.

———. 1991. "The Javanese Court Bedhaya Dance as a Tantric Analogy." In *Metaphor: A Musical Dimension,* ed. Jamie C. Kassler, 109–120. Sydney: Currency Press.

———. 1993. *Gamelan Stories: Tantrism, Islam, and Aesthetics in Central Java.* Monographs in Southeast Asian Studies. Tempe: Arizona State University Press.

Becker, Judith, and Alan Feinstein, eds. 1984, 1987, 1988. *Karawitan: Source Readings in Javanese Gamelan and Vocal Music.* 3 vols. Ann Arbor: Center for South and Southeast Asian Studies, University of Michigan.

Belo, Jane, ed. 1970. *Traditional Balinese Culture.* New York: Columbia University Press.

Bosch, F. D. K. 1951. "Guru, Drietand en Bron." *Bijdragen tot de Taal-, Land- en Volkenkunde* 107:117–134.

Brakel-Papenhuijzen, Clara. 1992. *The Bedhaya Court Dances of Central Java.* Leiden: E. J. Brill.

Brandon, James R. 1967. *Theatre in Southeast Asia.* Cambridge, Mass.: Harvard University Press.

———. 1970. *On Thrones of Gold: Three Javanese Shadow Plays.* Cambridge, Mass.: Harvard University Press.

Brandts Buys, J. S. 1921. "Over de ontwikkelingsmogelijkheden van de muziek op Java" (On the developmental possibilities of music in Java). *Djawa* 1, Praeadvies 2, 1–90.

———. 1926 "Over muziek in het Banjoewangische" (On music in Banyuwangi). *Djawa* 6:205–228.

———. 1928. "De Toonkunst bij de Madoereezen" (The music of the Madurese). *Djawa* 8:1–290.

———. 1929. "Een en ander over Javaansche muziek" (This and that about Javanese music). *Programma van het Vijfde-Congres ter gelegenheid van het tienjarig bestaan van het Java Instituut,* 45–63.

Brandts Buys, J. S., and A. Brandts Buys–van Zijp. 1925. "Oude Klanken" (Old Sounds). *Djawa* 5(1):16–56.

Brandts Buys, J. S., and A. Brandts Buys–van Zijp. 1929. "Inlandsche dans en muziek." *Timboel* 3(2):13–18.

Brinner, Benjamin E. 1989–1990. "At the Border of Sound and Silence: The Use and Function of Pathetan in Javanese Gamelan." *Asian Music* 21(1):1–34.

———. 1992. "Performer Interaction in a New Form of Javanese Wayang." In *Essays on Southeast Asian Performing Arts: Local Manifestations and Cross-Cultural Implications,* ed. Kathy Foley, 96–114. Berkeley: Centers for South and Southeast Asia Studies, University of California.

———. 1993a. "Freedom and Formulaity in the Suling Playing of Bapak Tarnopangrawit." *Asian Music* 24(2):1–37.

———. 1993b. "A Musical Time Capsule from Java." *Journal of the American Musicological Society* 46(2):221–260.

———. 1995a. "Cultural Matrices and the Shaping of Innovation in Central Javanese Performing Arts." *Ethnomusicology* 39(3):433–456.

———. 1995b. *Knowing Music, Making Music: Javanese Gamelan and the Theory of Musical Competence and Interaction.* Chicago: University of Chicago Press.

Carle, Rainer. 1981, 1982. *Die Opera Batak: Das Wandestheater der Toba-Batak in Nord Sumatra.* 2 vols. Berlin: Dietrich Reimer Verlag.

Choy, Peggy. 1984. "Texts through Time: The Golèk Dance of Java." In *Aesthetic Tradition and Cultural Transition in Java and Bali,* ed. Stephanie Morgan and Laurie Jo Sears, 51–81. Madison: University of Wisconsin Center for Southeast Asian Studies.

Clara van Groenendael, Victoria. 1985. *The Dalang behind the Wayang.* Verhandelingen van de Koninklijk Instituut voor Taal-, Land- en Volkenkunde, 114. Dordrecht, Holland, and Providence, R. I.: Foris Publications.

———. 1987. *Wayang Theatre in Indonesia.* Koninklijk Instituut voor Taal-, Land- en Volkenkunde, Bibliographical Series 16. Dordrecht, Holland; Providence, R. I.: Foris Publications.

———. 1990. "*Po-té-hi*: The Chinese Glove-puppet Theatre in East Java." Paper presented at the International Symposium on Indonesian Performing Arts, School of Oriental and African Studies, University of London, July–August 1990.

———. 1993. "*Po-té-hi*: The Chinese Glove-puppet Theatre in East Java." *In Performance in Java and Bali: Studies of Narrative, Theatre, Music, and Dance*, ed. Bernard Arps, 11–33. London: School of Oriental and African Studies, University of London.

Cornets de Groot, A. D. 1852. "Bijdrage tot de kennis van de zeden en gewoonten der Javanen" (Contribution to the knowledge of the manners and customs of the Javanese). *Tijdschrift voor Nederlandsch Indie* 14(2):257–280, 346–367, 393–424.

Covarrubias, Miguel. 1937. *The Island of Bali.* New York: Knopf.

Crawford, Michael. 1980. "Indonesia: East Java." *The New Grove Dictionary of Music and Musicians,* ed. Stanley Sadie. London: Macmillan.

Crystal, Eric, and Catherine Crystal. 1973. *Music of Sulawesi.* Ethnic Folkways FE 4351. Notes to LP disk.

DeVale, Sue Carole, and I Wayan Dibia. 1991. "Sekar Anyar: An Exploration of Meaning in Balinese Gamelan." *The World of Music* 33(1):5–51.

deBoer, Fredrik E. 1989. "Balinese Sendratari: A Modern Dramatic Dance Genre." *Asian Theatre Journal* 6(2):179–193.

de Zoete, Beryl, and Walter Spies. 1973 [1938]. *Dance and Drama in Bali.* Selangor, Malaysia: Oxford University Press.

Dewantara, Ki Hadjar. 1964. *Serat Sari Swara* (Essence of sound / voice). 2nd ed. Jakarta: P. N. Pradnjaparamita.

Ellis, Alexander J. 1884. "Tonometrical Observations on Some Existing Nonharmonic Musical Scales." *Proceedings of the Royal Society* 37:368–385.

Erb, Maribeth. 1988. "Flores: Cosmology, Art and Ritual." In *Islands and Ancestors: Indigenous Styles of Southeast Asia,* ed. Jean-Paul Barbier and Douglas Newton, 106–119. Munich: Prestel.

Falk, Catherine A. 1982. "The Tarawangsa Tradition in West Java." Ph.D. dissertation, Monash University.

Foley, M. Kathleen. 1979. "The Sundanese 'Wayang Golek': The Rod Puppet Theatre of West Java." Ph.D. dissertation, University of Hawaii.

———. 1984. "Of Dalang and Dukun-Spirit and Men: Curing and Performance in the Wayang of West Java." *Asian Theatre Journal* 1(1):52–75.

———. 1985. "The Dancer and the Danced: Trance Dance and Theatrical Performance in West Java." *Asian Theatre Journal* 2(1):28–49.

———. 1986. "At the Graves of the Ancestors: Chronicle Plays in the Wayang Cepak Puppet Theatre of Cirebon, Indonesia." In *Historical Drama,* ed. James Redmond, 31–49. Themes in Drama, 8. Cambridge: Cambridge University Press.

———. 1990. "My Bodies: The Performer in West Java." *The Drama Review* 34(2):62–80.

Forrest, Wayne Jeffrey. 1980. "Concepts of Melodic Pattern in Contemporary Solonese Gamelan Music." *Asian Music* 11(2):53–127.

Fox, James J. 1974. "Our Ancestors Spoke in Pairs: Rotinese Views of Language, Dialect and Code." In *Explorations in the Ethnography of Speaking,* ed. Richard Bauman and Joel Sherzer, 65–85. London: Cambridge University Press.

———. 1977. *Harvest of the Palm: Ecological Change in Eastern Indonesia.* Cambridge, Mass.: Harvard University Press.

———. 1979. "The Ceremonial System of Savu." In *The Imagination of Reality: Essays in Southeast Asian Coherence Systems,* ed. A. L. Becker and Aram Yengoyan, 145–173. Norwood, N. J.: Ablex Publishing.

———. 1979b. "Standing in Time and Place: The Structure of Rotinese Historical Narratives." In *Southeast Asian Perceptions of the Past no. 4,* ed. A. Reid and D. Marr, 10–25. Kuala Lumpur: Heinemann.

———. 1988. *To Speak in Pairs: Essays on the Ritual Languages of Eastern Indonesia,* ed. James J. Fox, 1–28. Cambridge: Cambridge University Press.

Frederick, William H. 1982. "Rhoma Irama and the Dangdut Style: Aspects of Contemporary Indonesian Popular Culture." *Indonesia* 34:103–130.

Geertz, Clifford. 1960. *The Religion of Java.* New York: Free Press.

Geirnaert, Danielle C. 1989. "The Pogo Nauta Ritual in Laboya (West Sumba): Of Tubers and Mamuli." *Bijdragen tot de Taal-, Land- en Volkenkunde* 145(4):445–463.

Gieben, Claartje, Renée Heijnen, and Anneke Sapuletej. 1984. *Muziek en dans Spelletjes en Kinderliedjes van de Molukken.* Hoevelaken, The Netherlands: Christelijk Pedagogisch Studiecentrum.

Gold, Lisa. 1992. "Musical Expression in the Gender Wayang Repertoire: A Bridge between Narrative and Ritual." In *Balinese Music in Context: A Sixty-Fifth Birthday Tribute to Hans Oesch,* ed. Danker Schaareman, 245–275. Winterthur: Amadeus.

Goldsworthy, David. 1978. "Honey-Collecting Ceremonies on the East Coast of North Sumatra." In *Studies in Indonesian Music,* ed. Margaret J. Kartomi, 1–44. Clayton: Centre of Southeast Asian Studies, Monash University.

———. 1979. "Melayu Music of North Sumatra." Ph.D. dissertation, Monash University.

———. 1986. "The Dancing Fish Trap (*Lukah Menari*): A Spirit Invocation Song and a Spirit-Possession 'Dance' from North Sumatra." *Musicology Australia* 9:12–28.

Groneman, J. 1890. *De Gamelan te Jogjakarta.* Amsterdam: Johannes Müller.

Harnish, David D. 1985. "Musical Traditions of the Lombok Balinese: Antecedents from Bali and Lombok." M.A. thesis, University of Hawai'i.

———. 1986. "Sasak Music in Lombok." *Balungan* 2(3):17–22.

———. 1988. "Religion and Music: Syncretism, Orthodox Islam, and Musical Change in Lombok." *Selected Reports in Ethnomusicology* 7:123–138.

———. 1990. "The Preret of the Lombok Balinese: Transformation and Continuity within a Sacred Tradition." *Selected Reports in Ethnomusicology* 8:201–220.

———. 1991. "Music at the Lingsar Temple Festival: The Encapsulation of Meaning in the Balinese / Sasak Interface in Lombok, Indonesia." Ph.D. dissertation, University of California at Los Angeles.

———. 1992. "The Performance, Context, and Meaning of Balinese Music in Lombok." In *Balinese Music in Context: A Sixty-Fifth Birthday Tribute to Hans Oesch,* ed. Danker Schaareman, 29–58. Winterthur: Amadeus.

———. 1993. "The Future Meets the Past in the Present: Music and Buddhism in Lombok." *Asian Music* 25(1-2):29–50.

———. 1994. "The Future Meets the Past in the Present: Music and Buddhism in Lombok." *Asian Music* 25(2):29–50.

Harrell, Max Leigh. 1974. "The Music of the Gamelan Degung of West Java." Ph.D. dissertation, University of California at Los Angeles.

———. 1975. "Some Aspects of Sundanese Music." *Selected Reports in Ethnomusicology* 2(2):81–100.

Hastanto, Sri. 1985. "The Concept of Pathet in Javanese Gamelan Music." Ph.D. dissertation, University of Durham.

Hatch, Martin. 1976. "The Song Is Ended: Changes in the Use of Macapat in Central Java." *Asian Music* 7(2):59–71.

———. 1979. "Towards a More Open Approach to the History of Javanese Music." *Indonesia* 27:129–154.

———. 1980. "Lagu, Laras, Layang: Rethinking Melody in Javanese Music." Ph.D. dissertation, Cornell University.

———. 1985. "Popular Music in Indonesia." In *Popular Music Perspectives,* vol. 2, ed. D. Horn, 210–227. Göteborg: International Association for the Study of Popular Music.

———. 1989. "Popular Music in Indonesia." In *World Music, Politics and Social Change: Papers from the International Association for the Study of Popular Music,* ed. Simon Frith, 47–67. Manchester: Manchester University Press.

Hatley, Barbara. 1971. "Wayang and Ludruk: Polarities in Java." *The Drama Review* 15(3):88–101.

———. 1980. *Ketoprak Theatre and the Wayang Tradition.* Melbourne: Monash University Press.

Hefner, Robert W. 1985. *Hindu Javanese: Tengger Tradition and Islam.* Princeton, N. J.: Princeton University Press.

———. 1987. "The Politics of Popular Art: Tayuban Dance and Culture Change in East Java." *Indonesia* 43:75–94.

Heins, Ernst L. 1967. "Music of the Serimpi 'Anglir Mendung'." *Indonesia* 3:135–151.

———. 1969. "Tempo (Irama) in de M.-Javaanse gamelanmuziek." *Kultuurpatronen* 10–11:31–57.

———. 1970. "Cueing the Gamelan in Javanese

Wayang Performance." *Indonesia* 9(April):101–127.

———. 1975. "Kroncong and Tanjidor: Two Cases of Urban Folk Music in Jakarta." *Asian Music* 7(1):20–32.

———. 1977. "*Goong Renteng:* Aspects of Orchestral Music in a Sundanese Village." Ph.D. dissertation, University of Amsterdam.

Heins, Ernst L., and G. van Wengen. 1979. "Maluku (Molukken)." In *Musikgeschichte in Bildern: Südostasien,* ed. Paul Collaer, 142–143. Leipzig: VEB Deutschen Verlag.

Heinze, R. von. 1909. "Über Batak-Musik." In *Die Batakländer,* ed. Wilhelm Volz, 373–381. Nord-Sumatra, 1. Berlin: D. Reimer.

Henschkel, Marina. 1994. "Perceptions of Popular Culture in Contemporary Indonesia: Five Articles from Tempo, 1980–90." *Review of Indonesian and Malaysian Affairs* 28(2):53–71.

Hicks, David. 1988. "Art and Religion on Timor." In *Islands and Ancestors: Indigenous Styles of Southeast Asia,* ed. Jean-Paul Barbier and Douglas Newton, 138–151. Munich: Prestel-Verlag.

Hidding, Klaas A. H. 1929. "Nyi Pohatji Sangjang Sri." Ph.D. dissertation, Rijksuniversiteit Leiden.

Hoffman, Stanley B. 1978. "Epistemology and Music: A Javanese Example." *Ethnomusicology* 22(1):69–88.

Holt, Claire. 1939. *Dance Quest in Celebes.* Paris: Les Archives Internationales de la Danse.

———. 1967. *Art in Indonesia: Continuities and Change.* Ithaca, N. Y.: Cornell University Press.

———. 1971a. "Dances of Sumatra and Nias: Notes." *Indonesia* 11:1–20.

———. 1971b. "Batak Dances: Notes." *Indonesia* 12:65–84.

———. 1972. "Dances of Minangkabau: Notes." *Indonesia* 14:73–96.

Hood, Mantle. 1954. *The Nuclear Theme as a Determinant of Paṭet in Javanese Music.* Groningen: J. B. Wolters.

———. 1963. "The Enduring Tradition: Music and Theatre in Java and Bali." In *Indonesia,* ed. Ruth McVey, 438–471. New Haven, Conn.: Human Relations Area Files.

———. 1966. "Sléndro and Pélog Redefined." *Selected Reports in Ethnomusicology* 1(1):28–48.

———. 1970. "The Effect of Medieval Technology on Musical Styles in the Orient." *Selected Reports in Ethnomusicology* 1(3):148–170.

———. 1971. "Aspects of Group Improvisation in the Javanese Gamelan." In *Musics of Asia.* Manila: National Music Council.

———. 1972. "Music of Indonesia." In *Music,* ed. Mantle Hood and José Maceda, 1–27. Leiden and Cologne: E. J. Brill.

———. 1975. "Improvisation in the Stratified Ensembles of Southeast Asia." *Selected Reports in Ethnomusicology* 2(2):25–34.

———. 1980. *The Evolution of Javanese Gamelan, Book I: Music of the Roaring Sea.* Wilhelmshaven: Edition Heinrichshofen.

———. 1984. *The Evolution of Javanese Gamelan, Book II: Legacy of the Roaring Sea.* Wilhelmshaven: Edition Heinrichshofen.

———. 1988. *The Evolution of Javanese Gamelan, Book III: Paragon of the Roaring Sea.* Wilhelmshaven: Edition Heinrichshofen.

Hornbostel, Erich M. von. 1908. "Über die Musik der Kubu." In *Die Orang-Kubu auf Sumatra,* ed. B. Hagen, 245–256. Frankfurt: Baer.

Hoskins, Janet. 1988a. "Arts and Cultures of Sumba." *Islands and Ancestors: Indigenous Styles of Southeast Asia,* ed. Jean Paul Barbier and Douglas Newton, 120–138. Munich: Prestel-Verlag.

———. 1988b. "The Drum Is the Shaman, the Spear Guides His Voice." *Social Sciences Medicine* 27(8):819–828.

———. 1993. *The Play of Time: Kodi Perspectives on Calendars, History and Exchange.* Berkeley: University of California Press.

Hughes, David. 1988. "Deep Structure and Surface Structure in Javanese Music: A Grammar of *Gendhing Lampah.*" *Ethnomusicology* 32(1):23–74.

Hughes-Freeland, Felicia. 1990. "Tayuban: Culture on the Edge." *Indonesia Circle* 52:36–44.

———. 1993. "*Golèk Ménak* and *Tayuban:* Patronage and Professionalism in Spheres of Central Javanese Culture." In *Performance in Java and Bali: Studies of Narrative, Theatre, Music, and Dance,* ed. Bernard Arps, 88–120. London: School of Oriental and African Studies, University of London.

Jacobson, Edward, and J. H. van Hasselt. 1975 [1907]. "The Manufacture of Gongs in Semarang." Translated by Andrew Toth. *Indonesia* 19:127–152, plates.

Jansen, Arlin D. 1980. "Gonrang Music: Its Structure and Functions in Simalungun Batak Society in Sumatra." Ph.D. dissertation, University of Washington.

Jessup, Helen Ibbitson. 1990. *Court Arts of Indonesia.* New York: The Asia Society Galleries Harry N. Abrams.

Joest, W. 1892. "Malayische Lieder und Tänze aus Ambon und den Uliase (Molukken)." *Internationales Archiv für Ethnographie* 5:1–34.

Jones, Arthur M. 1971. *Africa and Indonesia: The Evidence of the Xylophone and Other Musical and Cultural Factors.* Leiden: E. J. Brill.

Jordaan, Roy E. 1984. "The Mystery of Nyai Lara Kidul, Goddess of the Southern Ocean." *Archipel* 28:99–116.

———. 1991. "Text, Temple and Tirtha." In *The Art and Culture of South-East Asia,* ed. Lokesh Chandra, 165–180. New Delhi: International Academy of Indian Culture and Aditya Prakashan.

Kartomi, Karen S. 1986. "Mendu Theatre on the Island of Bunguran, Sumatra." Honors thesis, Monash University.

Kartomi, Margaret J. 1972. "Tiger-Capturing Music in Minangkabau, West Sumatra." *Sumatra Research Bulletin* 2(1):24–41. Reprinted as "Tigers into Kittens." *Hemisphere* 20 (5):9–15, 20(6):7–13.

———. 1973a. *Matjapat Songs in Central and West Java.* Canberra: Australia National University Press.

———. 1973b. "Music and Trance in Java." *Ethnomusicology* 17(2):163– 208.

———. 1976. "Performance, Music and Meaning in *Réyog Ponorogo.*" *Indonesia* 22:85–130.

———. 1979. "Minangkabau Musical Culture: The Contemporary Scene and Recent Attempts at its Modernization." In *What Is Modern Indonesian Culture?* ed. G. Davis, 19–36. Athens, Ohio: Ohio University Press.

———. 1980. "Musical Strata in Sumatra, Java, and Bali." In *Musics of Many Cultures,* ed. Elizabeth May, 111–133. Berkeley, Los Angeles, London: University of California Press.

———. 1981a. "Dualism in Unity: The Ceremonial Music of the Mandailing Raja Tradition." *Asian Music* 12(2):74–108.

———. 1981b. "Lovely When Heard from Afar: Mandailing Ideas of Musical Beauty." In *Five Essays on the Indonesian Arts,* ed. Margaret J. Kartomi, 1–16. Clayton: Centre of Southeast Asian Studies, Monash University.

———. 1981c. "Randai Theatre in West Sumatra: Components, Music, Origins, and Recent Change." *Review of Indonesian and Malaysian Affairs* 15(1):1–44.

———. 1981d. "His Skyward Path the Rainbow Is: Funeral Music of the Sa'dan Toraja." *Hemisphere* 25(5):303–309.

———. 1983a. *The Angkola People of Sumatra: An Anthology of Southeast Asian Music.* Bärenreiter Musicaphon BM30 SL2568. LP disk and liner notes.

———. 1983b. *The Mandailing People of Sumatra: An Anthology of Southeast Asian Music.* Bärenreiter Musicaphon BM30 SL2567. LP disk and liner notes.

———. 1986a. "Kapri: A Synthesis of Malay and Portuguese Music on the West Coast of North Sumatra." In *Cultures and Societies of North Sumatra,* ed. Rainer Carle, 351–393. Berlin and Hamburg: Dietrich Reimer Verlag.

———. 1986b. "Muslim Music in West Sumatran Culture." *The World of Music* 3:13–32.

———. 1986c. "Tabut—A Shi'a Ritual Transplanted from India to Sumatra." In *Nineteenth and Twentieth Century Indonesia: Essays in Honour of Professor J. D. Legge,* ed. David P. Chandler and M. C. Ricklefs, 141–162. Monash: Monash University Centre of Southeast Asian Studies.

———. 1988. "Ritual Music and Dance: Contact and Change in the Lowlands of South Sulawesi." In *The Twelfth Festival of Asian Arts,* ed. J. Thompson, 26–35. Hong Kong: Urban Council.

———, ed. 1990a. *On Concepts and Classifications of Musical Instruments.* Chicago Studies in Ethnomusicology. Chicago: University of Chicago Press.

———. 1990b. "Parallels between Social Structure and Ensemble Classification in Mandailing." In *On Concepts and Classifications of Musical Instruments,* 215–224. Chicago: University of Chicago Press.

———. 1990c. "Taxonomical Models of the Instrumentarium and Regional Ensembles in Minangkabau." In *On Concepts and Classifications of Musical Instruments,* 225–234. Chicago: University of Chicago Press.

———. 1991a. "Experience-Near and Experience-Distant Perceptions of the Daboih Ritual in Aceh, Sumatra." In *Von der Vielfalt musikalischer Kultur: Festschrift für Josef Kuckertz, zur Vollendung des 60 Lebensjahres,* ed. Rüdiger Schumacher, 247–260. Berlin: Free University.

———. 1991b. "Dabuih in West Sumatra: A Synthesis of Muslim and Pre-Muslim Ceremony and Musical Style." *Archipel* 41:33–52.

———. 1992. "Appropriation of Music and Dance in Contemporary Ternate and Tidore." *Studies in Music* 26:85–95.

———. 1993a. "The Paradoxical and Nostalgic History of 'Gending Sriwijaya' in South Sumatra." *Archipel* 44:37–50.

———. 1993b. "Revival of Feudal Music, Dance and Ritual in the Former 'Spice Islands' of Ternate and Tidore." In *Culture and Society in New Order Indonesia,* ed. Virginia Hooker, 185–220. New York, Oxford: Oxford University Press.

———. 1994. "Is Maluku Still Musicological Terra Incognita? An Overview of the Music-Cultures of the Province of Maluku." *Journal of Southeast Asian Studies* 25(1):141–171.

———. 1996. "Contact and Synthesis in the Development of the Music of South Sumatra." In *All Kinds of Music, in Honour of Andrew McCredie,* ed. Graham Strahle and David Swale, 234–253. Wilhelmshaven: Florian Noetzel Verlag.

———. 1997. "The Royal *Nobat* Ensemble of Indragiri in Riau, Sumatra, in Colonial and Post-Colonial Times." *Galpin Society Journal* 50(1):3–15.

Kaudern, Walter A. 1927. *Musical Instruments in Celebes.* Ethnographical Studies in Celebes, 3. Göteborg: Elanders Boktryckeri.

Keeler, Ward. 1975. "Musical Encounter in Java and Bali." *Indonesia* 19:85–126.

———. 1987. *Javanese Shadow Plays, Javanese Selves.* Princeton, N. J.: Princeton University Press.

Kornhauser, Bronia. 1978. "In Defence of Kroncong." In *Studies in Indonesian Music,* 104–183. Monash Papers on Southeast Asia, 7. Clayton: Monash University.

———. 1935. "De rijstgodin op Midden-Celebes, en de Maangodin." *Mensch en Maatschappij* 11(2):109–122.

Kunst, Jaap, and C. J. A. Kunst–Van Wely. 1924. *De Toonkunst van Bali.* Weltevreden: G. Kolff.

Kunst, Jaap. 1938. *Music in Nias.* Supplement 38. Leiden: Internationales Archiv für Ethnographie.

———. 1942. *Music in Flores: A Study of the Vocal and Instrumental Music among the Tribes Living in Flores.* Leiden: E. J. Brill.

———. 1945. *Een en Ander Over de Muziek en den dans Op de Keieilanden.* Mededeling 64. Amsterdam: Koninklijke Vereeniging Indisch Instituut.

———. 1950. "Die 2000-jährige Geschichte Süd-Sumatras gespiegelt in ihrer Musik." *Kongress-Bericht Lüneburg,* 160–167.

———. 1960 [1954]. *Cultural Relations between the Balkans and Indonesia.* 2nd ed. Afdeling Culturele en Physische Anthropologie, 47, Mededeling 107. Amsterdam: Koninklijk Instituut voor de Tropen (Royal Tropical Institute).

———. 1968 [1927]. *Hindu-Javanese Musical Instruments.* The Hague: Martinus Nijhoff.

———. 1973 [1934]. *Music in Java: Its History, Its Theory, and Its Technique.* 3rd ed. Revised and enlarged by Ernst L. Heins. 2 vols. The Hague: Martinus Nijhoff.

———. 1994. *Indonesian Music and Dance: Traditional Music and Its Interaction with the West: A Compilation of Articles (1934–1952) Originally Published in Dutch, with Biographical Essays by Ernst Heins, Elizabeth den Otter, Feliz van Lamsweerde.* Amsterdam: Ethnomusicology Centre "Jaap Kunst," Royal Tropical Institute and University of Amsterdam.

Lentz, Donald. 1965. *The Gamelan Music of Java and Bali: An Artistic Anomaly Complementary to Primary Tonal Theoretical Systems.* Lincoln: University of Nebraska Press.

Lindsay, Jennifer. 1985. "Klasik, Kitsch or Contemporary: A Study of the Javanese Performing Arts." Ph.D. dissertation, University of Sydney.

Lysloff, René T.A. 1986. "The *Bonang Barung* in Contemporary Gamelan Performance Practice." *Balungan* 2(1–2):31–40.

———. 1990a. "*Srikandhi* Dances *Lènggèr:* A Performance of Music and Shadow Theater in Banyumas (West Central Java)." 2 vols. Ph.D. dissertation, University of Michigan.

———. 1990b. "Non-Puppets and Non-Gamelan: Wayang Parody in Banyumas." *Ethnomusicology* 34(1):19–36.

———. 1993. "A Wrinkle in Time: The Shadow Puppet Theatre of Banyumas (West Central Java)." *Asian Theatre Journal* 10(1):49–80.

Lysloff, René T. A., and Deborah Wong. 1991. "Threshold to the Sacred: The Overture in Thai and Javanese Ritual Performance." *Ethnomusicology* 35(3):315–348.

Manuel, Peter, and Randal E. Baier. 1986. "Jaipongan: Indigenous Popular Music of West Java." *Asian Music* 18(1):91–110.

Manik, Liberty. 1973–74. "Eine Studienreise zur Erforschung der rituellen Gondang-Musik der Batak auf Sumatra." *Mitteilungen der Deutschen Gesellschaft für Musik des Orients* 12:134–137.

McDermott, Vincent. 1986. "Gamelans and New Music." *Musical Quarterly* 72(1):16–27.

McDermott, Vincent, and Sumarsam. 1975. "Central Javanese Music: The Paṭet of Laras Sléndro and the Gendèr Barung." *Ethnomusicology* 19:233–244.

McPhee, Colin. 1966. *Music in Bali: A Study in Form and Instrumental Organization in Balinese Orchestral Music.* New Haven, Conn., and London: Yale University Press.

Messner, Gerald Florian. 1989. "Jaap Kunst Revisited: Multipart Singing in Three East Florinese Villages Fifty Years Later: A Preliminary Investigation." *The World of Music* 21(2):3–50.

Moore, Lynette M. 1985. "Songs of the Pakpak of North Sumatra." Ph.D. dissertation, Monash University.

Morgan, Stephanie, and Laurie Jo Sears, eds. 1984. *Aesthetic Tradition and Cultural Transition in Java and Bali.* Madison: University of Wisconsin Center for Southeast Asian Studies.

Muller, Karl. 1991. *East of Bali: From Lombok to Timor.* Singapore: Periplus Editions.

Murgiyanto, Sal. 1991. *Dance of Indonesia.* New York: Festival of Indonesia Foundation.

Natapradja, Iwan. 1975. "Sundanese Dances." *Selected Reports in Ethnomusicology* 2(2):103–108.

Nizar, M. 1994. "*Dangdut:* Sebuah Perjalanan" (*Dangdut:* a journey). Five-part series. *Citra* 221–225.

Nooey-Palm, Clémentine H. M. 1988. "The Mamasa and Sa'dan Toraja of Sulawesi." In *Islands and Ancestors: Indigenous Styles of Southeast Asia,* ed. Jean-Paul Barbier and Douglas Newton, 86–105. New York: Metropolitan Museum of Art.

North, Richard. 1988. "An Introduction to the Musical Traditions of Cirebon." *Balungan* 3(3):2–6.

Notosudirdjo, R. Franki S. 1990. "European Music in Colonial Life in 19th Century Java: A Preliminary Study." M.A. thesis, University of Wisconsin-Madison.

Okazaki, Yoshiko. 1994. "Music Identity and Religious Change among the Toba Batak People of North Sumatra." Ph.D. dissertation, University of California at Los Angeles.

Onghokham. 1972. "The Wayang Topèng World of Malang." *Indonesia* 14:111–124.

Ornstein, Ruby Sue. 1971. "Gamelan Gong Kebjar: The Development of a Balinese Musical Tradition." Ph.D. dissertation, University of California at Los Angeles.

Pacholczyk, Józef M. 1986. "Music and Islam in Indonesia." *The World of Music* 28(3):3–12.

Peacock, James. 1968. *Rites of Modernization: Symbolic and Social Aspects of Indonesian Proletarian Drama.* Chicago: University of Chicago Press.

Pemberton, John. 1987. "Musical Politics in Central Java, or How Not to Listen to a Javanese Gamelan." *Indonesia* 44 (October):17–29.

———. 1994. *On the Subject of "Java."* Ithaca, N. Y.: Cornell University Press.

Perlman, Marc. 1983. "Notes on 'A Grammar of the Musical Genre Srepegan'." *Asian Music* 14(1):17–29.

———. 1993. "Unplayed Melodies: Music Theory in Post-Colonial Java." Ph.D. dissertation, Wesleyan University.

Phillips, Nigel. 1980. *Sijobang.* Cambridge: Cambridge University Press.

Pigeaud, T. 1938. *Javaanse Volksvertoningen: Bijdrage tot de Beschrijving van Land en Volk.* Batavia: Volkslectuur.

Piper, Suzan, and Sawung Jabo. 1987. "Indonesian Music from the 50's to the 80's." *Prisma* 43 (March), 25–37.

Powers, Harold. 1980. "Mode." *The New Grove Dictionary of Music and Musicians,* ed. Stanley Sadie. London: Macmillan.

Probohardjono, R. Ng. S. 1984 [1966]. *Sléndro Songs of the Dhalang.* Translated by Susan Pratt Walton. In *Karawitan: Source Readings in Javanese Gamelan and Vocal Music,* ed. Judith Becker and Alan Feinstein, 1:439–523. Ann Arbor: Center for South and Southeast Asian Studies, University of Michigan.

Purba, Mauly. 1997. "Gondang Sabangunan: Functions and Meaning of Performance in Contemporary Protestant Toba Batah Society." Ph.D. dissertation, Monash University.

Raffles, Thomas Stamford. 1978 [1817]. *The History of Java.* 2 vols. Kuala Lumpur: Oxford University Press.

Rai, I. Nyoman. 1996. "Balinese *Gamelan Semar Pegulingan Saih Pitu:* The Modal System." Ph.D. dissertation, University of Maryland, Baltimore County.

Ramseyer, Urs. 1977. *The Art and Culture of Bali.* Singapore: Oxford Press.

Rassers, W. H. 1959. *Pañji, the Culture Hero.* Koninklijk Instituut voor Taal-, Land- en Volkenkunde, translation series, 3. The Hague: Martinus Nijhoff.

Revel-Macdonald, Nicole. 1988. "The Dayak of Borneo." In *Islands and Ancestors: Indigenous Styles of Southeast Asia,* ed. Jean-Paul Barbier and Douglas Newton, 66–85. Munich: Prestel.

Ricklefs, M. C. 1981. *A History of Modern Indonesia: c.1300 to the Present.* Bloomington: Indiana University Press.

Rodgers, Susan. 1986. "Batak Tape Cassette Kinship: Constructing Kinship through the Indonesian National Mass Media." *American Ethnologist* 13(1):23–42.

Rogers-Aguiniga, Pamela. 1986. "Topeng Cirebon: The Masked Dance of West Java as Performed in the Village of Slangit." M.A. thesis, University of California at Los Angeles.

Schaareman, Danker, ed. 1992. *Balinese Music in Context: A Sixty-Fifth Birthday Tribute to Hans Oesch.* Winterthur: Amadeus-Verlag.

Schlager, Ernst. 1976. *Rituelle Siebenton-Musik auf Bali.* Bern: Franck.

Schnitger, F. M. 1937. *The Archaeology of Hindoo Sumatra.* Leiden: E. J. Brill.

Schumacher, Rüdiger. 1980. *Die Suluk-Gesang des Dalang im Schattenspiel Zentraljavas.* 2 vols. Munich and Salzburg: Musikverlag Emil Katsbichler.

Sears, Laurie Jo. 1984. "Epic Voyages: The Transmission of the Ramayana and Mahabharata from India to Java." In *Aesthetic Tradition and Cultural Transition in Java and Bali,* ed. Stephanie Morgan and Laurie Jo Sears, 1–30. Madison: University of Wisconsin Center for Southeast Asian Studies.

———. 1991. "Javanese *Mahabharata* Stories: Oral Performances and Written Texts." In *Boundaries of the Text,* ed. Joyce B. Flueckiger and Laurie J. Sears, 61–82. Ann Arbor: Center for South and Southeast Asian Studies, University of Michigan.

Sedana, I. Nyoman. 1993. "The Education of a Balinese Dalang." *Asian Theatre Journal* 10(1):81–100.

Seebass, Tilman. 1990. "Theory (English), Lehre (German), versus Teori (Indonesian)." *Report of the XIVth International Congress of the International Musicological Society held at Bologna 1987,* 200–211.

———. 1996. "Change in Balinese Musical Life: Kebiar in the 1920s and 1930s." In *Being Modern in Bali: Image and Change*, ed. Adrian Vickers, 71–91. New Haven, Conn.: Yale University Southeast Asian Studies.

Seebass, Tilman, I Gusti Bagus Nyoman Panji, I Nyoman Rembang, and I Poedijono. 1976. *The Music of Lombok: A First Survey.* Bern: Franke.

Siddique, Sharon. 1977. "Relics of the Past: A Sociological Study of the Sultanates of Cirebon, West Java." Ph.D. dissertation, Universität Bielefeld.

Simon, Artur. 1982. "Altreligiöse und soziale Zeremonien der Batak." *Zeitschrift für Ethnologie* 107(2):177–206.

———. 1984. "Functional Changes in Batak Traditional Music and its Role in Modern Indonesian Society." *Asian Music* 15(2):58–66.

———. 1984–1985. *Gondang Toba / Northern Sumatra.* Museum Collection Berlin (West) 12. 2 LP disks and liner notes.

———. 1985. "The Terminology of Batak Instrumental Music in Northern Sumatra." *Yearbook for Traditional Music* 113–145.

———. 1987. *Gendang Karo / Northern Sumatra, Indonesia—Trance and Dance Music of the Karo Batak.* Museum Collection, Berlin (West) 13. LP disk and liner notes.

———. 1993. "Gondang, Gods and Ancestors, Religious Implications of Batak Ceremonial Music." *Yearbook for Traditional Music* 25:81–88.

Sindoesawarno, Ki. 1987 [1955]. *The Science of Gamelan,* trans. Martin Hatch. In *Karawitan: Source Readings in Javanese Gamelan and Vocal Music,* ed. Judith Becker and Alan Feinstein, 2:389–407. Ann Arbor: Center for South and Southeast Asian Studies, University of Michigan.

Snelleman, J. F. 1918. "Muziek en Muziekinstrumentum in Nederlandsch Oost-Indië." In *Encyclopedie van Nederlandsch-Indië,* 24–26.

Snouck Hurgronje, C. 1906 [1893–c1894]. *The Acehnese.* Translated by A. W. S. O'Sullivan. 2 vols. Leiden: E. J. Brill.

Soedarsono. 1969. "Classical Javanese Dance: History and Characterization." *Ethnomusicology* 13(3):498–506.

———. 1974. *Dances in Indonesia.* Jakarta: Gunung Agung.

———. 1984. *Wayang Wong: The State Ritual Dance Drama in the Court of Yogyakarta.* Yogyakarta: Gadjah Mada University Press.

Sorrell, Neil. 1990. *A Guide to the Gamelan.* London: Faber & Faber.

Suanda, Endo. 1981. "The Social Context of Cirebonese Performing Artists." *Asian Music* 13(1):27–42.

———. 1986. "Cirebonese Topeng and Wayang of the Present Day." *Asian Music* 16(2):84–120.

———. 1988. "Dancing in Cirebonese Topeng." *Balungan* 3(3):7–15.

Suharto, Ben. 1990. "Dance Power: The Concept of Mataya in Yogyakarta Dance." M.A. thesis, University of California at Los Angeles.

Sumarsam. 1975a. "Inner Melody in Javanese Gamelan Music." *Asian Music* 7(1):3–13.

———. 1975b. "Gendèr Barung, Its Technique and Function in the Context of Javanese Gamelan." *Indonesia* 20:161–172.

———. 1981. "The Musical Practice of the Gamelan Sekatèn." *Asian Music* 12(2):54–73.

———. 1984a. "Gamelan Music and the Javanese Wayang Kulit." In *Aesthetic Tradition and Cultural Transition in Java and Bali,* ed. Stephanie Morgan and Laurie Jo Sears, 105–116. Madison: University of Wisconsin Center for Southeast Asian Studies.

———. 1984b. "Inner Melody in Javanese Gamelan." M.A. thesis, Wesleyan University. In *Karawitan: Source Readings in Javanese Gamelan and Vocal Music,* ed. Judith Becker and Alan Feinstein, 2:245–304. Ann Arbor: Center for South and Southeast Asian Studies, University of Michigan.

———. 1987. "Introduction to Ciblon Drumming in Javanese Gamelan." In *Karawitan: Source Readings in Javanese Gamelan and Vocal Music,* ed. Judith Becker and Alan Feinstein, 2:171–203. Ann Arbor: Center for South and Southeast Asian Studies, University of Michigan.

———. 1995. *Gamelan: Cultural Interaction and Musical Development in Central Java.* Chicago: University of Chicago Press.

Supanggah, Rahayu. 1985. "Introduction aux styles d'interpretation dans la musique javanaise." Ph.D. dissertation, University of Paris.

Surjodiningrat, R. M. Wasisto. 1970. *Gamelan, Dance and Wayang in Jogjakarta.* Yogyakarta: University of Gadjah Mada Press.

Surjodiningrat, R. M. Wasisto, P. J. Sudarjana, and Adhi Susanto. 1972. *Tone Measurements of Outstanding Javanese Gamelans in Jogjakarta and Surakarta.* Yogyakarta: Gadjah Mada University Press.

Suryabrata [Ijzerdraat], Bernard. 1987. *The Island of Music: An Essay in Social Musicology.* Jakarta: Balai Pustaka.

Susilo, Hardja. 1967. "Drumming in the Context of Javanese Gamelan." M.A. thesis, University of California at Los Angeles.

———. 1984. "Wayang Wong Panggung: Its Social Context, Technique, and Music." In *Aesthetic Tradition and Cultural Transition in Java and Bali,* ed. Stephanie Morgan and Laurie Jo Sears, 117–161. Madison: University of Wisconsin Center for Southeast Asian Studies.

———. 1989. "The Logogenesis of Gendhing Lampah." *Progress Reports in Ethnomusicology* 2(5).

Sutton, R. Anderson. 1975. "The Javanese Gambang and Its Music." M.A. thesis, University of Hawaii.

———. 1979. "Concept and Treatment in Javanese Gamelan Music, with Reference to the Gambang." *Asian Music* 9(2):59–79.

———. 1982. "Variation in Javanese Gamelan Music: Dynamics of a Steady State." Ph.D. dissertation, University of Michigan.

———. 1984a. "Who Is the *Pesindhèn?* Notes on the Female Singing Tradition in Java." *Indonesia* 37:118–131.

———. 1984b. "Change and Ambiguity: Gamelan Style and Regional Identity in Yogyakarta." In *Aesthetic Tradition and Cultural Transition in Java and Bali,* ed. Stephanie Morgan and Laurie Jo Sears, 221–245. Madison: University of Wisconsin Center for Southeast Asian Studies.

———. 1985a. "Musical Pluralism in Java: Three Local Traditions." *Ethnomusicology* 29(1):56–85.

———. 1985b. "Commercial Cassette Recordings of Traditional Music in Java: Implications for Performers and Scholars." *World of Music* 27(3):23–45.

———. 1986a. "The Crystallization of a Marginal Tradition: Music in Banyumas, West Central Java." *Yearbook for Traditional Music* 18:115–132.

———. 1986b. "New Theory for Traditional Music in Banyumas, West Central Java." *Pacific Review of Ethnomusicology* 3:79–101.

———. 1987. "Variation and Composition in Java." *Yearbook for Traditional Music* 19:65–95.

———. 1988. "Individual Variation in Javanese Gamelan Performance." *Journal of Musicology* 6(2):169–197.

———. 1989. "Identity and Individuality in an Ensemble Tradition: The Female Vocalist in Java." In *Women and Music in Cross-Cultural Perspective,* ed. Ellen Koskoff, 111–130. Urbana and Chicago: University of Illinois Press.

———. 1991a. *Traditions of Gamelan Music in Java: Musical Pluralism and Regional Identity.* Cambridge Studies in Ethnomusicology. Cambridge: Cambridge University Press.

———. 1991b. "Music of Indonesia." In *Aspects of Indonesian Culture,* ed. William Frederick. New York: Festival of Indonesia Foundation.

———. 1993a. *Variation in Central Javanese Gamelan Music: Dynamics of a Steady State.* Special reports, 28. De Kalb: Center for Southeast Asian Studies, Northern Illinois University.

———. 1993b. "Semang and Seblang: Thoughts on Music, Dance, and the Sacred in Central and East Java." In *Performance in Java and Bali: Studies of Narrative, Theatre, Music, and Dance,* ed. Bernard Arps, 121–143. London: School of Oriental and African Studies, University of London.

———. 1996. "Interpreting Electronic Sound Technology in the Contemporary Javanese Soundscape." *Ethnomusicology* 40(2):249– 268.

Suyenaga, Joan. 1984. "Patterns in Process: Java through Gamelan." In *Aesthetic Tradition and Cultural Transition in Java and Bali,* ed. Stephanie Morgan and Laurie Jo Sears, 83–104. Madison: University of Wisconsin Center for Southeast Asian Studies.

Taylor, Paul Michael, and Lorraine V. Aragon. 1991. *Beyond the Java Sea: Art of Indonesia's Outer Islands.* Washington, D.C.: National Museum of Natural History.

Tenzer, Michael. 1991. *Balinese Music.* Singapore: Periplus Editions.

Toth, Andrew F. 1970. "Music of the Gamelan Sekati." B.A. honors thesis, Wesleyan University.

———. 1975. "The Gamelan Luang of Tangkas, Bali." In *Selected Reports in Ethnomusicology* 2(2):65–80.

Tsuchiya, Kenji and James Siegel. 1990. "Invincible Kitsch or as Tourists in the Age of Des Alwi." *Indonesia* 50:61–76.

Turner, Ashley M. 1982. "Duri-Dana Music and Hoho Songs in South Nias." B.A. thesis, Monash University.

———. 1991. "Belian as a Symbol of Cosmic Reunification." In *Metaphor and Analogy: A Musical Dimension,* ed. Margaret Kartomi, 121–145. Sydney: Currency Press.

Valentijn, François. 1724–26. *Oud en Nieuw Oost-Indien, Vervattende een Naauwkeurige en Uitvoerige Verhandelinge van Nederlands Mogentheyd in die Gewesten, Benevens eene Wydlustige Beschryvinge der Moluccos, Amboine, Banda, Timor, en Solor, Java, etc.* 5 vols. Dordrecht: Joannes van Braam. Amsterdam: Gerard onder de Linden.

Valeri, Valerio. 1990. "Autonomy and Heteronomy in the Kahua Ritual: A Short Meditation on Huaulu Society." *Bijdragen tot de Taal-, Land- en Volkenkunde* 1:146:56–73.

van Dijk, Toos, and Nico de Jonge. 1990. "After Sunshine Comes Rain: A Comparative Analysis of Fertility Rituals in Marsela and Luang, South-East Moluccas." *Bijdragen tot de Taal-, Land- en Volkenkunde* 1:146:3–20.

van Hoëvell, G. W. W. C., Baron. 1875. *Ambon en Meer Bepaaldelijk de Oeliasers, Geografisch, Ethnographisch, Politisch en Historisch.* Dordrecht: Joannes van Braam. Amsterdam: Gerard onder de Linden.

van Zanten, Wim. 1984. "The Poetry of Tembang Sunda." *Bijdragen tot de taal-, Land- en volkendkunde* 140(2/3):289–316).

———. 1985. "Structure in the Panambih Pelog Songs of Tembang Sunda." In *Teken van Leven, Studies in Etnocommunicatie,* ed. Ad Boeren, Fransje Brinkgreve, and Sandy Roels, 187–198. Leiden: Instituut voor Culturele Antropologie en Sociologie der Niet-Westerse Volken.

———. 1986. "The Tone Material of the Kacapi in Tembang Sunda in West Java." *Ethnomusicology* 30(1):84–112.

———. 1989. *Sundanese Music in the Cianjuran Style: Anthropological and Musicological Aspects of Tembang Sunda.* Providence, R. I.: Foris Publications.

———. 1993. "Sung Epic Narrative and Lyrical Songs: Carita Pantun and Tembang Sunda." In *Performance in Java and Bali: Studies of Narrative, Theatre, Music, and Dance,* ed. Bernard Arps, 144–161. London: School of Oriental and African Studies, University of London.

———. 1994a. "Aspects of Baduy Singing." Paper presented at the workshop "Performing Arts in South-East Asia" at the Koninklijk Instituut voor Taal-, Land-, en Volkenkunde, Leiden University, Netherlands.

———. 1994b. "L'estétique Musicale de Sunda (Java-Ouest)." *Cahiers de Musiques Traditionnelles* 7:75–93.

———. 1995. "Aspects of Baduy Music in Its Sociocultural Context, with Special Reference to Singing and Angklung." *Bijdragen tot de Taal-, Land-, en Volkenkunde* 151:516–544.

van Zanten, Wim, and Marjolijn van Roon. 1995. "Notation of Music: Theory and Practice in West Java." *Oideion: The Performing Arts World-Wide* 2:209–233.

Vetter, Roger. 1977. "Formal Aspects of Performance Practice in Central Javanese Gamelan Music." M.A. thesis, University of Hawaii.

———. 1981. "Flexibility in the Performance Practice of Central Javanese Music." *Ethnomusicology* 25(2):199–214.

———. 1984. "Poetic, Musical and Dramatic Structures in a Langen Mandra Wanara Performance." In *Aesthetic Tradition and Cultural Transition in Java and Bali,* ed. Stephanie Morgan and Laurie Jo Sears, 163–208. Madison: University of Wisconsin Center for Southeast Asian Studies.

———. 1986. "Music for 'The Lap of the World': Gamelan Performance, Performers, and Repertoire in the Kraton Yogyakarta." Ph.D. dissertation, University of Wisconsin at Madison.

———. 1989. "A Retrospect on a Century of Gamelan Tone Measurements." *Ethnomusicology* 33(2):217–227.

Vetter, Valerie Mau. 1984. "In Search of Panji." In *Aesthetic Tradition and Cultural Transition in Java and Bali,* ed. Stephanie Morgan and Laurie Jo Sears, 31–50. Madison: University of Wisconsin Center for Southeast Asian Studies.

Vickers, Adrian. 1985. "The Realm of the Senses: Images of the Court Music of Pre-Colonial Bali." *Imago Musicae* 2:43–77.

Vitale, Wayne. 1990. "Kotekan: The Technique of Interlocking Parts in Balinese Music." *Balungan* 4(2):2–15.

Wagner, Frits A. 1959. *Indonesia: The Art of an Island Group.* New York: Crown.

Wallace, Alfred Russel. 1869. *The Malay Archipelago.* London: Macmillan.

Wallis, Richard Herman. 1979. "The Voice as a Mode of Cultural Expression in Bali." Ph.D. dissertation, University of Michigan.

Walton, Susan Pratt. 1987. *Mode in Javanese Music.* Athens: Ohio University Center for International Studies.

Warsadiningrat. 1987 [1972]. *Sacred Knowledge about Gamelan Music.* Translated by Susan P. Walton. In *Karawitan: Source Readings in Javanese Gamelan and Vocal Music,* ed. Judith Becker and Alan Feinstein, 2:1–170. Ann Arbor: Center for South and Southeast Asian Studies, University of Michigan.

Weijden, Gera van der. 1981. *Indonesische Reisrituale.* Basler Beiträge zur Ethnologie, 20. Basel: Ethnologisches Seminar der Universität und Museum für Völkerkunde.

Weintraub, Andrew. 1990. "The Music of Pantun Sunda: An Epic Narrative Tradition of West Java, Indonesia." M.A. thesis, University of Hawaii.

———. 1993. "Theory as Institutionalized Pedagogy and 'Theory in Practice' for Sundanese Gamelan Music." *Ethnomusicology* 37(1):29– 40.

———. 1993-94. "Tune, Text, and the Function of Lagu in Pantun Sunda, a Sundanese Oral Narrative Tradition." *Asian Music* 26(1):175–211.

Weiss, Sarah. 1993. "Gender and Gendèr: Gender Ideology and the Female Gendèr Player in Central Java." In *Rediscovering the Muses: Women's Musical Traditions,* ed. Kimberly Marshall, 21–48. Boston: Northeastern University Press.

Wenten, I. Nyoman. 1996. "The Creative World of Ki Wasitodipuro: The Life and Work of a Javanese Composer." Ph.D. dissertation, University of California at Los Angeles.

Wessing, Robert. 1977. "The Position of the Baduy in the Larger West Javanese Society." *Man* 12(2):293–303.

———. 1978. *Cosmology and Social Behavior in a West Javanese Settlement.* Athens: Ohio University Center for International Studies, Southeast Asia Program.

———. 1990. "Sri and Sedana and Sita and Rama: Myths of Fertility and Generation." In *Asian Folklore Studies* 49(2):235–257.

Wilken, G. A. 1912. "Het animisme bij de volken van den Indischen Archipel." In *De Verspreide Geschriften van Prof. Dr. G. A. Wilken,* ed. F. D. E. van Ossenbruggen, 3–287. Semarang: G. C. T. van Dorp.

Williams, Sean. 1989. "Current Developments in Sundanese Popular Music." *Asian Music* 21(1):105–136.

———. 1990. "The Urbanization of *Tembang Sunda,* an Aristocratic Musical Genre of West Java, Indonesia." Ph.D. dissertation, University of Washington.

Wolbers, Paul Arthur. 1986. "*Gandrung* and *Angklung* from Banyuwangi: Remnants of a Past Shared with Bali." *Asian Music* 18(1):71–90.

———. 1987. "Account of an *Angklung Caruk,* July 28, 1985." *Indonesia* 43:66–74.

———. 1989. "Transvestism, Eroticism, and Religion: In Search of a Contextual Background for the *Gandrung* and *Seblang* Traditions of Banyuwangi, East Java." *Progress Reports in Ethnomusicology* 2(6).

———. 1992. "Maintaining and Using Identity through Musical Performance: *Seblang* and *Gandrung* of Banyuwangi, East Java (Indonesia)." Ph.D. dissertation, University of Illinois at Urbana-Champaign.

Wongsosewojo, R. Ahmad. 1930. "Loedroek." *Djawa* 10:204–207.

Wright, Michael R. 1978. "The Music Culture of Cirebon." Ph.D. dissertation, University of California at Los Angeles.

———. 1988. "Tarling: Modern Music from Cirebon." *Balungan* 3(3):21– 25.

Yampolsky, Philip. 1987. *Lokananta: A Discography of the National Recording Company of Indonesia, 1957–1985.* Madison: University of Wisconsin Center for Southeast Asian Studies.

———. 1989. "*Hati Yang Luka:* An Indonesian Hit." *Indonesia* 47:1–17.

———. 1991a. *Music of Indonesia 2: Indonesian Popular Music.* Washington, D.C.: Smithsonian / Folkways SFCD 40056. Liner notes.

———. 1991b. *Music of Indonesia 3: Music from the Outskirts of Jakarta: Gambang Kromong.* Washington, D.C.: Smithsonian / Folkways SFCD 40057. Liner notes.

———. 1995a. *Music of Indonesia 8: Vocal and Instrumental Music from East and Central Flores.* Washington, D.C.: Smithsonian / Folkways SFCD 40424. Compact disc and liner notes.

———. 1995b. *Music of Indonesia 9: Vocal Music from Central and West Flores.* Washington, D.C.: Smithsonian / Folkways SFCD 40425. Compact disc and liner notes.

Yaningsih, Dra. Sri, Umar Siradz, and I Gusti Bagus Mahartha. 1988. *Peralatan Hiburan dan Kesenian Tradisional Daerah Nusa Tenggara Barat.* Mataram: Departemen Pendidikan dan Kebudayaan.

Borneo

Alman, J. H. 1961. "If You Can't Sing, You Can Beat a Gong." *Journal of the Sabah Society* 1:29–41.

Bastin, J. 1971. "Brass Kettledrums in Sabah." *Bulletin of the School of African and Oriental Studies* 24(1):132.

Brunei Delegation. 1974. "A Short Survey of Brunei Gulintangan Orchestra." In *Traditional Music and Drama of Southeast Asia,* ed. Mohd. Taib Osman, 198–308. Kuala Lumpur: Dewan Bahasa dan Pustaka.

Chong, Julia. 1989. "Towards the Integration of Sarawak Traditional Instruments into 20th Century Malaysian Music." *Sarawak Museum Journal* 40(61):125–130.

Crump, Juliette T. 1991. "Some Features of the Solo Dance that Maintain its Viability for Tribes in Transition in Sarawak." *Sarawak Museum Journal* 42(63):159–176.

Davis, G.C. 1960. "Borneo Bisaya Music in Western Ears." *Sarawak Museum Journal* 9(15-16):496–498.

Frame, Edward. 1975. "A Preliminary Survey of Several Major Musical Instruments and Form Types of Sabah, Malaysia." *Borneo Research Bulletin* 7(1):16–24.

———. 1976. "Major Musical Forms in Sabah." *Journal of the Royal Asiatic Society, Malaysian Branch* 49(2):156–163.

———.1982. "The Musical Instruments of Sabah, Malaysia." *Ethnomusicology* 26(2):247–274.

Galvin, A. Dennis. 1962. "Five Sorts of Sarawak and Kalimantan Kenyah Song." *Sarawak Museum Journal* 10:501–510.

———. 1966. "Some Baram Kenyah Songs." *Sarawak Museum Journal* 14:6–14.

———. 1968. "Mamat Chants and Ceremonies, Long Moh." *Sarawak Museum Journal* 32-33:235–248.

———. 1972. "A *Sebop* Dirge (Sung on the Occasion of the Death of Tama Jangan by Belawing Lupa)." *Brunei Museum Journal* 2(4):1–158.

———. 1975a. "Suket (Long Julan)." *Brunei Museum Journal* 3(3):13– 19.

———. 1975b. "Two Kenyah Love Songs." *Brunei Museum Journal* 3(3):20–26.

Georgie, E. 1959. "A Dayak (Love) Song." *Sarawak Museum Journal* 9(13-14):21–24.

Gorlinski, Virginia K. 1988. "Some Insights into the Art of Sapé Playing." *Sarawak Museum Journal* 39(60):77–104.

———. 1989a. "*Pangpagaq:* Religious and Social Significance of a Traditional Kenyah Music-Dance Form." *Sarawak Museum Journal* 40, 61, new series, part 3:280–301.

———. 1989b. "The Sampéq of East Kalimantan, Indonesia: A Case Study of the Recreational Music Tradition." M.A. thesis, University of Hawaii.

———. 1994 "Gongs among the Kenyah Uma' Jalan: Past and Present Position of an Instrumental Tradition." *Yearbook for Traditional Music* 26:81–99.

———. 1995. "Songs of Honor, Words of Respect: Social Contours of *Kenyah Lepo' Tau* Versification, Sarawak, Malaysia." Ph.D. dissertation, University of Wisconsin.

Harrisson, Tom. 1949. "Singing Prehistory." *Journal of the Royal Asiatic Society, Malayan Branch* 22(1):123–142.

———. 1966. "A Kalimantan Writing Board and the Mamat Festival." *Sarawak Museum Journal* 13:287–295.

Hood, Mantle. 1980. "Outer Islands: Borneo (Kalimantan)." *The New Grove Dictionary of Music and Musicians,* ed. Stanley Sadie. London: Macmillan.

Hudson, Judith M. 1971. "Some Observations on Dance in Kalimantan." *Indonesia* 12:133–150.

Koizumi, Fumio, ed. 1976. *Asian Musics in an Asian Perspective, Report of Asian Traditional Performing Arts.* Tokyo: Heibonsha.

Leach, Edmund. 1950. *Social Science Research in Sarawak.* London: Her Majesty's Stationery Office.

Liew, Richard. 1962. "Music and Musical Instruments in Sabah." *Journal of the Sabah College Borneo Society* 3:10.

Maceda, José. 1962. "Field-Recording Sea-Dayak Music." *Sarawak Museum Journal* 10(19-20):486–500.

———. 1977. "Report of a Music Workshop in East Kalimantan." *Borneo Research Bulletin* 10(2):83–103.

Masing, James Jemut. 1981. "The Coming of the Gods: A Study of the Invocatory Chant *(Timang Gawai Amat)* of the Iban of the Baleh Region of Sarawak." Ph.D. dissertation, Australian National University.

Matusky, Patricia. 1986. "Aspects of Musical Style among the Kajang, Kayan and Kenyah-Badang of the Upper Rejang River: A Preliminary Survey." *Sarawak Museum Journal* 36:185–229.

———. 1989. "Ethnomusicology and the Musical Heritage of Sarawak: Implications for the Future." *Sarawak Museum Journal* 40(61):131–149.

———. 1990. "Music Styles among the Kayan, Kenyah-Badang, and Malay Peoples of the Upper Rejang River (Sarawak): A Preliminary Survey." *Sarawak Museum Journal* 41(62):115–149.

———. 1991. "Musical Instruments of the Indigenous Peoples." In *Sarawak Cultural Legacy,* ed. Lucas Chin, 232–246. Kuching, Sarawak: Society Atelier Sarawak.

Maxwell, Allen R. 1989. "A Survey of the Oral Traditions of Sarawak." *Sarawak Museum Journal* 40(61):167–208.

Myers, Charles Samuel. 1913. "A Study of Sarawak Music." *Sammelbände der Internationalen Muzikgesellschaft* 15:296–308.

Ongkili, James P. 1974. "The Traditional Musical Instruments of Sabah." In *Traditional Music and Drama of Southeast Asia,* ed. Mohd. Taib Osman, 327–335. Kuala Lumpur: Dewan Bahasa dan Pustaka.

Revel-Macdonald, Nicole. 1978. "La danse des hudoq (Kalimantan-Timur)." *Objets et Mondes* 18(1–2):31–44.

———. 1981. "Masks in Kalimantan Timur." *The World of Music* 23(3):52–56.

Roth, Henry Ling. 1980 [1896]. *The Natives of Sarawak and British North Borneo.* 2 vols. London: Truslove and Hanson; Kuala Lumpur: University of Malaya Press.

Rousseau, Jérôme. 1989a. "The People of Central Borneo." *Sarawak Museum Journal* 40, 61 (new series), part 3:7–17.

———. 1989b. *Central Borneo: Ethnic Identity and Social Life in a Stratified Society.* London: Oxford University Press.

Rubenstein, Carol. 1973. "Poems of Indigenous Peoples of Sarawak: Some of the Songs and Chants." Special Monograph. *Sarawak Museum Journal* 21(42).

———. 1985. *The Honey Tree Song, Poems and Chants of Sarawak Dayaks.* Athens, Ohio, and London: Ohio University Press.

———. 1989a. "Some Notes and Long Songs of the Dayak Oral Literature." *Sarawak Gazette* 115(1508):21–28.

———. 1989b. "'For Marrying Lian during Durian Season': A Song of the Penan Urun." *Sarawak Gazette* 115(1509):22–30.

———. 1990a. *The Nightbird Sings: Chants and Songs of Sarawak Dayaks.* Dumfriesshire, Scotland: Tynron Press.

———. 1990b. "'Like Early Mist': Five Songs of the Penan Urun." *Sarawak Museum Journal* 41(62):151–188.

———. 1990c. "'So Unable to Speak Am I . . .': Sarawak Dayaks and Forms of Social Address in Song." *Asian Music* 21(2):1–37.

Sandin, Benedict. 1974. "Iban Music." In *Traditional Music and Drama of Southeast Asia,* ed. Mohd. Taib Osman, 320–326. Kuala Lumpur: Dewan Bahasa dan Pustaka.

Seeler, Joan DeWitt. 1969. "Some Notes on Traditional Dances of Sarawak." *Sarawak Museum Journal* 17:163–201.

———. 1975. "Kenyah Dance, Sarawak, Malaysia: A Description and Analysis." M.A. thesis, University of Hawai'i.

———. 1977. "Research on Kenyah Dance: Reason and Method." *Sarawak Museum Journal* 25:165–175.

Skog, Inge. 1993. *North Borneo Gongs and the Javanese Gamelan: Studies in Southeast Asian Gong Traditions.* Studies in Musicology, 2. Stockholm: Stockholms Universitet.

Soedarsono. 1968. *Dances in Indonesia.* Jakarta: P. T. Gunung Agung.

Strickland, S. S. 1988. "Preliminary Notes on a Kejaman-Sekapan Oral Narrative Form." *Sarawak Museum Journal* 39, 60, new series:67–75.

Wan Ulok, Stephen, and A. Dennis Galvin. 1955. "A Kenyah Song." *Sarawak Museum Journal* 6:287–289.

Williams, Thomas Rhys. 1961. "Form, Function and Culture History of a Borneo Musical Instrument." *Oceania* 32:178–186.

Philippines

Abubakar, Carmen. 1983. "Islamization of Southern Philippines: An Overview." In *Filipino Muslims: Their Social Institutions and Cultural Achievements,* ed. F. Landa Jocano, 6–13. Diliman: Asian Center, University of the Philippines.

Bañas y Castillo, Raymundo C. 1975. *Filipino Music and Theater.* Quezon City: Manlapaz Publishing.

Beyer, Henry Otley. 1948. "Philippine and East Asian Archeology." *National Research Council of the Philippines* 29 (December):1–82.

Blair, Emma Helen, and James Alexander Robertson, eds. 1973 [1903]. *The Philippine Islands 1493–1898.* 55 vols. Mandaluyong: Cachos Hermanosted.

Butocan, Aga Mayo. 1987. *Palabunibunyan: A Repertoire of Musical Pieces for the Maguindanaon Kulintangan.* Manila: Philippine Women's University.

Cadar, Usopay Hamdag. 1975. "The Role of Kulintang Music in Maranao Society." *Selected Reports in Ethnomusicology* 2(2):49–62.

———. 1980. "Context and Style in the Vocal Music of the Muranao in Mindanao, Philippines." Ph.D. dissertation, University of Washington.

———. 1996a. "The Role of Kolintang Music in Maranao Society." *Asian Music* 27(2):81–104.

———. 1996b. "Maranao Kolintang Music and Its Journey in America." *Asian Music* 27(2):131–148.

Cadar, Usopay Hamdag, and Robert Garfias. 1974. "Some Principles of Formal Variation in the Kolintang Music of the Maranao." *Ethnomusicology* 18(1):43–55.

Cadar, Usopay Hamdag, and Robert Garfias. 1996. "Some Principles of Formal Variation in the Kolintang Music of the Maranao." *Asian Music* 27(2):105–122.

Casiño, Eric. 1976. *The Jama Mapun: A Changing Samal Society in Southern Philippines.* Quezon City: Ateneo de Manila University Press.

Castro y Amadeo, Pedro de. 1790. "Historia de la Provincia de Batangas por Don Pedro Andrés de Castro y Amadeo en sus viajes y contraviajes en toda esta Provincia año de 1790." Madrid: MS Archivo Nacional, Códice 931, 7.

Chung, Lilia Hernandez. 1979. *Jovita Fuentes: A Lifetime of Music.* Manila: Jovita Fuentes Musicultural Society.

de la Concepción, Juan. 1788–1792. *Historia general de las islas Filipinas.* Manila: Agustín de la Rosa y Balagtas.

Conservatory of Music, University of the Philippines: 1916–1960. 1960. Quezon City: University of the Philippines Conservatory of Music.

de León, Felipe Padilla. 1977. "Banda Uno, Banda Dos." *Filipino Heritage: The Making of a Nation,* 8.

Dioquino, Corazón C. 1982. "Musicology in the Philippines." *Acta Musicologica* 54:124–147.

Dulawan, Manuel. 1970s. "Tuwali Oral Folk Literature." University of the Philippines, College of Music, Department of Music Research. Typescript.

Ellis, Henry T. 1856. *Hongkong to Manila and the Lakes of Luzon in the Philippine Islands in the Year 1856.* London: Smith, Elder.

Eugenio, Damiana. 1987. *Awit and Corrido: Philippine Metrical Romances.* Quezon City: University of the Philippines Press.

Fernández, Doreen G. 1978. *The Iloilo Zarzuela 1903–1930.* Quezon City: Ateneo de Manila University Press.

———. 1981 [1905]. "Introduction." In *The Filipino Drama,* ed. Arthur Stanley Riggs. Manila: Ministry of Human Settlements.

Fernando-Amilbangsa, Ligaya. 1983. *Pangalay: Traditional Dances and Related Folk Artistic Expressions.* Los Angeles: Philippine Expressions.

Fox, Robert. 1959. *The Philippines in Pre-Historic Times: A Handbook for the First National Exhibition of Filipino Prehistory and Culture.* Manila: UNESCO National Commission of the Philippines.

———. 1961. "Social Aspects of the Rice-Wine Complex among the Tagbanwa of Palawan Island, Philippines." Typescript.

———. 1977. "Manunggul Cave." *Filipino Heritage* 1:169–173.

Francisco, Juan R. 1993. "The Ramayana in the Philippines." In *Ang Paglalakbay ni Radiya Mangandiri.* Souvenir Program, Philippine Educational Theater Association Kalinangan Ensemble.

Georsua, Racquel. 1987. "Traditional Practices among the Subanen in Lapuyan, Zamboanga del Sur, with Special Reference to Music." M.A. thesis, University of the Philippines.

Kalundayan, Danongan S. 1996. "Instruments, Instrumentation, and Social Context of Maguindanaon Kulintang Music." *Asian Music* 27(2):3–18.

Kiefer, Thomas. 1970. *Music from the Tausug of Sulu.* Bloomington: Indiana University. LP disk and liner notes.

Lambrecht, Francis. 1967. "The Hudhud of Dinulawan and Bugan at Gondahan." *Saint Louis University Journal* 5(3–4):267–713.

Larkin, John. 1978. "The Capampangan Zarzuela: Theatre for a Provincial Elite." In *Southeast Asian Transitions: Approaches through Social History,* ed. Ruth T. McVey, 186–189. New Haven, Conn.: Yale University Press.

Laureola, Asuncion. 1971. "Musical References from Books Published before 1900 in the U.P. Filipiniana Library." M.Mus. thesis, University of the Philippines.

Maceda, José M. 1963. "The Music of the Maguindanao in the Philippines." Ph.D. dissertation, University of California at Los Angeles.

———, ed. 1971. *Musics of Asia.* Manila: National Music Council of the Philippines and UNESCO.

———. 1973. "Music in the Philippines in the 19th Century." In *Musikkulturen Asiens, Afrikas und Ozeaniens im 19. Jahrhundert,* ed. Robert Gunther, 216–232. Regensburg: Gustave Bosse.

———. 1974. "Drone and Melody in Philippine Musical Instruments." In *Traditional Drama and Music of Southeast Asia,* ed. Mohd. Taib Osman, 246–273. Kuala Lumpur: Kementerian Pelajaran Malaysia.

———. 1984. "A Cure of the Sick Bpagipat in Dulawan, Cotabato (Philippines)." *Acta Musicologica* 56:93–105.

———, ed. 1988. *Kulintang and Kudyapiq: Gong Ensemble and Two-String Lute among the Maguindanaon in Mindanao Philippines.* University of the Philippines. 2 LP disks and liner notes.

———. 1990. "In Search of a Source of Pentatonic Hemitonic and Anhemitonic Scales in Southeast Asia." *Acta Musicologica* 72(2–3):192–223.

Maceda, José M., and Alain Martenot. 1976. *Sama de Sitangkai.* Office de la Récherche Scientifique et Technique Outre-Mer (Société de la Récherche Linguistiques et Anthropologiques de France). LP disk and liner notes.

Majul, Cesar Adib. 1974. "The Muslims in the Philippines: An Historical Perspective." In *The Muslim Filipinos: Their History, Society and Contemporary Problems,* ed. Peter Gowing and Robert McAmis, 1– 12. Manila: La Solidaridad.

Mallat, Jean Baptiste. 1846. *Les Philippines: Histoire, Géographie, Moeurs, Agriculture, Industrie et Commerce des Colonies Espagnoles dans l'Oceanie.* 2 vols. Paris: Imprimerie de Madame Veuve Bouchard-Hazard.

Manuel, E. Arsenio. 1958. *The Maiden of the Buhong Sky, a Complete Song from the Bagobo Epic Tuwaang.* Quezon City: University of the Philippines.

———. 1978. "Towards an Inventory of Philippine Musical Instruments." *Asian Studies* 1978:1–72.

Mantaring, Melissa. 1983. "Philippine Musical References from the Lopez Museum 1601–1848."

M.Mus. thesis, University of the Philippines.

Maranan, Edgardo, E. Arsenio Manuel, and Jonathan Chua. 1994. "Epic." In *Philippine Literature,* ed. Nicanor G. Tiongson. CCP Encyclopedia of Philippine Art, 9. Manila: Cultural Center of the Philippines.

Martínez de Zúñiga, Joaquín. 1893. *Estadismo de las Islas Filipinas y mis Viajes por este País.* Madrid: Imprenta de la Viuda de M. Minuesa de los Rios.

Mas, Sinibaldo de. 1843. *Informe Sobre el Estado de las Islas Filipinas en 1842.* Madrid.

McFarland, Curtis D. 1983. *A Linguistic Atlas of the Philippines.* Manila: Linguistic Society of the Philippines.

Mednick, Melvin. 1957. "Some Problems of Moro History and Political Organization." *Philippine Sociological Review* 5(1):39–52.

de la Merced, Aniceto. 1852. *El libro de la vida: historia sagrado con santas reflexiones y doctrinas morales para la vida cristiana en verso tagalo* (The book of life: sacred history with pious reflections and moral teachings for the Christian life written in Tagalog verse). Manila: Librería y Papelaría de J. Martínez.

Molina, Antonio J. 1977. "The Sentiments of Kundiman." *Filipino Heritage* 8:2026–29.

Molina, Exequiel. 1977. "The Philippine Pop Music Scene." *Asian Culture* 15:21–24.

Ness, Sally A. 1995. "When Seeing Is Believing: The Changing Role of Visuality in a Philippine Dance." *Anthropological Quarterly* 68(1):1– 13.

Nicolas, Arsenio. 1987. "Ritual Transformations and Musical Parameters: A Study of Selected Headhunting Rites in the Southern Cordillera, Northern Luzon." M.A. thesis, University of the Philippines.

Otto, Steven W. 1985. *The Muranao Kakolintang: An Approach to the Repertoire.* Marawi City: Mindanao State University.

———. 1996. "Repertorial Nomenclature in Muranao Kolintang Music." *Asian Music* 27(2):123–130.

Paterno, Pedro. 1893. *El Individuo Tagalo y su Arte.* Madrid: Imprenta de los Sucesores de Cuesta.

Patricio, María Cristina. 1955. "The Development of the Rondalla in the Philippines." Research paper, University of the Philippines.

Pfeiffer, William. 1976. *Filipino Music: Indigenous, Folk, Modern.* Dumaguete City: Silliman Music Foundation.

Posner, Karen. 1996. "A Preliminary Analysis of Maguindanaon Kulintang Music." *Asian Music* 27(2):19–32.

Prudente, Fe. 1986. "Musical Process in the Gasumbi Epic of the Buwaya Kalinga People of Northern Philippines." Ph.D. dissertation, University of Michigan.

Puya y Ruiz, Adolfo. 1838. *Filipinas: Descripción General de la Provincia de Bulacan.* Manila: R. Mercantil de Diaz Puertas.

Reid, Laurence. 1961. "A Guinaang Wedding Ceremony, Dancing and Music." *Philippine Sociological Review* 9(3–4):1–84.

Revel, Nicole. 1987. *Philippines, Musique des Hautes Terres Palawan.* CNRS, Le Chant du Monde LDX 74 865. LP disk and liner notes.

Retana, Wenceslao Emilio. 1888. *El Indio Batnagueno.* 3rd ed. Manila: Tipo Litografía de Chofre y Cía.

———. 1895–1905. *Archivo del Bibliófile Filipino. Recopilación de documentos históricos, científicos, literarios y políticos, y estudios bibliográficos.* 4 vols. Madrid: Imprenta de la Viuda de M. Minuesa de los Rios.

Ronquillo, Wilfredo. 1987. "The Butuan Archeological Finds: Profound Implications for Philippines and Southeast Asian History." *Man and Culture in Oceania* 3:71–78.

Saint Scholastica's College. 1992. *A Harvest in Sprung Rhythm: St. Scholastica's College School of Music 1907–1992.* Anniversary pamphlet. Manila.

Samson, Helen. 1972. "Extant Music in the Zarzuelas of Severino Reyes." M.Mus. thesis, University of the Philippines.

San Nicolás, Fray Andrés de. 1973. "General History of the Discalced Augustinian Fathers." In *The Philippine Islands 1493–1898,* ed. Emma Helen Blair and James Alexander Robertson, 21:111–317. Mandaluyong: Cachos Hermanos.

San Agustín, Gaspar de. 1890. *Conquistas de las Islas Filipinas.* Villadolid: Luis N. de Gavira.

Santos, Ramón P. 1992. "Nationalism in Philippine Music during the Japanese Occupation: Art or Propaganda?" *Panahon ng Hapon* (Japanese Time) 2:93–106.

———. 1994. "The American Colonial and Contemporary Traditions." In *Music,* ed. Corazon C. Dioquino and Ramon P. Santos. CCP Encyclopedia of Philippine Art, 6. Manila: Cultural Center of the Philippines.

Scholz, Scott. 1996. "The Supportive Instruments of the Maguindanaon Kulintang Ensemble." *Asian Music* 27(2):33–52.

Stewart, A. M. 1831. *A Visit to the South Seas in the U.S. Ship Vincennes, during the Years 1829 and 1830 with Scenes in Brazil, Peru, Manilla, the Cape of Good Hope, and St. Helena.* Vol. 2. New York: John P. Haven.

Stone, Richard L. 1962. "Intergroup Relations among the Tausug, Samal and Badjaw of Sulu." *Philippine Sociological Review* 10(3–4):107– 133.

Terada, Yoshitaka. 1996. "Variational and Improvisational Techniques of Gandingan Playing in the Magindanaon Kulintang Ensemble." *Asian Music* 27(2):53–80.

Tiongson, Nicanor G., ed. 1991. *The Cultural Traditional Media of the Philippines.* Manila: ASEAN and the Cultural Center of the Philippines.

———, ed. 1994. *Philippine Literature.* CCP

Encyclopedia of Philippine Art, 9. Manila: Cultural Center of the Philippines.

Trimillos, Ricardo D. 1972. "Tradition and Repertory in the Cultivated Music of the Tausug of Sulu, Philippines." Ph.D. dissertation, University of California at Los Angeles.

Walls y Merino, Manuel. 1982. *La Musica Popular de Filipinas.* Madrid: Libreto de Fernando Fe. LP disk and liner notes.

A Guide to Recordings of Southeast Asian Music

MAINLAND SOUTHEAST ASIA

Collections

Music of Southeast Asia. 1956. Compiled by Harold Courlander. Commentary by Henry Cowell. Smithsonian/Folkways 04423. LP disk, cassette.

Cambodia

Apsara: The Feminine in Cambodian Art. 1987. Los Angeles: The Woman's Building Gallery. Cassette.

Cambodge. 1976. Recording and commentary by Jacques Brunet. Musiques de l'Asie Traditionnelle, 1. Playasound PS 33501. LP disk.

Cambodge: Musique classique khmère, théâtre d'ombres et chants de mariage. 1995. Recording and commentary by Loch Chhanchhai and Pierre Bois. Paris: Inedit, Maison des Cultures du Monde W 260002. Compact disc.

Cambodge: Musique instrumentale. 1973. Recording by Jacques Brunet and Hubert de Fraysseix. Commentary by Jacques Brunet. Musiques et Traditions du Monde. CBS 65522. LP disk.

Cambodia. 1990. Commentary in French by Catherine Basset, based on remarks by Jacques Brunet. Translated into English by Jeffrey Grice. Translated into Italian by Marie-Christine Reverte. Translated into German by Brigitte Nelles. Music of the Ramayana, 2. Ocora Radio France C 560015. Compact disc.

Cambodia: Folk and Ceremonial Music. 1996. Musical Atlas. Recording and commentary by Jacques Brunet. Auvidis-Unesco D-8068. Compact disc.

Cambodia: Music of the Exile. 1992. The Orchestra of the Khmer Classical Dance Troupe. Recording by Jean-Daniel Bloesch and Khao-I-Dang. Commentary by Giovanni Giurate with Jean-Daniel Bloesch. VDE-Gallo 698. Compact disc.

Cambodia: Music of the Royal Palace (The 1960s). 1994. Commentary in French by Jacques Brunet. Translated into English by Peter Lee. Translated into German by Volker Haller. Ocora Radio France C 560034. Compact disc.

Cambodia: Royal Music. 1971–1989. Recording and commentary by Jacques Brunet. Musics and Musicians of the World. International Music Council. Auvidis / Unesco D 8011. Compact disc.

Cambodian Mohori: Khmer Entertainment Music. 1991. Sam-Ang Sam Ensemble. World Music Institute WMI-015. Cassette.

Cambodian Traditional Music in Minnesota. 1983. World Music Enterprises. Cassette.

Court Dance of Cambodia. 1994. Recording by Teodor Octavio Graca. Commentary by Sam-Ang Sam. AVL 95001. Compact disc.

Echoes from the Palace: Court Music of Cambodia: Sam-Ang Sam Ensemble. 1996. Recording and commentary by Sam-ang Sam. Music of the World CDT-140. Compact disc.

Instrumental and Vocal Pieces. 1978. Recording and commentary by Chinary Ung. Cambodia Traditional Music, 1. Folkways FE 4081. LP disk.

Mohori: Sam Ang Sam Ensemble. 1997. World Music Institute and Music of the World. Latitudes LAT50609.

The Music of Cambodia. 196? Recording and commentary by Alain Daniélou. Musical Anthology of the Orient. Bärenreiter-Musicaphon BM 30 L 2002. LP disk.

Music of Cambodia. 1989. The Sam-Ang Sam Ensemble. The New Americans. World Music Institute WMI-0 007. Cassette.

Musicians of the National Dance Company of Cambodia: Homrong. 1991. Recording by Richard Blair. Lyrics transcribed by students of the Fine Arts University of Phnom Penh. Lyrics translated by Sam Phany and Bill Lobban. Real World Records 2–91734. Compact disc.

Musiques du Cambodge des Forêts. 1975. Commentary by Bernard Dupaigne. Anthologie de la Musique de Peuples. AMP 2902. LP disk.

9 Gong Gamelan Recorded inside Angkor Wat. 1993. Recording by David and Kay Parsons. Commentary by John Schaefer. The Music of

Cambodia, 1. Celestial Harmonies 13074–2. Compact disk.

Royal Court Music Recorded in Phnom Penh. 1992. Recording by David and Kay Parsons. Commentary by John Schaefer. The Music of Cambodia, 2. Celestial Harmonies 13075–2. Compact disc.

Solo Instrumental Music Recorded in Phnom Penh. 1994. Recording by David and Kay Parsons. Commentary by John Schaefer. The Music of Cambodia, 3. Celestial Harmonies. 13076–2. Compact disc.

Silent Temple, Songful Hearts: Traditional Music of Cambodia. 1991. Sam-Ang Sam and Ensemble. World Music Press WMP-008. Cassette.

Traditional Music of Cambodia. 1987. Sam-Ang Sam. Recording and commentary by Sam-Ang Sam. MC-SS-NR001. LP disk.

Tribe Music, Folk Music and Popular Dances. 1979. Recording and commentary by Chinary Ung. Cambodia Traditional Music, 2. Folkways FE 4082. LP disk.

Thailand

Ceremonial Music of Thailand: Music for Sacred Rituals and Theatre. 1989. Siamese Music Ensemble. Pacific Music Co. 8.260581. Compact disc.

Classical Music of Thailand. 1991. World Music Library. King Record Co. KICC 5125. Compact disc.

Dontri Chao Sayam—Traditional Folk Music of Siam. 1993. Produced by Saeng Arun Arts Centre. SAACI CD 001–006. 6 compact discs.

Drums of Thailand. 1974. Compiled by Princess Chumbhot of Nagor Svarga. Folkways FE 4215B. LP disk.

En Thaïlande: La Musique Traditionnelle des Môn. 1979. Ocora 558.535. LP disk.

The Flower of Isan: Songs and Music from North-East Thailand. 1989. Commentary by Ginny Landgraf. Ace Records CDORBD 051. Compact disc.

Instrumental Music of Northeast Thailand. 1991. World Music Library. King Record Co. KICC 5124. Compact disc.

Karenni: Music from the Border areas of Thailand and Burma. 1994. Recording and commentary by Fred Gales. Paradox Records. PAN 2040CD. Compact disc.

The La hu nyi of Thailand. 197? Recording by Gretel Schworer-Kohl and Hans Oesch. Commentary by Gretel Schworer-Kohl. Bärenreiter-Musicaphon BM 30 L 2572. LP disk.

Lao Music of the Northeast. 1981. Recording and commentary by Terry E. Miller. Lyrichord LLST 7357. LP disk.

Maan Mongkhon: an Auspicious Piece in the Burmese Style. 1997. Thai Music Circle (London). Pan Records 2049. Compact disc.

The Mahori Orchestra. 1994. Fong Naam. Commentary by Prasarn Wongwirojruk and Bruce Gaston. Siamese Classical Music, 5. HNH International. Marco Polo 8.223493. Compact disc.

Mo Lam Singing of Northeast Thailand. 1991. Chawiwan Damnoen and Thongkham Thaikla. World Music Library. King Record Co. KICC 5123. Compact disc.

Les Môns de Thaïlande. 1976. Hum Rong Krathai Ten. Musiques et Traditions du Monde. CBS 81389. LP disk.

Music of Minorities in the Northwestern Thailand. 1980. Recording and commentary by Ruriko Uchida. Translated by Gen'ichi Tsuge. Victor SJ 1010 2. LP disk.

Music of Northeast Thailand. 1992. Chagkachan. Commentary in Japanese by Sentoku Miho. Translated by Larry Richards. World Music Library. King Record Co. KICC 5159. Compact disc.

Music of Thailand. 1959. Recording and commentary by Howard K. Kaufman. Folkways FE 4463. LP disk.

Musique des Tribus Chinoises du Triangle d'Or. 1980. Recording and commentary by François Jouffa. Arion ARN 33535. LP disk.

The Nang Hong Suite: Siamese Funeral Music. 1992. Fong Naam. Commentary by Neil Sorrell and Bruce Gaston. Nimbus Records NI 5332. Compact disc.

The Piphat Ensemble before 1400 A.D. 1990. Fong Naam. Commentary by Bruce Gaston. Siamese Classical Music, 1. HNH International. Marco Polo 8.223197. Compact disc.

The Piphat Ensemble 1351–1767 A.D. (The Afternoon Overture). 1990. Fong Naam. Commentary by Montri Tramoj. Siamese Classical Music, 2. HNH International. Marco Polo 8.223198. Compact disc.

The Piphat Sepha. 1992. Fong Naam. Commentary by Prasarn Wongwirojruk and Bruce Gaston. Siamese Classical Music, 4. HNH International. Marco Polo 8.223200. Compact disc.

Royal Court Music of Thailand. 1994. Recording and commentary by M. R. Chakrarot Chitrabongs. Smithsonian / Folkways Recordings. SF 40413. Compact disc.

Shiva's Drum: Spiritual Music from the Beginning of Time. 1989. Siamese Music Ensemble. Commentary by Bruce Gaston. Pacific Music Co. 8.260582. Compact disc.

The Sleeping Angel: Thai Classical Music. 1991. Fong Naam. Commentary by Neil Sorrell and Bruce Gaston. Nimbus Records NI 5319. Compact disc.

The String Ensemble. 1992. Fong Naam. Siamese Classical Music, 3. HNH Interational. Marco Polo 8.223199. Compact disc.

Thai Classical Music. 1994. The Prasit Thawon Ensemble. Commentary by Somsak Ketukaenchan and Donald Mitchell. Nimbus Records. NI 5412. Compact disc.

Thailand: Classical Instrumental Traditions. 1993. JVC World Sounds (recorded in 1976). JVC Musical Industries. VICG 5262–2. Compact disc.

Thailand: The Music of Chieng Mai. 1988 [1975]. Recording and commentary by Jacques Brunet. Musics and Musicians of the World. International Music Council. Auvidis / Unesco D 8007. Compact disc.

Thaïlande: Musique Classique du Nord. 198? Recording and commentary by Jacques Brunet. Musiques de l'Asie Traditionnelle, 17. Playasound. PS 33522. LP disk.

Virtuosi of Thai Classical Music. 1991. Benjarong Thanakoset and Chaloem Muangphresis. Commentary by Adul Kananasin. World Music Library. King Record Co. KICC 5158. Compact disc.

Laos

Bamboo Voices: Folk Music from Laos. 1997. World Music Institute and Music of the World. Latitudes LAT50601.

Boua Xou Mua: The Music of the Hmong People of Laos. 1995. Produced by Alan Govenar for Documentary Arts. Arhoolie CD 446. Compact disc.

Lam lao sut phiset: Phouvieng & Malavanh. 1995. Huntington Beach, Calif: JKB Productions. Compact disc.

Laos. Recorded by Jacques Brunet. 1989. Ocora C 559 058. Compact disc.

Laos: Musique pour le khène / Lam Saravane. 1989. Recording and commentary by Jacques Brunet. Translation by David Stevens. Ocora C 559 058. Compact disc.

Laos: Musiques du Nord. 1976. Recording and commentary by Jacques Brunet. Musiques de l'Asie Traditionnelle. Playasound PS 33502. LP disk.

Laos: Traditional Music of the South. 1992 [1973]. Recording and commentary by Jacques Brunet. International Music Council. Musics and Musicians of the World. Auvidis / Unesco D 8042. Compact disc.

Mohlan of Siiphandon/Wannaa Keaopidom. 1997. King Record Co. KICC 5225. Compact disc.

Music from Southern Laos. 1994. Molam Lao. Recording by Robin Broadbank. Commentary in French by Jacques Brunet. Translated by Atlas Translations, Cambridge, England. Nimbus Records NI 5401. Compact disc.

The Music of Laos. 196? Recording and commentary in French by Alain Daniélou. Translated into English by John Evarts. Translated into German by Ingrid Brainard. A Musical Anthology of the Orient. Bärenreiter-Musicaphon BM 30 L 2001. LP disk.

Musique des Hmong du Laos: Cour d'Amour et Culte des Ancêtres. 1981. Commentary by Eric Mareschal. Translated by Marguerite Garling. Anthologie de las Musique des Peuples. AMP 2911. LP disk.

The Songs of the Lao. 1997. Musicians of the National Music School, Vientiane. King Record Co. KICC 5226. Compact disc.

Thinking about the Old Village: Traditional Lao Music. 1982. Khamvong Insixiengmai. Minneapolis: Lao Association. Cassette.

Virgins, Orphans, Widows, Bards: Songs of Hmong Women. 1987. Recordings by Amy Catlin. Angeles: The Woman's Building Gallery. Cassette.

Visions of the Orient: Nouthong Phimvilayphone: Music from Laos. 1995. Amiata Records ARNR 0195. Compact disc.

Burma (Myanmar)

Asian Percussions: Bali, Burma, China, India, Sri Lanka, Thailand. 1988. Commentary by Gerard Kremer. Playasound PS 65026. Compact disc.

Birmanie: Musique d'art. 1989. Recording and commentary by Jacques Brunet. Translation into English by Derek Yeld. Ocora 559019/20. 2 compact discs.

Burmese Folk and Traditional Music. 1953. Commentary by Maung Than Myint. Folkways FE 4436. LP disk.

La Harpe Birmane. 1980 Commentary by Jacques Brunet. Musiques de l'Asie Traditionnelle, 22. Playasound PS 33528. LP disk.

Hsaing Waing of Myanmar. 1992. World Music Library. King Record Co. KICC 5162. Compact disc.

Music of Myanmar. 1988. World Music Library. King Record Co. KICC 5132. Compact disc.

Piano Birman / Burmese Piano: U Ko Ko. 1995. UM MUS, SRC Radio (Canada) UMM 203. Compact disc.

White Elephants and Golden Ducks: Enchanting Musical Treasures from Burma. 1997. Newton, N.J.: Shanachie 64087. Compact disc.

Malaysia

Dream Songs and Healing Sounds in the Rainforests of Malaysia. 1995. Recordings and commentary by Marina Roseman. Smithsonian / Folkways SF CD 40417. Compact disc.

Malaisie. 1975. Recording by Hubert De Fraysseix. Commentary by Jacques Brunet. Musiques et Traditions du Monde: Musique Traditionelle. CBS 80934. LP disk.

Malaisie. 198? Commentary by Guy Saint-Clair. Musiques de l'Asie Traditionnelle, 13. Playasound PS 33517. LP disk.

Malaysia: Traditional Music of West Malaysia. 197?. Recording by Jacques Brunet. Commentary by Mubin Sheppard. Translated into German by Wilfried Sczepan. A Musical Anthology of the Orient. Bärenreiter-Musicaphon BM 30 L 2026. LP disk.

The Negrito of Malacca. 1977 [1963]. Recording and commentary by Hans Oesch. Translated by Nancy van Deusen. Anthology of South-East Asian Music. Bärenreiter-Musicaphon BM 30 L 2562. LP disk.

The Protomalayans of Malacca. 1977 [1963]. Recording and commentary by Hans Oesch. Translated by Nancy van Deusen. Anthology of South-East Asian Music. Bärenreiter-Musicaphon BM 30 L 2563. LP disk.

The Senoi of Malacca. 1977 [1963]. Recording and commentary by Hans Oesch. Translated by L.W. Vyse. Anthology of South-East Asian Music. Bärenreiter-Musicaphon BM 30 L 2561. LP disk.

Temiar Dream Songs from Malaya. 1955. Recording by Malaya Broadcasting System [1941]. Commentary by E. D. Robertson and H. D. Noone. Smithsonian / Folkways 04460. LP disk, cassette.

Singapore

New Music Compositions. 1993. Second ASEAN Composers Forum on Traditional Music, 1. ASEAN Committee on Culture and Information. Compact disc.

Traditional Music of Singapore. 1993. Second ASEAN Composers Forum on Traditional Music, 2. ASEAN Committee on Culture and Information. Compact disc.

Vietnam

The Art of Kim Sinh. 1992. Kim Sinh. Commentary in Japanese by Hoshikawa Kyoji. Translated by Larry Richards. World Music Library. King Record Co. KICC 5161. Compact disc.

The City of Huế. 1995. Commentary by Sten Sandahl. Music from Vietnam, 2. Caprice Records CAP 21463. Compact disc.

Dân Ca Cổ Truyền V. N. 1993. Hoàng Oanh. Hoàng Oanh Music Center HOCD 08. Compact disc.

Escale au Vietnam / A Journey to Vietnam. 1995. Commentary and recording by Gerard Kremer. Playasound PS 66509. Compact disc.

Eternal Voices: Traditional Vietnamese Music in the United States. 1993. Commentary by Phong Nguyễn and Terry E. Miller. New Alliance Records NAR CD 053. Compact disc.

Ethnic Minorities. 1995. Commentary by Sten Sandahl. Music from Vietnam, 3. Caprice Records CAP 21479. Compact disc.

Folk Songs of Viet Nam Sung by Pham Duy et al. 1991 [1968]. Smithsonian / Folkways 31303. LP disk, cassette.

From Rice Paddies and Temple Yards: Traditional Music of Vietnam. 1990. Phong Thuyết Nguyễn. Danbury, Conn.: World Music Press. Companion recording for the book by the same name, published by World Music Press. Book and tape set ISBN 0-937203-34-3. Cassette.

Imperial Court Music Recorded in Huế. 1994. The Music of Vietnam, 2. 13084–2. Celestial Harmonies Compact disc.

Instrumental Music of Vietnam. 1992. Commentary in Japanese by Hoshikawa Kyoji. Translated by Larry Richards. World Music Library. King Record Co. KICC 5160. Compact disc.

Introduction to the Music of Viet Nam. 1991 [1965]. Commentary and recordings by Pham Duy. Smithsonian / Folkways 04352. LP disk, cassette.

Landscape of the Highlands. 1997. Tran Quang Hai. Chapel Hill, N.C.: Music of the World. Latitudes LAT50612.

Mekong River: Traditional Music of Vietnam. 1992. Ngoc Lam and Que Lam. Recording by Oliver DiCicco. 1 L CD. Compact disc.

Music from Vietnam. 1991. Commentary by Nguyen Thuy Loan and Sten Sandahl. Caprice Records CAP 21406. Compact disc.

The Music of Vietnam: Volume 1.1. 1994. Recording by David and Kay Parsons. Commentary by John Schaefer. Celestial Harmonies 13082–2. Compact disc.

The Music of Vietnam: Volume 1.2. 1994. Recording by David and Kay Parsons. Commentary by John Schaefer. Celestial Harmonies 13083–2. Compact disc.

Nhạc Lễ, Ritual Music of Vietnam. 1997. King Record Co. KICC 5224. Compact disc.

Song of the Banyan: Folk Music of Vietnam. 1997. Phong Nguyen Ensemble. World Music Institute and Music of the World. Latitudes LAT 50607. Compact disc.

Stilling Time: Người Ngồi Ru Thời Gian. 1994. Recording by Philip Blackburn and Miranda Arana. Innova 112. Compact disc.

String Instruments of Vietnam. 1991. World Music Library. King Record Co. KICC 5121. Compact disc.

The Traditional Songs of Huế. 1997. King Record Co. KICC 5223. Compact disc.

Việt Nam Ca Trù: Tradition du Nord. Ensemble Ca Trù Thái Hà de Hanội. 1996. Paris: Inedit, Maison des Cultures du Monde W 260070. Compact disc.

Vietnam Hat Cheo: Traditional Folk Theatre. 1989 [1978]. Recording and commentary by Trần Văn Khê. Anthology of Traditional Musics. International Music Council. Auvidis / Unesco D 8022. Compact disc.

Viêt-Nam: Instruments et ensembles de musique traditionnelle. 1995 [1984]. Recorded by Maison des

Cultures du Monde, Paris. Arion ARN 64603. Compact disc.

Vietnam: Music of the Truong Son Mountains. 1997. Compiled by Dr. Phong Nguyễn and Dr. Terry E. Miller. White Cliffs Media, WCM 9990. Compact disc.

Viet Nam: Musiques de Huế. 1996. Paris: Inedit W 260073. Compact disc.

Viet-Nam: Musiques et chants des minorités du nord. 1997. Buda 92669-2. Compact disc.

Viet-Nam: Poésies et Chants. 1994. Trần Văn Khê and Trân Thi Thuy Ngoc. Commentary in French by Professor Trần Văn Khê. Translated into English by Jeffrey Grice. Translated into German by Volker Haller. Ocora C 560054. Compact disc.

Vietnam: Reviving a Tradition. 1993. Bibliographic References by Trần Văn Khê. Commentary in French by Bach Thai Hao and Patrick Kersale. Translated into English by Mary Pardoe. Auvidis Playasound PS 65116. Compact disc.

Viet Nam: Tradition of the South. 1993 [1975]. Recording by Hubert de Fraysseix. Commentary by Trần Văn Khê. Anthology of Traditional Musics. International Music Council. Auvidis / Unesco D 8070. Compact disc.

Vietnamese Folk Theatre: Hat Cheo. 1991. World Music Library. King Record Co. KICC 5122. Compact disc.

Vietnamese Zither: The Water and the Wind. 1993. Trân Quang Hai. Commentary in French by Tran Quang Hai. Translated into English by Mary Pardoe. Auvidis Playasound PS 65103. Compact disc.

ISLAND SOUTHEAST ASIA

Sumatra

The Angkola People of Sumatra: An Anthology of Southeast Asian Music. 1983. Bärenreiter Musicaphon SL 2568. LP disk.

Batak of North Sumatra. 1992. New Albion Records NA 046. Compact disc. Bärenreiter Musicaphon BM 30 SL 2567. LP disk.

Gondang Toba / Northern Sumatra. 1985. Museum Collection Berlin, ISBN 3 88 609 5126. LP disk.

Kartomi, Margaret J. 1979. *The Mandailing People of Sumatra: An Anthology of Southeast Asian Music.* Bärenreiter Musicaphon BM 30 SL 2567. LP disk.

Melayu Music of Sumatra and the Riau Islands: Zapin, Mak Yong, Mendu, Ronggeng. 1996. Music of Indonesia, 11. Smithsonian / Folkways SF 40427. Compact disc.

Music from the Forests of Riau and Mentawai. 1995. Music of Indonesia, 7. Smithsonian / Folkways SF 40423. Compact disc.

Music of Nias and North Sumatra: Hoho, Gendang Karo, Gondang Toba. 1992. Music of Indonesia, 4. Smithsonian / Folkways SF 40420. Compact disc.

Nias: Epic Songs and Instrumental Music. 1994. Pan Records PAN 2014CD. Compact disc.

Night Music of West Sumatra: Saluang, Rabab Pariaman, Dendang Pauah. 1994. Music of Indonesia, 6. Smithsonian / Folkways SF 40422. Compact disc.

Simon, Artur. 1984–1985. *Gondang Toba / Northern Sumatra.* Museum Collection Berlin (West) 12. 2 LP disks.

———. 1987. *Gendang Karo / Northern Sumatra, Indonesia—Trance and Dance Music of the Karo Batak.* Museum Collection, Berlin (West) 13. LP disk.

Sumatra: Gongs and Vocal Music. 1996. Music of Indonesia, 12. Smithsonian / Folkways SF 40428. Compact disc.

Java (including Cirebon, Sunda, and Madura)

Asmat Dream: New Music Indonesia, volume 1. 1992. Lyrichord LYRCD 7415. Compact disc.

Bêdhaya Duradasih—Court Music of Kraton Surakarta II. 1995. World Music Library KICC-5193. Compact disc.

Betawi and Sundanese Music of the North Coast of Java: Topeng Betawi, Tanjidor, Ajeng. 1994. Music of Indonesia, 5. Smithsonian / Folkways SF 40421. Compact disc.

Chamber Music of Central Java. 1992. World Music Library KICC-5152. Compact disc.

Court Music of Kraton Surakarta. 1992. World Music Library KICC-5151. Compact disc.

Detty Kurnia: Coyor Panon. 1993. Timbuktu Records FLTRCD519. Compact disc.

Gamelan Degung: Classical Music of Sunda, West Java. 1996. Pan Records Pan 2053 CD. Compact disc.

The Gamelan of Cirebon. 1991. World Music Library KICC-5130. Compact disc.

Gamelan Music from Java. 1963. Philips 831 209. LP disk.

Indonesia I: Java Court Music. 1970s. Bärenreiter Musicaphon BM SL 2031. LP disk.

Indonesian Music: From New Guinea, the Moluccas, Borneo, Bali, and Java. 1954. Columbia SL 210. LP disk.

Indonesian Popular Music: Kroncong, Dangdut, and Langgam Jawa. 1991. Music of Indonesia, 2. Smithsonian / Folkways SF 40056. Compact disc.

Jaipongan Java: Euis Komariah with Jugala Orchestra. 1990. Globestyle CDORB 057. Compact disc.

The Jasmine Isle: Javanese Gamelan Music. 1969. Nonesuch H-72031. LP disk.

Java: Gamelans from the Sultan's Palace in Jogjakarta. 1973. Music Traditions in Asia Series. Archiv 2723 017. LP disk.

Java: Historic Gamelans. 1972. UNESCO Collection, Musical Sources, Art Music from Southeast Asia Series, 9, 2. Philips 6586 004. LP disk.

Java: "Langen Mandra Wanara," Opèra de Danuredjo VII. 1987. Musiques Traditionelles Vivantes, 3. Ocora C559 014/15. Compact disc.

Java: Une Nuit de Wayang Kulit; Légende de Wahju Tjakraningrat. 1973. CDS 65.440. Compact disc.

Javanese Court Gamelan from the Pura Paku Alaman, Jogyakarta. 1971. Nonesuch H-72044. LP disk.

Javanese Court Gamelan Volume II, Recorded at the Istana Mangkunegaran, Surakarta. 1977. Nonesuch H-72074. LP disk.

Javanese Court Gamelan, Volume III, Recorded at the Kraton, Yogyakarta. 1979. Nonesuch H-72083. LP disk.

The Javanese Gamelan. 1987. World Music Library KICC-5129. Compact disc.

Javanese Music from Surinam. 1977. Lyrichord. LLST 7317. LP disk.

Klênêngan Session of Solonese Gamelan I. 1994. World Music Library KICC-5185. Compact disc.

Langêndriyan—Music of Mangkunêgaran Solo II. 1995. World Music Library KICC-5194. Compact disc.

Lolongkrang: Gamelan Degung Music of West Java. 1994. Sakti Records Sakti 33. Compact disc.

Music from West Java. 1992. Ethnic / Auvidis Series D8041. Compact disc.

The Music of K. R. T. Wasitodiningrat: Performed by Gamelan Sekar Tunjung. 1991. Creative Music Productions CMP CD 3007. Compact disc.

The Music of Madura. 1991. ODE Recording ODE CD 1381. Compact disc.

Music of Mangkunêgaran Solo I. 1994. World Music Library KICC-5184. Compact disc.

Music of the Venerable Dark Cloud: The Javanese Gamelan Khjai Mendung. 1967. Institute of Ethnomusicology (University of California at Los Angeles) IER-7501. LP disk.

Music from the Outskirts of Jakarta: Gambang Kromong. 1991. Music of Indonesia, 3. Smithsonian / Folkways SF 40057. Compact disc.

Musiques Populaires d'Indonesie: Folk Music from West Java. 1968. Ocora OCR 46. LP disk.

Musiques du Ramayana, vol. 3: Bali-Sunda. 1990. Ocora C560016. Compact disc.

Nasida Ria: Qasidah Music from Java. 1991. Piranha Music PIR 26-2. Compact disc.

Palais Royal de Yogyakarta, Musique de Concert. 1995. Ocora C560087. Compact disc.

Sangkala. 1985. Icon Records 5501. LP disk.

Songs Before Dawn: Gandrung Banyuwangi. Music of Indonesia, vol. 1. 1991. Smithsonian / Folkways SF 40055. Compact disc.

The Sound of Sunda. 1990. Globestyle CDORB 060. Compact disc.

Street Music of Central Java. 1976. Lyrichord LLST 7310. Compact disc.

Street Music of Java. 1989. Original Music OMCD 006. Compact disc.

The Sultan's Pleasure, Javanese Gamelan and Vocal Music. 1994. Music of the World CDT-116. Compact disc.

Sunda: Musique et chants traditionnels. 1985. Ocora 558 502. LP disk.

Sundanese Classical Music. 1991. World Music Library KICC-5131. Compact disc.

Sundanese Music from Java. 1976. Philips 6586 031. LP disk.

Tembang Sunda: Sundanese Classical Songs. 1993. Nimbus Records NI 5378. Compact disc.

Tonggeret. 1987. Electra / Nonesuch 79173-2. Compact disc.

Vocal Art from Java. 1979. Philips 6586 041. Compact disc.

Bali

Baleganjur of Pande and Angklung of Sidan, Bali. 1995. World Music Library KICC-5197. Compact disc.

Bali: Barong—The Dance Drama of Singapadu Village. 1992. JVC World Sounds. JVC VICG-5217. Compact disc.

Bali: The Celebrated Gamelans. 1976. Musical Heritage Society MHS 3505. LP disk.

Bali: Divertissements Musicaux et Danses de Transe. 1973. Ocora OCR 72. LP disk.

Bali: Gamelan and Kecak. 1989. Nonesuch 9-79204. LP disk.

Bali: Joged Bumbung. 1987. Ocora 558 501. LP disk.

Bali: Le Gong Gedé de Batur. 1975. Ocora 558 510. LP disk.

Bali: Musique de Danse. 1976. Playa Sound PS 33503. LP disk.

Bali: Musique et Théâtre. 1971. Ocora OCR 60. LP disk.

Bali: Musique pour le Gong Gedé / Gong Gedé de Batur. 1987. Ocora C559002. Compact disc.

Bali: Musique Sacrée. 1972. CBS 65173. LP disk.

Bali: Musiques du Nord-Ouest. 1992. Ethnic / Auvidis B 6769. Compact disc.

Bali: Stage and Dance Music. 1973. Philips 6586 015. LP disk.

Barong, Drame Musical Balinais. 1971. Vogue LD 763. LP disk.

Dancers of Bali. 1952. Columbia ML 4618. LP disk.

The Exotic Sounds of Bali. 1963. Columbia ML 5845. LP disk.

Fantastic and Meditative Gamelan: "Tirta Sari": Semar Pegulingan of Peliatan Village. 1988. JVC Ethnic Sound, 7. JVC VID 25024. Compact disc.

Fantastic Sound Art "Mahabharata" / "Wayang Krit": A Virtuoso Shadow Play in Bali. 1987. JVC Ethnic Sound, 14. JVC VID 25028. Compact disc.

Gamelan Batel Wayang Ramayana. 1990. Creative Music Productions CMP CD 3003. Compact disc.

Gamelan Gong Gedé of Batur Temple. 1992. World Music Library KICC-5153. Compact disc.

Gamelan Gong Kebyar of "Eka Cita," Abian Kapas Kaja. 1992. World Music Library. KICC-5154. Compact disc.

Gamelan Joged Bumbung "Suar Agung," Negara. 1994. World Music Library KICC-5181. Compact disc.

Gamelan Music of Bali. 1960s. Lyrichord LLST 7179. LP disk.

The Gamelan Music of Bali. 1991. World Music Library KICC-5126. Compact disc.

The Gamelan of Bali. 1975. Arion. FARN 91009. LP disk.

Gamelan Selonding "Guna Winangun," Teganan. 1994. World Music Library KICC-5182. Compact disc.

Gamelan Semar Pegulingan: Gamelan of the Love God. 1972. Nonesuch H-72046. LP disk.

Gamelan Semar Pegulingan "Gunung Jati," Br. Teges Kanginan. 1994. World Music Library KICC-5180. Compact disc.

Gamelan Semar Pegulingan of Binoh Village. 1992. World Music Library KICC-5155. Compact disc.

Gamelan Semar Pegulingan Saih Pitu: The Heavenly Orchestra of Bali. 1991. Creative Music Productions CMP CD 3008. Compact disc.

Geguntangan Arja "Arja Bon Bali." 1994. World Music Library KICC-5183. Compact disc.

Gendèr Wayang of Sukawati Village. 1992. World Music Library KICC-5156. Compact disc.

Golden Rain: Balinese Gamelan Music. 1969. Nonesuch H-72028. LP disk.

Golden Rain / Gong Kebyar of Gunung Sari, Bali. 1995. World Music Library KICC-5195. Compact disc.

Jegog: Dynamic Sound of the Earth: A Percussion Ensemble of Gigantic Bamboo in Sangkar Agung, Bali. 1987. JVC Ethnic Sound, 12. JVC VID 25026. Compact disc.

Jegog [II]: "Suar Agung," The Bamboo Ensemble of Sangkar Agung Village. 1992. JVC World Sounds. JVC VICG-5218. Compact disc.

Jegog of Negara. 1992. World Music Library KICC-5157. Compact disc.

Kecak: A Balinese Music Drama. 1990. Bridge BCD 9019. Compact disc.

Kecak and Sanghyang of Bali. 1991. World Music Library KICC-5128. Compact disc.

Kecak in the Forest of Anima: The Choral Spectacle of Singapadu Village in Bali. 1987. JVC Ethnic Sound, 13. JVC VID 25027. Compact disc.

Music for the Balinese Shadow Play: Gendèr Wayang from Teges Kanyinan, Pliatan, Bali. 1970. Nonesuch H-72037. LP disk.

Music for the Gods: The Fahnestock South Sea Expedition: Indonesia. 1994. Rykodisc RCD 10315. Compact disc.

Music from the Morning of the World: The Balinese Gamelan. 1967. Nonesuch H-22015. LP disk.

Music in Bali. 1991. World Music Library KICC-5127. Compact disc.

Musiques du Ramayana, vol. 3: Bali-Sunda. 1990. Ocora C560016. Compact disc.

Panji in Bali I. 1972. Bärenreiter Musicaphon BM 30 SL 2565. LP disk.

The Polyphony of South-East Asia; Court Music and Banjar Music. 1971. Philips 6586 008. LP disk.

Saron of Singapadu. 1995. World Music Library KICC-5196. Compact disc.

Scintillating Sounds of Bali. 1976. Lyrichord LLST 7305. LP disk.

Tektekan: The Dance Drama "Calonarang" of Krambitan Village. 1991. JVC World Sounds JVC VICG-5226. Compact disc.

Nusa Tenggara Barat

Cilokaq Music of Lombok. 1994. World Music Library KICC-5178. Compact disc.

The Music of Lombok. 1995. World Music Library KICC-5198. Compact disc.

Panji in Lombok I. 1972. Bärenreiter Musicaphon BM 30 SL 2560. LP disk.

Panji in Lombok II. 1970s. Bärenreiter Musicaphon BM 30 SL 2564. LP disk.

Nusa Tenggara Timur

Music of Sasandu. 1994. World Music Library KICC-5179. Compact disc.

Vocal and Instrumental Music from East and Central Flores. 1995. Music of Indonesia, 8. Smithsonian / Folkways SF 40424. Compact disc.

Vocal Music from Central and West Flores. 1995. Music of Indonesia, 9. Smithsonian / Folkways SF 40425. Compact disc.

Sulawesi

Indonesia, Toraja: Funerals and Fertility Feasts. 1995. Recordings by Dana Rappoport. Collection du Centre National de la Recherche Scientifique et du Musée de l'Homme, CNR 2741004. Harmonia Mundi HM 91.

Music of Sulawesi. 1973. Ethnic Folkways FE 4351. LP disk.

Borneo

Borneo: Musique Traditionelles. 1979. Playa P533506. Compact disc.

Dayak Lutes. 1997. Music of Indonesia, 13. Smithsonian / Folkways. Compact disc.

Dayak Festival and Ritual Music. 1997. Music of Indonesia, 14. Smithsonian / Folkways. Compact disc.

Murut Music of North Borneo. 1961. Folkways FE 4459. LP disk.

The Music of the Kenyah and Modang in East Kalimantan, Indonesia. 1979. UNESCO: University of Phillipines. LP disk.

Musique Dayak. 1972. Collection Musée de L'Homme. Disques Vogue LDM 30108. LP disk.

A Visit to Borneo. 1961. Capitol T 10271. LP disk.

Philippines

Gifts from the Past: Philippine Music of the Kalinga, Maranao, and Yakan People. 1996. Notes by Ramon Santos. P&C Ode Records CD MANU 1518. Compact disc.

Hanunoo Music from the Philippines. 1956. Folkways FE 4466. LP disk.

Kulintang: Ancient Gong / Drum Music from the Southern Philippines. 1994. World Kulintang Institute WKCD 72551. Compact disc.

Kulintang and Kudyapiq: Gong Ensemble and Two-String Lute among the Maguinanaon in Mindanao Philippines. 1989. College of Music, University of the Philippines UPCM-LP UP. Compact disc.

Muranao Kakolintang: Philippine Gong Music from Lanao; vol 1, The Villages of Romayas and Buribid. 1978. Lyrichord LLST 7322. LP disk.

Muranao Kakolintang: Philippine Gong Music from Lanao; vol 2, The Villages of Taraka, Molondo and Bagoaingud. 1970s. Lyrichord LLST 7326. LP disk.

Music from the Tausug of Sulu. 1970. Ethnosound EST 8000–8001. LP disk.

Revel, Nicole. 1987. *Philippines, Musique des Hautes Terres Palawan.* CNRS, Le Chant du Monde LDX 74 865. Compact disc.

A Guide to Films and Videos of Southeast Asian Music

CAMBODIA

From Angkor to America: The Cambodian Dance and Music Project of Van Nuys, California, 1984–1990. 1991. Directed by Amy Catlin. Video.

Khmer Court Dance. 1992. Produced by Sam-Ang Sam. Khmer Studies Institute. Video.

Samsara. 1990. Directed by Ellen Bruno. Video.

Vietnam and Cambodia. 1988. The JVC Video Anthology of World Music and Dance. Southeast Asia I, 6.

The Tenth Dancer. 1992. Directed by Sally Ingleton. Film.

THAILAND

The Diamond Finger. 1957. Film.

Hymn of Praise of Deity: Celestial Drama of Siam. N.d. Bangkok: Arts for Charity Foundation. Video.

Ladyboys. 1992. Produced and directed by Jeremy Marre. Video.

Land of Smiles: Thailand. 1995 [1973]. Produced by Deben Bhattacharya. Video-Forum V 72543. Film, video.

Miao Year. 1971. Produced by William Geddes. Two-part film.

Nang Yai: Thai Shadow Puppet Drama. N.d. Produced by Banhong Kosalawat and Stephanie Krebs. Film.

Rum Thai: Thai Classical Dance. N.d. Bangkok: Foto House Camera & Video Co. Video.

Sounds of Bamboo [Philippines and Thailand]. 1976. Produced by the Japan Foundation. Tokyo: Mitsu Productions, Japan Foundation. Film.

Thailand, Myanmar (Burma). 1988. The JVC Video Anthology of World Music and Dance. Southeast Asia II, 7, Video.

Thai Traditional Music and Classical Dance. 1961. Bangkok: Fine Arts Department. Film.

Two Faces of Thailand: A Musical Portrait. 1994. Newton, N. J.: Shanachie Entertainment Corp. SH 1214. Video.

LAOS

Between Two Worlds: The Hmong Shaman in America. 1985. 16mm. Produced by Taggart Siegel and Dwight Conquergood. Evanston, Ill.: Siegel Productions. Film, video.

Blue Collar and Buddha. 1987. Siegel Productions. Video.

Ib Hnub Hauv Hmoob Lub Neej (Daily life of the Hmong). 1991. CJV Video.

A New Year for the Mien. 1986. Guy Phillips Productions. Video.

BURMA

The Dancers and Musicians of the Burmese National Theatre. N.d. Asia Society. Written and narrated by Beate Gordon. Produced and directed by David W. MacLennan at the Brooklyn College Television Center. Video.

Dances and Rites at the Dispelling of Death Spirits. 1962. Film.

Myanmar: Buddhist Monks and Nuns. 1994? Win Tin Win Presentation. Yangon, Myanmar: Av Media. Video.

Myanmar: Theatrical Dances of Myanmar. 1994? Win Tin Win Presentation. Yangon, Myanmar: Av Media. Video.

Myanmar Traditional Marionette Dances. 1994? Thukuma Video Garden. Yangon, Myanmar: Onpa Trading Co. Video.

Myanmar (Burma). 1988. The JVC Video Anthology of World Music and Dance. Southeast Asia II, 7. Video.

Tribal Dances of Myanmar. 1994? Win Tin Win Presentation. Yangon, Myanmar: Av Media. Video.

MALAYSIA

Borneo Playback: A Sabah Story. 1984. Produced by Carol Kreeger Davidson. Video.

Brides of the Gods. 1986 [1956]. Produced by W. R. Geddes. Video.

Floating in the Air, Followed by the Wind. 1973. Produced by Ronald Simmons. Film.

The Ibans of Sarawak. 1983. Educational Images. 80 slides and audio tape.

Malaysia, Philippines. 1988. The JVC Video Anthology of World Music and Dance. Southeast Asia III, 8. Video.

VIETNAM

Ca Dao: The Folk Poetry of Vietnam. 1984. Produced and directed by David Grubin and Columbia University. David Grubin Productions. University Park, Penn.: Pennsylvania State Audio-Visual Services. Video.

Cultic Dances in a Buddhistic Pagoda near Hue. 1973. Film.

Music of Vietnam [Trần Văn Khe plays the *dan tranh*]. N.d. Filmed and recorded by Robert Garfias and Harold Schutz. Washington Films, Ethnic Music and Dance Series, University of Washington Press. Film.

Vietnam and Cambodia. 1988. The JVC Video Anthology of World Music and Dance. Southeast Asia I, 6. Video.

Vietnam Mission: Fifty Years among the Montagnards. 1994. Produced and directed by Douglas W. Smith. Video.

SINGAPORE

Singapore Street Opera. 1985. Atlanta: Super Station WTBS. Video.

INDONESIA

General

Indonesia: A Balinese Gong Orchestra. 1974. Film.

Indonesia: An Angklung Orchestra. 1974. Film.

Indonesia 1. 1988. The JVC Video Anthology of World Music and Dance. Southeast Asia IV, 9. Video.

Indonesia 2. 1988. The JVC Video Anthology of World Music and Dance. Southeast Asia V, 10. Video.

Sumatra

Karo-Batak—Die Zeremonie "Njujungi beras piher." 1994. Directed by Franz Simon and Artur Simon. Göttingen: Institut für den Wissenschaftlichen Film.

Karo-Batak—Erpangir kalau: Fest der Haarwaschung in Sukanalu. 1994. Directed by Franz Simon and Artur Simon. Göttingen: Institut für den Wissenschaftlichen Film.

Karo-Batak—Gendang-Musik "mari-mari" mit Röhrenzithern und Flöte. 1994. Directed by Artur Simon. Göttingen: Institut für den Wissenschaftlichen Film.

Karo-Batak—Gendang-Musik "mari-mari" und "patam-patam." 1994. Directed by Artur Simon. Göttingen: Institut für den Wissenschaftlichen Film.

Karo-Batak—Gendang-Musik "silengguri" mit Röhrenzither und Laute. 1994. Directed by Artur Simon. Göttingen: Institut für den Wissenschaftlichen Film.

Karo-Batak—Tanze anlasslich einer Haarwaschzeremonie in Kata Mbelin. 1994. Directed by Franz Simon and Artur Simon. Göttingen: Institut für den Wissenschaftlichen Film.

Pakpak-Batak—Genderang-Musik. 1994. Directed by Artur Simon. Göttingen: Institut für den Wissenschaftlichen Film.

Pakpak-Batak—Spielen auf der Längsflöte "sordam." 1994. Directed by Artur Simon. Göttingen: Institut für den Wissenschaftlichen Film.

Pakpak-Batak—Xylophonmusik "kuku endek-endek" und "tangis-tangis beru ikan." 1994. Directed by Artur Simon. Göttingen: Institut für den Wissenschaftlichen Film.

Simalungun-Batak—Gonrang-Musik "olob-olob" und "sabung-sabung anduhur." 1994. Directed by Artur Simon. Göttingen: Institut für den Wissenschaftlichen Film.

Simalungun-Batak—Gonrang-Musik (sidua-dua) "parahot." 1994. Directed by Artur Simon. Göttingen: Institut für den Wissenschaftlichen Film.

Simalungun-Batak—Spielen auf dem Reishalminstrument "ole-ole." 1994. Directed by Artur Simon. Göttingen: Institut für den Wissenschaftlichen Film.

Toba-Batak—Gondang-Musik "sampur marmeme." 1994. Directed by Artur Simon. Göttingen: Institut für den Wissenschaftlichen Film.

Toba-Batak—Gondang-Musik "somba-somba." 1994. Directed by Artur Simon. Göttingen: Institut für den Wissenschaftlichen Film.

Java

Karya: Video Portraits of Four Indonesian Composers. 1992. Produced by Jody Diamond. American Gamelan Institute. Video.

Gambyong Pangkur: Traditional Javanese Court Dance from Solo. 1993. Resonance Media. Video.

The Prosperity of Wibisana: A Performance of Wayang Kulit. 1995. Resonance Media. Video.

The Prosperity of Wibisana: A Study Guide and Analysis of Javanese Wayang Kulit. 1995. Resonance Media. Video.

Bali

Bali beyond the Postcard. 1991. Produced and directed by Nancy Dine, Peggy Stern, and David Dawkins. New York: Filmmakers Library.

Balinese Children Learn to Dance. N.d. Filmed by Gregory Bateson and Margaret Mead. New York: Filmmakers Library. Video.

Dance and Trance of Balinese Children. N.d. Produced by Madeleine Richeport-Haley and Jay Haley from the film *Learning to Dance in Bali.* Video.

Isle of Temples: Bali. 1995 [1973]. Produced by Deben Bhattacharya. Video Forum V72542. Film, video.

Kembali—To Return. 1991. Produced by Jim Mayer, Lynn Adler, and John Rogers. Berkeley: Center for Media and Independent Learning, University of California Extension. Video.

Learning to Dance in Bali. 1978 [1939]. Gregory Bateson and Margaret Mead. New York: Gregory Bateson and Margaret Mead. Film, video.

Nini Pantun: Rice Cultivation and Rice Rituals in Bali. 1988. Berkeley: Center for Media and Independent Learning, University of California Extension. Video.

Releasing the Spirits: A Village Cremation in Bali. 1981. Directed by Patsy Asch, Linda Connor, et al. Documentary Educational Resources. Video.

Taksu: Music in the Life of Bali. 1991. Jann Pasler. Berkeley: University of California, Extension Media Center. Video.

Trance and Dance in Bali. 1988 [1952]. Gregory Bateson, Jane Belo, and Margaret Mead. Institute for Intercultural Studies. Film, video.

Outer islands

A Celebration of Origins. 1992. Directed by Timothy Asch. Documentary Educational Recources. Video.

Trance of the Toraja. 1974. Eric Crystal and Lee Rhoads. Color, 21 min. Berkeley: University of California Extension Media Center. Video.

Borneo

Kayan-Dayak—Frauentanz "Karangarum" in Padua. 1990. Directed by Franz Simon and Sonja Balbach. Göttingen: Institut für den Wissenschaftlichen Film. Video.

Kayan-Dayak—Frauentanz "Tinaak Anaak" in Padua. 1990. Directed by Franz Simon and Sonja Balbach. Göttingen: Institut für den Wissenschaftlichen Film. Video.

Kayan-Dayak—Kriegstanz "Hivaar Peyitang" in Padua. 1990. Directed by Franz Simon and Sonja Balbach. Göttingen: Institut für den Wissenschaftlichen Film. Video.

PHILIPPINES

Hanunoo. 1958. Directed by H. C. Conklin. Film.

Ilocano Music and Dance of the Northern Philippines. 1971. Filmed and recorded by Robert Garfias and Harold Schutz. Washington Films, Ethnic Music and Dance Series, University of Washington Press. Film.

Maguindanao Kulintang Ensembles from Mindanao, the Philippines. 1971. Filmed and recorded by Robert Garfias and Harold Schutz. Washington Films, Ethnic Music and Dance Series, University of Washington Press. Video.

Music and Dance from Mindanao, the Philippines. 1971. Filmed and recorded by Robert Garfias and Harold Schutz. Washington Films, Ethnic Music and Dance Series, University of Washington Press. Film.

Music and Dance from the Sulu Islands, the Philippines. 1971. Filmed and recorded by Robert Garfias and Harold Schutz. Washington Films, Ethnic Music and Dance Series, University of Washington Press. Film.

Music and Dance of the Bagobo and Manobo Peoples of Mindanao, the Philippines. 1969. Filmed and recorded by Robert Garfias and Harold Schutz. Washington Films, Ethnic Music and Dance Series, University of Washington Press. Video.

Music and Dance of the Hill People of the Northern Philippines. 1971. Filmed and recorded by Robert Garfias and Harold Schutz. Washington Films, Ethnic Music and Dance Series, University of Washington Press. Two-part film.

Music and Dance of the Ibaloy Group of the Northern Philippines. 1971. Filmed and recorded by Robert Garfias and Harold Schutz. Washington Films, Ethnic Music and Dance Series, University of Washington Press. Film.

Music and Dance of the Maranao People of Mindanao, the Philippines. 1971. Filmed and recorded by Robert Garfias and Harold Schutz. Washington Films, Ethnic Music and Dance Series, University of Washington Press. Film.

Music and Dance of the Yakan People of Basilan

Island, the Philippines. 1971. Filmed and recorded by Robert Garfias and Harold Schutz. Washington Films, Ethnic Music and Dance Series, University of Washington Press. Film.

Samal Dances from Taluksangay. 1971. Filmed and recorded by Robert Garfias and Harold Schutz. Washington Films, Ethnic Music and Dance Series, University of Washington Press. Film.

Sounds of Bamboo [Philippines and Thailand]. 1976. Produced by the Japan Foundation. Tokyo: Mitsu Productions, Japan Foundation. Film.

Malaysia, Philippines. 1988. The JVC Video Anthology of World Music and Dance. Southeast Asia III, 8. Video.

Notes on the Audio Examples

1. Frogs (4:45)

   Although these sounds might seem merely curious, frogs in fact have great significance to Southeast Asian farmers. Frog sounds are welcome as an indication that generous rains have fallen, that the rice crop will be successful, and that the flooded fields are full of delicious fish, shrimp, insects, and frogs. Prosperity will follow, at least for that year.

   Recorded by Terry E. Miller on 14 September 1988 in Mahasarakham, Thailand

2. Chinese-Thai *sizhu* ensemble piece "*Chung we meng*" ("Moon Shining Brightly in the Spring") (4:55)

   The majority of Chinese-Thai trace their lineage to the Chaozhou area of Guangdong province. The amateur "silk and bamboo" *(sizhu)* ensemble heard here is distinguished by its lead fiddle (the nasal and piercing *tou xian)* and its stereotyped rhythmic variation patterns, some of which are heard in this piece. Amateur musicians, primarily local businessmen, play this music for recreation in a music room attached to one of the local Chinese temples. They use a variety of instruments, including—in this case—certain modern "bass" versions of traditional plucked and bowed lutes.

   Recorded by Terry E. Miller on 27 January 1974 at a Chinese temple in Roi-et, Thailand

3. Khmer classical *pinn peat* ensemble dance piece "*Thep monorom*" (4:48)
   Performed by musicians from the Royal University of Fine Arts, Phnom Penh

   During the years of the Khmer Rouge reign of terror (1975–1979), the city of Phnom Penh was emptied and thousands died or were exiled, including most musicians and dancers. After being liberated in 1979, the few surviving musicians and dancers began rebuilding Cambodia's classical traditions. The ensemble heard here consists of survivors—and young musicians trained by them—accompanying the great dance *thep monorom.* Instrumental sections alternate with vocal interludes.

   Recorded by Terry E. Miller on 13 December 1988 at the Royal Palace Dance Pavilion, Phnom Penh, Cambodia

4. Thai *salaw seung pi* ensemble music (4:20)
   Performed by musicians led by Sanit A-phai

   Northern Thai instrumental music is often called *salaw seung pi* after its three most important instruments (*salaw* being a family of bowed lutes, *seung* a plucked lute, and *pi* a free-reed pipe with finger holes). In this recording, a fipple flute *(khlui)* is substituted for the free-reed pipe. In addition, there are a pair of small cymbals *(ching)* and a drum *(klawng).* Playing in a tuning system distinct from those in both central and northeast Thailand, the instruments repeat a relatively short melody with continuous variations, producing heterophonic texture.

Recorded by Terry E. Miller on 2 July 1994 at Mae San Pakham village, Lamphun Province, Thailand

5. Thai *lam sing* repartee song (4:25)
Sung by Mawlam Rattri Si-wilai

Although *lam sing* is a northeastern Thai repartee genre created in 1989 by Mawlam Rattri and her brother, it has become the rage throughout Thailand. It combines the traditional accompaniment of free-reed mouth organ *(khaen)* with modern pop instruments such as electric lute *(phin)* and drum set to give it a driving, modern sound.

Recorded by Terry E. Miller on 20 June 1991 in Khon Kaen, Thailand

6. Laotian *lam salavane* repartee song ("Song of Salavane") (4:29)
Sung by Bounta Duang-panya, accompanied by *khene* 'free-reed mouth organ' (Mr. Bountem), *kajapi* 'lute' (Mr. Bountawee), *so i kang* 'fiddle' (Mr. Bounta Duang-panya), and *kong* 'drum' (Mr. Surat)

This vocal genre of southern Laos, performed by acculturated Lao of upland Mon-Khmer origin, is typically accompanied by a small ensemble or by *khene* alone. This recording includes only the male singer, but a full performance would consist of male-female repartee in which the singers test each other's wits with questions of knowledge and a feigned love affair.

Recorded by Terry E. Miller on 2 July 1991 in Salavane, Laos

7. Burmese *kyo* classical song (3:36)
Sung by Daw Yi Yi Thant, accompanied by *saùñ* 'harp' (played by Ù Myint Mauñ) and *siwa* 'cymbals and clapper' (played by Ù Mauñ Then)

Recorded during a government radio station recording session as part of the preparation for a national contest, this song is performed by two of the country's most senior artists. While the vocal melody and harp accompaniment sound somewhat free and are quite flexible, they fit into a regular metric pattern articulated by the cymbals and castanet-like hinged clapper.

Recorded by Terry E. Miller on 16 July 1994 at the National Theater, Rangoon, Burma

8. Vietnamese *nhạc lễ* ritual ensemble (5:45)
Musicians led by Nguyen Van Tam

Nhạc lễ music is associated with many kinds of rituals, both Buddhist and family centered, and is played by double reeds, fiddles, drum, gong, and a struck water buffalo horn. This recording is in the style typical of southern Vietnam, especially the delta area of the Mekong.

Recorded by Terry E. Miller on 23 June 1993 in Vinh Xuan, Vinh Long Province, Vietnam

9. Thai Dam *khắp* repartee singing (3:20)
Sung by Ha Long and Ngan Thi Quang

The Thai Dam (Black Thai) minority in northern Vietnam is closely related to upland Tai minorities in Laos. This special performance was given in a large stilted wooden house for a group of visiting ethnomusicologists, surrounded by a crowd of curious onlookers. Heard first is an excerpt of the male singer's part, followed by the opening of his female partner's song. Such unaccompanied singing consists of stanzas of poetry, with the melody being generated in part by the lexical tones of the words.

Recorded by Terry E. Miller on 23 June 1994 in Binh Son Village, Thanh Hoa Province, Vietnam

10. Jarai gong ensemble with song *"Yong Thoach"* ("Brother Thoach, Please Come Back") (3:28)
Sung by Y Yon

Accompanied by an ensemble consisting of individually held gongs played by members of the Jarai upland ethnic group, Y Yon sings: "Brother Thoach, please come home/ The village is waiting for you/ The rice fields are beautiful/ Please come home to a safe place." While he is singing, female dancers encircle him and the instrumental ensemble.

Recorded by Phong T. Nguyễn in February 1996 in Ae H'leo district, Dak Lak Province, in central Vietnam

11. East Javanese *"Srempeg, pelog patet wolu"* (4:30)
Gamelan ensemble directed by Pak Kasdu (drummer), managed by Pak Taslan Harsono

An example of East Javanese gamelan music used to accompany *wayang topèng* (masked dance drama) and *wayang kulit* (shadow puppetry) in the Malang region, *"Srempeg"* is similar to a Central Javanese piece of the same name used to accompany entrances, exits, and moderate levels of fighting in the theater. However, the structures are different, and East Javanese playing emphasizes crisp, highly syncopated drumming.

Recorded by R. Anderson Sutton on 10 July 1986 in Karang Tengah, Java

12. Accompanied *cakepung* song *"Pemungkah"* ("Opening") (3:41)
Sekaha Cakepung "Taat," co-directed by Ida Bagus Gede and Ida Bagus Djelantik

A recreational music-dance form that originated in Lombok, *cakepung* employs a group of male singers who imitate the sounds and functions of gamelan instruments. An unmetered introduction based on Hindu East Javanese romantic poems is followed by a metered section involving both instruments (flutes and bowed lute) and voices. Although such performances may accompany ritual, they can also be recreational, with much drinking of palm wine and a progressive lowering of players' inhibitions.

Recorded by David Harnish on 9 July 1983 in Amlapura, Bali

13. Sasak shadow play music *"Telaga dundan"* ("Eternal Pond") (3:30)
Musicians directed by I Gede Budiarta

The theatrical tales portrayed in the shadow-puppet theater of the Sasak people of Lombok derive from the *Menak* cycle concerning the hero Amir Hamzah and the early Islamic world. *"Telaga Dundan"* accompanies both the removal of the puppets from their box and the introduction of the main puppet, the *gunungan* (symbolizing the cosmic mountain), with two smaller puppets behind it representing Adam and Eve. The ensemble, tuned in *pelog,* is led by a flute *(suling).*

Recorded by David Harnish on 23 July 1989 in Cakranegara, West Lombok

14. Filipino ensemble pieces *"Te-ed"* and *"Kuriri"* (2:37)
Performed by members of the Ajijil family

These are two examples of instrumental music performed during a festival by members of the Yakan minority from Lamitan in the southern Philippines. The instruments used are the *kwintang* (set of five small bossed gongs in a rack), *agung* (set of three deep-rimmed hanging gongs), *gabbang* (five-key xylophone), and *gandang* (bamboo slit drum).

Recorded by Ramón P. Santos in 1994 in Davao City, Basilan Province, Philippines

15. Song *"Kulilal ni puguq"* ("Kulilal of the Quail") (3:50)
Performed by Bunjag (vocal) and Lamuna O (tube zither)

The *kulilal* love song is of recent origin and stems from contact with peoples of the Sulu Sea. The poetry, which mixes several languages, is made exceptionally intimate through severe simplification, allowing lovers to exchange messages in subtle and secret ways. The text is: "Oh, yes, I know it/ A weir of stones, a stony weir/ Tagperara is beyond/ I only have to walk/ And I went there/ For a graceful maiden."

Recorded by Nicole Revel-Macdonald, Charles Macdonald, and José Maceda in March 1972 in Kangrian, Palawan Highlands, Philippines

Index

Page numbers in *italic* indicate pages on which illustrations appear.
See page xvi for a guide to pronunciation.